Also by Robert Kimball

COLE
(editor)

REMINISCING WITH SISSLE AND BLAKE
(co-author)

THE GERSHWINS
(co-author)

THE UNPUBLISHED COLE PORTER
(editor)

THE COMPLETE LYRICS OF COLE PORTER
(editor)

THE COMPLETE LYRICS OF LORENZ HART
(co-editor)

CATALOG OF THE AMERICAN MUSICAL
(co-author)

THE COMPLETE LYRICS OF IRA GERSHWIN
(editor)

READING LYRICS
(co-editor)

The Complete Lyrics of

IRVING BERLIN

ALFRED A. KNOPF   NEW YORK   2001

The Complete Lyrics of

IRVING BERLIN

Edited by

ROBERT KIMBALL and LINDA EMMET

Grateful acknowledgment is made to the following for permission to reprint published and unpublished material:

Carl Sandburg's article in the *Chicago Times* (page 351). Used by permission of the Trustees of the Carl Sandburg Family Trust. All rights reserved. Dwight D. Eisenhower's letter (page 357). Used by permission of the Dwight D. Eisenhower Library. All rights reserved. Henry Morgenthau Jr.'s letters (pages 370 and 373). Used by permission of the Estate of Henry Morgenthau Jr. All rights reserved. Jerome Robbins's letter (page 401). Used by permission of the Estate of Jerome Robbins. All rights reserved.

Copyright information on the lyrics of Irving Berlin appears in the Index, starting on page 507.

Library of Congress Cataloging-in-Publication Data
Berlin, Irving, 1888–1989
[Lyrics]
The complete lyrics of Irving Berlin / edited by Robert Kimball and Linda Berlin Emmet.
p.   cm.
Includes index.
ISBN 0-679-41943-8 (lib. bdg.)
1. Songs, English—United States—Texts.   2. Popular music—Texts.   3. Musicals—Librettos.
I. Kimball, Robert.   II. Emmet, Linda.   III. Title.
ML54.6.B464 K55   2000
782.42164'0268—dc21   00-062890

Photographic Credits

Irving Berlin Music Company: 3, 16, 29, 46, 67, 85, 95, 164, 173, 183, 193 (right inset), 219, 227, 244 (bottom), 250, 272 (bottom), 292, 403, 446 (top left), 449, 480, 486; © Henri Cartier-Bresson/Magnum Photos: 502; Culver Pictures: 151, 193 (bottom), 282 (top left), 313 (bottom), 347, 439; Linda Emmet: title page, 370; The Kobal Collection: 265, 301, 304, 398; Museum of the City of New York: 110, 143, 233, 282 (bottom and top right), 425; New York Public Library/Billy Rose Theatre Collection: 29 (inset), 193 (left inset), 272 (top), 384; Photofest: 126, 244, 308, 313 (top), 315, 320, 333, 336, 356, 378, 410, 446 (bottom left and right), 467; Shubert Archive: xiv, 324 (top left and right and bottom right); Rex Hardy, Jr./TimePix: 324 (bottom left)

To the memory of

HILDA SCHNEIDER,

Irving Berlin's secretary from 1942 to 1989

Contents

Contents

a Senator with a Girl • In an Old-Fashioned Parlor • We Might Have Had a Future

HOLIDAY INN | 1942   347

I'll Capture Your Heart Singing • You're Easy to Dance With • White Christmas • Happy Holiday / Holiday Inn • Customers, I'm Here to Greet You • Let's Start the New Year Right • Abraham • Be Careful, It's My Heart • I Can't Tell a Lie • Let's Say It with Firecrackers • Song of Freedom • Plenty to Be Thankful For • Holiday Inn—Finale • This Is a Great Country

THIS IS THE ARMY | 1942   356

Opening (The Army and the Shuberts Depend on You) • Opening Chorus (Some Dough for the Army Relief) • This Is the Army, Mister Jones • I'm Getting Tired So I Can Sleep • My Sergeant and I Are Buddies • My Captain and I Are Buddies • Don't Sing, Go into Your Dance • I Left My Heart at the Stage Door Canteen • The Army's Made a Man out of Me • Yip, Yip, Yaphanker's Introduction • Ladies of the Chorus • That Russian Winter • That's What the Well-Dressed Man in Harlem Will Wear • How About a Cheer for the Navy? • Opening of Act II (Jane Cowl Number) • American Eagles • With My Head in the Clouds • Aryans Under the Skin • A Soldier's Dream • This Time (Closing) • Ve Don't Like It • What Does He Look Like (That Boy of Mine)? • Dressed Up to Kill / Dressed Up to Win • Officer's Speech • England and America • The Kick in the Pants • My British Buddy • Daddy's Coming Home on a Furlough • The Fifth Army Is Where My Heart Is • What Are We Going to Do with All the Jeeps? • There Are No Wings on a Foxhole • Misses the Army • Cozy Little Foxhole by the Sea • I Get Along with the Aussies • I'm Getting Old in New Guinea • Heaven Watch the Philippines • Oh, to Be Home Again • Oh, for a Dress Again • What Is a War Song?

Other Songs of 1940–1945   370

A Little Old Church in England • Everybody Knew But Me • In Old San Juan • When That Man Is Dead and Gone • Any Bonds Today? • Any Bombs Today? • Arms for the Love of America (The Army Ordnance Song) • When This Crazy World Is Sane Again • Angels of Mercy • I Paid My Income Tax Today • The President's Birthday Ball • This Time • Me and My Piano • Me and My Melinda • The Youth Parade • I Threw a Kiss in the Ocean • Till We Hang the Paper Hanger • Take Me

with You, Soldier Boy • If I Could Write the Nation's Laws • All My Life • Mona • Just a Blue Serge Suit • Eyes to See With

BLUE SKIES | 1946   378

A Serenade to an Old-Fashioned Girl • I'll See You in C-U-B-A • A Couple of Song-and-Dance Men • You Keep Coming Back Like a Song • We Keep Coming Back with a Song • (Running Around in Circles) Getting Nowhere • The Race Horse and the Flea • Wilhelmina • I'll Dance Rings Around You • It's a Lovely Day for a Walk • Have You Ever Tried Drinking Water? • I Want You to Meet My Girl • The Road to Yesterday • I'd Rather Not Dance Again • Mending the Old World (Making It New) • My Old Pal

ANNIE GET YOUR GUN | 1946   384

Colonel Buffalo Bill • I'm a Bad, Bad Man • Doin' What Comes Naturally • The Girl That I Marry • You Can't Get a Man with a Gun • There's No Business Like Show Business • They Say It's Wonderful • Moonshine Lullaby • I'll Share It All with You • My Defenses Are Down • I'm an Indian Too • I Got Lost in His Arms • Who Do You Love? I Hope • I Got the Sun in the Morning • Anything You Can Do • Take It in Your Stride (Whatever the Fates Decide) • With Music • Pardners • Something Bad's Gonna Happen ('Cause I Feel So Good) • Let's Go West Again • An Old-Fashioned Wedding • Who Needs the Birds and Bees?

EASTER PARADE | 1948   398

Happy Easter • Drum Crazy • It Only Happens When I Dance with You • A Fella with an Umbrella • Steppin' Out with My Baby • A Couple of Swells • Better Luck Next Time • Mr. Monotony/Mrs. Monotony • I Love You—You Love Him

STARS ON MY SHOULDERS | 1948 and Other Songs of 1946–1949   403

STARS ON MY SHOULDERS | 1948
Five O'Clock in the Afternoon • Beautiful Brooklyn • A Beautiful Day in Brooklyn • Funny When You're Left with Nothing More to Say • John Jacob Astor • If We Weren't Married • A Roof over My Head • Monohan and Callahan

OTHER SONGS OF 1946–1949
Help Me to Help My Neighbor • Kate (Have I Come Too Early, Too Late?) • Love and the Weather • The Freedom Train • Mister Jolson • Lyric Ideas for Professional Children's School Show • I Gave Her My Heart in Acapulco • Let's Keep in Touch While We're Dancing • I'm Beginning to Miss You • Jingle Bells • Thanks for the Memory (Parody) • Operation Vittles • Operation Fräulein

MISS LIBERTY | 1949   410

Extra! Extra! • I'd Like My Picture Took • The Most Expensive Statue in the World • A Little Fish in a Big Pond • Let's Take an Old-Fashioned Walk • Homework • Paris Wakes Up and Smiles • Only for Americans • Just One Way to Say I Love You • Miss Liberty • Consul Bows • The Train • You Can Have Him • The Policemen's Ball • Me and My Bundle • Falling out of Love Can Be Fun • Give Me Your Tired, Your Poor • The Hon'rable Profession of the Fourth Estate • I'll Know Better the Next Time • What Do I Have to Do to Get My Picture in the Paper? • Business for a Good Girl Is Bad • For a Good Girl It's Bad • The Pulitzer Prize • Sing a Song of Sing Sing • The Story of Nell and the *Police Gazette* • Only in America • A Woman's Place Is in the Home • If I Had Never Been Born • They Say It's Full of Indians

CALL ME MADAM | 1950   425

Mrs. Sally Adams • The Hostess with the Mostes' on the Ball • Washington Square Dance • Lichtenburg • Can You Use Any Money Today? • Marrying for Love • (Dance to the Music Of) The Ocarina • It's a Lovely Day Today • The Best Thing for You • Something to Dance About • Once upon a Time Today • They Like Ike • I Like Ike • I Still Like Ike • Ike for Four More Years • We Still Like Ike • You're Just in Love • What Did You Do to Me? • Free • Our Day of Independence • Our Town • Call Me Madam • You've Got to Be Way Out to Be In • Nuts to You • I Speak American • Lichtenburg Cheese • The Wild Men of Lichtenburg • Blintzes from Lindy's • What This Country Needs

WHITE CHRISTMAS | 1954   439

The Old Man • Sisters • The Best Things Happen While You're Dancing • Snow • I'd Rather See a Minstrel Show / Mandy • Count Your Blessings Instead of Sheep • Choreography • Love, You Didn't Do Right by Me • What Can You Do with a General? • Gee, I

Foreword

In 1935 my father, who at the time was out in California working on *Top Hat*, sent me a series of postcards—fifty-three in all. When finally assembled, their message read as follows:

Dear Linda Louise

You must put away these postals I'm sending with one
    word a day.

You'll have to be patient for weeks will have passed

Before this is over and you get the last.

So don't be discouraged, and please don't be bored.

But wait for the finish, and get your reward.

The reward, a doll, does not survive. But the postcards, pasted into a scrapbook, do. One small example of my father's versatility.

Because he worked frequently on movie projects in the thirties and went overseas with *This Is the Army* during the war, my father was absent throughout much of my childhood. And like many children, taken up with their own lives, I wasn't particularly focused on what he did for a living.

It wasn't until I agreed to do the research for this book, and started going through the office files, that I began to grasp the scope of his output. Many of the lyrics were unfamiliar, and the pleasure of discovering them propelled me forward, and made the sometimes tedious work worthwhile.

There is no way of knowing where the inspiration—the impetus to write lyrics—came from. Whether in the cabarets where my father worked as a singing waiter, or elsewhere. But it becomes evident after reading all the material that at an early age he developed an absolute need to write, which never left him.

Even during the final decades of his life, when he suffered recurring bouts of depression and became increasingly reclusive, he continued to turn out incisive and, at times, humorous verse.

This compilation not only traces the different stages of my father's evolution as a lyricist, but also reveals two enduring characteristics of his psyche—humor and melancholy. Above all, it is a chronicle of his life—and of his metamorphosis from immigrant to quintessential American.

—Linda Emmet

Introduction

Let me tell you about "All Alone." After the First World War I spent a lot of time in Atlantic City. I wrote many songs there including most of the songs for the Music Box Revues. *Anyway, I had written this song, but something was missing and I wasn't quite satisfied with it. Originally, the chorus began, "All alone / I am all alone." It wasn't bad, but I felt it needed something more. As I remember, I sat on the beach near the boardwalk for days, maybe weeks, before I got the one word that changed everything in the song. The word was "so." "All alone / I'm so all alone." It gave the song a big lift. It made all the difference. That and the good luck to have John McCormack sing and record it.*

—IRVING BERLIN

Beyond Irving Berlin's unceasing quest for inspiration were his uncommon persistence and a relentless tenacity. In 1972, when I was collaborating with Alfred Simon on a book called *The Gershwins*, Berlin, as was his custom in our many telephone conversations, asked me what I was working on. When I told him about the Gershwin book, he said, "I have a story for your book—no, a story and a song." The song, an obscure one, was Berlin's "That Revolutionary Rag," written in 1919. The story was about a young pianist, very gifted, Berlin noted, who worked for Max Dreyfus and his prestigious Harms Company. The pianist was George Gershwin. "The song," said Berlin, "is of no importance, except that George took it down for me. He wanted to be my musical secretary." After Berlin told me the story, he asked me to write up what he had said and send it to him so he could edit it—which he did, endlessly, making numerous changes, the most important and interesting of which was to alter the narration from the first person to the third. Days went by. Berlin continued to tinker with what was a pretty short story. Not only did he rework it, but over the next several days I had to recite the story for him as if I were doing a dramatic reading. Soon I knew it so well that I could almost recite it from memory. Finally, he stopped fussing with it, but knowing Mr. Berlin (which is what I always called him), I expected a telephone call and words I came to know well over the years. "Forget about it," is what he often said. Yet this time either he lost interest in revising it, or forgot about it altogether, or actually was ready to let the story remain as it was. Later, in exhaustion, disbelief that the "Revolutionary Rag" saga had come to an end, and gratitude for the story and the gift of the song for our book (and it was a gift), I thanked him and asked if he always worked the way he had worked with me. He laughed and replied, "Kid, you had it easy!"

•   •   •

Anyone who writes the history of twentieth-century America must give a place of honor to Irving Berlin (1888–1989), a musical bard whose work expressed his times as eloquently and unerringly as the poetry of Walt Whitman and the songs of Stephen Foster gave voice to the aspirations of nineteenth-century America. Not only because Berlin is one of our greatest songwriters, but also because he is one of our most important social chroniclers.

If all traces of our nation from the first half of the last century were to disappear except for Berlin's songs, our descendants would still have an extraordinarily rich and varied account of our customs and values. These songs offer us a treasure trove of insights into the ways America has lived and changed in times of war and peace, in tumult and euphoria, and in prosperity and depression. Admittedly, his world of music and dancing, love and the weather, heartache and optimism, and fads and fancies, reflects an earlier time when relationships had more solidity and durability than they seem to have in our own era. Yet from his early dialect songs and opera burlesques to the most beautiful ballads and the most poignant expressions of love of country, Berlin more than confirmed what Jerome Kern, a great composer in his own right, said of him, "Irving Berlin has no place in American music: he *is* American music."

Some lyricists have rhymed with more consistent cleverness and complexity than Berlin. Others have pitched their utterances more precisely to the intellectual tastemakers. There are those who have employed more symbolism and greater depth of allusion. And some are clearly more likely candidates for footnotes and the other trappings of scholarly exegesis.

Other composers have expanded the limits of the popular song more dramatically than Berlin. And many of his colleagues have had a surer knowledge of the textbook rules of harmony. (Although to the great orchestrator Robert Russell Bennett, "Berlin had the most uncanny intuitive knowledge of harmony. He worked tirelessly to get exactly the sound he wanted. If one note in a series of chords wasn't to his liking, he would sweat to get it right.")

Still, a great song is something quite apart from all this. It is an individual statement that makes its appeal in taking something personal, local, topical, perhaps transient, and transforming that notion through the skillful mating of words and music into a universal truth for millions. The ability to capture and represent the human experience in a simple, direct way is what the greatest songwriting is all about. And that is where Irving Berlin has few, if any, peers.

Berlin was born in Russia on May 11, 1888 (see the Chronol-ogy for more information on his life and career). It was the year in which Tchaikovsky wrote his Fifth Symphony, Wolf his *Mörike Lieder,* Strauss his *Don Juan,* and Rimsky-Korsakov his *Scheherazade.* Irving (born Israel Beilin, then changed to Baline) was the youngest of eight children; his father was a cantor in the local synagogue. Because Jews were harassed in Czarist Russia in the early 1890s, the family made the long journey to the United States and settled in New York's Lower East Side.

Singing with his father, who helped train a synagogue choir, gave Berlin his early involvement with music. He was thirteen when his father died; at fourteen, he ran away from home and earned a precarious living singing on street corners for pennies, selling newspapers, and working as a singing waiter in cafés. His first steady job was at Mike Salter's Pelham Café at 12 Pell Street in the heart of New York's Chinatown. Later he worked at Jimmy Kelly's place in Union Square. Throughout this boyhood, Berlin already was demonstrating a remarkable ear for speech patterns and dialects, an uncanny memory, and a keen intuitive grasp of music. He heard and absorbed the sounds of the turbulent city and its teeming population of immigrants and poured them all into his songs.

When he began his songwriting career in 1907 with the words for "Marie from Sunny Italy," Berlin was primarily a lyricist and vocalist; many of his early songs were written with others more skilled in composition. But soon he was working almost exclusively by himself. As the writer of such standouts as "Alexander's Ragtime Band" (1911), "When I Lost You" (1912)—written after the death of his first wife, Dorothy Goetz—and "When the Midnight Choo-Choo Leaves for Alabam'" (1912), he rose quickly to the top of his profession.

Later, he was sensitive about his early work. "I wrote more lousy songs than almost anyone else," he told me. "Some of them may have seemed clever when they were written but they embarrass the hell out of me now. I would be happier if people did not perform them. I have a running gag with Groucho Marx where I'll say I'll pay him if he stops singing my old song 'Stay Down Here Where You Belong.'"

Berlin took such a dim view of his youthful offerings that

when, late in his life, he assembled a special bound collection of 192 of his published songs to give to friends, he included only nine pre-1915 numbers ("Alexander's Ragtime Band," 1911; "Call Me Up Some Rainy Afternoon," 1910; "Everybody's Doin' It Now," 1911; "My Wife's Gone to the Country—Hurrah! Hurrah!" 1909; "Play a Simple Melody," 1914, "Snookey Ookums," 1913; That International Rag," 1913; "When I Lost You," 1912; and "When the Midnight Choo-Choo Leaves for Alabam'" (1912). That is an astonishingly low number considering how many wonderful songs he wrote during those early years.

Historian Charles Hamm has written that while "many of Berlin's . . . novelties appear insensitive and even offensive today, they were written in a different social climate," and there is no anger or hatred expressed in any of them. Humor, for racial and ethnic groups, was an important part of being initiated into the dominant Anglo-American culture. Hamm adds that these songs "carry the message just beneath the surface of their stereotyping, jesting and exaggeration, that American society—at least in New York City—was made up of peoples of varying racial and ethnic backgrounds, interacting with one another and finding some measure of common cause against those who would deny them full access to the American dream."

Eubie Blake (1883–1983), the great African-American ragtime and theater composer and pianist, knew Berlin during those early years. "I was playing piano in the summer of 1911 in Atlantic City," Blake recalled during a conversation we had during the 1960s. "I was working at a place called The Boat House. Sophie Tucker introduced me to him. When he said, 'Hey Eubie! Give me my song, kid!' I knew what he was talking about and I played 'Alexander's Ragtime Band.' I helped make it popular in Atlantic City. Izzy—we called him Izzy then—my partner Noble Sissle and I, many of us, also wrote songs that you couldn't write today. But they are a part of our history and we can't forget that."

Broadway naturally beckoned to Berlin. In 1914, after a number of his songs had already been interpolated in pre–World War I productions, he wrote his first complete Broadway score—*Watch Your Step*, which introduced "Simple Mel-ody." A year later he was back with *Stop! Look! Listen!*, which included such favorites as "I Love a Piano," "The Girl on the Magazine Cover," and "Everything in America Is Ragtime."

America's involvement in the war elicited many first-rate efforts from Berlin, most remarkable of which was his score for the Army revue *Yip, Yip, Yaphank*, featuring a cast of 350 doughboys from Camp Upton, Long Island. Among them was draftee-composer-lyricist Irving Berlin, who, early in the second act, sang his memorable solo "Oh! How I Hate to Get Up in the Morning," that universal lament of everyone who has ever been blasted prematurely from the arms of Morpheus. (Berlin's legendary contributions to America's war efforts culminated in *This Is the Army*, 1942, which he felt was personally and artistically the greatest experience of his life.)

After World War I, Berlin contributed generously to the *Ziegfeld Follies* of 1919 and 1920 (including the *Follies* theme song, "A Pretty Girl Is Like a Melody"). By 1921, he owned a publishing company and a theater, the Music Box, which remains one of the crown jewels of Broadway and for which he wrote four annual editions (1921–1924) of *Irving Berlin's Music Box Revue*. (The theater's theme song, "Say It with Music," made its appearance in the first of them.) The four *Music Box* shows were among the finest and most successful of revues assembled during this great age of the revue.

The 1920s also saw the creation of many of the greatest Berlin ballads: "What'll I Do?," "All Alone," "Remember," and "Always," written in 1925, which was a wedding present to Berlin's wife, the former Ellin Mackay. His friend Cole Porter aptly defined "a Berlin ballad" as "the top."

Over the next four decades, Berlin went on to continued triumphs. There were such fabulous shows as *Ziegfeld Follies of 1927*, *Face the Music* (1932), *As Thousands Cheer* (1933), *Louisiana Purchase* (1940), *This Is the Army* (1942), *Annie Get Your Gun* (1946), and *Call Me Madam* (1950). Berlin also wrote such memorable film scores as *Puttin' on the Ritz* (1929), *Top Hat* (1935), *Follow the Fleet* (1936), *On the Avenue* (1937), *Carefree* (1938), *Holiday Inn* (1942), and *Easter Parade* (1948).

As time passed, more and more of his songs were recognized as classics. He was astonished to see recordings of his work make the classical record charts, and he was amazed to learn that the words and music of his treasured miniatures had become the subject of school papers and master's and doctoral dissertations. Long before his death, he had been acknowledged as a great American master. And the popularity of his work continues.

Early in the morning of his one hundredth birthday, a group of friends and well-wishers stood outside Berlin's Beekman Place home in Manhattan and serenaded him quietly with "Happy Birthday" and his own "Always." He had been accorded the kind of tribute that Italian music lovers had given to Giuseppe Verdi, and he deserved no less for the lovely todays and tomorrows his work has brought to all of us.

. . .

My first telephone conversation with him was largely about his close friend and colleague Cole Porter. He greatly enjoyed *Cole*, the book I edited with Brendan Gill in 1971, and called to express his appreciation and to reminisce about Porter. "We met during World War I," he told me. "I think it was at a party given in Greenwich Village by the theater producer Bessie Marbury. He played the piano and sang some of his own songs and surprised me by knowing many of my songs, including quite a few of my big catalogue of non-hits. Cole could write easily in any style and could parody anything. I used to plead with him not to write like me or anybody else. 'Write in your own style,' I often said to him."

"Cole and Linda Porter," he said, "were among our best friends. When Ellin and I got married and went over to Europe—we wanted to get away from all the publicity over our marriage—it was the Porters who looked after us in Paris and introduced us to their friends and protected us as best they could from reporters and photographers."

Over the years (Berlin and I were telephone friends for nearly twenty of them), people often asked what he was like. The restless energy I had encountered when I met him in 1962 at a performance of his musical *Mr. President* at Washington's National Theater was one of the first things that came to mind. He was down-to-earth and easy to talk to, smart, funny,

shrewd, curious, enthusiastic, volatile. His interest in others was genuine; he was a big fan of people he liked and had an excellent memory, but only rarely chose to reminisce. His language was blunt, colorful, and occasionally peppered with profanity. He got upset when he thought people were trying to take advantage of him or were challenging his right to make artistic and business decisions about his own songs. Yet when artists performed his songs well or individuals wrote books or articles that he enjoyed, he was more than appreciative; his enthusiasm was heartwarming and deeply moving. All of us who were ever thanked by Irving Berlin know how deeply he expressed his gratitude.

Ideas, brainstorms—or angles as he liked to call them—poured out of him even in the final years of his life. His fellow composer and good friend Harold Arlen said that Berlin sent things airborne as if they were balloons and then usually popped them very quickly. When he heard singer Joan Morris's overdub of the countermelody to the refrain of "Pack Up Your Sins and Go to the Devil," he became excited for a couple of days about putting together an album of his double songs—and then something else drew his attention.

He loved newspapers. He had sold copies of the *New York World* as a boy, often shivering through the wintry Gotham days, and newspapers played a big role in such shows as *As Thousands Cheer* and *Miss Liberty*. Veteran New York publicist Gary Stevens, who first met Berlin in 1941, remembers seeing him in front of Lindy's. "He asked me to come in and sit down with him," Stevens recalls, "while he went through, page by page, at a very fast clip, all the New York newspapers."

Stevens also tells a story that demonstrates Berlin's humor. "In the mid 1950s," Stevens recalled, "I walked into a Chinese restaurant on West Forty-ninth Street called Sun Luck West. The manager, Tom Chung, asked me a question. He said, 'A man comes here maybe three times a week. I think he must be a big Seventh Avenue manufacturer. He is sitting over there. Do you know him?' I glanced over to the area he pointed out. There was Irving Berlin finishing his dinner in the company of one of his daughters. Seeing that Berlin was just about finished with his meal, I walked over and said hello. He asked me to sit down, whereupon I recounted Chung's conclusion about who Berlin was. He put his glasses down on the table and said, 'Gary, that's very funny. Most people think I look like an accountant.'"

He also was very curious. He always asked what I was working on. When I mentioned Lorenz Hart, he sang "My Funny Valentine" and said he thought it was a perfect lyric. He gave equal praise to Ira Gershwin, offered an expressive interpretation of "A Foggy Day," and wanted to be certain I knew how great George Gershwin and his brother Ira were.

He particularly loved Jerome Robbins. "He knew how to correct something that was wrong but he also knew when it was better to leave things alone," commented Berlin about the director-choreographer. Berlin often said that he wanted to write one more show for his beloved Music Box, the Broadway theatre on West Forty-fifth Street that he had built with his partner, producer Sam Harris. While the show never materialized, Berlin had a plan: it would have old songs and new songs, Robbins would direct and choreograph, Arthur Laurents would write the book, and Goddard Lieberson would record it. (Lieberson noted that every time CBS Records—now Sony—which he headed, prepared to undertake a Berlin retrospective, Berlin would encourage it for a while, but ultimtately stop it, saying that it would be his obituary.)

We had many conversations about his shows. He happily agreed to let the Goodspeed Opera House in East Haddam, Connecticut, revive *Louisiana Purchase, Miss Liberty,* and *Face the Music* (the revival of the latter still hasn't happened) and sent me over to the town house he owned at 29 West Forty-sixth Street, which later was to house his music company, to look for the scores for the shows. There was no electricity on the top floor where the music was stored. I brought a large flashlight and wore old clothes. On the cluttered, dusty floors were battered file boxes, suitcases, steamer trunks, and old steel cabinets that housed the songs and memorabilia of his extraordinary career. After various visits Ernie, from Mr. Berlin's shipping department, and I carried some of the music back to the music company offices.

Although Mr. Berlin was cautious in allowing his lesser-known works to be heard again, preferring instead to champion his huge roster of hits, he gradually yielded to entreaties from me and others to encourage a wider rediscovery to take place. While he did not see the Goodspeed's revivals, for example, he was happy with the results, the positive press reports, and the good word-of-mouth.

Of course, he continued to nurture his standards. Every year, at Christmastime, he called daily to check the sales figures for "White Christmas," comparing them to results from past years. As he grew older, he continued to run his business as he had for decades. Entering the office was like being transformed into a time capsule, complete with old switchboard and stockroom. Most of his staff, including his secretary and office manager Hilda Schneider and his chief arranger Helmy Kresa (who had been with him since 1926) had grown old with him. He said that building his own business, the Irving Berlin Music Company, and gradually reacquiring all his earlier copyrights were among the smartest things he had done. When he was too frail to come to his office, his associates brought checks and papers for him to sign at his home on Beekman Place, where he and his wife lived in virtual seclusion, seeking the privacy they had craved when as a young married couple their romance had been one of the most publicized events of the 1920s. "We had more press attention at that time," he said, "than anyone could have wanted for a lifetime."

• • •

Once, when Berlin was in his early nineties, we had a long talk about what had happened to American popular music since the late fifties and early sixties. Berlin, who had thought about this a great deal, simply said, "It was as if I owned a store and people no longer wanted to buy what I had to sell." His daughter Mary Ellin Barrett recorded his comment in her book, *Irving Berlin: A Daughter's Memoir:* "Everything changed. The world was a different place. The death of President Kennedy, the Vietnam War, the social protest. Music changed, too. The Beatles and other groups reached audiences. I couldn't. It was time to close up shop."

• • •

Robert Gottlieb has been my editor and friend for over twenty years. When we began work on what became *The Complete Lyrics of Cole Porter*, first published in 1983, he said there should be a series of the complete works of the great lyricists. When I mentioned this to Mr. Berlin and asked his permission to compile his lyrics for publication, he said, perhaps surprisingly, "All right, but not while I'm alive. When I'm gone, work with my wife and daughters." With his characteristic curiosity, the ninety-something Berlin fired many questions at me when the Cole Porter book was published. How would a publisher undertake such a book, he wanted to know; how would it be compiled and edited and produced.

The unusually large size of this book is a reflection of an extraordinary career that spanned more than eighty years and produced more than 1,250 lyrics, including 400 or so previously unpublished. They were gathered from the Berlin office files, published sheet music, unpublished copyright song files, and unpublished, uncopyrighted files. Some were found in a collection of manuscripts kept in a bank vault. Others came from scripts and recordings and from show and film files that included numbers not used in the productions. A few were located in Berlin's extensive office scrapbooks. Still others came from collectors. Many are individual songs from Berlin's Tin Pan Alley life. Those written for shows and films appear for the most part in the order in which they were first performed. Dropped and deleted songs follow the used material.

Hilda Schneider and I often spoke of her boss's aproval of a posthumous collection of his lyrics, and after his death she began work on it. (Hilda worked for Mr. Berlin for nearly fifty years, starting as a production secretary for *This Is the Army*.) So too did Linda Emmet, Mr. Berlin's middle daughter, who lives in Paris but commutes to New York for monthly family meetings. We began the project in 1991 with Hilda gathering and typing all of the approximately eight hundred published lyrics. Before Hilda's illness became terminal (she died of cancer in 1993), she started organizing and typing lyrics from the massive unpublished song files she had watched over for decades in her office. Soon after Berlin's death, his daughters, with their typical generosity and sense of responsibility, decided to donate his song, production, and business files to the Music Division of the Library of Congress. Their gift was announced at a 1992 Library ceremony.

—Robert Kimball

Chronology

1888

MAY 11   Israel Beilin is born in Russia to Moses Beilin, a cantor, and his wife, Leah Lipkin. His date of birth is approximate due to differences between the Julian and Gregorian calendars in the nineteenth century. Although the Beilin family is from Tolochin in Byelorussia, there is reason to believe that Israel's birthplace may have been Tyumen in Western Siberia.

1893

SEPTEMBER 23   Israel Beilin arrives in New York with his parents and six siblings (his eldest brother stays in Russia) aboard the S.S. *Rhynland*.

1893–1900

Upon arrival in New York, the family's name changes to Baline. The Balines live briefly on Monroe Street, then move to a tenement at 330 Cherry Street.

Israel Baline attends P.S. 147 on Monroe Street. After school he works at odd jobs—selling newspapers and peddling junk in a wheelbarrow.

1901

JULY 21   Moses Baline dies.

1901–1904

Israel Baline quits school and leaves home. He becomes a busker (street singer) and works for a time with Blind Saul.

1905

Israel Baline is hired by songwriter-publisher Harry Von Tilzer to plug songs at Tony Pastor's Music Hall on Fourteenth Street.

1906

Israel Baline works as a singing waiter at Mike Salter's Pelham Café in Chinatown. He begins writing parody lyrics.

1907

Israel Baline writes lyric (music by Mike Nicholson) of his first published song, "Marie from Sunny Italy." He earns 37 cents in royalties and changes his name to Irving Berlin.

1908

Irving Berlin works as singing waiter at Jimmy Kelly's in Union Square.

Irving Berlin writes "The Best of Friends Must Part," the first song for which he has written music and lyrics.

1909

Irving Berlin writes "Dorando." He leaves Jimmy Kelly's.

Irving Berlin is hired by Ted Snyder Co., music publishers at 112 West Thirty-eighth Street, Manhattan, as an in-house lyric writer. He begins collaboration with Ted Snyder. Berlin writes two of the year's popular successes: "My Wife's Gone to the Country (Hurrah! Hurrah!)" and "That Mesmerizing Mendelssohn Tune."

1910

Irving Berlin and Ted Snyder appear in *Up and Down Broadway* at the Casino Theatre, New York. They introduce "Oh, That Beautiful Rag" and "Sweet Italian Love."

APRIL   Irving Berlin writes "Call Me Up Some Rainy Afternoon," his first number-one-selling song.

1911

MARCH 28   "Alexander's Ragtime Band" is published.

APRIL   "Alexander's Ragtime Band" is introduced by Emma Corus in Chicago.

MAY 28   Irving Berlin sings "Alexander's Ragtime Band" at the Friars Club Fourth Annual Frolic.

JUNE 26   Irving Berlin contributes four songs to the *Ziegfeld Follies of 1911*.

The year's songs include: "Everybody's Doin' It Now."

Irving Berlin moves to apartment at 854 Hewitt Place, the Bronx.

1912

JANUARY   Name of Ted Snyder Company changed to Waterson, Berlin & Snyder.

FEBRUARY 2   Irving Berlin marries Dorothy Goetz, sister of songwriter E. Ray Goetz.

Irving and Dorothy Berlin take an apartment at 346 West Seventy-second Street.

JULY 17   Dorothy Berlin dies of typhoid fever contracted in Cuba on their honeymoon.

NOVEMBER 8   Irving Berlin writes "When I Lost You," his first important ballad.

NOVEMBER   Irving Berlin becomes a partner of the publishing house Waterson, Berlin & Snyder.

Songs include: "When the Midnight Choo-Choo Leaves for Alabam'."

1913

Irving Berlin moves to apartment at 235 West Seventy-first Street.

Irving Berlin travels to London. He is fêted as the "King of Ragtime."

JULY 7 Irving Berlin is featured in the revue *Hello Ragtime* at the Hippodrome Theatre, London. He introduces "That International Rag."

OCTOBER 19 The Friars Club in New York gives a dinner honoring Irving Berlin.

1914

Irving Berlin becomes a charter member of ASCAP.

MAY Waterson, Berlin & Snyder moves offices to Strand Theatre Building at Broadway and Forty-seventh Street in Manhattan.

DECEMBER Berlin opens Irving Berlin, Inc., at 1571 Broadway, the Strand Theatre Building.

DECEMBER 8 Opening of *Watch Your Step* at the New Amsterdam Theatre, New York: Irving Berlin's first complete musical score for theatre. It includes "Simple Melody (Musical Demon)."

1915

MAY 4 *Watch Your Step* opens at the Empire Theatre in London.

DECEMBER 25 Opening of *Stop! Look! Listen!* at the Globe Theatre, New York. Score includes "I Love a Piano" and "The Girl on the Magazine Cover."

1916

FEBRUARY 19 *Follow the Crowd*, the English title of *Stop! Look! Listen!* opens at the Empire Theatre, London.

NOVEMBER 6 *The Century Girl*, a revue written in collaboration with Victor Herbert, opens in New York.

1917

Irving Berlin establishes his own publishing house: Irving Berlin, Inc., at 1571 Broadway. He moves to apartment at 30 West Seventieth Street.

1918

FEBRUARY 26 Irving Berlin becomes a citizen of the United States.

Irving Berlin contributes songs to *The Canary*, a musical comedy.

MAY 8 Irving Berlin is inducted into the United States Army with the rank of private. He writes

army show *Yip, Yip, Yaphank* at Camp Upton, New York.

AUGUST 19 *Yip, Yip, Yaphank* opens at the Century Theatre, New York. Irving Berlin appears in the show and introduces "Oh! How I Hate to Get Up in the Morning."

1919

JANUARY 16 Irving Berlin is honorably discharged from the U.S. Army.

JUNE Irving Berlin, Inc., moves offices to 1587 Broadway, also at Broadway and Forty-seventh Street.

Irving Berlin writes most of the score for the *Ziegfeld Follies of 1919*, including "A Pretty Girl Is Like a Melody."

1920

Irving Berlin and Sam Harris become partners and build the Music Box Theatre in New York.

Irving Berlin contributes songs to the *Ziegfeld Follies of 1920*.

Irving Berlin makes frequent trips to London and Paris in 1920 and during the next few years. In Paris, he meets Les Six (the six French composers Georges Auric, Louis Durey, Arthur Honegger, Darius Milhaud, Francis Poulenc, and Germaine Tailleferre).

SEPTEMBER 22 Irving Berlin becomes a member of SACEM (the French Society of Authors, Composers, and Publishers).

1921

APRIL Irving Berlin, Inc., moves to 1607 Broadway.

SEPTEMBER 22 The *Music Box Revue of 1921* opens at the newly completed Music Box Theatre, New York. The score includes "Say It with Music" and "Everybody Step."

Irving Berlin buys a house at 29 West Forty-sixth Street.

1922

JULY 21 Leah Baline dies.

OCTOBER 22 The *Music Box Revue of 1922* opens at the Music Box Theatre, New York. The score includes "Lady of the Evening" and "Pack Up Your Sins and Go to the Devil."

1923

SEPTEMBER 22 The *Music Box Revue of 1923* opens at the Music Box Theatre, New York.

1924

MAY Irving Berlin meets Ellin Mackay, daughter of Clarence Mackay and Katherine Duer Blake.

Gilbert Seldes includes a profile of Irving Berlin in his book *The Seven Lively Arts*.

DECEMBER 1 The *Music Box Revue of 1924* opens at the Music Box Theatre.

Year's songs include "All Alone" and "What'll I Do."

1925

Publication of Alexander Woollcott's biography *The Story of Irving Berlin*.

DECEMBER 8 *The Cocoanuts* opens in New York.

Year's songs include "Always" and "Remember."

1926

JANUARY 4 Irving Berlin and Ellin Mackay are married at City Hall, New York.

JANUARY 8 Ellin and Irving Berlin sail for Europe aboard the S.S. *Leviathan*. After a month's honeymoon in Madeira, Portugal, the Berlins live in London and Paris for nearly eight months.

AUGUST Irving and Ellin Berlin return to New York.

OCTOBER–NOVEMBER The Berlins live at the Warwick Hotel in Manhattan.

NOVEMBER 25 Birth of daughter Mary Ellin Berlin.

NOVEMBER–DECEMBER The Berlins move to Irving Berlin's bachelor apartment at 29 West Forty-sixth Street in Manhattan shortly after the birth of their daughter Mary Ellin.

DECEMBER 28 "Blue Skies" is interpolated into the Ziegfeld show *Betsy*. It is introduced by Belle Baker.

1927

JANUARY–MARCH The Berlins spend part of the winter in Palm Beach, Florida.

APRIL–MAY The Berlins return briefly to 29 West Forty-sixth Street.

JUNE–SEPTEMBER   Irving Berlin rents house in Dobbs Ferry, New York.

AUGUST 16   The *Ziegfeld Follies of 1927*, with complete score by Irving Berlin, opens in New York. Songs include "Shakin' the Blues Away."

SEPTEMBER–DECEMBER   The Berlins return to the Warwick Hotel in Manhattan.

Year's songs include "Russian Lullaby" and "The Song Is Ended."

Al Jolson sings "Blue Skies" in first full-length-soundtrack film, *The Jazz Singer*.

1928

JANUARY–JUNE   The Berlins move to California. They rent houses in Palm Springs and Santa Monica.

MARCH 20   *The Cocoanuts* opens at the Garrick Theatre, London.

JUNE–SEPTEMBER   The Berlins rent a summer house in Port Washington, New York.

OCTOBER   The Berlins move to a rented house at 9 Sutton Place, Manhattan, where they live until June 1929.

Irving Berlin writes story outline for *Mr. Bones*, an unproduced ragtime opera.

Irving Berlin writes the theme songs for the films *The Awakening, Coquette,* and *Lady of the Pavement*.

DECEMBER 1   Birth of son Irving Berlin Jr.

DECEMBER 24   Irving Berlin Jr. dies and is buried at Woodlawn Cemetery, New York.

1929

Ellin and Irving Berlin spend a two-month summer holiday in Europe, including visits to Paris, Venice, and Baden-Baden, Germany.

SEPTEMBER   The Berlins return to California. They rent a house in Hollywood and live there until May 1930.

Irving Berlin writes two songs for the film *Hallelujah*.

Irving Berlin writes the score, which includes "Let Me Sing and I'm Happy," for the film *Mammy*.

Irving Berlin writes four songs, including "Puttin' on the Ritz," for the film *Puttin' on the Ritz*.

1930

Irving Berlin writes the score for the film *Reaching for the Moon*. With the exception of two songs, the entire score is cut from the film before it is released because movie musicals have become temporarily unpopular.

The Berlins move back to the Warwick Hotel in Manhattan, where they live on and off until November 1931.

1931

The Berlins move to penthouse apartment at 130 East End Avenue.

1932

FEBRUARY 17   *Face the Music* opens in New York. The score includes "Let's Have Another Cup of Coffee," "Manhattan Madness," and "Soft Lights and Sweet Music."

FEBRUARY 21   Birth of daughter Linda Louise Berlin.

Songs include "How Deep Is the Ocean" and "Say It Isn't So."

1933

MARCH   Irving Berlin, Inc., moves offices to 799 Seventh Avenue.

SEPTEMBER 30   *As Thousands Cheer* opens at the Music Box Theatre, New York. The score includes "Easter Parade," "Heat Wave," and "Supper Time."

NOVEMBER   Ellin and Irving Berlin and George, Leonore, and Ira Gershwin take a cruise to the West Indies.

1934

MAY–JUNE   Irving Berlin contributes material and appears on the Gulf Radio Shows.

MAY 28   Irving Berlin is on the cover of *Time* magazine.

Irving Berlin and Moss Hart embark on a working vacation sailing the Mediterranean. They begin writing *More Cheers*, a successor to *As Thousands Cheer*, but do not finish it.

1935

FEBRUARY 21   *Stop Press*, the English version of *As Thousands Cheer*, opens at the Adelphi Theatre in London.

MAY–SEPTEMBER   The Berlins rent a house for the summer in Santa Monica, California.

AUGUST 29   New York premiere of the film *Top Hat*. Score includes "Cheek to Cheek," "Isn't It a Lovely Day," and "Top Hat, White Tie and Tails."

1936

FEBRUARY 20   New York premiere of the film *Follow the Fleet*. The score includes "I'm Putting All My Eggs in One Basket," "I'd Rather Lead a Band," and "Let's Face the Music and Dance."

JUNE 16   Birth of daughter Elizabeth Irving Berlin.

Ellin and Irving Berlin take a summer holiday in Europe. It includes visits to Venice and Budapest.

1937

FEBRUARY 4   New York premiere of *On the Avenue*. The score includes "I've Got My Love to Keep Me Warm" and "Slumming on Park Avenue."

JUNE–SEPTEMBER   The Berlins spend the summer in a rented house on the beach in Santa Monica, California.

AUGUST   Irving Berlin charters a boat and takes his family to Alaska on a three-week fishing holiday.

1938

Irving Berlin writes material for a new, but never produced, *Music Box Revue* project.

AUGUST 3   Gala radio tribute on WABC to celebrate Irving Berlin's fiftieth birthday.

AUGUST 16   Release of the film *Alexander's Ragtime Band*. Score includes "Now It Can Be Told."

SEPTEMBER 2   Release of the film *Carefree*. The score includes "Change Partners" and "I Used to Be Color Blind."

SEPTEMBER–OCTOBER   Irving Berlin is in England for the United Kingdom premiere of the film *Alexander's Ragtime Band*.

NOVEMBER 10   "God Bless America" is introduced by Kate Smith on her Armistice Day radio program.

DECEMBER   Irving Berlin buys a country house in Lew Beach, New York.

1939

JULY 14   Release of the film *Second Fiddle*.

OCTOBER   Berlins move to house at 129 East Seventy-eighth Street.

1940

MAY 28   *Louisiana Purchase* opens at the Imperial Theatre, New York. The score includes "It's a Lovely Day Tomorrow."

JUNE   Irving Berlin receives an honorary doctorate of music from Bucknell University.

1941

Film version of *Louisiana Purchase* is released.

Irving Berlin writes three songs for the war effort and donates the royalties to the following organizations: the American Red Cross ("Angels of Mercy"); the Treasury Department ("Any Bonds Today"); and the Ordnance Department ("Arms for the Love of America").

1942

APRIL   Irving Berlin moves to Camp Upton, New York, and begins to work on *This Is the Army*.

JULY 4   *This Is the Army* opens at the Broadway Theatre, New York. Irving Berlin appears in the show and sings "Oh! How I Hate to Get Up in the Morning."

AUGUST 4   New York premiere of *Holiday Inn*. "White Christmas" is introduced in the film by Bing Crosby.

OCTOBER 1   National tour of *This Is the Army* opens at the National Theatre in Washington, D.C.

OCTOBER   Berlins move to apartment at 1 Gracie Square.

1943

APRIL   Irving Berlin receives an Oscar for "White Christmas" (Best Song) from the film *Holiday Inn*.

JULY 28   Premiere of film version of *This Is the Army*.

NOVEMBER 10   The stage version of *This Is the Army* opens at the Palladium in London.

1944

FEBRUARY   Final performance of *This Is the Army* in the United Kingdom.

MARCH 3   *This Is the Army* opens at the Teatro San Carlo in Naples, Italy.

JULY 23   Italian tour of *This Is the Army* ends in Bari. Irving Berlin leaves tour temporarily and returns to New York.

SEPTEMBER   Irving Berlin severs publishing relationship with his business partner Saul Bornstein and establishes the Irving Berlin Music Company.

NOVEMBER   The Irving Berlin Music Company opens at 1650 Broadway.

1945

JANUARY   Irving Berlin rejoins the *This Is the Army* tour in New Guinea.

MARCH 24   The South Pacific tour of *This Is the Army* ends in the Philippines. Irving Berlin returns to the United States.

JUNE–SEPTEMBER   The Berlins spend the summer in Beverly Hills, California.

OCTOBER   Irving Berlin is given the Medal of Merit by President Harry S. Truman.

1946

MAY 16   *Annie Get Your Gun* opens at the Imperial Theatre, New York. The score includes "There's No Business like Show Business."

JUNE–SEPTEMBER   The Berlins rent a house in Bermuda.

OCTOBER 16   New York premiere of the film *Blue Skies*. The score includes "You Keep Coming Back Like a Song."

Irving Berlin buys a house at 17 Beekman Place.

1947

JUNE 7   *Annie Get Your Gun* opens at the Coliseum Theatre in London.

JUNE–SEPTEMBER   The Berlins return to Santa Monica, where they spend the summer in a rented house on the beach.

DECEMBER   The Berlins move to 17 Beekman Place.

DECEMBER   Irving Berlin takes his wife and daughter Mary Ellin to Mexico for the Christmas holiday. Berlin meets the painters Diego Rivera and Jose Clemente Orozco.

1948

JUNE 30   New York premiere of the film *Easter Parade*. The score includes "Steppin' Out with My Baby."

Irving Berlin works on the unproduced show *Stars on My Shoulders*.

JULY 3   May Ellin Berlin marries Dennis Burden. Marriage later dissolved.

DECEMBER   Irving Berlin, accompanied by his wife, travels to Berlin, Germany, with Bob Hope, to entertain U.S. troops during the airlift.

1949

JULY 15   *Miss Liberty* opens at the Imperial Theatre, New York.

OCTOBER 18   Irving Berlin receives the Legion d'Honneur from the French government.

DECEMBER   Ellin and Irving Berlin and their daughters Linda and Elizabeth fly to Paris and Rome for the holidays.

1950

FEBRUARY 19   *Annie du Far West* opens at the Théâtre du Chatelet in Paris.

Irving Berlin flies to Paris and attends performance of *Annie du Far West*. He and his friend Irving Hoffman spend a brief holiday in Antibes. They meet Pablo Picasso and Françoise Gilot on Picasso's private beach.

Film version of *Annie Get Your Gun* is released.

OCTOBER 12   *Call Me Madam* opens at the Imperial Theatre, New York. The score includes "You're Just in Love" and "They Like Ike."

1951

MARCH–APRIL   Irving and Ellin Berlin, accompanied by their daughter Elizabeth, spend spring vacation in Cuba and Haiti.

Irving Berlin receives a Tony Award for the musical score of *Call Me Madam*.

1952

Irving Berlin writes new lyric "I Like Ike" for Dwight D. Eisenhower's presidential campaign.

MARCH 15   *Call Me Madam* opens at the Coliseum Theatre, London.

OCTOBER 14   Mary Ellin Berlin marries Marvin Barrett.

NOVEMBER   Irving Berlin starts preliminary work on the unproduced show *Palm Beach*, based on Cleveland Amory's book *The Last Resorts*.

DECEMBER   The Berlins, accompanied by their daughter Linda, fly to Sicily and spend Christmas with Mary Ellin and her husband.

1953

Film version of *Call Me Madam* is released.

NOVEMBER 11   Birth of granddaughter Elizabeth Esther Barrett.

1954

APRIL   Ellin and Irving Berlin, accompanied by their daughters Mary Ellin and Linda, and their son-in-law Marvin Barrett, fly to Madrid and spend spring holiday in Spain.

MAY 1   Irving Berlin receives an honorary degree from Temple University.

JULY 22   Irving Berlin is given the Congressional Medal of Honor by President Dwight D. Eisenhower.

Film *White Christmas* is released.

Release of film *There's No Business Like Show Business*.

1955

MAY 20   Birth of grandson Irving Berlin Barrett.

Irving Berlin works on unproduced show *Sentimental Guy*, based on *The Legendary Mizners* by Alva Johnston.

1956

Irving Berlin continues work on *Sentimental Guy*.

AUGUST 24   Birth of granddaughter Mary Ellin Barrett.

1957

"Sayonara," originally intended as part of the score of a book musical, is featured in the film *Sayonara*.

1959

APRIL 11   Linda Berlin marries Edouard Emmet.

1960

MARCH 14   Birth of granddaughter Katherine Leah Barrett.

1961

DECEMBER   Ellin and Irving Berlin spend Christmas in Paris with their daughter Linda and her husband.

1962

OCTOBER 20   *Mr. President* opens at the Imperial Theatre, New York.

DECEMBER   Ellin and Irving Berlin return to Paris for Christmas holiday with Linda and Edouard Emmet.

1963

Irving Berlin starts work on film project *Say It with Music* for MGM.

JULY 31   Birth of granddaughter Caroline Case Emmet.

AUGUST   Irving Berlin Music Company moves offices to 1290 Avenue of the Americas, between Fifty-first and Fifty-second Streets in Manhattan.

SEPTEMBER   Ellin and Irving Berlin travel to London for the wedding of their daughter Elizabeth to Edmund Fisher (marriage later dissolved).

1965

FEBRUARY 27   Birth of granddaughter Elizabeth Clare Fisher.

1966

MARCH 7   Death of Elizabeth Clare Fisher.

MARCH 15   Birth of granddaughter Ellen Emmet.

Revival of *Annie Get Your Gun* at New York State Theater at Lincoln Center, New York. Irving Berlin writes "An Old-Fashioned Wedding" for this production.

1967

JANUARY 7   Birth of granddaughter Emily Anstice Fisher.

1968

MAY 11   Irving Berlin is honored on a ninety-minute television tribute by Ed Sullivan.

MAY 22   Birth of grandson Edward Watson Emmet.

DECEMBER   Ellin and Irving Berlin fly to Paris for Christmas holiday with Linda and Edouard Emmet and their family.

1969

APRIL   MGM cancels production of *Say It with Music*.

JUNE 7   Irving Berlin receives an honorary degree from Fordham University.

1970

FEBRUARY 27   Elizabeth Berlin marries Alton Peters.

DECEMBER 13   Birth of granddaughter Rachel Canfield Peters.

1973

Irving Berlin sings "God Bless America" at a White House dinner honoring returning American prisoners of war from Vietnam. It is his last public appearance.

1977

JANUARY 10   Irving Berlin is given the Medal of Freedom by President Gerald Ford.

1986

MARCH   The television documentary *Irving Berlin's America* is broadcast on PBS.

Irving Berlin is one of twelve naturalized Americans to receive the Liberty Medal from President Ronald Reagan in celebration of the Statue of Liberty's hundredth anniversary.

1988

Irving Berlin Music Company moves its offices to Berlin's townhouse at 29 West Forty-sixth Street.

MAY 11   ASCAP tribute at Carnegie Hall to celebrate Irving Berlin's one hundredth birthday.

JULY 29   Ellin Berlin dies and is buried at Woodlawn Cemetery.

1989

FEBRUARY 26   Irving Berlin's song "Mr. Monotony" is introduced in *Jerome Robbins Broadway*.

SEPTEMBER 22   Irving Berlin dies at 17 Beekman Place and is buried at Woodlawn Cemetery.

1990

FEBRUARY 6   ASCAP memorial tribute at the Music Box Theatre, New York.

Acknowledgments

The editors, who have "plenty to be thankful for," express their gratitude for assistance in the preparation of this vast compilation to Hilda Schneider, secretary to Irving Berlin, who worked closely with us until shortly before she died in 1993. She was responsible for preserving the archival materials that document Berlin's life and work and for typing most of the lyrics that appear in this book. Sharing top billing with Hilda are the estate and family of Irving Berlin, notably Berlin's son-in-law Alton Peters who, until his death in May 1999, shepherded this endeavor and gave constant encouragement to the editors; daughter Mary Ellin Barrett, who carefully read the manuscript and page proofs and offered many helpful suggestions; daughter Elizabeth Peters for her wise counsel; son-in-law Edouard Emmet for his patience and editorial aid; son-in-law Marvin Barrett for his inspiration and guidance; granddaughter Ellin Emmet for her work on the book during its early stages; Robert J. Laughlin, Vice President of the Morgan Guaranty Trust Company, who guides the Estate of Irving Berlin for J. P. Morgan, and his predecessor, Frederic B. Ingraham, for all they have done to make this book possible.

Special thanks also to Amy Asch, archivist of the Irving Berlin Music Company, for her expert knowledge of the Berlin catalogue and her help in song and photo research; to Claudia Arenas and Caroline Shookhoff for their typing of the manuscript; to our many friends at the Rodgers and Hammerstein Organization, who manage the Irving Berlin Music Company: Theodore S. Chapin, President and Executive Director, and his colleagues Maxyne Lang, Victoria Traube, Bert Fink, Robin Walton, Vincent Scuderi, Flora Griggs, Jamie Polon, Bruce Pomahac, Cynthia Boyle, Tracy Burke, Kara Darling, D. Michael Dvorchak, Nicole

Harman, Michel Hidalgo, Juliet Abbott, Audrey Arnold, Wayne Blood, Tom Briggs, Kevin Cruse, Nancy DiTuro, John Elmer, Kathleen McCullough, Gina Scalia, and Charles Scatamacchia; to the Music Division of the Library of Congress, stewards of the Irving Berlin Collection: notably, Jon Newsom, Elizabeth H. Auman, Raymond White, Mark Eden Horowitz, and Thomas P. Barrick; to Miles Kreuger and the Institute of the American Musical for his prodigious knowledge of film and theater history, which he happily shared; to Charles Hamm for his trailblazing scholarship and his superb editing of early Berlin songs; to collectors James J. Fuld, Michael Feinstein, and Harvey Granat for sharing their lyric discoveries; to the Kimball family, Abigail, Philip, and Miranda, for their indispensable assistance at many stages; to the staff of the Billy Rose Theater Collection at the New York Library for the Performing Arts: led by Bob Taylor and including Sylvia Alicea, Dawnsheri Arroyo, David Bartholomew, Jacquin Bignon, Rod Bladel, Philip Craig, Pat Darby, Rosario De Jesus, Carmela Dee, Rhony Dostaly, Elisabeth Elkind, Christopher Frith, Patrick Hoffman, Nailah Holmes, Susan McArthur, Christine Karatnytsky, Ronald Limage, Mark Maniak, Annette Marotta, Jeremy Megraw, William Charles Morrow, Karen Nickeson, Brian O'Connell, Daniel Patri, Louis Paul, Mary Ellen Rogan, Amy Schwegel, Devin Slaton, Charles Squire, and Olive Wong; to archivist Maryann Chach and her colleagues at the Shubert Archive: Mark Swartz, Reagan Fletcher, and Sylvia Wang; to Judith B. Schiff and Richard Warren, Jr. of the Yale University Library; to Marty Jacobs and Marguerite Lavin of the Museum of the City of New York; to Geraldine Duclow of the Free Library of Philadelphia; to Jeanne Newlin of the Harvard University Library; to Stewart Desmond of the New-York Historical Society; to the Theatre Library in London, the American Library in Paris, and the New York Society Library; to photographer Pat Cuomo for his professional services and for important aid and permissions in photo research; to Culver Pictures, Inc. (Peter Tomlinson), the Kobal Collections (Bob Cosenza), Photofest (Ron Mandelbaum), and Magnum (Natasha O'Connor); also to a number of other individuals who helped along the way: Fred Astaire, Alan Anderson, Paulette Attie, Robert Baral, Robert Russell Bennett, Robert Barlow, Ken Bloom, William Bolcom, Gerald Bordman, Richard Brown, Carol Bruce, Rosemary Clooney, Bradford Conner, Robert Cornfield, Anna Crouse, Barry Daugherty, Lee Davis, Caroline Emmet, Edward and Jody Emmet, Ian Marshall Fisher, Philip Furia, Mark Trent Goldberg, Herbert Goldman, Mynna Granat, Stanley Green, Mary Cleere Haran, Kitty Carlisle Hart, Marilyn Horne, Dick Hyman, Edward Jablonski, Stacey Jackson, Stephen Kahan, Tom Lawson, Robert Lissauer, Tracy Loskoski, Alan Manson, Susannah McCorkle, Allyn Ann McLerie, Janet Merrill, Max Morath, Joan Morris, John Mueller, Russell Nype, Michael Price, Jack Raymond, Jerome Robbins, Bertram Ross, Anne Kaufman Schneider, Benjamin Sears, Anne Phipps Sidamon-Eristoff, Donald J. Stubblebine, John Wallowitch, Joel Whitburn, and Robert White. Finally, our deepest appreciation to everyone at Alfred A. Knopf who brought this book to life—our editors Robert Gottlieb and Katherine Hourigan, publisher Sonny Mehta, and their colleagues Leyla Aker, Kevin Bourke, Romeo Enriquez, Andy Hughes, Ralph Fowler, Nathan Chaney, Carol Devine Carson, William Loverd, Paul Bogaards, Ken Schneider, Kathryn Zuckerman, Nicholas Latimer, Patrick Dillon, Amy Stackhouse, Lisa Buonaiuto, and Kimo Bentley.

The Complete Lyrics of

IRVING BERLIN

Songs of 1907–1909

MARIE FROM SUNNY ITALY

Irving Berlin's first published song. Copyrighted May 8, 1907. Music by M. Nicholson. Written when Berlin was a singing waiter at "Nigger Mike" Salter's Pelham Cafe at 12 Pell Street in Lower Manhattan, in response to a song called "My Mariucci Take a Steamboat." There is an inscribed photo of a woman on the sheet music cover, signed "Sincerely, Leah Russell."

Irving Berlin, quoted by Ed Sullivan in an undated article from the late 1930s:

I never wanted to be a songwriter. All I wanted in those days was a job in which I could earn $25.00 a week. That was my idea of heaven. But a bartender in another Bowery saloon, Al Piantadosi, had written a song, an Italian type of tune, and "Nigger Mike" sneered at us and asked us why we didn't write something. So Mike Nicholson and myself wrote "Marie from Sunny Italy," and split it 33 cents apiece. That was in 1907. Joe Schenck, the drug clerk around the corner, bought a copy. I think he was the only one.

Irving Berlin, in a letter to Herbert E. Marks, December 6, 1967:

It is true that Julius Saranoff wrote the lead sheet of "Marie from Sunny Italy."

He played the fiddle at Mike Salter's cafe in Chinatown when I worked there as a singing waiter. Mike Nicholson, who wrote the music to the song, was the piano player but he couldn't write [down] the music.

Saranoff was the only one who could do it.

VERSE 1

Oh, Marie,
'Neath the window I'm waiting,
Oh, Marie,
Please don't be so aggravating,
Can't you see my heart just yearns for you, dear,
With fond affection,
And love that's true, dear?
Meet me while the summer moon is beaming,
For you and me the little stars are gleaming.
Please come out tonight, my queen,
Can't you hear my mandolin?

CHORUS

My sweet Marie from sunny Italy,
Oh, how I do love you,
Say that you'll love me, love me, too,
Forevermore I will be true.
Just say the word and I will marry you,

And then you'll surely be,
My sweet Marie from sunny Italy.

VERSE 2

Oh, Marie,
I've been waiting so patiently,
Oh, Marie,
Please come out and I shall happy be.
Raise your window, love, and say you're coming;
The little birds, dear,
Are sweetly humming.
Don't say no, my sweet Italian beauty,
There's not another maiden e'er could suit me.
Come out, love, don't be afraid,
Listen to my serenade,

REPEAT CHORUS

THE BEST OF FRIENDS MUST PART

Published. Copyrighted February 6, 1908. The first song for which Berlin was credited with music as well as lyrics. In a letter to music publisher Leonard Feist (May 13, 1980), Berlin described this as "the second song I wrote." "The only significance this song has," Berlin noted in the same letter, "is that it was published in Tin Pan Alley on 28th Street by the Selig Publishing Company. I think Selig later became a silent movie producer."

VERSE 1

What's that you say?
No work today?
Done lost your job?
Where is your pay?
Been shooting dice?
That's very nice,
Needn't apologize,
I'm cold as ice.
Pack up your clothes,
Lord only knows,
You've been the cause of my troubles and woes.
Don't ask me why,
Too late to cry,
Just bid yourself goodbye.

CHORUS

A friend in need is a friend indeed,
That's just the kind of friend I've been to you.

When poverty smiled down on thee,
I hung around and stuck like glue.
It's a long, long lane that has no turn,
You can never tell your finish when you start.
But when you find you can't make both ends
    meet,
Then the best of friends must part.

VERSE 2

Don't talk of love
Just like a dove,
Can't eat the stars
That shine above.
That stuff don't go,
You'd better blow,
Can't buy a meal with that lovin', you know.
I know it's hard
On your old pard,
But I can't help that you played your last card.
Don't hesitate,
Evaporate,
Hunt up another mate.

REPEAT CHORUS

QUEENIE

Published. Copyrighted February 29, 1908. Music by Maurice Abrahams (1883–1931), also known as Maurice Abrams, who was married to the vaudeville singer Belle Baker. Alternate title: "Queenie (My Own)."

VERSE 1

The moon above
Am shining, love,
I'm out here waiting.
Don't be so shy,
I can't see why,
You're hesitating.
Come out and meet me, lady,
You are my dark-eyed baby.
Come, love, don't be afraidy,
My little honey, do:
Here while the stars are peeping
And all the world am sleeping,
My promise I'll be keeping, love, to you.

CHORUS

Queenie, my own,
I'll build a nice little home

Where we can live all alone
And from you I'll never roam.
Say you'll be mine,
Oh! honey, please don't decline,
And all the stars will then shine
For you and me.

VERSE 2

Impatiently
I wait for thee
Here in the moonlight.
Don't be afraid,
My dusky maid,
This is a spoonlight.
Now, don't be hesitating,
The birds above are mating,
My love, I'll be relating
To you, my dusky queen.
Think, dear, of what you're missing,
Loving and lots of kissing,
Come out, my love, and listen to my plea:

REPEAT CHORUS

DORANDO

Published. Copyrighted March 11, 1909. The first Irving Berlin song to be published by the Ted Snyder Company. It also was the first Berlin song to achieve commercial success. He described how he wrote "Dorando" in a letter of October 19, 1951, to his friend and attorney, Godfrey Cohen, of the law firm Gilbert & Gilbert:

> I had written a recitation based on the marathon race run by Dorando, the Italian, and Longboat at Madison Square Garden. I recited it to Henry Waterson, who was interested in it for a vaudeville singer, who sang character songs, named Amy Butler. He asked me whether I had music to it. I told him I could give him music within an hour. At that time, a music arranger by the name of Schultz worked for Henry Waterson. (I think Schultz is still alive and working for one of the publishers.) I went into the piano room with Schultz and dictated to him a melody to "Dorando" and then sang the song to Henry Waterson. He liked it. So did Amy Butler. I made a deal with Waterson that if it was good for her as a number for her act, he would give me $25.00 for it. I got $15.00 as a first payment, and then after she sang it and it became a success with her I was given the other $10.00. He published the song

with the Ted Snyder Music Publishing Company and it became a moderate commercial success.

VERSE 1

I feel-a much-a bad, like anything;
All the night I nunga canna sleep;
It's-a my pizon Pasquale,
He say we take da car
And see Dorando race-a Long-a-ship.
Just like da sport, I sell da barber shop,
And make da bet Dorando he's a win.
Then to Madeesa Square,
Pasquale and me go there,
And just-a like-a dat, da race begin.

CHORUS

Dorando! Dorando!
He run-a, run-a, run-a like anything.
One-a, two-a hundred times around da ring,
I cry, "Please-a nunga stop!"
Just then, Dorando he's-a drop!
Goodbye, poor old barber shop.
It's no fun to lose da mon
When de sun-of-a-gun no run,
Dorando,
He's a good-a-for-not!

VERSE 2

Dorando, he's-a come around next day,
Say, "Gentlemen, I wanna tell-a you,
It's a one-a bigga shame,
I forgot da man's a-name
Who make me eat da Irish beef-a stew.
I ask-a him to give me da spaghett',
I know it make me run-a quick-a-quick,
But I eat da beef-a stew,
And now I tell-a you,
Just like da pipps it make me very sick."

REPEAT CHORUS

I DIDN'T GO HOME AT ALL

Published. Copyrighted March 13, 1909. Words and music by Edgar Leslie (1885–1976) and Irving Berlin. The sheet music cover states that this song was introduced by "England's Dainty Chanteuse—Alice Lloyd." Alternate title (cover): "I Didn't Go Home At All (I Heard the Clock Strike One A.M., One A.M.!)."

VERSE 1

Jack and May were newly wed,
A loving pair were they,
Until the other day
When Jack said to his May:
"Tonight I have to talk some business with some
    businessmen,
But rest assured that I'll return at ten."
That night he left the flat,
And simple wifey sat
Up with the cat for Jack, who never came;
The day was dawning when
He rambled home again
And said: "My darling, please let me explain."

CHORUS

"I heard the clock strike
One A.M., one a.m., one a.m.,
It told me of my promise
When I left you in the hall.
Before I knew 'twas
Two A.M., three a.m., four a.m.,
But you know I promised I'd be home at ten,
So I didn't go home at all."

VERSE 2

Jack remarked, "It's eas'ly seen
That I'm not all to blame.
My explanation's tame;
It's true, though, just the same.
Much rather than disturb you from your slumber
    so divine,
I lingered just to pass away the time,
And then again, you see,
I didn't take the key,
Which proves that my intentions were the best.
I even said a pray'r
That you might not despair,
Besides, I knew how much you needed rest."

REPEAT CHORUS

VERSE 3

Jack had been forgiven and
The future seemed so bright
Until the other night;
His May was not in sight.
She went to see a sick friend but had promised to
    come back,
At sixty minutes after nine, to Jack.
At sixty minutes past,
Next morn she came at last,
Her op'ning speech was "I've been with my
    friend.

Because they said she'd die,
I wanted to be nigh,
And so I waited for the coming end."

REPEAT CHORUS

NO ONE COULD DO IT LIKE MY FATHER

Published. Copyrighted April 2, 1909. Music by Ted Snyder (1881–1965).

VERSE 1

I hate to brag about my fam'ly, but I must say that
My father is the greatest man that ever wore a hat.
He always took things easy, in an easy sort of way,
And when it came to taking things, just kindly let me say:

CHORUS 1

No one could do it like my father!
Ever clever, stunning, cunning Father!
Other men might do the same,
But when it came to make a name,
No one could do it like my dad!

VERSE 2

At keeping servant girls, my father always was an ace!
He had a certain way to keep the ladies in their place.
Their place was in the kitchen, and his place to keep them there;
I don't know how he did it, but I really must declare:

CHORUS 2

No one could do it like my father!
Ever clever, stunning, cunning Father!
Servants liked the cops, of course,
So Father joined the police force:
No one could do it like my dad!

VERSE 3

One night, Papa went in to see that great Salome dance.

You talk about attention—say! he gave her ev'ry glance.
He has my mother dancing now, her brain is in a whirl,
And only here last week he came home with a string of pearls.

CHORUS 3

No one could do it like my father!
Ever clever, stunning, cunning Father!
Now he always stays at home,
Mamma has learned that dance Salome:
No one could do it like my dad!

VERSE 4

My mother weighs three hundred pounds, but don't give it away,
She bought a brand-new sheath gown and she wore it yesterday,
My father showed his dignity when my mother showed her sock,
Then just to make the two ends meet, he used a big padlock.

CHORUS 4

No one could do it like my father!
Ever clever, stunning, cunning Father!
Neighbor Jones and his neighbor Lee
Are hunting for my father's key,
And no one could do it like my dad!

VERSE 5

I haven't told you how my father and my mother wed,
She was an old maid, he a burglar underneath the bed,
She flashed a gun at Father and said, "I must be your wife."
My father wears a medal now for saving someone's life.

CHORUS 5

No one could do it like my father!
Ever clever, stunning, cunning Father!
Mother thinks a lot of Pa,
But Father drinks to think of Ma,
And no one could do it like my dad!

VERSE 6

The other night when Pa came home, he found to his surprise

The iceman and my mother on the sofa making eyes.
He did not get excited—no! not one word did he say,
But when the iceman's bill came due, Papa refused to pay.

CHORUS 6

No one could do it like my father!
Ever clever, stunning, cunning Father!
Father proved he was no slouch,
He fooled them all when he sold the couch,
And no one could do it like my dad!

VERSE 7

When Father went to school, they tell me, he was very bad,
They also say he had a purpose to make Teacher mad.
She'd make him stay in after school and Pa would ne'er refuse,
For when it came to helping Teacher tie her dainty shoes,

CHORUS 7

No one could do it like my father!
Ever clever, stunning, cunning Father!
Teacher knew a thing or two,
She always wore a low-cut shoe,
And no one could do it like my dad!

VERSE 8

We lived right near a railway station not so far from here,
And Father would make faces at the passing engineers.
They'd all throw coal at Father, yes they would, upon my soul,
And when the winter came around we never needed coal.

CHORUS 8

No one could do it like my father!
Ever clever, stunning, cunning Father!
First he got coal one by one,
And now he sells it by the ton,
And no one could do it like my dad!

VERSE 9

Around election time my father never knows his name,

Sometimes it's Breen, or Smith, or Green,
    Gilhooley, or McShane,
Then other times it's Harrigan, O'Connor, or
    O'Dell,
They ought to call him Winchester, 'cause he
    repeats so well.

CHORUS 9

No one could do it like my father!
Ever clever, stunning, cunning Father!
When you see him change his coat
You know that means another vote,
And no one could do it like my dad!

SADIE SALOME (GO HOME)

Published. Copyrighted April 2, 1909. Words and music by Irving Berlin and Edgar Leslie. Alternate title: "Sadie Salome Go Home!" Sung in vaudeville by Fanny Brice; many sources indicate that it played an important role in starting her career. Best-selling records by Edward M. Favor (Edison) and Bob Roberts (Columbia). An article in the New York *Telegraph* (October 8, 1911) included the following:

Henry Waterson, head of a music firm, tells a funny story about Berlin's . . . song, "Sadie Salome, Go Home." For two weeks previous to submitting the song Berlin, with a pianist, occupied the room adjoining Waterson's, and played and sang until Waterson said he dreamed of "Sadie Salome." At the expiration of two weeks Berlin called him into the piano room to hear the song; but at the conclusion of the introduction, and before he had heard a word of it, Waterson said he'd take it.

"Play it a tone lower, and I'll sing it for you," he said to the surprised writers, which he did, much to their embarassment.

Letter dated October 19, 1951, from Irving Berlin to Godfrey Cohen:

My next song that was published by the Ted Snyder Company was "Sadie Salome Go Home" which I wrote with Edgar Leslie, and Waterson paid one cent a copy royalty to Edgar Leslie and myself. We asked and received one cent a copy royalty, which was the standard rate of royalty paid to writers on the ten cents music of that day.

VERSE 1

Sadie Cohen left her happy home
To become an actress lady,

On the stage she soon became the rage,
As the only real Salomy baby.
When she came to town, her sweetheart Mose
Brought for her around a pretty rose;
But he got an awful fright
When his Sadie came to sight,
He stood up and yelled with all his might:

CHORUS

"Don't do that dance, I tell you, Sadie,
That's not a business for a lady!
Most ev'rybody knows
That I'm your loving Mose,
Oy, oy, oy, oy,
Where is your clothes?
You better go and get your dresses,
Ev'ryone's got the op'ra glasses.
Oy! Such a sad disgrace,
No one looks in your face;
Sadie Salome, go home."

VERSE 2

From the crowd Mose yelled out loud,
"Who put in your head such notions?
You look sweet but jiggle with your feet—
Who put in your back such funny motions?
As a singer you was always fine!
Sing to me 'Because the World Is Mine'!"
Then the crowd began to roar,
Sadie did a new encore,
Mose got mad and yelled at her once more:

REPEAT CHORUS

MY WIFE'S GONE TO THE COUNTRY (HURRAH! HURRAH!)

Published. Copyrighted June 18, 1909. Words by George Whiting (1884–1943) and Irving Berlin. Music by Ted Snyder. This was Berlin's first major hit song. It was so successful that Berlin wrote many additional lyrics for publication in the New York *Evening Journal*. On original sheet music covers there is a photo with the legend "Sung with great success by Netta Vesta." Best-selling recordings by the famous comedy singing team of Arthur Collins and Byron Harlan (Victor and Columbia) and by Bob Roberts (Indestructible).

Irving Berlin, quoted in a newspaper article, July 1910:

Songwriting all depends on the public. The thing it likes one minute, it tires of the next. Just now for some reason the public wants to have some fun with the marriage relation. Get up a song panning the husband or the wife, roast them, have some fun with them, show up some of the little funny streaks in domestic life and your fortune is made, at least for the moment. Pretty soon the public will tire of these and then you must be able to switch your lyre to something else. If not a new writer will take your place and your star which rose so suddenly will set as rapidly as it came up.

Irving Berlin, quoted in an article in the London *Daily Mirror*, 1911:

The song made an extraordinary stir. Four days after it was published everybody in New York was whistling or singing it. Everyone talked about it, ministers preached about it. It was known all through America.

The idea arose out of a most simple incident. I was in a barber's shop with a friend who told me that his wife had gone away to the country and had left him to his own devices. "Gee," said I, "that's a good title for a song!" And we went back to the office, wrote it, and sang it that night at a cafe before an audience of thirty people. And it went—so much so that the orders were pouring in the next day, while in four days it was about the best known song in America.

Irving Berlin, quoted in a Portland, Oregon, newspaper, October 17, 1915:

"My Wife's Gone to the Country" was my first big hit and I got the idea of that from a Chicago fellow. He and I were having a little drink and chat near dinner time and noting the clock I said to him "Almost supper time. Suppose you've got to be beating it home?" He said "Oh no! My wife's not in the city." Now you'll probably laugh, but right then and there it occurred to me that "My Wife's Gone to the Country" would be a capital name for a popular song. The music buzzed into my head. I got somebody to write it and there I was.

VERSE 1

When Mrs. Brown told Hubby,
"I just can't stand the heat,
Please send me to the country, dear,
I know 'twould be a treat,"
Next day his wife and fam'ly
Were seated on a train,
And when the train had started,
Brownie shouted this refrain:

CHORUS 1

"My wife's gone to the country,
Hurrah! Hurrah!
She thought it best,
'I need a rest,'
That's why she went away.
She took the children with her,
Hurrah! Hurrah!
I don't care what becomes of me,
My wife's gone away."

VERSE 2

He kept the phone a-going,
Told ev'ryone he knew,
"It's Mister Brown, come on downtown,
I have some news for you."
He told a friend reporter
Just why he felt so gay,
Next day an advertisement,
In the papers read this way:

REPEAT CHORUS

VERSE 3

He sang his joyful story
Into a phonograph,
He made a dozen records, and
I say it was to laugh.
For when his friends had vanished,
And Brown was all alone,
His neighbors heard the same old tune
On Brownie's gramophone:

CHORUS 3

"My wife's gone to the country,
Hurrah! Hurrah!
She thought it best,
'I need the rest,'
That's why she went away.
She took the children with her,
Hurrah! Hurrah!
Like Eva Tanguay, I don't care,
My wife's gone away."

VERSE 4

He went into the parlor
And tore down from the wall
A sign that read God Bless Our Home
And threw it in the hall.
Another sign he painted
And hung it up instead.
Next day the servant nearly fainted
When those words she read:

CHORUS 4

"My wife's gone to the country,
Hurrah! Hurrah!
She thought it best,
'I need the rest,'
That's why she went away.
She took the children with her,
Hurrah! Hurrah!
Now I'm with you, if you're with me,
My wife's gone away."

VERSE 5

He called on pretty Molly,
A girl he used to know;
The servant said, "She left the house
About an hour ago.
But if you leave your name, sir,
Or write a little note,
I'll give it to her when she comes,"
And this is what he wrote:

CHORUS 5

"My wife's gone to the country,
Hurrah! Hurrah!
She thought it best,
'I need the rest,'
That's why she went away.
She took the children with her,
Hurrah! Hurrah!
I love my wife but oh! you kid,
My wife's gone away."

VERSE 6

He went and bought a parrot,
A very clever bird,
The kind that always would repeat
Most anything she heard.
So when his voice grew husky
And Brownie couldn't talk,
While he'd be taking cough drops,
He would have the parrot squawk:

CHORUS 6

"My wife's gone to the country,
Hurrah! Hurrah!
She thought it best,
'I need the rest,'
That's why she went away.
She took the children with her,
Hurrah! Hurrah!
I knew my book, she left the cook,
My wife's gone away."

JUST LIKE THE ROSE

Published. Copyrighted July 2, 1909. Music by Al Piantadosi (1884–1955).

VERSE 1

In a garden fair
A lily rare
Was loved by a blushing rose.
They knew no woe,
He loved her so,
With love that a flower knows.
Until one day,
From o'er the way,
A hand plucked the lily fair;
The rose sighed and sighed,
'Til one day it died;
Nobody seemed to care.

CHORUS

Just like the rose, dear, I loved you,
Like the lily they stole you away,
Just like the rose I adored you,
Worshiped you night and day.
Tonight all alone I am sighing,
Sighing for sweet repose;
Just like the rose, my love's dying,
Dying just like the rose.

VERSE 2

In a garden fair
I wandered there.
Sweet memories of the past
Came back to me
So tenderly.
Would if they could only last.
The rose that sighed
And long since died
Seemed fresh from the morning dew,
Then close to my breast,
The sweet flow'r I pressed,
And cried alas for you.

REPEAT CHORUS

OH, WHAT I KNOW ABOUT YOU

Published. Copyrighted July 2, 1909. Words and music written originally by Joseph H. McKeon, Harry M. Piano, and W. Raymond Walker. A letter from Walker to music historian and collector James J. Fuld, dated November 23, 1954, says:

> I wrote the song with Joe McKeon and Harry Piani [sic] while playing at Kennedy's Cafe (formerly Kid McCoy's) and Harry Von Tilzer heard it there and liked the title and melody but not the lyric. Offered us $50.00 for it and said he would have a new lyric written for it but would put our names on as the writers when he published it. Berlin rewrote the lyric, maybe all of it or maybe part of it, but I do know it was a great deal different from the original lyric.

VERSE 1

Now sweet Flo and Joe,
With lights burning low,
Sat spooning as all lovers do;
Her wee sister Rose
Stood on her tiptoes
And eagerly kept peeping through.
Oh my, oh what bliss,
She soon heard them kiss,
As he gently called her "my dear."
The very next day
When Flo came her way
She whispered these words in her ear:

CHORUS

"Oh! What I know about you,
Oh! What I know about you.
Don't say you didn't,
'Cause I overheard.
Honest to goodness I won't say a word.
Oh! What I know about you,
Something that I wouldn't do,
Far be it from me
To repeat what I see,
But oh! What I know about you."

VERSE 2

Next evening when Joe
Called 'round to see Flo,
He found little Rose all alone.
In her cunning way
He soon heard her say,
"My sister said she's not at home."

Her face wore a grin,
She said, "Please come in,"
Poor Joseph, oh my what he saw.
There sat pretty Flo
With her other beau—
Rose cried to her sister once more:

REPEAT CHORUS

SOMEONE'S WAITING FOR ME (WE'LL WAIT, WAIT, WAIT)

Published. Copyrighted July 2, 1909. Words and music by Edgar Leslie and Irving Berlin. Alternate titles: "Someone's Waiting for Me 'We'll Wait Wait Wait' " (sheet music cover) and "We'll Wait Wait Wait Someone's Waiting for Me." Sheet music cover states that the words are by Edgar Leslie and the music is by Irving Berlin, but the title page of the song governs.

VERSE 1

Henpeck O'Johnson and Henpeck O'Day
Made an appointment with Molly and May,
Soon they were calling their wives on the
    phone,
"Don't cook my supper for I won't be home."
Then in a taxi to some swell café
They rode away to meet Molly and May,
Waited and waited, grew intoxicated,
O'Johnson then sang to O'Day:

CHORUS

"Someone's waiting for me,
Someone's waiting for you,
I'm waiting and you're waiting
And Wifey's waiting too.
Are we downhearted? No!
We have plenty of dough.
What! Go home to Wifey?
Well, not on your lifey—
We'll wait, wait, wait."

VERSE 2

While they were waiting a waiter named
    Binks
Waited for tips while they waited for drinks,
Manhattan cocktails and highballs galore,
Three extra waiters were put on the floor.

Music was playing, "I'm Coming Home Soon,"
O'Day was praying for some other tune,
Hours were flying, still they kept on buying,
O'Johnson was crying again:

REPEAT CHORUS

VERSE 3

Mrs. O'Johnson and Mrs. O'Day
Happened to stroll in the same swell café,
They had grown tired of waiting at home,
Went out and left both their flats all alone.
Soon from a corner a voice hollered loud,
"Give us another and treat the whole crowd."
Just then somebody broke up the whole party
'Twas Molly, and sweet little May.

REPEAT CHORUS

DO YOUR DUTY, DOCTOR! (OH, OH, OH, OH, DOCTOR)

Published. Copyrighted August 6, 1909. Music by Ted Snyder. Alternate title (sheet music cover): "Do Your Duty Doctor and Cure My Pain."

VERSE 1

Liza Green felt awf'ly sick,
Sent out for the doctor quick.
The doctor called around, these words to say:
"You're suff'ring from a love attack,
And if you want to bring health back,
A loving man must love you every day."
Then he turned to say goodbye,
Just to hear Eliza cry:

CHORUS

"Oh, oh, oh, oh, Doctor,
Won't you kindly hear my plea?
I know you know, Doctor,
Exactly what is best for me.
Hear me sigh, hear me cry,
Surely you ain't goin' to let me die,
For if some love will make me gain,
Do your duty, Doctor, cure my pain."

VERSE 2

Doctor said, "I can't decline,
Curing patients is my line,"
Then started lovin' Liza good and strong.
Soon she was feeling well once more.
The doctor then looked t'ward the door,
And said, "I guess I'd best be getting along."
But Eliza hollered quick,
"Oh, I fear I'm getting sick."

REPEAT CHORUS

GOODBYE, GIRLIE, AND REMEMBER ME

Published. Copyrighted August 6, 1909. Music by George W. Meyer (1884–1959), although on some sheet music covers it was incorrectly attributed to Ted Snyder.

VERSE 1

So you're leaving me, sweet girlie,
So it's true we have to part.
Let me whisper something, girlie,
To my own sweetheart;
It will worry me, sweet girlie,
And I'll be so lonesome too.
It will cheer me, dear,
When you're not near me,
Just to know your heart beats true.

CHORUS

Goodbye, girlie, and remember me
When you're far away.
I'll be thinking of you, dearie,
More and more each day.
Summer's coming,
Birds will soon be humming
Love's sweet melody.
Good luck!
Goodbye, girlie, and remember me.

VERSE 2

I can see a scene, sweet girlie,
As sweethearts can only do,
Where we'll sit and dream, sweet girlie,
In a home for two.
See just what it means, sweet girlie,
What it means for you and I.
So in June time, spoon time,

Honeymoon time,
We'll be happy, bye and bye.

REPEAT CHORUS

WILD CHERRIES (COONY, SPOONY RAG)

Published. Copyright August 12, 1909. Music by Ted Snyder. Introduced by Fanny Brice in *Ziegfeld Follies of 1910*. Published and copyrighted previously as an instrumental (piano rag), September 23, 1908. Alternate title: "Wild Cherries, That Cooney Spooney Rag."

VERSE 1

Talk of yo' loony coons,
Talk of yo' spoony coons,
Lover of coony tunes,
Jackson was the leader of a big brass band,
Understand!
While at a ball one night,
Lucinda Morgan White
Yelled out with all her might
When he started playing some familiar tune.
She just cried with delight:

CHORUS 1

"If you love yo' babe,
Play that tune for me.
Just because I feel so funny,
Honey, I don't care for money.
I'm goin' crazy, that rag's a daisy,
I just can't make my feeling behave.
Play that tune again,
Mighty soon again.
Honey, don't you start to scold,
I'm feeling like a two-year-old.
When I hear that strain,
Gwine to cry again,
Play me some 'Wild Cherry Rag.' "

VERSE 2

Talk of yo' weddin' chimes,
Talk of yo' champagne wines,
Talk of yo' scand'lous times,
Mister Jackson married Miss Lucinda White
Sunday night.
Just as the knot was tied,
Parson had blessed the bride,

Jackson stood by her side
When the music played that lovin' weddin' march,
Miss Lucinda just cried:

CHORUS 2

"If you love yo' babe,
Play that tune for me
No, I'm not a-blowin', hon,
But I just feel like goin' some.
I'm goin' crazy, that rag's a daisy,
I just can't make my feeling behave.
Play that tune again,
Mighty soon again.
Oh, you seven-come-eleven!
Hon, I'm goin' straight to heav'n.
When I hear that strain,
Gwine to cry again,
Play me some 'Wild Cherry Rag.' "

OH! WHERE IS MY WIFE TONIGHT?

Published. Copyrighted September 16, 1909. Music by Ted Snyder. Words by George Whiting and Irving Berlin. Original sheet music cover states: "Answer to 'My Wife's Gone to the Country' by the original writers."

VERSE 1

You've heard about foxy old Brownie,
Who sent his whole fam'ly away?
Well, you can just bet that I envied old Brown,
When I heard him shouting hooray!
I borrowed some money from Brownie,
Induced my old lady to pack,
It's now been a month and I can't raise the price
To pay for her fare coming back.

CHORUS

Oh, where is my wife tonight?
Oh, why did she leave my sight?
I'm sorry to say, I shouted hooray!
Oh, why did I ever let her go away?
She never would leave the town
If it hadn't have been for Brown,
Bring back, bring back,
Bring back my wifey to me.

VERSE 2

I've tried ev'ry way to raise money,
But none of my friends are in town
Excepting the one man that started this thing.
So I called around to see Brown.
He answered, "I'm sorry, old fellow,
I'll have to refuse you this time,
I just have enough money left in the bank
To send for that fam'ly of mine."

REPEAT CHORUS

SHE WAS A DEAR LITTLE GIRL

Published. Copyrighted October 5, 1909. Music by Ted Snyder. According to information on the sheet music cover, it was introduced by Marie Cahill in the 1908 musical *The Boys and Betty*, probably during the post-Broadway tour.

VERSE 1

Betsy Brown, a manicurist fair,
Dropped in town to get the city air,
Met the son of some millionaire
Who had lots of time to spare.
Same old case of "I remember you,"
Same old smile and same old howdy-do,
Same old look of innocence true
In her great big eyes so blue.

CHORUS 1

She was a dear little girl,
Dearest of dear little girls,
Dear little eyes, dear little size,
Dear little golden curls.
She murmered, "Dear, never fear,
I'll always hold you dear."
When she said so true
"I'm fond of wine," he knew
She was a dear, dear girl.

VERSE 2

Soon he took Miss Betsy out to dine
And they had the dearest little time,
For he bought the dearest of wine,
Till the pair were feeling fine.
Tho' it isn't altogether right
To remark about her appetite,

Seven waiters worked hard that night,
Serving what she called a bite.

CHORUS 2

She was a dear little girl,
Dearest of dear little girls,
Dear little eyes, dear little size,
Dear little golden curls.
She murmered, "Dear, never fear,
I'll always hold you dear."
To a check his pen
Was introduced, but then
She was a dear, dear girl.

SOME LITTLE SOMETHING ABOUT YOU

Published. Copyrighted October 14, 1909. Music by Ted Snyder.

VERSE 1

I've met lots of girlies who were just my style,
Girls whose charms most any boy would share,
Girls who captivate you with their roguish smile,
Girls you think beyond compare.
When I saw the love-light in your eyes, sweetheart,
When you smiled on me so tenderly,
Mischief-making Cupid pierced me with his
    dart,
Something told me you were meant for me.

CHORUS

Some little something about you,
Some little something, dear,
Means I can't live without you,
I always want you near.
Some hidden charm makes me love you,
Something I cannot see,
And I know one thing,
Some little something
Means you're the girl for me.

VERSE 2

Oft I've wondered if another boy like me
Thinks there's something sweet about you too.
I'll admit it's made me jealous as could be,
That's because I love you true.
Then again, I thought of what the poets say,
"Faint heart never won a lady fair."

So I don't intend to wait another day,
There's a cozy home that we can share.

REPEAT CHORUS

IF I THOUGHT YOU WOULDN'T TELL

Published. Copyrighted October 14, 1909. Music by Ted Snyder.

VERSE 1

A maiden pretty, from Jersey City,
Paid a visit to some cousins out of town.
She answered "Mercy" when Cousin Percy
Said, "I'd dearly love to show you all around."
Like bees a-buzzin'
She and her cousin
Were together ev'ry minute of the day.
One night he kissed her, she shouted "Mister,"
But he answered in a cute and cunning way:

CHORUS

"If I thought you wouldn't tell your mother,
I would try and take one more.
Promise not to tell your father or your brother,
And I'll make it three or four.
If I thought that you could keep a secret,
I would keep you busy, Nell.*
I'd forget that I'm your cousin
And I'd take half a dozen,
If I only thought you wouldn't tell."

VERSE 2

One evening early, he took the girlie
To a restaurant where drinks were often tried
He ordered porter, she ordered water,
Then she said, "I'll take a cocktail on the side."
She drank a dozen,
Just then her cousin
Whispered, "Dearie, don't you think we should go
    home?"
She answered, "Later, please call the waiter,"
Then she murmured in a rather husky tone:

REPEAT CHORUS

In the second chorus, this line is:
    "I would take all they would sell."

I WISH THAT YOU WAS MY GAL, MOLLY

Published. Copyrighted October 14, 1909. Music by Ted Snyder. On the sheet music cover there is a photo with the legend "Sung with great success by Amy Butler."

VERSE 1

I saw you, Molly, walking with your sweetheart,
And I only looked and wished that I was he.
You looked so swell, I couldn't help but wonder
If a gal like you would ever fall for me.
I know he thinks the world and all about you,
Well, I wish I had the chance to think so too.
He wouldn't be the same old boy without you,
Gee, it must feel great to have a gal like you.

CHORUS

I wish that you was my gal, Molly,
I only wish I was your beau,
To feel that you was my pal, Molly,
Would mean an awful lot, I know.
It isn't right, I know, to tell you,
But what's a fellow goin' to do?
I wish that you was my gal, Molly,
I only wish you loved me too.

VERSE 2

Come, tell me why you started crying, Molly.
Did I hurt you feelings? Tell me if I did.
I didn't mean to knock your other sweetheart,
On the level, I am awful sorry, kid.
I told me mother just how much I love you,
It was her that made me go to you and tell.
So let me be your pal, if not your sweetheart,
When you marry, I'll be there to wish you well.

REPEAT CHORUS

NEXT TO YOUR MOTHER, WHO DO YOU LOVE?

Published. Copyrighted October 26, 1909. Music by Ted Snyder. The popularity of the song led to two sheet music cover designs. Many years later, Berlin recalled the circumstances of writing the song in an undated letter to songwriter Harry Ruby:

In the WBS [Waterson, Berlin and Snyder] days, I wrote a song you may remember called, "Next to Your Mother, Who Do You Love?" A school teacher I knew gently and tactfully suggested that I should have said "whom do you love." I tried to make the change but Max Winslow, the professional manager, said, "Whom doesn't sing as well as who, besides whom asked you to change it?"

The song was published with "who" and sold about half a million copies which was pretty good in those days.

VERSE 1

Two loving sweethearts mid flowers in Maytime,
Two happy faces like children in playtime,
Two eyes of blue, gazing into
Eyes of her own sweetheart.
One cozy bench holds the couple within it,
Hours that passed only seemed like a minute,
Sweet maiden sighs,
Fellow replies,
"Tell me before we part,

CHORUS

"Next to your mother, who do you love?
Next to your brother, who do you love?
Next to your father and your sister Sue,
Tell me who looks good to you?
Next to your mother, who would you miss?
Next to your brother, who would you kiss?
Next to your own dear folks at home,
Tell me, now who do you love?"

VERSE 2

Five cozy rooms in a flat in the city,
One baby boy cute and cunning and pretty,
Parson had said, "You two are wed,
Bless you, my children, go."
"Come spend a week," so she wrote to her mother,
Mother replies, "I am bringing your brother."
Husband remarks,
"Me for the parks.
But first I want to know,

REPEAT CHORUS

STOP THAT RAG (KEEP ON PLAYING, HONEY)

Published. Copyrighted November 24, 1909. Music by Ted Snyder. Introduced by Stella Mayhew in Lew Fields's production *The Jolly Bachelors*, which opened on Broadway January 6, 1910, at the Broadway Theatre (84 performances). On the sheet music cover there is a tinted photograph of Mayhew. Alternate title: "Stop That Rag, Keep on Playing."

VERSE 1

Do my ears deceive me,
Or am I goin' mad?
Honey, please believe me
That my hearin' ain't bad,
But something seems to tell me
That I'm list'nin' to Rag.
I've been suspectin' so all night,
Tunes I've heard befo' was only music what
    ain't,
Melody like this is what an artist can't paint.
Go get me some ammonia, 'cause I fear I must
    faint,
I'm suffocating with delight.

CHORUS

Stop dat rag, keep on playin', honey,
Stop dat rag, hear me prayin', honey,
Run away, I feel that I must be alone,
But don't you dare to leave me
Till the cows come home.
Cease dat strain, please repeat it, honey,
Once again, and I'll meet it, honey,
Oh, I'm sad,
No, I'm glad,
Stop dat rag, I'm sayin',
I mean keep on a-playin',
Don't you dare to stop dat rag.

VERSE 2

Call in some physician
'Cause I feel that I'm ill;
Somehow or another,
Hon, my feet won't keep still.
Please request that leader man
To keep a-playin' till
I cry enough, enough some more;
Hon, I'll ne'er forgive you, just for takin' me
    here,
Take me miles and miles away from here,
    anywhere,

Just raise a hand to move me, Mister Man, if you
      dare,
I'm satisfied to die right now.

REPEAT CHORUS

YIDDLE, ON YOUR FIDDLE, PLAY SOME RAGTIME

Published. Copyrighted November 30, 1909. A type-script of the lyric acquired by James J. Fuld indicates that this song was "expressly written for Miss Lillian Shaw." Another artist, Sadie Cecil Weston, recalled her own association with the song in a letter to Berlin dated November 11, 1947:

Dear Irving,

   A few days ago, at the dentists, I picked up some magazines to help pass the time waiting. In two there were articles about you and your career. The next day being Sunday, I went to spend the day with life-long friends in Encino. On the piano was a sheet of music, with a picture of me as I looked in 1910 (no one will believe it's my picture, and I don't blame them). The name of the song is, "Yidel [sic] on Your Fiddle Play Some Rag-time." Do you recall how some of the notices spoke about my being Irish and putting over the Jewish accent? What they didn't know was that you coached me.

VERSE 1

Ev'ryone was singing, dancing, springing,
At a wedding yesterday.
Yiddle on his fiddle played some ragtime,
And when Sadie heard him play,
She jumped up and looked him in the eyes.
Yiddle swelled his chest way out,
Ev'ryone was taken by surprise,
When they heard Sadie shout:

CHORUS

"Yiddle in the middle of your fiddle, play some
      ragtime;
Get busy, I'm dizzy, I'm feeling two years
      young,
Mine choc'late baby, if you'll maybe play for
      Sadie,
Some more ragtime;
Yiddle, don't you stop,
If you do, I'll drop,

For I just can't make my eyes shut up,
Yiddle on your fiddle, play some ragtime."

VERSE 2

At the supper table Sadie thought
Yiddle must have flew the coop.
She looked all around, but could not find him
Till she heard him drinking soup.
Sadie waited till they served the fish,
Then she jumped upon the floor,
Put a quarter right on Yiddle's dish
And yelled to him once more:

REPEAT CHORUS

CHRISTMAS-TIME SEEMS YEARS AND YEARS AWAY

Published. Copyrighted December 2, 1909. Music by Ted Snyder.

VERSE 1

In a garden fair
Sat a happy pair
'Neath a shady maple tree.
She had promised him,
"We'll be married, Jim,
To the chimes of Trinity.
'Tis the month of May,
But next Christmas day
I will be your blushing bride.
Don't you worry, dear,
It will soon be here."
But he looked at her and sighed:

CHORUS

"Christmas chimes mean happy times,
For you and me, sweetheart,
Winter-time means you'll be mine,
And never more to part.
Honeymoon can't shine too soon,
I wish it were today.
Girlie mine, don't Christmas-time
Seem years and years away?"

VERSE 2

"There is nothing, dear,
That I have to fear.

If I can't afford the ring,
Santa Claus is kind
And I'm sure he'll find
Just a plain gold band to bring.
It's been just a year
Since I met you, dear,
But it seems just like a day.
If I only could,
Girlie dear, I would
Turn December into May."

REPEAT CHORUS

I JUST CAME BACK TO SAY GOODBYE

Published. Copyrighted December 8, 1909. Alternate title (sheet music cover): "I Just Come Back to Say Goodbye."

VERSE 1

"Who is that down below
A-pounding on my door?"
Said Liza Green,
"It's downright mean
To wake me from a pleasant dream!"
"It's Bill!" came the reply,
"Came back to say goodbye!
I overlooked it when I left,
That's just the reason why."

CHORUS

"I just came back to say goodbye,
Let me explain, I won't remain,
Besides, you see, I don't know when
I may have time to call again.
Been cooking, honey, I smell stew!
Don't look so cross, I know you're boss!
Just tell me how you're feeling now,
And then I'll say goodbye."

VERSE 2

"It's blowing up out here,
I'll catch a cold, I fear!
Now, Liza, please
Don't stand and tease!
How can you see your William freeze?"
But Liza said, "Go 'way!
Come round some other day."

Then as she closed the window down,
She heard poor William say:

REPEAT CHORUS

THAT MESMERIZING MENDELSSOHN TUNE

Published. Copyrighted December 22, 1909. Music "adapted" in part from Felix Mendelssohn's "Spring Song" ("Lied ohne Worte," op. 62, no. 6—"Früh-lingslied"). Title page lists the year of copyright as 1910. A huge success for Berlin; it sold over one million copies of sheet music. Top-selling recordings were by Arthur Collins and Byron Harlan (Victor, Columbia, Edison, Edison Amberol, Zonophone, and U.S. Ever-lasting). The sheet music cover bears the subtitle "Mendelssohn Rag."

VERSE 1

Honey, listen to that dreamy tune they're
    playin',
Won't you tell me how on earth you keep from
    swayin'?
Umm! Umm!
Oh, that Mendelssohn "Spring Song" tune.
If you ever loved me, show me now or never,
Lord, I wish they'd play that music on forever,
Umm! Umm!
Oh, that Mendelssohn tune,
My honey,

CHORUS

Love me to that ever-lovin' "Spring Song"
    melody,
Please me, honey, squeeze me to that
    Mendelssohn strain,
Kiss me like you would your mother,
One good kiss deserves another,
That's the only music that was ever meant
    for me,
That tantalizin', hypnotizin',
Mesmerizin' Mendelssohn tune.

VERSE 2

Don't you stand there, honey, can't you hear me
    sighin'?
Is you gwine to wait until I'm almost dyin'?
Umm! Umm!

Oh, that Mendelssohn "Spring Song" tune;
Get yourself acquainted with some real live
    wooin',
Make some funny noises like there's something
    doin',
Umm! Umm!
Oh, that Mendelssohn tune,
My honey,

REPEAT CHORUS

SPRING SONG MELODY

Not previously published. Exact date unknown. An-other bit of fun to Mendelssohn: this time Berlin wrote a duet for the well-known songwriters Ernest R. Ball (1878–1927) and Gus Edwards (1879–1945), possibly for a Friars Club dinner.

VERSE

There's a melody
Full of harmony
That was written long years ago,
And every modern composer
Stole that beautiful tune.
When you hear a strain
Of a sweet refrain
And you think that it sounds familiar,
Bet your life it was stolen
From that beautiful tune.

CHORUS

Poor old "Spring Song" melody,
Everyone has stolen thee.
Everyone who writes a song
Puts you where you don't belong.
You've been in almost every key,
Poor old "Spring Song" melody,
Every song you seem to be.
Seems to me that everyone
Picks on poor old Mendelssohn
And his poor old "Spring Song" melody.

Alternate version

VERSE

BALL: There is a certain melody
      In each composer's memory.
CHORUS: Hum . . .

EDWARDS: We love to play it all day long,
         Sometimes we use it for a song.
BALL: We'll try and show you while we hum it
      The different songs that were taken
        from it.

CHORUS*

BALL: Poor old "Spring Song" melody,
CHORUS: Hum . . .
EDWARDS: Everyone has stolen thee.
CHORUS: Hum . . .
BALL: Everyone who writes a song
      Puts you where you don't belong.
EDWARDS: You've been in almost every key,
CHORUS: Hum . . .
BALL: Poor old "Spring Song" melody.
CHORUS: Hum . . .
EDWARDS: Every song you seem to be.
CHORUS: Hum . . .
BALL: Seems to me that everyone[†]
      Picks on poor old Mendelssohn
EDWARDS: And his poor old "Spring Song"
         melody.

---

*Another, slightly different version of the chorus:
    BALL: Poor old "Spring Song" melody,
  EDWARDS: (Love me to that ever-loving)
    BALL: Everyone has stolen thee.
  EDWARDS: (Gee I wish I had my old girl)
    BALL: Everyone who writes a song
          Puts you where you don't belong.
          You've been in almost every key,
  EDWARDS: (Ev'ry little movement was that)
    BALL: Poor old "Spring Song" melody,
  EDWARDS: (Love me while the moon is beaming)
    BALL: Every song you seem to be.
  EDWARDS: (Gee I wish that I had a girl)
    BALL: Seems to me that everyone
          Picks on poor old Mendelssohn
  CHORUS: And his poor old "Spring Song" melody.

†Alternate version of the last three lines:
    BALL: Every other song you hum
          Seems to say "I'm stolen from—"
  EDWARDS: "—that poor old 'Spring Song' melody."

SOMEONE JUST LIKE YOU

Published. Copyrighted December 22, 1909. Music by Ted Snyder. Alternate title (sheet music cover): "Someone Just Like You Dear."

VERSE 1

Same old moon is shining, same old stars above,
Same old couple pining, same old tale of love,
Same game still we must explain,
The old, old story must be told.
Now to get their names, we'll call the fellow Joe,
We could call him Harry, but Joe rhymes with
    Flo;
Flo, Joe, now their names we know,
We'll have them say:

CHORUS

"Someone just like you, dear,
Just like you will do, dear,
When I tell you true, dear,
Can't you see?
Just your style, your size, dear,
Just your smile, your eyes, dear,
Someone just like you was meant for
Someone just like me."

VERSE 2

Same old couple tarried, same old coming spring,
Same old couple married, same old wedding
    ring.
Flo, Joe, on thro' life they go,
In clover now, the story's over.
Ev'ry song and story has a happy two,
Couldn't do without them, 'twould be something
    new.
Same tale never known to fail,
When someone sighs:

REPEAT CHORUS

BEFORE I GO AND MARRY, I WILL HAVE A TALK WITH YOU

Published. Copyrighted December 31, 1909. The title page lists the year of copyright as 1910.

VERSE 1

Jealous little maid was sadly crying,
Crying 'cause her little heart was hurt.
Told her fellow there was no denying,
She saw him flirt.
Fellow whispers, "Let your heart be cheery,
Won't you let me dry those tears away?
Be your own sweet self and cuddle near me,
There is something sweet I want to say.

CHORUS

"I may take a walk with Dolly,
I may smile at pretty May,
I may have a talk with Molly,
Or with Polly, or even Fay,
I may flirt with charming Carrie,
As another boy would do;
But before I go and marry,
I will have a talk with you."

VERSE 2

"When I noticed something sweet in Molly,
That's the time I loved your baby smile.
When I saw how cute and neat was Dolly,
I liked your style.
Fellows raved to me about a prize, dear,
Meaning Carrie's pretty eyes of blue,
So I went and gazed into her eyes, dear,
That's the day I fell in love with you.

REPEAT CHORUS

MY FATHER WAS AN INDIAN

Probably 1909. Words and music by Edgar Leslie and Irving Berlin. No music is known to survive. A typed copy of the lyric was found among the papers of the Broadway and vaudeville performer Lillian Shaw. These were purchased from a dealer by noted historian and sheet music collector James J. Fuld.

VERSE 1

Way out in the wild and wooly West,
Cohen took off his brand-new coat and vest,
Then to get some feathers he went and killed a
    chicken,
He dressed up just like an Indian.
But the day was very windy and
Cohen lost his feathers so he killed another
    chicken.
The Indians soon caught him—
And to the Big Chief brought him.
The Big Chief said, "Come tell us who you
    are!"
They grabbed him by the collar—and Cohen
    commenced to holler
As he lit up a swell five-cent cigar:

CHORUS

"My father was an Indian,
My mother was his wife,
My uncle almost died
Until a kind judge gave him life [Joke].
My brother was the president
Of every Ind'an Club,
My sister was a chambermaid,
So that made me a Hebrew."

VERSE 2

Cohen said, "You got a big mistake
Just because my Christian name is Jake.
That don't say that I should believe in Christian
    Science,
From my chicken heart I want to beg,
I'm the goose that lays the golden egg,
Let me duck away or I will kill another
    chicken!"
The Indians soon bound him—
And built a fire round him.
I think they tried to make it hot for Cohen,
But Cohen shouted, "No, sir—
That fire out must go, sir,
For I left my insurance papers home."

REPEAT CHORUS

OVERLEAF: *Irving Berlin and Ted Snyder*

Songs of 1910

TELLING LIES

Published. Copyrighted January 14, 1910. Music by Henrietta Blanke-Belcher.

VERSE 1

Moon was slyly peeping from above,
On a summer's night;
Sally Brown and Joe were making love
Neath the pale moonlight.
Sally said, "I think I'd better go,"
As she rolled her eyes;
But foxy little Joe said,
"There's a game I know called
Telling Lies.

CHORUS

"Telling lies, telling lies,
Say you never want to be
Near to me, dear to me,
Telling lies, close your eyes.
Then a kiss or two I'll steal
And give them back to you,
While telling lies."

VERSE 2

Little Sally Brown and Joe were wed,
She became his bride;
"I will never marry you," she said,
Then the knot was tied.
Ev'ry morn he kisses her goodbye,
Leaves her all alone,
But 'fore he goes away,
These words he'll always say,
"I won't come home."

REPEAT CHORUS

SWEET MARIE, MAKE-A RAG-A-TIME DANCE WID ME

Published. Copyrighted January 18, 1910. (The title of the printed sheet music lists the year of copyright as 1909.) Music by Ted Snyder. Introduced by Emma Carus during the pre-Broadway tryout of *The Jolly Bachelors*. Dropped before the New York opening when Carus was no longer in the show. There is a portrait of Carus on the cover of the sheet music. Alternate title: "Sweet Marie, Make-a-Rag-a-Time Dance with Me."

VERSE 1

Liss-a to the sweet-a rag-a-time,
Ain't it nunga make you feel-a fine?
Ev'ry body dance,
Sleep-a like-a trance,
Keep-a steady, get-a ready,
One, two, three, kid!
What's-a mat-ta, you no look-a wise?
Get-a busy, make-a googoo eyes.
Nunga make-a fake,
Just-a shake-a shake,
Make-a jealous for the other guys.

CHORUS

Sweet Marie,
Make-a rag-a-time dance wid me?
Take-a steam-a boat to Italy,
On the rag-a line.
Hey, you wop-a, nunga stop-a,
Kiss-a Tony call 'im Pop-pa,
One, two, three,
I'm-a feel-a like-a "hully gee,"
Come dance rag-time wid me,
Oh, my sweet-a Marie.

VERSE 2

What's-a mat-ta, you no wan-na dance?
Nunga feel afraid to take a chance.
Ev'rybody look,
Shout-a, "Get da hook!"
I'm-a sad-a, feel-a bad-a,
Shake yourself, kid!
If you love-a Tony nice-a fine,
Make-a noise-a like-a rag-a-time.
Hurry up-a quick,
Nunga take-a week,
If you nunga wanna never mind.

REPEAT CHORUS

IF THE MANAGERS ONLY THOUGHT THE SAME AS MOTHER

Published. Copyrighted February 15, 1910. Music by Ted Snyder. Introduced by Emma Carus during the pre-Broadway tryout of *The Jolly Bachelors*. Dropped before the New York opening when Carus was no longer in the show. On the original sheet music cover there is a large portrait of Carus and a smaller photo of Berlin and Snyder.

VERSE 1

There's no mistake that I can act,
I'm talented and that's a fact,
I know, because my mother told me so.
She kept a house for actor folks
And listened to their funny jokes,
So now I guess my mother ought to know.
But managers are awful dense,
It seems to me they have no sense;
I know my darling mother wouldn't lie.
She thinks I'm better than the best,
But managers think I'm a pest,
And all they say is, "Go somewhere and die."

CHORUS

If the managers only thought the same as
    Mother,
You bet I'd show them all a thing or three.
They'd have starred me in *The Thief*,
For it's Mother's firm belief,
Margaret Illington could never steal like me.
If the Shuberts only took a tip from Mother,
I'd be starring like a star was never starred;
Leslie Carter and that bunch
Would be at Child's a-serving lunch,
If the managers only thought the same as Ma.

VERSE 2

My mother goes to all the shows,
She knows *What Every Woman Knows*,
She knows Maude Adams knows a thing or two.
But when she saw her in that play,
She said to me that very day,
"My child, she doesn't know as much as you."
So I got busy with my pen
And wrote to Charlie Frohman then,
I asked him if he wouldn't star me quick.
His answer nearly knocked me dead;
For in his letter Charlie said,
"I didn't even know that you were sick."

CHORUS 2

If the managers only thought the same as Mother,
I'd act like Sarah Bernhardt never did,
Harry Miller would forget
Margaret Anglin, you bet,
He would want me as his real supporting kid.
If Frohman only took a tip from Mother,
He would label me as Frohman's only star,
Mrs. Fiske would take a drop
To some Broadway candy shop,
If the managers only thought the same as Ma.

OH, HOW THAT GERMAN COULD LOVE

Published. Copyrighted February 15, 1910. Music by
Ted Snyder. Introduced by Sam Bernard (Herman
Schultz, Lapidary) late in the New York run and during
the post-Broadway tour of his show *The Girl and the
Wizard.* Irving Berlin recorded the song for Columbia
in January 1910; it was his first commercial recording.
The sheet music cover has a photo with the legend "As
sung by Sam Bernard in his production of *The Girl and
the Wizard.*"

VERSE 1

Once I got stuck on a sweet little German,
And oh what a German was she;
The best what was walking,
Well, what's the use talking,
Was just made to order for me.
So lovely, and witty, more yet she was pretty,
You don't know until you have tried.
She had such a figure, it couldn't be bigger,
And there was some more yet beside.

CHORUS 1

Oh, how that German could love,
With a feeling that came from the heart;
She called me her honey,
Her angel, her money,
She pushed ev'ry word out so smart.
She spoke like a speaker,
And oh what a speech
Like no other speaker could speak.
And my, what a German,
When she kissed her Herman,
It stayed on my cheek for a week.

VERSE 2

This girl could squeeze and it never would hurt,
For that lady knew just how to squeeze;
Her loving was killing,
More yet, she was willing,
You never would have to say please.
I just couldn't stop her, for dinner and supper
Some kisses and hugs was the food;
When she wasn't nice it was more better twice,
When she's bad she was better than good.

CHORUS 2

Oh, how that German could love,
With a sweetness that's sweeter than sweet.
Just say what you please,
You would hug and you'd squeeze,
Just the shoes that she wore on her feet.
Her smile was like money
That somebody owed you,
That somebody wanted to give;
When you felt like dying
And she started sighing,
Ach my, it was worthwhile to live!

VERSE 3

Sometimes we'd love for a week at a time
And it only would seem like a day;
How well I remember
One night in December,
I felt like the middle of May.
I'll bet all I'm worth that when she came on earth,
All the angels went out on parade;
No other one turned up, I think that they
  burned up
The pattern from which she was made.

CHORUS 3

Oh, how that German could love,
With a love like you see in a play;
When she said "My dear,"
It would ring in my ear
For a year, and a week and a day.
Her no was like yes,
And her yes was like no,
It was something like yes, it was, well.
When we got together
Ach, Donner und Vetter,
'Twas love with a capital L.

WHEN I HEAR YOU PLAY THAT PIANO, BILL!

Published. Copyrighted March 16, 1910. Music by Ted
Snyder.

VERSE 1

Said Miss Eliza Johnson to William Brown,
"Up to my home you I invite,
Call around some Sunday night,
I'd love to have you play my piano upright."
Said Mister William Brown,
"The pleasure is mine, I can assure you, lady fair."
He called around next day
And started in to play,
Just to hear Eliza declare:

CHORUS

"When I hear you play that piano so sweet,
My blood runs cold way down to my feet.
You sure do bring forth music
Like I never heard before.
When you start in tearing rag by the streak,
I could hear you play that box for a week,
For it does most anything but speak,
When you play that piano, Bill."

VERSE 2

Said Mr. William Brown, "I can't help but blush,
Because, Miss Lize, you flatter so,
I only play the worst I know,
While at my best to beat me so they must go."
Then Miss Eliza answered,
"What's that you say? You only played the worst
  you knew!
Sweet William, I can guess
How you play at your best,
But the worst right now will do."

REPEAT CHORUS

IT CAN'T BE DID

Published only as a lead sheet. Copyrighted April 13,
1910. Apparently sung by Lillian Shaw in the Broadway
show *Jumping Jupiter.* According to a lyric typescript
now in the possession of James J. Fuld, this song was

"written expressly for Miss Lillian Shaw." The lyrics for the second verse and chorus were on the Lillian Shaw typescript.

VERSE 1

Julius Schultz and me were thick like brothers,
I think he is the thickest of the two,
He took me to a ball
And while inside the hall
I danced with him as any girl would do.
While dancing Julius stepp'd upon my dresses,
I felt that they were slipping to the floor;
So quick I took a seat,
But Julius said so sweet,
"Come, Lena, let us dance a little more."

CHORUS 1

"It can't be did," I told him,
But he answered, "Why not so?"
I said "Go on, you dumb kop
There is something you don't know.
I know you love to dance with me,
But if I let my dresses free,
I'll have to show my dignity,
You see, it can't be did."

VERSE 2

Yesterday our cat had one nice kitten,
And everybody blamed it all on me;
You see I found the cat
And brought her to the flat,
So now they're all as mad as they can be.
Mother said let's call the kitten Jenny,
Father said he'd like to call it Flo;
Julius said that Jane
Was such a pretty name,
I only looked at him and answered, "No!"

CHORUS 2

"It can't be did," I told him,
But he answered, "Yes it can!"
I said, "You talk so foolish, Julius,
Like a crazy man.
Eliza, Jane, Jenny, and Flo
Are very pretty names, I know,
But it's not that kind of kitten, so—
You see, it can't be did."

DRAGGY RAG

Published. Copyrighted April 13, 1910. Alternate title (sheet music cover): "Dat Draggy Rag."

VERSE 1

Honey darlin', take your time,
Don't you hurry, baby mine,
Throw your lovin' arms around me,
Oh! Oh! Oh! I'm feelin' so fine.
Won't you squeeze my hand again?
Squeeze it hard, I feel no pain,
Don't deny me, satisfy me
To that draggy strain.

CHORUS

Oh, that draggy rag!
Oh, that easy drag!
Don't you hurry, honey, or you'll cause me
    pain,
I want to go to heaven on an Erie train.
Slide, glide, not too fast,
Go slow to the last,
I love my quick decision, hon,
But oh, that draggy rag!

VERSE 2

I could almost swear I see
Two of you, and now it's three.
I believe my mind is wand'rin',
Oh! Oh! Oh! poor delicate me.
Honey, dear, I'm suff'rin' so,
Get your hat and we will go,
Don't decline, dear, take your time, dear,
Let us walk out slow.

REPEAT CHORUS

ANGELO

Published only as a lead sheet. Copyrighted April 13, 1910. Introduced in *Jumping Jupiter* by Lillian Shaw. According to a lyric typescript now in the possession of James J. Fuld, this song was "written expressly for Miss Lillian Shaw." The lyrics for the second verse were found in the Shaw typescript.

VERSE 1

I feel-a da blue, and I tell-a to you,
Up-a-stairs in da head I'm-a craze,
I make-a divorce wid my husband for course
He's asleep-a too much, he's a laze,
He make-a me work like a big-a da Turk,
While he sleep-a just like-a da King.
He think he's-a boss, just-a, just-a for course
He's-a give me da wedding-a ring.
But I nunga can stand-a for that,
So I tell-a the good-a-for-not:

CHORUS

"Angelo, Angelo,
Too-a much is-a plenty, you know,
I make-a you fat like-a dis, like-a dat,
But you lose-a da fat when I leave-a you flat.
Angelo, Angelo,
When I say I'm-a gone-a I go,
You make-a me sick,
And-a next-a da week
I'm-a run away quick
Wid the Irish-a Mick,
Nunga more-a you kick wid your meal-a da tick,
It's-a just what I speak-a for you."

VERSE 2

You make-a me scare but I nunga no care,
Just-a like-a da Eva-da Tang.
De Irish-a Mick, he's-a fix-a you quick,
He belong to the big-a da gang.
It's a shame-a for you when I make-a skidoo,
Everybody she laugh in her face;
Sleep-a sleep all the time, nunga care-a fer mine,
But you no can-a sleep in dis place.
Gone away nung' you ask fer da kiss,
It's-a better you liss-a fer dis.

REPEAT CHORUS

DEAR MAYME, I LOVE YOU

Published. Copyrighted April 18, 1910. Music by Ted Snyder.

VERSE 1

Dear Mayme: I want to explain
Why I sat down to write you this note.

Gee, Mayme, I do feel ashamed,
It's the first letter I ever wrote,
There's some little something way down in my
	heart
I haven't the nerve to say;
But sooner or later I must make a start,
So it might as well be today.

CHORUS

I love you, I love you, I love you, Mayme,
I'd like to be there with a real pretty spiel,
But three simple words can explain how I feel,
I love you, I want you, I need you,
Is all that I know.
My love to your ma,
Kind regards to your pa,
And kisses to you from Joe.

VERSE 2

P.S. Dear Mayme, can you guess
Who I saw? Well, it's old Parson Brown.
Gee whiz, he was chock full of biz,
And he wants you and me to come round.
Now I've bought a bargain, a nice wedding ring,
Worth twenty, I bought it for ten;
Jim Jones wants to buy it for fifteen next spring,
Do you want me to sell it again?

REPEAT CHORUS

GRIZZLY BEAR

Published. Copyrighted April 19, 1910. Music by
George Botsford (1874–1949). Alternate titles: "The
Grizzly Bear" and "The Dance of the Grizzly Bear."
Many reference books attribute this song to *Ziegfeld
Follies of 1910*, but programs seen by the editor do not
include this title. Popularized by Sophie Tucker. Top-
selling recordings by the American Quartet (Billy Mur-
ray and John Bieling, tenors; Steve Porter, baritone; and
William F. Hooley, bass) for Victor and Arthur Collins
(Indestructible). Sung by Alice Faye and danced by Jack
Oakie and June Havoc in the musical film *Hello Frisco,
Hello* (1943).

VERSE 1

Out in San Francisco where the weather's fair,
They have a dance out there
They call the Grizzly Bear.
All your other lovin' dances don't compare,

Not so coony,
But a little more than spoony;
Talk about yo' bears that Teddy Roosevelt shot,
They couldn't class with what
Old San Francisco's got.
Listen, my honey, do,
And I will show to you
The dance of the Grizzly Bear.

CHORUS 1

Hug up close to your baby,
Throw your shoulders t'ward the ceiling,
Lawdy, lawdy, what a feelin'
Snug up close to your lady,
Close your eyes and do some nappin',
Something nice is gwine to happen.
Hug up close to your baby,
Sway me everywhere;
Show your darlin' beau
Just how you go to Buffalo,
Doin' the Grizzly Bear.

VERSE 2

Let's sit down and rest a minute, honey, dear,
My head feels awful queer,
Please call the waiter near;
"Water, water, quick, the lady's gone, I fear."
Thank you, honey,
In my purse you'll find some money
Where's the man who showed me how to do that
	dance
That put me in a trance?
I'll take another chance,
Now that I've got my breath,
I'm his'n until death,
Come on with yo' Grizzly Bear.

CHORUS 2

Hug up close to your baby,
Hypnotize me like a wizard,
Shake yo'self just like a blizzard,
Snug up close to your lady.
If they do that dance in heaven,
Shoot me, hon, tonight at seven.
Hug up close to your baby,
Sway me everywhere;
You and me is two,
I'll make it one when we get through,
Doin' the Grizzly Bear.

CALL ME UP SOME RAINY AFTERNOON

Published. Copyrighted April 23, 1910. The first Irving
Berlin song to reach number one on the best-selling
popular music charts. The leading recording was by Ada
Jones and the American Quartet (Victor, Columbia, Edi-
son, Amberol, and Indestructible).

VERSE 1

Nellie Green met Harry Lee
At a masquerade the other night;
He liked she, and she liked he,
Just a case of love at single sight.
He took Nellie home that eve,
Also took the number of her phone.
Just before he took his leave
Nellie whispered in the cutest tone:

CHORUS

"Call me up some rainy afternoon,
I'll arrange for a quiet little spoon.
Think of all the joy and bliss,
We can hug and we can talk about the weather,
We can have a quiet little talk,
I will see that my mother takes a walk.
Mum's the word when we meet,
Be a Mason, don't repeat,
Angel eyes, are you wise?
Goodbye."

VERSE 2

He look'd wise, then looked for rain,
Sure enough, it rained that Saturday;
"Give me 3-4-5-6 Main—
Nellie dear, prepare, I'm on my way."
When he rang the front door bell
No one there responded to his call.
Soon he heard his pretty Nell
Singing to somebody in the hall:

REPEAT CHORUS

THAT OPERA RAG

Published. Copyrighted April 28, 1910. Music by Ted
Snyder. Introduced by May Irwin in *Mrs. Jim*, the pre-

Broadway title of *Getting a Polish*. The sheet music cover included a large photograph of Irwin and indicated that the production also included "My Wife Bridget" by Berlin and "He Sympathized with Me" by Berlin and Snyder. Both songs are missing.

VERSE 1

Sam Johnson was op'ra mad,
He sho' had the fever bad,
He said, "Those ordinary ragtime tunes are mild;
Some music from Verdi's hand,
Or any old op'ra grand,
Would never fail to set this op'ra darkie wild."
One ev'ning at a ball
They heard Sam Johnson call
Unto the leader man to play some *William Tell*;
The leader swelled his chest
And said, "I'll do my best."
So when he played they heard Sam Johnson yell:

CHORUS

"Hear dat strain,
Mister Verdi come to life again,
Oh, that operatic sweet refrain,
Sho' would drive a crazy man insane,
Just let me die and meet those brainy men
Who manufactured notes of opera grand,
Oh! Verdi, where, where, oh art thou?
Let me shake you by the hand,
Man, you know what's grand—
Good Lord, it's over,
They're playin' 'Home Sweet Home.' "

VERSE 2

Old Sam was a painter man;
One day with a brush in hand
He stood upon a scaffold way up in the air.
A German band down below,
Was playin' some *Rig'letto*,
Sam said, "I know that's op'ra, be it here or
    there."
While he daubed up the wall
He tried hard not to fall,
But in the street the band kept right on playin'
    fair,
They played some *Faust* below,
Just then old Sam let go,
He tumbled down below a-shouting in the air:

REPEAT CHORUS

I'M A HAPPY MARRIED MAN

Published. Copyrighted May 2, 1910. Music by Ted Snyder.

VERSE 1

"A fool there was," said Smith to Gray,
"And that same fool was me,
Not satisfied with bach'lor bliss,
I took a wife, you see."
Said Gray to Smith,
"You're crazy, man—why, married life is fine,
I have the dearest little wife
And let me say for mine:

CHORUS

"I'm a happy married man,
Yes, I am, yes, I am,
Married life was made for me,
I wouldn't choose another.
Betch yer life I love my wife,
Love my wife with all my life,
I'm a happy married man—
My wife lives with her mother."

VERSE 2

"I hate to hear the married men
Complaining all the time;
One would imagine married life
Was anything but fine.
They don't appreciate
The wife who helps to make life gay,
But far be it from me to frown,
I mean it when I say:

REPEAT CHORUS

I LOVE YOU MORE EACH DAY

Published. Copyrighted May 19, 1910. Music by Ted Snyder.

VERSE 1

Come, sit beside me, darling May,
And look into my eyes;

It seems as though 'twere yesterday
I won you for my prize.
The hand of time has turned
Your golden locks to silv'ry gray;
The silver threads have drawn you
Closer to my heart each day.

CHORUS

You were my queen at sweet sixteen,
You're my queen at sixty-three;
Your eyes that shone with gladness then
Still hold their charms for me.
And as I gaze into your eyes,
There's one thing I must say:
You're still the same sweet darling girl,
And I love you more each day.

VERSE 2

You cheered me up when I was blue,
You laughed when I was gay;
When trouble came you were the same,
You turned night into day.
You never measured what you gave
By what you thought I'd give;
You're still my little sweetheart,
And I'll love you while I live.

REPEAT CHORUS

ALEXANDER AND HIS CLARINET

Published. Copyrighted May 19, 1910. Music by Ted Snyder. On the cover of some of the original sheet music there is a photograph accompanied by a legend that reads: "Sung by Little Amy Butler." Alternate title: "Alexander and His Clarionet."

VERSE 1

Alexander Adams played a clarinet,
Brought out music that no one has brought out
    yet;
Miss Eliza Johnson was his angel pet,
And Alexander was her one best bet.
Strange to say, they quarreled on last Sunday
    night;
Monday ev'ning Alexander came in sight,
Played his clarinet beneath her window light,
To hear Eliza yell with all her might:

CHORUS

"Honey, is that you? Yes, yes,
Didn't even have to guess, my honey,
What brought you? Oh pet,
I see you brought your clarinet, my honey.
I'm angry, no, no,
For lawdy sake, don't dare to go,
My pet, I love you yet,
And then besides, I love your clarinet."

VERSE 2

Alexander played his clarinet with vim,
Up to Liza's door, then played himself right in;
When he got inside he played and played like sin,
Then played her cards to see who'd buy the gin.
When he left, Miss Liza tried some sleep to get,
Dreamt her Romeo came back to Juliet,
Also dreamt he brought with him his clarinet;
If no one woke her, she'd be shoutin' yet:

REPEAT CHORUS

SWEET ITALIAN LOVE

Published. Copyrighted June 9, 1910. Music by Ted
Snyder. Introduced by Irving Berlin (vocal) and Ted
Snyder (piano) in the musical *Up and Down Broadway*
(1910). There is a large photograph of Berlin on the
sheet music cover. In programs for the show this song is
listed as "Italian Love." Top recordings were by Byron G.
Harlan (Columbia) and Billy Murray (Edison).

From a review of *Up and Down Broadway* in the
New York *Morning Telegraph*, July 23, 1910:

> The screaming big hit of the evening, however,
> must be put down to the credit of Irving Berlin
> and Ted Snyder, who, when introduced quite ca-
> sually into the Cafe de l'Obster scene wearing eve-
> ning clothes and no make-up, proceeded first to
> get on friendly terms with the audience and then
> to turn them into a lot of college boys rah-rah-
> rahing for two men who were perfect strangers
> to them five minutes before, but who had sud-
> denly become personal friends. "Italian Love"
> and "O, That Beautiful Rag" were the two vehi-
> cles they used, to which they hitched the Pega-
> suses of their personalities and soared aloft with
> never a hitch nor a falter.

VERSE 1

Ev'ryone talk-a how they make-a da love,
Call-a da sweet-a name-a like-a da dove,
It make me sick-a when they start in to speak-a
'Bout the moon way up above.
What's-a da use to have-a big-a da moon?
What's-a da use to call-a dove?
If he no like-a she,
And she no like-a he,
The moon can't make them love;
But

CHORUS 1

Sweet Italian love,
Nice Italian love,
You don't need the moon-a-light your love to tell
    her
In da house or on da roof or in da cellar,
Dat's Italian love,
Sweet Italian love;
When you kiss-a your pet
And it's-a like-a spaghett',
Dat's Italian love!

VERSE 2

Ev'ryone say they like da moon-a da light,
There's one-a man up in da moon all-a-right,
But he no tell-a that some other nice feller
Was-a kiss your gal last night.
Maybe you give your gal da wedding-a ring,
Maybe you marry, like-a me,
Maybe you love your wife,
Maybe for all your life,
But that's only maybe.
But

CHORUS 2

Sweet Italian love,
Nice Italian love,
When you squeeze your gal and she no say,
    "Please stop-a!"
When you got dat twenty kids what call you
    "Papa!"
Dat's Italian love,
Sweet Italian love;
When you kiss one-a time
And it's-a feel like-a nine,
Dat's Italian love!

TRY IT ON YOUR PIANO

Published. Copyrighted July 7, 1910.

VERSE 1

Benjamin Manner played a grand piano,
And he cert'nly played it fine;
Played the piano all the time,
Like a reg'lar Rubinstein.
Sunday he called around
To see Miss Lucy Brown
And said, "My darling pet,
I have found a new way to make love
That hasn't been discovered yet,
Won't you let me show you how?"
But Miss Lucy cried, "Not now!

CHORUS 1

"Try it on your piano grand,
I don't care to understand
B- or I-flat, C- or Y-flat,
Try it, hon, but not in my flat.
While I don't doubt that what you say is true,
I'm not for taking chances with some love that's
    new,
So Mister Manner, try it on your piano,
But you can't try it on me."

VERSE 2

Benjamin Manner sold his grand piano,
And became a doctor fair,
One who cures your pain and care;
He was known most ev'rywhere.
Lucy took sick one day;
He called around to say,
"I've brought with me a pill,
It's a new discov'ry of my own
That surely ought to cure or kill,
It has never yet been tried."
But Miss Lucy loudly cried:

CHORUS 2

"Try it on your piano grand,
I don't care to understand
B- or I-flat, C- or Y-flat,
Try it, hon, but not in my flat.
Give me Peruna for my ev'ry pain,
For he who takes that will live to take again.
So try your brand upon a baby grand,
Because you can't try it on me."

OH, THAT BEAUTIFUL RAG

Published. Copyrighted July 9, 1910. Music by Ted Snyder. According to noted Berlin collector Vince Motto (*The Irving Berlin Catalog*, October 1988, pp. 19–20), it was introduced by Dale Fuller in *The Girl and the Kimono*, at the Ziegfeld Theatre, Chicago, beginning June 25, 1910. That show closed shortly after its Chicago opening. Introduced in New York in the musical *Up and Down Broadway* (July 18, 1910; Casino Theatre; 72 performances) by Irving Berlin (vocal) and Ted Snyder (piano), who were billed as "Entertainers at the Cafe de l'Obster." On some of the original sheet music covers there is a large photograph of Berlin. Apparently, the song also was sung in *The Jolly Bachelors*, although the artists who sang it are not known to the editors. Best-selling recording by Arthur Collins (Columbia and Zonophone). Also recorded by Arthur Collins and Albert Harlan (Indestructible). Alternate titles: "That Beautiful Rag" and "O That Beautiful Rag."

VERSE 1

Honey, that leader man
Leads like a leader can,
Just see him leadin' that band—
My honey, don't you understand,
That they're playin' music grand?
And
Just never mind the name,
Ragtime is all the same,
Music is music with me.
But I will say that it's beautiful, hon,
With a great big capital B.

CHORUS

Oh! Oh! Oh! Oh!
Oh! That beautiful rag,
It sets my heart a-reelin'.
Oh! Oh! Oh! Oh!
Oh! That beautiful drag,
That funny feeling stealing.
Hear that trombone blowin', hon,
Ain't dem fiddles goin' some?
Oh, sir! Oh, sir! Cuddle up closer,
Squeeze me like you would a flower,
Make a minute last an hour.
Oh! Oh! Oh! Oh!
Oh! That heavenly strain,
It makes me feel so funny.
If I ever cry, "Don't play it again,"
Just don't believe me, honey,
Oh, my dearie,
Can't you hear me callin'?

Come up near me,
Catch me, dear, I'm fallin',
Oh! Oh! Oh! Oh!
Oh! That beautiful rag.

VERSE 2

What does my honey want?
Go in a restaurant?
Now you is talkin' some sense,
And this here place is just immense,
I know you don't mind expense,
Hence,
Bring on yo' bill o' fare,
Honey, I do declare,
Somehow I'm feelin' forlorn—
Hear them playin' that old beautiful rag,
Now my appetite is gone.

REPEAT CHORUS

KISS ME, MY HONEY, KISS ME

Published. Copyrighted August 3, 1910. Music by Ted Snyder. According to noted Berlin collector Vince Motto, there are at least three early sheet music covers of this song. One has a tinted photograph with the legend "Sung with great success by Little Amy Butler." Another indicates that the song was featured by Emma Carus in the musical *Up and Down Broadway*. And yet another states that it was featured by Richard Carle in H. H. Frazee and George W. Lederer's production *Jumping Jupiter*. Top-selling recordings by Elida Morris (Columbia and Indestructible) and Ada Jones and Billy Murray (Edison Amberol).

VERSE 1

My little honey,
I must be leaving;
Be bright and sunny,
Now don't be grieving.
Just dry your tears, dear,
It's not for years, dear,
I'll soon return to you.

CHORUS

Kiss me, my honey, kiss me,
And say you'll miss me as I'll miss you.

Love me, my honey, love me,
Like stars above me,
Say you'll be true.
While away ev'ry day,
I'll be thinking of you,
Dearie, now don't grow weary,
Be bright and cheery, my honey, do.
So, dear, before I go, dear,
Come here and kiss me,
Honey, I love you.

VERSE 2

That same old moon, dear,
That shines above us
Will see us soon, dear,
As happy lovers
So don't you worry,
For I will hurry
Right back and marry you.

REPEAT CHORUS

"THANK YOU, KIND SIR!" SAID SHE

Published. Copyrighted August 31, 1910. Music by Ted Snyder. Introduced in *Jumping Jupiter* by Edna Wallace Hopper (Connie) and Richard Carle (Jupiter). Alternate title: "Thank You Kind Sir." The original sheet music cover has a large photograph of "Richard Carle (Himself)."

VERSE 1

Crowded thoroughfare,
People here and there,
Dashing up the avenue;
Maiden young and shy
Quickly passing by,
Something comes in contact with her shoe.
Someone's fallen down,
Slipped upon the ground,
It happens on a slipp'ry street.
Kind young gent,
Who saw the accident,
Helps the charming lady to her feet.

CHORUS 1

"Thank you, kind sir," said she.
"Welcome, sweet miss," said he,

"May I not escort you home?"
"You may not, I'll go alone,
I've a husband," said she;
"And I've a wife, miss," said he.
"You needn't call me up," said she,
"My phone is 1-2-3."
"Thank you," said he.

VERSE 2

Scene, a near café,
Couple chatting gay,
Same young maiden shy and sweet.
On the he-male end
Sits her fellow friend,
Same young man who helped her to her feet.
Maiden softly speaks,
"I've been sad for weeks,
My darling husband failed last year,
I'm in debt right up to here, you bet."
Fellow whispers something in her ear.

CHORUS 2

"Thank you, kind sir," said she.
"Welcome, sweet miss," said he,
"May I not escort you home?
I would hate to go alone."
"I live here, sir," said she.
"And so do I, miss," said he.
"Don't dare to call on me," said she,
"I'm always in at three."
"Thank you," said he.

YIDDISHA EYES

Published. Copyrighted September 8, 1910.

VERSE 1

Benny Bloom went to a swell affair,
Given by a real millionaire;
Jenny Golden Dollars was there.
Now comes the bus'ness end;
Benny, to a friend,
Said, "Introduce me to Miss Jenny, do!"
Soon he whispered, "Pleased to meet you too!"
Then young Benny winked at Jenny
With his Yiddisha eyes.

CHORUS 1

Oy, oy, oy, those Yiddisha eyes!
Benny had those Yiddisha eyes
That shone so bright, with an Israel light,
Eyes that could tell a diamond in the night.
Oy, oy, oy, those Yiddisha eyes!
Benny had those Yiddisha eyes!
He took a look in her bankbook
With his Yiddisha eyes.

VERSE 2

Ben looked at her finger with his eyes,
Next day bought a ring the proper size.
Jenny's bus'ness father got wise!
Now comes the finish part:
Benny, from his heart,
Began to shout, "I love your daughter fine!"
Jenny's pa cried, "That's how I got mine!"
Benny, bending, saw the ending,
With his Yiddisha eyes.

CHORUS 2

Oy, oy, oy, those Yiddisha eyes!
Benny had those Yiddisha eyes
That shone so bright, with an Israel light;
Eyes that could tell a diamond in the night.
Oy, oy, oy, those Yiddisha eyes!
Benny had those Yiddisha eyes!
He said, "Farewell," the teardrops fell
From his Yiddisha eyes.

IS THERE ANYTHING ELSE I CAN DO FOR YOU?

Published. Copyrighted September 8, 1910. Music by Ted Snyder. Major recording by Ada Jones (Columbia).

VERSE 1

Pretty young Mabel was helping her mother,
Clearing the table and dressing her brother,
Washing the dishes, feeding the fishes,
As ev'ry girl should do.
Johnny dropped in and soon made himself handy,
Helping his Mabel dear,
When all the work was through,
And nothing more to do,
He whispered in her ear:

CHORUS

"Is there anything else that I can do for you?
Tell me do, come on and ask me to,
I've got hours to spare, my dear, and then a few.
Tell me, Mabel,
I'm able to do anything else, so don't you be
    afraid.
Pretty maid,
I've learned the tailor trade,
And somehow I've been guessin'
That your lips need some pressin',
Tell me, dear, is there anything else?"

VERSE 2

Pretty young Mabel could not see the joke, so
Said, "In the stable there's wood to be broke," so
There was no stopping, John started chopping,
Chopped for an hour or two.
Soon work and Johnny became perfect strangers,
He did the best he could.
Calling his Mabel near,
He whispered, "Listen, dear,
I'm not so strong for wood!"

REPEAT CHORUS

COLORED ROMEO

Published. Copyrighted September 14, 1910. Music by Ted Snyder.

VERSE 1

Last winter Liza Snow
Picked up a book called *Romeo*.
She read a page or so,
Then hunted for a man;
Soon she was dreaming of
A beau who cooed just like a dove,
A man who sho' could love
Like a Romeo can.
She wandered out one night
Beneath the pale moonlight
And sang with all her might
This ancient cry:

CHORUS

"Where art thou, Romeo,
My colored Romeo?

The balcony wants to see
He and she, you and me.
Come out and pet your colored Juliet,
Don't linger, do it now,
Come kiss my fevered brow.
Shakespeare's love come and show me,
Colored Romeo."

VERSE 2

Miss Liza's father, Joe,
Did not approve of Romeo,
But Liza loved him so
They ran off in a car.
They made a mile or three
In almost nothing, don't you see;
The auto struck a tree,
Then they didn't go far.
Miss Liza from the ground
Kept gazing all around;
Her beau could not be found,
So Liza cried:

REPEAT CHORUS

STOP, STOP, STOP (COME OVER AND LOVE ME SOME MORE)

Published. Copyrighted September 17, 1910. Top recording by Elida Morris (Victor, Columbia, and Indestructible).

VERSE 1

Honey, there's something buzzin' round my
     heart,
Something that must be satisfied.
My dearie,
See that Morris chair
Standing over there?
There's some room to spare,
Now for some love prepare.
Make yourself comf'table before we start,
Tie yourself right up to my side,
Sing me that lovin' song
That goes something like
Umm-umm-umm-umm.

CHORUS

Cuddle and squeeze me, honey,
Lead me right to Cupid's door,
Take me out upon that ocean called the Lovable
     Sea,
Fry each kiss in honey, then present it to me.
Cuddle and please me, honey,
Anchor at that kissing shore;
My honey, stop, stop, stop, stop,
Don't dare to stop,
Come over and love me some more.

VERSE 2

Hon, did I hear you say you're going home?
Just 'cause the clock is striking nine,
My dearie—
That clock at its best
Is an hour fast,
Eight o'clock just past,
Stay, let the party last.
Surely you wouldn't leave me all alone
Just for to satisfy the time,
Sing me that lovin' song
That goes something like
Umm-umm-umm-umm.

REPEAT CHORUS

HERMAN, LET'S DANCE THAT BEAUTIFUL WALTZ

Published. Copyrighted September 24, 1910. Music by Ted Snyder. Sung by Belle Gold (who portrayed "Helena, who wants to 'yump her yob' ") in the pre-Broadway tryout of William A. Brady's *The Girl and the Drummer*. Also, according to some original sheet music covers, it was "successfully introduced by Belle Gold in William A. Brady and the Shuberts' (Limited) production of *Two Men and a Girl*." Both shows closed out of town.

VERSE 1

Miss Lena Kraussmeyer
With hair red as fire
Last Saturday went to a ball;
There stood Mister Herman,
A sweet little German,
The best that was dressed in the hall.
The music played dances like ragtime and lancers

But no one would go on the floor,
So quickly the band played a waltz that was
     grand,
A waltz that made sweet Lena roar:

CHORUS

"Herman, let's dance
To the tune of that beautiful waltz!
Now listen, you German, I'm talking to you,
I'll do something, dear, you don't want me to do,
So come on take a chance
And I'll know that your love isn't false.
A feeling that's healing
Comes stealing while spieling
That beautiful, beautiful waltz."

VERSE 2

"I heard that a coon
Who heard Mendelssohn's tune
Kissed the first man she saw, if it's true;
That very same feeling
I feel on me stealing
And Herman, I'm looking at you.
So close both your eyes, make believe you ain't
     wise,
Only pucker your lips into place,
Think of five hundred meld or a sweet Anna
     Held
While I kiss the hole in your face.

REPEAT CHORUS

PIANO MAN

Published. Copyrighted October 5, 1910. Music by Ted Snyder. Top-selling recording by Billy Murray (Edison Amberol).

VERSE 1

You all have your favorite masters,
The kind what music give;
Did you ever, ever meet my lovin' Piano Man?
No? Then you've yet to live.
He sits on his stool like a king on the throne
And plays and plays with ease;
Why, the melody just nestles in his fingertips
And oozes out in the keys.

CHORUS

Piano Man, Piano Man,
He brings forth notes like no one can.
Oh, what a feelin'
When his notes come a-stealin',
Why, I just feel like kneelin' and appealin'
To my Piano Man, Piano Man.
Lawdy, how his music lingers,
May the Heaven bless his fingers.
When he plays for days and days
It soothes me like a fan.
Just lend your ear, dear, here,
Near to my ever-lovin' Piano Man.

VERSE 2

You've listened to Verdi's music,
Beethoven's classy tune;
I'm alludin' to the fellows with the hair as long
As a rainy afternoon.
They all need love to inspire their notes,
Be it the spring or fall,
But my Piano Man, just have him meet a piano
    grand
Then listen, umm, umm, that's all.

REPEAT CHORUS

INNOCENT BESSIE BROWN

Published. Copyrighted October 5, 1910. On some of
the original sheet music covers there is a large photo-
graph with the legend "Sung with great success by Min-
dell Kingston."

VERSE 1

Innocent Bessie landed in the city,
From Kankakee, the sights to see.
Fellows looked at her saying, "What a pity
She's from the farm," meaning no harm.
Ev'ry maiden, ev'ry gent,
When discussing she,
Said she must be innocent,
'Cause she came from Kankakee.

CHORUS 1

Innocent Bessie Brown
Wanted to see the town,
Met upon the avenue one afternoon fair

A fellow who said, " 'Aven't you an hour to
    spare?"
So pretty innocent Bessie Brown
Went for an hour in town,
And when the day was breaking
They were still partaking
Of some frizzes of gin
That fizzed within
Innocent Bessie Brown.

VERSE 2

Bessie was stopping with her second cousin,
Who was a beaut, cunning and cute.
Fellows would call upon her by the dozen.
Innocent Bess never could guess
Where her cousin got such toys,
Diamonds more or less.
'Twasn't long before the boys
Made a jew'lry store of Bess.

CHORUS 2

Innocent Bessie Brown
Dressed in a country gown,
Bessie Brown was lonesome for a diamond or two,
But since she met the city she could loan some to
    you.
And she was innocent Bessie Brown,
Lived in a country town,
When Mrs. Morgan chubby
Missed her darling hubby,
She began talking war
While hunting for
Innocent Bessie Brown.

DREAMS, JUST DREAMS

Published. Copyrighted October 12, 1910. Music by Ted
Snyder.

VERSE 1

The sunbeams have taken their flight,
The day slowly turned into night;
All nature's at rest,
The birds in their nest
Sleep on neath the moon's silv'ry light.
The shadows of eve ease my heart,
For now that we've drifted apart,
I find joys anew while dreaming of you,
Dreams that can ne'er come true.

CHORUS

Dreams, just dreams,
My beautiful golden dreams,
It seems my dreams
Are missives of sweet consolation.
Each dream I dream
Turns gloom to a bright sunbeam;
Since the love that I gave
Found a grave, all I crave
Is dreams, just dreams.

VERSE 2

I wake with the morning, my dear,
The sun up above shining clear;
The flowers seem gay
To welcome the day,
A day that will seem like a year.
My goal is a land, so it seems,
Where night never turns to sunbeams,
The world I would give to go there and live,
Live with my golden dreams.

REPEAT CHORUS

I'M GOING ON A LONG VACATION

Published. Copyrighted October 12, 1910. Music by Ted
Snyder. Introduced by Beth Tate in *Are You a Mason?*
The show closed out of town during its pre-Broadway
tryout.

VERSE 1

Nellie Brown, stenographer,
Working on the second floor,
Writing letters for a man named Kelly.
Kelly's wife, a lady thin,
Calls around, is ushered in,
Sees her husband fondly kiss Miss Nellie.
Next morning Kelly whispered in Nell's ear;
She left the office singing loud and clear:

CHORUS

"I'm going on a long vacation,
Oh, you railway station,
First in years, so give three cheers,
Yea-bo, yea, hurray, hurray.
Everybody in creation

Needs some recreation;
My boss guessed I need some rest,
Yea, I'm going away."

VERSE 2

Nellie told the office boy;
He replied with shrieks of joy,
Then went in and said to Mister Kelly:
"Nellie told me where she'd go,
I can tell your wife, you know,
Don't you think I better go with Nellie?"
Next week the office boy and Nellie Brown
Were holding hands and singing out of town:

REPEAT CHORUS

BRING BACK MY LENA TO ME

Published. Copyrighted October 20, 1910. Music by Ted Snyder. On the original sheet music covers there is a photograph with a legend that reads: "Successfully interpolated by Sam Bernard in Sam S. and Lee Shubert's production of *He Came from Milwaukee*" (September 20, 1910; Casino Theatre; 117 performances). Alternate title (on theatre programs): "Lena."

VERSE 1

You know how you feel when your rich uncle
      dies
And leaves you a lot and a house?
Well, that's how I felt when I first met Miss
      Lena,
Sweet little neat Lena Kraus.
I just hate to think how she came in my life
Like a landlord that comes for the rent,
The rent was my heart when she took it apart,
Just how she came she went.

CHORUS 1

Oh, when I think of my Lena
My face turns so white, just like starch;
The hand organs play pretty love songs all day
But to me it's just plain fun'ral march.
It's bad to be sad,
To be glad when you're sad
Can't be did, as you all must agree.
If you feel like I feel

And you hear my appeal,
Oh, bring back my Lena to me!

VERSE 2

I cry when I think what a woman she was,
What cost dollars she bought for a cent.
When she broke a glass, why, it wouldn't be broke,
      Ach!
No, it would only be bent.
To cry over milk that's been spilt isn't good,
But the feeling that I'm feeling now,
It wasn't just one glass of milk that I spilt—
When Lena went, then went the cow.

CHORUS 2

Oh, when I think of my Lena,
I think of a girl who could cook
Some sweet sauerkraut that would swim in your
      mouth
Like the fishes that swim in the brook.
When I think of a meal
That was real I just feel
Like a ship with no sail on the sea;
There's no tears in my eyes,
But my appetite cries,
Oh, bring back my Lena to me!

WISHING

Published. Copyrighted December 17, 1910. Music by Ted Snyder. Introduced, possibly by Belle Gold, during the pre-Broadway tryout of William A. Brady's musical *The Girl and the Drummer*. The show closed out of town. Later sung by Elsie Ryan in the pre-Broadway tryout of William A. Brady and the Shuberts' production *Two Men and a Girl*. (Some of the original sheet music covers have a large photograph of Elsie Ryan.) This production also closed out of town.

VERSE 1

In the days of fairy tales
Most any wish was granted,
Granted by some fairy brave.
Let's suppose a fairy rose
In fairy clothes from head to toes
And granted us the wish we'd crave.
Would you wish for diamonds, dear,
Or would you wish for pearls;
Would you wish to rule the land and sea,

Would you wish a crown to rest upon your golden
      curls?
The maiden sweetly answered, "Not for me.

CHORUS

"I'd wish for a night in June,
A silv'ry moon real soon,
A moon that makes you want to spoon
And softly croon love's tune.
Then a tree that I could trust,
A bench that just holds two;
Then I'd wish for Cupid's loving dish
And then I'd wish for you."

VERSE 2

"Why should I profess to sigh
For precious pearls or diamonds
When my ev'ry sigh means you?
All the gold the world may hold,
Its wealth untold, I would unfold,
To hold a place that just holds two,
Hold a place that holds a face
That holds a case of bliss,
And that case of bliss would hold you too.
Such a place would make me trace upon your face
      a kiss."
The fellow answered, "Here's just what I'd do:

REPEAT CHORUS

THAT KAZZATSKY DANCE

Published. Copyrighted December 19, 1910. According to one newspaper report, Irving Berlin introduced this song in a vaudeville appearance at the Victoria Theatre, New York, on September 12, 1911.

VERSE 1

Abie, darling dear, can't you hear very clear
They're playing that Kazzatsky Dance?
Cohen with his hand leads the band, ain't it
      grand?
I tell you, Abie, take a chance.
Take me by the wrist with your fist, make a
      twist,
Or else I'll go right in a trance.
Come and give your baby just one glance
And we'll do that Yiddisha dance.

CHORUS

Oy, that Kazzatsky Dance,
It makes me lose my sense.
Come and get handy, it's dandy, dandy,
Kiss me, kid, I'm candy.
Oy, that Kazzatsky Dance,
I'm going in a trance,
I love my ham and cabbage, kid,
But oy, that Yiddisha,
That Yiddisha,
Oy, that Kazzatsky Dance.

VERSE 2

Abie, hurry up, take your time, hurry up,
I want to dance fast, please go slow.
Darling, run away, better stay, while they play,
Because I hate you, love you so.
Look at what you did, oh, you kid in the lid,
I'm going crazy like a loon.
Make some spooning with a silver spoon
While they play that Yiddisha tune.

REPEAT CHORUS

IT'S REALLY NONE OF MY AFFAIRS

Unpublished. No music is known to survive. According to a lyric typescript (with corrections in Berlin's hand) owned by James J. Fuld, this song was "written expressly for Miss Lillian Shaw." Only a verse and patter of the lyric survive.

VERSE

In me you see a lady
That would rather die than talk.
I mind my own affairs,
My troubles and my cares;
I never cared for knocking
For 'twas never known to pay,
Don't misconstrue my meaning
When this single word I say.
I don't intend to roast—
Oh no, far be it for me—
But this certain Mrs. Brown I'm working for,

PATTER

Her husband is a lovely man,
Does for her most all he can,
Works for her both night and day,
Gives her all his hard-earned pay.
Every morning at the gate
Kisses her good-bye at eight;
Nine o'clock a man named Jim,
Calls around, is welcomed in,
For this man she plays and sings,
Gives him tea and other things,
Feeds him on the best of sweets,
Hubby pays for all he eats.
Hubby dear will never miss
Just a teeney weeney kiss,
So she kisses him with pluck,
Throws a hug in just for luck,
Calls him lovey angel heart,
Curls his mustache à la carte,
Sits upon his lap and then
Hubby may come home at ten,
So she leads him to the gate,
Whispers, "Call next day at eight,"
He forgot his fountain pen,
So she takes him in again.
What I'd like to say would shock,
But I never care to knock,
And beside it's really none of my affairs.

Songs of 1911

DAT'S-A MY GIRL

Published. Copyrighted January 14, 1911.

VERSE 1

I'm in love
Like a dove,
Got no time to work-a with da pick and shov',
Feel so gay
That I say,
If I die tomorrow,
Honest, boss, I no feel sorrow
'Cause I feel so fine all the time,
Got-a such a feeling like da champagne wine.
Since I met-a
My sweet Annette-a
Much love I get-a for mine.

CHORUS

My gal,
She's-a got-a such a figure,
So big,
Maybe it's a little bigger.
Small feet
Just-a like-a Japanese-a;
Big waist,
It take me seven days to squeeze 'er.
My gal,
She's a dream-a, peach-a, cream-a,
Sweet to beat the band and
When you see a miss
Who got-a shape-a like-a dis,
Dat's-a my gal.

VERSE 2

My gal's pop,
He's nice wop,
He's-a got-a much-a swell-a barber shop.
Once he said,
When we wed,
If the business is rotten,
He's-a shave-a me for not'in'
And he's got
Some gal what
Manicure my fingers ev'ry day for not'.
Feel so glad that I can't get mad
And I feel yet better than that.

REPEAT CHORUS

THAT DYING RAG

Published. Copyrighted February 18, 1911. Music by
Bernie Adler. Alternate title (sheet music cover): "The
Dying Rag."

VERSE 1

Honey, I'm sinkin' fast,
Soon I will breathe my last;
Fever is very high,
Doctor said I will die.
'Fore I take my long, long rest,
Grant me, dear, one request.
'Member that afternoon
We heard that dreamy tune,
When you remarked to me,
Who wrote that melody;
That's the air I want to share
Before I die.

CHORUS

Honey dear,
I must be going, I fear,
I feel the finish is near,
Please bring your cello in here.
While I see
Just play the sweet melody
And, honey, call it for me
That Dying Rag.

VERSE 2

Honey, don't hesitate,
Soon it will be too late;
Heavenly gates I see,
St. Peter's calling me.
Thank the Lord I'm gwine to go
Up above, not below.
Right on my tombstone, dear,
Put this inscription clear:
"Buried without disgrace,
Died with a smiling face."
Honey, say I passed away
Without a care.

REPEAT CHORUS

ALEXANDER'S RAGTIME BAND

Published. Copyrighted March 18, 1911. One of the greatest successes in the annals of American popular music and the song that made Berlin famous all over the world. According to Berlin, who was quoted in a 1914 article in *Theatre Magazine*, "the melody came to me right out of the air. I wrote the whole thing in eighteen minutes surrounded on all sides by roaring pianos and roaring vaudeville actors." Berlin told the story of how "Alexander" was written to his friend Rennold Wolf, who recounted it for an article titled "The Boy Who Revived Ragtime," which he contributed to the *Green Book Magazine* (August 1913). As Wolf described it, "the greater portion of the song was written in ten minutes, and in the offices of the music publishing firm, Waterson, Berlin and Snyder (then known as Ted Snyder Co., Inc.), while five or six pianos and as many vocalists were making bedlam with songs of the day." Wolf continued:

> Berlin was not impressed by it when the melody first came to him. In fact, after playing it over a few times on the piano, he did not take the trouble to note the melody on paper. He might never have completed the song had it not been for a trip to Palm Beach, Florida, which months later he arranged to take with Jean Schwartz and Jack M. Welch. Just before train time he went to his offices to look over his manuscripts, in order to leave the best of them for publication during his absence. Among his papers he found a memorandum referring to "Alexander," and after considerable reflection he recalled its strains. Largely for the lack of anything better with which to kill time, he sat at the piano and completed the song.

The exact date of the trip to Palm Beach is unknown, but it almost certainly occurred during the winter of 1911. It is possible that the first public performance of "Alexander" took place in mid-April, possibly on April 15, in Atlantic City, New Jersey, when comedian Otis Harlan interpolated a whistled version of it into a performance of *Hell*, a segment of a three-part entertainment that later was presented in New York beginning April 27, 1911, at the Folies Bergere dinner theatre. According to Berlin scholar Charles Hamm, "Alexander" was probably given its first public performance by Emma Carus on April 17, 1911, when she began a week's engagement as headliner of the Big Easter Vaudeville Carnival at Chicago's American Music Hall. A week later she performed it in New York, and subsequently in other cities. Many of the original sheet music covers state that it was "successfully intruduced [*sic*] by Emma Carus." Other vaudevillians quickly included the song in their acts. Among them were Neil

McKinley (who may have been the second to sing it in New York), Eddie Miller, Adele Oswald, and Helen Vincent. Miss Vincent's photograph appears on some of the early sheet music covers of the song, as do photographs of, among others, Carl Cook, Belle Dixon, Mae Maxfield, and a woman billed simply as "Priscilla."

The next important date in the song's early history is May 28, 1911, when Berlin and Harry Williams offered it in the *Friars Frolic of 1911* at New York's New Amsterdam Theatre and during a subsequent two-week tour of eastern American cities that culminated with a return presentation at the New Amsterdam on June 8, 1911. As Berlin recalled his Friars rendition with Williams, for New York *Daily News* writer Danton Walker (July 29, 1938), "We sang, did a little dance and went off with a cartwheel."

Four days after the Friars tour ended, "Alexander" was offered at the Columbia Theatre, New York, as part of the burlesque entertainment *The Merry Whirl*, where it was sung by James C. Morton and Frank F. Moore. *The Merry Whirl* ran until mid-August and then toured. Throughout the summer and fall and beyond, "Alexander" became an increasingly huge sensation. The great ragtime pianist and theatre composer Eubie Blake told Robert Kimball in the late 1960s that "I helped make it popular in Atlantic City that summer when I played at the Boat House. Sophie Tucker brought Izzy—we called him that then—into the place and he thanked me for plugging his song." Finally, on September 11, 1911, Berlin, elevated to a kind of stardom by the fame of "Alexander," began a week as a vaudevillian at Hammerstein's Victoria Theatre in New York, where, of course, he included "Alexander."

Another important measure of the song's success was that Berlin's publisher ended its life as the Ted Snyder Co., for which Berlin was employed as a staff composer, and replaced it in January 1912 with the newly formed Waterson-Berlin-Snyder Company.

Many recordings spread and enhanced the fame of this song. The renowned comedy singing team of baritone Arthur Collins and tenor Byron Harlan (Victor, Columbia, Indestructible, Edison, Amberol, U.S. Everlasting, and Zonophone) had a huge success that occupied the top spot on the popular charts for ten weeks. Other notable early recordings were by Billy Murray (Edison and Edison-Amberol), Prince's Orchestra (Columbia), and the Victor Military Band (Victor). Over the years several other artists had successful recordings of the song, including Bessie Smith; the Boswell Sisters; Louis Armstrong; Bing Crosby and Connee Boswell (a number-one hit in 1938); Ray Noble; and Crosby and Al Jolson. It is not correct, as many have written, that Jolson was chiefly responsible for the song's fame; nor is it true that "Alexander" was first published as an instrumental (an instrumental was not published until September 6, 1911). On screen, Alice Faye sang it in *Alexander's Ragtime Band* (1938), and it was sung by Ethel Merman, Dan Dailey, Donald O'Connor, Mitzi

Gaynor, and Johnnie Ray in *There's No Business Like Show Business* (1954).

Over the years Berlin was often asked about the song. In 1938 he submitted the following to the publicity department of Twentieth Century–Fox to coincide with the release of the film *Alexander's Ragtime Band*.

I originally wrote the melody in 1910 as an instrumental number. By that I mean it was not intended to be a song with words, but it was to be my first instrumental piece. At that time there were many so-called ragtime instrumentals for the piano and "Alexander" was to be my first of that type. No one liked it in that form so I set a lyric to it. It then lay on the shelf for some time as everyone thought the chorus was too long and the range too large for the ordinary voice. However, Emma Carus liked the song and introduced it in Chicago. It was a big hit for her and before long many other vaudeville acts were singing it.

Before the song became very popular, I sang it as the close of a songwriter's act that was one of the features in the *Friars Frolic of 1911*. The number created quite a lot of talk in that performance and it wasn't long after then that it was a big hit both in America and abroad.

When it reached its height, I was booked for a week at Hammerstein's Victoria Theatre on the strength of the popularity of "Alexander's Ragtime Band."

I took my first trip abroad in 1912 and was delighted to hear it whistled by a newsboy as I stepped off the train at the station in London. I soon realized how big a hit "Alexander" was in England. Within a year or so it became an international song hit and was translated in almost every known language.

It has been credited for being the first ragtime song, but that is not true. There were many ragtime songs before "Alexander's Ragtime Band." The construction of the chorus was new at that time, and it was the key song for many ragtime songs to follow, among which were "Everybody's Doing It" and "Ragtime Violin."

While it was popular the first year and a half it sold about two million copies, and I would say it sold possibly 500,000 more copies since then.

On June 19, 1947, Berlin wrote the following to theatre critic Ward Morehouse for a book on which Morehouse was working at the time:

I checked with Jesse Lasky and here are the facts regarding the "Alexander's Ragtime Band" story in connection with the Folies Bergere: . . . [Sam Harris] and Jesse Lasky built what is now the Fulton Theatre, and, incidentally, it was the first theatre cabaret in America. They had engaged Ethel Levey to come over from England for this

show. Jesse Lasky asked me to write a song for her. I wrote a song called "I Beg Your Pardon Dear Old Broadway." Levey had been away from America for many years, and this was a special number to fit that situation. (By the way, it was a very bad song and never got anywhere, although Levey sang it beautifully.) I came to a rehearsal to hear Levey sing "I Beg Your Pardon Dear Old Broadway." Jesse told me they needed a spot-in-one for Levey and asked if I had a song that might be suitable. I said I had a new song and sang "Alexander's Ragtime Band" for him. He said, "This is a good song, but certainly not for Ethel Levey who's a contralto and needs a song that can be sung much slower." So "Alexander's Band" was not sung by Levey but instead was whistled by Oatis Harland [*sic*], the comedian of the show, for one performance. It was taken out of the show after the opening night of Folies Bergere. Later it was sung for the first time by Emma Carus in Chicago. This is particularly interesting because after the Folies Bergere flopped and Ethel Levey had returned to England, the song became a tremendous success and "Alexander's Ragtime Band" finally got to Levey in London. She sang it there and caused a sensation with it, singing it very slowly. Several years later, she played a return engagement in America at the Palace Theatre and sang "Alexander" in her act. I remember how upset I was at her rendition of it. The audience, of course, did not agree with me. She was a riot. Lasky just told me over the telephone that he likes to refer to himself as the man who turned down "Alexander's Ragtime Band." He added that had he been smart enough to choose it for Ethel Levey, the Folies Bergere might have been a big success . I doubt it very much. . . .

VERSE 1

Oh, ma honey, oh, ma honey,
Better hurry and let's meander,
Ain't you goin', ain't you goin',
To the leader man, ragged meter man?
Oh, ma honey, oh, ma honey,
Let me take you to Alexander's
Grand stand, brass band,
Ain't you comin' along?

CHORUS

Come on and hear, come on and hear
Alexander's Ragtime Band.
Come on and hear, come on and hear,
It's the best band in the land.
They can play a bugle call like you never heard
    before,

So natural that you want to go to war,
That's just the bestest band what am,
Honey lamb.
Come on along, come on along,
Let me take you by the hand
Up to the man, up to the man
Who's the leader of the band,
And if you care to hear the "Swanee River" played
  in ragtime,
Come on and hear, come on and hear
Alexander's Ragtime Band.

VERSE 2

Oh, ma honey, oh, ma honey,
There's a fiddle with notes that screeches
Like a chicken, like a chicken,
And the clarinet is a colored pet;
Come and listen, come and listen,
To a classical band what's peaches,
Come now, somehow,
Better hurry along.

REPEAT CHORUS

VIRGINIA LOU

Published. Copyrighted March 20, 1911. Berlin's revised lyric for an original song by Eddie Leonard and Earl Taylor (copyrighted December 7, 1910).

VERSE 1

I'm writing her a letter
To Virginia, where I met her,
And believe me I'll feel better
When she knows I'm coming home.
My heart will cease its aching;
If God grants tomorrow's waking
A train I will be taking to my own.
Let me hear a Southern tune,
For I'm going back to Virginia soon.

CHORUS

Virginia Lou,
I'm coming home to you,
Because I'm lonesome and blue
All through and through.
Southern jokes and Southern folks
Are good enough for me too
If they're for you.
If I remain I'll go insane,

I'm waiting now to bless the train
That carries me back to old Virginia.
Lou, Lou, I'm coming home to you,
Virginia Lou.

VERSE 2

If Southern blood flows in yer,
Take a map of old Virginia,
Look 'er over and then kin yer
Help but say that none compare?
The map is bound to find yer
Weeping tears of joy that blind yer,
If you left one behind yer, waiting there.
Pretty gals there's quite a few,
But there's only one Virginia Lou.

REPEAT CHORUS

THAT MONKEY TUNE

Published. Copyrighted March 25, 1911. On the cover of the original sheet music is the legend "Successfully introduced by Emma Carus," and her photograph.

VERSE 1

Down
In a sunny jungle town
Where the monkeys run around
Lived a crazy little monkey who loved to sing.
A chimpanzee
In a coconutty tree
Heard his nutty melody.
She
Fell in love with his singing,
From the branches a-clinging
She'd pitch her voice in a monkey key
And yell with all her might:

CHORUS

"Sing
That monkey tune,
You monkey loon
Don't dare to stop, hurry up, hurry up,
I want to hear
That strain so queer
Because I'm crazy
About that monkey tune."

VERSE 2

She
Kept a-shouting from the tree
For his nutty melody
Till the crazy little monkey looked up and said,
"I want to spoon
Neath the monkey honeymoon
To the nutty wedding tune
Soon."
Mister and Missus Monkey
Pitched their voices in one key
And now they can't get a wink of sleep,
The baby yells all night:

REPEAT CHORUS

WHEN I'M ALONE
I'M LONESOME

Published. Copyrighted March 25, 1911. Across the top of the original sheet music cover is the legend "Successfully introduced by Emma Carus."

VERSE 1

I feel blue,
Lonesome too,
Just because I'm all alone.
I confess
Lonesomeness
Seems to be the only friend I own.
No one cares to hear my woes;
Friendless like a faded rose.
I'm unhappy, goodness knows,
When I'm all alone.

CHORUS

When I'm alone I'm lonesome,
When I'm alone I'm blue.
Someone kindly listen to my sympathy plea,
Ev'ry other girl and brother
Has a pal just like a mother,
Whom they can tell their troubles,
Whom they can call their own.
Won't somebody kindly hear me,
Linger near me, come and cheer me,
I'm lonesome when alone.

VERSE 2

One-oh-oh,
Now you know
That's the number of my phone;
Five-six-eight
On the gate,
Now you know the number of my home.
Father tries to make me glad
When he thinks I'm feeling sad,
But there's things you can't tell Dad
When you're all alone.

REPEAT CHORUS

I BEG YOUR PARDON, DEAR OLD BROADWAY

Published. Copyrighted March 28, 1911. Introduced by Ethel Levey and ensemble in *Gaby* ("A Satirical Revuette in Three Scenes," says the program), the third part of the three-part spring 1911 show at the restaurant-theatre Folies Bergère. The original sheet music cover has a large photograph of Levey.

VERSE 1

Broadway, Broadway,
I've a message from a friend across the foam
From someone who loves you dearly
Though he's miles away from home.
Kind applause is not his cause,
Because I know he loves you true.
I'll feel better when I read his letter;
Here's the words he wrote to you:

CHORUS

"I beg your pardon, dear old Broadway,
For list'ning to a foreign song;
I thought I'd find a street
With you could compete,
I only found that I was wrong.
My hat's aloft to you, old Broadway,
You're in a class alone today.
And if I thought for a minute
That the others were in it,
Won't you pardon me, Broadway?"

VERSE 2

Broadway, I too
Said goodbye to all the sights across the sea.

Joy! once more, for soon I saw
The Statue of Old Liberty.
Hand in air, she greets you there,
To drive away all care and pain;
Joy smiles at you, while the great big statue
Seems to say, "Never again!"

REPEAT CHORUS

THE WHISTLING RAG

Published. Copyrighted March 31, 1911. Alternate title (sheet music cover): "Whistling Rag."

VERSE 1

Alexander Johnson had a music ear,
He could whistle any tune he'd ever hear;
Couldn't sing or hum,
He was good as dumb
When it came to singing,
But you bet he could whistle some.
Liza heard him whistling a ragtime air;
"Me for you," she whispered to him then and
    there.
Now he can't decline,
Be it rain or shine,
Liza keeps a-shouting all the time:

CHORUS

"Honey, whistle that Whistling Rag,
Fill your lungs with that whistling drag,
Blessings upon the fairy
Who revealed my black canary.
Honey, I
Can't reply,
Just 'cause my
Lips are dry,
So, honey, whistle that Whistling Rag,
That's the Whistling Rag."

VERSE 2

Alexander whistled till he caught a cold;
Pretty soon the fever got a stranglehold.
Doctor shook his head,
Looked at him and said,
"Cut the whistle out."
The doctor shouted, "And stay in bed."
Liza heard the doctor and began to shout,
"Doctor, if you're goin' to cut the whistle out,
Won't you kindly wait,

Ere it is too late,
Let me say before you operate:"

REPEAT CHORUS

WHEN YOU'RE IN TOWN

Published. Copyrighted April 11, 1911. Apparently performed in the musical *A Real Girl*, which closed out of town. Alternate title (sheet music cover): "When You're in Town in My Home Town." Popular recording by Henry Burr and Elise Stevenson (Victor, Columbia, Zonophone, U.S. Everlasting).

VERSE 1

One fine day, on Broadway,
Simple Sally Brown
Met a trav'ling salesman who was trav'ling around.
"Howdy do, how are you?
Let's go see the town."
Sally answered, "What a pity,
I would like to, but the city
Folks would talk, they would talk,
You know that they can;
But I'd like to know you better,
Mister Trav'ling Man.

CHORUS

"When you're in town,
In my home town,
Look me up, look me up,
I'll be happy to see you;
When you're passing my way,
Drop in and stay,
If you'll come, you're welcome as flowers in May,
And you can hang your samples on a sour apple
    tree,
And I'll see that no one's around.
For I'd much rather walk
Where the neighbors don't talk,
When in town call around, goodbye."

VERSE 2

Sally Brown settled down,
Wed her trav'ling man.
He said, "Dearie, I'll be home as much as I can."
Trav'ling men now and then
Get a telegram,
Their employer sends a wire,
"Go and see a certain buyer."

Looking round, Sally found
In her hubby's coat
Seven diff'rent notes that seven
Diff'rent females wrote:

REPEAT CHORUS

BUSINESS IS BUSINESS

Published. Copyrighted April 21, 1911. Alternate title (sheet music cover): "Business Is Business (Rosey Cohen)."

VERSE 1

Abie Bloom loved Miss Rosie Cohen;
Abie as a bus'ness man
Was in a class alone.
Rosie's family were satisfied;
Abie owned a clothing store, a business man.
Ev'ry month Rosie's father, Mose,
Walked in Abie's clothing store
And took a suit of clothes;
One day Abie drew Rosie near
And whispered these words in her ear:

CHORUS

"Business is business, Miss Rosie Cohen,
I've got to pay for ev'rything I own.
Seven suits of clothes your father took out from
    my store,
All he says is, 'Charge it to my future son-in-law.'
Tell your expensive father C.O.D.
Don't mean 'Come On Down' to my store, for
Ev'ry little dollar carries int'rest all its own;
Bus'ness is business, Rosie Cohen!"

VERSE 2

Abie said, "Listen, Rosie dear,
Ev'ry month a suit, means just
A dozen suits a year—
Seven years, and then your father, Mose,
He will have enough to start a clothing store.
Then again, Father is no fool,
He can tell a cotton suit
From one that's made of wool—
Since I fell in love with you, Rose,
Your father is so hard on clothes."

REPEAT CHORUS

SPANISH LOVE

Published. Copyrighted on April 24, 1911, and again on October 18, 1911. Music and lyrics by Vincent Bryan, Irving Berlin, and Ted Snyder. Introduced by Ethel Levey in *Gaby*. A photograph of Levey in Spanish costume appears on the original sheet music cover. Popular recording by Andrea Sarto (Columbia).

VERSE 1

Love, never dying,
Love, ever sighing,
Love, undenying love.
Love, ever yearning,
Love, ever burning,
Sweet fire from above.
Love's mighty flame
To my lonely heart came,
'Tis a flame that will burn there
Forever, evermore.
Heaven above
Never knew greater love
Than the dear Spanish love I adore.

CHORUS

Spanish love,
Love that burns while it's chilling me,
Through and through it is thrilling me,
I would die for you willingly.
Spanish love
With its fire is instilling me,
Flames of passion are filling me,
Burning love that is killing me.

VERSE 2

Dear one that I love,
You shall be my love
Through all eternity.
Time cannot change me,
Naught can estrange me;
My king you'll ever be.
Make me your own,
Let my heart be your throne,
You will reign there alone, dear
Forever and for aye.
While time endures
All my soul shall be yours,
As I bow to your love's mighty sway.

REPEAT CHORUS

DOWN TO THE FOLIES BERGERE

Published. Copyrighted April 24, 1911. Words and music by Vincent Bryan, Irving Berlin, and Ted Snyder. Probably introduced by ensemble in *Gaby*.

VERSE 1

Why do they rave about beautiful France,
Where the wine flows and the maidens entrance?
Why go to Berlin, Vienna, or Rome?
We can enjoy all their joys here at home,
In old New York up at Long Acre Square,
Turn round the corner you'll find yourself there,
Millions of miles from all trouble and care,
Two doors from Heaven, the Folies Bergere.

CHORUS

Down, down, down, down,
Down to the Folies Bergere,
Order a taxi, a cab, or a car,
Go where the girlies sing Ooh-la-la.
Girls, boys, joys, noise,
Laughter and music all there,
Ask me where? where? where?
Down to the Folies Bergere.

VERSE 2

Why do they sing of the Rathskeller's joys?
Why go to places just meant for the boys?
We'll get the girls and we'll bring them along,
Down to the Folies, they'll see nothing wrong.
Bring down your sweetheart and give her a treat;
If your wife's there, get a gallery seat.
Then if your wife and your sweetheart should
    meet,
Thirty-two exits lead out to the street.

REPEAT CHORUS

WHEN IT RAINS, SWEETHEART, WHEN IT RAINS

Published. Copyrighted April 29, 1911. On the original sheet music cover is the following: "Dedicated to my friend, Jack Welsh."

VERSE 1

So you want me to say that I love you.
In the words of a storybook man,
Little girl, what you ask
Is indeed quite a task,
Playing hero is more than I can.
I'm a stranger with flowery speeches,
As a poet I never could learn;
All that I ask of you is to love me,
This is all I can say in return:

CHORUS

"I'll make ev'ry Monday a Sunday,
I'll cover a wrong with a right,
I'll still wear a smile in the morning,
The smile that I wore last night.
I'll stick when the sunshine has vanish'd
And darkness is all that remains,
I'll hold an umbrella up over your head,
When it rains, sweetheart, when it rains."

VERSE 2

If I said that you look'd like a princess
Or a queen, I'd be telling you lies,
'Cause I never have seen
Any princess or queen,
Still I don't think I've cheated my eyes.
All the words Mister Webster made famous,
With "I love you" they never could start,
If the speaker is dead on the level
And the words come from down in his heart:

REPEAT CHORUS

MOLLY-O! OH, MOLLY!

Published. Copyrighted May 13, 1911. On the original sheet music cover are a photograph of Emma Carus and the legend "Successfully introduced by Emma Carus."

VERSE 1

Mike O'Toole on a stool
Sat one Sunday morning fair,
Molly-O, pure as snow,
Happened to be passing there.
She smiled and said, "I see you're all alone."
Listen to some blarney Michael brought from
    home:
"Maiden sweet, half my seat

You can have, sweet Molly-O.
Faith I'm glad that your dad
Wed your mother years ago;
They never thought their girl and Mike O'Toole
Would sit and talk upon the same old stool.

CHORUS

"Molly-O, oh, Molly, I adore you,
And I've got the spot,
A regular house and lot,
There's a great big future, dear, before you,
If you'll marry me.
I hate to be talking about myself,
But when it comes to being father,
I'm as gentle as could be.
You don't say no,
So now is me time to go,
Consider yourself engaged to me,
Good morning, Molly."

VERSE 2

Molly sighed, then she cried,
"Don't you think you'd rather stay?"
Michael winked—said, "I think
This will be a lovely day."
They sat for hours on the same old stool,
Spooning like the teacher never taught at school.
Michael read from his head
Seven chapters of a book,
Ev'ry line meant a fine
Irish kiss that Michael took.
At three A.M. beneath the smiling moon,
The milkman heard him sing the same old
    tune:

REPEAT CHORUS

WHEN YOU KISS AN ITALIAN GIRL

Published. Copyrighted June 16, 1911.

VERSE 1

I no rave about Italy,
I no talk about my country,
Any place is the same to me,
Just so long I got enough to eat.
But I'd like-a to tell you dis,
I'm-a kiss-a da plenty miss,

But of all-a da sweet-a kiss
There-a one-a got the world-a beat.

CHORUS 1

When you kiss an Italian gal, boss,
Oh! You feel-a,
Well, I don't know how to tell-a,
But you get so excite
You go home that night
And put your left-a shoe
Upon the foot what is right.
Let an Italian gal, boss,
Kiss-a you upon the cheek
And you won't wash your face for a long-a time,
'Cause it feel-a so swell
When you kiss an Italian gal.

VERSE 2

My sweetheart-a look like a freak,
Got a face-a just like next week,
But the minute I kiss the cheek,
Right away she look like Anna Hel'.
Married men, if you got da strife,
You can lead-a da happy life:
Ev'ry time that you kiss your wife,
Think of an Italian-a gal.

CHORUS 2

When you kiss an Italian gal, boss,
Oh! You feel-a,
Well, I don't know how to tell-a,
But before much-a long
You feel-a so strong,
You go and choke da monk,
Until he sing-a da song.
Let an Italian gal, boss,
Kiss-a you upon the cheek
And you won't wash your face for a long-a time,
'Cause it feel-a so swell
When you kiss an Italian gal.

EPHRAHAM PLAYED UPON THE PIANO

Published. Copyrighted June 20, 1911. Words and music by Irving Berlin and Vincent Bryan. Introduced by Fanny Brice in the *Ziegfeld Follies of 1911* at the Jardin de Paris atop the New York Theatre (June 20, 1911; 80 performances).

VERSE 1

Down below the Dixie line, in Alabam',
Lived a lovin' piano player, Ephraham.
'Cause he never took a lesson,
He had ev'rybody guessin'
How he played with such a lovin' tone.
Any old piano that he could annoy,
Ephraham would call an instrument of joy;
When it came to make a piano
Cry out in a fancy manner,
Ephraham was in a class alone.

CHORUS

Ephraham played upon the piano,
Ephraham, he had a great left hand,
Ephraham in his fancy manner
Made an upright sound like a baby grand.

VERSE 2

Any kind of music he could understand,
Still he didn't play by ear, he played by hand.
When he started fishin'
For the tune that you'd been wishin',
Ev'ry other good musician stepped aside.
Ephraham was never known to lose his head;
I remember once a certain lady said,
"Can you play a fiddle, mister?"
He looked up and answered, "Sister,
I don't know because I've never tried."

REPEAT CHORUS

YOU'VE BUILT A FIRE DOWN IN MY HEART

Published. Copyrighted June 20, 1911. On the original sheet music cover is the following: "As sung by Winona Winters in the musical comedy *The Fascinating Widow* [September 11, 1911; Liberty Theatre; 56 performances]." A notice was printed at the bottom of the title page: "The performing rights of this song has [*sic*] been restricted to F. Ziegfeld, Jr. Any infringement on the part of any performer will be prosecuted to the fullest extent of the law." This song also seems to have been given to Ziegfeld for the *Ziegfeld Follies of 1911* and is listed on other sheet music for that show.

VERSE 1

Dearest, the day that I gazed in your eyes,
That was the day that Cupid came;
Some joyous feeling makes me realize
My heart is wrapped up in a flame,
And you're piling coal of love, honey mine,
On my burning heart all the time.
Worried, unhappy, I'm going about,
Fearing you'll put this fire out.

CHORUS

You've built a fire down in my heart,
Dearest, it's burning higher
Than any house on fire,
Just like a live, live wire.
Right from the start,
Oh, my pretty heart's desire,
You have built a fire
Down in my heart.

VERSE 2

Dearest, I promise this fire will burn,
Burn on until the end of time.
All that I ask of you, dear, in return
Is lots of fuel, honey mine,
And if e'er a spark of love should depart
From this fire down in my heart,
Honey, I hope the spark travels to you,
And sets your heart on fire too.

REPEAT CHORUS

WOODMAN, WOODMAN, SPARE THAT TREE!

Published. Copyrighted June 27, 1911. Words and music by Irving Berlin and Vincent Bryan. Based on the George Pope Morris/Henry Russell song of 1837. Introduced by Bert Williams in the *Ziegfeld Follies of 1911* (June 20, 1911; Jardin de Paris; 80 performances). Top-selling recordings by Bert Williams (Columbia) and Bob Roberts (Victor and Edison Amberol).

VERSE 1

A great big tree grows near our house,
It's been there quite some time,
This tree's a slipp'ry elm tree
And very hard to climb.
But when my wife starts after me,

Up in that tree I roost;
I go up like a healthy squirrel
And never need no boost.
The other day a woodman came to chop the refuge down
And carve it into kindling wood, to peddle round the town.
I says to him, "I pray thee cease, desist, refrain and stop,
Lay down that forest razor, man, chop not a single chop.

CHORUS

"Woodman, woodman spare that tree,
Touch not a single bough,
For years it has protected me,
And I'll protect it now.
Chop down an oak, a birch or pine,
But not this slippery elm of mine—
It's the only tree that my wife can't climb,
So spare that tree."

VERSE 2

I said to him, "You see that hole,
Up near that old treetop?
I've got five dollars there that's yours
If you refrain to chop.
No beast but me can climb that tree,
'Cause it's too slippery;
I can't get up myself
Unless my wife is after me.
So get my wife, and I'll call her a very naughty word,
And then you'll see me give an imitation of a bird.
You may not know just where to go when my wife gets around,
But when she comes, remember this, if I'm not on the ground:

REPEAT CHORUS

RUN HOME AND TELL YOUR MOTHER

Published. Copyrighted June 29, 1911. On some of the covers of the original sheet music there are photographs of Berlin and a child holding a flower in her teeth, with the legend "Sung by Baby Edna Nickerson the Phenomenal Child Coon Shouter." On other covers, along with the photo of Berlin, there is a photograph of two children billed as "Rutan's Song Birds."

VERSE 1

The other day a pretty little maid,
Dressed in her Sunday clothes,
All alone went strolling up the avenue.
Fellows looked as fellows do;
A certain fellow stopped her as he said,
"I beg your pardon, miss,
I've been watching you for an hour or two,
And I've got to tell you this:

CHORUS

"Run home and tell your mother,
Your father, and your brother,
That they better keep their eyes on you.
Don't forget you're nothing but a pet,
And all the boys are saying that they'll get you
   yet.
If you don't watch out,
Some fellow will be stealing you,
As fellows often do;
Run home and tell your mother,
Your father, and your brother,
That they better keep their eyes on you."

VERSE 2

The maiden said, "How dare you talk to me?
I'll call an officer."
Pretty soon an officer was by her side.
"He insulted me," she cried.
The fellow started running down the street,
And pretty soon he fled;
While the fellow ran, Mister Policeman
Turned unto the maid and said:

REPEAT CHORUS

AFTER THE HONEYMOON

Published. Copyrighted August 23, 1911. Music by
Ted Snyder. Major recording by Walter Van Brunt
(Columbia).

VERSE 1

Before you get married your sweetheart
Is your sweetheart to the dot,
But after you marry your sweetheart, girls,
Becomes your sweetheart not.
Of course there are many exceptions
To most ev'ry rule, but then

In this very case, any time, any place,
Eleven times out of ten,

CHORUS

After the honeymoon, after the honeymoon
There's millions of women and millions of men*
Who'd give half their lives to be sweethearts
   again.
After it's Mister and Missus
There's often a year between kisses,
A sweet wedding cake only gives you an ache
After the honeymoon.

VERSE 2

Before your engagement you want your love
To stand and stand around,
But after the wedding, it changes to
"For goodness sake, sit down!"
You want who you want in the summer,
You get who you want that fall,
But after you've got who you wanted, it's not
The one whom you wanted at all.

REPEAT CHORUS

THAT MYSTERIOUS RAG

Published. Copyrighted August 31, 1911. Music by Ted
Snyder. According to various newspaper reports the
song was introduced by Berlin in a vaudeville appear-
ance he made during the week of September 12, 1911, at
Hammerstein's Victoria Theatre, New York, and was
written for the occasion. Leading recordings by Arthur
Collins and Albert Campbell (Columbia) and the
American Quartet (Victor) and, more recently, by Joan
Morris and William Bolcom (*The Girl on the Magazine
Cover*, RCA, 1979). This song also is listed on the origi-
nal sheet music cover for the song "Cuddle Up" as being
part of the score for *A Real Girl* (1911).

"That Mysterious Rag" was one of many American
songs about ragtime that captivated sophisticated Euro-
pean musicians. When Erik Satie was composing his bal-
let score *Parade* (1917) for Serge Diaghilev's Ballets
Russes, he used and parodied the rhythms and har-

---

*Alternate version of lines 2 and 3 (see *Hamm, vol. 2,
pp. 70–73*):*

   I'll wager my life there are millions of men
      Who wish that their wives were their sweethearts
         again.

monies of "Mysterious Rag" for the "Little American
Girl" section of his astonishing collaboration with Jean
Cocteau, Pablo Picasso, and Léonide Massine.

Irving Berlin, in a letter to Cole Porter, September 2,
1943:

   Years ago, I remember, the William Morris office
   booked me to play at the Winter Garden, where I
   came out and sang "Mysterious Rag," in a green
   spotlight, and the audience was very glad when I
   finished. I remember paying them ten per cent of
   my salary and would have been glad to give them
   the whole salary if they hadn't booked me there.

VERSE 1

Did you hear it? Were you near it?
If you weren't, then you've yet to fear it;
Once you've met it, you'll regret it,
Just because you never will forget it.
If you ever wake up from your dreaming,
A-scheming, eyes gleaming,
Then if suddenly you take a screaming fit,
That's it!

CHORUS

That mysterious rag,
While awake or while you're a-slumbering,
You're saying, "Keep playing
That mysterious drag."
Are you listenin'?
Are you listenin'?
Look! Look!
You're whistlin'
That mysterious rag,
Sneaky, freaky, ever melodious,
Mysterious rag.

VERSE 2

Any minute they begin it,
E'er you know what you're about you're in it;
Then a feeling, most appealing,
Comes a-stealing, sets your brain a-reeling.
When it's late and ev'ryone is yawning,
Good morning, day dawning,
Then if suddenly you hear a warning shout,
Look out!

REPEAT CHORUS

ONE O'CLOCK IN THE MORNING I GET LONESOME

Published. Copyrighted September 16, 1911. Music by Ted Snyder. Introduced by Berlin in a vaudeville appearance he made during the week of September 12, 1911, at Hammerstein's Victoria Theatre, New York. This song also is listed on the original sheet music for the song "Cuddle Up" as being part of the score for *A Real Girl* (1911). Major recording by Walter Van Brunt (Columbia).

VERSE 1

Jonesey with a frown
Was telling Mister Brown,
"Old pal, I'm just as sick as I can be.
Most ev'rything I've done,
The doctors, ev'ryone,
In vain have tried to find a cure for me.
They doctor me until I almost faint,
They help'd me not, for this is my complaint:

CHORUS 1

"One o'clock in the morning I get lonesome,
One o'clock in the morning I get blue,
But my wife and family won't stay up with me,
So I've got to leave the house and hunt for
    company.
Going in and out the diff'rent places,
Places where they've thrown away the key,
I just hunt until I'm wild
For a woman, man, or child,
Who is troubled with the same complaint as
    me."

VERSE 2

Many doctors thought
An operation ought
To be the very thing, without a doubt.
They ether'd him, the fools,
Then went to get their tools;
Came back at one to cut his lonesome out.
They found a dozen nurses by his side,
They ask'd him to explain, and he replied:

CHORUS 2

"One o'clock in the morning I get lonesome,
One o'clock in the morning I get blue;
All the ether neath the sun, ether by the ton,

Couldn't keep me sleeping when the clock is
    striking one.
So you'll have to wait until tomorrow,
Soon I'll be as busy as a bee,
For I've got an awful hunch
There's a nurse among the bunch
Who is troubled with the same complaint as
    me."

THERE'S A GIRL IN HAVANA

Published. Copyrighted September 19, 1911. Words and music by E. Ray Goetz (1886–1954), Irving Berlin, and Ted Snyder. Introduced by Will Archie and Helen Hayes in the Lew Fields musical *The Never Homes* (October 5, 1911; Broadway Theatre; 92 performances). The sheet music erroneously credits E. Ray Goetz and A. Baldwin Sloane as the writers of this song. Major recording by the Lyric Quartet (Victor), whose members were Harry MacDonaugh, Reinald Werrenrath, Olive Kline, and Elsie Baker.

VERSE 1

I'm in love with you, but I'll admit
I've told the same tale o'er
To a lot of girls, but I'll admit
'Twas never meant before.
Like ev'ry boy, I've loved a few, 'tis true,
But never with a love I feel for you;
So I think for future happiness
My past I should confess.

CHORUS

There's a girl in Havana,
There's a girl in Savannah,
I've wooed a few sweet girlies who
I promised to be true to,
But then I never knew, dear,
That I'd ever meet you, dear,
So let's forget the girls I met
Before I met you.

VERSE 2

If a fellow says he loves you,
And he's never said the same
To another girl, if you believe him,
You're the one to blame.
When love is true, each thought you would
    confide,

When love is true, there's naught that you could
    hide;
So to prove my love is not amiss
Is why I tell you this.

REPEAT CHORUS

DON'T TAKE YOUR BEAU TO THE SEASHORE

Published. Copyrighted September 22, 1911. Words and music by E. Ray Goetz and Irving Berlin. On the original sheet music cover is the following: "Sung by Julian Eltinge in the musical comedy *The Fascinating Widow* [September 11, 1911; Liberty Theatre; 56 performances]."

VERSE 1

Mother often said to me,
"Someday a beauty fair
You may or may not grow to be,
In any case beware.
Beside a fellow's side,
A gown your faults will always hide,
But not beside a fellow's side
Beside the oceanside;
He's there when you go in without a doubt,
He's liable to be gone when you come out.

CHORUS

"Don't take your beau to the seashore,
When bathing, don't take your beau to the shore,
For bathing suits reveal what petticoats conceal,
And if there's a slight defection,
You will never stand inspection,
When you go down to the seashore.
Take my advice and you won't go wrong:
Girls, when you go,
If you've nothing to show,
Don't take your beau along."

VERSE 2

Mother knew a thing or two,
She told me Father dear
Had never seen her bathing,
That's the reason I am here.
An ankle should be covered good
Until the show'r of rice,

And even then it's none too safe
To show it more than twice.
Although we know that love is blind, be wise!
A bathing suit may open up his eyes.

REPEAT CHORUS

DOGGONE THAT CHILLY MAN

Published. Copyrighted September 30, 1911. Introduced in the *Ziegfeld Follies of 1911* by Fanny Brice (June 20, 1911; Jardin de Paris, New York; 80 performances). The cover of the original sheet music states incorrectly that this song has "words and music by Vincent Bryan and Irving Berlin." The original cover lists the following Berlin songs as being from the *Ziegfeld Follies of 1911*: "Ephraham Played Upon the Piano," "You've Built a Fire Down in My Heart," "Woodman, Woodman, Spare That Tree," and "Doggone That Chilly Man."

VERSE 1

Did you ever fall in love with a bonehead,
A stoneheaded man,
A man who doesn't know that the lights a-burning
   low
Mean he should be most lovable?
That's the very kind of man that I'm in love
   with,
A dove with no heart.
When he should hug, snug like a bug within a
   rug,
That's the time he wants to part.

CHORUS

Doggone that chilly man of mine,
Overboard I'd shove him,
Just because he made me love him.
Doggone that chilly man of mine,
He's as cold a lover
As the pole that Cook discovered.
Doggone that icy man of mine,
With a heart just like a fan,
For when I'm all fussed up for an ever-lovin'
   spoon,
He's out in the garden making faces at the moon,
And I sigh, and I cry,
Doggone that chilly man.

VERSE 2

When your heart is jumping to your collar,
You holler for love,
And that's the time a man should be doing all he
   can
To love his gal most beautiful.
When I ask him for a kiss on his call days,
He'd always refuse.
What would you think of any man who talks of
   love
While he reads the daily news?

REPEAT CHORUS

RAGTIME VIOLIN!

Published. Copyrighted October 6, 1911. Top-selling recording by the American Quartet (Victor), who also recorded it as the Premier Quartet for Edison and Edison Amberol. Alternate title: "The Ragtime Violin." Later sung by Alice Faye, Dixie Dunbar, and Wally Vernon in the musical film *Alexander's Ragtime Band* (1938) and by Judy Garland and Fred Astaire in the musical film *Easter Parade* (1948).

VERSE 1

Mister Brown, Mister Brown had a violin,
Went around, all around with his violin.
Lawdy, how he play'd it, sway'd it,
Made it moan so beautiful.
Anna Lize, Anna Lize heard his violin,
Roll'd her eyes, roll'd her eyes at his violin,
Lawdy, how he lov'd 'er, turtle-doved 'er,
When Anna would cry:

CHORUS

"Fiddle up, fiddle up
On your violin;
Lay right on it, rest your chin upon it,
Doggone, you better begin
And play an overture upon your violin.
Hurry up, hurry up with your violin;
Make it sooner,
Don't you stop to tune 'er,
Fid-fid-fid-fiddle
The middle of your ragtime violin."

VERSE 2

Mister Brown, Mister Brown at a fancy ball,
Sat around, sat around, sat around the hall.
Wouldn't take a chance to dance,
Because the band was terrible.
Anna Lize, Anna Lize hit upon a plan,
Roll'd her eyes, roll'd her eyes at the leader man,
Took his fiddle down to Mister Brown, to
Just kiss him and cry:

REPEAT CHORUS

YIDDISHA NIGHTINGALE

Published. Copyrighted October 7, 1911.

VERSE 1

Miss Minnie Rosenstein
Had such a voice so fine,
Just like Tetrazzini;
Any time that Minnie sang a song,
You'd think of real estate seven blocks long.
Some song!
Young Mister Abie Cohn
Used to call to her home
Just to hear her singing;
Presents he was bringing, full of bliss!
One night young Abie proposed to the miss,
Like this:

CHORUS

"Yiddisha nightingale, sing me a song,
Your voice has got such sweetness
That it makes me strong.
Yiddisha nightingale, sing me a song,
I promise that I'll take you on a long honeymoon.
I'd give a dollar to hear you, my queen,
I wouldn't give a nickle to hear Tetrazzini—
Just to hear your cultivated voice good and strong,
I'd serve a year in jail,
Yiddisha nightingale,
Won't you sing me a song?"

VERSE 2

Then said young Abie Cohn,
"I'm goin' to buy a home,
One that's made of marble,
Dear, where you can warble harmony,

And I don't care for expenses, you see,
That's me!
I'll go and learn to play on the piano, say,
You'll sing while I'm playing,
People will be saying
As they pass
And they look in through the windowpane glass,
Some class!"

REPEAT CHORUS

MY MELODY DREAM

Published. Copyrighted October 14, 1911. On the original sheet music cover, which is black and white, "My Melody Dream" is described as "a song poem." It was "Respectfully Dedicated to My Pal Wilson Mizner."

While in slumberland I dreamed
A dream so beautiful;
While in slumberland I seemed
To hear the sweetest melody,
Sweetest melody.
It seemed that melody dear
Had journeyed year after year,
Then stopped to rest in my ear,
Seeming to know it was welcome.
But soon when I woke again,
I found that beautiful strain
Had left me crying in vain;
Come back, come back again.
Seems an angel from above
Had sent that melody
To remind me of my love
That vanished like my melody,
Like my melody dream.

YOU'VE GOT ME HYPNOTIZED

Published. Copyrighted November 2, 1911.

VERSE 1

Listen, honey dear,
I've been feeling queer;
I don't know what to do

Since I fell in love with you.
It's true,
I'm feeling so lonesome and blue too,
I'll go crazy soon,
Morning, night, and noon,
I'm just going around
With my eyes upon the ground,
And now, my honey, I've found

CHORUS

You've got me hypnotized,
I'm certainly mesmerized,
I thought that I was wise,
Till I gazed in your beautiful eyes.
That very day,
You stole my heart away;
I'm doing things I shouldn't do,
Things I wouldn't do,
Things I couldn't do,
I could do for you,
Just because you've got me hypnotized.

VERSE 2

Honey, just for you,
If you asked me to,
Like a baby I'd crawl
Ev'ry time I hear you call.
I'm all
Wrapped up in a heavenly shawl,
All that I do is fret
Till my eyes are wet.
If my love disappears,
I would sit and cry for years,
And weep an ocean of tears.

REPEAT CHORUS

EVERYBODY'S DOING IT NOW

Published. Copyrighted November 2, 1911. Alternate title (sheet music cover): "Everybody's Doin' It Now." Top-selling recordings by Arthur Collins and Byron Harlan (Victor, Columbia, and U.S. Everlasting), Arthur Pryor's Band (Victor), and the Peerless Quartet (Columbia). (The Peerless Quartet in 1911–12 consisted of tenors Henry Burr and Albert Campbell, baritone Arthur Collins, and bass John Meyer.) Many of the early sheet music covers bear the legend "As sung by Lydia Barry at the Winter Garden, New York." Later sung by Alice Faye, Dixie Dunbar, and Wally Vernon in the

musical film *Alexander's Ragtime Band* (1938) and by the ensemble in the musical film *Easter Parade* (1948). In an article from 1913 Berlin spoke about the song:

> I write words and music at the same time. Usually I sit at a piano and pick with one finger. I have in mind some phrase, some line or some idea. For instance the line "Everybody's Doin' It" was particularly fortunate. It was something universal. Analyze it and it means nothing. As a line that suggests something it is unlimited in possibilities. Everybody might be doing anything or everything. But everybody is doing something and that was the great catch line of that song. I might call it the spark of the song.

VERSE 1

Honey, honey, can't you hear?
Funny, funny music, dear;
Ain't the funny strain
Goin' to your brain?
Like a bottle of wine, fine,
Hon, hon, hon, hon, take a chance,
One, one, one, one little dance;
Can't you see them all
Swaying up the hall?
Let's be gettin' in line.

CHORUS

Ev'rybody's doin' it,
Doin' it, doin' it,
Ev'rybody's doin' it,
Doin' it, doin' it;
See that ragtime couple over there,
Watch them throw their shoulders in the air,
Snap their fingers—honey, I declare,
It's a bear, it's a bear, it's a bear.
There!
Ev'rybody's doin' it,
Doin' it, doin' it,
Ev'rybody's doin' it,
Doin' it, doin' it;
Ain't that music touching your heart?
Hear that trombone bustin' apart?
Come, come, come, come let us start,
Everybody's doin' it now.

VERSE 2

Baby, baby, get a stool,
Maybe, maybe I'm a fool;
Honey, don't you smile,
Let us rest a while,
I'm so weak in the chest, best,
Go, go, go, go get a chair,
No, no, no, no, leave it there;

Honey, if the mob
Still are on the job,
I'm as strong as the rest.

REPEAT CHORUS

BRING BACK MY
LOVIN' MAN

Published. Copyrighted November 16, 1911. The original sheet music cover bears a legend at the top that reads: "Successfully introduced by Little Amy Butler." The cover also has a photograph of Butler. Major recording by Ada Jones (Victor).

VERSE 1

Kindly lend an ear to my appeal;
I've lost the only man I had.
You will know just how I feel
When I tell you I'm sadder than sad!
Ever since he left I'm looking pale,
And ev'ry day I lose a pound.
Won't you help me look around
Till my ever-lovin' man is found?

CHORUS

Bring back my lovin' man,
Bring back my great big bunch of sweetness;
Bring back them kisses sweet,
Find 'em! Find 'em!
The kisses with the steam behind 'em!
Beneath the carpet in my hall,
I got a little money, take it all!
Take it all if you will bring back
To me my ever-lovin' man.

VERSE 2

All I do is worry, day and night;
I've lost the roses off my cheek,
And I've lost my appetite;
Haven't eaten a thing for a week.
If you saw the foolish things I do,
I know you'd stand right up and laugh.
I've just kiss'd away 'most half
Of his ever-lovin' photograph.

REPEAT CHORUS

SOMBRERO LAND

Published. Copyrighted November 17, 1911. Words and music by E. Ray Goetz, Irving Berlin, and Ted Snyder. On the original sheet music cover is the following: "As sung by Dolly Jardon at the Winter Garden, New York." There is evidence that it was sung in *La Belle Paree* (March 20, 1911; Winter Garden, New York; 104 performances).

VERSE 1

Starlight a-twinkling,
Mandolin tinkling
Sweet serenade,
Mid convent bells,
Of love sweetly tells
A Mexican maid;
Longing to go to,
Longing to know true
Love's paradise,
As he sings to eyes
That dim fairest golden skies:

CHORUS

"Sombrero Land,
Fair tropic strand
Beside the Rio Grande,
With love my heart command;
Eyes understand
What hearts demand,
Come, we'll delight some, quite some,
Bright Sombrero Land."

VERSE 2

Silently hiding,
Silently sliding
Down to his arms,
Two lips caress,
With kisses impress
Her heart in their charms;
Through gardens groping
They go eloping,
Silently flee,
As once more to her
He tenderly hums his plea:

REPEAT CHORUS

CUDDLE UP

Published. Copyrighted November 24, 1911. On the original sheet music covers is the following: "Bonita and Lew Hearn" in *A Real Girl*. Presumably they introduced it during the pre-Broadway tryout. The show closed out of town. Eight songs are listed on the cover, including four by Berlin: "Cuddle Up," "When You're in Town," "That Mysterious Rag," and "One O'Clock in the Morning."

VERSE 1

Dearie, dearie, linger nigh,
Hear me, hear me, hear me sigh;
Since you told me that you love me,
I've been feeling so fine.
Some sweet something round my heart
Has been thumping from the start,
I just feel like I've been bathing,
In an ocean of wine.

CHORUS

Cuddle up, my bunch of joy,
Cuddle up and hold me, fold me.
Come and build a nest
On my lovin' breast;
Nestle to your Venus,
Nothing can come between us.
Cuddle up, my bunch of joy,
Cuddle up, caress me, press me.
Oh, my darlin' beau,
I want to show
I love you so;
And if you want to know
Just how I love you, dear,
Come and cuddle up now.

VERSE 2

Peachy, peachy turtle dove,
Teach me, teach me how to love;
Tell me that you're glad you found me,
Oh, my lovable boy.
Meet me, greet me with a kiss,
Sweety, treat me to some bliss,
Throw your great big arms around me
Till I holler for joy.

REPEAT CHORUS

BRING ME A RING IN THE SPRING AND I'LL KNOW THAT YOU LOVE ME

Published. Copyrighted December 5, 1911.

VERSE 1

Spooning and crooning they sit,
Loving it quite a bit,
Telling lies by the pack;
See him steal a kiss from the pretty miss,
Watch him put it back, smack!
"Honey, oh, honey, I swear
By my hair that I care
For nobody but you.
Can't you tell the way I woo
That I love you, love you true?"
Then the maiden sings this chorus old,
But sings it oh, so new:

CHORUS

"Bring me a ring in the spring
And I'll know that you love me,
A simple band of gold,
Just like your father gave your mother in the days
    of old.
Say what you may, what you say
Doesn't mean that you love me,
So if you want me to love you true,
Bring me a ring in the spring
And I'll know that you love me.

VERSE 2

"Whispering nothings, my dear,
In my ear when I'm near
Is as sweet as can be;
But I sit and grieve when you have to leave,
That's what worries me, see!
When I'm just bathing in woe,
Don't you know that my beau
Should be right by my side?
Then again I've tried and tried
To become a blushing bride;
If you love me, tie it with a knot
That cannot be untied.

REPEAT CHORUS

HE PROMISED ME

Published. Copyrighted December 12, 1911.

VERSE 1

Kindly stop that music from playing,
"Oh, Promise Me";
Because it makes me sad, so sad,
It brings back to my memory
Years and years of misery,
Thoughts of one who promised me
A love I thought I had.

CHORUS

He promised me
That someday he would marry me;
He promised me
A beautiful home,
One down by the sea;
He promised that he'd pay
For the wedding day,
On the first of May;
Then he moved away, and all he left
Were the promises he promised me.

VERSE 2

Sealskins, autos, dresses, and diamonds
He promised me,
And told me that someday he'd pay;
My ringless fingers know he's gone,
All my rings he put in pawn,
Even took the tickets on
The day he went away.

REPEAT CHORUS

MEET ME TONIGHT

Published. Copyrighted December 12, 1911.

VERSE 1

Molly's dad and mother,
Sister and her brother,
Went to see an uncle,
Leaving Molly all alone.
Molly on her own hook
Took the telephone book,
Soon Miss Central heard this conversation o'er the
    phone:
"Now, Charlie dear, I need your company,
And if you want to prove your love for me:

CHORUS

"Meet me tonight, meet me tonight,
Bring down your kisses,
I'll be there with mine, all right.
We'll start out at seven,
Spoon until eleven,
Then we'll start for 'Home Sweet Home' 's a
    pretty ditty.
Meet me tonight, meet me tonight,
Don't disappoint me, honor bright.
Love and kisses we'll be pawning,
Till the yawning, dawning morning,
If you meet me tonight."

VERSE 2

Charlie met Miss Molly,
They got feeling jolly;
Talked a while, then walked a mile,
Then had another talk.
They grew tired of talking,
They grew tired of walking,
Then to make things lively, for a change they took
    a walk.
That morning when he left her at the door,
She whisper'd, "If you'd like to walk some more:

REPEAT CHORUS

YANKEE LOVE

Published. Copyrighted December 15, 1911. Words and music by E. Ray Goetz and Irving Berlin. The sheet music cover bears the legend "As introduced by Mabel McKinley," a large photograph of McKinley, and the following erroneous credit: "Words by E. Ray Goetz. Music by Irving Berlin."

VERSE 1

Girlie, cuddle near me,
Girlie, won't you hear me?
I've been feeling blue;
Ring the final curtain,
For I'm more than certain,
I'm in love with you.
Like my Yankee father,
Girlie, I would rather
Die than prove untrue.
Fearless, undenying,
Yankee never-dying
Love I bear for you.

CHORUS

Red, white, and blue love,
Real all-for-you love,
All-through-and-through love,
Real Yankee-Doodle Doo love,
Honest and true love,
I bring to you, love,
Old Kentucky, Alabama,
Mississippi, Lou'siana,
Yankee love.

VERSE 2

Girlie, flags are waving,
My poor heart's behaving
Like a house on fire;
Church bells gayly ringing
Mean I'll soon be bringing
Home my heart's desire.
Thoughts of care or sorrow
Will be dead tomorrow,
When you wear my ring;
Ere the morn arouses,
From the tops of houses
To the world I'll sing:

REPEAT CHORUS

HOW DO YOU DO IT, MABEL, ON TWENTY DOLLARS A WEEK?

Published. Copyrighted December 19, 1911. In recent years the song was recorded and frequently performed by Max Morath.

VERSE 1

Mabel Brown came to town,
All dressed up in her gingham gown,
And a ribbon in her hair,
In her eyes a vacant stare;
Joined a show, wrote her beau,
Mabel wanted to let him know
She was earning, so to speak,
Twenty dollars a week.
Her beau came down to New York town
To see Mabel dear,
The minute that he saw her flat,
He whisper'd in her ear:

CHORUS 1

"How do you do it, Mabel,
On twenty dollars a week?
Tell us how you are able,
On twenty dollars a week.
A fancy flat and a diamond bar,
Twenty hats and a motorcar;
Go right to it,
But how do you do it,
On twenty dollars a week?"

VERSE 2

Mabel's beau couldn't go,
Hung around for a week or so;
Till he'd written on a pad
All the things that Mabel had.
When he'd spent ev'ry cent,
Right to Mabel he quickly went
For a small financial loan;
Then he started for home.
Each girl he met down home, you bet,
He told them all he saw.
Next day a mob were on the job
At Mabel's flat to roar:

CHORUS 2

"How do you do it, Mabel,
On twenty dollars a week?
Tell us how you are able,
On twenty dollars a week.
We'd like to work in the chorus too,
Earn our twenty the same as you;
If we knew it,
We'd willingly do it,
On twenty dollars a week."

BEAUTIFUL CHORUS GIRLS

No music is known to survive. A lyric typescript found among Berlin's papers, now in the Irving Berlin Collection of the Music Division of the Library of Congress, bears the legend "Copyrighted 1911 by Ted Snyder Co." Yet the extensive 1993 Irving Berlin copyright search failed to show any prior copyright registration for this song.

VERSE

Musical plays of nowadays
For which the two-dollar audience pays
Never could open shop without some chorus girls.
Managers know that kind of show,
With twenty stars at a thousand a throw,
Never would mean success without some chorus
  girls.
The Tra-la-las behind the stars
With discord singing that often jars
Are really responsible for the success
Of many a musical show.

CHORUS 1

Beautiful dancing, most entrancing chorus girls.
What would the managers do without Maries and
  Pearls?
Gwendolyn, Polly, Estelle, and Cora
Figured a little in *Floradora*;
Many's the mess was made success
By beautiful chorus girls.

CHORUS 2

Beautiful dancing, most entrancing chorus girls.
What would the managers do without Maries and
  Pearls?
Gwendolyn, Polly, Estelle, and Anna
Hello'd the people to see *Havana*;
Many's the show was made a go
By beautiful chorus girls.

THE YIDDISHA BALL

No music is known to survive. A lyric typescript found among Berlin's papers, now in the Irving Berlin Collection of the Music Division of the Library of Congress, bears the legend "Copyrighted 1911 by Ted Snyder Co." Yet the extensive 1993 Irving Berlin copyright search failed to show any prior copyright registration for this song.

VERSE 1

Oy, oy, listen Rose—put on your fancy clothes,
I'm goin' to take you to the Yiddisha ball.
Hurry up, come down, dressed in your velvet
    gown,
You'll be the best in the hall.
We want to show, let them know
That we go in the latest style
Or we wouldn't go at all.
Call me a fancy name,
You'll be so glad you came
To the Yiddisha ball.

CHORUS

Come, come, come along, it isn't far,
Come, come, we can take a trolley car.
We will dance and sing, take in everything,
Like a fancy king, I'll spend the evening.
Maybe when it's over we can grab
Abie's second-handed taxicab.
Clean your jewelry, so the crowd can see
You've got diamonds, gee, when you dance
    with me
Down at the Yiddisha ball.

VERSE 2

Rosieneau, my own musical Sammy Cohen
His fancy orchestra is going to bring.
When he leads the band, you could just kiss his
    hand.
He wears a big diamond ring.
A friend of mine, Rosenstein,
Gave me balcony tickets, dear,
So we wouldn't have to stand,
And I'll propose to you
While we're listening to
Sammy's Yiddisha band.

REPEAT CHORUS

I MIGHT GO HOME TONIGHT

Written around 1911. Words and music by Vincent Bryan and Irving Berlin. No music is known to survive. A lyric typescript was found among Berlin's papers and is now in the Irving Berlin Collection of the Music Division of the Library of Congress.

VERSE 1

I've got a dear little wife at home,
She's waiting till I come in.
I'm afraid to go home, for I can't explain
When she asks me where I've been.
Although I may as well be hung for a sheep
As a blooming lamb,
I think I might go home tonight,
That's the kind of a man I am.

CHORUS

I think I might go home tonight,
My wife waits up for me,
But every night I come home tight
She'll give me the third degree.
My best excuse will be no use,
I'm tight all right, all right,
If I don't stay out until morning, boys,
I might go home tonight.

VERSE 2

The best excuses a man can make,
She's on to them all, I know.
And that is the reason my happy home
Is the last place I will go.
Although we've had six hundred scraps
And I never have won a fight,
I'd like to bet, I'll win one yet,
So I think I'll go home tonight.

REPEAT CHORUS

SPOONING IN THE NEW-MOWN HAY

Written around 1911. Words and music by Irving Berlin and Vincent Bryan. No music is known to survive. A lyric typescript found among Berlin's papers is in the Irving Berlin Collection of the Music Division of the Library of Congress.

VERSE

On a summer's day when your work is over,
Wait for the harvest moon,
In the new-mown hay and the fragrant clover,
That is the place to spoon.
Just you and he, with nothing but haystacks round
    to see.
You stray away, for you've lots of things to say;
A firefly comes round to spy (symphony),
He'll watch you two and all you do
When you're spooning in the new-mown hay.

CHORUS

When you spoon beneath the moon
At the closing of the day,
When the katydids are singing and the fireflies are
    winging,
Round your waist his arm is clinging in the same
    old way.
When all is still, the whippoorwill
Sings out his plaintive lay,
And the moon in all its glory listens to the same
    old story
When you're spooning in the new-mown hay.

DRINK, BROTHERS, DRINK

Written around 1911. Words and music by Vincent Bryan and Irving Berlin. No music is known to survive. A lyric typescript was found among Berlin's papers and is now in the Irving Berlin Collection of the Music Division of the Library of Congress.

VERSE 1

The best advice I can hope to give
Is to keep on drinking all the time you live;
If you never drink, you'll get so dry
That you'll burn twice as easy when at last you die.

CHORUS

Drink, brothers, drink—drink, I said;
When you die you'll be a long time dead.
Drink, brothers, drink, let your troubles pass;
Life looks better through the bottom of a glass.

VERSE 2

There's just two times when to drink it's right:
You can drink all day and you can drink all night.
But at other times don't taste or touch,
For you may be a drunkard if you drink too
    much.

REPEAT CHORUS

VERSE 3

Tom Jones drank hard till it came to pass
He cut his mouth upon a broken glass.
He drank very hard before that, but
He can drink twice as easy since his mouth was
    cut.

REPEAT CHORUS

VERSE 4

I knew a man and this man loved rum,
But he lost two fingers and he lost a thumb.
Every time he drank he said, said he,
"Well, I guess seven fingers will about do me."

REPEAT CHORUS

Songs of 1912

PICK, PICK, PICK, PICK ON THE MANDOLIN, ANTONIO

Published. Copyrighted January 2, 1912. On some of the original sheet music covers there is a photograph of Belle Blanche with the accompanying legend "As sung by Belle Blanche."

VERSE 1

Antonio
Long ago
Buy a mandolin
What can't be beat;
He right away
Learn to play
On the mandolin
So nice and sweet.
He's got a gal what's a swell and beautiful,
And ev'ry day
She make a drop in the shop
To Tony and say
Dis-a-way, dis-a-way:

CHORUS

"Pick, pick, pick, pick on the mandolin,
Antonio,
Swing wid da fing' on the string like dis,
Soon make a tune on da nice new mandolin;
Quick, quick, quick, quick wid da mandolin,
Antonio,
My sweet Italian love.
If you want a kiss from a miss, just like a dove,
Pick, pick, pick, pick on the mandolin, Antonio."

VERSE 2

Antonio,
He's a go
Wid his mandolin
To see his gal.
He sings a sing,
Some-a-thing
Like a serenade
So nice and swell;
He shake a shake
Till he wake a policeman
Who sleep in bed,
He break the thin mandolin
On Tonio's head,
Then he said, then he said:

REPEAT CHORUS

I WANT TO BE IN DIXIE

Published. Copyrighted January 14, 1912. Music by Ted Snyder. A big hit, this song was reported to have sold over one million copies. According to Rennold Wolf, in an article in the *Green Book Magazine* (August 1913), it was "written in the Friars Club when Berlin, to use his own expression, was 'dubbin' around the piano. Berlin had called at the club to meet Ted Snyder and Tom Penfold and found them earnestly engaged in a game of pool. To while away the time he sat down at the piano and fifteen minutes later 'Dixie' sprang into being."

First published under the title "I'm Going Back to Dixie," the song was introduced by May Irwin in *She Knows Better Now* (January 15, 1912; Plymouth Theatre, Chicago; closed out of town). The original sheet music covers of "I'm Going Back to Dixie" feature a large photograph of May Irwin and include the legend "Song Successes Introduced by May Irwin in Her New Farce Comedy, *She Knows Better Now*." The Berlin and Snyder songs listed on the cover are "I'm Going Back to Dixie," "The Ragtime Mockingbird," and "Brand New." No copy of the song "Brand New" has been discovered. Major recording of "I'm Going Back to Dixie" by Arthur Collins and Byron Harlan (Columbia and Zonophone). Under the title "I Want to Be in Dixie," the song was sung at the Winter Garden, New York, by the Courtenay Sisters in *A Night with the Pierrots*, the curtain raiser for *Whirl of Society*. The sheet music cover of "I Want to Be in Dixie" lists the publisher as "Ted Snyder Co.; Waterson, Berlin & Snyder Co. Proprietors," making this the first song to list the new company, Waterson, Berlin & Snyder, on the cover of a Berlin song.

VERSE 1

I'm very glad,
I'm very glad,
Because a train I'm takin'
To that ne'er forgotten or forsaken
Sunny land of cotton,
Down to the town I was born.
I'm glad I had,
I'm glad I had
Enough to buy a ticket.
Now I hope that there will be no pause;
Let me tell you the reason is because

CHORUS

I want to be,
I want to be,
I want to be down home in Dixie,
Where the hens are doggone glad to lay
Scrambled eggs in the new-mown hay.

You ought to see,
You ought to see,
You ought to see my home in Dixie.
You can tell the world I'm going to
D-I-X-I—I don't know how to spell it,
But I'm goin',
You bet I'm goin',
To my home in Dixieland.

VERSE 2

Conductor man,
Conductor man,
I'm kinda hard of hearin',
So just fix it when the train is nearin'
Dear old Dixie, better shout,
Holler out, good and loud.
Conductor man,
Conductor man,
I'm going to fall asleep now.
Tell the motor man to start the train;
Let me tell you when I wake up again:

REPEAT CHORUS

TAKE A LITTLE TIP FROM FATHER

Published. Copyrighted January 20, 1912. Music by Ted Snyder.

VERSE 1

Old man Wilson had quite a family,
Seven grown-up boys.
Handing out advice to his family
Was his only joy.
They would come to him for his good advice
Almost ev'ry day,
And when it came to the marriage game,
He'd light up his pipe and say:

CHORUS

"Take a little tip from Father,
Take a little tip from Dad,
Stay far away from the beautiful girls;
Each little peach is a full-grown lemon.
Wedding chimes seven times
Out of ten are bad—
But if you find a girl like Mother,
Get married like your dear old dad."

VERSE 2

Old man Wilson said to his family,
"I'm for married life
If a married man doesn't have to see
Too much of his wife!
Till you find a girl like your mother, dear,
Long you'll have to roam;
Your mother, dear, seven months each year
Would spend with her folks down home."

REPEAT CHORUS

RAGTIME MOCKINGBIRD

Published. Copyrighted January 25, 1912. According to a 1912 newspaper article, the song was written for May Irwin at the home of Berlin's fiancée, Dorothy Goetz, sister of E. Ray Goetz. On the sheet music this song is incorrectly credited to "Berlin and Snyder" and listed, along with "I'm Going Back to Dixie" and "Brand New," among the song successes introduced by May Irwin in her new farce comedy *She Knows Better Now* (January 15, 1912; Plymouth Theatre, Chicago; closed out of town). Major recording by Dolly Connolly (Columbia), the wife of composer Percy Wenrich.

VERSE 1

Honey dear, honey dear,
Can't you hear that ragtime mockingbird?
Lend an ear, lend an ear
To the dearest notes you ever have heard.
Here's the man, here's the man,
Here's the man who owns that mockingbird—
Hear him yell
That he'll sell it for a dollar bill,
Yes he will, yes he will.

CHORUS

Honey, won't you buy for me that mockingbird?
Just open up your pocketbook,
Can't you hear me holler?
Pay the man a dollar.
Honey, if you buy for me that mockingbird,
I'll call you names like King Louis the Third,
If you buy for me that ragtime mockingbird.

VERSE 2

Honey dove, honey dove,
Don't you love that feathered Tetrazzin'?

Ev'ry note in her throat
Is a boat chock'd full of peaches and cream.
If your heart cares for art,
Better part with that one-dollar bill.
Honey, why
Don't you buy that bird and keep me still?
Say you will, say you will.

REPEAT CHORUS

I'M AFRAID, PRETTY MAID, I'M AFRAID

Published. Copyrighted February 6, 1912. Major recordings by Ada Jones and Walter Van Brunt (Columbia) and by Ada Jones and Billy Murray (Edison Amberol and Zonophone).

VERSE 1

Two old sweethearts met the other day
On a crowded car and started talking.
"I'm so glad to see you," said the maid,
"Let's get off the car and do some walking."
"Pardon me," said the fellow with a sigh,
"Things that have happen'd don't allow—
Walks we had in the days gone by
Are walks we can't have now.

CHORUS 1

"I'd like to take you walking,
But I'm afraid, pretty maid, I'm afraid.
What's the good of talking
When I'm afraid, pretty maid, I'm afraid?
I'm married now, and my walking days are done,
My wife's right hand weighs a half a ton.
Gee! I'd like to have a little fun,
But I'm afraid, pretty maid, I'm afraid.

VERSE 2

"Please don't tempt me," said the married man,
"Knowing that my wife is strong and lively,
If she ever heard about the plan,
She'd decorate my room with poison ivy.
You'd enjoy if I took you out to dine,
But then it wouldn't be a joke.
I would think of that wife of mine
And then I know I'd choke.

CHORUS 2

"I'd like to take you walking,
But I'm afraid, pretty maid, I'm afraid.
What's the good of talking
When I'm afraid, pretty maid, I'm afraid?
My wife's right hand wears a bunch of pointed rings;
Any time she hits, you bet it stings.
Gee! I'd like to do a lot of things,
But I'm afraid, pretty maid, I'm afraid."

Hamm, vol. 2, p. 346, writes concerning "I'm Afraid, Pretty Maid, I'm Afraid" that the British Library has a deposit copy, dated February 1912, that has a different text for the second verse:

"I'm so sorry," said the married man
"I'd enjoy a couple of your kisses.
But my wife aims like nobody can;
Any time she throws she never misses
My wife went to a magic school to learn.
She's a magician, never fear!
If she knew, I'm afraid she'd turn
My nose into an ear."

The same source gives a different second half of the second chorus:

"My wife believes that a woman shouldn't talk
Only with a poker and a fork.
Gee I'd like to take you for a walk,
But I'm afraid, pretty maid, I'm afraid."

Hamm also notes (p. 346) that in "March of 1912, Ada Jones and Walter Van Brunt recorded a 'double' version for Columbia with the following first verse":

"How do, stranger, you're always on the go."
"Well, I must admit that I've been quite a stranger."
"Remember how we flirted years ago?"
"Yes, if we flirted now we'd only flirt with danger!"
"So let's go where we can have a quiet talk."
"Oh, excuse me, I must be on the run."
"Now for old time's sake let us take a walk."
"No, I said it can't be done."
"Why?"

ALEXANDER'S BAGPIPE BAND

Published. Copyrighted February 10, 1912. Words and music by E. Ray Goetz, Irving Berlin, and A. Baldwin Sloane. Introduced by Fay Templeton ("Bunty Bigger, with a talent for management") and ensemble in *Bunty Bulls and Strings*, part of Weber and Fields' All Star Jubilee Production *Hokey Pokey* (February 8, 1912; Broadway Theatre, New York; 108 performances).

VERSE 1

Last week when Alexander McIntosh
Returned from a trip to Yankee land,
He got a half a dozen pipers with their bagpipes
And organized a band.
He brought back with him a Yankee tune
That was written all about a coon;
Now he's playing it,
Crowds hurraying it,
Because he plays it grand:
You understand,
You understand
That it's a bagpipe, ragpipe band.

CHORUS

Come on and hear the bagpipes raggin' up a tune
In Alexander's Bagpipe Band.
Come on and see McPherson acting like a coon
In Alexander's Bagpipe Band.
Sandy McGregor is a ragtime Scot,
Come see him do the Hieland Turkey Trot,
The only ragtime Scotchman in the land.
Come on and see the lassies kicking up their
    kilties
When they do a ragtime fling;
Come on and hear the pipers play a Scottish rag
And hear the crowds begin to sing
"Should auld acquaintance be forgot" on the
    "Swanee River."
Come on along and take your lassie by the hand
To Alexander's Bagpipe Band.

VERSE 2

Ragtime was never meant for a Scotchman;
Just the same, Mister Alexander knows
Just how to play it till you feel as if a highball
Was going to your toes.
Come and hear the lassies all declare,
"Hoot mon, Sandy, it's a Hielan' Bear!"
On the heather
They dance together

With a Yankee ragtime air;
Come on along,
Come on along,
You'll see the Scotch Bonbuddies there.

REPEAT CHORUS

OPERA BURLESQUE

Published. Copyrighted February 24, 1912. Based on the sextet from Gaetano Donizetti's opera *Lucia di Lammermoor*. Introduced as "The Ragtime Sextette" in *A Night with the Pierrots*, curtain raiser for *Whirl of Society* (March 5, 1912; Winter Garden; 136 performances), by Violet Colby, Al Jolson, Willie Howard, Eugene Howard, Ernest Hare, and a sixth singer, unlisted (possibly Stella Mayhew), although it is possible that as a joke five singers sang six parts and Mayhew did not participate. Sung in Weber and Fields' All Star Jubilee Production *Hanky-Panky* (August 5, 1912; Broadway Theatre; 104 performances), billed as "a Jumble of Jollification in Two Acts," by Florence Moore ("Clorinda Scribblem, Wallingford's typewriter, with literary aspirations"), Vera Michelena ("Cleopatra, who has been in cold storage for a matter of two thousand years"), Harry Cooper ("Solomon Bumpsky, an angel"), Bobby North ("Herman Bierheister, partner and financial guide to Rausmitt"), Max Rogers ("Wilhelm Rausmitt, a capitalist"), and Hugh Cameron ("Sir J. Rufus Wallingford, a recent addition to the British peerage"). Top recording by Billy Murray and ensemble (Victor). Alternate titles: "Ragtime Opera *(Lucia)*" and "Opera Burlesque (On the Sextette from *Lucia di Lammermoor*)."

SOLO: [*Clem*] Let's sing
QUARTET: [*Danton, Nettie, Baker, and Sallie*]
    Let us sing, let us sing
SOLO: Some ragtime op'ra
QUARTET: Ragtime op'ra
SOLO: Let's sing
QUARTET: Let us sing, let us sing
SOLO: Some op'ra grand,
QUARTET: We understand
SOLO: About a man
QUARTET: Let us sing about a man
SOLO: Called Ephraham
QUARTET: Ephraham, Ephraham
SOLO: Who heard
QUARTET: Who heard
SOLO: The Sextet from *Lucia* so beautiful.
QUARTET: Beautiful!
SOLO: Ev'ry night you'd see him sitting in
    the gallery

QUARTET: At the op'ra house,
    Quiet as a mouse;
SOLO: He loved to hear Caruso sing his part
    so tenderly;
QUARTET: When he struck a high one,
    To-the-sky one,
SOLO: Ephraham would begin to holler,
QUARTET: That note alone is worth a dollar!
SOLO: Take it!
QUARTET: Take it!
SOLO: Make it!
QUARTET: Make it!
SOLO: Jump to the top of the house and
    shake it soon.
QUARTET: Very soon, very soon.
SOLO: This op'ra darkie,
QUARTET: Op'ra darkie,
SOLO: He bought
QUARTET: Yes, he bought, yes, he bought
SOLO: That score, you bet!
QUARTET: That sweet sextet!
SOLO: He hunted then
QUARTET: He went out and hunted then
SOLO: For colored men
QUARTET: Colored men, colored men
SOLO: Who could
QUARTET: Who could
SOLO: Sing that sextet he heard so beautiful.
QUARTET: Beautiful.
SOLO: Soon he found some coons who
    understood the harmony,
QUARTET: And they said:
    "We'll do it!
    Go right to it!"
SOLO: So he gave them parts and said,
    "The hard one is for me!"
QUARTET: Then they started turning up their
    voices
SOLO: Ephraham, at the old piano,
QUARTET: Struck at a chord in a fancy manner;
SOLO: Swaying,
QUARTET: Swaying
SOLO: Saying,
QUARTET: Saying
SOLO: "Start in to sing, never mind my
    playing," so
QUARTET: They began, they began
SOLO: To sing the sextet,
QUARTET: Sing the sextet.
SOLO: And say
QUARTET: Let us say, let us say
SOLO: It was a bird.
QUARTET: Then Ephr'am heard.
SOLO: He shouted, "Stop!"
QUARTET: But the singers wouldn't stop.
SOLO: They'd rather drop.
QUARTET: Rather drop, rather drop
SOLO: Than stop

QUARTET: Than stop

SOLO: That sextet from *Lucia*, so
 beautiful,

QUARTET: Beautiful.

SOLO: Ephraham cried out, "You all
 Are singing out of tune!"

QUARTET: But they kept on goin',
 Blowin', showin'

SOLO: How they could sing that ragtime
 op'ra!

QUARTET: Ephraham began to shout,

SOLO: "Stop!"

QUARTET: "No!"

SOLO: "Stop!"

QUARTET: "No!"

SOLO: "Stop!"

QUARTET: "No!"

SOLO: "Stop!"

QUARTET: "Keep it up, keep it up!
 Hon!"

SOLO: "Where's my gun, where's my
 gun?"

QUARTET: "We have only begun."

SOLO: "Better run, better run."

QUARTET: "Let us sing it for fun."

SOLO: "You're off the key!"

QUARTET: "Let it be, let it be."

SOLO: "Try and sing it right for me."

QUARTET: "Let's sing that melody."

SOLO: "Off the key, off the key!"

QUARTET: "It's as sweet as it can be,
 Like pickin' cotton."

SOLO: "Rotten!"

QUARTET: "No!"

SOLO: "Yes!"

QUARTET: "No!"

SOLO: "Yes!"

QUARTET: "No!"

SOLO: "Yes!"

QUARTET: "No!"

SOLO: "Yes, stop, I say!"

QUARTET: "Let us sing, let us sing."

SOLO: "I'd be willing to pay"

QUARTET: "Let us sing, let us sing."

SOLO: "If you stop right away"

QUARTET: "Let us sing, let us sing."

SOLO: "You'd better stop!"

QUARTET: "Keep it up!"

SOLO: "Please stop!"

QUARTET: "Keep it up!"

SOLO: "Please stop!"

QUARTET: "Keep it up!"

SOLO: "You'll stop!
 Don't you intend to ever stop?"

 [at the same time as:]

QUARTET: "We don't intend to ever stop!"

SOLO: "Please stop!"

QUARTET: "Keep it up,
 Keep it up,
 Keep it up,
 Keep it up!"

SPRING AND FALL

Published. Copyrighted February 24, 1912. On the sheet music cover Berlin described this composition as "A Tone Poem."

SPRING

The spring was here, the skies were blue,
The birds seem'd glad to sing
The very sweetest song they knew,
Ev'ry happiness to bring.
Sweet nature dressed in colors bright,
The flowers brought good cheer;
The spring was here,
The world was right,
And I knew that you were near.

FALL

The fall was here; alas! I found
That the birds had flown away;
The skies were dark for miles around,
And the whole world seem'd to pray, darling.
The sun had gone, the flowers died,
And all nature look'd forlorn;
It seem'd to me the angels cried,
And I knew that you had gone.

I'VE GOT TO HAVE SOME LOVIN' NOW

Published. Copyrighted March 4, 1912.

VERSE 1

My sweet honey, make a start,
See the longing in my eye,
Some sweet something round my heart,
Feels like I'm going to die.
Locked up in your lovin' arms I want to be,

Throw the key in the sea, gee!
Come up closer, till I know
Nothing can break us apart.

CHORUS

I've got to have some lovin' now;
Won't you let me show you how?
Now hug me like a bear,
Come and muss my hair,
Give me a kiss on the brow.
Come, be nice, sweet honey, like you should,
And love me while the lovin's good;
I may die in the morning,
So I want some lovin' now.

VERSE 2

My sweet honey, hear the chimes
Ringing out the hour of ten,
Kiss me double twenty times,
Then come and kiss me again.
One, two, three, four, wait a while, the four you
 passed
Came too fast, make 'em last, blast!
Goodbye, honey, call again,
Don't go, I'm changing my mind.

REPEAT CHORUS

SOCIETY BEAR

Published. Copyrighted April 1, 1912. On the cover of the original sheet music there is a photograph of Stella Mayhew and the accompanying legend "As sung at the Winter Garden by Stella Mayhew"—probably in the show *The Whirl of Society*, (opened March 5, 1912). Alternate title (sheet music cover): "That Society Bear."

VERSE 1

Millionaires, so the papers tell,
Learned a dance that we all know well;
Papers say that an extra-swell affair
Was given by a millionaire.
The rich four hundred, one and all, had gathered
 there;
Strange to say, some reporter men
Happened there with a pad and pen,
They wrote down what they saw, and when the news
Was printed in the papers, people were reading
 everywhere:

CHORUS

Doing that Society Bear,
Hetty Green and Rockefeller
Threw their shoulders up in the air,
Rocking like a big propeller.
Someone cried, "Cuddle up to your Vanderbilt,
Wrap me up in a beautiful di'mond quilt!"
Mister Schwab was on the job,
In a high-toned manner, playing the piano;
Morgan cried, "I don't give a care,
Let me spend another dollar!"
Throwing up his hands in the air,
Mister Gould began to holler,
"Stocks are going up, going up, going up,
Stocks are going up, going up, going up!
So come on, let's dance that Society Bear,
It's a bear, it's a bear."

VERSE 2

Papers say ev'rybody there
Laughed out loud when an heiress fair
Kissed John D. where he has no hair at all;
Then cunningly began to call
His head her lovin' bill'ard ball, around the hall.
Carnegie did the Turkey Trot
For an hour with a chicken that
Egged him on till he most forgot to care
A snap about his lib'ry, doing that rich Society
    Bear.

REPEAT CHORUS

LEAD ME TO THAT BEAUTIFUL BAND

Copyrighted April 18, 1912. Words and music by E. Ray
Goetz and Irving Berlin. Major recording by Stella May-
hew (Edison Blue Amberol). Apparently, the song was
sung in the post-Broadway tour of *Cohan and Harris
Minstrels*.

VERSE 1

Dear, lend an ear to the finest music in the land.
You'd better hurry and take a hand,
I want to linger beside that grandstand band, and
Hon, better run, just because I hear them tuning
    up.
I'm kind of hungry myself,
But we'll be late,

So please don't wait to sup.
Oh, hurry up!
I just kind of think that I'd rather drink
From a musical cup.

CHORUS

Just hear that slide trombone a-blowin' for me,
Just hear those sweet cornets all goin' for me,
Hear the piccoloer pick a melody,
See the clarionetter clarionetting me,
Hear that cello moan, moan,
Say what you may, but the way he plays that
    violin
Shows when he bows that he knows he throws his
    feelings in.
Come, come, honey, they're goin' some,
Drum, drum,
Lead me, lead me to that beautiful band.

VERSE 2

Dear, it's a year since you took your baby to a
    show,
I'm not complaining a bit, oh no!
I'm only telling you that you're oh so slow,
    beau.
I'm worth a dime, so come on, don't worry 'bout
    the fare.
We'll take some dinner along
In first-class style,
And eat it while we're there.
I'll bet my share
You'll be there all right with an appetite
Like a grizzly bear.

REPEAT CHORUS

THE MILLION-DOLLAR BALL

Published. Copyrighted May 6, 1912. Words and music
by E. Ray Goetz and Irving Berlin. Introduced in
Hanky-Panky (August 5, 1912; Broadway Theatre; 104
performances) by Carter de Haven ("Blackie Daw,
Wallingford's former pal, but present too") and Virginia
Evans ("Iona Can, formerly of the Lunch Counter Girl
Co. and now of the Peerage"). On the original sheet
music covers all songs from *Hanky-Panky*, including,
apparently, in error, "The Million Dollar Ball," are cred-
ited to E. Ray Goetz (lyrics) and A. Baldwin Sloane
(music).

VERSE 1

Dearie, hurry up, hurry up, hurry up,
I've a bit of wonderful news!
Pass your worry up, worry up, worry up;
It's the kind to drive away blues.
Tell me how you'd like to call
At the million-dollar ball
That's given by a rare millionaire, this affair,
Don't you dare to care to refuse.

CHORUS

Come on down,
There's a million-dollar ball in town,
Just chase away that frown,
Come on down,
You'll be the best little, dressed little lady,
With your diamond crown,
And your pretty little satin gown—
I'll bet that all in the ball
Start to fall in love with you,
You'll be beautiful.
Come with me
And hear that most appealing harmony,
That million-dollar feeling comes to you;
While the melody hums to you,
You'll be glad to be at that million-dollar ball.

VERSE 2

Dearie, there's a queen of a green limousine
On the outside, ready to go;
Dear, in this machine, to the scene that I mean
Only takes a minute or so.
Tell me that you understand;
Really, it's a wonderland,
And comf'table and snug like a bug in a rug,
We can hug our way to the show.

REPEAT CHORUS

ANTONIO

Published. Copyrighted May 13, 1912. Alternate title
(sheet music cover): "Antonio You'd Better Come Home."

VERSE 1

I can't explain-a how I feel, my heart no let me
    speak,
Antonio, he run away and leave me last-a week;

He take 'em all the money what I hide under the
floor,
He also take the Irish gal that live-a next-a door.
He thinks that I'm an easy mark, like what you
call the "Jay,"
I write-a him a letter and-a this is what I say:

CHORUS 1

"Antonio,
Don't you think that you can treat me so,
Because I sharp-a da stiletto till she look-a much-a
new,
And pretty soon the people walk-a slow behind-a
you;
Antonio,
Don't you think that you can treat me so,
I'm gonna give-a you a close-a shave,
So close-a that you shake-a hand-a with the
grave—
Antonio,
Better come back home."

VERSE 2

The minute what he sees-a me, he's gonna know I
sore,
And then he's gonna run-a like he never run
before.
I wrote-a him a dozen letters in the past-a week,
For ev'ry letter what I write, I'm gonna throw a
brick.
I lose 'em all the pity, and my heart she turn to
stone,
And here's the last-a letter what I write-a to
Antone:

CHORUS 2

"Antonio,
Don't you think that you can treat me so,
Because I go and see the tailor, and the tailor
he's-a guess
Why I go there and order up the nice-a black-a
dress.
Antonio,
Don't you think that you can treat me so,
I'm gonna cook for you some macaroni, you eat—
goodbye,
Antonio, Antonio,
Better come back home."

COME BACK, ANTONIO

Possibly written in 1912, but could be as late as 1914. No
music is known to survive. A lyric typescript was found
among Berlin's papers and is now in the Irving Berlin
Collection of the Music Division of the Library of
Congress.

VERSE

I feel-a much-a da sore,
My husband go to the war,
He take-a da gun and make-a da run
To Mexico.
It nearly make-a me sick,
I lose my meal-a da tick,
I'm worried like anything,
Because I miss-a him so,
I write-a him a letter last-a night,
And this is just exactly what I write:

CHORUS

Come back, Antonio,
Won't you come back from Mexico?
Better you go and sell your gun and run,
They shoot-a you in Vera Cruz,
You lose-a da hand what shine-a da shoes.
Come back, Antonio—please don't say no,
Look out somebody shoot-a you while you're
fighting in the woods,
And then when you come back-a to me,
You're goin'-a be damaged goods.
Tell me why you leave-a me alone, Antone,
Didn't we fight enough at home?
Antonio, you better come back.

Additional lyric sketches for
"Come Back, Antonio" or a related song

Better you leave the army flat—like that.
The devil wid all the Mexican,
Better come home and sell-a banan'.
The only way you ever could put the enemy in a
grave
Is if you take them one-a by one and give 'em a
close-a shave.
Hurry up—I don't want to dress the kids in black,
Jonny and Jenny and Mary and Jack;
There may be another when you come back.

I haven't got-a da cent
With which to pay-a da rent.
It isn't a joke, he leave-a me broke
Before he go.

If he would leave-a me mon'
Before he make-a da run,
I wouldn't be worried, he could stay in Mexico.
If he no answer my letter right away
I write-a him another one and say:

THAT'S HOW I LOVE YOU

Published. Copyrighted May 13, 1912.

VERSE 1

All my life I dreamed a wonderful dream,
A wonderful dream of someone;
All my life it seemed a wonderful love
Would be my possession from one.
Now that my dream is realized,
Now that you love me so;
Let me say this in my heart,
For I want you to know:

CHORUS

I love you, darling, I love you,
With a love as true as the heaven's blue;
All life through I will live for you,
There is nothing I would not do
If you asked me to,
That's how I love you.

VERSE 2

Ev'ry joy I dreamed of, I realize,
A thousand and one real pleasures;
Ev'ry hour with you I cherish and prize
Like so many golden treasures.
Tell me your love for me will grow
Stronger with ev'ry day,
And until the breath of life
Has gone, sweetheart, I'll say:

REPEAT CHORUS

A TRUE-BORN
SOLDIER MAN

Published. Copyrighted May 15, 1912.

VERSE 1

Sherman and Washington were fighting men,
Hip, hip, hurray for them, then, hip, hip again;
Grant and Lee in history
Proved they were true-born fighting soldiers.
Dewey, Hobson, and Schley as well
Were heroes at every go;
While on the subject, I'd like to tell
Of a real live soldier I know.

CHORUS

When he was three years old he wanted a pistol
Like a soldier man.
At the age of twenty he went to the war
And fought as a soldier only can.
When the war was over he came home again
And married a girl named Ann;
Now he stays at home and fights with his
      wife,
There's a true-born soldier man.

VERSE 2

Many a fellow went to war and then
Thought of his wife and never came back
      again;
Each one swore a real live war
Is nothing compared to being married.
War only lasts for a year or three,
And that's why this man took a wife;
Just to make sure of a battle he
Went and married to fight for life.

FIDDLE-DEE-DEE

Published twice. First copyrighted under the title "He Played It on His Fid-Fid-Fiddle-Dee-Dee" on May 27, 1912. Also copyrighted under "Fiddle-Dee-Dee" on June 12, 1912. Words and music by E. Ray Goetz and Irving Berlin. The two versions have slightly different lyrics (their second verses differ).

VERSE 1

Fiddler Joe from Kokomo
Took lessons on the piccolo;
After seven years or so
He could play a violin.
Beneath his whiskered chin
He'd tuck his violin,
And when you least expected,
Fiddler Joseph would begin:

CHORUS

On his fid-fid-fid-fid-fid-fid-fiddle-dee-dee
He played a melody
As plain as plain could be.
Now he might have played that tune
On a harp or a bassoon,
But he played it on his fid-fid-fiddle-dee-dee!

VERSE 2

Joe and Jim, like two big fools,
Went out one night to steal some jewels;
Joseph had no burglar tools,
So he brought his violin.
So Joseph said to Jim,
"This is the house, go in,
Go in and I'll accomp'ny you
Upon my violin."

REPEAT CHORUS

First version

VERSE 2

Joseph met a girl last spring
Who said, "Come up and bring a ring."
Joseph had no ring to bring,
So he brought his violin.
A cunning B-flat grin
Hung from his whiskered chin;
And when the maiden shouted,
"Mister fiddler man, begin."

Additional verses

Published in England in *Feldman's 18th Song Annual* (London: B. Feldman, 1912):

When Miss Stiles wed Farmer Giles,
The folks came round from miles and miles;
Fiddler Joe, with many smiles,
Brought along his violin!
The Wedding March, you see,
Had slipped his memory;
So as they walked the aisle, he played
This simple melody.

Joseph watched some people play
The game we call croquet one day;
Joseph couldn't play croquet,
So he played his violin.
A lady, tall and thin,
Took out a long hatpin
And, while Joe wasn't looking, stuck him
In his violin.

Joe's wife couldn't stand the breeze
That came from some Limburger cheese,
So she put the cheese and the breeze
Into Joseph's violin.
When first she put it in,
The cheese was weak and thin,
But when the cheese grew strong enough,
It choked the violin.

The doctor told poor Joseph's dad,
"Joe needs an operation bad,"
So they cut most all he had,
All except his violin.
The doc said with a grin,
"To stop would be a sin,
There's nothing left to cut,
So let's cut his violin."

BECKY'S GOT A JOB IN A MUSICAL SHOW

Copyrighted June 6, 1912. Alternate title (sheet music cover): "Becky Joined a Musical Show." Only two verses and the first chorus were printed in the original publication.

VERSE 1

Miss Becky Rosenstein
Met an actor from the stage who seemed to know a
      lot.
He said, "You're losing time
Working for your father with a shape like you have
      got.
What you ought to do," he said,
"Is go on the stage—you'll be a big success, I'll
      vow."*
She said, "I understand,"
Went to the Shuberts, and†
Let me tell you now:

CHORUS

Becky's got a job in a musical show;
She's showing off her figure in the very front row.
The fellows raise the dickens
When Becky starts a-kickin',

Alternate line:
   Is to go out and learn to sing a song and make a bow.

†*Alternate line:*
   Cleaned up her dresses, and

And all the boys are calling her a "Yiddisha
    chicken."
Becky's gettin' twenty dollars a week,
And how she does it no one seems to know:
She's got a coat made of seal, corsets with steel,
She comes to the theatre in an automobile;
And all of Miss Rebecca's relatives
Want to go with a musical show.

VERSE 2

Becky's got jewelry,
Lots of diamonds that she bought on the
    installment plan;
And let me tell you,
She smokes a Turkish cigarette as good as any man
    can;
And any night that she doesn't feel like working,
She stays home and there it ends.
Nobody bothers her:
She and the manager
Are the best of friends.

VERSE 3

Becky's got jewelry imitations
That the smartest experts couldn't tell.
And let me tell you,
She even knows the night clerk from the Albany
    Hotel, swell.
She's got a certain friend, and every night he takes
    her out,
And he and Becky dine.
Someone will shoot them yet;
Then Becky's going to get
A job in Hammerstein's.

CHORUS

Becky's got a job in a musical show.
She's showing off her figure in the very front
    row;
They say she's gay and airy,*
She's very, very merry,
She even drinks a cocktail now without the cherry.
Becky's getting twenty dollars a week,
And how she does it no one seems to know;
She uses big words to speak, paint on the cheek,
She's stuck up just because she takes a bath twice
    a week;

Alternate version of lines 3–5:
    She's entertaining monarchs,
    Drinking fancy tonics.
    And soon she's going to buy herself a home in the
        Bronnix.

And all of Miss Rebecca's relatives
Want a job in a musical show.

THE RAGTIME JOCKEY MAN

Published. Copyrighted June 11, 1912. Introduced in
The Passing Show of 1912 (July 22, 1912; Winter Gar-
den; 136 performances) by Willie Howard and chorus.
Major recording by Maurice Burkhardt and the Peerless
Quartet (Columbia). There is also a double or "conversa-
tion" version of this song. It was found among Berlin's
papers and is now in the Irving Berlin Collection of the
Music Division of the Library of Congress.

VERSE 1

Down upon the track,
On a horse's back,
Warming up his fingers, sits the ragtime jockey,
Smile upon his face,
Ready for the race,
In his colors so gay.
See 'em spread apart,
Now they're goin' to start;
Kindly keep an eye upon the ragtime jockey.*
Never mind your cold, don't stop to cough—
They're off!

CHORUS

Go, go, go, go,
I've got a bet upon you;
Go, go, go, go,
I'm betting heavy on you;
Pop, giddy-up, giddy-up, giddy-up,
Like I know you can.†
Run, run, run, run,
And leave the rest behind you;
Run, run, run, run,
Don't ever let 'em find you.
I'll bet a swag on the ragtime jockey man.

VERSE 2

Hear the people yell,
"Someone surely fell!"
"Did I hear you say it was the ragtime jockey?"
"Sure enough, you're right,

Earlier version of line:
    Better put a bet upon the ragtime jockey.

†*Earlier version of line, with different music:*
    And carry home that money fast as you can.

See me turning white,
All my money is gone!"
"No it isn't, boss!
See, he's on his hoss;
He was only kidding all the other jockeys,
He's just playing with them like a toy,
Good boy!"

REPEAT CHORUS

WHEN JOHNSON'S QUARTETTE HARMONIZE

Published. Copyrighted June 11, 1912. Alternate title (sheet
music cover): "When Johnson's Quartet Harmonize."

VERSE 1

Johnson Jones from Tennessee,
Father of sweet harmony,
Organized a quartette, goodness me!
And they sang so wonderful,
Kindly let me tell you, when
It comes down to singing men,
I've just got to say again,
They're wonderful!

CHORUS

Come on and hear that harmony sweet,
Come and have a musical treat,
From your head down to your feet
You'll be fairly hypnotized;
They harmonize most any old place,
Alto, Tenor, Baritone, Bass.
Ev'ry other chord
Is a message from the Lord,*
When you hear old Johnson's quartette
    harmonize.

VERSE 2

When you find you can't afford
To be paying for your board,
You can find a meal in ev'ry chord.
And it's most remarkable,
No one found their equal yet:

---

* *Earlier version of lines 7 and 8:*
    You can bet your room and board
    That you'll hear the angels chord

To go out and try to get
Men who sing like that quartette,
Impossible!

REPEAT CHORUS

CALL AGAIN!

Published. Copyrighted June 17, 1912.

VERSE 1

Charlie Brown, caught in the rain,
Stopped to call on Mary Jane,
Knocked upon the door and then explained,
"I've got no umbrella, help a fellow."
"Come right in," said Mary Jane.
Charlie did, and when the rain
Stopped outside, he softly cried,
"Goodbye, I can't remain,
I thank you much," he sighed.
And Mary Jane replied:

CHORUS 1

"Call again,
You're welcome as the flowers in the springtime,
Any time it showers and it rains like sin,
Come right in.
Sit down on my lap and cure your rheumatism.
I'll be up until the early hours,
Honey, maybe after then
I'll tell you the rest of the tale I didn't finish,
When you call again."

VERSE 2

Charlie married Mary Jane,
But at home he can't remain;
Charlie got a job that only gets him home ev'ry
   summer,
He's a drummer.
After Charlie makes a heap,
He comes home to take a peep.
One night Charlie heard his wifey talking in her
   sleep;
The name she called was Fred,
And this is what she said:

CHORUS 2

"Call again,
You're welcome as the flowers in the springtime,

Any time it showers and it rains like sin,
Come right in.
Sit down, hon, my husband won't be home till
   August,
I'll be up until the early hours.
Honey, maybe after then
I'll finish the song that my husband interrupted,
When you call again."

THE ELEVATOR MAN GOING UP! GOING UP! GOING UP! GOING UP!

Published. Copyrighted July 5, 1912. Alternate title: "Going Up Going Up Going Up Going Up (with the Elevator Man)."

VERSE 1

Andy Gray, young and gay,*
Was an elevator man;
Like an aviator, in his elevator,
All day long he was on the job,
Taking people up and down.
Mandy Brook as a cook
Started working in the place,
And they found her later
In the elevator
With Andy, so handy;
Said Mandy, "It's dandy!"

CHORUS

Going up, going up,
Going up, going up,
With the elevator man;
Going up, going up,
Going up, going up,
I feel like barrels of dynamite
Blowing up, blowing up,
Blowing up, blowing up.
Ev'ry pleasure in the land,†

---
*Earlier version of line:
   Andy Lee, Andy Lee

†Earlier version of lines 4–9:
   I feel like
   Blowin' up, blowin' up,
   Blowin' up, blowin' up,
   Just like a barrel of dynamite,
   Throwin' up, throwin' up,
   Throwin' up, throwin' up,

It makes me act
Just like a funny coon;
I could spend my honeymoon,
Going up, going up,
Going up, going up,
With the elevator man.

VERSE 2

Andy Gray, young and gay,
Went and married Mandy Brook;
We discovered later that the elevator
Was the place where the knot was tied,
Tied while they were going up.
Soon a gal known as Sal
Came to work in Mandy's place;
And they found her later
In the elevator
With Andy, so dandy,
And handy, like Mandy.*

REPEAT CHORUS

RAGTIME SOLDIER MAN

Published. Copyrighted July 12, 1912. Introduced in *Hello Ragtime* (London, 1912). Major recording by Arthur Collins and Byron Harlan (Victor and Columbia).

VERSE 1

My lovin' baby,
My lovin' baby,
You better dry your eyes and don't be grievin'.
You got to stop it,
You better drop it;
I told you once before,
I've got to go to war.
Now don't you worry,
I've got to hurry,
Because the regiment will soon be leavin';
Don't you feel blue,
Because I'm goin' off to war.

---
*Earlier version of lines 6–11:
   In a year, when the dear
   Little busy Mister Stork
   Knew what they'd be needin',
   Came and now they're feedin'
   A dandy—sweet candy—young Andy
   From Mandy.

CHORUS

I've got to go, I've got to go,
A soldier man I've got to be;
I've got to go, I've got to go,
I hear the bugle calling me.
Oh my hon, hurry up, hurry up,
Get my gun, hurry up, hurry up, hurry up.
Can't you see that
I've got to fight for love and liberty?
My honey dear,
My honey dear,
You better save your sympathy;
If you should hear,
If you should hear,
I got too near the enemy,
Kindly carry me back to old Virginia,
And when you get me there
Say a prayer for your ragtime soldier man.

VERSE 2

The time is flying,
I'm kind'a sighing,
'Cause I must say goodbye to my home cooking.
There's no denying
I leave you crying,
But don't you worry, hon,
As long as I can run,
They'll never find me,
They'll be behind me;
But if they shoot me, dear, while I'm not looking,
If so, you'll know
That I was wounded comin' home.

REPEAT CHORUS

Earlier version of chorus

The bugle call, the bugle call,
The bugle call is calling me;
I've got to fall, I've got to fall,
I've got to fall in line, you see.
Here they come—let me go, let me go.
Hear that drum—let me go, let me go.
Hear them calling me—they're calling me
To fight for love and liberty;
If you should hear, if you should hear.
A cannonball rolled under me,
You'll know, my dear, you'll know, my dear,
I got too near the enemy.
Oh my hon, hurry up, hurry up,
Get my gun, hurry up, hurry up,
Come and say goodbye to your
Ragtime soldier man.

Another earlier version of chorus

My honey, can't you hear that bugle calling me?
It means that I must go and fight for my country.
Hear that drum—get away, get away—
Hear them come—get away, get away—
I must run with my gun to the front,
Where I can fight for love and liberty.
If you should hear a cannonball rolled under me,
Why, then you'll know I got too near the enemy.
Oh my hon, hurry up, hurry up,
Get my gun, hurry up, hurry up,
You better say goodbye to your lovin'
Ragtime soldier man.

KEEP AWAY FROM THE MAN WITH THE AUTOMOBILE

Published. Copyrighted August 9, 1912. Hamm, vol. 2, p. 349, notes that the first few bars of the music to the verse of "Keep Away" are identical to the verse of Berlin's "It All Belongs to Me" (1927).

VERSE 1

There's a certain flirtin' man
With money in the bank;
The man I mean owns a machine,
The kind you have to crank.
His great delight
Is to invite
A girlie for a whirl
In his machine, and I just mean
To kinda warn each girl!

CHORUS

Keep away from the fellow who owns the
    automobile,
He'll take you far in his motorcar,
Too darn far for your pa and ma.
If his forty horsepower
Goes sixty miles an hour,
Say goodbye forever, goodbye forever.
There's no chance to talk, squawk or balk,
You must kiss him or get out and walk;
Keep away from the fellow who owns the
    automobile.

VERSE 2

Mary White went out one night
In Harry's new machine;

They rode quite far when Harry's car
Ran out of gasoline.
The hour was late,
And sad to state,
No gas could Harry get.
The latest word I overheard
Was that they're walking yet!

REPEAT CHORUS

WHEN I'M THINKING OF YOU

Published. Copyrighted September 27, 1912. Alternate title (original sheet music cover): "When I'm Thinking of You I'm Thinking of a Wonderful Love."

VERSE 1

A thousand times a day, sweetheart, I think of
    thee,
A thousand golden thoughts of you assure me
That you have come to linger in my memory,
Surrounded by all that's sweet and pure.

CHORUS

I think of the springtime when I think of you,
Springtime and sweet-scented flowers;
I think of the sunshine when I think of you,
Sunshine and happy hours;
I think of the angels when I think of you,
Angels and heavens of blue;
I'm thinking of a wonderful love
When I'm thinking, just thinking of you.

VERSE 2

A thousand times a day I hold your hands, it seems,
And whisper once again how much I love you;
A thousand times each night I see you in my
    dreams,
Surrounded by angels from above.

REPEAT CHORUS

COME BACK TO ME, MY MELODY

Published. Copyrighted October 8, 1912. Music by Ted Snyder.

VERSE

A man composed a sweet melody
One summer's night in June,
And he played that pretty tune
Till he learned to love it soon.
He ne'er wrote down that sweet melody,
And, very strange, one day
He found that pretty melody
Had vanished from his memory.
He cried as he tried to recall that tune,
Then sang to it tenderly:

CHORUS

"Come back to me, my melody,
Come back to where you ought to be,
I want you, don't you understand?
Locked up in my baby grand,
Just where I can lay my hand on thee.
Oh! I miss you so,
More than you may know;
Don't you know it's very wrong
To be where you don't belong?
Oh! Please come back to me, my melody."

VERSE 2

The man who wrote that sweet melody
Tried to recall the strain,
But it ne'er came back again,
So he gave it up in vain.
One night he heard an orchestra play
Strains of a sweet refrain;
He recognized his melody,
Although they changed it cleverly.
He ran to the man and loudly cried,
"That music belongs to me!"

REPEAT CHORUS

DO IT AGAIN

Published. Copyrighted October 9, 1912.

VERSE 1

My pulse is jumpin' so nice,
Oh! honey, can't you hear?
My heart is thumpin' so nice,
Oh! honey, cuddle near.
Don't you know the reason why I'm feeling so?
Can't you hear me sigh?
If you really want to know,
Here's the reason why.

CHORUS

I kinda liked it when you gave me a lovin' kiss,
Do it again, do it again!
Hold me steady, now I'm ready—
Umm! That's wonderful!
I kinda liked it when you covered me up with
    bliss;
Do it again, do it again!
Don't you fear,
Even if it rained and thundered,
Stay right here,
Kiss me till I count a hundred;
When I've counted to a hundred,
Do it again.

VERSE 2

You cert'nly do it so nice,
Your squeeze is like a dream.
You go right to it so nice,
Your kiss is full of steam.
Once somebody told me of a lovin' miss
Who such kisses tried;
I heard after just one kiss
She laid down and died.

REPEAT CHORUS

A LITTLE BIT OF EVERYTHING

Published. Copyrighted October 18, 1912. Introduced in the *Ziegfeld Follies of 1912*.

VERSE 1

Come, honey, come, honey,
Let me take you into swell society,
If you care for a share of a world of pleasure,
You better hurry up and come with me.
Come, honey, come, honey,
To the ball that's given by Miss Hannah Lee,
Where there'll be a large variety.
We'll see

CHORUS

A little bit of ev'rything,
Ev'rything, ev'rything,
A little bit of ev'rything,
Ev'rything, ev'rything.
We'll hear a band that's a dream, you bet,
From the drum to the clarinet,
We'll dance and drag and minuet.
Come along, come along,
And get a little bit of ev'rything,
Ev'rything, ev'rything,
A little bit of ev'rything,
Ev'rything, ev'rything.
We'll hear songs that'll make you sad,
We'll hear songs that'll make you glad,
We won't go home until we've had
A little bit of ev'rything, dear.

VERSE 2

Come, honey, come, honey,
We'll do ev'rything before the night is through,
We will sing ev'rything that the band starts
    playing,
We'll do the Texas Tommy black and blue.
Come, honey, come, honey,
I will treat you to a lemonade or two,
Hurry up and come, I promise you
We'll do

REPEAT CHORUS

HIRAM'S BAND

Published. Copyrighted October 24, 1912. Music and lyrics by Irving Berlin and E. Ray Goetz. (On the title page E. Ray Goetz is listed as Ed. Ray Goetz.) Introduced in *The Sun Dodgers* (September 30, 1912; Broadway Theatre). On the original sheet music covers several published songs from *The Sun Dodgers* are credited to E. Ray Goetz and A. Baldwin Sloane.

VERSE 1

Ev'ry nation, ev'ry land,
They own a band they think is grand,
And they all adore the hand
That leads the band around.
But of all the hurdy-gurdy bands I've
      heard,
I'll say a word of a certain funny bird,
Of a certain band I found.

CHORUS 1

You ought to hear the music queer
That comes from Hiram's band,
The notes of blue,
So blue that you
Could never understand.
It's worth a half a dollar
To hear old Hiram holler,
"One, two, three, go!"
You ought to be around
And see the faces that they make,
Each Ruben's face all out of place
With ev'ry note they take.
When they hear them passing by,
The ladies sigh, the babies cry,
Cats and dogs lay down to die,
When they hear old Hiram's band.

VERSE 2

Talk about your Creatores
Who get encores with opera scores,
Hiram plays them all outdoors
And makes them all look sick,
Sick enough sometimes to die, you can't
      deny,
And if you try any time you're passing by,
He can show you gosh darn quick.

CHORUS 2

You ought to hear the music queer
That comes from Hiram's band.
The notes of blue,

So blue that you
Could never understand.
He makes Philip Souser
Look like a march-abuser,
"One, two, three, go!"
You'd laugh, I swear, if you were there
And heard the way he cheered
When Hiram's thin old violin
Got tangled in his beard.
Any time the band appears,
Each neighbor clears away in tears,
Ma wears earmuffs on her ears,
After hearing Hiram's band.

DOWN IN MY HEART

Published. Copyrighted October 30, 1912. Introduced in *The Little Millionaire* (September 25, 1911; George M. Cohan Theatre) by Charles King. The published song is a duet.

VERSE

HE: Around my heart I've got the funniest,
      Honeyest, appealing feeling;
      It came the very day that I fell in love with
            you,
      Revealing a bunch of joy.
      I really can't explain the reason why;
      What's more, I don't intend to even try.
      I know it's there, and on the square,
      I'm as happy with it
      As a baby with a toy.

CHORUS 1

Down in my heart
You've played a prominent part
Right from the start,
When Cupid mixed a funny drink,
And the drink, I think,
Went to my heart,
And now it's bursting apart.
Somehow I feel so good
With my little Venus;
Nothing could
Ever come between us.
Honest, little girlie,
I am strong for you
Way down in my heart.

VERSE 2

SHE: Around my heart of late I've noticed
      The most peculiar something thumping
      When you're around; just like the funniest
            jumping jack,
      It's jumping on ev'ry side.
      If you could only look within its doors,
      You'd find conditions there the same as
            yours;
      Now all that I can say is,
      I'll be so happy, happy,
      When the loving knot is tied.

CHORUS 2

Down in my heart
You've played a prominent part
Right from the start,
When Cupid mixed a funny drink,
And the drink, I think,
Went to my heart,
And now it's bursting apart,
It's jumping all around
Like a champagne bubble
Burden'd down
With a happy trouble;
Honest, little fellow,
I am strong for you
Way down in my heart.

MY SWEET ITALIAN MAN
(First Version)

Published. There are two entirely different versions of this song, even though both have the same title and front cover. The first was published and copyrighted October 31, 1912; the second, on February 21, 1913.

VERSE 1

Pretty Annetta, she feel on the bum,
She call a doctor, and when he's-a come,
Right away da doctor look and say,
"I think Annetta's gonna die."
Pretty Annetta, she make-a da plea,
"Bring-a my sweet-a-heart, Tony, to me."
She keep mum, but when her Tony come,
Pretty Annetta she cry:

CHORUS

"My sweet Italian man,
I'm-a sick, I'm-a sick,
Love-a me much-a quick,
Come here and squeeze-a my hand;
Say you love me, wop-a,
Like you love your barber shop-a;
Don't you wait—
If I die, it's gonna be too late.
So you just betta
Come and pet-a
Your Annetta while you can,
My Italian man."

VERSE 2

Tony, he make-a da spoon wid Annette,
It make her feel-a much better, you bet,
Twenty time he kiss her nice-a fine,
Then Miss Annetta, she was well.
Tony, he sell-a da pick and da shov',
He got no time to work, he's got-a love.
Ev'ry week Annetta she get sick,
And to her Tony she yell:

REPEAT CHORUS

WHEN THE MIDNIGHT CHOO-CHOO LEAVES FOR ALABAM'

Published. Copyrighted November 2, 1912. A number-one-selling record was made of "Alabam" by Arthur Collins and Byron Harlan (Columbia, Victor, Edison Amberol, Indestructible, and U.S. Everlasting). Another major recording was made by the Victor Military Band (Victor) conducted by Walter B. Rogers. Alternate title (sheet music cover): "When That Midnight Choo, Choo, Leaves For Alabam." The song's popularity in later years was demonstrated repeatedly when Berlin revived it in several musical films. It was sung by Alice Faye in *Alexander's Ragtime Band* (1938); by Fred Astaire and Judy Garland in *Easter Parade* (1948); and by Ethel Merman, Dan Dailey, Mitzi Gaynor, and Donald O'Connor in *There's No Business Like Show Business* (1954). The funniest anecdote about the song was written by George S. Kaufman for *The New Yorker*:

> Not long before turning out "Always," Irving had written the song bearing the somewhat implausible title of "When the Midnight Choo-Choo Leaves for Alabam'." Like "Always," it swept the

country. Irving's lyric glorified the enchanted moment when that choo-choo pulled out of the station for Alabam'. With a view to checking up on the facts of the situation, so that I'd be able to make suggestions to Irving about the realism of this lyric, I turned up in Pennsylvania Station at a quarter to twelve one night for that wonderful and glorious departure.

> The first thing I found out was that there *was* no midnight choo-choo for Alabam'; the choo-choo for Alabam' left at twelve nineteen. Well, I was not too worried about that. Clearly, Irving could not have written a song entitled "When the Twelve-Nineteen A.M. Choo-Choo Leaves for Alabam'." Next I discovered that the platform was crowded with songwriters, slapping each other on the back and uttering shrill cries in praise of Alabam', "where the rhyming is easy." Between times, they were bidding tearful farewells to their dear old mothers, who had moved up from Alabam' twenty-five years before and were living contentedly on West Seventy-second Street. Some of the poorer songwriters, who had not yet had a big hit, were sad to behold. Getting a piano into an upper berth is, at best, a difficult job. But I did learn one thing about it—always get the stool up first, so you'll have some place to sit while you're waiting for the piano to get there. The moment of departure was noisy and gay. The happy songwriters, jauntily singing their songs, could be observed at every window as the train pulled out. The mothers went happily back to Seventy-second Street. I gave a lusty cheer myself, and was delighted to have witnessed the whole happy scene.

> I learned afterward that the songwriters all got off at Newark, took the Hudson Tube back to Manhattan, and were safely in Lindy's by one-thirty. I never told Irving about that, but ever since then I have not quite believed everything I heard in a song lyric.

VERSE 1

I've had a mighty busy day,
I've had to pack my things away,
Now I'm goin' to give the landlord back
    his key,
The very key
That opened up my dreary flat,
Where many weary nights I sat
Thinking of the folks down home who think
    of me;
You can bet you'll find me singing happily.

CHORUS

When the midnight choo-choo leaves for
    Alabam',
I'll be right there,
I've got my fare.
When I see that rusty-haired conductor man,
I'll grab him by the collar
And I'll holler,
"Alabam'! Alabam'!"
That's where you stop your train
That brings me back again,
Down home where I'll remain,
Where my honey lamb
Am.
I will be right there with bells,
When that old conductor yells,
"All aboard! All aboard!
All aboard for Alabam'."

VERSE 2

The minute that I reach the place,
I'm goin' to overfeed my face,
'Cause I haven't had a good meal since the day
I went away.
I'm goin' to kiss my pa and ma
A dozen times for ev'ry star
Shining over Alabama's new-mown hay;
I'll be glad enough to throw myself away.

REPEAT CHORUS

WHEN I LOST YOU

Published. Copyrighted November 8, 1912. This great ballad is believed to have been the first song that Berlin wrote after the tragic early death of his young bride, Dorothy Goetz, in July 1912, only five months after their wedding. Top-selling recordings were by Henry Burr (Victor and Edison Amberol) and Manuel Romain (Columbia). The Burr recording was a number-one seller.

VERSE 1

The roses, each one,
Met with the sun,
Sweetheart, when I met you;
The sunshine had fled,
The roses were dead,
Sweetheart, when I lost you.

CHORUS

I lost the sunshine and roses,
I lost the heavens of blue,
I lost the beautiful rainbow,
I lost the morning dew,
I lost the angel who gave me
Summer the whole winter through,
I lost the gladness
That turned into sadness,
When I lost you.

VERSE 2

The birds ceased their song,
Right turned to wrong,
Sweetheart, when I lost you;
A day turned to years,
The world seemed in tears,
Sweetheart, when I lost you.

REPEAT CHORUS

THEY ALL COME WITH YOU

This appears to be an earlier version of the lyric that became "When I Lost You." No music is known to survive. Berlin's handwritten lyric sheets were found among the songwriter's papers and are now in the Irving Berlin Collection of the Music Division of the Library of Congress.

VERSION A

Sunshine and heavens of blue,
Flowers and sweet morning dew,
Innocent birds gaily sing
Sweetest of all songs they knew,*
Gladness and happiness too,
Wonderful dreams that come true,
Heavenly pleasures, a world full of treasures,
My sweetheart, they all came with you.

VERSION B

Sunshine and roses and heavens of blue,
Springtime and flowers and sweet morning dew,
Birds in the treetops with nothing to do,

---

*Earlier version of lines 2–4:
    Roses and sweet morning dew,
    Robins with nothing to do,
    Nothing but sing like the angels,

Nothing but sing like the angels.
Hours of gladness and happiness too,
Wonderful dreaming of dreams that come true,
Heavenly pleasures, a world full of treasures,
My sweetheart, they all came with you.
My sweetheart, they all came with you.

THAT'S JUST WHY I LOVE YOU

This is almost certainly an earlier version of the song that became "When I Lost You." No music is known to survive. A lyric typescript was found among Berlin's papers and is now in the Irving Berlin Collection of the Music Division of the Library of Congress. The lyric was published in 1994 in Hamm, vol. 2, pp. 350–1.

VERSE

A thousand times you've asked me
Why I love you;
Come to my arms and I'll answer,
I'll tell you just why I do.

CHORUS

I love the flowers that bloom in the spring,
I love the birds in the treetops that sing,
I love the church bells that solemnly ring,
I love the sweet morning dew,
I love the angels who watch from above,
I love the cooing of each little dove,
I love the things God wants me to love,
That's just why I love you.

FATHER'S BEARD

Published. Copyrighted November 11, 1912. There is no music. This strophic poem—a dramatic recitation—was published as a pamphlet. Its last verse is "to be sung to the tune of 'The Rosary' (1898) by Ethelbert Nevin."

1

You ask why I treasure this bit of red hair
I sadly keep gazing upon;
I answer it's all there is left to recall,
Golden mem'ries of one who has gone.

2

Don't laugh till I tell you the saddest of tales;
I know you will cry when it's told:
The story I swear is attached to the hair
I keep in this locket of gold.

3

I once had a father, the finest of men,
A father like you might have had;
And if you hear me out, I will tell you about
The sad death of my poor old dad.

4

On Dad's manly shoulders a head calmly sat,
A head that was much to be feared.
On one end my dad wore a Panama hat,
On the other my dad wore a beard.

5

A more finer lace never hung from a face
That was proud of the beard it possessed.
Its color, 'twas said, often grew twice as red
As the tie it concealed on his chest.

6

The barbers in town often said that they would
Give a lot if my father appeared
And gave them a dear tiny red souvenir
Of his well-worn mysterious beard.

7

The sight of a comb to my father was just
Like a waving red flag to a bull.
He never would dare to untangle the hair
Of his beard, but when Father was full,

8

A mysterious stillness would creep o'er the
    house—
A stillness that everyone feared.
We shook in our shoes as we whispered the news:
"We're going to comb Father's beard."

9

And comb it we would, that is, much as we
    could,
For his beard was as thick as a track,
And combs by the score would just fall on the
    floor
And die of a broken back.

10

If one single hair would come out with the
comb,
My father would wake up and swear.
Why, he even could name just from where that
hair came,
For my dad had a name for each hair.

11

Emmanuel, Thomas, Sebastian, and Jake,
Eliza and Little Bo Peep.
We'd smile when a hair that he called
Camenbier
Would curl up and fall asleep.

12

A more useful beard on a face never grew;
It acted a prominent part:
When our napkins we found wouldn't quite go
around,
Father's beard played a napkin real smart.

13

Our dinners would start with some oysters or
clams;
Then soup would be served to the group:
And when Dad's consommé had been taken
away,
His beard sadly wept tears of soup.

14

And Dad would consume food enough for a
mob,
Though he didn't eat much, so to speak.
When the table was cleared, there was food in
his beard
That would last any man for a week.

15

The children would play with my father for
hours—
When a toy from the house disappeared,
There'd be some girl or boy who could tell you
that toy
Was concealed in my father's red beard.

16

How well I remember that sad day in June
When Father, all tired, poor man,
Lay down in his bed and forgot overhead
To turn off an electric fan.

17

While Dad slept the fan blew his beard to
and fro,
And Father grew shorter in breath,
For alas and alack, the beard blew down his
back
And tickled poor father to death.

18

The news spread around that my father would
soon
Be sleeping behind yonder hill,
And relatives came to be in on the game
For they knew that my dad had left a will.

19

They all gathered round when the lawyer
came in,
And when Father's last will appeared,
The lawyer's one call was "Your dad leaves
you all
A piece of his wiry red beard."

20

Eleven strong barbers were put on the job
To grant Father's one last request;
And after the beard from his face had been
cleared
We sadly laid Father at rest.

21

And now that I have told you my heartrending
tale
And now that my mystery is cleared,
I know you are glad if you never have had
A father who left you his beard.

22

If ever you happen to pass Father's grave,
Kindly look at the tombstone and see
In letters of red, like the beard that he shed,
You'll notice this sweet poetry:

[*To be sung to the tune of "The Rosary":*]

The hours I spent with Dad are in
My mem'ry, where they often stung.
I closed my eyes and seemed to see his chin
And there a beard is hung.

FOLLOW ME AROUND

Published. Copyrighted November 13, 1912. Introduced by Maude Raymond (Daphne Follette of the Moulin Rouge) in *My Best Girl* (September 12, 1912; 68 performances). Possibly added after the New York opening. On many theatre programs the composer-lyricist of "Follow Me Around" is listed as "Irwin Berlin." On the original sheet music cover there is a photograph of Maude Raymond with the following quotation: "Dat Certainly is Good!"

VERSE 1

Tell me, dear, would you like to see the town a bit?
Would you like to go around?
If you'd care to be where there's a whole lot doin',
Then you better come down.
Let's go down to where everybody's doin' it,
Where they never wear a frown.
You will have a tonful of fun, little hon,
If you follow me around.

CHORUS

Follow me around,
All around, all around,
Chasing, racing all around town;
Don't you make a sound,
Make a sound, make a sound,
And you'll be glad before the night is over
That you followed me around,
All around, all around.
We will cover lots of ground,
I've got the key to most ev'ry cabaret,
Where there's an hour of joy we can grab away.
We'll discover places that Columbus never found,
Dearie, if you follow me around.

VERSE 2

Let's go where everybody makes a night of it,
Where they've thrown away the key,
Where a steinful of wine starts your head
a-buzzin',
Like a troublesome bee.
Rest assured, ever since I got the sight of it,
There I always want to be,
Let me tell you, pet, that I've yet to regret,
So you better follow me.

REPEAT CHORUS

61

AT THE DEVIL'S BALL

There are three published editions. The first was registered for copyright on November 14, 1912; the second, on December 18, 1912; the third, on January 8, 1913. Leading recording by the Peerless Quartet with Maurice Burkhardt (Columbia).

VERSE 1

I had a dream last night
That filled me full of fright;
I dreamt that I was with the Devil, below,
In his great big fiery hall,
Where the Devil was giving a ball.
I checked my coat and hat and started gazing at
The merry crowd that came to witness the show;
And I must confess to you
There were many there I knew.

CHORUS

At the Devil's Ball,
At the Devil's Ball,
I saw the cute Mrs. Devil, so pretty and fat,
Dressed in a beautiful fireman's hat;
Ephraham, the leader man, who led the band last
 fall,
He played the music at the Devil's Ball.
In the Devil's Hall,
I saw the funniest devil that I ever saw
Taking the tickets from the folks at the door;
I caught a glimpse of my mother-in-law
Dancing with the Devil,
Oh! The little Devil,
Dancing at the Devil's Ball.

VERSE 2

The Devil's pa and ma
Were standing at the bar,
Conversing with the little fellow who first
Put the pain in champagne wine;
He was pouring it out in a stein.
I bought a round of ice for ev'rybody twice,
It wasn't long before I ordered a fan;
And before the break of dawn
I put my overcoat in pawn.*

REPEAT CHORUS

Verse 2, last four lines (1912 version):
 I saw the waiter, Jack, who never hurried back;
 He waited on the merry gathering there,
 And upon his two big horns
 He had grown a dozen corns.

IF ALL THE GIRLS I KNEW WERE LIKE YOU

Published. Copyrighted November 16, 1912.

VERSE 1

I often wonder and wonder
Just what I really would do,
How I would keep from a blunder,
If ev'ry girlie I knew
Happened to be just like you,
I'd be at a loss what to do.

CHORUS

If all the girls I knew
Were like you, like you,
I would swear to a thousand girls
That I'd be true.
I'd gaze in a thousand eyes,
I'd sigh a thousand sighs,
For I'd be in love with a thousand girls,
If they were all like you,
If they were all like you.

VERSE 2

If they were all fascinating,
I wouldn't know which to choose;
I'd set my poor heart debating
Over which one to enthuse,
Which one to take or refuse,
Which one to gain or to lose.

REPEAT CHORUS

DON'T LEAVE YOUR WIFE ALONE

Published. Copyrighted November 20, 1912.

VERSE 1

There are many married men who lead a double
 life,
One they lead in cabaret, the other with their
 wife.
Staying out till four
While wifey goes to bed at ten
Looks well on the surface,
But just listen, married men:

CHORUS 1

Don't leave your wife alone,
Waiting for you at home,
When you go out at nights; I'll tell you what,
Maybe she's waiting home and maybe she's not.
While you're with Flo or May,
Hunting a new café,
She may go out with a fella
And not drink sarsaparilla,
So don't leave your wife alone.

VERSE 2

What is good for Mister Gander's good for Missus
 Goose;
Wives can go as fast as husbands once you let
 them loose.
Wives can paint the town
And make their husbands look like skates;
They've got paint enough
To paint the whole United States.

CHORUS 2

Don't leave your wife alone,
Waiting for you at home,
When you go out nights; I'll tell you what,
Maybe she's waiting home, maybe she's not.
When you go out and chase
After a pretty face,
She may go and do some chasin'
With some wise brother Mason,
So don't leave your wife alone.

YIDDISHA PROFESSOR

Published. Copyrighted November 23, 1912. Alternate title (sheet music cover): "The Yiddisha Professor."

VERSE 1

Abie Cohen, Abie Cohen,
Went to Paris and Germany and learned how to
    play
On the piano; now he's making money out of
    sight,
Giving concerts ev'ry night.
Come along, come along,
For the half of a dollar you can get in the hall,
Sit in the gallery and you'll be glad to pay,
When you hear young Abraham play.

CHORUS

Come and hear the Yiddisha professor,
Mister Abie Cohen, Abie Cohen;
Come and hear him tickling the piano
In a first-class Yiddisha tone.
I would never kiss him on the lips,
But I'd kiss him on the fingertips.
Oy, such a much is the touch that lingers
In his Yiddisha fingers,
He can make a secondhand piano
Sound the same as new;
More yet too,
He can play some sentimental melody
And break the heart of a stone.
When his melody begins to pour,
Then your wishbone wishes for some more.
Come along and listen to the Yiddisha
    professor,
Mister Abie Cohen.

VERSE 2

Abie Cohen, Abie Cohen,
Wears his hair like an actor, it's as long as his
    arm,
He never cuts it off; and ev'ryone who sees his
    hair
Looks and hollers, "It's a bear!"
Come along, come along,
Have a look at the diamond that he wears on his
    hand
When he is fingering, and just to see the gent
Makes you think of seven percent.

REPEAT CHORUS

ONLY A GIRL

On November 19, 1946, a woman named Aimee V. Samuel, formerly Aimee Raudnitz, of Kingston, New York, wrote a leter to Berlin that begins as follows:

> You cannot possibly have any recollection of writing a lyric and giving it to me many, many years ago—I considered it very good and you copied it down for me one night when I met you with Maxie Winslow—November, 1912—to be exact. We all had a wonderful time, thanks to you, Ted Snyder and one other man and my fiancé or intended, Mr. B. Jackson Samuel.

She offered to send Berlin the lyric and did so after receiving a letter from him dated November 29, 1946. At first he did not recall writing the lyric, but after having his memory refreshed he wrote her again on December 4, 1946, as follows:

> Not alone do I remember it, but I recall how much I thought of it at the time. I sincerely felt I had written a great ballad. Viewing it today, I'm awfully glad I never published it. However, the thought and idea behind this song could—if written with the experience I have had since 1912—have been turned into a hit.

No music is known to survive.

VERSE

He met her one day, in a halfhearted way,
Because she was only a girl,
An innocent queen, yet to see seventeen,
Displaying a beautiful curl.
He studied her ways for a number of days,
And now it's a year since they met
Still he can't keep away, for he learned every day
Some things that he'll never forget.

CHORUS

She taught him the right from the wrong way,
And they said she was only a girl.
She showed him the short from the long way,
And they said she was only a girl.
In hours of trouble she pleaded his case,
She gave him the courage to win every race,
The Ten Commandments were stamped on her
    face,
And they said she was only a girl.

GOODY, GOODY, GOODY, GOODY, GOOD

Published. Copyrighted December 11, 1912.

VERSE 1

Oh my honey, don't be slow,
Honey, go and turn the lights down low;
Kindly hurry, don't you know
I've got something to tell you?
See that cozy Morris chair
Standing there? The chair will hold a pair;
If you've got some love to spare,
I'd like to have some now.

CHORUS

'Cause it's good, so good,
You bet that it's goody, goody, good.
No one else could do it like you could,
I want a little lovin', 'cause it's good,
So good,
You bet, even gooder that good.
Honey, when you press your ruby lips to mine,
I feel like an ocean full of wine.
Do I love it, do I? Umm! Umm!
Goody, goody, goody, goody, good.

VERSE 2

Hug me, honey, like a bear,
I don't care if you should muss my hair;
I'm all ready pay the fare
For a journey to heaven.
One kiss, honey, calls for two;
After two, I'd like to have a few;
When I get a few from you,
I'm goin' to holler more.

REPEAT CHORUS

WAIT UNTIL YOUR DADDY COMES HOME

Published. Copyrighted December 19, 1912. According to contemporary newspaper articles, Berlin introduced this song the week of September 12, 1911, in a vaudeville appearance at Hammerstein's Victoria Theatre, New York.

VERSE 1

Curly-headed pickaninny acting gay,
He's been bad all day, and he won't obey;
Talking back to Mammy in a sassy way,
Makes her look with much surprise,
Mammy starts to holler as a mammy would,
"Won't you please be good, like a good boy
    should?"
But it doesn't seem to do any good,
So she finally cries:

CHORUS

"Wait until your daddy comes home,
Wait until your daddy comes home,
I'll tell him how you've been talkin' to your
    mammy,
Since he started to roam.
Wait until I tell him the way
You've been misbehaving today;
He'll press your pants in a manner nice and fine,
Right on the spot where the sun will never shine.
Lawdy! How you're going to groan
When your loving daddy comes home."

VERSE 2

Curly-headed pickaninny jumps about,
Sticks his tongue way out at his mammy stout;
Steps upon his mammy's foot, the one with gout,
Till it almost breaks apart.
Mammy lays the pickaninny on her lap,
In her hand a strap, ready for the rap;
But she hollers as she lays down the strap,
"No, I haven't the heart!"

REPEAT CHORUS

THE FUNNY LITTLE MELODY

This song was transcribed by Charles Hamm from Victor 17213–A, recorded in 1912 by Walter J. Van Brunt and Maurice Burkhardt; published in Hamm, vol. 3, pp. 224–5.

VERSE 1

Ephraham, a fiddler full of harmony,
Wrote the most peculiar little melody;
Morning, night, and noon he would play the tune,
Till most everybody learned to love it.
Soon the little fascinating Hannah Lee,
She fell in love with Ephra'm and his melody;
Now most every night Hannah holds him tight,
Singing tenderly, "My honey,

CHORUS

"Play the funny little melody,
Play the little funny tune for me,
Play me just a teeny little weeny measure,
If you want to fill me up with pleasure,
Take your violin and tune 'er up, tune 'er up,
Tune 'er up, tune 'er up,
Play a most peculiar harmony,
In the most peculiar little key;
Look at everybody swayin' to that rhythm,
In a minute I'll be goin' with 'em—
Play the funny little melody."

VERSE 2

Ephraham played the funny melody.
Till the little fascinating Hannah Lee,
She whispered in his ear, "There's a parson near,
Lock your fiddle up and we'll get married."
Seven years of married life and now we see
Seven little fiddlers in his family,
Seven honey lambs, seven Ephrahams,
Singing all with glee, "Oh, Papa,

REPEAT CHORUS

IF IT WASN'T FOR MY WIFE AND BABY

No music is known to survive. A lyric typescript found among Berlin's papers and now in the Irving Berlin Collection of the Music Division of the Library of Congress bears the legend "Words and Music by Irving Berlin. Copyrighted 1912 by Ted Snyder Co. Waterson, Berlin & Snyder Co. Props." Yet the 1993 Irving Berlin Copyright Search failed to show any prior registration of this song.

VERSE 1

"I've got the dearest wife and child,"
Said Henry Wild. "My wife and child
Have made me what I am—
A peaceful married man.
I used to go out with the boys,
Make an awful lot of noise;
Now I'm pleased to say my joys
Are on a different plan.
I must confess, somehow,
Lord knows where I'd be now.

CHORUS 1

"If it wasn't for my wife and baby,
Lord knows what I'd be doin';
With a love so great, they have kept me
    straight
From the road that leads to ruin.
They're the two best pals I ever had,
And let me tell you maybe
I'd go out and have a devil of a time
If it wasn't for my wife and baby."

VERSE 2

Said Henry Wild, "I'll tell you what,
A tiny tot can do a lot
Towards keeping you quite clear
From trouble when it's near.
From eight to six I work all day;
Then with baby I must play,
Till I haven't strength to say,
'I'll take another beer.'
Who knows but what I might
Be good and drunk each night.

CHORUS 2

"If it wasn't for my wife and baby,
Lord knows what I'd be doin';

With a love so great, they have kept me
   straight
From the road that leads to ruin.
They're the two best pals I ever had,
And let me tell you maybe
I'd go out and spend a quarter at a time
If it wasn't for my wife and baby."

I'LL MAKE IT WARM FOR YOU

No music is known to survive. A lyric typescript found among Berlin's papers and now in the Irving Berlin Collection of the Music Division of the Library of Congress bears the legend "Words and Music by Irving Berlin. Copyrighted 1912 by Waterson Berlin and Snyder." Yet the 1993 Irving Berlin Copyright Search failed to show any prior registration of this song.

VERSE 1

"Winter is coming," said Mabel to Joe,
"Snowflakes will shortly appear;
Don't forget, my dear,
That I live right near,
I'm always here when the weather is cold;
I never go out at all.
So on the first blizzard, just pay me a visit,
I promise you, dear, when you call,

CHORUS

"I'll make it warm for you,
I'll make it warm for you;
Don't buy an overcoat, just call around.
We'll be squeezing, dear,
When you're freezing, dear,
I'll make it warm for you,
That's what I'll do.
I'll feed you on lovin',
You'll feel like an oven
When I make it warm for you."

VERSE 2

"I'd like to bet you," said Mabel to Joe,
"All that a millionaire spends,
That when winter ends
We'll be warm, warm friends.
Come around and I'll show all round the
   house;
After I've shown you about,

Your pulse will jump higher
Than any live wire,
My dear, should the fire run out,

REPEAT CHORUS

MIDNIGHT EYES

No music is known to survive. A lyric typescript and a holograph written on Hotel Cumberland (New York) stationery were found among Berlin's papers and are in the Irving Berlin Collection of the Music Division of the Library of Congress. The bottom of the lyric typescript bears the legend "Copyrighted 1912 by Waterson, Berlin and Snyder." Yet the 1993 Irving Berlin Copyright Search failed to show any prior registration of this song.

VERSE 1

Twelve o'clock 'most any night,
You can see them shining bright;
When you least expect,
They'll grab you—and nab you—then stab you.
It's an even-money bet,
Like a fish caught in a net
You'll wiggle and wiggle,
They'll get you yet.

CHORUS

Glancing, dancing, most entrancing midnight
   eyes,
Like sunny southern skies, they shine,
And bankers, bakers, undertakers
All fall when they shine;
Just like sparkling wine,
They fill you and thrill you
And they'll kill you in time,
Daring, tearing, glaring, scaring midnight
   eyes.
The wisest of the wise they keep
A-skipping, tripping, gee I'm slipping;
Goodbye—they're calling,
Goodbye—I'm falling,
Yes, falling for those midnight eyes.

VERSE 2

When it comes to married men,
Ev'ry ten times out of ten,

When they say they won't be falling
Or crawling, they're stalling.
Manuel, the king, was wise,
He was in a wise disguise;
But Naby Miss Gaby
Had midnight eyes.

REPEAT CHORUS

I HAD A DREAM LAST NIGHT

On the same holograph (Hotel Cumberland) that has a portion of "Midnight Eyes," the following verse appears which is very different metrically from the verses of "Midnight Eyes." No music is known to survive.

I had a dream last night
And it's given me an awful fright;
I dreamt a dozen people had me by the throat
For writing all the horrible songs I wrote.
Everybody seemed to cry,
"Now we've got him, he must die."
A healthy-looking fellow, six foot three,
Threw a bottle at me,
But then he missed me.
I'm glad he missed me;
If he ever kissed me
With the bottle he threw
[*Lyric breaks off here.*]

MUSICAL MOSE

No music is known to survive. Probably written in 1912. A lyric typescript found among Berlin's papers is now in the Irving Berlin Collection of the Music Division of the Library of Congress.

VERSE 1

Down in Lou'siana where the cotton grows
Lives a mighty genius by the name of Mose.
Anything around that can make a sound,
Say, without a lesson he can play it,
Clarinets and piccolos and big bassoons,

Any other instrument that's meant for tunes,
He makes 'em moan—down home he's
    known
As Musical Mose.

CHORUS

Musical Mose, from his head to his toes
He's a music center, harmony inventor;
From a ten-cent whistle
To a million-dollar
Fiddle-dee-dee, he was born, don't you see,
Where the instrumental blossom grows.
He's the brainy fellow
That put the O in "cello"—
That's Musical Mose.

VERSE 2

Talk about your fiddle players o'er the land—
Mose was born with seven fiddles in each hand.
Talk about your chin on a violin—
Mose can make a fiddle holler "uncle."
He can make a piano act just like a slave—
Lawdy, how he makes a baby grand behave!
America's best orchestra,
That's Musical Mose.

REPEAT CHORUS

PAINT ME A PICTURE
OF THE MAN I LOVE

No music is known to survive. At the bottom of a lyric typescript found among Berlin's papers and now in the Irving Berlin Collection of the Music Division of the Library of Congress is the legend "Words and Music by Irving Berlin. Copyrighted 1912 by Waterson Berlin Snyder Co." Yet the 1993 Irving Berlin Copyright Search failed to show any prior registration of this song.

VERSE 1

An artist sat working in his studio,
Painting a picture one day;
When he heard a knock upon his door,
He opened the door and there he saw
A beautiful maiden like a fairy queen.
"Pardon me, mister," she sighed.
And when he asked her what she wanted
    there,
The beautiful maiden replied:

CHORUS

"Paint me a picture, Mr. Artist Man,
A life-size photograph,

Of a man with eyes like the skies;
Make his shoulders the hero size;
Make him resemble Mr. Romeo,
A man a girl could love always.
I've hunted all around,
But that man can't be found;
So satisfied I must go to be with just
A picture of the man I love."

VERSE 2

The artist just whispered, "I know what you
    want;
I'll paint the picture for you."
Then he took his best paint from the shelf
And painted a picture of himself.
The maiden looked down upon the photograph,
Then took a step toward the hall,
Saying, "I'm sorry, but the picture don't
Resemble the fellow at all."

REPEAT CHORUS

THAT INTERNATIONAL RAG

WORDS AND MUSIC BY

IRVING BERLIN

SOPHIE TUCKER

WATERSON · BERLIN & SNYDER CO.
MUSIC PUBLISHERS
112 WEST 38TH ST. NEW YORK

HE'S SO GOOD TO ME

Published. Copyrighted January 4, 1913.

VERSE 1

I've got a lot of pretty diamond rings,
I've got a lot of other pretty things;
I've got a mortgage on a man's affections.
That's the reason why I
Don't have to worry if it rains or snows;
I'm always well supplied with pretty clothes;
I'm so extremely happy, goodness knows!
Night and day I cry:

CHORUS

That man, that man,
He's so good to me.
He's got a great big heart
Like a Christmas tree;
That man, that man,
He's all sympathy.
Night and day
I'm thinking of him,
And I've got to say,
He made me love him,
'Cause he's
Oh, oh, oh, oh, oh
So good to me!

VERSE 2

He comes around to see me when I'm sad,
He sends me flowers when I'm feeling bad,
You bet he's better than a million doctors
When he's holding my hand, and
He's got a lovin' way that's all his own,
He's got a lovin' kiss that reaches home,
He's goodness, from his tootsies to his dome
Oh, oh, oh so grand.

REPEAT CHORUS

ANNA LIZA'S WEDDING DAY

Published. Copyrighted January 15, 1913. In a letter to Spencer Vanderbilt (January 3, 1949), Berlin wrote: "I do remember 'Anna Liza's Wedding Day.' . . . 'Anna Liza' never amounted to much. It was just another song I had written which didn't come off."

VERSE 1

Oh, my honey, paint your face with a smile,
Wear a smile that they can see for a mile;
Get your Sunday clothes and dress up in style!
Honey, after a while I'll
Hire a rubber-tired carriage, so nice!
Don't you worry, honey, I've got the price;
Kindly hurry, honey, take my advice,
Shake it up and come along.

CHORUS

Ev'rybody's goin' to town,
Honey dear, we better go down,
It's Anna Liza's wedding day;
They're goin' to give the bride away.
My honey, come and see the cute little bride
With her lovin' man by her side;
Come and hear that parson say,
"Bless you, love and honor and obey."
Ev'rybody's happy and gay,
It's Anna Liza's wedding day.

VERSE 2

Oh, my honey darlin', don't you forget,
There's a wedding cake, and say, it's a pet!
Made by Anna Liza's mammy, you bet!
Sweetest you ever eat yet.
Oh, my honey, come and let's make a raid
On the healthy-looking hens that were slayed;
We'll devour them with red lemonade—
Hurry up and come along.

REPEAT CHORUS

AT THE PICTURE SHOW

Published. Copyrighted January 20, 1913. Words and music by E. Ray Goetz and Irving Berlin. Introduced in *The Sun Dodgers* (Broadway Theatre, New York; November 30, 1912) by Harry Clark ("A Lamb, man about town") and Maud Gray ("Trixie Turner, a 'broiler' ") and chorus. On the sheet music covers all of the songs printed from *The Sun Dodgers* were attributed, incorrectly, to E. Ray Goetz and A. Baldwin Sloane.

VERSE 1

Hurry up, hurry up, buy your ticket now,
Hurry up, hurry up, better come somehow;
Ev'rybody's going, all tiptoeing,
To the picture show.
Come along, come along, with a smiling face,
Come along, come along, to the happy place
Where the picture reelers, fun revealers,
A-flickering go.

CHORUS

At the picture show,
At the picture show,
Come and see the villain gay
Steal the hero's girl away;
Or ponies racing,
Just see them chasing
At the picture show
Owned by Marcus Loew,
Come on, you're just in time,
To see the latest crime,
All for a single dime,
At the picture show.

VERSE 2

Better run, better run, don't you miss the show;
Ev'ry one, ev'ry one has a thrill you know;
Lovers that you see, too, love as we do
At the picture show.
Come along, come along, to a world of fun;
Come along, come along, where the films, each one,
With the things revealing, they go reeling,
Love fonder will grow.

REPEAT CHORUS

WELCOME HOME

Published. Copyrighted January 23, 1913. There are two versions of this song, each with different music and lyrics. Only the first was published.

Published version

VERSE 1

Jack Jones left his wife and home,
Left his wife and home to roam,

Sunday night a year ago last May. The other day
He came back wrapped up in fear,
Wond'ring if his wifey dear
Would receive him in the same old way; and say,
As he slowly walked inside,
She looked at him and cried:

CHORUS

"I'm mighty glad that you came back,
Welcome home, welcome home, welcome home,
I'm mighty glad that you came back, Jack.
Night and day I thought about you,
'Twas hard to live without you.
I don't know of any braver life saver.
I need some brand-new winter clothes,
Welcome home, welcome home, welcome home,
To protect me when the winter snows blow.
Here's some bills that you can pay,
They've been due since way last May,
Landlord comes for rent today—
Welcome home."

VERSE 2

"Sit right down," said she to he,
"You look like a Christmas tree!
Hang your whiskers, Mister Santa Claus, upon
    your jaws.
Your voice sounds a trifle old,
I'm afraid you've got a cold,
Cough right up and don't you even pause,
    because
Wifey needs an Easter hood,
The stove needs coal and wood,

REPEAT CHORUS

Earlier version

VERSE

Mr. Gray, he ran away
From his home and wife and baby
Just a year last May. Yesterday
He thought he'd go around and look things over.
Nervously he went to see
If his wifey would forgive him.
When he slowly walked inside,
She looked at him and cried:

CHORUS

"Welcome home—
I'm awfully glad to see you, dear.
Welcome home—

I've lived a very lonesome year.
All I did was think and think about you,
It was awfully hard to live without you.
Welcome home—
The baby needs a pair of shoes
And I need a hat for my own dome.
Here's the grocer's and the butcher's bill to pay,
I expect the man aroun' for rent today,
I'm so overcome all that I can say is
Welcome home."

IN MY HAREM

Published. Copyrighted February 1, 1913. Top-selling recordings by Walter Van Brunt (Columbia) and Billy Murray (Edison). The following information was printed in an Edison record flyer for Murray's recording of the song:

> An interesting story of "In My Harem" is told by Clifford Hess, private secretary to Irving Berlin. Mr. Berlin has had little practical instruction in music, and, although he plays the piano exceptionally well, he plays by ear only. At the time "In My Harem" was written, Mr. Hess was working in the Chicago office of the Waterson, Berlin and Snyder Company. Berlin went to Chicago on the 20th Century Limited and worked out this tune in his head while on the train. When in Chicago he played it over (all on the black keys, as he always does) and Mr. Hess sat by him and wrote it down on paper as he played it. [Berlin played in the key of F-sharp, which has six black and two white notes.] This struck the composer as a great time-saving device, for Mr. Hess afterward transferred it into a simpler key, and arranged it in its less complicated commercial form.

VERSE 1

Down in Turkey-urkey, Pat Malone [Abie Cohen]
Was selling fancy clothes to anyone who'd wear
    'em.
When the Turks were called away to war,
A Turk asked Patrick [Abie] if he wouldn't watch
    his harem;
Patrick [Abie] said, "With pleasure;
I will cover ev'ry track,
I'll take care of ev'rything,
So don't you hurry back."
Patrick [Abie] then sat down and wrote a note
To all his friends at home,
And this is what he wrote:

CHORUS

In my harem, my harem,
There's Rosie, Josie, Posie,
And there never was a minute
King Solomon was in it.
Wives for breakfast,
Wives for dinner,
Wives for suppertime;
Lots of fancy dancing,
And it doesn't cost a dime.
In my harem, my harem,
There's Fanny, Annie, Jenny,
And the dance they do
Would make you wish that you
Were in a harem with Pat Malone [Abie Cohen].

VERSE 2

Patrick [Abie] said, "I've got a thousand wives,
And ev'ry one of them has got a perfect figure;
Small ones, tall ones, big as they could be,
There's some as big as that, and some are even
    bigger.
That young Turk ain't coming back
Until the war is won;
I don't wish him hard luck,
But I hope they steal his gun.
I am living many happy lives—
How can a man get lonesome
With a thousand wives?"

REPEAT CHORUS

MY SWEET ITALIAN MAN
(Second Version)

Published. Copyrighted February 21, 1913. A completely different lyric from the first version of "My Sweet Italian Man." This version really should be known as "My Sweet Italian Gal."

VERSE 1

Upon the day I take the steam-a-ship
And sail across the sea,
I make-a much-a grieve, because I leave
The gal I love in Italy.
You talk about your nice fine sweet-a gal,
They don't come one, two, three
With the first-class gal
I leave behind in Italy.

CHORUS

My sweet Italian gal,
She love her Italian fell',
And when she love me well,
I feel like I can't tell.
And say, she's got one great big heart,
Like a push-a-cart.
Just for her, I'd go and put my pick and shov' in
    hock,
I'd jump into the river and I swim-a like a
    rock;
That's how much I love my Italian gal.

VERSE 2

If I would meet a nice kind fairy queen
Who'd give my wish to me,
You bet your life I'd wish to be a fish
And swim right back to Italy,
Because the gal I love is over there
And waiting patiently,
'Cause she needs me there
To help her raise a family.

REPEAT CHORUS

SNOOKEY OOKUMS

Published. Copyrighted February 21, 1913. According to music historian Robert Lissauer (*Lissauer's Encyclopedia of Popular Music*), this song was introduced by Natalie Normandy. Some of the original sheet music covers bear the legend "As featured by Clark and Bergman." Leading recordings by Arthur Collins and Byron Harlan (Columbia, Edison Amberol, and Indestructible) and Billy Murray (Victor). Many years later Fred Astaire and Judy Garland sang the song in a medley in the musical film *Easter Parade* (1948). One of the interesting aspects of this song's history is Berlin's inconsistent spelling of snookey/snooky. The spelling on the title page and on the copyright notice is "snookey." The spelling in the text of the lyric is "snooky."

VERSE 1

There's a married couple happily
Living in apartment forty-three;
I live right next door
In apartment forty-four.
Gee, but they're a mushy he and she,
Mushing seems to be their specialty;

It would start you walking
If you heard them talking.

CHORUS

All day long he calls her
Snooky Ookums, Snooky Ookums.
All they do is talk like babies;
She's his jelly-elly roll,
He's her sugey-ugar bowl.
Here's the way they bill and coo:
Poogy-woo, poogy-woo, poogy-woo.
All night long he calls her
Snooky Ookums, Snooky Ookums;
All night long the neighbors shout,
"Cut it out! Cut it out! Cut it out!"
They cry, "For goodness sake!
Don't keep us all awake,
With your snooky-ookey-ookey baby talk!"

VERSE 2

If you ever heard their mushy song,
If you saw how well they get along,
You would bet your life
That they weren't man and wife.
He's a little fellow, four foot tall,
Weighing just a hundred, clothes and all;
She's a great big lady,
Weighs a hundred eighty.

REPEAT CHORUS

OOS SNOOKY OOKUMS IS OO

Probably an earlier version of the song that became "Snookey Ookums." No music is known to survive. Typed lyric sheets were found among Berlin's papers and are now in the Irving Berlin Collection of the Music Division of the Library of Congress.

VERSE

She just weighed two hundred pounds;
He just weighed the same:
Cupid had a great big target,
So how could he miss his aim?
Four hundred pounds in love,
Four hundred pounds of dear;

Did you ever hear four hundred pounds
Whisper in each other's ear:

CHORUS

"Oosums little snooky ookie ookums is oo,
Oosums little poogie woogie woo,
Oosums little pugie-nosed bunch of joy
Is oo—oo—oo.
Come my little jelly-elly-elly roll,
Snuggle to your sugie-ugie-ugar bowl,
And tell ums, please tell ums,
Oos snooky ookums is oo."

THE APPLE TREE AND THE BUMBLEBEE

Published. Copyrighted March 7, 1913.

VERSE 1

One night in June when the silv'ry moon
Shone down in all its glories,
Said a bumblebee to an apple tree,
"Let's tell each other stories.
'Twill be like a show, telling what we know.
Think of the fun we're missin'."
Said the apple tree,
"If it's up to me,
Just open your ears and listen:

CHORUS

"A he and she were seated under me,"
Said the apple tree to the bumblebee.
"Soon they drew up closer;
The rest I fear I'll have to whisper in your ear:
I saw them um, um, um, um, um, um, um
Beneath the silv'ry moon."
That's the tale the apple tree
Told the bumblebee, one night in June.

VERSE 2

Said the bumblebee to the apple tree,
"Gee, but your tale was dandy!
I'll remember you if you tell it to
My little brother Andy—
I would give a pile just to see him smile,
You know he's always gloomy."
Said the apple tree,

"Just leave it to me,
Go on, bring your brother to me.

REPEAT CHORUS

SAN FRANCISCO BOUND

Published. Copyrighted March 13, 1913. On the cover of the original sheet music there is a photograph with the legend "Successfully featured by Amy Butler." There was a major recording by the Peerless Quartet (Victor and Columbia).

VERSE 1

My little baby brother, sister, and my mother,
All my cousins and my uncles and dad
Live in a happy, happy little snappy, snappy
Little town where ev'rybody is glad:
San Francisco town,
That's where I am bound;
I'm drawing closer, closer on a train,
And oh sir, when I get there I'll be glad!

CHORUS

Oh you sixty-mile-an-hour choo-choo hound,
Rattle, rattle, rattle 'cause I'm Frisco bound;
You better hurry across the ground—
Don't you dare to be slow, go!
Oh you sunny, all-the-money, honey coast,
Oh you Mammy, Uncle Sammy loves you most.
Wake up, choo-choo, roar and roar,
Steam up, steam up more and more,
Rattle, rattle like you never did before,
'Cause I'm San Francisco bound.

VERSE 2

I've got a full lunch basket—if you care to ask,
You can share it if you're going my way.
I've got my choo-choo ticket—if you dare to pick it
From my pocket, there'll be murder to pay.
San Francisco shores,
Here's to you and yours—
Your sunny sons and daughters live in sunny
  quarters,
And I'll meet them all today.

REPEAT CHORUS

THE KI-I-YOUDLE-ING DOG

Published. Copyrighted April 4, 1913. Music by Jean Schwartz (1878–1956).

VERSE 1

I've got a cute little four-legged male,
Cute little ears and a cute little tail,
He's got a beaut of a cute little wail,
Ki-i-youdle, that poodle
Sings doggie words to a dog melody,
Warbles away all the day willingly;
I've grown attached to his dog harmony,
He made a hit with me.

CHORUS

With his ki-i-i-i-you-oodle you-oodle,
That ki-i-youdle-ing dog.
He'll go off his noo-oodle noo-oodle,
Ki-i-you-oodle-ing.
Morning, noon, and night he's around running
  loose,
Singing like a four-legged Mister Carus',
Ki-i-i-i—he's a wonderful
Ki-i-i-youdle-ing dog.

VERSE 2

Talk of your Melbas and singers of choice,
Talk of your voices that make you rejoice,
They don't compare with my pet's little
  voice—
You could pawn it, doggone it.
Queen Tetrazzin' sings as high as could be,
I've heard that she hits a C easily;
My little pet sings his dog melody
Ten notes above high C.

REPEAT CHORUS

KEEP ON WALKING

Published. Copyrighted April 14, 1913. Among the artists whose photographs appear on original sheet music covers are Sophie Tucker and "the Gypsy Countess."

VERSE 1

"Mother dear," said Carrie,
"I'd like to take a walk
Through the park with Johnny
And have a little talk.
Give me your permission;
Now don't you answer no."
Carrie's mother answered,
"My daughter, you may go,
Go ahead and have your little talk;
But the minute you and Johnny start to walk,

CHORUS

"Keep on walking, walking, walking,
Keep on walking, dear.
You may stroll through the park
With your beau after dark,
But whatever you do, my daughter,
Don't get tired,
Keep on walking, walking, walking,
When you start from here;
Walking through the park at ten
With your beau is lovely
When you keep on walking, dear."

VERSE 2

Carrie started walking
With Johnny by her side.
After they'd been walking
An hour Johnny cried,
"Carrie dear, I'm tired."
Now what could Carrie do?
Just to change the subject,
She said, "I'm tired too."
"There's a tree," he said, "with no one nigh."
But a couple neath the tree began to cry:

REPEAT CHORUS

THE OLD MAIDS BALL

Published. Copyrighted April 16, 1913. Alternate title (cover of original sheet music): "The Old Maid's Ball." Correct title probably should be "The Old Maids' Ball."

VERSE 1

Talk about your funny masquerades,
Talk about your funny-looking braids,

Did you hear of the four old maids
Who gave a fancy ball?
Old maids gathered there from every town,
Each one dressed up in a funny gown;
I was asked to go and so I hurried
Down to the Old Maids' Ball.

CHORUS 1

There were old maids short and tall
Dancing round the hall.
One who knew us drew up to us,
She was older than St. Louis;
Miss Melinda Rand
Led the female band,
And when they played "Here Comes the Bride,"
Four old maids sat down and cried;
Someone hollered, "There's a man outside!"
And broke up the Old Maids' Ball.

VERSE 2

Everybody in the hall was asked
Not to laugh and say, it was a task.
What I thought was a funny mask
Turned out to be a face;
Someone came to me and put me wise.
Fifty dollars was the standing prize
To the one who had a perfect figure;
Nobody won the prize.

CHORUS 2

There were old maids short and tall,
Dancing round the hall.
One who knew us drew up to us,
She was older than St. Louis;
Miss Melinda Rand
Led the female band,
And one old maid named Geraldine,
Oldest maid I've ever seen,
Said, "Tomorrow I'll be seventeen,"
And broke up the Old Maids' Ball.

YOU PICKED A BAD DAY OUT TO SAY GOODBYE

Published. Copyrighted April 25, 1913.

VERSE 1

I see you've packed your junk
Within that rusty trunk,

And it looks like you're going away;
I really don't know exactly what to say.
I've done the best I could,
You know that I've been good,
And to think that you're leaving me now
Almost takes my breath away,
And I've got to say:

CHORUS

You cert'nly picked a bad day out to say goodbye,
When meat and groc'ries are mighty high,
You had to wait till there were many things to buy.
You better take one long last look
At your honey when you leave me;
I'm goin' to crawl away
And lay right down and die,
And when my ghost comes back to you
You're goin' to turn red, white, and blue,
'Cause you picked this bad day out to say goodbye.

VERSE 2

If there should come a time
When you ain't got a dime
And you come back, remember that then
You're goin'-a walk in, then walk right out again.
When you come back to me
Expecting sympathy
I'll have earmuffs on both of my ears;
When the time comes you can bet
That I won't forget:

REPEAT CHORUS

THE PULLMAN PORTERS ON PARADE

Published. Copyrighted May 14, 1913. Music by Maurice Abrahams. Words by Ren G. May (a pseudonym for Irving Berlin: move around the letters R E N G M A Y and you get "Germany," which leads to "Berlin"). Alternate title (original sheet music cover): "Pullman Porters Parade." Al Jolson recorded it for Columbia on June 4, 1913; it was the first Berlin song he recorded.

VERSE 1

Here they come down the street,
See them comin';
Hear the drums, how they beat,
Hear the drummin'.

Oh, my one little hon,
Better run to the fun,
They're parading;
Hear the yell from the boys!
Honey, listen!
Can't you tell by the noise
That we're missing all the fun?
Come and see the big parade,
My honey.

CHORUS

Just see those Pullman porters
Dolled up with perfumed waters
Bought by their dimes and quarters;
Here they come, here they come, here they come.
Just see those starched-up collars,
Hear how that captain hollers,
"Keep time, keep time."
It's worth a thousand dollars
To see those tip collectors,
Those upper-berth inspectors,
Those Pullman porters on parade.

VERSE 2

Look at flat-footed Mose,
See him juggling
His hat as he goes;
See the struggling of bow-legged Joe,
Don't he go rather slow?
Watch him stepping
On the ground like a hen!
All in clover,
See those round-shouldered men,
Stoopin' over, oh my hon,
That's what I call some parade,
My honey.

REPEAT CHORUS

ABIE SINGS AN IRISH SONG

Published. Copyrighted May 15, 1913. Introduced in *All Aboard* (June 5, 1913; Lew Fields' 44th Street Roof Garden, New York City;); performer unknown. Copies of this song are very rare. According to Hamm, vol. 3, p. 206, "No illustrated cover has been located: song may not have been marketed; typed lyric sheet and lead sheet in LC-IBC [Library of Congress, Irving Berlin Collection]." But we have seen a photocopy of a published piano-vocal which indicates that the song was printed for general sale.

VERSE 1

In an Irish neighborhood
Abie kept a clothing store,
But business wasn't good,
No one came into the store
And Abe wondered why
But soon winked his eye,
Then bought up ev'ry Irish song that he could
    buy.
In an hour and a half
Someone taught him how to sing the Irish songs
    somehow,
He learned them all with ease,
These Irish melodies,*
He knows them all by heart, and now

CHORUS 1

When an Irishman looks in the window,
Abie sings an Irish song;
When a suit of clothes he sells,
He turns around and yells
"By Killarney's Lakes and Dells."
Any time an Irish customer comes in the place,
Thinking that it's owned by someone of the Irish
    race,
If he looks at Abie with a doubt upon his face,
Abie sings an Irish song.

VERSE 2

Ev'ry morning Abie goes
Through the store a-singing
"Where the River Shannon Flows";
Business it is bringing.
And he knows what is best,
He don't take a rest,
He sings "Killarney" when he sells a coat and vest.
Any time he gets a cold
Down his throat a bunch of fancy cough drops he
    will push;
When anyone is near,
He sings "Acushla Dear,"
With emphasis upon the "cush."

CHORUS 2

When an Irishman looks in the window,
Abie sings an Irish song;

*Published sheet music, probably in error, has "Then Irish melodies."

When a suit of clothes he sells,
He turns around and yells
"By Killarney's Lakes and Dells."
Any time an Irishman comes in to pick a bone,
If he looks at Abe and hollers in an angry tone,
"I would like to wrestle with a Levi or a Cohn,"
Abie sings an Irish song.

THE MONKEY DOODLE DOO

Published. Copyrighted May 15, 1913. Introduced in *All Aboard* (June 5, 1913; Lew Fields' 44th Street Roof Garden;) by Will Philbrick ("Russel, a customs officer"). In 1925 Berlin wrote a totally different song with the same title for his musical *The Cocoanuts*.

VERSE 1

Oh my honey, do come and hurry to the zoo,
Where the funny little monkeys are;
If you want to laugh for an hour and a half,
Better hurry up and take a car.
Come and see them dance
That peculiar little prance;
You'll be crazy over every bar;
Come and see them do that Monkey Doodle Doo.

CHORUS

Watch those monkeys monkey doodle all around,
All around, all around;
Watch those monks go off their noodle as they
    bound
Round.
Look, look, look, look,
Look at the funny little monkeys in the cage,
Eating peanuts while they're monkey doodling.
Watch those monkeys throw their shoulders in the
    air,
In the air, in the air,
See them snap their claws and holler,
"It's a bear there!"
See that monkey on the bench
Lead the band with a monkey wrench,
While the rest are dancing
That Monkey Doodle Doo.

VERSE 2

Honey, hear that pure little monkey overture
Coming from the little monkey band;
Can't you see the tails winding all around the rails,

Hear the leader of them all command,
Listen to his moan,
In a language of his own,
"Take your monkey ladies by the hand,
Take your partners for that Monkey Doodle Doo."

REPEAT CHORUS

SOMEBODY'S COMING TO MY HOUSE

Published. Copyrighted May 15, 1913. Introduced in *All Aboard* (June 5, 1913; Lew Fields' 44th Street Roof Garden;); performer unknown. Alternate title: "Someone Is Coming to My House." "When I last saw him," wrote Rennold Wolf of Berlin in the *Green Book Magazine* (August 1913), "with the faithful Hess by his side, he was engaged in writing a song somewhat different from his previous themes. The lyric related to the arrival of a baby in the house."

VERSE 1

Ev'ryone's excited down at my house,
Ev'ryone's delighted there;
Soon you'll be invited down to my house,
Down to a joyous affair.
Can't you see I'm happy, happy and gay,
See the look of joy in my eye;
You'll never guess why I'm feeling this way,
So here's the reason why.

CHORUS

Somebody's coming to my house,
Somebody's coming to stay.
Father feels so happy he's jumping with joy;
All he keeps saying is "I hope it's a boy!"
Welcome is waiting the stranger
Who'll come to brighten our lives,
I can hear Mother croon,
"He'll be president soon,"
When the cute little stranger arrives.

VERSE 2

Ev'rything is quiet down at my house,
We must tiptoe through the hall;
Soon there'll be a riot down at my house
When someone starts in to bawl.
Auntie said, "We'll call it Lizabeth Jane";
Sister looked at Auntie and smiled.

Dad said, "Elizabeth's fine, but I hope
It's not that kind of a child."

REPEAT CHORUS

HAPPY LITTLE COUNTRY GIRL

Published. Copyrighted May 21, 1913. Introduced by Lillian Russell at a vaudeville engagement (date unknown) at the Colonial Theatre, New York City.

VERSE 1

I know a girl,
Sweet little pearl,
Doesn't know a thing about the city whirl,
Lives on a farm,
Where nature's arm
Wraps around her all day;
Early to bed,
Early to rise,
Keeps the light of heaven shining in her eyes,
Happily she spends the hours,
Among the butterflies and flow'rs.

CHORUS 1

Happy, happy, happy little country girl,
Much too good for any duke or earl,
Simple dress and ten-cent ribbon round her
    curl,
She's a beautiful lady.
Reuben lover, loves her to her fingertips,
Loves her kisses just like honey drips;
He doesn't taste a drugstore on her ruby lips,
Happy little country girl.

VERSE 2

Birds on their way
Linger to stay
Long enough to sing to her a fond "Good day."
As she goes by,
Roses all sigh,
How they envy her cheeks!
Early each day,
Crowing away,
Mister Rooster wakes her and he seems to
    say,
"Dress yourself, for goodness' sake!
We'll all be glad when you awake."

CHORUS 2

Happy, happy, happy little country girl,
Much too good for any duke or earl,
Simple dress and ten-cent ribbon round her curl,
She's a beautiful lady.
Nine o'clock her tired eyes refuse to peep,
Then into her cozy bed she'll creep;
She doesn't miss a minute of her beauty sleep,
Happy little country girl.

HAPPY LITTLE CHORUS GIRL

A preliminary or alternate version of "Happy Little Country Girl." Lyric published in Hamm, vol. 3. A typed lyric sheet found among Berlin's papers is now in the Irving Berlin Collection of the Music Division of the Library of Congress.

VERSE 1

There she goes,
Flashy clothes,
Dressed up like a circus from her head to her toes;
See those rings,
Flashy things,
You would surely swear her father was a
    millionaire.
But that's not so—'cause I know
She's just one of many in a musical show:
She's the little girl in blue,
The one who made an awful hit with you.

CHORUS

Happy, happy, happy little chorus girl,
Polish up your imitation pearl;
Go to sleep and dream about a duke or earl
Who may marry you someday.
Powder up for Harry, Johnny, Jack, and Bob;
Make up pretty for the front-row mob;
Lose your figure and you lose your job,
Happy little chorus girl.

VERSE 2

Manager
Dresses her,
But it's all subtracted from her seventeen per;
After he
Gets his fee,
Half her salary she sends home to her mother,
And an empty purse
Makes it worse

When for seven weary weeks she has to rehearse.
After much rehearsing nights
She's fired, 'cause she doesn't fit her tights.

REPEAT CHORUS

WE HAVE MUCH TO BE THANKFUL FOR

Published. Copyrighted May 21, 1913. Major recording by Manuel Romain (Edison).

VERSE 1

Sweetheart, I love but you,
I know you love me too,
And we could not hope to ask for more;
We should bless this world of ours,
With its sunshine and its show'rs:
We have much to be thankful for.

CHORUS

We have eyes to behold one another,
We have voices to say, "I love you,"
We have ears to hear love's tender story,
We have hearts that are fond and true,
We have arms to embrace one another,
We have lips just to kiss o'er and o'er;
With such wonderful treasures from heaven,
We have much to be thankful for.

VERSE 2

When things go wrong, my dear,
When sunbeams disappear,
And the world looks dark from shore to shore,
Don't give way to feeling blue:
You have me, and I have you,
And there's much to be thankful for.

REPEAT CHORUS

THEY'VE GOT ME DOIN' IT NOW

Published. Copyrighted June 17, 1913.

VERSE 1

Doctor, hurry,
Won't you hurry up and stop my worry,
Can't you see that I am all aflurry?
I've been troubled with an ailment greatly
Here lately;
Headache fixer,
Oh, you wonderful prescription mixer,
Won't you tell me why my shoulders
Keep going in the air?

CHORUS

Any little rag will start me doin' it,
Doin' it against my will;
Ev'ry orchestra seems to say,
"Go, go, go, go to it, do it";
Any little swinging, ringing melody
Makes me dance somehow;
When they start that rhythm,
I've got to hurry up and do it with 'em,
I just can't pause, because
They've got me doin' it now.

VERSE 2

Doctor, cure me,
Won't you hurry up and temperature me?
Of a quick recovery assure me,
Tell me what's the matter, don't deceive me,
Relieve me;
Capsule maker,
Oh, you friend of ev'ry undertaker,
Won't you tell me why my shoulders
Keep going in the air?

REPEAT CHORUS

THEY'VE GOT ME DOIN' IT NOW MEDLEY

Published. Copyrighted July 11, 1913. Written for Berlin's trip to England in the summer of 1913, this number uses "They've Got Me Doin' It Now" as the foundation for a medley that also includes portions of the following Berlin hits: "When the Midnight Choo-Choo Leaves for Alabam'," "That Mysterious Rag," "I Want to Be in Dixie," "Ragtime Violin," "Grizzly Bear," "Alexander's Ragtime Band," and "Everybody's Doin' It Now."

Doctor, hurry,
Won't you hurry up and stop my worry,
Can't you see that I am all aflurry?
I've been troubled with an ailment greatly
Here lately;
Headache fixer,
Oh, you wonderful prescription mixer,
Won't you tell me why my shoulders
Keep going in the air?

Any little rag will start me doing it,
Doing it against my will.
Ev'ry orchestra seems to say,
"Go! Go! Go! Go, to it! Do it!"
Any little swinging, ringing melody
Makes me dance somehow;
When they start that rhythm,
I've got to hurry up and do it with 'em;
I just can't pause, because
They've got me doin' it now.

When the midnight choo-choo leaves for Alabam',
So snappy, it makes me happy, and
That mysterious ra-ag,
It fills me with a jumping jag,
It's the drag of the rag.
And you really ought to see,
You ought to see,
How I perform when they play "Dixie."
Doctor, doctor,
I must hurry near them,
Doctor, doctor,
Any time I hear them
Fiddle up, fiddle up on their violins,
Some peculiar something sets my feet a-jumping
Most any time that I listen to a ragtime violin.
I've got to go, I've got to go,
I've got to go right to it;
First I snap my fingers,
Then I hug up close to my baby.
Doctor, you can tell me maybe
Why I hug up to my baby
When the music starts playing,
And when I hear, and when I hear
"Alexander's Ragtime Band,"
I've got to dance, I've got to dance,
Just because my feet demand,
I just find myself doing it
Before the band is through,
So natural that I don't know what to do;
Doctor, I see you're doing it too,

You! You! You! You! You!
Doctor, I'm afraid I've got you doing it,
Doing it against your will;
And I thought that you'd cure me sure,
Go! Go! Go! Go to it! Do it!
Doctor, when I came I wanted medicine,
But I've changed my mind somehow;
I came here because I was sure
With your help it couldn't endure—
Now I know there is no cure:
Ev'rybody's doing it now.

THAT HUMMING RAG

Published in Hamm, vol. 3, p. 246. Written to order at the office of Berlin's English publisher, Bert Feldman, before an audience of newsmen, several of whom described how Berlin did it. One such account appeared in the *Daily Express*; it is undated but it is from around June 21, 1913.

RAGTIME WHILE YOU WAIT

MR. BERLIN MAKES 500 POUNDS IN TWO HOURS, TUNE HUSTLING

If any one could have peeped into a top room in the premises of Messrs. Feldman, the music publishers, yesterday, he would have seen a young man walking up and down with the steps of a cat on broken glass, and with his hand to his ear as though suffering from a severe pain.

It was only Mr. Irving Berlin earning 500 pounds by making a new ragtime melody.

Irving Berlin is the man of twenty-five who cannot write or read a note of music, or play the piano with any efficiency, and yet has made a fortune by "dictating" ragtime to an "arranger."

He showed how he did it for the benefit of the *Express* representative yesterday. "Usually," he said, "I get my rhythm and melody complete before I give them to the 'arranger.' This is a pretty hard test but I'll try."

He did. He walked about four miles doing it, in the course of two hours. He was never still a moment.

At the finish a new ragtime had grown before its listeners, all complete, from the introduction and vamp to the final chord of the chorus. Afterwards, he made up the words.

GENIUS ON WIRES

This is how he did it. The "arranger" sat at the piano, pencil and paper ready. Irving Berlin started a one-step up and down the room, snapping his fingers and jerking his shoulders as he went. He did this for some time. It was the divine afflatus on marionette wires.

Suddenly he stopped, leaned over the "arranger" and "La-ta-ta-ta-tatata," he began. "That's the opening line."

The "arranger" wrote down the precious notes and played them.

"Fine," said Irving Berlin; and off he went again, up and down, to and fro, dancing a one-step to imaginary tunes rollicking through his mind.

"Play it again," he said with a snap of his fingers. A minute passed. Irving Berlin clapped his hands to his ears and changed the direction of his walk. It came slowly but when it did come there was a burst of half a dozen bars.

So, gradually, the ragtime is built up.

"Play it once more. I want to get back to the key," he says, after a half-hour's ineffectual "lum-tum-tums."

Finally, the chorus, the most difficult of all. It has to be catchy; it has to trip and slide and stop and drop from key to key and be lifted back again. It has to "Go."

With a rush the thing is finished. It has been fitted together like a puzzle, intricate little pieces of melody running haphazard nowhere and fading abruptly as other strains follow, with just a semblance of the motif to keep it together.

READY FOR THE MARKET

Impudent repetitions of a musical phrase like the tune to "Everybody's doing it—doing it—doing it"; isolated notes and quick changes of time—he has only whistled and hummed these things, as a child makes up his own artless songs, and the whole is a ragtime ready for the market. In an hour the words are set to it:—

> Down in Georgia there lived a funny little
> coon
> Named Mose;
> All day long he was humming a funny little
> tune;
> It was wonderful!
> But no one knew the name of the funny
> little strain,
> So, they gave it a name—
> "That Hummin' Rag."

Ragtime words read as nonsense when you take away the music, but when Irving Berlin, with a twitch of his shoulders, and knees working loosely, sang the words and the music of the ragtime that is made while you wait, one saw the whole thing complete.

One saw audiences all over the world in vast theatres humming the song he had just snatched out of nowhere.

One saw Irving Berlin collecting 500 pounds or *more* as royalties for a couple of hours work on a June afternoon in a top room in the Charing Cross Road.

VERSE

Down in Georgia there lived a funny little coon
Named Mose;
All day long he was humming a funny little
tune;
It was wonderful!
But no one knew the name of that funny little
strain,
So they gave it a name—
"That Hummin' Rag."

CHORUS

You ought to see them dance around
While funny little Mose hums the "Hummin'
Rag."
Before a week we found that
Everyone was hummin' it.
The folks in town are crazy 'bout that tune.
"It's a cute little beaut of a melody,
'That Hummin' Rag,' so tuneful."
Every time they see him coming up the street
They just follow him,
And fill up on a hummin' ja-ag.
He's got them all in an awful fix,
They act like so many lunatics,
They're simply daffy over
"That Hummin' Rag."

THE INTERNATIONAL RAG

Published. Copyrighted August 12, 1913. Written in London during the first week of July 1913. Introduced by Irving Berlin in the English musical revue *Hello, Ragtime* during the week of July 7, 1913. Presented in the Broadway musical *All Aboard*, sometime after its New York opening (June 5, 1913; Lew Fields' 44th Street Roof Garden;) by Carter de Haven and chorus. Alternate title (original sheet music cover): "That International Rag." Top-selling recordings by Arthur Collins and Byron G. Harlan (Victor), the Victor Military Band (Victor), and Prince's Orchestra (Columbia). Among the artists whose photographs appear on the original sheet music cover is Sophie Tucker.

In 1914 Irving Berlin described the origins of the song to a writer for an unnamed newspaper:

I was in London. I had a grip full of stuff; nothing especially new, nothing characteristic enough, they said. I composed the melody and wrote the first verse of "International Rag" in the Hotel Savoy at 4 o'clock the morning of the day before I opened, having thrown all my bath towels into the piano to deaden its resonance. I wrote the next verse the following morning and sang the song that afternoon.

Some time after his return to New York in July 1913, Berlin reflected on both the song and his craft as follows:

I was treated nicely in London. I also brought back a new ragtime song that I wrote for my engagement at the Hippodrome, and if those who heard the number weren't kidding me it looks like a big hit. It is called "The International Rag" and the London public liked it very much.

I am now back on the job, rhyming rag and drag, and spoon and coon, and with the help of those original rhymes I hope to eke out a meager livelihood this winter.

Another unnamed reporter described the fortunes of this new Berlin hit in an undated article in an unnamed newspaper:

Irving Berlin's latest composition, "The International Rag," has taken New York by storm, judging from the way it is being sung in vaudeville, musical comedy and cabaret. The new number is being featured by Sophie Tucker, Belle Baker and other prominent vaudevillians, and is the big number in Lew Fields' *All Aboard* show. Next week at the New Brighton Theatre, Pauline Welsh will feature the song, together with another recent composition of Mr. Berlin, entitled "You've Got Your Mother's Big Blue Eyes."

VERSE 1

What did you do, America?
They're after you, America.
You got excited and you started something,
Nations jumping all around;
You've got a lot to answer for,
They lay the blame right at your door,
The world is ragtime crazy from shore to shore.

CHORUS

London dropped its dignity,
So has France and Germany,
All hands are dancing to
A raggedy melody
Full of originality.

The folks who live in sunny Spain
Dance to a strain
That they call the Spanish Tango;
Dukes and lords and Russian czars,
Men who own their motorcars,
Throw up their shoulders to
That raggedy melody
Full of originality.
Italian opera singers
Have learned to snap their fingers,
The world goes round to the sound
Of the International Rag.

VERSE 2

In every land, America,
Most every band, America,
Has started everybody dancing daily,
Prancing gaily all around;
There's syncopation in the air,
They've got the fever everywhere,
Each happy, snappy chappy cries "It's a bear."

REPEAT CHORUS

Alternate version

When Berlin decided to include this song in the film version of *Call Me Madam*, he republished the number with a new title—"That International Rag"—and changed the "Russian czars" couplet to:

Dukes and lords and diplomats
Dressed in tails and opera hats

He also supplied a new lyric for the second half of the repeat of the chorus:

That was nineteen-thirteen;
Still today each Eu-ro-pean
Throws up his shoulders
To that raggedy melody
Full of originality.
All Harrys, Dicks, and Tommies
And someday even commies
Will dance around
To the sound
Of the International Rag.

KISS YOUR SAILOR BOY GOODBYE

Published. Copyrighted August 15, 1913.

VERSE 1

My honey dear, my honey dear,
You hear the steamboat whistle blowin';
My honey dear, my honey dear,
The whistle means I must be going
Far across the sea,
Hear them calling me,
It's the captain's orders,
I must go, so

CHORUS

Kiss your sailor boy goodbye,
Now don't you cry,
Just dry that tear from your eye, my honey.
Don't feel so blue,
I'll write to you;
If I don't I hope to die.
When I'm away
You bet I'll stay
All by my ownsome,
Real lonesome for you, honey.
Sweet letters I'll be sending
With crosses on the ending,
Kiss your sailor boy goodbye.

VERSE 2

My honey dear, my honey dear,
You better save up all your lovin',
Remember, dear, remember, dear,
My heart'll be just like an oven;
When my ship comes in,
Honey, we'll begin
To make up for lost time,
Don't forget, pet,

REPEAT CHORUS

TAKE ME BACK

Published. Copyrighted September 8, 1913. "Successfully introduced" in *All Aboard* (June 5, 1913; Lew Fields' 44th Street Roof Garden;) by Claire Rochester.

There is a photograph of Rochester on the cover of the original sheet music.

VERSE 1

Sweetheart, the day we parted
Somehow I never knew
You'd leave me brokenhearted,
Pining away for you.
All that I really cared for,
All that I wanted near,
All that made life worth living,
Vanished with you, my dear.

CHORUS

Take me back, won't you take me back?
Every joy I knew will return with you;
I'm so sad, you are all I had,
Can't you hear my broken heart calling you?
Take me back.

VERSE 2

Sweetheart, since we've been parted
Seems like a thousand years;
For every hour of gladness
I've paid an hour of tears.
Come back and make me happy;
Why should we live apart?
Come to my arms and answer
The call of my broken heart.

REPEAT CHORUS

YOU'VE GOT YOUR MOTHER'S BIG BLUE EYES!

Published. Copyrighted September 12, 1913. Sung in vaudeville in New York during the summer of 1913 by Pauline Welsh. On some of the original sheet music covers there is a large photograph accompanied by the legend "Successfully introduced by Helene Vincent." Top-selling recording by Marguerite Dunlop (Victor) under the pseudonym Lillian Davis.

VERSE 1

Baby Mabel, seven years old,
Sitting on her daddy's knee,
Cried, "I've been a good little girl,
Please give a penny to me."

Daddy softly sighed,
Gave her the penny and cried:

CHORUS

"You've got your mother's big blue eyes,
You've got your mother's teeth, like pearl!
I must confess you are
The image of your ma,
From your nose to your toes to your curls.
The way you ask for pennies shows
You know just what your mother knows.
And when you grow to be a great big lady,
Like your daddy wants you to,
If you're half the lady that your mother is,
I'll be mighty proud of you."

VERSE 2

Soon her mother came in the room,
Whisper'd, "Mabel, go to bed."
When her ma unbuttoned her dress,
Babe looked at Mother and said:
"Here's the latest thing
My daddy taught me to sing:

REPEAT CHORUS

IF YOU DON'T WANT ME (WHY DO YOU HANG AROUND)

Published. Copyrighted September 24, 1913. Introduced by Harry Clark and Gladys Bergman in Jesse Lasky's *Trained Nurses*, a vaudeville act. Alternate title (from sheet music covers): "If You Don't Want Me."

VERSE 1

Honey, something's wrong with my eyes,
And it makes me blue:
Ev'ry time I open my eyes
I'm looking at you.
Why should you be haunting me
All the livelong day?
Honey, if you don't want me,
Why don't you keep away?

CHORUS

If you don't want me,
Why do you hang around,

Why do you hang around?
Why do you haunt me
Just like a haunting melody?
What did I do to you,
What did I do to you?
I can't forget you;
What am I goin' to do,
What am I goin' to do?
I sailed the ocean blue
To get away from you;
In ev'ry foreign place
I met you face to face.
If you don't want me,
Why do you hang around?

VERSE 2

I looked at your picture, my dear,
And it seemed to speak.
When I saw your beautiful face,
I cried for a week.
I tore up your picture, dear,
Threw it on the floor;
Then I saw you standing there
More lovely than before.

REPEAT CHORUS

TRA-LA, LA, LA!

Published. Copyrighted September 24, 1913. Introduced by Artie Mehlinger at the Winter Garden in New York. Major recording by Billy Murray (Edison). The following information was printed in an Edison flyer for Murray's recording of the song:

Irving Berlin, one of the youngest and most successful of song writers, and his even younger secretary, Clifford Hess, live together in a New York apartment house. They generally work only at night, Berlin composing, and Hess writing down the melodies as they are evolved. Consequently having worked during the night, they like to sleep during the morning.

Now as everyone knows, the walls of a New York apartment house are anything but sound proof. Next door to Berlin and Hess (where they used to live, they have moved now) was a singing teacher who did not work nights and consequently was not interested in sleeping in the mornings. The tra, la, la's that came through the wall were too much for Berlin and Hess. They were repaid for the trouble of moving, however, by the inspiration for this song.

VERSE 1

Once a vocal teacher
Said to Mabel Beecher,
"I think your singing voice is very canary!
It needs cultivation
For a demonstration:
I'll charge you ten to cultivate it."
She paid it.
Twice a week Miss Mabel scrapes the money up
    somehow;
Twice a week he teaches her to vocalize, and now:

CHORUS

All day long she's singing
Tra-la, la, la! Tra-la, la, la!
When her voice starts ringing
Tra-la, la, la! Tra-la, la, la!
All the neighbors get together and cry:
"It's most unbearable, terrible!
Why do they let her suffer?"
Ev'rybody hollers,
"Tie a can-o to her soprano!"
All her aunts and uncles
When they heard her
Holler'd "Murder!"
Ev'ry day a neighbor moves away
From her tra-la, la, la!
Tra-la, la, la!
Tra-la, la, la, la!

VERSE 2

Landlord sent a cable
Saying, "Dear Miss Mabel,
Your voice is good for breaking leases to pieces.
My advice, Miss Beecher,
Is give up your teacher;
Your singing voice needs no improving."
They're moving!
June, July, and August finds her relatives in tears,
Just because they must go round with earmuffs on
    their ears.

REPEAT CHORUS

WHAT AM I GONNA DO?

Three months after Berlin returned from London, the Friars Club held a dinner in his honor. The celebration, complete with after-dinner speeches and entertainment, took place at the Hotel Astor in New York on October 19, 1913. For the occasion Berlin wrote and delivered a song-speech, accompanied by Clifford Hess, which was recorded privately and printed in several newspapers. Hamm published the song in volume 3 of his three-volume edition of Berlin's early songs. Before Berlin's song-speech, Friar Abbot John W. Rumsey and Friar Rennold Wolf delivered the following speeches, which appear in a surviving typescript.

Address Delivered at a Complimentary Dinner Given to Friar Irving Berlin by the Friars Club at Hotel Astor, Sunday, October 19, 1913, at 7 p.m.

FRIAR ABBOT JOHN W. RUMSEY: Ladies, Mr. Berlin, Friars and Guests:

It is my agreeable duty as presiding officer of the organization that is responsible for this gathering tonight to pave the way for the post-prandial feast that is before us. The list of speakers, although not lengthy, contains the names of men who have done and are doing big things in our community and country.

Among those who have been the recipients of dinners in their honor by the Friars are many men who have climbed to the top of our profession. We have honored managers, players and dramatists, but we have never met before to show our appreciation to one whose works have met with such widespread recognition. Music, they say, has charms to soothe the savage breast. And certainly Mr. Berlin's melodies have done much to dispel gloom from the face of the globe.

Berlin is a great boy. Napoleon was a great man. He won many battles and gained great renown. Napoleon made a couple of million people fight for him. Berlin has made over fifty million people sing. (Applause) I leave it to you to decide which man has made the most people happy. (Applause)

Our guest this evening strikes me as bearing a strong resemblance to Halley's comet. Half a dozen years ago no one on Broadway had ever heard of Mr. Berlin. He had not arrived, and no one expected him. A little light began to twinkle in the sky, the eastern side of the sky I believe, and Berlin unannounced began to give us the benefit of his brains and personality. He began to make them both felt. Finally, like Halley's comet, Berlin burst forth in a scintillating blaze of glory, startling his followers with his brilliancy.

I need not dwell upon the triumphs this young man has had during the past few years. They are so recent that they are still part of Broadway's seven wonders.

Of Mr. Berlin's early life, his struggles, his trials and tribulations, I leave all that to some one more capable than myself. I therefore turn our guest of honor over to the kind and tender mercies (laughter) of a gentleman who, by reason of his peculiar fitness and his wide experience in such matters, is best able to throw the searchlight upon Irving Berlin's past performances. I take great pleasure in introducing to you Friar Rennold Wolf.

MR. WOLF: Friar Abbot, Mr. Berlin, Ladies and Gentlemen:—

At the outset it is only fair to explain that although our guest of honor is a music publisher, his parents were honest. (Laughter) Expecting him to grow up as a theatrical manager they christened him Isidore. Shortly after the christening many thefts were reported in the baby's nursery. The family physician missed his watch, and it was traced to the baby's cradle. "The boy," declared his father, "is going to be a music publisher." (Laughter) The next day the nurse's outfit, including some towels and a wash rag, strangely disappeared. Young Isidore had hidden them away. That was the origin of "That Mysterious Rag." (Laughter) From that beginning sprang the firm of Waterson, Berlin and Snyder.

Our guest was born in Russia. He acquired his first knowledge of rag-time by endeavoring to speak the Russian language. (Laughter) He just took a few Russian words and set them to music, and he had a good rag-time tune.

While learning to walk, with the assistance of his nurse, he frequently tumbled over and floundered upon the floor, pulling his nurse down with him, and that gave him the idea for The Dip and the Bunnie Hug and the Turkey Trot.

Immediately after our guest arrived in New York he adopted an alias. Isidore Belein became Irving Berlin. Then he took a job over at Nigger Mike's (laughter). No. 12 Pell Street, a resort frequented exclusively by burglars. He did this in order to get into the music publishing atmosphere. (Laughter) Unprejudiced patrons of Nigger Mike still say that when Berlin quit to enter the song writing profession the world lost a great waiter. (Laughter)

Perhaps a word of explanation is due the lay members present tonight. There are two degrees of larceny, known in the criminal statutes,—embezzlement and music publishing. The first music publisher mentioned in history is Captain Kidd. You can always distinguish a music publisher by his automobile. He rides in a 1914 sixty horse power Mercedes. Those two ragged men on foot you see trying to get out of the way of the automobile are the composer and lyric writer. (Laughter) Their brains are paying for the car. Now, you understand what Mr. Berlin meant when he wrote the song "Keep Away From the Man Who Owns an Automobile."

One and all tonight, I urge you to avoid the music publisher as you would a show girl. (Laughter) He is a wizard with figures. Two and two in royalties do not with him neccessarily make four. Oh, shun him. He biteth like a serpent and stingeth in his addition. (Laughter and applause) He is the siren who lures you on to false hopes, deferred payments and rag-time arithmetic. I speak with feeling because I have met him, and he holds a mortgage on my right eye. He will promise you anything, and will show you the house on Riverside Drive that you are to purchase with your royalties. Then you sign a contract, and he publishes your song. Pretty soon

every cabaret sings with its melody, the pianola and phonograph spread its infection, the whole world is singing it. Six months later you get your statement. You open it feverishly to read that four copies of the song have been sold, and that you owe the publisher $11. For postage.

After leaving Nigger Mike's our guest moved over to Jimmy Kelley's in 14th Street for a post graduate course. There his industry and scholarly attainments advanced him rapidly, and I am happy to say that he was promoted to the proud eminence of assistant headwaiter. Mr. Berlin having come from Russia and being named Isidore was very frugal in those days. It is said of him that he was so close that he wouldn't pay ten cents to see a revival of the Battle of Waterloo with the original cast. (Laughter) Also it is told of him that while serving the customers at Kelley's he was in the habit of giving them counterfeit twenty-five cent pieces in change. In Mr. Berlin's behalf I indignantly deny that story. They were fifty cent pieces. (Laughter)

In further exposing our guest, it is possible tonight to reveal to the world his first lyric. It was only a couplet, and the song never was completed nor published because the author could not maintain the poetic pace set in the first two lines. The song was about a girl and the couplet goes:

> She stood in the moonlight on the plaza,
> No one in the world was as beautiful as her.

(Great laughter)

Perhaps Mr. Berlin's most conspicuous quality is his wonderful memory. Up to date he has remembered over two hundred tunes, almost note for note. Were it not for him, Wagner, Mendelssohn, and the other old masters probably would never have been revived. One always enjoys a new Berlin tune. It is like meeting an old friend. Listening to one of his melodies is as good as attending "Old Home Week." A good tune dropped carelessly near Irving Berlin has the same chance as a piece of raw meat in a cage of lions. Largely due to Mr. Berlin's influence, food has nearly been eliminated in the restaurants. (Laughter) For an entree, one gets "Snooky Ookums," and for the roast, "Everybody's Doin' It."

We all like Irving Berlin. The Friars are very proud of him. We like him not only because he is the greatest song writer of all time, but because he is a fine, manly, modest boy. (Hearty applause) Due to his influence the Star Spangled Banner has been replaced in the schools by "My Wife's Gone to the Country." And tender mothers sing their babies to sleep to the tune of "The Old Maid's Ball."

Mr. Berlin is young. In fact, he is growing younger all the time. Two years ago he told me he was twenty-five. Tonight he says he is twenty-two. If he continues growing younger at this rate he will wake up some morning and find his name among the birth notices. (Laughter)

As for the ladies, they all love him. In fact, wherever he goes he is surrounded by them. Doubtless he intended us to accept as his autobiography his song "In My Harem." (Very great applause.)

Mr. Berlin then arose, and after very hearty and continued applause, sang the following:

Friar Abbot! Brother Friars! Ladies and guests!
Don't expect too much of me:
I'm confined to melody,
And furthermore, I must confess,
I don't know just how to express
The depth of my appreciation.
Just why you honor me,
In vain I've tried to figure out;
I don't know what it's all about.
Nevertheless, I want to thank you;
While I syncopate, I appreciate your wonderful
  kindness
Making what you'd call a speech
Is away beyond my reach,
All I can do is shout a bit,
'Twill bore you, there's no doubt of it,
But it's the only way out of it.
For days and days I worried as to what I'd have to
  say—
So worried that I hurried to Rumsey one day and
  shouted:
"What am I going to do! What am I going to do?
I never made a speech. Tell me,
What am I going to do! What am I going to do?"
John Rumsey answered: "Don't you let that worry
  you!
I'll tell you what to do.
I know a certain Friar whose speeches are surefire.
Go to Havez! Jean Havez!
Ren Wolf, Sam Harris, and the rest of them
Went to Havez, Jean Havez;
He's written speeches for the best of them."
And so I went to Jean for my routine.
He said: "Don't worry, sonny,
I'll write you something funny."
The speech he wrote was like the *Morning
  Telegraph:*
It didn't have a laugh;
The jokes he wrote were all so solemn,
Like the ones in Ren Wolf's column.
All I could do was write a rag;
I had a rag, the same old gag,
But I can't express my feelings to a rag:
The minute that I begin ragtiming,
I've got to keep on rhyming.
My rhymes, if there are any, are not so very many.
You'd bet I'd keep on goin' if I could rhyme like
  Cohan,
But now I must be stopping before my speech
  starts flopping.
Here's to the Friars! Here's to them!
Kind applause, kind applause, kind applause.
With apologies to Victor Herbert,

Here's to the Friars, ladies, guests, and music
  buyers:
All I can say is I thank you,
Thank you with all my heart!

FRIAR ABBOT: We are now to hear from a gentleman who has spent his life exploiting both our City and our Country.

And this, ladies and gentlemen, is a particularly happy occasion for us, because it marks the return to us assembled here, of a wonderful man who lately, in spite of a terrible accident, was returned to us by the grace of Almighty God.

I take great pleasure in introducing to you the only man who really owns Broadway, Friar George M. Cohan. (Hearty applause, all rising)

MR. COHAN: Friar Abbot, Mr. Berlin, ladies and gentlemen:—It is going to be very short and sweet. The first time I met the young man, or rather heard of the young man, he had written the song Mr. Wolf referred to, "My Wife's Gone to the Country, Hurray." So I naturally pictured him as an old married man with a grey beard. You can imagine how surprised I was when I walked into the Friars Club one day and was introduced to this little boy.

I don't know whether to boost Irving or roast him. I feel the same toward Irving as a whole lot of other song writers feel. (Laughter) Of course you know I was a song writer. That is, I thought I was a song writer until this young man came along. He didn't do me a great deal of good. Up to the time he put in an appearance I was able to collect some advanced royalties from several music publishers and was considered rather a handy little fellow to have around. But he spoiled my graft. And in fact he—well, he drove me out of musical comedy, that is all. I discovered that Berlin's songs were being whistled wherever mine were being played.

Berlin is a great little fellow. His specialty is Italian song writing. He called them "Wop" songs, I think. I heard all these Italian songs before I met him, and I thought he was a "Dago," but afterward I discovered he was a Jew boy, who named himself after an English actor and a German city. (Laughter)

I remember about ten years ago a music publisher to whom I brought a coon song, told me that rag-time was dead. I guess it was until Irvy resurrected it. And it has been an awful thing ever since. It is almost impossible to get a night's sleep. The turkey-trotting orchestras and phonographs go all night, and then the brass bands and hand organs haunt you all day.

I have heard people say they wished rag-time would go and so would Berlin. But I think he proved that he was not confined to rag-time entirely when he wrote that little love song "When I Lost You." I think it is the prettiest song I have ever heard in my life. (Applause)

Irving is to the music business now what Barnum was

[*Text of speech breaks off.*]

Alternate opening

Some lines but no music survive of what might have been an earlier attempt to write something for the Friars Club dinner.

Friar Abbot—Brother Friars—Ladies and Guests,
I have tried to figure out
Just what this is all about;
I must confess I'm all at sea,
I don't know why you picked on me:
What have I done,
What have I done
That's worthy of your generosity?
I must confess
I'm in an awful plight,
I can't express
Just how I feel tonight.

DOWN IN CHATTANOOGA

Published. Copyrighted November 21, 1913. Introduced by Belle Baker. Major recording by Arthur Collins and Byron Harlan (Victor and Columbia).

VERSE 1

Goodbye, I'm leaving town,
I've sent my baggage down
To the railway station;
I've had my vacation.
Before I go away
This much I want to say:
I would like to have you call
On me someday.

CHORUS

When you're down in Tennessee,
Stop at Chattanooga,
Stop at Chattanooga.
Don't forget to call on me
Down in Chattanooga,
Down in Chattanooga.
Accept my invitation,
You can make yourself at home;
I'll meet you at the station
With a "Giddyap, giddyap, Napoleon."
You'll find hospitality
Down in Chattanooga,
Down in Chattanooga,
You're just as welcome as you can be;
You'll find a menu, a menu,

With a lot of things to eat upon it when you
Come to Chattanooga,
Chattanooga, Tennessee.

VERSE 2

What's mine you'll find is yours,
My folks keep open doors,
Anyone who will come
Is entirely welcome.
And you'll be glad to stay
Where healthy chickens lay
Sixty-cents-a-dozen eggs
The livelong day.

REPEAT CHORUS

DADDY COME HOME

Published. Copyrighted December 16, 1913.

VERSE 1

Hello, Central dear!
Central, listen here:
Please connect me with my father.
Number one-two-three!
Daddy, this is me;
Come home right away.
Since you left this morning, Daddy dear,
Many, many things have happen'd here.

CHORUS

Daddy, come home!
Close the factory and hurry up home!
Won't you come to me?
Johnny stole my mittens,
My brand-new Sunday mittens;
Outside of that,
The cat just lost her kittens.
Daddy, come home!
Johnny's punching me and
I can't hold my own.
Ma found a locket
Of a girl in your pocket,
Daddy, so you better come home.

VERSE 2

Daddy, hurry up!
Johnny broke the cup
That we borrowed from our neighbor.

Harry stubbed his toe
Playing Buffalo;
Mabel fell downstairs;
Willie's chasing Jack around the flat;
Ev'rything is fine outside of that.

REPEAT CHORUS

DOWN ON UNCLE
JERRY'S FARM

Published 1994 in Hamm, vol. 3, pp. 230–1. Lead sheet
and typed lyric sheets were found in Berlin's papers and
are now part of the Irving Berlin Collection of the
Music Division of the Library of Congress. The lyric
sheets have the notation "Copyrighted 1913 by Water-
son Berlin & Snyder Co."; yet the extensive 1993 Irving
Berlin Copyright Search failed to show any prior regis-
tration of this song. Hamm notes (p. 279) that the
"music and text of the first four lines of the first verse
are largely identical to 'He's a Devil in His Own Home
Town.' " See page 87.

VERSE 1

I've got an uncle by the name of Jerry;
He's got a farm, a great big farm—
Three thousand acres of the very, very
Best land in the whole United States.
All from a turnip to a huckleberry
Grows on his farm, his great big farm—
When you come to town, you must go down to
Uncle Jerry's farm.

CHORUS

Great big watermelons, extra-size
Heads of cabbages that took first prize,
Nice fat healthy-lookin' hens that lay
Fresh sixty-cent-a-dozen eggs all day,
Milk and butter from the speckled cow,
Green grass growing way up to your brow—
You can bet your life I'd like to be right now
Down on Uncle Jerry's farm.

VERSE 2

Come hear the crowing of the great big rooster
Down on the farm, the great big farm;
My uncle Jerry had a cow that used to
Give milk to the whole United States.
He's got a farmer by the name of Brewster

Down on his farm, his great big farm;
Brewster has a share of taking care of
Uncle Jerry's farm.

REPEAT CHORUS

I COULD LIVE ON
LOVE AND KISSES

Published 1994 in Hamm, vol. 3, pp. 232–3. Lead sheet
and typed lyric sheets were found among Berlin's papers
and are now part of the Irving Berlin Collection of the
Music Division of the Library of Congress. One of the
lyric sheets bears the notation "Copyrighted 1913 by
Waterson Berlin & Snyder Co."; yet the extensive 1993
Irving Berlin Copyright Search failed to show any prior
registration of this song.

VERSE

I like you, yes I do.
I'd like to settle down
And have a home that's furnished up nice,
If I had the price;
I must confess I haven't got a cent.
But the rent must be paid,
My pretty maid;
Where there is love, the money doesn't matter.
I'll explain it all to you.

CHORUS

I could live on love and kisses
In a furnished four-by-two;
I would have to wash the dishes—
I'd be glad to do it, too.
I could walk the floor with baby
If it cried the whole night through.
I could even live in Brooklyn
With a beautiful girl like you.

I WANT A HAREM
OF MY OWN

Published 1994 in Hamm, vol. 3, pp. 234–5. A lead sheet
and typed lyric sheet were found among Berlin's papers
and are now in the Irving Berlin Collection of the Music
Division of the Library of Congress. The lyric sheet in-

cludes the notice "Copyrighted 1913 Waterson Berlin & Snyder Co."; yet the extensive 1993 Irving Berlin Copyright Search failed to show any prior registration of this song.

VERSE 1

Old Man Murad had a harem down in Turkeyville;
He had wives enough to fill a village in Brazil.
When his only son
Grew to twenty-one,
Old Man Murad, he could hardly keep him still.
One day the Turkish lad
Shouted to his dad:

CHORUS 1

"I want a harem of my own,
One with lots of tone;
I want my female stables
Filled up with Flos and Mabels.
Father, don't say no:
You've got one and—oh, oh—
Every single time I see them do Salome,
Something tells me I should have a harem of my
    own."

VERSE 2

Christmas comes around in Turkey just the same
    as here;
Mister Santy Claus pays them a visit every year.
And would you believe
That on Christmas Eve
Murad's son hung up a dozen stockings near;
He then sat down and wrote
Santy Claus this note:

CHORUS 2

"I want a harem of my own,
One with lots of tone;
I want a flock of fillies—
Elizas, Janes, and Tillies.
Santy Claus, be kind
And if you don't mind, find
Twenty pretty girls who understand Salome—
My ambition is to have a harem of my own."

I'VE GOT A LOT OF LOVE FOR YOU

Published 1994 in Hamm, vol. 3, pp. 236–7. A lead sheet and three typed lyric sheets were found among Berlin's papers and are now in the Irving Berlin Collection of the Music Division of the Library of Congress. One lyric sheet bears the notice "Copyrighted 1913 by Waterson Berlin & Snyder Co."; yet the extensive 1993 Irving Berlin Copyright Search failed to show any prior registration of this song. A double version exists under the title "I Love Your Ma."

VERSE

You are the best of the rest of the girls;
You're a little nicer than the others.
Right from your toes to your nose to your curls
You're everything that calls for wedding bells.
I love your style and your smile and your eyes;
I'm in love with everything about you.
I love your dress and your cute little hat;
I must confess outside of that

CHORUS

I love your ma,
I love your pa,
I love your sister Sue—I do—
I love your little baby brother,
I love your granny and your grandfather too,
And besides the love I've got for your family,
I've got a lot of love for you.

VERSE 2 (FROM DOUBLE VERSION)

SHE: Don't make a move till you prove you're
        sincere.
HE: Anything you say, I'll do to prove it.
SHE: Go ahead, bring me a ring in the spring of
        the year.
HE: And?
SHE: Then put an order in for wedding bells.
HE: I'm willing.
SHE: My family will agree right away.
HE: Honey, that's the reason why I love them.
SHE: Do you think your family dear will be good
        to me?
HE: I represent my family.

REPEAT CHORUS

I'VE GOT TO CATCH A TRAIN, GOODBYE

Published 1994 in Hamm, vol. 3, pp. 238–9. A lead sheet and three lyric sheets were found among Berlin's papers and are now in the Irving Berlin Collection of the Music Division of the Library of Congress. Two lyric sheets bear the notice "Copyrighted 1913 by Waterson Berlin Snyder & Co."; yet the extensive 1993 Irving Berlin Copyright Search failed to show any prior registration of this song.

VERSE 1

Everybody has their troubles,
Everybody has their cares;
And I know I have no right to
Trouble you with my affairs.
But if you'll listen to me awhile,
Just like I know you can,
You'll hear a story very sad—
It's all about a man.

CHORUS 1

He came around and bought me candy,
As any nice young man will do;
He held my hand and called me pet names:
"Poogy-woo, Poogy-woo, Poogy-woo."
I started mapping out my future—
I really did, I hope to die—
But then when I spoke of wedding bells,
He said, "I've got to catch a train, goodbye."

VERSE 2

When it came to playing hero,
He was simply joy and bliss.
Didn't have a beard or mustache,
Just the kind you like to kiss.
But there is one thing I'm certain of,
I'd like to bet my life
That if there were no railroad trains,
I would have been his wife.

CHORUS 2

One afternoon he drank a cocktail
And then he promised me the earth;
He called me up one night from Pittsburgh
And we talked twenty-four dollars' worth.
I thought I had him line and sinker—
I really did, I hope to die—
But then when I spoke of wedding bells,
He said, "I've got to catch a train, goodbye."

Earlier version of first chorus

The music appears to have been somewhat different.

He started telling me his troubles
Which made me think I had him right,
But then when I spoke of wedding bells,
He asked for his hat and cane;
Said, "I can't remain—
I've got to catch a train, good night."

Earlier version of second chorus

With different music.

He sent me flowers every morning,
And when he'd leave me all alone,
The minute that he reached his office
He'd call me up on the telephone.
I started mapping out my future,
I builded castles to the sky;
But when I spoke of wedding bells,
He jumped up and looked about;
Then he hollered out,
"I've got to catch a train, goodbye."

SOMEWHERE
(BUT WHERE IS IT?)

Published 1994 in Hamm, vol. 3, pp. 240–1. A lead sheet and three typed lyric sheets were found among Berlin's papers and are now in the Irving Berlin Collection of the Music Division of the Library of Congress. One lyric sheet bears the notice "Copyrighted 1913 by Waterson Berlin Snyder Co."; yet the extensive 1993 Irving Berlin Copyright Search failed to show any prior registration of this song.

VERSE 1

Often in my heart there comes a feeling of
disgrace
When I wake up and find the same world looks me
in the face;
But consolation do I find in dreaming of a place,
Somewhere.
The Good Book says it's not the world but those
who live within,
The Good Book knows I'm one of those who often
flirts with sin;

But let me tell you here and now a new life I'll
begin,
Somewhere.

CHORUS 1

Somewhere the sun always shines in the sky;
Somewhere there's a Washington who wouldn't
lie;
Somewhere you needn't deposit your eye
When you borrow a dollar or two.
Somewhere a heart goes along with the hand
That shakes you, and makes you feel happy and
grand;
Somewhere you love your own wife, understand;
Somewhere but tell me, where is it?

VERSE 2

A fool there was, a fool there is, a fool there still
remains,
And while there's nothing in my head that ever
causes pains,
And though I've never found them yet, I know I
must have brains
Somewhere.
I say all that because there's something in me
makes me sure
This world of ours is not all stained, there's spots
in it what's pure;
For every pain and care that is, I know there is a
cure,
Somewhere.

CHORUS 2

Somewhere there's lots that have never been sold;
Somewhere there's jokes that have never been
told;
Somewhere there's girls who admit that they're
old
When the wrinkles break out on their faces.
Somewhere, with lantern if you look around,
Honest and square politicians are found;
Somewhere up north there's a pole in the ground;
Somewhere but tell me, where is it?*

---

*Earlier version of last four lines:
    Somewhere a ride in the car is a treat
    Because you don't have to stand up on your feet;
    Somewhere you just put your hand on a seat
    And you find someone sitting on it.

YIDDISHA WEDDING

No music is known to survive. A lyric typescript found among Berlin's papers and now in the Irving Berlin Collection of the Music Division of the Library of Congress bears the notice "Copyrighted 1913 by Waterson Berlin & Snyder Co."; yet the extensive 1993 Irving Berlin Copyright Search failed to show any prior registration of this song.

VERSE 1

Sunday night Rebecca Klein
Married Abie Rosenstein;
I was invited to the wedding—
Oy, oy, what a wonderful time!
Such a sight I never saw:
Taxicabs were at the door;
So many high hats,
Way-up-to-the-sky hats,
I never saw before.

CHORUS

Oy, such a wedding!
Yiddle in the middle played upon the fiddle.
Oy, such music!
Everybody started dancing.
Jackie Bloom from Birmingham
Sent the groom a telegram:
"I wish you happiness for ages,
Make heavy wages."
Oy, such a supper!
Chicken and potatoes, stuffed-up tomatoes.
Oy, such presents!
Everything was sterling silver.
Cohen sent them dishes,
I sent my best wishes,
At that Yiddisha wedding Sunday night.

VERSE 2

Goldstein gave them something swell,
Spoons of silver polished well:
Some of the spoons were made in Tiff'ny's
Some were marked "Knickerbocker Hotel."
Rosenthal sent them a bed,
But they sent it back and said,
"We must refuse it
'Cause we couldn't use it,
We'll take a check instead."

REPEAT CHORUS

YOU'RE GOIN' TO LOSE YOUR BABY SOMEDAY

Published 1994 in Hamm, vol. 3, appendix pp. 244–5. A lead sheet and two typed lyric sheets were found among Berlin's papers and are now in the Irving Berlin Collection of the Music Division of the Library of Congress. There is no date on these lyric sheets, but Hamm notes that the material is "in same hands and format" from other lyrics dated 1913, "so probably from 1913."

VERSE 1

Honey, I've been feeling blue,
And it's on account of you

Acting like the way you do.
You've been mean for days,
You've been acting mighty cold,
And while I don't like to scold,
My complaint I must unfold.
If you don't change your ways,

CHORUS

You're goin' to lose your baby someday,
Someday your baby's going away.
You better love me, honey, like you should;
Honey, if you don't be good,
You're goin' to wake up early some morn
And find your lovin' baby is gone.
I'm goin' to go so far you'll find it hard
To reach me with a million-dollar postal card.

So if you don't obey, right away,
You're goin' to lose your baby someday.

VERSE 2

When your baby disappears,
You'll weep oceansful of tears,
Like you haven't wept for years,
And I mean to go.
You've turned to a cake of ice,
You've forgotten to be nice;
I won't tell you more than twice:
If you continue so,

REPEAT CHORUS

Left to right: *Jerome Kern, Louis A. Hirsch, A. Baldwin Sloane, Rudolf Friml.* Seated: *Oscar Hammerstein I, Alfred Robyn, Gustave A. Kerker, Hugo Felix, John Philip Sousa, Leslie Stuart, Raymond Hubbell, John L. Golden, Silvio Hein, Irving Berlin*

Songs of 1914

THIS IS THE LIFE

Published in two editions. The first was copyrighted January 26, 1914; the second, on February 21, 1914. On some of the covers of the second edition there are photographs of Al Jolson, bearing the legend "Successfully introduced by Al Jolson"; on others there are photographs of Belle Baker. Top-selling recordings by the Peerless Quartet (Columbia) and Billy Murray (Victor and Edison Amberol).

First edition

VERSE 1

Farmer Brown came to town,
Started to take in the sights:
Cabarets, swell cafés
Took up most of his nights.
After seven days or so,
After seeing ev'ry show,
After meeting May and Flo,
Farmer Brown remarked:

CHORUS

"I love the cows and chickens,
But this is the life,
This is the life!
I love to raise the dickens
While I'm cabareting,
Where the band is playing!
I love the trees and flowers,*
But I'd rather while away the hours
Picking daisies from a musical comedy—
That's the life for me!
I love the homemade cider,
But I'd rather have wine;
No more picking berries,
Me for cocktail cherries!
This is the life,
This is the life,
This is the life for mine!"

VERSE 2

Missus Brown, out of town,
Wrote to her husband and said:
"Please come home, I'm alone!"
When her letter he read,
Farmer Brown took off his coat,

In the second edition, lines 7–10 of the chorus were deleted.

Sat right down and then he wrote
To his wife a little note;
This is what he said:

REPEAT CHORUS

FOLLOW THE CROWD

Published. Copyrighted January 30, 1914. Introduced in *Queen of the Movies* (January 12, 1914; Globe Theatre, New York City) by Frank Moulan (Professor Josiah Clutterbuck, "a rich and famous inventor of artificial food, known as the Wizard of the Market Basket") and ensemble. Recorded by Irving Berlin for Columbia in 1914; unreleased until included in the anthology *Music for the New York Stage, 1890–1920*, vol. 3, 1913–1917 (Pearl GEMM 9056–8).

VERSE 1

Look at the crowd up the avenue—
Oh, don't you know where they're going to?
They're on their merry way
To turn night into day;
Dressed in their best, they're a happy mob,
Soon to a tune they'll be on the job.
If you care to join them,
Just hurry along.

CHORUS

Follow the crowd, follow the crowd,
Come with me, you're goin' to be so proud.
Don't stay behind,
Go where you'll find
Thousands of dreamy tango dancers.
Come, my honey, come!
The drummer's drum
Will make things hum!
The whole night long
We'll dance away the blues—
Take an extra pair of shoes!
Come, come, come, come and follow the
crowd.

VERSE 2

You'll hear a jew'l of an orchestra!
Best of the rest in America!
Each syncopated beat
Just goes right to your feet.
Heirs, millionaires, all the best of them
Glide side by side with the rest of them;

They'll be glad to meet you,
Just hurry along.

REPEAT CHORUS

IT ISN'T WHAT HE SAID, BUT THE WAY HE SAID IT

Published. Copyrighted February 10, 1914.

VERSE 1

Happy, I'm so happy
I could throw myself away.
Some peculiar something
Keeps my heart a-jumping
Both night and day.
Say!
Stupid Mister Cupid
Went and pierced me through the heart.
I've been fascinated,
Simply captivated,
Captured from the start.

CHORUS

It isn't what he said,
But the way he said it
Made me fall.
He spoke of wedding bells
Until it seem'd the knot was tied;
He described an automobile
And it was just as good as taking a ride.
The way he spoke of love
Set my heart a-bouncing
Like a ball;
He told me of a kiss last week
So natural I could feel it on my cheek.
It isn't what he said,
But after he said it
I had to love him, that's all.

VERSE 2

Clever, he's so clever
You could never understand.
Ev'ry word they carry
In the dictionary
Is at his command.
And
Peaches are his speeches,
They're the finest in the land.

He'll describe a jewel
In a way that you will
Feel it on your hand.

REPEAT CHORUS

I LOVE TO QUARREL WITH YOU

Published. Copyrighted February 10, 1914. Some of the original sheet music covers have a photograph of Belle Baker and the legend "Successfully Introduced by Belle Baker."

VERSE 1

Honey, cuddle near,
Come on over here!
Pick a fuss with me,
Pick a fuss with me!
There's a reason, my dear.
Try and make me cross,
Act just like a boss!
Pick a fuss with me,
Pick a fuss with me,
My honey, because

CHORUS

I love to quarrel with you,
Quarrel with you;
Making up is so nice.
I love to make you cry,
To kiss the tears away from your eye.
I'm wild about you!
Can't live without you!
That's just the reason why I tease you.
I love to hear myself saying
"I didn't mean it,
I didn't mean it!"
When I've had a quarrel with you.

VERSE 2

Honey, ain't it nice
To be cold as ice?
To be cold and then
To get warm again:
Gee, it's nicer than nice!
Say that I'm to blame,
I will say the same.
Let's get mad, and then

Let's make up again:
It's all in the game.

REPEAT CHORUS

HE'S A DEVIL IN HIS OWN HOME TOWN

Published. Copyrighted March 14, 1914. Words by Grant Clarke (1891–1931) and Irving Berlin. Hamm, vol. 3, writes that "Down on Uncle Jerry's Farm" (see page 81) is a preliminary version of this song, with a quite different chorus. Top-selling recordings by Billy Murray (Victor) and Eddie Morton (Columbia).

VERSE 1

I've got an uncle by the name of Jerry;
He's got a farm, a great big farm,
Two thousand acres of the very, very
Best land in the whole United States.
He's got a reputation in the village,
Known as a dude, a gosh-darn dude;
He would never do in New York City,
But in his home town

CHORUS

He's a devil,
He's a devil,
He's a devil in his own home town.
On the level,
On the level,
He's as funny as a clown.
He spends a five-cent piece,
Thinks nothing of it;
His pants all creased,
Red vest above it.
And when it comes to women, oh!
Oh! Oh! Oh!
He's a devil,
He's a devil,
Telling stories in a groc'ry store,
On the level,
On the level,
Has 'em rolling on the floor.
Down at the fair
With all the other heckers
He received first prize for playing checkers;
And he cheated,
Can you beat it?
He's a devil in his own home town.

VERSE 2

He's got an overcoat that's fine and furry,
Gold-headed cane that came from Spain.
They've even got him saying "I should worry"
Just like all the sporty city folks.
You ought to see the way he spends his money:
He bought a box of hole-proof socks;
They would never do for New York City,
But in his home town

REPEAT CHORUS

Hamm notes (vol. 3, p. 220) that Billy Murray on his recording sings the following at the end of the second chorus:

In Philadelphia he had a high old time:
He stayed out one night till a quarter past nine.
He's a devil,
He's a devil,
He's a devil in his own home town.

GOD GAVE YOU TO ME

Published. Copyrighted April 20, 1914. Black-and-white edition; no cover art or photographs.

VERSE 1

For ev'ry care there's an angel
Who makes the care seem small;
For ev'ry pray'r there's an answer
From one who answers all.

CHORUS

The flowers pray'd for sunshine,
So God gave the flowers the sun;
The birds pray'd to be merry,
So God gave a song to each one;
The trees pray'd for the springtime,
So God gave the spring to each tree;
My lonely heart pray'd for someone,
So God gave you to me.

VERSE 2

For ev'ry heart there is gladness,
When eyes are wet with tears;
For ev'ry care there's an answer,
From one who always hears.

REPEAT CHORUS

ALONG CAME RUTH

Published. Copyrighted May 1, 1914. According to a news clipping preserved in Berlin's scrapbook, the song was introduced by Billy Schaefer between the first and second acts of the show (play with music) *Along Came Ruth* (February 23, 1914; Gaiety Theatre, New York). On the cover of some of the original sheet music there is a photograph with the legend "Successfully introduced by Claire Rochester." On the cover of other original sheet music there is a photograph of a woman with the legend "Irene Fenwick as Ruth Ambrose in Henry W. Savage's production *Along Came Ruth.*" Major recording by Arthur Fields (Victor). In 1926 Christy Walsh (who was Babe Ruth's agent), Addy Britt, and Harry Link, with Berlin's approval, wrote new lyrics to Berlin's 1914 song to accompany Babe Ruth's vaudeville appearances.

VERSE 1

I had girls by the score,*
Yes, a hundred or more,
Each one as nice as could be.
It was hard to decide
Which I'd want for my bride;
They all looked lovely to me.
While I was trying to choose one,
I met a wonderful girl;
She came tripping along
Like a beautiful song,
Setting my brain in a whirl.

CHORUS

I was growing very fond of Molly
When along came Ruth,
Along came Ruth.
I thought an awful lot of Dolly;
When Ruth came along,
My head began to merry-go-round.
I almost married Polly,
I was making love to May,
When along came Ruth,
And to tell the truth,
She stole my heart away.

Alternate version of lines 1–6:
>   There's a fellow I know
>   Who was some Romeo;
>   Girlies he had by the score.
>   It was hard to decide
>   Which he'd take for his bride;
>   He had a hundred or more.

VERSE 2

There's a right little girl
With the right little curl
For ev'ry right little boy.
When she comes you'll forget
All the others you've met;
Sorrow will turn into joy.
She doesn't have to be pretty;
She doesn't have to be wise,
When she comes you will find
Though they say love is blind,
She'll make you open your eyes.

REPEAT CHORUS

IF I HAD YOU

Published. Copyrighted May 1, 1914.

VERSE 1

I never envied the rich millionaires,
I never wanted to have what was theirs,
I never bother about their affairs,
As the others do.
All that I want is a chance to be glad;
I've grown so tired of being so sad.
There's only one thing I wish that I had:
That's you, just you.

CHORUS

If I had you
To just be around when I'm blue,
A four-by-two
Would be like a mansion on Fifth Avenue.
I wouldn't change places with Carnegie
Or anyone else that I know;*
There'd be hours and hours
Of sunshine and flowers
If I had you.

In some printed versions, the last four lines of the chorus are:
>   And that goes for Rock'feller too!
>   They could keep all their troubles
>   And "Automobbles"
>   If I had you.

VERSE 2

I never envied those rich millionaires
Who sit around in their silk-cover'd chairs:
Any old sofa, with someone who cares,
It would more than do.
Just you and me and I'd want nothing more;
Maybe a baby to play on the floor.
I'd have a whole lot to be thankful for
If I had you.

REPEAT CHORUS

THEY'RE ON THEIR WAY TO MEXICO

Published. Copyrighted May 2, 1914. This is the first Berlin song to list the Waterson, Berlin & Snyder Co. as having its offices at "Strand Theatre Building, Broadway at 47th Street, N.Y." In 1915 Berlin was quoted about this song as follows:

> The height of my ambition was to write a popular and patriotic song to the new syncopated style of melody. The trouble with Mexico and the fact that our boys were on their way to the front gave me the needed inspiration and I immediately sat down and wrote the words of "They Are on Their Way to Mexico."

VERSE 1

They're gettin' ready,
They're gettin' ready:
We've had a row
And now they're going to war.
They've got their orders
To sail the waters;
With heavy heart
They start for a foreign shore.
They're not excited,
They're just delighted
To go and shake them,
Make them stand up and roar
Like they never did before.

CHORUS

They're on their way
To Mexico—
Just see those Yankee fighters, foe exciters,
Gettin' ready to go!
They're on their way

To win the day.
Just take a look at those Yankee brothers
Waving to their gray-hair'd mothers!
Goodbye, they're leaving;
Goodbye, stop grieving;
Don't cry, they're glad to go.
They'll make them run like a herd of cattle,
They'll know they've had some battle,
Way down in Mexico.

VERSE 2

Come over near them,
Come on and cheer them!
They've got a right
To fight this battle because
They've been invited
To go and fight it,
And so they're in
To win and they'll never pause
Until they take 'em
And then they'll make 'em
With head erect
Respect America's laws—
Give three cheers for them because

REPEAT CHORUS

IF YOU DON'T WANT MY PEACHES (YOU'D BETTER STOP SHAKING MY TREE)

Published. Copyrighted May 9, 1914.

VERSE 1

Mary Snow had a beau
Who was bashful and shy;
She simply couldn't make the boy propose,
No matter how she'd try.
Mary grew tired of waiting,
So she called her beau one side,
While he stood there biting his fingernails,
Mary cried:

CHORUS

"If you don't want my peaches,
You'd better stop shaking my tree.
Let me say that you're mighty slow;
You're as cold as an Eskimo.
There's a thousand others waiting,

Waiting to propose to me;
So if you don't want my peaches,
You'd better stop shaking my tree."

VERSE 2

Mary's pa and her ma
Soon came into the room;
They took a look at Mary's beau and cried,
"You ought to be a groom!
Or course it's none of our bus'ness,
But she'd make a lovely bride."
He just answered, "I'll think it over," but
Mary cried:

REPEAT CHORUS

THE HAUNTED HOUSE

Published. Copyrighted May 27, 1914. It has been suggested that the "bony skeleton" who wrote "That Mysterious Rag" is Ted Snyder, that song's coauthor with Berlin, but it also could be a reference to Berlin himself.

VERSE 1

You see that vacant house,
As quiet as a mouse?
It's chock-full of myst'ry;
Besides, it has a hist'ry:
The man who occupied
That building strangely died;
No one wants to buy it, because
That house is

CHORUS

Haunted, haunted—
Lanky hanky-panky skeletons
Go sneakin' around.
You see that bony crony,
I mean that bony skeleton,
Hiding behind that statue?
Look out, he's looking at you!
Listen! Listen!
Tell me, can't you hear him whistling
"That Mysterious Rag," so noted?
He wrote it
In that rickety haunted house.

VERSE 2

I often have been told
That there's a bag of gold
In the house that's haunted.
I'm poor but I don't want it:
The doors are open wide,
But no one steps inside;
No one needs the money, because
That house is

REPEAT CHORUS

IF THAT'S YOUR IDEA OF A WONDERFUL TIME (TAKE ME HOME)

Published. Copyrighted June 22, 1914. Alternate title (original sheet music cover): "If That's Your Idea of a Wonderful Time—Take Me Home." Major recording by Ada Jones (Victor).

VERSE 1

Johnny took Geraldine out one night
To show her a wonderful time;
When they sat down in a cabaret,
He bought two cigars for a dime.
"Bring us a couple of sodas," Johnny cried
When the waiter drew near;
After an hour Miss Geraldine
Whispered in Johnny's ear:

CHORUS

"If that's your idea of a wonderful time,
Take me home,
Take me home.
I want you to know that I'm choking
From that five-cent cigar that you're smoking.
You came out with a one-dollar bill;
You've got eighty cents left of it still—
If that's your idea of a wonderful time,
Take me home."

VERSE 2

Johnny looked foolish and said, "My dear,
The evening has only begun;
I'll take you down to a picture show,
Where we'll have a barrel of fun.
I know the fellow who owns the place;

I'll ask him to pass us inside."
Geraldine looked into Johnny's face;
Shaking her head, she cried:

REPEAT CHORUS

I WANT TO GO BACK TO MICHIGAN (DOWN ON THE FARM)

Published. Copyrighted July 30, 1914. Alternate title (original sheet music cover): "I Want to Go Back to Michigan Down on the Farm." Written for the vaudevillian Belle Baker to sing at the Palace Theatre, New York. Top-selling recordings by Elida Morris (Columbia) and Morton Harvey (Victor). In 1915 Berlin told a writer for the Detroit *Journal:*

> I always think of phrases of words and phrases of music together. That's how I happened to write "I Want to Go Back to Michigan." That's a wonderfully musical word, Michigan. I understand those rhymes of wish again and fish again have been used before, but I had never heard them when I wrote the song.

VERSE 1

I was born in Michigan,
And I wish and wish again
That I was back
In the town where I was born.
There's a farm in Michigan,
And I'd like to fish again
In the river
That flows beside the fields of waving corn.
A lonesome soul am I;
Here's the reason why:

CHORUS

I want to go back,
I want to go back,
I want to go back to the farm,
Far away from harm,
With a milk pail on my arm.
I miss the rooster,
The one that useter
Wake me up at four A.M.
I think your great big city's very pretty;
Nevertheless, I want to be there,

I want to see there
A certain someone full of charm.
That's why I wish again
That I was in Michigan,
Down on the farm.

VERSE 2

You can keep your cabarets,
Where they turn nights into days;
I'd rather be
Where they go to bed at nine.
I've been gone for seven weeks,
And I've lost my rosy cheeks;
That's the reason
I'd rather have the country life for mine.
My thoughts are far away,
That's just why I say:

REPEAT CHORUS

Double version

VERSE 1

A: I was born in Michigan
B: Michigan?
A: And I wish and wish again—
B: What?
A: —that I was back—
B: Where?
A: In the town where I was born.
B: You don't say.
A: I do say. There's a farm in Michigan.
B: Michigan?
A: And I'd like to fish again—
B: Where?
A: In the river.
B: The one that flows beside the fields of corn?
A: A lonesome soul am I.
B: Won't you tell me why?

CHORUS 1

A: I want to go back.
B: You want to go back?
A: I want to go back to the farm.
B: Far away from harm?
A: With a milk pail on my arm.
B: You miss the rooster?
A: The one that useter—
B: What?
A: —wake me up at four A.M.
B: You told me that you liked the great big city.

A: Nevertheless, I want to be there.
B: Who will you see there?
A: A certain someone full of charm.
B: That's why you wish again—
A: That I was in Michigan—
BOTH: —down on the farm.

VERSE 2

A: I don't like your cabaret—
B: You're a jay.
A: —where they turn night into day.
B: Why?
A: I'd rather be—
B: Where?
A: —where they go to bed at nine.
B: You're lazy.
A: You're crazy. I've been here for seven weeks.
B: Seven weeks?
A: And I've lost my rosy cheeks.
B: Have you been dissipating?
A: Yes, I drank a glass of wine.
B: Fine.
A: My cheeks have lost their pink.
B: All from just one drink?
A: Yes.

CHORUS 2

B: You oughta go back.
A: I want to go back.
B: You ought to go back to the farm.
A: Far away from harm.
B: With a milk pail on your arm.
A: I'm on the level.
B: He's [She's] such a devil.
A: But I can't stay up so late.
B: You ought to go and move to Philadelphia—
A: Nevertheless—
B: —with a milk pail on your arm.
A: I've dissipated.
B: So you have stated.
A: I've stayed out till half past ten.
B: You ought to go and move to Philadelphia.
A: Nevertheless, I'm on the level.
B: You've been a devil.
A: I've got cause to be alarmed.
B: That's why you wish again—
A: —that I was in Michigan—
BOTH: —down on the farm.

I WANT TO GO BACK TO THE FARM

This lyric appears to be an early version of the song that became "I Want to Go Back to Michigan." No music survives for this number. Holographs and typed lyrics were found among Berlin's papers and are now in the Irving Berlin Collection of the Music Division of the Library of Congress.

VERSE 1

I'm tired of everything here;
It's just been exactly a year
I left the farm in Louisville, Kentucky.
Didn't know that I was mighty lucky
To be where I wish I was right now—
Somehow

CHORUS

I want to go back,
I want to go back,
Back down on the farm.
I miss the great big rooster—
It's the one that used ter
Wake me up down on the farm.*
Don't begin to think I'm raving
When I tell you that I'm craving
For the corn that's waving—
It's as long as your arm.
I want to go back,
I want to go back,
Far away from harm.
I
Just love to hear the farmer stutter
While
He sells his healthy milk and butter.
I want to go back,
I want to go back,
Back down on the farm.†

Earlier version of lines 5 and 6 of chorus:
    And the gal who used ter
    Walk around tied to my arm.

†*Earlier version of ending of chorus:*
    I've been a lonesome chappy,
    And I won't be happy
    Till I go back
    Down on the farm.

VERSE 2

I'm tired of dressed-up affairs
Where everyone's puttin' on airs.
And that's because I'm just a human being
And my eyes were simply made for seeing
Everything that's close to nature's hand,
So grand.

REPEAT CHORUS

ALWAYS TREAT HER LIKE A BABY

Published. Copyrighted August 24, 1914. There is also a double version of an earlier lyric with the same title.

VERSE 1

See those sweethearts?
They've just been married.
They'll be leaving soon;
They're getting ready to begin
A lifelong honeymoon.
See the old folks crowding around them?
Gladness fills the room.
Just hear the bride's old mother
Whispering to the groom:

CHORUS

"Treat her like a baby,
For she's only a baby.
When you take her with you, lad,
You are taking all we had.
I know she'll be a comfort to you
Like she's always been to me.
So do be kind,
And keep unhappiness away;
And when you find
Her golden hair is turning gray,
Continue to treat her like a baby."

VERSE 2

See those sweethearts
Rocking a cradle
With a baby boy?
After a year of wedded bliss,
He came to bring them joy.
Listen to them planning his future,
Hear his father say,

"I picture some girl's mother
Saying to him someday:

REPEAT CHORUS

Double version of earlier lyric

VERSE

HE: I would like to marry you, honey.
SHE: You don't mean it, dear.
HE: Honest and truly, won't you have me?
SHE: You won't do, I fear.
HE: I've saved up a bundle of money.
SHE: Love you cannot buy.
HE: How can I make you love me?
SHE: Dear, would you like to try?
HE: Yes.

CHORUS

SHE: Treat me like a baby.
HE: You'll grow tired of it maybe.
SHE: Baby names just set me wild.
HE: I think you're a spoiled child.
SHE: At night when I grow tired and weary—
HE: I'll hold you on my knee.
SHE: And while I sleep—
HE: I'll keep the boogeyman away.
SHE: I'll never weep.
HE: And when your hair is turning gray—
SHE: —continue to treat me—
BOTH: —like a baby.

HE'S A RAGPICKER

Published. Copyrighted September 28, 1914. Major recording by the Peerless Quartet (Victor, Columbia, and Edison Amberol). Among the artists whose photographs appear on the original sheet music covers are Sophie Tucker and Ban-Joe Wallace.

VERSE 1

Down in Alabama where the cotton grows
Lives a funny fellow by the name of Mose.
He hasn't anybody he can pick upon,
So he picks on a grand piano;
Morning, noon, and night you'll find him
    picking rags.
I don't mean the kind of rags they put in
    bags,

He doesn't own a junk shop,
Just the same

CHORUS

He's a rag picker, a rag picker,
All the livelong day
He bangs upon the piano keys
In search of raggy melodies.
All day he's at the ivories,
And while he dozes he composes.
Mister Moses makes an ordinary ditty
Sound so pretty,
Like nobody can.
Most any time of the day
You'll find him picking away;
He's a rag picker, a rag picker,
A ragtime picking man.

VERSE 2

Moses' father told me that upon the morn
When his little piano-playing boy was born,
They didn't have a cradle they could put him in,
So he slept on the grand piano.
In a week they found him there upon his knees,
Chewing on the highly polished piano keys;
That very day his father
Loudly cried:

REPEAT CHORUS

FURNISHING A HOME FOR TWO

Published. Copyrighted October 8, 1914. Introduced by Gladys Clark and Henry Bergman in Jesse Lasky's vaudeville production *The Society Buds*. On the original sheet music covers there is a photograph of Clark and Bergman.

VERSE 1

Honey, I've been thinking
About the cozy little flat,
The one we'll soon be looking at,
To furnish up with this and that;*

*Earlier version of lines 3–4:
    All furnished up with this and that
    Where you and I will soon be at.

Honey, I can picture,
The happy smile upon your face
When we both get started
Furnishing up the place,
My dearie,

CHORUS

I'll hang the picture on the wall;
You'll hold the chair so I don't fall.*
My honey,
While I lay the carpet in the dining room,
You'll be busy with a broom.
I'll place the dishes on the shelf;
You'll change them, dear, to suit yourself.
When ev'rything is furnished there,
We'll cuddle in the morris chair;
We'll be such a happy pair,
Furnishing a home for two.

VERSE 2

You'll do all the shopping;
'Twill help you pass the time away:
That's how you'll spend most of the day,
Including all my hard-earned pay.
We will have a parrot,
So when I have to go away,
You will think I'm near you—
I'll teach the bird to say,
"I love you."

REPEAT CHORUS

THAT'S MY IDEA OF PARADISE

Published. Copyrighted October 10, 1914. Introduced by Gladys Clark and Henry Bergman in Jesse Lasky's vaudeville production *The Society Buds*. On the cover of the original sheet music there is a photograph of Clark and Bergman.

VERSE 1

It doesn't take a lot of time to make me happy;
I'm easily satisfied.

*Earlier version of lines 1 and 2:
    I'll buy a hammer at the store;
    You tack the carpet on the floor.

I never cared for grand affairs
Where ev'rybody puts on airs.
I wouldn't pay a lot to own a mansion;
It wouldn't be worth the price.
Come and hear of my idea of paradise.

CHORUS

A little moonlight upon a June night;
A little bench beneath a tree;
One little squeeze of the hand;
A squeeze in return, meaning "I understand";
A sigh of "Oh, sir, come over closer";
A little kissing, oh so nice;
And then a goodbye, dear—
That's my idea of paradise.

VERSE 2

I never doubted anyone who told me
That heaven is up above;
Still, I would wager all I'm worth
That there's a heaven here on earth.
The gates of Paradise are ever open;
Just listen to my advice:
Any lover can discover Paradise.

REPEAT CHORUS

STAY DOWN HERE WHERE YOU BELONG

Published. Copyrighted October 20, 1914. Apparently at one time intended for *Watch Your Step*. Championed over the years by Groucho Marx, who maintained a running gag with Berlin over the song. In a letter to Marx (April 23, 1956), Berlin wrote:

Let me tell you of my favorite Groucho Marx story the way I tell it. There's a song I wrote during the First World War called "Stay Down Here Where You Belong" of which Groucho knows all the lyrics. Anytime he sees me when I am trying to pose as a pretty good song writer, he squares off and sings it. I've asked him how much money he will take not to do this but so far he will not be bribed.

VERSE 1

Down below,
Down below,

Sat the Devil talking to his son,
Who wanted to go
Up above,
Up above.
He cried, "It's getting too warm for me
Down here, and so
I'm going up on Earth,
Where I can have a little fun."
The Devil simply shook his head and answered
    his son:

CHORUS

"Stay down here where you belong;
The folks who live above you don't know right
    from wrong.
To please their kings they've all gone out to
    war,
And not a one of them knows what he's
    fighting for.
Way up above they say that I'm a devil and
    I'm bad;
Kings up there are bigger devils than your
    dad:
They're breaking the hearts of mothers,
Making butchers out of brothers—
You'll find more hell up there than there is
    down below."

VERSE 2

"Kings up there,
They don't care
For the mothers who must stay at home,
Their sorrows to bear.
Stay at home,
Don't you roam;
Although it's warm down below,
You'll find it's warmer up there.
If e'er you went up there, my son,
I know you'd be surprised,
You'll find a lot of people who are not
    civilized."

REPEAT CHORUS

THE POPULAR SONG

A poem written by Berlin in (probably) 1914. Registered for copyright as an unpublished work April 18, 1962. The occasion for the verse was a dinner by the United Song Writers of America at Keen's Chop House, New York; exact date unknown. The "arrangers" of the dinner were E. Ray Goetz (chairman), Bert Grant, James V. Monaco, Joseph McCarthy, and Edgar Leslie. On the evening's program Berlin's poem was billed as "A Bully Number." The officers of the United Song Writers of America were Stanley Murphy (president), L. Wolfe Gilbert (vice-president), George W. Meyer (secretary), and Theodore Morse (treasurer). In a letter to Abel Green (September 7, 1954) Berlin noted that this was "the first song writers' organization that was in existence."

Born just to live for a short space of time,
Often without any reason or rhyme;
Rated by highbrows who call it a crime;
Loved by the masses who buy it;
Made by the fellows who stay up at night,
Sweating and fretting while getting it right—
Publisher pleading with all of his might
With some performer to try it;

Heard by the critic without any heart—
One of those fellows who pick it apart,
Cares for the finish but don't like the start,
Makes many worthless suggestions;
Sold to the public—that is, if they'll buy—
Sometimes they do, and the royalty's high—
Most times the statement brings tears to your
    eye—
Take it without any questions:

Popular song, you will never be missed
Once your composer has ceased to exist,
While Chopin, Verdi, Beethoven, and Liszt
Live on with each generation.
Still, though you die after having your sway,
To be forgotten the very next day,
A rose lives and dies in the very same way—
Let that be your consolation.

TIP THE WAITER

Music with this title was filed among the unpublished material in Irving Berlin's office. Typed lyric sheets and a holograph lyric sketch of an early version of the refrain were found among Berlin's papers and are now in the Irving Berlin Collection of the Music Division of the Library of Congress. One lyric sheet bears the notice "Copyrighted 1914 by Waterson Berlin & Snyder"; yet the extensive 1993 Irving Berlin Copyright Search failed to show any prior registration of this song.

VERSE

Mabel's brother was a waiter in a cabaret,
And he always would cater
To the folks who left the largest tip upon his tray,
Like a regular waiter.
Mabel and her beau one day
Walked into a cabaret;
Her brother started waiting on her sweetheart—
Here's what happened that day:

CHORUS

Every drink he'd buy,
She'd holler, "Tip the waiter, dearie,
Tip the waiter."
Every time she caught his eye,
She'd loudly cry, "I'm getting dry";
He'd order up another in a hurry.
The waiter was her brother, so she would worry;
When he changed a dollar,
She would loudly holler,
"Tip the waiter, my dear."

Earlier version of chorus

Every drink he'd buy,
She'd holler, "Tip the waiter, sonny,
Tip the waiter."
And the minute she got dry,
She'd yell to her brother,
"You can bring us another."
When the drink was brought,
She'd make him change a dollar
Like a sport,
And then she'd loudly holler,
"Tip the waiter,"
And when he did it she'd holler,
"Tip the waiter again."

REVIVAL DAY

Published 1994 in Hamm, vol. 3, appendix pp. 226–7. Music and lyrics transcribed from Al Jolson's September 19, 1914, recording (Columbia), the only surviving source for this song. Alternate title: "On Revival Day."

VERSE

Brothers and sisters,
Misters and misses,
Good people all in song,

Come on down
And jine the congregation
At the old town hall;
Johnson the speaker,
He was the speaker,
Come hear what he will say.
Don't be slow,
Come let's go,
This is revival day.

CHORUS

Come and hear the congregation shouting,
"Hallelujah! Hallelujah!"
If you misbehave,
Come, sinners, and you'll be saved.
Ring your voices up to heaven, shouting
"Hallelujah! Hallelujah!"
Don't forget to bring your Bible;
You won't regret,
You know you're liable
To have your sins forgiven
In that revival day.

REPEAT CHORUS

[*Substitute "Raise your voices" for "Ring your voices."*]

HEY, WOP

Published 1994 in Hamm, vol. 3, appendix pp. 228–9.
Typed lyric sheet found among Berlin's papers is now in
the Irving Berlin Collection of the Music Division of
the Library of Congress. The lyric sheet bears the notice
"Copyrighted 1914 by Waterson, Berlin & Snyder Co.";
yet the extensive 1993 Irving Berlin Copyright Search
failed to show any prior registration of this song. The
music was transcribed by Hamm from a 1915 recording
by Rhoda Bernard (Pathé), which included only the first
verse and the chorus; the second verse was found on
Berlin's typed lyric sheet. There is also a recording by
L. Thompson for Edison Blue Amberol.

VERSE 1

I got da hus-a-band, he's so lazy,
Sleep all da time and he make me crazy;
Seven o'clock he's still in bed—
Dead!
Good-a-ness me, but he make me sore-a,
Like-a da cannon he make da snore-a,
Every morning I
Got to wake him up and cry:

CHORUS

"Hey, wop, it's seven o'clock, get up,
Sleep-a no more, sleep-a no more,
You wake-a da kids when you make-a da snore.
Hey, wop, go to the barber shop,
Take-a da razor and make-a da skip,
Shave-a da face and collect-a da tip.
What's dat?
You want your breakfast brought in da bed?
Shut up, wop!
I think you got the swell-a da head.
You can sleep just as much as you like when you're
    dead—
It's seven o'clock, get up!"

VERSE 2

While I get up and put on my clothes,
He sing an op-e-ra through his nose-a,
All-a da kids they holler, "Pop—
Shut up!"
When he begin-a to make-a da snore-a,
All da neighbors who live next door-a
Holler, "Holy Mose,
Put a clothespin on his nose!"

REPEAT CHORUS

Unpublished Songs of 1907–1914

ALL ABOARD FOR MATAWAN

No music is known to survive. Berlin's pencil holograph of the lyric was found among his papers and is now in the Irving Berlin Collection of the Music Division of the Library of Congress. The last lines of the chorus are missing.

VERSE

I know a place where people chase
Each other night and day,
Where poor men, rich men,
Brakemen, switchmen,
While the hours away.
The song I sing was written there,
As you can easily tell;
From noon to sun there is this one
And only college yell:

CHORUS

"All aboard for Matawan,
All aboard for Matawan!
Please help me sing this foolish thing;
It was written by a brother.
All aboard for Matawan,
All aboard for Matawan!
The reason that I sing this song
Is because I know no other.
You needn't brains to board the trains
That go from here to there;
You need no sense, there's no expense—
They'll even pay your fare.
Would you believe the other eve
A lady tried to put
The smallest shoe, a number two,
Upon a seven foot [*Song breaks off here.*]

ALL DAY LONG I SIGH

No music is known to survive. Berlin's holograph of this lyric fragment, found among his papers, is now in the Irving Berlin Collection of the Music Division of the Library of Congress.

All day long I sigh,
All night long I cry,

And the reason why
Is just because I need
Someone's company,
Someone just to be
Acting loving
To poor neglected me.

ALL MY LOVE AND KISSES

No music is known to survive. A holograph of what appears to be a completed chorus was found among Berlin's papers and is now in the Irving Berlin Collection of the Music Division of the Library of Congress.

I love you, dear, with all my heart,
And I have loved you from the start;
In my lonesome life,
Full of care and strife,
You play a most important part.
Just say the word and we will fly
Into the little church nearby;
If you change from Miss to Missus,
I will know what bliss is.
All my love and kisses—goodbye.

ALL THAT I WANT

No music is known to survive. A holograph of what appears to be a first draft of a chorus was found among Berlin's papers and is now in the Irving Berlin Collection of the Music Division of the Library of Congress.

All that I want is someone near
To whisper nothings in my listening ear;
That's really all that I want from year to year:
A cozy morris chair, someone there,
Someone I can tell my troubles to.
All that I want is someone near,
Someone to call me dear—
That's all I want.

AT THE ACROBATIC BALL

No music is known to survive. A typed lyric sheet found among Berlin's papers is now in the Irving Berlin Collection of the Music Division of the Library of Congress.

VERSE

Said Mister Barnum to Mister Bailey,
"The acrobats worked well last fall!
And I thought
We really ought
To give a ball
To one and all!"
Said Mister Bailey to Mister Barnum,
"You've got the right idea, old man!"
So they told the acrobats all about their plan;
What a sight
On the night
That the swell affair began!

CHORUS

At the Acrobatic Ball,
To the hall, one and all, came the acrobats.
When they marched into the hall,
They were dressed in their best like aristocrats.
Like jumping jacks on the flyin' rings,
The diff'rent acts, they were tryin' things;
We all expected them to fall
They were wonderful:
At that Acrobatic Ball,
Old and young, there they hung from the
    chandeliers,
Just like flies upon the hall wall.
Barnum hollered to the freaks,
"You're all booked for forty weeks!"
While they acrobated at the Acrobatic Ball.

BE CAREFUL

No music is known to survive. A typed lyric sheet was found among Berlin's papers and is now in the Irving Berlin Collection of the Music Division of the Library of Congress.

VERSE

Mary Green
Seventeen,

No experience—
Got a lecture from an older girl
Who had more sense:
"Soon, no doubt,
You'll go out
With a boy or two;
I've been through the mill
And here's some good advice for you:

CHORUS 1

"When a young man takes you out to dine,
Be careful.
If you mean to stay out after nine,
Be careful.
Should he carry a flask on his hip,
No matter how he may ask, take a tip—don't sip.
If you find he has the gift of gab,
Be careful.
Should you go home in a taxicab,
Be careful.
If he whispers, 'What a pity'
That you should work 'when you're so pretty,'
Be careful, my dear."

CHORUS 2

"When an aviator calls around,
Be careful.
If he urges you to leave the ground,
Be careful.
He may fly like a hawk, don't you care—
You cannot get out and walk in the air up there.
When a young man orders food for you,
Be careful.
If he tries to leave before you're through,
Be careful.
Should he say 'I'll come back later,'
And if he hasn't paid the waiter,
Be careful, my dear."

A BEAUTIFUL PHOTOGRAPH

No music is known to survive. An ink holograph of the lyric was found among Berlin's papers and is now in the Irving Berlin Collection of the Music Division of the Library of Congress.

A summer's night in June;
A loving couple neath a silvery moon;
Two arms entwining around each other,
Clinging like a mother

Clings to her baby boy;
A beating heart at play,
Beneath a nice bouquet
Of sweet forget-me-nots:
Believe me, that's
A beautiful photograph.

BRAINS

No music is known to survive. A typed lyric sheet was found among Berlin's papers and is now in the Irving Berlin Collection of the Music Division of the Library of Congress.

VERSE

My father was a businessman, who had the poorest
    sight;
Still he saw a couple of fortunes through his specs.
He had no education, Father couldn't read or write;
Still he signed his name on the back of many
    checks.
The day that I was born, my father sat beside
    my cot
And said, "I'm glad that it's a boy, and now I hope
    he's got

CHORUS

"Brains—brains!
My father's father's father
Had a lot of brains.
He took after them,
I take after him,
And that is just the reason why I'm always in the
    swim.
To know just how to do, and when to do, and when
    to not,
To figure out the surest way to figure out a plot,
You need no college education if you've only got
Brains."

BRING YOUR MONEY TO ME

No music is known to survive. An ink holograph of this lyric, written on Hotel Plymouth, New York, stationery, was found among Berlin's papers and is now in the Irv-

ing Berlin Collection of the Music Division of the Library of Congress. Alternate title: "Cuddle Up to Any Other Girl."

Cuddle up to any other girl,
But bring your money to me.
Saturday when you come home,
Pony up your seven-thirty;
Spend the other dime with Gertie.
Take your marriage vows and tear 'em;
Go ahead and have a harem:
Cuddle up to any other girl,
But bring your money to me.

THE CALL OF MY BROKEN HEART

No music is known to survive. An ink holograph of this unfinished lyric was found among Berlin's papers and is now in the Irving Berlin Collection of the Music Division of the Library of Congress.

Sweetheart, since we've been parted
Seems like a thousand years;
For every hour of gladness
I've paid an hour of tears.
Come back and make me happy;
Why should we live apart?
Come to my arms and answer
The call of my broken heart.

EIGHT LITTLE SONGWRITERS

No music is known to survive. A typed lyric sheet was found among Berlin's papers and is now in the Irving Berlin Collection of the Music Division of the Library of Congress. This lyric might have been written for a special evening or a benefit at a place such as the Friars Club.

VERSE

We are the pick of the clique of popular
Ragtime song composers:

We are the smart full-of-art little fellows,
We write your popular songs;
We are the men with the pen that scribbles
Away the whole night long;
We admit we're wonderful
When it comes to a popular song.

CHORUS

Eight little great little writers of melody—
Wait till we state how we figure out harmony.
We hear a ditty that sounds pretty, then we
    write it;
We take a plea that we're here to apologize
To all of you, for we can't help but realize
It's simply awful—most unlawful—
To write a popular song.

EVER SINCE I MET YOU I'M A NUT

No music is known to survive. This song is attributed on the typed lyric sheet to Grant Clark (1891–1931; correct spelling of last name is "Clarke"), Jean Schwartz (1878–1956), and Irving Berlin. Typed lyric sheets were found among Berlin's papers and are now in the Irving Berlin Collection of the Music Division of the Library of Congress.

VERSE 1

Honey, honey,
I've been feeling funny;
There is something wrong with me.
Listen, listen,
There is something missin'
Where my thinking cap should be.
Call a doctor quick—
I'm a lunatic.

CHORUS

Ever since I met you
I'm a nut, I'm a nut, I'm a nut, honey;
Ever since you gave me that hug,
I'm a bug, I'm a bug.
Sometimes my head feels like a merry-go-round;
Voices seem to holler,
"Come, come, come to a sanitarium!"
Ever since you kissed me,
I'm a nut, I'm a nut, I'm a nut, honey;
Bees within my bonnet
Buzz around, buzz around, buzz around.

Reserve a room in Matawan,
For I'm going, going, gone:
Ever since I met you
I'm a nut, I'm a nut, I'm a nut.

VERSE 2

I'm so nervous,
'Cause my thinking service
Isn't acting very well.
Honey, kiss me,
'Cause you're gonna miss me
When they lock me in a cell,
When they slam the door,
I'll begin to roar.

REPEAT CHORUS

Extra lines

I'm just the worst you ever saw,
Even worse than Harry Thaw.

Just where my senses ought to be
There is solid ivory.

A thousand bees have made their home
In the center of my dome.

Beneath my new fedora hat
There's a German acrobat.

My honey, tell the judge for me
That I plead insanity.

I fear my common-sense machine
Has run out of gasoline.

I'm like a great big chestnut tree:
There are squirrels after me.

My little baby brother Bert
Wants to serve me for dessert.

My head is full of bees that buzz
And recite "A Fool There Was."

THE GARDEN OF GIRLS

No music is known to survive. Typed lyric sheets were found among Berlin's papers and are now in the Irving Berlin Collection of the Music Division of the Library of Congress.

You're the very most beautiful flower
That blooms in the garden of girls.
You're ev'ry sweet thing that comes with the
    spring;
You're all that sweet nature unfurls.
You're the queen of the green-coated summer
All covered with dewdrops like pearls;
You are the very most beautiful flower
That blooms in the garden of girls.

GEE, BUT IT'S GREAT TO BE A CHORUS GIRL

No music is known to survive. A typed lyric sheet was found among Berlin's papers and is now in the Irving Berlin Collection of the Music Division of the Library of Congress. Alternate title: "Opening Chorus."

VERSE

We're here because the manager pays twenty
    dollars a week,
Twenty dollars a week, twenty dollars a week.
We paint and powder and dance and sing,
We do a little of everything;
And some of us get our salary every week—
    maybe.
We get up at nine in the morning, work at home all
    day,
Then go out and play
A hard-earned matinee;
There's lots of other things we have to do to earn
    our pay—
You bet that it's a wonderful life,
Hurray!

CHORUS

Gee, but it's great to be a chorus girl,
To sing and dance for you.
Gee, but it's great to be a chorus girl,
A chorus girl with really nothing to do—but
Rehearse for seven weeks or more
For a manager who's a bore,
Spend your salary for paint,
Try to look what you really ain't,
Make up nice before the mob,
Lose your shape and you lose your job.
Oh—oh—oh—oh,
Gee, but it's great to be a chorus girl.

HE NEVER COMES HOME AT ALL

No music is known to survive. Typed lyric sheets with Berlin's pencil corrections were found among his papers and are now in the Irving Berlin Collection of the Music Division of the Library of Congress. One of the lyric sheets has the alternate title "He Never Goes Home at All." Because the lyric includes a quotation from Berlin's song "This Is the Life," it probably was written in 1914.

VERSE 1

Mrs. Brown and Mrs. Grey
Met upon the street one day.
"How's your husband?" said Mrs. Brown;
"Tell me, is he out of town?
I haven't seen him since way last fall;
He's never in any time I call—
Is he ever home at all?"
Then Mrs. Grey replied:

CHORUS 1

"He's a Mason, he's there every day;
He belongs to the YMCA;
He's a BPOE and a good one too,
Although his dues have been overdue.
He belongs to the Friars;
He's a member of Tammany Hall.
We never get a single chance to fight:
He's at a different clubhouse every night,
Singing 'This Is the Life,' 'This Is the Life'—
He never comes home at all."

VERSE 2

Mrs. Brown said, "Mrs. Grey,
You don't look so well today;
You're dressed up in your last year's clothes,
From your head down to your toes.
I thought that your husband's salary
Could keep you dressed as a wife should be.
Is he short financially?"
Then Mrs. Grey replied:

CHORUS 2

"He's a Mason, he's there every day;
He belongs to the YMCA;
With the dough that we saved from a ton of coal
He bought a badge for his buttonhole.
He belongs to the Friars;
He's a member of Tammany Hall.

With part of what he earns he buys my shoes;
He spends the balance of it paying dues,
Singing, 'This Is the Life,' 'This Is the Life'—
They're keeping him broke, that's all."

HE WALKS IN HIS SLEEP

No music is known to survive. A holograph written on the songwriter's stationery was found among Berlin's papers and is now in the Irving Berlin Collection of the Music Division of the Library of Congress.

You better lock the door,
Lock the door,
'Cause he walks in his sleep:
Should he leave the house behind him,
There's no telling where you'll find him.
It's very strange, I know;
Still, it's so—
You can never tell where he may go:
Sometimes it's the YMCA,
Most times it's a Broadway café.
You better lock the door,
Lock the door,
Because he walks in his sleep.

HERE'S TO FLO

Probably not a song lyric, this might have been a verse that Berlin wrote on some special occasion for Ziegfeld and his then leading lady, Lillian Lorraine. The reference to "Row, Row, Row," a song that Lorraine sang in the *Ziegfeld Follies of 1912*, dates these lines as sometime after the middle of 1912. A typed lyric sheet written on *Follies* stationery with some corrections by Berlin is now in the Irving Berlin Collection of the Music Division of the Library of Congress.

Here's to Flo,
Lillian's beau;
He loves her so,
As we all know.
In Ziggy's show
At two a throw
His Lil must go,
Though Abe says no.
Now here's to Lil,
Who buys her fill

And sends the bill
To Flo, until
He takes the pill,
As suckers will.
Been through the mill
Till almost ill;
The place may kill,
Yet he loves her still.

She goes although
Little Abe says no
Let her "Row, Row, Row,"
With [*Rest of line illegible.*]

HE'S JUST THAT KIND OF A MAN

No music is known to survive. An ink holograph of the lyric was found among Berlin's papers and is now in the Irving Berlin Collection of the Music Division of the Library of Congress.

He's just the kind o' man you like to have around
When your brain begins to blast;
He's just the kind of man you want to feel your
    pulse
When your heart is beating fast.
And when you find your features growing slim,
Losing all your health and vim,
Don't send for the doctor—send for him,
Because he's just that kind of a man.

HONEY, I FEEL BLUE

No music is known to survive. Ink holograph lyric sheets of the duet version, which follows, were found among Berlin's papers and are now in the Irving Berlin Collection of the Music Division of the Library of Congress.

SHE: Honey, I feel blue.
 HE: What's the matter with you?
SHE: All account of you.
 HE: What's the matter with you?
SHE: The way you're acting lately makes me sad.
 HE: Why, what's the matter?
SHE: There's lots the matter.
 HE: Tell me what I've done.

SHE: It's the things you're saying.
HE: They were just in fun.
SHE: I don't like your playing.
HE: What have I said, dear?
SHE: You said you don't love me.
HE: Let me take back what I said.
SHE: No.
HE: I didn't mean it.
SHE: Yes you did.
HE: I didn't mean it.
SHE: Yes you did.
HE: I was joking, honey.
SHE: Let me tell you that your jokes aren't
      funny.
HE: I didn't mean it.
SHE: Yes you did.
HE: I didn't mean it.
SHE: Yes you did.
HE: I'm always thinking of you.
SHE: Swear by the stars above you.
HE: Cross my heart, I love you.
SHE: Well, did you mean it?
HE: I didn't mean it.
      If I did, I hope to die.

HOW DID I EVER LIVE WITHOUT YOU?

No music is known to survive. A holograph of the following stanzas of this unfinished lyric was found among Berlin's papers and is now in the Irving Berlin Collection of the Music Division of the Library of Congress.

I don't know quite how I lived without your
   love.
There is only one thing that I'm certain of:
I didn't live before I met you;
I only existed, that's all.

How did I ever live without you?
All these years—all those years—
I never knew we had to meet
To make my happiness complete.

I HEARD YOU SAY

No music is known to survive. A pencil holograph of this unfinished lyric was found among Berlin's papers

and is now in the Irving Berlin Collection of the Music Division of the Library of Congress.

I heard you say that you didn't love me, dear;
I heard you say that you didn't want me near.
You keep refusing me, but never fear—
I'll make you love me.
I don't know why I fell in love with you;
I can't explain it, but I know I do.
And now you simply have to love me too,
As I love you.

I LOVE A SMALL TOWN

No music is known to survive. A typed lyric sheet with Berlin's ink corrections was found among his papers and is now in the Irving Berlin Collection of the Music Division of the Library of Congress.

VERSE

I love the Ruben and the Jay;
I love the country and the new-mown hay;
I love the nice fat hens who lay
Fresh sixty-cent-a-dozen eggs all day;
I love the homemade apple pie
Made from the apples that were picked by Si.
From the tree that grows close by—
That's just the reason why

CHORUS

I love a small town,
Where the girls—perfection—
Wear their own complexion.
Keep your know-it-all town;
Give me cows and chickens,
Home at ten and raise the dickens.
I love the Jay folks,
Plain everyday folks;
Rosy cheeks and healthy faces
Come from a small, small town.

I WANT TO MARRY YOU

No music is known to survive. A typed lyric sheet was found among Berlin's papers and is now in the Irving

Berlin Collection of the Music Division of the Library of Congress.

I want to marry you, marry you;
I've made up my mind
To go and carry you, carry you
To the first church I can find.
I mean to marry you, marry you,
If it's the last thing I do.
I won't be happy till the knot is tied;
I know I never will be satisfied
Till I'm M-A–double R–I-E-D
To Y-O-U.

I'LL HANG AROUND

No music is known to survive. A typed lyric sheet was found among Berlin's papers and is now in the Irving Berlin Collection of the Music Division of the Library of Congress.

Although you're far above me,
I'll have you thinking of me;
I'll make you turtle-dove me—
You've simply got to love me.

I'll hang around—
You'll never lose me.
I'll hang around—
You can't refuse me.
Right by your side I'm going to stay;
An army couldn't drive me away.
Sixty minutes every hour each day
I'm gonna be on the ground—
I'll never part
Until I've got you
Locked in my heart.
I'm gonna watch you
Until I'm well connected,
Until I've been elected,
I'm gonna hang around.

These other lyrics were found on the same page as the above:

So keep yourself protected,
For when you least expect it
I'm gonna be elected;
Our hearts will be connected,
I'd like to bet you—until I get you.
Honey, I'm sad today
Just 'cause I heard you say

You couldn't care for me,
You wouldn't spare for me
A cozy corner of your heart.
I've grown to love you so
'Twould break my heart to go.
I'm gonna make you love me,
I want you to know

My honey, I feel blue;*
It's on account of you.
You're just as cold as you could be
And I'm afraid you don't love me.
I've grown to love you so,
I mean to let you know—
Until I get you
I'll never go.

I'LL MAKE YOU LOVE ME

No music is known to survive. A typed lyric sheet was found among Berlin's papers and is now in the Irving Berlin Collection of the Music Division of the Library of Congress.

I'll make you love me,
I'll make you love me.
Although
I know that I'm rejected,
I won't go,
And when you least expect it
You'll rest in my arms, dear,
And you won't know why.
As sure as there's a heaven up above me,
It won't be long ere you'll be thinking of me—
Just rest assured I mean to make you love me
Bye and bye.

I'M GOING BACK, BACK, BACK TO HADES

No music is known to survive. An ink holograph and typed lyric sheets were found among Berlin's papers and are now in the Irving Berlin Collection of the Music

*See also "Honey, I Feel Blue," pages 99–100.

Division of the Library of Congress. Similar to "Stay Down Here Where You Belong" (1914), page 92.

VERSE

The Devil grew tired of his place below;
Things down below were getting mighty slow.
He told his family, "I'm going to go
Up on earth this very night."
He packed up his grip and kissed his wife
goodbye;
Soon he was standing underneath the sky.
After eyeing everything he could eye,
He yelled with all his might:

CHORUS

"I'm going back, back, back to Hades—
It's much too warm for me up here!
Kings are sending everyone to war,
And they don't know what they are fighting for;
Just because they want to reign above the others,
Kings are making butchers out of brothers.
I can see they're bigger devils than me—
I'm going back where I came from."

IN THE TWILIGHT

No music is known to survive. An ink holograph lyric sheet was found among Berlin's papers and is now in the Irving Berlin Collection of the Music Division of the Library of Congress.

If your heart is all aglow,
Tell her so—
In the twilight;
When the shadows come and go,
Let her know—
In the twilight.
There's a saying very old:
Darkness makes a heart grow bold,
Love's sweet story turns to gold
When it's told
In the twilight.

IS EVERYBODY SATISFIED?

No music is known to survive. An ink holograph lyric sheet was found among Berlin's papers and is now in the Irving Berlin Collection of the Music Division of the Library of Congress.

VERSE

The Lincoln Social Club gave a beefsteak Sunday
night;
Jones, the president of the lodge,
Was the fellow they put in charge.
Exactly one A.M., when the fun was at its height,
Jones stepped out upon the floor and yelled with
all his might:

CHORUS

"Is everybody satisfied?
Is everybody satisfied?
Are you satisfied with the talent I selected,
And has the bunch come up to what you
expected?
If there's a single soul inside
Who's not entirely satisfied,
I want to warn him that I never miss my aim,
Hitting what I aim at is my middle name,
And I'll make him sorry that he came—
Is everybody satisfied?"

IT'S ALL IN THE GAME

No music is known to survive. Ink and pencil holograph lyric sheets were found among Berlin's papers and are now in the Irving Berlin Collection of the Music Division of the Library of Congress. Alternate title: "Come on and Make Me Angry."

VERSE

Come over here, my honey;
Honey, I want you near.
Come and hold my hand;
Don't you understand,
There's a reason, my dear.
Say something just to tease me;
Honey, try and make me cross;
Pick a fuss with me,
Pick a fuss with me,
My honey, because:

CHORUS

Come on and make me angry,
Say you don't want me near;
When you've told me so,
I will turn to go,
Then you'll follow me, dear.
Honey, when I forgive you,
Call me by a funny name.
We'll get mad and then
We'll make up again—
It's all in the game.

Double version

VERSE

SHE: Come over here, my honey.
HE: Why do you want me near?
SHE: Come and hold my hand.
HE: I don't understand.
SHE: Don't you understand,
    There's a reason, my dear.
HE: What is it?
SHE: Say something just to tease me;
    Honey, try and make me cross.
HE: I don't want to.
SHE: Pick a fuss with me.
HE: That's no way to be.
SHE: Pick a fuss with me,
    My honey, because—
HE: Tell me.

CHORUS

SHE: Come on and make me angry.
HE: Where do you buy your hair?
SHE: Do you like my dress?
HE: It's an awful mess.
SHE: Tell me just what you think of me, dear.
HE: I never use such language.
SHE: Call me something funny, do.
HE: You're my lemon drop.
SHE: You're my barber shop.
HE: I'm angry with you.
SHE: Let's make up.

I'VE WRITTEN ANOTHER MELODY

No music is known to survive. Ink holograph lyric sheets were found among Berlin's papers and are now in the Irving Berlin Collection of the Music Division of the Library of Congress. See also "I've Written Another Song."

The minute that she shuts her eyes,
He pokes her in the ribs and cries,
"Wake up, I've got an inspiration;
You're gonna be proud of me—
I've written another melody!"
She cries with all her might,*
"Your song may be all right,
But if it's like the one you wrote last night,
I don't want to hear it,
I don't want to hear it!"
One night while asleep at her mother's home
He hollered over the telephone,
"Come home, I've got an inspiration;
There's gonna be royalty—
I've written another melody!"
All night he's up composing;
The minute she starts dozing,
He gets another inspiration.

I'VE WRITTEN ANOTHER SONG

No music is known to survive. A typed lyric sheet was found among Berlin's papers and is now in the Irving Berlin Collection of the Music Division of the Library of Congress. See also "I've Written Another Melody."

CHORUS

He wakes her up and cries,
"I've written another song,
You've got to listen to it!"
She rubs her eyes and answers,
"I don't want to hear it,
I don't want to hear it."
He keeps it up all morning,
Until the day is dawning,
And when he sees her yawning,
He starts to holler louder—
She takes a sleeping powder.
And then he wakes her up and cries,

---

*Alternate version of opening lines:
    The minute that she shuts her eyes,
    He pokes her in the ribs and cries,
    "Wake up, I've written another melody!"
    She answers,
    "I don't want to hear it.

"I've written another song!"
She has to listen to it;
She simply cannot keep him shut—
He's a nut, he's a nut, he's a nut.
One night she went to her mother's home;
While she was sleeping there all alone,
He called her up on the telephone
And cried, "I've written another song . . . !"

JUST FOR YOU

No music is known to survive. A typed lyric sheet was found among Berlin's papers and is now in the Irving Berlin Collection of the Music Division of the Library of Congress.

Just for you,
Just for you,
I would do
Anything you requested,
I'd be so interested.
If you asked me to,
I'd go through
Most anything that I could stand;
I'm waiting now for your command.
If I but knew,
I'd make your every dream come true:
I'd fly higher than the highest flyer,
I'd hold on to a live live wire,
I'd jump into a house on fire,
Just for you.

KENTUCKY RYE

No music is known to survive. A pencil holograph lyric sheet was found among Berlin's papers and is now in the Irving Berlin Collection of the Music Division of the Library of Congress. Alternate title: "They All Took a Drink of It."

VERSE

Andy Brown came to town
With a bottle of Kentucky rye.
Soon he saw three or four
Of his coon friends slyly gazing
At his hand with the brand
Of that bottle of Kentucky rye.

6666666

Andy, kind and free, good-naturedly
Just passed the bottle around.

CHORUS

They all took a drink of it
To see what they would think of it,
That Kentucky rye.
They all started wiggling
And soon began a-giggling;
Then they all began to cry.
Jackson ate a clarinet;
Ephraham is sleeping yet;
They put Alexander Fox
Within a fancy wooden box
And carried him back to old Virginia,
Where the kids who called him Pop
Never touch a drop
Of old Kentucky rye.

LET ME LOVE YOU JUST A LITTLE BIT

No music is known to survive. Typed lyric sheets and pencil holograph manuscripts were found among Berlin's papers and are now in the Irving Berlin Collection of the Music Division of the Library of Congress.

VERSE

Don't you be so stingy, dear;
Won't you come and cuddle near?
Don't you know I haven't had some lovin'
For 'most a year?
There's a feeling round my heart
Like it wants to bust apart—
Can't you hear it beating like a drum?
Come

CHORUS

Let me love you just a little bit,
A little bit, a little bit.
Won't you let me hold your hand
Like I did before?
Let me kiss you just a little bit,
A little bit, a little bit;
When we've loved a little bit,
You'll want a little bit more.

Second "Little Bit" song

VERSE

Come over here, my honey, please,
Now don't you be a great big tease—
Come on and sit down on my knees,
Because I want to love you.
You're just as mean as you can be,
You're keeping all your love from me;
My lovin' baby, can't you see
I only want to love you?

CHORUS

Don't be stingy,
Let me love you just a little bit.
I don't want much,
Just a little bit,
A tiny little bit.
Don't be a tantalizer;
I need a sympathizer;
Come on, don't be a miser:
Open up your heart, let it part
With a little love.
Don't be stingy,
Let me kiss you just a little bit.
Love me, honey,
Come over here and show me
How you can Romeo me.
Don't be stingy—
Give me a little love right now.

Double version of second "Little Bit" song

VERSE

A: My lovin' baby, don't you tease.
B: What's the matter? Tell me, please.
A: Come on and sit down on my knees, because—
B: What do you want? I'm afraid we'll disagree.
A: —I want to love you.
B: But—
A: You're just as mean as you can be.
B: What do you want to do to me?
A: I only want to love you.

CHORUS

A: Don't be stingy.
B: What do you want?
A: Let me love you just a little bit.
B: Do you want much?
A: Just a little bit.

B: A tiny little bit?
A: Don't be a tantalizer.
B: I'm not a sympathizer.
A: Come on, don't be a miser,
   Open up your heart.
B: Wide apart?
A: Just a little bit.

ANOTHER CHORUS

A: Don't be stingy.
B: What do you want?
A: Let me kiss you just a little bit.
B: Don't you love it?
A: Gee, it's awf'ly good.
B: You mean it's goody good.
A: Yes.
B: You know I haven't got much.
A: I only want just that much.
B: Don't be stingy.
BOTH: Give

Another "Little Bit" song

CHORUS

Won't you love me,
If it's only just a little bit?
I'll be satisfied.
Now don't you be a tantalizer;
I need a sympathizer;
Come on, don't be a miser:
Open up your heart,
Let it part with a little love.
Won't you kiss me,
If it's only just a little bit?
I'll be glad, I vow.
I'll have you loving me before I'm through,
But I can't wait until you do.
Won't you let me have a little bit
On account right now?

Still another chorus

I want a little bit, a little bit,
Just a little bit, that's all. Can't you see
That much will do for me?
I want a little bit, a little bit,
Just a little bit, oh my honey bee.
No one ever misses
One-two-three-four-five-six kisses.
Don't forget, don't forget,
Save a little bit for me.

MILLION-DOLLAR GIRL

No music is known to survive. A typed lyric sheet was found among Berlin's papers and is now in the Irving Berlin Collection of the Music Division of the Library of Congress.

All you need is a twenty-dollar dress
Without any frills upon it.
A ten-cent ribbon in your pretty golden hair,
Covered by a simple bonnet.
Some girls wear million dollars' worth of clothes
Beneath a twenty-dollar curl,
But all you need is a twenty-dollar dress
And you're a million-billion-dollar girl.

MY DREAMS WERE OF A WONDROUS LOVE

No music is known to survive. A pencil holograph manuscript was found among Berlin's papers and is now in the Irving Berlin Collection of the Music Division of the Library of Congress.

CHORUS

My dreams were of a wondrous love,
A love I knew
Someday would come and take me from
The darkness to heavens of blue.
For years it seems I dreamed my dreams
Till I met you,
And now I know that all my dreams
Of love came true.

VERSE

Thousands of hours I spent all alone,
Dreaming a wonderful dream;
Thousands of visions I planned as my own,
All with the same golden theme.

REPEAT CHORUS

MY GAL IN ITALY

No music is known to survive. A pencil holograph lyric manuscript was found among Berlin's papers and is now in the Irving Berlin Collection of the Music Division of the Library of Congress. This lyric is similar to the lyric for the second version of "Sweet Italian Man" (1913), page 69.

VERSE

Upon the day I take da steam-a-ship
To come to dis country,
I make much-a grieve because I leave
The gal I love in Italy.
I've seen a lot of girls since I've been here,
And I talk honestly:

CHORUS

My gal in Italy,
She's nice as nice could be.
She got a face like Lilly Russell;
She don't need a bustle
To look very good to me:
She's got a shape, you see,
Just like the number 3.
I'd cut off both my knees
If I could go and squeeze
My gal in Italy.

MY TANGO MAN

No music is known to survive. A typed lyric sheet was found among Berlin's papers and is now in the Irving Berlin Collection of the Music Division of the Library of Congress.

CHORUS

I'm thinking of him;
He made me love him
When he taught me
How to do the dreamy tango.
My heart departed
The day we started
Dancing-prancing;
While he showed me,
He Romeo'd me.
He popped the question

At my suggestion;
Now he loves me
The way nobody can.
I've given my answer
To a wonderful dancer,
And I'm crazy about him,
Can't do without him,
My dreamy tango man.

PATTER OR VERSE

Oh, have you seen that movement
Mary brought from Spain?
When Mary passes,
Put on your glasses—
Put them on, then take them off again.
For Mary's gotten bolder
With her shoulder blade;
It could not stand improvement,
Mary's movement
That she brought from Spain.

ORIENTAL WAYS

No music is known to survive. A typed lyric sheet was found among Berlin's papers and is now in the Irving Berlin Collection of the Music Division of the Library of Congress.

Oriental ways—
She has a sentimental gaze;
The country jays
Are in a maze:
Her way betrays
That she's been to Cairo,
And any time the music plays
A Turkish tune, her body sways.
She says it pays
To spend your days
Out in Cairo
And get on to their funny little
Oriental ways.

POOR LITTLE CHAMBERMAID

No music is known to survive. A typed lyric sheet was found among Berlin's papers and is now in the Irving Berlin Collection of the Music Division of the Library of Congress.

VERSE

With a pass key and a dustpan
We're a weary lot who must pan
The one who invented the chambermaid;
We must declare it's a rotten trade,
Making beds up for the drummers,
Doing towel-juggling feats,
Spending winters, falls, and summers
Shaking the sheets.

CHORUS

Poor chambermaid,
With a very romantic soul,
Poor chambermaid,
How you treasure the pleasure
Of peeping through a keyhole.
Making the bed
Where a love-making couple had laid,
With a sigh you say, "Gee,
Why wasn't it me?"
Poor little chambermaid.

RAGTIME PREACHER

Probably written in 1914. A copyist's ink manuscript of lyrics and music was found among Berlin's papers and is now in the Irving Berlin Collection of the Music Division of the Library of Congress. The lyric includes references to "Everybody's Doin' It" (1911), "That International Rag" (1913), "This Is the Life" (1914), and "He's a Devil in His Own Home Town" (1914).

Even ragtime preachers love to bend and sway
Their congregations in a ragtime way.
Sisters, brothers, loving congregation,
While the organ peals a little syncopation,
Before I start my sermon long,
Turn to page six and raise your voice in song:
Char idi da,

Char idi da,
Char idi da.
Today that loving message that I'm bringing to
    you
Is just a little passage from the ancient Hebrew:
Itchy coo,
Itchy coo,
Itchy coo.
Love your neighbors like you do yourself,
Love the ladies,
Love the ladies,
But don't you steal your neighbor's wife
Nor his ox nor his cows and chickens.
This is the life, this is the life,
And we shall meet just as sure as shooting
When Gabriel's horn starts in a-tooting
That raggedy melody
Full of originality.
Kind friends, you'd better begin
To lead a life that's free from sin
Or the Devil on the level
Is goin' to get you in his own home town.
So be good and kind,
Forgive your enemies and bear in mind
The contribution, please,
For old Saint Peter's watching you—
Every little change'll
Bring him another angel.
Don't forget that on the Judgment Day
You've got to make your bow;
Do unto others like they would do—
Ev'rybody's doing it,
Ev'rybody's doing it,
Ev'rybody's doing it now.

SAMUEL BROWN
(THE OPERATIC WAITER)

No music is known to survive. A typed lyric sheet was found among Berlin's papers and is now in the Irving Berlin Collection of the Music Division of the Library of Congress.

Samuel Brown, Samuel Brown
Was a waiter in a table d'hôte restaurant
Where an Italian orchestra played grand opera.
Melodies fine
By Rubinstein
They would play night and day;
They were serving the music
While Samuel was serving the wine.

Samuel Brown hung around, hung around, hung
    around
The orchestra; any time they started playing opera
    grand,
He would lay down his tray and keep time with his
    musical feet,
Dancing all around, dancing up and down
The restaurant, when Samuel Brown,
He couldn't wait upon the table—he wasn't able,
Because that music went to his feet,
Against his wishes—he'd have to hop while he
    dropped
Some dishes.
Samuel, he slipped and he tripped and he skipped
Around that place, until the boss became real
    cross,
And said to Samuel Brown, "You're sacked—
It's time that you went and packed."
Just then the band struck this operatic tune so
    grand,
Samuel began to shout
To the rest'rant mister man,
"For the love of your sister,
Please go 'way, let me stay,
I'll work here without any pay!"
Just then they crowded all around him and began
    to pound him
To the Anvil Chorus; they just beat him up as
    sore as
Any man could be—still that opera orchestra kept
    playing.
Samuel fell exhausted, crying "my opera'
    busted"—
Then he just laid down and died.
And the orchestra changed its tune, to
"Heart and Flowers"—they played for hours,
As they shipped his coffin to the land of cotton.
Now old Samuel's forgotten, all alone, all alone;
He is sleeping in an alley.

SAVE A LITTLE BIT FOR ME

No music is known to survive. An ink holograph manuscript was found among Berlin's papers and is now in the Irving Berlin Collection of the Music Division of the Library of Congress.

VERSE

One night in May
Young Harry Gray
While going through the park

Spied neath a tree
A he and she
Gaily spooning in the dark.
They hugged up snug like a bug in a rug;
While they moaned just like a cello,
Young Harry Gray
Stopped on his way
And whispered to the fellow:

CHORUS

"Save a little bit for me,
Save a little bit for me.
Go ahead and take her,
Shake her, make her
Love you some more,
Just like before.
Sting her like a bumblebee
Underneath the shady tree;
Squeeze her like a log—
But don't be a hog:
Save a little bit for me."

SELL MY SHACK IN HACKENSACK

No music is known to survive. A typed lyric sheet with Berlin's corrections was found among his papers and is now in the *Irving Berlin Collection* of the Music Division of the Library of Congress.

VERSE

Ebenezer Black
Down from Hackensack,
Stopping at a big New York hotel—
After spending several nights
Taking in the sights,
He made up his mind the place was swell.
He sent his lawyer a note,
And this is what he wrote:

CHORUS

You can sell my shack in Hackensack,
The cows and chickens as well;
It's a lovely place to dwell,
But not as nice as this hotel.
Sell the horses and cart;
Take out your part
And send the balance to me.
This life was meant for Ebenezer—

Through the glasses on my sneezer
I can see, each girl here is a gem.
They wink at me—
I wink right back at them.
The ladies all have pretty faces
And they let you tie their laces.
You better sell my shack in Hackensack,
For I'm never coming back.

SO NICE

No music is known to survive. A pencil holograph manuscript was found among Berlin's papers and is now in the *Irving Berlin Collection* of the Music Division of the Library of Congress.

VERSE

My pulse is jumpin' so nice;
Oh, honey, can't you hear
My heart a-thumpin' so nice?
Oh, honey, cuddle near.
Don't you know the reason why I'm feeling so,
Can't you hear me sigh?
If you really want to know,
Here's the reason why:

CHORUS

You certainly do it so nice;
Your squeeze is like a dream.
You go right to it, so nice;
Your kiss is full of steam.
Once somebody told me of a lovin' miss
Who such kissin' tried;
I heard after just one kiss
She laid down and died.
[*Lyric breaks off here.*]

SOMEDAY YOU'LL COME BACK TO ME

No music is known to survive. A pencil holograph manuscript was found among Berlin's papers and is now in the *Irving Berlin Collection* of the Music Division of the Library of Congress.

VERSE

Sweetheart, I'm lonesome without you;
I miss you night and day.
Each golden memory about you
Seems to console me and say:

CHORUS

Someday you'll come back to me;
Somehow I feel it must be.
Someday you'll start mending my broken heart;
Someday you'll know how I love you.
Memories will come to remind you
Of one you left far behind you.
Just as I lost you, I'll find you;
Someday you'll come back to me.

SOMETHING WAS GOING TO HAPPEN

No music is known to survive. A pencil holograph manuscript was found among Berlin's papers and is now in the *Irving Berlin Collection* of the Music Division of the Library of Congress.

VERSE

"Nothing ventured, nothing gained" has been said
    by men of brain,
But it doesn't prove that everyone who ventures
    always gains.
I ventured once to wink my eye at a gal who
    looked so grand,
When all at once a man appeared
With a razor in his hand.

CHORUS

I felt that something was going to happen,
Just what I could not say;
A peculiar feeling crept over me
In the most peculiar way.
A voice within me seemed to croon,
"There's something going to happen soon"—
I've got a scar as large as a spoon
To show it happened.

SWEETHEART, IF I HAD YOU

No music is known to survive. A typed lyric sheet was found among Berlin's papers and is now in the Irving Berlin Collection of the Music Division of the Library of Congress. This is not the same song as "If I Had You" (1914) (see page 88).

VERSE

I had begun to think the sun stopped shining,
The world seemed dark and drear,
Until I met you, dear;
Then through the clouds there came a silver
    lining,
And now I realize
As I gaze in your eyes,
My search for joy would soon be through,
Sweetheart, if I had you.

CHORUS

If I had you,
I would ask for nothing more;
You'd bring to view
All that gladness has in store.
Somehow I feel
Things would be real,
Things that were just dreams before.
A four-by-two
Anyplace or anywhere
Would more than do
If I knew that you were there.
Life would be dearer,
Heaven would seem nearer,
Sweetheart, if I had you.

TAKE ME BACK TO THE GARDEN OF LOVE (PARODY)

A parody of the well-known popular song of 1911 written by E. Ray Goetz (words) and Nat Osborne (music). A typed lyric sheet was found among Berlin's papers and is now in the Irving Berlin Collection of the Music Division of the Library of Congress.

VERSE

I went in a rest'raunt to satisfy
What an appetite demands;
The waiter who brought my soup to me
Wore gloves upon his hands.
Just out of mere curiosity,
I called him to my side;
I asked him why he wore the gloves,
And he nervously replied:

CHORUS

"I must ask you to pardon my glove, sir,
I must ask you to censure me not;
For the soup that I'm serving to you, sir,
Believe me, is terribly hot;
And when I put my thumb in the soup, sir,
It burns like the hot sun above;
If you must have soup with your dinner,
I must ask you to pardon my glove."

TEACH ME TO CUDDLE UP

No music is known to survive. An ink holograph lyric fragment was found among Berlin's papers and is now in the Irving Berlin Collection of the Music Division of the Library of Congress.

Teach me to cuddle up nice and cozy,
The kind of cuddling I adore—and more.
When I have cuddled up to my Rosey,
Kiss me, I've never been kissed before

THAT GARDEN OF BEAUTIFUL GIRLS

No music is known to survive. A typed lyric sheet was found among Berlin's papers and is now in the Irving Berlin Collection of the Music Division of the Library of Congress.

CHORUS

I know a lovely garden
Blooming with pretty girls,
Lovable little queens,

Beautiful seventeens,
Maisies and Daisies and Pearls.
There in that lovely garden
With the golden curls,
Right from the start
I had to part with my heart
In that garden of beautiful girls.

THAT TIRED MELODY

No music is known to survive. An ink holograph manuscript was found among Berlin's papers and is now in the Irving Berlin Collection of the Music Division of the Library of Congress.

There's a melody in town—
I believe it just came down
To kinda hound you,
And I just want you to hear it:
When you do, you will declare
It's a different kind of air.
You're liable to hear it
Most anywhere.
What'll they play?
Something that goes like this;
You're gonna say
It's a tune heaven kissed.
When it's away, I'm afraid 'twill be missed.
It's called "that tired melody";
You'll declare it's sugar-coated.
Without any doubt
I think the one who wrote it
Was all tired out.
After a while you'll be crazy about
That weary tired melody.

THAT'S HOW I LOVE YOU, MIKE

Special material written for the well-known comedians Joe Weber and Lew Fields. No music is known to survive. An ink holograph manuscript was found among Berlin's papers and is now in the Irving Berlin Collection of the Music Division of the Library of Congress.

VERSE

FIELDS: We've been friends for many years.
WEBER: We've been good friends, everybody
    knows it.
FIELDS: From my heart there comes big tears
    Every time I think of how I love you.
WEBER: Do you love me?
FIELDS: Do I love you? Oh, I simply can't
    explain it.
    Tell me, ain't it time you knew I love you?
WEBER: You love me?
FIELDS: I love you!
WEBER: You love me?
FIELDS: Mike!
WEBER: Meyer!
    [*They kiss.*]

CHORUS

FIELDS: My friend Mike!
WEBER: You love me?
FIELDS: Do I love you? How can you doubt it, my
    friend Mike?
WEBER: You love me?
FIELDS: So much so I can't do without it, Mike.
WEBER: What, what?
FIELDS: By heaven above you, Mike—
WEBER: Yes, yes?
FIELDS: —I swear that I love you.
WEBER: How much?
FIELDS: So much—
WEBER: How much?
FIELDS: —I could soak you, poke you, croak you,
    choke you, my friend Mike.
WEBER: You love me?
FIELDS: In my heart there comes such a gladness,
    my friend Mike—
WEBER: You love me?
FIELDS: —so much so it's turning to madness,
    Mike.
WEBER: What, what?
FIELDS: I'll pay what I owe you, Mike.
WEBER: Yes, yes?
FIELDS: I'm going to show you how I love you,
    Mike.
WEBER: You love me, Meyer, don't you?
FIELDS: Yes.
WEBER: Then come and choke me, won't you?
FIELDS: Mike.
WEBER: Why don't come and share me—
FIELDS: Why?
WEBER: —and show me how you love me.
FIELDS: [*choking Weber, sings*]
    That's how I love you, that's how I love
      you,
    That's how I love you, Mike—I love you—
      I love you.

WAIT'LL YOU LAND IN DEAR OLD TEXAS

No music is known to survive. This appears to have been an early attempt to write a Texas song. A pencil holograph lyric was found among Berlin's papers and is now in the Irving Berlin Collection of the Music Division of the Library of Congress.

Wait'll you land in dear old Texas,
Out where they brand the cows with X's;
Strangers don't know the dangers
That haunt those cattle rangers
When you start to skedaddle
Upon a horse without a saddle.
Open your ear to what I'm telling:
Wait'll you hear a cowboy yelling—
For days and days you'll carry it;
You'll see him throw his lariat
Way out west in Texas
Out on a ranch.

WE HAD A WONDERFUL HONEYMOON

No music is known to survive. A typed lyric sheet with Berlin's pencil corrections was found among his papers and is now in the Irving Berlin Collection of the Music Division of the Library of Congress.

VERSE

Little Sally Brown was married,
To the Mendelssohn tune;
After Sally Brown was married,
She went on a honeymoon.
She came back the other day,
Husband by her side,
"What's the news?" her mother asked,
And Sally Brown replied:

CHORUS

"We had a wonderful honeymoon,
We had a wonderful honeymoon;
Folks knew we were bride and groom,
So we never left the room.
We'd have our breakfast served and then
We'd go right back to sleep again.
He called me wonderful baby names;

We played some wonderful baby games.
I was oh so very shy;
I guess that's the reason why
The hotel bellboy winked his eye—
We had a wonderful time."

WE'LL MEET AGAIN

No music is known to survive. A pencil holograph manuscript was found among Berlin's papers and is now in the Irving Berlin Collection of the Music Division of the Library of Congress.

We'll meet again,
We'll meet again,
And never more we'll have to part.
I'll kiss you then
As I did when
You came to dwell within my heart.
A little rain,
A little pain,
A little happiness, and then
A gentle sigh,
A fond goodbye,
Just to meet and to love again.

WHAT'S GOOD ENOUGH FOR YOUR FATHER IS GOOD ENOUGH FOR YOU

No music is known to survive. Typed lyric sheets were found among Berlin's papers and are now in the Irving Berlin Collection of the Music Division of the Library of Congress. Alternate title on one lyric sheet: "It Was Good Enough for Your Father."

VERSE

"Don't you talk back to your mother,"
Said Mrs. Dan MacVey
To her son, who wouldn't eat the food
She cooked for him that day.
She cried, "This is no restaurant,
And don't forget, young man,
For fifty years I did the cooking
For your father, Dan.

CHORUS

"Corn beef and cabbage,
Potatoes and corn,
Was good enough for your father
Before you was born.
He thought it was a holiday
When I gave him Irish stew—
What was good enough for your father
Is good enough for you."

WHEN THEY BEGIN TO PLAY

No music is known to survive. The lyric is unfinished. A pencil holograph of the lyric, written on Hotel Algonquin (New York) stationery, was found among Berlin's papers and is now in the Irving Berlin Collection of the Music Division of the Library of Congress.

When they begin to play,
I add to my vocabulary
Words not in the dictionary.
I'm sure the things I say
Are anything but sensible
Or even comprehensible.
Last night my dancing partner said to me,
"You swing a nasty pedal extremity."
She said my step
Was full of salt, full of salt,
Full of some kind of seasoning.
Although I try my best
To carry on a conversation
Free from any syncopation,
I go right with the rest
And change the English language so
I would give the king an awful blow
[*Lyric breaks off here.*]

WHERE MY HEART OUGHT TO BE

No music is known to survive. A pencil holograph manuscript was found among Berlin's papers and is now in the Irving Berlin Collection of the Music Division of the Library of Congress.

Where my heart ought to be there's a fire
Blazing up higher and higher.
Its funny sensation is rocking me,
Knocking me, shocking me;
It beats with a sixty horsepower,
Ten thousand beats to an hour.
Lead me right to the altar,
The rock of Gibraltar
Is down where my heart ought to be.

YOU WILL NEVER GROW OLD

No music is known to survive. An ink holograph manuscript was found among Berlin's papers and is now in the Irving Berlin Collection of the Music Division of the Library of Congress.

VERSE

Old Man Brown was eighty-three,
Just as spry as he could be,
Did all the devilish things that young folks do,
Mingled with the younger men,
Told a story now and then;
Sometimes his stories were a trifle blue.
They asked him to explain just how he
Kept so young and gay;
He ran his fingers through his beard
And then they heard him say:

CHORUS

"Just as long as you can keep loving,
You will never grow old. You'll never grow old.
There may be wrinkles on your face,
But if your heart's in the proper place
You're just a baby, a baby.
No matter how bad your . . . may be,
Take a fool's advice and see:
Keep lovin';
Don't you let your heart grow cold.
When the last hair from your head disappears,
Don't you go around sheddin' tears;
If the rustle of a skirt is music to your ears,
You will never grow old."

VERSE 2 (POSSIBLE)

Though you may be way past eighty-three,
Just as weak as any man could be,
If you're strong enough to hold a gal upon your knee
[*Lyric breaks off here.*]

YOUR AUTOMOBILE IS BURNING, ABIE

No music is known to survive. A typed lyric sheet found among Berlin's papers is now in the Irving Berlin Collection of the Music Division of the Library of Congress.

VERSE

Abie Cohen bought an automobile,
And he insured it right away.
Morris Rosenthal, his partner,
Borrowed the car one day.
Upon the road something happened:
The automobile caught fire.
He called up Abie Cohen
On the telephone
And he shouted over the wire:

CHORUS

"Your automobile is burning, Abie—
What shall I do, what shall I do?
I know that it's insured for twice as much as it cost;
In another minute I'm afraid it will be lost.
What's that? You want me to keep talking,
And you'll pay for the telephone call.
Well, how's da Mamma, How's da Mamma?
Better get the fire insurance papers from her,
For your automobile is burning, Abie—
Congratulations, goodbye. . . ."

OVERLEAF: *Irene Castle*

WATCH YOUR STEP | 1914

WATCH YOUR STEP (1914)

Tryout: Empire Theatre, Syracuse, New York, beginning November 25, 1914, and the Detroit Opera House, Detroit, Michigan, beginning November 30, 1914. New York run: New Amsterdam Theatre; opened December 8, 1914; 175 performances. Lyrics and music by Irving Berlin. Produced by Charles Dillingham: "A Syncopated Musical Show in Three Acts (Made in America)." Staged by R. H. Burnside. "Plot (if any)" by Harry B. Smith. Originally titled *Round the Clock*. Orchestra under the direction of Dewitt C. Coolman. Orchestrations uncredited. Cast: starring Vernon Castle (Joseph Lilyburn), "who invented the steps you watch"), Irene (Mrs. Vernon) Castle (Mrs. Vernon Castle), Frank Tinney (A Carriage Caller at the Opera, A Pullman Porter, A Coat Room Boy), Elizabeth Murray (Birdie O'Brien, "of the Comedie Française, Dublin"), Elizabeth Brice (Stella Sparks), Charles King (Algy Cuffs, "a matinee idol"), Sallie Fisher (Ernesta Hardacre, "too good to be true"), Harry Kelly (Ebenezer Hardacre, "a thrifty sport"), Sam Burbank (Willie Steele, "a tango lawyer"), William J. Halligan (Silas Flint, "a Maxixe lawyer"), Justine Johnstone (Estelle, "a hestitating typewriter"), Dama Skyes (Iona Ford), Hariette Leidy (Anne Marshall, "the lovely laundress"), Al Holbrook (Howe Strange), and Harry Ellis (The Ghost of Verdi). W. C. Fields and his billiard scene were dropped from the show during the Syracuse tryout. A complete piano-vocal score was published and registered for copyright on January 27, 1915. London production: Empire Theatre; opened May 4, 1915; 275 performances.

OFFICE HOURS

Published only as part of the show's piano-vocal score, which was registered for copyright January 27, 1915. Introduced by ensemble (chorus). Alternate titles: "Typewriter Song" and "Entrance of Relatives."

Office hours,
Office hours—
From the moment you arrive,
Keep alive from nine till five—
It's a strain
On one's brain,
For dictation brings vexation
When you've been out

Dancing about
Out on a spree such as we've been out on.

Bright lights shining,
Gay folks dining—
What a night!
Oh, what a lovely night!
Shoulder shakers,
Merrymakers—
What a sight!
Oh, what a lovely sight!
I got home at half past four;
Father started in to roar,
"You've got to go to work at seven o'clock
This morning." How I grumbled
As I tumbled out of bed,
I tumbled out of bed;
No more laughter
Morning after—
What a head!
Oh, what an awful head!
In the dizzy business world
Heaven help a working girl
After having had such a wonderful night.

BOYS: I've a little note that I'd like to send—
       Won't you take it down for me?
       It's a little note to a lady friend—
       I'm in love with her, you see.
GIRLS: If 'twill make you feel much better,
       I'll typewrite your little letter.
BOYS: Keep it in the dark, not a word—
           I depend
       That you treat it confidentially.
[GIRLS *place paper in typewriters.*]
GIRLS: Dictate, sir—dictate, sir;
       Please dictate your letter.
       Don't wait, sir—don't wait, sir;
       I'm quite ready now.
BOYS: [*dictating to girls*]
       Dear little girl, just a sweet word or two;
       First I'll explain why I'm writing to you.
       I couldn't say what is wrapped in my
           heart;
       That's why I'm sending this letter,
       My tale of love to impart.

       I love you, dear, with all my heart,
       And I have loved you from the start.
       In my lonesome life,
       Full of care and strife,
       You play a most important part.
       Just say the word and we will fly
       Into the little church nearby.
       If you change from Miss to Missus,
       I will know what bliss is—
       All my love and kisses,
       Goodbye!

GIRLS: Now will you give me the address?
BOYS: Address it to yourself, dear.
GIRLS: This is quite sudden, I confess.
BOYS: Say yes, say yes, say yes, dear.
GIRLS: Have you bought the ring?
BOYS: I have ev'rything.
GIRLS: Where will I get my wedding dress?
BOYS: Wear the dress your mother wore.
GIRLS: Will you be near me night and day?
BOYS: I'll never leave your sight, dear.
GIRLS: Will you do everything I say?
BOYS: I may.
GIRLS: I can hear the choir singing.
BOYS: Bells will soon be ringing,
ALL: Ting-a-ling-a-linging away!

WHAT IS LOVE?

Published individually and as part of the show's piano-vocal score. Copyrighted December 5, 1914, and in the piano-vocal score on January 27, 1915. Introduced by Sallie Fisher (Ernesta Hardacre), who replaced Renee Gratz during the pre-Broadway tryout. First sung by Ms. Gratz in the Syracuse and Detroit performances. Dropped during the New York run in March 1915 and replaced by "Lead Me to Love."

VERSE 1

Love, love,
Won't you come out from your hiding place,
Let me see a trace of your hidden face?
Love, love,
Wrapped in your mantle of mystery,
Makes me ponder,
Ponder and wonder,
What you may be.

CHORUS

What is love?
Is it gladness?
Or a form of sadness?
Or a sign of madness?
Should we meet face to face?
Will it frighten me?
Kindly enlighten me,
What is love?
I keep guessing
Whether it's a blessing
Or a thing distressing;
Should it come to me,
What will it prove to be,
When I'm head and heels in love?

VERSE 2

Love, love,
Out of the darkness I call to thee;
Won't you let me see what you hold for me?
Love, love,
I want to have you within my reach,
For I'm yearning
Just to be learning
The things you teach.

REPEAT CHORUS

LEAD ME TO LOVE

Published. Copyrighted April 14, 1915. Music by Ted Snyder. Added to the show on March 8, 1915, it replaced "What Is Love?" Introduced by Sallie Fisher (Ernesta Hardacre) and William J. Halligan (Silas Flint) and ensemble. Not printed in the piano-vocal score.

VERSE 1

SHE: Tell me all about the game of love,
All about the love I'm dreaming of.
HE: Ah, go on, ah, go on,
I believe you're only fooling.
SHE: I'm so very stupid at that game,
Stupid Mister Cupid never came.
HE: Ah, go on, ah, go on,
I'm afraid you need no schooling.
SHE: I'd like to take a lesson from you.
HE: Just tell me what you want me to do.

CHORUS 1

SHE: Lead me, oh, lead me to love.
HE: Get away, get away,
For I'm on to you.
SHE: Come be my own turtle dove.
HE: Not today, not today,
You will never do.
SHE: Come here and Romeo me.
HE: I fear that you don't know me.
SHE: I'll learn if you just show me how.
HE: Now?
SHE: Yes!
HE: No!
SHE: Please help a poor lovesick miss.
HE: Let me look, let me look
Till I find a cure.
SHE: I've never yet had a kiss.
HE: Get the hook, get the hook,
She's an amateur.

SHE: Loved I must be, dear.
HE: Why pick on me, dear?
SHE: Lead me!
HE: Go on.
SHE: I want to be loved.

VERSE 2

SHE: Take me in your arms and call me dear;
Whisper little nothings in my ear.
HE: Don't you dare, don't you dare
Take advantage of a stranger.
SHE: Listen to a maiden's earnest plea:
Won't you come and flirt with
lovesick me?
HE: I'm afraid, I'm afraid,
I'm afraid to flirt with danger.
SHE: I'd like to know just what it's about.
HE: I'll show you if the lights will go out.

CHORUS 2

SHE: Lead me, oh, lead me to love.
CHORUS: Give her a kiss, give her a kiss,
While the lights are low.
SHE: Come be my own turtle dove.
CHORUS: Watch your step, watch your step
Or you'll stub your toe.
SHE: I'm sure when you will know me,
You'll want to Romeo me—
Come over here and show me how.
HE: Now?
SHE: Yes!
HE: No!
SHE: Please, help a poor lovesick miss.
CHORUS: Better look, better look
Till you find a cure.
SHE: I've never yet had a kiss.
CHORUS: Get the hook, get the hook,
She's an amateur.
SHE: Kiss me, I'm anxious.
HE: Not while I'm conscious.
SHE: Lead me!
HE: Come on!
SHE: I want to be loved.

I'M A DANCING
TEACHER NOW

Published only as part of the show's piano-vocal score, which was registered for copyright January 27, 1915. Introduced by Vernon Castle (Joseph Lilyburn). Alternate titles: "The Dancing Teacher" and "Since I Became a

Dancing Teacher." Although the song was listed on sheet music covers for the show as having been published, it was never printed separately for publication, and only the first two verses and choruses were published in the piano-vocal score.

VERSE 1

My parents weren't wealthy, so I had to go to
work;
For years I earned a sal'ry working as a lawyer's
clerk.
My wife said, "Get a million dollars quick and
don't you fail."
I didn't want to rob a bank and serve a year in jail.

CHORUS 1

So I became a dancing teacher,
And the very next day
A class of eighty-three were paying me a fee
And every one of them were better dancers
than me.
I used to ride in crosstown trolleys
Every day with my frau;
But now I know how it feels
To ride in automobiles,
For I'm a dancing teacher now.

VERSE 2

When I was told I had to sing this ditty in the
show,
I sang it over to a friend to see how it would go.
I asked him if he didn't think the song was very
nice.
He said, "I only thank you for your very good
advice."

CHORUS 2

And now my friend's a dancing teacher
With a class of his own.
I told him what they pay;
He started in next day;
He's cutting prices now to steal my pupils away.
The twelve young fellows in this chorus
Have been raising a row:
They own their own motorcars
And want to dress with the stars,
Because they're dancing teachers now.

VERSE 3

Since I became a teacher, all my relatives agree
That Jesse James the outlaw was a saint compared
to me.

It's fifty dollars for a lesson, and they're glad
  to pay;
On bargain days it's forty-nine, and that's my
  busy day.

CHORUS 3

Since I became a dancing teacher
I've been rolling in wealth
[*lines missing*]
My German chauffer taught me all the steps that
  I do.
A class of married ladies pay me
All their husbands allow;
They pay me barrels of dough
To let them step on my toe,
For I'm a dancing teacher now.

VERSE 4

My dancing partner used to be a certain lady fair;
The people said we made a very lovely dancing
  pair,
My arm encircled round her waist as we would
  dance away.
My wifey watched us dance one night, and soon I
  heard her say:

CHORUS 4

"I'm going to a dancing teacher;
I must learn how to dance.
Your arm was placed, I see,
Around her waist," said she,
"And if you've got an arm to waist, you'll waist it
  on me."
And now my wife's a dancing teacher;
There's no chance for a row.
I lead a miserable life:
I have to dance with my wife,
For she's a dancing teacher now.

THEY'RE DANCING
TEACHERS

No music is known to survive. Unused. This number ap-
pears to have been intended for the spot in the show ulti-
mately occupied by "I'm a Dancing Teacher Now," but
the lyric would appear to have been set to slightly differ-
ent music.

VERSE 1

I went into a well-known restaurant a week ago;
I found the service awful and I told the owner so.
I said, "I see no waiters here; I wish you'd tell me
  why."
The cafe owner burst in tears and made me this
  reply:

CHORUS 1

"They're dancing teachers, dancing teachers.
I had thirty of the best;
Two are lame, and all the rest
Are dancing teachers, dancing teachers.
No more headwaiters—
They're all becoming hesitaters.
Old hash-slingers snap their fingers;
If you've got the price they'll show you how.
We have empty dining rooms,
For all our waiters, cooks, and grooms
Are dancing teachers now."

VERSE 2

I walked into a barbershop and found nobody
  home
Except the barber's parrot, who was chewing on a
  comb.
I cried "Where are the barbers?" when I saw the
  empty shelves;
The parrot said, "They are not here; we'll have to
  shave ourselves.

CHORUS 2

"They're dancing teachers, dancing teachers,
Whiskers growing to the ground,
Not a barber to be found.
They're dancing teachers, dancing teachers,
Each one's a master;
The only man they'll shave is Astor.
No shampooing—nothing doing—
In society they've made their bow;
All of our brilliant wops
Who used to work in barbershops
Are dancing teachers now."

VERSE 3

A foreign nation sent a call to her ambassador
To mobilize her subjects and send them home
  to war.
He cabled back, "Postpone the war, or fight it out
  alone;
Your subjects here are mobilizing classes of their
  own.

CHORUS 3

"They're dancing teachers, dancing teachers;
Dancing here is worse than war:
Folks are crippled by the score
By dancing teachers, dancing teachers.
Foxy sharpshooters
Are working here as tango-tutors;
High-toned scholars pay them dollars—
They don't want a European row.
Europe's war will stop, I fear,
For all her soldiers over here
Are dancing teachers now."

EXTRA CHORUS

"They're dancing teachers, dancing teachers;
Dentists in the tenderloin
Are now extracting lots of coin
As dancing teachers, dancing teachers.
Full-dressed headwaiters
Are all becoming hesitaters,
All directing and collecting
Twenty dollars for an hour.
Don't forget that most of our
Tango instructors
Were streetcar conductors—
Hurrah for the Red, White, and Blue!"

THE MINSTREL PARADE

Published individually and as part of the show's piano-
vocal score. Copyrighted December 5, 1914, and in the
piano-vocal score on January 27, 1915. Introduced by
Elizabeth Murray (Birdie O'Brien) and ensemble. Lead-
ing recording by the team of Arthur Collins and Byron
Harlan (Victor).

VERSE 1

It's eleven-forty-five,
Just as sure as you're alive.
Just see those minstrel folks
Parading up the avenue
Two by two.
They've been billed all over town,
Ev'ry one of them a clown;
Why, I can hear them coming up the street—
Honey, you better come down.

CHORUS

Here they come,
Here they come,

Marching to the big brass drum.
Come and see those minstrels parade
In their costumes covered with braid.
Hear those coons
Playing tunes
Like they should be played.
From ev'ry dwelling
Folks will come to hear them telling
Lots of funny riddles at the old town hall.
One and all,
Come on and watch the minstrel parade.

VERSE 2

Get your tickets for the show;
Oh, my honey, if you go,
You'll know the reason why
A chicken goes across the street—
It's a treat.
Paint your face up with a smile;
Get yourself rigged up in style;
They're only here to play a one-night stand—
Honey, you better come down.

REPEAT CHORUS

LET'S GO AROUND THE TOWN

Published individually and as part of the show's piano-vocal score. Copyrighted December 5, 1914, and in the piano-vocal score on January 27, 1915. Introduced by the entire company, led by Sallie Fisher (Ernesta Hardacre), William J. Halligan (Silas Flint), Harry Kelly (Ebenezer Hardacre), Sam Burbank (Willie Steele), Al Holbrook (Howe Strange), and Vernon Castle (Joseph Lilyburn). Alternate titles: "Let's Go Round the Town" and "Around the Town."

VERSE 1

ERNESTA: Where can we go to pass the time away?
FLINT: I know a very lively cabaret.
HARDACRE: You'll have to lead me to it, I'm a jay.
STEELE: Show me the sight of it,
I'll make a night of it.
STRANGE: Let's go round and take in the show.
LILYBURN: I'm with you wherever you go.

CHORUS

ALL: Let's go round the town,
And where a band is playing
We'll go hip-hurraying
And we'll turn things upside down.
Our heads will grow dizzy
Keeping headwaiters busy;
I promise you
We'll discover places that Columbus
never found.
Come on and drown your troubles
In champagne bubbles
While we're going around the town.

VERSE 2

ERNESTA: I'd like to go and see the town a bit.
FLINT: I'd like to be where they're all doing it.
HARDACRE: I'd like to listen to the latest hit.
STEELE: I'd run a mile or two
Just for a smile or two.
STRANGE: Let's go where they gladden the heart.
LILYBURN: I'm with you whenever you start.

REPEAT CHORUS

THEY ALWAYS FOLLOW ME AROUND

Published individually and as part of the show's piano-vocal score. Copyrighted December 2, 1914, and in the piano-vocal score on January 27, 1915. Introduced by Charles King (Algy Cuffs) and ensemble ("The Matinee Girls").

VERSE 1

There must be something nice about me,
Because the girls can't do without me.
I refuse them but can't lose them;
They always follow me.
I never dare to go out riding;
I've always got to keep in hiding.
I'm a chappy most unhappy,
Just because the girls

CHORUS

They follow me around, all around, all around,
Follow me around, all around, all around.
I don't know why
They hound me, surround me;
Wherever I may be, I can see two or three—

Ev'ry other she wants to be on my knee.
And any time they find me,
They drag along behind me—
It keeps me dodging in hallways,
Because they always follow me around.

VERSE 2

I'm followed by young girls good-looking;
And even cooks who do their cooking
Leave their stoves and come in droves,
Demanding my autograph.
The matinee I play on Wednesday
Is what I've nicknamed "My Old Hens' Day"—
Each old maid is on parade,
And when they see me come,

REPEAT CHORUS

Earlier version of verse 2

I'm better known than George M. Cohan;
I always pack the house I show in—
Every show, it's SRO,
And girls are my audience.
But that's the very thing that torments,
For at the end of my performance
There's a mob right on the job,
And when I start for home,

Earliest version of verse 2

I really don't know what there is in me
That makes the ladies try to win me—
Honestly, in me you see
The pet of the petticoats.
It's pretty bad not to have any,
But then it's worse to have too many.
My popularity arouses;
I always play packed houses—
Every show is SRO.

SHOW US HOW TO DO THE FOX-TROT

Published individually and as part of the show's piano-vocal score. Copyrighted December 5, 1914, and in the piano-vocal score on January 27, 1915. Introduced by Irene (Mrs. Vernon) Castle, who portrayed herself, and ensemble ("Pupils").

VERSE 1

BOYS: Dancing teacher, give us a chance—
We came here to learn how to dance
That brand-new dance they call the
fox-trot.
The lovin' fox-trot.
If you'll kindly show us the way,
Any price we're willing to pay.*
Take us each in turn—
We're all ready to learn.

CHORUS

BOYS: Dancing teacher, show us how to do the
fox-trot.
MRS. C: You'll have to watch your step.
BOYS: Won't you come and show us how to do
the fox-trot?
MRS. C: You'll have to watch your step.
BOYS: Tell us what to do!
MRS. C: You must follow me.
BOYS: Can we do it too?
MRS. C: Very easily.
BOYS: Kindly show us.
MRS. C: Watch me, watch me.
BOYS: That dance is simply great,
And it's so up to date—
It beats the tango, one-step,
And the others we know:
So,
Dancing teacher, once again
Show me how it's done, and then
We'll do the fox-trot
The whole night long.

VERSE 2

BOYS: Dancing teacher, do it some more—
Glide us gently over the floor
Until we learn to dance the fox-trot,†
The lovin' fox-trot.
Really, it's a barrel of fun,
Though it's not so easily done.
If you'll see us through,
We'll be doing it too.

REPEAT CHORUS

*Earlier version lines 5 and 6:
Teaching us might be quite a task,
But we'll pay whatever you ask.

†Earlier version of line:
We simply love to dance the fox-trot,

WHEN I DISCOVERED YOU

Music and lyrics by Irving Berlin and E. Ray Goetz. Published individually and as part of the show's piano-vocal score. Copyrighted December 2, 1914, and in the piano-vocal score on January 27, 1915. Introduced by Elizabeth Brice (Stella Spark), Charles King (Algy Cuffs), and ensemble ("Dancing Teachers"). The published version includes only the two verses and the first chorus.

VERSE 1

HE: History proves since the world first
began,
Wonderful things have been discovered
by man.
Though to discover has not been my
plan,
I'm a discoverer too—
Though I know my name
Won't be known to fame,
This much is true:

CHORUS 1

HE: Columbus discovered America;
Hudson discovered New York.
Benjamin Franklin discovered the
spark
That Edison discovered would light up
the dark.
Marconi discovered the wireless
telegraph
Across the ocean blue;
But the greatest discovery
Was when you discovered me
And I discovered you.

VERSE 2

SHE: History proves since the world first
began,
Ev'rything great was not discovered
by man.
Girls can discover what men never can;
I'm a discoverer too—
Though I'll never be
Known to history,
This much is true:

CHORUS 2

SHE: Salome discovered the evening gown;
Venus discovered good form.
Lillian Russell discovered the tights

That managers discovered keep men
out at nights.
Miss Gaby discovered that chicken à
la king
Would bring a pearl or two;
But the greatest discovery
Was when you discovered me
And I discovered you.

CHORUS 3

The Castles discovered the turkey trot;
Munyon discovered there's "Hope."
Wrigley discovered the gum that we chew,
And Georgie Cohan discovered the Red, White,
and Blue.
Rockefeller discovered that making millions
Was an easy thing to do;
But the greatest discovery
Was when you discovered me
And I discovered you.

THE SYNCOPATED WALK

Published individually and as part of the show's piano-vocal score. Copyrighted December 2, 1914, and in the piano-vocal score on January 27, 1915. Introduced by the entire company and reprised late in Act III under a title listed in programs as "Look at Them Doing It," which is nearly identical to "Look at 'em doin' it," the opening line of the chorus of "The Syncopated Walk." Successfully recorded by Prince's Orchestra (Columbia).

VERSE 1

Strange,
But there's a change
In how the people walk these days.
Yes!
You must confess
That ever since the dancing craze
Ev'rybody has a syncopated walk.
Where?
It's in the air—
You'll find them swaying as they go.
Smile,
But all the while
You must admit that it is so.
For they do,
They do,
If you don't think it's true,

CHORUS

Look at 'em doin' it,
Look at 'em doin' it,
That syncopated walk.
Look at 'em doin' it,
Look at 'em doin' it,
I know who introduced it.
Wait'll he reaches you,
Wait'll he teaches you
That syncopated walk.
You'll be doing it too,
Because it's done
By ev'ryone.
You'll find it's international,
That irrational step,
It's full of pep, full of pep;
And in the morning when they rise
For their morning exercise
They take a syncopated walk.

VERSE 2

Say
Whate'er you may,
It's in the air without a doubt.
You
Will do it too;
Before you know what you're about,
You'll be walking with a syncopated walk.
Don't
You say you won't,
Because you don't know what you say.
Friend,
You can depend
That it will strike you some fine day;
Ere you know,
You'll go—
If you don't think it's so,

REPEAT CHORUS

TRIO OR PATTER SECTION

MR. C: Come, come, come, come,
My little dear;
Won't you come, come, come, come,
Come over here?
Would you like
To go walking
To a syncopated tune?
MRS. C: I would enjoy it greatly.
MR. C: You must admit
That it's up-to-dately.
MRS. C: I'd be delighted to go, dear,
So, dear,
Let us get started for a syncopated walk.
MR. C: Come along, come along.

MRS. C: And while we walk—
MR. C: —hum a song, hum a song.
MRS. C: Where will we go?
MR. C: Follow me, follow me.
MRS. C: I want to know.
MR. C: You will see, you will see.
MRS. C: I simply cannot resist that meter.
MR. C: Follow your raggy leader.
Come—
MRS. C: Don't you hesitate.
MR. C: —with—
MRS. C: Let us syncopate.
MR. C: —me.
MRS. C: What'll we do, what'll we do?
MR. C: We'll have a syncopated walk.
MRS. C: A syncopated walk.
MR. C: The best we ever had.
MRS. C: We will have a little talk.
MR. C: A syncopated talk.
MRS. C: I know 'twill make me glad.
MR. C: Drag your feet.
MRS. C: You must show me how.
MR. C: Follow me, follow me,
Come.
MRS. C: Must I do it now?
MR. C: Certainly, certainly.
MRS. C: I'm
So elated.
MR. C: You're
Fascinated
MRS. C: With
That syncopated walk.
MR. C: Come, come, come,
My little dear.
Won't you come, come, come, come,
Come over here?
Hurry up,
Let's get started
For a syncopated walk.
CHORUS: Come, come, come, come,
My little dear.
Won't you come, come, come, come,
Come over here?
Hurry up,
Let's get started
For a syncopated walk.

METROPOLITAN NIGHTS

Published only as part of the show's piano-vocal score, which was registered for copyright on January 27, 1915. Listed in the piano-vocal score as "Opening Chorus Act II." Introduced by ensemble.

Metropolitan nights,
Metropolitan nights—
Fashion and wealth go parading
In the glare of the Metropolitan lights,
Metropolitan lights.
Down at the Opera House
If you want to see Metropolitan sights,
Metropolitan sights,
You'll have to stand to be bored a bit
By some classical song
Mid the suffering throng—
Fashion demands it
On Metropolitan nights.

I LOVE TO HAVE THE BOYS AROUND ME

Published individually and as part of the show's piano-vocal score. Copyrighted December 5, 1914, and in the piano-vocal score on January 27, 1915. Introduced by Elizabeth Brice (Stella Spark) and ensemble ("Chappies"). Only the two verses and the first chorus were published.

VERSE 1

When I was a baby,
I used to sit on my daddy's knee;
When I was a schoolgirl,
The fellows always appealed to me.
My dad said, "Don't scold her,
She'll change when she's older."
But strange to say,
To this very day
I've never changed.

CHORUS

I love to have the boys around me,
Around me all the time.
I'm never happy till I'm with the men,
Then I'm unhappy till we meet again—
I simply couldn't live without them.
There's something makes me wild about them.*
All kinds,
The very large and very small kinds—
I love to have them chasing me,
Embracing me,
All of the time.

*Earlier version of lines 5 and 6:
    No matter if he came from Hades,
    I love the boy who loves the ladies.

VERSE 2

I'm hoping for heaven,
But let me tell you in any case,
If boys aren't up there,
I want to go to the other place.
I never will marry
A Tom, Dick, or Harry—
Just one, you see,
Wouldn't do for me:
I love them all.

REPEAT CHORUS

Earlier version

VERSE 2

I went to a doctor
And asked him if he could help a miss
Who always was lovesick.
He felt my pulse, then he told me this:
"You're suffering ment'ly."
I answered him gently,
"I'm glad I came."
Then I put his name
Down on my list.

CHORUS 2

I love to have the boys around me,
Around me all the time.
He doesn't have to be a duke or lord—
I'd even love him if he owned a Ford.
I'd holler from the tops of houses—
I'm strong for anything in trousers.
Show me a fellow who can Romeo me,
And soon I'll have him chasing me,
Embracing me,
All of the time.

SETTLE DOWN IN A ONE-HORSE TOWN

Published individually and as part of the show's piano-vocal score. Copyrighted December 5, 1914, and in the piano-vocal score on January 27, 1915. Introduced by Elizabeth Brice (Stella Spark) and Charles King (Algy Cuffs).

VERSE 1

I'm getting tired of the glare and light,
I've had enough of staying out at night,

There's nothing in it, honey, honor bright,
I'm through—all through.
A little cottage in a one-horse town:
That's where I'd like to go and settle down;
I'd be as proud as if I wore a crown
If I had you.

CHORUS

Come, let's settle down
In some small country town
Away from all this care and strife.
Far, far away from cabarets,
We'll stay among the jays
And live the quiet simple life.
And from the time the rooster calls
I'll wear my overalls
And you'll wear a simple gingham gown.
So if you're strong for a shower of rice,
We could make a paradise
Out of a one-horse town.

VERSE 2

I love the city with its buildings tall,
I love apartments with a great big hall;
The place you speak of would be much too small
For me, sweetheart.
I'd rather live upon Fifth Avenue;
The simple life for me would never do;
I really couldn't go away with you—
When do we start?

REPEAT CHORUS

I'VE GOTTA GO BACK TO TEXAS

Published. Copyrighted January 17, 1916. Added to the show during the post-Broadway tour, where it was introduced by Bernard Granville (Joseph Lilyburn). Alternate title: "I've Got to Go Back to Texas." This song was "respectfully dedicated to Miss Madeleine Cochran." Not printed in the published piano-vocal score.

VERSE 1

Far away out west in Texas,
By the Rio Grande,
There's a ranch of many acres
On the prairie land.
And I want you to be knowing,

That's exactly where I'm going.
In just a day or so
You'll see a satchel in my hand.

CHORUS

I gotta go back, I gotta go back,
I gotta go back to dear old Texas,
To the ranch I left behind
And the girl who's on my mind,
I couldn't remain; I'm taking a train,
The Southern Pacific bound for Texas.
I'm simply aching to skedaddle
Upon a horse without a saddle;
And ev'ry letter that I get from Texas
Is covered with a lot of X's.
I gotta go back, I gotta go back
To the girl I left behind.

VERSE 2

Where the western sun is blazing
By the Rio Grande,
I can see the cattle grazing
On the prairie land,
And it fills me with a yearning
That I ought to be returning—
If you were ever there,
I'm pretty sure you'd understand.

REPEAT CHORUS

RAGTIME OPERA MEDLEY

Published, in a black-and-white edition, probably in 1914; exact date unknown, since this number was not registered separately for copyright. Registered for copyright as part of the show's piano-vocal score on January 27, 1915. A ragtime treatment of the famous quartet from Verdi's *Rigoletto* and snippets from other well-known operas. Introduced by entire company, led by Elizabeth Brice (Stella Spark), Sallie Fisher (Ernesta Hardacre), Charles King (Algy Cuffs), Harry Kelly (Ebenezer Hardacre), Elizabeth Murray (Birdie O'Brien), and Harry Ellis (the Ghost of Verdi). Alternate titles: "Old Operas in a New Way" and "Finale Act II—Opera Medley."

VERSE 1

STELLA: *Aida*,
There's not a melody sweeter,
But you'll be sweeter when we begin

Turning you into a rag.
Aida,
We're gonna chop up your meter;
We're getting tired of you, and so
Here's where we're going to.
Hurdy-gurdy Mister Verdi
Op'ra, you always sound like an
    uproar,
And that's the reason it's not a sin
Turning you into a rag.
You'll soon be placed with the
    popular taste,
For we're going to rearrange you,
Change you to a rag.

ERNESTA: Dreamy *La Bohème,*
We will hesitate you;
Though we aggravate Puccini,
He may roar and scream,
Nevertheless we will hesitate to
    La Bohème.

ALGY: Op'ra lovers, if you grant us your
    pardon,
We'll take the garden scene from
    Faust

HARDACRE: And we'll rearrange the Flower Song
And call it our song,

ALGY: Because its melody makes a dreamy
    maxixe.
Op'ra lovers, if you do not approve of
What we remove of *Faust,*
Just roust and occupy back seats
While we maxixe
To the Flower Song from *Faust.*

BIRDIE: Everybody's doing it,
So we'll do the tango to the strains of
    Carmen
O'er the floor—
Let ev'ry Carmen take a toreador
And throw her arms around him
While they go dancing
To that entrancing melody.
There's something in the rhythm
Of that refrain that suits us
    perfectly—
That's the reason
We do the tango
To the *Carmen* melody.

CHORUS 1

Oh, you *Pagliacci,*
You make a wonderful one-step,
A barrel-of-fun step,
And so before we're through
We'll make a one-step out of you.
We like you, *Pagliacci,*
Because your melody mellow
By Leoncavallo

Affords us something new,
And so we'll one-step to you.

VERSE 2

VERDI: Please don't rag my melody.
CHORUS: We hate to tantalize you,
    But we mean to modernize you.
VERDI: Let my *Rigoletto* be.
CHORUS: We want you syncopated
    Even though we know you hate it.
VERDI: Tell me why you pick on me.
CHORUS: Because you're out of fashion—
    Syncopation is our passion.
VERDI: Really I'm as mad as a man can be.
CHORUS: So are we, so are we.
VERDI: You know it's wrong.
CHORUS: What's wrong? What's wrong?
VERDI: To change my song.
CHORUS: Your song is wrong.
VERDI: 'Twill drive me mad.
CHORUS: Too bad, too bad.
VERDI: You'll have to stop.
CHORUS: No! No! No! No!
VERDI: I ask you not to rag my melody.
CHORUS: You'll never recognize it
    From the way that we'll disguise it.
VERDI: Tell me why, oh why, does it have
    to be?
CHORUS: We're growing weary of your dreary
    little melody—
    That's why we play it the way it ought
    to be.
VERDI: You needn't bother—
    I would rather you let it be.
CHORUS: There's nothing to it;
    We'll do it easily.
VERDI: Please don't.
CHORUS: We will.
VERDI: Don't rag my *Rigoletto.*
CHORUS: We will.
VERDI: Again I say—
CHORUS: What do you say? What do you say?
VERDI: —you'll have to stop.
CHORUS: No!
VERDI: Yes!
CHORUS: No!
VERDI: Yes!
CHORUS: No!
VERDI: Yes!
CHORUS: No! No!
VERDI: Yes! You'll have to stop.
CHORUS: No! No! No! No!
VERDI: Why are you tired of my melody?
CHORUS: We hate to pay admission
    For your dreary composition.
VERDI: It don't sound the same to me.
CHORUS: You'll notice in a minute

That we put some ginger in it.
VERDI: You have changed the harmony.
CHORUS: You must admit it's sweeter
    Even though we change the meter.
VERDI: Won't you spare my poor *Rigoletto?*
CHORUS: Oh, you know, it's slow, and so
    We'll sprinkle on your melody
    A bit of originality.
VERDI: Kindly spare it.
CHORUS: We will tear it.
VERDI: Don't you dare it.
CHORUS: You must bear it.
VERDI: Stop!
CHORUS: We're goin' to rag it.
VERDI: Stop!
CHORUS: We're goin' to rag it.
VERDI: Stop!
CHORUS: We're goin' to rag it.
VERDI: Stop!
CHORUS: We're goin' to rag it.
VERDI: No!
CHORUS: Rag, rag, rag, rag your *Rigoletto.*
VERDI: No!

CHORUS 2

Oh, you *Pagliacci,*
You make a wonderful one-step,
A barrel-of-fun step,
And so before we're through
We'll make a one-step out of you.
We like you, *Pagliacci,*
Because your melody mellow
By Leoncavallo
Affords us something new,
And so we'll one-step to you.

MOVE OVER

Published individually and as part of the show's piano-vocal score. Copyrighted December 5, 1914, and in the piano-vocal score on January 27, 1915. Introduced by Elizabeth Brice (Stella Spark). Dropped during the New York run and replaced by "Homeward Bound" on March 8, 1915.

VERSE 1

A married couple stepped one night
Upon a Pullman train;
It near drove them insane
To hear the man explain:
"An upper berth for both of you

Is all that we can spare,
And so if you don't care,
You both may sleep up there."
They tumbled in that upper berth
At ten o'clock that night,
And soon the porter heard somebody
Yell with all their might:

CHORUS 1

"Move over,
Move over,
Move over, over, over.
This berth is much too small;
I'll fall, I fear—
I'll tumble out, in, under,
Just like a roar of thunder.
Can't you see you're crowding me?
Move over, my dear."

VERSE 2

The other people in the train,
Yelled out, "For goodness' sake!
That awful noise you make
Is keeping us awake."
But just the same they kept it up;
And while they moved around,
We heard an awful sound:
The berth came tumbling down.
They fell upon a fellow
Who was in the lower berth;
He woke up suddenly and yelled
For all that he was worth:

CHORUS 2

"Move over,
Move over,
Move over, over, over!"
The man began to shout,
"Get out of here!"
The porter started grinning;
He shouted, "Seventh inning!"
They stretch'd and then cried out again,
"Move over, my dear."

HOMEWARD BOUND

Published. Copyrighted April 14, 1915. Added to the show on March 8, 1915, replacing "Move Over." Introduced by Elizabeth Brice (Stella Spark) and Charles King (Algy Cuffs) and ensemble.

VERSE 1

When you've packed your grip for a homeward
    trip
And you've started for the train,
There's a feeling grand of a happy brand
That you really can't explain.
"All aboard!" you hear with a welcome ear
As the train speeds o'er the ground.
There's a happiness that you can't express
When you're homeward bound.

CHORUS

Happy, happy, happy, happy,
When you're homeward bound,
Homeward bound.
That's the time you love the rattle of the choo-
    choo hound
O'er the ground.
Doggone, how lovely it feels
To hear those rattling wheels;
It's the grandest kind of sound:
"All aboard, all aboard, step lively!"
Happy, happy, happy, happy,
When you're homeward bound,
Homeward bound.
As you travel on your way,
The rhythm of the engine seems to say,
"We're gettin' nearer to it,
We're gettin' nearer to it,"
When you're homeward bound.

VERSE 2

I have tried to doze but my eyes won't close;
Can't you guess the reason why?
When the clock strikes ten, I'll be home again,
Nevermore to say goodbye.
I don't like the jar of the Pullman car,
As it speeds along the ground;
Still, a Pullman berth is the best on earth
When you're homeward bound.

REPEAT CHORUS

SIMPLE MELODY/ MUSICAL DEMON

Published individually and as part of the show's piano-vocal score. Copyrighted December 2, 1914, and in the piano-vocal score on January 27, 1915. Introduced by Sallie Fisher (Ernesta Hardacre) and Charles King (Algy

Cuffs). During the pre-Broadway tryout the role of Ernesta Hardacre was played by Renee Gratz. Alternate title: "A Simple Melody." The song later was retitled "Play a Simple Melody." The first of Berlin's great double songs. In an early version of the script for *Watch Your Step*, "Musical Demon" (the opening words of the lyric for the countermelody) is listed as a freestanding title. Over the years "Play a Simple Melody" became the most famous song from the score. Successfully recorded by Walter Van Brunt and Mary Carson (Edison Amberol), by Billy Murray and Elsie Baker (under the pseudonym "Edna Brown") (Victor), and years later (1950) by Bing Crosby and Gary Crosby (Decca) and many others.

Simple Melody

VERSE 1

The diff'rent lays of nowadays
All set my brain awhirl;
They're not the kind of songs they sang
When Mother was a girl.
Your spoony rags and coony drags
All made my poor heart ache;
Bring back the rhymes of olden times
And just for old times' sake

CHORUS

Won't you play a simple melody
Like my mother sang to me,
One with good old-fashioned harmony?
Play a simple melody.

VERSE 2

In the days of yore before the war
When hearts now old were young,
At home each night by the firelight
Those dear old songs were sung.
Sweet melodies their memories
Around my heart still cling.
That's why I long to hear a song
Like mother used to sing.

REPEAT CHORUS

Musical Demon

VERSE

I don't care for longhaired musicians
With their classy melodies;

They're all full of high-toned ambitions,
But their music doesn't please.
Give me something snappy and popular,
The kind the darkies play—
Lots of rhythm and I go with 'em,
That's why I say:
Oh you

CHORUS

Musical demon,
Set your honey a-dreamin',
Won't you play me some rag?
Just change that classical nag
To some sweet beautiful drag.
If you will play from a copy
Of a tune that is choppy,
You'll get all my applause,
And that is simply because
I want to listen to rag.
[*The choruses of "Musical Demon" and "Simple Melody" are then sung in counterpoint.*]

WATCH YOUR STEP

There are two surviving songs with this title. The second was published and registered for copyright on April 14, 1915. It was added to the show on March 8, 1915. Introduced by Vernon Castle (Joseph Lilyburn) and ensemble. Not printed in the published piano-vocal score.

Published version

VERSE

Subway guards and motormen
Congregated once again
At the streetcar conductors' annual ball.
Just watch them dancing round the slippery floor,
As they did the year before.
While the band is playing,
The subway guards are saying:

CHORUS

"Watch your step!
Watch your step!"
How those conductors all shout!
"Watch your step!
Watch your step!"
As they go dancing about.
They're such a jolly mob,
That crosstown trolley mob.

Soon they'll all be drinking
Fine Rhine wine.
Look at the fellows who collect your fare—
See them there,
Having the time of their lives;
One and all
At the ball,
Dancing around with their wives.
See the children that they bring up
On the nickels they forget to ring up;
And while the band is playing,
They are saying,
"Watch your step!"

Earlier version

Probably dropped during rehearsals. A lyric typescript was found among Berlin's papers and is now in the Irving Berlin Collection of the Music Division of the Library of Congress.

CHORUS

Watch your step—
I'll introduce you to it.
Watch your step—
I'll teach you how to do it.
Follow me—
One, two, three.
Go slow—
Everybody does it.
If you watch your step,
You'll soon be dancing with 'em.
Watch your step—
You'll find it's in the rhythm
Of that melody—
Just follow me,
But you've got to watch your step.

LOOK AT 'EM DOING IT

Published only in the complete piano-vocal score, which was registered for copyright on January 27, 1915. A new lyric to the melody of the refrain to "The Syncopated Walk." Introduced by entire company. Alternate titles "Finale Act III" (piano-vocal score) and "Look At Them Doing It."

Look at 'em doing it,
Look at 'em doing it,
That syncopated walk.

What do you think of it,
What do you think of it?
We really hope you like it.
Look at the lady fair
Doing it over there—
Don't look at her because
You'll be doing it too.
Before you roam
Back to your home
There's really no denying
That you'll be trying that step;
It's full of pep, full of pep.
And in the morning when you rise
For your morning exercise
You'll take a syncopated walk.

DROPPED AND UNUSED SONGS

WHEN IT'S NIGHTTIME IN DIXIELAND

Published. Copyrighted December 5, 1914. Introduced during the pre-Broadway tryout by Elizabeth Murray (Birdie O'Brien). Dropped before the New York opening.

VERSE 1

Talk about your Arabian Nights,
I must admit they're grand;
But if you long for wonderful nights,
Come down to Dixieland.
That's the dearest place of all,
Listening to the crickets call
When the evening shadows fall
Down in Dixieland.

CHORUS

Nighttime in Dixieland,
Darkies strolling hand in hand,
Southern melodies
Floating on the breeze—
Let me tell you, it's grand;
For when you hear those darkies harmonize,
Tears of gladness fill your eyes:
Baritones and basses

Lounging round the places;
Dixieland embraces the happiest of races—
All you see is smiling faces
When it's nighttime in Dixieland.

VERSE 2

Through the air float the wonderful tunes
Of Mister Whippoorwill.
On the ground dance the bow-legged coons;
They simply can't keep still.
Vet'rans of the Civil War
Telling stories by the score
How they fought in 'sixty-four
Down in Dixieland.

REPEAT CHORUS

I HATE YOU

Published. Copyrighted December 5, 1914. Dropped during rehearsals. Intended for Vernon Castle (Joseph Lilyburn) and Renee Gratz, who was the original Ernesta Hardacre. Berlin used some of the same lyric ideas and phrases of this song in "Outside of That I Love You" from *Louisiana Purchase* (1940).

VERSE

HE: I couldn't love you if I tried for years.
SHE: I never asked you to.
HE: I think that you're the cause of all my fears.
SHE: I think the same of you.
HE: There's quite a lot I despise about you.
SHE: I'm very sorry that we met.
HE: I'd get along very well without you.
SHE: You'd be very easy to forget.

CHORUS

HE: I hate the very ground you walk upon.
SHE: I hate your great big eyes of blue.
HE: I hate the very phone you talk upon.
SHE: I don't give a rap for you.*
HE: I hope you never do.
SHE: I hate the color of your curly hair.

———————

Earlier version of line:
   I don't care if you do.
Another early version of same line:
   I do—I do.

HE: I hate the clothes you wear all through.
SHE: Then besides, I must hate someone,*
      And it might as well be you.

VERSE 2

HE: You're not the girl I want to be my wife.
SHE: I'd never marry you.
HE: You don't mean anything in my young life.
SHE: I never wanted you.
HE: I hate your dress just because you wear it.
SHE: I hate the place where you reside.
HE: Don't ever fret—you will never share it.
SHE: Rest assured I'll never walk inside.

REPEAT CHORUS

LOCK ME IN YOUR HAREM AND THROW AWAY THE KEY

Published. Copyrighted December 5, 1914. Intended for Elizabeth Murray (Birdie O'Brien). Dropped during rehearsals. Alternate title (sheet music cover): "Lock Me in Your Harem and Throw the Key Away."

VERSE 1

In the heart of Cairo the Sultan one day
Nearly lost his life when his horse ran away.
Pat McCann, an Irishman, who happened to be there,
Stopped the horse and saved the Sultan's life by a hair.
The Sultan said, "I'll give you anything I can afford."
Patrick answered, "If you want to give me a reward,

CHORUS

"Lock me in your harem and throw the key away!
Let me cuddle-uddle up to Rosie and May;
Let me see the fat one, who dances all the day.
My eyes were made for seeing,
Honest, I'm a human being;
Down in your harem
There's Rosie, Josie, Posie, and

———————

Earlier version of line:
   For you see I must hate someone

I know that you could spare 'em—
So won't you let me stay
Locked in the harem with the keys thrown away?"

VERSE 2

When the Sultan brushed off his clothes and could speak,
He replied, "You're welcome to stay for a week."
Pat walked in the harem with a smile from ear to ear.
Though the Sultan said a week, he stayed for a year.
The morning after Pat came home his wife began to weep;
He could not explain why he was singing in his sleep:

REPEAT CHORUS

COME TO THE LAND OF THE ARGENTINE

Published. Copyrighted December 2, 1914. Probably dropped during rehearsals.

VERSE 1

Down in the land of the Argentine,
That's where you'll see the fandango
Done in a way that you've never seen;
That's where they started the tango.
But outside of their dancing,
It's a land of entrancing
Romancing as well.

CHORUS

Come to the land of the Argentine,
Where ev'ry girl is a tango queen,
And ev'ry boy is a star with his guitar;
He can play it till you get a thrill with ev'ry bar.
You haven't lived till you've gone and seen
The sunny home of the tambourine,
Where the Spanish Romeos and their Juliets
Lovey-dovey to the tune of their castanets—
I'm pretty certain that you'll be keen
About the land of the Argentine.

VERSE 2

Down in the land of the Argentine,
Home of the fair señorita,

They are the loveliest ever seen,
No girl could ever be sweeter.
Neath the wonderful moonlight
Ev'ry night is a June night
And spoon night as well.

REPEAT CHORUS

I'M GETTING STRONG
FOR YOU

An unused number intended for Elizabeth Brice (Stella Spark) and Charles King (Algy Cuffs). No music is known to survive. A holograph lyric was found among Berlin's papers and is now in the Irving Berlin Collection of the Music Division of the Library of Congress.

VERSE

HE: Honey, I've been exercising
All day long, getting strong.
Every morn I'm in the hall
With a medicine ball.
SHE: Tell me why you're exercising;
I would like to hear.
Kindly put me wise—
Why the exercise?
Tell me, my dear.

CHORUS

I'm getting strong for you,
Strong for you;
I'm throwing a medicine ball
To be in condition when we marry next fall.
You may want to stay out late some night*
And I may not think it right.
In case you ever want to start a fight
I'm getting strong for you.

VERSE 2

SHE: Honey, I've been exercising
Every day, strange to say;
While you played your healthy game,
I was doing the same.

---

*Alternate version of last four lines:
There'll be lots of heavy work for me;
I'll be busy as a bee;
I may have to support a family—
I'm getting strong for you.

HE: Honey, I can't understand it;
Won't you make it clear?
I can't realize
Why you exercise—
Tell me, my dear.

Earlier version

VERSE

Johnny Jones kept exercising,
All day long, getting strong.
You'd always find him in the hall
With a medicine ball.
Johnny's sweetheart called one morning;
Standing by his side,
She said with surprise
And Johnny replied:

CHORUS

"I'm getting strong for you,
Strong for you;
I'm throwing this medicine ball
To be in condition when we marry next fall.
There'll be lots of heavy work to do,
Furnishing a home for two;
My little honey, can't you see it's true
I'm getting strong for you?"

EVENING EXERCISE

Unused. No music is known to survive. A typed lyric was found in Berlin's papers and is now in the Irving Berlin Collection of the Music Division of the Library of Congress. Probably intended for *Watch Your Step*.

CHORUS

Come and take your evening exercise,
Everybody
Come and throw your shoulders to the skies,
Everybody
Cuddle-uddle up to your baby,
Gaze into her eyes.
When you hear those fiddlers
Fiddle-ing, fiddle-ing, on their violins,
You'll be dancing with those other guys.
Everybody
Takes their partners when the leader cries "Rise."
They'll have you doing the one-step,
That brand-new son-of-a-gun step—
Come and take your evening exercise. . . .

THERE'S A FIRE BURNING
DOWN IN MY HEART
(PUT IT OUT—PUT IT OUT—
PUT IT OUT)

Unused. A typed lyric sheet and a pencil sketch of music were found in the *Watch Your Step* folder among Berlin's papers and are now in the Irving Berlin Collection of the Music Division of the Library of Congress.

VERSE

Mister Fireman, Mister Fireman,
Come to me, I implore you.
Mister Fireman, Mister Fireman,
Come, come, there's work before you.
Won't you hurry up, won't you hurry up,
Come quick and I'll adore you.
Heed you—I need you—
Come to me right away.

CHORUS

There's a fire burning down in my heart:
Put it out—put it out—put it out.
Won't you come to my assistance?
I'll make no resistance.
Before it burns to a cinder
Hurry up—hurry up—hurry up.
Get your engine working on it,
Turn the hose of love upon it;
Help—help—help—help,
Fireman, save my heart.

THERE'S A GIRL
ON MY MIND

Unused. Two typed lyric sheets and a pencil sketch of music dated July 13, 1914, were found in the *Watch Your Step* folder among Berlin's papers and are now in the Irving Berlin Collection of the Music Division of the Library of Congress.

VERSE

I'm in a fearful condition;
Something is wrong with my brain.
Don't recommend a physician;
It would be only in vain.

I'll break the news to you gently:
Something has happened of late.
It keeps me suffering ment'ly;
I'm in a terrible state.

CHORUS

There's a girl on my mind,
There's a girl on my mind.
Somehow she made me love her,
And now I'm thinking of her.
No hope for me—where my brain ought to be,*
There's a lady who moved in there,
"A rag, a bone, a hank of hair."
If you could only look inside,
I know that you would find
I'm a chappy unhappy
With a girl on my mind.

WHEN I'M IN LOVE

Unused. Typed lyric sheets and ink lead sheets of music were found in the *Watch Your Step* folder among Berlin's papers and are now in the Irving Berlin Collection of the Music Division of the Library of Congress.

VERSE

I find myself repeating constantly,
"What does the mystic future
Hold in store for me?"
Will I be loved by someone
Just as I hope to be?
Should love become my gift from one,
What will it mean to me?

CHORUS

Will it make me happy
Or will I be sad?
Will it bring thousands of pleasures,
Pleasures that I never had?
Will it come revealing
All that I dreamed of?
Will I find it a blessing
Or very distressing
When I'm in love?

*Alternate version of lines 5 and 6:
    Within my dome there's nobody home
    But a lady who moved in there,

IF THEY WERE ALL LIKE YOU

Unused. A holograph manuscript, an earlier version of the lyric for the chorus, typed lyric sheets, and a copyist's lead sheet of music were found among Berlin's papers and are now in the Irving Berlin Collection of the Music Division of the Library of Congress.

VERSE

I've often wondered, little girlie,
Just exactly what I'd do
If there were many little girlies
In the world as sweet as you.
I've thought the whole thing over;
Now that my thinking's done,
I've come to this conclusion:
I'm glad there's only one.

CHORUS

If every little girl I knew
Happened to be just like you,
I wouldn't know which way to turn
Or just what to do.
If they were all as sweet and charming,
My position would be most alarming,
For I'd be in love with a thousand
If they were all like you.

HUSBANDS—WIVES—SWEETHEARTS

Unused number for station scene. Typed lyric sheets and a copyist's ink piano-vocal score, with lyrics, were found in the *Watch Your Step* folder among Berlin's papers and are now in the Irving Berlin Collection of the Music Division of the Library of Congress.

HUSBANDS: Off to the country Wifey has to
        go—
        Doctor told her so,
        Doctor ought to know—
        Up in the mountains where the
        breezes blow;
        Hubby hates to see her go.
WIVES: Poor little husband must stay in
        town,
        Working the whole day long.
HUSBANDS: He doesn't mind it,
        knowing that his wife

Is in the country getting good and
        strong.
WIVES: Send the check each week and
        don't you make it less, dear.
HUSBANDS: Yes, dear.
WIVES: Don't you leave the children out of
        sight.
HUSBANDS: All right.
WIVES: Don't forget to pay the tailor for
        my dress, dear.
HUSBANDS: Yes, dear.
WIVES: Promise that you won't go out at
        night.
HUSBANDS: I promise.
WIVES: Don't go to a Broadway chorus
        show, dear.
HUSBANDS: No, dear.
WIVES: Should the baby cry, give her a pill.
HUSBANDS: I will.
WIVES: Don't you linger near a bar.
HUSBANDS: I won't go where they are.
WIVES: And now I want to hear you say
        You hate to see me go away.
HUSBANDS: Now that you're leaving the parting
        gives me pain—
        Hurry or you'll miss the train.
PORTERS: All aboard, all aboard!
HUSBANDS: [*wiping eyes with kerchiefs*]
        Goodbye, dear.
WIVES: Don't cry, dear.
PORTERS: All aboard, all aboard!
HUSBANDS
& WIVES: Goodbye.
HUSBANDS: They're gone—they're gone—my
        wife's gone to the country.
        They're gone—they're gone—my
        wife's gone to the country.

[WIVES *have entered gates to train.*]

HUSBANDS: [*taking telephones*]
        Hello, central?
        It's the same old fellow, central.
        Won't you please connect me
        With you-know-who-I-mean?
        Is that you, dear?
        This is Mr. You-Know-Who, dear.
        I'm a lonesome hubby—be clubby
        And hurry to the scene.
        I'm at the station, dear—
        A cab will bring you here.

CHORUS

Won't you please come over—come over—come
over?
I'll be all in clover the moment you arrive.
We'll take in all the sights,

For tonight's the night of nights—
We'll paint the city so pretty.
My wife's gone to the country, hurray, hurray—
So won't you please come over,
Come over right away?

HUSBANDS: [*pounding on their receivers*]
Hello, central?
It's the same old fellow, central.
Won't you please contact
    me with Rector's cabaret?
That you, Rector?
This is Mr. Home Neglector.
Please reserve a table—I'm able
To more than pay my way.
Put lots of wine on ice—
The devil with the price.

[HUSBANDS *hang up receivers. A piano plays as the second half of chorus swells out and the* HUSBANDS *greet their* SWEETHEARTS.]

SWEETHEARTS: Here we are, dear.
HUSBANDS: Come and jump into a car, dear.
SWEETHEARTS: Let us know the program.
HUSBANDS: It's all of that, you bet.
SWEETHEARTS: That's exciting.
HUSBANDS: Don't you think it sounds
    inviting?
SWEETHEARTS: We had better hurry.
HUSBANDS: Don't worry.
SWEETHEARTS: You're married, don't forget.
HUSBANDS: Of that there is no doubt.
SWEETHEARTS: Your wifey may find out.
HUSBANDS: She will not discover.
SWEETHEARTS: You love 'er.
HUSBANDS: [*sarcastically*]
I love 'er.
SWEETHEARTS: Keep it under cover.
HUSBANDS: Don't let that bother you.
SWEETHEARTS: 'Twould make her very cross.
HUSBANDS: Don't forget that I'm the boss.
SWEETHEARTS: Somehow I'm leery.
HUSBANDS: But, dearie,
I sent her to the country.
SWEETHEARTS: Hurrah.
HUSBANDS: I'm glad that you came over.
ALL: [*starting to exit*]
Now let's be on our way.

[WIVES, *having missed their trains, enter through the gates and catch* HUSBANDS *and* SWEETHEARTS *as they are about to exit arm in arm.*]

WIVES: Stop!
SWEETHEARTS: [*to* HUSBANDS, *who haven't seen* WIVES]
Look!
WIVES: Listen, what does all this mean?

HUSBANDS: Holy mackerel, it's our wives!
WIVES: You will pay us with your lives.
HUSBANDS: We sent you to the country.
WIVES: But we missed the train.
HUSBANDS: Another train leaves later, dear.
WIVES: The train will leave but we'll
    stay here.
Won't you please come over—
    come over—come over?
Thought you was in clover
But now you're just in bad.
Who are those dressed-up
    squabs?
HUSBANDS: They're just asking us for jobs.
They all typewrite, dear.
WIVES: What? At night, dear?
HUSBANDS: It's lovely in the country.
WIVES: Nay, nay—we stay.
Come home—we'll talk it over.

[*Exit to funeral march.*]

WHEN I GET BACK TO MY HOMETOWN

Typed lyric sheets and pencil holograph manuscripts were found among Berlin's papers and are now in the Irving Berlin Collection of the Music Division of the Library of Congress. There are two versions of this lyric and an earlier lyric with the same title set to different music. A folder of material related to *Watch Your Step* contained a music manuscript (probably in the hand of Clifford Hess) titled "Home Town," which fit verse and chorus of the later version.

VERSE

I left home a year ago
To go trouping with a show.
If I knew then what I know,
I'd have stayed home with my mother.
Traveling with a number-three
Small-town-playing company
Isn't what it's cracked to be;
I should have picked another.
But playing towns not on the map
Will bring me home again;
I'm waiting for this troupe to play
My own hometown, and then:

CHORUS 1

When I get back to my hometown,
I'll tell my mother that I'm through with traveling
    round.
I'm tired of sneaking out of boardinghouses
Through the side-street door;
Working in the chorus
Is what Sherman said about war.
I wasn't meant to be a clown;
I've had enough, and now
I'm strong for settling down.
So if the boy I left behind
Hasn't gone and changed his mind,
I'll be married in my hometown.

CHORUS 2

When I get back to my hometown,
I'll tell my mother that I'm through with traveling
    round;
I'm tired of dancing in the chorus
With the merry, merry mob.
You must keep your figure if
You want to keep your job.
I'm very strong for settling down;
Although my mother thought
I'd make a regular clown,
I'll tell my ma the manager
Didn't think the same as her
When I get back to my hometown.

Alternate version

VERSE 1

Simple little Mary Snow,*
Living out in Kokomo,
Thought that traveling with a show
On the road could not be grander.
Though her friends said "No, no,
Mary, you stay home and sew,"
Mary left her home to go
Out with a one-night-stander.
I met her in a one-horse town
Where everything looked dead;†

---

*Earlier version of lines 1–4:
    Simple little Mary Snow
    Thought she'd like to join a show,
    So she left her home to go
    With a patched-up one-night-stander.

†Earlier version of lines 9 and 10:
    I met her in a town where even
    Angels fear to tread;

I asked her how she liked the life,
And simple Mary said:

CHORUS 1

"When I get back to my hometown,
I'll tell my mother that I'm through with traveling
    round;
I'm tired of sneaking out of boardinghouses
Through the side-street door—
Traveling with this troupe
Is just what Sherman said of war.
I'm very strong for settling down;
Although my mother thought I'd make a regular
    clown,
I'll tell my ma the manager
Didn't think the same as her
When I get back to my hometown."

VERSE 2

Mary said, "What can I do?
I am understudy to
Our prima donna, who
Doesn't know what I've forgotten.
Go and ask most any jay
Who has been to see the play
How he liked it and he'll say,
'Gosh, but the show was rotten!'
But playing towns not on the map
Will bring me home again;
I'm waiting for this troupe to play
My own hometown, and then:

CHORUS 2

"When I get back to my hometown,
I'll tell my mother that I'm through with traveling
    round.
I'm tired of dancing in the chorus,
With the merry, merry mob;
You must keep your figure
If you want to keep your job.
I wasn't meant to be a clown;
Just bet your life that there'll be no one keeping
    me down
As understudy to a she
Who should understudy me
When I get back to my hometown."

Earlier version with different music

Give my regards to Hiram Brown, the grocery
    man;

Just shake his hand—he'll understand.
Remember me to Hiram's daughter, Miss Mary
    Ann;
Tell her if she sent me a letter
I'd surely feel much better.
Go and see my father, Joe,
And let him know
I need a hundred or so.
Now, don't forget, tell them all you can.
Kiss my mother for me
When you get back
When you get back
To my hometown.

CARUSO SONG

Probably intended for the opera scene in *Watch Your Step*. Early versions of the script indicate that there was a Caruso song in that scene and that it involved a jewelry theft. No music appears to have survived. Ink holograph manuscripts of the lyric were found among Berlin's papers and are now in the Irving Berlin Collection of the Music Division of the Library of Congress. Alternate title: "Finale."

CARUSO: Tell me, what does all this mean?
CHORUS: We're here to separate you
    From your dough or 'ssasinate
        you.
CARUSO: You're the worst I've ever seen.
CHORUS: Our home is in the ghetto
    Where they swing a mean stiletto.
CARUSO: But you cannot frighten me.
CHORUS: If you refuse to pony,
    You'll eat no more macaroni.
CARUSO: I'm as tough, as tough
    As a guy could be.
CHORUS: So are we—so are we.
CARUSO: Go on your way.
CHORUS: Nay, nay, nay, nay.
CARUSO: You mean to say?
CHORUS: Until you pay.
CARUSO: On that you're set?
CHORUS: You bet—you bet.
CARUSO: You'd better go.
CHORUS: No, no, no, no.
CARUSO: I'll call assistance here
    With my high C.
CHORUS: We'll put you on a diet
    Made of bullets if you try it.

CARUSO: There's a dozen cops
    Always watching me.
CHORUS: Now stop your stalling—
    We're not falling
    For the copper salve.
    So don't get funny—
    The money
    We've got to have.
CARUSO: You'll never get it
    To your credit—
    I refuse to pay.
CHORUS: We'll send your body
    To Scotti
    Without delay.
CARUSO: Stand back.
CHORUS: We won't.
CARUSO: Don't lay a hand upon me.
CHORUS: We will.
CARUSO: Again I say—
CHORUS: What do you say?
    What do you say?
CARUSO: —you'll have to go.
CHORUS: No, no, no, no.
CARUSO: This strain will give my voice
    An awful blow.
CHORUS: We've got an ear for music,
    Even though it's making you
        sick.
CARUSO: Otto Kahn will fail, I know.
CHORUS: The Century show's a hit;
    The managers admitted it.
CARUSO: Why do you advertise that
        show?
CHORUS: It's in the lyric, damn it—
    Berlin wants to Dillingham it.
CARUSO: Really, this attack is an outrage.
CHORUS: Show the dough and out we go,
    Or we'll cut out your melody
    That's full of originality.
CARUSO: I can't bear you.
CHORUS: We will tear you.
CARUSO: I just dare you.
CHORUS: We won't spare you.
CARUSO: Stop.
CHORUS: We're gonna kill him.
CARUSO: Stop.
CHORUS: We're gonna kill him,
    We're gonna kill him.
CARUSO: Stop.
CHORUS: We're gonna kill him.
CARUSO: No.
CHORUS: Yes, yes, yes, yes—
    Get ready to die.
CARUSO: Pagliacci———
[*Curtain.*]

Songs of 1915 and
STOP! LOOK! LISTEN! | 1915

ALL SHE DOES IS SIT AROUND THE HOUSE

Written in early 1915. No music is known to survive. A typed lyric sheet was found among Berlin's papers and is now in the Irving Berlin Collection of the Music Division of the Library of Congress.

VERSE 1

I've got a sister and she's an old maid;
No men have kissed her, because they're afraid.
Wrinkled and houseworn is she,
Old-fashioned as she can be.
Mother and father would like her to wed,
But she would rather stay single instead.
Other folks have son-in-laws,
But they'll never have one, because:

CHORUS

All she does is sit around the house,
Driving ev'ryone mad.
There she sits as quiet as a mouse,
Dressed in a calico apron and blouse.
Mother takes a fit around the house;
So does Brother and Dad.
Loudly they shout, "Mary, go out!
You can't raise a family sitting around the house."

VERSE 2

We had a neighbor, a very nice man,
Willing to labor for our Mary Ann.
Somehow he soon changed his mind,
Leaving these few words behind:
"Mary needs airing, without any doubt
She would be wearing my furniture out."
He had the wedding ring bought
But wasn't as brave as we thought.

REPEAT CHORUS

Joseph Santley and the Magazine Girls: Autumn (Evelyn Conway), Winter (Hazel Lewis), Spring (Eleanor St. Clair), and Summer (Marion Davies) in Stop! Look! Listen!

THE VOICE OF BELGIUM

Published. Copyrighted March 9, 1915.

VERSE 1

There's a land where hearts are aching
And eyes are wet with tears;
It's the land where hearts start breaking
When the smoke of battle clears.
There's a voice that seems to haunt me
When the shades of night appear;
'Tis the mournful voice of Belgium
Ringing in my ear.

CHORUS

I hear the voice of Belgium
Calling far across the sea.
I speak of wives and mothers
Waiting patiently;
I hear the cries of children praying,
Sad as they could be;
I can hear them say,
"Please send my daddy back to me."

VERSE 2

Hear a voice that rings with sorrow;
It mournfully imparts
That the news of each tomorrow
Means a thousand broken hearts.
See a hand stretched out for mercy
With a plea to every man;
'Tis the call of help from Belgium—
Answer, if you can.

REPEAT CHORUS

I'M GOING BACK TO THE FARM

Published. Copyrighted March 23, 1915. According to *Variety*, the song was first sung in public by Irving Berlin during an afternoon at the Strand Roof Garden on February 28, 1915; it was sung again by Berlin in *Watch Your Step* on March 6, 1915, the hundredth performance of the show. The number did not remain in the show and was not printed in the published piano-vocal score.

VERSE 1

Down into town with a grip on his arm,
Boob, Mister Rube, landed in from the farm;
He came to see if the farmer was right
Who said, "This is the life."
Soon, like a loon, he was dancing about;
One week of fun found him all tired out.
They asked him what he thought of the city
And they heard old Reuben shout:

CHORUS 1

"Dancing around till the break of day
Never was meant for a rube or a jay.
I've seen it all and I'm ready to say,
I'm going back to the farm.
Cabaret life is an awful disgrace;
I've checked my hat till I'm blue in the
    face—
I've handed out a fortune
For a Prince Albert and an old fedora.
I love the cows and the chickens,
The chickens you love to eat,
Not those you have to treat—
I'm going back to the farm."

VERSE 2

Si said goodbye, for he couldn't remain,
Thought that he ought to be taking a train,
Glad that he had just enough for a ticket
To take him back home.
When home again all the neighbors appeared,
Ate until late, when the table was cleared.
He told them what he thought of the city
As he gently milked his beard:

CHORUS 2

"Dancing around till the break of day
Never was meant for a rube or a jay.
I've seen it all and I'm ready to say,
I'm going back to the farm.
Cabaret life is an awful disgrace;
I've checked my hat till I'm blue in the
    face—
I went to wash my hands with water;
I had to give the boy a quarter.
What good are Broadway chickens
With beautiful fancy legs
'Less they can lay some eggs?
I'm going back to the farm."

SI'S BEEN DRINKING CIDER

Published. Copyrighted March 25, 1915.

VERSE 1

"What's the matter? What's the matter?"
Shouted Farmer Brown
As he saw a crowd of people
Rushing through the town.
"Is the town on fire
Or has someone met* their death?"
One old rube looked up at him
And cried all out of breath:

CHORUS 1

"Si's been drinking cider,
And he's acting like a fool!
Take his wife and hide 'er,
For he's li'ble to treat her cru'l.
He's acting mighty gay;
He gave his Ingersoll away.
Oh! Oh! Oh! Oh!
What will the neighbors say?
He told a naughty story
To the parson in the hall;
Parson knew the answer,
So he didn't laugh at all.
The constable and sheriff
Have locked him in the barn;
But Si's been drinking cider,
So he don't give a good gosh-darn."

VERSE 2

Hiram Perkins heard the news and
My, but he was vexed!
Mumbled to himself, "I wonder
What will happen next?"
Told his wife that right before
She rang the dinner bell;
"No use talking, Mary Jane,
The country's gone to hell."

CHORUS 2

"Si's been drinking cider,
And he's acting like a fool!
Take his wife and hide 'er,
For he's li'ble to treat her cru'l.
He's acting mighty gay;

The word "next," which appeared instead of "met" in the published sheet music, is clearly incorrect.

He gave his Ingersoll away.
Oh! Oh! Oh! Oh!
What will the neighbors say?
He told an untrue story
Of a chicken with one leg
Drinking boiling water
And it laid a hard-boiled egg.
The sheriff won't believe it;
He claims it is a yarn.
But Si's been drinking cider,
And he don't give a good gosh-darn."

MY BIRD OF PARADISE

Published. Copyrighted April 2, 1915. Introduced by Blossom Seeley at the Winter Garden Theatre, New York. A big hit. Number-one-selling recording by the Peerless Quartet (Victor). Sung in the London Production of *Watch Your Step* by Ethel Levey.

VERSE 1

In Honolulu far away
A maiden who could not be gay
Is feeling so much better
Since she received a letter.
From her Hawaiian lover came
A little tender note;
She's so excited and so delighted,
For this is what he wrote:

CHORUS

Wait for me,
My Honolulu girl,
My hula-hula girl,
I'm coming back to you.
That sunny skyland Hawaiian island
Will soon be my land.
I hear a ukulele strumming gaily;
In my dreams you seem to say to me,
"Come back and play to me
That melody oh, so nice!"
So if you love me still,
My things I'll pack again;
Then I'll be coming back again
To you, my bird of Paradise.

VERSE 2

In Honolulu by the sea
A maiden's waiting patiently;
And as a ship goes past her,

Her little heart beats faster.
He'll soon be landing at the pier;
She's waiting for the boat.
He won't forget her, for in his letter
Her sweet Hawaiian wrote:

REPEAT CHORUS

WHILE THE BAND PLAYED AN AMERICAN RAG

Published. Copyrighted April 7, 1915.

VERSE 1

I had a wonderful dream last night;
I never saw such a lovely sight.
I dreamt that the warring nations were at a ball.
There wasn't anyone talking fight;
They realized that it wasn't right.
And this is just what I noticed
In the hall:

CHORUS

The king of England danced
With the president of France;
The crown prince of Germany
Danced with the king of Hungary.
They all laid down their swords
While the diff'rent dukes and lords all shouted,
"We don't want any more talk of war talk."
They started drinking to each other
Like brothers;
They drank a toast to each other's flag.
The Russian czar said to the Kaiser,
"Let's drink some Budweiser";
Then he shook his hand while a German band
Played an American, made-in-America,
An American rag.

VERSE 2

The Russian czar wet his lips with wine,
Then started whistling the "Wacht am Rhein."
The Kaiser sang "Tipperary" without a pause.
They kept it up till the break of day;
Then when they started to go away,
The whole world rang out with gladness,
Just because

REPEAT CHORUS

WHEN I LEAVE THE WORLD BEHIND

Published. Copyrighted May 15, 1915. "Respectfully dedicated to the memory of Charles Lounsbury whose legacy suggested this song." On the original sheet music covers there is a large photograph of Al Jolson. Leading recordings by Henry Burr (Victor) and Sam Ash (Columbia).

Irving Berlin, in the *New York Times*, January 2, 1916:

Some years ago Wilson Mizner and I were discussing verse. We often get together and talk about unusual poems we have seen, not the poems of the big poets, but stray selections we have run across. Mizner told me that night of one he had read of a pauper who, when he died, left a will in which he bequeathed the sunshine, flowers, and other beautiful things of the world to various classes. "There's a great idea for a song in that!" I told him, "and I would give a lot for the rights to it." But he didn't remember where he had read it and although he tried to locate it he couldn't find it.

Then last year at the Selwyn party Bob Davis, editor of *Munsey's*, and I were talking about the same subject and I told him of the pauper and his strange will. "You don't have to look any further for that," he said, "I published it myself and will send you a copy of the magazine it was in." It was not a poem, but an article that told the story of Charles Lounsbury, a Chicago lawyer who died penniless and left such a will. So I dedicated my ballad to Charles Lounsbury, because I had borrowed his idea and put it in bad verse to catch the royalties.

Irving Berlin, letter to Abel Green, editor of *Variety*, May 21, 1945:

Many years ago Wilson Mizner told me of a famous will that was made by one Charles Lounsberry [*sic*].

He was an attorney and after giving away his law books, which were his only possessions, he proceded to give away the stars, the moon, the milky way for children to wonder at, and "all the best things in life that were free." This was the inspiration for a song I wrote many years ago called "When I Leave the World Behind." I believed there had been a Charles Lounsberry so dedicated the song, and all the copies bear this inscription: "Respectfully dedicated to the memory of Charles A. Lounsberry [*sic*]." You can imagine the great shock and disillusionment when I found out that the will had been written by someone to be included in a pamphlet for an insurance company! This story is included in the Alexander Woollcott biography.

On December 12, 1967, Philip C. Duschnes, a New York rare-book dealer, wrote Berlin as follows:

Dear Mr. Berlin,

I have followed with interest Earl Wilson's comments on Charles Lounsbury and his will, which inspired your great song, "When I Leave the World Behind."

I was particularly interested in Friday's *New York Post*, December 8 and that statement that Alexander Woollcott concluded that there never was such a will nor any Charles Lounsbury.

As you will see on pages 47 to 57 of the accompanying book, *The New Colophon*, January, 1948, there was such a will and it was written by Williston Fish and it was first published in *Harper's Weekly*, September 3, 1898. There were many subsequent publications, all cited by the author of this fine article, Jacob Blanck, 19 Riverside Road, Chestnut Hill, Mass.

It is surprising that Alexander Woollcott came to his unusual conclusion, "that the story was a piece of advertising copy written for a bank." The text and many printings were known in many bookshops for a great many years. I hope that you will find Mr. Blanck's authoritative article of interest.

With all good wishes for the holiday season,

Very sincerely yours,
Philip C. Duschnes

VERSE 1

I know a millionaire
Who's burdened down with care;
A load is on his mind.
He's thinking of the day
When he must pass away
And leave his wealth behind.
I haven't any gold
To leave when I grow old;
Somehow it passed me by.
I'm very poor, but still
I'll leave a precious will
When I must say goodbye.

CHORUS

I'll leave the sunshine to the flowers,
I'll leave the springtime to the trees;
And to the old folks I'll leave the mem'ries
Of a baby upon their knees.
I'll leave the nighttime to the dreamers,

I'll leave the songbirds to the blind;
I'll leave the moon above
To those in love
When I leave the world behind,
When I leave the world behind.

VERSE 2

To ev'ry wrinkled face
I'll leave a fireplace
To paint their fav'rite scene:
Within the golden rays
Scenes of their childhood days
When they were sweet sixteen.
I'll leave them each a song
To sing the whole day long
As toward the end they plod.
To ev'ry broken heart
With sorrow torn apart
I'll leave the love of God.

REPEAT CHORUS

ARABY

Published. Copyrighted July 28, 1915. Leading recording by Harry MacDonough (Victor).

VERSE

Tonight I'm dreaming of Araby;
That's where my dreams seem to carry me—
Where ev'rything is Oriental
And ev'ryone is sentimental.
There in the shade of the shelt'ring palms
I met a maiden fair;
I long to hold her gently in my arms—
Oh, how I wish I were there!

CHORUS

Araby, when shades of night appear
I seem to hear you calling;
Araby, you seem to beckon, and I reckon
I'll be hurrying back again.
Seems to me a maiden's face appears;
I see her tears are falling, falling,
Because I left her there.
That's why I long to be
Where all those happy faces wait for me
Beside the fair oasis.
Soon you'll see,

Within a caravan, an Arab man will take me
Over the desert back to Araby.

VERSE 2

Someday you'll find me in Araby,
Where someone's waiting to marry me.
I can't forget the day we parted;
She said I left her brokenhearted.
I helped her onto a camel's back;
Before she rode away,
She made me promise that I would come back—
I'll keep my promise someday.

REPEAT CHORUS

COHEN OWES ME NINETY-SEVEN DOLLARS

Published. Copyrighted August 27, 1915. In a letter of April 27, 1967, to theatre historian Marian S. Thompson, author of *The Palace*, Berlin wrote that Belle Baker introduced this song during a vaudeville engagement at the Palace Theatre, New York.

VERSE 1

Old Man Rosenthal lay sick in bed;
Soon the doctor came around and said,
"No use crying, the man is dying,
He can't live very long."
"Send my son here to my side,"
They heard the old man say;
"I've got something to tell him
Before I pass away."
Soon his son was sitting by his bed;
"What's the matter, Papa dear?" he said.
The old man said,
"My son, before my days are done, I want you to
    know,

CHORUS 1

"Cohen owes me ninety-seven dollars,
And it's up to you to see that Cohen pays.
I sold a lot of goods to Rosenstein and Sons
On an IOU for ninety days;
Levi Brothers don't get any credit—
They owe me for a hundred yards of lace.
If you promise me, my son,
You'll collect from every one,
I can die with a smile upon my face."

VERSE 2

Old Man Rosenthal is better now;
He just simply wouldn't die somehow.
He is healthy and very wealthy
Since he got out of bed.
Such a change you never saw;
He's got such rosy cheeks.
He picks up in just one week—
That should take weeks and weeks.
Everyone who knew that he was sick
Couldn't tell why he got well so quick.
They went and asked him to explain
How he pulled through; Rosenthal replied:

CHORUS 2

"Cohen owed me ninety-seven dollars,
And my son went out and made poor Cohen pay.
A bill was owed to me by Rosenstein and Sons,
And they settled on that very day.
What could my son do with all that money*
If I should leave it all and say goodbye?
It's all right to pass away;
But when people start to pay,
That's no time for a businessman to die."

I LOVE TO STAY AT HOME

Published. Copyrighted August 30, 1915.

VERSE 1

I don't go out nights;
I'm not about nights.
I'll tell you why I never roam:
I love my home, so cozy.
The dizzy nightlife
May be the right life,
But I don't like that kind of fun
At night when my work is done.

CHORUS

I just love to stay at home in the evening
When the winter nights are cold.

Earlier version of lines 5–9:
    What would my son do with all that money
    If I should die and leave it all behind?
    I made up my mind to die;
    But when the money caught my eye,
    I jumped up from the bed and changed my mind."

I love to sit around the fire harmonizing
"Darling, I Am Growing Old."
While Mother darns
My father's woolen hosiery,
He's telling yarns
Of how he fought in 'sixty-three.
I don't envy the cocktail sippers—
Give me my carpet slippers,
For I love to stay at home.

VERSE 2

My cousin Mary,
She's a canary;
Each night she sings the Rosary—
It sounds to me like Melba.
When Uncle Louie,
Who looks like Dewey,
Recites "The Picture on the Wall,"
It's simply heaven, that's all.

REPEAT CHORUS

WHEN YOU'RE DOWN IN LOUISVILLE CALL ON ME

Published. Copyrighted November 19, 1915. Leading recording by vaudeville singer Anna Chandler (Columbia).

VERSE 1

Goodbye, ev'rybody,
I'm on my way to Louisville.
I feel oh, so happy,
I hardly can keep still.
Although my home is very small,
I invite you all;
If you will come,
You'll be welcome
Any time you call.

CHORUS

Don't forget, don't forget,
When you're down in Louisville,
Louisville, Louisville,
Just call around—
I'll be found in the town directory.
I'll have the table set,
No fancy dishes,
But the things you get will all be delicious;

And you're just as welcome as can be.
When you get there, take a jitney bus,
Call on us;
I'll have you see the family.
If you're ever so lucky to be down in Kentucky,
Don't forget to stop at Louie-, Louie-,
Louisville, and call on me.

VERSE 2

Listen, ev'rybody,
We've got the fairest women there—
Lovely dispositions
And locks of golden hair;
They've got complexions like the rose,
Ev'ry body knows.
Nature made them;
We parade them,
Dressed in simple clothes.

REPEAT CHORUS

STOP! LOOK! LISTEN! (1915)

Tryout: Forrest Theatre, Philadelphia, December 1, 1915. New York run: Globe Theatre; opened December 25, 1915; 105 performances. Lyrics and music by Irving Berlin. Produced by Charles Dillingham. Book by Harry B. Smith. Staged by R. H. Burnside. Orchestra under the direction of Robert Bowers and Frank E. Tours. Orchestrations by Frank Saddler. Cast: starring Gaby Desiys and featuring Walter Wills, Frank Lalor, Justine Johnstone, Florence Morrison, James Doyle and Harland Dixon, Harry Fox, Joseph Santley, Florence Tempest and Marion Sunshine, Harry Pilcer and Blossom Seeley. One of the Magazine Girls was Marion Davies. London production under the title *Follow the Crowd* opened at the Empire Theatre, February 19, 1916.

THESE ARE THE COSTUMES THE MANAGER SELECTED

The only source for the music and lyrics is the original piano-vocal score in the R. H. Burnside Collection of the Music Division of the New York Public Library for the Performing Arts. Introduced by ensemble. Alternate title: "Opening Chorus Act I."

GIRLS: These are the costumes the manager
    selected.
    They all have been inspected;
    They had to be corrected
    Before they were perfected.
    The manager knows
    That the shows that are successes
    Are made so by the dresses
    That are worn by the chorus girls.
    They must be of the latest fashion,
    And each a perfect fit;
    They help to bring the cash in
    And make the show a hit.
    If the show's a bloomer,
    They blame the costumer:
    So you see how very necessary
    The costumes are for the merry,
      merry chorus.
    And now we'll bring on the dear
      little fellows
    Who designed them;
    We're pretty sure you'll find them
    The nicest little fellows you've ever
      seen.

DESIGNERS: That costume is a perfect fit, my dear,
    And you're a perfect dream in it, my
      dear.
    'Twill make them notice you a bit,
      my dear—
    I'm glad you left it all to Percy.
    Oh, mercy!
    I'm simply mad about the color
      scheme:
    The lines bring out your—you know
      what I mean.
    That costume's a creation;
    'Twill be a big sensation—
    Wait till they see it, my dear.

PAGES: There are some gentlemen outside
    To see the ladies.

GIRLS: Show them in here,
    Show them in here,
    Show them in here, do!

PAGES: They wish to take them for a ride,
    The charming ladies.

GIRLS: Show them in here,
    Show them in here,
    Show them in here, do!

BOYS: Good afternoon, dear, won't you
      come for a ride?
    There's an automobile outside.
    Won't you come for a spin
    In my brand-new runabout?

GIRLS: No thank you!
    Sir, I couldn't go for a ride,
    Because I must be careful,
    Mother told me,
    To keep away from the fellow
    Who owns an automobile.

BOYS: There's really nothing to fear.

GIRLS: The neighbors may observe us.

BOYS: Don't worry, dear.

GIRLS: Joyriding makes me nervous.

BOYS: I promise not to go fast.

GIRLS: That's what the last one said,
    And he went sixty miles an hour.

BOYS: You drive the car.

GIRLS: I fear I'd make a blunder.

BOYS: We won't go far.

GIRLS: Then you'd get out and get under.

BOYS: Don't be nervous;
    I'm here at your service
    To take you for a motor ride—
    It's a lovely day outside.

GIRLS: Good afternoon!

BOYS: Come along, dear.

GIRLS: Good afternoon!

BOYS: Come along, dear.

GIRLS: Good afternoon!

ALL: Goodbye!

BLOW YOUR HORN

Published. Copyrighted December 10, 1915. Introduced by Walter Wills (Owen Coyne) and girls.

VERSE 1

Barnum and Bailey were wonderful showmen—
In the theatrical world, there are no men
Who would claim to be their equal;
And the sequel
Was they made the tin, packed them in ev'ry
    season.
I know it well, and I'll tell you the reason:
They were a pair of handbill throwers,
Horn blowers—
You must talk about yourself
Or they'll put you on the shelf.

CHORUS

Blow your horn,
Let 'em know you're comin';
Blow your horn,
That'll start 'em hummin'.
Just make a whole lot of noise;

The only way to collar ev'ry dollar
Is to holler.
Mister Barnum said,
Ev'ry other minute
There's another one born.
You'll strike it
Just like Barnum;
Make 'em like it,
Gosh darn 'em—
Yell out, you'll sell out
If you'll only blow your horn.

VERSE 2

Some people argue against advertising;
How they can feel as they do is surprising.
I'm a walking eight-sheet poster—
I'm a boaster.
The Red, White, and Blue and its value was
    doubted
Till Georgie Coh'n started singing about it;
Now ev'ryone who was against it
Commenced it.
You will be a household word
If you just make yourself heard.

REPEAT CHORUS

WHY DON'T THEY GIVE US A CHANCE

Introduced by Gaby Deslys (Gaby, "only a chorus girl now, but just wait") and girls. The only source for the music and lyrics is the original piano-vocal score in the R. H. Burnside Collection of the Music Division of the New York Public Library for the Performing Arts. According to musical theatre historian Steven Suskin (*Show Tunes* [New York: Dodd, Mead, 1986], p. 82), this song was "advertised" on the cover of sheet music for *Stop! Look! Listen!* "but not published." Alternate title (program): "Give Us a Chance."

VERSE

Why don't they give the chorus girl
A chance to make a start?
Why do they say "Don't bore us, girl,
You couldn't play a part"?
Why do they hide us behind a star
Who hums around in her motorcar?
She was a merry "tra-la-la"
Before she played a part.

CHORUS

Why don't they give us a chance?
Why don't they give us a chance?
Why don't they do something for us
And take us out of the chorus?
Managers don't seem to care;
Why don't they help us to advance?
To be a chorus girl is oh such a bore;
It's just what Sherman said about war.
They may discover another Ethel Barrymore
If they give us a chance.

I LOVE TO DANCE

Music alone published in the piano selections for the 1916 London production of *Follow the Crowd*. The only source for both music and lyrics is the original piano-vocal score in the R. H. Burnside Collection of the Music Division of the New York Public Library for the Performing Arts. According to musical theatre historian Steven Suskin (*Show Tunes* [New York: Dodd, Mead, 1986], p. 82), this song was "advertised" on the cover of sheet music for *Stop! Look! Listen!* "but not published." Introduced in *Stop! Look! Listen!* by Gaby Deslys (Gaby), Harry Pilcer (Anthony St. Anthony), and ensemble.

VERSE

HE: How do you like the way I make love?
    Isn't it simply divine?
SHE: Love's not the only thing a man must know
    To be a sweetheart of mine.
HE: Oh, tell me what I have to do
    My value to enhance.
SHE: The man who wants to be my beau
    Must know how to dance.

CHORUS

I love to dance,
I love to dance—
I'd rather two-step than eat.
Give me a partner and a ballroom floor
And I'd ask for nothing more.
Show me a step
Full of the pep,
Show me and I'll take a chance.
I love to spin around until I'm all out of breath,
Vernon Castle myself to death—
Twirl me about,
Tire me out,
Because I'm simply crazy to dance.

AND FATHER WANTED ME TO LEARN A TRADE

Published. Copyrighted January 13, 1916. Introduced by Harry Fox (Abel Connor).

VERSE 1

When I was young, my father said to me,
"Learn a trade, learn a trade.
Do me a favor and become an engraver,
For engravers are well paid."
If I'd have done what Father wanted,
Imagine what I'd miss.
There is no doubt
I was cut out
For a life like this.

CHORUS 1

I come around to the theatre in my automobile
Singing, "This is the life, this is the life."
Surrounded by chorus ladies in the troupe,
I spend all my time in a chicken coop.
They come to my dressing room, as cute as can be,
Saying, "Won't you hook up my dress for me?"
And it makes me mad to think my dear old dad
Wanted me to learn a trade.

VERSE 2

When I come out with lots of powder
Upon my sleeve, on my sleeve,
Somebody rested on my new double-breasted,
I believe you've got me, Steve.
I always kiss the prima donna
In ev'ry scene we act:
Leave it to me,
That has to be—
It's in my contract.

CHORUS 2

I leave the show ev'ry evening in my automobile
Singing, "This is the life, this is the life."
My supper consists of chicken à la king;
I get indigestion and ev'rything.
A ring on my finger with a four-carat stone—
Twenty payments more and it's all my own.
And it makes me mad to think my dear old dad
Wanted me to learn a trade.

THE GIRL ON THE MAGAZINE

Published. Copyrighted December 21, 1915. Introduced by Joseph Santley (Van Cortlandt Parke) and the "Four Seasons"—Eleanor St. Clair (Spring), Marion Davies (Summer), Evelyn Conway (Autumn), and Hazel Lewis (Winter). Top-selling recording by Harry Mac-Donough (Victor), the flip side of Billy Murray's number-one hit "I Love a Piano": this coupling was the first double-sided number-one hit record. Alternate title: "The Girl on the Magazine Cover."

Letter from Eileen (Mrs. Harry) Ruby to Irving Berlin. Her stage name was Eileen Percy:

Dear Irving:

A few years ago, 1914 to be exact, when I was posing for Harrison Fisher in his studio, you stopped in for a visit. Several weeks later you again came in when I was posing. At this time you told me that on our previous meeting you got an idea for a song: "The Girl on the Magazine Cover," and that you had incorporated it into a score you were doing for Charles Dillingham called *Stop , Look and Listen* [sic]. You asked me if I might like to be in it. You gave me a note of introduction to Mr. Dillingham. Thanks to you I was in it for the entire run of the show. Now then, what I'm getting at is, when last I saw you several years ago, I asked if by chance you had a printed copy of this song. If you do, Irving, I would so love to have it. Autographed of course, and be forever grateful.

My fondest love to you and Ellen.

Affectionately,
Eileen

Irving Berlin's letter of December 19, 1967, to Eileen Ruby:

Dear Eileen:

I was glad to get your letter and am enclosing an autographed copy of "The Girl on the Magazine Cover." Also a copy of the program which I am sure you'll be interested in seeing.

Your letter brought back memories of Charles Dillingham—both pleasant and sad. He was one of the kindest and most generous men I ever knew. As you know he gave me my first chance at a show—*Watch Your Step.*

I saw him many times during the last years of his life when he lived at the Astor Hotel with his valet, Martin. He had lost everything and a few months after he died, Martin, who had been with him for many years, died of a broken heart.

VERSE 1

My head's in a dizzy whirl
Since I met a certain girl;
There isn't another like her—
She's a matchless pearl.
Since I met this maid divine,
I do nothing else but pine,
Because I know she never could be mine.

CHORUS

The girl I love
Is on a magazine cover;
It seems they painted her just for me.
I'd fall in love
If I could ever discover
A little girl quite as nice as she.
If I could meet
A girl as sweet,
I'd simply claim her
And name her
My queen;
For if she ever came,
I would love her the same
As I love her
On the cover
Of a magazine.

VERSE 2

My home is a picture book;
If ever you came to look,
You'd find her in ev'ry corner
And in ev'ry nook.
She's fairer than all the queens,
And loving her simply means
That I'm kept busy buying magazines.

REPEAT CHORUS

I LOVE A PIANO

Published. Copyrighted December 10, 1915. Introduced by Harry Fox (Abel Connor). According to one newspaper report, "I Love a Piano" "introduced six pianists who played one instrument, which was almost as long as the stage was wide. The chorus and the orchestra produced a rush of vocal and instrumental melody which filled the theatre like an operatic finale." Top-selling recording by Billy Murray (Victor), the flip side of Harry MacDonough's number-one hit "The Girl on the Magazine": this coupling was the first double-sided number-one hit record.

VERSE 1

As a child
I went wild
When a band played;
How I ran
To the man
When his hand swayed!
Clarinets
Were my pets,
And a slide trombone
I thought was simply divine.
But today
When they play,
I could hiss them;
Ev'ry bar
Is a jar
To my system;
But there's one musical instrument
That I call mine:

CHORUS

I love a piano,
I love a piano;
I love to hear somebody play
Upon a piano,
A grand piano—
It simply carries me away.
I know a fine way
To treat a Steinway;
I love to run my fingers
O'er the keys,
The ivories,
And with the pedal
I love to meddle.
When Paderewski comes this way,
I'm so delighted,
If I'm invited
To hear that longhaired genius play.
So you can keep your fiddle and your bow,
Give me a P-I-A-N-O, oh, oh—
I love to stop right
Beside an upright
Or a high-toned baby grand.

VERSE 2

When a green
Tetrazzin'
Starts to warble,
I grow cold
As an old
Piece of marble;
I allude
To the crude
Little party singer
Who doesn't know when to pause.

At her best
I detest
The soprano;
But I run
To the one
At the piano—
I always love the accompaniment,
And that's because:

REPEAT CHORUS

I LOVE TO SIT BY THE FIRE

Introduced by principals led by Florence Tempest (Willie Chase), Marion Sunshine (Vera Gay), Joseph Santley (Van Cortlandt Parke), and ensemble. The only source for the music and the lyrics is the original piano-vocal score in the R. H. Burnside Collection of the Music Division of the New York Public Library for the Performing Arts. This number includes an entirely new lyric to the melody of the chorus to "I Love a Piano" and a reprise of the chorus to "I Love to Dance." Alternate title: "Finale Act I."

WILLIE
& VERA: I love to sit by the fire,
Far from the cabaret throng,
Happy the whole evening long,
Singing an old-fashioned song.
CHORUS: Watching the flames burning higher—
No sweeter pleasure I know.
WILLIE
& VERA: Painting my own heart's desire
CHORUS: There in the firelight's glow.

PARKE: I love to spoon
'Neath the silvery moon
While all the world is at rest;
Under a tree
With a lovable she,
Holding her close to my breast.
CHORUS: There is nothing as nice as the
moonlight
To sit with somebody and spoon.
PARKE: Love tales you tell
Never sound quite as well
CHORUS: As they do 'neath the silvery moon.

I could stay far away from the
movies
And I never would miss them at all.
I wouldn't walk across the hall

To see them play a game of ball.*
I would rather be list'ning to Sousa
Than to shake any king by the hand.
I wouldn't walk across the street to see
the Kaiser
But I'd run a hundred miles to hear a
band.

The song continues with the following section, set to the melody of "I Love a Piano."

VERSE

I love the movies,
I love the movies;
I love to go there ev'ry night.
I love the movies,
The movie-oovies;
It simply fills me with delight.†
That big sensation
Birth of a Nation—
So thrilling I forgot
Where I was at.
A couple sat
Next to me loving;
I started shoving
Until they fell upon the floor.
'Twas so exciting
To see them fighting
The way they did in 'sixty-four.
And when it comes to laughing
merrily,
Give me a M-O-V-I love to see
What's happ'nin'
To Charlie Chaplin
At the moving picture show.

CHORUS

I love to dance,
I love to dance—

Earlier version of the four lines beginning "I could stay far away from the movies":
When a band starts to play I go dippy,
For a band simply drives me insane;
It seems to go right to my brain
Just like a glass of old champagne.

†*Earlier version of the first six lines:*
I love the movies,
I love the movies;
It simply fills me with delight
To see the movies,
The movie-oovies,
I love to go there ev'ry night.

I'd rather two-step than eat.
Give me a partner and a ballroom floor
And I'd ask for nothing more.
Show me a step
Full of the pep,
Show me and I'll take a chance.
I love to spin around until I'm all out of breath,
Vernon Castle myself to death—
Twirl me about,
Tire me out,
Because I'm simply crazy to dance.

OH, WHAT A PLACE IS DREAMY HONOLULU

The only source for the music and the lyrics is the piano-vocal score in the R. H. Burnside Collection of the Music Division of the New York Public Library for the Performing Arts. Introduced by "Tourists and Natives." Alternate title: "Opening Chorus Act II."

Oh, what a place
Is dreamy Honolulu!
It puts a smile on your face
To be in Honolulu,
For there is something that pleases—
Those tropical breezes,
They're oh so gentle,
It makes you sentimental.
Home of romance
Is dreamy Honolulu,
And there's a wonderful dance
They do in Honolulu.
It simply fills you with something
That you cannot understand;
And you say what is it
That makes you visit
That wonderful land?
Home of romance
Is dreamy Honolulu,
And there's a wonderful dance
They do in Honolulu.
It simply fills you with something
That you cannot understand;
And you say what is it
That makes you visit
That wonderful land?

THAT HULA-HULA

Published. Copyrighted December 10, 1915. Introduced by Blossom Seeley (Lilla Kiliana, "a Hula Hula girl") and ensemble. Alternate title: "The Hula Hula."

VERSE 1

Underneath the sad Hawaiian moon,
Where the sad Hawaiians love to spoon,
While the ukuleles strum a tune,
Ev'ry evening you can see them doing

CHORUS

That hula-hula—
Have you seen them do the hula
In Honolula
The way they do?
I know if you knew
How to do the hula-hula,
You'd be in Honolula
Doing the hula too.

VERSE 2

I can teach you how to do the dance—
Tell me, would you like to take a chance?
Shake your hands, quietly advance;
In another minute you'll be doing

REPEAT CHORUS

A PAIR OF
ORDINARY COONS

The only source for the music and lyrics is the original piano-vocal score in the R. H. Burnside Collection of the Music Division of the New York Public Library for the Performing Arts. Musical theatre historian Steven Suskin (*Show Tunes* [New York: Dodd, Mead, 1986], p. 82) writes that this song was published in a "separate edition." The editors have never seen a published copy of this song. Introduced by James Doyle (Rob Ayers) and Harland Dixon (Frank Steele).

VERSE 1

We were born in New Orleans;
Our mammies raised us there.

We represent a race of dusky face
And kinky, inky hair.
We've traveled all around the map,
We've been to ev'ry place,
And we find it most convenient
To be trav'ling with a dark-brown face.

CHORUS

In Honolulu
We pass as Hawaiians,
Though we come from New Orleans.
When we go to South America
We're a couple of Argentines.
They think we're natives
While passing through India;
We sing their native song.
And in Araby
We make them think we're Arabians.
We pass through all those places
On the faces
Of a pair of ordinary coons.

VERSE 2

Once while in Arabia
We tried to pass but failed;
They were all wise to us, made an awful fuss,
And soon we both were jailed.
Of course, it scared us half to death,
But soon we both were free;
For the jailor came from Georgia—
That was southern hospitality.

REPEAT CHORUS

WHEN I'M OUT
WITH YOU

Published. Copyrighted February 15, 1916. Introduced by Gaby Deslys (Gaby), Joseph Santley (Van Cortlandt Parke), and ensemble.

VERSE 1

Let's take a stroll up the avenue;
Dearie, I love to be seen with you.
Showing off is one of my joys;
Let me show you off to the boys—
You'll never guess what they say and do
When I am out with you.

CHORUS

I've seen them stare as we're passing by;
I've seen them glare with a jealous eye.
Let me tell you that I'm all in clover
When I notice how they look you over.
I've heard them cry, "It's the very best!"
Now you know why I throw out my chest.
You beautiful thing,
I'm as proud as a king
When I'm out with you.

VERSE 2

I like your clothes, 'cause I think they're great;
You're the original fashion plate:
Always something diff'rent to show,
All dressed and someplace to go.
If I'm conceited, don't think it queer;
There's a reason, dear.

REPEAT CHORUS

TAKE OFF A
LITTLE BIT

Published. Copyrighted February 2, 1916. Introduced by Gaby Deslys (Gaby) and girls.

VERSE 1

The girls are overdressing;
It keeps the fellows guessing,
I've heard them say
The gowns today
Are really most distressing.
Your ankle is detested
If you have overdressed it;
A man must see
An inch or three
To keep him interested.
An ankle now and then
Will catch the best of men.

CHORUS

So take off a little bit,
A tiny little bit and nothing more.
Just raise your dress up a little bit;
Don't let it drag upon the floor,
Because a banker or broker, a lawyer, a sport,
They always look longer when dresses are short.

So take off a little bit;
If you don't make a hit,
Take off a little bit more.

VERSE 2

You'll be the main attraction
And put the boys in action:
They'll linger nigh;
You'll catch them by
Removing just a fraction.
The chicken-pickin' jury
Will go into a fury
If they can't see
An inch or three—
They all come from Missouri.
'Twas said by someone wise,
"It pays to advertise."

REPEAT CHORUS

TEACH ME
HOW TO LOVE

Published. Copyrighted January 13, 1916. Introduced by Florence Tempest (Willie Chase), Marion Sunshine (Vera Gay), and ensemble. According to one unnamed newspaper report, "Miss Tempest was the boy and Miss Sunshine the girl who wanted to be taught and who liked the lesson so well that she shouted in comic ecstasy 'Steady! Steady! Very good, Eddie!' " Dropped in early 1916 when Tempest and Sunshine left the show.

VERSE 1

GIRL: I had a diff'rent teacher ev'ry year;
    They taught me ev'rything, and yet
        I fear
    My education's been neglected,
        dear—
    They never taught me to love.
BOY: I don't know much about geography,
    Grammar, arithmetic, or history;
    But I know
    Ev'rything about love from A to Z.

CHORUS

GIRL: Teach me how to love;
    I'd like to know, sir.
BOY: If you want to love, come over closer.
GIRL: Do you know the game, dear?

BOY: That's my middle name, dear.
GIRL: Call me turtle dove;
    I'd like to hear it.
BOY: It will fit you like a glove.
GIRL: I'd like to know a teeny weeny bit
    about it.
BOY: I could explain it to you
    If your lips were pouted.
GIRL: I'm all ready.
CHORUS: Look at 'em doing it!*
BOY: Hold steady!
CHORUS: Look at 'em doing it!
GIRL: Oh, oh, it's very good, Eddie—
    Won't you teach me some more?

VERSE 2

GIRL: How many lessons do you think I'll
    need?
BOY: Not many lessons, if you'll only
    heed.
GIRL: You know a lot about it, yes, indeed.
BOY: I've taken lessons for years.
GIRL: I'd like to understand it through and
    through.
BOY: Practice makes perfect, so it's up to
    you.
GIRL: I'm waiting.
BOY: 'Twon't be long before you're a teacher
    too.

REPEAT CHORUS

THE LAW MUST
BE OBEYED

Published. Copyrighted February 25, 1916. Introduced by James Doyle (Rob Ayers) and Harland Dixon (Frank Steele).

VERSE 1

Do you know just who we are?
If you don't, look at this star:
We're the constabules,
And we're no darned fools.
There are speeders in the town,
And we're here to run them down;

*The line is a reference to Berlin's "The Syncopated Walk" in Watch Your Step (1914).

They ran like the dickens,
And they killed four chickens
That belonged to Farmer Brown.
We've got a darned good clue:
The car was painted blue.

CHORUS

We're the county sheriffs,
And the law must be obeyed.
When they speed in an automobile,
You can hear us holler, "Whoa, Bill!"
Any time we catch them
There's a fine that must be paid,
So we must arrest those gents:
The jailhouse needs a fence;
It'll cost us sixty cents,
So the law must be obeyed.

VERSE 2

We will catch them yet, by heck,
If it makes us both a wreck!
When we do, you bet
They'll be all upset.
There was one that wore a cap
Like a gosh-darned sporty chap:
No doubt from the city,
'Cause a gal quite pretty
Was a-sittin' on his lap.
Don't be one bit surprised—
You may find us disguised.

REPEAT CHORUS

RAGTIME
MELODRAMA

The only source for the music is the original piano-vocal score in the R. H. Burnside Collection of the Music Division of the New York Public Library for the Performing Arts. Introduced by principals and ensemble. This extended number is the finale to Act II. Alternate title: "Ragtime Finale (Melodrama)." An earlier version of the lyric with a different opening section for the heroine is in an early version of the script in the Billy Rose Theatre Collection of the New York Public Library for the Performing Arts.

HEROINE: I'm so sad,
    I don't know what to do:
    A desp'rate villain follows me around.

It almost drives me mad;
I'm worried through and through:
He wants to carry me
Off and marry me—
What shall I do?

[VILLAIN *enters.*]

VILLAIN: There you are, my proud beauty!
There you are, my little cutie!
You must marry me—
I'm gonna watch you
Until I've got you.
I've laid a careful plan,
So don't tarry—
I'm the man
You've got to marry.
You can't get away;
You must become my wife today.
HEROINE: Desp'rate Desmond,
Haven't I told you that I love another
man?
VILLAIN: Curses on him!
I'll have him murdered
And you know damn well I can.
HEROINE: When we meet I'm going to tell him
All about your desp'rate plan.
VILLAIN: Give me your answer now before I go.
HEROINE: A thousand times I answer no!
VILLAIN: You know I hold a mortgage on this
house and lot.
HEROINE: Wait—I'll get the money and I'll pay.
VILLAIN: You know that I could turn you out as
well as not.
HEROINE: Think of my father, who is old and gray.
VILLAIN: If you refuse I'll gag and bind you with
a cord.
HEROINE: What'll you do to me when I'm that
way?
VILLAIN: I'll kidnap you in my one-and-a-half-
cylinder Ford.
HEROINE: Oh, Gawd!
VILLAIN: You're gonna be my pris'ner locked up
in a tower—
You're in my power.
HEROINE: I won't be kept there long,
Because my faithful lover
Will soon discover.
VILLAIN: I haven't much more time to lose.
HEROINE: I refuse.
VILLAIN: You'd better hurry up and choose.
HEROINE: I refuse.
VILLAIN: Then I intend to carry out my
desp'rate scheme.
HEROINE: I'll scream.
Father! Father!

[HEROINE *and* VILLAIN *struggle.* FATHER *enters.*]

FATHER: Stop!

Villain, I'd rather you would stop!
I am her father and I'd like to know
Just why you called today.
HEROINE: He tried to trap me—kidnap me!
FATHER: Oh! From what she mentions, sir,
I know that your intentions were
To carry her away.
HEROINE: Into a dungeon I'd plunge in.
VILLAIN: If your daughter doesn't consent,
I mean to throw her into a cell.
FATHER: Touch one hair on this lady's head
And you will eat your supper in hell!
VILLAIN: There's no need of raising a scene—
She'll occupy a comf'table flat.
FATHER: Damn you, sir, I know what you mean—
For your insinuations, take that!

[FATHER *slaps* VILLAIN. *Then* VILLAIN *shoots* FATHER,
who staggers to the couch and collapses.]

HEROINE: Oh! Father! Please do not die!
I want to have you near.
VILLAIN: [*running up and down the stage*]
I'm in an awful scrape;
I must escape—
The cops are coming!
HEROINE: Oh! Father! Don't say goodbye!
That awful man I fear.
VILLAIN: I'm gonna hide right here!

[VILLAIN *hides under the couch. The music changes and*
the HERO *enters.*]

HERO: I heard a shot—
'Twas followed up with a shout;
I wonder what
The trouble could be about.
This is the home of my sweetheart;
A year ago we had to part—
I went to work so I could help her pay
the mortgage.
Oh, Mary dear,
Why are you hiding away?
Come over here;
Your lover's come back to stay—
Come to me, for I love you so.
HEROINE: Oh! Father! 'Tis an awful blow.

[HEROINE *and* HERO *see each other for the first time.*]

HERO: Mary!
HEROINE: Hero!
HERO: What is the matter, hon?
Didn't I hear a gun?
HEROINE: Father's been shot!
HERO: What?!?

[HERO *and* HEROINE *run to sides of the stage, calling,*
and crowds gather.]

BOTH: Help! Help! Help!
CROWD #1: What's the matter?

What's the matter?
We heard somebody shout, holler
out "Help!"
CROWD #2: What's the matter?
What's the matter?
We heard somebody shout, holler
out "Help!"
CROWD #3: What's the matter?
What's the matter?
We heard somebody shout, holler out
"Help!"
CROWD #4: What's the matter?
What's the matter?
We heard somebody shout, holler out
"Help!"
HEROINE: I fear my poor old father's days are
done.
CHORUS: What's been done? What's been done?
What's been done?
HEROINE: A desp'rate villain shot him with a gun.
CHORUS: With a gun, with a gun, the son of a
gun.
HERO: If there's a doctor here—
CHORUS: He's here!

[DOCTOR *enters.*]

HERO: —I wish he'd hurry near—
CHORUS: Hurry near.
HERO: —and take him to the hospital on the
run.
CHORUS: Better run, better run, better run.
DOCTOR: He's got a bullet in his head.
CHORUS: In his head!
DOCTOR: And I believe the man is dead!
CHORUS: Is he dead?
DOCTOR: Yes! He's dead.
CHORUS: The poor old man is dead.

[CAPTAIN OF POLICE *enters.*]

CAPTAIN: Who committed this crime?
I'd like to know.
CHORUS: We'd like to know the villain,
The one who did the killin'.
CAPTAIN: I must capture that man before I go.
CHORUS: We're here to help you find him—
Maybe he left a clue behind him!
CAPTAIN: Someone must have seen him from
below!
CHORUS: Before the lady shouted,
No one knew a thing about it.
CAPTAIN: It's an awful blow!
CHORUS: Quite so, quite so, quite so.
CAPTAIN: He must be hiding somewhere in this
place.
CHORUS: For all we know, the feller
May be hiding in the cellar.
CAPTAIN: This is quite a most peculiar case!
CHORUS: But then we won't be baffled;

CAPTAIN: Soon we'll have him on the scaffold.

CAPTAIN: Where's the old man's daughter?

CHORUS: Question her you oughter.

CAPTAIN: Come here, girl, and tell the story through.

CHORUS: Yes, do!

HEROINE: Just like a cat he sneaked up those back stairs.*

CHORUS: Like a cat, like a cat, like a cat.

HEROINE: Before I knew he caught me unawares.

CHORUS: Where's that? Where's that? Where's that?

HEROINE: He wore a look so vicious—

CROWD: Yes?

HEROINE: —it made me grow suspicious.

CROWD: Well?

HEROINE: He tried to . . .

CHORUS: What?

HEROINE: He tried to . . .

CHORUS: What?

HEROINE: To marry me against my wishes.

CHORUS: Oh!

HEROINE: He offered me a diamond and a pearl.

CHORUS: What did you do? What did you do? What did you do?

---

*On December 19, 1967, Irving Berlin, in a letter to Eileen (Mrs. Harry) Ruby, who (as Eileen Percy) had appeared in Stop! Look! Listen!, recalled an amusing story of Gaby Deslys and "Ragtime Melodrama."

I wonder if you remember the *second act finale*. I had written a ragtime melodrama which ran about fifteen minutes. It was one of those tapeworms that really wasn't too good. However, there was one big laugh in it that I never planned. Harry Fox played the villain who pursued Gaby Deslys. Joseph Santley was the hero. At one point Gaby was telling the story about the villain to the following lyrics:

GABY: Just like a cat he crept up those back stairs.

CHORUS: Like a cat, like a cat, like a cat.

GABY: Before I knew he caught me unawares.

CHORUS: Where was that, where was that, where was that?

The opening night, Gaby sang the first line thus: "Youst like a cat he 'CRAPPED' up those back stairs"

I could never get her to pronounce the word correctly but it got such a laugh that Dillingham decided to keep it in.

In preparing a finished piano-vocal score for the number, Berlin changed the four lines he recalled from memory in 1967 (he did not know about the piano-vocal score in the New York Public Library) to what appears above in the complete lyric.

HEROINE: I told him I was not that kind of girl!

CHORUS: Bully for you! Bully for you! Bully for you!

HEROINE: My father shouted, "Sir—"

CHORUS: Yes, yes.

HEROINE: "—don't lay a hand on her!"

CHORUS: Yes, yes.

HEROINE: 'Twas then I heard the desp'rate villain shoot!

CHORUS: The brute!
Where's the villain, where's the villain?
He must be found.
We'll search all around
From top to bottom;
When we've got 'im
He won't live long, we vouch.

CAPTAIN: Imagine such a plan.

CHORUS: It's terrible!

CAPTAIN: Killed an innocent man.

CHORUS: Unbearable!
Where's the villain who did the killin'?

FATHER: He's under the couch.

[*Pause.*]

VILLAIN: Ouch!

CHORUS: Grab him!

FATHER: Make him pay the penalty!

CHORUS: Nab him!

FATHER: Take him where he ought to be!

CHORUS: Jab him!

FATHER: He's the man who murdered me.

CHORUS: Pounce upon him!
Put the handcuffs on him!
While you take him—

FATHER: He's the villain, that's a fact.

CHORUS: —make him.

FATHER: He shot me in the second act.

CHORUS: Think of that, think of that—
He shot him in the second act
And says is it not
A terrible spot,
A terrible spot,
For a man to be shot?
Away with the villain,
Away with the villain,
Away!

An earlier version of the opening section

HEROINE: I'm so sad,
I don't know what to do.
I'm worried through and through;
I fear that I'll go mad,
And if you only knew,
You would be worried too:

A desp'rate villain is taunting me;
For some strange reason he's wanting me;
Where'er I go he is haunting me.
All night long I seem to see him stare—
I never sleep a wink,
I lay awake and think.
And now I must beware—
He wants to carry me
Away and marry me,
And I'm in love with Nero,
The hero
Of this melodrama.

Earlier version of closing pages

CHORUS: Grab him!
There, he is the murderer!
Nab him!
There, he is the dirty cur!
Jab him!
Do your duty, officer—
Pounce upon 'im,
Put the handcuffs on 'im,
While you take him
Where the villains ought to be—
Make him,
Make 'im pay the penalty.
Officer, officer,
Take heartless murderer
Away—
Lock 'im up
Away—
Lock 'im up
Away—
Lock 'im up, lock 'im up
Away—
Lock 'im up, lock 'im up
Away.

WHEN I GET BACK TO THE U.S.A.

Published. Copyrighted December 10, 1915. Introduced by Joseph Santley (Van Cortlandt Parke) and ensemble. Sung as a countermelody to "America," or, as it is often known, "My Country! 'Tis of Thee!" Leading recording by Billy Murray (Victor, Edison, and Edison Amberol). For the London production of *Stop! Look! Listen!*, which was titled *Follow the Crowd*, the lyric was changed to "When I Get Back to London Town," and the lyric of the countermelody changed to "God Save the King" (which uses the same tune as "America"). The lyric to "When I Get Back to London Town" is missing.

VERSE 1

I've been on the go for a month or so;
Now my heart begins to yearn
For the U.S.A., many miles away,
And I'm anxious to return.
I have been around, covered lots of ground,
But it don't appeal to me;
Seeing sights abroad is an awful fraud—
I'm as homesick as can be.

CHORUS 1

When I get back home again
To the U.S.A.,
In the land of peace and freedom
I intend to stay.
Somehow I never feel at home
When I'm away from there, anywhere;
No other nation
In this creation
Would ever do for me.
I guess I'm cranky
'Cause I'm a Yankee,
But then I'm proud to be;
On the pier you'll hear me shouting
"Hip hip hooray!"
When I get back to the U.S.A.

VERSE 2

There is not a thing in the song I sing
That has not been sung before;
It's a story old that has oft been told
In a thousand songs or more.
But when I salaam to my Uncle Sam
In the good old U.S.A.,
It is not because I would ask applause,
But because I feel that way.

REPEAT CHORUS

[*With the music and lyrics to "America" sung in counterpoint*]

My country! 'Tis of thee,
    When I get back home again
    To the U.S.A.,
Sweet land of liberty,
    In the land of peace and freedom
    I intend to stay.
Of thee I sing:
    Somehow I never feel at home
    When I'm away from there, anywhere;

Land where my fathers died,
    No other nation
    In this creation
    Would ever do for me.
Land of the pilgrim's pride,
    I guess I'm cranky
    'Cause I'm a Yankee,
    But then I'm proud to be;
From every mountain side let freedom ring!
    On the pier you'll hear me shouting
    "Hip hip hooray!"
    When I get back to the U.S.A.

STOP! LOOK! LISTEN!

Published. Copyrighted January 13, 1916. Introduced by Walter Wills (Owen Coyne, "a manager of musical comedy"), Frank Lalor (Gideon Gay, "a tired businessman"), James Doyle (Rob Ayers, "a librettist"), Harland Dixon (Frank Steele, "a composer"), Harry Fox (Abel Conner, "a press agent"), and Joseph Santley (Van Cortlandt Parke, "who wants to do people good"). Alternate title: "Sextette—Stop! Look! Listen!"

VERSE 1

Love will make a fool of any man, it has been said;
No one can advise him, for his heart will rule his
    head.
He names the wedding day, just throws himself
    away;
Before the wedding all his friends will come to
    him and say:

CHORUS 1

"Stop! Look! Listen to a friend's advice;
Better look before you leap,
Or you'll be in water deep.
For God's sake don't get married;
Don't give up your name."
Then he'll stop, look, listen to his friend's
    advice—
But he'll go out and marry just the same.

VERSE 2

Mister Brown, a widower, was handing out advice
To his son, who fell in love with someone very
    nice.
He whispered to the lad, "To marry would be bad;
I know just what I'm saying—take a tip from your
    old dad:

CHORUS 2

"Stop! Look! Listen to your dad's advice;
She's a nice girl, that is true,
But she'll never do for you.
So tie a can to Cupid;
Lay him on the shelf."
Then he stopped, looked, listened to his dad's
    advice—
While his dad went and married her himself.

VERSE 3

There's a railroad on Long Island, not so far away;
Accidents occur there almost every other day.
The man who owns the line said, "The fault's not
    mine,
Because at every railroad crossing you will find
    this sign:

CHORUS 3

"Stop! Look! Listen! Always safety first;
If there were no such display,
You would pass right on your way.
But they insist you linger
By the railroad track;
So you stop, look, listen, then you hear a crash;
And the next day your family's dressed in black."

SKATING SONG

According to musical theatre historian Steven Suskin (*Show Tunes* [New York: Dodd, Mead, 1986], p. 82) this song was "advertised but not published." The only source for the music and lyrics is the original piano-vocal score in the R. H. Burnside Collection of the Music Division of the New York Public Library for the Performing Arts. Introduced by Harry Pilcer (Anthony St. Anthony, "a leading man"). Alternate title: "I'll Be Coming Home With a Skate On."

VERSE

Skating seems to be the craze;
Ev'rybody nowadays
Is learning how to skate,
Because it's up to date.
I've engaged a teacher who
Knows his business through and through;
Soon I will be skating too,
And when I do

CHORUS

I'll be coming home with a skate on,
Feeling mighty nice.
I'll throw all of my weight on
The slip'ry-ipry ice.
I'll crack the ice and put it in
A glass of Mister Gordon's gin
And then I'll start for home with a skate on.
[*Dance.*]

EVERYTHING IN AMERICA IS RAGTIME

Published. Copyrighted January 13, 1916. Introduced by Gaby Deslys (Gaby, "only a chorus girl now, but just wait") and ensemble. According to the New York *Herald* (December 26, 1915), the following occurred on opening night:

> In the last scene a large stairway in the center of the stage is utilized as a background for the biggest ensemble number in the piece, "Everything in America is Ragtime." Miss Gaby Deslys, star of the company, and the entire organization had been dancing up and down the stairway, when suddenly the brassy glories of Mr. Sousa's musicians echoed the lively melody, and to the amazement of every one in the body of the theatre Mr. Sousa appeared at the top of the flight of steps and led his band down the stairway.
>
> "Oh's!" and "Ah's" which had followed the other innovations for the evening, gave way to shouts of pleasure and astonishment at the climax of the performance, and the curtain fell on a "first night" which Broadway will remember for some time.

VERSE 1

People here are going wild;
Every woman, man, and child
Has some ragtime on the brain.
Every band and orchestra
Playing in America
Plays a syncopated strain.
It's floating in the air;
You hear it everywhere.

CHORUS

Everything in America is ragtime.
They talk in ragtime,
It seems to be the fashion;

Their only passion
Is swaying to and fro,
Snapping fingers so,
Acting as though they were having a jagtime.
The U.S.A. is a land of syncopation;
It seems the nation
Is just a million acres of shoulder shakers.
Composers, just as thick as bees,
Writing raggy melodies—
They're even making Gaby Deslys
Sing ragtime.

VERSE 2

In the subway every night
Folks start swaying left and right
While they read the evening news.
When a baby starts to cry,
Longing for a lullaby,
Mother sings the "Memphis Blues";
You can't drive it away,
Because it's here to stay.

REPEAT CHORUS

SAILOR SONG

Published. Copyrighted December 10, 1915. Dropped before the New York opening.

VERSE 1

A pair of sailor boys are we;
We sail across the angry sea—
Ya ho! Ya ho!
To prove we're sailor boys all right,
We smoke a hornpipe every night—
Ya ho! Ya ho!
We really hate the ocean, 'cause it's all around the place;
We only use it when we have to wash the captain's face.
Of that we really shouldn't speak;
He only washes once a week—
Ya ho! Ya ho!

CHORUS

While we go sailing, sailing,
Over the ocean blue,
We're sailors through and through,
The best you ever knew!
If you doubt the story we're telling you,

Any chorus girl can tell you we're sailors.
As we go sailing, sailing,
What do you think we do?
We flirt with ev'ry mermaid on Fifth Avenue.
Our fathers lost a fortune down on Wall Street;
So they both insisted we become a couple of sailors too.

VERSE 2

It makes no difference where are we;
We always like to strike a bar—
Ya ho! Ya ho!
We stand in line to quench our thirst;
The second mate is always first—
Ya ho! Ya ho!
The steward has an anchor tattooed near his vocal cord,
So when we want to stop the ship, we throw him overboard;
We tie him to an iron chain,
So we can pull him up again—
Ya ho! Ya ho!

REPEAT CHORUS

UNTIL I FELL IN LOVE WITH YOU

Published. Copyrighted December 10, 1915. The lyric for the second chorus is not in the published sheet music; it is included in an early version of the script at the Billy Rose Theatre Collection of the New York Public Library for the Performing Arts. A duet for Florence Tempest (Willie Chase) and Marion Sunshine (Vera Gay). It was intended for late in Act I, after "I Love a Piano." Dropped before the New York opening.

VERSE 1

HE: Come over closer, my dear,
Come over here;
I've a confession to make:
Long before I met you,
I have loved quite a few.
There have been many sweet girls I cared for;
Though 'twas all long ago,
It's only fair you should know:

CHORUS 1

I loved a lovely girl in London;
I loved a peach in Spain.
I used to pet a brunette while in Gay Paree;
I was fond of a blonde while in Germany.
While in Japan I met a geisha;
I thought I loved her too.
I've loved a diff'rent girl in ev'ry land;
I've sampled kisses, dear, of ev'ry brand;
But I never really fell in love, dear,
Until I fell in love with you.

VERSE 2

SHE: I'm very glad you confessed,
    Though I'd have guessed—
    You're only human, dear boy.
    Don't you worry, my dear,
    There is nothing to fear;
    Ev'ryone flirts till they meet the right
        one.
    It's all in the game;
    I have been doing the same.

CHORUS 2
[*not in the published sheet music*]

SHE: I loved a lovely boy in London;
    I loved a peach in Spain.
    Upon the lap of a chap out in Gay Paree
    I would sit quite a bit while he fondled me.
    I loved a curly-headed Russian;
    I loved a German too.
    I've loved a different boy in ev'ry land;
    I've sampled kisses, dear, of ev'ry
        brand;
    But I never really fell in love, dear,
    Until I fell in love with you.

OOZUMS LITTLE SNOOZUMS IS OO

No music is known to survive. Added to the score during the New York run. Introduced by Florence Morrison (Mrs. Singer) and Frank Lalor (Gideon Gay, "a tired businessman"). This number, presented in Act II, Scene 2, replaced the non-Berlin "On the Beach at Waikiki." Two holograph manuscripts of the lyric were found among Berlin's papers and are now at the Irving Berlin Collection of the Music Division of the Library of Congress. Alternate titles: "Oozums" and "Oozums Little Snoozums Is Oo, Oo, Oo?"

VERSE 1

SHE: We would make a happy couple, don't you
        think we would?
HE: Honestly, I never thought of that.
SHE: We would rent a flat within a quiet
        neighborhood.
HE: You'd require more than just a flat.
SHE: The neighbors all would envy us—we'd be
        so happy, dear.
HE: I'd like to bet they all would move away.
SHE: The whole day long I'd whisper pretty
        nothings in your ear.
HE: Tell me just exactly what you'd say.

CHORUS 1

SHE: "Oozums little snoozums is oo, oo, oo?"
HE: Lovey, turtle dovey, that's how we'll coo.
SHE: On the morris chair I'd sit.
HE: I'd hate to be in under it.
BOTH: Singing "Oozums little snoozums is oo,
        oo, oo?"

VERSE 2

SHE: We'd enjoy the happiness that money
        cannot buy.
HE: I would sell my portion for a dime.
SHE: Every night I'd sing to you a pretty lullaby.
HE: I'd be wearing earmuffs all the time.
SHE: We'd play a lot of baby games and you
        would let me win.
HE: I'd have to pay, and that would keep me
        broke.
SHE: If you behave, I'd let you stroke me under-
        neath the chin.
HE: Which one of the seven would I stroke?

CHORUS 2

SHE: "Oozums little snoozums is oo, oo, oo?"
HE: Mumsy, you're too clumsy to bill and coo.
SHE: I would sit upon your knee
HE: And that would be the last of me.
SHE: Singing "Oozums little snoozums is oo,
        oo, oo?"

HUNTING FOR A STAR

No music is known to survive. The lyric is included in an early version of the script at the Billy Rose Theatre Collection of the New York Public Library for the Performing Arts. The number was intended as the final number

of the first scene of Act I and was intended for James Doyle (Rob Ayres), Harland Dixon (Frank Steele), Harry Fox (Abel Connor), Gaby Deslys (Violette, which was changed to Gaby), and ensemble. Dropped either in rehearsals or during the Philadelphia tryout. Alternate title: "In Search of a Star."

VERSE

MANAGER: We must hunt up a star to play the
        leading role.
LIBRETTIST: To speak the lines I wrote, she must
        be full of soul.
COMPOSER: To sing my music she must reach a
        clear high C.
PRESS AGENT: I'll find it for you if you'll leave it
        to me.
VIOLETTE: I'm just the girl for you.
ALL: We know you'll never do.

CHORUS

So we'll go hunting for a star,
A prima donna with art
Who just suits the part,
With a voice just like Farrar.
To reach a high C very nicely,
We must go hunting near and far;
Until the lady is found
We'll search all around.
The costumes are all up to date;
The book and the music are great;
But then we can't begin,
They won't come in,
Unless we have a star.

DON'T YOU REMEMBER MARY BROWN

No music is known to survive. Probably introduced by Eva Francis (Mary Brown) during the Philadelphia try-out. Dropped before the New York opening. One version of the lyric is in an early version of the script, in the Billy Rose Theatre Collection of the New York Public Library for the Performing Arts. The song was reintroduced in the midnight revue *Dance and Grow Thin* on January 18, 1917, at the Cocoanut Grove Roof of the Century Theatre, by Rita Boland with "Miss Bliss" (full name unknown) and Harry Kelly. A copy of the lyric (date unknown) with a different verse in Berlin's hand was written on stationery from The Breakers, the celebrated Palm Beach, Florida, hotel.

VERSE

How do you do, Mr. Chicken Chaser!
I remember you—
Bet your life I do!
Don't act as though you didn't know me—
One night you tried to Romeo me.
Looking you over, I must confess, dear,
You look good to me—
Like a Christmas tree.
We don't require an introduction;
I'll refresh your memory.

CHORUS

Don't you remember Mary Brown?
You surely ought to remember Mary Brown.

I met you one night at Rector's;
You called upon your queen;
You took me riding in your yellow limousine—
Don't you remember?
You promised to buy me a gown;
You whispered, "Don't refuse it,"
But I did.
And now that I can use it,
Oh, you kid,
You better slip me one or else I'll raise a row.*
Don't you remember now?

———————————

*Alternate version of line:
    You better slip me one or else I'll tell your frau.

Alternate "Palm Beach" verse

Jonesy went out with his wife last Sunday
To a cabaret.
Right across the way
A girl kept looking him over.
His wife said, "Dear, do you know her?"
Jonesy cried out, "She's a perfect stranger—
I don't know her, dear."
But the girl could hear;
She walked up to his table
And she whispered in his ear:

Top: *Women of the Ages: Barbara Fritchie (Evelyn Conway), Queen Boadicea (May Leslie), Helen of Troy (Marjorie Cassidy), and Joan of Arc (Hazel Lewis) in* The Century Girl. *Bottom: Leon Errol and Elsie Janis, "The Chicken Walk"*

Songs of 1916
and
THE CENTURY GIRL | 1916

SONGWRITER'S SPEECH

Written for a Friars Club dinner, March 29, 1916. Registered for copyright as an unpublished song May 2, 1991. Alternate titles: "What Am I Goin' a Do" and "Brother Choosers—Rhyme Abusers."

Brother Choosers—Rhyme Abusers,
I don't intend to make a speech.
But if I may, I'd like to say
That I am mighty glad to be here today.
It's been a damn bad season—that's the reason
I feel so happy that I came
To hear your new songs.
I may strike one or two songs
That I like—
And if I like your songs I'll go right home and
    write them—rewrite them.
Nowadays it's hard to write a song that makes a hit
Unless the publisher pays everyone for singing it.
I asked a singer the other day
Who works in a cabaret
If he would sing my latest thing
And I heard the singer say,
"Sing a song for sixpence? Never on your life!
A Taylor trunk for me, sir, and pictures for the
    wife."
That's what I call a bad condition.
Then there's competition:
Ribbon clerks and fighters
Want to be songwriters—
And the songs that they write are as good as those
That you and I compose.
What am I gonna do? What am I gonna do?
I can't find a spot that has not been written about.
What am I gonna do? What am I gonna do?
The songs about the good old levee
Used to bring a statement heavy;
But now somehow
The "Swanee Rivers"
Are surefire flivvers.
It's true, I vow,
They won't buy a ditty
About a city.
But that's not really what I wanted to say.
I would not throw a damper on this scamper
For anything in the world;
But I would like to propose a silent toast
To our absent Brothers . . .
Let's drink a toast to the fellows
Who have been taken away;
For we lost the gladness that turned into sadness
When we lost . . .
The man who wrote "My Gal Sal,"
A peculiar sort of a gal,

With a heart that was mellow an all-round good
    fellow
Was Paul Dresser, our old pal.
"Roses, roses, roses" reminds us of Ingraham.
"Someone thinks of someone" holds a mem'ry
    dear,
For it makes us think of
Fred Helf and Ed Gardenier.
"In the Good Old Summertime"
Takes us all back to the time
When Georgie Evans and Ren Shields
Both were in their prime.
I know you feel the same as I,
So drink a toast from your stein
To our absent Brothers,
Lew Muir and the others,
For Auld Lang Syne.

THE FRIARS' PARADE

Published. Copyrighted May 27, 1916. "By Friar Irving Berlin." From the *Friars Frolic of 1916*. "Written for and dedicated to 'The Friars.' "

VERSE 1

Hear the sound of shuffling feet
On the pavements of the street;
Look up the avenue,
Hear that shout—tell me, haven't you
Heard about the Friars coming into town?
Ev'rybody come on down.

CHORUS

Come and see the Friars—
Here they come, here they come—
See that mob go marching four in a row,
On the job to give a wonderful show.
Look at those live wires
In their dusters arrayed;
Just hear that snappy rhythm
From the band.
Come on and march right with 'em;
Understand
You'll see the best show ever played
If you follow the Friars' Parade.

VERSE 2

See those coppers on the track,
Holding ev'rybody back;
They've stopped the trolley cars

To make room for a hundred stars.
Like a broom they'll sweep the town of all dull
    care;
Ev'rybody should be there.

REPEAT CHORUS

I'VE GOT A SWEET TOOTH BOTHERING ME

Published. Copyrighted June 2, 1916. Introduced in the musical *Step This Way* (Shubert Theatre, New York; May 29, 1916; 88 performances) by Gladys Clark (Susie Scraggs, "assistant cashier of the Universal, an American department store in London") and Henry Bergman (Dudley Cheatter, "cashier of the Universal and inbred with the American idea of high finance").

VERSE 1

"Take me to the dentist right away!"
Shouted little Johnny Jones one day;
"I've got a tooth that's hurting me,
And I simply can't delay."
In about an hour he was there,
Standing right beside the dentist's chair;
And when they sat him inside,
To the dentist Johnny cried:

CHORUS

"I've got a sweet tooth bothering me—
Pull it out, pull it put, pull it out!
It isn't candy or molasses,
It isn't honey, jam, or cake;
But when a sweet young lady passes,
My tooth begins to ache like the dickens.
I don't use sugar at all
In my coffee or my tea;
But when I meet Rosie, Flo, or May,
My wisdom tooth says, 'Keep away,'
But my sweet tooth starts bothering me."

VERSE 2

Johnny hollered out, "There's no one home
In the second story of my dome
Except a thousand ladies fair,
And it's like a honeycomb.
Ev'ry night when I sit down to eat,
First I have my oysters, soup, and meat;

And then my favorite dessert
Is the rustle of a skirt.

REPEAT CHORUS

HURRY BACK TO MY BAMBOO SHACK

Published. Copyrighted June 30, 1916.

VERSE 1

A geisha girl is waiting for
Her little sailor man;
He sailed up on his man-of-war
And left her in Japan.
All day she watches anxiously,
And when the night appears,
She sadly gazes toward the sea
And murmurs through her tears:

CHORUS

"Hurry back
To my lonely little bamboo shack,
Where your lonely little geisha
So patiently waits for you.
Though my heart is grieving,
I'm still believing
That all the things that you said were true.
Here in Japan, behind my fan,
I'm thinking of my sailor man.
So won't you hurry back
To my lonely little bamboo shack?
All by my ownsome
I'm lonesome for you."

VERSE 2

The geisha girl will never see
Her little sailor man;
Never again she'll pour his tea
As only geishas can;
Because the handsome sailor boy
Who sailed across the sea
Will soon forget his broken toy
Who murmurs tenderly:

REPEAT CHORUS

HE'S GETTING TOO DARN BIG FOR A ONE-HORSE TOWN

Published. Copyrighted June 30, 1916.

VERSE 1

Hiram Perkins, sittin' by the fire,
Talking to his wife,
Hollered out, "Now looka here, Maria,
A farmer's life
Was never meant for our son!
The boy is almost twenty-one;
I've been closely watching him of late,
And something's gotta be done.

CHORUS

"He's getting too darn big for a small town;
He ought to be in New York.
He has seen a champagne cork;
He's even eating with his fork.
He knows at least a dozen of troopers;
He's got a tie from Siegel and Cooper's;
And his name stamped on the inside of his hat—
Think o' that, think o' that!
Down there on Broadway is the place where he
    belongs;
He knows 'Bedelia' and the other latest songs.
He's got a watch with an open crystal
And a walking cane with a pistol—
He's getting too darn big for a one-horse town."

VERSE 2

Hiram Perkins bought a railroad ticket
On the B and O;
When they warned him New York town was
    wicked,
He said, "I know,
But then my boy can hold his own;
Of late he's actin' too high-tone.
Why, he combs his hair three times a day—
He even uses cologne!

REPEAT CHORUS

IN FLORIDA AMONG THE PALMS

Published. Copyrighted August 18, 1916. A note by Berlin on the original lyric manuscript states that this song was written on July 16, 1916. According to a note by Berlin on the published sheet music, it was dedicated to Mr. Leland Sterry. Introduced in the *Ziegfeld Follies of 1916* after its New York opening (New Amsterdam Theatre; June 12, 1916). In the post-Broadway tour it was sung late in Act II by Bernard Granville and chorus. Leading recording by the Sterling Trio (Victor), whose members were Henry Burr, Albert Campbell, and John Meyer.

VERSE 1

Everybody sings of the sunny South;
That's the song that clings to the singer's mouth—
They ragtime it and boost the climate way up to
    the sky.
I never cared a lot for the Swanee shore;
There's another spot that I'm rooting for—
I've been there and I declare,
It can't be praised too high.

CHORUS

If I had my way, I'd always stay
In Florida among the palms,
With its peaceful air of "I don't care"
And lazy atmosphere that calms.
My one favorite haunt is a palm tree,
And all I want is someone
Just to rest in my arms.
I'd love to live among the bamboo huts, the
    coconuts,
There's something in the climate that charms;
Heaven's corridor is sunny Florida,
Home of the shelt'ring palms.

VERSE 2

Florida was named very prettily
By the man who claimed its discovery;
He spent hours among the flowers and called it
    God's Land.
And nature seems to sigh, "It's my favorite";
That's the reason why heaven gave her it—
It was born from a diamond worn upon an angel's
    hand.

REPEAT CHORUS

WHEN THE BLACK SHEEP RETURNS TO THE FOLD

Published. Copyrighted September 11, 1916. The sheet music covers state that this song was introduced by Belle Baker. There also is a note that states, "Respectfully Dedicated to my pal, Wilson Mizner."

VERSE 1

When the robin returns to the nest
After straying away from the rest,
There's a welcome that waits
From its feathery mates,
A welcome that can't be expressed.
So it is with the boy who decided
From his father and mother to roam:
Through his travels he may be misguided,
But when finally the black sheep comes
    home,

CHORUS

Everything that he did is forgotten,
And they welcome him back to the fold.
He knows by their sad wrinkled faces
That the pain of his absence has told.
Once again they all sit round the table
As they did in the days of old;
And they'll weep tears of joy,
As they whisper "My boy,"
When the black sheep returns to the fold.

RECITATION

Every homestead has a black sheep;
Every black sheep has a home.
Though the fear of being censured holds him
    back,
You will find there's always one
Who don't care what he's done.
There's a kind, forgiving mother
For every wayward son.
Every child is glad on Christmas;
Everybody knows the cause:
They expect a kind old Santa
At their fireside to pause.
There's a present for the old folks
Who say "God is Santa Claus"
When the black sheep returns to the fold.

VERSE 2

When the smile of a fool starts to fade,
When he finds out the errors he made,
Then the old-fashioned truth
That he heard in his youth
Says, "Go home," but he is afraid.
As he stands on the threshold of sorrow
With the doors of the world closed up tight,
He compares yesterday with tomorrow
And decides that he'll go home that night.

REPEAT CHORUS

I'M DOWN IN HONOLULU LOOKING THEM OVER

Published. Copyrighted October 25, 1916. George Gershwin made a piano roll of this song for the Aeolian Company, probably in the fall of 1916. It was issued in December 1916 under the Metro-Art and Universal Uni-Record brand names.

VERSE 1

You know my uncle Jeremiah,
Who disappeared a month ago;
We got a letter from Hawaii,
And I declare, my uncle's there.
The atmosphere set him on fire;
It simply went right to his head.
What do you think he wrote
In his little note?
This is what he said:

CHORUS

"I'm down in Honolulu looking them over,
I'm down in Honolulu living in clover.
Try and guess the way they dress;
No matter what you think it is, it's even less.
Their language is hard to understand,
Because it's so tricky;
I've got them teaching me
To say 'wicky wicky.'
I don't know what it means,
But it's the best that ever was;
And if it means just what I think it does,
I'll be in Honolulu looking them over
For a long, long time."

VERSE 2

My brother said, "It's very nifty,
Our uncle's got the right idea."
Although my brother's very thrifty,
He sent a wire to Jeremiah;
He said, "I'll go you fifty-fifty
With every hula girl you see."
My brother nearly died;
Uncle just replied,
"Please don't bother me.

REPEAT CHORUS

I'M NOT PREPARED

Published. Copyrighted December 4, 1916.

VERSE 1

Jack McCoy, a soldier boy,
Was taken from the battle wounded;
A pretty Red Cross nurse
Was there to see that he wouldn't get worse.
From the start she won his heart;
So when he started to get better,
He called her to his side
And in a pleading voice he cried:

CHORUS

"Don't make me love you,
Because I'm not prepared;
My heart is weak,
And I'm a trifle scared.
Oh, can't you see I'm in a bad condition,
With no ammunition,
So please don't attack me
With those bewitching eyes.
Each time your fingers touch my wrist,
I can't resist,
I fear that I must surrender.
You've got me in your power;
I'm weak'ning ev'ry hour,
For when I gaze into your great big eyes,
It seems my temp'rature begins to rise.
Please don't make me love you,
Because I'm not prepared."

VERSE 2

Jack cried out, "There is no doubt,
If you continue your attack, dear,

You'll soon capture my fort,
Then I'll be left with a wife to support.
That won't do, I'm warning you,
It won't be easy for your Jack, dear,
To raise a family,
Upon a soldier's salary.

REPEAT CHORUS

SANTA CLAUS—A SYNCOPATED CHRISTMAS SONG

Published in the New York *World Magazine*, December 24, 1916. Rediscovered by Brad Conner and Benjamin Sears.

VERSE

Soon he'll be coming down the chimney
With a bag on his back where he carries a pack of
I don't have to tell you what.
Soon every kid'll holler "Jim'ny!"
If Mister Santa Claus forgets to pause
And leave them this or that.

CHORUS

So you'd better be good,
Just like a good baby should,
Or he will fly right by
To another neighborhood.
He don't give his toys
To bad little boys
Or bad little girls, that's understood;
So don't act like a fool
And don't play hooky from school:
If you're forgotten, you'll know the cause.
If you do anything that's shocking,
You'll find an empty stocking,
And you'll say, "Where is it?"—
You won't get a visit
From Santa Claus.

THE CENTURY GIRL (1916)

Produced by Charles Dillingham and Florenz Ziegfeld Jr. "For the first time on any stage" at the Century Theatre, New York, November 6, 1916. Closed April 28, 1917; 200 performances. Lyrics and music by Irving Berlin and music by Victor Herbert with lyrics by Henry Blossom. Staged by Edward Royce, Leon Errol, and Ned Wayburn. Scenery by Joseph Urban. Orchestra under the direction of Max Hoffman. Orchestrators unknown. Cast: starring Hazel Dawn, Irving Fisher, Marie Dressler, Sam Bernard, Elsie Janis, James Doyle and Harland Dixon, Frank Tinney, Gus Van and Joe Schenck, Billie Allen, and Harry Kelly, and featuring Cathryne Rowe Palmer, Adelaide Bell, Gertrude Rutland, Arthur Cunningham, Maurice and Florence Walton, the Barr Twins, Evelyn Conway, Hazel Lewis, Vera Maxwell, Lilyan Tashman, Marion and Madeline Fairbanks, and John Slavin. Artists came and went during the frequently changing sequences of the "musical entertainment," which on its opening night lasted from 8:25 p.m. until 12:58 a.m. In the words of *Variety:* "As there are only about 90 to 100 minutes to be taken out, it doesn't require much of a knife, just a hydraulic dredger."

THE MUSIC LESSON

Music and lyrics were found among Berlin's papers and are now in the Irving Berlin Collection of the Music Division of the Library of Congress. Introduced in Scene 2 of Act I of *The Century Girl* by Arthur Cunningham (Victor Herbert) and John Slavin (Irving Berlin). This number segued into Herbert's "Kiss Me Again." Alternate title: "Herbert-Berlin Duet."

HERBERT: I'm a composer with a reputation.
  BERLIN: I never heard of you—
        A single word of you.
HERBERT: I have a master mind for orchestration.
  BERLIN: I couldn't orchestrate—
        But I can syncopate.
HERBERT: My music fills them with delight.
  BERLIN: What did you ever write?
CHORUS: Kiss me, etc.

KISS ME ONCE MORE

Possibly intended by Berlin as a countermelody to Victor Herbert's "Kiss Me Again." It may have been sung in this spot in *The Century Girl.*

CHORUS

Kiss me once more, dear,
Kiss me once more;
My love grows stronger
With every kiss, so make them last longer.
Rub off my lip rouge
Just like before—
Oh, sir! Come closer
And kiss me once more.

IT TAKES AN IRISHMAN TO MAKE LOVE

Published. Copyrighted January 11, 1917. Lyric by Irving Berlin and Elsie Janis. Introduced by Elsie Janis (Peggy O'Brien), James Doyle (Will B. Rich), Harland Dixon (Wood B. Rich), and the Sunshine Girls in Scene 4 of Act I of *The Century Girl.*

VERSE 1

It takes a German to make lager beer;
It takes the French to make wine.
It takes a pale-faced man from old Japan
To make a nice embroidered fan;
It takes a Turk to make the cigarettes
For you American men.
It takes a black-eyed Hawaiian lad
To make ukuleles, but then

CHORUS

It takes an Irishman to make love;
It seems to fit them just like a glove.
I know you moneymakers are here in New York,
But all the heartbreakers are over in Cork.
It is not the things that they do,
But how they do them fascinates you;
And when it comes to kissing, sure they stand alone—
For years they've practiced on the Blarney Stone.
And you'll discover

THE COMPLETE LYRICS OF IRVING BERLIN

That the world's great lover
Came from Ireland.

VERSE 2

You've heard them sing in all their Irish songs,
"Ireland fell from the skies";
And I believe it's true their eyes of blue
Are little bits of heaven too.
Talk of your gentlemen from foreign lands
And the polite things they do,
But it's the honey-toned Irish voice
That steals the heart right out of you.

REPEAT CHORUS

THE CHICKEN WALK

Published. Copyrighted November 11, 1916. The Act I finale of *The Century Girl*. The scene is titled "Hunting for a New Dance." Introduced by Arthur Cunningham (the Lion), Hazel Dawn (the Lame Duck), Cathryne Rowe Palmer (the Turkey), John Slavin (the Fox), the Barr Twins (the Two Foxes), Irving Fisher (the Hunter), Billie Allen and Vera Maxwell (the Hunteresses), Elsie Janis (the Chicken), and an ensemble of Lame Ducks, Turkeys, Foxes, and Chickens. Alternate titles: "That Broadway Chicken Walk" and "Jungle Ball Finale." In addition to the published version, there is a more extended show version.

Published version

VERSE

There's a dance that soon will be the talk.
Won't you kindly name it?
It is called the Broadway Chicken Walk.
Who's the one to claim it?
Young and pretty girlies with Mary Pickford curlies
First started doing it in New York.
That Chicken Walk, it's full of fun.
Won't you tell us how it's done?

CHORUS

Scratch the ground with your feet
And then you gaze around.
Should you meet a millionaire,
Don't stare—
Just tell him you won't stop.
Don't stop—
Flap your wings,
Start to talk about engagement rings.
And then you fly back to your coop;
When you get there, gently perch—
Don't forget to leave him in the lurch.
You can bet he'll hang around;
He's found
Wherever you're going, crowing,
"Look out for auto racers
And Broadway chicken chasers
Doing that Broadway Chicken Walk."

Show version

[*The* LION *is directing* MONKEY *waiters.*]

LION: Hurry up and sprinkle the wax on
the ground—
Pretty soon the guests will be
gathered around
To dance at the Jungle Ball;
They're gonna prance all around
the hall.
Make it good and slipp'ry and
hustle along—
Can't you hear them coming and
humming a song?
I vow—here they all come now!

[*The* TIGER, *as butler, announces guests.*]

TIGER: I beg to announce the Grizzly Bears.
CHORUS: Show them in—show them in—show
them in.
GRIZZLY
BEARS: We're the Grizzly Bears,
And we're as proud as millionaires,
Because all over the map
We caused your fingers to snap.
Almost everywhere
They threw their shoulders in the air.
We feel just as toney
As Edison and Marconi,
For didn't we invent the Grizzly Bear?
TIGER: I beg to announce the Lame Ducks.
CHORUS: Show them in—show them in.
LAME
DUCKS: We're the weary lame ducks—
Lame ducks—lame ducks.
Our fate—is to hesitate.
We were known as game ducks—
Game ducks—game ducks.
Now we are lame,
And you are to blame,
And you are to blame,
For you made us walk this way.
TIGER: I beg to announce the Turkeys.
CHORUS: Show them in—show them in.

TURKEYS: Turkey trot, turkey trot—
We're the originators, are we not?
Sorry to say, we must answer
For ev'ry professional dancer.
Just for that, on the spot
All of us should be shot.
Though we're among the living,
Never mind, because on next
Thanksgiving
You will find us in a great big pot,
Steaming hot,
Doing the turkey trot.

[*Note: A portion of the lyric that would follow "Doing the turkey trot" is missing.*]

LEADER: We're not here to hunt for game.
ANIMALS: We'd like to take your word,
But you would break your word.
LEADER: Really that's not why we came.
ANIMALS: Then won't you make it clear
Just what you're doing here?
LEADER: The jungle is the home
Of ev'ry dance except Salome.
So have no fear, we're just here
To learn your latest dance.
LION: If that's really so,
Then a new dance we will show.
HUNTERS: Go!
LION: There's a dance that soon will be
the talk.
HUNTERS: Won't you kindly name it?
LION: It is called the Broadway Chicken
Walk.
HUNTERS: Who's the one to claim it?
LION: Young and pretty girlies
With Mary Pickford curlies.
First started doing it in New York.
That Chicken Walk,
It's full of fun.
HUNTERS: Won't you tell us how it's done?
LION: Scratch the ground with your feet
And then you gaze around.
Should you meet a millionaire,
Don't stare—
Just tell him you won't stop.
Don't stop—
Flap your wings;
Start to talk about engagement
rings.
And then you fly back to your
coop;
When you get there, gently
perch—
Don't forget to leave him in the
lurch.
You can bet he'll hang around;
He's found
Wherever you're going, crowing,

148

"Look out for autoracers
And Broadway chicken chasers
Doing that Broadway Chicken
Walk."
CHORUS: Bring on the chickens,
The cute little chickens,
And we'll show you how to do it.
LION: And when it's done by the
chickens,
The cute little chickens,
You will see there's nothing to it—
You simply
ALL: [*while* CHICKENS *do dance*]
Scratch the ground with your feet
And then you gaze around.
Should you meet a millionaire,
Don't stare—
Just tell him you won't stop.
Don't stop—
Flap your wings;
Start to talk about engagement
rings.
And then you fly back to your
coop;
When you get there, gently
perch—
Don't forget to leave him in the
lurch.
You can bet he'll hang around;
He's found
Wherever you're going, crowing,
"Look out for autoracers
And Broadway chicken chasers
Doing that Broadway Chicken
Walk."
CHICKENS: Look out—look out.
CHORUS: While you walk
CHICKENS: Look out—look out,
For you've got to get used to
Looking out for the rooster
ALL: While you're doing the Chicken
Walk.

[*Curtain.*]

ALICE IN WONDERLAND

Published. Copyrighted November 11, 1916. Introduced by Hazel Dawn (Eva Brown) and Irving Fisher (Howell Lauder), with Yvonne Shelton (Alice) and a huge ensemble of playing cards and children, among them Lilyan Tashman (King of Hearts), Marion Fairbanks (Jack of Diamonds), and Madeline Fairbanks (Jack of Clubs). Berlin wrote a different song with the same title for the *Music Box Revue of 1924* (page 216).

VERSE 1

BOY: Come, little girlie, let's fly away
Into the land of dreams;
Far from the whirly gay cabaret,
Up with the bright sunbeams.
Just let's suppose we are children again;
Just to the past let us gaze.
Come take a trip on a nursery train
Back to our childhood days.

CHORUS

Let's wander hand in hand
To dreamy Wonderland.
Upon a cloud we'll glide;
Side by side we'll stand.
We'll float right through the air,
And when we're landed there,
I'll build a fairy palace
For you, my Alice in Wonderland.

VERSE 2

GIRL: Most every Christmas I used to spend
Hours in Wonderland;
Happy was this miss just to pretend
She was a princess grand.
There with my playthings I dreamed of a
boy,
Hoping my dreams would come true;
I used to say things I thought he'd
enjoy—
That boy resembled you.

REPEAT CHORUS

ON THE TRAIN OF A WEDDING GOWN

Lyrics were found among Berlin's papers and are now in the Irving Berlin Collection of the Music Division of the Library of Congress. No music is known to survive. Introduced by Hazel Dawn and Irving Fisher, Billie Allen and Harry Kelly, Marie Dressler, and Leon Errol, Elsie Janis and Sam Bernard, James Doyle and Harland Dixon, the Barr Sisters, and ensemble as part of Scene 5 of Act III of *The Century Girl*, titled "Procession of the Laces of the World."

HE: How would you like to take a ride
with me

In my automobile?
I'd love to have you sitting side of
me—
Oh, how lovely 'twould feel!
SHE: I would like to go riding with you,
But an automobile wouldn't do.

CHORUS 1

SHE: I used to sigh for a joy ride,
HE: A girl-and-boy ride in my machine.
SHE: My, how we'd fly, 'twas alarming.
HE: You looked as charming as any
queen.
SHE: We would buzz by a dozen
policemen.
HE: How they chased us all over town!
SHE: But now as a bride
HE: You long for a ride
BOTH: On the train of a wedding gown.

CHORUS 2

HE: I love to ride on a freight train.
SHE: A never-late train—they come on
time.
HE: I love to ride on a mail car.
SHE: A never-fail car—a rotten rhyme.
HE: I depend on the Twentieth Century.
SHE: As a train it won great renown.
HE: The one train I find
That's always behind
BOTH: Is the train of a wedding gown.

CHORUS 3

HE: I do the one-step and two-step.
SHE: That's not a new step, you can't deny.
HE: I could just die while I'm waltzing.
SHE: That's what they all sing, but never
die.
HE: I have made quite a large reputation
As a stepper all over town.
SHE: But you'll lose your rep
If ever you step
On the train of my wedding gown.

FINALE

MEN: Come, let us all be wedded.
LADIES: That is the plot and we've got to
thread it.
MEN: No show is ever over until the lovers
are married.
MINISTERS: Promise to honor and obey.
PRINCIPALS: Yea, yea.

MINISTERS: Now we can finish up the play.
ALL: Hurray!
No matter how the actors hate each other and fight,
They've got to get married each night.
CHORUS: That's right.
PRINCIPALS: Now the show is over, good night.
CHORUS: Good night.

MY ONCE-IN-A-CENTURY GIRL

Both Berlin and Victor Herbert wrote "Century Girl" numbers for the opening of Act I of the show. It appears that the version used in the production was by Herbert and Harry Blossom. Berlin's song was probably not used. Lyrics were found among Berlin's papers and are now in the Irving Berlin Collection of the Music Division of the Library of Congress. Earlier title: "My Wonderful Century Girl."

VERSE 1

HE: How can I ever express my feelings,
Wonderful girl, wonderful girl?

Long before I knew of you
I had started to love you;
All my life I've been dreaming
Of a girl like you.

CHORUS 1

Once in a century
A certain girlie appears;
Somehow it happens,
Just once in one hundred years.
She's the fairest and the smartest,
Just an ideal model for an artist.
They pursue her, come to view her,
And say,
"She's like a dainty piece of china,
No finer
We'll see for many a day.
Angels design her,
Then throw the model away.
And as I stand here gazing
Upon your lovely charms,
It's so amazing
I want to throw my arms
Around you—
I've found you,
My once-in-a-century girl."

VERSE 2

SHE: Wonderful compliments you have paid me,
Lovely to hear—thank you, my dear.
I must give you my OK
For each beautiful bouquet.
You tell old-fashioned stories,
But they sound so new.

CHORUS 2

Once in a century
A certain fellow appears;
Somehow it happens,
Just once in a hundred years.
He is charged with Cupid's batt'ry,
And he makes a specialty of flatt'ry.
He's a master, working faster
Each day.
There's something wonderful about him,
Without him
Your life would be such a bore.
Sometimes you doubt him,
Which makes you love him the more.
And as you stand there phrasing
Your pretty tale in rhyme,
It's so amazing
I must confess that I'm enraptured—
You've captured
Your once-in-a-century girl.

Lillian Lorraine and ensemble in "The Blue Devils of France" from Ziegfeld Follies *of 1918*

Songs of 1917–1918

SOMEONE ELSE MAY BE THERE WHILE I'M GONE

Published. Copyrighted January 4, 1917. Probably written in September 1916, since the top-selling (number two on the charts) recording by Al Jolson (Columbia) was made on September 19, 1916.

VERSE 1

I left my darling the other day,
We started quarreling, I went away;
But now I wish that I was back.
I love my baby, indeed I do,
And who knows, maybe she loves me too,
But that's just maybe,
And that won't do.

CHORUS

All that worries me
Is someone else may be there while I'm gone:
In my dreams I see
A couple spooning on the lawn.
That very thought just keeps me worried;
I lay awake till the break of dawn.
I must hurry back,
'Cause someone else may be there while I'm gone.

VERSE 2

I'm wild about her; that is why I'm blue—
I hate to doubt her the way I do;
I may be wrong, I may be right.
Although I worry an awful lot,
If I should hurry back to the spot,
She may be waiting,
She may be not!

REPEAT CHORUS

THE ROAD THAT LEADS TO LOVE

Published. Copyrighted January 9, 1917.

VERSE 1

Once a boy met a man who was famous;
Filled with envy, the boy sadly sighed,

"Oh, how happy I'd be
If such fame smiled on me."
Then the famous man replied:

CHORUS

"The road that leads to fortune and fame
Is paved with gold in your dreams;
But after you've journeyed and reached your aim,
It seldom is all that it seems.
To have, to hold, to love and caress,
Is all we can ask from above;
For the road that leads to happiness
Is the road that leads to love."

VERSE 2

On the highway of love every milestone
Is an angel from heaven above;
All the world will be bright
If you turn to the right,
To the road that leads to love.

REPEAT CHORUS

FROM HERE TO SHANGHAI

Published. Copyrighted January 23, 1917. Probably written in December 1916, as Al Jolson's recording (Columbia), which reached number four on the charts, was made on December 11, 1916.

VERSE 1

I've often wandered down
To dreamy Chinatown,
The home of Ching-a-ling.
It's fine, I must declare,
But now I'm going where
I can see the real, real thing.

CHORUS

I'll soon be there
In a bamboo chair,
For I've got my fare
From here to Shanghai.
Just picture me
Sipping oolong tea
Served by a Chinaman,
Who speaks away up high:
"Hock-a-my, hock-a-my."
I'll eat the way they do,

With a pair of wooden sticks,
And I'll have Ching Ling Foo
Doing all his magic tricks.
I'll get my mail
From a pale pigtail,
For I mean to sail
From here to Shanghai.

VERSE 2

I'll have them teaching me
To speak their language, gee!
When I can talk Chinese,
I'll come home on the run,
Then have a barr'l of fun,
Calling people what I please.

REPEAT CHORUS

DANCE AND GROW THIN

Published. Copyrighted February 6, 1917. Music by George W. Meyer. Introduced in *Dance and Grow Thin*, the midnight revue presented by Charles Dillingham and Florenz Ziegfeld at the Cocoanut Grove Roof of the Century Theatre, New York, beginning on January 18, 1917, by Gus Van, Joe Schenck, and the entire company.

VERSE 1

Some folks who are stout
Worry, there's no doubt;
Doctors come and shout,
"Cut your eating out!"
I just have to grin
At the double chin;
Really, it's a sin—
They could all be thin.

CHORUS

It's very simple if you care to try it;
A million people are reducing by it.
You needn't bother 'bout a silly diet;
Try a one-step or a fox-trot.
Go right ahead and eat a great big luncheon;
I guarantee that you will soon have one chin
Instead of two or three—
Just take a tip from me:
Dance and grow thin.

VERSE 2

Throw your diet book
In the nearest brook;
Chase that weary look;
Fox-trot with your cook.
Starving is abuse;
There is no excuse;
You can all reduce
Your—well, what's the use!

REPEAT CHORUS

THE KIRCHNER GIRL

Unpublished. A typed lyric sheet and a copyist's (possibly Cliff Hess's) lead sheet of the melody were found among Berlin's papers and are now in the Irving Berlin Collection of the Music Division of the Library of Congress. Introduced in *Dance and Grow Thin*, the midnight revue presented by Charles Dillingham and Florenz Ziegfeld at the Cocoanut Grove Roof of the Century Theatre, beginning on January 18, 1917, by Irving Fisher with Leonora Kohler (the Gibson Girl), Florence Cripps (the Brinkley Girl), and Ethel Davies (the Harrison Fisher Girl) and the Kirchner Girls: Evelyn Conway ("Through the Heart"), Elizabeth Chase ("A Feather in Her Hat"), Yvonne Shelton ("Rosalba"), Agnes Jepson ("the Scout Girl"), Beatrice Hughes ("Pierrot"), Lois Gardner ("Spoils of the Chase"), Geraldine Alexander ("Hatched"), Billie Allen ("Temptation"), Lilyan Tashman ("Merry Christmas"), Mlle Semone ("Eve"), Dorothy Leeds ("Little Sister"), Eileen Percy ("Intermezzo"), Vera Maxwell ("Shopping"), Marie Wallace ("Morning Call"), Edna Chase ("Sailor Boy"), and Rosa Davies ("Innocence").

VERSE

We've seen the Gibson Girl,
The Brinkley Girl,
The Harrison Fisher too;
Back in their heyday
We used to say they
Were just the finest a pen ever drew.
But a new girl has come into style
Who has them all beaten a mile.

CHORUS

Sweet Kirchner Girl,
A million hearts are in a whirl
With your grace and your face so fair

You have captured,
Enraptured the boys everywhere.
Your perfect form
Has taken all the world by storm.
To your splendor
We all surrender,
Oh, you beautiful Kirchner Girl.

THE GIBSON GIRL

Don't you remember the Gibson Girl,
Gibson Girl, Gibson Girl?
She made a star out of Miss Suratt.
Outside of that,
Everyone noticed
That from Maine to Frisco
Every Mary Jane and Pearl
Walked with a bend in her back,
Imitating the Gibson Girl.

THE BRINKLEY GIRL

You know the Nell Brinkley Girl,
Who wears a cute, careless curl—
William Randolph Hearst
Says he saw her first,
The beautiful Brinkley Girl.

THE HARRISON FISHER GIRL

Lovely Fisher Belle,
So many wish 'er well—
Her ruby lips just seem to say,
"Come on and woo me,
Snuggle-uggle-uggle to me."
With her baby face
She's worthy of a duke or earl
And we know she's a peach-a-re-no,
Harrison Fisher Girl.

Of all the girls they've shown
There's one who stands alone:

REPEAT CHORUS

LET'S ALL BE AMERICANS NOW

Published. Copyrighted February 17, 1917. Music and lyrics by Irving Berlin, Edgar Leslie, and George W. Meyer. Leading recording by the American Quartet (Victor). The members of the American Quartet in 1917

were Billy Murray, John Young, Steve Porter, and William F. Hooley.

VERSE 1

Peace has always been our pray'r;
Now there's trouble in the air:
War is talked of ev'rywhere.
Still, in God we trust;
Now that war's declared,
We'll show we're prepared,
And fight if we must.

CHORUS

It's up to you!
What will you do?
England or France will have your sympathy
Over the sea,
But you'll agree
That now is the time
To fall in line.
You swore that you would,
So be true to your vow:
Let's all be Americans now.

VERSE 2

Lincoln, Grant, and Washington,
They were peaceful men, each one;
Still, they took the sword and gun
When real trouble came,
And I feel somehow
They are wond'ring now
If we'll do the same.

REPEAT CHORUS

THERE'S SOMETHING NICE ABOUT THE SOUTH

Published. Copyrighted April 2, 1917. The program for the midnight revue *Dance and Grow Thin* (Cocoanut Grove Roof of the Century Theatre, beginning January 18, 1917) lists a song titled "Way Down South," introduced by Gus Van and Joe Schenck and ensemble. It is almost certainly the same song as "There's Something Nice About the South."

VERSE

I've been a traveling chap,
Traveled all over the map,
From London to Jamaica,
Where they make the ginger snap.
I've seen America through,
Right down to Kalamazoo,
And talking 'bout America,
Let me say to you:

CHORUS

There's something nice about the South;
A paradise is way down South.
It seems that nowadays
They love to sing its praise;
A song of Dixie lingers in ev'ry singer's mouth.
There's something sweet about their ways;
The girls you meet are oh! so different.
Tennessee, Florida, Alabam',
Fav'rite children of Uncle Sam—
There's something nice about the South.

THERE ARE TWO EYES IN DIXIE

Published. Copyrighted May 5, 1917.

VERSE 1

When I left the old folks
Down in Dixieland,
From that very moment
I could understand
Why they put two i's in "Dixie"
When they spell that word.
Here's the simple reason;
It's the best you've ever heard.

CHORUS

There are two i's in "Dixie,"
D-I-X-I-E,
Two eyes in Dixie
Always watching me;
And while I'm straying,
By day and night,
They keep on saying,
"Turn to the right."
Makes no diff'rence where I wander
Or where I happen to be;
I simply can't go wrong,

Because the whole day long,
There are two eyes in Dixie
Watching me.

VERSE 2

Ev'ry night you'll find me
With a pen in hand,
Writing them a letter
Down in Dixieland.
I can see two eyes in Dixie,
Reading what I write;
And I ask their blessing
When I say my pray'rs each night.

REPEAT CHORUS

FOR YOUR COUNTRY AND MY COUNTRY

Published. Copyrighted May 8, 1917. Listed on sheet music as "The Official Recruiting Song." Leading recordings by the Peerless Quartet (Columbia) and by the opera star Frances Alda (Victor). Sung in the film version of *This Is the Army* (1943) by Frances Langford and ensemble.

VERSE 1

We know you love your land of liberty;
We know you love your U.S.A.
But if you want the world to know it,
Now's the time to show it;
Your uncle Sammy needs you one and all—
Answer to his call.

CHORUS

It's your country, it's my country,
With millions of real fighting men;
It's your duty and my duty,
To speak with the sword, not the pen.
If Washington were living today,
With sword in hand he'd stand up and say,
"For your country and my country,
I'll do it all over again."

VERSE 2

America has opened up her heart
To ev'ry nationality,
And now she asks of ev'ry nation

Their appreciation;
It makes no difference now from where you came,
We are all the same.

REPEAT CHORUS

HOW CAN I FORGET (WHEN THERE'S SO MUCH TO REMEMBER)?

Published. Copyrighted May 25, 1917. Featured in England, according to a photo and information on the sheet music of the United Kingdom edition, by Derickson and Brown.

VERSE 1

When the morn bids me rise,
And I open my eyes,
I begin with a sweet thought of you;
Then the rest of the day,
While at work or at play,
I'm thinking, just thinking of you.

CHORUS

How can I forget
When there's so much to remember:
Your smiling face,
Your fond embrace,
Your voice so sweet and tender?
After all these years,
I'm afraid I love you yet;
When there's so much to remember,
How can I forget?

VERSE 2

Through the heartbreaking years
I have smiled through my tears;
To have met you is well worth the pain.
Though we've drifted apart,
You'll remain in my heart
As long as my heart will remain.

REPEAT CHORUS

SMILE AND SHOW YOUR DIMPLE

Published. Copyrighted August 20, 1917. Leading recording by Sam Ash (Columbia). In 1933 Berlin used part of the melody of the chorus as the principal source for the music of "Easter Parade."

VERSE 1

Little girlie, you look sad;
I'm afraid you're feeling bad
Because he's leaving.
But stop your grieving, little girl;
He don't want you to feel blue,
For it's not the thing to do.
It will soon be over;
Then he'll come marching back to you.

CHORUS

Smile and show your dimple;
You'll find it's very simple:
You can think of something comical
In a very little while.
Chase away the wrinkle;
Sprinkle just a twinkle:
Light your face up,
Just brace up and smile.

VERSE 2

Little girlie, don't you know
That your pearly teeth will show
If you start smiling?
So keep on smiling, little girl;
You can cut your cares in half
If you only try to laugh.
Look into my cam'ra—
I'm goin' to take your photograph.

REPEAT CHORUS

WHOSE LITTLE HEART ARE YOU BREAKING NOW?

Published. Copyrighted August 27, 1917. Leading recording by Albert Campbell and Henry Burr (Columbia). Lyric rewritten by Berlin in 1947. Alternate titles of later version: "Whose Foolish Heart Are You Breaking Now?" and "Whose Loving Heart Are You Breaking Now?"

VERSE 1

Butterfly,
You're like a butterfly,
Baby vampire:
Through the year
You're sipping honey here
And there.
Your love is like a blushing rose;
It just comes and goes.
Butterfly,
You're just a butterfly,
With your string of helpless beaux.

CHORUS

Whose little heart are you breaking now,
Little butterfly?
Who is the one that you're shaking now,
Little butterfly?
Who keeps on ringing your telephone,
One-two-three-four?
Who keeps on singing,
"What do you want to make those eyes at me for?"
Who sends you candy and flowers now,
Little butterfly,
Spending above what his folks allow?
I wonder whose feelings you're hurting
When he catches you flirting;
Whose little heart are you breaking now?

VERSE 2

Seems to me
You're like a bumblebee,
Baby vampire:
Buzzing round,
But never settling down,
That's you!
Why don't you give up stinging hearts?
Don't you know it smarts?
Taking them
And simply breaking them
In a thousand diff'rent parts?

REPEAT CHORUS

Revised version of chorus, c. 1947

Whose little heart are you breaking now?
Who is the one you are shaking now?
Whose tears are falling
While you're with a new romancer?
Who keeps on calling
Just to hear the central say "No answer"?
Who spends his evenings without you now,
Wond'ring whose arms are about you now?
I wonder whose feelings you're hurting
When he catches you flirting;
Whose little heart are you breaking now?

Unfinished chorus, c. 1947

Whose foolish heart are you breaking now?
Who is the one you are shaking now?
Whose tears are falling
While everyone's deep in slumber?
Who keeps on calling
Wondering why the central says "Wrong number"?
Whose loving kiss are you tired of now?
Who's winding up with a broken vow?

MR. JAZZ HIMSELF

Published. Copyrighted August 27, 1917. Performed in recent years and recorded by Max Morath.

VERSE 1

I know a certain young fellow
Who's filling people with joy;
How would you like to say hello
To this remarkable boy?
Ev'ryone's talking about him,
He's been the topic for days;
He's just a winsome gent
With an instrument that plays—
I'd like to have you meet him.

CHORUS

Shake hands with Mister Jazz himself!
He took the saxophone from off the shelf,
And when you hear him play,
You'll say that he's been taking lessons up in heaven.
That dreamy moan is his own 'riginality;
He knows a strange sort of change in a minor key.
I don't know how he does it,
But when he starts to play the blues,
He's like a messenger of happy news;
No one else could ever do it as
My friend Mister Jazz.

VERSE 2

I never cared about discords,
They never cared about me;
But when I listen to his chords,
We both agree to agree.
He's not a Wagner or Verdi,
He's not a classy highbrow;
He's just the boy who has
Put the joy in jazz—and now
I'd like to have you meet him.

REPEAT CHORUS

MY SWEETIE

Published. Copyrighted October 11, 1917.

VERSE 1

I never felt so happy before;
A little rascal knocked at my door.
It's Cupid that I'm speaking of—
I'm in love,
So in love.
I must confess that right from the start
I went and lost my heart.

CHORUS

Wait till you see me with my sweetie,
Showing her off to the crowd;
Looking so dreamy at my sweetie,
Feeling so terribly proud.
She makes a specialty
Of looking good to me;
She ought to be right in Tiffany's window—
She's a jewel,
I know that you'll agree.
Wait till I'm married to my sweetie,
How happy I'll be;
I've got the bungalow paid for,
I've had it specially made for
My sweetie,
Sweetie-eetie-eetie,
My sweetie and me.

VERSE 2

You've seen an exhibition where they
Charge you a large admission to stay.
Fine, I know,
But don't go;

I've got a picture and it's a treat—
You needn't buy a seat.

REPEAT CHORUS

I'LL TAKE YOU BACK TO ITALY

Published. Copyrighted October 13, 1917. Introduced in the musical *Jack O'Lantern* (Globe Theatre, New York; October 16, 1917; 265 performances) by Fred Stone and Teresa Valerio. Alternate title (out-of-town tryout): "Sunny Italy." Revived in recent years by John Wallowitch and Bertram Ross.

VERSE 1

TONY: I like-a you, Marie.
MARIE: I like-a you, Tony.
TONY: We gonna make-a marriage soon.
MARIE: Make-a da nice-a honeymoon.
TONY: After I marry you—
MARIE: What are you gonna do?

CHORUS 1

TONY: I'll take-a you back with me,
    Back to sunny Italy.
MARIE: That's where I would like to be,
    In the old country.
TONY: Across the sea.
MARIE: No more you make the organ grind.
TONY: I leave the org' behind.
MARIE: I'll cook spaghetti.
TONY: That's very good, Eddie.
MARIE: The nice Italian kind.
TONY: We'll raise-a da family.
MARIE: They will look like you and me.
TONY: How many we have, Marie?
MARIE: One, two, or three.
TONY: Plenty enough for me.
MARIE: What will we do with the monk'?
    They'll never let him pass.
TONY: We'll give the monk' to Missus Vernon
    Cas'
BOTH: And sail back to sunny Italy.

VERSE 2

TONY: We'll have a little wop.
MARIE: Someone to call you "Pop."
TONY: He'll look like his daddy did.

MARIE: Gee, but he'll be a homely kid!
TONY: We'll call-a him Tony.
MARIE: Maybe he'll be a she!

CHORUS 2

TONY: I'll take-a you back with me,
    Back to sunny Italy.
MARIE: That's where I'd like to be,
    In the old country.
TONY: Across the sea.
MARIE: No more you make the organ grind.
TONY: I leave the org' behind.
MARIE: I'll cook spaghetti.
TONY: That's very good, Eddie.
MARIE: The nice Italian kind.
TONY: We'll tell-a da family—
MARIE: They must never cross the sea.
TONY: The money in this country—
MARIE: Is not so free—
TONY: As it's supposed to be.
MARIE: We'll sell the barbershop business,
    It never pays;
TONY: Ev'ryone here, they use the safety raz'.
BOTH: So we came to sunny Italy.

POOR LITTLE RICH GIRL'S DOG

Published. Copyrighted October 13, 1917. Introduced by Joseph Cawthorn (Joseph Guppy) in the musical comedy *Rambler Rose* (Empire Theatre, New York; September 10, 1917; 72 performances).

VERSE 1

Ev'ry time I see you sitting in your daddy's lap,
My heart fills up with sympathy for you;
I am pretty sure that you would be a far more
    happy chap
If you could do what other doggies do.
They say it's blissful to be dumb, and if that's
    really so,
I'm mighty glad that ignorance is bliss;
It's better that they meant you to be dumb,
    because I know
'Twould break your heart if you knew what you
    miss.

CHORUS 1

You've never had a horseshoe or a can tied to your
    tail;

You never yet have stuck your nose into a garbage
pail.
You're not allowed to chase the cat around the
place
Or come home in the evening with a lovely dirty
face.
While all the other human dogs go round without
a care,
A-hunting for their breakfast and their dinner
here and there,
They feed you indigestion from a Plaza bill of
fare,
Poor little rich girl's dog.

VERSE 2

Ev'ry day an English butler dolls you up in style,
And you and Madam motor off to tea;
Then you have to sit up straight and look your
very grandest while
Your mistress lies about your pedigree.
They pick you out a soul mate that they purchase
at the store,
You're not allowed to choose your future wife;
You have to marry someone that you never met
before—
My God, but you do lead a rotten life!

CHORUS 2

You've never sunk your teeth into a hobo's trouser
patch;
They chase the fleas so you can't have a good old-
fashioned scratch.
You're not allowed to greet a dog upon the street;
The straight-and-narrow path for yours—you
can't be indiscreet.
You don't know what it means to have a great big
juicy bone;
Your mistress doesn't think it right to let you out
alone;
Her husband, who wears corsets, has to be your
chaperone—
Poor little rich girl's dog.

WASN'T IT YESTERDAY

Published. Copyrighted October 29, 1917.

VERSE

Grandma is seventy-four;
Grandpa is eighty or more.

Through all sorts of weather
Those dear souls grew old together,
Ofttimes like children at play;
I hear Grandpa say;

CHORUS

"Wasn't it yesterday
When first I met you?
Wasn't it yesterday
When you became my bride?
I drove to town in a hack
And brought the minister back
To your father's rickety shack,
Where the knot was tied.
It seems just yesterday,
And now we're old and gray;
When you're in love,
How the time does fly!"

IF I HAD MY WAY, I'D LIVE AMONG THE GYPSIES

Written in 1917. Never published. This song has an in-
teresting story, much of which was set down in a press
release issued in 1943 by 20th Century–Fox to herald
a film on the life of the famed American aviator and
war hero Captain Edward Vernon Rickenbacker
(1890–1973):

Irving Berlin's re-discovery of "If I Had My Way,
I'd Live Among the Gypsies," a song of his which
has been a hit for twenty-six years without his
knowledge, was disclosed here yesterday.

Berlin's Gypsy song was the most popular song
among the American flyers in France in 1918 and
was adopted as the official song of the Ninety-
fourth Squadron, or Hat-In-The-Ring Squadron,
which was commanded by Capt. Edward V. Rick-
enbacker.

Before he could publish the song, Berlin was
in Camp Yaphank with the Seventy-seventh Divi-
sion. In the Army he forgot all about life among
the Gypsies, and left the only copy of the song in
a trunk, where it remained from that day until
yesterday. One of the few who had heard Berlin
sing it was a young unknown Greenwich Village
youngster named Cole Porter, who memorized
the words and music. Porter, who went to France
as an ambulance driver about the same time that
soldier Berlin went to Yaphank, made the Gypsy
song a part of his routine in army camps. It was a
hit everywhere he played it.

When he heard it, Capt. Rickenbacker asked

for a copy of the song for the Ninety-fourth
Squadron, but there was no copy. The American
Ace of Aces memorized it and introduced it in a
cracked falsetto voice to his comrades. It became
the hit of hits with American flyers of the
Ninety-fourth and other squadrons. Since the war
it has been sung with vim and gusto at reunions of
American World War pilots.

Winfield Sheehan, producer of *Rickenbacker,
The Story of An American*, wanted to use "If I
Had My Way, I'd Live Among the Gypsies" as the
theme song of the Rickenbacker picture and tele-
phoned Berlin for a piano copy of it.

"I think you've got me mixed up with some-
body else," said Berlin. "I didn't write any Gypsy
song for the American flyers in 1917."

Sheehan said that the World War pilots, who
had been singing it for years, all said it was an Irv-
ing Berlin song. He started to repeat some of the
lyric lines.

"Oh, yes," said the startled Berlin, "I had for-
gotten all about that. I wrote that to fit the charac-
ter of Douglas Fairbanks, who was living in New
York at the Hotel Algonquin at the time. He was a
great roamer and world traveler, always on the
move, and I got the idea of putting his love of
wandering into a song. I forgot it and thought
everybody else had."

Remembering that Cole Porter had been en-
thusiastic about it, Berlin telephoned him and
asked if he recalled the lyric.

"Do I? I'll sing it to you now," said Porter. He
played and sang it for Berlin over the phone.

"I sang it everywhere I went in France,"
said Porter later. "It was always a hit. It would
have been a sensation everywhere if it had been
published."

There was no radio then, and without any
sheet music, its circulation was limited to those
who memorized it. The song has terrific gusto and
all the natural Berlin swing and rhythm. Irving
had forgotten about it, but after returning to
France, Cole Porter told him what a hit it has
been, but he just let it lie in his trunk.

The song was introduced to the Ninety-fourth
at Toul, France, when they were battling against
the famous von Richtofen Flying Circus. One of
the piano-thumpers who sang it in France was
John G. Winant, now American Ambassador to
England, who was flying with a squadron which
had a hangar beside that of the Ninety-fourth.
The song was sung for General Billy Mitchell,
Major Carl A. Spaatz, and visiting French Gener-
als by a quartet of pilots of the Ninety-fourth
consisting of Rickenbacker; Le Roy Prinz, now a
motion picture director in Hollywood; Jimmy
Meissner, an American ace now in Africa; and
Hamilton Coolidge, President Coolidge's nephew,

who was killed in combat after downing eight German fighting planes.

Berlin didn't even copyright the song. He found his old piano copy yesterday in the trunk in Hollywood. The song will be featured in the Rickenbacker picture.

Berlin offered a succinct version of the story in a letter of June 10, 1943, to Harry Brand of 20th Century–Fox:

The simple facts are:—I wrote a song in 1917 that was never published, very much as "God Bless America" was written and put aside until 1938. In the case of the Rickenbacker song, I had never done anything about it nor never intended to. Cole Porter, for whom I played the song, memorized it and took it overseas. It became the theme song for the Rickenbacker flying squad—something I didn't know about until he told Winnie Sheehan about it. I now find myself with an important manuscript. We have yet to see whether it will become an important song. If the song doesn't become a hit, it will wind up as just a good, true story—and nothing more.

On September 2, 1943, Fox executive Sheehan wrote Berlin to tell him that they had decided, after all, not to use the song in the Rickenbacker film. In a letter to Sheehan of September 15, 1943, Berlin accepted the decision with good grace.

If I had my way,
I'd live among the Gypsies;
If I had my way,
That's where I'd love to stay.
I'd hear the call of the wild;
They'd call me Nobody's Child.
I'd love to stop at farms
And stretch my arms
And breathe the new-mown hay.
If I had my way
I'd travel with the Gypsies,
Where they laugh and play
And everything's okay.
I'd love to give my face a coat of tan,
Trav'ling through the country in a caravan
All day,
If I had my way.

DOWN WHERE THE JACK-O'-LANTERNS GROW

Published. Copyrighted February 23, 1918. Introduced in *The Cohan Revue 1918* (New Amsterdam Theatre, New York; December 31, 1917; 96 performances). The artists who first sang it are unknown, as the show's programs listed only the titles and authors of the songs presented, not the performers who first introduced them. Alternate title (program): "Down Where the Pumpkins Grow." Other Berlin songs presented in *The Cohan Revue 1918* were "Pretty Polly" (music only), "Show Me the Way," "A Man Is Only a Man," "King of Broadway," "The Wedding of Words and Music," and "A Bad Chinaman from Shanghai." They are lost.

VERSE 1

I really think that Broadway
Is just a false alarm;
It's just a great big fraudway
Compared to a farm.
A lot of folks may like it,
But I could not agree;
It may be good enough for them,
But not for me.

CHORUS

I'm gonna stay right here where the jack-o'-
lanterns grow;
I'm gonna wake each morn when the rooster starts
to crow.
Then when I'm through milking the cow,
I'll be out working the plow,
While the birds sing a little hello.
I'm gonna settle down with a certain gal I know,
Until the day comes round when I must really go;
Then, should the angels whisper,
"What have you been?"
I'll say, "I've been a Reuben,
Down where the jack-o'-lanterns grow."

VERSE 2

I stop my work at sundown,
And if I want to roar,
I comb my hair and run down
To Si's grocery store.
I hear the latest songs there,
I've got them all down pat;
I know "Poor Butterfly" by heart—
Just think of that!

REPEAT CHORUS

WHEN THE CURTAIN FALLS (FIRST ACT, SECOND ACT, AND THIRD ACT)

Published. Copyrighted March 1, 1918. Introduced in *Going Up* (Liberty Theatre, New York; December 25, 1917; 351 performances) by Frank Craven (Robert Street) and Edith Day (Grace Douglas).

VERSE 1

SHE: I have a cute idea for a play.
HE: Tell me about it, do.
SHE: It's just a story of ev'ry day.
HE: Nothing today is new.
SHE: There isn't much to my little plot.
HE: I'm sure it's more than you say.
SHE: Maybe you will not like it a lot.
HE: Tell me about your play.

CHORUS

In the first act a girl and boy appear;
In the second act their fam'lies interfere:
A row is started, they're brokenhearted,
And soon they're parted, for one long year.
In the third act the lovers meet again,
And before they take their curtain calls,
We see them spending a happy ending
In the last act when the curtain falls.

VERSE 2

SHE: What do you think of my little play?
HE: I think it simply great.
SHE: Somebody may produce it someday.
HE: I'll bet you just can't wait.
SHE: I wonder what the critics will say.
HE: I'm sure 'twill fill them with joy.
SHE: I'd love to be the girl in the play.
HE: I'd love to be the boy.

REPEAT CHORUS

THEY WERE ALL OUT OF STEP BUT JIM

Published. Copyrighted March 9, 1918. Leading recording by Billy Murray (Victor). Revived by Max Morath.

VERSE 1

Jimmy's mother went to see her son
Marching along on parade;
In his uniform and with his gun,
What a lovely picture he made!
She came home that ev'ning
Filled up with delight,
And to all the neighbors
She would yell with all her might:

CHORUS 1

"Did you see my little Jimmy marching
With the soldiers up the avenue?
There was Jimmy just as stiff as starch,
Like his daddy on the seventeenth of March.
Did you notice all the lovely ladies
Casting their eyes on him?
Away he went
To live in a tent;
Over in France with his regiment.
Were you there, and tell me, did you notice?
They were all out of step but Jim."

VERSE 2

That night little Jimmy's father stood
Buying the drinks for the crowd;
You could tell that he was feeling good:
He was talking terribly loud.
Twenty times he treated—
My, but he was dry!
When his glass went empty,
He would treat again and cry:

CHORUS 2

"Did you see my little Jimmy marching
With the soldiers up the avenue?
There was Jimmy just as stiff as starch,
Like his daddy on the seventeenth of March.
Did you notice all the lovely ladies
Casting their eyes on him?
It made me glad
To gaze at the lad;
Lord help the Kaiser if he's like his dad.
Were you there, and tell me, did you notice?
They were all out of step but Jim."

THE DEVIL HAS BOUGHT UP ALL THE COAL

Published. Copyrighted March 14, 1918.

VERSE 1

Ev'ryone's hollering, "Me oh my,
We're in a terrible hole!"
Ev'ryone's hollering, "Tell us why
There is a shortage of coal."
I have the whole thing figured out;
Really it isn't so bad.
I know the cause without a doubt,
Why there's no coal to be had.

CHORUS 1

The Devil has bought up all the coal;
He's goin' to save it, I swear,
Until the Kaiser gets there—
He means to make it warm for Mister William.
The Devil has spent his little roll
For all the coal from ev'rywhere;
He's piling it up by the ton,
And oh, what he'll do to that Hun!
There'll be a hot time in Hades
When the Kaiser gets there.

VERSE 2

Satan is freezing way down below;
He feels a terrible chill.
Still he won't use up his coal—oh, no!
Satan is waiting for Bill.
If he can stand it, why can't we?
Tell all the grumblers to pause:
Although we freeze, let's shout with glee—
It's for a wonderful cause.

CHORUS 2

The Devil has bought up all the coal;
He's going to save it, I swear,
Until the Kaiser gets there—
He means to make it warm for Mister William.
I'd give Mister Rockefeller's roll
To see the Kaiser, I declare,
And whisper in his little ear,
"You don't know the half of it, dear."
There'll be a hot time in Hades
When the Kaiser gets there.

DEAR DOCTOR

Verse (there is no music) written by Berlin on March 25, 1918, and sent to his physician, Otto M. Schwerdtfeger. Thirty-five years later Schwerdtfeger wrote to Berlin as follows:

March 2, 1953

Dear Irving:

After forty-two years of living at 54 East 58th St., we have been obliged to move because the old houses are being renovated. One collects a great many things in the course of years and a treasure was found way back in the top drawer of my desk. It was sent to me 35 years ago and enclosed is a copy which I thought would interest you and remind you of an old friend.

Trusting that you and yours are well and happy, I am

Very sincerely yours,
Otto M. Schwerdtfeger

March 25th, 1918

Dear Doctor:

I'm writing you this letter
To say that I'm better,
As far as my stomach is concerned;
I keep to my diet
And profit much by it:
Three pounds and a half I have earned.
At sleeping, however,
My every endeavor
Is meeting with failure; what's more
A nasal musician
Makes worse the condition,
And God! How that fellow can snore!
He's my next-door roomer,
Whose idea of humor
Is snoring bass solos at night.
The walls are like tissue,
So his every issue
Of thunder just fills me with fright.
I've swallowed up oceans
Of strong sleeping potions,
But never a wink can I get;
With every new powder
His snoring gets louder—
I haven't tried ether as yet,
So me for the latter,
If that doesn't matter
I'm going to dig him a grave,
Then, armed with a saber,

I'll visit my neighbor
And give him a very close shave.

Sleeplessly yours,
Irving Berlin

December 7, 1953

Dear Doctor:

Your letter enclosing the verse I sent you in 1918 was forwarded here to me. Many thanks.

I had forgotten all about having sent this to you and was, of course, glad to get a copy. It is interesting to note how far back I was complaining about my insomnia.

Sometime after I get back, I'll give you a ring and maybe we might meet for a cocktail.

Again my thanks—and with my very best wishes, I am

Sincerely,

OVER THE SEA, BOYS

Published. Copyrighted May 7, 1918.

VERSE 1

In uniform we represent
The navy of our President,
Yo-ho! Yo-ho!
We try to be as Dewey was,
The fearless man we knew he was,
Yo-ho! Yo-ho!
With watchful eye we take our post
To guard our uncle Sammy's coast,
Yo-ho! Yo-ho!
We'll fill our guns with navy beans
And shoot the German submarines,
Yo-ho! Yo-ho!

CHORUS

Over the sea, boys, we're assigned,
With the land we love ever in mind;
Over the ocean, full of devotion
For the girls we left behind.

VERSE 2

We're each a son of Washington,
And each a man behind a gun,
Yo-ho! Yo-ho!
The fun'ral march is all rehearsed,

If we should see the Kaiser first,
Yo-ho! Yo-ho!
We don't get much for what we do,
But what we do means much to you,
Yo-ho! Yo-ho!
We have to leave our wives behind
For fighting of a diff'rent kind,
Yo-ho! Yo-ho!

REPEAT CHORUS

I'M GONNA PIN A MEDAL ON THE GIRL I LEFT BEHIND

Published. Copyrighted July 2, 1918. Introduced by Frank Carter (a Private) with Gus Minton (a General), Martha Mansfield (the Girl I Left Behind), and male ensemble in the *Ziegfeld Follies of 1918* (New Amsterdam Theatre; June 18, 1918; 151 performances). Leading recording by the Peerless Quartet (Victor). Alternate title (program): "I'll Pin My Medal on the Girl I Left Behind."

VERSE 1

Over there in France
In a big advance
Little Johnny stood the test.
Johnny held his ground;
Now he struts around
With a medal on his chest.
There's a happy look in his eyes,
And ev'ry now and then he cries:

CHORUS

"I'm gonna pin my medal on the girl I left behind;
She deserves it more than I,
For the way she said goodbye.
You should have seen her try
To keep away the tears that blind;
A braver hero would be hard to find.
She puts a smile in ev'ry letter that she signs,
But I can read what's in her heart between the
lines,
And when I get back,
Yes, when I get back,
I'm gonna pin my medal on the girl I left behind."

VERSE 2

When the boys come home
From across the foam

To the girls they love the best,
There'll be more than one
Little Yankee son
With a medal on his chest.
When the drive is over this spring,
A lot of soldier boys will sing:

REPEAT CHORUS

THE CIRCUS IS COMING TO TOWN

Published. Copyrighted August 27, 1918. Introduced in Charles Dillingham's production *Everything* (Hippodrome, New York; August 22, 1918; 461 performances) by the Elm City Four and ensemble in the "2nd Thing" (each scene was listed as a "thing").

VERSE 1

Honey, did you see that bill,
Pasted there on yonder hill?
Kindly pay attention
To what the letters mention;
'Twill give you a wonderful thrill.
Chase away those weary blues—
Ain't you heard the happy news?

CHORUS

Circus is coming to town,
Circus is coming to town:
Two dozen acrobats from o'er the foam,
And Salome, Hip-Hip-Hippodrome.
Come see the comical clown
Turning himself upside down;
Come and purchase a photograph
Of the freaks and the big giraffe;
Open your dining room and start to laugh—
The circus is coming to town.

VERSE 2

Come and see the big parade;
Jazzy music will be played.
Just before we're seated,
I'll see that you are treated
To peanuts and red lemonade.
Barnum had the right idea—
Come and give him one big cheer.

REPEAT CHORUS

COME ALONG TO TOY TOWN

Published. Copyrighted August 27, 1918. Introduced in *Everything* by Belle Story and ensemble in the "4th Thing."

VERSE 1

We have heard the wise men say,
Each working day
Should have an hour of play.
So if you'll come with me,
I'll show the way
Where all the playthings are—
It's not so very far.

CHORUS

Come along to Toy Town,
Let me take you there;
It's a wond'rous joy town,
Free from ev'ry care.
Come join the curly heads
That glisten with gold;
There's room for silver threads,
No matter how old.
When you see the playthings,
You will dance and sing;
Come and hear them say things
When you pull the string.
'Twill take you back to the shack
Where you played upon the floor—
Come to Toy Town
And be a kiddy once more.

VERSE 2

If your hair is tinged with gray,
A toy each day
Will keep the gray away.
We really never grow too old to play;
The land of harmless joys
Makes old folks girls and boys.

REPEAT CHORUS

DING DONG

Published. Copyrighted August 27, 1918. Introduced in *The Canary* (Globe Theatre, New York; November 4,

1918; 152 performances) by the entire company. Also performed in *Yip, Yip, Yaphank* (1918) in a slightly different version (page 167).

VERSE 1

I'm so happy today;
Things are coming my way.
There's a wonderful reason
Why I'm feeling so gay.
Now you never will guess,
So I'd better confess
Why I'm so happy:
My Melinda said yes.

CHORUS

Ding dong, ding dong,
Hear those joy bells ring?
Ting-a-ling-a-ling.
My little Lindy whispered in my ear,
"Set the date, honey, don't you wait,"
And ever since, all I can hear is
Ding dong, ding dong.
Listen to those joy bells chime.
I've had my fortune read,
And here's what the Gypsy said:
"You're gwine to be happy for a long, long
    time."

VERSE 2

Come and follow the crowd,
Ev'rybody's allowed;
Come and look at the reason
Why I'm feeling so proud:
She's a picture to see,
Just as nice as could be,
A bunch of sweetness
Made to order for me.

REPEAT CHORUS

THE BLUE DEVILS OF FRANCE

Published. Copyrighted September 4, 1918. Introduced in Act II of *Ziegfeld Follies of 1918* (New Amsterdam Theatre, New York; June 18, 1918; 151 performances) by Lillian Lorraine and ensemble. Alternate title (program): "The Blue Devils."

VERSE

I've seen many diff'rent pictures
Of the Devil down below,
And he doesn't stand a show
With a certain devil I know.
Let me introduce you to him;
You'll be happy when I do.
He's a devil dressed in blue
And a soldier through and through.

CHORUS

High up in the Alpine Mountains
Are the Blue Devils,
Where the rain of shrapnel fountains
Scar the Blue Devils.
With their glistening sabers,
Amid the shot and shell,
They visit their Austrian neighbors
And give them H-E–double L,
H-E–double L.
Strong and active, most attractive
Are the Blue Devils.
They came here the Liberty Loan to advance;
We entertained them with the best;
And now they've gone back to the trenches to rest,
Those Devils, the Blue Devils of France.

I WOULDN'T GIVE "THAT" FOR THE MAN WHO COULDN'T DANCE

Published. Copyrighted October 15, 1918. Introduced in *The Canary* by Julia Sanderson (Julie), James Doyle (Dodge), and Harland Dixon (Fleece).

VERSE

SHE: The Tom, Dick, or Harry
    That I ever marry
    Will have to be a dancer
    Before he gets my answer.
HE: I'm not much at dancing,
    But as for romancing,
    I know a thing or two.
SHE: But that would never do.
HE: Why wouldn't it?

CHORUS

I wouldn't give "that"
For the man who couldn't dance,

If only a little bit.
He'd have to take a chance,
For when the band starts playing a lively air,
That's when he'll have to be there,
With a light fantastic, very elastic.
I wouldn't waste one little tiny little glance,
No matter how very much he spoke about
romance;
He may be handsome, wealthy, full of
personality—
I wouldn't give "that"
For the man
Who couldn't dance with me.

IT'S THE LITTLE BIT OF IRISH

Published. Copyrighted October 15, 1918. Not listed in New York programs of *The Canary*. Apparently dropped from the show before the New York opening.

VERSE 1

When Irish meets Irish,
They will seldom disagree;
There's a perfect understanding,
Like a chord of harmony.
They talk the same;
And they walk the same;
They think the same, they do—
That's just why you fancy me
And I fancy you.

CHORUS

Why do you love what I do?
It's the little bit of Irish
That's in your heart.
When McCormack sings,
Why do you shout with joy?
If a band should start
Playing an Irish rhythm,
You'd go with 'em.
Why do you speak as I do,
With a little bit of brogue,
From which you'll never part?
When you see a three-leaf clover,
Why do you smile all over?
It's the little bit of Irish in your heart.

VERSE 2

When Irish meets Irish,
Should they ever start a fight,

They will leave it to a German
To decide which one is right.
Lord help the Hun,
The lucky one
Who's picked out to decide;
Hist'ry tells us that's just how
A thousand Huns died.

REPEAT CHORUS

GOODBYE, FRANCE (YOU'LL NEVER BE FORGOTTEN BY THE U.S.A.)

Published. Copyrighted November 23, 1918.

VERSE 1

I can picture the boys over there
Making plenty of noise over there,
And if I'm not wrong,
It won't be long
Ere a certain song will fill the air;
It's all very clear,
The time's drawing near
When they'll be marching down to the pier,
singing:

CHORUS

"Goodbye, France,
We'd love to linger longer, but we must go home;
Folks are waiting to welcome us across the foam.
We were glad to stand side by side with you,
Mighty proud to have died with you,
So goodbye, France,
You'll never be forgotten by the U.S.A."

VERSE 2

They are waiting for one happy day
When the word comes to start on their way;
With a tear-dimmed eye
They'll say goodbye,
But their hearts will cry, "Hip hip hooray!"
The friends that they made
Will wish that they stayed
As they start on their homeward parade, singing:

REPEAT CHORUS

I HAVE JUST ONE HEART FOR JUST ONE BOY

Published. Copyrighted November 23, 1918, and again on December 7, 1918. Introduced in *The Canary* (Globe Theatre, New York; November 4, 1918; 152 performances) by Julia Sanderson (Julie) and Florence Bruce, Evelyn Conway, Pauline Hall, Doris Faithful, Albertina Marlowe, and Mildred Sinclair (Johnnies). Alternate title (program): "I Have Just One Heart."

VERSE 1

JOHNNIES: We've been busy running after you,
Hoping that you'll part
With a corner of your heart.
JULIE: That is something I will never do;
I could not divide my heart
And give it to a few.

CHORUS

JULIE: I have just one heart,
It's for just one boy;
I mean to keep it until some day
When he comes along—then I'll give
it away.
It is plain to see
I'm not fancy free;
I have just one heart for one little boy
Who has one little heart for me.

VERSE 2

JOHNNIES: Till you meet him, have a little fun,
Just a little kiss
He will never, never miss.
JULIE: All my kisses, ev'ry single one,
I am nursing, no rehearsing,
Though it's been done.

REPEAT CHORUS

YOU'RE SO BEAUTIFUL

Written in late 1918. Published. Copyrighted January 4, 1919. Introduced in *The Canary* (Globe Theatre, New York; November 4, 1918; 152 performances) by Maude Eburne (Mary Ellen) and Joseph Cawthorn (Timothy).

VERSE 1

SHE: You and me would happy be as man and
     wife.

HE: Don't tempt me so—I beg of you to stop it.

SHE: I would make you comf'table, I know,
     through life.

HE: I'm comf'table enough, so kindly drop it.

SHE: Why don't you come and marry me?

HE: It's just as plain as ABC.

CHORUS

HE: You're so beautiful, so beautiful,
    I'm a little bit afraid of you;
    I'd hang around till you had me pat,
    And then some millionaire would come
    And you'd leave me flat.
    Can you blame me for being cautious?
    I'm afraid, pretty maid, that's why;
    It would be a pleasant duty,
    But I fear your fatal beauty
    Makes it impossible—goodbye.

VERSE 2

SHE: Simple clothes would hide my beauty, that is
     true.

HE: The face is there, and nothing could remove
     it.

SHE: I would make my face up very plain for you.

HE: No matter what you do you can't improve it.

SHE: I'll give you all my love, don't fear.

HE: I couldn't be so selfish, dear.

REPEAT CHORUS

YIP, YIP, YAPHANK 1918

YIP, YIP, YAPHANK (1918)

Presented by Uncle Sam at the Century (August 19–31, 1918) and the Lexington (September 2–14, 1918) Theatres in New York City for a total run of 32 performances. Billed as "A Military 'Mess' Cooked up by The Boys of Camp Upton (In Aid of the Fund to Establish a Community House at Camp Upton For the Wives, Mothers and Sweethearts Who Visit Their Boys at Camp)." "Authorized and Given Through the Courtesy and Co-operation of Major-General J. Franklin Bell." Words and music by Sergeant Irving Berlin. Staged by Private William H. Smith. "Entire production under the Personal Direction of Sergeant Irving Berlin." Orchestra under the direction of Sergeant Dan Castler. Orchestrations by, among others, Harry Ruby and Oscar Radin. Cast included Danny Healy, Sammy Lee, and Irving Berlin.

WE LIVE AT UPTON WITH MAJOR GENERAL BELL

Written at Camp Upton, Yaphank, Long Island, on or just before May 10, 1918, by "Private Irving Berlin" as a tribute to the post's commanding officer, Major General J. Franklin Bell. Lead sheet and holograph of lyric were found among Berlin's papers and are now in the Irving Berlin Collection of the Music Division of the Library of Congress. Alternate title: "General Bell Song."

Some time after World War II, Berlin received music and lyrics of the song from a "Mr. Larkin." What follows is a draft of a letter he sent in response.

Again, many thanks for sending me copies of the manuscripts of "Hate to Get Up" and "We Live at Camp Upton With Major General Bell."

I was particularly glad to get the lead sheet and lyrics of the General Bell song because I did not have a copy in my files. These lyrics are in my handwriting.

I hope we can meet sometime so I can tell you of what a great man General Bell was. When I came to Camp Upton as a private, he very quickly realized that I wasn't fit to be a soldier, so I was assigned to furnish the entertainment for the camp.

You may be interested in my first meeting

Ensemble: "We're on Our Way to France." Inset: Sergeant Irving Berlin and chorus "girls" in "Kitchen Police (Poor Little Me)"

with him. I was called to his headquarters on the hill. I entered his office, stood at attention and gave him my best salute. He put me at ease and asked me to sit down. There were two women sitting at the end of his desk. He said, and I'm not quoting him exactly, "Berlin, these women are here to ask you to change your name from Berlin to something else." (At that time the hatred for the Germans was so great that Sauerkraut we renamed "liberty cabbage.") General Bell continued, "It's up to you, Berlin, but you've been pretty successful with that name, so I wouldn't change it."

VERSE 1

We kissed the folks goodbye
And heard a parting sigh,
Then congregated at our local boards.
They sent us on our way;
We shouted "Hip hurray"
Loud enough to strain our vocal cords.
Now we're with the happy, scrappy mob,
Each and every one of us on the job.

CHORUS

We live at Upton with Major General Bell,
Where we're preparing to give the Kaiser hell.
Upton is not what you'd call a modern hotel,
But what do we care
As long as we're there
With Major General Bell?

VERSE 2

They jabbed us in the arm,
Then sent us out to farm;
We started digging stumps with pick and axe.
They kept us on the go,
And in a week or so
We developed humps upon our backs.
When the war is over o'er the foam,
Upton will be somebody's summer home.

REPEAT CHORUS

HELLO, HELLO, HELLO

Introduced by the entire company. Alternate title: "Opening Chorus." It was followed immediately by "Hesitation Blues."

Hello, hello, hello,
We need the dough and so
We came up from Upton
With a musical show.
We'd like to have you know
It's not that kind of a show
That you've been in the habit of seeing
At two dollars a throw.
But we'll try and entertain you just the same
With a song and joke about the army game.
We were drafted by our President,
With a hip hurray away we went
To be placed into a regiment
To drill, drill, drill
Until they shipped us over there.

HESITATION BLUES

Introduced by the entire company. Although not listed in the program, it directly followed "Hello, Hello, Hello."

VERSE 1

We're stationed at Upton, just a short way from home;
We're waiting for orders to be shipped across the foam.
Tell us, how long do we have to wait?
Oh, will we get there soon, or must we hesitate?

VERSE 2

With rifles and bayonets we have all been rehearsed,
And Lord help the Kaiser if we ever see him first.
Tell us, how long do we have to wait?
Oh, will we get there soon, or must we hesitate?

VERSE 3

We're drilled by a sergeant; we won't tell you his name—
He thinks he's the general and we've got to think the same.
Tell us, how long do we have to wait?
Oh, will we get there soon, or must we hesitate?

VERSE 4

Now Upton, Long Island, is a wonderful place,
A million mosquitoes digging trenches in your face.

Tell us, how long do we have to wait?
Oh, will we get there soon, or will we have to
hesitate?

VERSE 5

Our second lieutenant is a regular beaut,
But Lord help the private who goes by and don't
salute!
Tell us, how long do we have to wait?
Oh, will we get there soon, or must we hesitate?

VERSE 6

There's one regulation that we've got to obey:
We must sign the payroll, but we don't get the pay.
Tell us, how long do we have to wait?
Oh, will we get there soon, or must we hesitate?

All we do is sign the payroll,
All we do is sign the payroll,
All we do is sign the payroll,
But we don't get a gosh-darn cent.

Now you've heard the op'ning chorus,
So let the show begin.
We know that you'll be walking in,
So we tried to kill time
With some music and rhyme.
We have lots of work before us
To please blasé Broadway.
But we hope ere we stop
We'll go over the top
With a hip, hip, hooray,
Hooray, hooray,
With a hip, hip, hooray!

BEVO

Published twice. First printed and copyrighted August 19, 1918. Introduced in *Yip, Yip, Yaphank* by Private Schor and chorus. Printed and copyrighted again September 30, 1919. Probably sung by Eddie Cantor in the *Ziegfeld Follies of 1919*. Possibly added during the New York run.

VERSE

I used to own a vicious-looking dog
Who wouldn't bite;
I used to know a dangerous-looking man
Who couldn't fight.
My brother trained wild animals,

But they were really tame;
And now I've tasted a drink
That strikes me just the same.

CHORUS 1

Bevo, oh, oh, oh, Bevo,
You're the grandest imitation that we know.
You're the only drink that a soldier can pick;
You taste like lager, but you haven't got the kick—oh!
Bevo, oh, oh, oh, Bevo,
Though you haven't got a punch up your sleeve-o,
All the soldiers insist
That a Christian Scientist
Could easily come staggering home on Bevo.

CHORUS 2

Bevo, oh, oh, oh, Bevo,
You're the grandest imitation that we know.
You may taste like beer but you're only a bluff,
You may be near it but you ain't near enough—
oh!
Bevo, oh, oh, oh, Bevo,
When Prohibition hits the town we will grieve.
Married men may stay home;
From their wives they'll never roam,
For who would want to stay up all night on Bevo?

SILVER THREADS (PARODY)

Irving Berlin lyric parody of the well-known song "Silver Threads Among the Gold" (1873; music by Hart Pease Danks [1834–1903] and original lyric by Eben E. Rexford [1848–1916]). Introduced by the Service Dollars Quartette (Privates Johnson, Brennan, Kline, Jorn) and chorus. Alternate title (piano-vocal score): "Darling, I Am Growing Older (Parody)."

Darling, I am not too old;
I am only twenty-three.
There's no silver 'mongst the gold,
And the draft is after me.
Soon they'll send me where the bugle calls
Ev'ry morn at half past four;
Wrap my dress suit up in camphor balls
I won't need it anymore.
One more drink to wet my vocal cords;
I received my card today.
Drink a toast, dear, to my local Board;
Tell them that I'm on my way.

EVER SINCE I PUT ON A UNIFORM

Introduced by Private Clark and chorus. Alternate title (program): "What a Difference a Uniform Will Make."

VERSE

The ladies never cared for me;
Somehow we never could agree.
I always try my best to satisfy,
But they always pass me by.
They wouldn't fall for me nohow,
But things are mighty diff'rent now.

CHORUS 1

Ever since I put on a uniform,
Oh, what a difference it's made!
Since I've been dressed up in the olive drab,
They come to meet me in a taxicab.
I get a dozen letters ev'ry day
Saying, "We'd like to know you."
Before the war they never noticed me,
But now I've got 'em sitting on my knee—
Isn't it wonderful, simply remarkable,
What a uniform will do?

CHORUS 2

Ever since I put on a uniform,
Oh, what a difference it's made!
I'm just a riot with the petticoats;
They send me angel cake and perfumed notes.
When I go home upon a Sunday pass,
I kiss a dozen or two.
Before the war they used to pass me by,
But now they think that I'm a handsome
guy—
Isn't it wonderful, simply remarkable,
What a uniform will do?

THE STERLING SILVER MOON

Published. Copyrighted August 19, 1918. Original title of the song that, revised and retitled, became "Mandy." Introduced by Private Murphy, Private Danny Healy, and chorus. Alternate title: "Under the Sterling Silver Moon." Listed as "Mandy" in *Yip, Yip,*

Yaphank programs. Also see "Mandy" with other songs from the *Ziegfeld Follies of 1919* (page 184).

VERSE

I was strolling out one evening
Neath the sterling silv'ry moon;
I could hear somebody singing
A familiar tune.
So I stopped awhile to listen;
Not a word I wanted to miss.
It was just somebody serenading
Something like this:

CHORUS

Mandy,
Sweeter than a bushel of candy,
Don't you know the summer is dandy
For a sterling silver spoon?
My pretty Mandy,
Don't you know the parson is handy,
Come and talk it over with Andy
Neath the sterling silver moon.

RAGTIME RAZOR BRIGADE

Published. Copyrighted August 19, 1918. Introduced by "Rookie Trio" (Privates Clark, Snyder, Reilly) and chorus.

VERSE

Have you heard of the Razor Brigade
And the reputation they've made?
Ever since they came to France,
They've been used in ev'ry advance.
They are noted for capturing Huns,
And they never go out with their guns—
When the captain takes his stand,
He gives them this command:

CHORUS

"Take your trusty razor by the hand;
Lead him gently into no-man's-land.
Keep a-dancing while advancing,
And the first Hun that you meet,
Hold up your razor and cut off his retreat.
They'll surrender when they see your blade—
Razors make those German lads afraid.
And when you bring your prisoners back,

You can make them ball the jack,
And the world will say
Hip hip hooray
For the Ragtime Razor Brigade."

DING DONG

Registered for copyright as an unpublished song August 27, 1918. Introduced by Privates Higgins (Man), Howard Friend (Girl), Louis Grant (Preacher), and chorus. Also performed in *The Canary* (1918) in a slightly different version (page 161).

VERSE

I'm so happy today;
Things are coming my way.
There's a wonderful reason
Why I'm feeling so gay;
Now you never will guess,
So I'd better confess
Why I'm so happy:
My Melinda said yes.

CHORUS

Ding dong, ding dong
Hear those joy bells ring?
Ting-a-ling-a-ling.
My little Lindy whispered in my ear,
"Set the date, honey, don't you wait,"
And ever since, all I can hear is
Ding dong, ding dong.
Listen to those joy bells chime;
I've had my fortune read,
And here's what the Gypsy said:
"You're gwine to be happy for a long, long time."

PREACHER: Do you take this woman for your
          lawful wedded wife?
MAN: Betcha life I do.
PREACHER: Will you love and honor and obey him
          all your life?
GIRL: If he wants me to.
PREACHER: Will you ever want to be freed?
MAN: No indeed.
PREACHER: Then the marriage service I'll read.
MAN: Show some speed.
PREACHER: Let the loving knot be tied.
MAN: And now I'll kiss the bride.

PAGE BOYS

Introduced by chorus. Not listed in the program.

VERSE 1

Ladies and gentlemen,
In a revue every now and then
It's necessary to change the scene—
You know very well what I mean.
That is the reason we came along
Now with a specialty:
We'll introduce a little pal
Who'll do Joe Jackson on his bicycle.

VERSE 2

Ladies and gentlemen,
Sorry to say we are here again;
They're not quite ready behind this drop.
Just hold steady—the show won't stop.
Be patient one and all;
Help us along with our little stall.
We'll introduce a fellow who
Would like to juggle-uggle up for you.

VERSE 3

Ladies and gentlemen,
Some of the boys must appear again,
Dressed up like ladies, and that's some job—
They were part of the minstrel mob.
Changing from black to white
Isn't a cinch if you do it right;
So while they don their skirts and hats,
We'll introduce a troupe of acrobats.

COME ALONG, COME ALONG, COME ALONG

Introduced by "Girls and Boys" (chorus). Alternate title (piano-vocal score): "Floradora Sextette."

GIRLS: It's a terrible job to be a dame,
       To dress in girlie clothes.
       With hands and feet like those,
       It's a very hard job to play the game;
       Before it's over
       We will all be lame.

For we've been rehearsing nightly,
And it has been no cinch;
We're squeezed in corsets tightly,
And lordy, how they pinch!
When it's over we'll never feel the
    same,
And we'll tell of the terrible job
    it was to be a dame.

CHORUS

I was a plumber;
I quit work last summer—
My bus'ness was hitting the pipe.

I was a printer;
I quit work last winter—
They didn't want men of my type.

I was a stoker,
A furnace-door choker;
I sailed in the billowy sea.

I'm a longshoreman;
My dad is a Mormon—
I've ninety-two sisters at home.

Now we're in the chorus—
Don't you agree we are brave?
All that we need is a shave;
We ought to be in a cave.
Twelve young Floradoras
Doing our darn'dest to please:
On the farm we all split lumber;
Now we're here to do a number
A la Florador,
As with twelve dirty guys like these.

BOYS: Hello, Miss Jasbo.
    Would you like to do a little song and
        dance with me?
GIRLS: I'd like it, I would.
    But my dancing isn't very good.
BOYS: Don't worry, dear.
GIRLS: Keep off my tootsies.
BOYS: Oh. I promise not to step upon your
        number eights.
    Please play some music for us,
    A Floradora chorus—
    Come along, come along, come along.
GIRLS: Come along, come along, come along.
BOYS: That's all they ever say in this kind of a
        song.
BOTH: Come along, come along, come along.
GIRLS: They never say just where they're going.
BOYS: But they holler "Come along," and so
BOTH: Come along, let's go.

[Dance.]

BOTH: Come along, come along, come along.
    Come along, come along, come along.
    They never say just where they're going,
    But they holler "Come along," and so
    Come along, let's go.

Extra lyrics for chorus

I was a copper,
A motorcar stopper;
I'll give you a summons or die.

I was a watchman;
I worked for a Scotchman—
He'd drink every time that I'd buy.

I was a burglar,
An alibi gurgler;
I took everything I could swipe.

I was a farmer,
Potato embalmer,
I picked them before they were ripe.

I was a chauffeur,
A regular loafer;
The clock on my taxi would fly.

I was a rubber,
A busy back scrubber;
A Turkish bath artist was I.

I was a porter,
A baggage assorter;
To smash every trunk I know how.

I was a packer;
I chewed plug tobaccer—
I wish I had some of it now.

LOVE INTEREST

Introduced by Private Brennan (Boy), Private Bob Higgins (Girl), and Private Grey (Mother). Alternate title (piano-vocal score): "Love Interest (I Love You)."

VERSE

You and I are very important
In a musical play,

For we represent the love interest,
As the managers say.
It's very necessary
To have a sweet melodious lay
For the boy and girl in the plot;
It always helps a lot
To have them sing
A pretty thing
Of which the chorus goes this way:

CHORUS

I love you,
Only Y-O-U.
There's a cozy spot up in Yonkers
For just us two.
All day through
We will bill and coo,
And we'll teach the parrot to say,
"Darling, I love you."

SEND A LOT OF JAZZ BANDS OVER THERE

Published. Copyrighted August 19, 1918. Introduced by Private Snyder, jazz band, and entire company. Alternate title (program): "Jazz Land."

VERSE 1

Mister Wilson, Mister Wilson,
Will you kindly lend an ear
To what I think is a bright idea?
It is very necessary
That the boys are in good cheer
So that they can do their best,
And here's what I suggest:

CHORUS

Send a lot of jazz bands over there
To make the boys feel glad.
Send a troupe of Alexanders
With a ragtime band to Flanders
And make 'em play a lot of snappy airs,
The kind that make you dance.
It isn't just ammunition and food;
You gotta keep 'em in a happy mood—
So hurry up and send
A lot of jazz bands over to France.

CHORUS, SECOND ENDING

To data, data, data,
Data-data-data-data-data-data-da—
Give 'em a lot of jazz.

VERSE 2

Mister Wilson, Mister Wilson,
Syncopation of today
Is the music of the U.S.A.
It is snappy, very happy,
And the only kind to play
For the sailors out in France;
'Twill help the big advance.

REPEAT CHORUS

OH! HOW I HATE TO GET UP IN THE MORNING

Published. Copyrighted July 23, 1918. According to a notation by Berlin on the earliest surviving piano-vocal score of this song, it was "written and composed at Camp Upton, June 20, 1918." Introduced in *Yip, Yip, Yaphank* by "Sergeant Irving Berlin." Number-one-selling recording by Arthur Fields (Victor, Columbia, Edison Amberol, Pathé, and Empire). Alternate title (program): "How I Hate to Get Up in the Morning." "Dedicated," according to a note by Berlin on the sheet music, "to my friend 'Private Howard Friend' who occupies the cot next to mine and feels as I do about the 'bugler.'"

More than any other of his works, this song is linked with Berlin as a performer. Nearly a quarter of a century later Berlin sang it in *This Is the Army* (1942), and his "original cast" recording is justly acknowledged as the definitive version of the song. He also sang it in the 1943 film of the show.

Over the years Berlin was often asked about the song. In August 1967 he was quoted about it in an article in *American Heritage:*

I found out quickly I wasn't much of a soldier. There were a lot of things about army life I didn't like, and the thing I didn't like most of all was reveille. I hated it. I hated it so much that I used to lie awake nights thinking about how much I hated it. To make things worse I had this assignment that kept me working late into the evening, so I didn't get too much sleep. But I wanted to be a good soldier. So every morning when the bugle blew I'd jump right out of bed just as if I liked getting up early. The other soldiers thought I was a little too eager about it and they hated me. That's why I finally wrote a song about it.

Arguably the funniest anecdote that Berlin frequently relayed about the song was first set down in an April 10, 1943, letter to his friend and attorney Francis Gilbert during work on the film version of *This Is the Army.*

Today they finished shooting my portion of the picture and I am certainly glad it's over with. All I do is sing "Hate to Get Up in the Morning" as I did in the show, but the camera is a severe judge and I am afraid even with the great amount of care and fuss they can't improve what the Fates decreed to be a homely face. As for my voice, I made a recording. When the record was first played on the set, one of the electricians, who didn't know whose voice it was, said, "If the guy who wrote that song could hear the record, he would turn over in his grave"—which gives you a fair idea. However I am hoping it won't be too bad.

In 1945, near the end of the war, Berlin made a number of efforts to set down his memories of Camp Upton and "Oh! How I Hate to Get Up in the Morning," but apparently he never completed any of the following accounts:

I arrived in Camp Upton and was put through the usual routine of questions and checkups before they gave me a uniform. I remember little of that first day but I will never forget that first night. Ten o'clock found me lying on an army cot in the dark. The large wooden barracks was filled with dozens of men who would soon be asleep. As a civilian I never went to bed before two in the morning. The thought of having to lie there awake for hours depressed me. Up to now I had taken it all in my stride. Somehow none of it seemed real. All day I was so busy being agreeable and doing what was asked of me in a manner that assured them I was going to be a good sport about it. Everyone was so nice and polite. This wasn't going to be bad at all. But lying there that night listening to the strange sounds that came from the other cots made me realize for the first time that I wasn't going to like army life.

My cot was in a corner next to a window. I got up and looked out. A guard holding a rifle on his shoulder was pacing back and forth in front of the barracks. I went back and stretched out on my cot again. The next few hours were the longest I ever spent in my life. Suddenly, I got very hungry. I knew it was one o'clock because I always get hungry at that hour of the morning. I thought of my apartment in New York. The night before some friends had been there for a farewell dinner. What was left of a turkey was still in the ice box when I started for camp. Nothing could have brought home the seriousness of my position more than the fact that I couldn't be in my kitchen at one o'clock in the morning. I have no idea what time I fell asleep but I awoke with a start and heard for the first time the bugler who was to become my pet aversion and be the inspiration for "Oh How I Hate to Get Up in the Morning."

. . .

I arrived at Camp Upton and went through the usual army routine of questions before a uniform was issued to me. I remember little of that first day but I will never forget that first night. The clock found me stretched out on an army cot in the dark. The large wooden barracks where I was quartered was filled with dozens of soldiers falling off to sleep. As a civilian I would be out somewhere or at home working. I never went to bed before two in the morning. The prospect of lying there all night waiting for reveille depressed me. My cot was in a corner next to a window. After stewing a while I got up, sat on the edge of my cot and looked out the window. I saw a soldier with a rifle. The other men were asleep. I sat there listening to the strange sounds that . . .

. . .

No story of *T.I.T.A.* [*This Is the Army*] would be complete without beginning at the beginning and the beginning is *Yip, Yip, Yaphank*. When I received that little card from my draft board in the early part of 1918, I was surprised. I had gone through two physical examinations because the case history I gave them of my state of health called for a double check up. Much has been written of my early struggles when I was a singing waiter on the Bowery and in Chinatown. True, the life I led then was not one a family doctor would have prescribed for a growing boy but my health was good. I ate any and everything with no bad effects. I would go to bed at six or seven in the morning after a hard night's work and sleep like a [*word unclear*] until 6 or 7 that night. I weighed more than I do today and hardly ever saw a doctor. Not until after I became a successful songwriter did I develop all sorts of ailments—insomnia, indigestion, and all the by-products of what was known in the trade as composers' stomach. Many kinds of medicines were prescribed which I would buy but never take. I kept going to one doctor for days and finally convinced him I had ulcers. He sent me to bed where I was given a strict dairy diet—the whites of eggs and cream at ten minute intervals. After two weeks he pronounced me cured. I got up feeling no better and no worse than before. Then followed a series of rest cures. After every stretch of work I would go to bed for some kind of diet. Of course, my ills were mostly imagined, but I managed to leave the impression that a nervous breakdown was just around the corner. So when my draft board assured me there was nothing to worry about where my health was concerned, I was surprised. Joe Schenck was indignant. "It's ridiculous," he said. "What does the Army want with Irving." Wilson Mizner cracked, "Up to now the Allies had a chance."

VERSE 1

The other day I chanced to meet
A soldier friend of mine;
He'd been in camp for sev'ral weeks,
And he was looking fine.
His muscles had developed,
And his cheeks were rosy red,
I asked him how he liked the life,
And this is what he said:

CHORUS 1

"Oh! How I hate to get up in the morning!
Oh! How I'd love to remain in bed!
For the hardest blow of all
Is to hear the bugler call:
'You've got to get up,
You've got to get up,
You've got to get up this morning!'
Someday I'm going to murder the bugler;
Someday they're going to find him dead—
I'll amputate his reveille,
And step upon it heavily,
And spend the rest of my life in bed."*

VERSE 2

A bugler in the army
Is the luckiest of men:
He wakes the boys at five and then
Goes back to bed again.
He doesn't have to blow again
Until the afternoon;
If ev'rything goes well with me,
I'll be a bugler soon.

CHORUS 2

"Oh! How I hate to get up in the morning!
Oh! How I'd love to remain in bed!
For the hardest blow of all

Alternate version of last three lines:
    And then I'll get that other pup,
    The one that wakes the bugler up,
    And spend the rest of my life in bed."

Is to hear the buglar call:
'You've got to get up,
You've got to get up,
You've got to get up this morning!'
Oh, boy! the minute the battle is over,
Oh, boy! the minute the foe is dead,
I'll put my uniform away
And move to Philadelph-I-A
And spend the rest of my life in bed."

Show version of verse 1

I've been a soldier just a while*
And I would like to state
The life is simply wonderful,
The army food is great.
I sleep with ninety-seven others
In a wooden hut;
I love them all; they all love me—
It's very lovely, but

DOWN FROM THE FOLLIES

Introduced by Privates Snyder (Lillian Lorraine), Fervesier (W. C. Fields), Gordon Newman (Will Rogers), Belles (Marilyn Miller), S. Cutner (Eddie Cantor), Loher (Joe Frisco), Kay Kendall (Ann Pennington), and ensemble. Alternate title: "Follies Opening."

VERSE

GIRLS: Down from the Follies,
    Where we merrily tra-la-la,
    We just came in a special train,
    And here we are.
    All for the soldiers
    Who are doing their little share,
    To cheer them,
    Be near them,
    Before they go over there.
    With kind permission
    Of our manager Ziegfeld:

CHORUS

GIRLS: We left the bright lights of Broadway
    And came to Upton
    To sing and dance
    Just as we do in the Follies

Original version of line 1:
    I've been a soldier just a month

For the boys who are going to France.
It's the least we can do for the soldiers
Who are fighting for Uncle Sam;
They can't come to town,
So we came down
To let them see the show
We're giving
Down at the Amsterdam.

BOYS: We don't know how to thank you
    For coming here today
    To let us see the play
    You're doing on Broadway.
GIRLS: You needn't stop to thank us;
    We're mighty glad we came.
BOYS: Where's the rest of your organization?
GIRLS: They're on their way from the station.
BOYS: We were worried that perhaps
    The special train you missed.
GIRLS: That's not a disappointment;
    Here is the list.

Unused verse

The following section of "Down from the Follies," intended for two soldiers portraying Savoy and Brennan, was dropped during rehearsals.

SAVOY: You don't know the half of it, dearie;
    You don't know the half of it, dear.
BRENNAN: What has happened to Margie?
    Has she gone to war?
SAVOY: Margie got married
    To a big stevedore,
    And you don't know the half of it,
        dearie.
BRENNAN: Let's go get a bottle of beer.
SAVOY: I'm so glad you asked me.
    I'm so glad you asked me,
    For you don't know the half of it, dear.

THE MILITARY POLICE

Introduced by Privates Seyster, McCrystal, Barnett, White, Martin, Bryde, W. O'Brien, Meidel. The first number in the "Our Boys!" sequence, which culminated in Sergeant Irving Berlin and chorus singing "Kitchen Police."

BOYS: We're the military police;
    We keep the soldiers at peace.
    The guardhouse makes them
    Just as peaceful as can be.

When they start guarding,
We teach them how to sing
"Nearer, my guard, to thee,
Nearer, my guard, to thee,
Nearer, my guard, to thee."

THE ARMY COOKS

Introduced by Privates Ward, Schor, Joe Kelly, York, Brennan, Johnson, Weisberg, and Brena. The second number in the "Our Boys!" sequence.

COOKS: We're the cooks, we're the cooks;
We don't need any books,
For cooking in the army only means
You get up at four and then you
Begin to work and when you
Make up your little menu,
Don't forget the beans—
You get beans.

Earlier version of above

COOKS: We're the cooks, we're the cooks,
We don't need any books,
For cooking in the army only means
To get up at dawn
And then you begin to work,
Make up your little menu—
Don't forget the beans.

CHORUS: You get up at dawn and then you
Begin to work, and when you
Make up your little menu,
Don't forget the beans.

THE ARMY DOCTORS

Introduced by Privates Cline, Balton, Cronin, Welsh, A. Kelly, Talbot, Schonegold, and Reiss. The third number in the "Our Boys!" sequence.

DOCTORS: We're the doctors, the army doctors;
We're stationed down at the infirmary.
When a soldier has a chill,
We give him a little pill,
And we give him the same
When he has a broken knee.

PRISONERS

Introduced by Privates Turner, Rosenberg, Moon, Mc-Kanneany, Johnston, Nacht, A. Brown, and Phillips. The fourth number in the "Our Boys!" sequence.

PRISONERS: We're the prisoners, the army prisoners,
The only kind who never get out on bail.
They just let us come on to sing a song;
We won't be with you very long,
For when the song is over,
We've got to go back to jail.

BUGLERS

Introduced by Privates J. O'Brien, Robinson, A. Clark, Grossman, Fields, McGinness, McNamara, and Ewell. The fifth number in the "Our Boys!" sequence, it segued into "Kitchen Police."

BUGLERS: We're the buglers, the buglers;
We bugle-oogle-oogle with a grin.
But the hardest job of all,
Yes, the hardest job of all,
Is waking Irving Berlin,
Waking Irving Berlin,
Waking Irving Berlin.

KITCHEN POLICE (POOR LITTLE ME)

Published. Copyrighted September 19, 1918. Introduced (as "Poor Little Me") in the *Ziegfeld Follies of 1918* by Marilyn Miller. Sung by Sergeant Irving Berlin and chorus in *Yip, Yip, Yaphank*.

VERSE

There's dirty work to be done in the army,
And it's not much fun;
It's the kind of work that's done
Without the aid of a gun.

The boys who work with the cooks in the kitchen
Holler out for peace;
For they have to do the dirty work,
And they're called the kitchen police.

CHORUS 1

Poor little me,
I'm a KP.
I scrub the mess hall
Upon bended knee;
Against my wishes
I wash the dishes,
To make this wide world
Safe for democracy.

In Berlin's lyric sheets for the show the following additional material is included for this song:

CHORUS 2

CHORUS: Poor little he,
He's a KP.
He scrubs the mess hall
Upon bended knee;
Against his wishes
He scrubs the dishes,
To make this wide world
Safe for democracy.

[*While chorus is being played by orchestra,* BERLIN *walks to* FOLLIES GIRLS. *Business of shaking hands, saying hello, etc.*]

SERGEANT: [to BERLIN]
Berlin? Back to the kitchen.

[BERLIN *exits slowly while* CHORUS *sings:*]

CHORUS: Against his wishes
He scrubs the dishes,
To make this wide world
Safe for democracy.
[*Slow curtain.*]

I CAN ALWAYS FIND A LITTLE SUNSHINE IN THE YMCA

Published. Copyrighted August 26, 1918. Introduced by Private Johnson and chorus. Alternate title (program): "The Y.M.C.A."

VERSE

Mother dear, I've just finished mess,
And I'm here in the YMCA.
How I've missed your tender caress,
Since the day when I marched away!
But don't worry, dear,
I'm contented here;
What is more, I'm feeling fine.
Ev'rything's all right, dear,
And ev'ry night I will drop you a line.

CHORUS

You can picture me ev'ry ev'ning,
At the close of the day,
Writing a little letter
In the YMCA.
Don't you worry, Mother darling,
For while the skies are gray,
I can always find a little sunshine
In the YMCA.

WE'RE ON OUR WAY TO FRANCE

Published. Copyrighted August 19, 1918. Introduced by Private Brennan and entire company. This was the finale of Act II. Sung by ensemble in the film version of *This Is the Army.*

VERSE 1

All is ready, so just hold steady;
We'll soon be going to the pier.
No more waiting or hesitating—
The time to sail is here.
Bye-bye, mothers and all the others
Who'll come to shed a little tear—

Don't cry,
Bye-bye,
Give us a parting cheer.

CHORUS

We're on our way to France;
There's not a minute to spare—
That's why.
For when the Yanks advance,
You bet we wanna be there—
Goodbye.

VERSE 2

Old Hoboken is bent and broken
From soldiers marching on the pier;
While you slumber, a great big number
Of soldiers disappear.
To the millions of brave civilians
That we are leaving over here
We say,
Day-day,
Give us a parting cheer.

REPEAT CHORUS

KISS ME, SERGEANT

Unused. Dropped from the show before its New York opening. No music is known to survive. A typed lyric sheet was found among Berlin's papers and is now in the Irving Berlin Collection of the Music Division of the Library of Congress.

CHORUS

Kiss me, Sergeant—
I don't want you to be

Angry with me,
For that would make me most unhappy.
Let's be playmates;
You and me shouldn't fight.
Be a goody-goody, Sergeant,
And kiss me good night.

WAIT UNTIL WE GET OVER THERE

Unused. Dropped during rehearsals. A typed lyric sheet was found among Berlin's papers and is now in the Irving Berlin Collection of the Music Division of the Library of Congress. On the lyric sheet the title is listed as "My Country 'Tis of Thee," indicating perhaps that Berlin considered setting it as a double song with "America," the famous song more familiarly known by that title. It seems unlikely that Berlin would have called his song that knowing the confusion it was likely to cause.

Wait until we get over there,
Over there in France.
On the western front you'll find us
For the big advance.
Just wait until we get
The order to go
Over the top;
We won't stop:
We'll knock him silly
And place a lily
Right in the Kaiser's hand;
And then we'll come back
And bring the bum back
Behind a big brass band.
In the words of Georgie Cohan
We'll do our share
Till the scrap is over, over there.

Songs of 1919 and
Unpublished Songs of 1915–1919

THAT REVOLUTIONARY RAG

Published by T. B. Harms Company. Copyrighted February 20, 1919. Introduced in George M. Cohan and Sam Harris's "musical romance" *The Royal Vagabond* (Cohan and Harris Theatre, New York; February 17, 1919; 208 performances).

In early 1973 Irving Berlin told Robert Kimball the following story about the song for inclusion in Kimball and Alfred Simon's book *The Gershwins* (New York: Atheneum, 1973; p. 20).

After World War I Irving Berlin had severed his relations with the music-publishing firm Waterson, Berlin and Snyder. Before he established his own firm in 1919, he considered tying up with Max Dreyfus, head of T. B. Harms. One day he came to Dreyfus with a song called "That Revolutionary Rag" and asked if he wanted to publish it. Dreyfus said he was interested and Berlin told him he needed someone to take the song down for him. Dreyfus said, "I have a kid here who can do it."

The kid, George Gershwin, took the song down, made a lead sheet, and played it for Berlin, improvising to such a degree that Berlin hardly recognized his own song. Yet he could see that the young man was a brilliant pianist. Gershwin had heard that Berlin was looking for a musical secretary and he said he would like the job.

Berlin replied that his plans were unsettled and asked him what he really wanted to do. Gershwin said he wanted to write songs. Berlin listened to some Gershwin songs (later to become part of the show *La*, *La*, *Lucille*) and said, "What the hell do you want to work for anybody else for? Work for yourself!"

VERSE 1

Where the Russian breezes blow
There's a piece of calico,
Ev'ry thread dyed in red.
You can see it on a pole
Or in Trotsky's buttonhole;
Long-haired Russian foxes
Wave it from old soapboxes.

CHORUS 1

That Revolutionary Rag—
'Twas made across the sea
By a tricky, slicky Bolsheviki.
Run with your little moneybag
Or else they'll steal it all away, wheel it away,

As they go raving, madly waving
That Revolutionary Rag.
It's not a melody,
It's a crimson flag:
All the royalties across the seas
Shake in their BVDs
When they see that Revolutionary Rag.

VERSE 2

Little Mary Antoinette
Was a lovely queen, you bet,
Till one day, sad to say,
From her window she could see
Little Miss Democracy.
Mary's brain was whirling
When France began unfurling

CHORUS 2

That Revolutionary Rag—
'Twas made across the sea
By a tricky, slicky Bolsheviki.
Run with your little moneybag
Or else they'll steal it away, wheel it away,
As they go raving, madly waving
That Revolutionary Rag.
It's not a melody,
It's a crimson flag;
All the kings and queens in foreign scenes
Know that they've spilled the beans
When they see that Revolutionary Rag.

THE HAND THAT ROCKED MY CRADLE RULES MY HEART

Published. Copyrighted July 18, 1919. Previously registered for copyright as an unpublished song June 27, 1919. Dedicated "To My Mother." Leading recording by Irving Kaufman and Jack Kaufman (Columbia). This was the first song Berlin published with his newly formed company, Irving Berlin, Inc.

VERSE 1

How can I ever pay the debt I owe you,
Mother o' mine,
Mother o' mine?
What is there I could ever do to show you
How much I love you,
Mother o' mine?

CHORUS

I kiss the hand, the wrinkled hand,
That rocked my cradle in babyland.
A mem'ry lingers of bygone years
When gentle fingers would dry my tears.
Her face will ever be my guiding light;
She'll whisper tenderly,
"Turn to the right":
No harm can come to me
By day or night,
For the hand that rocked my cradle rules my
    heart.

VERSE 2

Close to my side you stand whate'er betide me,
Mother o' mine,
Mother o' mine.
How can I come to harm with you beside me
Ever to guide me,
Mother o' mine?

REPEAT CHORUS

NOBODY KNOWS AND NOBODY SEEMS TO CARE

Published. Copyrighted September 30, 1919. Previously registered for copyright as an unpublished song July 16, 1919. Sung by Irving Berlin in vaudeville at the Palace Theatre, New York, during the week of October 13, 1919.

VERSE 1

I'm sad and lonely;
There's a good reason why.
Nobody cares about me;
That's why I'm sad as can be.
I long for someone,
Somebody, yes indeed:
Lovin' kisses from one
Is exactly what I need

CHORUS

Many's the time I feel so lonesome,
But nobody knows
And nobody cares.
I've grown so tired of being on-my-own-some;
I want somebody to hug,

Cuddle and snug,
As comfy as a bug in a rug.
Many's the time I feel like spooning,
But nobody knows
And nobody cares.
I guess I'll make out a little ad
That I want some lovin' so bad,
'Cause nobody knows
And nobody seems to care.

VERSE 2

I'd love a sweetie
Hanging around the place,
Someone to worry about;
I'd never want to go out.
My home is gloomy;
Nobody's there, that's why.
I feel bride-and-groomy—
Can't you see it in my eye?

REPEAT CHORUS

THE NEW MOON

Published. Copyrighted July 18, 1919. A note on the cover of the original sheet music reads "Inspired by the Norma Talmadge movie *The New Moon*."

VERSE 1

Beneath a sky of gray
The lovers stroll along.
The flow'rs have died away;
The birds have hush'd their song;
There's a teardrop in her eye,
For he's come to say goodbye.
He whispers, "Dearie, don't you cry,
For I won't be long:

CHORUS

"When the new moon is shining,
I'm coming back to you.
Clouds have a silvery lining;
Soon the silver will be peeping through.
Angel hands will be mending
A broken romance soon;
They will bless us with a happy ending
'Neath the bright new moon."

VERSE 2

"The clouds will roll away,
And then we'll meet again;
A happy wedding day
Will dawn upon us then.
Little sweetheart, don't you pine;
Soon you'll see the new moon shine—
A little patience, girl of mine,
Till we meet again."

REPEAT CHORUS

I LOST MY HEART IN DIXIELAND

Published. Copyrighted October 30, 1919. Previously registered for copyright as an unpublished song July 26, 1919.

VERSE 1

I'm always losing something, ev'ryplace I go;
Just why I don't know,
And it worries me so.
Last year I lost a diamond ring that used to shine;
And the other day while trav'ling
Below the Mason-Dixon line

CHORUS

I lost my heart in Dixieland,
Where the cotton grows
And the Swanee flows.
I lingered long enough to see
That a home in Dixie
Would appeal to me.
There's something real
About the people there;
They make you feel
So welcome ev'rywhere.
I went out walking with a Tennessee kid;
She kissed me, and the minute she did,
I lost my heart in Dixieland.

VERSE 2

I'm going back to Dixie and look for my heart;
You and I must part—
I'm all ready to start.
Send all my mail to Dixie, that's where I am
      bound;

I may stay down there forever,
Because my heart may ne'er be found.

REPEAT CHORUS

I'VE GOT MY CAPTAIN WORKING FOR ME NOW

Published. Copyrighted September 30, 1919. Previously registered for copyright as an unpublished song July 26, 1919. Number-one-selling recording by Al Jolson (Columbia). Other leading recordings by Billy Murray (Victor, Emerson, Vocalion, and Paramount) and Eddie Cantor (Pathé). It is believed that this song was also sung by Cantor in the *Ziegfeld Follies of 1919*.

VERSE 1

Johnny Jones was a first-class private
In the army last year.
Now he's back to bus'ness in his father's place;
Sunday night I saw him with a smiling face.
When I asked why he felt so happy,
Johnny chuckled with glee;
He winked his eye and made this reply:
"Something wonderful has happened to me:

CHORUS 1

"I've got the guy who used to be my captain
      working for me!
He wanted work, so I made him a clerk in my
      father's factory,
And by and by I'm gonna have him wrapped in
      work up to his brow.
I make him open the office ev'ry morning at eight;
I come around about four hours late;
Ev'rything comes to those who wait—
I've got my captain working for me now.

VERSE 2

"He's not worth what I have to pay him,
But I'll never complain;
I've agreed to give him fifty dollars per—
It's worth twice as much to hear him call me 'sir.'
While I sit in my cozy office,
He's outside working hard,
Out in the hall at my beck and call
With a feather duster standing on guard.

CHORUS 2

"I've got the guy who used to be my captain
    working for me!
He wanted work, so I made him a clerk in my
    father's factory,
And by and by I'm gonna have him wrapped in
    work up to his brow.
When I come into the office, he gets up on his feet,
Stands at attention and gives me his seat—
Who was it said 'Revenge is sweet'?
I've got my captain working for me now."

SWEETER THAN SUGAR (IS MY SWEETIE)

Published. Copyrighted September 30, 1919.

VERSE 1

Listen to me,
Listen to me—
I've got a whole lot to say.
Listen to me,
Listen to me—
Things have been coming my way.
I met somebody;
That's why I'm so happy today.
Listen to me,
Listen to me—
I want to holler and shout.
Wait'll you see,
Wait'll you see,
Wait'll you see me step out
With a load of charm
On my arm
Well worth raving about.

CHORUS

Sweeter than sugar is my sweetie,
Sweeter than honey or jam;
So sweet is she
That when she kisses me
I don't put sugar in my coffee or tea.
Candy, molasses, and sweet cookie,
Sweeter than all of the three;
I would have that sweet little soul
Living in a sugar bowl—
Sweeter than sugar is my sweetie.

VERSE 2

Listen to me,
Listen to me—
She's such a sweet little pet.
Listen to me,
Listen to me—
Right from the moment we met,
My sweet tooth pained me;
It hasn't stopped hurting me yet.
Way out of town,
Way out of town
We'll spend the rest of our days;
We'll settle down,
We'll settle down
Just like a couple of jays.
We'll start raising Cain—
Sugar cane,
That's not all that we'll raise!

REPEAT CHORUS

EVERYTHING IS ROSY NOW FOR ROSIE

Published. Copyrighted October 25, 1919. Words by Irving Berlin and Grant Clarke.

VERSE 1

Hear the dickey birds singing—
What a beautiful song!
Serenading a couple—
See them strolling along.
Hear them talking it over,
Hear them naming the day.
The little chappy looks happy—
Listen, can't you hear him say:

CHORUS

"Ev'rything is rosy now for Rosie;
Ev'rything is rosy now for me!
The bells are pealing—
Oh, what a feeling!
The future looks so flowery.
There's a little cottage nice and cozy,
Ev'rything was paid for COD.
Now Rosie's busy with her wedding duds;
Soon there'll be a lot of baby buds
Hanging around my Rosie and me."

VERSE 2

Hear the wedding bells ringing,
With a lovely ding dong;
Hear the choirboys singing—
What a beautiful song!
Hear the minister saying,
"Honor, love, and obey."
They're all in clover; it's over—
Listen to the bridegroom say:

REPEAT CHORUS

EYES OF YOUTH

Published. Copyrighted October 25, 1919. Introduced in *The Eyes of Youth*. Not the same song as "The Eyes of Youth See the Truth," which is credited to George M. Cohan.

VERSE 1

There's a wonderful glow in the eyes of youth,
As over the crystal she bends,
For she's anxious to know what the eyes of youth
Will see when her journey ends.

CHORUS

Gazing in the future
Through the eyes of youth,
Wond'ring what awaits
Behind the mystic gates;
Will she find a bluebird
When she learns the truth,
Or will the years
Bring sadness and tears
To the eyes of youth?

VERSE 2

May the finger of fate point the crimson way
And guide her to happiness soon;
May it open the gate to a perfect day
That ends in a honeymoon.

REPEAT CHORUS

I LEFT MY DOOR OPEN AND MY DADDY WALKED OUT

Published. Copyrighted October 25, 1919.

VERSE 1

What'll I do?
What'll I do?
I'm just as sad as can be;
Something awful happened to me.
What'll I do?
What'll I do?
I'm in a terrible plight;
Like a great big fool I did
A very silly thing last night.

CHORUS

I left my door open and my daddy walked out.
Without a doubt
Worried am I
Wondering why
He never stopped to say goodbye.
I can't live without my loving daddy about;
That's why I shout.
He must come back or I'll lose my mind;
A good man's mighty hard to find.
He must have some lovin' now and then;
Maybe that'll bring him back again—
I'm gonna keep my door wide open
Till my daddy comes back.

VERSE 2

What'll I do?
What'll I do?
I'm in a terrible rage;
Like a bird he flew from his cage.
Daddy of mine,
Send me a line;
Say that you'll come back to me.
When you do, I'll lock the door
And try my best to lose the key.

REPEAT CHORUS

WAS THERE EVER A PAL LIKE YOU?

Published. Copyrighted November 29, 1919. Previously registered for copyright as an unpublished song November 10, 1919. Leading recording by Henry Burr (Victor).

VERSE 1

Mother dear, it's lonely here without you:
Days and nights are long;
Ev'rything goes wrong.
All I seem to do is think about you,
Dearest friend I knew—
Oh, how I miss you!

CHORUS

Was there ever a pal like you?
Was there ever a gal like you?
You taught me the right from the wrong way;
You showed me the short from the long way.
Was there ever a flow'r that grew
Half as pure as your heart so true?
They needed an angel in heaven,
So they sent for a pal like you.

VERSE 2

Mother dear, my love for you grows dearer,
Dearer day by day,
Since you went away.
Ev'ry day an angel draws us nearer;
Just a while and then
We will meet again.

REPEAT CHORUS

I WONDER

Published. Copyrighted January 13, 1920. Previously registered for copyright as an unpublished song December 9, 1919.

VERSE 1

We talked it over
Neath a cloudy sky;
Love's dream was ended,
And we said goodbye.
You decided just as I did
That it could not go on;
But I'm lonely for you only,
And now that you are gone

CHORUS

I wonder
If you still remember;
I wonder
If you could forget.
I often wonder
If it's really over
Or if you love me
Just a little bit yet.
I wonder
If you ever miss me;
I wonder
If you're ever blue.
I wonder
When we'll meet again,
And I wonder
If you wonder too.

VERSE 2

I miss the evenings
That we spent alone,
The sweet "good morning"s
On the telephone.
How I yearn to just return to
The days beyond recall;
And the kisses that you gave me—
I miss them most of all.

REPEAT CHORUS

WHEN MY BABY SMILES

Published. Copyrighted December 24, 1919. Not the same song as "When My Baby Smiles at Me" (words by Andrew B. Sterling and Ted Lewis, music by Bill Munro), made famous by Ted Lewis in 1920.

VERSE 1

I don't care
If the weather's fair
Or if skies are gray;
I don't frown
When the rain comes down
On a rainy day.
It may storm and thunder for the longest while;
Still I'll say it's a lovely day
When I see my baby smile.

CHORUS

When my baby smiles at me,
Oh, what a beautiful day!
All my troubles go hurrying by;
Just like bubbles they fly to the sky.
And I never ask the weatherman
Whether it's fair or warmer;
Rain or shine, the weather's fine
When my baby smiles.

VERSE 2

I don't brood
When the price of food
Goes away up high;
Didn't mind
When I woke to find
That the town went dry.
Let the skies be cloudy for the longest while;
Blue or gray, ev'rything's okay
When I see my baby smile.

REPEAT CHORUS

UNPUBLISHED SONGS OF 1915–1919

AT THE POKER BALL

No music is known to survive. A typed lyric sheet was found among Berlin's papers and is now in the Irving Berlin Collection of the Music Division of the Library of Congress.

Pack your grips with your poker chips
And come to the ball—
The cards are giving a ball.
They'll soon be on the loose
To raise the deuce.
The King and Queen of Hearts are seen
In front of the deck;
Around her beautiful neck
Is a string of diamonds.
When she snubs the Queen of Clubs,
There'll be an awful crush;
Then for weeks upon her cheeks
You'll see a royal flush.
Take your places
With the aces down at the hall—
The Queen of Spades and the joker
Will dance at the Poker Ball.

BECKY IS SHIMMYING NOW

A typed lyric sheet and a leadsheet were found among Irving Berlin's papers and are now in the Irving Berlin Collection of the Music Division of the Library of Congress.

VERSE

Becky Cohn and her brother
Went to a vaudeville show;
Ever since that afternoon
Becky has acted like a loon.
Sunday night her brother
Before he went to bed

Walked up to his mother
And this is what he said:

CHORUS

"Mamma, Becky saw Bea Palmer;
She took a lesson from her,
And she shimmies now,
She shakes her shoulder
Every time she hears the jazz band play—
Somebody told her that she makes a wicked
    lingerie.
Papa, better go and stop her,
Because it isn't proper
To dance that way.
Last week her sweetheart Abie
Gave her the sack;
She shimmied just a little bit
And he came back.
Oy, Mama, Bea Palmer
Has got Becky shimmying now!"

THE HAWAIIAN BLUES

No music is known to survive. A holograph manuscript of the lyric was found among Berlin's papers and is now in the Irving Berlin Collection of the Music Division of the Library of Congress.

Play for me that mournful refrain,
Play for me that melancholy strain—
On your ukulele play it again.
I'm sentimental.
That gentle Oriental melody
Has entered into my brain—
Seems to me
That's where it will remain.
I'm in love with it, so don't refuse—
Play me that tune you call the
Hawaiian Blues.

THE SAD HAWAIIAN BLUES

No music is known to survive. A typed lyric sheet was found among Berlin's papers and is now in the Irving Berlin Collection of the Music Division of the Library of Congress.

All day long he plays the ukulele—
He wrote a mournful song
Upon his ukulele.
One day she left him brokenhearted;
That night he started
Composing the sad Hawaiian Blues.
He's thinking of the day
They met in Honolulu
And of the dreamy way
She did the hulu-hulu.
So when the evening comes,
That Hawaiian fellow, he
Pours out his heartbreaking melody,
The tune he calls
The sad Hawaiian Blues.

I KNOW THAT LADY

No music is known to survive. An ink holograph manuscript of the lyric was found among Berlin's papers and is now in the Irving Berlin Collection of the Music Division of the Library of Congress.

VERSE

In a cabaret
Not so far away
There's a fancy lady doing the hulu.
All over town's she's advertised
And she's recognized
As the finest one from Honolulu.
Morris Rosenthal went up the other night;
He just took one look and yelled with all his
    might:

CHORUS

"I know that lady—
She knows me too!
She doesn't come from where the hula-hula do:
Her father keeps a store on Seventh Avenue;
Her name is Sadie,
And what is more,

She used to work at Siegel and Cooper's store.
She does the hulu
But she's not from Honolulu,
And if she tells you so,
Just tell that it's not true.
I know her family,
You bet I do,
And if they took a look
In her bankbook,
They'd be doing the hulu too!"

IF I HAD MY WAY
(I'D BE A FARMER)

No music is known to survive. A typed lyric sheet was found among Berlin's papers and is now in the Irving Berlin Collection of the Music Division of the Library of Congress.

VERSE

I grow so weary living in the city;
The fields of clover all over
Are calling me.
I have a cozy flat that's very pretty,
But still my life is full of care;
I'm unhappy there.

CHORUS

If I had my way,
I'd be a farmer;
If I had my way,
I'd be a jay.
For there's a fortune in a cow,
The kind they're milking now;
A rube is not a boob
When it comes to making you pay.
If I had my way,
I'd own some chickens,
And I'd make them lay
Ten times a day.
I'd buy a certain girl a wedding ring
And raise potatoes and everything
On a great big farm,
If I had my way.

LET EVERY TRUE
AMERICAN MAN

No music is known to survive. A pencil holograph manuscript of the lyric, written on Pat Morris Chemical Works, Inc., New York, stationery, was found among Berlin's papers and is now in the Irving Berlin Collection of the Music Division of the Library of Congress.

Let every true American man
Do what he can for peace;
Their admiration
For our nation
Will surely then increase.
Let's stretch our hands across the sea
For everlasting harmony,
And when it's over they'll take their hats off
To the good old U.S.A.

LOVE'S LABOR LOST

A rare Berlin poem. Typed lyric sheets were found among Berlin's papers and are now in the Irving Berlin Collection of the Music Division of the Library of Congress.

1.

A poet sat down with pencil in hand
To write for his loved one a poem;
A thousand and one little lovable terms
Lay concealed in the back of his dome.

2.

He likened her eyes to the blue of the skies,
And her cheeks to the blush of the rose;
Her throat was the throat of a beautiful swan,
And a Grecian creation, her nose.

3.

Her hair was the sunset, her teeth were the pearls
That made Gaby the brightest of stars;
Her voice was canarylike, heavenly sweet,
And her touch was a message from Mars.

4.

Her lips were the rubies the Orient claims,
While her form was the last word in pose.
He summed up her charms, and the maiden to
    him
Was a Venus de Milo in clothes.

5.

The springtimey verse when received by the maid
Caused her innocent heart to grieve;
She gazed in her mirror, then looked at the poem,
Saying, "Which one am I to believe?"

THE NIGHT IS FILLED WITH JAZZBOWS

An unusual Berlin poem, which at one time bore the
title "Manhattan Madness." Interestingly, a typed lyric
sheet of the poem, bearing that title, was found in
Berlin's *Face the Music* file, reinforcing the idea that he
took from the poem the title for the published song in-
troduced in *Face the Music*. In addition to the typed
poem, a two-page ink holograph manuscript was found
among Berlin's papers and is now in the Irving Berlin
Collection of the Music Division of the Library of
Congress.

The night is filled with jazzbows
As I sit writing here,
And through the mystic hokum
I hear you calling, dear.

Your voice so sweet and jentum
Speaks words of love to me;
Oh, would I were a dofauh,
That I might fly to thee!

The hours are fastly fasting,
The weeks are growing weak,
The months are monthing madly,
Because they heard you speak.

Ah, love, could you but knew it,
Then you would understood
Our parting caused me painless—
It hurt me oh so good.

Come back if you still hate me,
Because I hate you too.
I weep and weep and giggle;
My eyes are wet with dew.

The flowers in the gardam
Don't blossom as of young;
The birds have ceased their birding—
They simply will not sung.

Upon your moving picture
I gaze with both eyes shut
As sadly I keep sipping
My cup of coconut.

And now goodbye-the-way, dear,
I go from whence I came;
My head is full of nothing—
I hope you feel the same.

SHAKESPEARE SPEECH

A speech written by Berlin and probably delivered by
him at the Friars Club, New York. Date unknown. An
ink holograph manuscript was found among Berlin's
papers and is now in the Irving Berlin Collection of the
Music Division of the Library of Congress.

Friar Abbot, Mr. Shakespeare, Brother Friars,
Don't expect too much of me;
I'm confined to melody,
And making speeches in that way
Is not so easy, let me say,
Because I have to keep on rhyming.
However, I'm delighted to be here with all the
    rest
And meet our friend the honored guest.
Nevertheless I'm at a loss
To understand just why this Shakespeare guy
Has started them talking.
Giving dinners is all right;
I'd attend one every night.
I think when any he or she
Does something very wonderfully,
They should be showered with eulogy.
But in this case I'm forced to be truthful, and so
I don't know why we're giving this dinner to
    Mr. S.
What did he ever do?
I'd really like to know, tell me,
What did he ever do
Outside of saying once
"My kingdom for divorce"?
He was a married man, of course;
And any married man would have said it
Without expecting credit.
They say his plays were written by a man named
    Bacon,

And I have figured out that they are not
    mistaken:
Shakespeare was an actor,
And an actor is known as a ham—
Ham is the same as bacon.
I'm very smart, I am,
But as a Friar and a host
I must not start to roast
A man the world will praise
For many years and many days,
Who had the world before his gaze
And wrote a score or more of plays:
The Taming of the Shrew,
King John and *Much Ado*,
All's Well That Ends Well, too,
And these are just a few.
There's *Romeo*, *Juliet*,
And *Othello* black as jet,
As You Like It, *Julius Caesar*,
Hamlet and *Macbeth*,
King Henry Number Eight,
The Wives of Windsor—great
King Lear, *Love's Labor's Lost*—
He never wrote a frost.
His name will surely live forever,
For I think the kid was clever.
Mr. Bill Shake,
If you will shake,
Let me shake your writing hand.

SONGWRITERS

During the 1910s Berlin frequently wrote special mate-
rial for himself and other well-known songwriters of the
era to perform at benefit concerts. Pencil holograph
manuscripts of this lyric were found among Berlin's pa-
pers and are now in the Irving Berlin Collection of the
Music Division of the Library of Congress. The song-
writers featured on this occasion were Herbert Spencer
("Underneath the Stars"); George Botsford (who with
Berlin wrote "The Grizzly Bear"); Harry Carroll ("The
Trail of the Lonesome Pine"); James V. Monaco ("You
Made Me Love You"); Ernest R. Ball ("Love Me and the
World Is Mine"); Berlin ("Alexander's Ragtime Band");
and Gus Edwards ("School Days").

INTRODUCTION

Ladies and gentlemen,
I'll introduce to you
A few sentimental men
Who write your different popular songs.
These temp'ramental men would like the chance

To syncopate and demonstrate
The things that they can do.

HERBERT SPENCER

I'm sure you've heard his melody mellow—
It's played by every fiddle and cello.
I'm sure you'd like to look at the fellow
Who wrote "Underneath the Stars."

GEORGE BOTSFORD

Hug up close to your baby—
Though the song has been forgotten,
Every boy was turkey-trottin'
With some beautiful lady
To this syncopated ditty;
It was played in every city.
Even Diamond Jim Brady
Danced it everywhere—
So you ought to know
The man who started girl and beau
Doin' "The Grizzly Bear."

HARRY CARROLL

Now I'll introduce the young composer
Who wrote "The Trail of the Lonesome Pine."
It made him the pet of each brunette,
And outside of that, it's selling yet.
He proved by the money he made
Writing songs is a very good trade;
So you really ought to meet the fellow
Who wrote "The Trail of the Lonesome Pine."

JAMES V. MONACO

You made me love you,
You didn't want to do it,
But you were dancing to it—
You know you sang it too,
Yes you do, yes you do, you know you do.
Played by every hurdy-gurdy—
I'm sure you'd like to meet the little Verdi
Who wrote "You Made Me Love You."

ERNEST R. BALL

We never will forgive the man
Who started every Mary Ann
Uncorking her soprano
With "Love Me and the World Is Mine."

IRVING BERLIN

And now we'll hear,
And now we'll hear

From "Alexander's Ragtime Band."
It may appear
A trifle queer,
But he wants you to understand
Although he wrote the song
He never saw the Swanee River—
He's just a chap
Whose fingers snap
To "Alexander's Ragtime Band."

GUS EDWARDS

School days, school days—
You remember "School Days."
When the composer had written it,
He knew that there was a hit in it;
One day while he was fast asleep,
Into his books I took a peep—
I found that it earned enough to keep
A wife and a couple of kids.

TUM-TIDDLE-DEE-UM-TUM

No music is known to survive. Typed lyric sheets, one with handwritten revisions, were found among Berlin's papers and are now in the Irving Berlin Collection of the Music Division of the Library of Congress.

VERSE

Somebody wrote an ABC melody
With a tum-tiddle-dee-um-tum,
Tiddle-dee-um-tum.
The people living next to me
Seem to be full of
Tum-tiddle-dee-um-tum,
Tiddle-dee-um-tum.
Morning night and noon
They keep playing that tune
On the pianola,
And mighty soon

CHORUS

I'll go insane
'Cause that refrain
Gives me a pain
Right in my tum-tiddle-dee-um-tum,
Tiddle-dee-um-tum.
All that belongs to me
I'd give to charity
To lay my hands upon the throat
Of the man who wrote

That melody.*
And what is more,
I never swore
Until next door
They began to
Tum-diddle-dee-um-tum,
Tiddle-dee-um-tum;
I've called them names,
But the worst is yet to come:
Some evening late
I'll amputate
Their tum-tiddle-dee-um-tum-tum.

UNDER THE PALMS

No music is known to survive. An ink holograph manuscript of the lyric was found among Berlin's papers and is now in the Irving Berlin Collection of the Music Division of the Library of Congress.

Under the palms
In sunny Pensacola
With someone else in my arms
And just an old Victrola
To play a sentimental tune,
The kind that makes you want to spoon,
While I'm
Fanned by the breezes that gently blow
From the Gulf of Mexico:
Someday I'll go
To sunny Pensacola
With some sweet someone I know
To act as a consoler;
It won't be long ere you find me resting
In someone's arms
Drinking milk from a coconut
In a little hut
Under the palms.

On one typed lyric sheet Berlin crossed out lines 6–10 and replaced them with:
    I haven't slept a wink;
    My nerves are on the blink;
    I'm a fella
    With an empty cellar
    And it's driving me to drink.

UNTIL

No music is known to survive. An ink holograph manuscript of the lyric, on Strand Theatre Building stationery, was found among Berlin's papers and is now in the Irving Berlin Collection of the Music Division of the Library of Congress. Because there are quotation marks at the beginning and the end of both stanzas, it is possible that the words are not Berlin's but someone else's.

No rose in all the world until you came,
No star until you smiled upon life's sea,
No song in all the world until you spoke,
No hope until you gave your heart to me.

O rose, bloom ever in my lonely heart,
O star, shine steadfast with your light divine,
Ring out, O song, your melody of joy,
Life's crowned at last, and love is ever mine.

WE'RE WITH MR. WILSON

Published in 2000 in Barry Dougherty's book *New York Friars Club Book of Roasts* (M. Evans and Company, New York). It was written for the New York Friars Club's *1916 Friars Frolics* and performed in Baltimore, Maryland, on May 20, 1916, with President Woodrow Wilson in attendance. Along with other Berlin lyrics of 1916, it also marked the opening of the new Friars Clubhouse (the Friars call their clubhouses "monasteries") at 106–110 West Forty-eighth Street in Manhattan. (The current Friars Clubhouse is at 57 East Fifty-fifth Street.) This lyric was brought to the editors' attention by Michael Feinstein and Paulette Attie.

VERSE

We're with Mr. Wilson,
Yes we are, yes we are;
He's the only candidate in the swim.
Abraham Lincoln would have voted for him.
Give three cheers for Wilson.
As Americans can,

Let every man remember, when he votes
Sometime in the next November, sending notes
Is safer than a fighting plan.
Mr. Wilson, we know you're the man!

Above: *Fanny Brice.* Below: *Bert Williams*

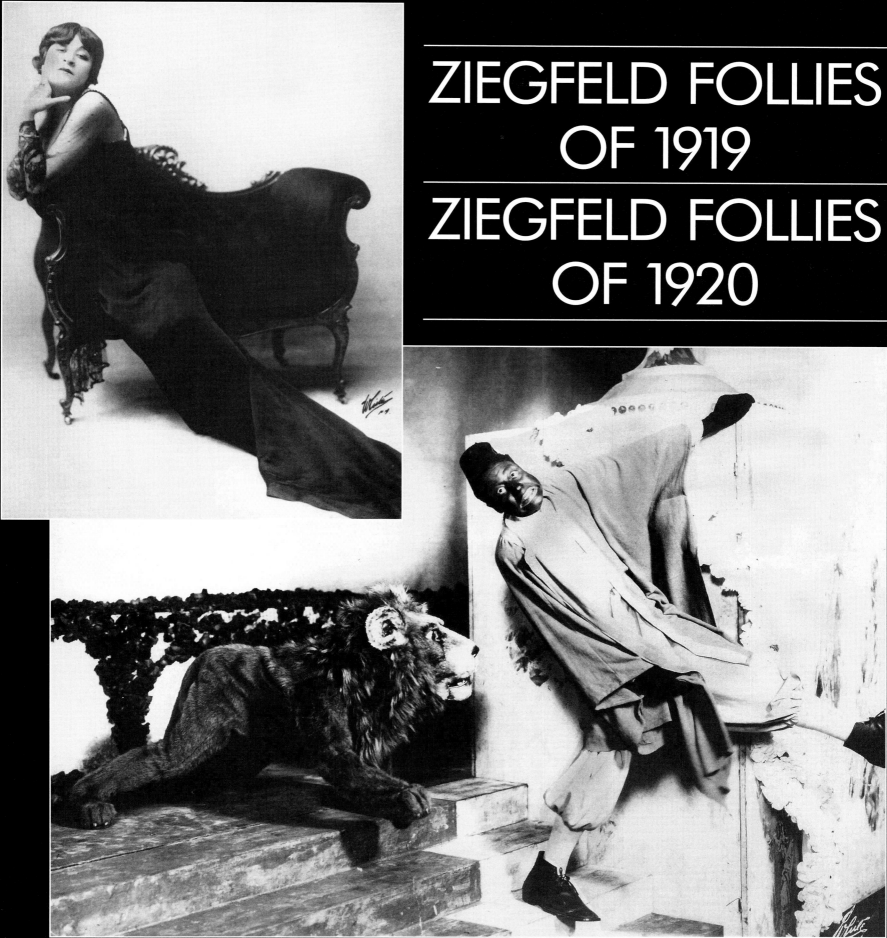

ZIEGFELD FOLLIES OF 1919
ZIEGFELD FOLLIES OF 1920

ZIEGFELD FOLLIES OF 1919

Tryout: Nixon's Apollo Theatre, Atlantic City, New Jersey; June 10, 1919. New York run: New Amsterdam Theatre; June 16–August 12 and September 10–December 6, 1919 (temporary shutdown because of the Actors Equity strike); 171 performances. Lyrics and music by Irving Berlin, Gene Buck and Dave Stamper, Harry Tierney and Joseph McCarthy, Rennold Wolf (lyrics), and Victor Herbert (ballet). Produced under the direction of Florenz Ziegfeld Jr. Scenery by Joseph Urban. Staged by Ned Wayburn. Orchestrations and musical direction are uncredited. Cast headed by Marilyn Miller, Eddie Cantor, Bert Williams, John Steel, Delyle Alda, Gus Van and Joe Schenck, Johnny and Ray Dooley, Mary Hay, the Fairbanks Twins, Lucille Levant, Eddie Dowley, Hazel Washburn, and George LeMaire.

I'D RATHER SEE A MINSTREL SHOW

Published. Copyrighted September 30, 1919. Previously registered for copyright as an unpublished song July 9, 1919. Introduced by Eddie Cantor with Bert Williams, George LeMaire, and a quartet (Joe Schenck, first tenor; John Steel, second tenor; Johnny Dooley, baritone; and Gus Van, bass) at the start of the Act I finale (listed in the program as "Episode 13—'The Follies Minstrels' "), which also included Berlin's song "Mandy."

VERSE

I never cared about the drama;
The drama always got my hammer—
I came from sunny Alabama,
Home of the minstrel show.
I think revues are always bloomers;
They all depend upon costumers.
You can have the plays
That are all the craze
At two dollars a throw.

CHORUS

I'd rather see a minstrel show
Than any other show I know.
Oh, those comical folks

With their riddles and jokes!
Here is the riddle that I love the best:
"Why does a chicken go . . . ?"
You know the rest.
I'd pawn my overcoat and vest
To see a minstrel show.

MANDY

Published. Copyrighted June 26, 1919. Previously registered for copyright as an unpublished song June 10, 1919. Derived from Berlin's song "The Sterling Moon," written in 1918 for *Yip, Yip, Yaphank* (see page 166). Introduced in the *Ziegfeld Follies of 1919* by Gus Van and Joe Schenck, with Marilyn Miller, Lucille Levant, Mary Hay, Ray Dooley, and entire company (listed in programs as "Entire Aggregation"). Top-selling recording by Gus Van and Joe Schenck (Victor). An exchange of letters in 1967 between Gus Van and Irving Berlin elicited the following from Berlin: "One of the thrills of my memory is you and Joe singing 'Mandy' in the *Ziegfeld Follies of 1919.* Everyone still thinks that was the best *Follies* Ziegfeld had and the Minstrel Finale was the high spot."

VERSE 1

I was strolling out one evening
By the silv'ry moon;
I could hear somebody singing
A familiar tune.
So I stopped a while to listen;
Not a word I wanted to miss.
It was just somebody serenading
Something like this:

CHORUS

Mandy, there's a minister handy,
And it sure would be dandy
If we'd let him make a fee.
So don't you linger;
Here's the ring for your finger—
Isn't it a humdinger?
Come along and let the wedding chimes
Bring happy times
For Mandy and me.

VERSE 2

Honey gal, I'm getting nervous
And I can't keep still.
We can hear that marriage service

For a dollar bill.
Come along, my dear, and promise
That you'll honor, love, and obey.
Let the parson take the dollar from us—
What do you say?

REPEAT CHORUS

MINSTREL SHOW FINALE

Introduced in "Episode 13—'The Follies Minstrels' " by the "Entire Aggregation" led by Eddie Cantor (Tambo), Bert Williams (Bones), George LeMaire (Interlocutor/Middle Man), the quartet of Joe Schenck (first tenor), John Steel (second tenor), Johnny Dooley (baritone), and Gus Van (bass), Marilyn Miller (George Primrose), Ray Dooley ("Mandy"), and the ensemble of "Mandys," "Dandies," and "Follies Pickaninnies," headed by Lucille Levant and Mary Hay. "I'd Rather See a Minstrel Show" and "Mandy" were part of the extended production number that closed the first act, which included lyric sequences that were not in the published versions of "Minstrel Show" and "Mandy." No music is known to survive for these additional sequences. The "Minstrel Show Finale" lyrics are part of the May 27, 1919, typed compilation of the lyrics completed by that date.

INTERLOCUTOR: Ladies and gentlemen, be seated.
Mister Bones, Mister Bones—
How do you feel, Mister Bones?
BONES: Rattling.
INTERLOCUTOR: Mister Bones feels rattling.
COMPANY: Ha, ha, ha, ha—that's a good one.
INTERLOCUTOR: Tell a little story, Mister Bones.
COMPANY: A funny little story, Mister Bones.
BONES: How can you keep an angry dog
From biting you on Monday?
INTERLOCUTOR: That joke is old;
The answer is to kill the dog on
Sunday.
BONES: That's not the way to stop a dog
From biting you on Monday.
INTERLOCUTOR: How would you bring that about?
BONES: Have the doggy's teeth pulled out.
INTERLOCUTOR: Oh, Mister Bones, that's terrible.
COMPANY: Yes, Mister Bones, that's terrible.
INTERLOCUTOR: [*rising*]
And now we'll hear the ballad
singer's pet,
A song we'll never forget,
By the Barnyard Quartet.

[*The* QUARTET *steps downstage from the front row and harmonizes.*]

QUARTET: Yes, my darling, you will be, will be
Always young and fair to me.
That's a song that never grows old:
"Silver Threads Among the Gold."

TAMBO: Mister Interloc'tor.

INTERLOCUTOR: What is wrong with you?

TAMBO: I know a doctor.

INTERLOCUTOR: Tell about him, do.

TAMBO: Sad to say, one day he fell
Right into a great big well.

HAREM LIFE (OUTSIDE OF THAT EVERY LITTLE THING'S ALL RIGHT)

Published. Copyrighted September 30, 1919. Previously registered for copyright as an unpublished song July 9, 1919. Two versions survive of this lyric: the published version and the show version. Introduced in "Episode 1" of Act II by Hazel Washburn and members of the ensemble, featuring, as "Ladies of the Harem," Mauresette and May Graney, Helen Jesmer, Gladys Colby, Lillian McKenzie, Betty Morton, and Florence Crane; Marthe Pierre as Cleopatra; Lucille Levant as "A Dancer"; Jessie Reed, Caroline Erwin, Alta King, Hazel Washburn, Ethel Hallor, Ruth Taylor, Nan Larned, and Margaret Irving as "Favorite Wives"; and Bernice Dewey, Kathryn Perry, Mary Washburn, Edna Lindsay, Alma Braham, and Marcelle Earle as "Dancers of the Harem." Alternate title (program): "Harem Life."

VERSE 1

While trav'ling through Turkey in my dreams,
I chanced to stray
Right into a harem, and it seems
They let me stay.
I spoke to the sultan's fav'rite wife
Before I fled;
I asked her how she liked harem life—
Here's what she said:

CHORUS

"Living in a harem, what a life!
Ne'er a thought of care or strife.

Waiting on the Sultan night and day,
Ever ready to obey.
He keeps me dancing morning, noon, and night;
Dancing fills 'im with delight.
I am black and blue
From the dance I do,
But outside of that
Ev'ry little thing's all right."

VERSE 2

I wanted to know how many wives
The Sultan had;
She answered, "Each day a wife arrives
Fresh from Baghdad."
How did he continue on that plan
So many years?
She answered "He's just a poor old man
With young ideas.

REPEAT CHORUS

Show version (as of May 27, 1919) Act II, Episode 1

[*At rise, seven beautiful* HAREM GIRLS *are discovered.*]

GIRLS: Living in a harem—what a life!
Ne'er a thought of care or strife.
Waiting on the Sultan night and day,
Ever ready to obey.
He keeps us dancing morning, noon, and night;
Dancing fills 'im with delight.
We are black and blue
From the dance we do,
But outside of that
Ev'ry little thing's all right.

WIVES: Eight of the Sultan's wives are we,
And there are a whole lot more;
Weekdays he marries two or three,
And Sundays he marries four.
He has a hundred agents who
Lead very busy lives;
He pays them such a salary to
Keep him supplied with wives.
And now we'll tell the rhyme
Just how we spend our time:

WIFE 1: Every morning to his bed I bring his toast and tea.

WIFE 2: I prepare his bath, for that's the job he gave to me.

WIFE 3: I massage his brow, because he likes my gentle touch.

WIFE 4: I then manicure his nails and never hurt him much.

WIFE 5: I bring him his slippers every evening after eight.

WIFE 6: I then fetch his cigarettes upon a silver plate.

WIFE 7: I arrange his bed at nine; he gets so sleepy then.

WIFE 8: I begin to dance and then he's wide awake again.

ALL: And then we all dance the vision of Salome.

According to the May 27, 1919, lyric sheet this was to have been followed by a dance with six special dancers, an Oriental dance by Evan Burrows Fontaine, and a burlesque dance by Johnny Dooley.

I'M THE GUY WHO GUARDS THE HAREM (AND MY HEART'S IN MY WORK)

Published. Copyrighted September 30, 1919. Previously registered for copyright as an unpublished song July 9, 1919. Introduced by Johnny Dooley. Listed in the program as "Episode 2" of Act II. Alternate title (program): "I Am the Guy Who Guards the Harem." This number replaced "Who Was King Solomon's Favorite Wife?" during the pre-Broadway tryout.

VERSE

When the Sultan goes out on a spree,
He presents me with the harem key.
Ev'ry Turk in Turkey envies me,
For I've got the best job in Turkey.

CHORUS

I'm the guy who guards the harem
When the Sultan goes away.
I'm a conscientious Turk,
And my heart is in my work.
The Sultan tells me that I earn my pay;
While he's gone I keep them happy,
And it keeps the wheels a-working in my nob.
If the Sultan ever saw the way I guard the harem,
He would go out and engage someone
To stand guard over me.
I'm the guy who guards the harem,
And I wouldn't take a million for my job.

A PRETTY GIRL IS LIKE A MELODY

Published. Copyrighted June 26, 1919. Probably written just before the Atlantic City tryout. Introduced by John Steel with Mary Washburn, Mauresette ("Humoresque"), Hazel Washburn ("Spring Song"), Marthe Pierre ("Elegy"), Jessie Reed ("Barcarolle"), Alta King ("Serenade"), and Margaret Irving ("Traumerei") in "Episode 5" of Act II. Number-one-selling recording by John Steel (Victor).

Over the years Berlin provided several accounts of the creation of what became not only the theme song of the *Follies* but the song played everywhere a beautiful woman walks across a stage. On the *Good Gulf Program* of May 13, 1934, Berlin said:

One of my best songs was written because the late Flo Ziegfeld needed a song to show off five [sic] of his most beautiful showgirls. . . . One day Mr. Ziegfeld called me into his office and showed me designs for costumes to be worn by five of his famous showgirls, including Jessie Reed, Alta King, and Martha Mansfield [sic]. Then he said, "All I need is an idea to introduce them." Well, I finally hit on the notion of having each girl represent one of the old melody classics, such as Mendelssohn's "Spring Song," Schubert's "Serenade," etc. The *last* thing that was thought of was an original song to introduce the famous old melodies. But finally I wrote one.

Another description occurs in Berlin's letter of May 21, 1945, to *Variety* editor Abel Green.

I had agreed to write one act for the *Ziegfeld Follies of 1919*. After I had finished it, Ziegfeld called me into his office and asked me to write one more song. He needed a spot to show off his famous Ziegfeld show girls. This was the so-called Ziegfeld Girl number in every *Follies*. He had some costume plates for this number. This was John Steel's first appearance, and having him in mind I thought of an idea to have each girl represent a famous classical number like "Traumerei," Mendelssohn's "Spring Song," Schubert's "Serenade," etc. There were five [sic] of these melodies, each representing a girl. I wrote a special lyric for each classic so Steel could sing it. I then found it was necessary to have some kind of a song that would serve as the springboard for these old classics. The result was "A Pretty Girl Is Like a Melody." It is interesting to note that the last thing I thought of was this song. In other words, I had no idea that it would be anything more than a "special material" song.

Another Berlin account of the genesis of the song (Cleveland *News*, October 14, 1954):

I had written one act of that *Follies* and was all through with the show when Flo Ziegfeld came to me and said "I have to have another song! Look at these costumes"—and he showed me five color plates of beautiful gowns with the names of the beauties that were to wear them. "I have to have a number for them" Flo said.

So I went home. I looked at the costume plates. I thought of melodies to go with each girl and gown. But I had to have a song to introduce the number and close it. Then I wrote lyrics and music to fit the action. It wasn't the hit of the show—"Tulip Time" was the hit then—"Pretty Girl" has become the hit.

Today they play it when a pretty girl walks across a stage. And strip teasers disrobe to it. That's show business.

On March 1, 1974, three years after the death of her husband, John Steel, Janette Hackett Steel wrote Berlin of how Steel had recalled the *Follies* theme song, which his performance had helped make famous.

As John told me, it was in Atlantic City where the show was playing prior to the New York premiere that he was not satisfied with his allotted time as the singer. His background was of a classical nature and he felt he did not show to advantage unless he had more chance to show off the quality of his voice. He said he spoke to Ned Wayburn about that, and he said he would speak to you about it, because he needed about seven minutes in one to prepare a big setting behind it. This was arranged, and you and John somehow were in a taxi cab and he sang some songs for you. Out of this taxi cab audition you selected the following numbers, that were interpolated into the song. "Humoresque" . . . "Mendelssohn Spring Song" . . . Massenet "Elegy" . . . [Offenbach's] "Barcarolle" . . . "Serenade" by Schubert . . . [Schumann's] "Traumerei." . . . There were some delightful lyrics you wrote for the sixteen bar interludes, which John did not remember entirely but the idea was that each girl got away from him, and left him with with her memory—melody. He said the costumes were faked for Atlantic City when it was produced, but that "Lucille" . . . Lady Duff Gordon, created new gowns for the opening at the New Amsterdam Theatre in New York.

The lyrics Berlin wrote for the "classical" interludes do not survive.

VERSE 1

I have an ear for music,
And I have an eye for a maid;
I link a pretty girlie
With each pretty tune that's played.
They go together like sunny weather
Goes with the month of May;
I've studied girls and music,
So I'm qualified to say:

CHORUS

A pretty girl is like melody
That haunts you night and day;
Just like the strain of a haunting refrain,
She'll start upon a marathon
And run around your brain.
You can't escape, she's in your memory
By morning, night, and noon;
She will leave you and then
Come back again:
A pretty girl is just like a pretty tune.

VERSE 2

Most every year we're haunted
By some little popular tune;
Then someone writes another—
The old one's forgotten soon.
A pretty maiden with beauty laden
Is like that kind of song:
Just when you think you love her,
Another one comes along.

REPEAT CHORUS

YOU CANNOT MAKE YOUR SHIMMY SHAKE ON TEA

Published. Copyrighted June 26, 1919. Words by Irving Berlin and Rennold Wolf. Introduced by Bert Williams in "Episode 7—'Prohibition' " of Act II. The extended "Prohibition" sequence, whose music and lyrics were credited to Berlin, undoubtedly included much more material, but it does not survive.

VERSE

'Tis a sad, sad day for me,
This day of lemonade and tea,
For now my dancing aspirations

Haven't got a chance.
In the Harlem cabarets
I used to spend my nights and days
Partaking of my fav'rite indoor sport,
The shimmy dance.
On the day they introduced their Prohibition laws
They just went and ruin'd the greatest shimmy
    dancer, because:

CHORUS 1

You cannot make your shimmy shake on tea;
It simply can't be done.
You'll find your shaking ain't taking
Unless you has the proper jazz
That only comes with such drinks as
Green River, Haig and Haig, and Hennessy.
Way out in China among the pale Chinese,
There's nothing finer than good old China teas;
But then you never saw a Chinaman a-shaking his
    chemise,
'Cause you cannot make your shimmy shake on
    tea.

CHORUS 2

You cannot make your shimmy shake on tea;
It simply can't be done.
You'll find your shaking ain't taking.
The shimmy, it is intricate,
And so you needs a little bit
Of Scotch or rye to lubricate your knee.
A cup of Ceylon, it may be strong or weak,
Won't help you spiel on, because it's much too
    meek;
Besides, a drink that's soft will very often ruin
    your technique—
No, you cannot make your shimmy shake on tea.

A SYNCOPATED COCKTAIL

Published. Copyrighted July 18, 1919. Introduced during "Episode 7" of Act II ("Prohibition") by Marilyn Miller and ensemble of "China Dolls": Martha Wood, Marcelle Earle, Mary Washburn, Viola Clarens, Madeleine Wales, Mabel Hastings, Monica Boulais, Lois Davison, Mildred Sinclair, Alma Braham, Olive Vaughn, Kay Mahoney, Lola Lorraine, Heloise Sheppard, Helen Shea, and Edna Lindsey. It is quite possible that "Bevo" also was sung during this scene titled "A Saloon of the Future," which also featured a number by Berlin (apparently lost) entitled "The Near Future," performed by John Steel ("A Customer"), Eddie Cantor ("The

Waiter"), Ethel Hallor ("Coca-Cola"), Jessie Reed ("Sarsaparilla"), Betty Francesco ("Grape Juice"), Hazel Washburn ("Lemonade"), Mauresette ("Bevo"), and Delyle Alda ("Lady Alcohol").

VERSE

Now that your drinking days are through,
Come along with me;
I've got a brand-new jag for you—
It's a melody.
Syncopated music
Goes right to your head;
I'd like to treat you to a cocktail
Before you go to bed, so

CHORUS

Come along, oh, come along,
And have a syncopated cocktail.
Come along, oh, come along with me—
You'll find that anyone can get a bun
On a jazzy melody.
Never mind your cocktail shakers;
Just shake your lingerie [your shimmies].
Come along and hum a song
That's bound to make you kind of dizzy.
Get a jag upon a raggy melody;
They're fascinating, intoxicating—
Come along and have
A syncopated cocktail with me.

MY TAMBOURINE GIRL

Published. Copyrighted September 30, 1919. Previously registered for copyright as an unpublished song July 9, 1919. Introduced in "Episode 9" of Act II by John Steel, with Jessie Reed and ensemble featuring Hazel Washburn, Betty Morton, Ethel Hallor, Caroline Erwin, Alta King, Marthe Pierre, Florence Crane, and Margaret Irving as the "Salvation Lassies."

VERSE

I'm in love with a beautiful maid,
Sweet as a girlie could be;
Out in Flanders she came to my aid—
A Salvation lassie is she.
Strange to say, I'd met her before,
In the city's mad whirl;
Ere we thought of going to war,
I called her my tambourine girl.

CHORUS

I met her on Broadway
With a tambourine in her hand;
"Follow on, follow on"
Was her solemn cry
To the passersby.
I wanted to tell her,
But I feared she'd not understand;
I bid a fond goodbye to her then.
One day in France I met her again
And I told her that I loved her
Out in no-man's land.

YOU'D BE SURPRISED

Published. Copyrighted October 28, 1919. Previously registered for copyright as an unpublished song September 27, 1919. Introduced by Eddie Cantor. Sung in vaudeville by Irving Berlin. Added to the show during the New York run, probably in September 1919. Top-selling recording by Eddie Cantor (Emerson).

VERSE 1

Johnny was bashful and shy;
Nobody understood why
Mary loved him—
All the other girls passed him by.
Ev'ryone wanted to know
How she could pick such a beau;
With a twinkle in her eye
She made this reply:

CHORUS 1

"He's not so good in a crowd,
But when you get him alone,
You'd be surprised.
He isn't much at a dance,
But when he takes you home,
You'd be surprised.
He doesn't look like much of a lover,
But don't judge a book by its cover.
He's got the face of an angel,
But there's a devil in his eye.
He's such a delicate thing,
But when he starts in to squeeze,
You'd be surprised.
He doesn't look very strong,
But when you sit on his knee,
You'd be surprised.
At a party or at a ball,

I've got to admit, he's nothing at all,
But in a morris chair
You'd be surprised."

VERSE 2

Mary continued to praise
Johnny's remarkable ways
To the ladies;
And you know, advertising pays.
Now Johnny's never alone;
He has the busiest phone;
Almost ev'ry other day
A new girl will say:

CHORUS 2

"He's not so good in the house,
But on a bench in a park
You'd be surprised.
He isn't much in the light,
But when he gets in the dark
You'd be surprised.
I know he looks as slow as the Erie,
But you don't know the half of it, dearie;
He looks as cold as an Eskimo,
But there's fire in his eyes.
He doesn't say very much,
But when he starts in to speak,
You'd be surprised.
He's not so good at the start,
But at the end of a week
You'd be surprised.
On a streetcar or in a train
You'd think he was born without any brain,
But in a taxicab
You'd be surprised."

LOOK OUT FOR THE BOLSHEVIKI MAN

Published by T. B. Harms and Co. Copyrighted June 30, 1919. Introduced during the pre-Broadway tryout by Johnny and Ray Dooley and ensemble. Alternate title (out-of-town programs): "The Bolsheviki Man." Dropped before the New York opening.

Published version

VERSE

Far across the ocean blue
There's a dang'rous boogyboo;

He'll be after me and you
By and by.
He's as bad as he can be;
When I spell his name you'll see:
B-O-L-S-H-E-V-I-K-I.

CHORUS

Look out for the Bolsheviki man!
You can tell him anyplace
By the whiskers on his face.
He's a slippery fellow from Russia
Seeking fortune and fame;
Be careful of his game—
It's full of bull just like his name,
So look out for the Bolsheviki man.
To the speeches that he makes
Tie a little can;
He hasn't got a single sou,
And he wants to share it all with you—
Look out! Look out
For the Bolsheviki Man!

Show version as of May 27, 1919

VERSE

You've seen the boogyboo,
The yama-yama too;
We warned you to be careful when they came.
And now another face
Has come to take their place—
Just listen and I'll try and spell his name:
B-O-L-S-H-E-V-I-K-I.
I know well, you'll agree he's an awful guy.

CHORUS, SECOND ENDING
[*Last four lines*]

He hangs out with a bunch of guys
Who spell their names with S-K-Y's.
Look out! Look out
For the Bolsheviki man!

WHO WAS KING SOLOMON'S FAVORITE WIFE?

Introduced by Eddie Cantor after the harem comedy scene ("Episode 2") in Act II during the pre-Broadway tryout. Dropped before the New York opening. No music is known to survive.

VERSE

Old King Solomon wrote a column and
A half about his thousand wives;
History put his name in the hall of fame
With all the other famous lives.
While I admire him so,
There's one thing I'm anxious to know.

CHORUS 1

Who was King Solomon's favorite wife?
Gee, but she must have been a peach!
Who did he feature in his all-star cast?
Who did he always say good night to last?
Who was the pride and joy of his life
When he was full of care and strife?
He had a thousand at his beck and call—
I wonder who he beckoned most of all.
I'd give up all my dough
To spend a day or so
With Solomon's favorite wife.

CHORUS 2

Who was King Solomon's favorite wife?
Gee, but she must have been a peach!
Who did he give the most of all his love?
Who was the one the rest were jealous of?
Who was the pride and joy of his life
When he was full of care and strife?
I wouldn't give a rap to wine and dine
The other nine hundred and ninety-nine,
But I would give my legs
To have some ham and eggs
With Solomon's favorite wife.

BEAUTIFUL FACES NEED BEAUTIFUL CLOTHES

Published. Copyrighted October 7, 1920. Introduced in *Broadway Beauties of 1920* (Winter Garden, New York; September 29, 1920; 105 performances) by Edith Hallor and "the girls." Previously registered for copyright as an unpublished song on January 3, 1920, having been sung in the pre-Broadway tryout (Nixon's Apollo Theatre, Atlantic City; June 10, 1919) of *Ziegfeld Follies of 1919* by Nancy Brown with John Daly, William Conrad, Jack Natter, Ray Klages, Jack Waverly, Frederick Easter, Otis Harper, and Bruce Buddington and interpreted by Ziegfeld showgirls Mauresette and Nan Larned ("Early Morning,"), Margaret Irving and Marthe Pierre ("Forenoon"), Alta King and Hazel Washburn ("Tea Time"), and Jessie Reed and Ethel Hallor ("At the

Opera"). In a list of numbers dated May 27, 1919, located among Irving Berlin's papers, "Beautiful Faces" was originally to have been sung by Delyle Alda. It was dropped from the *Follies of 1919* before the New York opening.

VERSE

Lonesome little shopgirl
Sitting home alone,
No boy about
To take her out.
She is very pretty,
But nobody knows:
Lonesome little rose
Hasn't any clothes.

CHORUS

Beautiful faces need beautiful clothes,
Satins and laces, nice ribbons and bows.
An ankle may be a joy,
But any boy who gazes
Won't warble its praises
Unless it's covered by attractive hose.
Many a shopgirl whom nobody knows
Would be the top girl in musical shows
If she were dressed in the best
From her head right down to her toes,
For beautiful faces need beautiful clothes.

ZIEGFELD FOLLIES OF 1920

Tryout: Nixon's Apollo Theatre, Atlantic City, New Jersey; June 15, 1920. New York run: New Amsterdam Theatre; June 22–October 16, 1920; 123 performances. Lyrics and music by Irving Berlin and others, including Gene Buck and Dave Stamper, Harry Tierney and Joseph McCarthy, Bert Kalmar and Harry Ruby, Ballard MacDonald, and Victor Herbert. Produced under the personal direction of Florenz Ziegfeld Jr. Scenery by Joseph Urban. Staged by Edward Royce. Orchestra under the direction of Frank Tours. Orchestrations by Frank Saddler, Maurice de Packh, Steve Jones, and Charles Grant. Cast headed by Fanny Brice, W. C. Fields, Jack Donahue, Ray Dooley, Gus Van and Joe Schenck, John Steel, Mary Eaton, Bernard Granville, Delyle Alda, Doris Eaton, Carl Randall, Charles Winninger, Lillian Broderick, Moran and Mack, Margaret Irving, Jessie Reed, Addison Young, and Art Hickman's Famous Midnight Frolics Orchestra.

CHINESE FIRECRACKERS

Published. Copyrighted June 23, 1920. Previously registered for copyright as an unpublished song May 24, 1920. Introduced by Gus Van and Joe Schenck and "Firecracker Girls." This number is listed in programs for the *Follies of 1920* as "Chinese Fantasy."

VERSE

Charlie Younge lay smoking on his bunk one
    night;
Something happened, filling Charlie Younge with
    fright:
Someone placed a bunch of firecrackers under his
    bunk
And touched the stem of each of them
With a piece of lighted punk.
Charlie jumped up in the air;
Filled with rage, he started to swear:

CHORUS

"Hop Toy, Ming Foy,
Sing Goy, Ung Loy,
Suey Pow, Yenshee Gow Main!"
That bunch of crackers exploded
With a bing, bang, boom,
And so did Charlie Younge
In his native tongue
With a "Hop Toy, Ming Foy,
Sing Goy, Ung Loy,
Hunka Chinee punk!"
Which means, "Who the hellee
Put those firecrackers under my bunk?"

THE GIRLS OF MY DREAMS

Published. Copyrighted June 21, 1920. Previously registered for copyright as an unpublished song May 18, 1920. Introduced in the *Ziegfeld Follies of 1920* by John Steel and ensemble ("Cloud Girls"). Original cast recording by John Steel (Victor).

VERSE

When the shadows fall
And the crickets call,
I can hear the voice of Dreamland,
Calling to me from afar,
Where my little dream girls are.

When the lights are low,
Silently I go
To the girls I know in Dreamland;
Happiness awaits me in the land of dreams,
For the girls I love are there.

CHORUS

I'd love to meet
The girls of my dreams;
They're all so sweet,
The girls of my dreams.
When I need sympathy,
They cheer and comfort me;
And I call my little girls
My string of pearls,
My precious rosary.
When day draws near,
The girls of my dreams
All disappear,
To heaven, it seems.
In the morning they are gone,
But they're mine till break of dawn,
And I love every one
Of the girls of my dreams.

THE GIRL OF YOUR DREAMS

An earlier version of "The Girls of My Dreams." The lyric fits the same music. A pencil holograph of the lyric was found among Berlin's papers and is now at the Irving Berlin Collection of the Music Division of the Library of Congress.

VERSE

High up in the clouds,
Far away from crowds,
Living in an airy castle
Isn't really what it seems—
After all, they're only dreams.
There's a greater joy
For a dreamy boy
In a little cozy cottage.
When the little smoke clouds all have cleared
    away,
Happiness will come to stay.

CHORUS

Someday you'll meet
The girl of your dreams;
She's oh so sweet,

The girl of your dreams.
Someday she'll come to you
And in her eyes of blue
You'll see a wonderful glow;
Then you will know
That all your dreams came true.
Close to your breast
The girl of your dreams
Will gently rest
While happiness beams;
You'll be glad to say goodbye
To your castles in the sky
For a cottage for two
With the girl of your dreams.

BELLS

Published. Copyrighted June 23, 1920. Previously registered for copyright as an unpublished song December 9, 1919. Introduced in the *Ziegfeld Follies of 1920* by Bernard Granville (Groom) with Jane Carroll (Bride), Charles Winninger (Bishop), Gus Van and Joe Schenck (Storytellers), Helen Shea and Doris Eaton (Bridesmaids), and ensemble ("Bell Girls"). In the summer of 1953, when Berlin was preparing "Bells" for use in the film musical *White Christmas*, to win approval of the censors he changed the last line of the song to: "Have the sweetest little sound of them all."

VERSE

Very many years ago,
Mister Edgar Allan Poe
Wrote a little poem I know
Called "Bells."
When I read those clever rhymes
Of the many different chimes,
I could almost hear them ringing,
Ding-dong-dinging.

CHORUS

Phone bells, sleigh bells,
And very merry Christmas-day bells;
The brazen firebells
That ring with fear,
And happy New Year bells
That ring out once a year.
Cowbells, doorbells,
For all I know there may be more bells;
But the poet tells
That wedding bells
Have the sweetest little ding-dong of all.

TELL ME, LITTLE GYPSY

Published. Copyrighted June 21, 1920. Previously registered for copyright as an unpublished song May 20, 1920. Introduced by John Steel and Delyle Alda. The most popular song in the *Follies of 1920*. Original cast recording by John Steel (Victor). Another original cast recording by Art Hickman and His Orchestra (Columbia).

VERSE

Deep down in my heart there's a burning
    question;
Maybe you can answer it, Gypsy maid.
Have I searched in vain for that little bluebird?
Tell me how much longer 'twill be delayed.
Will my dreams come true?
Tell me my fortune, do.

CHORUS

Tell me, little Gypsy,
What the future holds for me.
"Kindly cross my palm with silver,
And I'll try and see-ee."
Tell me, is there someone
In the days that are to be?
There's a girl for every boy in the world;
There must be someone for me.

THE LEG OF NATIONS

Published. Copyrighted July 29, 1920. Previously registered for copyright as an unpublished song June 28, 1920. Introduced by Carl Randall. On the original sheet music the title is mistakenly listed as "The Leg of Nation's."

VERSE

I'd like to form a League of Nations
Without any obligations
Composed of girls, and each a beautiful one.
'Twould be a very novel treaty,
Represented by a sweetie
From each and ev'ry country under the sun.
Don't think I'm asking for your kind applause,
But I think a Yankee girl
Should be its president
Because:

CHORUS

Her eyes are a little bit brighter,
Her teeth are a little bit whiter,
She's just a little more lively,
Which makes her more attractive;
The rest are not as active
At a party or ball.
Her smile is a little bit sweeter,
Her style is a little bit neater,
And from her toes up to her knees
The ankle gazer sees she's
Got the leg of nations,
My girl of the U.S.A.

COME ALONG SEXTET

Published. Copyrighted July 29, 1920. Previously registered for copyright as an unpublished song June 28, 1920. Added after New York opening. Introduced by ensemble. Alternate title (sheet music cover): "Come Along."

VERSE

BOY: How do you do?
GIRL: How do you do?
BOY: Do you think the weather's
    Nice enough to do a sextet?
GIRL: I think so, don't you?
BOY: If you think so, I've got to think so too!
GIRL: What'll we sing?
BOY: Any old thing.
GIRL: Is the music very pretty to your little
    sextet?
BOY: It was written especially for us.
GIRL: Let us hear the chorus:

CHORUS

BOY: Come along, come along, come along!
    Come along, come along, come along!
    That's all they ever sing in this kind of a
        song.
BOTH: Come along, come along, come along!
    Come along, come along, come along!
    They never say just where they're going,
    But they holler "Come along!" and so
    Come along, let's go inside
    And we'll take a little ride.
    You will sit right by my side—
    Come along, let's go!

THE SYNCOPATED VAMP

Published. Copyrighted June 23, 1920. Previously registered for copyright as an unpublished song June 7, 1920. Introduced by Bernard Granville, Carl Randall, Jack Donahue, Lillian Broderick, Florence Ware, and Ray Dooley with ensemble ("All the Little Vamps") and Art Hickman's Famous Midnight Frolics Orchestra.

VERSE

There she goes—
Just take a glance at her.
There she goes—
Go have a dance with her.
'Ere she goes—
She's got a devil in her dancing toes.
Beneath her stylish clothes
A little bit of her ankle shows,
Which makes a hit with her dancing beaus,
And that's the reason ev'rybody knows:

CHORUS

She's a syncopated vampire,
Just a syncopated vamp;
Among a hundred thousand acres
Of American shoulder shakers
She's the champ.
This little jazzy Cleopatra
Has the people gazing at her;
She sticks to her partner
Like a penny postage stamp.
If you ever had a fox-trot
With the syncopated vamp,
You'd say it's like a lot of liquor,
For your vision begins to flicker like a lamp.
She doesn't wink at the boys—she's much
   bolder:
She only flirts with her shoulder.
So they call her
The syncopated vamp.

I LIVE IN TURKEY

Dropped before the New York opening, either during rehearsals or during the pre-Broadway tryout. Listed on sheet music covers for the *Ziegfeld Follies of 1920* but apparently, according to Donald J. Stubblebine and other well-known collectors, never published. No music is known to survive. A typed lyric sheet was found among Berlin's papers and is now in the Irving Berlin Collection of the Music Division of the Library of Congress.

VERSE

My father's name is Ben Ali;
He is a terrible Turk.
He and the Sultan are pally;
That's why he don't have to work.
I lead a wonderful life;
I'm the Sultan's favorite wife.

CHORUS

I live in Turkey
Oi-oi-oi-oikey—
Turkey, where the harems are.
I sleep on a Turkish rug;
If I don't I hope to choke.
I drink from a Turkish jug,
And the cigarettes I smoke
Are made in Turkey
Oi-oi-oi-oikey.
Turkey is my favorite fowl;
On every Saturday night
When I take my bath,
I dry myself with a Turkish towel.

TURKEY

This lyric appears to have been a forerunner of "I Live in Turkey." Not used in the *Ziegfeld Follies of 1920*. No music is known to survive.

VERSE 1

Turkey is the place where Sally
Met a young Turk named Ben Ali.
He and she became quite pally,
Ta-da-da-da-dum.
Very many wives had Benny;
She became one of his many.
She was there a year and then 'e
Sent her home to invite her lady friends to

CHORUS 1

Turkey—ever since Sally came from Turkey,
Sally is not the same.
She sleeps upon a rug,
Drinks water from a jug,
Sits on her pa's veranda
Spreading Turkish propaganda.

Turkey, all that she eats is turkey,
That's her fav'rite fowl.
Ev'ry morning sharp at ten
She takes a Turkish bath, and then
She dries herself with a Turkish towel.

VERSE 2

Sally has become a dancer—
If you don't believe she can, sir,
Ask a question and she'll answer
With her da-da-dum.
Sally's husband sent a cable
Saying, "Come back when you're able;
Bring along your sister Mabel—
She'll be nice company for you while you're in—"

CHORUS 2

Turkey—ever since Sally came from Turkey,
Sally is not the same.
Dressed in her harem pants,
She does her fav'rite dance;
That's only one of many
That she has to do for Benny.
Turkey, all that she eats is turkey,
That's her fav'rite fowl.
One night at a masquerade,
Imagine what a hit she made—
All that she wore was a Turkish towel.

STAGE DOOR SONG

No music is known to survive. A typed lyric sheet was found among Berlin's papers and is now in the Irving Berlin Collection of the Music Division of the Library of Congress. Possibly intended for the *Ziegfeld Follies of 1920* as the apparent reference to "Tell Me, Little Gypsy" indicates.

VERSE

I'm the stage door man at the Amsterdam,
Where the *Ziegfeld Follies* play.
Though he don't give me much pay,
I'm a wealthy man today;
You may think it's strange, but I make more
   change
Than the actors in the troupe—
I receive much more, for I guard the door
Of Mr. Ziegfeld's chicken coop.

CHORUS 1

If you saw what I saw at the stage door each
night,
You'd get what I get to keep my mouth shut tight.
I feel just like the Gypsy that the fellow sings
about—
They've crossed my palm with silver till they've
almost worn it out.
They drive up in taxis and I must shut my eyes;
I mustn't mention it, sir, but if you knew who
they were,

You'd be surprised.
I don't go to the smart hotels
To meet the famous social swells;
I meet them and greet them
At the stage door each night.

CHORUS 2

If you saw what I saw at the stage door each night,
You'd get what I get to keep my mouth shut tight.
If Ziegfeld saw the bankbook that I keep on my
shelf,

I'd soon lose my position—he would take the job
himself.
My social acquaintance is enormous in size;
The millionaires that I've met who come to meet
the sextet—
You'd be surprised.
I know some men with naked domes
Who'd lose their wives and happy homes
If I told what I saw
At the stage door each night.

*Wilda Bennett and ensemble in "The Legend of the
Pearls," from* Music Box Revue *of 1921. Left inset:
Bobby Clark and Fanny Brice. Right inset: Claire
Luce, "Wild Cats." Both from* Music Box Revue *of
1924*

MUSIC BOX
REVUES
1921–1924

From an undated, unidentified newspaper clipping:

"I'll never forget that town," he reminisced [about Atlantic City]. "I wrote the Music Box Revues of 1921, 1922, 1923, and 1924 locked in a suite at the Traymore. The only breath of salt air I got for weeks at a time was when I leaned out of a window and flew a kite."

MUSIC BOX REVUE 1921

Tryout: None. New York run: Music Box; September 22, 1921; 440 performances. Music and lyrics by Irving Berlin. Produced by Sam H. Harris. Sketches by Frances Nordstrom, William Collier, George V. Hobart, and Thomas J. Gray. Staged by Hassard Short. Orchestrations by Frank Tours, Maurice de Packh, Steve Jones, Charles Grant, Alfred Dalby, Oscar Radin, and Harry Akst. Orchestra under the direction of Frank Tours and Anton Heindi. Cast: starring Joseph Santley, Wilda Bennett, Ivy Sawyer, Paul Frawley, William Collier, Sam Bernard, and Irving Berlin, and featuring Florence Moore, Rose Rolando, Emma Haig, Hugh Cameron, and the Three Brox Sisters. All the previously unpublished lyrics that follow can be found in Berlin's complete piano-vocal score in the Irving Berlin Collection of the Music Division of the Library of Congress.

WHAT'S IN THE QUEER-LOOKING BUNDLE? and WHERE AM I ? and WE WORK WHILE YOU SLEEP and WE'LL TAKE THE PLOT TO ZIEGFELD and EIGHT LITTLE NOTES

These linked segments constitute the opening to Act I. Introduced by the ensemble. Alternate titles: "Opening Act I" and "Opening Chorus—Act One." Alternate title of the segment titled "We Work While You Sleep" is "Burglar Song." The original "Eight Little Notes" were

Mary Milford, Virginia Dixon, Helen Clare, Betsy Ross, Helen Newcombe, Claire Davis, Miriam Hopkins, and Jeanne St. John.

What's in the Queer-looking Bundle?

[*Scene: Roof of Music Box Theatre. After business of cats, etc., stork flies over roof and drops bundle. Four stagehands pick up bundle and go into following:*]

STAGEHANDS: What's in the queer-looking bundle?
Why did they leave it here?
It looks like somebody's baby.
That's what it is, I fear.
Who is the poor little kiddie,
Somebody's pride and joy?
Where is its father and mother?
Is it a girl or boy?
Looks like a plot for a drama
Or a good comedy;
But it begins like a problem.
Looks like a farce to me.
Let me examine the bundle,
Look for a clue.
Goodness, gracious,
What is it?
It's a revue!
A revue?
Good God, another revue!

Where Am I?

[*Bundle opens, disclosing a little* GIRL *who stretches arms and yawns, saying:*]

GIRL: Where am I, where am I?
STAGEHAND: This is the Music Box.
GIRL: Please let me in—
I'm anxious to begin.
STAGEHAND: Who are you, who are you?
GIRL: I'm called the Music Box.
STAGEHAND: Is that what they christened you?
GIRL: Yes, the Music Box Revue.
STAGEHAND: Who sent you here?
GIRL: My father.
STAGEHAND: Is he near?
GIRL: He'd rather not appear.
STAGEHAND: Is he ashamed of you?
Please tell us, do!
GIRL: My father and mother are weary and worn;
They fought with each other before I was born.

STAGEHAND: Perhaps that's why you don't look very strong.
GIRL: All day I've trembled.
STAGEHAND: Don't weaken or you won't live very long.
GIRL: Those folks assembled out there—
Who are they?
STAGEHAND: They're the customers—
The hims and hers who pay—to stay.
Can you dance?
GIRL: I can dance a little bit.
STAGEHAND: Can you sing?
GIRL: Just enough to make a hit.
STAGEHAND: Do you know just how to dress?
GIRL: I can dress.
STAGEHAND: Yes, yes!
GIRL: More or less.
STAGEHAND: Make it less.
GIRL: There's a lot
For the first and second act.
STAGEHAND: Have you got
What'll keep the theatre packed?
GIRL: Do they want much for their money?
STAGEHAND: You must make them think you're funny.
GIRL: If I'm not?
STAGEHAND: They will want their money back.
GIRL: I think you'd better take me home.
STAGEHANDS: [*rocking* GIRL]
Rockabye, baby,
And while you rock,
You must be good
Or else they will knock.
If you behave,
They'll stay till you're through—
But if you're bad,
They'll walk out on you.

[*After* GIRL *deposits book in music box she goes to sleep at the right corner of the music box. Enter nine* BURGLARS *who sing the following number:*]

We Work While You Sleep

VERSE

With burglar tools we represent a certain class of men
Whose business is to sneak right in and sneak right out again.
We don't advise young men to take a course in burglary,
For cracking safes is not as safe as it is cracked up to be.

CHORUS

At night when all is quiet
We come around to take a little peep.
Sometimes we profit by it;
Then again there are times
When it isn't what we thought it was.
The only time we try it
Is when you're wrapped in slumber deep;
Just like a famous patent medicine,
We work while you sleep.

We'll Take the
Plot to Ziegfeld

[*A* BURGLAR *takes the plot from the music box and joins other* BURGLARS *downstage.*]

OTHER BURGLARS: What's that?
FIRST BURGLAR: It's the plot.
OTHER BURGLARS: Of what?
FIRST BURGLAR: Of a new revue.
OTHER BURGLARS: Do you think it's worthwhile stealing?
FIRST BURGLAR: It's worth quite a bit if the show is a hit.
OTHER BURGLARS: Let's try and think of someone whom we can take it to.
FIRST BURGLAR: There's Dillingham and Ziegfeld.
OTHER BURGLARS: That's just what we'll do.

CHORUS

ALL: We'll take the plot to Ziegfeld—
He's got an office at the Amsterdam.
If Ziegfeld doesn't want it,
We'll go round to the Globe
And we'll visit Charlie Dillingham.
If Charlie doesn't buy it,
We'll go and tie it up in knots
And throw it in the Hudson River
With the rest of the plots.

[*They exit.*]
[*Baby* GIRL *wakes and sees* BURGLARS *go off with plot.*]

GIRL: There goes the plot,
The only one we've got.
It was really very thin;
You'd have hated every bit of it—

Now that we're rid of it,
Let the show begin.

[*She winds up music box. The* EIGHT LITTLE NOTES *appear and go into number.*]

Eight Little Notes

Eight little notes are we,
Useful as we can be.
You know and we know
What do-re-mi-fa-sol-la-ti-do
Mean to a melody.
Eight little notes can't fail
When they are placed on sale;
Songwriters claim us—
We are the very famous
Eight little notes of the scale.
Speaking of notes—
Eight little notes—
We represent the music of the *Music Box Revue*,
The little notes of the music that were written just for you.
The pretty girls and costumes are important, there's no doubt,
But even more important is the tune that you whistle going out.
Nobody likes the lyrics that the chorus ladies yell—
Nobody ever hears them, and perhaps it's just as well.
We've got a lot of music in the *Music Box Revue*;
Somebody has to hear it, and it might as well be you.
And now before we leave you to let the show advance,
We'll present the little gent who taught us how to dance.

[*Enter* DANCE.]

DANCE: 1–2–3–No!
1–2–3–Oh!
1–2–3–So!
1–2–3–Go!

DANCE YOUR
TROUBLES AWAY

Introduced by Beth Meakins, Richard W. Keene, and Emma Haig. According to show programs, the number in this spot was titled "Dancing the Seasons Away," but the unpublished piano-vocal score and typed lyric sheets

preserved by Berlin indicate "Dance Your Troubles Away." There remains a possibility that at some point "Dance Your Troubles Away" replaced a different song called "Dancing the Seasons Away," or vice versa.

VERSE

GIRLS: We're feeling mighty blue;
We don't know what to do.
HE: I'd like to know just what's the matter with you.
GIRLS: The sun up in the sky
Has bid us all goodbye.
HE: It seems you're very sad; I'd like to know why.
GIRLS: We're overtaken by the weary blues;
That's why the heavens are gray.
HE: They shouldn't be so very hard to lose.
GIRLS: How can we chase 'em away?

CHORUS

Dance when you're blue
To a lively little melody;
That's what to do—
You'll discover it's the remedy.
Off with the blues,
On with the shoes,
Shoes that were only made for dancing!
One step or two
And you're feeling like you ought to be,
I'm telling you—
If you're looking for a recipe
When you're lonely
There is only
One thing to do:
Make 'em play a lively melody
And dance your troubles away.

BEHIND THE FAN

Published. Copyrighted October 5, 1921. Previously registered for copyright as an unpublished song September 12, 1921. Introduced by Wilda Bennett and ensemble.

VERSE

Be careful of the señorita
Who knows the value of a fan—
That's how a beautiful chiquita
Becomes acquainted with a man.
I've seen them flirting with a stranger,

And when the game of love began,
He didn't realize the danger
Behind her fan.

CHORUS

Eyes of brown are peeping at you
From behind the fan;
No one knows just what they can do
To the heart of a man.
There behind a shelter of lace
Lies a hidden plan;
You may find a heavenly face
With the heart of a devil
Behind the fan.

IN A COZY KITCHENETTE APARTMENT and DINING OUT

The "In a Cozy Kitchenette Apartment" section of the "Dining Out" scene was published separately. Copyrighted October 6, 1921. Previously registered for copyright as an unpublished song September 12, 1921. Introduced by Joseph Santley and Ivy Sawyer. The complete "Dining Out" scene, according to the opening-night program (which names the characters in the scene somewhat differently from the piano-vocal score, from which the text of the lyric was drawn), was introduced by Santley and Sawyer (Boy and Girl Diners), Hugh Cameron (Headwaiter), Lucretia Craig (Coatroom Girl), Richard W. Keene (Coatroom Boy), the Misses Dixon, Clare, Davis, Ross, Newcombe, and Mahan (the Oysters), Emma Haig (the Chicken), Mary Milford (the Cauliflower), Miss Aleta (the Mushroom), Mlle Marguerite (the French Pastry), Rose Rolando (the Cigar), Renie Riano (the Check), the Misses Duffy, Wylie, Foune, Meakins, Haver, Cox, Shea, and Lowry (the Tips), and Messrs Quinlivan, Hylan, Mays, and Mendelssohn (the Waiters).

In a Cozy Kitchenette Apartment

Published version

VERSE

I'm getting tired of eating in restaurants;
They don't appeal to me.
If we could own a cute apartment,
I'd know just what a joyful heart meant.
I hate to think of waiters and bill of fares
When evening time draws near.
Three little rooms will be just like heaven
When we are married, dear.

CHORUS

In a cozy kitchenette apartment for two
I'll be setting the table
While you're cooking a stew for me and you.
I'll be there to help you put the dishes away;
Then together we'll listen
To the phonograph play
The tuneful "Humoresque"—
And oh, what bliss
When it's time to kiss
In a cozy kitchenette apartment for two!

Show version

Dining Out Scene (A Full-Course "Word-and-Musical Meal")

[*At rise of curtain a* COATROOM BOY *and a* COATROOM GIRL *are discovered, along with the* HEADWAITER. *Enter* BOY AND GIRL DINERS.]

COATROOM BOY:	Let me take your hat and coat, sir. Let me take your walking cane.
COATROOM GIRL:	Please give your wrap to me; I'll guard it carefully.
BOY DINER:	In an hour we'll be going— You can bring them to us then.
COATROOM BOY AND GIRL:	When you're ready to go, For a dollar or so You can buy them back again.
HEADWAITER:	Take a seat, sir—here's a chair. You may order when you please.
GIRL DINER:	I'm as hungry as a bear.
BOY DINER:	Let me see the menu, please.

[HEADWAITER *hands menu to* BOY DINER, *who orders as follows:*]

BOY DINER:	Oysters on the half-shell.
HEADWAITER:	The large or small?
BOY DINER:	Any kind at all.
HEADWAITER:	Will you have some consommé?
BOY DINER:	Never mind the soup, and no entrée.

HEADWAITER:	What else will you have, sir?
BOY DINER:	A chicken—fat!
HEADWAITER:	No, you can't have that.
BOY DINER:	Can't you pick us out a fat one?
HEADWAITER:	There was only one and I ate that one.
GIRL DINER:	I'd like some cauliflower and mushrooms.
BOY DINER:	Me too.
GIRL DINER:	And then a nice dessert.
HEADWAITER:	What will I bring you?
GIRL DINER:	Some nice French pastry I would adore.
BOY DINER:	Bring some pastry.
HEADWAITER:	Anything more?
BOY DINER:	Repeat what I ordered— Perhaps I can't afford it.
HEADWAITER:	[*repeating order*] Oysters, chicken, vegetables, pastry— You've not gone too far.
BOY DINER:	[*as* HEADWAITER *starts to exit*] Waiter!
HEADWAITER:	Yes, sir!
BOY DINER:	And a good cigar.

[HEADWAITER *exits.* BOY AND GIRL DINERS *sing the following duet:*]

VERSE

I'm getting tired of eating in restaurants;
They don't appeal to me.
If we could own a cute apartment,
I'd know what a joyful heart meant.
I hate to think of waiters and bill of fares
When evening time draws near.
Three little rooms will be just like heaven
When we are married, dear.

CHORUS

In a cozy kitchenette apartment for two
I'll be setting the table
While you're cooking the stew for me and you.
I'll be there to help you put the dishes away;
Then together we'll listen
To the phonograph play
The tuneful "Humoresque"—
And oh, what bliss
When it's time to kiss
In a cozy kitchenette apartment for two!

GIRL DINER:	Where's the waiter? Call him, dear, For we haven't long to stay.
BOY DINER:	I can see him coming near With the oysters on a tray.

[*As the food is being served to couple, characters representing the different courses appear and sing the following choruses:*]

OYSTERS: Six little oysters surrounded by
pearls,
Three of us gentlemen and three
of us girls.
This morning we pounded our
heads
In our cute little comfortable
oyster beds;
Someone awoke us and now we
are cross—
Soon we'll be covered with red
catsup sauce.
We're unhappy to be so far away
From our home down in Oyster
Bay.

CHICKEN: I was born
Way out in Michigan on a farm;
I'd have sworn
That no one ever would do me
harm.
Like a baby I was fed
Till I grew fat; then I was led
Out to the barn,
And in a minute I lost my head.
"Oh, how I wish again
That I was in Michigan
Back on the farm."

MUSHROOM AND
CAULIFLOWER: We grew in a beautiful garden
Till one day
Without even asking our pardon
They pulled us up and carried us
away.
In that lovely garden
A happy life we planned;
Now we own a tin kimona—
We were canned,
We were canned.

FRENCH PASTRY: I came here from gay Paree—
Can't you see
When you look at me
That I'm as tasty as can be?
And I'll agree
With any little he
If he'll agree
With a bit of French pastry.

CIGAR: Clear Havana
I'm supposed to be;
But I'm not, you see—
You'll get wise to me
When you smell a real panatela.
In Havana
They would all agree
I'm really not worth more than a

Five-cent banana
I'm not a panatela.

[*Afterward:*]

BOY DINER: Anything else, my dear? Before
we get out of here?
GIRL DINER: I've had so much, dear, really
I couldn't eat another speck.
BOY DINER: Waiter!
HEADWAITER: Yes, sir!
BOY DINER: Bring along the check.

[*Enter the* CHECK.]

CHECK: When your meal is ended
And you've been attended
By a waiter splendid
Who hung around your neck,
You begin to stutter
As you sadly utter
The greatest after-dinner speech:
"Bring me the check."
I'm the bad news,
The bad news,
That hangs about when you're
dining out.
I'm the sad news,
The sad news
That comes at the end of a
perfect meal
When the dinner check must be
paid.

[BOY DINER *pays* CHECK, *then addresses* COATROOM BOY
as follows:]

BOY DINER: Let me have my hat and coat,
boy!
Let me have my walking cane!
And like a nice young chap
Please bring the lady's wrap—
We are anxious to be going,
For we must be home by ten.
COATROOM BOY
AND GIRL: If you're ready to go,
For a dollar or so
You can buy them back again.

[*At this point eight little* TIPS *enter from behind trees
and sing the following:*]

TIPS: Tip, tip, tip, tip—
Don't forget the little
Tip, tip, tip, tip.
Never let the little
Tip
Slip

Out of your grip.
It's a total loss,
But you've got to come across
With the
Tip, tip, tip, tip.
To the bottom of your pocket
Take a dip;
Hear us holler, "Please change a
dollar!"
And give us a little
Tip, tip, tip, tip.

[*After* BOY DINER *is cleaned out thoroughly tipping,
scene changes to kitchenette apartment.* BOY AND GIRL
DINER *sing chorus of kitchenette song,* "In a Cozy
Kitchenette Apartment."]

MY LITTLE BOOK OF POETRY

Published. Copyrighted October 6, 1921. Previously
registered for copyright as an unpublished song September 15, 1921. Only the verse and chorus of the song were
printed in the published edition. Introduced by Joseph
Santley (the Singer) with Margaret Irving (Annabel Lee), Emma Haig (the Vampire), Helen Lyons
(Evangeline), the Eight Little Notes (the Storytellers), Richard W. Keene (Paul Revere), Beth Meakins
(Maud Muller), Frank Gill (Gunga Din), Chester Hale
(Hiawatha), Irene Duffy (the Raven), and ensemble.

VERSE

Some folks who don't know what to do with their
evenings,
Up till dawn with their dress clothes on they will
roam,
Dancing round in a cabaret,
Homeward bound at the break of day—
I have found that it doesn't pay,
So I'd rather stay at home.

CHORUS

With my little book of poetry
Let me while the hours away
Reading the poets of olden times,
Meeting the girls they dressed up in rhymes.
I will never ask for company
When the skies of blue turn gray;
Mister Kipling and Poe
Are the best friends I know
At the end of a weary day.

[*As* SINGER *continues, a girl representing each poem appears. Enter Edgar Allan Poe's* ANNABEL LEE.]

It was many and many a year ago
In my book of poetry
When I first met the maid whom you all may know
By the name of Annabel Lee.
And often since then have I met her again
In her kingdom by the sea.
For the moon never beams
Without bringing me dreams
Of the beautiful Annabel Lee.

[*Enter Rudyard Kipling's* VAMPIRE.]

SINGER: A fool there was and he made his
            prayer—
VAMPIRE: I'm the little Vampire Kipling wrote
            about;
          I go through the ages vamping in and
            out.
SINGER: To a rag and a bone and a hank of
            hair—
VAMPIRE: Theda Bara used to do it too;
          I'm the one who taught her everything
            she knew.
SINGER: They called her the woman who did not
            care—
VAMPIRE: Ever since I started in to vamp,
          Every other woman winks a wicked
            lamp.
SINGER: But the fool he called her his lady fair—
VAMPIRE: Once you're in my clutches,
          You'll know what "in dutch" is.
SINGER: Even as you and I.

[*Enter Henry Wordsworth Longfellow's* EVANGELINE.]

SINGER: Evangeline, Evangeline,
          My queen of poetry,
          A simple maid of seventeen
          Who lived in Arcady,
          And it seems when Longfellow found
            her,
          He placed a halo around her:
          With magic paint
          He drew a saint
          And he called her Evangeline.

[*The* SINGER *retells Longfellow's story of Paul Revere and Maud Muller—in ragtime—as it is acted out in background. Enter* PAUL *and* MAUD, *followed, at the appropriate cues, by Kipling's* GUNGA DIN, *Longfellow's* HIAWATHA, *and Poe's* RAVEN.]

SINGER: Listen, my children, and you shall hear
          About the famous ride of Paul Revere.
          Out in the country he rode one day

And met Maud Muller, who raked the
  hay.
There they sat, just he and she,
Under the spreading chestnut tree.
The stag at noon had drunk his fill
From the babbling brook beside the hill;
Paul and Maud were thirsty too,
And they knew just what to do:
They hollered, "Din-ding, Gunga Din,
Hurry up and bring a jug of water in!"
And after Maud Muller and Paul Revere
Drank their cups of water clear,
Paul said, "My dear,
I've waited now for about a year;
Let's marry, now don't you tarry—
The wedding bells I'd like to hear."
And as he started to say,
"Let's name the day,"
Who came along but Hiawatha.
He said to Paul, "She'll never fall—
To win the farmer's daughter
You need some firewater.
Here is my flask, you needn't ask—
Give her a drink," said Hiawatha.
Paul just answered, "Stand aside—
I've got no use for an Indian guide."
Up in the tree above,
Watching the couple love,
Sat a foxy little Raven,
List'ning to Paul Revere
Telling his sweetie dear
Of the money he was savin'.
"Make up your mind," he said,
"And marry me, Maud."
She answered, "Yes,"
And then he shouted, "Gawd,
I've never been so happy before."
Quoth the Raven: "Nevermore."
And then the bells—bells—bells—
The rhyming and the chiming
Of the bells—bells—bells—
Were ringing, ting-a-ling-ing,
With a happy ding-dong
All the day long.
To the tune of those bells,
Edgar Allan Poe's bells,
That afternoon the lovin' knot was tied.
The people say she made a lovely bride
And they both lived happily ever after.

REPEAT CHORUS

SAY IT WITH MUSIC

Published. Copyrighted March 21, 1921, six months before the *Music Box Revue of 1921* opened on Broadway. Previously registered for copyright as an unpublished song January 17, 1921. Written as a theme song for the Music Box Theatre. Introduced by Wilda Bennett and Joseph Santley. Number-one-selling recording by Paul Whiteman and His Orchestra (Victor). Other major recordings by Ben Selvin and His Orchestra (Vocalion), John Steel (Victor), and the Columbians (Columbia). The published version is followed by the song as it was routined in the revue.

Published version

VERSE 1

GIRL: Music is a language lovers understand;
        Melody and romance wander hand in
          hand;
        Cupid never fails assisted by a band—
        So if you have something sweet to tell
          her:

CHORUS

Say it with music,
Beautiful music;
Somehow they'd rather be kissed
To the strains of Chopin or Liszt.
A melody mellow
Played on a cello
Helps Mister Cupid along;
So say it with a beautiful song.

VERSE 2

BOY: There's a tender message deep down in
        my heart,
      Something you should know—but how
        am I to start?
      Sentimental speeches never could
        impart
      Just exactly what I want to tell you.

REPEAT CHORUS

Show version

VERSE 1

GIRL: Music is a language lovers understand;
    Melody and romance wander hand in
        hand;
    Cupid never fails assisted by a band—
    So if you have something sweet to tell me:

CHORUS

Say it with music,
Beautiful music;
Somehow I'd rather be kissed
To the strains of Chopin or Liszt.
A melody mellow
Played on a cello
Helps Mister Cupid along;
So say it with a beautiful song.

VERSE 2

BOY: There's a tender message deep down in
        my heart,
    Something you should know—but how
        am I to start?
    Sentimental speeches never could
        impart
    Just exactly what I want to tell you.

CHORUS

GIRL: Say it with music,
    Beautiful music;
    Somehow I'd rather be kissed
    To the strains of Chopin or Liszt.
BOY: How can I impart, dear,
    What's in my heart, dear?
GIRL: Music will help you along,
    So say it with a beautiful song.

[Orchestra plays the first two lines of the chorus of
"Say It with Music."]

BOY: Just a little love, a little kiss.

[Orchestra plays the second line of the chorus of "Just
a Little Love, a Little Kiss."]

GIRL: Somehow I'd rather resist;
    Music makes me want to be kissed.
BOY: Kiss me again, kiss me again.

[Orchestra plays the next few bars of "Kiss Me
Again."]

BOY: Say it with music,
    Beautiful music.
GIRL: You made me love you—
    I didn't want to do it,
    I didn't want to do it.
BOY: Music will help you along,
GIRL: So say it with a beautiful song [high note].

ENCORE

BOY: Say it with music,
    Beautiful music.
GIRL: Somehow I'd rather be kissed
    To the strains of Chopin or Liszt.
BOY: A melody mellow
    Played on a cello
GIRL: Helps Mister Cupid along,
    So say it with a beautiful song.

EVERYBODY STEP

Published. Copyrighted October 6, 1921. Previously registered for copyright as an unpublished song September 12, 1921. The finale of Act I, it was introduced by the Brox Sisters (Kathlyn, Dagmar, and Lorraine) and entire company. Leading recording by Ted Lewis (Columbia). Other major recording by Paul Whiteman and His Orchestra (Victor). Cited by the distinguished American composer John Alden Carpenter (1876–1951) as one of the greatest works of music, the only American composition on a list that also included works by Bach, Beethoven, Chopin, Debussy, Mussorgsky, Stravinsky, and Wagner.

VERSE

Soon
You'll hear a tune
That's gonna lift you out of your seat.
It could be sweeter,
But then the meter
Was written espec'lly for your feet.
Fly
Away up high
Upon a syncopated balloon;
A little ginger
Will never injure.
Hear them tuning up—
They'll be playing soon.

CHORUS

Ev'rybody step
To the syncopated rhythm;

Let's be goin' with 'em
When they begin.
You'll be sayin' "Yessir,
The band is grand"—
He's the best professor
In all the land.
Listen to the pep
That emerges
From the middle
Of the jazzy fiddle
Under his chin.
Oh, what music!
The clarineter
Could not be better;
Hear that strain—
I don't know just what it is, but it's great.
They simply ruin it;
Look at 'em doin' it.
Come, come, don't hesitate—
Ev'rybody step.
If you want to see a glutton
When it comes to struttin'
Over the ground,
Wait'll you see
My little sweetie and me
Step-step-stepping around.

PATTER

There's the instep and the doorstep,
There's the one-, two-, three-, and the four-step,
My step and your step,
Stepping up the stepladder,
There's the left step and the right step,
There's the heavy step and the light step,
There's the fatal step and the stepbrother,
And the watch-your-step and the stepmother;*
But the greatest step we know
Is the step full o' pep and go—so

REPEAT CHORUS

_____

*Alternate version of line:
    And the awful rep of the stepmother;

I'M A DUMBBELL

This number was listed on original sheet music covers for the show as having been published, but no printed copies are known to exist. Introduced by Renie Riano.

VERSE

Many, many tears
My folks have shed for years;
My family is mourning me,
For I'm dead above my ears.
My cra-ni-um
Is really on the bum.
They all agree that I should be
In a gym-na-si-um.

CHORUS 1

I'm a dumbbell,
Just a dumbbell;
Underneath my hat you'll find a wooden ball.
It makes no difference just how hard
I rap upon my dome;
I never get an answer,
Just because there's no one home.
I'd gladly marry
Dick or Harry,
But I know that Dick or Harry wouldn't fall;
For no man wants to marry me,
Because no man would like to see
A baby dumbbell on his knee—
I'm a dumbbell, that's all.

CHORUS 2

I'm a dumbbell,
Just a dumbbell;
Underneath my hat you'll find a wooden ball.
I asked a man to take me out,
And this is what he said:
"There's something in your figure,
But there's nothing in your head."
And ev'ry summer
I get dumber,
And I don't find much improvement in the fall.
My education isn't swell;
The only word that I can spell
Is D-U-M-B-G—oh, hell!
I'm a dumbbell, that's all.

THE SCHOOLHOUSE BLUES

Published. Copyrighted November 25, 1921. Previously registered for copyright as an unpublished song October 7, 1921. Introduced by the Three Brox Sisters, whose "original cast" recording (Brunswick), accompanied by Bennie Krueger's Orchestra, was a leading seller on the popular music charts.

VERSE

Hooky, hooky—
Oh, how we love to play
Hooky, hooky—
There'll be no school today.
Our lesson kept us guessin';
That's why we ran away.
Say—
Mother, Father,
Wants us to go to school,
But we'd rather
Be in a swimming pool
When the sun is in the sky;
That is just the reason why

CHORUS 1

We've got the schoolhouse blues,
We've got the schoolhouse blues.
Tired of reading history,
Don't care for geography;
We're getting oh so sick
Of grammar and arithmetic.
That's why we gave the teacher the sack,
And we're never gonna go back—
If she doesn't like it,
She can sit on a tack.
We've got the schoolhouse blues.

CHORUS 2

We've got the schoolhouse blues,
We've got the schoolhouse blues.
Tired of reading history,
Don't care for geography;
We're getting oh so sick
Of grammar and arithmetic.
So then if we don't pass our exam,
Oh, we're going to be in a jam!
Mother's going to spank us,
But we don't give a damn.
We've got the schoolhouse blues.

FAIR EXCHANGE, including AT THE COURT AROUND THE CORNER

"At the Court Around the Corner," a section of the "Fair Exchange" scene, was published separately but was not listed as a separate song in the show programs. Copyrighted October 6, 1921. Previously registered for copyright as an unpublished song September 12, 1921. The complete "Fair Exchange" sequence was introduced by Joseph Santley and Ivy Sawyer (First Couple), Hugh Cameron (Judge and Minister), Florence Moore (Lawyer), and Paul Frawley and Wilda Bennett (Second Couple).

At the Court Around the Corner

Published version

VERSE

What a beautiful morning!
What a wonderful day!
We can hear the birds singing
As we go on our way.
Like a couple of children,
We're so happy and gay,
For we've been married two years now—
And we're gonna be divorced today.

CHORUS

The judge is waiting
At the court around the corner
For the wife and me
With the final decree.
You'll see a happy groom and bride
Standing side by side
Receiving congratulations
When the knot is untied.
A foxy lawyer
At the court around the corner
Will collect his fee
The minute we're free;
We'll be divorced and then
We'll soon be married again
At the court around the corner,
The little wife and me.

Show version

Fair Exchange Scene

[*Enter the* FIRST MARRIED COUPLE, *who sing "At the Court Around the Corner" in front of a drop curtain.*] [FIRST COUPLE *exit. Curtain rises on courtroom.* FIRST COUPLE *reenter scene and walk up to the* JUDGE.]

JUDGE: What do you want?
FIRST COUPLE: A divorce.
JUDGE: Do you really want it?
FIRST COUPLE: Of course!
JUDGE: Are you tired of him?
And you of her?
FIRST COUPLE: We would rather not discuss it, sir!
JUDGE: But you must have a very good reason—
And you cannot keep it mum.
FIRST COUPLE: We have two very good reasons—
And here they come!

[*Enter* SECOND COUPLE, *who walk up to* JUDGE *as* FIRST COUPLE *did.*]

JUDGE: What do *you* want?
SECOND COUPLE: A divorce.
JUDGE: Do you really want it?
SECOND COUPLE: Of course!
JUDGE: Have you both agreed to disagree?
SECOND COUPLE: We're the best of friends, as you can see.
JUDGE: But you must have a very good reason—
Or you would not go this far.
SECOND COUPLE: We have two very good reasons—
And there they are!

[*They point to the other two.*]
[LAWYER *rises and addresses* JUDGE *and* JURY *as follows:*]

LAWYER: Your Honor, Ladies of the Jury,
I represent this case.
There's no complaint on either side;
Everybody is satisfied.
The husbands are the best of friends;
They've been so all through life—
In fact, when they're not with each other,

They're with each other's wife.
And the wives are very clubby,
As the evidence has shown:
They adore each other's hubby
And they share everything they own.
It's useless going into every detail of this case
When the facts are as plain
As the nose on Your Honor's face.
JUDGE: I see! I see!
It's a happy little family.
I see! I see!
But it really isn't up to me.
The Constitution laid out a course
From which I cannot budge.
There's not sufficient grounds for divorce.
LAWYER: You don't know the half of it, Judge.
JUDGE: I see! I see!
But it isn't up to me.
Let us hear the jury's verdict.

[JURY *whispers among itself, then rises in a body and shouts the following:*]

JURY: Divorce—in the first degree!
BOTH COUPLES: We're free! We're free! We're free!

[*The two* COUPLES *exchange partners and address their new spouses-to-be:*]

COUPLES: And now let the wedding bells ring out
Just for you and for me.
The parson's waiting
At the church around the corner—
Come along, my dear,
For the hour is near.
You'll see a happy groom and bride
Standing side by side
Receiving congratulations
When the knot has been tied.
The congregation
At the church around the corner
Will be there to see
How happy we'll be.
Once more we're on our way,
To honor, love, and obey,
At the church around the corner.

We better hurry!
CONGREGATION: Here come the bride and bridegroom
Dressed in their best to be married.

[*Scene changes to church. Both* COUPLES *walk arm in arm up to* MINISTER, *who addresses them in same manner as he did as the* JUDGE *in the courtroom scene.*]

MINISTER: What do you want?
BOTH COUPLES: We want to be united.
MINISTER: What do you mean?
BOTH COUPLES: Now don't you get excited.
MINISTER: You were here before and I gave you my consent—
I must say you're a glutton for punishment.
BOTH COUPLES: The other marriage didn't take somehow,
Though you tied us up for life.
MINISTER: Do you promise to honor and obey each other now?
BOTH COUPLES: We do.
CONGREGATION: They do.
MINISTER: You do?
BOTH COUPLES: We do.
MINISTER: Then I pronounce you man and wife.
EVERYBODY: The flat is waiting
At the house around the corner.
BOTH COUPLES: For the wife and me—
How happy we'll be!
LAWYER: A little while and then
We'll change the scenery again
To a court around the corner—
EVERYBODY: And we will set them free.

THEY CALL IT DANCING

Published. Copyrighted October 6, 1921. Previously registered for copyright as an unpublished song September 12, 1921. Introduced by Sam Bernard, with Emma Haig and Richard W. Keene presenting the fox-trot, Mlle Marguerite and Frank Gill presenting the waltz, and Renie Riano and Sam Bernard "Dancing, That's All." Leading recording by Paul Whiteman and His Orchestra (Victor). In January 1957 Berlin rewrote some of the lyrics because, as he explained in a January 10, 1957, letter to his friend and attorney A. L. Berman, he "was afraid some of it would be censored." The new version, dated January 10, 1957, was to have been sung by George Gobel and girls in a *Music Box Revue* television spectacular which Berlin was preparing but never completed.

VERSE

Years ago when I was just a wee little thing,
A man never squeezed a girl till she got the
  ring;
They were both engaged before the boy took a
  chance—
But now all he has to do is ask her to dance.

CHORUS 1

They call it dancing;
You see them cuddled up tight—
They're only dancing,
So ev'rything is all right.
Until the midnight cabaret closes
You can see he and she rubbing noses.
She calls him mister—
They're only friends, it appears—
And then he'll twist her
Like they've been married for years.
A man can squeeze all the shes
With his arms and his knees
And they call it dancing, that's all.

CHORUS 2

They call it dancing;
You see them cuddled up tight—
They're only dancing,
So ev'rything is all right.
Until the midnight cabaret closes
You can see he and she rubbing noses.
If it's a ballroom,
She doesn't mind his embrace;
But in a hall room
She'd slap him right in the face.
A man can grab someone's wife,
Have the time of his life,
And they call it dancing, that's all.

1957 revision

VERSE

Years ago when I was just a wee little thing,
A man never squeezed a girl till she got the
  ring;
They were both engaged before the boy took a
  chance—
But now all he has to do is ask her to dance.

CHORUS 1

They call it dancing;
You see them cuddled up tight—
They're only dancing,
So ev'rything is alright.
Until the midnight dancing place closes
You can see he and she rubbing noses.
She calls him mister—
They're only friends, it appears—
And then he'll twist her
Like they've been married for years.
The boys can squeeze all the shes
Just as much as they please
And they call it dancing, that's all.

CHORUS 2

They call it dancing;
You see them cuddled up tight—
They're only dancing,
So everything is all right.
The latest dance the youngsters think graceful
Grown-ups stare and declare it's disgraceful.
His arms around her,
She gets as warm as a bath;
And then he'll pound her
Just like an osteopath.
He's quite a gent, even more,
Till they get on the floor—
And they call it dancing, that's all.

THE LEGEND OF THE PEARLS

Published. Copyrighted October 6, 1921. Previously registered for copyright as an unpublished song September 15, 1921. Introduced by Wilda Bennett (Pearl) and ensemble, featuring the Misses Adair, Irving, Bateman, Van Pelt, Rich, Taylor, Wylie, and Sterling (Strings of Pearls) and Helen Lyons (Dancer).

VERSE

"Pearls mean tears" is a saying old;
Years ago it was found, I'm told,
In a legend I'll disclose—
Here's how the story goes:
Once a maid on her wedding day
Lost her love, who sailed away.
His ship, returning home,
Disappeared in the angry foam.
Beside the sea she sat and cried,
A most unhappy girl;
And ev'ry tear that fell below
Became a precious pearl.

CHORUS

Strings of teardrops
That you and I call pearls
Fell from the eyes of a beautiful bride
Who sat and cried by the seaside;
And when a crown of silver
Replaced the golden curls,
She had spent all her years
Shedding sad little tears
Just to make your string of pearls.

AN INTERVIEW

Introduced by Irving Berlin and the Eight Little Notes (Mary Milford, Virginia Dixon, Helen Clare, Betsy Ross, Helen Newcombe, Claire Davis, Miriam Hopkins, and Jeanne St. John). Alternate title (piano-vocal score): "The Irving Berlin Interview." "An Interview" concluded with Berlin singing "All by Myself." This number includes references to several prior Berlin hits, including "The Ragtime Violin," "I Want to Be in Dixie," "Oh, How I Hate to Get Up in the Morning," "Alexander's Ragtime Band," "You'd Be Surprised," and "Nobody Knows and Nobody Seems to Care."

REPORTERS: Eight reporters with work to do,
  We came here for an interview:
  We would like to see the man who
  Says it with music.
  At the office they told us to
  Make a note of the interview
  And find out just exactly how he
  Says it with music.
  Now we're here with pad and pencil,
  Ready to begin—
  For a word or two of an interview
  With Irving Berlin.

BERLIN: Good morning, ladies.
REPORTERS: Good morning, Mister Berlin.
BERLIN: What can I do for you?
REPORTERS: We'd like an interview.
BERLIN: Won't you be seated?
REPORTERS: We thank you, Mister Berlin.
BERLIN: If you'll be good enough to give me
  some suggestions
  Of what you'd like to know, I'd answer any question.

REPORTERS: Tell us how you say it with music.

BERLIN: I write my songs very easily.
When I need a melody,
If I hear of a tune that appeals to me,
I go right home and write it.

REPORTERS: He goes right home and writes it.

BERLIN: Fiddle up, fiddle up
On your violin.
I remember
It was in December,
Another fellow and me
Heard somebody fiddling this melody.
I admit writing it in a hurry—
If I didn't do it,
He would beat me to it.
That's how I happened to write
About the ragtime violin.

I want to be, I want to be,
I want to be down home in Dixie.
If you're in the business very long,
You'll wind up with a Dixie song.
I don't know why, but every guy
Who has the knack for words and
music
Wants to tell the world he's going to
D-I-X-I don't know how to spell it.
But I know there's lots of dough
In a song of Dixieland—and

Oh! How I hate to get up in the morn-
ing!
Oh! How I'd love to remain in bed!
Let me tell you from the start
That was one came from the heart—
I had to get up.

REPORTERS: He had to get up!

BERLIN: I had to get up each morning.
Oh! How I wanted to murder the
bugler!
Oh! How I wanted to find him dead!
A soldier's life is nice, I'm sure,
But since I'm out like Florence
Moore,
I've spent the most of my time in
bed.

REPORTERS: We'd like to hear, we'd like to hear
How you wrote "Alexander's Band,"
How it became a song of fame.

BERLIN: That's very hard to understand.
For about a year or so
It was lying on the shelf—
Nobody liked it, and I hated it myself.
But soon it turned out to be my
Money lamb.

REPORTERS: We heard you got an awful lot
For "Alexander's Ragtime Band."

BERLIN: I must admit, 'twas quit a bit.
But when the Music Box was planned,
I never knew how many songs it took
to build a theatre,
So every night I try to write
An "Alexander's Ragtime Band."

REPORTERS: And does it cost very much
A pretty theatre to build?

BERLIN: You'd be surprised.

REPORTERS: And will you lose very much
If every seat isn't filled?

BERLIN: You'd be surprised.

REPORTERS: It must be very hard on the bosses.
Who's gonna pay all the losses?

BERLIN: Nobody knows and nobody seems to
care.

REPORTERS: And now before we run along
We'd like to hear your latest song.

BERLIN: All by myself in the morning,
All by myself in the night;
I sit alone in a cozy morris chair,
So unhappy there,
Playing solitaire.
All by myself I get lonely,
Watching the clock on the shelf.
I'd love to rest my weary head
On somebody's shoulder;
I hate to grow older
All by myself.

LADIES AND GENTLEMEN, EVERY REVUE

Introduced by William Collier with Wilda Bennett, Sam Bernard, Florence Moore, and entire company. Alternate titles: "Finale" and "Finale—Act Two."

Ladies and gentlemen, every revue
Has a finale, and we have one too.
Someone must hear it before we are through,
And it might as well be you.
Everyone knows the success of a show
Often depends on the finish, and so
The finale has got to be sung
By a tenor who's handsome and young.
We have that kind of a tenor
Who reaches a clear high C;
With a face and a form like Apollo,

A beautiful thing is he.
He's the only one here with a beautiful voice,
So you have to hear him—there's no other choice.
So we'd like to present to you
The tenor of this revue,
Singing like John McCormack,
And very handsome too.

[*Business with orchestra.*]

MR. COLLIER: Ladies and gentlemen, you have
been told,
Told of a tenor who's handsome
and bold,
One who can sing with a voice
made of gold—
But he has an awful cold.
Somebody must take the gentle-
man's place,
Somebody old with a young-
looking face
And a voice that can reach high C,
So they gave the finale to me.
We thank you all for your kindness
And you ought to thank us too:
We have three hundred jokes on
Prohibition
That we might have told to you,
So we too have been kind,
Just like you have been kind.
And now that I've gotten that
much off my mind,
I would like to present to you
The payroll of this revue,
Harris and Berlin's *Worries of
1922*

Solly Ward and Miss Moore,
Wilda Bennett and Santley and
Sawyer,
Marguerite and her partner Gill,
Haig and Keene, and there's
Cameron—
I had to stop rhyming because
Berlin claims
The principals haven't got
rhymable names.
Mr. Frawley and Riano,
Rose Rolando and Hale Aleta,
But the greatest of all in the
play—

MR. BERNARD: If you point to yourself,
There'll be murder to pay.

MR. COLLIER: I was speaking about the girls,
The Tips and the Notes and the
Pearls—
We must admit that the girls are
the hit.

Now we'll just raise the curtain a
bit,
And we'll start the finale and bring
on the—
TIPS: Tip, tip, tip, tip—
Don't forget the little
Tip, tip, tip, tip,
Never let the little
Tip
Slip
Out of your grip.
They become so lean
Working in the dinner scene,
For the fancy kicking
Took the wrinkles out of
Each and every hip.
Hear them holler,
"We earn each dollar
By being a little tip, tip, tip!"
PEARL GIRLS: Strings of teardrops
That you and I call pearls—
MISS MOORE: When a pearl disappears,
Hassard Short is in tears.
PEARL GIRLS: It took years to count our pearls.

NOTES: Do, re, mi, fa, sol, la, ti, do,
Eight little notes are they,
Dancing their lives away.
You know and we know that
Do, re, mi, fa, sol, la, ti, do
Step full of pep through this play.
With loud applause we hail
[applause]
Each little blond female—
We're wild about them,
Just couldn't do without them,
Our little notes of the scale.

MISS BENNETT: And now before you leave us
To go upon your way,
Kindly tell your friends about us,
And whate'er you say, won't you
Say it with music,
Beautiful music—
Somehow we're hoping that soon
You'll be buying this little tune:
The sale of each copy
When times are choppy
Helps Irving Berlin along,
So say it with a beautiful song.

MUSIC BOX REVUE 1922

Tryout: none. New York run: Music Box; October 23, 1922; 330 performances. Lyrics and music by Irving Berlin. Produced by Sam H. Harris. Sketches by Frances Nordstrom, George Hobart, Walter Catlett, and Paul Gerard Smith. Staged by Hassard Short. According to the opening-night program, "The Red Lacquer Cage," "Diamond Horseshoe," "Under the Sea" (this number is lost), and "Ballet" orchestrated by Frank Tours; other orchestrations by Steve Jones, Charles Grant, Alfred Dalby, Arthur Gutman, Will Vodery, and Roy Webb, under the personal direction of Harry Akst. Orchestra under the direction of Frank Tours. Cast: starring Charlotte Greenwood, Grace La Rue, John Steel, William Gaxton, Bobby Clark and Paul McCullough, Margaret and Dorothy McCarthy, and the Fairbanks Twins, and featuring Margaret Irving, Robinson Newbold, William Seabury, Mrs. Estar Banks, Helen Rich, and Ruth Page. Lyrics and music for the following numbers are missing: "Prologue" (introduced by Margaret Irving, William Gaxton, and ensemble); "Dance Your Troubles Away" (introduced by the Fairbanks Twins, William Seabury, and ensemble); "Three Cheers for the Red, White, and Blue" (introduced by Bobby Clark and Paul McCullough; this number was listed on the sheet music covers as having been published, but no copies are known to exist); "Dancing Honeymoon" (introduced by Olivette, William Seabury, and ensemble); "Too Many Boys" (introduced by Charlotte Greenwood and the Music Box Boys); and "Finale" (introduced by Charlotte Greenwood, Grace La Rue, and the entire company).

TAKE A LITTLE WIFE

Published. Copyrighted December 27, 1922. Previously registered for copyright as an unpublished song December 15, 1922. Introduced by Margaret and Dorothy McCarthy.

VERSE

Parson Brown was preaching,
Preaching to his flock,
And his little sermon
Gave them quite a shock.
Ev'ry single fellow
In the church that day
Bowed his head

And then turned red
To hear the parson say:

CHORUS

"Take a little wife—
Hurry up, take a wife, hurry up,
Don't you wait.
Tommy, Dick, and Harry
Ought to go marry:
Ev'ry little bee that's a he
Takes a bee that's a she
For a mate,
And what is plenty good enough for a bee
Is good enough for you and me.
Living in a flat with a dog and a cat
Is a great big mistake.
So go and take a little wife—
But when you take a little wife,
Be careful whose wife you take."

PATTER

"The doggies on the street get together and play;
They talk things over and get married right away.
A chicken lays its eggs, but they wouldn't be
found
If old Mister Rooster didn't come around.
The ants get married ev'ry time they get a chance,
And so do their sisters and their cousins and their
aunts.
A bull couldn't do without a lady cow,
Nor a female cat without a cat's meow—
They've got the right idea.
And ev'ry little bee that's a he
Takes a bee that's a she
For a mate;
So go and take a little wife—
But when you take a little wife
Be careful whose wife you take."

PORCELAIN MAID

Published. Copyrighted November 2, 1922. Previously registered for copyright as an unpublished song October 9, 1922. Introduced by Helen Rich, Eva Sobel, and ensemble, which included Ruth Page. Leading recording by Paul Specht and His Orchestra (Columbia).

VERSE

BOY: Porc'lain boy is feeling so terribly lonely
Just because he's fallen in love with a maid.

Though she's very near him,
She don't seem to hear him
When he sings his little sad serenade:

CHORUS 1

Porc'lain maid,
I'm calling to you
From my teakwood stand.
Porc'lain maid,
I'm feeling so blue;
Please let me hold your hand.
How I long to cuddle and coo
Neath a bamboo shade;
I
Wanna design a
Home
Over in China
For my porc'lain maid.

CHORUS 2

GIRL: Porc'lain boy,
I'm list'ning to you
From my teakwood stand.
Porc'lain boy,
If you're feeling blue,
Come here and hold my hand.
If you long to cuddle and coo
Neath a bamboo shade,
Why
Don't you design a
Home
Over in China
For your porc'lain maid?

LADY OF THE EVENING

Published. Copyrighted November 2, 1922. Previously registered for copyright as an unpublished song October 4, 1922. Introduced by John Steel (the Pierrot) with Leila Ricard, Sherry Marchall, Fraun Koski, Trudde Marr, Dorothy Durland, Helen Lyons, Claire Hooper, Evelyn Oliphant, Helene Gardner, and Myrtle Thoreau as the Ladies of the Evening. Original cast recording by John Steel (Victor). Other leading recording by Paul Whiteman (Victor).

VERSE 1

After the gray
Of a long dreary day

Comes the evening.
Peaceful and calm
As a sheltering palm
Is the evening.
Daytime has gone to rest
There in the golden west;
Soon little stars will appear in the sky,
Seeming to say,
"We are here, hush-a-bye."

CHORUS

Evening,
Lady of the evening,
I can hear you calling me,
Calling
While the shades are falling,
Falling over land and sea.
You can make the cares and troubles
That followed me through the day
Fold their tents just like the Arabs
And silently steal away.
Evening,
Lady of the evening,
I hear you calling me.

VERSE 2

After the sun,
When its day's work is done,
Comes the evening.
Then with the night
Come the angels who light
Up the evening.
There in the sky they stand,
Each with a torch in hand.
Then one by one
Little stars in the sky
Look down and say,
"We are here, hush-a-bye."

REPEAT CHORUS

I'M LOOKING FOR A DADDY LONGLEGS

Published. Copyrighted December 27, 1922. Previously registered for copyright as an unpublished song December 15, 1922. Introduced by Charlotte Greenwood. Soon after the New York opening the song was moved to Act II. Alternate title (program): "Daddy Long Legs."

Performed in recent years by cabaret singer Karen Akers.

VERSE

I'm so worried, oh so worried;
I can't sleep a wink at night,
I've lost my appetite,
And it's all on account of my height.
I'm a Yankee, long and lanky,
And that's where the trouble lies:
For a little lovin' my heart cries,
But I can't find a man my size.

CHORUS

I'm looking for a daddy longlegs
Who's gonna measure up to me.
A little fellow has the wrong legs
To have me sitting on his knee.
I had a sweetheart, short and thin,
And when the spooning would begin,
He was there
Standing on a chair,
But he'd only get as far as my chin.
I want a daddy who can teach me
The kind of love I can't resist.
I want a daddy who can reach me
When I get ready to be kissed.
I want a nice young man to woo me,
But I don't want a man that has to climb up to me.
It's gonna take a daddy longlegs
To love a long-legged lady like me.

CRINOLINE DAYS

Published. Copyrighted November 2, 1922. Previously registered for copyright as an unpublished song October 4, 1922. Introduced by Grace La Rue (the Girl in the Crinoline) with the Fairbanks Twins (the White Crinolines) and ensemble. Major recording by Paul Whiteman (Victor) reached number two on the popular music charts.

VERSE

Back to the olden
Days that were golden
Memory often strays,
Before anyone could gaze
At Molly's and May's
Little ankle displays.
Time with its changes

Often arranges
Styles that become the craze;
But I am yearning
To be returning
Back to those crinoline days.

CHORUS

In those dear old crinoline days,
Old-fashioned people with their old-fashioned
    ways,
When the girl a fellow courted
Was the girl he married and supported.
Back in eighteen seventy-four
Rosy complexions weren't bought in a store.
Granny and Granddaddy longingly gaze
Back to those crinoline days.

PACK UP YOUR SINS AND GO TO THE DEVIL

Published. Copyrighted October 11, 1922. Previously registered for copyright as an unpublished song September 25, 1922. Introduced by Margaret and Dorothy McCarthy and ensemble. This song was the finale of Act I. Leading recording by Emil Coleman and His Orchestra (Vocalion). Later recorded by Joan Morris (who overdubbed the countermelody) and William Bolcom. Berlin was so enthusiastic about the Morris/Bolcom performance that for a time he considered preparing an entire album of his double songs.

VERSE

Oh,
I got a message from below—
'Twas a man I used to know,
About a year or so ago,
Before he departed.
He
Is just as happy as can be;
I'll tell you what he said to me:
He said,
"If ever you get heavy hearted,

CHORUS

"Pack up your sins and go
To the Devil in Hades.
You'll meet the finest of gentlemen
And the finest of ladies;
They'd rather be down below than up above—

Hades is full of thousands of
Joneses and Browns, O'Hoolihans, Cohens, and
    Bradys.
You'll hear a heavenly tune
That went to the Devil
Because the jazz bands,
They started pickin' it,
They put a trick in it,
A jazzy kick in it.
They've got a couple of old reformers in Heaven
Making them go to bed at eleven—
Pack up your sins and go to the Devil,
And you'll never have to go to bed at all."

PATTER

"If you care to dwell where the weather is hot,
H-E-double-L is a wonderful spot.
If you need a rest and you're all out of sorts,
Hades is the best of the winter resorts.
Paradise doesn't compare;
All the nice people are there.
They come from ev'rywhere
Just to revel with Mister Devil.
Nothing on his mind but a couple of horns,
Satan is waitin' with his jazz band
And
His band
Came from Alabam' with a melody hot.
No one gives a damn
If it's music or not;
Satan's melody
Makes you want to dance forever,
And you never have to go to bed at all."

[Then the patter and the refrain are sung in counterpoint.]

THE LITTLE RED LACQUER CAGE

Published. Copyrighted November 2, 1922. Previously registered for copyright as an unpublished song October 13, 1922. Introduced by Mrs. Estar Banks (Little Old Lady) and Helen Rich (Canary) as part of a sketch entitled "The Story of the 'Little Red Lacquer Cage.'" It is possible that the song was deleted from the script before or during the New York run.

VERSE

Locked in a cage, I'm as sad as can be,
Singing my song

All the day long.
It seems I can hear the forest calling me—
How I keep longing
Just to be free!

CHORUS

I'd love to leave
My little red lacquer cage
And fly
Away out there
Where
I
Could sing my beautiful song
In
The forest where I belong.
The little birds that live in a tree
Would love to hear my sweet melody.
I hate to sing
The song that God gave to me
In a little red lacquer cage.

WILL SHE COME FROM THE EAST? (EAST, WEST, NORTH, OR SOUTH)

Published. Copyrighted November 2, 1922. Previously registered for copyright as an unpublished song October 9, 1922. Introduced by John Steel with Hilda Ferguson (East), Helen Lyons (North), Evelyn Oliphant (West), and Mary O'Brien (South). Original cast recording by John Steel (Victor).

VERSE

Four little crossroads lie before me;
One of the four I must choose,
Whether the way be fair or stormy,
Whether I win or I lose.
Which of the four shall I make my way?
I wish I knew where to start.
Which little road shall be the highway
Leading to my heart?

CHORUS

Will she come
From the East,
Where the Broadway peaches grow?
Will she come
From the North,
From the land of ice and snow?

Or will she come
From the heart of the West,
There where the sun goes to rest?
Will she come
Trottin' from the land of cotton,
From away down South?

DIAMOND HORSESHOE

Published. Copyrighted December 27, 1922. Previously registered for copyright as an unpublished song December 15, 1922. Introduced by John Steel and ensemble, including many showgirls displayed as opera heroines. Alternate title (program): "My Diamond Horseshoe of Girls."

VERSE

Metropolitan nights bring to me memories dear;
Voices clear
Keep ringing in my ear.
Metropolitan girls with their sweet musical themes
Haunt my dreams,
And ev'ry night it seems

CHORUS

I see a horseshoe set with diamonds,
A diamond horseshoe set with girls,
And ev'ry lovely maiden I see
Is calling to me with a sweet melody.
I hear them saying it with music
Until each tragic tale unfurls,
And my heart is laden
With love for each maiden
In my diamond horseshoe of girls.

BRING ON THE PEPPER

Published. Copyrighted November 2, 1922. Previously registered for copyright as an unpublished song October 4, 1922. Introduced by Margaret and Dorothy McCarthy, with Sylvia Jocelyn and the Eight Music Box Dancers (Viola Fraas, Florence Barry, Gladys Reith, Miriam Miller, Louise Dale, Olga Borowski, Gloria Gale, and Nellie Roberts).

VERSE

Snappy music is the only music
That was ever meant for me;
A little spice
Is very nice
In ev'ry melody.
Let me mingle with a peppy jingle
That the jazz bands love to play.
I'm a swifty,
Very nifty,
That's why I say:

CHORUS

Bring on the pepper;
We need a lot of pepper—
You've got to be a stepper
With a barrel of speed.
Make it good and snappy
If you want to get by;
Make 'em think you're happy
Though you're ready to die.
When you begin it,
Put lots of ginger in it—
About a mile a minute
Is the tempo we need;
Slow folks are no folks
To trouble with, no indeed!
Lots of pep will make an undertaker
Rock with joy and laughter;
If you can sprinkle a cute little twinkle,
You'll find that's the wrinkle we're after.
Just keep a-goin'
And don't forget to throw in
A bit of Georgie Cohan, that we know;
Lots of Tabasco,
That's all we ask, so
Bring on the pepper—let's go!

MONTMARTRE

Published. Copyrighted November 2, 1922. Previously registered for copyright as an unpublished song October 10, 1922. Not listed in the programs for the show. It was probably dropped before the New York opening. Also see page 457.

VERSE

When all is still in Paris,
And evening shadows creep,
Upon a hill in Paris
The people never sleep.
They bid a royal welcome
To ev'ry restless heart;
Champagne bubbles
Drown their troubles
While they are in Montmartre.

CHORUS

Montmartre,
Playground of France;
Montmartre,
Wrapped in romance;
Montmartre,
On with the dance,
While the violin
Plays a song of sin
With love dreams
Luring you on
Till the
Vision is gone.
Young hearts
Break with the wake of each dawn.
How tragic is the magic of Montmartre!

MUSIC BOX REVUE 1923

Tryout: none. New York run: The Music Box; September 22, 1923; 273 performances. Lyrics and music by Irving Berlin. Produced by Sam H. Harris. Sketches by Edwin Burke, Robert Benchley, Bobby Clark and Paul McCullough, Stanley E. Rauh and Irving Strouse, George S. Kaufman, and Bertram Block. Staged by Hassard Short. Orchestrations by Frank Tours, Maurice de Packh, Steve Jones, and Charles Grant. Orchestra under the direction of Frank Tours. Cast: starring Frank Tinney, Joseph Santley, Ivy Sawyer, John Steel, Grace Moore, Robert Benchley, Solly Ward, Phil Baker, the Brox Sisters, and Florence Moore, and featuring Lora Sanderson, Mme Dora Stroeva, Hugh Cameron, Charles Columbus and Nelson Snow, Florence O'Denishawn, and Dorothy Dilley. No music or lyrics are known to survive for the opening, the finale, and the song "Your Hat and My Hat" (which was sung by Joseph Santley and Ivy Sawyer).

WHEN YOU WALKED OUT, SOMEBODY ELSE WALKED IN

Published. Copyrighted May 10, 1923. Previously registered for copyright as an unpublished song April 23, 1923. Introduced in the *Music Box Revue* by the Brox Sisters, but popular before the show opened. Leading recordings by Isham Jones (Brunswick) and Frank Crumit (Columbia).

VERSE 1

My honey, do you remember, 'twas a December day,
I said that you would repent the day that you went away.
You turned as red as a ruby, much too good to be true;
You thought I'd sit around lonely, thinking of only you.
Little you knew that

CHORUS

When you walked out,
Someone else walked right in.

Someone else with good news
Stepped right in your shoes.
Somebody else took your place on my knee,
Another sweetie in clover fussin' all over me.
I saw that you grew so cold, love,
So what could I do?
Off with the old love
And on with the new!
When you walked out,
Honey, I just had to grin:
You left the door wide open and
Somebody else walked in.

VERSE 2

A happy couple were we two while you were sweet to me,
But now I'm sending bad news to my little used-to-be.
You thought the minute you'd shake me that it would make me blue
And I would sit around lonely, thinking of only you.
Little you knew that

REPEAT CHORUS

ONE GIRL

Published. Copyrighted October 6, 1923. Previously registered for copyright as an unpublished song September 13, 1923. Introduced by John Steel with Helen Lyons and ensemble, featuring Maida Palmer, Adele McHatton, Joan Clement, Teddy Gill, and Katherine Ardell as the girls the singer met in Spain, Holland, Italy, France, and Ireland, respectively.

VERSE 1

Round the world I've roamed
As a roaming Romeo,
But my roaming Romeo days are done:
My heart used to beat for a dozen girls or so,
But now my heart is beating for only one.

CHORUS

One girl
Down in my heart,
And we
Never will part.
One girl
With a certain something

Won me from the very start,
Because there's one girl
Who will agree
To grow
Older with me.
I mean to go through life with,
Sharing ev'ry joy and strife with,
Just one girl.

VERSE 2

Ev'ry fellow has
His romances—I've had mine,
Sweet romances that I must now forget.
I must say goodbye to them all, but auld lang syne
Gives them each a mem'ry that lingers yet.

REPEAT CHORUS

TELL ME A BEDTIME STORY

Published. Copyrighted October 6, 1923. Previously registered for copyright as an unpublished song September 13, 1923. Introduced by Grace Moore and ensemble.

VERSE 1

Pretty little Flo,
Sitting with her beau
In the parlor, list'ning
To a radio.
Twelve o'clock is striking,
And there's no more radio;
Tenderly the maiden whispers,
"Dear, before you go

CHORUS

"Tell me
A bedtime story
Before you kiss me goodnight.
Before you go away
I'd like to hear you say
That your love is everlasting—
Please begin broadcasting,
And maybe
Your tired baby
Will go and turn down the light.
Before I climb the stairs
And say my evening prayers,
Won't you tell me
A bedtime story?"

VERSE 2

"Hold me closer, dear;
Whisper in my ear
Just a little story
That I long to hear.
Dawn will soon be breaking,
For the skies are growing pale;
Rock-a-bye your baby with
A pretty fairy tale.

REPEAT CHORUS

MAID OF MESH

Published. Copyrighted October 30, 1923. Previously registered for copyright as an unpublished song October 16, 1923. Introduced by Ivy Sawyer (Maid) and Joseph Santley (Boy) and ensemble. Shortly after the opening of the show, the scene that featured this number was moved from Act I to Act II.

VERSE

I have seen each and ev'ry queen
In the fashion shows;
I've seen them pose
In lovely clothes.
But the best is the maiden dressed
In a costume made of mesh—
Dressed in her new creation,
She'll cause a big sensation.

CHORUS

Maid of mesh,
In a gown all made of mesh,
All the boys are
Wild over you.
Maid of mesh
In a plat'num setting,
You will soon be getting
All the love and petting too:
You'll find that Tommy, Harry, Freddy, and Paul
Have tripped and slipped
And now they're getting ready—
Right from the start
Ev'ry fellow lost his heart
To the pretty little maid of mesh,
All made of mesh.

AN ORANGE GROVE IN CALIFORNIA

Published. Copyrighted July 14, 1923. Previously registered for copyright as an unpublished song June 15, 1923. Introduced by John Steel (Boy) and Grace Moore (Girl). Original cast recording by John Steel (Victor). Other leading recording by Paul Whiteman (Victor). Whiteman featured this song, among other Berlin numbers, in his Aeolian Hall concert of February 12, 1924, in which he introduced George Gershwin's *Rhapsody in Blue*.

VERSE 1

I've a longing to go
Where the oranges grow—
I know a cozy nest
Way out west,
And I miss it so.
California my own,
Oh, how lonely I've grown!
That's why I'm on the run
To the one I left there all alone:

CHORUS

Arm in arm we will rove
Through a sweet orange grove
Far away in California.
Like a bird I mean to fly west again,
And I'll hold her close to my breast again.
When the blossoms unfold
And the green turns to gold,
Some fine day in California
You'll see a happy girlie and a happy fellow
Mid the fields of yellow
In an orange grove.

VERSE 2

What a beautiful day
For a bridal bouquet!
Where orange blossoms bloom,
Bride and groom
Honor and obey;
Where the heavens are blue,
All my dreams will come true—
I just received a note
And he wrote I'm coming back to you.

REPEAT CHORUS

LEARN TO DO THE STRUT

Published. Copyrighted October 6, 1923. Previously registered for copyright as an unpublished song June 23, 1923, and September 21, 1923. Introduced by the Brox Sisters and the entire company as the closing number of Act I. Original cast recording by the Brox Sisters (Victor). Other leading recording by Vincent Lopez and His Orchestra (Okeh).

VERSE

There's a brand-new step
That they call the strut—
Listen, my dear,
You'll make a dancing rep
If you do the strut.
Anyone here can do it;
There's nothing to it.
I know that you have done
Every one of the diff'rent dances,
The waltz and the lancers,

CHORUS

But
You oughta learn to do the strut—
You'd better leave your house or hut
Before the dancing halls are shut,
And you will go right off your nut
'Bout that new step,
That easy-to-do step.
If you'll be led,
I'll show you how it's done:
Just throw back your head and then
You step around just like a hen.
To all the girls and dancing men
I wanna say just once again
It isn't hard to do so when
You've begun it;
Don't stop till you've done it—
A jazzy tune and pretty soon
You're gonna find yourself struttin' around.

LITTLE BUTTERFLY

Published. Copyrighted October 6, 1923. Previously registered for copyright as an unpublished song September 13, 1923. Introduced by John Steel (Man) with Dorothy Dilley (Butterfly) and Nelson Snow and Charles Columbus (Two Admirers). Alternate (earlier) title "Butterfly." Original cast recording by John Steel

(Victor). The second verse is the same as the verse to "Too Many Sweethearts" (page 224).

VERSE 1

Butterfly, without a single care
You flit from here to there;
Your heart is ev'rywhere,
Fluttering about from boy to boy,
Filling your heart with joy,
Playing with each new toy.

CHORUS

Butterfly,
Little butterfly,
Flitting round from flow'r to flower—
Each time you change your mind,
You leave a lonely heart behind.
You play your part
With a new sweetheart
Till you have him in your power,
And then you flutter away
To leave him crying all day—
Come back, little butterfly.

VERSE 2

Butterfly, take warning while you may:
Youth only lasts a day,
Blossoms and fades away.
There will come a morning when you'll cry,
Poor little butterfly—
You know the reason why.

REPEAT CHORUS

THE WALTZ OF LONG AGO

Published. Copyrighted October 6, 1923. Previously registered for copyright as an unpublished song September 13, 1923. Introduced by Grace Moore (Hostess) with Dorothy Burgess (Little Girl at the Party), Gayle Mays (Boy with the Ukulele), Joseph Santley (Host and Grandfather), and Ivy Sawyer (Grandmother). Leading recording by Paul Specht and His Orchestra (Columbia). Alternate title: "A Waltz of Long Ago."

VERSE

Jazz dancing nowadays does not appeal to me;
I never cared about the jazzy melody.

I'd love to dance around a while,
But my kind of dance is out of style.

CHORUS

I love to dance
The dreamy waltz of long ago,
When Grandmama and Grandpapa
Were girl and beau:
I can see them there dancing,
Such a happy pair romancing
While gliding o'er the ballroom floor
To the waltz of long ago.

CLIMBING UP THE SCALE

Published. Copyrighted October 6, 1923. Previously registered for copyright as an unpublished song September 13, 1923. Introduced by Florence Moore and ensemble.

VERSE 1

Singing is part of ev'ry creature;
Ev'rybody likes to hum a tune.
Let me be your little singing teacher:
I've prepared your lesson;
You can learn it soon.

CHORUS

Strike a key and begin with do,
Do-re-mi and the rest you know,
One-two-three come along, let's go
Climbing up the scale.
Oh, what fun going up, and when
That's all done you go down and then
Ev'ryone should begin again,
Climbing up the scale.
A tenor or a soprano
Can try it on a piano.
Strike a key and begin with do,
Do-re-mi and the rest you know,
One-two-three, come along, let's go
Climbing up the scale.

VERSE 2

In this very ordinary chorus
There's an old effect that never fails.
So we'll ask you to do something for us:

While we sing the chorus,
You go up the scale.

REPEAT CHORUS

"YES! WE HAVE NO BANANAS" OPERA BURLESQUE

Irving Berlin's "opera" treatment of the hugely popular novelty song "Yes! We Have No Bananas!" (written in 1923 by Frank Silver and Irving Cohn). Introduced by Florence Moore, Grace Moore, Lora Sanderson, Frank Tinney, John Steel, and Joseph Santley. Arranged by Arthur Johnston. (On the first page of the piano-vocal score the song is billed as "a concoction by Irving Berlin mixed up with Arthur Johnston.") Programs for the *Music Box Revue* list this number as "A Bit o' Grand Opera." Alternate titles: "Opera Sextette" and "Bananas Sextette." A second version of this number was written for Al Jolson to sing in the film *Mammy*.

First version

Yes, we have no bananas!
Yes, we have no bananas!
Yes, oh yes, we have no,
We have no bananas—no bananas,
Yes, we haven't any.
If you want bananas,
If you want bananas,
You can't get 'em 'cause we haven't any.
B-A-N-A-N-A—
Yes, we know just how to spell it;
If we had one we would sell it,
But we haven't got no bananas.
Yes, oh yes, we must confess
We're in distress with no bananas,
No bananas—no bananas—no bananas—no
    bananas.
We have a bunch or three
Of good celery,
But we have no bananas.
Yes, we have no bananas,
Bananas—bananas,
Yes, oh yes, we have no bananas,
No more bananas, yes,
Bananas—
Yes, oh yes, we have to confess
We have no bananas, yes,
Bananas.

We have lots of apricots
And lots of watercress—
Bananas—
But we haven't got no bananas,
No more bananas,
'Nanas, bananas, bananas, bananas,
Yessir, we have no bananas—no bananas,
Yessir, we have no bananas—no bananas,
Yessir—we have, I said we have,
I said we have—oh yes, we have,
Oh yes, we have no bananas,
Yes, oh yes, oh yes, oh yes, we have no bananas,
    yes,
We must confess we're in distress
Because we haven't got bananas, yes.
Oh yes, oh yes—oh yes, oh yes—oh yes, oh,
YES, WE HAVE NO BANANAS,
We have no bananas today.

Second version

Yes, we have no bananas,
Yes, we have no bananas,
Yes, oh yes, we've no bananas,
We have no bananas, yes, oh yes.
We have lots and lots
Of pears and apricots,
Yes, but we
Have positively
No bananas.
Oh, we hate to disappoint you, but we have to
    answer yes,
Yes, oh yes, we've no bananas and we're in an
    awful mess.
So if you want a bunch of nice bananas,
You must do without them, 'cause we haven't no
    bananas, yes
(Bananas—bananas).
Yes, I'm afraid we have no bananas, yes
(Bananas—bananas).
Yes, if you ask us, that's what we must confess
(Bananas—bananas).
Teardrops may pour
But dry them with your
Bandanas
(Bananas—bananas).
It's really so—
Yes, we haven't no
Bananas
('Nanas bananas bananas bananas
Bananas bananas bananas etc.).
Yessir, we have no bananas—no bananas,
Yessir, we have no bananas—no bananas,
Yessir, we have—I said we have—I said we
Have—no bananas.
Yes, we have no banans—
You'll have to make other plans

'Cause we have no bananas,
No bananas—no ba-nan-as
Yes—yes—yes—yes,
Yes, oh yes,
We will have to confess
No ba-nan-as,
Yes—oh yes, oh yes—oh yes, oh yes—oh yes, oh
Yes, we have no bananas,
We have no bananas today.

MUSIC BOX REVUE 1924

Tryout: None. New York run: The Music Box; December 1, 1924; 184 performances. Lyrics and music by Irving Berlin. Produced by Sam H. Harris. Sketches by Bert Kalmar and Harry Ruby, Bobby Clark and Paul McCullough, Gilbert Clark, Ned Joyce Heaney, and others. Staged by John Murray Anderson. Orchestrations by Frank Tours, Maurice de Packh, and Steve Jones. Vocal arrangements by Arthur Johnston. Orchestra under the direction of Frank Tours. Cast: starring Fanny Brice, Bobby Clark and Paul McCullough, Grace Moore, Oscar Shaw, Claire Luce, Carl Randall, and the Brox Sisters and featuring Hal Sherman, Ula Sharon, Joseph Macaulay, Tamiris and Margarita, Bud and Jack Pearson, Helen Lyons, and the Runaway Four. No copy has been found for the music and lyrics to "Sixteen, Sweet Sixteen," which was introduced by Carl Randall and ensemble. "Polly from Hollywood," which might not be by Berlin, is also missing.

EXCERPTS OF LETTERS FROM IRVING BERLIN TO ELLIN MACKAY

September 26, 1924

Had my first session with [John Murray] Anderson last night (he is going to stage the new show) and he likes the numbers very much. Am beginning to make some headway and hope to be fairly well set in another week—Since returning from Philadelphia I have done nothing but grind out music (God knows whose).

October 23, 1924

The past week I have been on the go every second. I have talked the new show until I am blue in the face. We go to rehearsal in the morning and then the fight begins. . . . Here's a verse for my feelings tonight:

This little song I send your way
The beard is long and tinged with gray
So e'er I write what's in my head
I'll say goodnight and go to bed

. . . which is terrible, thank God.

October 28, 1924

. . . I could go on for pages and talk about the show, which is progressing nicely, but that would be very dull. Please don't think I am being coy or modest when I speak so lightly about the new revue. I really am delighted with a good deal of my stuff, but I have lived with it so long and gone over the numbers so often that they have become stale. Then again, as I told you so many times, the thrill of the Music Box has gone and now it has become a job that I love most when it's finished. . . .

November 5, 1924

The rehearsals have been on for a week and a half and they are very much "Three Ring Circus"— The show (as usual) started out to be small and simple and has grown so large that it frightens me a bit. Anderson works very slowly and having started quite late we will all be on the job every second to get the show on. We are working under an entirely different system this year (trying to keep the expenses down) and a good deal of the scenes and costumes have not been put in work yet—then again there have been so many changes made—there are so many in the cast to take care of and place which is not very easy, however I am hoping for the best and feel pretty certain about most of the material. . . .

November 22, 1924

. . . We had a very hard week of rehearsals and just tonight I finished the finale, which cleans up everything in the way of words and music to be written. We are trying hard to open on Thanksgiving eve. or night. A good deal of scenery or costumes are still in work and we will have little time for dress rehearsal. We assembled the show last night for the first time and it looks fine. I feel sure we have sufficient material for a great show. Everybody seems to think (judging from rehearsals) that it will be our best revue; I hope so. A lot of interest is shown in the show from the outside and the demand for opening night seats is greater than we ever had. . . .

I am sure your "Alice in Wonderland" will be one of the best numbers. It's my favorite and has turned out better than I expected. . . .

December 3, 1924

With the exception of Allen Dale's (and his isn't bad) I think they are fine notices. We took about 15 minutes out of the show tonight and it went like wildfire. We also broke the record of the Music Box Theatre for the second night with the receipts which is a very good sign. . . .

January 11, 1925

. . . Mrs. Cushings's summing up of the show was quite fair. She evidently saw the show the first week before we made the necessary changes and cuts. "Listening," the Brox Sisters' song, and "Unlucky in Love," are out. They slowed up the performance along with some of the dialogue in the sketches and we took them out of the show. Mr. Harris and I saw Saturday night's performance and agreed it is the best *Music Box Revue* since the first. In any case we are doing the biggest business we ever did and that is the final criticism and proof. I hope it continues. . . .

Since the show opened I have been at the theatre every night as we keep changing things around. . . .

I don't think we will do another *Music Box Revue*. They're too hard and not worth the hard work and money we have to spend to make them good. . . .

CATSKILL MOUNTAINS SCENE and BROADWAY SCENE and WHERE IS MY LITTLE OLD NEW YORK?

Only "Where Is My Little Old New York?," the third of the three linked numbers that comprised the opening of *Irving Berlin's Fourth Annual Music Box Revue*, was published. It was copyrighted December 29, 1924, and had been previously registered for copyright as an unpublished song December 6, 1924. Introduced by Joseph Macaulay (Rip Van Winkle). Music and lyrics for the "Catskill Mountains" and "Broadway" scenes were found among Berlin's papers and are now in the Irving Berlin Collection of the Music Division of the Library

of Congress. The three-part opening sequence featured Macaulay (Rip Van Winkle), Oscar Shaw (Mountain Climber), Margarita (Miss Bronx), Helen Lyons (Miss Riverside Drive), Phyllis Pearce (Miss Fifth Avenue), Pansy Maness (Miss Tenth Avenue), Claire Luce (Miss Broadway), and Tamiris (Miss Greenwich Village). "Catskill Mountains Scene" also was known as "Catskills Opening."

Catskill Mountains Scene

MOUNTAIN
CLIMBER: Wake up,
Mr. Rip Van Winkle!
Wake up,
Chase away that wrinkle
From your brow—right now!
You must forget your trouble and
strife—
Come down from the Catskill
Mountains,
Come down to the soda fountains
On Broadway, and say,
I'm gonna show you the time of your
life!
The man who wrote this melody
Has sent me after you;
He'd like to have you come and see
The *Music Box Revue*.*
So won't you
Wake up?
Can't you hear me roaring
"Wake up!"?
While you're up here snoring,
Wrapped in dreams, it seems
Somebody else paid the rent for your
wife.

[*Rip wakes.*]

RIP: Why do you wake me from my
slumber?
So very tired am I.
CLIMBER: We had to have an opening number,
That is the reason why.
This is as good a way as any other way
To begin a revue.

---

*Earlier version of lines 9–12:
For twenty years you've slumbered on,
And my, how things have changed!
We'd like to have you gaze upon
A new revue that we've arranged.

RIP: Are you a revue?
CLIMBER: A brand-new show, and here's a ticket
for you.
Come along, do.
RIP: But I don't want to see a lot of scenery,
And I don't care to hear a song.
CLIMBER: But do you care for women?
RIP: Yes!
CLIMBER: Then you'd better come along.
Just come with me and I will
Show you to a front-row seat—
I know you will be glad to meet
Those lovely queens "Sixteens,"
And you'll forget your trouble and
strife.
Come down
From the Catskill Mountains
Come down
To the soda fountains
On Broadway, and say
I'm gonna show you the time of your
life!

Broadway Scene

MOUNTAIN
CLIMBER: This, Mr. Rip Van Winkle, is
Broadway!
These are the lights that twinkle on
Broadway!
New York City comes here every
evening for a smile—
Pretty girls from different sections of
Manhattan Isle.

There's Miss Bronx, from the Bronx—
You can tell that she comes from
the Bronx:
She walks with her hand in the air,
and perhaps
She got that way hanging on subway
straps.

Miss Riverside Drive is hardly alive;
The trains wake her up every
morning at five
In her cozy little bedroom
Looking out on Grant's Tomb.

But Miss Fifth Avenue,
She doesn't live in a four-by—two;
She's living so grand with the
Vanderbilts and the Astors.
Just watch her take a sip
From what she carries upon her hip—
She's a flapper, a finger snapper,

Who never wore an apron or a
    wrapper.

On Tenth Avenue, on Tenth Avenue,
You can tell all the girls by the gum
    that they chew.
They know how to treat a romancer
Who doesn't take no for an answer:
A wallop or two will knock 'em
    cuckoo—
They're all perfect ladies on Tenth
    Avenue.

You'll be happy to meet
The Broadway stepper—
She's full of pepper and go.
We would like to repeat
She's full of ginger—
Which doesn't injure the show.
When the show is over, she'll cabaret
Until the morning, jazzing her life
    away;
From her head to her feet
You'll find her active—
And so attractive to know!

In a little studio where there's dust
    upon the shelf
Lives the girl from Washington
    Square.
We'll let her speak for herself:

MISS
GREENWICH
VILLAGE: Down in Greenwich Village
We're very moody, living in a
    studi-o
That used to be a stable.
We spend our weeks making nice
    antiques,
And we tell the art collectors
That they're buying something
    rare.
Living in a stable where the cobwebs
    cling,
Breathing little microbes, makes us
    pale and int'resting—
Way down in Greenwich Village,
Better known as Washington Square.

So, if you'd like to be artistic,
Come along and join us there.
Go and cut your hair off up around
    your ears,
Loosen up your morals, drape your
    shape in red portières,
And come to Greenwich Village,
Better known as Washington Square.

Where Is My Little Old New York?

VERSE

RIP: So this is Manhattan Isle,
    Where everythin's gay—
    And these are the pretty girls
    That visit Broadway!
    They're beautiful, more or less,
    Be that as it may—
    But speaking about your city,
    I've got to say, What a pity!

CHORUS

Where is the little old New York,
The one that I used to know, long, long ago?
What has become of all the people
That used to go to the church with the steeple?
Oh, how I'm longing to see
New York as it used to be—
Bring back my little old New York,
The one that I used to know long ago!

MOUNTAIN
CLIMBER: Wake up,
    Mr. Rip Van Winkle!
    Wake up,
    Chase away that wrinkle
    From your brow—right now!
    I'm gonna take you through
    The new *Music Box Revue*.

TOKIO BLUES

Published. Copyrighted December 29, 1924. Previously registered for copyright as an unpublished song December 15, 1924. Introduced by the Brox Sisters and ensemble. Danced by Tamiris and Margarita.

VERSE

Oh,
Why did we ever roam,
Oh,
Far away from our home?
Oh,
Why did we ever plan
To
Run away from Japan?

CHORUS

What'll we do? We've got those Tokio Blues—
Tokio Blues are not so easy to lose.
Where the lotus flowers grow,
That's where we would like to go—
To our home in Tokio.
How we yearn to return to sunny Japan,
The home of almond-eyed queens
Looking like those you see embroidered on
    screens—
Three unhappy little shes
Kneeling on their Japan knees
Singing the Tokio Blues!

A COUPLE OF SENSELESS CENSORS

Introduced by Bobby Clark and Paul McCullough. Incomplete lyric sheets in Berlin's handwriting were found among his papers and are now in the Irving Berlin Collection of the Music Division of the Library of Congress. Only portions of the lyric survive. Alternate titles: "Censor Song" and "We're a Couple of Senseless Censors."

We just read a story that's hard to believe,
About a naked lady who was known as Mother
    Eve.
If we knew who wrote the Bible
We'd be suing him for libel,*
For a couple of senseless censors are we.

We censor the drama and soon we'll decide
To censor all the ladies who are being glorified.
They call it artistic to dance like a faun,
But dancing isn't dancing when it's done with
    nothing on.

We censor all the movies and we censor all the
    plays;
We censor all the dancing in the different
    cabarets;
We censor the music that's known as the blues;
We censor all the pictures in the lobbies of revues;
We censor the dresses with so much to see;
We censor all the postal cards that come from gay
    Paree;

*Alternate version of lines 3 and 4:
    And so some day we're liable
    To go censoring the Bible,

We censor *What Price Glory?*
As we would a dirty story,
For a couple of senseless censors are we.

DON'T SEND ME BACK TO PETROGRAD

Published. Copyrighted January 13, 1925. Previously registered for copyright as an unpublished song December 18, 1924. Introduced by Fanny Brice in a sketch entitled "The Immigrant." Alternate title (program): "Don't Send Me Back."

VERSE

Poor little immigrant feeling oh so sad,
I came from Petrograd with ev'rything I had.
Now that I'm over here, they won't let me stay;
That's why I'm so unhappy today—
Please don't send me away!

CHORUS 1

Don't send me back—
I don't want to go back to Petrograd.
Don't send me back—
I don't want to go back to my hometown.
There's millions of people on the shore;
Why can't you make room for just one more?
There's a boy that I love waiting out on the
        pier—
How can I go when my heart is over here?
Give me the chance
That you gave all my friends from Petrograd:
I want to be
In the land of the free and settle down.
The Liberty Statue down the bay
Is looking right at you and seems to say,
"Oh! Don't send her back!"
It's terrible in my hometown.

CHORUS 2

Don't send me back—
I don't want to go back to Petrograd.
Don't send me back—
I don't want to go back to my hometown.
The very best people that you know
Were foreigners not so long ago:
When they came over here, they were all
        immigrants—
So were their cousins and their uncles and their
        aunts.

Give me the chance
That you gave all my friends from Petrograd.
I want to be
In the land of the free and settle down.
I'll promise to work the best I can—
I'll even wash sheets for the Ku Klux Klan.
Oh! Don't send me back!
It's terrible in my hometown.

Earlier version

VERSE

Poor little immigrant feeling oh so sad,
I crossed the ocean and came from Petrograd.
I was so happy the day I sailed away;
Now that I'm over here,
They won't let me stay.

CHORUS 1

Don't send me back—
I don't want to go back to Petrograd.
Please let me stay
With the people from my hometown.
There on the shore
There's a million or more from Petrograd:
When they came over here they were all
        immigrants—
So were their cousins and their uncles and their
        aunts.
Oh, give me the chance
That you gave all my friends from Petrograd
When they came here
With their bundles and settled down!
The Liberty Statue across the bay
Is looking right at you and seems to say,
"Oh, don't send her back!"
It's terrible in my hometown.

CHORUS 2

Don't send me back—
I don't want to go back to Petrograd.
Please let me stay
With the people from my hometown.
There on the shore
Is a Yiddisher boy from Petrograd.
We'll get married and he'll pay my room and my
        board—
He runs an agency for Mr. Henry Ford.
And after a while
We'll get busy and raise a family,
Just like my friends
Who came over and settled down.
I promise to work the best I can—

I'll even wash sheets for the Ku Klux Klan.*
Oh! Don't send me back!
It's terrible in my hometown.

UNLUCKY IN LOVE

Published. Copyrighted December 15, 1924. Previously registered for copyright as an unpublished song October 28, 1924. Introduced by Oscar Shaw. Dropped from the show after the first week of the run.

VERSE 1

I always win at the races—
Very strange, but it's true.
Ev'ry time I play roulette,
Seems I cash in ev'ry bet;
And I get plenty of aces
Playing poker, I do.
Winning in a gambling game
Seems to be my middle name,
But

CHORUS

I'm so unlucky,
Unlucky in love.
There's something about me
That makes a girl do without me.
I'm always finding
Somebody to love;
I find her, and then
I lose her again.
Meet her on Monday and say hello,
Take her out Tuesday to see a show,
Tell her on Wedn'sday how much I care,
Call her up Thursday and get the air.
And then it's all over on Friday—
Friday's my day, my goodbye day.
I'm so unlucky,
Unlucky in love.

VERSE 2

I've got a dozen addresses
In my little red book;
Ev'ry time I make a call,
I'm quite welcome, but that's all.

*Alternate version of lines 13 and 14:
    I wanna stay here and build a nest
    With Jake and Lee and Morris Gest.

For when it comes to caresses,
They just give me a look;
Someone that they're wild about
Walks right in as I go out.
For

REPEAT CHORUS

TELL HER IN THE SPRINGTIME

Published. Copyrighted December 15, 1924. Previously registered for copyright as an unpublished song October 28, 1924. Introduced by Grace Moore; danced by Ula Sharon. Original cast recording by Grace Moore (Victor). Other leading recording by Paul Whiteman and His Orchestra (Victor).

VERSE 1

The time for beaux to propose
Is the springtime;
Ev'ry girl becomes sentimental then.
A girl will part with her heart
In the springtime,
To the lovesick boy who proposes
With the bloom of the roses.

CHORUS

Tell her in the springtime,
In May or June;
Tell her in the springtime,
The best time to spoon,
When ev'rything begins blossoming,
You'll hear Mendelssohn's "Spring Song" tune.
When the moon is shining,
You speak of her charms;
Then is when she's pining
To rest in your arms.
Don't worry so—
She won't answer no
If you play Romeo
In the spring.

VERSE 2

A sweet romance has a chance
In the springtime;
That's the only time when the peaches fall.
Because we find love is blind
In the springtime,

And your tale of love overpowers
If you say it with flowers.

REPEAT CHORUS

WHO

Published. Copyrighted December 23, 1924. Previously registered for copyright as an unpublished song August 15, 1924. Introduced by the Brox Sisters.

VERSE 1

Ever since I met you
I haven't been the same;
I don't sleep a wink at night,
And I've lost my appetite.
Seems I can't forget you
And you are all to blame.
Don't say no,
You know it's so,
You can't deny it—
Please don't try it.

CHORUS

Who
Gave me that lovesick feeling?
Who
Started my senses reeling?
Who
Was it when I was blue
Gave me a kiss that grew
Into a red-hot furnace,
The kind that burns us?
And you know
Who
Cuddled up closer to me,
Who
Made me feel bride-and-groomy,
Who
Gave me that notion
To
Jump in the ocean—
Nobody else but you.

VERSE 2 (NOT IN PUBLISHED SHEET MUSIC)

I wrote you a letter
You haven't answered yet.
Seems you just refuse to be
Sweethearts like we used to be.
It would be much better

If we had never met;
Then if you'd flirt,
It wouldn't hurt.
There is no doubt, dear,
Figure out, dear,

PATTER (NOT IN PUBLISHED SHEET MUSIC)

It wasn't the man with the barrel of cash;
It wasn't the man with the sandy mustache;
It wasn't the man who could reach a high C
When he sang "What'll I Do?" all off the key;
It wasn't the man who would make a bad
    crack,
Who had a nice car—but you had to walk
    back;
It wasn't the man who was always well
    dressed,
Nor the big butter-and-egg man from the
    West.

LISTENING

Published. Copyrighted December 15, 1924. Previously registered for copyright as an unpublished song October 28, 1924. Introduced by Grace Moore and Oscar Shaw. Dropped from the show after the first week of the run. Original cast recording by Grace Moore (Victor).

VERSE 1

I'm so lonely, dear,
Lonely waiting here,
Waiting for you in the gloaming.
While you are far away,
I long for the day
When you'll weary of your roaming.

CHORUS

Listening,
Listening for you,
All alone,
Feeling kind o' blue.
Listening
For a knock upon the door,
Growing weary waiting for
Your returning, yearning,
Missing you more and more each day,
Wanting you more than I can say.
Listening because there is nothing else to do,
Just a lonely thing,
Listening for you.

VERSE 2 (NOT IN PUBLISHED SHEET MUSIC)

How I long for you
When the day is through
And the shades of night are falling!
How I miss you, dear,
For I want you near,
And I seem to hear you calling.

REPEAT CHORUS

THE CALL OF THE SOUTH

Published. Copyrighted December 15, 1924. Previously registered for copyright as an unpublished song August 15, 1924. Introduced by Oscar Shaw, Grace Moore, and ensemble. More than thirty years later, Berlin considered using "The Call of the South" in a proposed *Music Box Revue* television special, but that show was never produced.

VERSE

A gentle voice is calling me;
I hear it night and day.
It seems to whisper tenderly,
"You should be on your way."
I'm going back without a doubt
To where my heart belongs,
The land that Jolson sings about
In all his "Mammy" songs.

CHORUS

Southland,
All night long your banjos ring in my ear
And I can hear
The call of the Southland.
Cornfields
Seem to say it's just the time of year,
Come on and hear
The call of the South.
I'll be so happy when I open the gate
To see my sweetie there who promised to wait;
And then when I deliver
The kiss I'm gonna give 'er,
Trouble will drown way down
In the Swanee River.
Southland,
I must go back to somebody I've missed—
I can't resist
The call of the South.

Berlin wrote the following lyrics to Stephen Foster's "Old Folks at Home" to be sung as a countermelody to the chorus of "The Call of the South":

Way down upon the Swanee River
I feel so blue.
Oh, how my heart is yearning ever,
Yearning to welcome you!
All the world is sad and dreary,
Dreary while you roam;
So won't you please return, my dearie,
Back to the old folks at home.

BANDANNA BALL

Introduced by Fanny Brice and company. This number was the Act I finale. Music and lyrics were found among Berlin's papers and are now in the Irving Berlin Collection of the Music Division of the Library of Congress.

VERSE

I've got a ticket for the ball,
Hannah;
Come, come along.
We'd better hurry to the hall,
Hannah;
Come, come along.
There's a bevy of brownskins there
From the levee, and I declare,
You'll be the swellest of 'em all,
Hannah;
Come, come along.

CHORUS

Hannah,
Put on the bandanna
You wore in Savannah
And come to the ball.
Ev'rybody's gonna be there:
Sammy is bringing his mammy;
She came from Miami
Dressed up in a shawl.
You'll see lots of Hottentots
All dolled up in polka dots—
Hannah,
Put on your bandanna
And come to the Grand Bandanna Ball.

PATTER

I feel so grand—
Come hold my hand

To that jazz band,
Hannah.
And when you've met
My pet cornet
You'll get all set,
Hannah.
They've got a lot
Of that stuff what
I call red-hot
Rhythm—
I know your beau
Feels so—Oh! Oh!
Come, dear—let's go
With 'em
To that rhythm.

ALICE IN WONDERLAND

Published. Copyrighted January 14, 1925. Previously registered for copyright as an unpublished song October 30, 1924. Introduced by the Brox Sisters, Ula Sharon, Carl Randall, and ensemble. Alternate title (program): "Come Along with Alice." This is not the same song as the "Alice in Wonderland" number in *The Century Girl* (1916).

VERSE

You know the tale of the girl who was sittin'
By the fire with her kitten—
It's a story that was written long ago.
You know that she was about to retire
When the glass above the fire
Seemed to suddenly expire like the snow.
You know when the way was cleared
That she disappeared
Through the looking glass.
You know that her name was Alice.
So come along if you care;
We'll take you there.
You must prepare
To be a kiddie like you were
When you read of the girl who was sittin'
By the fire with her kitten
In the story that was written long ago.

CHORUS

Come along with Alice
Into Wonderland,
To the lovely palace
Where they're all so grand.
See the funny people

Strolling hand in hand.
Come along and pass
Through the looking glass
Into Wonderland.

I WANT TO BE A BALLET DANCER

Registered for copyright as an unpublished song October 28, 1924. Introduced by Fanny Brice with Bobby Clark and ensemble.

VERSE

I'm a dancer, that's what I am,
Like the girls who don't give a damn
When they dance to the toot of a flute
In their undershirts.
Ev'rybody thinks I'm a fool
Just because I go to school
Where they teach me to pose
On the tips of my toes
Till it hurts—oh!

CHORUS

I want to be a ballet dancer!
If you don't believe I can, sir,
Look at me stand on my toe—oh!
It isn't so easy to do.
I want to dance around all over
On my toes just like Pavlova;
She's a ballet dancer,
And I want to be one too.

ROCKABYE, BABY

Published. Copyrighted December 15, 1924. Previously registered for copyright as an unpublished song August 15, 1924. Introduced by Grace Moore and ensemble. Original cast recording by Grace Moore (Victor). The lyric of the medley section was not part of the published song; a copy was found among Berlin's papers and is now in the Irving Berlin Collection of the Music Division of the Library of Congress. Except for "School Days," no music for the medley section is known to survive.

VERSE

Little baby,
Can't you hear the call
Of the sandman
While the shadows fall?
Let him lead you by the hand
Into drowsy slumberland.
Soon the morning
Will be on its way
To my baby
With a brand-new day.
Go to sleep, my dear, while I
Sing a tender lullaby.

CHORUS

Rockabye, baby,
Hushabye, dear,
Slumber, my sweetheart,
Mother is near,
Dreaming of baby
All of the night,
Planning a future
Rosy and bright:
Dollies and schoolbooks
Waiting for you,
Beautiful dresses,
Wedding bells too,
Plenty of sunshine
Crowning each year—
Rockabye, baby,
Hushabye, dear.

MEDLEY

I can see you at the age of four
With your playthings scattered on the floor
In your pretty nursery,
Sitting on your mother's knee.
I'll be reading little nursery rhymes
To my baby—oh, what happy times
We'll be having, you and me!
Till the years begin to
Roll right into:

School days, school days,
Dear old golden-rule days—
I see you there with your books and slate,
Standing alone at the schoolhouse gate.
Baby is sad and feeling blue,
Lessons are oh so hard to do.
But your lessons at school will soon be
    through;
Then parties and dresses
And sweethearts' caresses.

I can see you with your first romance
At a party while the others dance.
You are seated with your beau
Who has learned to love you so;
He proposes and you answer yes—
You are dreaming of a wedding dress.
In another little while
I can see you marching down the aisle.

Bells ring, the organ's playing
"Here come the bride and groom."
Kind friends are softly saying,
"Gee, isn't he mighty lucky!"
Preacher is by their side,
And then when the knot is tied,
The bridegroom will kiss the bride.
And after a year I can see baby dear
Over a cradle, and I seem to hear:

REPEAT CHORUS

WILD CATS

Introduced by Carl Randall; danced by Claire Luce and ensemble. Music and lyrics were found among Berlin's papers and are now in the Irving Berlin Collection of the Music Division of the Library of Congress. Alternate title: "Oh, Those Wild Cats." In a letter to Irving Berlin, dated August 6, 1982, Claire Luce recalled the song: "Do you by any chance," she wrote, "remember the 'Wild Cat' number in the *Music Box Revue*? Oh well, dear Sam gave us a backdrop of lovely girls in 'leopard skin' and a magnificent (background drop) leopard curtain—and dear Carl Randall caught me in his elegant tux at the end of the number and I left his suit covered with my body makeup!!"

VERSE

I'm a good aim;
Hunting wild game
Used to take me out to Africa.
The tiger cats there
Never could scare
A hunter like me.
Very brave, yes—
Nevertheless,
When it comes to hunting in the city
For the wild cats
Living in flats,
I'm scared as can be.

CHORUS

Oh, those wild cats!
I wonder what makes them wild.
No one seems to know who's to blame.
Homemade sweeties who should be tame
Are oh, such wild cats!
It used to be "angel child"
But the angel child is a wild cat now.
And when you're near 'er
You'll hear 'er meow.
Oh, those wild cats!
I wonder what makes them wild.

IN THE SHADE OF A SHELTERING TREE

Published. Copyrighted December 15, 1924. Previously registered for copyright as an unpublished song October 28, 1924. Introduced by Oscar Shaw, Grace Moore, and ensemble.

VERSE

Here and there
A loving pair
Will go and share
A morris chair to spoon.
Jack and Jill
Preferred the hill,
And there's a thrill
Beneath the silv'ry moon;
But there's only one place
For a lover's embrace:

CHORUS

In the shade of a sheltering tree,
That's the place for a couple to be.
You will find that they always agree
In the shade of a sheltering tree.
All the tales Adam whispered to Eve
Mother Eve simply had to believe.
What was hers was his—the reason is
They happened to be
In the shade of a sheltering tree.

DON'T WAIT TOO LONG

Published. Copyrighted September 25, 1925. Previously registered for copyright as an unpublished song September 11, 1925. Added during the post-Broadway tour, where it was introduced in Act II by Grace Moore and Oscar Shaw. Later during the tour Lottice Howell replaced Moore.

VERSE 1

You may have a certain someone in mind,
Someone that someday you're hoping to find.
The one that you'll adore
Is worthwhile waiting for,
But the rest of the world is mating
While you sit there waiting, so

CHORUS

Don't wait too long
With your castles in the sky.
Don't wait too long;
While you're waiting, time will fly.
Love songs are best when they're sung
In the springtime, when ev'rything's young;
So don't wait too long—
Happiness may pass you by.

VERSE 2

So much time is wasted waiting around
Just for someone who may never be found
And when the years have flown
You may be all alone
Looking back on the days you wasted,
Leaving life untasted; so

REPEAT CHORUS

YIDDISHA ESKIMO

Intended for Fanny Brice but not used in the show. Music and lyrics were found among Berlin's papers and are now in the Irving Berlin Collection of the Music Division of the Library of Congress.

VERSE

Someone told my father
If he went up to the North Pole
He would make a million
From the natives, selling them coal.
So he went in business
Where it's just as cold as could be;
But I'll tell you what—it's not the spot
For a red-hot mama like me!

CHORUS 1

Oh, oh, oh, I'm a Yiddisha Eskimo!
Where the weather is cold as ice,
Take my advice, don't go,
Because there ain't much fun
In the land of the midnight sun.
Living in a house of snow without a steeple,
I'm one of God's frozen people.
It's too cold for a couple of hands to hold,
So I play with the seals all day—
And does it pay? Oh, no!
I don't like playing with a seal;
A seal ain't got no sex appeal.
Oh, oh, I'm a Yiddisha Eskimo.

CHORUS 2

Oh, oh, oh, I'm a Yiddisha Eskimo!
Where the weather is always cold,
It's hard to hold a beau,
Because a frozen breath
Nearly freezes a man to death.
While you're kissing Eski-Jake or Eski-Moses,
There's icicles on their noses.
What a life! When a lady becomes a wife,
She must sleep on a cake of ice;
And is that nice? Oh, no!
It's awful when a girl goes wrong—
The nights up here are six months long
Oh, oh, I'm a Yiddisha Eskimo.

I'LL SEE YOU IN C-U-B-A

Published. Copyrighted January 20, 1920. Registered for copyright as an unpublished song January 5, 1920. Introduced in the *Ziegfeld Midnight Frolic* (1919); artist[s] unknown. According to the published sheet music, the song was featured by Ted Lewis in the *Greenwich Village Follies*. Leading recordings by Billy Murray (Victor), Ted Lewis (Columbia), and Jack Kaufman (Emerson). Revised by Berlin in June 1945 for the 1946 musical film *Blue Skies*, where it was sung by Bing Crosby and Olga San Juan (see page 379).

VERSE 1

Not so far from here
There's a very lively atmosphere;
Ev'rybody's going there this year,
And there's a reason; the season
Opened last July.
Ever since the U.S.A. went dry
Ev'rybody's going there,
And I'm going too;
I'm on my way to

CHORUS

Cuba—
That's where I'm going.
Cuba—
That's where I'll stay.
Cuba,
Where wine is flowing
And where dark-eyed Stellas
Light their fellers' panatelas.
Cuba,
Where all is happy;
Cuba,
Where all is gay.
Why don't you plan a wonderful trip
To Havana? Hop on a ship
And I'll see you in C-U-B-A.

VERSE 2

Take a friend's advice:
Drinking in a cellar isn't nice;
Anybody who has got the price
Should be a Cuban. Have you been
Longing for the smile
That you haven't had for quite a while?
If you have, then follow me
And I'll show the way;
Come on along to

REPEAT CHORUS

AFTER YOU GET WHAT YOU WANT, YOU DON'T WANT IT

Published. Copyrighted April 29, 1920. Previously registered for copyright as an unpublished song March 31, 1920. Popularized by the singing team of Gus Van and Joe Schenck, whose recording of the song for Columbia was, according to Joel Whitburn in *Pop Memories*, number two on the best-seller list. More than thirty years later the song was sung by Marilyn Monroe in the 1954 film musical *There's No Business Like Show Business*.

VERSE 1

Listen to me, honey dear,
Something's wrong with you, I fear—
It's getting harder to please you,
Harder and harder each year.
I don't want to make you blue,
But you need a talking to;
Like a lot of people I know,
Here's what's wrong with you:

CHORUS

After you get what you want you don't want it.
If I gave you the moon,
You'd grow tired of it soon.
You're like a baby—
You want what you want when you want it,
But after you are presented
With what you want, you're discontented.
You're always wishing and wanting for something;
When you get what you want,
You don't want what you get.
And though you sit upon my knee,*
You'll grow tired of me,
'Cause after you get what you want,
You don't want what you wanted at all.

VERSE 2

Don't you say that I'm unkind;
Think it over and you'll find
You've got a changeable nature:
You're always changing your mind.
There's a longing in your eye
That is hard to satisfy;

---

*Alternate line for girl:
And though I sit upon your knee,

You're unhappy most of the time.
Here's the reason why:

REPEAT CHORUS

BUT! (SHE'S JUST A LITTLE BIT CRAZY ABOUT HER HUSBAND, THAT'S ALL)

Published. Copyrighted May 26, 1920. Previously registered for copyright as an unpublished song March 31, 1920.

VERSE 1

All the boys are feeling blue;
Seems they don't know what to do.
One little wonderful girl
Set all their hearts in a whirl;
Ever since she came to town,
She has turned things upside down.
They'd love to speak of romance,
But they never get the chance.

CHORUS

She's so beautiful,
Oh, so beautiful!
But!—
She's just the least bit crazy.
She's so wonderful,
Oh, so wonderful!
But!—
She's a nut, she's a nut.
She looks like Tiffany's window
When she's got her jewels on;
In her limousine,
She looks like a queen;
But!—
She's just a little bit gone.
All the boys in town
Follow her around,
But!—
She doesn't seem to know it;
They have never met,
For they never get
An invitation to call.
She's got a husband who is eighty years old;
He's got a million and a terrible cold.
She's just a little bit crazy

About her husband,
That's all.

VERSE 2

All the other girls in town
Wear a rather jealous frown;
She has upset their affairs,
Taken the boys unawares.
Still the boys are feeling blue;
They are puzzled what to do.
Her beauty drives them insane;
Still they pursue her in vain.

REPEAT CHORUS

LINDY

Published. Copyrighted November 3, 1920. Previously registered for copyright as an unpublished song October 19, 1920.

VERSE 1

Big pale moon
Was shining down on Tennessee;
Birds in tune
Sang love's sweet melody;
Lovesick coon
Was sighing tenderly;
And pretty soon
I listened to this plea:

CHORUS

Lindy, Lindy, how much longer must I wait?
The Good Book says that man
Must take unto himself a mate.
You'll need somebody who
Will cuddle up close to you
Next winter, Lindy,
When the weather is windy.
You know the birds and the bees
And chickens raise a family,
And what was meant for them
Was meant for Lindy and for me.

VERSE 2

Big pale moon
Still shining down on Tennessee;
Birds in tune
Hum that same melody;
Honeymoon

Will come eventually;
And that same coon
Is urging hopefully:

REPEAT CHORUS

HOME AGAIN BLUES

Published. Copyrighted November 24, 1920. Music and lyrics by Irving Berlin and Harry Akst (1894–1962). Akst was Irving Berlin's musical secretary from c. 1919 to c. 1921. The leading recording (number two on the popular music charts) was by the Original Dixieland Jazz Band (Victor).

VERSE 1

I've been known to be a rolling stone for many
    years;
Now alone I sit around and moan when night
    appears—
Thoughts of my home fill me with regrettable
    tears.
Ev'ry year, oh, how I long to hear a bit of news!
Friends appear to offer words of cheer, but I
    refuse.
Pack up my trunk, 'cause I've got those Home
    Again Blues.
I'm going

CHORUS

Home, knock at the door,
Home, just like before,
Roam never no more.
"No place like home"—
Oh, what a song!
Home where I belong—
Oh, I've got those Home Again Blues.

VERSE 2

I can't wait until I reach that gate and home I see;
Sure as fate I know they're gonna wait to welcome
    me.
I want to state that's the end of my misery.
If I knew I'd ever feel so blue, I'd never roam,
But it's true we learn a thing or two away from
    home:
I'm telling you I've ceased to be a rollable stone—
I'm going

REPEAT CHORUS

DROWSY HEAD

Published. Copyrighted January 20, 1921. Previously registered for copyright as an unpublished song December 24, 1920. Words and music by Irving Berlin and composer-singer Vaughn DeLeath (1896–1943), the first woman to broadcast on radio.

VERSE 1

Shadows fall on nursery wall;
It is the end of the day.
Mammy comes and softly hums
To her child at play:

CHORUS

"Drowsy head,
Drowsy head,
Close your eyes and go to bed.
Go put your toys away;
You've played enough today.
Shadows are falling;
Sandman is calling.
Go to sleep,
Go to sleep,
Pray the Lord your soul to keep,
Hush-a-bye, my baby, don't you dare to peep,
Mammy's little drowsy head."

VERSE 2

Shadows fall on nursery wall;
Daylight is passing by.
Baby calls to her dolls
That same lullaby.

REPEAT CHORUS

I LIKE IT

Published. Copyrighted February 1, 1921. Previously registered for copyright as an unpublished song January 5, 1921.

VERSE

Mary Green, seventeen,
Mother's only child;
Mother's cross just because
Mary's running wild.

Sits and spoons afternoons
With the boy next door;
Mother cries, "You mustn't do it!"
And Mary starts to roar:

CHORUS

"I'm gonna do it
If I like it—
And I like it.
I'll let him hold me
Though you scold me
When I'm through.
I hate to make Mother and Dad
So terribly mad,
But there are times
When it's good to be bad.
I'm gonna hold hands
If I like it—
And I like it.
A little squeezing
Is so pleasing
If you're blue.
And since the boy next door first realized
I'd let him kiss me, well, you'd be surprised . . .
I'm gonna do it
If I like it—
And I do."

PICKANINNY MOSE

Published. Copyrighted February 28, 1921. Previously registered for copyright as an unpublished song January 31, 1921.

VERSE

Little speck of midnight,
That's his other name;
Mammy croons her darky tunes
With much more feeling since he came:

CHORUS

Pickaninny Mose,
Precious little lamb,
Mighty like a rose
Sure enough you am.
Angels in the night
Made you black as coal,
But a lily white
Blossoms in your soul.
Playin' in the sun

By the cabin door,
Makin' ev'ryone
Love you more and more;
Sweeter is the song
Where the Swanee flows
Since you came along,
Pickaninny Mose.

THERE'S A CORNER UP IN HEAVEN

Published. Copyrighted March 24, 1921. Previously registered for copyright as an unpublished song March 9, 1921.

VERSE 1

So Mammy's curly head is feeling blue,
So many troubles, don't know what to do;
Feels like he wants to cry,
And what is the reason?
All just because the little white boy said:
"Can't get to heaven with a kinky head."
White boy done tole a lie:

CHORUS

There's a corner up in heaven
That the angels put aside
Just for little pickaninnies,
And the gates are open wide.
Pickaninny will be welcome;
They'll be glad to have him too:
Plenty angels up in heaven
Just as black as you.
There's a corner up in heaven
Just for you.

VERSE 2

The angels brought you in the blackest night,
And I believe they meant to make you white,
Just like the winter snows.
But you needn't worry;
Although they made my honey black as coal,
A snow-white lily blossoms in her soul—
That's why your mammy knows:

REPEAT CHORUS

ALL BY MYSELF

Published. Copyrighted April 27, 1921. Previously registered for copyright as an unpublished song April 6, 1921. Introduced by Charles King at the Palace Theatre in New York. Ted Lewis's recording (Columbia) reached the number-one spot on the popular music charts on October 21, 1921, where it remained for four weeks, until it was displaced on November 26, 1921, by Paul Whiteman's recording (Victor) of Berlin's "Say It with Music." Included in "An Interview" in the first edition of the *Music Box Revue* (1921), where it was sung by Irving Berlin.

VERSE 1

I'm so unhappy;
What'll I do?
I long for somebody who
Will sympathize with me;
I'm growing so tired of living alone.
I lie awake all night and cry;
Nobody loves me, that's why.

CHORUS

All by myself in the morning,
All by myself in the night;
I sit alone in my cozy morris chair,*
So unhappy there,
Playing solitaire.
All by myself I get lonely,
Watching the clock on the shelf.
I'd love to rest my weary head
On somebody's shoulder;
I hate to grow older
All by myself.

VERSE 2

My name and number
Are in the book,
The one that hangs on a hook
In almost every drugstore;
Why don't someone bother to look?
My central tells me all day long,
"Sorry, the number is wrong."

REPEAT CHORUS

Later changed to:
  "I sit alone with a table and a chair."

THE PASSION FLOWER

Published. Copyrighted May 6, 1921. Previously registered for copyright as an unpublished song April 21, 1921.

VERSE

Once a human rose was born,
But she grew to be a thorn,
Piercing hearts of loving men—
One who will never love again.
He who dies won't feel the loss;
She must live and bear the cross.
Fortune holds a tearful hour
For him who'd love the passion flower.

CHORUS

Passion flow'r, the fates have spoken:
You alone must pay the cost.
Passion flow'r, your heart is broken,
Aching for the one you loved and lost.
But angel hands are ever mending
Broken hearts within their pow'r;
Heaven holds a happy ending
For a lonely passion flow'r.

SOME SUNNY DAY

Published. Copyrighted March 25, 1922. Previously registered for copyright as an unpublished song March 10, 1922. Leading recordings by Marion Harris (Columbia) and Paul Whiteman (Victor).

VERSE 1

My heart goes pitter patter;
No one knows what's the matter:
Just received a telegram
From Alabam', my home.
That's why I'm gonna worry
Till the time when I hurry
Right back to that cabin door,
Never more to roam.

CHORUS

Some sunny day,
With a smile on my face,
I'll go back to that place

Far away.
Back to that shack
And that red-headed hen—
She'll say "How have you be'n?"
Then go back to the hay
And lay me my breakfast.
Some sunny day
I'll be on that express
Flying away to my
Little bunch of happiness.
Oh, how I pine
For those lips sweet as wine!
They'll be pressed close to mine
Some sunny day.

VERSE 2

Sunny spring is the season
When birds sing; there's a reason
Rolling stones who hear their song
Begin to long for home.
Lohengrin, Mister Verdi,
Don't begin with a birdie
Telling you to go back home,
Never more to roam.

REPEAT CHORUS

HOMESICK

Published. Copyrighted August 25, 1922. Previously registered for copyright as an unpublished song August 10, 1922. Leading recording by Nora Bayes (Columbia).

VERSE 1

I feel very blue, yes, I do—can't you tell?
Worry quite a lot, 'cause I'm not feeling well.
Friends have come to me
Saying, "We can see
You need company."
But I'm not lonely,
I'm only

CHORUS

Homesick.
I know just what's the matter—
I'm homesick, that's all.
I see that cozy little shack
And the little red school,

Daddy on the back of a funny old mule,
"God Bless Our Home" on the wall,
The fields of clover—
They seem to say,
"Why don't you come over, pay us a call."
I miss the cows and the chickens
And the apple tree shady,
And there's that little old lady—
Do you wonder why I'm homesick?

VERSE 2

My poor heart will stop when I hop off the train,
Such a happy soul when I stroll down the lane.
I can't wait'll then,
To be there again
In the twilight when
The sun is setting,
I'm getting

REPEAT CHORUS

DON'T BLAME IT ALL ON THE MUSIC

Written in 1922. No music is known to survive. In a May 2, 1955, letter to *Variety*'s editor-in-chief, Abel Green, Berlin recalled this song as follows: "If you will go back to some of your 1922 issues, you will find that there was an awful lot of noise made about jazz being the cause of the 'cheek to cheek' dancing at the time. I remember writing a special material song called 'Don't Blame It All on the Music' which was never published."

VERSE

The people who believe that modern dancing is a
    shame
Are saying jazzy music is entirely to blame.*
I don't approve or disapprove of how they dance
    today,
But if there's cause for criticism, I'd like to say:

CHORUS 1

Don't blame it all on the music,
Because the music is not to blame.

Earlier version of lines 1 and 2:
    If you will read your paper, you will notice that it has
    A lot of things to say about the people who jazz.

If you took all the benches out of Central Park,
The park would still be crowded when the night is
    dark.
Don't blame the saxophones. If Mary Jones
Gets a thrill by shaking ev'rything she owns,
She would get just as far
If you played a guitar
Or without any music at all.

CHORUS 2

Don't blame it all on the music,
Because the music is not to blame.
There was no jazzy music back in history;
Still Cleopatra made a mark of Antony.
They had no saxophones with jazzy tones
When the people lived in houses made of stones;
And those cave-dwelling men
They were much wilder then
Without any music at all.

TOO MANY SWEETHEARTS

Published in a black-and-white professional edition.
Copyrighted March 23, 1923. Previously registered for
copyright as an unpublished song February 7, 1923. The
verse is the same as the second verse to "Little Butter-
fly" (page 209).

VERSE

Butterfly, take warning while you may:
Youth only lasts a day,
Blossoms and fades away.
There will come a morning when you'll cry,
Poor little butterfly—
You know the reason why.

CHORUS

Too many sweethearts
Call you their sweetheart,
But when your day is done,
You'll wish that you had only one;
For someday you may be nobody's baby—
Instead of many,
You'll find you won't have any
Sweetheart at all.

TELL ME WITH A MELODY

Published in a black-and-white professional edition.
Copyrighted May 11, 1923. Previously registered for
copyright as an unpublished song April 23, 1923. Writ-
ten for the London production of the *Music Box Revue*.
(Palace Theatre; May 15, 1923; 119 performances). In-
troduced by Ethelind Terry and Gregory Stroud. It
replaced "Say It with Music," which had already become
very well known in England after being heard in
the Charles B. Cochran revue *Mayfair and Mont-
martre* (1922).

VERSE

The world goes round to the sound of a love song;
Love goes hand and hand with a sweet refrain.
A girl will part with her heart for a love song,
Telling her what words never could explain.

CHORUS

Tell me
With a melody,
With a love song—
Tell me
That you care for me.
If you want to win my petting,
Wrap your loving in a dreamy musical setting.
Woo me
With a pretty tune;
Sing a love song
To me
While we sit and spoon.
If you would cast a spell
Around the things you tell,
Tell me with a pretty melody.

TELL ALL THE FOLKS IN KENTUCKY (I'M COMIN' HOME)

Published. Copyrighted August 28, 1923. Previously
registered for copyright as an unpublished song Au-
gust 2, 1923.

VERSE 1

So you're goin' back to Kentucky?
Let me say that you're mighty lucky.

Gee, I wish I were you—
I would like to go too.
Time for leavin' is gettin' shorter;
Give your grip to the Pullman porter.
You're very anxious, I see—
Please do a favor for me.

CHORUS

Tell all the folks down at home in Kentucky
That I'm comin';
Say that a lonely old rollin' stone
Wants to come home.
And don't forget to tell those darkies
To keep their banjos strummin'—
I'd like to have them welcome me
With a Dixie melody.
Oh, how I long to be back in Kentucky
With my mammy!
Oh, how I wish that I never had started to roam!
I feel so blue I could almost cry.
Here comes your train—goodbye.
Tell all the folks down home in Kentucky
That I'm comin' home.

VERSE 2

You'll be very glad in Kentucky;
No one's ever sad in Kentucky.
It's a land without care;
Sunshine follows you there.
Flocks of bluebirds are always singing;
Happiness they are always bringing.
You will forget how to cry
When you get back to K-Y.

REPEAT CHORUS

THE HAPPY NEW YEAR BLUES

Published in a black-and-white professional edition.
Copyrighted January 16, 1924. Previously registered for
copyright as an unpublished song January 3, 1924. Pos-
sibly intended for the *Third Annual Music Box Revue*
(1923). Berlin remembered it somewhat differently. In a
May 20, 1965, letter to Paul Hollister, Berlin recalled that
"I originally wrote this for the second *Music Box Revue*
[1922], but never got around to using it. It was one of
Bob Sherwood's favorites, and still is one of mine." See
note for "Manhattan Madness" (page 277).

Out in the street hear that beat of a drum—
It's twelve o'clock and the New Year has come.
Just hear them yell as they welcome the news!
I should be glad but I'm not, 'cause I'm sad,
'Cause I've got the Happy New Year Blues.
The very first of each January keeps getting
    worse,
'Cause I have to carry one more year
With nobody near who feels just the same as I.
A wedding ring, a sweet bridal bouquet,
And ev'rything, I know, would be OK,
But each day it's further away,
And my, how the time does fly!
Counting the days until
Someone gives me their sympathy,
Hoping to get a thrill
From one who'll get a thrill from me,
Year after year I grow older;
Soon they all will be gone—
Going through life with no shoulder
To lay my head upon.
Out in the street the crowd walking,
Shouting a hip hurray,
Filling the night with loud talking;
I seem to hear them say:
"Here comes old Father Time
Bringing plenty of happy news."
Ev'ryone's glad while I'm singing
The Happy New Year Blues.
"Ring out the old year and ring in the new"
Means nothing to someone who feels so blue.
There goes my phone, but it's not happy news;
Central is ringing my phone just to wish me
A very Happy New Year Blues.

WHAT'LL I DO?

Published. Copyrighted March 10, 1924. Previously registered for copyright February 21, 1924. Written in Palm Beach, Florida, where Berlin was vacationing with E. Ray Goetz. In an article that appeared in the Boston *Daily Globe* (October 5, 1954), Berlin said: "Sometimes music comes first like 'What'll I Do?' That began as a musical phrase and I had to work hard to find the words to fit the melody." Recording by Paul Whiteman and His Orchestra (Victor) was number one on the popular music charts. Added to the score of the *Third Annual Music Box Revue* in March 1924, where it was sung by Grace Moore and John Steel. Introduced to London by Norah Blaney in *The Punch Bowl* (Duke of York's Theatre; May 21, 1924).

VERSE 1

Gone is the romance that was so divine;
'Tis broken and cannot be mended.
You must go your way and I must go mine,
But now that our love dreams have ended,

CHORUS

What'll I do
When you are far away
And I am blue,
What'll I do?
What'll I do
When I am wond'ring who
Is kissing you,
What'll I do?
What'll I do
With just a photograph
To tell my troubles to,
When I'm alone
With only dreams of you
That won't come true,
What'll I do?

VERSE 2

Do you remember a night filled with bliss?
The moonlight was softly descending.
Your lips and my lips were tied with a kiss,
A kiss with an unhappy ending.

REPEAT CHORUS

LAZY

Published. Copyrighted March 19, 1924. Previously registered for copyright as an unpublished song February 21, 1924. Leading recordings by Al Jolson (Brunswick), Blossom Seeley (Columbia), Paul Whiteman (Victor), and the Brox Sisters (Victor). Sung by Bing Crosby in the film musical *Holiday Inn* (1942). Marc Connelly, in his memoir *Voices Off Stage* (New York: Holt, Rinehart & Winston, 1968; pp. 79–80), recalled that he and George S. Kaufman wrote a play titled *The Deep Tangled Wildwood*. "Our play quickly faded from the public memory," Connelly wrote, "but the title stayed alive in the words of Irving Berlin's popular 'Lazy.' If you ever sang:

> I wanna peep
> Through the deep
> Tangled wildwood
> Counting sheep

'Till I sleep
Like a child would

you may have thought Berlin had Samuel Woodworth in mind."

VERSE 1

Ev'ry time I see a puppy
Upon a summer's day,
A puppy dog at play,
My heart is filled with envy—
That's because my heart is yearning
To pass the time away
Like that pup, 'cause I'm all fed up,
And tho' it's wrong to be,
I long to be

CHORUS

Lazy—
I want to be lazy.
I long to be out
In the sun
With no work
To be done,
Under that awning
They call the sky,
Stretching and yawning,
And let the world go drifting by.
I wanna peep
Through the deep
Tangled wildwood,
Counting sheep
Till I sleep
Like a child would,
With a great big valise full
Of books to read where it's peaceful
While I'm
Killing time
Being lazy.

VERSE 2

Life is short and getting shorter
With each day that goes by,
And how the time does fly!
Before you know it's over.
That's why I'm in such a hurry
To pack my things and fly
To a spot where it's nice and hot
And hear the birdies sing
While I'm being

REPEAT CHORUS

WE'LL ALL GO VOTING FOR AL

Published in a black-and-white professional edition. Copyrighted May 16, 1924. Previously registered for copyright as an unpublished song April 10, 1924. Written for New York governor Alfred E. Smith's 1924 campaign for the Democratic nomination for President. Apparently, Berlin auditioned the song for Franklin Delano Roosevelt, Smith's campaign manager. Roosevelt okayed the song, but it was never used, because Al Smith did not win the Democratic Party's nomination. Berlin also was believed to have written special lyrics for Smith to the tune of "East Side, West Side," but they do not survive.

VERSE 1

The bands will all be playing
As we go hip-hooraying,
Inviting ev'rybody to come along—
With ev'rybody cheering
We'll go electioneering
And sing the chorus of this little song.

CHORUS

In the fall
We'll all go voting for Al;
In the fall
We'll all be there.
In November
We'll remember
To be with Smith—
He's a member
Of the "East Side, West Side."

Ev'ry fellow and gal
From Maine to Texas
They'll mark their X's
In the Democratic circle for Al.

VERSE 2

The White House will be ready;
The room where dear old Teddy
Made history is waiting for our pal.
The servants are preparing
To give the place an airing;
They're dusting off the furniture for Al.

REPEAT CHORUS

ALL ALONE

Published. Copyrighted September 9, 1924. Previously registered for copyright as an unpublished song August 15, 1924. Berlin wrote this song over a period of several weeks while he was in Atlantic City, New Jersey, in the summer of 1924 starting work on the songs for the *Fourth Music Box Revue*. Remarkably, recordings of "All Alone" by three different artists—Al Jolson (Brunswick), Paul Whiteman and His Orchestra (Victor), and John McCormack (Victor) reached the top of the popular music charts. Interpolated into the *Third Music Box Revue*'s post-Broadway tour, where it was first presented to theatre audiences by John Steel and Ruth Thomas. By March 1925 Grace Moore and Oscar Shaw were singing it during the New York run of the *Fourth Annual Music Box Revue*. Introduced to London by Norah Blaney in *The Punch Bowl* (third edition, March 1925). Sung by Alice Faye in the film musical *Alexander's Ragtime Band* (1938).

VERSE 1

Just like the melody that lingers on,
You seem to haunt me night and day.
I never realized till you had gone
How much I cared about you—
I can't live without you.

CHORUS

All alone,
I'm so all alone;
There is no one else but you.
All alone
By the telephone,
Waiting for a ring,
A ting-a-ling,
I'm all alone ev'ry evening,
All alone feeling blue,
Wond'ring where you are
And how you are
And if you are
All alone too.

VERSE 2

Just for a moment you were mine, and then
You seemed to vanish like a dream.
I long to hold you in my arms again;
My life is very lonely,
For I want you only.

REPEAT CHORUS

Newlyweds Ellin and Irving Berlin

Songs of 1925–1926

REMEMBER

Published. Copyrighted July 27, 1925. Previously registered for copyright as an unpublished song on February 26, 1925, under the title "Remember" and again on March 26, 1925, under the title "You Forgot to Remember." Another alternate title: "Remember (You Forgot To)." This song took several months to achieve wide acclaim. Berlin's partner Max Winslow believed in the song, and by the end of 1925 it became one of Berlin's most successful ballads. The first recording to become popular was by Jean Goldkette and His Orchestra (Victor), which featured a vocal by Seymour Simon and Tommy Dorsey on trombone. In mid-December 1925 the recording by Isham Jones and His Orchestra (Brunswick) became the number-one seller in America.

VERSE 1

One little kiss,
A moment of bliss,
Then hours of deep regret.
One little smile
And after a while
A longing to forget.
One little heartache
Left as a token,
One little plaything
Carelessly broken.

CHORUS

Remember the night,
The night you said,
"I love you,"
Remember?
Remember you vowed
By all the stars
Above you,
Remember?
Remember we found a lonely spot
And after I learned to care a lot
You promised that you'd forget me not,
But you forgot to remember.

VERSE 2

Into my dreams
You wandered, it seems,
And then there came a day
You loved me too,
My dreams had come true,
And all the world was May.
But soon the Maytime
Turned to December;

You had forgotten—
Do you remember?

REPEAT CHORUS

HE DOESN'T KNOW WHAT IT'S ALL ABOUT

Published. Copyrighted November 6, 1925. Previously registered for copyright as an unpublished song April 22, 1925.

VERSE

I've got a beau so very slow—
Gee, but he makes me cross!
My Romeo don't seem to know
That he's a total loss.
He has lips that I adore,
But he don't know what they're for.

CHORUS 1

He's just as handsome as could be,
But he doesn't know what it's all about.
He lets me sit upon his knee,
But he doesn't know what it's all about.
He's got the face and form of Apollo,
The kind of man the women all follow,
But when I pucker up my lips and pout,
He doesn't know what it's all about.
He comes around and holds my hand,
But he doesn't know what it's all about.
I've tried to make him understand,
But he doesn't know what it's all about.

CHORUS 2

I plan to see him all alone,
But he doesn't know what it's all about.
I disconnect my telephone,
But he doesn't know what it's all about.
He comes around at night and he's handsome,
But if you ever looked through the transom,
It wouldn't take you long to figure out
He doesn't know what it's all about.
He sits with me till break of dawn,
But he doesn't know what it's all about.
I stretch my arms and start to yawn,
But he doesn't know what it's all about.

ALWAYS

Published. Copyrighted September 16, 1925. Previously registered for copyright as an unpublished song July 2, 1925. Given as a wedding present by Berlin to his bride Ellin Mackay. (They were married January 4, 1926.) According to a notation by Berlin on the earliest known piano-vocal manuscript of the song—found among his papers and now in the Irving Berlin Collection of the Music Division of the Library of Congress—"Always" was written in Atlantic City in July 1925. Yet there is evidence that composition was begun even earlier. A notation on a Berlin copyright card indicates that the title "Always" was registered with the Music Publishers Protection Association (MPPA) on May 28, 1925.

The lyric on that earliest piano-vocal manuscript, as Berlin mentioned in an undated contemporary article, was intended to be a "dummy," or temporary lyric:

I'll belong to you
Always
Will you love me too
Always
Should there come a day
When the sky is gray
Love will find a way
Always.
Always
In the spring or fall
Always
At your beck and call
Always
Not for just an hour
Not for just a day
Not for just a year
But always.

In discussing those last four lines—the only lines carried over to the final version—Berlin told an unnamed newspaper, "Those were the dummy lines—and I really thought at the time that they weren't good enough. Now I believe that without those lines the song would never have been half as popular as it was. Now I think they're just right—but I didn't know at the time."

Over the years it has been frequently but incorrectly claimed that "Always" was written for the musical *The Cocoanuts*. Actually, "Always" was written before Berlin began work on that score. In a letter to Groucho Marx, a star of that show, dated June 2, 1959, he wrote: "Now, regarding my song 'Always' where *The Cocoanuts* is concerned, I didn't write it to be part of the score of this show, but I did write it during that period. I remember singing it for George Kaufman and he didn't seem too enthusiastic." In an earlier letter to Marx (May 23, 1958), Berlin wrote, "Thinking back, if I had put it in the show, I wonder who could have sung it outside of yourself."

According to the Boston *Record* of July 9, 1943, "Always" was introduced by Belle Baker at the Bushwick Theatre in Brooklyn (date unknown). Over the years there have been many successful recordings of the song, two of which became number-one sellers two weeks apart in 1926: the first, by George Olsen and His Orchestra (Okeh), on April 24, and the second, by Vincent Lopez and His Orchestra (Okeh), on May 8.

VERSE

Ev'rything went wrong,
And the whole day long
I'd feel so blue.
For the longest while
I'd forget to smile;
Then I met you.
Now that my blue days have passed,
Now that I've found you at last:

CHORUS

I'll be loving you
Always,
With a love that's true
Always.
When the things you've planned
Need a helping hand,
I will understand
Always, always.
Days may not be fair
Always;
That's when I'll be there
Always—
Not for just an hour,
Not for just a day,
Not for just a year,
But always.

IT'S A WALK-IN WITH WALKER

Published in a black-and-white professional copy. Copyrighted September 17, 1925. Previously registered for copyright as an unpublished song August 29, 1925. A campaign song for James J. Walker, who was elected to his first term as mayor of New York City in November 1925. A printed version of this song appeared "by special arrangement with Irving Berlin Inc. New York City," in the November 1, 1925, issue of *World* magazine. Also see the songs "Jimmy" and "My New York" in the *Ziegfeld Follies of 1927*.

VERSE

Ev'ryone's invited to the City Hall
In the fall—if you call,
There's a royal welcome waiting
One and all
From the mayor's chair.
Will we put him there?

CHORUS

Why, it's a "walk-in" with Walker—
It's a walk-in with Jim!
He's a corker and one of the mob,
A real New Yorker who's fit for the job.
Let the others keep running,
But they're in for a trim
When we walk in with Walker,
For they're all out of step but Jim.

VENETIAN ISLES

Published. Copyrighted October 14, 1925. Previously registered for copyright as an unpublished song September 24, 1925. In late 1931 Berlin set a new lyric to the "Venetian Isles" tune. It became "I'll Miss You in the Evening." Berlin described the origins of "Venetian Isles," which he wrote for a Florida land development, in a February 17, 1956, letter to his friend Irving Hoffman.

> I was paid $25,000.00 to write "Venetian Isles" as a popular song and plug it and the development to adopt it as a theme song with the understanding that after a certain number of years (I think it was five) the tune was returned to me.
>
> It was a good waltz melody, a la the waltzes I was writing then, so I took another try at it with "I'll Miss You in the Evening," but again no dice. . . .
>
> Both songs became part of my large no-hit list.

VERSE 1

There's a sunny land
Calling to me,
Seeming to say,
"Don't you delay."
You would understand
Why I'm gloomy,
Why I'm so blue,
If you but knew.

CHORUS

I long to be returning
Back to the Venetian Isles.
A spark of love is burning
Down in the Venetian Isles.
I can see a setting sun across the bay,
And a little lonely one who seems to say,
"Come back, my heart is yearning,"
Down in the Venetian Isles.

VERSE 2

Soon I'm gonna be
Like the daisy
Gazing up high,
Up at the sky.
Can't you picture me
Being lazy
Under a palm,
Peaceful and calm?

REPEAT CHORUS

WE'LL NEVER KNOW

Published May 22, 1926; previously registered for copyright as an unpublished song April 10, 1926. Published again December 19, 1938; previously registered for copyright as an unpublished song November 16, 1938.

VERSE 1

After all these years I can't forget
The happiness that I once knew;
Maybe there's a spark that's burning yet
And filling me with thoughts of you.
Gone is the treasure we found and let go—
Was it worth keeping?
We never will know.

CHORUS

There might have been a sky of blue
For me and you;
We'll never know.
There might have been a garden too,
Where roses grew;
We'll never know.
We might have built a castle high,
For you were young and so was I,
But we just kissed and said goodbye,
And so we'll never know.

VERSE 2

Maybe we had found the thing we sought,
And maybe it was worth the cost,
Leaving it behind without a thought
What happiness we might have lost.
Maybe the rose that we covered with snow
Wanted to blossom;
We never will know.

REPEAT CHORUS

AT PEACE WITH
THE WORLD

Published. Copyrighted May 19, 1926. Previously registered for copyright as an unpublished song April 23, 1926. Written during the Berlins' honeymoon. According to press clippings dated April 28, 1926, Al Jolson overheard the song, memorized it, and sang it at a private dinner on April 27, 1926. He received so many requests for encores that at first he claimed to have written it himself; but later he confessed it had been written by Berlin and that he had promised to keep it a secret until it was broadcast. The song was formally introduced by John Quinlan in early May 1926 in a musical program at the Strand Theatre, New York. According to one report, the song crossed the Atlantic in the *Leviathan*, which sailed from Liverpool to New York; Berlin entrusted the song to the ship's purser during the voyage. Jolson's recording (Brunswick) of May 3, 1926, reached number three on the popular charts.

VERSE

The day is done;
The golden sun
Is sinking behind the blue.
And on its way
It seems to say,
"I'm glad that my work is through."
Night is drawing near;
Stars will soon appear;
Buildings are beginning to light up their windows.
And as for me,
I'm glad to be
At peace with the world with you.

CHORUS

I love to spend the evening
At peace with the world with you:

A cozy room,
A comf'table chair,
And never a care
As long as you're there.
The day may have its worries,
For skies are not always blue;
But when the day has flown,
How sweet to be alone,
At peace with the world,
In the evening with you.

HOW MANY TIMES?

Published. Copyrighted June 21, 1926. Previously registered for copyright as an unpublished song May 20, 1926. Top recording—number three on the popular charts—by Benny Krueger and His Orchestra (Brunswick). Sung by the Brox Sisters in the 1929 film musical *The Time, the Place and the Girl*.

VERSE 1

A fellow and his lady friend
Walking and talking of love;
A moon that has a silvery lining
Is shining above.
The girlie says, "You certainly do like
To coo like a dove."
A nervous youth; a jealous miss
Who wants the truth is asking this:

CHORUS

"How many times have you said 'I love you'?
How many times have you said, 'I'll be true'?
How many wonderful sweeties have you told
  that to?
How many times has a certain feeling
Troubled you so that you hit the ceiling?
How many hands have you held all alone?
How many lips have you pressed to your own?
I'd hate to think that you kissed too many,
But I'd feel worse if you hadn't kissed any.
Please tell me how many times."

VERSE 2

"A certain thing has puzzled me greatly,
Just lately, my dear:
Why does a fellow always get stupid
When Cupid is near?
Although I was the smartest at college,
That knowledge, I fear,

Could never bring a Romeo
The only thing he wants to know:

REPEAT CHORUS

THAT'S A GOOD GIRL

Published. Copyrighted September 26, 1926. Previously registered for copyright as an unpublished song August 18, 1926. Leading recording by Ben Selvin and His Orchestra (Brunswick).

VERSE 1

Sweet little girlie and her beau
Sittin' in the parlor with the lights down low;
Things are progressing mighty slow—
Too much delayin',
Fellow keeps sayin':

CHORUS

"Come on over here
From way over there—
There's nobody near
And room in the chair
For two.
That's a good girl!
You never will miss
A sweet little smack,
So give me a kiss
And I'll give it back
To you.
That's a good girl!
I've got a present here to show you
Before I start to Romeo you:
It's only a ring;
I bought it today—
It don't mean a thing
Unless you will say
'I do.'
That's a good girl!"

VERSE 2

Sweet little girlie tells her beau
That she won't say yes, but then she won't say no.
Things are progressing mighty slow;
Moments are flyin',
Fellow is sighin':

REPEAT CHORUS

BECAUSE I LOVE YOU

Published. Copyrighted September 29, 1926. Previously registered for copyright as an unpublished song August 28, 1926. Leading recording by Henry Burr (Victor).

VERSE 1

Why am I lonely and why am I blue,
And why am I thinking, just thinking of you?
Why should I care if you've broken your vow,
And why do I wonder who's kissing you now?

CHORUS

Because I love you—
I've tried so hard but can't forget.
Because I love you—
You linger in my mem'ry yet.
Because I miss you—
I often wish we'd never met.
And though you left a tear
As a souvenir,
It doesn't matter, dear,
Because I love you.

VERSE 2

"Off with the old love and on with the new"
Is easy to say but not easy to do.
What does it matter how far we're apart?
You're out of my life, dear, but still in my heart.

REPEAT CHORUS

I'M ON MY WAY HOME

Published. Copyrighted October 5, 1926. Previously registered for copyright as an unpublished song August 28, 1926.

VERSE 1

I was blue and melancholy,
And I knew that it was folly
To be feeling so sad
When I ought to be glad.
So I sent a little letter;
Off it went—I'm feeling better:

Got an answer today,
Ev'rything's okay.

CHORUS

Why is the sun shining brighter?
I'm on my way home,
I'm on my way home.
Why is my heart feeling lighter?
I'm on my way home,
I'm on my way home.
Why did I buy something nice at the store,
Something that she'll adore?
Can't you guess who it's for?
It's for someone with hair growing whiter,
Who's happy because I'm on my way home.

VERSE 2

Not so sweet are things that you chew
When you eat upon a choo-choo;
They keep opening cans—
I've got different plans:
When it's time to get to supper,
I'll just climb into an upper
Till the morning, and then

PATTER

I've been shopping and I'll put you wise;
I've got packages of ev'ry size.
Here's a half a dozen knitted ties
For my brother and another.
Here's a parasol that's very plain
For my pretty little sister Jane.
Here's a nifty little walking cane
For my father,
But I'd rather not tell you what
But there's one package more
That I bought at the store.
Can't you guess who it's for?
It's for someone with hair growing whiter,
Who's happy because I'm on my way home.

MY BABY'S COME BACK TO ME

Registered for copyright as an unpublished song August 28, 1926. Lyric is missing.

JUST A LITTLE LONGER

Published. Copyrighted October 19, 1926. Previously registered for copyright as an unpublished song September 30, 1926. Probably written in August 1926. Major recordings by Phil Spitalny and His Orchestra (Victor), Fred Rich and His Orchestra (Columbia), and Rudy Vallee (Victor).

VERSE 1

Hold me fast, for the time has passed
And we have to say goodbye;
In my arms let me hold your charms
While the precious moments fly.
How I hate to go, for I love you so!
Let me gaze in your eyes, and then
Lonely days till we meet again,
So

CHORUS

Just a little longer
Let me hold you close to my heart,
And that little longer
I'll remember while we're apart.
Just another moment of bliss
And just another wonderful kiss;
My love keeps growing stronger
Lingering longer with you.

VERSE 2

Soon, I know, I must let you go,
From my arms, where you belong,
Leaving me with a memory
Of an interrupted song.
It will linger on after you have gone.
Hold me fast while we kiss, and then
It's the last till we meet again,
So

REPEAT CHORUS

BLUE SKIES

Published January 14, 1927. Previously registered for copyright as an unpublished song December 27, 1926. Written, according to copyright cards in the Berlin office, on or about December 16, 1926. Introduced by Belle Baker in the Ziegfeld production *Betsy* (New Amsterdam Theatre, New York; December 28, 1926; 39 performances), whose score was otherwise written by Richard Rodgers and Lorenz Hart. Al Jolson sang it in *The Jazz Singer* (1927), the first talking picture. While the song may have always been intended for Belle Baker, it certainly was not written overnight to rescue *Betsy*, which was first presented at the National Theatre, Washington, D.C., on December 20–25, 1926. Top-selling recordings by Ben Selvin and His Orchestra (Columbia) and George Olsen and His Orchestra (Victor). Sung by Bing Crosby in the musical film *Blue Skies* (1946). More recently—1978—the song received a successful recording by Willie Nelson.

VERSE 1

I was blue,
Just as blue as I could be;
Ev'ry day
Was a cloudy day for me.
Then good luck
Came a-knocking at my door;
Skies were gray,
But they're not gray anymore.

CHORUS

Blue skies
Smiling at me
Nothing but blue skies
Do I see.

Bluebirds
Singing a song,
Nothing but bluebirds
All day long.
Never saw the sun
Shining so bright,
Never saw things
Going so right.
Noticing the days
Hurrying by—
When you're in love,
My, how they fly!
Blue days,
All of them gone—
Nothing but blue skies
From now on.

VERSE 2

I should care
If the wind blows east or west;
I should fret
If the worst looks like the best;
I should mind
If they say it can't be true;
I should smile—
That's exactly what I do.

REPEAT CHORUS

Parody version

Written on June 5, 1975. The lyric refers, of course, to the discomfort the younger Richard Rodgers and Lorenz Hart must have felt when Ziegfeld interpolated "Blue Skies" by the veteran Berlin into *Betsy* (1926)—especially since it became the hit of the show.

"Blue Skies," we'd like to know
Why is that "Blue Skies" in our show?
Ziegfeld, tell him we're sore
Putting that "Blue Skies" in our score.
Never saw a more happier crowd,
Cheering the song, clapping so loud;
Though we don't enjoy making a fuss,
Why should this thing happen to us?
"Blue Skies," wish it was gone—
Curses on Berlin from now on!

The Marx Brothers

THE COCOANUTS | 1925–1926

THE COCOANUTS (1925–1926)

Tryout: Tremont Theatre, Boston, Massachusetts, October 26, 1925, and Forrest Theatre, Philadelphia, November 23, 1925. New York run: Lyric Theatre; December 8, 1925; 375 performances. Return engagement: Century Theatre, New York; May 16, 1927; 16 performances. Music and lyrics by Irving Berlin. Produced by Sam H. Harris. Book by George S. Kaufman. Directed by Oscar Eagle. Musical numbers staged by Sammy Lee. Orchestrations by Frank Tours, Maurice de Packh, and Stephen Jones. Orchestra under the direction of Frank Tours. Cast: starring the Marx Brothers (Groucho, Chico, Harpo, and Zeppo) and featuring George Hale, Frances Williams, Margaret Dumont, Henry Whittemore, Janet Velie, Mabel Withee, Jack Barker, Bernice Speer, Boris Ruysdael, Antonio and Nina De Marco, and the Breen Brothers. London production: Garrick Theatre; March 20, 1928; 16 performances.

FLORIDA BY THE SEA

Published. Copyrighted November 10, 1925. Previously registered for copyright as an unpublished song August 12, 1925. Introduced by Zeppo Marx (Jamison) and ensemble. Originally it was the opening number of Act I. Soon after the New York opening it became the sixth number, following "A Little Bungalow."

VERSE

Down in the land of cocoanuts
Before the welcome season shuts
A million million-dollar-huts will be found.
Down in the land where the trees are tall,
We're asking you to pay a call
And live where it is summer all the year round.
Buy a lot,
Any piece
That we've got
Will increase
Ev'ry season;
Ask us why
Ev'ryone
Wants to lie
In the sun;
There's a reason.
One little ride in a Pullman car,
A night and day and there you are—
Come on, it's time you should be Florida bound.

CHORUS

In the lovely land of Florida,
Sunny Florida by the sea—
All the sunshine in America
Is in Florida, you'll agree.
When they're freezing up north,
Sneezing up north,
Always it's July the Fourth
In the lovely land of Florida,
Sunny Florida by the sea.

PATTER (NOT IN PUBLISHED VERSION)

ZEPPO: How many lots have you sold today?
BOYS: The crowds don't seem to come our way.
ZEPPO: Perhaps you don't know what to say to the crowds.
BOYS: We tell them all that the sun is here.
ZEPPO: But do you say it is here all year?
BOYS: We try to make that very clear to the crowds.
ZEPPO: Every lot,
Any piece
That we've got,
Will increase
Every season.
BOYS: That's just what
They were told.
That they're not
To be sold,
What's the reason?
ZEPPO: I've got a plan and it can't go wrong.
BOYS: Perhaps your plan will help along.
ZEPPO: Why don't you sing this little song to the crowd?

THE GUESTS and THE BELL HOP

These linked numbers, introduced by Zeppo Marx (Jamison), George Hale (Eddie), and ensemble, became the opening sequence soon after the New York opening. "The Bell Hop" also was variously known as "The Bellhops" and "Bellboy Opening."

The Guests

So this is Florida,
Where flow'rs are blooming,
The sunny land where
Ev'rybody thinks they're swell.

So this is Florida,
Where land is booming
And ev'rybody has a little lot to sell.
The climate is delightful,
The natives tell us so;
But living here is frightful—
We'd like to have you know
That lovely Florida,
The land of sunshine,
Is not so lovely
Stopping at a bum hotel.

The rooms are very beautiful,
They're furnished lovely, but
The service is enough to drive
A cocoa off its nut;
We find that ev'ry bellboy
Is a Johnny-off-the-spot—
Oh, is it *not* a nice hotel,
You bet your life it's not!
So this is Florida—
The land of sunshine
Is not so lovely
Stopping at a bum hotel.

PATTER

ADELE: Is there a note in the box for me?
ZEPPO: There's nothing there that I can see.
BONNIE: I wish you'd let me have my key.
BOY: Would you like to go out
And have a nice walk, dear?
MARGIE: When does the two-thirty train arrive?
ZEPPO: It always gets here after five.
MARGIE: The clerk don't know that he's alive.
BOY: Would you like to go out
And finish our talk, dear?
MAXINE: Where's my trunk?
ZEPPO: There's a wreck.
MAXINE: That's the bank.
ZEPPO: Give the check to the porter.
MAXINE: What's the time?
ZEPPO: Nearly three.
MAXINE: Here's a dime.
ZEPPO: Pardon me, try a quarter.
FLOSSIE: I'll tell the world it's a bum hotel.
MARGIE: No wonder it's not doing well.
ADELE: The whole day long you'll hear us yelling
With all our might:
ENSEMBLE: Service! Service!
ADELE: Day and night.
ENSEMBLE: Service! Service!
ZEPPO: Don't get nervous.
ENSEMBLE: We want service!

[ZEPPO *rings bell eight times.*]

The Bell Hop

VERSE

Listen to the bellboys' little tale of woe—
Morning, noon, and night they keep us on the go,
And bringing ice water to mother and daughter
Is nothing to write home about.
Talk about your dances that have lots of pep,
Nothing is as tiring as the lively step
The people—the bell hop—the busy hotel hop—
The step that is wearing us out.

CHORUS

Jump in your clothes,
Then on your toes
Doing the bell hop.
All out of breath,
We're worked to death
Doing the bell hop.
And oh, the man who made a million in cotton,
Oh, will go and leave a lot o' forgotten
Jerrys and Toms
With empty palms
Doing the bell hop all day.

PATTER

BELLBOYS 1–4: The gentleman in ninety-four
Has ordered once or twice—
He wants the morning papers
And a highball glass of ice.
BELLBOYS 5–8: Go tell the man in parlor A
Who left a call for ten
It's only twenty after eight
But you'll be back again.
BELLBOYS 9–12: Go tell the girl in sixty-five
She must turn down the light—
A man across the court
complained
He couldn't sleep all night.
BELLBOYS 13–16: The bridal couple occupying
Eighty-four and -five
Have not been out since
Wednesday—
Go and see if they're alive.

REPEAT CHORUS

A HOTEL OF OUR OWN

Registered for copyright as an unpublished song August 12, 1925, under the title "When We're Running a Little Hotel of Our Own." Introduced in the pre-Broadway (Philadelphia and Boston) tryout by George Hale (Eddie) and Bernice Speer (Tony). Dropped before the New York opening. Alternate title: "Running a Little Hotel of Our Own."

VERSE

HE: My ambition, honey, is to own a hotel.
        I know just the one
        You and I could run.
SHE: Save up all your money and you'll own a
            hotel—
        It's as good as done;
        We'll have lots of fun.

CHORUS 1

When we're running a little hotel of our own,
It will probably be the finest ever known.
We'll advertise that it's
Much nicer than the Ritz,
And our slogan will be "Ev'rything high-tone."
Ev'ry courtesy to the patrons will be shown:
We won't bother them when they want to be alone;
We'll have several clerks, all young and handsome,
Bridal suites without a transom,
In the little hotel of our own.

CHORUS 2

When we're running a little hotel of our own,
It will probably be the finest ever known.
We'll see that ev'ry pair
Arrive with baggage there,
And each chambermaid will have a chaperone.
We'll have plenty of rooms with walls all made of
    stone
For the people who practice on the saxophone;
And the drummer's plans will all be wrecked if
He don't tip the house detective,
In the little hotel of our own.

WITH A FAMILY REPUTATION

Printed in a professional edition only. Registered for copyright as an unpublished song August 12, 1925. In-
troduced by Mabel Withee (Polly) and ensemble. Alternate title (program): "Family Reputation." Earlier title: "My Family Reputation."

VERSE 1

My ancestors were shrewd investors,
Making millions at speculation;
When they counted their gold, they mounted
On the high horse of reputation.
Now it seems I've inherited
A responsibility;
Though it never was merited,
I must act accordingly.

CHORUS 1

With a family reputation,
Oh, you can't do this,
And you musn't do that.
What an awful situation
When you can't do this,
And you mustn't do that!
I'm looking for a Washington who'll agree
To come and chop down my family tree.
Oh, my family reputation
Is making a wreck of me!

VERSE 2

In a restaurant, should a debutante
Depart from the dull convention?
Scandal papers review her capers
With a curt little hurtful mention.
But the pretty stenographer
When she starts to slip a bit,
There's no spying photographer,
And she gets away with it.

CHORUS 2

With a family reputation
You must sacrifice
What is naughty but nice.
You must say no to temptation
Though you must confess
That you'd rather say yes.
The others have been doing for months and
    months
The things that I'd like to try just once;
For my family reputation
Is making a wreck of me.

Alternate version

Prepared "for print" by music editor Albert Sirmay

VERSE

My ancestors were shrewd investors,
Making millions in speculation;
When they counted their gold, they mounted
On the high horse of reputation.
There's no doubt it was merited,
But the thing that bothers me
Is I'm supposed to inherit it
And act accordingly.

CHORUS

With my family reputation
You can't do this,
And you mustn't do that.
There's a certain elevation
That goes with the wealth
Of the past generation.
Washington, won't you hear my plea?
Come and chop down my family tree,
For my family reputation
Is making a wreck of me!

WHY AM I A HIT WITH THE LADIES?

Introduced by Groucho Marx (Henry W. Schlemmer) and female ensemble. Alternate title—"A Hit with the Ladies."

VERSE 1

At the early age of four
I had nurses by the score;
They were all so fond of me,
Wouldn't take a salary.
That's how I began as a ladies' man—
It continues ev'ry season,
Though I hardly know the reason.

CHORUS 1

Why am I a hit with the ladies?
Tell me, why do I just fit with the ladies?
They go wild over me—
Oh, what can it be?
Now is it my figure or my personality?
Why am I the center attraction
When I never even try?
If they're cold as could be,

With one look at me they seem to fry—
I wonder why.

VERSE 2

I'm not what you'd call a dude;
Still it seems that I'm pursued
By a dozen on my staff
Asking for my autograph.
I keep signing checks
For the weaker sex;
Juliets who hardly know me
Whisper, "Won't you Romeo me?"

CHORUS 2

Why do I appeal to the ladies?
Tell me, why am I ideal for the ladies?
Tell me, is it the meal,
The automobile,
Or is it my dancing or my fatal sex appeal?
Why am I the center attraction?
Any time I start to buy,
While I'm paying the check
They hang on my neck, just like a tie—
I wonder why.

A LITTLE BUNGALOW

Published. Copyrighted November 10, 1925. Previously registered for copyright as an unpublished song August 12, 1925. Introduced by Jack Barker (Bob), Mabel Withee (Polly), and ensemble.

VERSE 1

HE: If you told me that I'm the lucky young man,
From that moment I'd know my future began.
I'd get busy attending
To the happy ending—
Let me tell you about my wonderful plan.

CHORUS

A little bungalow,
An hour or so
From anywhere;
A little cozy nest,
The kind that's best for two,
Among the shady trees,
With birds and bees
And lots of air
And just enough o' ground
To fool around with you.

Away from all the crowds,
We'll watch the clouds
Go drifting by;
And when the moon above
Presents a lovely view,
There'll be a room in blue,
The one that you would occupy—
It's understood that I would occupy it too.

VERSE 2

SHE: If you're anxious to make me part of your plan,
I'm quite ready to tell the world that you can.
If the plan that you're laying
Just needs my okaying,
Don't let anyone try to stop you, young man.

REPEAT CHORUS

THE MONKEY-DOODLE-DOO

Published. Copyrighted November 10, 1925. Previously registered for copyright as an unpublished song August 14, 1925. (This is not the same song as the "Monkey Doodle Doo" published in 1913). Introduced by George Hale (Eddie), the Breen Brothers, and ensemble.

VERSE

Monkeys upon a tree
Never are
Very blue;
They never seem to be
Under par,
That is true,
Not like the ones you see
On a bar
In the zoo.
Monkeys upon a tree
Do the Monkey-Doodle-Doo.

CHORUS

Oh, among the mangoes
Where the monkey gang goes,
You can see them do
The little Monkey-Doodle-Doo.
Oh, a little monkey
Playing on his one key
Gives them all the cue
To do the Monkey-Doodle-Doo.

Let me take you by the hand
Over to the jungle band;
If you're too old for dancing,
Get yourself a monkey gland,
And then let's go, my little dearie,
There's the Darwin the'ry
Telling me and you
To do the Monkey-Doodle-Doo.

PATTER

We did the Turkey Trot, the Grizzly Bear,
The Bunny Hug, and everywhere
The Texas Tommy was so popular for a year or two.
We used to Ball the Jack and Camel Walk,
The Eagle Rock was all the talk,
The Lazy Lame Duck and the Tango were danced
   when they were new.
We used to do the Hula-Hoo,
And quite a few would Shimmy too,
And now the Charleston we've got, so hot,
The Oceana Roll, the Peacock Strut;
To Walk the Dog was lovely too:
They don't compare with what we're calling
The Monkey-Doodle-Doo.

Alternate patter

Turkey Trot, Grizzly Bear,
Bunny Hug everywhere,
Texas Tommy,
Ball the Jack, Camel Walk,
Eagle Rock, all the talk;
Lazy Lame Duck,
Hula-Hoo,
Shimmy too,
And now the Charleston—Hey, hey! Ho, ho!
The Oceana Roll, the Peacock Strut,
Walk the Dog—over the top,
Now get ready for the monkey's little Monkey-
   Doodle-Doo.

LUCKY BOY

Published. Copyrighted November 16, 1925. Previously registered for copyright as an unpublished song August 12, 1925. Introduced by Jack Barker (Bob) and ensemble.

VERSE 1

Your smiling face is an open book, young man;
We know that look, young man—

You must be oh so happy.
It's just a case of a love that took, young man;
There are quite a few
Who envy you.

CHORUS 1

Lucky boy,
She's a beautiful thing.
Lucky boy,
You will give her a ring.
Lucky boy,
We suppose in the spring
You will take your pride and joy
On a train,
And her leather suitcase
Will contain
Bits of satin and lace—
It's as plain
As the nose on your face—
How we envy you,
Lucky boy!

VERSE 2

I must confess that you pave the way for me;
You really say for me
The things I want to tell you.
You'll never guess what a lucky day for me
When I found that she
Had chosen me.

CHORUS 2

Lucky boy,
She's a beautiful thing.
Lucky boy,
I'm as proud as a king.
Lucky boy,
When I give her the ring,
Can't you see me jump with joy?
With a cheer
And "Whatta we care?"
We'll appear
In a bungalow where
In a year may be three of us there.
How we envy you,
Lucky boy.

Earlier version of verse 2

You needn't guess, but go out and say for me—
Go pave the way for me
And tell the world I'm happy:
She answered "Yes"—what a lucky day for me
When I found that she
Had chosen me!

Reprise (not used in show)

VERSE

I saw you dancing around last night, young man,
You held her tight, young man,
And I could see she liked it.
No one need tell you that you're in right, young
   man—
There were quite a few
Who envied you.

CHORUS

Lucky boy,
She's a beautiful thing.
Lucky boy,
Did you give her that ring?
Lucky boy,
I suppose in the spring
You will take your pride and joy
On a train
And her leather suitcase
Will contain
Something covered with lace—
It's as plain
As the nose on your face—
How I envy you,
Lucky boy!

FIVE O'CLOCK TEA

Published. Copyrighted December 28, 1925. Previously registered for copyright as an unpublished song October 10, 1925. Introduced by Antonio and Nina De Marco and ensemble.

VERSE

BOYS: Five o'clock in the afternoon
   Means nothing over here,
   But across the sea
   It means a little cup of tea.
GIRLS: It means a cup of tea,
   Does five o'clock across the sea,
BOYS: No one works in the afternoon
   When five o'clock draws near,
   For they all agree
   To have a little cup of tea.
GIRLS: That's when they all agree
   To have a little cup of tea.
BOYS: They go about their labors
   Without a single sound
   And speak well of their neighbors

Till five o'clock comes round;
Then they grab a teacup handle
And they breathe a breath of scandal,
For it seems that custom sets the gossips
    free
To say it with a cup of tea.
GIRLS: It sets the gossips free
To say it with a cup of tea.
BOYS: An ambassador has reached the shore
With a note from Puerto Rico,
But affairs of state will have to wait
For a cup of orange pekoe.
So you see that a cup of tea
Is an awful lot to them and ought to be
An awful lot to you and me.
GIRLS: A little cup of tea
Should mean a lot to you and me.

CHORUS

One o'clock, two o'clock, three o'clock, four
    o'clock,
Five o'clock and we ought to have some tea,
Like the folks across the sea.
Come along, here's a cup,
Won't you please fill it up,
Fill it up for me
With a drop of five o'clock tea?
A cup of oolong is so easy to sip;
You don't have to carry it on your hip.
One o'clock, two o'clock, three o'clock, four
    o'clock,
Five o'clock and we
Should go and have a cup of
L-M-N-O-P-Q-R-S- tea,

GIRLS: A little more or less of
    M-N-O-P-Q-R-S-T-E-A tea.
BOYS: T-E-A tea.

THEY'RE BLAMING THE CHARLESTON

Published. Copyrighted December 22, 1925. Previously registered for copyright as an unpublished song November 25, 1925. Added during the Philadelphia tryout. Introduced by Frances Williams, George Hale (Eddie), Antonio and Nina De Marco, and ensemble. In the "summer edition" of 1926 it was replaced by "Everyone in the World Is Doing the Charleston."

VERSE

Gone are the times
When they blamed all the crimes
On the old cafés.
They used to blame
Ev'rything you could name
On the drinking days.
Drinking is still in season;
But there's another reason
Things that are done
That would make anyone
Feel ashamed today
Are blamed today

CHORUS 1

Upon the Charleston.
They're blaming the Charleston.
What happens at night
That isn't quite right,
It's blamed on the Charleston,
And each reformer
Gets warmer and warmer
When he discovers that his wife has gone
With his best friend, he blames it on
The Charleston.
They tell us that the girls who dare
To do the Charleston
Are going to the Lord knows where;
Instead of blaming
The girls who need taming,
When Mabel and Kate
Refuse to go straight
It's blamed on the Charleston.

CHORUS 2

Upon the Charleston.
They're blaming the Charleston
Whenever a wife
Says "This is the life"
It's blamed on the Charleston.
They love it so much,
That's why they're not home much,
Those high-toned ladies from Fifth Avenue
Who think they're wicked when they do
The Charleston.
The ladies in the big revues
All do the Charleston;
It helps to chase away the blues.
They shake a leg when
Those butter-and-egg men
Come into the hall,
And if they should fall,
It's blamed on the Charleston.

WE SHOULD CARE

Published in two different versions. The first was published November 10, 1925; previously registered for copyright as an unpublished song October 27, 1925. The second was published December 14, 1925; previously registered for copyright as an unpublished song November 25, 1925. The first version was sung during the out-of-town tryout at the Tremont Theatre, Boston, by Jack Barker (Bob), Mabel Withee (Polly), and ensemble. The second version was introduced during the New York run by Barker, Withee, George Hale (Eddie), Bernice Speer (Tony), and ensemble.

First version

VERSE

Whether the day is clear,
Whether it's cloudy, dear,
Let it be any kind of weather—
Never a single fuss,
Nothing can bother us
Long as we agree to be together:

CHORUS

Let the lazy sun refuse to shine,
We should care.
Long as I am yours, and you are mine,
We should care.
Should there come a day
When the sky is gray,
Love is blind, but never mind,
It's bound to find a way.
Business may be bad or may be fine,
We should care,
Just as long as we remain a pair,
For as long as we keep caring,
The world may go on tearing out its hair,
We should care.

Second version

VERSE 1

Whether the day is clear,
Whether it's cloudy, dear,
Let it be blue or gray above,
Never a single fuss,
Nothing can bother us,
Long as we remain in love.

CHORUS

Let the sky
Start to cry,
What does it matter?
Let it pitter-patter,
We should care.
Hand in hand
We can stand
Any old weather
Long as we're together,
We should care.
Let the lazy sun refuse to shine
Long as I am yours and you are mine,
Long as we keep on caring,
The world may go tearing its hair,
We should care.

VERSE 2

Nothing is ever sure,
Happiness can't endure;
Trouble comes creeping up the stairs
That is when things look blue
But if I'm there with you,
And you're there with me, who cares?

REPEAT CHORUS

MINSTREL DAYS

Registered for copyright as an unpublished song October 2, 1925. Introduced by Janet Velie (Penelope) and ensemble.

VERSE

I recall
When I was small
And the minstrels came to town
I was glad
Because my dad
Always used to take me down.
Often my memory strays
Back to those wonderful days.

CHORUS 1

Those good old minstrel days—
My heart is yearning
For those minstrel days.
My thoughts are turning
To those old-fashioned scenes,

Semicircles and tambourines—
It used to be a treat
To hear just why a chicken crossed the street.
Remember when the fellow in the middle
Would ask that riddle
Way back in those minstrel days?

CHORUS 2

Those good old minstrel days,
When McIntyre and Heath were all the craze.
Remember how we laughed at Primrose and West,
Lew Dockstader and all the rest?
They came from near and far
To Eddie Leonard with his "wah-wah-wah."
I wish that I could go and search the heavens
For Georgie Evans
And bring back those minstrel days.

Earlier version of chorus

Those good old minstrel days of long ago,
Those minstrel days we used to know—
Bring back those funny scenes,
Bring back those tambourines.
Before the cabarets and saxophones
Became the craze, old Mr. Bones
Used to tell us why a chicken goes across the
     street,
Back in those minstrel days.

TANGO MELODY

Published. Copyrighted December 23, 1925. Previously registered for copyright as an unpublished song December 10, 1925. Introduced by Janet Velie (Penelope); specialty dance by Antonio and Nina De Marco. Alternate titles: "To a Tango Melody," "A Tango Melody." This song was featured on the soundtrack of the film *The Bad One* (1930), in which Dolores Del Rio sang a few bars of it.

VERSE

Spain!
A lonely refrain,
A glass of champagne,
A heart that is yearning—
Spain!
The story is plain:
A maiden in vain
Awaits his returning.

CHORUS

They met one night
When the moon shone bright,
And they soon romanced
As together they danced
To a tango melody.
He praised her charms
As within his arms
She was held and kissed,
For she couldn't resist,
To a tango melody.
Dawn!
And soon he was gone,
But lingering on
Was a tender memory.
He left a tear
As a souvenir,
For she waits in vain
With a broken refrain
Of a tango melody.

Additional refrain (from script)

Sung by Groucho Marx (Schlemmer) and ensemble.
[MRS. POTTER *enters. Then* SCHLEMMER *enters. They are both dressed in Spanish regalia.* PENELOPE *exits.*]

SCHLEMMER: They met one night
          At a rooster fight
          And they soon romanced
          As she hemmed up his pants
          To a tango melody.
          He praised her charms
          And her manly arms.
          He was held and kissed
          But her lip had a cyst
          From a tango malady.
ENSEMBLE: Dawn!
          And soon he was gone,
          But lingering on
          Was a tender memory.
SCHLEMMER: He left a tear
          In her glass of beer
          As she waits in vain
          With a clog in her drain
          From a tango malady.

THE TALE OF A SHIRT

Music based on the "Habanera" from Georges Bizet's opera *Carmen* (1875), which itself was derived from "El Arreglito" by Sebastian de Yradier, one of Yradier's

Fleurs d'Espagne, published in 1864. Introduced by Basil Ruysdael (Hennessy). Piano specialty by Chico Marx. Harp specialty by Harpo Marx.

HENNESSY: I want my shirt, I want my shirt,
I can't be happy without my shirt!
ENSEMBLE: He wants his shirt, he wants his shirt,
He can't be happy without his shirt!
HENNESSY: I don't want food, I don't want drink,
Because my feelings are more than hurt!
ENSEMBLE: He don't want food, he don't want drink,
He don't want anything except his shirt!
HENNESSY: My shirt! My shirt!
ENSEMBLE: Not his hat and not his tie
And not his shoes covered up with dirt.
HENNESSY: My shirt! My shirt!
ENSEMBLE: Not his coat and not his vest
And not his pants, but he wants his shirt.
HENNESSY: I want my shirt, I want my shirt,
Because my feelings are more than hurt.
ENSEMBLE: He wants his shirt, he wants his shirt,
He don't want anything except his shirt!

[SAM *reveals the shirt*.]

He's got it. He's got it.
He's got it. He's got it.
He's got it. He's got it.
He's got it. He's got it.
HENNESSY: I've got my shirt, thank God I've got my shirt!
I've got my shirt, I've got my shirt.
You'll never know how deeply I was hurt;
I thought that I'd lost my shirt—
'Twas given to me by my brother Bert.
ENSEMBLE: His brother Bert.
HENNESSY: That's why I love this shirt.
My shirt, my shirt, my shirt!
ENSEMBLE: His shirt, his shirt, his shirt.
He has found his shirt,
He has found his shirt!
HENNESSY: Now that I've found my shirt—
ALL: Goodbye!

Version in script

HENNESSY: I want my shirt, I want my shirt.

I can't be happy without my shirt.
PRINCIPALS: He wants his shirt, he wants his shirt.
He can't be happy without his shirt.
HENNESSY: I don't want food, I don't want drink,
Because my feelings are more than hurt.
PRINCIPALS: He don't want food, he don't want drink,
He don't want anything except his shirt,
Except his shirt.
HENNESSY: How can a man be happy without his shirt?
PRINCIPALS: Without his shirt?
HENNESSY
AND POLLY: How, won't you tell me how
Can a fellow flirt
PRINCIPALS: Without his shirt?
HENNESSY: How can a man make love to a pretty skirt
PRINCIPALS: Without his shirt?
HENNESSY
AND POLLY: Oh, life is not worth living
Without his shirt.
PRINCIPALS: Tell us about it, tell us about it.
HENNESSY: Listen, won't you listen
To a story.
CHICO: To the tale of a shirt.
JULIUS: It's a shirt tale—just a shirt tale.
PRINCIPALS: It's the tale—the tale of a shirt.
HENNESSY: I want my shirt.
PRINCIPALS: He wants his shirt.
HENNESSY: I want my shirt.
PRINCIPALS: He wants his shirt.
Not his hat, not his tie, not his shoes
Covered up with dirt—
Not his coat, not his vest, not his pants,
But he wants his shirt.
HENNESSY: I want my shirt.
ALL: He wants his shirt. He wants his shirt.
He won't be happy till he gets his shirt.

[*Business of putting on* HENNESSY's *shirt*.]

ALL: He's got it, he's got it, he's got it, he's got it.
HENNESSY: I've got my shirt.
Thank God I've got my shirt,
I've got my shirt, I've got my shirt.
You'll never know how deeply I was hurt;
I thought that I'd lost my shirt.
It was given to me by my brother Bert;

That's why I love this shirt.
ALL: The beautiful shirt.
HENNESSY: My shirt.
ALL: The wonderful shirt.
HENNESSY: My shirt.
ALL: The beautiful shirt.
HENNESSY: Now that I've found my shirt—
ALL: Goodbye.

WHY DO YOU WANT TO KNOW WHY?

Published. Copyrighted June 28, 1926. Previously registered for copyright as an unpublished song May 20, 1926. Introduced in the 1926 "summer edition" by Jack Barker (Bob), Phyllis Cleveland (Polly), and ensemble. Reprised in the second act by Barker, Cleveland, the Brox Sisters, and ensemble.

VERSE

Ev'ry now and then you ask me why I love you,
Why is it that I'm forever thinking of you?
Ev'ry now and then I pause,
Trying hard to find the cause;
And tho' it's true
That I love you,
It's hard to say just why I do,
But

CHORUS

Why
Do you want to know why?
Does it matter just why I love you
Long as I do?
Hope to die,
I'd be willing to try
But I couldn't tell why,
I only know that I do.
Maybe it's because you came my way
When I was blue;
Maybe it's because I heard you say,
"I'm lonely too."
Maybe away up high
In the blue of the sky
They could tell you just why I love you
Much as I do.

Duet chorus

POLLY: Why?
BOB: Do you want to know why?
POLLY: Doesn't matter just why you love me
Long as you do.
BOB: Yes I do, hope to die.
POLLY: Tell me, why don't you try?
BOB: 'Cause I couldn't tell why—
I only know that I do.
POLLY: Tell me why.
BOB: Maybe it's because you came my way
When I was blue.
POLLY: Maybe it's because you heard me say,
"I'm lonely too."
BOB: Maybe away up high
POLLY: In the blue of the sky
BOB: They could tell you just why I love you
Much as I do.

GENTLEMEN PREFER BLONDES

Published. Copyrighted June 28, 1926. Previously registered for copyright as an unpublished song May 20, 1926. Introduced in the 1926 "summer edition" by Groucho Marx (Schlemmer) and girls. Inspired by the Anita Loos novel of the same name.

VERSE

Girls with golden hair
Seem to have a flair
That makes a kind old gentleman respond.
Since the world began,
Ev'ry gentleman
Is just a man who's gentle to a blonde.

CHORUS 1

The most neglected girls in town
Are those with hair of black or brown,
'Cause gentlemen prefer blondes.
The redheads and the sweet brunettes
Make very lovely household pets,
But gentlemen prefer blondes.
A curly head of yellow
Without any sense
Can always make a fellow
Pay all the expense.
A girlie with a golden crop
Can take the Scotchman out to shop
'Cause gentlemen prefer blondes.

CHORUS 2

A girl with Mary Pickford curls
Will live to see her string of pearls
'Cause gentlemen prefer blondes.
It takes a fairhaired MaryAnn
To catch a Cinderella man
'Cause gentlemen prefer blondes.
Those golden heads that flutter
With so many faults
Make men of eggs and butter
Go down to their vaults.
If you don't think it means a lot,
Just see what Peggy Hopkins got,
'Cause gentlemen prefer blondes.

CHORUS 3

A married redhead or brunette
Will soon discover with regret
That gentlemen prefer blondes.
The hair she finds on hubby's sleeve
When he comes home makes her believe
That gentlemen prefer blondes.
A girl with golden tresses
Who touched up her hair
Is wearing all the dresses
The wife ought to wear.
Peroxide on a lady's dome
Will help to keep her husband home
'Cause gentlemen prefer blondes.

TING-A-LING
THE BELLS'LL RING

Published. Copyrighted June 28, 1926. Previously registered for copyright as an unpublished song on May 20, 1926, and June 15, 1926. Introduced in the 1926 "summer edition" by Jack Barker (Bob), Phyllis Cleveland (Polly), and ensemble. Alternate title: "Ting-a-Ling." According to a newspaper article of June 3, 1926, this song was written in Paris and sent to *Cocoanuts* producer Sam Harris in New York. It was inspired by anticipation of the arrival of the Berlins' first baby.

VERSE 1

HE: I've composed a happy jingle for you, my dear,
And I filled it with conventional rhymes;
It will tell you what I'm thinking, so lend an ear
To my song of love and wedding bell chimes.

CHORUS

Ting-a-ling
The bells'll ring
And as they swing
The crowd'll sing.
The queen and king
Are entering,
So ting-a-ling.
Down the aisle
That seems a mile
We'll walk in style
And try to smile;
Then in a while
A domicile
And ev'rything.
When it's done and two are one forever,
We've begun a life that none can sever.
Ting-a-ling
The bells'll ring
And in the spring
The stork may bring
A tiny thing
That we can swing
To ting-a-ling.

VERSE 2

SHE: I adore the happy jingle you wrote for me,
And I wish I could remember those rhymes;
Maybe I could learn the words and the melody
If I heard it sung a couple of times.

REPEAT CHORUS

EVERYONE IN THE WORLD IS DOING THE CHARLESTON

Published. Copyrighted June 28, 1926. Previously registered for copyright as an unpublished song May 20, 1926. Introduced in the 1926 "summer edition" by the Brox Sisters and girls, with specialty dance by Antonio and Nina De Marco. It replaced "They're Blaming the Charleston." Edwin Knopf, who saw Berlin in Paris in the spring of 1926, remembered him writing a Charleston song for producer Charles B. Cochran; yet there is no evidence that a Berlin Charleston song written for Cochran survives. Knopf's May 7, 1968, letter to Berlin contains an amusing anecdote:

> It was forty-two years ago this spring, in Paris in 1926, that George Gershwin brought me up to your suite at the Crillon. You were working on a revue for Mr. Cochran and had just written "Some-son—of a some-one—took the Charles-ton—into Lon-don and they're all doing it now." (The rest of the lyrics on request.) I, of course, was enormously impressed at being in the presence of genius at work. But George, without taking his cigar from his mouth, said:
>
> "Why do you always establish a theme and then repeat it one-third higher?" And you replied:
>
> "Because I'm just a little Jewish boy from Tin Pan Alley and leave Carnegie Hall to you."

VERSE

I've been trav'ling far and wide
Over on the other side,
And it's strange
What a change
Is happ'ning all around.
Years ago it used to be
Shaking hands across the sea;
Now we meet
Shaking feet,
For that is what I found.

CHORUS

Ev'ryone in the world is doing the Charleston.
They do it in London,
They do it in France;
In Spain and Italy
And in Germany they all Charleston.
No matter how far you roam
Away from home,
You'll find them doing that dance.
That certain step that was all the craze
With those Lenox Avenue sheiks
Is being done by the Portugese,
The Armenians, and the Greeks.
Papers say that most ev'ry day
There's a European
Who sprained his knee in the
Charleston, Charleston,
Because they're all doing it now.

WHEN MY DREAMS COME TRUE

Published. Copyrighted March 12, 1929. Previously registered for copyright as an unpublished song July 27, 1928. Sung in the film version of *The Cocoanuts* (1929) by Mary Eaton and Oscar Shaw.

VERSE

Ever since I met you
All that I seem to do
Is dream wonderful dreams.
Heaven's before my eyes;
When will I realize
My dreams, wonderful dreams?

CHORUS

The skies will all be blue
When my dreams come true,
And I'll be smiling through
When my dreams come true.
That Spanish castle I built in my mind
Will be a love nest, the practical kind,
And I'll be there with you
When my dreams come true.

TAKE 'IM AWAY (HE'S BREAKIN' MY HEART)

Registered for copyright as an unpublished song August 12, 1925. Intended for *The Cocoanuts* but dropped during rehearsals.

VERSE

Feel my pulse,
Does it beat very fast?
Something must be wrong with me, yes, sir,
Ever since I heard the professor
Playing on his fiddle so grand.
Feel my heart,
Do you think it will last
Long as he continues to jazz, sir?
'Cause that melody has, sir,
Something that I never could stand.

CHORUS

Take 'im away, away,
He's breakin' my heart.
People who play that way,
They never should start.
What's that piece that he plays so grand?
It hasn't got any faults.
Make him cease,
'Cause I just can't stand it—
Bring me my smelling salts.
Oh! Take 'im away, away,
Whoever you are.
Take 'im away,
But don't you take 'im too far.
What'll I do, 'cause it's gettin' me,
That melody blue is upsettin' me.
So take 'im away, away,
'Cause he's breakin' my heart.

WHAT'S THERE ABOUT ME?

Registered for copyright as an unpublished song August 12, 1925. Intended for *The Cocoanuts* but dropped during rehearsals. This song evolved into "Why Am I a Hit with the Ladies?"

VERSE

At the early age of four
I had nurses by the score;
They were all so fond of me,
Wouldn't take a salary.
Ever since, I've been a treat
To the female eye,
Stopping traffic on the street—
I wonder why.

CHORUS

What's there about me
That makes the ladies hang around?
There's always a gang around.
They seem to hound me, surround me,
No matter what time it is,
Or whatever the climate is,
The reason that I'm it is,
I really shouldn't say, but—
Why is it
When I visit
Most any public place
I'm followed
And soon swallowed
By satin, silk, and lace?

I've been caressed
By the best of femininity
In this vicinity—
I wonder why.

CAN'T YOU TELL?

Registered for copyright as an unpublished song December 11, 1925. Alternate title: "Can You Tell?" Possibly intended for *The Cocoanuts*.

VERSE

Listen, honey, I've been told
That you think I'm getting cold
Just 'cause I never sigh
When you hold my hand.
You say that I've changed my mind—

Honey dear, you must be blind;
Why you say I'm that way
I can't understand.

CHORUS 1

Must I feel very blue
Like the sad babies do
Just to prove I love you—
Can't you tell?
Must I bill and coo just like a turtle dove
Just to prove to you I'm head and heels in love?
Must I sit by the phone
Singing "I'm all alone,"
Full of mush,
Till I'm thrown in a cell
Just to prove I mean to do right by our Nell?
When you gaze in my eyes, can't you tell?

CHORUS 2

Must I feel very blue
Like the sad babies do

Just to prove I love you—
Can't you tell?
Just to prove to you exactly how I feel,
Must I cough myself to death just like Camille?
Must I be on the spot
With the love that I've got
When I'm tired and I'm not feeling well?*
Every time I kiss you must I ring the bell?
When you gaze in my eyes, can't you tell?

---

*Alternate version of lines 7–9:
    Must I go into shops
    Buying sweet lollipops
    Or those nice chocolate drops that they sell?

ZIEGFELD FOLLIES OF 1927

ZIEGFELD FOLLIES OF 1927

Tryout: Colonial Theatre, Boston, Massachusetts; August 2, 1927. New York run: New Amsterdam Theatre; opened August 16, 1927; 167 performances. Music and lyrics by Irving Berlin. Produced by Abraham L. Erlanger and Florenz Ziegfeld Jr. Sketches by Harold Atteridge and Eddie Cantor. Dances staged by Sammy Lee. Dialogue by Zeke Colvan. Ballets by Albertina Rasch. Orchestrations by Frank Tours, Roy Webb, Paul Lannin, Louis Katsman, and Arthur Gutman. Orchestra under the direction of Frank Tours. Scenery by Joseph Urban. Costumes designed by Joseph Harkrider. Cast: starring Eddie Cantor and featuring Irene Delroy, Claire Luce, Andrew Tombes, Franklyn Baur, Frances Upton, Peggy Chamberlin, the Brox Sisters, Phil H. Ryley, William H. Powers, Ruth Etting, Fanny Watson, Lora Foster, Cliff Edwards, Harry McNaughton, Dan Healy, the Banjo Ingenues, and the Albertina Rasch Girls. Lyrics are missing for the following numbers: "Tickling the Ivories" (introduced by Ruth Etting, with Frances Upton, Lora Foster, Edgar Fairchild, and Ralph Rainger at the piano, and ensemble), "Now We Are Glorified" (the closing number), and two unused numbers, "What Makes Me Love You" and "Why I Love My Baby."

WE WANT TO BE GLORIFIED

Introduced by ensemble. No music is known to survive.

And now we seek to reach a higher plane,
A job that isn't easy to attain.
We want to be glorified
By Mr. Ziegfeld,
As only Mr. Ziegfeld can.
It would be thrilling
To share his billing
And he'd be willing—
He's a generous man.
We want to be advertised
By Mr. Ziegfeld,
And when we're known both far and wide,
We'll keep the salesman and the drummers
Looking forward to their summers
While we're in the Follies
Being glorified.

RIBBONS AND BOWS

Listed on sheet music covers for the *Ziegfeld Follies of 1927* as having been published, but apparently never printed. Registered for copyright as an unpublished song August 12, 1927. Introduced by Irene Delroy and ensemble.

VERSE

When the doctor yells with joy,
Glad to tell you it's a boy,
Everybody's glad except the maker of dresses.
When a little girl is born
Very early on that morn,
Every costumer hearing the rumor
Hurries around because—

CHORUS

All the babies cry for ribbons and bows;
Mama has to buy the ribbons and bows.
And then when baby grows older,
Some Harry or John
Lifts up his shoulder
For baby to cry upon.
More and more and more of ribbons and bows—
Take her to the store before they all close.
Between her twinkles
She sprinkles
A river that flows
From her eyes
As she cries ribbons and bows.

SHAKING THE BLUES AWAY

Published. Copyrighted August 15, 1927. Previously registered for copyright as an unpublished song June 8, 1927. Introduced by Ruth Etting, with Dan Healy and ensemble (the Jazzbow Girls, the Albertina Rasch Girls, and the Banjo Ingenues). Original cast recordings by Ruth Etting (Columbia), Edgar Fairchild and Ralph Rainger (Victor), and Franklyn Baur (Brunswick). Other leading recording by Paul Whiteman and His Orchestra (Victor). According to show programs, the orchestration was by Ferde Grofé, "with the kind permission of Paul Whiteman." Years later, with a slightly revised lyric, it was sung and danced by Ann Miller in the 1948 film musical *Easter Parade*. Sung by Doris Day, as Ruth Etting, in the 1955 film musical *Love Me or Leave Me*.

VERSE

There's an old superstition
Way down south—
Ev'ry darkie* believes that trouble
Won't stay
If you shake it away.
When they hold a revival
Way down south,
Ev'ry darkie* with care and trouble
That day
Tries to shake it away.

CHORUS

Shaking the blues away,
Unhappy news away.
If you are blue,
It's easy to
Shake off your cares and troubles.
Telling the blues to go,
They may refuse to go;
But as a rule they'll go
If you'll shake them away.
Do like the darkies do
List'ning to
A preacher way down south:†
They shake their bodies so
To and fro—
With ev'ry shake
A lucky break,
Proving that there's a way
To chase your cares away.
If you would lose
Your weary blues,
Shake 'em away.

OOH, MAYBE IT'S YOU

Published. Copyrighted August 15, 1927. Previously registered for copyright as an unpublished song June 8, 1927. Introduced by Irene Delroy and Franklyn Baur with the Ziegfeld Dancing Girls and the Brox Sisters. Original cast recordings by Franklyn Baur with Ben Selvin and His Orchestra (Brunswick), Baur with Nat

For the film musical Easter Parade *(1948), Berlin changed "Ev'ry darkie" in lines 3 and 8 to "Ev'rybody."*

†*For* Easter Parade, *Berlin changed lines 10–12 of the chorus to:*

Do like the voodoos do
List'ning to
A voodoo melody.

Shilkret and the Victor Orchestra (Victor), and the Brox Sisters (Victor). Alternate title (program): "Maybe It's You."

VERSE

I wonder what's the matter with me,
Losing my appetite,
Lying awake at night;
I wonder what the trouble can be,
Watching the days go by,
Caring not whether I live or die.

CHORUS

Ooh! Maybe it's you
Making me blue,
Maybe it's you.
Ooh! What would I do
If it were you
Making me blue?
I went and had my fortune read;
Someone's to blame, the Gypsy said,
But she wouldn't say who.
Maybe it's you
Making me blue,
Maybe it's you.

RAINBOW OF GIRLS

Published. Copyrighted August 25, 1927. Previously registered for copyright as an unpublished song June 30, 1927. Introduced by Franklyn Baur with ensemble featuring the Albertina Rasch Girls. Original cast recording by Baur with Nat Shilkret with the Victor Orchestra (Victor).

VERSE

While you hurry through life and worry,
I'm painting fanciful pictures;
A dreamer am I—
My home is the sky.
You may treasure each earthly pleasure
While I keep roaming the heavens;
I'd rather be there,
Just walking on air.

CHORUS

I'm living up in the clouds,
Chasing a rainbow of girls;
Far from the maddening crowds,

Gathering dewdrops for pearls.
Castles in the air
Up there to screen us;
Nothing but the stars and Mars and Venus
Coming between us.
I'm happy up in the clouds,
Chasing a rainbow of girls.

IT ALL BELONGS TO ME

Published. Copyrighted August 25, 1927. Previously registered for copyright as an unpublished song July 15, 1927. Introduced by Eddie Cantor with Lora Foster. Original cast recordings by Ruth Etting with Johnny Hamp's Kentucky Serenaders (Columbia) and Franklyn Baur, the Brox Sisters, and Fairchild and Rainger (Victor).

VERSE

Take a look at the flower in my buttonhole—
Take a look say and ask me why it's there.
Can't you see that I'm all dressed up to take a
    stroll?
Can't you tell that there's something in the air?
I've got a date can hardly wait:
I'd like to bet she won't be late:

CHORUS 1

Here she comes, come on and meet
A hundred pounds of what is mighty sweet,
And it all belongs to me.
Flashing eyes, and how they roll!,
A disposition like a sugar bowl,
And it all belongs to me.
That pretty baby face,
That bunch of style and grace,
Should be in Tiff'ny's window
In a platinum jewel case.
Hey there, you, you'll get in dutch—
I'll let you look
But then you mustn't touch,
For it all belongs to me.

CHORUS 2

Here she comes, come on and meet
A hundred pounds of what is mighty sweet,
And it all belongs to me.
Rosy cheeks and red-hot lips
And polished nails upon her fingertips,
And it all belongs to me.
Those lips that I desire
Are like electric wire;

She kissed a tree last summer
And she started a forest fire.
I'm in love with what she's got,
And what she's got
She's got an awful lot,
And it all belongs to me.

IT'S UP TO THE BAND

Published. Copyrighted August 25, 1927. Previously registered for copyright as an unpublished song June 30, 1927. Introduced by the Brox Sisters and male ensemble. This number led to "Melody Land," the title (not a Berlin song) of the hugely populated, scenically splendid Joseph Urban–designed Act I finale. Original cast recording by the Brox Sisters (Victor).

VERSE

I can feel my spirits change
In a manner very strange;
It happens so unexpected.
My temperature is affected
By the music of a band;
I could never understand
Why each melody makes a change in me,
So when I hear you asking:

CHORUS

How do I feel?
I'll answer you by saying
It depends a good deal
On what the band is playing
As to whether I'm blue or I'm happy—
It's up to the band.
Why am I glad?
I heard a jazzy melody.
And why am I sad?
It's 'cause they played "The Rosary."
So whether I'm laughing or crying,
It's up to the band.
I want those sad musicians to play,
But after they start
I feel like shouting "Take 'em away,
They're breaking my heart!"
And then a rhythm that's new
Will give the gloomy tune a kick,
And what do I do?
I act just like a lunatic,
And I'm not to blame for what happens—
It's up to the band.

JIMMY

Published. Copyrighted August 29, 1927. Previously registered for copyright as an unpublished song February 25, 1927. Introduced by Ruth Etting and ensemble as part of a scene titled "At the City Hall Steps," in which Eddie Cantor portrayed New York's popular mayor, James J. Walker.

VERSE

There's a man who's full of personality and
    charm,
And he's heading for the Hall of Fame.
Father Knickerbocker came and took 'im by the
    arm;
Now we feel the magic of his name.

CHORUS

Jimmy—we simply had to fall for,
One and all for, Jimmy;
And now we're singing of him
'Cause we love him.
Who told Broadway not to be gay,
Who gets his picture taken three times a day—
Jimmy, we're very glad to show
That we all know that Jimmy is doing fine.
Can't you hear those old New Yorkers hollering,
"Gimme gimme gimme Jimmy for mine!"?

LEARN TO SING
A LOVE SONG

Published. Copyrighted August 25, 1927. Previously registered for copyright as an unpublished song July 15, 1927. Introduced by Franklyn Baur and ensemble.

VERSE

The world goes round
To the sound of a love song,
A melody for you and me.
In ev'ry heart
There's a part of a love song;
'Twas ever so, 'twill ever be.

CHORUS

Learn to sing a love song
And you'll remain forever young.

Learn it in the springtime,
When ev'ry song of love is sung.
Time will fly and by and by,
When dreary winter comes along,
You can sit beside your fireside
Humming an old love song.

THE JUNGLE JINGLE

Registered for copyright as an unpublished song July 20, 1927. Introduced by the Brox Sisters with Claire Luce, the Albertina Rasch Girls, and ensemble. Recorded by the duo-piano team of Fairchild and Rainger (music only) as part of an extended medley of songs from the score featuring Nat Shilkret and the Victor Orchestra (Victor).

VERSE

In the heart of Africa
There's a jungle orchestra,
And you ought to hear them play.
At the close of ev'ry day,
When the night is clear,
You can plainly hear
Tom-toms beating away.

CHORUS

Listen to the jungle jingle,
The jungle jingle,
The rum-tum-tingle they play.
Listen to the tom-toms beating
A welcome greeting;
The tribes are meeting today.
Each native in a state of ecstasy,
Monkeys and bears—tigers, and there's—Jumbo!
Better come along and mingle
And hear them tingle
The jungle jingle they play.

YOU HAVE TO HAVE "IT"
IN HOLLYWOOD

Listed on the sheet music covers for the *Ziegfeld Follies of 1927* as having been published, but apparently never printed. Registered for copyright as an unpublished song August 12, 1927. Sung in the Boston tryout by Eddie Cantor but dropped before the New York opening. Alternate title: "You Got to Have 'It' in Hollywood."

VERSE

I just returned from dear old Hollywood,
And it's mighty good to be back here, because
No matter how you love the movie game,
It's not the same, because you miss the
    applause.
No matter how big you are,
No matter how small,
Out there on the coast,
Ask me,
What's the most important thing of all?

CHORUS

You've got to have "it" in Hollywood,
"It" in Hollywood—
"It" is a wonderful thing.
Clara Bow has lots of "it" in her romantic
    scenes;
Baby Peggy has "it," but she don't know what it
    means.
You got to have oh so much of it;
Just a touch of it
Won't get you into the ring.
I have four kiddies and that is no salve;
If I had "it," can you imagine all the kiddies I'd
    have?
You got to have "it" in Hollywood:
It is understood
"It" is a wonderful thing.

MY NEW YORK

Published. Copyrighted October 26, 1927. Previously registered for copyright as an unpublished song September 30, 1927. Added to the show after the New York opening. Introduced by Eddie Cantor. According to the sheet music, "Respectfully dedicated to His Honor the Mayor James J. Walker." The lyrics to choruses 3, 4, 5, and 6 were not printed in the sheet music.

VERSE

Let me place a crown
On my favorite town;
Let me sing its praises to the sky.
Not because I'm there
As its humble mayor,
But because you feel the same as I.

CHORUS 1

There's a spot in my heart
That's becoming a part
Of my New York.
There's a warm little beat
For each corner and street
Of my New York.
I gaze at Father Knickerbocker resting on the
    map,
With seven million children sitting pretty in his
    lap,
And there's something inside
That is bursting with pride
For my New York.

CHORUS 2

Money talks and it speaks
To the Turks and the Greeks
In my New York.
The Armenians too
Soon found out that it grew
In my New York.
The Irish sing of Ireland being heaven with a tear;
Well, Ireland may be heaven, but they all come
    over here—
If their coming should cease,
We would have no police
In my New York.

CHORUS 3

If you looked you would find
There's no thought in my mind
But my New York;
And it's part of my plan
To do all that I can
For my New York:
To regulate the traffic and to widen all the streets,
A ventilated subway with a lot of extra seats,
And a nickel's the fare
If it's up to the mayor
Of my New York.

CHORUS 4

I've been over the foam
And I'm glad to be home
To my New York.
They were all very nice,
And they've heard once or twice
Of my New York.
They treated me most royally, but this is what I
    think:
They're sore at us in Europe 'cause there's
    nothing there to drink.
There's no more, I was told,

All they had has been sold
To my New York.

CHORUS 5

For our next President
Keep your eye on a gent
From my New York.
He's the joy and the pride
Of the Lower East Side
Of my New York.
He'll get the nomination, which is just as it
    should be,
And Washington is waiting for the man from
    Albany
That we all used to meet
Down on Oliver Street
In my New York.

CHORUS 6

Every nation, it seems,
Sailed across with their dreams
To my New York.
Every color and race
Found a comfortable place
In my New York.
The Dutchmen bought Manhattan Island for a
    flask of booze,
Then sold controlling interest to the Irish and the
    Jews—
And what chance has a Jones
With the Cohens and Malones
In my New York?

WALKER GLORIFIED NEW YORK

A tribute in verse, no music, written by Berlin in December 1927.

Ziegfeld glorified the flapper,
Cohan glorified the flag,
Woolworth glorified the nickel,
Gershwin glorified the rag,
Barnum glorified the sucker,
Roosevelt glorified the stork,
Lindbergh glorified the airship—
Walker glorified New York.

IN THOSE GOOD OLD BOWERY DAYS

Registered for copyright as an unpublished song July 15, 1927. Not used in the show.

VERSE

Serving nut sundaes and pink lemonade
Isn't exactly what I'd call a trade;
This kind of job, you'll agree,
Is not for a fellow like me.
I can remember when I was a star
Down on the Bowery, where I tended bar.
Days were much happier then,
I wish I could see them again.

CHORUS 1

In those good old Bowery days,
In those good old Bowery days,
When the Bowery was crowded with ten-dollar
    clerks
Who mixed with the ladies who stopped at
    McGuirks,
On the Bowery, the Bowery.
And often my memory strays
To the sightseeing gang
And the waiters who sang
In those good old Bowery days.

CHORUS 2

In those good old Bowery days,
Long before the cabarets,
When a guy made a date with his peaches-and-
    cream
And showed her the sights in a nickel museum,
On the Bowery, the Bowery,
Where gold bricks were bought by the jays,
And a gal who got tight
Was the sailors' delight,
In those good old Bowery days.

WHY SHOULD HE FLY AT SO MUCH A WEEK (WHEN HE COULD BE THE SHEIK OF PAREE)

Registered for copyright as an unpublished song June 11, 1927. Not used in the show. Charles Lindbergh completed his nonstop solo flight from New York to Paris on May 20–21, 1927.

VERSE

He's done it, it's over—
He flew from here to Dover
And across the Channel into Paree.
And now that it's over,
The town is all in clover
And they wonder what his future will be.
They want him to keep flying in his plane
But if he does, I think that he's insane.

CHORUS 1

Why should he fly at so much a week
Since they gave him a peek at Paree?
Why should he fly at his salary
Since they gave him the key to Paree?
Way over there they're hot for Lindy;
Up in the air it's very windy—
So why should he fly at so much a week
When he could be the Sheik of Paree.

CHORUS 2

Why should he fly at so much a week
Since they gave him a peek at Paree?
Why should he fly at his salary
Since they gave him the key to Paree?
Mademoiselle and even Madam
Started to yell, "Just let me at 'im!"
So why should he fly at so much a week
When they kiss on the cheek in Paree?

Songs of 1927–1929 and
Unpublished Songs of the 1920s

SHADOWS

The lyric is dated "very early 1927." It was written on the back of a January 17, 1927, letter from Joseph Schenck to Berlin. No music is known to survive. "Shadows" evolved into "What Does It Matter?," the lyric that follows.

VERSE

Shadows will darken the happiest day;
Trouble frightens the gladness away,
And the sunshine will hasten away.
No one can tell what tomorrow may be,
But as long as there's you and there's me:

Heaven is smiling because we've begun
Living your life and my life as one;
Nothing can happen to change it, I know,
So if some little wind wants to blow:

Springtime may vanish and turn into fall;
Care and sorrow may pay us a call.
Trouble may frighten the sunshine away;
Tiny shadows may darken the day.

Troubles and worries may darken the day;
Shadows may frighten the sunshine away.

WHAT DOES IT MATTER?

Published. Copyrighted February 15, 1927. Previously registered for copyright as an unpublished song January 29, 1927. Performed by Al Jolson. Recordings by Henry Burr (Victor), Jesse Crawford (Victor), and Harry Richman (Brunswick).

VERSE 1

Troubles and worries may darken the day;
Shadows may frighten the sunshine away;
Winds may blow over the land and the sea;
But as long as there's you and there's me—

CHORUS

What does it matter
If the sun won't shine;
Long as you are mine,

Irving Berlin and Al Jolson

What does it matter?
What does it matter
If the clouds appear;
Long as you are near,
What does it matter?
Life is never one sweet song;
Things are liable to go wrong.
What does it matter?
Long as I love you
And you love me too,
What does it matter?

VERSE 2

Morning may wake us with unpleasant news;
Things may go wrong, just as wrong as they
    choose;
Skies may be cloudy or skies may be blue;
But as long as there's me and there's you—

REPEAT CHORUS

RUSSIAN LULLABY

Published. Copyrighted April 7, 1927. Previously registered for copyright as an unpublished song March 4, 1927. Written for the opening of S. L. Rothafel's Roxy Theatre in New York, March 11, 1927. Introduced by Douglas Stanbury, baritone in Roxy's Gang. Number-one-selling recording by Roger Wolfe Kahn and His Orchestra (Victor), vocal by Henry Garden.

VERSE

Where the dreamy Volga flows,
There's a lonely Russian Rose
Gazing tenderly
Down upon her knee
Where a baby's brown eyes glisten.
Listen—

CHORUS

Ev'ry night you'll hear her croon
A Russian lullaby,
Just a little plaintive tune
When baby starts to cry.
Rock-a-bye, my baby,
Somewhere there may be
A land that's free
For you and me
And a Russian lullaby.

TOGETHER WE TWO

Published. Copyrighted October 26, 1927. Previously registered for copyright as an unpublished song under the title "Together" on May 26, 1927, and published under that title September 26, 1927. Leading recordings by Ruth Etting (Columbia), Vaughn DeLeath and Ed Smalle (Victor), and Isham Jones and His Orchestra, with vocal by the Keller Sisters (Brunswick). It is likely that Berlin changed the title of this song to "Together We Two" to help distinguish it from "Together," the hit song by DeSylva, Brown, and Henderson of the same year.

VERSE

Happiness, happiness
All the day long;
Ev'rything's rosy,
And my heart keeps singing a song.
Nevermore troubles or nevermore strife,
And I keep thinking
Of the happiest day of my life.

CHORUS

Bells were tolling and we were strolling together;
I was telling where we'd be dwelling together:
Down at the bottom of a little hill
Where we could live and love
And hear the trill of a whippoorwill.
We were happy, we looked so snappy together;
No mistaking what we were aching to do.
You gave your love undivided,
Just as I did;
Then and there we both decided,
Ev'ry weather we'd share together, we two.

THE SONG IS ENDED (BUT THE MELODY LINGERS ON)

Published. Copyrighted November 11, 1927. Previously registered for copyright as an unpublished song October 20, 1927. Leading recordings by Ruth Etting (Columbia), "Whispering" Jack Smith (Victor), and Reinald Werrenrath (Victrola).

VERSE

My thoughts go back to a heavenly dance,
A moment of bliss we spent;

Our hearts were filled with a song of romance
As into the night we went
And sang to our hearts' content.

CHORUS

The song is ended,
But the melody lingers on;
You and the song are gone,
But the melody lingers on.
The night was splendid,
And the melody seemed to say,
"Summer will pass away;
Take your happiness while you may."
There neath the light of the moon
We sang a love song that ended too soon;
The moon descended
And I found with the break of dawn,
You and the song had gone,
But the melody lingers on.

SUNSHINE

Published. Copyrighted February 14, 1928. Previously registered for copyright as an unpublished song January 25, 1928. Leading recordings by Paul Whiteman, with vocal by Bing Crosby (Victor), and Nick Lucas (Brunswick).

VERSE

A lot of cobwebs in your head;
You're getting rusty, so you said;
You're feeling badly
And ev'rything looks gray;
You're getting worried, yes indeed—
I know exactly what you need:
A little sunshine
Will make you feel okay.

CHORUS

Give the blues a chase;
Find a sunny place;
Go and paint your face
With sunshine.
Pay your doctor bills;
Throw away his pills;
You can cure your ills
With sunshine.
Why don't you take your teardrops one by one,
Before it gets too late—

Hang them up out in the sun
And they'll evaporate.
When the troubles start
Pounding at your heart,
Rub the injured part
With sunshine.

I CAN'T DO WITHOUT YOU

Published. Copyrighted March 20, 1928. Previously registered for copyright as an unpublished song March 7, 1928. Registered for copyright as an unpublished song February 21, 1928, under the earlier title "Without You." Recordings by Gene Austin (Victor), Jesse Crawford (Victor), and James Melton (Columbia).

VERSE 1

There was I,
Satisfied to live and die
In a little world
Where life was all arranged;
There were you
In a world I never knew—
Suddenly we met
And ev'rything was changed.

CHORUS

All my life I did without you,
But now I can't do without you.
All my life I never missed you;
Until I kissed you,
I never missed you.
All through life I went
And thought that I was meant
To live and be content
Without you;
Then I put my arms about you,
And now I can't do
Without you.

VERSE 2

There was I,
Gazing at the cloudy sky,
Thinking that the clouds
Were all there was to see;
There were you,
Pointing to a sky of blue,

Showing me how bright
A day could really be.

REPEAT CHORUS

MY LITTLE FELLER

Registered for copyright as an unpublished song May 16, 1928. Apparently intended at one time for the Al Jolson film *The Singing Fool*; replaced by "Sonny Boy," by De Sylva, Brown, Henderson, and Jolson. Alternate title: "Little Feller."

VERSE

What care I if the sun refuses to shine!
Let the weather be bad or let it be fine,
I get lots of sun when my work is done
And I'm home with that little feller of mine.

CHORUS 1

Sweet as can be,
Climbing my knee—
Wait'll you see
My little feller.
Back of my chair,
Pulling my hair—
Who is it there?
My little feller.
I love that gleam in his eyes
When I bring home a surprise;
He grabs the bundle and cries,
"Whatcher bring me, Daddy?"
Presents galore
Bought at the store—
Who are they for?
My little feller.

CHORUS 2

Cute as can be,
Climbing my knee—
Wait'll you see
My little feller.
Back of my chair,
Pulling my hair—
Who is it there?
My little feller.
A tiny room and my board
Is all that I can afford,

But I'm as rich as a lord
When he calls me Daddy.
Having a lot
Worries me not
Long as I've got
My little feller.

TO BE FORGOTTEN

Published. Copyrighted November 22, 1928. Registered for copyright as an unpublished song on June 24, 1928, and again on June 29, 1928, under the earlier title "Forgotten (A Memory That's Soon to Be)." Registered for copyright as an unpublished song on August 28, 1928, under the title "A Memory That's Soon to Be Forgotten."

VERSE 1

Love is a flow'r that blooms in May,
Fresh for a moment, then fades away.
Love is a vow while springtime hums,
To be forgotten when winter comes.

CHORUS

To have, to hold,
To live just for a moment in ecstasy
And then to be forgotten.
To laugh at life
And learn to sing a love song, a melody
That's soon to be forgotten.
When love is ended, to cry;
But when your heart is mended,
To love again—
A night of bliss,
But when the dawn is breaking, a memory
That's soon to be forgotten.

VERSE 2

Love makes the sweetest dreams come true,
Then brings you gloom as it bids adieu.
Love is a vow when skies are clear,
To be forgotten when clouds appear.

REPEAT CHORUS

ROSES OF YESTERDAY

Published. Copyrighted August 31, 1928. Previously registered for copyright as an unpublished song on June 29, 1928, under the title "Roses," and again on August 14, 1928, as "Roses of Yesterday." Leading recording by Fred Waring's Pennsylvanians (Victor).

VERSE

Where are the roses of yesterday?
Where are the flowers that bloomed in May?
Where are the skies that were blue?
Where are the joys that I knew?
Gone with the roses of yesterday.

CHORUS

Roses of yesterday,
Faded and thrown away—
Love is a pale bouquet
Of yesterday's roses.
Roses were once in bloom
Here in my lonely room;
Now there's a faint perfume
Of yesterday's roses.
Roses of crimson red
Faded when love was dead;
Quickly the summer fled
And winter discloses
That it was not to be,
And all that's left for me
Is a sweet memory
Of yesterday's roses.

YASCHA MICHAELOFFSKY'S MELODY

Published. Copyrighted August 17, 1928. Previously registered for copyright as an unpublished song July 27, 1928. According to an August 8, 1928, article (newspaper unknown), Berlin wrote this song in Port Washington, New York. It was thought to be partly autobiographical. "All my life," noted Berlin, "I've been hearing nothing but stories about when I was a poor immigrant. Everybody is too ready to censure and scorn, no one gives credit where it is due. I am happy and very much in love so why shouldn't I write in a humorous vein?"

VERSE 1

Yascha Michaeloffsky, Russian lad—
He came over from Petrograd
With a fiddle in his hand,
Organized a first-class band.
Right away he wrote a melody
Just as Russian as it could be;
Ev'rybody hummed it soon,
Yascha Michaeloffsky's tune.

CHORUS 1

All night long they keep requesting
Yascha Michaeloffsky's melody;
People say it's interesting
How the music goes from key to key.
Many, many copies have been sold;
Yascha's rolling around in gold.
But with all his wealth and fame,
Yascha hasn't changed his name;
You can tell who wrote the music:
On the copy stands the name
Of Yascha Michaeloffsky.

VERSE 2

All the relatives that Yascha had
Came right over from Petrograd;
And they heard his music played,
Saw the money that he made.
Right away they said, "Oh gosh, oh gee,
Yascha did it, so why can't we?"
They were imitating soon
Yascha Michaeloffsky's tune.

CHORUS 2

All night long they're improvising
Yascha Michaeloffsky's melody;
It is really quite surprising
How they jump around from key to key.
Finally they wrote a tune one night,
But it didn't come out quite right;
So they tore it up and said,
"Better we should go to bed."
No one writes such music like where
On the copy stands the name
Of Yascha Michaeloffsky.

I LOVE MY NEIGHBOR

Registered for copyright as an unpublished song July 27, 1928.

Went to church one day,
Heard the preacher say,
"Love thy neighbor."
I turned crimson red
When the preacher said,
"Love thy neighbor."
My neighbor happens to be
Sweet seventeen, so just
Take it from me—
She lives next door, what's more,
When I come home from my labor,
I love my neighbor.
First kiss I gave her was her life saver;
She kissed me "smack" right back
And said I did her a favor—
I love my neighbor.

GOOD TIMES WITH HOOVER, BETTER TIMES WITH AL

Published. Copyrighted October 17, 1928. Previously registered for copyright as an unpublished song September 29, 1928. A campaign song for New York governor Alfred E. Smith's run for the presidency as the Democratic Party's 1928 standard bearer. Alternate title: "Better Times with Al." Many years later, a newspaper article (March 25, 1966) indicated that Berlin also had written special lyrics for Smith's campaign to the melody of "Back in Your Own Backyard," which included:

We have everything, never fear,
We have Al Smith right here
Back, back in your own backyard.

VERSE

Whether we elect a GOP
Or the man who comes from Albany,
We'll remain okay
In a business way.
Looking at the future, we can see:

CHORUS 1

Good times with Hoover,
Better times with Al;
Blue skies with Hoover,
Bluer skies with Al.
Prosperity does not depend
On who's in the chair;
We're bound to have prosperity
No matter who's there.
So we'll have good times with Hoover,
Better times with Al.

CHORUS 2

Good times with Hoover,
Better times with Al;
Blue skies with Hoover,
Bluer skies with Al.
They tell us that the future
Will be rosy and bright;
But they don't have to tell us—
We admit that they're right
That we'll have good times with Hoover,
Better times with Al.

HOW ABOUT ME?

Published. Copyrighted November 13, 1928. Previously registered for copyright as an unpublished song October 17, 1928. Leading recording by Fred Waring's Pennsylvanians (Victor). Widely performed and recorded in recent years.

VERSE 1

Too long
I held you close to my heart;
Too much
I loved you right from the start;
Too soon
You vanished out of my dreams;
Too late
To start all over, it seems

CHORUS

It's over, all over,
And soon somebody else
Will make a fuss about you—
But how about me?
It's over, all over,
And soon somebody else
Will tell his friends about you—

But how about me?
You'll find somebody new,
But what am I to do?
I'll still remember you
When you have forgotten.
And maybe a baby
Will climb upon your knee
And put its arms about you—
But how about me?

VERSE 2

Moonlight
Was beaming down from the skies;
Love light
Was gleaming deep in your eyes;
Sunlight
For just a moment, and then
Twilight
And I was lonely again.

REPEAT CHORUS

AT THE COCONUT GROVE

Typed lyric sheets and a one-page copyist lead sheet of music were found among Berlin's papers and are now in the Irving Berlin Collection of the Music Division of the Library of Congress.

VERSE

Down where the coconuts are growing,
Just as sure as you're living,
The monkeys are giving a ball
In jungle town.
They all want you to be knowing
They keep an open door,
And what is more,
You're welcome one and all.

CHORUS

Hustle along,
Hear the coconuts knocking,
See the monkeys all mocking
All the folks who are flocking
To the coconut grove.
Hustle along,
Everybody is rocking
There'll be a supper served by a flunkey;
He's the monkey butler.
You'll hear the band playing those monkey blues;

Put lots of wax on your new dancing shoes.
Hustle along—
There's a barrel of peanuts
For the he- and the she-nuts
At the coconut grove.

THE BRIDE WENT HOME WITH HER MOTHER (AND THE GROOM WENT BACK TO HIS WIFE)

No music is known to survive. A typed lyric sheet was found among Berlin's papers and is now in the Irving Berlin Collection of the Music Division of the Library of Congress.

VERSE

Poets have told us that wedding days
Are always merry and bright,
But I discovered Sunday night
The poets aren't always right—
Because I happened to be at a wedding
With all the rest who were there,
And goodness me, it turned out to be
A very, very sad affair.

CHORUS

The wedding bells were ringing
As they marched down the aisle;
The choirboys were singing,
And the world seemed to smile.
The minister was ready
To tie them up for life,
When someone shouted to the groom
In a nervous tone,
"Your wife would like to speak to you
On the telephone!"*

_____

Additional versions of lines 7–10:
   When suddenly a baby's voice
   Shouted to the groom,
   "Mama would like to see you, Dad,
   In the other room."

   When someone shouted to the bride,
   "Let that man alone!
   If you must have a husband, dear,
   Get one of your own."

So the bride went home with her mother
And the groom went back to his wife.

DANCE

No music is known to survive. A typed lyric sheet was found among Berlin's papers and is now in the Irving Berlin Collection of the Music Division of the Library of Congress.

CHORUS

Dance—
Come on along and dance.
Dance—
Upon your toes advance.
Dance—
While you have got the chance.
Why double
Your trouble?
It's just a
Soap bubble.
So
If you just point your toe,
Whoa—
We'll soon be on the go.
Oh,
Come be a stepper
With a lotta pepper
While you've got a chance—
Come on along and dance.

DON'T FORGET TO REMEMBER

Copyist's pencil score (lyrics and music) in the hand of Albert Sirmay was found among Berlin's papers and are now in the Irving Berlin Collection of the Music Division of the Library of Congress. Alternate title (found with different melody, no lyric): "Don't Forget to Remember Me."

VERSE

Soon you'll be going your way
And I'll be going mine;
I wish we could stay longer,
Because I think you're fine.

Much too quickly the moments flew;
I have so much to say to you—
But I'll have to save it for
Some other time.

CHORUS

Don't forget
To remember me;
We have met
Because it had to be.
Just a thought
Ev'ry now and then;
There's no telling when
We may meet again.
So remember to remember me
And I won't forget to remember you.

DON'T KNOW WORDS ENOUGH

No music is known to survive. A typed lyric sheet was found among Berlin's papers and is now in the Irving Berlin Collection of the Music Division of the Library of Congress.

Don't know words enough to tell it,
Couldn't write it out or spell it—
I mean the way I love my honey.
Many times I think I know it;
Maybe my expression shows it—
I mean the way I love my honey.
Go and measure the ocean,
That's the depth of my love;
And I cherish the notion
It was sent from above.
And if the angels choose to bless it,
Don't care if I can't express it—
I mean the way I love my honey.

HOW WAS I TO KNOW?

Typed lyric sheet and a separate melody (which does not seem to fit the lyric) with the same title were found among Berlin's papers and are now in the Irving Berlin Collection of the Music Division of the Library of Congress.

How was I to know
Love is like the winter snows—
It comes and goes,
But how was I to know,
How was I to know?
We said goodbye,
I thought you cared for me;
But here am I
With just a memory—
How was I to know?
Promises at night are gone
With break of dawn;
But how was I to know,
How was I to know?

I COULDN'T SPEAK
ANY ENGLISH

No music is known to survive. An ink holograph of the lyric was found among Berlin's papers and is now in the Irving Berlin Collection of the Music Division of the Library of Congress.

I couldn't speak any English,
And he couldn't speak any French.
I tried to make him understand
That I thought him simply grand;
I made gestures with my hand
And he said, "You lead a band."
I never felt so embarrassed
As together we sat on the bench.

I WANT TO JAZZ MY
TROUBLES AWAY

No music is known to survive. Typed lyric sheets, some bearing the title "I Want to Dance My Troubles Away," were found among Berlin's papers and are now in the Irving Berlin Collection of the Music Division of the Library of Congress.

VERSE

Mr. Headwaiter, come over here,
Give me your hand.
Here is a dollar—go take it to
The leader of your jazz band.

Tell him that I'm sad,
Feeling mighty bad,
And his band
Could make me feel glad.
Tell him to

CHORUS

Play me a little jazz music—
I want to jazz my troubles away.
I'm so unhappy,
So make it good and snappy—
A draggy slow tune
Is no tune for you today.
Play me a little jazzy fox-trot;
Perhaps a dance
Will make me feel gay.
Can't drown my troubles
In champagne bubbles,
Because the town is dry,
So I'll jazz my troubles away.

IN NAPOLI

No music is known to survive. A typed lyric sheet was found among Berlin's papers and is now in the Irving Berlin Collection of the Music Division of the Library of Congress.

In Napoli
They live happily
With a moon shining down,
With Italy
Dressed up prettily
In her best summer gown.
Two romantic hearts
In a sunny clime,
Like a tale that starts,
"Once upon a time."
In Napoli
They lived happily
Ever after.

LADY

Typed lyric sheets and copyist's piano-vocal score with lyrics were found among Berlin's papers and are now in the Irving Berlin Collection of the Music Division of the Library of Congress.

VERSE

I'm on the ground
Just spinning around
All on account of a lady I found.
Oh, oh, oh, oh,
She worries me so—
She won't say yes
And she won't say no.

CHORUS 1

Oh, lady—
You're gonna drive me off my nut!
Lady,
I'd love to fool around you, but
Your look is such
I mustn't touch—
You know a man can only stand so much.
Oh, lady—
You make me think you'd like to pet;
Lady—
Then you give me the hard-to-get.
Stop flirting—
Can't you see that it's hurting?
If you can't be yourself,
Be a lady.

CHORUS 2

Lady—
Why do you make me worry so?
Lady—
Please let me be your Romeo.
Come here to me,
Sit on my knee;
I'll be a gentleman if you will be
A lady.
You pucker up your lips and then,
Lady,
You snatch your lips right back again.
Stop teasin'—
Won't you listen to reason?
If you can't be yourself,
Be a lady.

ON ACCOUNT OF YOU

Registered for copyright as an unpublished song December 5, 1977. According to a February 16, 1954, letter from Helmy Kresa to Irving Berlin, this song had been copyrighted in 1927, but there is no other evidence to support that claim. Typed lyric sheets and copyist's (Arthur Gutman's) piano-vocal score (which includes music for a verse, but no lyrics) were found among Berlin's papers and are now in the Irving Berlin Collection of the Music Division of the Library of Congress.

On account of you
I'm so very blue;
How was I to know
I'd be feeling so
On account of you?
Maybe if I knew
You could not be true,
I would not be here
Brushing off a tear
On account of you.
I would not be longing for your kiss;
What we've never had, we never miss.
What am I to do
Now that you are through?
Guess I'll have to start
Patching up my heart
On account of you.

TELL ME WHEN

No music is known to survive. A typed lyric sheet was found among Berlin's papers and is now in the Irving Berlin Collection of the Music Division of the Library of Congress.

VERSE

Mr. Fortune Teller,
Gaze into my hand—
You're a clever feller,
So I understand
You can tell the future
And the past as well.
If you can,
Fortune Teller Man,
I'd like to have you tell

CHORUS

When, tell me when will I wander
Way down yonder, far away?
When, tell me when
Will I shake hands again
With that bald-headed hen
Who supplied my breakfast ev'ry morning?
When, tell me when,
When will I start to roam
Back to the shack that I call home sweet home?
One thing I know—
Pretty soon I must go,
And if that's really so,
Tell me, when?

WHEN

No music is known to survive. A typed lyric sheet was found among Berlin's papers and is now in the Irving Berlin Collection of the Music Division of the Library of Congress.

VERSE 1

Dearie, I miss you, dearie,
And I grew weary waiting for you,
Grieving, forever grieving
But still believing that you are true.

CHORUS

When will the sun shine brighter?
When will the skies turn blue?
When will my heart turn lighter?
When will my dreams come true?
When will the days grow shorter,
Just as they used to be?
When, tell me when
Will I smile once again?
When will you come back to me?

VERSE 2

Lonely, I feel so lonely—
I want you only, that's why I'm blue.
Yearning, forever yearning
For your returning—what will I do?

REPEAT CHORUS

WHEREVER YOU ARE

Copyist's (Albert Sirmay's) pencil piano-vocal score with lyrics was found among Berlin's papers and is now in the Irving Berlin Collection of the Music Division of the Library of Congress.

VERSE

We were meant to be together and so
Together we shall be, fair weather or no.
Let them take you, dear—no matter how far,
I will come to you wherever you are.

CHORUS

No matter where
They try to hide you,
I'll soon be there,
Right there beside you.
There may be oceans between us;
The skies may be all gray,
Mountains to screen us,
But love will find a way.
So have no fear,
I'll surely find you;
It may be near,
It may be far.
Your eyes will smile at me,
They'll pilot me to you,
They'll guide me to
Wherever you are.

WHY CAN'T YOU BE SWEET MORE OFTEN?

Typed lyric sheet and copyist's pencil lead sheet of music were found among Berlin's papers and are now in the Irving Berlin Collection of the Music Division of the Library of Congress.

When you're sweet, dear,
You're so sweet, dear,
No one could be sweeter—
Why can't you be sweet more often?
When you're nice, dear,
No one could be nicer—
Why can't you be nice more often?
When you're mean, dear,
You're so mean, dear,
And that makes me blue;

When I'm blue, dear,
I'm so blue, dear,
So it's up to you.
When you tell me
That you love me,
Nothing could be sweeter—
Why can't you be sweet more often?

YOU'RE AN UPTOWN GAL WITH A DOWNTOWN HEART

No music is known to survive. A handwritten holograph of the lyric on New York, New Haven & Hartford Railroad Co. stationery was found among Berlin's papers and is now in the Irving Berlin Collection of the Music Division of the Library of Congress.

VERSE

I've given you the once-over
And my conclusion is this:
Living uptown all in clover
Hasn't affected you, miss.
Don't think I'm throwing this bouquet
Just to be swelling your lid—
I'm simply placing my okay
On what I call a regular kid.

CHORUS

You're an uptown gal
With a downtown heart.
Though it's not just what
Your lady friends call smart,
Washing dishes, scrubbing floors,
And eating with your knife—
You could do them all
As though you've done them all your life.
I can't imagine you tango-teaing;
It seems you're more like a human being.
Honest, pal—you're an uptown gal
With a regular downtown heart.

MISTER BONES

Sometime in 1927 Berlin began work on a play with music that he had called *Mister Bones*. It was, as can be seen from Berlin's own synopsis, conceived as a serious, almost *Pagliacci*-like work. Was this to be the ragtime opera he often referred to in interviews? The star of the piece, not surprisingly, was to have been Al Jolson.

At any rate, two years passed while Berlin worked with author-actor James Gleason on *Mister Bones*. Gleason fashioned various versions of a script which altered and extended Berlin's original idea. After a while, the still-uncompleted *Mister Bones* was abandoned as a stage property and transformed into the film *Mammy*, in which, of course, Jolson starred.

Here is Berlin's synopsis for *Mister Bones* (it is undated):

MISTER BONES

Synopsis of Play with Music
Story by
Irving Berlin

The action of the play occurs in a small town of, say, approximately fifty thousand inhabitants—a town which plays one-night stands—and the story centers about a minstrel troupe such as the Al G. Fields Minstrels.

The first act shows the intersection of two streets in the town which come to an apex at the center of the stage. This is Hobson's Opera House. The box office is in the center—in the corner of the building—and the stage entrance is at the right. It is daytime and the rise of the curtain reveals a line of townspeople at the box office waiting for their tickets. Others drift in and stand with their backs to the audience looking at the billboards and posters advertising the minstrel show to be given that evening.

The opening chorus shows the anticipation of these people and their high expectations regarding the show. This is interrupted by Hobson, the owner of the Opera House, who comes out hurriedly looking at his watch. The people crowd about him with various complaints about their seats, queries and general chatter. Excitement runs high. He assures them that everyone will be taken care of in due time, but now he must hurry down to the station to meet the minstrel troupe and conduct them with proper ceremony to the Opera House. He invites them all to join him in giving the minstrels a rousing welcome and they exit singing the finish of the opening chorus—"When the Minstrels Come to Town."

As they exit, a young couple enter, Phyllis

Allen, daughter of the Mayor and belle of the town, and her childhood sweetheart, Jack Porter, home from college on his summer vacation. They are fond of one another and although not formally engaged, it has always been taken for granted by their parents and the townspeople in general that they will ultimately marry. They talk about going to the show that night and also about the party Phyllis' father is giving after the show. The scene ends with a duet—a light romantic number.

The next scene shows the three censors of the town coming to the box office to call for their tickets, which are, of course, complimentary. On discovering that they have been placed in the twelfth row, they complain that they cannot give a just criticism of the show unless they are seated at least as far in front as the third row. They recall that the last show—*Mary's Garter*—which was reported to be somewhat risque, was found by them to be entirely respectable from their seats in the second row; but in the present instance, they fear they will be forced to delete a great number of lines and situations from the minstrel show. The scene finishes with a trio on small-town censorship.

Phyllis reenters the scene with a group of girls all talking about the party that night. Another character enters announcing that the minstrels have arrived in town and are on their way to the Opera House. This leads into a lively number for Phyllis—"The Minstrel Parade."

Presently, offstage is dimly heard the minstrel band, which gradually becomes louder and louder. More of the townspeople gather expectantly and finally Bob Meadows, manager and owner of Meadows' Merry Minstrels, enters with a great flourish, followed by the minstrel band and the entire troupe amid wild cheering from the crowd, and general ensemble.

Meadows is a typical old-time showman—high hat and all. He addresses the populace in the fluent, pompous manner à la circus ballyhoo, with the old line about how delighted and touched he is to return to the home of his youth—the line he uses in every town that the troupe plays in. The fact that no one remembers him Meadows easily explains by saying he moved away when a small boy—but always cherishes fond memories of his boyhood home.

After the short speech, he introduces the principals of his company: the ballad singer, the quartet, the yodeler and the dancers; also Tambo (the heavy in the story); the interlocutor, Frank Gordon; and last and greatest of all—the sensational Mister Bones, famous throughout two continents and greatest minstrel of all time. To this elaborate introduction, Mister Bones does not respond for the good reason that Mister Bones is not there. Somewhat embarrassed, Meadows starts repeating his introduction to give Bones time to show up, but is interrupted by one of the men, who remarks that Bones was waylaid by a pretty girl, who said she wanted his autograph, and that Bones remained to talk to her. The remainder of the troupe react as if this were one of Bones' well-known failings.

Meadows is even more embarrassed now, but before he finishes his third introduction, Bones enters with a flourish, takes the center of the stage, and the scene leads into what will be the theme song, entitled: "Let Me Be a Troubadour."

At the conclusion of this number the troupe starts filing into the stage entrance of the Opera House and the townspeople disperse. Mister Bones is about to enter with the troupe when he is stopped by Hobson, accompanied by Phyllis, Jack, and Phyllis' father, Mayor Allen. Hobson says he would like to introduce Bones to the Mayor of the town and to his daughter and her sweetheart. Allen welcomes him and Phyllis shows she is flustered and embarrassed to be presented to such a celebrity. Gordon, the interlocutor, who is at the end of the line going into the stage entrance, calls to Bones, warning him not to be long—that this is one town where he will have to unpack his own trunk.

Bones shows he is interested in the pretty girl and Hobson remarks that Phyllis and Jack are engaged. Phyllis is embarrassed and to break the tension mentions that they are eager to see the show. This reminds Jack to ask about his seats and Hobson assures him that he is holding the three tickets in his own office. Hobson and Jack exit to get the tickets and Allen also leaves, pleading a business engagement.

Left alone Bones plays up to the girl facetiously, mentioning her reported engagement. Phyllis half denies it, explaining that it has always been an accepted fact—but she is not married yet and isn't in a hurry to be. Bones shows that he is a fast and experienced worker and completely fascinates the girl. Phyllis mentions the party that her father is giving that evening and wishes she could invite him, but apologetically intimates that small-town people are narrow-minded and are more or less prejudiced against theatrical people. Bones assures her he understands. They go into duet—"There Is Always One Girl." This number is interrupted by Jack returning for Phyllis. After a conventional goodbye the two leave as Gordon comes out.

Gordon and Bones are a onetime vaudeville team of straight man and comic—Bones being the comedian and Gordon the straight man, or "feeder." They have foresaken vaudeville for the minstrel life. There is a deep, sincere affection between the two. Bones is the lovable, irresponsible, irresistible one and gets all the applause and credit and Gordon is the steady balance wheel, pulling Bones out of holes, trying to keep him straight, doing all the work—getting new gags and none of the glory.

Bones is looking off after the girl with a rapt expression as Gordon comes to him and speaks sharply to him, telling him to snap out of it—keep his mind on business and remember what happened last month in Paducah, when the Sheriff all but compelled him to remain behind. Bones talks back and, for a minute, there is a heated argument, during which Tambo, unseen by either of them, walks through the scene in the background to get his bag which he had left behind. Tambo witnesses this part of the argument and shows his interest in it. After he reenters through the stage door, the argument subsides and the real affection between Bones and Gordon comes to the surface when Bones realizes that all of Gordon's sometimes unwelcome advice is for his own good.

The three censors enter with Hobson, who introduces them to the two actors, the seat matter having been straightened out to the entire satisfaction of the three. Bones and Gordon decide to have some fun with these "longhairs" and tell them they are eager to have their advice on certain gags or jokes they intend to try out that evening. Bones starts to tell a very risqué story, but one of the censors interrupts and regretfully says he is afraid that is a little too strong, This is repeated several times, using well-known openings of familiar stag stories; Gordon pretending to industriously make notes as to what may be objectionable. They all exit.

The next scene is between Tambo and Meadows. In this scene Meadows complains that Tambo is falling down—that he isn't funny anymore and unless he snaps out of it, he'll have to give him notice. Tambo tries to excuse his deficiency by asserting that his gags got over well enough before Gordon and Bones came with the troupe, but that Gordon, the interlocutor, doesn't feed him right, giving all the breaks to Bones. During this scene, Tambo clearly establishes his hatred and jealousy of the successful team. The manager promises to have a talk with Gordon and try to remedy this difficulty.

Bones enters in the midst of a bevy of the town's girls, which leads into a big ensemble finale with the remainder of the troupe joining them and the entire number on the stage. The number of the finale is—"The Big Show Tonight."

CURTAIN

ACT II

There are three scenes.

1. Scene—Dressing Room
2. Scene—Before Curtain
3. Scene—Full Stage Minstrel Show

The dressing room shown is the one occupied jointly by Bones and Gordon. It is a typical dressing room of a small-town theatre—dimly lighted, bare and bleak—not too clean, probably cracked mirrors and broken-down chairs. There is no running water, but instead a couple of pails with which to remove the cork.

Gordon comes on to make up for the show. Tambo enters immediately after him. Gordon greets him with a half-hearted polite "Hello," but Tambo immediately lets him know that he has not come for any polite conversation—but for a showdown. Tambo belligerently accuses Gordon of trying to crab his gags and not feed him properly, with the result that Meadows has just given him the devil, when in reality it isn't his fault at all. Tambo becomes more and more abusive, but Gordon calmly ignores it and continues carefully making up. This angers Tambo more and more and gives him added courage to become more abusive. Gordon pleasantly suggests that perhaps the entire difficulty could be remedied very simply—namely, that Tambo be funnier. This irritates Tambo to the point of insult and the scene is interrupted by a knock on the door. "Props" enters with the various articles to be used in the show by Bones and Gordon. These props consist of a tambourine, a little clown cap, a trick cigar and a revolver. Gordon remarks that the trick cigar did not work last night, which killed a laugh, and hopes that "Props" has had it fixed. Tambo looks interestedly at the props, particularly at the revolver. As the boy leaves, Tambo starts in again and Gordon, having taken about all he can, tells him to shut up or he will throw him out. Tambo returns with a nasty crack and Gordon strikes him. The fight is short, but realistic, ending in Gordon picking up the offender and tossing him out of the door.

As Gordon walks back to the makeup table, Bones enters, grinning back over his shoulder and remarking that Gordon seems to be playing a little rough. This leads into light repartee with Gordon warning Bones that he better be good and funny tonight or he'll treat him the same way. They decide to rehearse a new gag they are going to try out tonight for the finish of their act. This is the old minstrel gag where the comedian tells a hard-luck story. The interlocutor follows up by saying: "If you think *you've* had hard luck, listen to this." He then goes into a long lingo of misfortunes—at the start of which the comedian breaks into tears of sympathy. As each added misfortune is related, the comedian's grief increases. The interlocutor says that the day he paid the mortgage on the house, the house burned down; the only reason his wife wasn't burned up with it was that she eloped that morning with the iceman; last night the doctor told him he could not live a year. He then produces a telegram from his pocket and says dramatically—"And an hour ago, I got this telegram saying that my father is dead." Bones by this time is convulsed with grief. He takes a revolver from his pocket and shoots the interlocutor, who falls to the ground. Bones faces the audience and explains—"I had to kill him—he was breaking my heart!" At the end of this Gordon rises and they both take a bow. They rehearse this a couple of times. After they decide they have it perfect, they sit down and start to make up.

There is a knock on the dressing room door. Bones calls "Come in" and Phyllis enters, flushed and embarrassed. Bones goes quickly to greet her and she explains that she slipped away from her father and Jack, who are out front, in order to just have a word with him before the show. She is all aflutter and hopes she has not been too bold in coming back. Bones assures her that she's a joy and an inspiration and he hopes she will enjoy the performance. She leaves with Bones gazing after her.

Gordon berates him for having his mind on anything but the show and as Bones closes the door, he tells him that he is going to give the greatest performance of his career that evening. Gordon laughs at him and tells him that if he had a dollar for every time he has heard him say that, they both could retire.

They are interrupted again by a call boy announcing that Mr. Meadows wants to see them both on the stage immediately. Bones hopes that Meadows is not going to ask them to cut their salaries again. A moment after they exit, Tambo sneaks cautiously in, still bearing some evidence of his encounter with Gordon. He quickly picks up the gun, extracts the blank cartridges, puts them in his pocket and substitutes real cartridges. He places the gun where he found it and sneaks hurriedly out. A moment later Bones and Gordon return and their remarks indicate that Meadows has asked them to "give Tambo a break." They again sit down and hurriedly finish their makeup, Bones humming the Troubadour air. There is an affectionate "pally" interchange of wise cracks between the two and they start out, but Gordon reminds Bones that he has forgotten his props. Bones hurriedly picks up the props, puts the gun in his pocket and exits as drop curtain of Hobson Opera House comes down. This is a typical small-town Opera House curtain with the local advertise-

ments. After the curtain is lowered, Meadows steps before it in full evening dress. He addresses the audience much as he did in the first act in his flowery, pompous manner, enthusiastically praising the show and promising the spectators an evening of undiluted entertainment. As he exits, the curtain rises, revealing the minstrel show, composed of fifty men, including the band. After the opening chorus, there follows twenty or twenty-five minutes of a real minstrel show, including numbers by the ballad singer, the quartet, the yodeler, a song-and-dance number à la "Mandy," which introduces six boys doing the Virginia Essence, a wedding number called "In the Morning," finishing with a bride appearing (female impersonator), the minister and four little pickaninnies.

After this number, Gordon, as interlocutor, introduces Tambo and Bones to the Tambourine Chord by entire company. They come on from their entrance, cross—shake hands in the center of the stage and then walk to their places and sit down.

Gordon starts his gag with Tambo and shows that he is trying to help him. The first gag falls flat, principally because it is an old one and partially because Tambo is extremely nervous. They try another with the same result. He then turns to Bones and introduces Bones in a song, which can be any good lively number.

After this they go into the hard luck gag, which is the same as they had rehearsed in the dressing room. During this Tambo is increasingly nervous. At the end Bones produces the gun, aims it at Gordon, fires, and Gordon falls. Bones then steps downstage and has his line—"I had to kill him, he was breaking my heart." The entire company laugh heartily. Bones takes his bow and looks back for Gordon to rise, but Gordon fails to do so. Bones waits again and then murmurs in an undertone that is audible to the audience, "Get up, Bozo, you are killing the laugh," and still Gordon remains where he fell. The entire company sense that something is wrong. Tambo rushes over to Gordon, stoops to him, feels his shoulder, and raises his hand, on which blood is seen. Instantly there is great confusion and pandemonium on the stage. Tambo rises, exclaiming accusingly as he points to Bones—"He has killed him—I heard them quarreling this afternoon." Bones, confused, bewildered, horror struck, kneels down beside Gordon's body and has touching scene. The entire company crowd around as Meadows enters hurriedly from the wings—sees what has happened, tries to restore order—calls "Curtain" and as curtain falls, veiling the scene, Meadows is before it. He addresses the audience calmly, trusting they approve of the finish to the act and explaining that

he felt the need of a certain element of drama even in a minstrel show. He goes on to say that the second act will continue after the regular intermission and he promises them just as much enjoyment as they experienced from the first act. He walks off bowing and smiling as the house lights come on.

MAMMY (1930)

A film produced by Warner Bros. Released in March 1930. Lyrics and music mostly by Berlin. Screenplay by Gordon Rigby and Joseph Jackson based on a story by Berlin. Directed by Michael Curtiz. Music conducted by Louis Silvers. Cast: starring Al Jolson (Al Fuller) and featuring Lois Moran (Nora Meadows) and Louise Dresser (Al's mother). Lyrics are missing for the unused song "Here We Are."

(ACROSS THE BREAKFAST TABLE) LOOKING AT YOU

Published November 4, 1929. Previously registered for copyright as an unpublished song on May 18, 1927, and again on May 16, 1929. Written for *Mister Bones*. Introduced by Al Jolson in the musical film *Mammy* (1930). Original cast recording by Al Jolson (Brunswick).

VERSE

Never saw such perfect beauty before;
Never saw such charming manners; what's more,
Never saw such eyes of heavenly blue;
Never saw what I see looking at you.

CHORUS

I could never weary
Looking at you,
Looking at you,
All through life, my dearie,
Looking at you,
Looking at you.
Wish that I were able
To make you say "I do"
And sit across the breakfast table
Looking at you.

LET ME SING AND I'M HAPPY

Published. Copyrighted June 10, 1929. Previously registered for copyright as an unpublished song August 8, 1928. Originally titled "Let Me Be a Troubadour" and intended for *Mister Bones*. Introduced by Al Jolson in the 1930 film *Mammy*. Original cast recording by Jolson with Louis Silver's Orchestra (Brunswick; recorded January 10, 1930). Other leading recordings by Ruth Etting (Columbia), Gene Austin (Victor), and Ben Selvin's Orchestra, vocal by Smith Ballew (Columbia). Lyric slightly revised by Berlin for Jolson to sing in a 1938 radio broadcast celebrating Berlin's fiftieth birthday. Jolson also presented this song on the sound track of the 1946 film *The Jolson Story* and recorded it again for Decca.

VERSE

What care I who makes the laws of a nation;
Let those who will take care of its rights and
    wrongs.
What care I who cares
For the world's affairs
As long as I can sing its popular songs.

CHORUS

Let me sing a funny song
With crazy words that roll along,
And if my song can start you laughing,
I'm happy, happy.
Let me sing a sad refrain
Of broken hearts that loved in vain,
And if my song can start you crying,
I'm happy.
Let me croon a low-down blues
To lift you out of your seat;
If my song can reach your shoes
And start you tapping your feet,
I'm happy.
Let me sing of Dixie's charms
Of cotton fields and Mammy's arms*
And if my song can make you homesick,
I'm happy.

When Berlin returned to this song in 1938, he added a patter for Al Jolson to sing on the fiftieth-birthday broadcast.

Alternate line:
    The Swanee shore and Mother's arms

PATTER

Let me sing a funny song
'Bout a girl in a fortune-telling place
Who read my mind and slapped my face,
And if my song can start you laughing,
I'm happy, so happy.
Let me sing a sad refrain
'Bout a lover who found a lonely spot
And said, "Remember," but she forgot,
And if my song can start you crying
I'm happy.
Let me croon a rhythm,
A snappy little rhythm,
A syncopated afterbeat
That gets to ev'rybody's feet,
And if my little rhythm
Can start you going with 'em
And make you loosen up a bit,
You bet that I'm just loving it—
Oh, let me sing on bended knee
"Rock-a-Bye Your Baby to a Dixie Melody."

Revised verse

In 1959 Berlin rewrote the verse for Gene Kelly to sing on a television spectacular.

What care I who makes the laws of a nation;
Let those who will take care of the world's
    advance.
What care I who cares
For the world's affairs
As long as I can just go into my dance.

LET ME SING

According to Berlin (in a November 5, 1963, letter to his friend Irving Hoffman), "I wrote ['Let Me Sing'] about forty years ago and later rewrote it into a song for Jolson called "Let Me Sing and I'm Happy." Berlin published the original poem under the title "Let Me Sing" after registering it for copyright December 17, 1963. Many years earlier he had also submitted it to *Stage* magazine for publication in its August 1938 issue.

Let me sing a simple song
That helps to jog the world along,
Along its weary way,
And I'll be glad today.

Let me mold a homely phrase
For those who sit through wintry days

Before a fireside
And I'll be satisfied.

Let me be a troubadour
And I will ask for nothing more
Than one short hour or so
To sing my song and go.

MY CASTLE

Registered for copyright as an unpublished song August 15, 1928. Written to be sung in counterpoint with "Nora" (the name of the heroine) in *Mammy*, but not used.

VERSE

I built my castle in Spain
Just at the end of the lane,
And it's especially made for
A girl and a boy—and it's paid for.

CHORUS

Just a cottage small
Behind a garden wall,
It's what I call my castle.
Just a little ground
With flowers to be found
Blooming all around my castle.
When the day is done and the setting sun
Slowly sinks in the West,
You can picture me very comf'tably
Cuddled up in my nest.
When it's time for prayers,
I climb a flight of stairs
With the one who shares my castle.

NORA

Registered for copyright as an unpublished song August 15, 1928. Written to be sung in counterpoint with "My Castle."

VERSE

I fell in love with a sweet little miss
Fair as a girl could be,
And what is much more important is this:

She fell in love with me.
I went and bought her a ring;
Now when I meet her I sing:

CHORUS

Skies of gray or skies of blue,
I love you, Nora;
And forever I'll be true,
True to you, Nora.
There's a cottage by the sea
Built for two and maybe three;
Oh, how happy we will be,
You and me, Nora.

TO MY MAMMY

Published. Copyrighted December 2, 1929. Previously registered for copyright as an unpublished song April 30, 1929. Introduced by Al Jolson in the 1930 film *Mammy*. Original cast recording by Al Jolson (Brunswick). Berlin later took the lyrical phrase of the release (lines 9–12 of chorus) and used it as the kernel of "How Deep Is the Ocean?"

VERSE

Mammy mine, there's a light divine
In your eyes that shines for me
And that light tells me I'm all right,
Though the world may not agree.
Whatever they say or do,
I know how I stand with you.

CHORUS

Who cares what the world may say?
No matter what comes my way,
I'm ev'rything
To my mammy.
Who cares if I lose the race?
No matter who takes my place,
I'm still the king
To my mammy.
How much does she love me?
I'll tell you no lie:
How deep is the ocean?
How high is the sky?
Who cares if my friends have gone?
You'll find me still holding on,
'Cause I can cling
To my mammy.

IN THE MORNING

Published in a black-and-white professional edition. Copyrighted December 4, 1929. Previously registered for copyright as an unpublished song May 16, 1929. Intended for *Mister Bones*. Introduced by the minstrel chorus in the 1930 film *Mammy*.

CHORUS

I may not sleep all night
But I'll be all right
In the morning.
I'll get right up and shout
When the sun comes out
In the morning.
It won't be long
Till the clock strikes eight,
But just the same
I can hardly wait:
Those wedding bells will chime
Around breakfast time
In the morning.
A happy ding-dong-ding
Will begin to sing
As a warning.
I've got the ring
And she'll have a bouquet,
And ev'rything is bound to be okay
With Malinda
Early in the morning.

KNIGHTS OF THE ROAD

Published. Copyrighted December 2, 1929. Previously registered for copyright as an unpublished song September 19, 1929. Introduced by Al Jolson and chorus in the 1930 film *Mammy*.

VERSE

When knighthood was in flower, 'twas grand—
The knights lived on the fat of the land.
The talents that they had were bestowed
On you and me, the knights of the road.

CHORUS

Life is like a song
As we march along,
Loyal knights of the road.

Clothes all torn to shreds,
Still we raise our heads,
Royal knights of the road.
Work may come but we step aside,
Knowing that the Lord will provide.
Let each man who strays
Drink to happy days
To the knights of the road.

OTHER EARLY FILM SONGS

PUTTIN' ON THE RITZ

Published with two different lyrics. Written in May 1927. First published December 2, 1929, after being registered for copyright as an unpublished song August 24, 1927, and again on July 27, 1928. The first, or "Lenox Avenue," version was introduced by Harry Richman and chorus in the 1930 United Artists film *Puttin' on the Ritz*. It was the first song in film to be sung by an interracial ensemble. Later sung by Clark Gable and "Les Blondes" in the 1939 MGM film *Idiot's Delight*. Richman's recording (Brunswick) became the number-one-selling record in America. Later, Berlin rewrote the lyric with the locale changed to Park Avenue. This version was published after being registered for copyright on August 28, 1946. Introduced by Fred Astaire in the 1946 Paramount film *Blue Skies*. Later sung by Peter Boyle (Monster) and Gene Wilder (Dr. Frankenstein) in the 1974 20th Century–Fox film *Young Frankenstein*. Revived by the Dutch/Indonesian singer Taco, whose recording (RCA) was a 1983 best-seller.

Original version

VERSE

Have you seen the well-to-do
Up on Lenox Avenue?
On that famous thoroughfare
With their noses in the air,
High hats and colored collars,
White spats and fifteen dollars,
Spending ev'ry dime
For a wonderful time.

CHORUS

If you're blue and you
Don't know where to go to,
Why don't you go where Harlem sits
Puttin' on the Ritz.
Spangled gowns upon a bevy
Of high browns from down the levee,
All misfits
Puttin' on the Ritz.
That's where each and ev'ry Lulu Belle goes
Ev'ry Thursday ev'ning with her swell beaus,
Rubbing elbows—
Come with me and we'll attend
Their jubilee and see them spend
Their last two bits
Puttin' on the Ritz.

Revised version

VERSE

Have you seen the well-to-do
Up and down Park Avenue?
On that famous thoroughfare
With their noses in the air
High hats and Arrow collars,
White spats and lots of dollars,
Spending ev'ry dime
For a wonderful time.

CHORUS

If you're blue and you
Don't know where to go to,
Why don't you go where fashion sits,
Puttin' on the Ritz.
Diff'rent types who wear a day coat,
Pants with stripes and cut-away coat,
Perfect fits,
Puttin' on the Ritz.
Dressed up like a million-dollar trouper
Trying hard to look like Gary Cooper,
Super duper.
Come let's mix where Rockefellers
Walk with sticks or umbrellas
In their mitts
Puttin' on the Ritz.

WITH YOU

Published. Copyrighted December 2, 1929. Previously registered for copyright as an unpublished song Janu-ary 31, 1929. Introduced by Harry Richman and Joan Bennett in the 1929 film *Puttin' on the Ritz*. Leading recordings by Guy Lombardo (Columbia), Harry Richman (Brunswick), and Fred Waring (Victor).

VERSE

I could find the road to happiness
With you close to me, dear.
I could turn a failure to success,
If you always were near.
I could make my dreams come true,
But it will depend on you.

CHORUS

With you, a sunny day;
Without you, clouds in the sky.
With you, my luck will stay;
Without you, fortune will fly.
With you, I'll never stop
Until I've reached the top;
Without you, I will never get by.
With you, a happy song;
Without you, castles that fall.
With you, I can't go wrong;
Without you, chances are small.
With you, my banner's unfurled
Right there on top of the world;
Without you, I'm just nothing at all.

MARIE (THE DAWN IS BREAKING)

Published. Copyrighted July 24, 1928. Previously registered for copyright as an unpublished song June 4, 1928. The theme song of the Samuel Goldwyn film *The Awakening*, which starred Vilma Banky. It is widely but erroneously asserted that "Marie" did not become popular until Tommy Dorsey's legendary 1937 recording. Yet Rudy Vallee's 1928 recording (Harmony) was the number-two-selling recording in America in early 1929, and there were other leading late-1920s recordings of "Marie" by Nat Shilkret (Victor), Franklyn Baur (Victor), the Troubadours (Victor), and others. Eight years later, Tommy Dorsey, changing the time signature from 3/4 to 4/4, made his famous fox-trot recording. Dorsey's disc (Victor) became the number-one seller in America. The musicians' "filler" lyrics behind Jack Leonard's vocal were an added treat. Also featured on that recording was a trumpet solo by Bunny Berigan. Dorsey's recording was so widely celebrated that Berlin published the song in the bandleader's "fox-trot ar-rangement" with its instruction that it be performed in "moderate swing tempo." Alternate title: "Marie."

VERSE

There's a gleam in your eyes, Marie,
And the meaning is plain to see,
But you'll find romance
Is a game of chance
That is not all it seems to be.

CHORUS

Marie,
The dawn is breaking;
Marie,
You'll soon be waking
To find
Your heart is aching,
And tears will fall
As you recall
The moon
In all its splendor,
The kiss
So very tender,
The words
"Will you surrender
To me, Marie?"

WHERE IS THE SONG OF SONGS FOR ME?

Published. Copyrighted July 13, 1928. Previously registered for copyright as an unpublished song June 22, 1928. Introduced by Lupe Velez in the D. W. Griffith film *Lady of the Pavements*. Leading recording by Franklyn Baur (Victor). Other recordings by Lupe Velez (Victor), Johnny Hamp's Kentucky Serenaders (Victor), and Paul Small (Velvetone). Many years later, Berlin used the opening musical phrase of the chorus as the start of "Is He the Only Man in the World?" from *Mr. President* (1962).

VERSE

Most of the world seems to be
List'ning to love's melody;
Each has a love song divine—
When will I listen to mine?

CHORUS

Where is the song of songs for me?
Beautiful song of ecstasy,
When will I hear the melody?
When will I hear the words "I love you"?
Where is the one I long to see?
Close to my heart in days to be,
Singing the song of songs to me,
Saying the words of words, "I love you."

COQUETTE

Published. Copyrighted November 30, 1928. Previously registered for copyright as an unpublished song October 27, 1928. Theme song of the film *Coquette*, starring Mary Pickford. Recordings by Rudy Vallee and His Connecticut Yankees (Victor) and the Paul Whiteman Orchestra, vocal by Bing Crosby (Columbia).

VERSE 1

Just a sweet coquette,
So they say, and yet
I know how true you can be.
Just a butterfly,
So they say, but I
Know just how much you love me.

CHORUS

The others you've met
May call you coquette,
But I'll always call you sweetheart.
They think of coquette
As something to pet,
But I think of you as sweetheart.
They say you're a devil with wonderful charms,
But I held an angel that night in my arms.
So try and forget
The name of coquette
And only remember sweetheart.

VERSE 2

Now that I love you
And you love me too,
I'll keep you close to my heart.
Now that I can see
You belong to me,
Nothing can keep us apart.

REPEAT CHORUS

SWANEE SHUFFLE

Published. Copyrighted August 21, 1929. Previously registered for copyright as an unpublished song August 16, 1928. Introduced by Nina Mae McKinney in the 1929 MGM King Vidor film *Hallelujah*.

VERSE

The Benevolent Order of the Flat-Footed Waiters
Gave their annual ball;
With the price of admission only one half a dollar
They just crowded the hall.
Flat-footing around,
They suddenly found
An original movement that they call Swanee
   Shuffle;
It's for one and for all.

CHORUS

Learn to do the Swanee Shuffle,
Nothing to the Swanee Shuffle—
Against the beat
You make your feet
Swanee Shuffle along.
If they're flat just make 'em flatter,
Like a pancake on a platter.
I'm telling you
It's easy to
Swanee Shuffle along.
Just imitate the way a waiter
Walks with a plate of chow;
You needn't wait, you'll do it later,
So why not now?
I'll show you how.
Come with me where Dixie marches,
Marches on its fallen arches,
And see them Swanee Shuffle along.

WAITING AT THE END OF THE ROAD

Published. Copyrighted June 10, 1929. Previously registered for copyright as an unpublished song April 30, 1929. Introduced by Daniel J. Haynes and the Dixie Jubilee Singers in the 1929 MGM King Vidor film *Hallelujah*. Original cast recording by Haynes and Dixie Jubilee Singers (Victor). Other leading recording by Paul Whiteman (Columbia).

VERSE

Weary of roaming on,
Yearning to see the dawn,
Counting the hours till
I can lay down my load;
Weary, but I don't mind,
Knowing that soon I'll find
Peace and contentment
At the end of the road.

CHORUS

The way is long,
The night is dark,
But I don't mind,
'Cause a happy lark
Will be singing
At the end of the road.
I can't go wrong;
I must go right—
I'll find my way,
'Cause a guiding light
Will be shining
At the end of the road.
There may be thorns in my path,
But I'll wear a smile,
'Cause in a little while
My path will be roses.
The rain may fall
From up above,
But I won't stop,
'Cause the ones I love
Will be waiting
At the end of the road.

Douglas Fairbanks and Bebe Daniels, center

REACHING FOR
THE MOON | 1930

REACHING FOR THE MOON (1930)

A film produced by Joseph M. Schenck and Douglas Fairbanks for United Artists Studio. Released in December 1930. Music and lyrics by Irving Berlin. Screenplay by William Anthony McGuire, credited to Edmund Goulding, with additional dialogue by Elsie Janis. Based on a story by Irving Berlin. Earlier title: *Love in a Cottage*. Directed by Edmund Goulding. Music conducted by Alfred Newman. Cast: starring Douglas Fairbanks Sr. (Larry Day) and Bebe Daniels (Vivien Benton) and featuring Edward Everett Horton (Roger, the Valet), Claud Allister (Sir Horace Partington Chelmsford), Jack Mulhall (Jimmy Carrington), Walter Walker (James Benton), June MacCloy (Kitty), Helen Jerome Eddy (Larry's Secretary), and Bing Crosby (an unnamed singer).

Irving Berlin, quoted in the *New York Times Magazine*, May 11, 1958:

> I had just come back from Hollywood. I'd written a lot of songs for a picture called *Reaching for the Moon*. This was after the stock market crash. Musicals were the rage out there and all of a sudden they weren't. Out went the songs. I developed the damnedest feeling of inferiority.

Reaching for the Moon was one of several film musicals of this period that lost their songs before their release.

BROKERS' ENSEMBLE (DON'T SELL AMERICA SHORT)

Registered for copyright as an unpublished song April 1, 1930. Intended for the ensemble as the opening number of *Love in a Cottage*. A slightly revised version, with an added introduction and coda, was projected as the second number in *Reaching for the Moon*. Dropped when most of Berlin's score was deleted after the press screening but before the film was released.

They're going up, up,
Stocks are going up—
They're goin' way up.
They're going up, up,
Stocks are going up—
They're gonna stay up.

They're going up
Without a stop.

There doesn't seem
To be a top.
And what is more, my son,
They've only just begun,
So don't sell America short.
They're going up,
You better buy;
Although they seem
A trifle high,
They're cheap at any price—
But take a friend's advice
And don't sell America short.
Someone that we know very well,
Someone who's in the know,
Bought a lot of
IT&T and Tel & Tel,
Motors, and Radio—so
Go out and get
A lot of shares
And be among
The millionaires.
You'll get your pockets full
If you become a bull
And don't sell America short.

They're going up, up,
Stocks are going up—
They're goin' way up.
They're going up, up,
Stocks are going up—
They're gonna stay up.

Earlier version

They're going up the hill
And going further still,
So don't sell America short

Just take a look at Radio,
Motors, and Tel & Tel—
Who'd have even thought that folks who shouted
    "Buy"
Soon would begin to yell "Sell"?

A telegram to Mr. Day:
"You must come back
And right away.
We need a large amount
To cover your account.
We sold all your stocks
And you're still ninety thousand dollars short."

DO YOU BELIEVE YOUR EYES OR DO YOU BELIEVE YOUR BABY?

Registered for copyright as an unpublished song February 17, 1930, and again on March 29, 1930. Intended for the characters Joe, Gladys, and Louis and ensemble, it was the second number in *Love in a Cottage*. Retained in early drafts of *Reaching for the Moon* but dropped before the film's production.

VERSE

When you accuse me of being untrue, my dear,
It hurts me so,
You'll never know.
There's no one else that I'm loving but you, my
    dear,
That's true, and so
You ought to know.

CHORUS

I don't go out with other guys.
I saw you myself with my own eyes.
Do you believe your eyes
Or do you believe your baby?
Whoever told you told you lies.
I saw you myself with my own eyes
Do you believe your eyes
Or do you believe your baby?
You saw me dancing around until three.
But I was home with mother, so it wasn't me.
It must have been two other guys
I saw you myself with my own eyes.
Do you believe your eyes
Or do you believe your baby?

SHE: The stock we bought is going to go up, I hear.
HE: I know just where you're getting your tips
        from, my dear.
SHE: It isn't quite what you surmise.
HE: I saw you myself with my own eyes.
SHE: Do you believe your eyes
        Or do you believe your baby?

HOW MUCH I LOVE YOU

Registered for copyright as an unpublished song on three occasions: January 22, 1930; March 29, 1930; and November 30, 1977. Intended for Larry and Joyce in

Love in a Cottage. Dropped in April 1930. Replaced by "It's Yours." Berlin later used the verse to this number for "How Deep Is the Ocean?"

VERSE

How can I tell you what is in my heart?
How can I find the proper way to start?
How can I tell you of the things I've planned?
How can I ever make you understand?

CHORUS 1

I've got a lot of pretty words
To whisper in your ear,
But that won't tell you, dear
How much I love you.
I've got a sentimental song
To sing when lights are low,
And still you'd never know
How much I love you.
I've got the violets
To send you each day,
But they couldn't say
How much I love you.
I've got to take you in my arms
And hold you close to me,
And then perhaps you'll see
How much I love you.

CHORUS 2

I'd love to hear the pretty words
You'd whisper in my ear,
But that won't tell me clear
How much you love me.
I'd love a sentimental song
You'd sing when lights were low,
And still I'd never know
How much you love me.
I'd love the violets
You'd send me each day
But they couldn't say
How much you love me.
You'd better take me in your arms—
So much I love you

CHORUS 3

HE: If you will try to understand
And just believe in me,
My darling, you will see
How much I love you.
If you will wait a little while,
The skies will all be blue
And I will prove to you
How much I love you.

SHE: I'm tired of honeymoons
Where I spend the day
Just hearing you say
How much you love me.
Why don't you take me in your arms
When lights are burning low
And then perhaps I'll know
How much you love me?

UNFINISHED ADDITIONAL CHORUS

I've got a lot of Tel & Tel
And lots of Radio
And that will help me show
How much I love you.
I've got a little pot of gold
That's piling up each year;
It's all for you, my dear—
So much I love you.
I've got a lot of stocks and bonds
To buy the things for you
That you're accustomed to,
How much I love you . . .

IT'S YOURS

Registered for copyright as an unpublished song May 14, 1930. Intended for *Reaching for the Moon*, in which it was to have been sung by Larry (played by Douglas Fairbanks). On April 29, 1930, Berlin wrote the following about this song to his colleague and friend Max Winslow:

> Everyone is crazy about "It's Yours" and personally I feel that it's the best number in the piece. I am planning to take out the Love Song and use this in its place, because as the story is developed I can reprise it at least three times. The two numbers that will be plugged will be "It's Yours" and "Little Things in Life."

During the summer of 1930 the song appears to have been retitled "Ask for the Moon." Dropped from *Reaching for the Moon* when most of Berlin's score was deleted just prior to the commercial release of the film.

VERSE

You've heard tell about Aladdin's lamp;
After you've rubbed it your wishes come true.
From now on I'm your Aladdin's lamp
Rub me the right way and I'll do it too.

CHORUS

Ask for the moon,
I won't deny it—
If I can buy it,
It's yours.
Ask for the stars,
If I can reach one
I'll see that each one
Is yours.
Most anything
To please you, honey—
I'll take a swing
At Mr. Dempsey or Tunney.
Ask for my heart,
And though you break it,
If you will take it,
It's yours.

WHAT A LUCKY BREAK FOR ME

Registered for copyright as an unpublished song March 3, 1930, and again on April 1, 1930. Intended for Larry and ensemble in *Love in a Cottage.* Dropped before the script was retitled *Reaching for the Moon.* Alternate title: "Lucky Break."

VERSE

I was rather slow
As a Romeo;
I would give but they would never take.
That's all in the past;
Things have changed at last—
Love has given me a lucky break.

CHORUS 1

Clouds breaking,
Rainbows in the making—
What a lucky break for me!
Dawn breaking
Means a happy waking—
What a lucky break for me!
I said to my baby,
"How soon will the day be?"
"Any day you say," said she.
You'll find that she's breaking
Dates that she was making—
What a lucky break for me!

CHORUS 2

ENSEMBLE: Clouds breaking,
Rainbows in the making—
What a lucky break for you!
Dawn breaking
Means a happy waking—
What a lucky break for you!

LARRY: I said to my baby,
"How soon will the day be?"
"Any day you say will do."

ENSEMBLE: You'll find that she's breaking
Dates that she was making—
What a lucky break for you!

THEY'RE GOING DOWN (BROKERS' AND CUSTOMERS' SONG)

Included in the script for *Love in a Cottage* and in *Reaching for the Moon*. Dropped when most of the score was deleted from the film after the press screening but before the commercial release.

BROKERS: They're going down
Without a stop—
We never thought
They'd ever drop.
They're going down, but then
They're coming back again,
So don't sell America short.

CUSTOMERS: They're going down
Without a doubt—
And what is more,
They sold us out.
There's nothing left to do
But kill the fellow who
Said "Don't sell America short."

Just look at Radio,
Motors and Tel & Tel—
Who'd have ever thought
That the folks who shouted "Buy"
Soon would begin to yell
"Sell"?

JOE: A telegram
To Mr. Day:
"You must come back
And right away.

We need a large amount
To cover your account.
We sold all your stocks
And you're still ninety thousand dollars short."

LARRY: I've got a little pot of gold
That's piling up each year—
It's all for you, my dear,
So much I love you.

BROKERS: They're going down
Without a stop.
We never thought
They'd ever drop.
They're going down, but then
They're coming back again,
So don't sell America short.

LARRY: I've got a lot of stocks and bonds
Increasing every year—
They're all for you, my dear,
So much I love you.

HEALY: They're going down
Without a doubt,
And what is more,
They sold me out.
There's nothing left to do
But kill the fellow who
Said "Don't sell America short."

LARRY: I've got some Radio
I bought very cheap
I'll give you to keep
To prove I love you.

JOE: [*to* STENOG]
Please send a wire to Mr. White.
Tell him about the smash:
Tell him that a couple of hundred
thousand might
Carry him through the crash—
Cash.

LARRY: I've got a little pot of gold
To buy the things for you
That you're accustomed to,
So much I love you.

WEDDING AND CRASH

Unused. A later version of the "Brokers' Song."

They're going down, down,
Stocks are going down—
They're goin' way down.
Down, down,
Stocks are going down—
They're gonna stay down.

They're going down
Without a stop.
We never thought
They'd ever drop.
They're going down,
But then
They're coming back again,
So don't sell America short.
They're going down
Without a doubt,
And what is more,
They sold us out.
There's nothing left to do
But kill the fellow who
Said "Don't sell America short."

Just take a look at Radio,
Motors, and Tel & Tel—
Who'd have ever thought
That the folks who shouted "Buy"
Soon would begin to yell
"Sell"?

ENDING

Go have a talk
With Larry Day—
And do it now
Without delay.
We need a large amount
To cover his account
Or else we'll have to sell him out.
Sell him out,
Sell him out.
They're going down, down,
Stocks are going down—
They're goin' way down.
Down, down,
Stocks are going down—
They're gonna stay down.

A telegram
To Mr. Day:
"You must come back
And right away.
We need a large amount
To cover your bank account—
You're just ninety thousand dollars short."

Ask for the gold
Down in the mint, dear,

Just drop a hint, dear,
It's yours.

EARLIER ENDING

Clouds breaking,
Rainbows in the making—
What a lucky break for me!
Dawn breaking
Means a happy waking—
What a lucky break for me!

I've got a little pot of gold
That's piling up each year—
It's all for you, my dear,
So much I love you.

IF YOU BELIEVE

Published March 21, 1933; February 14, 1940; and February 5, 1954. Registered for copyright as an unpublished song February 17, 1930; April 1, 1930; July 8, 1931; February 25, 1933; and December 5, 1939. It was to have been sung in various versions of *Love in a Cottage* and *Reaching for the Moon* by a black southern preacher and his congregation, but was not in the released version of *Reaching for the Moon*. Introduced at the 1954 publication by Johnnie Ray, who sang it in the film *There's No Business Like Show Business* (1954).

1930 version

VERSE

Nonbelievers, listen—
You don't know what you're missin'
Until you start to believe.
'Stead of being doubters,
Be hallelujah shouters,
Or else you're going to grieve.
Those who say 'tain't so
Must go down below—
Those who live accordin'
Will cross the river Jordan,
So better start to believe.

CHORUS

If you believe
That there's a heaven,
You'll get to heaven,
If you believe.
If you believe

That there are angels,
You'll see the angels,
If you believe.
I'm not making promises
To the doubting Thomases,
But if you believe
The Lord can help you,
The Lord'll help you,
If you believe.

PATTER

Jonah went out one night in a gale.
Do you believe that?
We do!
Soon he was swallowed up by a whale.
Do you believe that?
We do!
Daniel lay down with the lions that roared;
Moses looked up and spoke to the Lord.
Do you believe that?
We do.

REPEAT CHORUS

1933 version

VERSE

All that I bring to you is love,
And all that I ask in return is love;
And long as there's love you'll find
Clouds will be silver lined.
All that I am and all that I'll be
Depends on the faith that you have in me;
The grandest of dreams come true
If you believe they do!

CHORUS

If you believe that we'll be happy,
I know that I can make you happy,
If you believe.
If you believe that a home can be a heaven,
We'll be in heaven,
If you believe.
Faith in our love and in each other
Will bring the happiness
That only love can achieve.
If there's a doubt in your heart,
The way is stormy,
But there's a rising sun before me
If you believe.

1940 and 1954 versions

VERSE

Listen, you nonbelievers,
Listen—you better start to believe.
Doubters, be hallelujah shouters,
Or else you're going to grieve.
There's no time to wait;
You may be too late.
Listen, you don't know what you're missin'
Until you start to believe.

CHORUS (SAME AS 1930 CHORUS)

THE LITTLE THINGS IN LIFE

Published. Copyrighted November 14, 1930. Written in August 1927. Registered for copyright as an unpublished song August 25, 1927; February 17, 1930; and April 1, 1930. Dropped from *Reaching for the Moon* when most of Berlin's score was deleted from the film just before its commercial release. Leading recordings by Gus Arnheim and His Orchestra (Victor) and Ted Wallace and His Campus Boys, vocal by Dick Dixon (Columbia).

VERSE

Great big houses with great big rooms
Were not fashioned for brides and grooms—
A little place is where we should be.
Great big troubles and great big cares
Come from houses with marble stairs—
A little place for you and for me

CHORUS 1

Just a little room or two
Can more than do
A little man and wife;
That's if they're contented with
The little things in life.
Living on a larger scale
Would soon entail
A lot of care and strife.
We could be so happy with
The little things in life:
A little rain,
A little sun,
A little work,
A little fun,
A little time for loving

When the day is done,
And a little thing that cries
For lullabies
Could make a man and wife
Tell the world how much they love
The little things in life.

CHORUS 2 (FROM RELEASE)

SHE: A little can,
 A little jar—
HE: A little tin
 Of caviar—
SHE: A little biscuit and some
 Pâté de foie gras—
HE: Just a little food that's canned—
SHE: Some dishes
 And a little fork and knife—
BOTH: We'd be happy living on
 The little things of life.

WHEN THE FOLKS HIGH UP DO THE MEAN LOW-DOWN

Published. Copyrighted January 23, 1931. Previously registered for copyright as an unpublished song February 17, 1930, and April 1, 1930. Introduced in *Reaching for the Moon* by Bing Crosby, Bebe Daniels, June MacCloy, and ensemble, the only song to be sung in the commercially released picture.

VERSE

Lenox Avenue is known
For doing the low-down,
But you'll find they're not alone
In doing the low-down.
Fifth Avenue's learning how
They had to fall.
Fifth Avenue does it now
And that's not all.

CHORUS

Whenever the folks high up
Do the mean low-down,
There is no low-down
Lower than that.
Whenever the swells slow down
And become low-down,
There is no low-down
Lower than that.
You may believe it or not,

When they start getting hot
There is no Hottentot
That's hotter than that.
So you can lay your dough down
When they go low-down—
There is no low-down
Lower than that.

REACHING FOR THE MOON

Published. Copyrighted December 22, 1930. Previously registered for copyright as an unpublished song December 4, 1930. Heard as background music on the soundtrack for *Reaching for the Moon*. Intended to have been sung by Joyce (Bebe Daniels). Leading recording by Ruth Etting (Columbia).

VERSE

A pale new moon,
A sky of blue,
And here am I,
But where are you?
A dream of love
Would soon come true
If I could reach
The moon and you.

CHORUS

The moon and you appear to be
So near and yet so far from me,
And here am I
On a night in June
Reaching for the moon and you.
I wonder if we'll ever meet;
My song of love is incomplete—
I'm just the words
Looking for the tune,
Reaching for the moon and you.

A TOAST TO PROHIBITION

Registered for copyright as an unpublished song July 24, 1930. Earlier title: "The Bootleggers' Song." Dropped from *Reaching for the Moon* when most of Berlin's score was deleted from the film just prior to its commercial release. This number was used later in *Face the Music* (1932), where, under the title "Drinking

Song," it was introduced by Joseph Macaulay and "the boys."

VERSE

Fill your glasses high
With the best of scotch or rye;
Raise your elbows to the right position—*
Now let's drink a toast
To the land we love the most
And the law that gave us Prohibition.†

CHORUS

Here's to the Eighteenth Amendment—
Long may America be dry!
Things are going very well
For the gentlemen who sell
To the many thirsty gentlemen who buy.
Here's to my pal Mr. Volstead
And to the members of his crew—
Just as long as there's a throat
For what just come off the boat
Three cheers for the red, white, and blue!

YOU'VE GOTTA DO RIGHT BY ME

Probably written for *Reaching for the Moon*. Unused.

CHORUS

When the lights were low
You called me baby
And parked me on your lap;
I believed you like a sap—
Now you gotta do right by me.
When the lights were low
You called me baby
And bounced me on your knee;
Make an honest girl of me—
Say you gotta do right by me.
I'm not the least bit shady;
Although I like to pet,
I'm not an ermine lady
That gentlemen forget.

Alternate version of line 3:
 Let me hear your highball glasses clinking—

†*Alternate version of line 6:*
 And the law that started people drinking.

Don't forget that rags
Are royal raiments
When worn for virtue's sake;
Give a decent girl a break—
Say you gotta do right by me.

(I ASK YOU) IS THAT NICE?

Registered for copyright as an unpublished song January 3, 1927. Intended for *Reaching for the Moon* but unused.

VERSE 1

Johnny, pleading with Jane,
Said: I hate to complain;
I've attracted you—
Still, you act that you
Think it's all in vain.
I'm beginning to see
You're just playing with me;
Your canoodling isn't everything
It's cracked up to be.

CHORUS 1

You're in my arms
But soon I find
Another sweetie's on your mind—
Is that nice?
I ask you,
Is that nice?
I sit with you
When lights are dim,
But all you do
Is speak of him—
Is that nice?
I ask you,
Is that nice?
I take you out
And spend everything I make;
Then I notice my angel cake
Turns right into a cake of ice—
Is that nice?
I know you're good as you can be;
You're good to everyone but me—
Is that nice?
I ask you,
Is that nice?

CHORUS 2

We made a date
To change your name;
I waited but you never came—
Is that nice?
I ask you,
Is that nice?
I had the ring,
The preacher too,
And I was there
But where were you?
Is that nice?
I ask you,
Is that nice?
They all grew tired of waiting
And hurried out,
And the preacher began to shout,
"Don't let the same bee
Sting you twice!"
Was that nice?
On that night I occupied
A bridal suite without a bride—
Is that nice?
I ask you,
Is that nice?

OVERLEAF: *Mary Boland makes a grand entrance.*
Inset: *Mary Boland, J. Harold Murray, Katherine Carrington, Hugh O'Connell, and Andrew Tombes*

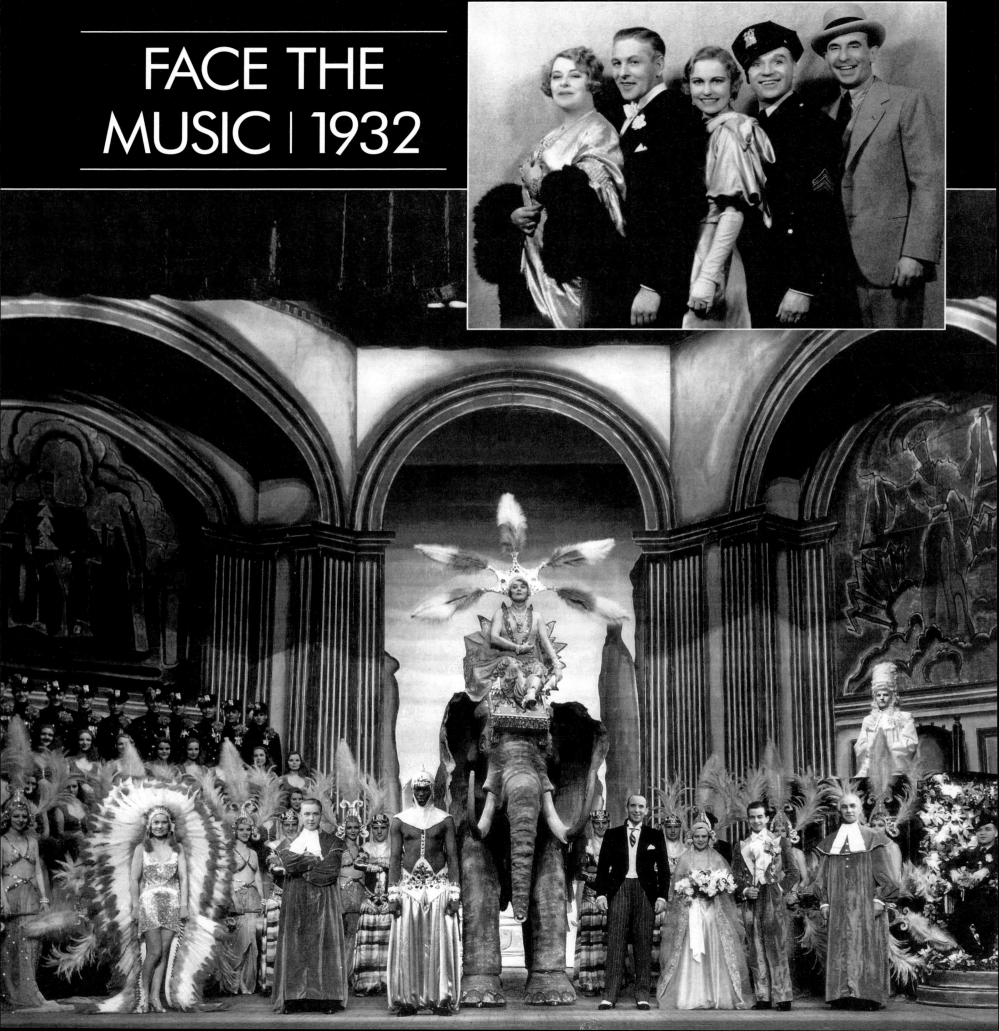

FACE THE MUSIC | 1932

FACE THE MUSIC (1932)

Tryout: Shubert Theater, Philadelphia, beginning February 3, 1932. New York: New Amsterdam Theatre; February 17, 1932; 165 performances. After a tour in late 1932 and early 1933, the show returned to New York on January 31, 1933, at the Forty-fourth Street Theatre; 32 performances. Billed as "a Musical Comedy Revue by Irving Berlin and Moss Hart." Actually, it was a book show, not a revue. Lyrics and music by Irving Berlin. Book by Moss Hart, with an uncredited assist by Morrie Ryskind. Produced by Sam H. Harris. Production staged and lighted by Hassard Short. Book directed by George S. Kaufman. Dances "created and arranged" by Albertina Rasch. Orchestrations by Robert Russell Bennett, Frank Tours, and Maurice B. de Packh. Orchestra under the direction of Frank Tours. Cast: starring Mary Boland (Mrs. Meshbesher) and J. Harold Murray (Pat Mason, Jr.), Andrew Tombes (Hal Reisman), Hugh O'Connell (Martin Van Buren Meshbesher), Katherine Carrington (Kit Baker), Joseph Macauley (Rodney St. Clair), Margaret Lee (Pickles), Jack Good (Joe), Jean Sargent (A Lady of the Evening), David (Dave) Burns (Louis), and the Albertina Rasch Dancers. Earlier titles: *Off the Beat*, *This Town of Ours*, and *Curtain Going Up* (credited to Moss Hart and Morrie Ryskind).

LUNCHING AT THE AUTOMAT

Registered for copyright as an unpublished song September 8, 1970. Introduced by ensemble; the opening number of the show. Alternate title: "Automat Opening."

Times are not so sweet,
But the bluebloods have to eat,
So the best of families meet
At the Automat.
All the millionaires
Who were lunching at Pierre's
Have been occupying chairs
At the Automat.
The Morgans and the Whitneys
And other big shots
Change dollars into jitneys
And drop them in the slots.
Times are on the fritz,

So they all have left the Ritz
And the social column sits
In the Automat.

Take your lunch at the Automat
And you'll find that it's become high-hat.
You'll see
Members of society,
Missus Belmont passing by,
Putting mustard on a Swiss-on-rye;
Ev'ry day with a tray in hand,
You can see those high-toned babies stand
In line.
Take a look at Missus Ryan
Pushing Missus Randolph Hearst,
Saying, "That's my place—I got here first."*
The Goulds and Biddles
And the Rockefellers too
Enjoy their griddles
Like the rest of us do,
And a plate of beans will fill their hearts with glee.
Come along and you will see
Missus Astor with a grin
And a dab of ketchup on her chin.
With pearls around her neck
Missus Woolworth eats her mutton,
And then she splits the check
With her girlfriend Missus Hutton;
And the scandal that will be spilt
When a Gould and Vanderbilt
Take a bit of a Swiss-cheese sandwich
And begin to chat
While lunching at the Automat.

Times are not so sweet,
But the bluebloods have to eat,
So the best of families meet

Before Berlin wrote the lyrics for the last "Times are not so sweet" section, there were two earlier versions of lyrics for the six lines beginning "Ev'ry day with a tray in hand":

First version:
Otto Kahn says it's very nice—
You should see him with a great big slice
Of ham.
Otto doesn't give a damn,
For it's really his belief
That it isn't ham, that it's just corned beef.

Second version:
Otto Kahn loses self-control—
You should see him dunking in a bowl
Of soup.
Otto doesn't give a whoop,
For he wants it understood—
If it isn't dunked, then it isn't good.

In the Automat.
While the panic's on,
If you look for Otto Kahn,
You will find that Otto's gone
To the Automat.
A Whitney with a pickle
Is not very swell,
But pickles for a nickle
Are cheap, so what the hell!
Times are on the fritz,
So they all have left the Ritz,
And the social column sits
In the Automat.

LET'S HAVE ANOTHER CUP OF COFFEE

Published. Copyrighted February 17, 1932. Previously registered for copyright as an unpublished song July 8, 1931. Introduced by J. Harold Murray (Pat Mason Jr.) and Katherine Carrington (Kit Baker). Leading recording by Fred Waring's Pennsylvanians, with vocal by Chick Bullock and Three Waring Girls (Victor). Historian Robert Lissauer (*Lissauer's Encyclopedia of Popular Music in America*) notes that this was "the theme song of the long-running radio show, *The Maxwell House Show Boat*, starring Lanny Ross and Annette Hanshaw." Later, Ethel Merman sang it in the 1954 film musical *There's No Business Like Show Business*.

VERSE

Why worry when skies are gray—
Why should we complain?
Let's laugh at the cloudy day;
Let's sing in the rain.
Songwriters say the storm quickly passes;*

Earlier versions of lines 1–5:

First version:
Tin Pan Alley meets every crisis
With a popular hit;
Each songwriter says, "My advice is
Don't be worried a bit."
In every song, the storm quickly passes;

Second version:
Songwriters are always gay;
They never complain:
Whenever the skies are gray,
They sing in the rain.
In every song, the storm quickly passes;

That's their philosophy.
They see the world through rose-colored glasses;
Why shouldn't we?

CHORUS

Just around the corner
There's a rainbow in the sky,
So let's have another cup o' coffee
And let's have another piece o' pie!
Trouble's just a bubble,
And the clouds will soon roll by,
So let's have another cup o' coffee
And let's have another piece o' pie!
Let a smile be your umbrella,
For it's just an April show'r,
Even John D. Rockefeller
Is looking for the silver lining.
Mister Herbert Hoover
Says that now's the time to buy,
So let's have another cup of coffee
And let's have another piece o' pie!*

REISMAN'S DOING A SHOW

Not listed in programs for the show. Introduced by, among others, Margaret Lee and Jack Good (Pickles and Joe), Aïda Conkey and Dorothy Walker (the Pratt Sisters), Dave Burns (Louis), Frances Halliday (Madame Elise), and Jean Sargent (A Lady of the Evening).

PICKLES AND JOE [a vaudeville team]

PICKLES: Reisman's doing a show.
JOE: Reisman's doing a show?
PICKLES: It says so in Variety—
He has a backer at last.
JOE: Suppose we call him up and see
If we can get in the cast.

THE PRATT SISTERS [a sister act]

FIRST: Reisman's doing a show.
SECOND: Reisman's doing a show?

---

*In early versions of the script, the Automat scene ended as follows:
Just around the corner
There's an eight- or ten-week buy,
So let's have another cup of coffee
And let's have another piece of pie.

FIRST: I understand the show is backed
And opens up in the fall.
SECOND: He may require a sister act,
So let's go pay him a call.

TWO HOOFERS

FIRST: Reisman's doing a show—
My agent told me so.
He needs a pair of hoofers that the
Public hasn't seen.
SECOND: Suppose we call around and let him
See the new routine.

LOU SHURR [an agent on phone]

Hello—hello—
Trafalgar seven oh oh—
Hello—Joe?
Reisman's doing a show.
He's looking for a tenor—
But you'll have to be content
To give him an audition
And to give me ten percent.

COSTUMER [dictating to STENOGRAPHER]

HE: Take a letter to Mr. Reisman.
Tell him I need the dough—
I mean the money that Reisman
owes me.
SHE: Reisman's doing a show.
HE: Reisman's doing a show?
SHE: Reisman's doing a show.
HE: Never mind the money he owes me—
Tell him I've heard the news.
Say that I've got a set of costumes
That he can use.

STREETWALKER [to POLICEMAN, who is about to arrest her]

Say, listen—
Reisman's doing a show.
He needs a ballad singer,
So you'll have to let me go.
Instead of walking pavements
I will soon be glorified;
I owe it to the public
And to Tyson and McBride.
Besides, I've had a rotten life:
If you'll release my hand,
I'll let you hear my story
And I think you'll understand.

[Segue to "Torch Song."]

Earlier version of final section

FIVE CHORUS GIRLS [one girl reading from the Mirror]

Girls, listen—
Reisman's doing a show.
It's here in Winchell's column,
So it really must be so.
Rehearsals start this morning,
So let's all be glorified;
We owe it to the public
And to Tyson and McBride.

Another earlier version of final section

LILLIAN SHADE [talking to two CHORUS GIRLS]

SHADE: Girls, listen—
Reisman's doing a show.
It's here in Winchell's column,
So it really must be so.
CHORUS GIRLS: Let's go join the chorus.
SHADE: But you haven't got a chance—
Outside of being beautiful
You must know how to dance.
FIRST GIRL: I studied with Wayburn.
SECOND GIRL: I studied with Madam Rasch.
FIRST GIRL: He taught me to buck-dance.
SECOND GIRL: She taught me to wave a sash.
CHORUS GIRLS: They said we had rhythm—
We paid them a lot of cash.
SHADE: Who said you had rhythm?
CHORUS GIRLS: Ned Wayburn and Madam Rasch.
SHADE: Rhythm is something that cannot
be bought—
It is the one thing that cannot be
taught.
You must be born with it, born
with it.

[Segue to "You Must Be Born with It."]

TORCH SONG

Registered for copyright as an unpublished song September 3, 1931. Introduced by Jean Sargent (A Lady of the Evening). Dropped from the show during the New York run.

VERSE

I'm just one of those women,
But I have no regret;
Let me tell you what made me

A girl that men forget.
Listen please while I tell you
How I happened to fall:
Someone sang me a torch song—
That's the cause of it all:

CHORUS

I wanted to sing a torch song,
So I got a man to break my heart,
And though I soon became a tart,
I did it for the sake of Art
And a torch song.
I needed a faithless lover
Who would give me all except his name,
A gigolo that I could blame,
And I was paid for all my shame
With a torch song.
I longed to sit upon a piano or an organ
Pouring out my heart, the same as Helen Morgan.
I wanted to sing a torch song
So I walked the streets where lights were pale
And shouted, "I've got love for sale"—
And now I'm winding up in jail
Singing a torch song.

YOU MUST BE BORN WITH IT

Registered for copyright as an unpublished song July 8, 1931. Introduced by Margaret Lee (Pickles) and Jack Good (Joe).

VERSE

Dancing schools
Are filled with fools
Who think they're gonna learn rhythm.
It's funny how much money
Is wasted that way:
Schools with reps
Will show them steps
And claim they're teaching them rhythm;
I'm saying what they're paying
Is just thrown away.

CHORUS

Rhythm is something
That's not to be bought;
It is the one thing
That cannot be taught:
You must be born with it—

You either have it
Or you simply haven't got it
On the day
That you're born.

Notice a place full
Of dancers get hot:
Some that are graceful
While others are not.
You must be born with it—
You either have it
Or you simply haven't got it
On the day
That you were born.

All the saxophoning men
The rhythm bands employ—
They're the ones who had it when
The doctor said, "It's a boy."

You won't be lifted
Whenever they play
Unless you are gifted
And gaited that way.
You must be born with it—
You either have it
Or you simply haven't got it
On the day
That you're born.

(CASTLES IN SPAIN) ON A ROOF IN MANHATTAN

Published February 17, 1932. Previously registered for copyright as an unpublished song July 8, 1931. Introduced by J. Harold Murray (Pat Mason Jr.) and Katherine Carrington (Kit Baker); danced by the Albertina Rasch Girls and ensemble. Alternate title (program): "A Roof in Manhattan."

VERSE

A cottage by the sea
Is not for you and me;
The time would soon arrive
When it would drive us frantic.
A little bungalow
Would never do, I know;
What I am hoping for
Is something more romantic.

CHORUS

We'll build a castle in Spain
On a roof in Manhattan,
And in our lofty domain
We'll pretend to be Latin.
You'll sing a sweet little tune
While I sit and strum my guitar;
We'll be so close to the moon,
I'll reach up and pluck you a star,
And through the night we'll remain,
Wrapped in velvet and satin,
And dream of castles in Spain
On a roof in Manhattan.

MY BEAUTIFUL RHINESTONE GIRL

Registered for copyright as an unpublished song September 3, 1931. Advertised for publication on sheet music covers for the show but never printed. Introduced by Joseph Macauley (Rodney St. Clair). Alternate title: "My Rhinestone Girl."

VERSE

Not like a glittering diamond,
Not like a pearl from the sea,
Not like the greenest of emeralds
Are you, my darling, to me.
Not like a beautiful topaz,
Not like a sapphire of blue,
Not like a rosy red ruby,
But like a rhinestone are you.

CHORUS

My beautiful rhinestone girl,
You're setting my heart awhirl.
In your eyes there's a light divine
And like rhinestones they seem to shine.
Bless the miners who mine stones
That turn out to be rhinestones,
For they sparkle like dew
And remind me of you,
My beautiful rhinestone girl.

SOFT LIGHTS AND SWEET MUSIC

Published. Copyrighted December 12, 1931. Previously registered for copyright as an unpublished song August 21, 1931. Introduced by J. Harold Murray (Pat Mason Jr.) and Katherine Carrington (Kit Baker). Leading recording by Fred Waring's Pennsylvanians, vocal by Three Waring Girls (Victor).

VERSE

I can't resist the moan of a cello;
I can't resist the light of the moon.
So place me in a light that is mellow
And let me hear a beautiful tune.
The music must flow;
The lights must be low.

CHORUS

Soft lights and sweet music
And you in my arms;
Soft lights and sweet melody
Will bring you closer to me.*
Chopin and pale moonlight
Reveal all your charms;
So give me velvet lights and sweet music
And you in my arms.

WELL, OF ALL THE ROTTEN SHOWS

Introduced by ensemble. Alternate title: "Opening—Second Act."

Well, of all the rotten shows!
Why it opened, heaven knows.
Did you ever see such scenery?
Did you ever see such clothes?
What a reminiscent score—
And the book was such a bore!
And that awful rhinestone number—
That was done before the war.
I wonder who produced it,
For the program doesn't say;

---

*In the script this line reads:
    Bring out the gypsy in me.

It's not the Minsky brothers—
They denied it yesterday.
Ev'ry sketch was much too long,
And the curtains all went wrong:
Did you ever hear such silence
At the end of every song?

What an awful mess!
Who would ever guess
That a thing like this
Could reach an opening night?
Such a disrespect
For your intellect!
I can just imagine
What the critics will write.
Any wonder why
The theatre's going to hell?
After looking at this show
It's easy to tell.
It's the worst in weeks,
And the wise old Greeks
Had a word for it,
And that word is "lousy."

I SAY IT'S SPINACH (AND THE HELL WITH IT)

Published. Copyrighted February 29, 1932. Previously registered for copyright as an unpublished song September 3, 1931. Introduced by J. Harold Murray (Pat Mason Jr.) and Katherine Carrington (Kit Baker).

VERSE

We must keep smiling and play the game
While life keeps hurrying on,
For there was trouble before we came,
'Twill be here after we're gone,
So we'll just have to prepare
To snap our fingers at care.

CHORUS

Long as there's you,
Long as there's me,
Long as the best things in life are free,
I say it's spinach
And the hell with it,
The hell with it,
That's all!
Long as I'm yours,
Long as you're mine,
Long as there's love and a moon to shine,

I say it's spinach
And the hell with it,
The hell with it,
That's all!
There must be rain to pitter-patter;
Things don't come on a silver platter—
What does it matter?
Long as there's you,
Long as there's me,
Long as the best things in life are free,
I say it's spinach
And the hell with it,
The hell with it,
That's all!

I DON'T WANNA BE MARRIED (I JUST WANNA BE FRIENDS)

Registered for copyright as an unpublished song September 3, 1931. Introduced by Margaret Lee (Pickles) and Jack Good (Joe). Alternate title: "I Don't Want to Be Married."

VERSE

You're compromising me,
But that's exactly as it ought to be:
I simply fell for you because I wanted to fall.
Don't speak of wedding chimes,
Because we mustn't be behind the times;
Besides, a wedding isn't necessary at all.

CHORUS 1

Don't worry because I fell—
You don't have to do right by Nell,
'Cause I don't wanna be married,
I just wanna be friends.
Don't worry 'cause I gave in—
Best of families live in sin,
'Cause they don't wanna be married,
They just wanna be friends.
While all the happy married couples sit and fight,
We'll be still going strong;
And fifty million Frenchmen say it's quite all right,
And that many can't be wrong.
I never would change my name
Even after the baby came,
'Cause I don't wanna be married,
I just wanna be friends.

CHORUS 2

BOY: My father would give me hell
    If I didn't do right by Nell.
GIRL: But I don't wanna be married,
    I just wanna be friends.
BOY: Please grant me my father's wish—
    Shotgun weddings are just his dish.
GIRL: 'Cause I don't wanna be married,
    I just wanna be friends.
BOY: The kiddies wouldn't like it, they'd be
        awfully mad,
    'Twould be known near and far.
GIRL: To be a little "who's this" isn't really bad,
    For some of my best friends are.
BOY: If not for the family,
    Make an hon'rable man of me!*
GIRL: But I don't wanna be married,
    I just wanna be friends.

MANHATTAN MADNESS

Published February 29, 1932. Previously registered for copyright as an unpublished song September 23, 1931. Introduced by J. Harold Murray (Pat Mason Jr.). The section beginning "Subways below . . ." is very similar musically to the section of "The Happy New Year Blues" (page 224) that begins "Counting the days . . ."

Manhattan, Manhattan,
Manhattan, Manhattan,
Manhattan madness,
You've got me at last.
I'm like a fly upon a steeple
Watching seven million people
Do a rhythm
That draws me with 'em.
Manhattan, Manhattan,
Manhattan, Manhattan,
Manhattan madness,
You're going too fast.
I'm like a baby on a rocker
Watching Father Knickerbocker
Being busy,
I'm getting dizzy.

*Earlier version of lines 13 and 14:
    BOY: Through life will I have to go
        Father to a cute so-and-so?

When shadows creep,
In my bed I tumble
But never sleep,
For I hear the rumble
In the street.
The tramping of feet
That haunt me the whole night long,
And through the day
I'm watching the drama
That people play
In your panorama,
And I hear,
In tones very clear,
The sound of your restless song.

Subways below and trains above racing,
Packed with humanity, chasing
Taxis and trucks and trolley cars,
Busy as they can be,
Steaming machines and riveters grating,
Motors instead of men,
Buildings go up with wrecking crews waiting
To tear them down again.
Newsies that shout sensational headlines,
Peddlars with things to sell
Noisy cafés and whispering breadlines,
Children that scream and yell,
Whistles and bells and siren horns blowing,
Pistols that crack and roar,
Traffic that stops and goes without knowing
What's all the shootings for.

Manhattan, Manhattan,
Manhattan madness,
You've got me at last.
I'm like a fly upon a steeple
Watching seven million people
Do a rhythm
That draws me with 'em,
And it's mad.

INVESTIGATION

Introduced by Andrew Tombes (Hal Reisman) and entire company. Also titled: "Investigation After Scene in One."

PROSECUTOR: Your Honor and ladies of the
        jury,
    At the outset let me say
    We are gathered here today
    To convince the prisoner at the
        bar

That a life of crime don't pay.
    He has broken, in effect,
    All the laws he should respect.
    He produced a show that glori-
        fied a bathroom.
DEFENSE: I object.
    The prisoner isn't guilty,
    And the prosecutor lies.
    He never saw a bathroom;
    Can't you see it in his eyes?
PROSECUTOR: But the evidence will show
    He's a villain mean and low,
    And before the trial is over
    Off to jail he'll have to go.
    Here's exhibit A,
    And I'd like to say
    It's the manuscript I put in
        evidence here:
    It's as full of dirt
    As the prisoner's shirt,
    And he hasn't changed his shirt
        for over a year.
DEFENSE: Now the prosecutor's mind
    Is narrow and small,
    For so help me, Judge,
    That book ain't dirty at all.
PROSECUTOR: It is most obscene.
DEFENSE: I insist it's clean.
JUDGE: I have read this book
    And I think it's lousy.
PRATT SISTERS: [singing in harmony]
    Lousy, lousy,
    That manuscript he read is
    Lousy, lousy,
    That's what His Honor said,
    So it really must be so,
    For His Honor ought to know,
    Yes, a lousy judge should
        know
    What's really lousy.
PROSECUTOR: One scene in Sweden
    In a Garden of Eden
    The girls were naked, I know.
    One girl, Your Honor,
    Who had nothing upon 'er
    Is here to prove that it's so.

[KIT enters on horse as Lady Godiva, à la Marilyn Miller in the Ziegfeld Follies.]

PROSECUTOR: [continues, to KIT]
    Please tell the jury
    How you came from Missouri
    And joined this terrible show.
KIT: When I came from Cincinnati
    And I joined this company,
    I was happy as can be,
    For it meant a salary.

When the op'ning night was
     over,
The producer came to me—
That's the night I lost my
     modesty.
He said, "We're flopping,
And the business is dropping—
The show's not liked by the
     mob."
There's no denying
That he soon had me crying;
I'm such a softhearted slob.
He said, "You'll have to take your
     clothes off
Or the show's off—here's why:
Having girls with no apparel
Is how Carroll gets by.
You must go naked;
Either leave it or take it"—
And Judge, I needed the job.

PROSECUTOR: So you see the prisoner's plot was
     carefully planned.
DEFENSE: I would like to have the
     prisoner step to the stand.
CLERK: Mr. Meshbesher,
     Mr. Meshbesher,
     Mr. Meshbesher will kindly step
     to the stand.
DEFENSE: [to PRISONERS]
     Tell the judge of your crippled
          aunt,
     That whatever she may want, you
          grant
     Her wish.
PRISONER: Me no speaka Eng-a-lish.
JURY: Yes, he always grants her wish,
     But he no speaka Eng-a-lish.
DEFENSE: Tell the judge you're a
          Christian true,
     That on every Friday evening
          you
     Eat fish.
PRISONER: Me no speaka Eng-a-lish.
JURY: Every Friday he eats fish
     But he no speaka Eng-a-lish.
DEFENSE: For this fair city
     He would give up his life.
     He loves his kiddie
     And his home and his wife,
     And he helps her wash the
          dishes—
     Every dish.
PRISONER: But me no speaka Eng-a-lish.
JURY: Yes, he washes every dish,
     But he no speaka Eng-a-lish.
PROSECUTOR: The counselor's plan is quaint;
     I object to his suggestions.

The prisoner's not a saint,
And I'd like to ask some
     questions.

[to PRISONER]

Didn't you sign a lot of checks
For a show that was full of sex?
Didn't you make a decent girl
Undress against her wish?
PRISONER: But me no speaka Eng-a-lish.
JURY: She undressed against her wish,
     But he no speaka Eng-a-lish.
DEFENSE: There is one more witness
     I will call to the stand;
     It's the prisoner's wife,
     And give this girl a big hand.
CLERK: Mrs. Meshbesher,
     Mrs. Meshbesher,
     Mrs. Meshbesher will kindly step
     to the stand.

[MRS. MESHBESHER enters on trunk of elephant.]

MRS.
MESHBESHER: Your Honor and ladies of the
     jury,
     I am here to testify,
     And believe me, I won't lie—
     But whatever else my husband
          is,
     He's as harmless as a fly.
     It's a falsehood when they say
     That he produced a sexy play—
     If it was, he didn't know it,
     For his mind don't run that
          way.
     Believe me, Judge, my husband
     Doesn't know the facts of life,
     And if he's been enlightened,
     Then it's news to me, his wife.
     On my wedding night
     I looked like Lill'an Gish
     But he no speaka Eng-a-lish.
JURY: Yes, she looked like Lill'an
     Gish,
     But he no speaka Eng-a-lish.
PROSECUTOR: She's trying to protect
     The defendant in this action.
DEFENDANT: Your Honor, I object;
     I demand a quick retraction.
JUDGE: Your objection is quite okay.
DEFENDANT: That is just what I thought
     you'd say.
PROSECUTOR: If His Honor had only gone to
     see that play,
     I wonder what he *then* would say.

JUDGE: Long as you've asked,
     Long as I may,
     Long as you must know what I
          would say,
     I'd say it's spinach and the hell
          with it.
JURY: The hell with it, that's all.
JUDGE: But I've weighed the evidence
          well
     And it's very easy to tell
     That the jury will agree with
          me—
     The prisoner's guilty as hell.
     The prisoner is guilty, yes,*
     For really I must confess
     In his eyes there's that certain
          look
     Tells me he's a dirty crook.
     Don't believe his attorney;
     Off to jail he must journey—
     From that verdict don't budge.
REISMAN: [rushing on]
     No you don't, Mister Judge!
     Your sentence will need
          amending,
     For we must have a happy
          ending—
     My productions, you see,
     Must end happily.
JURY: Your sentence will need
          amending,
     For he must have a happy
          ending.†
JUDGE: So I'll have to agree
     To let you go free.

---

*The Judge's first five lines replaced the following:
     But my duty to the State
     Is as solemn as it's great,
     And before I charge the jury
     To decide the prisoner's fate,
     I wish to say to the jury:
     Judge this unfortunate man—
     Don't you go into a fury,
     But be as kind as you can.
     First, there must be no confusion;
     Just weigh the evidence well.
     Then you must reach this conclusion:
     Meshbesher's guilty as hell.
     The prisoner's guilty, yes,

†Earlier version of four lines beginning "My productions, you see":
     So you'll have to agree
     To let him go free.
JURY: We must have a happy ending
     Or the curtain won't be descending.

KIT and PAT: And we'll sing the happy
ending,
Blending . . .

[*Segue into "Soft Lights and Sweet Music." Entire
company finishes chorus.*]*

---

*Earlier version of ending of scene, following "The
prisoner's guilty as hell":*

ALL: He's guilty, he's guilty.
He's guilty, he's guilty.
PROSECUTOR: The prisoner's guilty,
He's guilty as hell,
And off to jail he'll have to
journey.
DEFENSE: No he won't, with an attorney
Who is clever.
PROSECUTOR: To jail forever.
DEFENSE: Never!
ALL: He's guilty, he's guilty.
He's guilty, he's guilty.
JUDGE: The prisoner's guilty,
He's guilty as hell,
And in the morning when he's risen,
Take him to the nearest prison—
Throw him in it.
REISMAN: Just a minute!
A term in jail
He must not be spending—
This show would fail
With that kind of ending.
Set him free
And end happily,
For that's what they want today.
A tragedy
Would mean my destruction;
It wouldn't be
A Reisman production.
Happiness
Has been my success,
And this show must end that way.
JURY: We've got to have a happier ending,
That's what it has to be.
COPS: We've got to have a happier ending,
That's what they want to see.
DEFENSE: [*to* JUDGE]
We've got to have a happier ending—
Surely you must agree.
JUDGE: If there must be a happier ending,
I'll set the prisoner free.
DEFENSE: And now it's up to me
To sing the happy ending,
Blending . . .

[*Segue into "Soft Lights and Sweet Music."*]

THE NUDIST COLONY

Registered for copyright as an unpublished song September 11, 1931. Sung by Katherine Carrington (Kit Baker); danced by the Albertina Rasch Girls. Dropped from the show before the New York opening and replaced by "Crinoline Days" (see page 205). In *This Town of Ours*, an earlier version of the script, the following title is listed: "We'll Start a Colony of Nudists in Central Park." No lyric carrying out that idea is known to survive. Alternate titles of this song: "The Nudist Song" and "Let's Start a Nudist Colony."

VERSE

In a certain book I'm reading
About sex psychology
There are pictures you can see
Of a nudist colony.
It is somewhere out in Sweden,
Where they laugh at modesty;
Maybe that's the place for you and me.

CHORUS

Somewhere in Sweden
There's a Garden of Eden
Where men and women are one.
They dress each morn with
Just the clothes they are born with
And stay all day in the sun.
If you would care to see those Adams
And their madams
Turn brown,
If you'd care to see them stand up
To be tanned up
And down,
Go out to Sweden
To the Garden of Eden
And take your place in the sun.

REISMAN'S PUTTING IT ON

No music is known to survive. Unused. Intended for late in Act II but not part of any of the early scripts.

Reisman's putting it on,
Reisman's putting it on.
He's staging the investigation
With the biggest of names;

It's gonna be a revelation—
So the governor claims.
Reisman's putting it on,
Reisman's putting it on.
He's picked a sexy jury,
Fifty blondes with beautiful curls,
And Ziegfeld's in a fury,
For he's taken all of his girls.
Reisman's doing it right,
And on the opening night
There won't be any critics,
For we'll put them all in jail;
The mayor will write the notices,
Which ought to help the sale.
Reisman said that investigations
Ought to be made to pay
And that is why the administration's
Letting him have his way.
Reisman's having his way
And he's making it pay.
Reisman knew the city's condition
Wasn't so very hot;
Charging the public an admission
Would help a lot,
And that's the real reason
Reisman's putting it on.
Go out and get your tickets now,
For soon they'll all be gone.
Come on and see America's policemen glorified—
You owe it to the public
And to Tyson and McBride.

TWO CHEERS
INSTEAD OF THREE

Registered for copyright as an unpublished song July 8, 1931. Included in early versions of *Face the Music* when the script was titled *Off the Beat* and *This Town of Ours*. Intended for Act I soon after "Let's Have Another Cup of Coffee," but not used in the version tried out in Philadelphia and performed on Broadway.

In the *Off the Beat* and *This Town of Ours* scripts, this song is introduced as follows:

With a great fanfare of trumpets, the Parade comes on. The Parade proper consists of various symbolic American figures carrying banners bearing such well-known [slogans] as "Don't Sell America Short, etc." This banner, for instance, is carried by an American Indian. Another banner is carried by an almost nude lady, which says: "Don't Forget Our Natural Resources." And so forth. The final figure is Uncle Sam flanked on each side by a soldier and a sailor; he is standing behind a large sign which says: "It's Smart To Be Thrifty." As he steps from behind the sign it is revealed that he wears kilts. Great applause from the crowd, a blare of trumpets and he sings, with patriotic fervor: "We'll Just Have Two Cheers Instead of Three."

VERSE

It's smart to be thrifty
When times are so bad.
Let's be patriotic,
But let's not go mad;
We must cheer the colors we prize,
But here's what I strongly advise:

CHORUS 1

We'll just have two cheers
Instead of three
For the land of the brave and the free.
Instead of three cheers
We'll just have two
For the red and the white and the blue,
So when we cheer the Stars and Stripes,
Here's what we'll do:
We'll cheer the red and cheer the white,
But not the blue,
And just have two cheers
Instead of three
For the land of the brave and the free!

PATTER

Why give them three cheers
When two will more than do?
If there must be cheers,
Then let there just be two.
And the speeches that you make to Uncle Sam,
Cut 'em down to "Unaccustomed as I am."

CHORUS 2

And give them two cheers
Instead of three

[*Continue as in chorus 1*]

THE POLICE OF NEW YORK

Registered for copyright as an unpublished song July 8, 1931. Intended for the ensemble to perform in the Act I finale in the earliest version of the script, *Off the Beat*. Also included in *This Town of Ours*, but not in the final version as tried out in Philadelphia and performed on Broadway.

In *Off the Beat*, this song is introduced as follows:

The policemen pour out of the station houses, and the song "The Police of New York" starts. It is played for a rousing Finale and built up with the girls and groups of old time policemen with helmets and walrus mustaches. While the number is being sung, the stage runs riot behind them. All sorts of gangster and guerrilla warfare take place as the boys continue to sing.

VERSE

New York's finest,
That's exactly what we are,
And a finer bunch of men you never saw.
New York's finest,
We are known both near and far
As the men who keep the crooks within the law.

CHORUS

The police of New York,
Mister Ryan and O'Brien and O'Rourke,
Keep the crooks out of sight
Till they learn how to turn to the right.
When we put soft pedals
On the racketeers,
They'll give us gold medals
And a big three cheers!
There's a fight in the dark
As we stroll on patrol through the park;
There's a punch in the jaw
That we aim in the name of the law—
And there are more of us
In the County Cork
To increase the police of New York.

PATTER

When a guy demands
That you raise your hands,
If you think that he's a crook,
Just call the police.
If he takes your purse,
Don't begin to curse:
Let him take your pocketbook—

Then call the police.
If a burglar wakes you up
And flashes his light,
'Twould be very foolish
If you started to fight.
You can take a peep,
Then go back to sleep,
But before you say good night,
Just call the police.

REPEAT CHORUS

Earlier patter (with different music)

When a thief demands
That you raise your hands
And he holds you up at night,
We'll be lurking near
So you needn't fear—
It'll all turn out all right.
When the gashouse gang
Does a bang-bang-bang
And you hear a pistol shot,
In the news next day
You will find they say
We were right there on the spot.
When a nasty crook
Takes your pocketbook
And you don't know what to do,
Don't begin to curse;
We will get your purse
And we'll give it back to you.
When you wake at night
From a burglar's light
And you know he's come to rob,
You can take a peep,
Then go back to sleep—
We'll be right there on the job.

REPEAT CHORUS

This Town of Ours includes this description following the lyric:

While the patter is being sung by the cops downstage, we show behind them a hold up—a couple of gangsters shooting at each other—a man hit on the head with a blackjack—another's pocket is picked, etc. This Finale is played strictly for comedy until the last chorus when eight of the boy dancers come on in the Gay Nineties police costumes with walrus mustaches and helmets and the finale finishes with general dancing [by the] ensemble. An effect may be gotten by having flash lights in the nightsticks.

THE DANCING COPS

No music is known to have survived. Intended for Act II of *This Town of Ours*, but not included in any subsequent version of the script.

The following note on the lyric appears to have been written by Berlin:

This is an idea for 2 great dancers, like Doyle + Dixon used to be, to have them come on in 3 different spots, each time with a different lyric pertaining to the plot and, if it works out, it may be very valuable for spots in one while making changes. The following is their first entrance, after the board meeting scene. They dance while singing this lyric and continue with a routine that should be good enough for applause.

FIRST COP: How do you like to be backing a
    show?
SECOND COP: It's not very hard,
    For there's not much to know.
FIRST COP: I know better ways of investing your
    dough—
    The wife must never find out.
SECOND COP: What do you think of the third from
    the end?
FIRST COP: If you're stepping out,
    She's what I recommend.
SECOND COP: She's coming tonight
    And she's bringing a friend—
    The wife must never find out.

FIRST COP: Let's take them to the Casino and
    dance—
    The finest music is there.
SECOND COP: Not the Casino; we can't take a
    chance—
    We may run into the mayor.
FIRST COP: Let's take them into the park for a
    chat.
SECOND COP: We may meet the sergeant,
    So I'm not for that.
FIRST COP: The sergeant will be in the hot
    singer's flat.
BOTH: The wife must never find out.

HOW CAN I CHANGE MY LUCK?

Registered for copyright as an unpublished song November 24, 1931. Probably intended for *Face the Music*, as copies of this song were found along with other songs from the show.

VERSE

I've looked round for a lucky charm
Of the popular kind
That would keep me away from harm—
They're not easy to find.
Four-leaf clovers and rabbit's feet,

Lucky as they may be,
May help others, but I repeat,
They have never helped me.

CHORUS

The rabbit's foot that I found one day
Was on a rabbit that ran away—
Ooh, ooh, what'll I do?
How can I change my luck?
The four-leaf clover I stooped to pick
Was poison ivy and made me sick—
Ooh, ooh, what'll I do?
How can I change my luck?
I hung a horseshoe
Right over my bed;
Down came the horseshoe
On top of my head.
The lucky star that I long to see
Is shining somewhere, but not for me—*
Ooh, ooh, what'll I do?
How can I change my luck?

REPEAT CHORUS

Tag for repeat of chorus, lines 13 and 14:
    The lucky goldpiece, the one I had,
    I tried to spend it, but it was bad—

AS THOUSANDS CHEER | 1933

AS THOUSANDS CHEER (1933)

Tryout: Forrest Theatre, Philadelphia; September 9, 1933. New York run: Music Box; opened September 30, 1933; 400 performances. A musical revue by Irving Berlin (lyrics and music) and Moss Hart (sketches). Produced by Sam H. Harris. Staged and lighted by Hassard Short. Dances arranged by Charles Weidman. Orchestrations by Adolph Deutsch, Frank Tours, Eddie Powell, Russell Wooding, and Helmy Kresa. Philadelphia programs also credited orchestrations to Hans Spialek. Orchestra under the direction of Frank Tours. Cast: starring Marilyn Miller, Clifton Webb, Helen Broderick, and Ethel Waters, and featuring Leslie Adams, Hal Forde, Jerome Cowan, Harry Stockwell, Thomas Hamilton, Hamtree Harrington, Peggy Cornell, Harold Murray, and the Charles Weidman Dancers led by Letitia Ide and José Limón. A post-Broadway tour, with Dorothy Stone replacing Marilyn Miller, continued into 1935.

Irving Berlin, from an undated, untitled newspaper article:

> Most of the songs and choruses in my new revue *As Thousands Cheer* were written to fit the newspaper idea around which the show was built. As a result, the lyrics came first nearly every time.

MAN BITES DOG

Registered for copyright as an unpublished song September 14, 1970, and December 23, 1977. Introduced in the Prologue by Harry Stockwell (Reporter), Jerome Cowan (Editor), and ensemble. Alternate title: "Man Bites Dog Opening."

PART ONE [*after sketch blackout*]

[*Editor's office.*]
REPORTER: I've got a headline—oh, what a
    headline—
    Off the beaten track:
    A dog bit a man and the man bit the
    dog right back.
EDITOR: [*on phone*]
    You can print what Roosevelt said

Clockwise from top left: Dancers José Limón and Letitia Ide in "Revolt in Cuba" ballet; Marilyn Miller; Clifton Webb as Gandhi and Helen Broderick as Aimee Semple McPherson; Ethel Waters as Josephine Baker

On the front page for a great big
    spread.
REPORTER: But I've got a headline—oh, what a
    headline—
    Off the beaten track:
    A dog bit a man and the man bit the
    dog right back.
EDITOR: [*on phone*]
    Hold the wire, it's hard to hear—
    There is someone screaming in my
    ear.

[*To* REPORTER:]

    What the hell is the matter with you
    And why the big enthuse?
REPORTER: A man was bitten by a dog.
EDITOR: I know, but that's not news.
REPORTER: But the man bit the dog right back.
EDITOR: What's that you say?
    Got no time for gags today.
REPORTER: But this is no gag—it's on the square;
    I just this minute came back from
    there.
EDITOR: You just this minute came back from
    where?
REPORTER: From the swell Park Avenue shack
    Where a dog bit a man and the man
    bit the dog right back.
EDITOR: [*on phone*]
    Never mind the Roosevelt speech—
    I've a headline now that is a peach.
    It's a most important story
    That'll set the town agog.
    Kill the Roosevelt spread;
    Print this instead:
    MAN—BITES—DOG.

PART TWO

[*In the dark.*]
NEWSBOYS: Extra! Extra! Man bites dog!
    Extra! Extra! Man bites dog!
    Extra! Extra! Man bites dog!
    Extra! Extra! Man bites dog!

[*Times Square.*]

    Man bites dog!
    Extra! Extra! Man bites dog! Extra!
    Extra!
    Here's a headline off the beaten
    track:
    MAN BITES DOG!
    A dog bit a man and the man bit the
    dog right back.
    Extra! Extra! Extra! Extra!
    MAN BITES DOG!
    Extra! Extra! Extra! Extra!
    Man bites dog.
    Extra! Extra! Extra! Extra!

BOYS AND
GIRLS WITH
NEWSPAPERS: [*before curtain*]
    At last—at last—
    Something new in the news at last,
    Something else in the news
    Besides that the drys will lose,
    Besides that we'll soon have booze,
    Besides that we'll all be a bunch of
    stews.
    At last—at last—
    Something else in the news at last.
    A man bit a dog, and that's news.
    Arthur Brisbane in his column
    says
    That this will lift the fog:
    For years he has been waiting for
    A man to bite a dog.
    He says this proves we're cavemen
    Of the prehistoric sort,
    And proving that, Mister Brisbane
    says,
    "Don't sell America short."
    At last—at last—
    A man bit a dog at last.
    And it seems to Heywood Broun
    That the world is out of tune,
    That if things don't happen soon
    We'll be biting dogs next June.
    A man bit a dog, and that's news.
    Mister Walter Lippmann tells us he
    was told
    That the tooth that bit the dog was
    filled with gold,
    And while the politicians roll each
    other's logs,
    The nation's gold is going to the
    dogs.
    At last—at last—
    A man bit a dog at last,
    And Mister Hearst has a chance
    To kick the French in the pants:
    He says the man who bit the dog
    Was a native of France.
    And Winchell's all agog;
    He interviewed the dog,
    And he says that the pretty Pom
    Was soon to become a mom.
    He says 'twas a dog you hate to be
    with,
    The kind you see with the rich—
    Not a great big manly he-dog,
    A little she-dog—a bitch—which
    Gives us a headline off the beaten
    track:
    A bitch bit a man and the man bit
    the bitch right back.

HOW'S CHANCES

Published. Copyrighted September 22, 1933. Previously registered for copyright as an unpublished song July 6, 1933. Introduced in the scene titled "Woolworth Declares Regular Dividend—Barbara Hutton to Wed Prince Mdivani" by Marilyn Miller (Barbara Hutton) and Clifton Webb (Prince Mdivani). Original cast recording by Webb with Leo Reisman's Orchestra (Victor). When the show began its Philadelphia tryout (September 11), this number was presented fairly late in the second act. There are two versions, the show version and the published version. According to the New York *Sunday News* (January 21, 1934), Barbara Hutton was so pleased with "How's Chances" that she frequently asked orchestra leaders to play it.

Published version

VERSE

When I want to see the boys,
I know where to find the boys.
I don't go through a club or two;
I just find you
And there are the boys.
To get you alone I strive;
You ask me to tea at five.
I find you then
With other men
And wonder when
My chance will arrive.

CHORUS

How's chances,
Say, how are the chances
Of making you love me
The way I love you?
How many young men must I fight with
To be in right with,
In right with you?
How's chances
For one of those glances?
A glimpse of the heaven
I'm longing to see.
How's chances
To end all your romances
And start taking your chances with me?

Show version

VERSE 1

SHE: The nickels and dimes I got
       Have bought me an awful lot:

A great big box
Of bonds and stocks,
A hundred frocks,
A car and a yacht.
But having so much, and more,
Is getting to be a bore;
It's not much fun
When day is done
Without someone
To love and adore.

CHORUS 1

How's chances,
Say, how are the chances
Of making you love me
The way I love you?
I'd give up the things I'm possessing
To be caressing
Someone like you.
How's chances
For one of those glances,
A glimpse of the heaven
I'm longing to see?
How's chances
To end all your romances
And start taking your chances with me?

VERSE 2

HE: My tailor's the best, but he
      Is dear as a man can be;
      My shoes and spats,
      My opera hats,
      And my cravats
      Are made just for me.
      I like an expensive car,
      And when at my favorite bar,
      I think it's fine
      To order wine,
      And when I dine,
      I love caviar.

CHORUS 2

How's chances,
Say, how are the chances
Of making you love me
The way I love you?
My castle will need some restoring,
Ceiling and flooring,
Furniture too.
How's chances
For one of those glances,
A glimpse of the heaven
I'm longing to see?
How's chances

To end all your romances
And start taking your chances with me?

HEAT WAVE

Published. Copyrighted September 22, 1933. Previously registered for copyright as an unpublished song June 27, 1933. Introduced in the scene titled "Heat Wave Hits New York" by Ethel Waters; danced by Letitia Ide, José Limón, and the Charles Weidman Dancers. Earliest recordings to achieve wide popularity were by Ethel Waters (Columbia); Glen Gray and the Casa Loma Orchestra, vocal by Mildred Bailey (Brunswick); and Meyer Davis and His Orchestra, vocal by Charlotte Murray (Columbia). Performed in films by Ethel Merman (*Alexander's Ragtime Band*, 1938); Olga San Juan and Fred Astaire (*Blue Skies*, 1946); Bing Crosby and Danny Kaye (*White Christmas*, 1954); and Marilyn Monroe (*There's No Business Like Show Business*, 1954).

VERSE

A heat wave
Blew right into town last week;
She came from
The island of Martinique.
The cancan
She dances will make you fry;
The cancan
Is really the reason why:

CHORUS

We're having a heat wave,
A tropical heat wave.
The temp'rature's rising—
It isn't surprising:
She certainly can cancan.
She started the heat wave
By letting her seat wave,
And in such a way that
The customers say that
She certainly can cancan.
Gee!
Her anatomy
Made the mercury
Jump to ninety-three—
Yes sir!
We're having a heat wave,
A tropical heat wave.
The way that she moves that
Thermometer proves that
She certainly can cancan.

It's so hot,
The weatherman will
Tell you a record's been made.
It's so hot,
A coat of tan will
Cover your face in the shade.
It's so hot,
The coldest maiden
Feels just as warm as a bride.
It's so hot,
A chicken laid an
Egg on the street—and it fried!

REPEAT CHORUS

DEBTS

Registered for copyright as an unpublished song August 4, 1933. Introduced in the scene titled "*Majestic* Sails at Midnight" by Leslie Adams, Hal Forde, Harry Stockwell, and Jerome Cowan (the representatives of England, Italy, Germany, and France), and Helen Broderick (Statue of Liberty). During the Philadelphia tryout the scene was titled "*Leviathan* Sails at Midnight." While no musical number is listed in the program for this scene, "Debts" is part of the script and the conductor's score. Alternate title: "We'll All Be in Heaven When the Dollar Goes to Hell."

VERSE 1

England and Italy and Germany and France,
We came here to discuss the debts,
And we're leaving with no regrets;
For England and Italy and Germany and France,
We have more than reached our aim,
And we're mighty glad we came.

CHORUS 1

We had a lovely conference
With the U.S.A.
We'll pay our debts in silver and
We'll be glad to pay.
In a month or two, we think,
We can pay our debts in zinc,
And the next year we'll begin
Paying off what's left in tin.
Oh, how we love America,
For she never makes a fuss—
That's why we love America,

And America loves us!
We'll tell our countries what we did
And they're bound to say,
"If you think we could
Pay them off in wood,
Go back to the U.S.A."

[STATUE OF LIBERTY *steps off her pedestal and sings the following verse and chorus.*]

VERSE 2

England and Italy and Germany and France,
Here's some news that you ought to know:
Off the gold standard we must go;
Like England and Italy and Germany and France,
We are going to inflate,
And we're very glad to state,

CHORUS 2

Let the pound go up,
The franc go up,
The mark go up as well—
Uncle Sam will be in heaven
When the dollar goes to hell.
For the stocks go up,
The bonds go up—
When no one wants to sell,
Uncle Sam will be in heaven
When the dollar goes to hell.
Of course, our friends won't like it
Across the ocean blue,
But we can greet our neighbors
With a hey-nonny-nonny and the nuts to you!
Let them call us this
And call us that,
But while they scream and yell,
Uncle Sam will be in heaven
When the dollar goes to hell.

LONELY HEART

Published. Copyrighted September 22, 1933. Previously registered for copyright as an unpublished song July 14, 1933. Introduced in the scene titled "Lonely Heart Column" by Harry Stockwell; danced by Letitia Ide, José Limón, and ensemble. During the Philadelphia tryout the number was presented during Act II.

Miss Lonely Heart,
What will I do?
I am a lonely heart

Writing to you,
Hoping that through your column you
Will drop me a line
Saying you know a lonely heart
As lonely as mine.
Miss Lonely Heart,
Hear my appeal—
You seem to know the way
Lonely hearts feel:
That's why I'm writing and
I'm asking for a reply;
That's why I'm hoping you
Know someone lonely as I.
I'm so blue returning to my lonely room
Every night, for nothing's quite
As lonely as a lonely room.
Miss Lonely Heart,
I'm by myself,
Watching the clock that stands
Upon the shelf,
Hoping to hear the news
That you know somebody who
Watches a clock and whispers,
"I'm a lonely heart too."

THE FUNNIES

Published. Copyrighted September 22, 1933. Previously registered for copyright as an unpublished song July 28, 1933. Introduced by Marilyn Miller and ensemble.

VERSE

Sunday is Sunday to my family,
But Sunday is not simply Sunday for me,
For Sunday's the one day
When I love to see
The funnies.
Breakfast is nothing of which you can boast,
But breakfast to me isn't coffee and toast,
It's coffee and toast
And what I love the most,
The funnies.

CHORUS

Oh,
I love the funnies!
A cup o' coffee to my lips,
And in between the sips,
The papers with the capers
That are in the comic strips,

Which means I'm simply mad about,
I mean I couldn't do without,
The funnies.
Oh,
In my pajamas,
I love to read the Katzenjammers,
A little coffee in a cup,
And Bringing Father Up.
I'm dippy over Skippy
And his little yellow pup,
Which means I'm simply mad about,
I mean I couldn't do without,
The funnies.
I'm not concerned with the news of the day,
The stories of who murdered who;
And as for what Mister Hearst has to say,
I have no need of,
I don't want to read of,
The Dempseys or the Tunneys,
The wealthy daughters or the sonnies,
The news about the lovely trips
That people take in ships—
I'd rather read about the people
In the comic strips,
Which means I'm simply mad about,
I mean I couldn't do without,
The funnies.

TO BE OR NOT TO BE

Registered for copyright as an unpublished song July 20, 1933. Introduced by Ethel Waters in the scene titled "*Green Pastures* Starts Third Road Season"; sung to Hamtree Harrington as a would-be Hamlet.

VERSE

Listen, Mister Actor,
Listen till I'm through—
Since you spoke that one line in *Green Pastures*
There ain't no holding you;
Now you speak of Hamlet,
And you says to me,
That the question is to be or not to be.
For years you ain't been home much,
And now you're on your way
To be a Harlem Hamlet—
Well, here's what I've got to say:

CHORUS 1

To be or not to be,
That's what you've got to be,

To be or not to be my man.
To do or not to do,
That's what you've got to do—
I mean to do the things you can.
I hear you speaking of Ophelia
But I know you don't mean me,
'Cause if you think I'll get me to a nunnery,
You're crazy,
Because I'm not that kind—
So just make up your mind
To be or not to be my man.

CHORUS 2

To be or not to be,
That's what you've got to be,
To be or not to be my man.
To do or not to do,
That's what you've got to do—
I mean to do the things you can.
I know John Barrymore played Hamlet
In a way it should be played;
But you're no Barrymore—
Let's call a spade a spade.
Remember,
For years we've been apart—
Take off your tie and start
To be or not to be my man.

EASTER PARADE

Published. Copyrighted September 22, 1933. Previously registered for copyright as an unpublished song July 20, 1933. Introduced in the Act I finale, titled "Rotogravure Section—Easter Parade on Fifth Avenue—1883," by Marilyn Miller and Clifton Webb. (In the programs the song is titled "Her Easter Bonnet.") The melody for the refrain to this song was derived from Berlin's 1917 song "Smile and Show Your Dimple." The first recording of "Easter Parade" to achieve wide popularity was by Clifton Webb with Leo Reisman's Orchestra (Victor). Later performed in films by Don Ameche (*Alexander's Ragtime Band*, 1938), Bing Crosby (*Holiday Inn*, 1942), and Judy Garland and Fred Astaire (*Easter Parade*, 1948).

VERSE

Never saw you look
Quite so pretty before;
Never saw you dressed
Quite so lovely—what's more,
I could hardly wait

To keep our date
This lovely Easter morning,
And my heart beat fast
As I came through the door,
For

CHORUS

In your Easter bonnet
With all the frills upon it
You'll be the grandest lady
In the Easter Parade.
I'll be all in clover
And when they look you over
I'll be the proudest fellow
In the Easter Parade.
On the Avenue—Fifth Avenue—
The photographers will snap us,
And you'll find that you're
In the rotogravure.
Oh, I could write a sonnet
About your Easter bonnet
And of the girl I'm taking to
The Easter Parade.

EASTER PARADE—SONNET

In April 1947 Berlin received the following letter:

> Women's Emergency Housing
> University of Missouri
> Columbia, Missouri
> April 24, 1947
>
> Dear Mr. Berlin,
>   You claim and we quote, "I could write a sonnet about your Easter bonnet." Frankly we would like to see you do it, preferably in the Italian style.
>   We have spent the entire evening attempting to write one with very little success and therefore we decided to let you take over.
>
> Sincerely,
> Billie Florence Stewart
> Dorothy G. Wilson

He replied on May 1, 1947:

> Dear Billie Stewart & Dorothy Wilson:
>
> If you can't write a sonnet
> About her Easter Bonnet
> Why don't you write some verse
> About her satin purse
> Or write a page of prose
> About her silken hose

Or just dash off a "pome"
About her empty dome
Or maybe just a rhyme
Of how she wastes her time
Or leave it up to some
Who aren't quite so dumb
That they can't write a sonnet
About her Easter Bonnet.

Sincerely,
Irving Berlin

METROPOLITAN OPENING

Registered for copyright as an unpublished song August 4, 1933. Introduced in the scene titled "Metropolitan Opens in Old-Time Splendor," which opened Act II, where it was sung by Jerome Cowan (Radio Announcer), Clifton Webb (Monsieur Peppiton), Leslie Adams (Mr. Williams), Helen Broderick (Mrs. Williams), and Marilyn Miller (Miss Williams, their daughter). Alternate title: "Opening Scene Act II."

Who are we,
And what are we doing here?
Wait and see—
We're going to make it clear.
We're the new millionaires
Who will sit in the chairs
That were once occupied
By the old millionaires.
Where are they,
The people who had the cash?
They can't pay—
They lost it all in the Crash.
Their sables and their foxes
Have all been put in pawn;
So we bought up their boxes,
For the opera must go on!
And instead of Mister Belmont, Mister Gould,
   and Mister Kahn,
There's Mister Rubin,
A Cuban,
Who runs a delicatessen store,
The man which
A sandwich made famous.
And there is Mister Klein—
You've seen the sign
On Union Square;
The women's wear
He sells made him a millionaire
And a first-night patron of the opera.
The most expensive box

Was bought by William Fox;
A fellow named Nat Lewis
Who deals in ties and socks
Will occupy the chair
A Vanderbilt sat upon—
He'll be there
To help them all carry on.
Those gentlemen who force you
To buy their Scotch and rye
Are in the Diamond Horseshoe;
Would you like to know just why?
It seems a large delegation
Couldn't get a donation
From Otto Kahn,
And so the racket
Said, "We will back it"—
They came across
Because the opera must go on.

SUPPER TIME

Published. Copyrighted September 22, 1933. Previously registered for copyright as an unpublished song June 27, 1933. Introduced by Ethel Waters in the scene titled "Unknown Negro Lynched by Frenzied Mob." Original cast recording by Waters (Monmouth-Evergreen).

Supper time—
I should set the table,
'Cause it's supper time;
Somehow I'm not able,
'Cause that man o' mine
Ain't comin' home no more.
Supper time—
Kids will soon be yellin'
For their supper time;
How'll I keep from tellin' that
That man o' mine
Ain't comin' home no more?
How'll I keep explainin'
When they ask me where he's gone?
How'll I keep from cryin'
When I bring their supper on?
How can I remind them
To pray at their humble board?
How can I be thankful
When they start to thank the Lord?
Lord!
Supper time,
I should set the table,
'Cause it's supper time;
Somehow I'm not able,
'Cause that man o' mine

Ain't comin' home no more,
Ain't comin' home no more.

SOCIETY WEDDING

Registered for copyright as an unpublished song July 14, 1933. Introduced in the scene titled "Society Wedding of the Season—Outside St. Thomas" by Marilyn Miller, Clifton Webb, and ensemble. During the Philadelphia tryout it was presented early in Act I. In programs for the show this song is listed as "Our Wedding Day."

BRIDESMAIDS
AND USHERS: Ten little bridesmaids, ten little ushers,
   Marching side by side—
   We gave our promises
   To come to St. Thomas's
   And usher for the bridegroom
   And bridesmaid for the bride.
   From a hundred we were chosen,
   And we're very glad we were,
   For this is the most important
      wedding
   Of the *Social Register*.

   It's a perfect match:
   He was quite a catch,
   For the bridegroom is a member
   Of the best of families;
   And the lovely bride,
   On her mother's side,
   Is a first or second cousin
   Of the Astors, if you please.
   Cholly Knickerbocker says
   This is a smart affair;
   Cholly will be there,
   Knee-deep in Vanderbilts.
   It is plain to see
   Why we're proud to be
   The selected few
   Picked from *Who's Who*
   To come here side by side
   And usher for the bridegroom
   And bridesmaid for the bride.

   Now we must go into church
   And see the groom and bride
   Standing side by side
   Knee-deep in Vanderbilts—
   For the happy pair
   Will be waiting there,
   So we can't be late,

We mustn't wait;
The knot will soon be tied.
Champagne for the bridegroom
And babies for the bride!

HE: Wake up, sleepyhead,
Tumble out of bed,
Wake up—don't be so slow.
Bells go ting-a-ling,
Let's be hurrying—
Off to church we must go.

CHORUS

Sun's in the sky;
Don't you know why?
This is our wedding day.
Birds in their nest
Are singing their best,
For we're going to be married.
Flowers are in bloom,
And the perfume
Speaks of a bride's bouquet.
Spread the good news
With rice and old shoes,
For this is our wedding day!

SHE: I'm so sleepy, dear—
Won't you make it clear
Why you're shaking me so?
Please, dear, cut it out—
What's it all about?
HE: Off to church we must go.

REPEAT CHORUS

HARLEM ON MY MIND

Published. Copyrighted October 18, 1933. Previously registered for copyright as an unpublished song September 29, 1933. Introduced by Ethel Waters (Josephine Baker) in the scene titled "Josephine Baker Still the Rage of Paris." Listed in programs as "I've Got Harlem on My Mind." Added to the show during the Philadelphia tryout. Original cast recording by Waters (Columbia).

VERSE

Emeralds in my bracelets,
Diamonds in my rings,
A Riviera chateau
And a lot of other things,
And I'm blue,

So blue
Am I.
Lots of ready money
In seven different banks
I counted up this morning—
It's about a million francs,
And I'm blue,
So blue,
And I know why:

CHORUS

I've got Harlem on my mind,
And I'm longing to be low-down;
And my parlez-vous will not ring true
With Harlem on my mind.
I've been dined and I've been wined,
But I'm headin' for a showdown,
'Cause I can't go on from night till dawn
With Harlem on my mind.
I go to dinner with a French marquis
Each evening after the show;
My lips begin to whisper "mon chéri,"
But my heart keeps singing hi-de-ho.
I've become too damned refined,
And at night I hate to go down
To that highfalutin flat
That Lady Mendl designed
With Harlem on my mind.

TAG CHORUS (HALF CHORUS)
[to the same music as last nine lines of first chorus]

And when I'm bathing in my marble tub
Each evening after the show,
I get to thinking of the Cotton Club
And my heart starts chirping hi-de-ho.
I've become too damned refined,
And at night I hate to go down
To my flat with fifty million
Frenchmen tagging behind
With Harlem on my mind.

THROUGH A KEYHOLE

Introduced by Clifton Webb in the scene titled "Broadway Gossip Column." Dropped from the show during the Broadway run.

VERSE

My mother was frightened by
A snoopy neighbor who poked his eye

Through mother's keyhole, and that is why
I am what I am today,
The man who looks through the keyholes along
    Broadway.
My job is to be alert
And get the lowdown on all the dirt,
The dirt that gathers on Broadway's skirt,
For that's how I earn my pay,
The man who looks through the keyholes along
    Broadway.

CHORUS 1

Would you like to take a look
Through a keyhole?
If you'd like to get the in
On the latest bit of sin,
Have a look.
Life is like an open book
Through a keyhole.
If you wonder what occurs
Ere the lady gets her furs,
Have a look.
Angry people who think they're tough
Start to threaten, but that's a bluff—
They may holler but they won't stuff
Up their keyholes.
So come on and have a look
Through a keyhole.
If you'd like to get a view,
View of who is cheating who,
Have a look!

CHORUS 2

Would you like to take a look
Through a keyhole?
If you want to get a load
Of the husband on the road,
Have a look.
Life is like an open book
Through a keyhole.
If you want to see New York
Getting ready for the stork,
Have a look.
Lovely ladies of every kind
Think they're safe when they pull the blind;
I see just what is on their mind
Through a keyhole.
So come on and have a look
Through a keyhole.
If you'd really like to know
How she got into the show,
Have a look.

NOT FOR ALL THE RICE IN CHINA

Published. Copyrighted October 18, 1933. Introduced by Marilyn Miller, Clifton Webb, and entire company. A portion of the Act II finale; the verse was not sung in the show. Added to the production during the Philadelphia tryout. Original cast recording by Webb with Leo Reisman's Orchestra (Victor). Sung later in the film *Blue Skies* (1946).

In a letter to Richard Rosenblueth (April 16, 1969), Berlin wrote: "It may interest you to know that 'Rice in China' was put at the end of the show because we had no headline to go with it, and I liked it well enough to include it in the score."

VERSE

I've got a song I want to sing to you,
To bring to you, my love,
Hoping it may reveal
Something of how I feel.
It's not a sentimental tune, with lines
Of moon that shines above—
Still, it's a love song, dear,
That I want the world to hear.

CHORUS

Not for all the rice in China,
Not for all the grapes in France,
Would I exchange the pleasure
That I get from ev'ry measure
When we dance.
Not for all the kilts in Scotland,
Not for all the bulls in Spain,
Would I give up arriving
At your house, although you're driving
Me insane.
Not for all the onions in Bermuda
Or the cheeses that are made by the Swiss
Would I exchange that first kiss
That you gave me.
Not for all the beans in Boston,
Not for all the steaks in Moore's,
Would I agree to part with
All the joy you filled my heart with
When you said, "I'm yours."

AT LAST, AT LAST (FINALE, ACT II)

Introduced by principals and ensemble led by Margaret Adams, Ethel Waters, Helen Broderick, Marilyn Miller, and Clifton Webb. The finale featured the chorus (without the verse) of "Not for All the Rice in China."

ENSEMBLE: At last! At last!
Something new in the show at last,
Something new if you please!
We won't pull the same old wheeze—
We mean that we won't reprise
The chorus of one of the melodies.
At last! At last!
Here's a show that'll end at last
Without a reprise—
And that's news!
They looked up the Constitution
And they couldn't find a word
That said we had to sing a song
That you'd already heard.
The finest legal minds have met,
And every one agrees
That when we reach the finale,
We don't have to sing a reprise.
At last! At last!
We've come to the end at last.
It'll be over soon,
But we don't intend to croon
The composer's favorite tune,
The one they sang beneath the moon.
Now we'll explain a reprise:
It's that certain song they sing all through the show
And the one they sing again before you go.
But the judges met and every one agrees
That we will have to end without a reprise—
Yes! We will have to end without a reprise.

[LESLIE ADAMS *sings eight bars of "Easter Parade."*]

ENSEMBLE: Now you can't do that, you can't do that—
You can't sing again about your Easter hat.

[ETHEL WATERS *sings eight bars of "Heat Wave."*]

No, you can't repeat, you can't repeat,
You can't sing again about the cancan heat.

[HELEN BRODERICK *sings eight bars of "Debts."*]

No, you don't! You're through—
We mean you're through
With hey-nonny-nonny and a nuts to you!

[MARILYN MILLER *and* CLIFTON WEBB *sing eight bars of "How's Chances."*]

No, you can't do that, you can't do that,
Because if you do, we're gonna leave you flat.
MILLER: Never mind that introduction,
For we don't intend to sing
The chorus of "How's Chances,"
As it wouldn't mean a thing.
WEBB: We'd like to sing a song
That wasn't written for the score
A simple little chorus
That they haven't heard before—
ENSEMBLE: A simple little chorus
That you haven't heard before.
WEBB: [*to* MILLER]
Not for all the rice in China, etc.

SKATE WITH ME

Registered for copyright as an unpublished song August 1, 1933. Introduced by Marilyn Miller, Clifton Webb, and entire company during the Philadelphia tryout as part of the scene titled "Park Avenue Takes Up the Skating Craze." Dropped before the New York opening. Seven years later, for the show *Louisiana Purchase*, Berlin used the same music with a new lyric titled "Dance with Me (Tonight at the Mardi Gras)."

VERSE

HE: The party is stuffy.
SHE: I won't come again.
HE: The women are boring.
SHE: And so are the men.
HE: The liquor is awful.
SHE: The food's only fair.
BOTH: Let's look for the hostess and tell her
We're taking the air.

CHORUS

Won't you make a date with me
To skate with me—
Way out—
And stay out
Till late with me?
We can go just as far
As we can in a car.
Won't you take your place with me
To race with me—
Sprawl on—
And fall on—
Your face with me?
Arm in arm through the park we'll roll—
Honest, I promise to lose my control
If you make a date with me
To skate with me,
You won't have to walk back home.

MIDGET NUMBER

Possibly sung by Helen Broderick (Little Francine) in
the Act II scene titled "United States Closes Morgan In-
vestigation." Dropped from the show during the Phila-
delphia tryout.

VERSE

I just came from the big investigation;
They brought me there to bolster up the show.
My press agent planted me
On Mister Morgan's knee,
Saying to the cam'raman, "Let's go."
My presence there created a sensation,
But as for me, it didn't have a punch.
I kept thinking as I sat
On Mister Morgan that
Bankers are a stony-hearted bunch.

CHORUS 1

I sat on the lap of Mister Morgan,
But it didn't mean a thing to me.
You'd think a pretty midget
Could make a banker fidget,
But not a rise could I get from old J.P.
Sitting on the lap of Mister Morgan
Ain't as nice as sittin' with your beau.
They say the upper classes
Go in for making passes,
But I sat on the lap of Mister Morgan
And I know
It ain't so—it ain't so.

CHORUS 2

I sat on the lap of Mister Morgan,
But it didn't mean a thing to me.
My romance with a banker
Just laid there like an anchor,
For not a rise could I get from old J.P.
All my life I dreamed of getting closer,
Closer to a man with lots of dough.
I thought that he'd get funny,
But his mind was on his money;
They say the House of Morgan can be reached,
But now I know
It ain't so—it ain't so.

CHORUS 3

I sat on the lap of Mister Morgan,
But it didn't mean a thing to me.
As I was there a-sittin',
I purred just like a kitten,
But Mister Morgan wouldn't purr back at me.
All my life I dreamed of getting closer,
Closer to a man with lots of dough.
I thought that he'd get funny,
But his mind was on his money;
They say the House of Morgan can be reached,
But now I know
It ain't so—it ain't so.

MR. AND MRS. HOOVER

Probably intended for Helen Broderick (Mrs. Herbert
Hoover) in the Act I scene titled "Franklin D. Roosevelt
Inaugurated Tomorrow." Dropped during rehearsals.

VERSE

Cheer up, darling, though skies are gray,
Soon they're bound to be blue.
I can picture a brighter day
Both for me and for you.
Though they told us to go,
Are we downhearted? No!

CHORUS

Twenty million people didn't want you;
Twenty million people said you're through;
Twenty million voters said, "The country's on the
    bum—
What we want is someone new."
We must leave this luxury behind us;
In a humbler place we'll have to dwell.

But a silk hat or a derby,
You will always be my Herbie,
And those twenty million people can go to hell.

EIGHTEENTH AMENDMENT REPEALED

Registered for copyright as an unpublished song Au-
gust 25, 1933. Intended for Marilyn Miller and girls.
Dropped before the Philadelphia tryout.

[MILLER and GIRLS are discovered in front of the Ritz-
Carlton, at little tables, rather depressed, having their
cocktails out in the open.]

Gone are the days
When a girl could have some fun
In Tony's bar
And the bar in "21."
Gone are the joints
Where a lady could let go,
And now the future looks as black
As Old Black Joe.

For there ain't no kick
Getting tight as a tick
When you know that you're not breaking the
    law,
And there ain't no thrill
To be dipping your bill
In a place without a lock on the door.
Getting tight meant
Excitement;
With each drink you had,
Somehow you felt it was good to be bad.
But they took the sin
Out of orange and gin;
It was much more fun
Going home with a bun
Supplied by Enemy Number
One—oh!

Gone are the days
When the liquor had a kick;
One drink of Scotch
Made you either drunk or sick.
Those were the days
When a lady could let go,
But now the future looks as black as Old
    Black Joe.

[Business: They take several drinks from the table as
music plays softly the strains of "Old Black Joe." They

then go into an Old Virginia Essence to the tune of "Old Black Joe." At the end of dance they look behind their shoulders to see that no one is watching and take flasks from their stockings and take a good long drink out of them, then go into hot dance to the rhythm melody.]

CAPONE IN HIS CELL

Dropped during rehearsals.

VERSE

After doing a stretch of time,
Here's what I've got to say—
The profession that's known as crime
Can always be made to pay.
It pays if you've got a machine gun
To point at your enemies' backs—
But after they're dead,
Don't lose your head
And forget to pay your income tax.

CHORUS

If I had paid the tax upon my income,
I know that I would not be here today;
I would still be in Miami
Letting all the cops goddamn me—
That could all be settled in the usual way.
If I had only stuck to racketeering,
By now I could retire and relax.
I had no opposition—
They all took it on the jaw;
They'd put me on the spot,
But I was quicker on the draw.
And still I wasn't satisfied—
I had to break the law
And forgot to pay my income tax.

AIN'T YOU COMIN' TO THE FAIR?

Unused. No music is known to survive. Found with *As Thousands Cheer* material. An evocation of the Chicago World's Fair, "A Century of Progress," which opened on May 27, 1933.

VERSE

Go west, young man,
Dressed up in your best, young man—
Don't wait for the rest, young man,
Go now!
Prepare, young man,
To go to the fair, young man—
You better get there, young man,
Somehow!

CHORUS

Ain't you comin' to the fair
In Chicago?
Things are hummin'—
Ain't you comin' to the fair?
Ev'rybody will be there
In Chicago,
Out in Illinois,
They'll be hummin'—
Ain't you comin' to the fair?
Get your ticket and come with me
On the Twentieth Century—
Twenty hours, and then we'll be
In Chicago.
Better hurry to the fair
In Chicago,
Out in Illinois,
Things are hummin'—
Ain't you comin' to the fair?

GOOD GULF
PROGRAM | 1934
and Other Songs of 1930–1934

GOOD GULF PROGRAM (1934)

On five Sunday-night broadcasts during the spring of 1934 (May 6 through June 3), Irving Berlin was a featured guest on Gulf Oil's *Good Gulf Program*. The shows were aired on the National Broadcasting Company's station WJZ. The broadcasts featured, in addition to Berlin, Al Goodman's Orchestra, the Revelers, the Pickens Sisters, and Frank Parker in cavalcades of Berlin's song hits as well as new Berlin songs and special material Berlin wrote for the Gulf programs.

SO HELP ME

Published. Copyrighted May 1, 1934. Previously registered for copyright as an unpublished song April 7, 1934. No script survives, but according to a newspaper article (date and paper unknown), when Berlin made his radio debut May 6, 1934, he introduced his new song "So Help Me" and sang and played many of his other compositions.

VERSE

I met you, and ever since,
You've been on my mind;
I'm getting nowhere, and it's not my fault—
You seem to take me with a grain of salt.
You're not easy to convince;
You're the doubting kind.
Why don't you believe me?
Nothing's up my sleeve.

CHORUS

Ooh, I'm head and heels in love with you,
So help me!
Ooh, I'm gonna stick to you like glue,
So help me!
Though you never told me where I stand,
You're a part of ev'rything I've planned, and
Ooh, I'm gonna make your dreams come true,
So help me!
Ooh, I'm gonna make you love me, too,
But darling, maybe I've bitten off

Ira Gershwin, Leonore Gershwin, George Gershwin, Ellin Berlin, and Irving Berlin relaxing in Nassau

Much more than I can chew,
And I may need a lot of help,
So help me!

SAY IT WITH MUSIC

The second show, May 13, 1934, opened with the Revelers, a singing group, presenting a slightly rewritten "Say It with Music."

Say it with music,
With words and music.
Please listen and we'll begin
Introducing Irving Berlin.
That songwriting fellow
Wants to say hello,
So we will help him along
To say it with a beautiful song.
With the captain who done him wrong.

[*Near the close of the show the Revelers returned and sang:*]

Say it with music,
With words and music.
Next Sunday if you tune in,
We'll be here with Irving Berlin.

HOW DOES A SONGWRITER WRITE?

After being introduced, Berlin offered the following song.

How does a songwriter write?
Is it by day or by night?
Does he work hard till he grinds out a song,
Or wait till that certain idea comes along?
Most times he works till he's tired,
But sometimes a song is inspired:
When I was a soldier at Yaphank,
Where each one was doing his part,
One morning in June
Came the words and the tune
Of a song that came straight from the heart.
I'll ask you to picture the scene—
Camp Upton in nineteen eighteen.
But the Armistice came along,
Which inspired a different song:

'Twas the private getting even
With the captain who done him wrong.

[*Segue into Berlin's song "I've Got My Captain Working for Me Now."*]

ONCE MORE MY MEMORY STRAYS

On May 20, Berlin returned to discuss and sing about the *Music Box Revues*, which he wrote for the Music Box Theatre.

Once more my memory strays
Back to those Music Box days
When Sam Harris said, "I have purchased the
     ground;
We're building a theatre, so just stick around."
September nineteen twenty-one—
The Music Box Theatre was done.
I'll always remember that evening
When Sam Harris whispered, "Let's go"—
The hour had struck,
So we just said "Good luck"
As the curtain went up on that show.
The theatre was crowded, and soon
The orchestra started this tune. . . .

[*Segue into "Say It with Music."*]

IN THAT FIRST REVUE

After Al Goodman's Orchestra played an introduction to Berlin's "Everybody Step," Berlin offered the following:

In that first revue
We had a tune they said was new.
With a peppy swing
That had a certain thing
That new rhythm has.
I don't mean to boast,
But it was played from coast to coast,
And I really think
'Twas the connecting link
Between ragtime and jazz.
Here's the little tune I mean
From the big finale scene:

[*Segue into chorus of "Everybody Step."*]

MOST OF THE SONGS THAT YOU HEAR

The fourth program, on May 27, 1934, began with Berlin singing this song.

Most of the songs that you hear
Will be forgotten next year;
They come and they go, and the songwriters say
A rose lives and dies in the very same way.
The life of a popular hit
Is very short, I'll admit;
But still there are songs we'll remember,
With melodies that linger on.
It's hard to explain
Why a certain refrain
Seems to stay when the others have gone.
I'm proud to have written a few
That still are remembered by you,
And these are my favorites above all the rest—
Not because they sold the most,
But because you like them best.

[*Segue into a number of Berlin favorites.*]

THIS IS MY FINAL BROADCAST

The final program, on June 3, 1934, opened with Berlin thanking all who made the shows possible.

This is my final broadcast;
This is my fifth and the last.
At first I was frightened and all out of breath,
And now that it's over, I'm still scared to death.
But terribly grateful am I
To those who helped me get by.
So thanks to the three little Pickens,
And thanks to the Revelers too,
And thanks to my pal,
To the musical Al,
Who presented my music to you.
And thanks to the friends I can't see,
The people who've listened to me,
And thanks to my sponsors in Pittsburgh, PA.—
I've thought of my sponsors by night and by day.
I've written a chorus for my final show,
A song to my sponsors, for I'd like to know:

HOW MANY GALLONS OF OIL HAVE YOU SOLD?

How many gallons of oil have you sold
Since I've been on the air?
Are you selling less or more
Than you did the month before?
I'd like to know if you're still doing well
And if I've done my share.
Do they rush up to a station
And yell, with a grin,
"Fill her up with Gulf Oil,
We just heard Berlin"?
I've told you just how I write all my songs,
And so it's only fair
That I should be told
How much oil you've sold
Since I've been on the air.

[*This song led to the following colloquy between Berlin and the program's announcer:*]

ANNOUNCER: That's very good, Irving. The sponsors ought to be pleased.
BERLIN: Well, it's all in fun, Joe.
ANNOUNCER: Maybe they won't think it's so funny.
BERLIN: Oh now, they've got a sense of humor.
VOICE IN DISTANCE: Telegram for Mr. Berlin . . . telegram for Mr. Berlin.
BERLIN: Joe, you better take it.
ANNOUNCER: Here, give it to me, boy. . . .

[*Sound of telegram being opened.*]

BERLIN: What is it, Joe . . . from a fan?
ANNOUNCER: No, it's from the Gulf Refining Company.
BERLIN: What, an answer already?
ANNOUNCER: Yes, only this is a question, too. They're asking you a question.
BERLIN: Well, read it!
ANNOUNCER: No, I haven't the heart. . . . You better read it yourself.
BERLIN: All right. Give it to me. Listen, Joe, here's the question they're asking me:

[*Berlin then picked up his previous tune:*]

HOW MANY COPIES OF SONGS HAVE YOU SOLD?

How many copies of songs have you sold
Since you've been on the air?
Are you selling less this spring
Since the people heard you sing?
We'd like to know if you're still doing well
And if we've done our share.
Do they rush up to the counter
And yell, with a grin,
"Give us Gershwin's music;
We just heard Berlin"?
We'll gladly tell how much Gulf Oil we sell,
A statement we'll prepare,
If in turn we're told
Of the songs you sold
Since you've been on the air.

ANNOUNCER: Well, Irving . . . there's nothing like giving your sponsors a break. What's next?
BERLIN: Well . . . I've got a new song.
ANNOUNCER: What . . . another new song? Swell.
BERLIN: Yes, Frank Parker's going to introduce it now . . . for the first time.
ANNOUNCER: What's it called?
BERLIN: "I Never Had a Chance."

I NEVER HAD A CHANCE

Published. Copyrighted June 25, 1934. Previously registered for copyright as an unpublished song March 30, 1934. Introduced by Frank Parker. Leading recordings by Eddy Duchin and His Orchestra (Victor) and Glen Gray and the Casa Loma Orchestra (Brunswick).

VERSE

I guess there's nothing to do
And nothing to say
But simply go on my way
And call it a day.
I guess I'm ready to go
Right back on the shelf,
Because at last I've learned
Where you're concerned,
I've just been fooling myself.

CHORUS

I never had a chance;
I thought you cared for me,
But now I see
I never had a chance.
I never had a chance;
Though you never told me so,
Somehow I know
I never had a chance.
I knew we'd have to part,
For I could always reach your lips
But I could never reach your heart.
My dream about romance
Ended in a friendly chat,
But more than that,
I never had a chance.

GULF OIL FINALE, including GULF OIL and I GOT GULF OIL and DEAR, MAY I SUGGEST GULF OIL?

After Frank Parker sang "I Never Had a Chance" on the final program, the following exchange occurred:

ANNOUNCER: At this point in the program it's customary for somebody to step forward and say a few kind words about that Good Gulf Gasoline. However, just for a change . . . tonight, we're going to do it in song. Irving Berlin will tell you about it.

BERLIN: Well, tonight I thought I'd like to show how three American songwriters might have written a theme song for Gulf Gasoline. First . . . as George M. Cohan might have written it:

Gulf Oil

Gulf Oil—Gulf Oil—
Gulf Oil—Gulf Oil—Gulf Oil.
I was born on the Fourth of July:
That's the reason why I buy
Gulf Oil—Gulf Oil.
Oh, the tanks are coming,

The tanks are coming.
Johnny get a can—get a can—get a can
Of Gulf Oil—Gulf Oil,
And we'll bring it back flowing over with Gulf Oil.

BERLIN: Next, as George Gershwin might have written it:

I Got Gulf Oil

REVELERS: I got Gulf Oil—I got Gulf Oil.
I haven't got a palace or a hut;
I haven't got a lot of money, but
I got Gulf Oil—
Could you ask for anything more?
What do I care
If Mister Morgan has just bought a yacht,
Just as long as I got
Good Gulf Oil.

BERLIN: And finally . . . as I myself might have written it—in the form of a beautiful, heart-throbbing duet.

Dear, May I Suggest Gulf Oil?

JANE PICKENS: Darling, I am blue,
Don't know what to do.
I feel so bad:
Everything goes wrong,
And the whole day long
I'm oh so sad.
Blue skies are turning to gray—
How can I chase them away?

BERLIN: Dear, may I suggest Gulf Oil?
Really, it's the best, Gulf Oil.
Maybe you can lose
Your unhappy blues,
Darling, if you use
Gulf Oil—Gulf Oil.

JANE PICKENS: All alone in the evening
After my daily toil,
Wond'ring where you are
And how you are
And if you are using Gulf Oil—

[In a coda finish:]

REVELERS
AND PICKENS: If you are using Gulf Oil.

OTHER SONGS OF 1930–1934

ALL I NEED IS LOVE

An unfinished lyric. No music is known to survive. On a holograph manuscript now in the Irving Berlin Collection of the Music Division of the Library of Congress, someone, possibly Berlin, has written "About 1930" at the bottom of the page.

I've got my health
And my share of wealth,
And now—all I need is love.

I've got all the things that do not matter;
They were handed to me on a silver platter.
Life would be sweet,
But it's not complete
Because—all I need is love.

JUST A LITTLE WHILE

Published. Copyrighted September 18, 1930. Previously registered for copyright as an unpublished song on August 13, 1930, and again on August 29, 1930. Written in late 1927. According to a letter from Berlin (April 30, 1931) to his attorney Francis Gilbert: "As near as I can remember, I wrote this idea about three years ago. At that time it was constructed along the lines of 'What'll I Do,' meaning that I began and finished the first phrase with the title. . . . I started working on the song again while in California, about two months before it was copyrighted and registered."

VERSE

Romance seemed to beckon the first time we met;
Together we strolled neath the moon.
'Twas sweet while it lasted, and I've no regret,
Although it was over too soon.

CHORUS

Just a little while 'twas so divine
To see the sun come out and shine

When I was yours and you were mine,
Just a little while.
Just a little while the moments passed,
And soon my heart was beating fast
About a love I knew would last
Just a little while.
Now that we're apart
Guess I'd better start
Patching up my heart with a smile,
But I never knew that happy day
A broken heart would have to pay
For dreams of love that came to stay
Just a little while.

I WANT YOU FOR MYSELF

Published. Copyrighted February 5, 1931. Previously registered for copyright as an unpublished song January 13, 1931.

VERSE

You are the sweetest thing in all creation,
But when you fool around the way you do,
I must keep my eye on you.
I'm goin' to take you out of circulation,
Because it seems to be the only thing to do.

CHORUS

I don't want to share you
With somebody else;
I want you for myself,
Entirely for myself.
I could never spare you
To somebody else;
I want you for myself,
Entirely for myself.
There is only one of you;
No other could be found.
I want all or none of you;
Don't pass yourself around.
I don't want to share you
With somebody else;
I want you for myself,
Entirely for myself.

ANY LOVE TODAY?

Registered for copyright as an unpublished song January 14, 1931. Amy Asch, in her 1995 report, *Unpublished: Uncopyrighted Songs by Irving Berlin*, notes in her description of "Any Love Today?" (page 2) that "the melody for the title words matches the melody of 'Any Bonds Today?' (published 1941) but is otherwise different. The chorus of 'Any Love Today?' is similar, however, to the verse of 'The Yam' (published 1937)." Also see "Any Bonds Today?" (page 371) and "The Yam" (page 317).

VERSE

You know the man who once used to say,
"Any rags, any bones, any bottles today?"
I saw him out again;
I heard him shout again—
He's on the job, but he doesn't say,
"Any rags, any bones, any bottles today?"
There's a love light in his eyes
And he sighs as he cries:

CHORUS

Any love today?
If you've got any kisses that no one demands,
I'll take them off your hands.
Any love today?
If you're stuck with an old second-handed
  romance
That needs another chance,
Here's your chance today.
Pleading
For love that I'm needing,
The world is unheeding—
Don't send me away.
Hear me shouting,
Any love today?
If you're left with a heart that is broken in two,
I'll patch it up for you—
Any love today?

BEGGING FOR LOVE

Published. Copyrighted July 21, 1931. First registered for copyright as an unpublished song under the title "Just Begging for Love" on June 24, 1931. Registered for copyright as an unpublished song under the title "Begging for Love" on June 29, 1931. Introduced by George Murphy and Julie Johnson in the New York production

of the revue *Shoot the Works* (George M. Cohan Theatre; July 21, 1931; 87 performances).

VERSE

I said goodbye to you
With head unbowed;
I couldn't cry to you—
I was too proud.
I said I'm through with you,
So unconcerned,
No more to do with you,
But I've returned

CHORUS

I'm here under your window,
A mis'rable beggar
Begging for love.
All of my skies are gray
Since we parted;
Don't send me away
Empty-hearted.
So humbly I stand,
My heart in my hand,
Just begging for love.

SLEEP, BABY

Registered for copyright as an unpublished song July 8, 1931. The copyright registration date suggests that this song might have been intended for the show that became *Face the Music* (1932). The lyric idea of this song is similar to that of the later song "Chase All Your Cares (and Go to Sleep, Baby)."

Sleep, baby, and soon maybe
You'll sleep your troubles away.
Put your cares all on the shelf,
And let each care take care of itself.
Dream, baby, and soon maybe
You'll be in daisies knee-deep.
Say goodbye to the sun,
Count your sheep one by one,
Till you sleep, baby, sleep.

ME

Published. Copyrighted August 6, 1931. Previously registered for copyright as an unpublished song July 9, 1931. Leading recordings by Ruth Etting (Perfect, Conqueror, British Imperial) and the High Hatters, vocal by Frank Luther (Victor).

VERSE

We took a walk, we had a talk,
And let me tell you very confidentially,
The little walk, the little talk
Has made me just as glad, as glad as I can be.
I simply wanted to know
Who she was loving, and so
We took a walk and had a talk,
And I discovered pretty soon that it was me.

CHORUS

Me—
She gave her attention
Not to him, not to her,
Not to them, not to those,
But to me.
Her family,
They held a convention,
Not for him, not for her,
Not for them, not for those,
But for me.
I'm delighted, yes sir!
And I have to laugh—
Standing on my dresser
Is a photograph
Which proves that
She gives all her attention
Not to him, not to her,
Not to them, not to those,
But to me.

In 1955 Berlin revised and reprinted this song. He deleted the verse, added the masculine pronouns "he" and "his" as alternates to "she" and "her" in line 2 and "his" as an alternative to "her" in line 6, and revised the lyric to lines 15–16 of the chorus to:

Inscribed to
Me with all his affection

CHASE ALL YOUR CARES (AND GO TO SLEEP, BABY)

Registered for copyright as an unpublished song December 9, 1931. No music is known to survive. Typed lyric sheets were found among Irving Berlin's papers and are now in the Irving Berlin Collection of the Music Division of the Library of Congress.

VERSE

You're sad today;
The skies are gray—
You're worrying, baby.
But cares, like a dream,
Are not like they seem;
They're false alarms—
Here in my arms
They'll disappear, maybe.
Tomorrow, my dear,
The skies may be clear.

CHORUS

Chase all your cares
And go to sleep, baby,
And soon you'll sleep your little cares away.
Don't count your troubles,
Count your sheep, baby,
And say, "Tomorrow is another day."
Remember, things always look black at night,
And what seems wrong, you'll agree,
May turn out to be all right—
So won't you chase all your cares
And go to sleep, baby,
And soon you'll sleep your little cares away.

I'LL MISS YOU IN THE EVENING

Published. Copyrighted January 27, 1932. Previously registered for copyright as an unpublished song December 9, 1931. The music for the chorus is the same as the music for the chorus of "Venetian Isles." See "Venetian Isles" (page 229).

VERSE

What am I to say?
You are leaving;
Seeing you go
Worries me so.
At the close of day
I'll be grieving,
Lonely and blue,
Thinking of you.

CHORUS

I'll miss you in the evening,
When the heavens turn to blue.
I'll miss you in the evening,
When my daily work is through.
When I see the setting sun behind the hill,
When the busy day is done,
I wonder, will you miss me in the evening,
Just as much as I'll miss you?

A LITTLE SYMPATHY

Typed lyric sheet dated August 2, 1932. No music is known to survive.

I want your love,
But if I can't get your love,
A little sympathy,
A little sym-pa-thy, will do.
I want your kiss,
But if I can't get your kiss,
A little sympathy,
A little sym-pa-thy, will do.
I wish you could adore me,
But if you can't,
Try to be sorry for me—
I want your love,
But if I can't get your love,
A little sympathy,
A little sym-pa-thy, will do.

SAY IT ISN'T SO

Published. Copyrighted September 9, 1932. Previously registered for copyright as an unpublished song August 23, 1932. Introduced on the radio by Rudy Vallee. Number-one-selling recording by George Olsen and His Orchestra, vocal by Paul Small (Victor). Other leading recordings by Ozzie Nelson and His Orchestra (Brunswick), Connee Boswell (Brunswick), and Rudy Vallee (Columbia).

Berlin told the story of this song and of "How Deep Is the Ocean (How High Is the Sky)" in a May 21, 1945, letter to *Variety* editor Abel Green:

> I wrote them during a period of my career when I felt I was all through. It was right after I had lost almost everything I had in the market, along with everybody else, and I had gotten rusty as a songwriter. I hadn't been working at my trade for quite some time. I developed an inferiority complex. No song I wrote seemed right. I struggled to pull off a hit. I became very self-critical. The result was that I was afraid to publish any song. I had written "How Deep Is the Ocean?" but didn't like it and convinced everyone in the office it wasn't good enough. Soon after, I wrote "Say It Isn't So," which I also discarded. While I was in the Adirondacks, someone in the office let Rudy Vallee hear "Say It Isn't So" and he sang it on his broadcast. The reaction was good, so Max Winslow went after it and the song became a hit. I then re-examined "How Deep Is the Ocean?" and thought better of it. I think these two songs are important because they came at a critical time and broke the ice.

VERSE

You can't stop people from talking,
And they're talking, my dear;
And the things they're saying
Fill my heart with fear.
Now, I could never believe them
When they say you're untrue.
I know that they're mistaken;
Still, I want to hear it from you.

CHORUS

Say it isn't so,
Say it isn't so;
Ev'ryone is saying you don't love me—
Say it isn't so.
Ev'rywhere I go,
Ev'ryone I know
Whispers that you're growing tired of me—
Say it isn't so.
People say that you
Found somebody new
And it won't be long before you leave me—
Say it isn't true.
Say that ev'rything is still okay,
That's all I want to know,
And what they're saying,
Say it isn't so.

HOW DEEP IS THE OCEAN (HOW HIGH IS THE SKY)

Published. Copyrighted September 27, 1932. Previously registered for copyright as an unpublished song September 3, 1932. Leading recordings by Guy Lombardo and His Royal Canadians (Brunswick); Paul Whiteman and His Orchestra, vocal by Jack Fulton (Victor); Rudy Vallee and His Connecticut Yankees (Columbia); and Ethel Merman, accompanied by Nat Shilkret's Orchestra (Victor). The song is derived from two sources. According to Berlin (1971),

> In the early days of sound films I wrote a very awful movie for Al Jolson. One of the songs was a true horror called "To My Mammy." But in the middle of it I had a couple of nice lines. . . . Years later I took out those nice lines and wrote a new song around them called "How Deep Is the Ocean." . . . I think it's one of my best songs—taken from one of my worst.

The verse of "How Deep" is recycled from "How Much I Love You" from *Reaching for the Moon*. See also the headnote to "Say It Isn't So."

VERSE

How can I tell you what is in my heart?
How can I measure each and ev'ry part?
How can I tell you how much I love you?
How can I measure just how much I do?

CHORUS

How much do I love you?
I'll tell you no lie:
How deep is the ocean,
How high is the sky?
How many times a day
Do I think of you?
How many roses
Are sprinkled with dew?
How far would I travel
To be where you are?
How far is the journey
From here to a star?
And if I ever lost you,
How much would I cry?
How deep is the ocean,
How high is the sky?

A NEW WAY TO SAY "I LOVE YOU"

Typed lyric sheet dated September 16, 1932. No music is known to survive.

CHORUS

I found a brand-new way
To say "I love you"—
I simply grab my girl
And kiss my girl
And just say nothing at all.
Instead of wasting time
To say "I love you,"
Instead of all that gab,
I simply grab
And just say nothing at all.
After raving from the tops of houses
After wearing out the knees in all my trousers
I found a brand-new way,
To say "I love you"—
I simply grab my girl
And kiss my girl
And just say nothing at all.

I'M PLAYING WITH FIRE

Published. Copyrighted December 23, 1932. Previously registered for copyright as an unpublished song November 21, 1932.

VERSE

I've heard about you,
Each word about you
That ev'ryone has spoken;
And from the things I hear,
I should be careful, dear.
They come and find me
And then remind me
Of all the hearts you've broken;
But I'm in love with you,
So what am I to do?

CHORUS

I'm playing with fire,
I'm gonna get burned—
I know it, but what can I do?
I know my heart must be content to go

Where it is sent, although
I may repent when I'm through,
But what can I do?
I'm playing with fire,
I'm gonna get burned,
While merry-go-rounding with you.
But I go for my ride
With my eyes open wide—
I'm playing with fire,
I know it, but what can I do?

MAYBE IT'S BECAUSE I LOVE YOU TOO MUCH

Published under the title "Maybe I Love You Too Much." Copyrighted March 9, 1933. Previously registered for copyright as an unpublished song under that title on February 23, 1933. Leading recordings by Rudy Vallee and His Connecticut Yankees (Columbia); Guy Lombardo and His Royal Canadians (Brunswick); and Leo Reisman and His Orchestra, vocal by Fred Astaire (Victor). Published again in 1951 under the title "Maybe It's Because I Love You Too Much." In a letter to his friend Irving Hoffman (July 24, 1951), Berlin commented on the new attention that the song received:

> The present excitement is due to a record made by Paul Weston for Columbia. The disc jockeys are very enthusiastic about this recording and after it was played for about a week, we received some very healthy orders for copies of the sheet music. Present indications are that this song will become a big hit as a revival.

VERSE

Something has vanished,
Something has gone—
I know it, I feel it,
We're not getting on.
I seem to please you less
The harder I try.
Something has happened,
What can it be?
I know it, I feel it,
You're tired of me;
I love you much too much,
And maybe that's why.

CHORUS

Maybe it's because I love you too much,
Maybe that is why you love me so little.

Maybe when I answered yes,
Maybe I became a bore;
Maybe if I loved you less,
Maybe you would love me more.
Maybe it's because I've kissed you too much,
Maybe that is why my kiss means so little;
Maybe with a love so great and a love so small,
Maybe I'll be left with no love at all.

I CAN'T REMEMBER

Published. Copyrighted March 25, 1933. Previously registered for copyright as an unpublished song March 10, 1933. Leading recording by Eddy Duchin and His Orchestra (Victor).

VERSE

I met you, I remember,
But try as I may,
I can't seem to remember
The time or the day.
I met you, I remember,
That's all I can say.
Was it August or September
Or April or May?

CHORUS

I can't remember
The first time we met;
Was it cloudy or beautiful?
I can't remember
The first words I spoke;
Did I say you were beautiful?
Was it Sunday?
Was it Monday?
Were you dressed in gray or in blue?
I can't remember,
For all I remember is you.

ALL I BRING TO YOU IS LOVE

Written March 13, 1934. Registered for copyright as an unpublished song December 23, 1977. Alternate title: "The World Will Be Yours and Mine." The lyric is based on the lyric to "If You Believe."

CHORUS

All I bring to you is love,
And all that I ask in return is love,
And as long as you love
And as long as I love,
The sun will forever shine.
All I bring to you is me,
And all that I ask in return is you,
And as long as there's you
And as long as there's me,
The world will be yours and mine.

BUTTERFINGERS

Published. Copyrighted March 29, 1934. Previously registered for copyright as an unpublished song March 15, 1934. According to a newspaper item (March 3, 1934), Berlin returned from an eight-week vacation in Nassau with this song plus part of the score for a musical to be produced in the fall.

VERSE

You were always a careless kid,
Letting ev'rything fall.
No one blamed you for what you did—
You were careless, that's all.
Butterfingers was your nickname
Even when you were small;
You grew up and you're still the same,
Letting ev'rything fall.

CHORUS

When we were five,
Butterfingers,
I gave you my toys,
Butterfingers;
You let my toys
Slip through your fingers and break.
When we were ten,
Butterfingers,
I gave you my books,
Butterfingers;
They slipped right through your hand
And fell in the lake.
When we were seventeen,
You still were careless,
But I loved you so.
Though I knew that you were careless,
I couldn't let you go.
At twenty-one,
Butterfingers,

I gave you my heart,
Butterfingers;
You let my heart
Slip through your fingers and break.

MOON OVER NAPOLI

Published. Copyrighted September 6, 1934. Previously registered for copyright as an unpublished song August 22, 1934. Written for the unfinished revue *More*

Cheers, planned as a sequel to *As Thousands Cheer* (1933). According to one article, Berlin and Moss Hart left for Naples on July 21, 1934, aboard the *Rex.* The trip was a working holiday with a new satirical revue in mind.

Moon over Napoli,
I am thinking of the night I spent so happily
When a dark-eyed maid invited me
To see Naples and die.
Moon over Napoli,
I am thinking of the day she said farewell to me,
And I see her as my ship went out to sea

Waving goodbye.
That she'd be ever true
Was her solemn vow;
Still, I am wond'ring who
Is kissing her now.
Moon over Napoli,
Does that dark-eyed signorina ever think of me?
Does she know that once again I long
To see Naples and die?

Fred Astaire and Ginger Rogers, "Cheek to Cheek"

TOP HAT | 1935

TOP HAT (1935)

A film produced by Pandro S. Berman for RKO Radio Pictures. Released in August 1935. Lyrics and music by Irving Berlin. Screenplay by Dwight Taylor and Allan Scott. Adapted by Karl Noti from the play *The Girl Who Dared* by Alexander Farago and Aladar Laszlo. Directed by Mark Sandrich. Dances directed by Hermes Pan. Orchestrations and arrangements by Edward Powell, Maurice de Packh, Gene Rose, Eddie Sharpe, and Arthur Knowlton. Music conducted by Max Steiner. Cast: starring Fred Astaire (Jerry Travers) and Ginger Rogers (Dale Tremont) and featuring Edward Everett Horton (Horace Hardwick), Helen Broderick (Madge Hardwick), Erik Rhodes (Alberto Beddini), and Eric Blore (Bates).

When interviewed by John Wilson of the New York *Times* (November 19, 1976), Berlin spoke warmly of his association with Fred Astaire.

"You give Astaire a song, and you could forget about it. He knew the song. He sang it the way you wrote it. He didn't change anything.

"And if he did change anything"—Mr. Berlin's sly chuckle rattled over the telephone line—"he made it better. He might put a different emphasis on the lyric. He'd do things that you hoped other singers wouldn't do.

"Once I started writing for the Astaire-Rogers films, I was writing dance music. Even the lyrics were about dancing—'Cheek to Cheek,' 'Change Partners,' 'Let's Face the Music and Dance.' This was not true of other singers I wrote for."

NO STRINGS
(I'M FANCY FREE)

Published. Copyrighted July 24, 1935. Previously registered for copyright as an unpublished song March 22, 1935, under the title "Fancy Free." Introduced by Fred Astaire (Jerry Travers). Original cast recordings by Astaire with Leo Reisman's Orchestra (Brunswick) and Ginger Rogers with Victor Young's Orchestra (Decca).

VERSE

I wake up ev'ry morning with a smile on my face,
Ev'rything in its place as it should be.
I start out ev'ry morning just as free as the breeze,
My cares upon the shelf,
Because I find myself with—

CHORUS

No strings and no connections,
No ties to my affections—
I'm fancy free
And free for anything fancy.
No dates that can't be broken,
No words that can't be spoken,
Especially
When I am feeling romancy.
Like a robin upon a tree,
Like a sailor that goes to sea,
Like an unwritten melody,
I'm free—
That's me.
Bring on the big attraction;
My decks are cleared for action—
I'm fancy free
And free for anything fancy.

ISN'T THIS A LOVELY DAY (TO BE CAUGHT IN THE RAIN)?

Published. Copyrighted July 2, 1935. Previously registered for copyright as an unpublished song March 8, 1935. Introduced by Fred Astaire (Jerry Travers) and Ginger Rogers (Dale Tremont). Original cast recordings by Astaire with Johnny Green and His Orchestra (Brunswick) and Rogers with Victor Young's Orchestra (Decca). Probably in mid-1926, Berlin had written the following lines on the back of a business letter dated July 1, 1926:

Long as I have you
And long as you have me,
Let the raindrops patter
What does it matter
As long as I have you
And long as you have me.

VERSE

The weather is fright'ning;
The thunder and light'ning
Seem to be having their way.
But as far as I'm concerned,
It's a lovely day.
The turn in the weather
Will keep us together,
So I can honestly say
That as far as I'm concerned,
It's a lovely day,
And ev'rything's okay.

CHORUS

Isn't this a lovely day
To be caught in the rain?
You were going on your way;
Now you've got to remain.
Just as you were going,
Leaving me all at sea,
The clouds broke,
They broke, and oh,
What a break for me!
I can see the sun up high
Though we're caught in the storm.
I can see where you and I
Could be cozy and warm.
Let the rain pitter-patter,
But it really doesn't matter
If the skies are gray;
Long as I can be with you,
It's a lovely day.

TOP HAT, WHITE TIE AND TAILS

Published. Copyrighted July 24, 1935. Previously registered for copyright as an unpublished song February 28, 1935. Introduced by Fred Astaire (Jerry Travers) and male ensemble. Original cast recording by Astaire with Johnny Green and His Orchestra (Brunswick). Other leading recording by Ray Noble and His Orchestra (Victor), vocal by Al Bowlly. Apparently, this song was written in 1934 for the unfinished musical *More Cheers*.

VERSE

I just got an invitation through the mails:
"Your presence requested this evening; it's
     formal"—
A top hat, a white tie and tails.
Nothing now could take the wind out of my sails,
Because I'm invited to step out this evening
With top hat and white tie and tails.

CHORUS

I'm
Puttin' on my top hat,
Tyin' up my white tie,
Brushin' off my tails.
I'm

Dudin' up my shirt front,
Puttin' in the shirt studs,
Polishin' my nails.
I'm steppin' out, my dear,
To breathe an atmosphere
That simply reeks with class;
And I trust
That you'll excuse my dust
When I step on the gas,
For I'll be there
Puttin' down my top hat,
Mussin' up my white tie,
Dancin' in my tails.

CHEEK TO CHEEK

Published. Copyrighted July 2, 1935. Previously registered for copyright as an unpublished song December 19, 1934. Introduced by Fred Astaire (Jerry Travers) and danced by Astaire and Ginger Rogers (Dale Tremont). Original cast recording by Astaire with Johnny Green and His Orchestra (Brunswick) was the number-one seller in America for eleven weeks. Also recorded by Rogers with Victor Young's Orchestra (Decca). Nominated for an Academy Award.

Heaven,
I'm in heaven,
And my heart beats so
That I can hardly speak,
And I seem to find
The happiness I seek
When we're out together dancing
Cheek to cheek.
Heaven,
I'm in heaven,
And the cares that hung around me
Through the week
Seem to vanish
Like a gambler's lucky streak
When we're out together dancing
Cheek to cheek.
Oh! I love to climb a mountain

And to reach the highest peak,
But it doesn't thrill me half as much
As dancing cheek to cheek.
Oh! I love to go out fishing
In a river or a creek,
But I don't enjoy it half as much
As dancing cheek to cheek.
Dance with me—
I want my arm about you.
The charm about you
Will carry me through
To heaven—
I'm in heaven
And my heart beats so
That I can hardly speak,
And I seem to find
The happiness I seek
When we're out together dancing
Cheek to cheek.

THE PICCOLINO

Published. Copyrighted July 24, 1935. Previously registered for copyright as an unpublished song January 28, 1935. Introduced by Ginger Rogers (Dale Tremont), Fred Astaire (Jerry Travers), and ensemble. Original cast recordings by Astaire with the Leo Reisman Orchestra (Brunswick) and Rogers with Victor Young's Orchestra (Decca). Other leading recording by Ray Noble and His Orchestra (Victor), vocal by Al Bowlly. According to Berlin scholar Amy Asch, "The Lido" was an earlier title for the music that became "The Piccolino."

John Wilson, in his New York *Times* interview with Berlin of November 19, 1976, wrote:

Although Mr. Berlin may settle on "Top Hat, White Tie and Tails" as the best of the songs he wrote for the Astaire-Rogers films, the one that is closest to his heart is "The Piccolino." This was a follow-up to the big production numbers that Mr. Astaire and Miss Rogers had done in two earlier films—"The Carioca" in *Flying Down to Rio* and "The Continental" in *The Gay Divorcee*.

"I wrote it because it was a tradition," Mr. Berlin explained. "It was the thing to do for an Astaire-Rogers production. I hadn't done a tune like that since the Music Box Revues in the 1920's. I think it's one of my best, both as an instrumental and for the lyric. Go over it sometime. Look at it, measure by measure. Go over the lyric, and you'll find the phrases are very carefully worked out. I love it, the way you love a child that you've had trouble with. I worked harder on 'Piccolino' than I did on the whole score."

By the Adriatic waters,
Venetian sons and daughters
Are strumming
A new tune
Upon their guitars.
It was written by a Latin,
A gondolier who sat in
His home out
In Brooklyn
And gazed at the stars.
He sent his melody
Across the sea
To Italy,
And we know
They wrote some words to fit
That catchy bit
And christened it
The Piccolino.
And we know that it's the reason
Why ev'ryone this season
Is strumming
And humming
A new melody.
Come to the casino
And hear them play the Piccolino.
Dance with your bambino
To the strains of the catchy Piccolino.
Drink your glass of vino,
And when you've had your plate of scallopino
Make them play the Piccolino,
The catchy Piccolino,
And dance to
The strains of
That new melody,
The Piccolino.

FOLLOW THE FLEET | 1936

FOLLOW THE FLEET (1936)

A film produced by Pandro S. Berman for RKO Radio Pictures. Released in February 1936. Lyrics and music by Irving Berlin. Screenplay by Dwight Taylor and Allan Scott, adapted from the play *Shore Leave* by Hubert Osborne. Directed by Mark Sandrich. Dances directed by Hermes Pan. Orchestrations and arrangements by Maurice de Packh, Gene Rose, Clarence Wheeler, Walter Scharf, and Roy Webb. Music conducted by Max Steiner. Cast: starring Fred Astaire (Bake Baker) and Ginger Rogers (Sherry Martin) and featuring Randolph Scott (Bilge Smith), Harriet Hilliard (Connie Martin), and Astrid Allwyn (Iris Manning). Among others in smaller roles: Lucille Ball, Betty Grable, and Tony Martin.

WE SAW THE SEA

Published. Copyrighted January 10, 1936. Previously registered for copyright as an unpublished song September 12, 1935. Introduced by Fred Astaire (Bake Baker) and male ensemble. Original cast recording by Astaire with Johnny Green and His Orchestra (Brunswick).

We joined the Navy
To see the world,
And what did we see?
We saw the sea.
We saw the Pacific and the Atlantic,
But the Atlantic isn't romantic,
And the Pacific
Isn't what it's cracked up to be.
We joined the Navy
To do or die,
But we didn't do
And we didn't die.
We were much too busy looking
At the ocean and the sky,
And what did we see?
We saw the sea.
We saw the Atlantic and the Pacific,
But the Pacific
Isn't terrific,

Fred Astaire and Ginger Rogers, "I'm Putting All My Eggs in One Basket"

And the Atlantic
Isn't what it's cracked up to be.
They tell us that the admiral
Is as nice as he can be;
But we never see the admiral,
Because the admiral has never been to sea.
We joined the Navy
To see the girls,
And what did we see?
We saw the sea.
Instead of a girl or two in a taxi,
We were compelled to look at the Black Sea;
Seeing the Black Sea
Isn't what it's cracked up to be.
Sailing, sailing home again
To see the girls upon the village green;
Then across the foam again
To see the other seas we haven't seen.
We owe the Navy an awful lot,
For they taught us how to do the sailor's hornpipe,
And they showed us how to tie a sailor's knot,
But more than that, they showed us the sea.
We never get seasick sailing the ocean;
We don't object to feeling the motion—
We're never seasick,
But we are awful sick of seas.

LET YOURSELF GO

Published. Copyrighted January 10, 1936. Previously registered for copyright as an unpublished song August 30, 1935. Introduced by Ginger Rogers (Sherry Martin) and singing trio (Joy Hodges, Betty Grable, and Jeanne Gray). Dance reprise by Fred Astaire (Bake Baker) and Rogers. Solo dance reprise by Rogers. Original cast recordings by Rogers with Jimmy Dorsey and His Orchestra (Decca) and Astaire with Johnny Green and His Orchestra (Brunswick).

VERSE

As you listen to the band,
Don't you get a bubble?
As you listen to them play,
Don't you get a glow?
If you step out on the floor,
You'll forget your trouble;
If you go into your dance,
You'll forget your woe—
So:

CHORUS

Come get together,
Let the dance floor feel your leather,
Step as lightly as a feather—
Let yourself go.
Come hit the timber,
Loosen up and start to limber,
Can't you hear that hot marimba?—
Let yourself go.
Let yourself go,
Relax
And let yourself go,
Relax.
You've got yourself tied up in a knot;
The night is cold
But the music's hot;
So come cuddle closer,
Don't you dare to answer "No, sir,"
Butcher, banker, clerk, and grocer—
Let yourself go.

GET THEE BEHIND ME, SATAN

Published. Copyrighted January 10, 1936. Previously registered for copyright as an unpublished song July 12, 1934, and again on September 21, 1934. Introduced by Harriet Hilliard (Connie Martin). As Harriet Nelson, Hilliard later achieved fame on radio and television on the long-running *Adventures of Ozzie and Harriet*. Apparently, this song originally had been intended for Ginger Rogers in *Top Hat* (1935). Original cast recording by Harriet Hilliard with Ozzie Nelson's Orchestra (Brunswick).

Get thee behind me, Satan.
I want to resist,
But the moon is low
And I can't say no—
Get thee behind me.
Get thee behind me, Satan.
I mustn't be kissed,
But the moon is low
And I may let go—
Get thee behind me.
Someone I'm mad about
Is waiting in the night for me,
Someone that I mustn't see—
Satan, get thee behind me.
He promised to wait,
But I won't appear
And he may come here—

Satan, he's at my gate,
Get thee behind me—
Stay where you are,
It's too late.

I'D RATHER LEAD A BAND

Published. Copyrighted January 10, 1936. Previously registered for copyright as an unpublished song September 12, 1935. Introduced by Fred Astaire (Bake Baker) and ensemble. Original cast recording by Astaire with Johnny Green and His Orchestra (Brunswick).

VERSE

I haven't
Ambitions
For lofty
Positions
That wind up with the wealth of the land.
I'd give you the throne that a
King sat on
For just a
Small baton,
Providing you included a band.

CHORUS 1

If I could be the wealthy owner
Of a large industry,
I would say
"Not for me"—
I'd rather lead a band.
If I could be a politician
With a chance to dictate,
I would say
"Let it wait"—
I'd rather lead a band.
My ev'ry care ceases,
I'm rich as old Croesus
When I've got ten pieces
In hand.
If I could have a millionairess
With a whole flock of banks,
I would just
Whisper "Thanks,
I'd rather lead a band."

PATTER

A saxophone,
A slide trombone,
A bass fiddle and a drum,

A guy at the piano who makes it hum,
A violin,
A clarinet,
A hot trumpet and guitar,
And me with the baton
And there you are.

CHORUS 2

If I could be the wealthy owner
Of a large industry,
I would say
"Not for me"—
I'd rather lead a band.
If I could be a politician
With a chance to dictate,
I would say
"Let it wait"—
I'd rather lead a band.
Give me a band, yessir,
And not a thing lesser—
To be that professor
Is grand.
If Josephine had left Napoleon
And climbed in my lap,
I'd say "Go back to Nap"—
I'd rather lead a band.

BUT WHERE ARE YOU?

Published. Copyrighted January 10, 1936. Previously registered for copyright as an unpublished song August 16, 1935. Introduced by Harriet Hilliard (Connie Martin). Original cast recording by Hilliard with Ozzie Nelson's Orchestra (Brunswick). According to Berlin (letter to Francis Gilbert, January 10, 1938), an earlier version of this lyric was written in 1927.

VERSE

All alone I am yearning,
To be with you again;
For a spark is still burning,
It will ever remain—
But I'm yearning in vain.

CHORUS

The moon is high,
The sky is blue,
And here am I,
But where are you?
A night like this

Was meant for two,
And I am here,
But where are you?
Have you forgotten
The night that we met?
With so much to remember,
How could you forget?
The dreams I dream,
Have yet to come true;
My dreams and I are here,
But where are you?

Earlier version

The moon is high,
The sky is blue,
And here am I,
But where are you?
The way is clear
To bill and coo,
And I am here,
But where are you?
Have you forgotten all you promised
On the day we met?
I mean, with so much to remember
How could you forget?
The dreams I dreamed
Have yet to come true;
The moon and I are here,
But where are you?

I'M PUTTING ALL MY EGGS IN ONE BASKET

Published. Copyrighted January 10, 1936. Previously registered for copyright as an unpublished song November 8, 1935. Introduced by Fred Astaire (Bake Baker) and Ginger Rogers (Sherry Martin). Original cast recording by Astaire with Johnny Green's Orchestra (Brunswick) was the number-one-selling record in America. Also recorded by Rogers with Jimmy Dorsey and His Orchestra (Decca).

VERSE

I've been a roaming Romeo [Juliet];
My Juliets [Romeos] have been many,
But now my roaming days have gone—
Too many irons in the fire
Is worse than not having any.
I've had my share, and from now on:

CHORUS

I'm putting all my eggs in one basket;
I'm betting ev'rything I've got on you.
I'm giving all my love to one baby;
Lord help me if my baby don't come through.
I've got a great big amount
Saved up in my love account,
Honey, and I've decided
Love divided
In two
Won't do.
So I'm putting all my eggs in one basket;
I'm betting ev'rything I've got on you.

LET'S FACE THE MUSIC AND DANCE

Published. Copyrighted January 10, 1936. Previously registered for copyright as an unpublished song June 14, 1935. Introduced by Fred Astaire (Bake Baker) and Ginger Rogers (Sherry Martin). Original cast recording by Astaire with Johnny Green and His Orchestra (Brunswick).

There may be trouble ahead,
But while there's moonlight and music
And love and romance,
Let's face the music and dance.
Before the fiddlers have fled,
Before they ask us to pay the bill,
And while we still have the chance,
Let's face the music and dance.
Soon
We'll be without the moon,
Humming a diff'rent tune,
And then,
There may be teardrops to shed.
So while there's moonlight and music
And love and romance,
Let's face the music and dance.

MOONLIGHT MANEUVERS

Not used in film. Registered for copyright as an unpublished song August 3, 1935, and again on September 7, 1935.

CHORUS

Oh, the night is getting dark, co-oo,
Near the benches in the park, co-oo—
Each and ev'ry little gob
Is on the job
For moonlight maneuvers.
There'll be birds on ev'ry tree, co-oo,
Just to see what they can see, co-oo,
For a lot of open necks
Have cleared the decks
For moonlight maneuvers.
Arms waiting to be filled up,
Lips yearning for a kiss,
Ears list'ning to a buildup—
Lord help the Navy on a night like this!
They'll be rowing on the lake, co-oo,
Keeping ev'ryone awake, co-oo—
Tell the copper on the beat
It's just the fleet
At moonlight maneuvers.

THERE'S A SMILE ON MY FACE

Not used in film. Registered for copyright as an unpublished song July 29, 1935.

VERSE

Why don't you, why won't you see
What I want you to see?
Surely by now you've guessed
All that I've not expressed.*
Why don't you, why won't you see
What has happened to me?
Must I explain what appears
Just as plain as can be?

CHORUS

There's a smile on my face
And a kiss on my lips
And a place in my arms for you.
Leave the smile on my face;
Take the kiss from my lips
And your place in my arms, please do.
Here's my love—
Promise you won't forsake it.
Here's my heart—
Even if you should break it,
I'll take it,
With a smile on my face
And a kiss on my lips
And a place in my arms for you.

---

*Alternate version of lines 3 and 4:
  Why don't you try to guess
  Thoughts that I can't express?

ON THE AVENUE | 1937

ON THE AVENUE (1937)

A film produced by Darryl F. Zanuck and Gene Markey for 20th Century–Fox. Released February 1937. Lyrics and music by Irving Berlin. Screenplay by Gene Markey and William Counselman, based on an original story by Irving Berlin and William Counselman. Directed by Roy Del Ruth. Dances directed by Seymour Felix. Music conducted by Arthur Lange. Orchestrations by Herbert W. Spencer. Cast: starring Dick Powell (Gary Blake), Madeleine Carroll (Mimi Caraway), and Alice Faye (Mona Merrick) and featuring the Ritz Brothers (Al, Harry, and Jimmy) as themselves, George Barbier (Commodore Caraway), Alan Mowbray (Frederick Sims), Cora Witherspoon (Aunt Fritz), Walter Catlett (Jake Dibble), Joan Davis (Miss Katz, Dibble's secretary), Stepin Fetchit (Herman Step), Sig Ruman (Haufstangl), and Billy Gilbert (Joe Papalopoulos).

Many sources indicate that Berlin wrote a song titled "On the Avenue" for this film. While it is logical that the film would have a title song, no lyric with that title has come to our attention.

HE AIN'T GOT RHYTHM

Published. Copyrighted January 13, 1937. Previously registered for copyright as an unpublished song December 5, 1936. Introduced by Alice Faye (Mona Herrick), the Ritz Brothers, and ensemble. Leading recording by Benny Goodman and His Orchestra, vocal by Jimmy Rushing (Victor). According to Michael Feinstein, a manuscript of this song exists on RKO music paper, which indicates that it might have been written as early as late 1934 or 1935.

VERSE

I know a professor of great renown,
And he is the loneliest man in town.
He's as smart as a man can be,
But he never has company.
Why is he the loneliest man in town?

CHORUS 1

He ain't got rhythm—
Ev'ry night he sits in the house alone,

Alice Faye, Dick Powell, and Madeleine Carroll between takes

'Cause he ain't got rhythm;
Ev'ry night he sits there and wears a frown.
He attracted some attention
When he found the fourth dimension,
But he ain't got rhythm,
So no one's with 'im,
The loneliest man in town.
A lonely man is he,
Bending over his books;
His wife and family
Keep giving him dirty looks,
'Cause he ain't got rhythm—
When they call him up,
It's to call him down.
With a daring aviator
He encircled the Equator,
But he ain't got rhythm,
As no one's with 'im,
The loneliest man in town.

CHORUS 2

He ain't got rhythm.
Ev'ry night he sits in the house alone,
'Cause he ain't got rhythm;
Ev'ry night he sits there and wears a frown.
With a problem scientific
He's colossal and terrific,
But he ain't got rhythm,
So no one's with 'im,
The loneliest man in town.
A lonely man is he,
Bending over his books;
His wife and family
Keep giving him dirty looks,
'Cause he ain't got rhythm—
When they call him up,
It's to call him down.
In the month of January
He compiled a dictionary,
But he ain't got rhythm,
As no one's with 'im,
The loneliest man in town.

Ritz Brothers Specialty

[*After* MONA *sings a verse and chorus before the curtain with the twelve girls of the ensemble, we go into the Wilson Observatory set.* HARRY RITZ *is discovered at a long telescope.* JIMMY RITZ *is bending over a textbook.* AL RITZ *is examining an astronomical chart.*]

HARRY: I know every planet up in the sky;
    I've measured them all with my naked eye.

I've seen everything up in Mars;
I know all about falling stars.
But still I'm a very unhappy guy—
I wonder why.
JIM & AL: You ain't got rhythm.

[CHORUS enters to four bars of vamp.]

HARRY: I can read the tea leaves in my cup.
JIM, AL, &
CHORUS: But you ain't got rhythm.
HARRY: And I just found out how high is up.
JIM, AL, &
CHORUS: But you ain't got rhythm.
HARRY: I discovered once while sober
    Where the flies go in
      October;
    For what I found out about the flies,
    I got the Nobel Prize.
JIM, AL, &
CHORUS: But you can't do the Charleston,
    And you don't know how to do the
      Black Bottom—the new rhythm.
HARRY: [*after peeping through telescope*]
    Heaven—I see heaven
    Through my telescope while gazing
    From Mount Wilson's
      highest peak.
    I'll explain it all in Latin or in Greek.
JIM, AL, &
CHORUS: But you're not so hot while dancing
    cheek to cheek.
HARRY: I've mastered relativity,
    But when the Astors give a tea,
    They never think of asking me—
    I wonder why.
JIM, AL, &
CHORUS: 'Cause you don't know how to do the
    rumba—
    That's the reason you're a lonely guy.
HARRY: Ah, Venus is lovely tonight,
    And so is Jupiter.
    Jupiter is skipping from planet to
      planet,
    Jumping Jupiter!
JIM, AL, &
CHORUS: But you couldn't be stupider
    'Cause you ain't got rhythm.
HARRY: I discovered liquid air.
JIM, AL, &
CHORUS: But you ain't got rhythm.
HARRY: I've got a cure for falling hair.
JIM, AL, &
CHORUS: But you can't get hot.
HARRY: What!?
JIM, AL, &
CHORUS: No, you can't get hot.

HARRY: What!?
I'm a scientist to my fingertips.

JIM, AL, &
CHORUS: But you can't do nothing with your hips,
And that's the thing we miss.

HARRY: [business of shaking hips]
Do you mean like this?

JIM, AL, &
CHORUS: He's got it,
He's got it,
He's got it,
He's got it—
The man's got rhythm.

THE GIRL ON THE *POLICE GAZETTE*

Published. Copyrighted January 13, 1937. Previously registered for copyright as an unpublished song June 21, 1935. Introduced by Dick Powell (Gary Blake) and male ensemble. Original cast recording by Powell with Victor Young and His Orchestra (Decca).

VERSE

Some fellows see the girl that they love in a dream;
Some fellows see their love in a rippling stream.
I saw the girl that I can't forget
On the cover of a *Police Gazette*—
If I could find her, life would be peaches and cream.

CHORUS

Oh, my search will never cease
For the girl on the *Police Gazette*,
For the pretty young brunette
On the pink *Police Gazette*.
And above my mantelpiece
There's a page of the *Police Gazette*
With the pretty young brunette,
On the pink *Police Gazette*.
I love to stop
At my favorite barbershop
Just to take another look at
The girl that I haven't met—
Yet—
And my longing will increase
For the girl on the *Police Gazette*,
For the pretty young brunette
On the pink *Police Gazette*.

YOU'RE LAUGHING AT ME

Published. Copyrighted January 13, 1937. Previously registered for copyright as an unpublished song May 14, 1936. Introduced by Dick Powell (Gary Blake). Original cast recording by Powell with Victor Young and His Orchestra (Decca). Other leading recordings by Thomas "Fats" Waller (Victor) and Wayne King and His Orchestra (Victor).

VERSE

I love you,
Which is easy to see,
But I have to keep guessing
How you feel about me.
You listen
To the words that I speak,
But I feel that you listen
With your tongue in your cheek.

CHORUS

You're
Laughing at me—
I can't be sentimental,
For you're
Laughing at me, I know.
I want to be romantic,
But I haven't a chance;
You've got a sense of humor,
And humor is death to romance.
You're
Laughing at me—
Why do you think it's funny when I
Say that I love you so?
You've got me worried and I'm all at sea,
For while I'm crying for you,
You're
Laughing at me.

THIS YEAR'S KISSES

Published. Copyrighted January 13, 1937. Previously registered for copyright as an unpublished song May 22, 1936. Introduced by Alice Faye (Mona Merrick). Original cast recordings by Faye with Cy Feuer and His Orchestra (Brunswick) and Dick Powell with Victor Young and His Orchestra (Decca). Two recordings—by Hal Kemp and His Orchestra, vocal by Skinnay Ennis (Brunswick), and Benny Goodman and His Orchestra,

vocal by Margaret McCrae (Victor)—reached the top spot on the popular music charts.

VERSE

I didn't cry when romance was through;
I looked around for somebody new.
Since my romance I've kissed one or two,
But I'm afraid their kisses won't do.

CHORUS

This year's crop of kisses
Don't seem as sweet to me.
This year's crop just misses
What kisses used to be.
This year's new romance
Doesn't seem to have a chance,
Even helped by Mister Moon above.
This year's crop of kisses
Is not for me,
For I'm still
Wearing last year's love.

I'VE GOT MY LOVE TO KEEP ME WARM

Published. Copyrighted January 13, 1937. Previously registered for copyright as an unpublished song May 14, 1936. Introduced by Dick Powell (Gary Blake) with a brief assist from Alice Faye (Mona Merrick) and ensemble. Original cast recordings by Powell with Victor Young and His Orchestra (Decca) and Faye with Cy Feuer and His Orchestra (Brunswick). Other leading recordings by Ray Noble and His Orchestra (Victor) including Glenn Miller (trombone) and Charlie Spivak (trumpet), and Howard Phillips (vocal); Billie Holiday and Her Orchestra (Brunswick); Red Norvo and His Orchestra (Brunswick); and Glen Gray and the Casa Loma Orchestra (Decca). Twelve years later, in 1949, the recording by Les Brown and His Orchestra (Columbia) reached the top spot in the popular music charts.

The snow is snowing,
The wind is blowing,
But I can weather the storm.
What do I care how much it may storm?
I've got my love to keep me warm.
I can't remember
A worse December—
Just watch those icicles form.
What do I care if icicles form?

I've got my love to keep me warm.
Off with my overcoat,
Off with my glove;
I need no overcoat—
I'm burning with love.
My heart's on fire,
The flame grows higher,
So I will weather the storm.
What do I care how much it may storm?
I've got my love to keep me warm.

SLUMMING ON PARK AVENUE

Published. Copyrighted January 13, 1937. Previously registered for copyright as an unpublished song May 14, 1936. Introduced by Alice Faye (Mona Merrick), the Ritz Brothers, and ensemble. Original cast recording by Faye with Cy Feuer and His Orchestra (Brunswick). Other leading recordings by Red Norvo and His Orchestra, vocal by Mildred Bailey (Brunswick); Fletcher Henderson and His Orchestra, vocal by Jerry Blake (Vocalion); and Jimmie Lunceford and His Orchestra (Decca).

VERSE

Put on your slumming clothes
And get your car—
Let's go sightseeing where
The high-toned people are.
Come on, there's lots of fun
In store for you—
See how the other half lives
On Park Avenue.

CHORUS 1

Let's go slumming,
Take me slumming—
Let's go slumming on Park Avenue.
Let us hide behind a pair of fancy glasses
And make faces when a member of the classes
Passes.
Let's go smelling
Where they're dwelling,
Sniffing ev'rything the way they do.
Let us go to it;
They do it—
Why can't we do it too?
Let's go slumming,
Nose thumbing,
At Park Avenue.

CHORUS 2

Let's go slumming,
Take me slumming—
Let's go slumming on Park Avenue.
Where the social hearts for Broadway lights are
    throbbing,
And they spend their nights in smart cafés
    hobnobbing,
Snobbing.
Come, let's eye them,
Pass right by them,
Looking down our noses as they do.
Let us go to it;
They do it—
Why can't we do it too?
Let's go slumming,
Crumb bumming,
On Park Avenue.

The second chorus lyric was written in February 1957 and published in what became the "standard edition" of the song. Lyrics for two other choruses also were written at that time. The typed lyric sheet is dated February 25, 1957.

CHORUS 3

Let's go slumming,
Take me slumming—
Let's go slumming on Park Avenue.
Let's scrutinize them through a silver lorgnette
And make faces at their children who haven't been
    born yet.
When they're talking,
Hillside walking,
Let us look them up and down and through.
Let us go to it;
They do it—
Why can't we do it too?
Let's go slumming,
Chew gumming,
On Park Avenue.

CHORUS 4

Let's go slumming,
Take me slumming—
Let's go slumming on Park Avenue,
Where they won't see shows unless it's from the
    front row,
Paying prices that make actors call the front row
Grunt row.
Let's go find them
And remind them
That they live there though the rent is due.
Let us go to it;
They do it—

Why can't we do it too?
Let's go slumming.
Ho-humming,
On Park Avenue.

ON THE STEPS OF GRANT'S TOMB

Not used in film. Registered for copyright as an unpublished song May 14, 1936.

VERSE

There's an old inscription that will always survive
On a monument that stands on Riverside Drive.
It's a motto we could shout
When the wedding bells ring out,
And if I should live to see that moment arrive—

CHORUS

You'll be the bride,
I'll be the groom
When we are married on the steps of Grant's
    Tomb.
We'll tell the world
When we are one
That all our quarreling is over and done.
What greater news could we release,
What greater marriage vows than "Let there be
    peace"
When you're the bride
And I'm the groom?
And while the birds are singing "Love is in
    bloom,"
We'll say "I do" on the steps of Grant's Tomb.

SWING, SISTER!

Not used in film. Registered for copyright as an unpublished song May 14, 1936.

VERSE

The saxophones are saxophoning,
Phoning you to be there—
Swing is in the air.
The slide trombones are slide tromboning,

311

Meaning only one thing—
It's this year of swing.

CHORUS

Swing, sister—
Swing, brother—
Cuddle up to one another
And swing.
Come on, get close to one another
And swing it.
Swing, uncle—
Swing, auntie—
Raise the roof right off your shanty
And swing.
Come on, get close to one another
And swing it.
Let there be music,
Music to dance to.
Here is the music;
Now's your chance to
Swing, sister—
Swing, brother—
Cuddle up to one another
And swing.
Come on, get close to one another
And swing it.

CUSTOMERS, WE GREET YOU

Not used in film. No music is known to survive. Berlin's ink holograph manuscript and typed lyric sheets are in the Irving Berlin Collection of the Music Division of the Library of Congress. Alternate title: "Opening Chorus." This number evolved through a number of Berlin projects. See also *Music Box Revue of 1938–1939*. The earliest version follows.

Customers, we greet you
With a "Very pleased to meet you"
And an op'ning chorus you could do without;
But an op'ning chorus
Is a job that lies before us,
So we'll try to tell you what it's all about.
We greet you ev'ry season
At the start of each revue
Without much rhyme or reason,
And we know we're boring you,
But an op'ning must be spoken—
That's why we are here,
For until the ice is broken,
The stars won't appear.
So read your programs and gaze behind;
It's not unkind,
For we don't mind.
We'll struggle through this opening somehow;

Just bang your seats—we're used to it by now.
The opening is long,
So we brought along our knitting;
We aren't very strong,
So they let us do it sitting.
We'd enjoy it if we didn't have to sing;
Still, we're happy, for you can't have ev'rything.
Customers, it's boring—
Did we hear somebody snoring?
Go ahead—we promise not to even peep.
Go ahead—keep dozing,
For we haven't reached the closing:
You've exactly one more minute left to sleep.
We know that you first-nighters
Want the opening to go,
But op'ning-chorus writers
Have a union that says no,
So we often cross our fingers
And pray on our knees
That their children may be singers
Of op'nings like these.
And now it's over, we're leaving you;
You're glad it's through—
We're happy too.
So just forget we ever came to call—
In other words, we weren't here at all.*

When working on the unproduced Music Box Revue of 1938–1939, *Berlin changed the last two lines to read:*
 But really it was simply too divine
 To start the *Music Box Revue of 1939*.

Jack Haley (drums), Alice Faye, Don Ameche (piano), Tyrone Power (violin). Inset: Ethel Merman sings "Everybody Step."

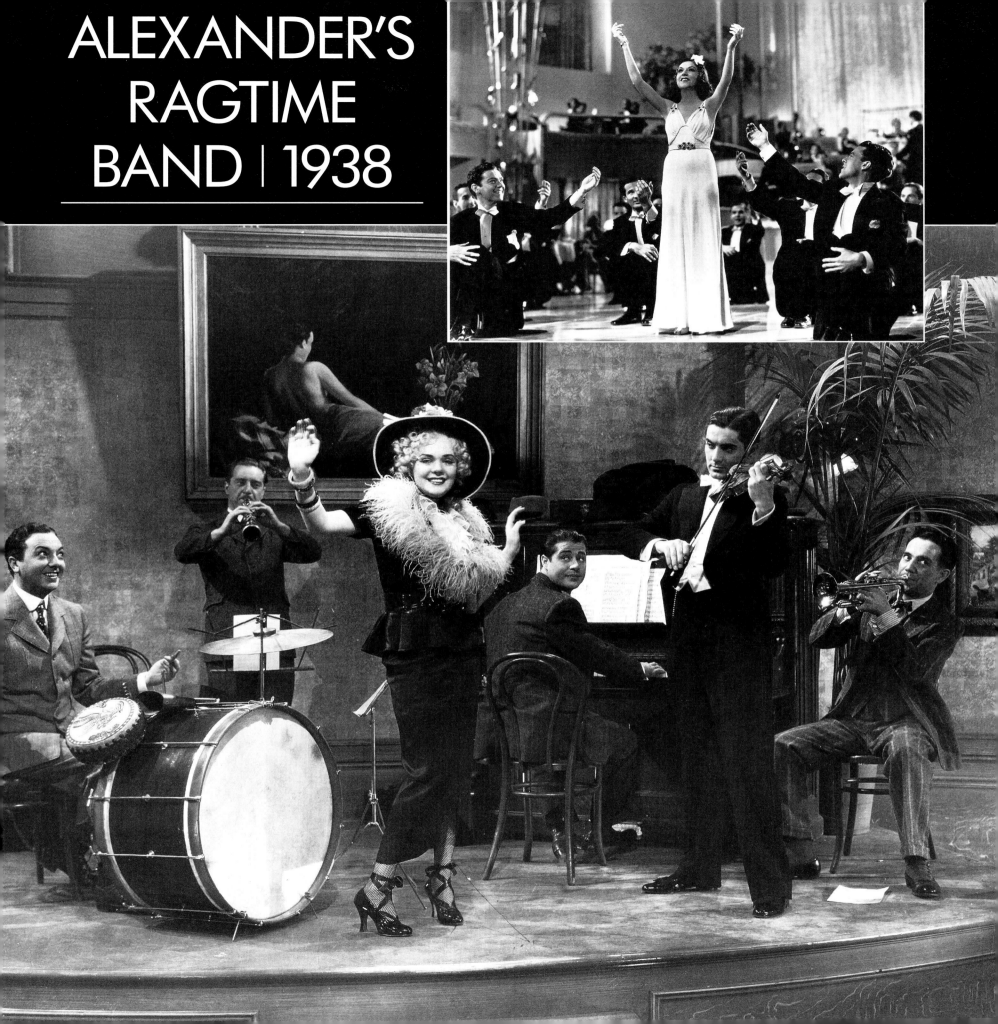

ALEXANDER'S
RAGTIME
BAND | 1938

ALEXANDER'S RAGTIME BAND (1938)

A film produced by Darryl F. Zanuck and Harry Joe Brown for 20th Century–Fox. Released in August 1938. Lyrics and music by Irving Berlin. Screenplay by Kathryn Scola, Lamar Trotti, and Richard Sherman, based on a story idea by Irving Berlin. Directed by Henry King. Dances directed by Seymour Felix. Orchestrations by Walter Scharf. Music conducted by Alfred Newman. Cast: starring Tyrone Power ("Alexander" Roger Grant), Ethel Merman (Jerry Allen), Alice Faye (Stella Kirby), and Don Ameche (Charlie Dwyer) and featuring Jack Haley (Davey Lane), Jean Hersholt (Professor Heinrich), Helen Westby (Aunt Sophie), John Carradine (Cab Driver).

Alexander's Ragtime Band, the first of Berlin's song cavalcades on film, also was the first musical film in which old and new songs all by the same composer were used. The movie included a total of twenty-nine Berlin songs, of which three were written expressly for the film.

Darryl Zanuck had wanted originally to make the film biographical. But Berlin vetoed the idea and the movie became a musical retrospective of the songwriter's work; thinly disguised episodes from his professional life were woven into the plot.

Alexander's Ragtime Band received an Academy Award for best score (Alfred Newman). It got five additional nominations, including Best Picture, Best Original Story (Irving Berlin), and Best Song ("Now It Can Be Told," Irving Berlin).

NOW IT CAN BE TOLD

Published. Copyrighted May 20, 1938. Previously registered for copyright as an unpublished song May 8, 1938. Introduced by Don Ameche (Charlie Dwyer) and Alice Faye (Stella Kirby). Top recording—number two on the popular music charts—by Tommy Dorsey and His Orchestra, vocal by Jack Leonard (Victor). Other leading recordings by Bing Crosby with John Scott Trotter's Orchestra (Decca) and Tony Martin with Ray Noble's Orchestra (Brunswick). Berlin wrote his partner Saul Bornstein (January 13, 1938) that "Now It Can Be Told" was spotted better than any song he'd ever "had in any picture and will be reprieved [*sic*] several times, with a 16-bar vocal finish at the end of the picture. If there ever was a chance for a song being a big hit, this is it."

VERSE

All the world's great lovers have been glorified;
Hist'ry placed them in a romantic set.
In between book covers they are side by side,
But the real thing hasn't been written yet.

CHORUS

Now it can be told,
Told in all its glory;
Now that we have met
The world may know the sentimental story.
The greatest romance they ever knew
Is waiting to unfold.
Now it can be told
As an inspiration;
Ev'ry other tale of boy-meets-girl
Is just an imitation.
The great love story has never been told before,
But now,
Now it can be told.

MY WALKING STICK

Published. Copyrighted May 20, 1938. Previously registered for copyright as an unpublished song February 4, 1938. Introduced by Ethel Merman and ensemble. Leading recordings by Tommy Dorsey and His Orchestra, vocal by Jack Leonard (Victor), and Ray Noble and His Orchestra, vocal by Tony Martin (Brunswick).

VERSE

Take away my high hats,
Take away my fav'rite tie,
Take away my white spats,
I'll still get by.
But my walking stick,
You simply must let that be—
I mean, you can't take that away from me.

CHORUS

Without my walking stick
I'd go insane;
Can't look my best,
I'd feel undressed,
Without my cane.
Must have my walking stick,
'Cause it may rain;
And when it pours,
Can't be outdoors
Without my cane.

If I ever left my house
Without my walking stick,
It would just be something
I could never explain;
The thing that makes me click
On lovers' lane
Would go for naught
If I were caught
Without my cane.

MARCHING ALONG WITH TIME

Published. Copyrighted May 20, 1938. Previously registered for copyright as an unpublished song February 4, 1938. Intended for Ethel Merman (Jerry Allen) but dropped from the score during production.

VERSE

This world of ours is ever changing;
The hand of time keeps rearranging.
With ev'ry change I'm right on the beat,
Won't let the grass grow under my feet—I'm

CHORUS

Marching along with time,
I'll be marching from time to time,
For I'm not gonna let the parade go by—
You know that time marches on, and so do I.
One day I changed my horse for a motor,
And now of course
I'll be changing my car for a plane to fly—
You know that time marches on and so do I.
There'll be a change in music,
A change in rhythm,
A change in dancing,
But I'll be right with 'em.
Watch me and you will find
That I just won't be left behind—
Father Time marches on with his head up
    high
And so do I.

Fred Astaire and Ginger Rogers doing "The Yam"

CAREFREE | 1938

CAREFREE (1938)

A film produced by Pandro S. Berman for RKO Radio Pictures. Released in August 1938. Lyrics and music by Irving Berlin. Screenplay by Ernest Pagano and Allan Scott, adapted by Dudley Nichols and Hagar Wilde from a story by Marian Ainslee and Guy Endore. Directed by Mark Sandrich. Dances directed by Hermes Pan. Orchestrations and arrangements by Robert Russell Bennett, Conrad Salinger, Gene Rose, Leonid Raab, and Max Reese. Music conducted by Victor Baravelle. Cast: starring Fred Astaire (Tony Flagg) and Ginger Rogers (Amanda Cooper) and featuring Ralph Bellamy (Stephen Arden) and Luella Gear (Cora Cooper).

SINCE THEY TURNED LOCH LOMOND INTO SWING

Registered for copyright as an unpublished song April 12, 1938. "Golf Solo" to this music was danced by Fred Astaire. Not sung in film. Considered later for the score of the unproduced *Music Box Revue of 1938–1939*.

Since they turned Loch Lomond into swing,
Out in Scotland they don't Highland fling—
Every bonny, bonny lassie
Now has rhythm in her chassis
Since that thing they call swing hit Loch Lomond.

Since they made Loch Lomond sweet and hot,
What it takes now every Scot has got—
Every clerk and every woodman
Wants to be a Benny Goodman
Since that thing they call swing hit Loch Lomond.

THE NIGHT IS FILLED WITH MUSIC

Published. Copyrighted June 13, 1938. Previously registered for copyright as an unpublished song December 3, 1937. Not sung in film. Danced by Fred Astaire (Tony Flagg) and Ginger Rogers (Amanda Cooper).

The night is filled with music,
The sky is filled with blue;

The air is filled with fragrant perfume,
Telling me that spring is in bloom;
The path is filled with moonlight,
The grass is filled with dew;
And I'd be filled
With a heavenly feeling
If my arms were filled with you.

I USED TO BE COLOR BLIND

Published. Copyrighted June 13, 1938. Previously registered for copyright as an unpublished song December 3, 1937. Introduced by Fred Astaire (Tony Flagg) and Ginger Rogers (Amanda Cooper). Original cast recordings by Astaire with Ray Noble and His Orchestra (Brunswick) and Rogers with an orchestra conducted by Hal Boone (Bluebird).

Berlin's reflections on this song were captured in a July 14, 1938, article in the New York *Post:*

Today you must have ideas. This used to be a world of singers, but now it's a world of listeners. So much is thrown at people's ears that a song must have a special quality of its own to be remembered, even for a little while. An example of an idea song is a number I've written for *Carefree*, the new Astaire-Rogers picture that will be brought out soon.

They were going to do it in Technicolor, and I wanted to write a Technicolor song that would be good in and out of the picture. The title that occurred to me was "I Used to Be Color Blind." But how to treat it? Here's the natural way to write it up:

I used to be color blind,
I never could see
The green in the grass, the gold in the moon, the blue in the skies;
Then you came along . . .

I don't remember how it went. But I do remember that they liked it, and I had a hard time unselling it. It was written the natural way. The natural way is often the best way, but not always. The song went along the beaten path.
This is how I changed it:

I used to be color blind,
But I met you and now I find
There's green in the grass,
There's gold in the moon,
There's blue in the skies . . .

Much better, isn't it? The first version was roundabout and negative; the second is direct and

positive. They finally decided not to use Technicolor, but the song is still O.K.

VERSE

Strange
How a dreary world can suddenly change
To a world as bright as the evening star.
Queer
What a diff'rence when your vision is clear
And you see things as they really are.

CHORUS

I used to be color blind,
But I met you and now I find
There's green in the grass,
There's gold in the moon,
There's blue in the skies.
That semicircle that was always hanging about
Is not a storm cloud, it's a rainbow—
You brought the colors out.
Believe me, it's really true,
Till I met you I never knew a setting sun
Could paint such beautiful skies;
I never knew there were such lovely colors—
And the big surprise
Is the red in your cheeks,
The gold in your hair,
The blue in your eyes.

Earlier version

VERSE

Strange
How a dreary world can suddenly change
To a world as bright as any star.
Queer
What a difference when your vision is clear
And you see things as they really are.

CHORUS

I used to be color blind,
But now I can see
The green in the grass,
The gold in the moon,
The blue in the skies.
The heavens were always gray,
And still I believed
That nothing was wrong—
Till love came along
And opened my eyes.
I can see all the storm clouds
That were hanging about
Turning into a rainbow—

You brought the colors out.
I used to be color blind,
But now I can see
A lovely you,
An open fire,
A room in blue
Where I'll admire
The red in your cheeks,
The gold in your hair,
The blue in your eyes.

THE YAM

Published. Copyrighted July 14, 1938. Previously registered for copyright as an unpublished song March 29, 1938. Introduced by Ginger Rogers (Amanda Cooper) and Fred Astaire (Tony Flagg). Original cast recordings by Astaire with Ray Noble and His Orchestra (Brunswick) and by Rogers with an orchestra conducted by Hal Boone (Bluebird).

VERSE

Come on and hear the Yam man cry,
"Any Yam today?"
The sweet potatoes that he'll fry
Will be Yam today.
The little step that you'll see him do
With ev'ry Yam that he sells to you,
It's something that you ought to try—
Come and Yam today.

CHORUS

Come get what I've got—
It will hit the spot—
Get your sweet and hot
Yam.
Raise your hand and sway
Like you hold a tray
When you're on your way—
Yam.
Come on and shake your depression
And let's have a Yam session:
There's that long note—
One, two, three, Yam—
Ev'ry orchestra
In America
Will be doing the
Yam.

PATTER

I didn't come to do the Charleston,
I didn't come to Ball the Jack,
I didn't come to do
The Suzy-Q
Or do the Bottom they call Black.
I didn't come to do Big Apple,
I didn't come to do the Shag,
But, honey, here I am
To do the Yam,
Because the Yam is in the bag.

On June 15, 1938, Berlin completed a new patter lyric, which he sent to Dave Dreyer, a songwriter, longtime Berlin musical assistant, and Hollywood arranger.

You can do it without a doubt:
Spread your toes, put your arms way out;
Now you know what it's all about—
Yam.
Walk awhile till you get the feel;
Turn around, then you toe and heel;
There's that long note with sax appeal—
Yam.

In reply to Berlin, Dreyer wrote that Fred Astaire and director Mark Sandrich were happy with this patter but asked that the second line read, "Put your toes together and your arms way out." Astaire also was not happy with the phrase "sax appeal."

An earlier version of the song, called "Jam," shows in the first two lines of the verse that the song was derived from "Any Love Today," page 296.

VERSE

I'm not the feller who used to say,
"Any rags, any bones, any bottles today?"
But I'm a salesman and here I am
Crying out, "Any Jam?"
Yah, man, I'm the Jam Man
And I'm right down from the stars,
But the Jam I'm talking about
Don't come in jars.

CHORUS

It isn't strawberry jam,
It isn't raspberry jam,
But it's a step that I call
Jam.
I've really got something new,
And it is not hard to do,
The little step that I call
Jam.
You better shake off your depression,
We're going into a jam session:

One, two, three—
Follow me—
Jam.
You know the band is compelled
To play a long note that's held,
And when they do,
Everybody Jam.

CHANGE PARTNERS

Published. Copyrighted June 13, 1938. Previously registered for copyright as an unpublished song December 3, 1937. Introduced by Fred Astaire (Tony Flagg) and Ginger Rogers (Amanda Cooper). Original cast recording by Astaire with Ray Noble and His Orchestra was the number-one seller on the popular music charts. The recording by Jimmy Dorsey and His Orchestra, vocal by Bob Eberly (Decca), also was number one on the charts. Nominated for an Academy Award as Best Song.

On July 5, 1938, Dave Dreyer wrote Berlin about this song and others in the score.

I thought you would be interested to know that we recorded the vocal on "Change Partners" Saturday. When Fred and Mark [Sandrich] heard the orchestra play it the first time, they jumped up and hugged each other. I never saw them show so much enthusiasm about a number before. You will probably receive a wire or a call from Mark about it. They both seemed to think it is even better than "Cheek to Cheek."

I am particularly pleased about this reaction because frankly, Irving, as you may have felt, there was no great enthusiasm on the lot for this score although they all admitted the songs were good, but there was not much confidence or assurance as to the ultimate success of the songs. However, since we have recorded "The Yam" and "Change Partners," also "The Night Is Filled with Music," the old spirit is back once more. Everyone is ready to lay the odds that these three songs will be one, two and three on the list. Personally, I don't see how they can miss. The only way these songs could be kept off the HIT PARADE would be NOT to publish them.

Must you dance ev'ry dance
With the same fortunate man?
You have danced with him since the music
    began—
Won't you change partners and dance with me?
Must you dance quite so close
With your lips touching his face?

Can't you see I'm longing to be in his place?
Won't you change partners and dance with me?
Ask him to sit this one out,
And while you're alone,
I'll tell the waiter to tell him
He's wanted on the telephone.
You've been locked in his arms
Ever since heaven knows when—
Won't you change partners, and then
You may never want to change partners again.

CAREFREE

Not used in film. Registered for copyright as an unpublished song December 3, 1937.

VERSE

As a student of psychology I find
A perfect state of health depends
On a perfect state of your mind.
As a student of psychology I say,
Rid yourself of all your cares
And do it right away.

CHORUS

Carefree—
Free from care—
Order that from your bill o' fare.
Only thing to be careful about
Is to be carefree.
All's well—
Have no doubt,
No self-pity, it wears you out—
Only people to pity are those
Who are not carefree.
Father Time will catch up with you,
So hurry and decide—
Take that lady to sup with you
And let your conscience be your guide.
Happy
With your lot—
Don't you try to be what you're not.
Only thing to be caring to be
Is to be carefree.

YOU CAN BE MY CAVE MAN

Not used in film. Intended for Mitzi Green, who at one time was slated to appear in the film. Registered for copyright as an unpublished song March 12, 1938.

VERSE

Get your slippers and your pipe;
I'm the strictly indoor type—
"Home Sweet Home" is the sweetest song ever
    composed.
If you want to make me yours,
Let's forget the great outdoors—
Unless you can fix it so the great outdoors are
    closed.

CHORUS 1

You can be my cave man,
And I will be true,
If you build me a cave on the top of a building
On Park Avenue.
I won't mind the stone age,
Whatever it brings,
If the stones are all diamonds and emeralds and
    rubies
And set in platinum rings.
You can be my Boy Scout,
I'll never say quits;
We can spend our summers
Roughing it at the Ritz.
You can be my Tarzan
And swing from a tree,
But you'll have to come down in the evening
If you want to go swinging with me.

CHORUS 2

You can plan a fox hunt—
I'll come along too,
If the foxes we hunt are in Jaeckel's, the furrier
On Fifth Avenue.
You can make it tigers
And still I won't mind,
If the tigers we hunt have been working in
    pictures—
I mean the Hollywood kind.
You can go exploring
In faraway Nome;
Darling, I'll be with you—
With you when you come home.
You can catch a whale, dear,
Somewhere in the sea,

But you'll have to go fishing for goldfish
If you want to go fishing with me.

LET'S MAKE THE MOST OF OUR DREAM

Not used in film. Written for a second dream sequence. Registered for copyright as an unpublished song December 3, 1937.

VERSE

Little did I know
When I counted sheep
And fell asleep,
I'd see the moon again,
But there's the moon,
And strange as it all may seem,
Little did I know
When we said goodbye
That you and I
Would meet so soon again,
But here we are—
You've come to me in a dream.

CHORUS

In the morning the sun will shine;
You'll go your way and I'll go mine.
Till the morning
Let's make the most of our dream.
I've got kisses, they're yours to take;
You can't have them when I'm awake.
Don't be frightened—
Anything goes in a dream.
You know that dreams are elastic;
There's really nothing you can't make them do.
Let's be fantastic and maybe
Some of the things that we dream will come true.
Far away from the noisy crowd,
We can drift on our fav'rite cloud;
Till the morning life can be simply supreme—
The dawn will come with coffee and toast,
So let's make the most of our dream.

WHAT THE WELL-DRESSED MAN WILL WEAR

Dropped from the film before production began. Intended for Fred Astaire (Tony Flagg). Registered for copyright as an unpublished song December 3, 1937.

VERSE

Stop talking about the foreign situation;
Stop saying that very soon we'll have inflation.
Incomes have shortened,
But there's no reason to fuss—
Something important
Is what I'd like to discuss.

CHORUS 1

I'm not interested in
The stocks that you've invested in;
I'm just interested in
What the well-dressed man will wear.
I don't want to know about
That blonde with whom you go about;
I just want to know about
What the well-dressed man will wear.
Let me mingle with the dudes;
Let my name repose
In the blue book that includes
The who's who in clothes.
I would not give up a cent
To be the nation's president;
I just want to represent
What the nation's well-dressed man will wear.

PATTER

[Men's Fashion Parade]
And now I'd like to show you what is part of next
    year's plan—
What summer, winter, spring, and fall will bring
    to the well-dressed man.

When spring arrives in April, you will find the
    season's catch—
A symphony in purple with his tie and socks to
    match.

When summer comes, his bathing trunks
    designed to keep him cool,
The envy of the other men around the swimming
    pool.

When fall arrives, a morning suit that's different
    will appear—
You'll find a dash of color in his cutaway this year.

When winter comes, the well-dressed man will
    weather every storm.
He doesn't need his love—he's got his underwear
    to keep him warm.

CHORUS 2

[Pajamas]
Here's a suit for when you rise,
In any shade or any size,
Blue or brown to match your eyes—
What the well-dressed man will wear.

[Sack Suit]
Here is something for the Ritz;
I hope you notice that it fits.
As a new creation it's
What the well-dressed man will wear.
Here's the latest thing in town
For the bridal path.
Here's a red-hot dressing gown
To wear to your bath.
Here is something for your arm;
We raised her on a chicken farm.
Something cute with lots of charm—
It's what every well-dressed man will wear.

WORDS

Not used in film. Lyric typed February 23, 1938. Music sketch in hand of Helmy Kresa dated April 30, 1937.

I've got words dipped in honey,
But they would not reveal how I feel about you.
I've got words set to music,
But they won't mean a thing when my singing is
    through.
I've got words down on paper,
But what I really think, pen and ink wouldn't
    show—
So if you want to know how I love you,
Just press those lips divine
Close to mine
And you'll know.

Earlier version

VERSE

Unaccustomed as I am to making pretty speeches,
You'll pardon me if I don't rave about you.
Not that I don't qualify at making pretty
    speeches,
But where there's love, those pretty speeches
    won't do.

CHORUS

I could whisper words dipped in honey,
But they would not reveal how I feel about you.
I could warble words set to music,
But it won't mean a thing when my singing is
    through.
I could scribble words on paper,
Saying what is in my heart,
But the most important part won't show—
So
If you want to know how I love you,
Just let me hold your charms
In my arms and you'll know.

WHY DO I LOVE YOU?

Not used in film. Lyric "dictated and typed . . . April 21, 1937." No music is known to survive.

CHORUS

Why do I love you
When I know you don't love me?
When I know you don't want me,
Why do I want you?
Each day you're colder
Than you were the day before;
Each day you throw me out—
Still I come back for more.
Tell me, why do I call you
When I know you don't listen?
When I know you won't answer,
Why do I call you?
Why do the flowers grow?
Why do the rivers flow?
Why do I love you so?
I don't know why—
But I do.

GOD BLESS AMERICA
and Other Songs of 1935–1939

YOU'RE THE TOP (PARODY)

Written in early January 1935. Berlin wrote the parody as a bon-voyage present for Cole Porter and Moss Hart at the start of the world cruise on which they wrote their musical *Jubilee*.

You're the top!
You're Miss Pinkham's tonic.
You're the top!
You're a high colonic.
You're the burning heat of a bridal suite in use,
You're the breasts of Venus,
You're King Kong's penis,
You're self-abuse.
You're an arch
In the Rome collection.
You're the starch
In a groom's erection.
I'm a eunuch who
Has just been through an op—
But if, baby, I'm the bottom,
You're the top.

WHEN YOUR HEART IS FULL O' TROUBLE

A tribute in verse (there is no music) to the songwriters Bert Kalmar and Harry Ruby. Written for *The Kalmar and Ruby Song Book*, published by Random House in 1936. Berlin's verse precedes the song "A Tulip Told a Tale" and is one of many introductions to the songs. The other contributors to this song book were Franklin P. Adams, Robert Benchley, Marc Connelly, Moss Hart, Ben Hecht, Nunnally Johnson, Groucho Marx, and James K. McGinness.

When your heart is full o' trouble
And when ev'rything goes wrong,
You can find a heap o' comfort
In a sentimental song.
So a rousing cheer for Harry

Kate Smith

And a rousing cheer for Bert
And another for good measure,
For another cheer won't hurt.
Let the ballad baiters snicker,
Let them aim their pointed darts,
Unafraid were Bert and Harry
Of the Kaufmans and the Harts
When they wove their tender heartthrobs
Into songs that have a spark,
Music worthy of the masters,
Lyrics worthy of Dave Clark.
Songs of home and songs of mother,
Songs of fishes and romance,
Songs of fifty million Frenchmen
Dreaming of the south of France,
Songs of love that like the rose is,
Songs of tulips on the hill,
Songs that even Irving Berlin
Would be glad to write—and will.
There is cheering in the alley,
In the word and music mart,
Where they've money in their pockets
For the song that's in your heart.
And I echo their three-cheering
Ere I go back on the shelf:
One for Bert and one for Harry
And the other for myself.

FOR GEORGE GERSHWIN

A poem written May 16, 1938, for Merle Armitage's book *George Gershwin*. Registered for copyright as an unpublished work June 24, 1970.

I could speak of a Whiteman rehearsal
At the old Palais Royal when Paul
Played the "Rhapsody" that lifted Gershwin
From the "Alley" to Carnegie Hall.
I could dwell on the talent that placed him
In the class where he justly belongs,
But this verse is a song-writer's tribute
To a man who wrote wonderful songs.

His were tunes that had more than just rhythm,
For just rhythm will soon gather "corn,"
And those melodies written by Gershwin
Are as fresh now as when they were born.
As a writer of serious music,
He could dream for a while in the stars,
And step down from the heights of Grand
    Opera

To a chorus of thirty-two bars.
And this morning's *Variety* tells me
That the last song he wrote is a hit
It's on top of the list of best sellers,
And the air-waves are ringing with it.
It remains with the dozens of others,
Though the man who composed them is
    gone;
For a song-writer's job may be ended,
But his melodies linger on.

GOD BLESS AMERICA

Published. Copyrighted February 20, 1939. Previously registered for copyright as an unpublished song October 27, 1938; completed some time after September 29, 1938, the date of the Munich Conference, in which Neville Chamberlain, Edouard Daladier, Adolf Hitler, and Benito Mussolini agreed to transfer the Sudetenland, a piece of Czechoslovakia, to Germany. Berlin wrote the song on his way back to America after attending the London premiere (September 30, 1938) of his film *Alexander's Ragtime Band*. Introduced by Kate Smith on her CBS radio show, *The Kate Smith Hour*, on November 10, 1938. Smith premiered the song late in the show and prefaced it with the following words:

And now it's going to be my very great privilege to sing for you a song that's never been sung before by anybody. One that was written especially for me by one of the greatest composers in the music field today. It's something more than a song—I feel it's one of the most beautiful compositions ever written, a song that will never die. The author—Mr. Irving Berlin. The title—"God Bless America."

Berlin described how he wrote "God Bless America" in a letter of July 19, 1954, to Abel Green, editor of *Variety:*

I wrote "God Bless America" at Camp Upton in 1918 to be the finale of *Yip, Yip, Yaphank.* As you may remember, the show opened on August 19th at the Old Century Theater. The finale—the boys were alerted in the scene before that they were going overseas, and in overseas outfits, including helmets, they marched through the Theater, went out to the street and backstage where they boarded a transport, and as the lights lowered, the transport, on wheel, slowly moved off stage. It was a very touching and emotional scene.

As I remember, the song they sang was "In the Y.M.C.A." as the curtain came down.

Having that finale in mind, it seemed painting the lily to have soldiers sing "God Bless America" in that situation, so I didn't use it.

Of course, I always had it in back of my mind to use someday on the right occasion. That occasion came after I returned from London in 1938 where I had gone to see the opening of *Alexander's Ragtime Band*, the picture. I was there during Chamberlain's visit to Hitler and the beginning of the Munich pact. On my way back, I tried to write a song that I felt at that time. I remember finishing a chorus of a song called "Thanks America" which I tore up because it was very bad. It seemed a bad editorial set to music. I then recalled "God Bless America" and *rewrote* it. I underline rewrote because that is a very important part of the story of "God Bless America." The original version was as follows:

God Bless America, land that I love
Stand beside her
And guide her
To the right with a light from above
Make her victorious on land and foam
God Bless America, my home sweet home

It is obvious that the word "right" had to be changed because in 1918 "guide her to the right" meant the right road. In 1938, there was a right and a left and it had a different significance. So in changing it the song was improved when I said "stand beside her and guide her, thru the night with a light from above." Then again, in 1918 it was written as a war song, which the phrase "make her victorious on land and foam" indicates. In 1938, I didn't want it to be a war song. I wanted it to be a song of peace. On Armistice Day, 1938, I spoke to Ted Collins [Smith's manager] and he wanted a song for Kate Smith to sing on that program, where she introduced it.

Over the years Berlin and his longtime friend and onetime (1918) musical secretary, songwriter Harry Ruby, frequently exchanged humorous letters. On October 26, 1971, Berlin wrote to Ruby about "God Bless America" as follows:

I was interviewed a few weeks ago about "God Bless America," and one of the questions was, "Is it true that Harry Ruby helped you keep it away from the public for twenty years?" That came out of left field, but he evidently read it somewhere and, Harry, as an old friend, I defended you. I told him that the one and only time I played and sang it was at a rehearsal where you were present. The reaction from the boys was a thunderous silence and that you, as a civilian, were the only one who stood up and saluted.

Seriously, Harry, I told the interviewer the simple facts—that the song was never taken down, that I did let the boys hear it and decided that 350 soldiers in overseas outfits marching down the aisle of the Century Theater going off to war, singing "God Bless America," was wrong.

So, as you will remember, I replaced it with a little thing called "We're On Our Way To France."

If the late Ted Collins, who was Kate Smith's manager, hadn't come to me in 1938 for a patriotic song to be sung by her on Armistice Day, I'm afraid "God Bless America" would still be a war song, unpublished and unsung.

The response to "God Bless America" was overwhelmingly positive. It received enormous attention in the press and from the public. Yet there was sharp criticism as well. In answer to those who questioned the sincerity of his lyric and his reference to God, Berlin had this to say: " 'God Bless America' is a patriotic song written so it can be sung and understood by everyone. It is not a hymn or an anthem. It is just a song. What's wrong with a patriotic song?"

Berlin's response was simple and eloquent: "All that I hope for 'God Bless America,'" he told the New York *Herald-Tribune* (October 10, 1940), "is that it will continue to be popular, especially in these days when so many people feel a need for some vocal expression of their patriotism."

The tremendous success and popularity of the song led to some unanticipated controversy. In the summer of 1940, both major national parties sought to appropriate it for their conventions. In a July 16, 1940, letter to W. F. Maloney, an official of the Democratic Party, Berlin wrote:

In reply to your inquiry, no political party has the exclusive rights to the song "God Bless America."

In our grant to the Republican Party Campaign Committee for Wendell L. Wilkie [*sic*] we specifically mentioned the fact that we could not give the exclusive rights to any political party to a song that is so obviously for all Americans.

Many Americans, in fact, found the song so powerful and compelling that they lobbied for it to replace "The Star-Spangled Banner" as the United States national anthem. In an August 16, 1943, letter to the well-known author Dale Carnegie, Berlin wrote:

I think it would be a mistake to suggest changing our National Anthem. I am, of course, touched and flattered that you think so highly of GOD BLESS AMERICA, but in my opinion, the Star Spangled Banner cannot be replaced.

Berlin also offered a more detailed response to those who wish to make the song our national anthem. He said:

A national anthem is something that develops naturally through age, tradition, historic significance, and general recognition. There is no such thing as a new national anthem. We can't legislate one. They arise alone and stand the test of time. We've got a good national anthem. You can't have two.

In 1940 Berlin established the God Bless America Fund, a trust that over the years has turned all income for the song over to the Girl Scouts and Boy Scouts of America.

As the years passed, "God Bless America," despite the objections of its creator, became our unofficial de facto national anthem. Of course, there were notable recordings, none more impressive than those by Kate Smith, who also sang it thrillingly in the 1943 film version of *This Is the Army*. Deanna Durbin sang it in the 1943 film *Hers to Hold*; and the great opera singer Lotte Lehmann and a young Marni Nixon, dubbing for Margaret O'Brien, sang it in the 1948 film *Big City*. For many years a Kate Smith recording was played at Philadelphia Flyers hockey games, and for especially key contests Smith was on hand to sing it in person.

Berlin himself sang it on television in 1968 during an eightieth birthday tribute presented on *The Ed Sullivan Show* and sang it again, most movingly, at the White House in 1974 in honor of returning Vietnam War prisoners. It was his last public appearance.

VERSE

While the storm clouds gather
Far across the sea,
Let us swear allegiance
To a land that's free;
Let us all be grateful
For a land so fair,
As we raise our voices
In a solemn prayer.

CHORUS

God bless America,
Land that I love,
Stand beside her and guide her
Through the night with a light from above.
From the mountains, to the prairies,
To the oceans white with foam,*

---

*At one time Berlin contemplated a second half-chorus that would have included the following as lines 5 and 6:

From the green fields of Virginia
To the gold fields out in Nome,

God bless America,
My home sweet home.

On November 7, 1969, Berlin added to the lore of "God Bless America" when he sent the following to his friend A. L. Berman:

> Now about Yip Harburg's comment suggesting a sequel to "God Bless America." . . . How about a sequel for Irving—entitled "God Help America." He can use the same tune. . . .

I like Yipper. Above all, I respect his talent as a lyric writer and since he has asked for a sequel to "God Bless America," I have written a special version just for him. Here it is:

> God bless America,
> Land I enjoy,
> No discussions with Russians
> Till they stop sending arms to Hanoi.
> Martha's Vineyard, dear old ASCAP,
> And a flat near Central Park—

God bless America
When skies are dark,
God bless America,
My Noah's ark.

OVERLEAF: *Irving Berlin at his transposing piano, and a glimpse of the Broadway season*

MUSIC BOX REVUE OF 1938–1939

MUSIC BOX REVUE OF 1938–1939

After completing the songs for the films *Alexander's Ragtime Band* and *Carefree*, Berlin began work on a new revue for his Music Box Theatre. On June 29, 1938, he wrote an outline of what he had in mind.

We open in the lobby of the Music Box Theatre. A sign in the lobby plainly shows that the current attraction is *Of Mice And Men*. A man and woman, dressed in evening clothes suggesting 1924, step up to the door man. The door man examines their seats and in surprise says, "These tickets are for the *Music Box Revue*." The man answers, "Yes, that's right." "Well, the last one we did was in 1924. What kept you all these years?" The man explains he was held up in the traffic. He insists on seeing the *Music Box Revue*, that's what the tickets call for. A conference is held between Harris and Berlin. They must do something about it. They decide on the only plan that can be carried out quickly, a dancing act. Harris tells the couple who are waiting to see the *Music Box Revue* that they can go inside and everything will be all right. From here on we play about three-quarters of an hour of the vaudeville show.

We then go back to the lobby of the theatre. The couple who came to see the *Revue* come out furious. Harris and Berlin are called. There is an argument. They did not come to see a vaudeville show. They want to see a revue. "But we cannot put on a revue just like that. There is no scenery. We have got to get scenery and costumes." The couple won't hear any explanations. It isn't their fault if there is no scenery and costumes. They have two tickets calling for a revue and that is what they want to see. Harris says, "All right, go in—we'll do the best we can." For the balance of this act we play a revue on a bare stage a la *Our Town*. A master of ceremonies like Frank Craven explains everything as they do it in that show. They never lower the curtain. A short comedy sketch is introduced in that way, also two numbers, and we finally get to the grand finale, which could be "Marching Along with Time." This is explained in great detail. He describes a super–Hazzard [*sic*] Short production of "Marching Along with Time." The number is done with the girls and boys in practice clothes.

Now Act 2—We open again in the lobby of the theatre. Harris asks the couple what they thought about it. "Thought about it? It stinks—no costumes, no scenery." That isn't what they paid their good money for. Harris explains that's the

latest thing. It's really up to the minute. That is the theatre of today—that's what everybody is doing today. The couple answer, "If that's what they are doing today, God knows what we will be seeing tomorrow." Harris says, "That's an idea—tomorrow. What they'll be doing tomorrow." The couple go inside. From here on we do the rest of the revue in the future idea, finishing with the back to back number.

At the end of this number, the couple interrupt the show, rushing down the aisle and on the stage—they want to see the management. They have been cheated. They paid $50.00 to a speculator to see the *Music Box Revue*, and by God they're going to see it. The man reads a newspaper advertisement, "Sam H. Harris presents Irving Berlin's *Music Box Revue* with Grace Moore, John Steele, Clark & McCullough, Collier & Bernard, the Brox Sisters, etc." That's what they came to see. Harris comes on the stage and says, "Please go back to your seats. I have never broken faith with my public and if that's what you came to see, that's what you'll see." We then do the rest of the show, showing high spots of all the *Music Box Revues*, with our own cast playing Grace Moore, John Steele, Clark & McCullough, the Brox Sisters, etc., finishing with entire company doing "Say It with Music."

("Marching Along with Time" had been dropped from the 1938 film *Alexander's Ragtime Band*. The "back to back number," actually titled "Back to Back," became part of the score for *Second Fiddle* [1939].)

A few months later (November 9, 1938), Berlin wrote his friend Harry Ruby: "I lost my enthusiasm for the revue Sam Harris and I were planning to do most because it is awfully tough to get a cast now and we decided that a revue without personalities is a hopeless proposition."

By the spring of 1940, with his chores on the film *Second Fiddle* and the show *Louisiana Purchase* behind him, Berlin returned to the idea of a revue. He told Ward Morehouse, the "Broadway After Dark" columnist (May 20, 1940):

I'm definitely done with Hollywood for the next year. I went there after the crash and it was a godsend. I'm now staying in our theater for a while. . . . I hope to do a revue in the fall with the Playwrights' Company.* Fine lot of fellows.

Founded in 1938 by playwrights Maxwell Anderson (1888–1959), S. N. Behrman (1893–1973), Sidney Howard (1891–1939), Elmer Rice (1892–1967), Robert Sherwood (1896–1955), and their attorney John F. Wharton (1894–1977). Sidney Howard died August 23, 1939, in an accident on his farm and, therefore, was not mentioned in Berlin's lyric "The Crystal Ball–Opening Chorus." The Playwrights Company dissolved in 1960.

They'd write the book material and I'd do the music and lyrics. We've talked of a show in three parts: The first act in the present, the second act in the future and the third act in the past.

On December 4, 1940, *Variety* reported that "Irving Berlin has postponed his movie project [see *Holiday Inn*] because he is planning a Broadway review [*sic*] entitled *Crystal Ball* starring Jessie Matthews and Dick Powell provided that they are available for projected Spring 1941 opening."

In the spring of 1943, when it was unclear whether *This Is the Army* would be going overseas, Berlin briefly turned again to the idea of a new *Music Box Revue*. "I postponed the Crosby–Astaire picture [which would become *Blue Skies*] until next year," he wrote his attorney Abe Berman in June, "so I would like very much to do a Music Box show as my next job." He added that

Louis Shurr [the well-known agent] dropped in to see me with Victor Moore yesterday, and I told him of my plan. I find that [William] Gaxton, [Grace] Moore, [Vera] Zorina, and Bert Lahr are all free. I told Shurr and [Victor] Moore that if I could make a package deal for Gaxton, Moore, Zorina, and Leana Horn [*sic*] for a *Music Box Revue* to charge $5.50, I would consider it, if it were practical. He is going to try to work it out. Victor Moore seemed very enthusiastic about it. Shurr tells me that Gaxton, Moore and Zorina are completely free and that he can get a release for Lena Horn [*sic*] from MGM. Please give me your reaction to this. You might also figure out how this can be done money-wise. At $5.50 we could do around $30,000. a week at the Music Box.

Even though Berman described Berlin's proposal as "terrific," Berlin once again put the project on the back burner, and he continued his tour with *This Is the Army*.

He turned to it again in 1945 while he was completing the score for *Blue Skies*. "In going over the material that I had already written for this particular show in the past six years," he wrote Berman on July 14, 1945, "I find that the best way to do it is as a *Music Box Revue*. It was originally planned as such." Various press reports in 1945 indicated that the show was to be called *Tea Leaves*, that Hassard Short was slated to stage the revue, that Hermes Pan was to do the choreography, and that Danny Kaye had been contacted as a possible star. But once again the show was set aside.

Eight years later it was announced under a new title—*Say It with Music*. "I've been trying to get to it for so many years," he told the New York *Herald-Tribune* (July 22, 1953), "and have announced it so many times, I'm ashamed to announce it again but I think we're ready to roll now with one big if—if we can get the right people." Press reports during 1953 and

1954 mentioned Kaye, Mary Martin, and Shirley Booth, but the show didn't materialize.

Yet the idea of doing one more show for the Music Box Theatre remained with him. He spoke about it over the years and indicated that he wanted to collaborate on the project with Arthur Laurents and Jerome Robbins. Writing to Robbins on December 20, 1968, he said, "Now about the *Music Box Revue*, Jerry. In spite of my present great enthusiasm, I would be very reluctant to do it unless we both felt it could be 'one of those things' before we started. My reason for getting in touch with you originally was that I would like to do one more show and I would like to do it with you." The show never happened.

TICKETS, PLEASE

No music is known to survive. Berlin's ink holograph lyric manuscript with pencil notations and his typed lyric sheets are in the Irving Berlin Collection of the Music Division of the Library of Congress. Alternate title: "*Music Box Revue—Opening.*"

[*The lobby of Music Box Theatre. Prominent sign bearing the title* Of Mice and Men. *Onstage are a* MAN, *a* WOMAN, *and the* DOORMAN.]

DOORMAN: Tickets, please.
MAN: Here they are—
  I thought we would never get here.
WOMAN: Oh, I hope we've not missed an awful
   lot.
  Come along, let's hurry up, dear.
DOORMAN: Not so fast—take your time.
  I can't let you enter with these.
MAN: They were sold to me by an agency.
  Step aside and let us in, please.
DOORMAN: These tickets, sir, were sold to you
  In 1923.
  They're for a *Music Box Revue*.
MAN: That's what we came to see.
DOORMAN: But you're fifteen years too late, sir—
  I'm afraid these seats are no good.
MAN: We were held up by the traffic
  And we got here as fast as we could.
DOORMAN: You were held up by the what?
MAN: Not by the what—by the traffic.
  And we got here fast as we could.

[MANAGER *enters.*]

MANAGER: What's all this? Something wrong?
DOORMAN: As wrong as it can be—

  They have seats for the *Music Box
   Revue of 1923*.
MAN: And that's what we came to see.
MANAGER: Now let me get this straight:
  You say you came to see the show
  That played here at the Music Box
  Just sixteen years ago?
  Won't you let me call a doctor?
  Are you sure you're feeling quite good?
MAN: We were held up by the traffic
  And we got here as fast as we could.
MANAGER: You were held up by the what?
MAN: Not by the what—by the traffic.
  And we got here as fast as we could
MANAGER: I believe you, sir—but this is strange,
  For it's sixteen years since then.
  We'll gladly offer an exchange—
  Give him two for *Mice and Men*.
MAN: But we don't want to see a drama—
  We came here to see a revue.
MANAGER: Not so loud—you'll disturb the crowd,
  Who have paid admissions too.
  Just step inside with your charming
   bride
  And I'll see what I can do.

[*They enter as curtains are drawn.* MANAGER *steps in front of curtains.*]

MANAGER: Ladies and gentlemen,
  It happens to be my lot
  To tell you that the management
  Is in a terrible spot.
  You came to see *Of Mice and Men*—
  I know you're drama fans—
  But with regret I must announce
  A sudden change in our plans.
  We've got to do a revue,
  A *Music Box Revue*.
  We know you're gonna hate it,
  And we're gonna hate it too,
  But we've got to do a revue.
  Two seats for the show that played here
  Back in 1923
  Turned up with a charming couple,
  And that's what they want to see.
  They were held up by the traffic,
  Which may or may not be true,
  But it gives us a damn good reason
  To do another revue.
  And now let me throw some light
  On the kind of show you're going to
   see tonight.
  It's in three acts
  Instead of the usual two,
  And in each act
  We're doing a separate revue:
  A first act, a second, and a last—

  The present, the future, and the past.
  In the first act
  The present is what we'll depict.
  In the second act
  The future we'll try to predict.
  The last act will show
  The long, long ago.
  In a nutshell, this revue
  Is planned so we can do
  A first act, a second, and a last—
  The present, the future, and the past.

IN THE EARLY GRECIAN DAYS

At one point Berlin revised the lyrics of "Tickets, Please," substituting what follows for the lines that began with "We know you're gonna hate it."

So kindly settle down;
Overlook what the show may lack—
The treasurer left town,
And you can't get your money back.
So I'm afraid you'll have to sit through
Anthoer, yes, another goddamn *Music Box Revue*.

[*Scene: In front of a Greek restaurant. One one side of window, a sign:* FRIED CHICKEN. *On the other side of window, a sign:* GREEK CHORUSES FURNISHED. *Sixteen* GIRLS *enter, dressed in conventional Greek costumes, carrying bags which contain knitting and each dragging a small stool.*]

GIRLS: In the early Grecian days
  The Greeks began their plays
  With an opening chorus
  That told you what it was all about.
  And the custom seems to last;
  A relic of the past
  Is the opening chorus
  That you could easily do without.

THE CRYSTAL BALL— OPENING CHORUS, including IN THE EARLY GRECIAN DAYS and WE KNOW THAT YOU FIRST-NIGHTERS and SHERWOOD, BEHRMAN, ANDERSON, AND RICE and IT'S IN THREE ACTS INSTEAD OF THE USUAL TWO

This opening number of the Playwrights' Company's projected revue of late 1940 or early 1941 evolved from material written for the *Music Box Revue of 1938–1939.* Typed lyric sheets are in the Irving Berlin Collection of the Music Division of the Library of Congress. The chorus segues continuously from one sequence to the next.

In the Early Grecian Days

[*A drop in two. Exterior, Greek restaurant. Sign* JOE POPOLOPELES GREEK RESTAURANT *is prominently seen in center. Eight* GIRLS *dressed in Grecian costumes enter through cut door in drop.*]

GIRLS: In the early Grecian days
  The Greeks began their plays
  With an opening chorus
  To tell you what it was all about.
  Though a relic of the past,
  The custom seems to last:
  There's the opening chorus
  That you could easily do without.
  We greet you ev'ry season
  At the start of each revue
  Without much rhyme or reason,
  And we know we're boring you.
  But an op'ning must be spoken;
  That's why we are here:
  For until the ice is broken,
  The stars won't appear.
  So read your programs and gaze behind;
  It's not unkind, for we don't mind.
  We'll struggle through this opening
    somehow;
  Just slam your seats—we're used to it
    by now.
  The opening is long,
  So we brought along our knitting;

We aren't very strong,
So they let us do it sitting.
We'd enjoy the opening
If we didn't have to sing,
But they let us do it sitting,
And you can't have ev'rything.
Customers, it's boring—
Did we hearing somebody snoring?
Go ahead—we promise not to even peep.
Go ahead, keep dozing,
For we haven't reached the closing.
You've exactly two more minutes
  left to sleep.

We Know That You First-Nighters

We know that you first-nighters
Want the opening to go,
But opening-chorus writers
Have a union that says no;
So we often cross our fingers
And pray on our knees
That their children may be singers
Of op'nings like these.
And now we think that you ought to know
How the Playwrights happen to be doing this
  show.

Sherwood, Behrman, Anderson, and Rice

Mister Berlin while in Hollywood
Tried to find an author who
Would write the different sketches
For the *Crystal Ball* revue.
He would go to them each day,
But they'd look at him and say,
"Do you think we'd leave our Spanish homes
And our lovely swimming pools
And write those lousy sketches?
Do you think we're goddamn fools?"
So what could Berlin do?
He told his troubles to
Sherwood, Behrman, Anderson, and Rice.
Those playwright fellows were extremely nice;
They said there's nothing to it:
"We'll be very glad to do it—
We'll be very glad to do it for a price."
Sherwood, Behrman, Anderson, and Rice—
Now Berlin didn't have to ask them twice;
They shouted, "We are willing

If you straighten out our billing."
They settled it like gentlemen—with a pair of
  dice.
And now we're going to throw some light
On the kind of a show you're going to see tonight.

It's in Three Acts Instead of the Usual Two

[*They step downstage and sing with emphasis:*]

It's in three acts
Instead of the usual two,
And in each act
We're doing a separate revue:
A first act, a second, and a last—
The *present,* the *future,* and the *past.*
In the first act
The *present* is what we'll depict.
In the second act
The *future* we'll try to predict.
The last act will show
The long, long ago.
In a nutshell, this revue
Is planned so we can do
A *first* act, a *second* act, and a *last*—
The *present,* the *future,* and the *past.*
So let's start our first act on its way
As we see things and people today.

[*Blackout as* Crystal Ball *curtain drops to announce first sketch.*]

COLUMNISTS' SONG

No music is known to survive. Berlin's ink holograph manuscript and typed lyric sheets are in the Irving Berlin Collection of the Music Division of the Library of Congress. Alternate titles: "*The Crystal Ball—Opening in Two Scenes,*" "*The World Is in a Mess,*" and "*See You Tomorrow.*" According to Berlin:

The first act is played behind a proscenium arch on which is prominently printed TO-DAY—also a curtain which in some ways suggests the present—The first item (a sketch) in this act should be a subject that immediately is recognized as of today—1940—and all the following items both sketches and numbers must be topical and up to date—in other words the first act must live up to its title—TO-DAY.

[*Eight well-known* COLUMNISTS *seated at their type-writers. A card is hung over each desk visible to the audience bearing the columnist's name and the subject he writes about.* WALTER LIPPMANN: Politics. DOROTHY THOMPSON: Foreign. WALTER WINCHELL: Broadway. LOUELLA PARSONS: Movies. CHOLLY KNICKERBOCKER: Society. DOROTHY DIX: Love. B. C. FORBES: Finance. MRS. ROOSEVELT: Everything.]

[*They step down from their typewriters and sing the following lyric:*]

ALL: The world is in a mess;
It's very hard to guess
Where the world is going to.
But without a doubt
We will soon find out,
And we'll pass it on to you.
We simply won't be licked,
And shortly we'll predict
What the future has in view.
We're about to see
What is yet to be,
And we'll pass it on to you.

LIPPMANN: Lippmann knows exactly what is
coming.
THOMPSON: Thompson sees the writing on
the wall.
WINCHELL: Winchell always looked into the
future.
PARSONS: Parsons sees ahead and tells it
all.
KNICKERBOCKER: Cholly Knickerbocker, too, is
psychic.
DIX: Mrs. Dix can see what there's in
store.
FORBES: Mr. Forbes can tell what's gonna
happen.
MRS. ROOSEVELT: If they can do it, so can Eleanor.

[*They exit as scene changes. A* SEER *is bending over a crystal ball.* COLUMNISTS *enter. Each addresses the* SEER *with a question.*]

LIPPMANN: Can you see just one Republican
in the future?
THOMPSON: Will those European dictators
ever quit?
WINCHELL: Will the newly wedded Ickes
have a baby?
PARSONS: Will Marion's latest picture be a
hit?
KNICKERBOCKER: Will they ask me to the Vincent
Astor party?
DIX: Will love remain the thing that
conquers all?
FORBES: What goes on with Tel & Tel and
Anaconda?

MRS. ROOSEVELT: Can you see a White House in
the crystal ball?
SEER: Not so fast—take your time!
There is so much I can see;
Many strange and startling
things
Present themselves to me.
So meet me in the future;
I'll be there when you arrive—
See you tomorrow,
In 1955.
COLUMNISTS: We'll see you tomorrow,
In 1955.

THIS PATTER THAT WE DO

This number appears to be incomplete. No music is known to survive. Berlin's ink holograph manuscript is in the Irving Berlin Collection of the Music Division of the Library of Congress.

This patter that we do
May disagree with you,
But you will have to listen
To much more before we're through:
The whole first act is written to words and
music—
We haven't got dialogue in this first act.

HOW'D YOU LIKE WHAT YOU SAW?

No music is known to survive. Berlin's ink holograph manuscript and typed lyric sheets are in the Irving Berlin Collection of the Music Division of the Library of Congress. An early version of an Act II opening, it was revised to become "Now How'd You Like What You Saw So Far?"

MANAGER: How'd you like what you saw?
I hope that you thought it was good.
For the time we had, it was not so bad;
We just did the best that we could.
MAN: What we saw wasn't bad,
But whether it's worth it depends:
We will let you know
How we like the show
Later on when the second act ends.

MANAGER: The second act has been designed
For patrons who come late;
The songs and sketches will predict
A distant future date.
If you're held up by the traffic—
I mean, if there is a delay—
We'll show you now what'll happen
Twenty years from today.
In other words, the future
Is what we mean to define,
As we see things and people
In 1959—
The future *Music Box Revue*
of 1959.

NOW HOW'D YOU LIKE WHAT YOU SAW SO FAR?

No music is known to survive. Berlin's ink holograph manuscript and his typed lyric are in the Irving Berlin Collection of the Music Division of the Library of Congress. A revised Act II opening, it replaced "How'd You Like What You Saw?"

MANAGER: Now how'd you like what you saw
so far?
MAN: What we saw so far wasn't bad.
MANAGER: If what you saw wasn't up to par,
It's the little time we had;
We do want you to be satisfied—
I assure you that's a fact.
MAN: I hope you do, but we can't decide
Till we've seen your second act.
MANAGER: The second act has been conceived
For patrons who are late;
It's written in the future,
Just to keep you up to date.
If you're held up by the traffic—
I mean, if there's a delay—
We'll show you now what'll happen
Twenty years from today.
In other words, the future
Is what we plan to design,
As we see things and people
In 1959.
MAN: You mean a revue in the future?
MANAGER: That's right.
MAN: That's fine.

MANY ARE THE CHANGES

No music is known to survive. Unfinished portion of an Act II opening to *The Crystal Ball*. Berlin's ink holograph is in the Irving Berlin Collection of the Music Division of the Library of Congress.

[*The same Greek restaurant drop and same Greek chorus.*]

Customers, we greet you
With a "Very pleasant to meet you"
And an op'ning chorus you have heard before.
Many are the changes
That the hand of time arranges,
But the op'ning chorus still remains a bore.

HEY THERE, YOU— MANAGER

No music is known to survive. Berlin's ink holograph manuscript and his typed lyric sheets are in the Irving Berlin Collection of the Music Division of the Library of Congress. Intended as an opening to Act III.

MAN: Hey there, you—Manager,
You'll just have to listen to me.
What we saw tonight
May be quite all right,
But it's not what we came here to see.
We have seats—
For the *Music Box Revue of 1923*.
MANAGER: Well, that's what it's gonna be—
So just go back to your seat,
And for the finish we will choose
The most familiar songs of all
The *Music Box Revues*.
In a mood that's reminiscent
We will come to the end of our show
With the songs and those who sang
    them
Not so many years ago.
Remember in the Music Box
Three sisters by the name of Brox—
When they came out full of pep
And sang "Everybody Step"?

PATTER TO VAUDEVILLE SHOW

No music is known to survive. Typed lyric is in the Irving Berlin Collection of the Music Division of the Library of Congress.

Ladies and gentlemen,
In a show ev'ry now and then
The scenery must be changed,
Entirely rearranged;
And while that's being done,
Someone has to come out in one
To keep things on the go—
We must kill time, and so
With your consent
We'll now present
A military vaudeville show.

[*After the curtain falls on a juggler:*]

Ladies and gentlemen,
Sorry, but here we are again.
The juggler that appeared
Used props that must be cleared;
Stagehands that we engage
Are at work cleaning up the stage,
And just in case they're slow,
We must kill time, and so
To stop a wait
We separate
Our military vaudeville show.

[*After the curtain falls on a magician:*]

Ladies and gentlemen,
Glad to see you, and how've you been?
We hope you're feeling well;
And how's your sister Nell?
No reason and no rhyme—
Maybe so, but we're killing time.
Now smilingly we go;
We smile because we know
You're bound to love
The finish of
Our military vaudeville show.

[*Verse following acrobats not written; lyric ends here.*]

COMMERCIAL PHOTOGRAPHY

No music is known to survive. Berlin's ink holograph manuscript and typed lyric sheets are in the Irving Berlin Collection of the Music Division of the Library of Congress. Alternate title: "In the Magazines."

[*Two men and three girls advertising* LISTERINE, PIANO PLAYING, STOCKINGS, UNION SUITS, *and* BRASSIERES. *In front of curtain:*]

ALL: Good morning.
An introduction would be a bore;
We have met many times before,
In the magazines,
For we're a very famous crew
With important work to do—
We're the ones who smile at you
From the magazines.
Our business
Is called commercial
    photography.
We're the faces you always see
In the magazines,
The faces that they photograph
For the advertising staff,
And it puts at least one laugh
In the magazines.
LISTERINE: Now I'm that most unhappy girl
In every magazine
Whom no one wants to dance with
'Cause I don't use Listerine.

PIANO PLAYING: "They laughed when I sat down to
    play"—
That caption makes me wince,
For everyone who knows me
Has been laughing ever since.

STOCKINGS: They photograph my Dietrichs,
For these stockings made of lace.
A million people know my legs
Who've never seen my face.

UNION SUITS: I advertise this union suit
That weathers every storm.
ALL: He doesn't need his love—
He's got his overcoat to keep him
    warm.

BRASSIERES: Good morning.
An introduction would be a bore;
I believe we have met before,
In the magazines,

For I'm the girl who gives three
    cheers
For the pair of cute brassieres—
Life is not all it appears
In the magazines.

ALL: But let that be as it may be;
    Come along and you can see
    How they do photography
    For the magazines.

[*Full stage. A bed with sign* SIMMONS BED. *A* PHOTOG-
RAPHER *with camera all set up; a* CLERK; *a* GIRL *in
nighty; and a* BOY *in pajamas.*]

CLERK: Miss Wilson, Mister Jones.
GIRL: How do you do?
BOY: How do you do?
CLERK: Kindly get into bed and pose—
    The photographer is ready for
    you.

[*They get into bed.*]

Mr. Jones, a little smile
And a twinkle in your eyes.
Remember, the caption's going to
    read,
"A Simmons Bed Satisfies."
Miss Wilson, a little closer—
Snuggle up and look cute.
That's fine—now hold it.
Ready—shoot!

[PHOTOGRAPHER *takes picture. He and* CLERK *exit,
leaving couple alone in bed.*]

BOY: Pardon me, I didn't catch your
    name.
GIRL: The name is Wilson and I'm glad
    I came.
BOY: I've been looking high and low for
    you.
GIRL: I'm glad you found me, for I like
    you too.

CHORUS

BOY: Fancy meeting you here—
    It's unbelievable, dear,
    That here we are head to head
    In a Simmons bed.
    I was ready to say
    I guess I'll call it a day
    When suddenly romance led
    To a Simmons bed.
    A hundred times I've crossed
    The blue Atlantic,

And after hope was lost,
I find you here—isn't it romantic?
Life is terribly grand;
You'll have to marry me, and
We'll tell our great-grandchildren
That we met in a Simmons bed.

NOW HERE IS THE WRITTEN ENDORSEMENT

No music is known to survive. Berlin's holograph manu-
script is in the Irving Berlin Collection of the Music Di-
vision of the Library of Congress.

Now here is the written endorsement,
And this is what you've said:
"You won't need a bill of divorcement
If you just use a Simmons bed."
Now sign on the dotted line,
And on your way out, if you ask for Mr. Peck,
He'll see that you get your check.

ENDORSEMENT SONG

No music is known to survive. Quite possibly this is part
of the same number as "Commercial Photography."
Berlin's pencil holograph manuscript and typed lyric
sheets are in the Irving Berlin Collection of the Music
Division of the Library of Congress. Alternate title: "In
the Ads."

Good morning—
Have you endorsed anything today?
Have you read what they have to say
In the ads?
We mean the ladies that they choose
From the smarter avenues
To endorse the things we use
Every day.
Good morning—
Did you know young Missus Allen Ryan
Tells the world that it's divine
In the ads?
She has some good advice to give,
Tells us just how long we'll live
If we use the laxative
She endorses.

And young Missus Gould,
Missus Anna Gould,
Endorses Chesterfields because she says
It's fun to be fooled.
Good morning—
You know Marie the Rumanian queen?
She's just crazy for Listerine.
But she agrees to split the fee—
Ten percent to charity
And the rest to Queen Marie
For endorsing.
And Elsa Maxwell, it appears,
Signs her names and gives three cheers
For a pair of tin brassieres
She endorses for horses.

HITLER AND MUSSOLINI

No music is known to survive. Typed lyric is in the Irv-
ing Berlin Collection of the Music Division of the Li-
brary of Congress. It was Berlin's intention in this
number to depict the leaders of Germany and Italy as a
pair of sidewalk comedians.

BOTH: We're a couple, just a couple of
    dictators,
    But we've not been working at it here
    of late.
    We're as good as we ever were,
    But there's no stenographer
    To take down the things that we
    dictate.
    We could handle almost anything
    with England,
    And we used to scare the daylights
    out of France;
    When it looked like we owned the
    place,
    We stooped down to tie a lace
    And somebody kicked us in the pants.
    Heigh ho—the future's very vague.

[*Dance.*]

Heigh ho—regards to Mayor Hague.

[*Dance.*]

HITLER: I would rather, so much rather, be in
    Berlin.
MUSSOLINI: I would rather, so much rather, be in
    Rome.
BOTH: But enough they have had of us

And while they're so mad at us
It's safer to stay away from home.

[*Dance.*]

JOSEPH P. KENNEDY AND PROMINENT AMERICAN WOMEN

No music is known to survive. Berlin's ink holograph manuscript and typed lyric are in the Irving Berlin Collection of the Music Division of the Library of Congress.

We want to be presented at court, dear Joe;
We'd like to be presented to the king.
Be a darling and don't say no—
It means just everything.
We've ordered lovely dresses,
The best that they can make;
So be a sport
And let us have our day in court
For old times' sake.

LOST AND FOUND BUREAU

No music is known to survive. Typed lyric sheet is in the Irving Berlin Collection of the Music Division of the Library of Congress.

VERSE

I'm forever finding things,
Imitation diamond rings
Or a watch with broken springs
Or an old nail file.
Night and day I stroll around
With my eyes glued to the ground,
But the other day I found
Something really worthwhile.

CHORUS

Found a pair of panties,
And I know they're not my auntie's—
Who lost the panties that I found?
Found a pair of panties
Near the tomb where General Grant is—

Who lost the panties that I found?
I want to be a Prince Charming
To the Cinderella who'll call
And claim the pair of combinations
That she let fall at the ball.
I'm a lonely lover
And I'm anxious to discover
Who lost the panties that I found.

[*This number goes into a full stage scene where we do the Cinderella story, using a pair of panties as the slipper, with the obvious finish of finally finding the girl they fit.*]

QUINTUPLETS' SONG

No music is known to survive. Berlin's ink holograph manuscript and typed lyric sheet are in the Irving Berlin Collection of the Music Division of the Library of Congress.

CHORUS

Poor little quints,
We appear in the prints,
But we think the stork's
A piece of cheese
For making us celebrities—oh, yes.
Oh, it's a crime
To come five at a time,
For we hate the crowds
And all the fuss;
It simply bores the pants off us—oh, yes.
For weeks we're in a panic,
But it's all for Canada's sake,
And then comes Darryl Zanuck
With another picture to make.
Poor little quints,
We've been sad ever since,
For we have to eat
At least one course
Of everything that we endorse—oh, yes.

SOCIETY BUMS

No music is known to survive. Berlin's ink holograph manuscript and typed lyric sheet are in the Irving Ber-

lin Collection of the Music Division of the Library of Congress.

VERSE 1

Oh, it's lovely, lovely to be poor;
To be broke is easy to endure.
For a Vanderbilt relaxes
While the others pay the taxes—
Gee, it's nice, worth the price,
To be without money.

VERSE 2

We salute when labor leaders pass,
For we're friendly with the working class.
To the men who dig the ditches
We're no longer sons of riches—
Gee, it's nice, worth the price,
To be without money.

PUT SOME CLOTHES ON, DEAR

No music for the first part of this lyric is known to survive; the second section fits the music to "America" ("My Country 'Tis of Thee"). Typed lyric sheet is in the Irving Berlin Collection of the Music Division of the Library of Congress.

Won't you put some clothes on, dear?
For I love you so—
We're alone and no one's looking,
And the lights are low.
Somehow it seems to me that ev'rytime
I want to kiss, you're like this.
It isn't normal to be so formal
When there is no one near;
I know it's shocking to wear a stocking,
But we're engaged, my dear.
Won't you make me happy? If it's only a glove,
Put some clothes on, dear, and we'll make love.

[*Martha Washington appears.*]

My Country, 'twas of thee,
Sweet land of modesty,
Of thee I sing.
Where is the blushing bride,
Dressed up and dignified?
She took those dresses off and cried,
"Let freedom ring!"

THIS WORD-AND-MUSIC PATTER

Berlin took "Customers, We Greet You," which was intended for but not used in *On the Avenue* (see page 312), deleted its last twelve lines, which began "We know that you first-nighters," and wrote a new section in its place, beginning "This word-and-music-patter." Intended for the *Music Box Revue—Crystal Ball*. No music is known to survive.

This word-and-music patter
May disturb you quite a lot—

But then it doesn't matter
If you care for it or not.
These lyrics that we do
May disagree with you,
But you will have to listen
To much more before we're through.
The whole first act is written to words and music;
We haven't got dialogue.
In this first act
You'll have to stand for nothing but words and
    music;
We couldn't get dialogue,
And that's a fact.
Mister Berlin while in Hollywood
Tried to find an author who
Would write some funny sketches

For the *Music Box Revue.*
He would go to them each day,
But they'd look at him and say,
"Do you think we'd leave our Spanish homes
And our lovely swimming pools
And write those lousy sketches?
Do you think we're goddamn fools?"
That's why this act has nothing but words and
    music.
And now if you'll excuse us, we'll be gone,
For heaven knows why, but the show must go on.

Sonja Henie

SECOND FIDDLE | 1939

SECOND FIDDLE (1939)

A film produced by Darryl F. Zanuck and Gene Markey for 20th Century–Fox. Released in July 1939. Lyrics and music by Irving Berlin. Screenplay by Harry Tugend, based on a story by George Bradshaw. Directed by Sidney Lanfield. Orchestrations by Walter Scharf. Music conducted by Louis Silvers. Cast: starring Sonja Henie (Trudi Hovland) and Tyrone Power (Jimmy Sutton) and featuring Rudy Vallee (Roger Maxwell), Edna May Oliver (Aunt Phoebe), Mary Healy (Jean Varick), Lyle Talbot (Willie Hogger), Alan Dinehart (George "Whit" Whitney), Minna Gombell (Jenny), Stewart Reburn (Henie's skating partner), and the Brien Sisters.

Berlin's confidence in the songs he had written for *Second Fiddle* was expressed in a February 1, 1939, letter he sent to his music publishing partner Saul Bornstein, in which he said, "I think it is the freshest bunch of ideas I've had in any score."

AN OLD-FASHIONED TUNE ALWAYS IS NEW

Published. Copyrighted May 12, 1939. Previously registered for copyright as an unpublished song February 3, 1939. Introduced by Rudy Vallee (Roger Maxwell) and ensemble. Original cast recording by Vallee and His Connecticut Yankees (Decca). Other leading recording by Jimmy Dorsey and His Orchestra, vocal by Don Matteson (Decca). Written and originally intended for the unproduced *Music Box Revue of 1938–1939*.

VERSE

Nothing's as old as last year's rhythm;
Nothing's forgotten so soon—
Nothing's as dated as last year's syncopated tune.
Ragtime is dead and so is jazz,
And swing will leave us cold;
There's only one kind of music that never grows
old.

CHORUS

An old-fashioned tune always is new;
It never seems to go out of style.
For just when you start thinking it's through,
It comes down from the shelf with a smile.
A simple melody will always linger—
I mean the kind you pick out with one finger.

If you have some thoughts rhyming with "June,"
Express them in an old-fashioned tune.

Earlier version of chorus

An old-fashioned tune always is new,
So try and write an old-fashioned tune.
And old-fashioned words always ring true,
So rhyme your thoughts with "June" and with
"moon."
A verse with simple words will always linger,
A tune that you can pick out with one finger.
That old boy-meets-girl never goes wrong,
But place them in an old-fashioned song.

THE SONG OF THE METRONOME

Published. Copyrighted May 12, 1939. Previously registered for copyright as an unpublished song July 13, 1938. Introduced by the Brien Sisters and ensemble of children led by Sonja Henie (Trudi Hovland). Original cast recordings by Mary Healy accompanied by Cy Feuer and His Orchestra (Brunswick) and Rudy Vallee and His Connecticut Yankees (Decca). Written and originally intended for the unproduced *Music Box Revue of 1938–1939*.

Listen to the song of the metronome—
Tick-tock, tick-tock—
Simple little song of the metronome—
Tick-tock, tick-tock.
Listen to it telling you that life is sublime,
Life is sublime if you just take your time,
Just keep in time with the song of the metronome.
Listen to it tick-tock an even beat—
Tick-tock, tick-tock—
Beating out a warning to anxious feet—
Tick-tock, tick-tock—
Telling you a turtle had a race with a hare,
And at the finish the turtle was there,
Keeping in time with the song of the
metronome—
Tick-tock, tick-tock.
You may be passed—
Tick-tock, tick-tock—
But you will last;
Better to be late than to not arrive—
Tick-tock, tick-tock—
Four o'clock has gone but you still have five—
Tick-tock, tick-tock.

When your day is over you'll be up on the shelf,
So, brother, don't run away with yourself,
Don't run away from the song of the metronome.

BACK TO BACK

Published. Copyrighted May 12, 1939. Previously registered for copyright as an unpublished song February 3, 1939. Introduced by Mary Healy (Jean Varick) and ensemble. Leading recordings by Glenn Miller and His Orchestra, vocals by Marion Hutton and Tex Beneke (Bluebird); Jimmy Dorsey and His Orchestra, vocal by Helen O'Connell (Decca); and Horace Heidt and His Musical Knights, vocal by Heidt's High Lights (Brunswick). Written and originally intended for the unproduced *Music Box Revue of 1938–1939*.

VERSE

There's nothing new beneath the sun
Except the new dance I've invented,
And it's really lots of fun.
Come on now, take your place,
And soon you'll get the knack;
You don't stand face to face—
You do it back to back.

CHORUS

Dancing back to back
Takes you off the beaten track;
You don't look at your partner at all
When you dance back to back—
That's that new attack
That the other dances lack.
You can see what goes on in the hall
When you dance back to back.
Your partner
Won't see you
Make eyes at who dances by.
Your partner
Won't mind it;
She's doing the same—
That's why
You must dance back to back.
Let me place you in the pack;
Cut the cards
And I'll deal you a queen and a jack
Back to back.

WHEN WINTER COMES

Published. Copyrighted May 12, 1939. Previously registered for copyright as an unpublished song February 3, 1939. Introduced by Rudy Vallee (Roger Maxwell); skated to by Sonja Henie and Stewart Reburn. Original cast recording by Mary Healy accompanied by Cy Feuer and His Orchestra (Brunswick).

VERSE

Winter is coming, and soon
There will be frost on the moon;
Snow will be falling, and what am I going to do?
I'll need somebody to hold,
Someone to hold when it's cold,
Someone to love, and I hope that that someone is
  you.

CHORUS

The sun will shine in the summer,
And I'll be fine in the summer,
But then I've gotta have you
To cuddle up to
When winter comes.
It's nice and warm in the summer,
I'll be in form in the summer;
But then I've gotta have you
To cuddle up to
When winter comes.
All summer I'll be playing
Out on a tennis court,
But in the winter
Just like a groundhog
I'll turn into an indoor sport.
I'll pull an oar in the summer
And hug the shore in the summer,
But then I've gotta have you
To cuddle up to
When winter comes.

An earlier, rejected verse with different music

Oh, I hate the winter—
I wear the warmest of clothes
Until the wintery snows depart.
Oh, I hate the winter;
I long for someone to hold.
The very minute the cold winds start,
I get as cold as a banker's heart.

I POURED MY HEART INTO A SONG

Published. Copyrighted May 12, 1939. Previously registered for copyright as an unpublished song January 5, 1939, and again on February 4, 1939. Introduced by Tyrone Power (Jimmy Sutton); reprised by Rudy Vallee (Roger Maxwell) and skated to by Sonja Henie (Trudi Hovland). Original cast recordings by Vallee and His Connecticut Yankees (Decca) and Mary Healy, accompanied by Cy Feuer and His Orchestra (Brunswick). Other leading recordings by Artie Shaw and His Orchestra, vocal by Helen Forrest (Bluebird); Jimmy Dorsey and His Orchestra, vocal by Bob Eberle (Decca); and Horace Heidt and His Musical Knights, vocal by Larry Cotton and the High Lights (Brunswick).

I poured my heart into a song,
And when you hear it, please remember from the
  start,
You won't be hearing just the words and tune of a
  song,
You will be list'ning to my heart.
I poured my heart into a song,
And I'm afraid the words I chose are not so
  smart;
I couldn't think of clever things to say in my
  song—
I had to say it with my heart.
If it's never played on the *Hit Parade*,
It will still contain a heart that is beating true.
If it's not a hit,
I won't mind a bit,
Long as it conveys the love that I bear for you.
Here is my heart wrapped in a song,
And if you take it, please don't tear my song
  apart;
For if you do, you won't be just destroying a
  song,
You will be tearing up my heart.

I'M SORRY FOR MYSELF

Published. Copyrighted May 12, 1939. Previously registered for copyright as an unpublished song July 26, 1938. Introduced by Mary Healy (Jean Varick). Original cast recordings by Healy, accompanied by Cy Feuer and His Orchestra (Brunswick), and Rudy Vallee and His Connecticut Yankees (Decca). Other leading recording by Guy Lombardo and His Royal Canadians, vocals by Carmen Lombardo, Larry Owen, and Fred Henry (Decca). Written and originally intended for the unproduced *Music Box Revue of 1938–1939*.

CHORUS 1

I'm sorry for myself,
So sorry for myself.
Someone I love said goodbye,
And no one's sorry for me; that is why
I'm so sorry for myself.

CHORUS 2

I'm blue as I can be;
My man walked out on me.
I'd go home and end it all,
But fourteen stories is an awful fall—
I'm so sorry for myself.

CHORUS 3

I'm feeling mighty sad;
I never looked so bad.
I have lost my appetite;
I couldn't eat my second steak last night,
I'm so sorry for myself.

CHORUS 4

So very blue am I,
I wish that I could die;
Wish I had a nasty cough—
I'd buy a gun, but then it might go off.
I'm so sorry for myself.

CHORUS 5

I soon could end my woes
Down where the river flows;*
I would jump right in the sea,
But no one may be there to rescue me.
I'm so sorry for myself.

*Original version lines 1 and 2:
  I don't know what to do;
  My baby said she's through.

LOUISIANA
PURCHASE
1940

LOUISIANA PURCHASE (1940)

Tryout: Shubert Theatre, New Haven, Connecticut, May 2, 1940; National Theatre, Washington, D.C., May 6, 1940; Forrest Theatre, Philadelphia, Pennsylvania, May 13, 1940. New York run: Imperial Theatre; opened May 28, 1940; 444 performances. Music and lyrics by Irving Berlin. Produced by B. G. De Sylva. Book by Morrie Ryskind, based on a story by B. G. De Sylva. Book staged by Edgar MacGregor. Ballets by George Balanchine. Dances by Carl Randall. Orchestrations by Robert Russell Bennett; additional orchestration by N. Lang Van Cleve. Vocal arrangements by Hugh Martin, assisted by Ralph Blane. Orchestra under the direction of Robert Emmett Dolan. Cast: starring William Gaxton (Jim Taylor), Vera Zorina (Marina Van Linden), Victor Moore (Senator Oliver P. Loganberry), and Irene Bordoni (Madame Yvonne Bordelaise), and featuring Carol Bruce (Beatrice), Nick Long Jr. (Lee Davis), April Ames (Emmy-Lou), Robert Pitkin (Colonel Davis D. Davis Sr.), Ray Mayer (Davis D. Davis Jr.), Ralph Riggs (Dean Manning), and Edward H. Robins (Police Captain Whitfield). A Paramount film version, released in November 1941, starred Bob Hope, Zorina, Moore, and Bordoni.

The original stage production toured the United States from September 1941 to May 1942. A revival with the original cast was presented by the Los Angeles Civic Light Opera and the San Francisco Light Opera in 1947. The Goodspeed Opera House revived it in July 1975. Carnegie Hall presented several concert performances at its Weill Recital Hall in June 1996 with a cast headed by Judy Blazer, Taina Elg, Debbie Gravitte, George S. Irving, and Michael McGrath. The Carnegie Hall presentation was recorded by DRG.

One song, tentatively titled "Without Romance" or "A Little Romance in My Life," seems never to have been written.

APOLOGIA

Published only in a special vocal selection. Registered for copyright as an unpublished song April 1, 1940, under the title "It's News to Us (Opening)." Introduced by Georgia Carroll (Secretary), John Eliot (Sam Liebowitz), and ensemble. Part one is called "The Letter" (alternate title: "Opening Letter"). Part two is "It's News to Us (Opening)" (alternate title: "Opening Chorus: It's News to Us").

Left: Vera Zorina and Victor Moore. Right: William Gaxton and Irene Bordoni. All in Mardi Gras costumes

Part One—The Letter

SECRETARY: Mr. Liebowitz's office . . .
He's busy . . .
Who shall I say? . . .
Yes, sir.
I'll be glad to.
I'll tell him.
Okay.
LIEBOWITZ: Take a letter to Mr. B. G. De Sylva.
My dear Mr. De Sylva,
I've read the book of your show,
And as your legal adviser,
I'm writing to let you know
That you're skating on very thin ice,
And since you've asked my advice,
Let me warn you it can't be done.
I know it's all in fun,
But there is a state called Louisiana,
And anyone can tell
That both your acts
Are based on facts,
And they're gonna be sore as hell.
You won't get away with it;
They'll sue
You and Ryskind and Berlin too,
Because
There are laws,
Laws that specifically say
You can't write a book or a play
Based on characters living today,
And that's what you've done.
I know it's in fun,
But for instance the very first scene,
The character you call the Dean—
You've changed the name,
But just the same,
They're going to know who you mean,
And you won't get away with it—
Oh no,
The minute you open, they'll close the show,
And they'll sue—
They'll sue
You and Ryskind and Berlin too,
And the cast will go to jail,
Of that I have no doubt.
But speaking as your attorney,
Let me say that there is a way out;
You can make the whole thing legal
Without changing a line in your book.
It can still be Louisiana;

You can call a crook a crook—
But you must say "It's based on fiction,"
And ev'rything will be fine.
Yours truly,
Sam Liebowitz
Of Rafferty, Driscoll, and O'Brien.

Part Two—It's News To Us: Opening

ENSEMBLE: Before we start the show
We'd like to have you know
The characters portrayed
In our musical charade
Have not been based on persons living or dead—
They've all been made up out of the author's head
Instead.
The things that we reveal
Never happen, they're not real,
In spite of what you've heard or what you've read.
The politicians we investigate
Would come from Maine or Kansas or Montana,
So we laid our story in a mythical state,
A mythical state we call Louisiana.
Within our simple plot
You'll notice quite a lot
Of reference to crooks
Who have monkeyed with their books,
And with those gentlemen we're not too gentle.
If they seem like men you've read about,
It's purely accidental.
The law says shows like this one can get by
With one restriction—
It must be fiction.
We've tried to stay within the law; that's why
We laid the scenes
In New Orleans,
A city we've invented so that there would be no fuss—
If there is such a place,
It's certainly news to us.
Again the same old word,
No matter what you've heard,
The villains in our show
Are just characters, and so

If an arrow seems to strike
Someone who's investigated,
If he looks to you just like
Someone to whom you're related,
Don't go out and sue;
We don't mean you—
It's fiction,
So don't be temperamental.
If you're sons of millionaires,
Don't start trembling in your breeches
When a character declares
That you're dirty sons-of-riches.
Don't go out and sue;
We don't mean you—
The likeness
Is purely accidental.
So please bear this in mind:
Our show is of the mythical kind.

The book is mythical,
The score is mythical;
To make them mythical was our only
    chance.
The girls are mythical,
The boys are mythical;
And now we'll let our mythical show
    advance
And go into our mythical dance.

SEX MARCHES ON

Published. Copyrighted May 15, 1940. Previously registered for copyright as an unpublished song March 24, 1940. Published only in a black-and-white professional edition and in the special vocal selection. Introduced by William Gaxton (Jim Taylor), Robert Pitkin (Colonel Davis D. Davis Sr.), Ray Mayer (Colonel Davis D. Davis Jr.), Ralph Riggs (Dean Manning), and Edward H. Robins (Police Captain Whitfield). Written for and originally intended for the *Music Box Revue of 1938–1939*.

VERSE 1

The horse-and-buggy has had its day,
The trolley has passed away,
The bicycle built for two is gone,
But sex, S-E-X, marches on.
The town is crowded with gentlemen
Who'll never be rich again;
They're putting their overcoats in pawn,
But sex, S-E-X, marches on.
The op'ra can't make money at the Met,
And no one gives a hoot,
But Billy Rose made a million dollars net

Out of a tank and a one-piece bathing suit.
The moon looks down from among the stars,
Where lovers are parked in cars,
And couples are strolling on your lawn*
While sex, S-E-X, marches on.

CHORUS 1

Glasses across the table—
Drink till the break of dawn.
Drink to Lamarr and Betty Grable—
Long may their oomph march on.
And here's to Sheridan,
To Garbo and to Dietrich
And to Crawford and the others on the coast—
Here's to Hollywood,
For sex marches on,
And that's where it marches on the most.
This may be yours and my day,
But we will soon be gone;
Ten thousand kids were born last Friday—
Sex marches on,
Sex, S-E-X, marches on.

VERSE 2

The revolution was fought and won
By General Washington;
The rebels who fought with him are gone,
But sex, S-E-X, marches on.
The bankers dealing in high finance
Went into their final dance;
They ended up with the dying swan,
But sex, S-E-X, marches on.
Professor Einstein's relativity
Is lying on the shelf,
But Sally Rand always draws capacity
Any old time she decides to fan herself.
Most ev'ry artist in town, they say,
Is painting a girl today
Instead of the fanny of a faun,
For sex, S-E-X, marches on.

CHORUS 2

Glasses across the table—
Drink till the break of dawn.
To Robert Taylor and Clark Gable—
Long may their oomph march on.
And here's to beauty shops,
To lip rouge and mascara
And to perfume that is worth its weight in gold.
Times are terrible,
But sex marches on,

*Alternate version of line 15:
    And couples make whoopee on your lawn.

And ten million girdles have been sold.
Fill up your empty glasses;
Drink till the last drop's gone.
Grandfather's old but still makes passes—
Sex marches on,
Sex, S-E-X, marches on.

EXTRA FINISH

Washington grinds its axes;
Incomes will soon be gone;
Ladies of leisure don't pay taxes—
Sex marches on,
Sex, S-E-X, marches on.

LOUISIANA PURCHASE

Published. Copyrighted May 10, 1940. Previously registered for copyright as an unpublished song February 17, 1940. Introduced by Carol Bruce (Beatrice), the Martins (Hugh Martin, Ralph Blane, Jo Jean Rogers, and Phyllis Rogers), and the Buccaneers (John Panter, John Eliot, Don Cortez, and James Phillips), and ensemble.

Louisiana Purchase—
I'll tell you what it means:
It means I'd like to sell you New Orleans.
Come on, come on,
And you all can go
To town
Way down
In New Orleans.
Louisiana salesman
With nothing in his jeans—
That's why I'd like to sell you New Orleans.
Come on, come on,
And do all the things
There are
To do
In New Orleans.
Where does that heat come from,
That rhythmic beat come from,
And that red meat come from?
New Orleans.
Louisiana Purchase—
I told you what it means:
So won't you let me sell you New Orleans?
Come on, come on,
And you all can go
To town
Way down
In New Orleans.

IT'S A LOVELY DAY TOMORROW

Published. Copyrighted January 11, 1940. Previously registered for copyright as an unpublished song December 16, 1939. Listed in programs for the show as "Tomorrow Is a Lovely Day." Introduced by Irene Bordoni (Madame Yvonne Bordelaise). According to an article in the London *Daily Sketch*, it "was especially written for the English—a song of hope. For the first time an American song is a success here before it is over there. In fact it has not been heard in America." An article by Jonah Barrington in the London *Daily Express* (January 31, 1940) said that "Paul Holt (January 25) headlined a song called 'It's a Lovely Day Tomorrow'— written in a taxi by Irving Berlin and prompted by Alexander Korda somewhere between Fifty-Eighth Street and Fifty-Second Street, New York. Tomorrow in 'Guest Night' Binnie Hale hands it out to B.B.C. customers, which will be its first airing—except when 'Hutch' [singer-pianist Leslie Hutchinson] sang it to a crowd of would-be travellers during the first big hold-up on Monday night."

In an early English edition of the published song on which "Hutch" is pictured on the cover, there is no verse to the song. The English edition with Binnie Hale's photograph on the cover includes a verse, which in turn was replaced by the verse (with different music) used in *Louisiana Purchase*.

> *English verse*
> When I was young my mother would watch
> me
> On the days when it would rain.
> She'd see me so unhappy,
> My nose against the dripping window pane,
> And I would hear her singing this refrain.

In May 1940, as Hitler's armies smashed through Holland and Belgium and drove the British and French forces back to the coastal ports of Nieuwpoort and Dunkerque, the great Gallic musical star Irene Bordoni, for many Americans the embodiment of France, stood on the stage of New York's Imperial Theatre. Her voice breaking, her eyes filled with tears, night after night Bordoni sang Berlin's poignant song of hope "It's a Lovely Day Tomorrow" while friends and family—their fate uncertain—were trapped behind enemy lines. Among notable recordings of the song were those by Vera Lynn and Gladys Swarthout.

VERSE

The front page of your paper is bound to make
  you sad,
Especially if you're the worrying sort;
So turn the front page over where news is not so
  bad—
There's consolation in the weather report.

CHORUS

It's a lovely day tomorrow;
Tomorrow is a lovely day.
Come and feast your tear-dimmed eyes
On tomorrow's clear blue skies.
If today your heart is weary,
If ev'ry little thing looks gray,
Just forget your troubles and learn to say,
Tomorrow is a lovely day.

OUTSIDE OF THAT, I LOVE YOU

Published. Copyrighted May 10, 1940. Previously registered for copyright as an unpublished song April 3, 1940. Introduced by William Gaxton (Jim Taylor) and Vera Zorina (Marina Van Linden). This song appears to have been influenced by Berlin's song from *Watch Your Step* (1914) called "I Hate You."

VERSE

What makes you think I'm crazy about you?
What makes you think I can't do without you?
I've looked you over carefully,
And if I never see you again,
It's soon enough for me.

CHORUS 1

I hate the ground you walk upon,
I hate the phone you talk upon,
I hate most ev'rything that you do,
I hate that funny little mouth you drink with,
That peanut on your shoulders that you think
  with,*
I hate the rouge upon your lips,
The polish on your fingertips,
I hate your eyes of heavenly blue,
I hate the way you sigh,
Honest I do—
Outside of that, I love you.

---

*Alternate version of lines 4 and 5 sung in the 1996
revive:
  I hate the table and the cloth you eat on,
  I hate the sofa that you rest your seat on,

CHORUS 2

I hate the way you comb your hair,
I hate the flashy clothes you wear,
I hate the patent shine on your shoe,
I hate the closet that you keep your clothes in,
I hate the handkerchief you blow your nose in,
I hate the smell of your cigar,
The way you lean against a bar,
I hate the jokes you tell that are blue,
I hate that fancy tie,
Honest I do—
Outside of that, I love you.

CHORUS 3

I hate the notes you write to me,
The verses you recite to me,
Your conversation flowing like glue,
I hate the way you watch me through your
  lorgnette,
I hate your children that have not been born yet,
I hate the dimple in your chin,
The bath you dunk your body in,
I hate the way you bill and you coo,
I hate those eggs you fry,
Honest I do—
Outside of that, I love you.

CHORUS 4

I hate the song you sing to me,
I hate the flow'rs you bring to me,
I hate your phony "How do you do?,"
I hate the way you always break my dance up,
I hate those rubber things that keep your
  pants up,
I hate the dates you fix for me,
The cocktails that you mix for me,
Those etchings you may want me to view,
I hate the way you lie,
Honest I do—
Outside of that, I love you.

CHORUS 5

I hate the cigarette you smoke,
The way you kill a funny joke,
I hate the brand of gum that you chew,
I hate your office with the door you swing
  through,
I hate that funny little nose you sing through,
I hate the tray you eat upon,
The chair you rest your seat upon,
I hate the way you go for a stew,
I hate the shirts you buy,
Honest I do—
Outside of that, I love you.

YOU'RE LONELY AND I'M LONELY

Published. Copyrighted May 10, 1940. Previously registered for copyright as an unpublished song July 19, 1939. Introduced by Vera Zorina (Marina Van Linden) and Victor Moore (Senator Oliver P. Loganberry). Leading recording by Tommy Dorsey and His Orchestra (Victor).

VERSE

We're all alone and we're sad,
Like two little babes in the wood;
But things would not seem so bad
If we weren't quite so good,
If we cuddled up as we should.

CHORUS

You're lonely and I'm lonely,
So why can't we be lonely together?
The night is young, and while it grows older,
We can forget crying on each other's shoulder.
The sky's cloudy 'cause we're lonely,
But soon we'll see a change in the weather;
Two lonely hearts beating as one
Can be mis'rable and still have a lot of fun.

DANCE WITH ME (TONIGHT AT THE MARDI GRAS)

Published. Copyrighted June 5, 1940. Previously registered for copyright as an unpublished song under the titles "Tonight at the Masquerade" on April 19, 1940, and "Tonight at the Mardi Gras" on April 23, 1940. Introduced by the Martins (Hugh Martin, Ralph Blane, Jo Jean Rogers, and Phyllis Rogers), Vera Zorina (Marina Van Linden, as Queen of the Mardi Gras and Queen of the Creoles), and Charles Laskey (Premier Danseur). The music for this song was originally the music for the song "Skate with Me," which was written for and dropped from *As Thousands Cheer* (1933). See page 289.

VERSE

Tonight I'll take you to the Mardi Gras,
Where we will dance and sing.
Tonight we'll hitch our wagon to a star

And be a queen and king.
Tonight I'll take you to the masquerade,
And all that I will ask
Tonight is that I meet you unafraid
When you remove your mask.

CHORUS

Come along and dance with me,
Dance with me,
And into my arms to romance with me.
As we waltz down the street,
Hear my heart miss a beat.
Maybe you could fall for me,
Fall for me,
And be the belle of the ball for me.
We could be such a happy pair;
Honest, I promised my heart we'd be there—
So come on and dance with me,
Dance with me
Tonight at the Mardi Gras.

ACT I FINALE

Introduced by Vera Zorina (Marina Van Linden), Victor Moore (Senator Oliver P. Loganberry), William Gaxton (Jim Taylor), and ensemble.

MARINA: Congratulations are in order,
For I'm soon to become a wife.
I met the man that I love
From heaven above
And I will go with him through life.
ENSEMBLE: Congratulations are in order;
She's in love and her heart is gone.
MARINA: I met a wonderful man;
That's how it began.
ENSEMBLE: Proving sex, S-E-X, marches on.

LOGANBERRY: I don't know just what happened
In that private dining room;
I entered as a senator
And came out as a groom.
MARINA: We were two lonely hearts beating as one.
ENSEMBLE: Being miserable is oh, such a lot of fun.

JIM: [*to* LOGANBERRY]
Cut out those happy yells;
Your dream of wedding bells
Is perfect for a laugh,
But you'll never stand the gaff.

If you marry her,
I swear that you will rue it—
After marriage there's a honeymoon,
And you will not live through it.

MARINA: You're jealous just because I love him so;
I mean sincerely.
ENSEMBLE: She loves him dearly.
JIM: You can't make me believe it, 'cause I know
That this antique
Won't last a week.

MARINA: He got me all excited
When he sat upon my knee.
LOGANBERRY: If I did such a thing,
It's certainly news to me.

JIM: [*to* MARINA]
I hate the lies you told to me,
The bill of goods you sold to me,
I hate the things that make you untrue,
I hate your last goodbye,
Honest I do.
MARINA: [*to* LOGANBERRY]
Outside of that, I love you.

LOGANBERRY: Everybody drink with me,
Drink with me,
Under the table
Come sink with me;
Very happy am I,
And I wish I knew why.
ENSEMBLE: We'll be glad to drink with you,
Drink with you,
Glasses of champagne
To clink with you.

[*Dialogue.*]

JIM: I'll be glad to drink with you,
Drink with you
A toast
To the bride and groom.

ENSEMBLE: Louisiana Purchase—
I'll tell you what it means:
It means I'd like to sell you
New Orleans.

Alternate version

ENSEMBLE: What's this we hear?
Please make it clear.

Are we to understand
A wedding is near?

JIM: Congratulations are in order;
She's in love and her heart is gone.

MARINA: I met a wonderful man—
That's how it began.

ENSEMBLE: Proving sex, S-E-X, marches on.

LOGANBERRY: I don't know just what happened
In that private dining room;
I entered as a senator
And came out as a groom.

MARINA: We were two lonely hearts beating as
one.

ENSEMBLE: Being miserable is oh, such a lot of
fun.

JIM: I hate the lies you told to me,
The bill of goods you sold to me,
I hate the things that make you
untrue,
I hate your last goodbye,
Honest I do.

MARINA: Outside of that, I love you.

LOGANBERRY: Everybody drink with me,
Drink with me;
Under the table
Come sink with me.
Very happy am I,
And I wish I knew why.

ENSEMBLE: We'll be glad to drink with you,
Drink with you—

JIM: A toast to the bride and groom.

ENSEMBLE: Louisiana Purchase—
I'll tell you what it means:
It means I'd like to sell you
New Orleans.

LATINS KNOW HOW

Published. Copyrighted May 10, 1940. Previously registered for copyright as an unpublished song February 17, 1940. Introduced by Irene Bordoni (Madame Yvonne Bordelaise) and ensemble. Helen Lawrenson had written an article for the October 1939 issue of *Esquire* magazine titled "Latins Are Lousy Lovers."

VERSE

In a magazine I read
Where a certain author said

That Latins are lousy lovers,
And it's a lie,
A libelous lie,
And who,
Tell me who,
Should know better than I?

CHORUS

Latins,
They don't play baseball;
They're not so good
With a rake or a plow;
They're not experts at making money—
But when it comes to making love,
A Latin knows how.
Latins,
They don't like farming;
You seldom see Latins milking a cow.
In the daytime they're always sleepy;
But with guitars beneath the stars,
A Latin knows how.
Englishmen and Yankees,
They've got quite a lot;
But that extra something,
They just haven't got.
Latins,
They're so romantic—
They've got more oomph
Than the law will allow.
If you're married to a Latin,
Life is just as smooth as satin,
For a Latin knows how.

WHAT CHANCE HAVE I?

Published. Copyrighted May 10, 1940. Previously registered for copyright as an unpublished song April 1, 1940. Introduced by Victor Moore (Senator Oliver P. Loganberry). Alternate title: "What Chance Have I with Love?" Conceived as early as 1931 as a possible song idea for an early version of *Face the Music*.

VERSE

Love is beautiful, love is swell,
Love is as sweet as a nut.
Love is grander than tongue can tell,
Love is remarkable, but

CHORUS

Look at what it did to Antony—
It made a fool out of Antony.

If love could do that to Antony,
What chance have I with love?
Look at what it did to Romeo—
It dealt poor Romey an awful blow.
If love could do that to Romeo,
What chance have I with love?
Look what it did to Samson—
Till he lost his hair he was brave.
If a haircut could weaken Samson,
They could murder me with a shave.
Look at what it did to Bonaparte—
He lost his head when he lost his heart.
If he kicked over the apple cart,
What chance have I, an ordinary guy,
What chance have I with love?

Alternate version

CHORUS 1

Look at what it did to Romeo—
It dealt poor Romey an awful blow.
If love could do that to Romeo,
What chance have I with love?
Look at what it did to Antony—
It made a Mark out of Antony.
If love could do that to Antony,
What chance have I with love?
Look at what it did to Samson—
Till he lost his hair he was brave.
If a haircut could weaken Samson,
They could murder me with a shave.
Louie Number Fifteen, king of France—
They say he suffered with each romance.
If love kicked him in the royal pants,
What chance have I,
An ordinary guy,
What chance have I with love?

CHORUS 2 [*from release*]

Look what it did to Adam—
From that bite he could not escape.
If an apple could finish Adam,
They could knock me off with a grape.
Miss Lucrezia Borgia, deep in sin—
She poisoned her lovers when they dropped in.
If they wound up with a Mickey Finn,
What chance have I,
An ordinary guy,
What chance have I with love?

CHORUS 3 [*from release*]

Look what love did for Reno—
It put Reno on the map.
When a woman goes to Reno,

It's because some man is a sap.
Tommy Manville's love is not returned—
He sells asbestos and he has learned
That with asbestos he still gets burned:
What chance have I,
An ordinary guy,
What chance have I with love?

And we'll ask the Forgiver
For his praise on Judgment Day
And we'll bless the Lord and say:

REPEAT CHORUS

Old man's darling or a young man's slave?"?

[*Ballet.*]

REPEAT CHORUS

THE LORD DONE FIXED UP MY SOUL

Published. Copyrighted May 15, 1940. Previously registered for copyright as an unpublished song March 25, 1940. Introduced by Carol Bruce (Beatrice), Nicodemus (Abner), the Buccaneers (John Panter, John Eliot, Don Cortez, and James Phillips), and ensemble.

VERSE

I had a mammy for a nurse;
When she could not be feeling worse,
She'd take her troubles into church,
And while the bells were ringing,
She'd come out singing.

CHORUS

The Lord done fixed up my eyes;
I see heaven way up there in the skies—
Bless the Lord for fixin' my eyes.
The Lord done fixed up my ears;
I hear music like I ain't heard in years—
Bless the Lord for fixin' my ears.
The Lord done fixed up my heart.
I got courage now,
Ain't afraid somehow—
The Lord done fixed up my soul.
It was broken and the Lord made it whole.
Bless the Lord for makin' my soul
Whole—
Bless the Lord,
Bless the Lord,
Bless the Lord.

REPEAT CHORUS

INTERLUDE

Down to the river,
We'll go down to the river
And we'll wash our sins away.
Down to the river

FOOLS FALL IN LOVE

Published. Copyrighted May 10, 1940. Previously registered for copyright as an unpublished song March 29, 1940. Introduced by William Gaxton (Jim Taylor) and Vera Zorina (Marina Van Linden). The song led directly into the ballet "Old Man's Darling—Young Man's Slave."

VERSE 1

Why do I allow my heart to make decisions
    for me?
Why do I keep listening to my heart?
Why do I get so involved when I would rather be
    free?
Maybe it's because I'm not so smart.

CHORUS

Fools fall in love;
Only lunatics fall in love,
And I'm a fool.
Fools seek romance;
Only idiots take a chance,
And I'm a fool.
I should be able
To put all my feelings aside;
I should be able
To take one free ride—
In my stride.
But fools cannot play,
They get serious right away
And break the rule;
My heart's on fire
When I know I ought to keep cool.
Fools fall in love,
And I'm such a fool.

VERSE 2

Why do you get so involved when you would
    rather be free?
Why not give your heart what it may crave?
Why not let your heart decide the question
    "Which will it be—

YOU CAN'T BRUSH ME OFF

Published. Copyrighted May 10, 1940. Previously registered for copyright as an unpublished song February 17, 1940. Introduced by April Ames (Emmy-Lou), Nick Long Jr. (Lee Davis), and the Martins (Hugh Martin, Ralph Blane, Jo Jean Rogers, Phyllis Rogers). During the pre-Broadway tryout this was the third number in Act I.

VERSE

Why don't you please give in?
Just like a Siamese twin,
I mean to stick to you
Until you do.
I won't take it on the chin;
You'll never leave me flat,
I'm not a last year's hat
That you can cast aside—
I've got my pride,
And I won't stand for that.

CHORUS 1

You can't brush me off
As you would a speck of powder.
You may try,
But you can't brush me off.
You can't shout me down;
You can yell, but I'll yell louder.
You can try,
But you can't brush me off.
You can say you're out,
But I'll keep phoning.
You can tell me goodbye;
You can tell me, but I won't go.
No, you can't leave me cold
As you would a plate of chowder.
You can try,
But you can't brush me off.

VERSE 2

What is this all about?
You've got me wrong, no doubt.
I give you all my time, believe me.
I'm not looking for some way out;

I want you for my wife,
Sharing my care and strife,
And that may not be fun,
For when it's done,
You're stuck with me for life.

CHORUS 2

You can't brush me off
As you would a fresh mosquito.
You can try,
But you can't brush me off.
You can't rub me out
Like a spot on my tuxedo;
You may try,
But you can't brush me off.
You can cut me dead,
But I won't mind it.
You may injure my pride;
Still, I'll never decide to go.
No, you can't drop me fast
As you would a live torpedo;
You may try,
But you can't brush me off.

CHORUS 3

You can't brush me off
Like a colored Pullman porter.
You may try,
But you can't brush me off.
You can't lock me out
Like a frightened farmer's daughter;
You may try,
But you can't brush me off.
You can drop a hint,
But I won't take it.
You can tell me bad news;
I intend to refuse to go.
No, you can't give me back
As you would a leaden quarter—
You may try,
But you can't brush me off.

Alternate version of chorus 2

You can't brush me off
As you would a poor relation.
You may try,
But you can't brush me off.
You can't leave me flat
Like a train down at the station;
You may try,
But you can't brush me off.
You can drop a hint,
But I won't take it.
You may injure my pride;

Still, I'll never decide to go.
No, you can't send me out
As you would an invitation;
You may try,
But you can't brush me off.

ACT II FINALE

Introduced by entire company. On the original lyric sheet, Berlin had written at the end of the song: "Going into some chorus of the score which Berlin is a very anxious to plug."

[PICKETS *march on, carrying banners and singing.*]

ENSEMBLE: Somebody handed us a ticket
To picket,
And we're marching as to
war.
We know the only way to lick it
Is picket,
Though we don't know what
We're picketing for.
Here we'll remain,
And if you should complain
When we ask you to sign,
You can take your complaint
Against the picket
And stick it,
But we won't let you cross the
line.

LOGANBERRY: What's this, a picket line?
I really must decline.
Whatever else I do,
Let me say to you and you,
As a candidate for President,
I simply can't go through.
ENSEMBLE: As a candidate for President,
I simply can't go through.
LOGANBERRY: A candidate can leave his party
flat,
And wind up on the opposition
ticket.
He can double-cross his other
brother rat,
But he mustn't hurt the feelings
of a picket.
ENSEMBLE: No, he mustn't hurt the feelings
of a picket.

MME BORDELAISE: What is this picket stuff?
We've waited long enough.

The villains must be tried;
Let us hurry up inside.
LOGANBERRY: Please remember, dear,
My place before the nation;
And as long as there are pickets,
There is no investigation.
ENSEMBLE: No investigation,
No investigation.
As long as there are pickets,
There can be no investigation.

MARINA: The senator was dreaming, but
we knew
That he'd awaken.
ENSEMBLE: He's been mistaken.
JIM: And now it seems that he in-
tended to
Investigate
Another state.
Louisiana's not the place where
Crime could ever be.
LOGANBERRY: If there is such a thing,
It's certainly news to me.

MARINA: And now without a doubt
This thing is
straightened out.
MME BORDELAISE: And everybody ends
As the very best of friends.
JIM: [*to* LOGANBERRY]
All that I've got to say
Is I'm certainly delighted
LOGANBERRY: [*to* JIM]
You can name your wedding
day—
JIM: Bet your life and you're invited.
MARINA: [*to* MME BORDELAISE]
You're invited too—
[*to* ENSEMBLE]
And you and you.
ALL: Which makes it a very happy
ending.

[*Few lines of dialogue, ending with a laugh about going to New Jersey for another investigation.*]

ALL: Which makes it a very
happy ending.
PRINCIPALS: [*step down and sing to audience*]
And now before you go,
We hope you liked our mythical
show.

Alternate version

ENSEMBLE: Somebody handed us a ticket
To picket—

They want pickets,
So here we are.
LOGANBERRY: Pickets?
ENSEMBLE: Yes, pickets.
It's a trick, a trick.
JIM: You know that it's a fact
That since the Wagner Act
The head of labor says
That a candidate for Prez
Mustn't cross a picket line.
ENSEMBLE: Mustn't cross a picket line.
MME BORDELAISE: With labor you'll be through—
They will never vote for you
If you cross a picket line.
ENSEMBLE: If you cross a picket line—
Yes, a candidate for President
Must never cross a picket line.
MME BORDELAISE: Listen to the pickets, Ollie dear.
Let's go inside—it means your
whole career.
LOGANBERRY: A candidate can leave his party
flat
And wind up on the opposition
ticket.
He can double-cross his other
brother rat,
But he mustn't hurt the feelings
of a picket.
ENSEMBLE: No, he mustn't hurt the feelings
of a picket.
Louisiana Purchase—
I told you what it means:
So won't you let me sell you
New Orleans?
Come on, come on,
And you all can go to town
Way down
In New Orleans.

IT'LL COME TO YOU

Published. Copyrighted June 5, 1940. Previously registered for copyright as an unpublished song April 3, 1940. Sung in the pre-Broadway tryout during Act I by Irene Bordoni (Madame Yvonne Bordelaise) and the "Louisiana Belles" (Georgia Carroll, Marion Rosamond, Judy Ford, Patricia Lee, Veva Selwood, Edith Luce). Dropped during the tryout.

VERSE

When life catches up with our flaming youth,
Someone tries to tell them the awful truth.

I would send them ignorant on their way;
To those little innocents I would say:

CHORUS 1

Don't worry so
About the things that you don't know.
When the time comes and you find yourself in
love,
It'll come to you,
You'll know what to do,
It'll come to you.
Don't be concerned
About the things you haven't learned;
If you can't express just what you're thinking of,
It'll come to you,
You'll know what to do,
It'll come to you.
No one teaches a duck how to swim
Or a bird how to fly;
They're not taught to do
What they ought to do—
Why should you and I?
Don't be afraid
Because you're such a bashful maid.
When you're strolling neath the silv'ry moon,
You may be shy, but pretty soon
It'll come to you,
You'll know what to do,
It'll come to you.

CHORUS 2

Don't start to plan
How to rebuff a fresh young man.
When you're in a cab and he starts making free,
It'll come to you,
You'll know what to do,
It'll come to you.
Don't lie awake
And think of answers you might make.
When he starts to put his hand upon your knee,
It'll come to you,
You'll know what to do,
It'll come to you.
No one teaches a mule how to kick
Or a dog how to bite;
They know what to do
And what not to do
When they're out at night.
Don't be undone
Because the first round has been won.
He begins to think that you're a dunce,
It seems you're lost,
Then all at once
It'll come to you,
You'll know what to do,
It'll come to you.

ADDITIONAL LINES

Don't be concerned
About the things you haven't learned.
When you're in his arms beneath the moon above,
It'll come to you,
You'll know what to do,
It'll come to you.

Don't be afraid
If you're a newly married maid.
When you start upon your honeymoon,
You may be dumb, but pretty soon
It'll come to you,
You'll know what to do,
It'll come to you.

I'D LOVE TO BE SHOT OUT OF A CANNON WITH YOU

Published in a black-and-white professional edition May 15, 1940. Previously registered for copyright as an unpublished song April 5, 1940. Sung late in Act II during the pre-Broadway tryout by Nick Long Jr. (Lee Davis), April Ames (Emmy-Lou), and the Martins (Hugh Martin, Ralph Blane, Jo Jean Rogers, Phyllis Rogers). Dropped before the New York opening. Alternate title (program): "I'd Love to Be Shot from a Cannon with You."

VERSE

I'm tired of doing the same things over and over
again;
You must admit that it's a bore.
I keep longing for a change,
Something diff'rent, something strange
That we have never done before.

CHORUS 1

I'd love to be shot from a cannon with you;
Now that's something diff'rent that I'd like
to do.
We'd float through the air in a way that
I never could forget the day that
I was shot from a cannon with you.

CHORUS 2

I'd love to be tried for a murder with you;
The trial goes against us and we're feeling blue.
And just when we couldn't have won it,

The judge stands up and says "I done it,"
When I'm tried for a murder with you.

CHORUS 3

I'd love to fall down in a coal hole with you;
We'd fall on a mattress and that's something new.
It's dark and we think we're in clover
When Winchell's voice says, "Please move over,"
When I fall in a coal hole with you.

CHORUS 4

I'd love to be caught in a mousetrap with you;
We're hungry, and so there is one thing to do.
We soon hear a couple of mouses
Yell out, "They ate our cheese, the louses,"
When I'm caught in a mousetrap with you.

CHORUS 5

I'd love to escape a hotel room with you;
We open the window and quickly jump through.
And just when we get to the bottom,
The cameraman says, "Cut—I got 'em,"
When I'm in a hotel room with you.

WILD ABOUT YOU

Published. Copyrighted June 5, 1940. Previously registered for copyright as an unpublished song December 31, 1934. Conceived as a duet for Victor Moore (Senator Oliver P. Loganberry) and Vera Zorina (Marina Van Linden). Dropped during rehearsals. Written originally for the film *Top Hat* (1935) but not used.

VERSE

I'm not a McCormack;
I haven't a voice.
I loosen my vocals,
But never by choice.
Still, I've a song to sing,
And I long to sing it for you.
It isn't a ballad
With plenty of heart;
It hasn't the rhythm
That's clever and smart.
Just a tune with words that rhyme
That I wrote to say that I'm—

CHORUS

Wild about you—
The child about you
Makes me wild about you.
If I were a native of Borneo,
I couldn't be wilder about you.
Mad about you—
The bad about you
Makes me mad about you.
If I were the Hatter in Wonderland,
I couldn't be madder about you.
That's my story
And I'll stick to it, dear.
In case you didn't listen,
In case you didn't hear.
Wild about you—
The child about you
Makes me wild about you.
If I were a tiger in Africa,
I couldn't be wilder about you.

I'M A QUAKER'S DAUGHTER FROM THE LATIN QUARTER

Written December 12, 1939. Not used. No music is known to survive. Typed lyric is in the Irving Berlin Collection of the Music Division of the Library of Congress.

VERSE

I was born in Pennsylvania,
But my mother had a mania
For art—my mother was smart.
So one morning she told Father
That she loved him, but she'd rather
Be free—delighted was he.
She bought a palette and brush and started to
    paint
And made me just what I am and just what I ain't.

CHORUS

I'm a Quaker's daughter from the Latin Quarter
And I'm hot,
And I'll flatten any Latin who says I'm not.
You can treat me, mister, as you would your sister
    or your aunt
And I'll weaken any deacon who says he can't.
When I wear satin,
I look like a Latin;

But when I "thee" and "thou,"
I'm a Quaker and how.
I am well acquainted for I'm being painted quite a
    lot,
And everything I started out with I've still got,
And I'll flatten any Latin who says I've not.

THE WALTZ OF OLD VIENNA

Registered for copyright as an unpublished song February 3, 1939. Intended for Vera Zorina (Marina Van Linden). Not used. Earlier title: "Nobody Dances in Vienna (You Can't Goose-step to a Waltz)."

VERSE

I just came from Vienna;
Ev'rything still is Viennese,
But those beautiful melodies
That we used to adore
Are not heard anymore.

CHORUS

The waltz of old Vienna
Has gone beyond recall,
Vanished from most ev'ry house
Kalman and Lehár and Strauss.

The waltz of old Vienna
You heard at ev'ry ball—
They still play them, it's true,
But the feeling is false;
You can't do the goose step to a waltz.

Earlier lines that evolved into the final song

Nobody dances in Vienna,
Nobody dances in Vienna.
They get out on the floor,
But the feeling is false;
You can't do a goose step to a waltz.

YOU MUST CATCH A SENATOR WITH A GIRL

Written c. October 10, 1939. Intended for William Gaxton. Not used. In an October 10, 1939 letter to Buddy De Sylva, Berlin described the song as follows: "See if you like the enclosed as a song for Gaxton at the end of the scene where the boys are going to be investigated. I wrote up as a 64-bar chorus and I think I've got a pretty good tune for it." No music is known to survive. Earlier title: "You Can Always Get a Senator with a Girl."

You catch a fly with honey;
A fly likes honey,
Prefers it to a diamond or a pearl.
A fish in a brook
With a worm you can hook,
But you must catch a senator with a girl.
You catch a dog with biscuits;
A dog likes biscuits—
A ginger snap will set his tail awhirl.
A mouse you can seize
With a small piece of cheese,
But you must catch a senator with a girl.

Back in history
Cleopatra took a fall
Out of Antony,
The greatest senator of them all.
You catch a horse with sugar;
A horse likes sugar—
A single lump will make his mustache curl.
If you want a quail,
Put some salt on his tail;
But if you want a senator, get a girl.

IN AN OLD-FASHIONED PARLOR

Intended for Irene Bordoni (Madame Yvonne Bordelaise). No music is known to survive, and only the following lines of the lyric.

Far, far away from care and strife,
I will spend the twilight of my life
In an old-fashioned parlor
On an old-fashioned street,
A setting for old-fashioned love.

WE MIGHT HAVE HAD A FUTURE

Written December 12, 1939. Not used. No music is known to survive. Typed lyric is in the Irving Berlin Collection of the Music Division of the Library of Congress.

CHORUS

We might have had a future
If I didn't have a past,
If I hadn't done so many things
That you consider fast.
If I had not stayed up nights
And gone home to bed,
If only I had caught up
With my reading instead.
We might have been in heaven
If I hadn't raised such hell.
If I hadn't kissed so many men
The kind who kiss and tell.
You are a perfect angel;
You've done everything you should
And
It's just too bad
That I'm so bad
And you're so god damn good.

Bing Crosby and Marjorie Reynolds

HOLIDAY INN | 1942

HOLIDAY INN (1942)

A film produced by Mark Sandrich for Paramount Pictures. Released August 1942. Music and lyrics by Irving Berlin. Screenplay by Claude Binyon, based on an idea by Irving Berlin; adaptation by Elmer Rice. Directed by Mark Sandrich. Dances directed by Danny Dare, assisted by Babe Pearce. Orchestration and arrangements by Joseph J. Lilley, Paul Wetstein, Gilbert Grau, Herbert Spencer, and Walter Scharf. Music conducted by Robert Emmett Dolan. Specialty accompaniments by Bob Crosby's Band. Cast: starring Bing Crosby (Jim Hardy) and Fred Astaire (Ted Hanover) and featuring Marjorie Reynolds, singing dubbed by Martha Mears (Linda Mason), Virginia Dale (Lila Dixon), Walter Abel (Danny Reed), Louise Beavers (Mamie), and Harry Barris (man at nightclub table). Original cast recordings (Decca and Sunbeam Sountrak).

During the late 1930s, Berlin and Moss Hart discussed writing a revue based on the major holidays. Berlin wrote down his idea for this revue and then filled it out in a version he sent to his lawyer Dennis F. O'Brien for copyrighting on February 16, 1939.

FEBRUARY 16, 1939

Happy Holiday by Irving Berlin

This is a first rough draft for a revue to be done entirely with lyrics and music. Through some mechanical device such as a calendar, an hour glass, or anything denoting time, the important holidays in a year will be shown in rotation as they naturally fall; each holiday as an individual item in the revue. The point of view will be the debunking of the holiday spirit. Each holiday will be announced through whatever medium we have a la the headline announcements in *As Thousands Cheer*.

We open with a small set in about two—a flower shop. Two characters behind the counter wrapping flowers will sound the keynote of the revue. They want more holidays; they suggest *crazy* ones—Dog Day: "Send a Posey to your Doggie," etc.

1. NEW YEAR'S: It is two minutes before twelve o'clock and the chorus of boys and girls are assembled in a New York cafe waiting for the sound of twelve. They are taking cracks at one another— "Mrs. So-And-So at the other end is having an affair with her chauffeur"—"Do you know Mr. Who's-This gave Mrs. What's-This that sable coat she is wearing." These cracks become quite vicious and when they reach an almost censorable point, lights go out, bells ring and ensemble go into "A Happy New Year to Everybody." Much kissing and "best wishes" and a complete opposite to what we heard before. This finishes with the entire chorus down in one, singing a "New Year's Resolution" finale.

2. INAUGURATION DAY 1956: The Republicans have finally elected a new president, but the Roosevelts won't get out of the White House. They have barricaded themselves in. A short item that would take the place of the opening sketch.

3. LINCOLN'S BIRTHDAY: A number done by a colored choir or an Ethel Waters. Some angle on emancipation day. Not too heavy, but a sincere emancipation number—a tentative title "Father Abraham."

4. VALENTINE'S DAY: This will be the first full stage production number. A fresh angle on the Valentine song, finishing with a dance.

5. WASHINGTON'S BIRTHDAY: Some new angle on a historical incident on Washington's life—or a comment on some topical incident to which Washington's birthday can be applied. This will be in a sketch form.

6. ST. PATRICK'S DAY: A drop representing the exterior of a row of apartment houses in an Irish neighborhood, with several practical windows. A male character dressed ultra-Irish and with a brogue singing "When Irish Eyes Are Smiling." A woman, his wife, also dressed Irish to the teeth, picking up the coins that are being dropped from the windows. At the finish of his song she goes into an Irish reel. They then start counting the silver that she collected and do it in pure, unadulterated Yiddish. If it is impossible to cast the man in this act, we can cut out the song and let him play an Irish reel on the organ while his wife dances. This should be very short and is only good, if at all, as a black-out.

7. EASTER: It will be hard to get anything as good as "Easter Parade" for this spot, but there is possibly a good angle in an egg-hunt or in a Mr. & Mrs. Bunny duet, finishing with 32 children before the chorus is over.

8. MOTHER'S DAY: The returning black sheep is singing a heart-breaking Mother song written along the lines of "M is for the different things she gave me, etc." This is done in front of the little white gate leading into the cottage where he knows Mother is waiting to kill the fatted calf. When he enters, we find a very sophisticated Mother with platinum hair, polished fingernails, a long cigarette holder and a young gigolo. She is sore as hell at being surprised by a middle-aged son.

9. DECORATION DAY: This is a number à la the "Debts" in *As Thousands Cheer*. The French Ambassador is decorating four great Americans with the Legionne [*sic*] of Honor. We will choose four types and show how promiscuous France is in handing out these decorations. It will be done very seriously and part of the song given over to some ridiculous service that each of our types has rendered to France. This will be a patter chorus against the French national anthem, "Marseillaise," which the Four Americans sing very reverently while the Ambassador repeats his part of the lyric enumerating their deeds and how proud France is to honor them. For this scene it may be a good idea to have the words "Decoration Day" somewhere prominently shown in the scene.

10. INDEPENDENCE DAY—JULY 4TH: This suggests a peppy, colorful, fire-cracker ballet and should be done entirely to music with no lyrics at all.

11. LABOR DAY: A sit-down strike of the Capitalists showing their point of view, including the DuPonts, Morgans, Rockefellers, Fords, Chryslers, etc. They refuse to make any more money and demand the same privileges that Labor has today. They will no longer be sent off on their yachts to Palm Beach while Labor is given the chance to make speeches and have fun. Let Labor eat those rich French dishes and get indigestion for a change. Let them drink Magnums of Vintage champagne and have a terrible hangover the next day and see how they like it. In a nut-shell, this is the legitimate squawk of the so-called privileged, proclaiming the hardships of the Capitalists.

12. COLUMBUS DAY: A communist meeting in Columbus Circle in front of the statue of Christopher Columbus. In the midst of fighting among themselves the statue comes to life and asks "Where are those peaceful Indians I left here in 1492?" This is just a suggestion.

13. HALLOWEEN: A Jack O'Lantern Ghost number, or a ballet to music with no lyrics. (Note: This kind of a revue done completely with words and music can stand two ballets—one in each act, especially if you can get Ballenchine [*sic*] to do something very arty and good.)

14. ARMISTICE DAY: This will be a number in one, sung in front of a moving picture screen done by male voices. During the number, different newsreel shots will be thrown on the screen. The number will be a stirring, patriotic Armistice Day song, sung as it might have been on Armistice Day in 1918, beginning something like "A war to end all wars has been fought, hurray, hurray. At last a world with one single thought, Armistice Day." The lyric will continue and in turn mention all the warring nations, predicting peace from now on and good will to all men. "The world has learned its lesson, hurray, hurray, And every heart is singing Armistice Day." As the

song goes on a series of newsreel shots will be thrown on the screen of what's happening in Europe today, finishing with that pathetic newsreel of a little wounded Chinese baby, after the Japanese had bombed the town. Here is another version of the Armistice Day lyric idea:

The war to end all wars has been fought,
Hurray, hurray.
At last a world with one single thought
Hurray—for Armistice Day.
Now every land is a land of the free.
The world is safe for democracy.

15. THANKSGIVING: A love duet—"Plenty to Be Thankful For."

16. CHRISTMAS and FINALE of the show: This will sum up our whole idea and point of view. An enormous Christmas tree in back of the stage with Santa Claus handing out presents to the cast.

All this is a rough draft and many of the items can be improved on. However, the structure of the revue will have to remain as is. There will be an advantage of being confined to the holidays in their rotation.

The following are notes by Berlin found in his *Holiday Inn* files.

I was in Washington one day and accidentally ran into Mark Sandrich. Mark had directed most of the Astaire-Rogers movies at RKO and he was now producing as well as directing at Paramount. I told him about my idea of a musical revue based on holidays and he thought it would make a perfect movie for Bing Crosby. But first there would have to be a story line since the revue format was considered unsuitable for the screen. I went out to Hollywood and worked on the general outline with Mark, just a thread of a story about an easygoing fellow who works only on holidays. We also thought it would be a great opportunity to co-star the screen's number one male singer with the screen's number one male dancer, Fred Astaire. Then we had a meeting with Frank Freeman, the president of Paramount, and Buddy De Sylva, the studio production chief. They liked the idea for Bing but when Mark proposed co-starring him with Fred, De Sylva shook his head. "I can get George Murphy for $50,000," he said. "Why do I need Astaire for $100,000?" Mark, who was one of the most self-effacing guys in the world and who never liked throwing his weight around, simply said, "If we don't get Fred Astaire, we don't do the picture." I was to get a 10% royalty of the gross but no one asked for my opinion. Everyone was just looking at Mark. Finally, Freeman said, "Mark, if that's what *you* want, we'll get Fred Astaire."

[undated]

April 17, 1941

IRVING BERLIN'S NOTES ON *HOLIDAY INN*

This is an idea for a picture based on the revue *Happy Holiday* by Irving Berlin.

The character, Bing Crosby, around whom this idea motivates, is very much like Bing Crosby without Crosby's ambition. When he saved enough money he bought a farm, and finding it tough going he hit on the idea of turning the farm into an Inn that would only be open on holidays. His philosophy was to work on the days when other people didn't work. All he wanted out of life was enough to live on—and only that.

We learn about his story and idea through Fred Astaire, who plays himself. He is on his way to Hollywood to do a couple of dances in an important picture (very much as Astaire really started). He stops off to see Bing, who he knew in show business. He thinks Bing's idea is crazy. Bing, however, is intent on going through with it.

The girl, Mary Martin, is the daughter of very rich parents, who have an estate in the neighborhood of Bing's farm. They give her everything her heart desires—a large house where she can entertain her friends, clothes; in fact all the luxuries that a young girl in her position would ask for, with one exception—money. It is a phobia with her father, and the result is that Mary really hasn't any spending money. In some way she finds out about Bing's idea, and having a voice she agrees to go to the Inn on holidays and sing. No one, of course, knows her background or who she is. We later find it out on Mother's Day when everyone has to bring his mother to the Inn.

In Hollywood, Fred's dance is so good that the star of the picture insists on it being cut out. He comes back with his tail between his legs and arrives at Holiday Inn a few minutes before twelve on New Year's Eve. Bing is holding a watch in his hand waiting for the stroke of twelve when the lights will go out and the usual hilarity and kissing in the New Year will begin. Fred enters just as the lights go out. When they are turned on again he finds himself in Mary Martin's arms. This introduction gives Fred a reason to want to stay on and help Bing with his idea.

From here on our story will be told through the characters. It will obviously be a two boys and a girl setup. In it we will use as many holidays as are possible. It is important that Bing's character conceives some appropriate angle for each holiday. This becomes an important attraction for the place. For instance, on New Year's everyone has to make a resolution, but of course will not keep. Washington's Birthday everyone has to tell the truth. Mother's Day everyone brings his mother. Etc.

Numbers already written and ideas for those still to be written:

Of the old songs, so far the two that fit are "Lazy," which will be more or less Bing's theme song, and "Easter Parade" for Easter.

"Happy New Year Blues"—New Year's
"White Christmas"—Christmas
"Plenty to Be Thankful For"—
    Thanksgiving
"This Is a Great Country"—4th of July

Ideas for other numbers:

"The Wedding of Capital and Labor"—
    Labor Day
"Father Abraham"—Lincoln's Birthday

Also any of the ideas in the original revue that may fit into the picture.

x x x

SONGS IN *HOLIDAY INN*

1. Special Musical Opening for Main Title
2. "You're Easy to Dance With"—(Only song without Holiday idea)
3. "Happy New Year's Blues"—New Year's Day
4. "Father Abraham"—Lincoln's Birthday
5. "Be Careful, It's My Heart"—Valentine's Day
6. "I Can't Tell a Lie"—Washington's Birthday
7. "A Little Bit of Irish"—St. Patrick's Day
8. "Easter Parade"—Easter
9. "I Pledge Allegiance to My Flag" (Musical Version)—Decoration Day and Flag Day
10. "This Is a Great Country"—July 4th
11. "The Wedding of Capital and Labor"—Labor Day
12. "If Columbus Came Back Today"—Columbus Day
13. "Jack O'Lantern"—Halloween
14. "We Fought the War to End All Wars, Hurray For Armistice Day"—Armistice Day (1918)
15. "Plenty to Be Thankful For"—Thanksgiving Day
16. "White Christmas"—Christmas Day

[undated, probably September 1941]

I'LL CAPTURE YOUR HEART SINGING

Published. Copyrighted May 12, 1942. Previously registered for copyright as an unpublished song November 18, 1941. Earliest registration as an unpublished song, under the title "Sing and Dance," October 22, 1941. Introduced by Bing Crosby (Jim), Fred Astaire (Ted), and Virginia Dale (Lila), who also can be heard singing it on the original sound track recording (Sunbeam Sountrak). Crosby, Astaire, and Margaret Lenhart with Bob Crosby and His Orchestra perform this song on *Song Hits from "Holiday Inn"* (Decca).

Published version

VERSE

Crosby sings pretty swell;
Fred Astaire dances well.
I'm that combination,
That's my reputation.

CHORUS

I'll capture your heart singing
And then I'll take you down the road with my
    dancing.
Just wait till I start singing
And wait until you get a load of my dancing.
I can't go wrong—
A tender song
And you'll discover my charms.
And then some taps
And you'll collapse
And fall right into my arms.
I'll capture your heart singing
And then we'll start a romance
When I go into my dance.

Film version

VERSE

TED: Here she comes down the street.
JIM: My oh my, ain't she sweet!
TED: Why, here comes my hot toddy.
JIM: Over my dead body.

CHORUS 1

JIM: I'll capture her heart singing.
TED: Just wait until she gets a load of my
    dancing.

JIM: Just wait till I start singing.
TED: I'll take her strolling down the road with
    my dancing.
JIM: I can't go wrong—
    A tender song
    And she'll discover my charms.
TED: Some fancy taps
    And she'll collapse
    And fall right into my arms.
JIM: I'll capture her heart singing.
TED: Oh, no, you haven't got a chance
    When I go into my dance.

CHORUS 2

JIM: I'll take you through life singing.
TED: I'll make you my wife dancing.
LILA: [to JIM]
    If you could dance
    Instead of sing,
    I'd learn to love you somehow.
    [to TED]
    If you could sing
    Instead of dance,
    I'd take you home with me now.
    [to TED]
    The way you sing
    Don't mean a thing—
    You'd better stick to your dance.
    [to JIM]
    And as for you,
    Your dance won't do—
    You'll have to sing for romance.
JIM &
    TED: I'll capture her heart—
    I'll capture her heart—
JIM: Singing.
TED: Dancing.

YOU'RE EASY TO DANCE WITH

Published. Copyrighted April 30, 1942. Previously registered for copyright as an unpublished song July 12, 1941. Introduced by Fred Astaire (Ted) and vocal ensemble; danced by Astaire and Virginia Dale (Lila); dance reprise by Astaire and Marjorie Reynolds (Linda). Sung by Astaire both on the original sound track recording (Sunbeam Sountrak) and in *Song Hits from "Holiday Inn"* (Decca). This was actually the third number in the score. The second was "Lazy," sung by Bing Crosby (Jim).

I could dance nightly
Just holding you tightly, my sweet;
I could keep right on,
Because you're so light on my feet.*
You're easy to dance with.
There is no doubt in
The way we stand out in the crowd.
Though it's called dancing,
To me it's romancing out loud.
You're easy to dance with.
Loving you
The way I do
Makes you easy to dance with;
That is why I'm always right on the beat.
All those charms
In one man's arms
Make you easy to dance with;
I can hardly keep my mind on my feet.
Let's dance forever;
Come on, say we'll never be through—
It's so easy to dance with you.

WHITE CHRISTMAS

Published. Copyrighted May 6, 1942. Previously registered for copyright as an unpublished song December 4, 1940. Written in 1938 or 1939 either in New York or possibly at the Arizona Biltmore Hotel in Phoenix or perhaps in both places. Introduced by Bing Crosby (Jim) with Marjorie Reynolds, singing dubbed by Martha Mears (Linda); reprised by Reynolds/Mears and Crosby. Crosby and Mears sing it on the original sound track release (Sunbeam Soundtrak). Crosby's recording with the Ken Darby Singers on *Song Hits from "Holiday Inn"* (Decca), often rereleased, frequently number one on the popular music charts, is one of the best-selling recordings of all time and was Berlin's biggest hit. Winner of the Academy Award (Oscar) for Best Original Song of 1942.

As Berlin recalled in the Los Angeles *Examiner* (December 14, 1954):

I wrote it for a revue I intended producing, changed my mind and put it away until it was used in a Bing Crosby picture. At the time I had no idea "White Christmas" would be a perennial hit or that Paramount would add to its popularity with a movie of the same name.

*In the film this line was:
Because you're so light on your feet.

When the song first became popular, I attributed it to the War and the fact that Christmas means peace. I felt that since people were singing it I ought to write another verse. But I couldn't do it. New words would not come.

"Much as I'd like to take a bow and say I anticipated its future success, I must admit I didn't," Berlin told the Jamaica (Long Island) *Press* (September 24, 1954). "Maybe because it was so easy, comparatively, to write I didn't realize its potential. I wrote it in two rather brief sessions and that's fast for a song. Some take a lot more work."

According to Erskine Johnson (Los Angeles *Mirror*, December 21, 1954), the melody was written in August 1938, then left on the shelf for four years (actually two years) until Berlin was signed by Paramount to write *Holiday Inn*. Berlin told Johnson: "I took it off the shelf and polished the lyrics a little, and went to Bing's dressing room at Paramount to get his okay on all the songs for the picture. I was nervous as a rabbit smelling stew. I sang several melodies and Bing nodded quiet approval. But when I did 'White Christmas' he came to life and said 'Irving, you won't have to worry about that one.' "

"We didn't even think 'White Christmas' was the big song of the picture," Berlin told Earl Wilson (December 12, 1953). "We started exploiting 'Be Careful It's My Heart,' which was the Valentine song. But the public liked 'White Christmas' and it became a runaway. You see, a war song doesn't have to be about wars. This is really a peace song."

In December 1942 Carl Sandburg wrote the following for the Chicago *Times:*

> We have learned to be a little sad and a little lonesome without being sickly about it. This feeling is caught in the song of a thousand juke boxes and the tune whistled in streets and homes. "I'm Dreaming of a White Christmas." When we sing that we don't hate anybody. And there are things we love that we're going to have sometime if the breaks are not too bad against us. Way down under this latest hit of his Irving Berlin catches us where we love peace.

VERSE

The sun is shining,
The grass is green,
The orange and palm trees sway.
There's never been such a day
In Beverly Hills, L.A.
But it's December the twenty-fourth,
And I am longing to be up north.

CHORUS

I'm dreaming of a white Christmas
Just like the ones I used to know,
Where the treetops glisten
And children listen
To hear sleigh bells in the snow.
I'm dreaming of a white Christmas
With ev'ry Christmas card I write:
"May your days be merry and bright
And may all your Christmases be white."

HAPPY HOLIDAY and HOLIDAY INN

Two linked numbers written separately and combined. "Happy Holiday": Published. Copyrighted May 12, 1942. Previously registered for copyright as an unpublished song November 3, 1941. "Holiday Inn" was registered for copyright as an unpublished song May 2, 1942. The combined numbers were introduced by Bing Crosby (Jim), Marjorie Reynolds, singing dubbed by Martha Mears (Linda), and ensemble. They can be heard on the original sound track release (Sunbeam Sountrak). The recording by Crosby with the Music Maids is part of the album *Song Hits from "Holiday Inn"* (Decca).

Happy Holiday

Happy holiday,
Happy holiday—
While the merry bells keep ringing,
May your ev'ry wish come true.
Happy holiday,
Happy holiday—
May the calendar keep bringing,
Happy holidays to you.

Holiday Inn

Original version

VERSE

A strange idea kept lurking
In the mind of a strange young man;
To keep away from working,
He discovered a simple plan.
He found the means and found the ways

To only work on holidays,
So he turned his farm
To a house of charm
And he called it Holiday Inn.

CHORUS

If you're burdened down with trouble,
If your nerves are wearing thin,
Park your load down the road
And come to Holiday Inn.
If the traffic noise affects you
Like a squeaky violin,
Kick your cares down the stairs
And come to Holiday Inn.
If you can't find somebody who
Will set your heart awhirl,
Get in a car and motor to
"The home of boy-meets-girl."*
If you're laid up with a breakdown,
Throw away your vitamin—
Don't get worse,
Grab your nurse
And come to Holiday Inn.

Combined version

Happy holiday,
Happy holiday—
While the merry bells keep ringing,
May your ev'ry wish come true.
Happy holiday,
Happy holiday—
May the calendar keep bringing
Happy holidays to you.

If you're burdened down with trouble,
If your nerves are wearing thin,
Park your load down the road
And come to Holiday Inn.

If the traffic noise affects you
Like a squeaky violin,
Kick your cares down the stairs
And come to Holiday Inn.

Original version of lines 9–12:
    If you can't get the world's okays,
    [*or:* If you can't find the means and ways,]
    If you're a beaten thing,
    Just meet us here on holidays
    And join us when we sing:
    [*Segue directly to:*]
    Happy holiday, etc.

If you can't find somebody who
Will set your heart awhirl,
Get in a car and motor to
"The home of boy-meets-girl."

If you're laid up with a breakdown,
Throw away your vitamin—
Don't get worse, grab your nurse
And come to Holiday Inn.

Happy holiday,
Happy holiday—
While the merry bells keep ringing,
May your ev'ry wish come true.
Happy holiday,
Happy holiday—
May the calendar keep bringing
Happy holidays to you.

CUSTOMERS, I'M HERE TO GREET YOU

Unused. Two early versions of the number that became "Happy Holiday" and "Holiday Inn." Both versions were intended for Marjorie Reynolds, singing dubbed by Martha Mears (Linda) and Bing Crosby (Jim).

LINDA: Customers, I'm here to greet you
With a "Very pleased to meet you"
And an op'ning chorus to explain Holiday
    Inn.
A strange idea kept lurking
In the mind of a strange young man;
To keep away from working,
He thought of a plan.
While you worked, he would play,
But on every holiday,
While you were on a spree,
He'd be busy as a bee.
So he turned his farm to a house of charm,
Put his troubles on the shelf,
And thereby found the means and ways
To live the only life that pays
And only work on holidays—
And here's the guy himself.
JIM: Customers, I'm glad to see ye
With a very best "How be ye?"
And a first-class royal welcome to Holiday
    Inn.

Happy holiday,
Happy holiday—

While the merry bells keep ringing,
May your ev'ry wish come true.
Happy holiday,
Happy holiday—
May the calendar keep bringing
Happy holidays to you.

Version dated November 11, 1941

LINDA: Customers, we greet you
With a "Very pleased to meet you"
And an op'ning chorus you could do
    without,
But I've got to tell you what it's all about.

A strange idea kept lurking
In the mind of a strange young man;
To get away from working,
He thought of a brilliant plan.
While you worked, he would play;
When you laid off on a holiday,
His labors would begin.
So he turned his farm
To a house of charm
And called it Holiday Inn.
This fellow isn't crazy,
He hasn't got a quirk;
It's not because he's lazy—
He just don't like to work.
So his year consists of fifteen working
    days;
That's why this inn will only be opened on
    holidays.

From New Year's to Christmas,
When you come for a song and a laugh,
You'll be ably taken care of
By a most efficient staff.
Gus,
Who drives the bus,
Any holiday you come,
Will meet you at the station
To take you to and from.
Mamie, the cook,
Fries chicken by instinct,
Not by a book. And look,
A couple of youngsters;
They both belong to Mame:
Daphne and Vanderbilt—
Don't be fooled by the name.
Now a great big hand
For the Maestro and his band,
And a final curtain call
For the guy who thought of it all—
Jim.
We owe it all to him.

[JIM enters and sings.]

Customers, we greet you
With a "Very pleased to meet you"
And a royal welcome to Holiday Inn
And a "Happy holiday" before we begin.

Happy holiday,
Happy holiday—
While the merry bells keep ringing,
May your every wish come true.
Happy holiday,
Happy holiday—
May the calendar keep bringing
Happy holidays to you

[All join in second chorus to musical finish.]

LET'S START THE NEW YEAR RIGHT

Published. Copyrighted May 5, 1942. Previously registered for copyright as an unpublished song September 11, 1941. Introduced by Bing Crosby (Jim). Crosby's original sound track recording on Sunbeam Sountrak. Original cast studio recording by Crosby with Bob Crosby and His Orchestra (Decca).

VERSE

One minute to midnight,
One minute to go,
One minute to say goodbye
Before we say hello.

CHORUS

Let's start the New Year right—
Twelve o'clock tonight,
When they dim the light, let's begin
Kissing the old year out,
Kissing the new year in.
Let's watch the old year die
With a fond goodbye
And our hopes as high as a kite.
How can our love go wrong if
We start the New Year right?

ABRAHAM

Published. Copyrighted May 5, 1942. Previously registered for copyright as an unpublished song September 10, 1941. Written by June 9, 1941. Introduced by Bing Crosby (Jim), Louise Beavers (Mamie), Marjorie Reynolds, singing dubbed by Martha Mears (Linda), and ensemble. Sung by Crosby with the Ken Darby Singers on *Song Hits from "Holiday Inn"* (Decca).

Upon a February morn
A tiny baby boy was born—
Abraham, Abraham.
When he grew up, this tiny babe,
The folks all called him Honest Abe—
Abraham, Abraham.
In eighteen sixty he became
Our sixteenth President,
And now he's in the Hall of Fame,
A most respected gent.
And that is why we celebrate
This blessed February date—
Abraham, Abraham.

When black folks lived in slavery,
Who was it set the negro free?*
Abraham, Abraham.
When trouble came down from the shelf,
Whose heart was bigger than himself?
Abraham, Abraham.
"The country's going to the dogs!"
They shouted loud and strong;
Then from a cabin made of logs
The right man came along.
And that is why we celebrate
This blessed February date—
Abraham, Abraham.
The U.S.A.'s united thanks
To one whose name was Nancy Hanks—

Originally this couplet read:

When black folks lived in slavery
Who was it set the darky free?

The Baltimore Afro-American *objected, telling Berlin that "the term 'd———y' [is] offensive to colored people. The piece is sung by Bing Crosby . . . and came to the attention of the* Afro *after it was blatantly rendered in its naked aspect by Fred Waring." Berlin responded by changing "darky" to "negro" in all future printed copies of "Abraham." "No song is important enough to offend a whole race," Berlin told* Time *magazine (November 23, 1942). "I should never have released it had I known the epithet was objectionable."*

Abraham, Abraham.
She gave this land the finest son
Who ever went to Washington—
Abraham, Abraham.
When someone told him Gen'ral Grant
Was drinking ev'ry night,
He answered, "Go see if you can't
Get all my gen'rals tight."
And that is why we celebrate
This blessed February date—
Abraham, Abraham.

BE CAREFUL, IT'S MY HEART

Published. Copyrighted April 30, 1942. Previously registered for copyright as an unpublished song July 9, 1941. Introduced by Bing Crosby (Jim); danced by Fred Astaire (Ted) and Marjorie Reynolds (Linda). Crosby's original sound track recording appears on Sunbeam Sountrak. His original cast studio recording (Decca) was number two on the popular music charts for several weeks. Another leading recording was by Tommy Dorsey and His Orchestra (Victor), with vocals by Frank Sinatra.

VERSE

Sweetheart of mine,
I've sent you a Valentine.
Sweetheart of mine,
It's more than a Valentine.

CHORUS

Be careful, it's my heart.
It's not my watch you're holding,
It's my heart.
It's not the note I sent you
That you quickly burned;
It's not the book I lent you
That you never returned.
Remember, it's my heart,
The heart with which so willingly I part.
It's yours to take
To keep or break,
But please, before you start,
Be careful, it's my heart.

I CAN'T TELL A LIE

Published. Copyrighted June 5, 1942. Previously registered for copyright as an unpublished song August 9, 1941. Introduced by Fred Astaire (Ted); danced by Astaire and Marjorie Reynolds (Linda). Sung by Astaire on the album *Song Hits from "Holiday Inn"* (Decca).

I could say that you're homely,
Just as homely as pie;
But this is Washington's Birthday,
And I've got to say
You're beautiful,
'Cause I can't tell a lie.
I could say that you're stupid,
Nothing up in your crown;
But this is Washington's Birthday,
And the truthful he
Of the cherry tree
Would look down on me and frown.
I could say that I hate you if I try,
But I've got to say I love you,
'Cause it's February the twenty-second
And I can't tell a lie.

LET'S SAY IT WITH FIRECRACKERS

Published. Copyrighted June 5, 1942. Previously registered for copyright as an unpublished song under the title "Say It with Firecrackers" on October 22, 1941. Introduced by ensemble; danced by Fred Astaire (Ted). This number segued directly to "Song of Freedom."

VERSE

On this Day of Independence,
On this Independence Day,
Let's speak of our independence,
But no matter what we say—

CHORUS

Let's say it with firecrackers
And banners held high;
Let's have a real old-fashioned
Noisy Fourth of July.
Let's say it with firecrackers,
Down south and up north;
Let's have the kind we used to call

A glorious Fourth.
Let's salute our native land,
Roman candles in each hand,
While the Yankee Doodle band
Gets hotter than a firecracker.
Don't need any long speeches
Or shouts of hurray;
No words can say as much as
Firecrackers can say.

SONG OF FREEDOM

Published. Copyrighted July 8, 1942. Previously registered for copyright as an unpublished song March 5, 1942. Introduced by Bing Crosby (Jim) and ensemble. Original sound track recording by Crosby (Sunbeam Sountrak). Crosby and the Ken Darby Singers present the song on *Song Hits from "Holiday Inn"* (Decca).

VERSE

Freedom,
Freedom—
That's my song for today.
Listen to an American troubador
From the U.S.A.

CHORUS

I'm singing a song of freedom
For all the people who cry out to be free—
Free to sail the seven seas,
Free to worship as we please.
If the birds up in the trees can be free,
Why can't we?
I'm bringing a song of freedom
To all people, wherever they may be—
Free to speak and free to hear,
Free from want and free from fear.
Sons of freedom far and near who agree,
Sing with me
That all God's people shall be free.

PLENTY TO BE THANKFUL FOR

Published. Copyrighted October 6, 1942. Previously registered for copyright as an unpublished song under the title "I've Got Plenty to be Thankful For" on April 19, 1941. Typed lyric sheet dated March 10, 1941. Introduced by Bing Crosby (Jim). Crosby can be heard singing the song on the original sound track recording (Sunbeam Sountrak) and on *Song Hits from "Holiday Inn"* (Decca).

I've got plenty to be thankful for.
I haven't got a great big yacht
To sail from shore to shore;
Still, I've got plenty to be thankful for.
I've got plenty to be thankful for.
No private car, no caviar,
No carpet on my floor;
Still, I've got plenty to be thankful for.
I've got eyes to see with,
Ears to hear with,
Arms to hug with,
Lips to kiss with,
Someone to adore.
How could anybody ask for more?
My needs are small;
I buy them all
At the five-and-ten-cent store—
Oh, I've got plenty to be thankful for.*

---

*Original version of last four lines:
My tiny flat
Was furnished at
The five-and-ten-cent store—
Still, I've got plenty to be thankful for.

HOLIDAY INN—FINALE

Introduced by Bing Crosby (Jim), Fred Astaire (Ted), Virginia Dale (Lila), Marjorie Reynolds, singing dubbed by Martha Mears (Linda), and ensemble. A portion of the finale can be heard on the original sound track recording (Sunbeam Soundtrak).

JIM: Here she comes down the street.
TED: I'll admit my defeat.
JIM: I won my hot toddy.
TED: Over my scarred body.

JIM: I knew that I'd win, singing.
TED: But wait until she gets a load of
your dancing.
JIM: We'll stay at the inn, singing.
TED: All by myself, I'll have to stick to
my dancing.
LILA: Oh, no, my friend—I'm here to
end
Your dancing trouble and strife.
TED: This will be fun—Miss Hit-and-
Run
Has come back into my life.
JIM: We'll stay at the inn.
TED: We'll have to begin—
JIM: Singing.
TED: Dancing.
JIM: [to LINDA]
We've each other to cling to;*
You'll be easy to sing to.
TED: [to LILA]
And you're easy to dance with.

JIM &
LINDA: So let the old year die
With a fond goodbye
And our hopes as high as a kite—
How can our love go wrong, dear,
If we start the New Year right?

---

*Earlier version of this line through end of song:
JIM: We'll sing and they will dance—
While they're hoofing, we'll just romance.
They'll shake a nimble foot—
While they're traveling, we'll stay put,
For we'll have each other to cling to,
You'll be oh so easy to sing to.
TED: And you're easy to dance with.
[JIM *sings last half of* "Careful, It's My Heart" *to* LINDA *as* TED *dances with* LILA.]
[End.]

THIS IS A GREAT COUNTRY

Registered for copyright as an unpublished song December 21, 1940. Written aboard the *America* during a Caribbean cruise, November 10–21, 1940. Intended for *Holiday Inn*, first as a July Fourth song, and then either as a possible Labor Day or Columbus Day song. Not used in *Holiday Inn*. Two decades later a different song (words and music) with the same title was written for and used in Berlin's last musical, *Mr. President* (1962).

Berlin wrote at least four different versions of this song. The patter in this lyric was used later in the lyric to "The Freedom Train" (page 406).

VERSE 1 (FOURTH OF JULY)

Say that I am raving,
Speaking boastfully.
Say that I'm flag-waving.
That's all right with me,
For I know that you will have to agree.

VERSE 2 (LABOR DAY)

We have our quarrels in the U.S.A.
I fight with you and you with me.
But we're together on this Labor Day
Because we all of us agree.

VERSE 3 (COLUMBUS DAY)

Columbus landed in the U.S.A.
And found a home for you and me.
So let's not quarrel on Columbus Day,
Because we all of us agree.

VERSE 4

We don't always agree, we Americans.
Our minds differ on how things should go.
But deep down in our hearts we're Americans
And deep down in our hearts we all know.

CHORUS

This is a great country.
A great country,
And we're feeling O.K.
This is a great country,
A great country,
And we'll keep it that way
Over here—here in America.
Counting our blessings, we say,
This is a great country,
A great country.
And we'll weather the show'rs
'Til the skies clear and the sun shines
On this great country of ours.

Earlier version of chorus

This is a great country,
A great country,
And we're feeling O.K.
This is a great country,
A great country,
And we'll keep it that way.
You can shout your anger from a steeple.
You can say the system's full of holes.
You can always question "We the People."
You can get your answer at the polls.
This is a great country,
A great country,
And we'll weather the showers
'Til the sun shines on this great country of ours.

PATTER 1

You can shout your anger from a steeple.
You can say the system's full of holes.
You can always question "We the People."
You can get your answer at the polls.

PATTER 2

You can say, "I'm just one of the many."
You can say the system's got you down.
You can start without a single penny
And become the richest man in town.

PATTER 3

You can hate the laws that you're obeying.
You can yell your head off to the crowd.
They may disagree with what you're saying,
But they'll fight to let you say it loud.

PATTER 4

You can write your President a letter.
You can criticize him to his face.
If you think that you can do it better,
Next election you can take his place.

THIS IS THE ARMY | 1942

THIS IS THE ARMY (1942)

On March 11, 1942, Irving Berlin received a letter from the War Department in Washington asking him to consider a Broadway revival of his World War I show, *Yip, Yip, Yaphank*, to raise funds for Army Emergency Relief. The letter concluded:

> We believe your direction of and possible participation in such a project would insure its success. Your situation is unique in that you did during the last world war what we are asking you to do in this. Your experience and your position today would be of the greatest value to us. . . . We should like to discuss plans with you soon so that the project if you consider it favorably can get underway at the earliest possible moment. . . .

Berlin had already been exploring the possibility of such an undertaking, and in his reply of March 12, 1942, he wrote: "I am delighted to accede to your request and I need not assure you that I will give this all my time because nothing could be closer to my heart."

The end of April 1942 found Berlin back at Camp Upton, Long Island, where, as a sergeant in 1918, he had put on *Yip, Yip, Yaphank*. In a letter dated May 2, 1942, to Colonel H. C. Brenizer, he wrote: "First let me tell you how wonderful it is to be back at Upton and how much I appreciate the abundant hospitality of the officers and men. I am afraid all this attention will spoil me for my eventual return to civilian life."

"I am sure," he added, "you will be pleased to know that my writing on the show has come ahead with leaps and bounds. The entire structure is now complete and close to 50% of it is written. This I am sure has been largely due to the comfortable and inspirational surroundings so generously afforded by yourself. . . ."

Along with writing the show, Berlin took charge of all the other aspects of its production. The entire company, excluding Berlin, was recruited from army camps throughout the United States. The cast included a number of black performers, and thus the show was destined to become the first integrated army unit in the United States.

There is no clear indication of when Berlin came up with the title *This Is the Army*. Yet as early as March 12, 1942, he had written the following in a letter to a friend: "There has been some talk about doing a soldier show, but if it is done I am afraid we will have to forget about the *Yip Yip Yaphank* title. I went to Upton several times

---

Irving Berlin, "Oh, How I Hate to Get Up in the Morning"

and it isn't Yaphank any longer. Also it would have to be done nationally with soldiers from all camps. . . ." And the New York *Times* of April 5, 1942, wrote: "Irving Berlin this week will begin his labors for *This Is the Army*—the revival, plus, of *Yip Yip Yaphank*." In another article Berlin described the show as "the *Yip Yip Yaphank* formula brought up to date."

This Is the Army opened at the Broadway Theatre, New York, on July 4, 1942; 113 performances. Music and lyrics by Irving Berlin. Produced by the United States Army, in cooperation with Irving Berlin, for the benefit of Army Emergency Relief. Staged by Sergeant Ezra Stone. Dances directed by Private Robert Sidney and Corporal Nelson Barclift. Orchestrations uncredited. Orchestra under the direction of Corporal Milton Rosenstock.

Upon closing in New York on September 26, 1942, the show went on a national tour, which opened at the National Theatre in Washington, D.C., on October 1, 1942; President Franklin D. Roosevelt attended a special matinee. After Washington the show played in Pittsburgh, Philadelphia, Baltimore, Boston, Cleveland, Cincinnati, St. Louis, Detroit, Chicago, and Los Angeles; the tour ended in San Francisco, with a final performance on February 1, 1943.

The movie version of *This Is the Army* was filmed at Warner Bros. studios March through June 1943. It was produced by Jack L. Warner and Hal B. Wallis for Warner Bros. Directed by Michael Curtiz. Screenplay by Casey Robinson and Claude Binyon. Orchestral arrangements by Ray Heindorf. Musical direction by Leo F. Forbstein. The cast included George Murphy, Joan Leslie, Lieutenant Ronald Reagan, George Tobias, Alan Hale, Charles Butterworth, Dolores Costello, Una Merkel, Frances Langford, Gertrude Niesen, Kate Smith, Sergeant Joe Louis, and Irving Berlin. The film had its premiere on July 28, 1943. All profits from the movie went to the Army Emergency Relief Fund.

In January 1943 Berlin wrote to his lawyer, "Regarding the show going abroad, there has been and continues to be serious talk along those lines. As you know when we were in Washington the War Department and the White House thought we should finish the picture quickly and get overseas."

On November 10, 1943, *This Is the Army* opened in London at the Palladium, where it ran until November 27. The show then toured the United Kingdom (Glasgow, Manchester, Liverpool, Birmingham, Bristol, and Bournemouth) before returning to London for a command performance for General Dwight D. Eisenhower on February 6, 1944, at His Majesty's Theatre. In a letter of February 8, 1944, Eisenhower wrote the following to General George C. Marshall:

> Your great show *This Is the Army* has had its final performance here in the U.K. . . . It has

been a real success not only in sustaining a high morale but in cementing British-American friendship. . . . I am sure that the show under Irving Berlin has tremendous and continuing possibilities for showing to our troops in all theaters. . . . After seeing this show I feel that the 150 men who comprise this well-led, smoothly working team are of immeasurably greater value to our forces if held together rather than dissipated into groups of individual performers. . . .

Thus, with the encouragement of the general staff, the show entertained troops in different war zones. At times they were close to the battle line, as in Italy and the South Pacific. In other instances they performed in areas of logistical importance such as Egypt and Iran. The company was in Italy from February to July 1944, then went on to Egypt, Iran, New Guinea, and the Philippines. The final performance of the tour took place in Hawaii in late October 1945.

In 1945 President Harry S Truman presented Berlin with the Medal for Merit, with the accompanying citation:

> For the performance of extraordinary service to the United States Army in building and maintaining morale among soldiers and civilians, and in contributing generously of his talent for the support of the dependents of fighting men. Beginning in February, 1942, Mr. Berlin volunteered and gave his time, the facilities of his organizations, and the earnings of his genius for the benefit of Army Emergency Relief, all without remuneration. Having written the book and lyrics and composed the music for the review, *This Is the Army*, he assembled from various units of the Army a company of talented soldiers, perfected their organization, and personally staged the review. After the company had played a highly successful engagement in New York City, he accompanied it on a nation-wide tour. He then supervised the production of the film, *This Is the Army*. Having reorganized his company to meet the requirements of over-sea travel, he led its tour into six theaters of operation, taking his entertainment to hundreds of thousands of United States and British soldiers and contributing substantially at the same time to British War Relief. For more than three years Mr. Berlin devoted all of his time and energy to this project, with the result that more than six million dollars has been added to the funds of Army Emergency Relief. He has set a high standard of devotion to his country and has won for himself the thanks and appreciation of the United States Army for highly meritorious service.

OPENING (THE ARMY AND THE SHUBERTS DEPEND ON YOU)

Published in special vocal selections. Copyrighted October 8, 1942. Introduced by ensemble (Minstrel Men).

[*Spoken:*]
Men,
For the past four weeks
You've been drilled and trained
For a fight that must be won;
And now we meet on the battlefield
To see that the job is done.
Out there is your enemy;
There they sit with their hands in their laps—
Tougher than the Germans
And tougher than the Japs.
But they can be licked—it won't be easy;
They've paid to get in.
But this is a fight you've got to win,
And you'll win it.
Not because you're soldiers helping a worthy
     cause,
Not because you're in uniform,
Will they give you their applause;
But you've got to be good,
And you will be good,
If you meet them unafraid.
They're plenty tough,
But you've got the stuff
Of which soldier shows are made.
So up and at 'em
And on with the show,
But this in conclusion
Before I go:

[*Sung:*]
As actors you've a duty to the theatre,
As soldiers to the red, white, and blue,
So march right into battle and remember—
The army and the Shuberts depend on you.

OPENING CHORUS (SOME DOUGH FOR THE ARMY RELIEF)

Published in special vocal selections. Copyrighted October 8, 1942. Introduced by ensemble (Minstrel Men).

You thought that many, many years ago
You saw the last of ev'ry soldier show;
But here we are, yes, here we are again.
A lot of water's gone across the dam
Since we put makeup on for Uncle Sam.
To greet you as our fathers greeted you then
We were drafted by our President,
And we marched with banners unfurled;
We were drilled and trained to represent
The greatest army in the world—
Yes, the greatest army of actors in the world!
But don't get us wrong;
We're not here for long—
Our stay in the theatre is brief.
We're here with the show
To help get some dough,
Some dough for the Army Relief,
The much-needed Army Relief.
Oh, beneath the powder
And beneath the paint
There's a soldier brave and true;
If some guy in Congress
Tells you that we ain't,
Let him do what we had to do
And go through what we went through.

THIS IS THE ARMY, MISTER JONES

Published. Copyrighted June 23, 1942. Previously registered for copyright as an unpublished song February 28, 1942. Introduced by Privates Ross Elliot, Nicholas Sassi, Henry Jones, Charles Blake, Sydney Robin, William Roerick, Stanley Saloman, Kenneth Bates (Selectees), Private John Draper and Corporal Chester O'Brien (Guards), Private Alan Manson (Second Interlocutor), and ensemble (Minstrel Men).

"People have been asking me to write a new war song, a marching song," Berlin told the New York *Post* (July 19, 1943). "Well, I like 'This Is the Army, Mr. Jones.' It's certainly a marching song. You may not realize it is a so-called war song because it has a comedy twist. But thank heaven we are not a nation to take things so seriously that we ever give up our sense of humor." Leading recordings by the orchestras of Hal McIntyre (Victor) and Horace Heidt (Columbia).

VERSE

A bunch of frightened rookies
Were list'ning filled with awe;
They listened while a sergeant
Was laying down the law.

They stood there at attention,
Their faces turning red.
The sergeant looked them over,
And this is what he said:

CHORUS

This is the army, Mister Jones—
No private rooms or telephones;
You had your breakfast in bed before,
But you won't have it there anymore.
This is the army, Mister Green—
We like the barracks nice and clean;
You had a housemaid to clean your floor,
But she won't help you out anymore.
Do what the buglers command;
They're in the army and not in a band.
This is the army, Mister Brown—
You and your baby went to town;
She had you worried, but this is war,
And she won't worry you anymore.

I'M GETTING TIRED SO I CAN SLEEP

Published. Copyrighted June 18, 1942. Introduced by Private William Horne and an "Octette" consisting of Sergeant Zinn Arthur, Corporal James Burrell, and Privates Orville Race, James Farrell, Thomas Chetlin, William Collier, Earl Lippy, and Donald McCray. The idea for the song came from the *Yip, Yip, Yaphank* song "Dream On, Little Soldier Boy." Leading recording by Jimmy Dorsey and His Orchestra (Decca).

VERSE

Out on a hike all day, dear—
Part of the army grind.
Weary and long the way, dear,
But really I don't mind.

CHORUS

I'm getting tired so I can sleep;
I want to sleep so I can dream;
I want to dream so I can be with you.
I've got your picture by my bed;
'Twill soon be placed beneath my head
To keep me company the whole night through.
For a little while,
Whatever befalls,
I will see you smile
Till reveille calls.

I hope you're tired enough to sleep,
And please sleep long enough to dream,
And look for me, for I'll be dreaming too.

MY SERGEANT AND I ARE BUDDIES

Published. Copyrighted June 22, 1942. Introduced by Private Pinkie Mitchell with Private First Class James MacColl (End Man) assisted by Private Leonard Berchman and Private First Class Louis Salmon (Messenger). Dropped from the show after the U.S. tour.

VERSE

All the talk you've heard
Of sergeants being terrible,
I say it's absurd.
They really aren't terrible;
In fact they're just as nice as they can be—
At least there's one who's very nice to me.

CHORUS 1

My sergeant and I are buddies;
It's funny how well we mix.
He lets me sleep till half past five;
The others get up at six.
Whenever we're out together,
He lets me supply the gals.
I pay for ev'ry drink that we buy;
My sergeant and I are pals.

CHORUS 2

My sergeant and I are buddies;
He sticks to me like a stamp.
On Sunday when the boys go home
He lets me remain in camp.
I loaned him my car last weekend
To motor around with gals,
And in exchange he loaned me his tie;
My Sergeant and I are pals.

MY CAPTAIN AND I ARE BUDDIES

Earlier version of "My Sergeant and I Are Buddies."

VERSE

Every now and then
You hear about an officer
Bawling out his men
To prove that he's an officer;
But officers are nice as they can be—
At least there's one who's very nice to me.

CHORUS 1

My captain and I are buddies;
It's funny how well we mix.
He lets me sleep till half past five;
The others get up at six.
He watches me like a father;
He keeps me away from gals.
I give him all my pay—what's more,
He's saving it for me till after the war.
I couldn't deny
My captain and I are pals.

CHORUS 2

My captain and I are buddies;
It's funny how well we mix.
He lets me sleep till half past five;
The others get up at six.
He watches me like a father;
He keeps me away from gals.
He drills me till the sun has set
And drills me all evening so I won't forget.
I couldn't deny
My captain and I are pals.

DON'T SING, GO INTO YOUR DANCE

Introduced by Private Pinkie Mitchell and ensemble in the London presentation of *This Is the Army*, which began at the Palladium, November 10, 1943.

MITCHELL: I think I could sing like Crosby
If only I had the chance,
For I can sing as good as Bing.

COMPANY: But don't sing, go into your dance—
Don't sing, go into your dance.
MITCHELL: I've listened to Frank Sinatra;
His singing invites romance.
I sing like Sinatra—
COMPANY: We heard you—you stank.
So don't sing, go into your dance—
Don't sing, go into your dance.

I LEFT MY HEART AT THE STAGE DOOR CANTEEN

Published. Copyrighted June 15, 1942. Introduced by Corporal Earl Oxford and company. This number also featured Private First Class Louis Salmon and Private Ross Elliot (Guards), Corporal Philip Truex (Third Interlocutor), and Private Julie Oshins and Sergeant Ezra Stone (End Men). Leading recordings by Sammy Kaye and His Orchestra, vocal by Don Cornell (Victor), and Charlie Spivak and His Orchestra, vocal by Garry Stevens (Columbia).

VERSE

Old Mister Absentminded, that's me,
Just as forgetful as I can be.
I've got the strangest sort of a mind;
I'm always leaving something behind.

CHORUS

I left my heart at the Stage Door Canteen;
I left it there with a girl named Eileen.
I kept her serving doughnuts
Till all she had were gone;
I sat there dunking doughnuts
Till she caught on.
I must go back to the army routine—
And ev'ry doughboy knows what that will mean.
A soldier boy without a heart
Has two strikes on him from the start,
And my heart's at the Stage Door Canteen.

THE ARMY'S MADE A MAN OUT OF ME

Published. Copyrighted July 2, 1942. Introduced by Sergeant Ezra Stone, Corporal Philip Truex, and Private Julie Oshins.

VERSE

To look at me you wouldn't think
That I was once a skinny gink;
The doctors thought I never would last.
They thought I had so many ills,
And I was always taking pills,
But that is all a thing of the past.

CHORUS 1

The army's made a man out of me,
A man out of me,
A man out of me.
My mother and my father agree
The army has made me a man.
I used to sleep with brother,
But now I sleep alone.
I used to be a tenor,
But now I'm a baritone.
My girl said when she sat on my knee
The army has made me a man.

CHORUS 2

The Army's made a man out of me,
A man out of me,
A man out of me.
My mother and my father agree
The army has made me a man.
My mind was all confusion,
But now my mind is clear;
My face was like a baby,
But now I can raise a beard;
And I can drink a strong cup of tea—
The army has made me a man.

YIP, YIP, YAPHANKER'S INTRODUCTION

Published in the special vocal selections. Copyrighted October 9, 1942. Introduced by Peter O'Neill, Peter J. Burns, Dan Healy, John Murphy, Jack Riano, and Harold Kennedy, all former members of the *Yip, Yip,* *Yaphank* company of 1918. Dropped from *This Is the Army* at the end of its U.S. tour. It segued directly to Berlin singing, "Oh, How I Hate to Get Up in the Morning." That number remained in *This Is the Army* after "Yip, Yip, Yaphander's Introduction" was deleted.

No doubt you wonder why we're in this show
Dressed in these uniforms of long ago,
So kindly listen and we'll make it clear.
You've seen us in a soldier show before,
The *Yip, Yip, Yaphank* of the First World War,
And so we really have a right to be here.
When the call came for emergency,
We were for emergency too,
So we quickly came around to see
If there was something we could do—
That's the only reason we wished ourselves on
    you.
And so we are here,
We're here to appear
And dance in an old-fashioned scene.
We'd like you to see
The number that we were in
Back in nineteen eighteen.

LADIES OF THE CHORUS

Published in special vocal selections. Copyrighted October 9, 1942. Originally in *Yip, Yip, Yaphank*. Rewritten for *This Is the Army* (1942). Introduced by Privates Burl Ives, Alan Manson, Alfred Lane, Robert Moore, Anthony Ross, Scott Fansworth, Larry Weill, and Sydney Robin ("Girls") and Privates Edward O'Connor, Stanley Saloman, Richard Browning, Kenneth Bates, Richard Reeves, John Draper, Alan Bandler, and Daniel Longo ("Boys").

Ladies of the chorus,
That's what we are, it appears.
We were inducted and we took a vow;
We joined the army, but look at us now.
We're ladies of the chorus,
Dolled up as girls to our ears,
With cute golden tresses,
In corsets and dresses,
But don't get any strange ideas.

[*The* GIRLS *introduce themselves one by one:*]

I was a plumber;
I quit work last summer—
My number was picked at the start.
I was a printer;
I quit work last winter—
They okayed my lungs and my heart.
I was a barber;
I worked at Bar Harbor—
They sent me to camp with the rest.
I was a baker,
An angel-cake maker—
The army put hair on my chest.
I was a foreman
Of fifty longshoremen—
My office was down at the docks.
I was a burglar,
An alibi gurgler—
An expert at splitting up rocks.
I was a farmer
For Swift and for Armour—
My business was nursing a cow.
I was a packer;
I chewed plug Tobaccar—
I wish I had some of it now.

ALL: Now we're in the chorus,
    Poured into girdles that squeeze.
    We're here to romance with,
    To sing and to dance with,
    A bunch of dirty guys like these.
BOYS: Pardon me, but aren't you the farmer's
    daughter?
GIRLS: Pardon me, but aren't you the city chap?
BOYS: Cuddle closer if you please—
    I'm about to take a squeeze.
GIRLS: You do and I will give your face a slap.
BOYS: I would like to take you home to see my
    etchings.
GIRLS: I would love to, but my mother says I can't.
BOYS: They're the best you've ever seen.
GIRLS: But I'm only seventeen.
BOYS: If you're a seventeener, so's my aunt.
GIRLS: Heigh ho, it's very warm for May.
BOYS: Heigh ho, it's cooler in the hay.
    How about a little stroll up in the country?
GIRLS: If you promise to keep walking, I'd be
    glad.
BOYS: Let's go strolling through the wood.
GIRLS: But suppose you aren't good?
BOYS: If I'm not good, it really won't be bad.

THAT RUSSIAN WINTER

Published. Copyrighted June 15, 1942. Introduced by Pvt. Julie Oshins and ensemble. Dropped from the show during or after the U.S. tour.

VERSE

Tanks and bombers are needed to win the war;
Guns and rifles are part of an army corps.
Old Man Winter is greater than all of those;
Ask the man with the little mustache—he knows.

CHORUS

The German troops heard Hitler shout,
"We'll win this war without a doubt,"
But they were never told about
That Russian winter.
The German troops heard Hitler swear;
He puffed and puffed and tore his hair,
But somehow Hitler couldn't scare
That Russian winter.
There was the German staff running from the
    storm,
For Hitler's photograph couldn't keep them
    warm.
When Hitler cried, "This cannot be,"
Napoleon's ghost beneath a tree
Looked up and yelled, "You're telling me!"—
That Russian winter.

THAT'S WHAT THE WELL-DRESSED MAN IN HARLEM WILL WEAR

Published. Copyrighted July 6, 1942. Introduced by Sergeants Clyde Turner and Jack Brodmax, Corporals Orlando Johnson, Arthur Hatchett, George Anderson, and Earl Allen, and Privates John Johnson, John Riley, Randolph Culley, Steve Ramos, and George Watson. Specialties by Corporal James A. Cross and Privates Marion Brown and William Wyckoff.

VERSE

There's a change in fashion that shows
In the Lenox Avenue clothes:
Mister Dude has disappeared with his flashy tie;
You'll see in the Harlem *Esquire*

What the well-dressed man will desire
When he's struttin' down the street with his
    sweetie pie.

CHORUS

Suntan shade of cream
Or an olive-drab color scheme—
That's what the well-dressed man in Harlem will
    wear.
Dressed up in ODs
With a tin hat for overseas—
That's what the well-dressed man in Harlem will
    wear.
Top hat, white tie and tails no more;
They've been put away till after the war.
If you want to know,
Take a look at Brown Bomber Joe—
That's what the well-dressed man in Harlem will
    wear.

HOW ABOUT A CHEER FOR THE NAVY?

Published. Copyrighted June 15, 1942. Introduced by the entire company. This number is not listed in programs for the show. According to Alan Manson, a member of the company, it was Berlin's idea to omit the song from the program; he wanted the audiences to be surprised when they heard it.

CHORUS 1

The army this, the army that,
Is all we heard from where we sat;
Now how about a cheer for the navy?
The army's great, the army's tough,
But don't you think we've heard enough?
So how about a cheer for the navy?
We know that Mister Stimson
Is solid as the rocks,
But how about an orchid
For Secretary Knox?*

According to Ben Washer's diary (May 5, 1944), Berlin replaced the Stimson-Knox lines with the following lines. Washer was the personal assistant to Berlin and press agent for the European tour of the show.

    A soldier is surrounded
    By girls of every sort;
    But remember that a sailor
    Has one in every port.

The army may be in the groove,
But Walter Winchell won't approve
Unless you give a cheer for the navy.
Hip, hip, hooray!
We haven't got long to stay,
So how about one bouquet for the navy?
One word of praise,
Let it flow from your lips;
One cheer and then
We'll go back to our ships.
Hip, hip, hooray!
The army has had its say;
You're letting them get away
With the gravy.
Just let them know
That an army show
Could never be a hit without the navy.

Material added for film version

CHORUS 2

COMPANY: The army's what you may prefer,
        But in the Social Register
        Is where you'll have to look for the
            navy.
        If you would like to touch the gilt
        Of Astor or of Vanderbilt,
        You'll have to come around to the navy.
        The show was in the alley;
        It simply wouldn't do
        Until the big finale
        Was navy, white and blue.
        The army sails across the foam;
        The navy always brings them home—
        So how about a cheer for the navy?
SAILORS: Hip, hip, hooray!
        The army has had its say;
        So how about one bouquet
        For the navy?
        Just let them know
        That an army show
        Could never be a hit
        Without the nay-ay-vee,
        The nay-ay-vee—
        The show could never click without
        The N-A-V-Y,
        The nay-ay-ay-veeeee.

OPENING OF ACT II (JANE COWL NUMBER)

Published in special vocal selections. Copyrighted October 9, 1942. Originally the fourth number in Act II. By the start of the national tour it had become the Act II opening. Introduced by Private Alan Manson (Jane Cowl), Sergeant Ezra Stone (Sergeant), Private First Class Joe Cook Jr. (Joe Cook), Corporal Nelson Barclift (Vera Zorina), Private Hayden Rorke (Noël Coward), Private Julie Oshins (Gypsy Rose Lee), Private Tileston Perry (Lynn Fontanne), Private First Class James Mac-Coll (Alfred Lunt), Private Louis De Milhau (Eileen), Corporal Earl Oxford (Soldier), Private Charles Blake and Corporal Chester O'Brien (Mirror Girls), and ensemble (Hostesses and Stage Door Canteen Soldiers).

HOSTESSES: Merrily we appear on the scene,
Hostesses of the Stage Door Canteen,
Sponsored by a lady with the wisdom
of an owl,
Waiting for instructions from our
Captain Cowl.
MISS COWL: Good evening, ladies.
HOSTESSES: Good evening, Miss Cowl.
MISS COWL: Tonight's a special occasion,
So be espec'lly bright:
The cast of *This Is the Army*
Will be our guest tonight.
They must have fun,
But don't be fools—
It must be done
According to the rules.
A hostess mustn't dance too long
With any one man.
Don't congregate in groups;
Spread out as much as you can.
You mustn't eat the food;
It's not intended for you.
The Theatre Wing's responsible for
what you do.
If a soldier boy looks tired, suggesting
slumber,
Make his coffee stronger—
You know what I mean.
And if he should ask you for your
telephone number,
You must change the subject
And keep it clean.
When meeting on the street,
You mustn't linger too long:
A hostess may be weak;
The army has to be strong.
You must obey the rules
That your profession demands;

The honor of the Theatre Wing
Is in your hands.
You must be ladies.
HOSTESSES: Don't worry, Miss Cowl.
Merrily we appear on the scene,
Hostesses of the Stage Door
Canteen,
Entertaining soldiers who are going
off to war,
Glad to be of service,
But we could do much more.
We could do more for the boys
And greatly add to their joys,
But we don't get very far;
The rules and regulations are
We mustn't be seen
Outside the canteen with a soldier.
We know that
They each could do with a gal;
'Twould greatly help their morale.
But we simply must resist;
We take an oath when we enlist
To answer the call
But never give all to a soldier.
The boys may want to be kissed,
But we have got to resist.
We can go and have a fling
With some guy in the Theatre
Wing
But never be found
Canoodling around with a
soldier.

AMERICAN EAGLES

Published. Copyrighted July 23, 1942. Introduced by ensemble (Ground Crew).

Eagles,
American Eagles—
America sings
Of her wings
In the sky.
Eagles,
American Eagles—
America's strong
Just as long
As they fly.
More bombers to attack with,
More bombers till the skies are black with,
Eagles,
American Eagles—
America sings

Of her kings
In the sky.

WITH MY HEAD IN THE CLOUDS

Published. Copyrighted June 18, 1942. Introduced by Private Robert Shanley and ensemble (Air Pilots).

VERSE

What does a flyer think of
When he's up there in the sky?
Ask any army pilot
And he'll answer with a sigh:

CHORUS

While I'm there in the air
With my head in the clouds,
I think of someone I love,
And I know down below
She is thinking of me
While I am up there above.
When the night is clear
And the bombardier
Drops a bomb that's wired for sound,
How I yearn to return
With my head in the clouds
To the one I love on the ground.

ARYANS UNDER THE SKIN

Published in special vocal selections under the title "Jap-German Sextette." Copyrighted October 9, 1942. Previously registered for copyright December 23, 1941, under the title "Welcome, Yellow Aryans." Introduced by Corporal Philip Truex and Privates Robert Moore, Pinkie Mitchell, and Arthur Atkins (Japs) and Privates Richard Reeves, Norman VanEmburgh, Burl Ives, and Roger Kinne (Germans). This song was dropped from the show some time during the New York run. It had been written around the time Berlin was working on the score for the film *Holiday Inn*. In a letter of December 22, 1941, to its director, Mark Sandrich, Berlin wrote: "You probably read the official announcement from Goebbles [sic], that the Japs were a pure race and therefore Goebbles considered them 'Yellow Aryans.' It suggested the following song. Have Bobby [probably

Holiday Inn's conductor, Robert Emmett Dolan] play it for you. If you like it, we may be able to create a new Holiday—say 'Aryan Day,' and use it in the picture."

JAPS: Six little Japanese from Tokyo—
GERMANS: Six little German Fräuleins from
         Berlin—
ALL: We were told to get together
    For a talk about the weather;
    We'll be out all night,
    But it's quite all right—
    We're Aryans under the skin.
JAPS: Six Japanese are knocking at your door.
GERMANS: Six German maids are glad to let you in.
JAPS: We are proud to take our places
    With the purest of races.
    You may rest with ease
    On our Japanese knees—
    We're Aryans under the skin.
GERMANS: We used to go out with Italians,
    But that was before the war;
    We don't ever see the Italians—
    They're not Aryans anymore.
ALL: Hitler and Hirohito said okay,
    And what our leaders tell us, we obey.
    There's a shining dagger neath each
       coat,
    And till they cut each other's throat
    We'll sing our song of sin,
    Aryans under the skin.

A SOLDIER'S DREAM

Introduced by Private Stewart Churchill and ensemble led by Sergeant Arthur Steiner (Sergeant) and including "Soldiers," "Gypsy Violinists," "Valets," "Waitresses," and "Dream Girls."

What does a soldier dream of
When he wearily goes to bed?
Of a shady nook, a babbling brook,
And a blue sky overhead?
Of a fireside and a mother
When the evening lamp is lit?
Is that what a soldier dreams of?
Not a goddamn bit!
But here's what runs through his head
When he wearily goes to bed.

[*Sketch follows.*]

THIS TIME (CLOSING)

Published under the title "Closing" in the special vocal selections. Copyright October 9, 1942. Introduced by the entire company. This number was derived from "This Time," written earlier in 1942. (See "This Time," page 374.)

[*Spoken:*]
Men!
For the past two hours you have battled on,
And the foe is weary and tired.
So now we come to the end of the fight,
When the final shot must be fired.

[*Sung:*]
As actors we have tried to entertain you,
But soon our days of acting will be done;
And we are not forgetting that we're soldiers,
And there's a final battle that must be won.
And this time we will make certain
That this time is the last time;
This time we will not say "Curtain"
Till we ring it down in their own hometown,
For this time
We are out to finish
The job we started then,
Clean it up for all time this time,
So we don't have to do it again.

VE DON'T LIKE IT

Published. Copyrighted March 8, 1943. Introduced on ABC's *Lux Radio Theater* broadcast of *This Is the Army* in February 1943. According to various newspaper articles, Berlin got the idea for this song while lunching with Cecil B. De Mille; they talked about Goebbels whining about Nazi reverses on the Russian front and the reaction of the German people. "I'll bet they don't like it," remarked De Mille.

VERSE

Herr Doktor Goebbels
Is on the air today.
Let's tune in and get Berlin
And hear what he has to say.

CHORUS 1

Ven the Russians push us back,
Ve don't like it.
In the vinter they attack;
Ve don't like it.
Ven they called us ruthless murderers,
Ve didn't make a fuss;
But now they're invading—
They can't do that to us!
Casablanca's full of Yanks;
Ve don't like it.
They've got ships und planes und tanks;
Ve don't like it.
Vile ve're vinning as ve should,
Hitler speaks,
Und das ist gut!
But ven Hitler don't make speeches,
Ve don't like it.

CHORUS 2

Ven the RAF begin,
Ve don't like it.
Ven they fly above Berlin,
Ve don't like it.
Ven they showered us mit paper,
Vy, ve didn't make a fuss;
But bombs mit explosives,
They can't do that to us!
Ev'ry cupboard here is bare;
Ve don't like it.
Und ve've got no clothes to vear;
Ve don't like it.
Hermann Goering had to speak
In the same suit tvice last veek;
Und ven Goering can't change costumes,
Ve don't like it.

CHORUS 3

Ven the German troops retreat,
Ve don't like it.
Ven the allied nations meet,
Ve don't like it.
They've got soldiers who are not afraid
Of Heinie, Fritz, und Gus.
That's not how ve planned it—
They can't do that to us!
In Japan our hands are tied;
Ve don't like it.
Mussolini's on our side;
Ve don't like it.
Und ve cannot come to terms
Mit the French, the dirty vorms,
For it seems the vorms are turning—
Ve don't like it.

WHAT DOES HE LOOK LIKE (THAT BOY OF MINE)?

Published. Copyrighted April 26, 1943. Written in March 1943. Introduced by Frances Langford in the film version of *This Is the Army*.

VERSE

Johnny Doughboy overseas,
Filled with pride and joy,
Stopping ev'ryone he meets
And shouting, "It's a boy!"

CHORUS

What does he look like,
That boy of mine?
Since the news came,
I can't get him off my mind.
Does he resemble
His homely dad?
Does he look like the girl that I left behind?
Bring on the Germans
And bring on the Japs,
Bring on the first two you can find—
One for the rascal
I haven't seen
And one for the girl that I left behind.

DRESSED UP TO KILL and DRESSED UP TO WIN

Dressed Up to Kill

Written to be part of the finale of the film version.

We're dressed up to kill,
We're dressed up to kill,
We're dressed up for Victory.
We don't like killing,
But we won't stop killing
Till the world is free.

Dressed Up to Win

Because of objections to the word "kill," Berlin changed the lyric, which was used as part of the "This Time" closing of the film.

Dressed up to win,
We're dressed up to win,
Dressed up for Victory.
We are just beginning,
And we won't stop winning
Until the world is free.

OFFICER'S SPEECH

Written during 1943. No music is known to survive.

Men,
You joined this show
Many months ago
For a job you thought would be brief.
The towns you played
And the movie you made
Will earn millions for army relief.
So far it's been wonderful,
But now that's done and you're here overseas
To play for a bunch that is hard to please,
And they'll have to be shown.
It won't be easy. They're getting it free.
And something for nothing, you must agree,
Is viewed with suspicion.
They know that you've been busy
Helping a common cause,
But that's no earthly reason
To give you their applause.
So you've got to be good,
And you will be good,
If you meet them unafraid.
They're plenty tough
But you've got the stuff
Of which soldier shows are made.
So up and at 'em
And on with the show,
But this in conclusion
Before I go—

'Twas easy when you entertained civilians
They sympathised and so you couldn't miss.
But now you're out here doing it for soldiers
And Heaven help an actor on a night like this.

ENGLAND AND AMERICA

Typed lyric sheet dated October 12, 1943. No music is known to survive. A forerunner of "My British Buddy."

England and America
Standing side by side,
Bound together with ancient ties
That the oceans can't divide.
Brighter days for all of us;
All men will be free
Long as England and America
Clasp hands across the sea.

THE KICK IN THE PANTS

Published. Copyrighted October 13, 1943. Added to Act II during the overseas tour. Introduced by Private Max Showalter at the Palladium, London, November 10, 1943. Later sung by Sergeant Zinn Arthur and ensemble. According to Ben Washer's diary of the tour, Berlin wrote new lyrics for the song when the show was presented at the Allied Military Theatre in Santa Maria, Italy.

VERSE

We Carioca'd,
We Continentaled,
And we Charlestoned for a while;
We Black-Bottomed and Eagle-Rocked
While those dances were in style.
But now prepare for the very latest dance—
It's in the air, and it's called
The Kick in the Pants.

CHORUS

Norway, Denmark, and Holland,
Poland, Belgium, and France,
They're holding steady,
Getting ready
To do the Kick in the Pants.
Out there in the Pacific,
They just wait for the chance;
They aren't cursing,
Just rehearsing
To do the Kick in the Pants.
Mister Tojo, if you please,
Step out in the light,
Bend down on your Japan knees—

That's our target for tonight.
Grab a Jap or a German;
Point your toe and advance:
The happy ending,
Catch 'em bending
And do the Kick in the Pants.

MY BRITISH BUDDY

Published. Copyrighted November 12, 1943. Introduced by Irving Berlin November 9, 1943, at a previous performance of *This Is the Army* at the Palladium, London. The song remained in the show during the United Kingdom tour only. Recorded by Berlin November 22, 1943 (H.M.V.). According to the *London Daily Mail* of November 9, 1943, "My British Buddy" was inspired by a stroll in Piccadilly one evening when Berlin saw groups of British and Americans waiting in movie queues together. The song was written the next day. Berlin told the *Daily Mail:* "I hope the song will be a big hit, not only because of the money it will bring into the British services, but because it means something more to me. I want it to bring about a still closer relationship between our two countries."

VERSE

I just read a letter from across the foam
Written by a doughboy to his folks back home.
He told them of the army life he led,
And speaking of the British boys, he said:

CHORUS 1

My British buddy,
We're as diff'rent as can be;
He thinks he's winning the war,
And I think it's me.
But we're in there pitching,
And on one thing we agree:
When the job is done
And the war is won,
We'll be clasping hands across the sea.

CHORUS 2

My British buddy,
We're as diff'rent as can be;
I like my coffee and rolls,
And he likes his tea.
But we're in there pitching
Till we get to Germany,
When we've licked the Hun

And the Japs are done,
We'll be clasping hands across the sea.

DADDY'S COMING HOME ON A FURLOUGH

Introduced in the overseas tour of *This Is the Army* by Privates First Class Ray Goss and Frank d'Elia and Private William MacIllhargey (Children) in a scene that also featured Private Julie Oshins (Their Daddy), Corporal William Roerich (Their Mommy), Corporal Hank Henry (Her Mommy), and ensemble (WACs). First sung at the Palladium, London, November 10, 1943.

Daddy's coming home on a furlough;
Daddy's coming home on a pass.
Daddy doesn't realize
There will be a big surprise;
He'll wish he were a couple of other guys.
After Daddy's through with his furlough,
He must sail away 'cross the foam;
He'll be glad to meet a bomb
When he takes a look at Mom—
There'll be hell when Daddy comes home.

REPRISE

After Daddy's through with his furlough,
He must sail away 'cross the foam.
He will sail without a fuss;
There are only three of us—
There'll be four when Daddy comes home!

Wartime Journal

JANUARY–FEBRUARY 1944

Irving Berlin seldom kept a diary or journal. Yet when the *This Is the Army* company toured the United Kingdom (November 1943–February 1944), Berlin jotted down some impressions over a two-week period that began in Belfast, Northern Ireland, on January 30, 1944, and ended in mid-February on an ocean liner in the Atlantic on his return to the United States.

One high spot was a two-day reunion in Dublin with the great tenor John McCormack (1884–1945), Ireland's "Ambassador of Song." Over the years, McCormack had

sung some Berlin songs, and he made a memorable recording of "All Alone" (see page 226) in 1924. "I hadn't seen John for many years," Berlin wrote in his journal, and "I was deeply touched by his welcome. At the cocktail party, McCormack played a record he had made of 'God Bless America' [and] we spent a very pleasant evening reminiscing and speaking of old times." McCormack suffered from emphysema and died less than two years after Berlin's visit.

The next day, January 31, Berlin spent a half hour with Eamon De Valera (1882–1975), the U.S.-born prime minister and later president of the Republic of Ireland. Among the people they spoke about were Victor Herbert and George M. Cohan.

The following morning Berlin traveled to London via airplane and train. The main purpose of his London visit was a special performance of *This Is the Army* given on the afternoon of February 6 for General Dwight D. Eisenhower (1890–1969) at His Majesty's Theatre. "I was brought to General Eisenhower's box during intermission," Berlin wrote,

and met him for the first time. He wanted to know all about the show and the boys and told me how much he liked the first act. He asked me to tell the boys that he thought it was grand. . . . After the second act, General Eisenhower was so enthusiastic that he asked to come back and speak to the boys. . . . With all the many great men and women who have come backstage to see us since the show opened, this was the real high spot. We were all so moved and emotional I could think of nothing to say as an introduction, so just sputtered out, "Boys," and then pointing to the General I said, "General Eisenhower."

He put the boys at their "ease" and then made the most inspirational talk that had been made up to that time. We all regretted that there wasn't someone there who could have recorded his speech. In substance, he said that he wasn't going to tell us how great a show we had, we knew all that and he expected it, but he did want to tell the men of what a grand job they were doing. He said that if there was anyone who had any doubts as to how important he was as a soldier he should ease his mind of those doubts. He continued this particular angle, which of course meant more to the boys in *This Is the Army* than anything that could possibly have been said to them. He closed his talk with "It's a great show. You're doing a great job. And what is more, you're fine soldiers." When he finished, the boys were called to attention and he left.

The next day, February 7, Eisenhower arranged to give Berlin a photo with the following inscription: "To Irving Berlin— With my lasting appreciation for the great job he has done in the United Kingdom with his show THIS IS THE ARMY." Berlin was thrilled. Berlin was then told that General Eisenhower had decided to recommend to Army Chief of Staff General George C. Marshall that *This Is the Army* should tour the world and Berlin should lead the tour.

It was during his London visit that Berlin also met General James Doolittle, commander of the Eighth Air Force in its assaults on Germany, and William (Wild Bill) Donovan, chief of the Office of Strategic Services.

On February 9, Berlin was invited to lunch with British Prime Minister Winston Churchill (1874–1965). Their meeting is remembered for being one of the most amusing anecdotes of mistaken identity. Churchill apparently believed he was having lunch with Isaiah Berlin (1909–1987), the Riga-born liberal philosopher. While the meeting was recorded by Churchill's secretary Jack Colville, Irving Berlin's account follows:

Wednesday, February 9th: I arrived at 10 Downing Street at one-twenty-five (the lunch was for one-thirty). I was ushered into the Prime Minister's private sitting room on the ground floor. Mrs. Churchill received me. The guests had not arrived. Soon they all came—I think about ten of them.

Mrs. Churchill introduced me to her guests, but, as usual, I failed to get their names. There was a British officer (a General I think), a Lady Somebody, a young girl, her cousin, and two other men, one of them a member of the Cabinet, and another woman.

Mr. Churchill soon came in, dressed in his "zipper" suit. We were served some Sherry and then went in to lunch. The British Officer sat at Mrs. Churchill's right, and I sat between her cousin and the Lady Somebody. Mr. Churchill sat on the other side of her.

During lunch, Mr. Churchill did most of the talking, and it was interesting to note how Mrs. Churchill helped things along by asking the questions. He held forth on early British history and was very amusing in portions of it that were not too complimentary to the British.

I spoke to Mrs. Churchill's cousin about the show and what we had done in the provinces. We also discussed the ENSA, the British Service Shows organization.

At one point Mr. Churchill turned and asked me what reaction I got during the tour through the provinces. I didn't quite know what he meant, so I made a general answer about how well we were received, etc. We discussed the amount of money earned for British Service Charities. He heard the figure wrong. I told him of the song I had written, "My British Buddy." He thought I said "My British Brother." We then talked about Anglo-American relationship where the soldiers were concerned and he said that the most impor-

tant complaint was the difference in pay. I said casually that it was a little thing compared to the all-over picture of winning the war, and he disagreed saying that there were only so many things to buy in the stores and there are only so many girls. He added that he tried to do something about it—to have the British Government raise the pay of the British soldier and to have the American Government hold back some of the pay of our boys—but he failed. He said that there was always a complaint about differences in soldiers' pay, even during the last war when the British got more than the French.

After lunch the women left the dining room and we stayed behind for coffee. Mr. Churchill asked me to move over next to him. He turned and very abruptly asked what I thought of the political situation in America. I was fussed and told him very frankly that I knew little about politics, but he seemed interested to know how I felt about the election. I told him that if Mr. Roosevelt wanted to be our next president, he would be elected; that instinctively I felt that most people would vote for him. I turned and asked him whether he didn't think so, and he said, quite seriously, "I'm not allowed to say." He asked about Dewey's chances and said that he had a good name. I gathered that he referred to his name being the same as that of Admiral Dewey. I said, "Speaking of that name, you remember what happened to Admiral Dewey." He immediately knew I was referring to the incident of Admiral Dewey putting the house which was given to him by public subscription in his wife's name and the criticism that resulted from this act. He told me that Peter Finley Dunne wrote a piece about it. I told him that of all the Republican candidates I thought Willkie had the best chance. He felt that Willkie had been anti-British for the past year and a half. At one point he asked me whether they still felt that the war would be over in 1944. I didn't realize he meant the American people and thought he was asking me that question. I looked at him and said, "This is something for my grandchildren—to have the Prime Minister of Britain ask me when the war will be over." He smiled at this. He asked me how I felt about the Zionist movement. I told him I knew very little about it and then proceeded to tell him the Belfast incident of the Jewish gentleman who came to me with an Irish brogue, and after he had told me that there were only 300 Jewish families in Belfast, I said, "Then there surely can be no Jewish problem here." He answered, "Oh, no. We have no problem. But we have a big job an our hands patching things up between the Catholics and the Protestants." I think he was amused at this story.

All in all, he was very pleasant and I was, of course, delighted to have had this opportunity to

sit and talk with him, but disappointed that we couldn't have spoken a little more about *This Is the Army* and the tour through the provinces. Perhaps it was my fault in not telling him more about it.

After we joined the ladies in the sitting room, Mr. Churchill left. In saying goodbye to me he said, "Well, you didn't answer any of my questions and I don't think you had a chance to ask any." He said this with a twinkle. The rest of the guests were leaving and I, too, thanked Mrs. Churchill and left.

Two days later, February 11, Berlin, having traveled by train from London to Glasgow, Scotland, was on an ocean liner with, among others, William Donovan, heading back to the United States.

THE FIFTH ARMY IS WHERE MY HEART IS

Published. Copyrighted June 10, 1944. Introduced by Irving Berlin at the Allied Military Theatre, Santa Maria, Italy, April 20, 1944. On May 14, 1944, when Berlin sang the song on the Fifth Army's Mobile Expeditionary Radio Station, General Mark Clark announced that it had been dedicated to the Fifth Army.

VERSE

I met her in America about a month ago;
She asked me if I'd give her love
To a certain GI Joe.
She said, "When he returns, I'll be his bride";
I asked her where he was, and she replied:

CHORUS 1

"Not the First, not the Second,
Not the Third, not the Fourth,
But the Fifth Army's where my heart is.
He's somewhere on a beachhead,
Which must be lots of fun.
I can see him in a bathing suit
Basking in the sun.
From a cute signorina he's been learning
To talk like a real native of Rome;
She's a very tasty dish,
But my baby no capish
Till the Fifth Army comes home."

CHORUS 2

Not the First, not the Second,
Not the Third, not the Fourth,
But the Fifth Army's where my heart is.
We landed in Salerno
And kept right on the go
As we fought our way through Napoli
Into Anzio.
Mile by mile we've been soldiering
The hard way, it seems,
On the road leading to Rome;
And without a single doubt
There'll be things to shout about
When the Fifth Army comes home.

WHAT ARE WE GOING TO DO WITH ALL THE JEEPS?

Published. Copyrighted November 6, 1944. Previously registered for copyright as an unpublished song August 31, 1944. According to Ben Washer's diary, Berlin got the idea for the song while driving from Santa Maria to the 56th Station Hospital and back April 24, 1944. He sang the song for the first time at a party in Naples, May 6–7, 1944. According to Washer's diary, Berlin worked on new lyrics in Bari, July 14–16, 1944. The song was originally titled "When the Boys Come Home." Published. Copyrighted August 28, 1944.

VERSE

The men who fight the war until it's won
Are making plans for when the job is done.
They all agree that it will be a task,
But here are sev'ral questions that they ask.

CHORUS 1

What are we gonna do with all the jeeps?
Thinking about the jeeps gives us the creeps.
What'll the army do with our old mess kits?
How will you squeeze your foot into a shoe that fits?
Where will we put the army blankets when
Fellows begin to sleep in sheets again?
How will we use the flannels
That we got through army channels
When the boys come home?

CHORUS 2

Who's gonna eat the meat that comes in cans?
Millions of soldier boys have other plans.
How will we use the junk that we all sent back,
Beautiful silver souvenirs that soon turned black?
How will we have the heart to say farewell
To signorina and to mad'moiselle?
How will you tell your Mary
Of that walking dictionary
When the boys come home?

CHORUS 3

What are we gonna do with all the chaps,
Strategists who were busy reading maps?
How will we use the gents who were never there,
Fellows who talked invasion from a rocking chair?
What are we gonna do with all the bars,
All of the leaves, the eagles, and the stars?
How will we face conditions
In a world without commissions
When the boys come home?

Alternate version of chorus 2

What'll we do with all the empty cans?
Where will we burn the papers filled with plans?
How will we use the junk that we all sent back,
Beautiful silver souvenirs that soon turned black?
What are we gonna do with all the bars,
All of the leaves, the eagles, and the stars?
How will we face conditions
In a world without commissions
When the boys come home?

Additional lyric about Spam

What are we gonna do with all the Spam,
Where will it go and who will give a damn?
What are we gonna do with all the jeeps?
Speaking about the jeeps gives me the creeps.
How'll we use the guys who were never there,
Fellows who talked invasion in a rocking chair?
What are we gonna do with all the bars,
All the leaves, the eagles and the stars?
How'll we face conditions
In a world without commissions*
When the boys come home?

For special stag audiences there was a line:
  What'll we tell relations about prophylactic stations?

THERE ARE NO WINGS ON A FOXHOLE

Published. Copyrighted August 14, 1944. Written in Santa Maria, Italy, and introduced by Irving Berlin on the *This Is the Army* company's opening night at the Rome Opera House, June 15, 1944. Presented to General George C. Marshall and dedicated to the infantrymen of the U.S. Army.

There are no wings on a foxhole
If it's where you happen to be.
While the shells are flying,
It's doing or dying
For the men of the infantry.
There are no wheels on your tootsies
When you march from night till the dawn.
Twenty miles of hiking
Is not to your liking,
But the foot soldier marches on;
From the night till the dawn
The foot soldier marches on.
There's a sharp end on your rifle
When you're close to your enemy;
At that close-up meeting
There is no retreating
For the men of the infantry.

MISSES THE ARMY

Written by Berlin for the 6719th WAC Headquarters Platoon, Foggia, Italy, July 8, 1944. Penned earlier that day on a beach near Foggia.

This is the army, Miss McCloud—
No dates with officers allowed.
There's a lieutenant with nice blue eyes;
You can look but you can't fraternize.
This is the army, Miss O'Day—
If he's your cousin it's okay.
Pick out a cousin with lots of charm;
Take him out, but don't walk arm in arm.
Don't kiss your date in the street
Come in the lobby and get off your feet.
This is the army, Miss Lamarr—
Two WACs at least in every car.
You are a private, but this is war,
And there's no privacy anymore.

COZY LITTLE FOXHOLE BY THE SEA

Introduced by Irving Berlin at the 55th Station Hospital, Foggia, Italy, July 10, 1944.

In my cozy little foxhole on the beachhead,
In my comfy little haven by the sea,
I'm as lonely, just as lonely, as can be
With your pinned-up picture looking down at me.
How I miss you while I'm waiting till it's over,
Finding comfort in a pleasant memory!
With my rifle aimed at Jerry
I am trying to be merry
In my foxhole by the sea.

I GET ALONG WITH THE AUSSIES

Written in December 1944 when there was a possibility that *This Is the Army* would be presented in Australia. It wasn't.

I get along with the Aussies,
And the Aussies get along with me.
When there's drinks, we drink 'em
And say "Fair dinkum"
Espec'ly when drinks are free.
When there's just one girl between us,
Do we fight for her kisses? No siree!
I stand guard for the Aussie
And he does the same for me.

I'M GETTING OLD IN NEW GUINEA

Introduced by Irving Berlin on January 14 or 15, 1945, on the Armed Forces radio station (WVTC) at Base "A" Beach Club in New Guinea. No music is known to survive. The *This Is the Army* company was in New Guinea from December 23, 1944, to March 28, 1945.

VERSE

Private Wilson was a youngster once.
He's been here for thirty-seven months.
When I asked what he was doing here,
He looked up and whispered in my ear:

CHORUS

"I'm getting old in New Guinea.
I left my home long, long ago.
There's romance in the tropics I'm sure,
But what good are the tropics without Dorothy
    Lamour?
Once I was fat, now I'm skinny.
I miss my mother's cooking so.
When it's over I'll be glad to leave New Guinea,
And they'll be glad to see me go.

HEAVEN WATCH THE PHILIPPINES

Published. Copyrighted April 5, 1945. Introduced by Irving Berlin in Leyte, backed by 150 schoolchildren. Dedicated to General Douglas C. MacArthur in commemoration of his liberation of the Philippines.

On May 27, 1945, Berlin introduced Kate Smith when she gave the first American performance of the song, on the CBS Radio show *We the People*.

BERLIN: Thank you, Kate Smith, and thanks for the swell job you've done on all my songs in the past. Right now, I'd like to tell *We the People* about another song—a song which could only come out of the suffering and hopes of a country at war. About ten weeks ago I arrived in Leyte, during my tour with *This Is The Army*. I heard the Filipinos singing "God Bless America"—only they were singing "God Bless the Philippines." This touched me very deeply and I felt they might like to have a song of their own. I tried to combine the spiritual quality of "God Bless America" with their feeling of friendship for America and their desire to be free as I wrote this song. When I finished the song I taught the school children of Leyte to sing it and when "This Is The Army" opened there I sang it for the first time as the finale of our show. We had a hundred and fifty Filipino children dressed in their native costumes singing the song with us. I dedicated the song to General MacArthur in commemoration of his liberation of the Philippines. Incidentally, a few days later I stood on the steps of the capitol of Leyte—and there in the mud and rain, fifteen hundred children and townspeople gathered and we sang the song which I was sure was in the hearts of all of us. This song has never been played in America and tonight for the first time on the air I'm going to ask my dear friend Kate Smith to sing it for us. The song is called "Heaven Watch the Philippines." All right, Kate.

Heaven watch the Philippines;
Keep her safe from harm.
Guard her sons and their precious ones
In the city and on the farm.
Friendly with America
Let her always be.
Heaven watch the Philippines
And keep her forever free.

OH, TO BE HOME AGAIN

Published. Copyrighted May 22, 1945. Previously registered for copyright as an unpublished song April 10, 1945. Members of the Army Nurse Corps recalled the song as "Oh, for a Dress Again" or "Oh, Give Me a Skirt Again."

VERSE

I received a V-mail yesterday;
This is what the GI's have to say:
"Stay here till it's over, that's our aim,
That's what we will do,
But just the same—"

CHORUS 1

Oh, to be home again,
Cross the foam again
And be home again—
Just one morning pounding my head,
Just one breakfast served in my bed.
Oh, to emerge again
In a blue serge again
For a splurge again;
To spend a week off your feet
With a napkin and a sheet—
Oh, how I long to be home!

CHORUS 2

Oh, for a tub again,
Just to scrub again
In a tub again—

Just one shave with water that's hot,
Just one drink of water that's not.
Oh, for a place again
To erase again
Last night's face again;
A looking glass and a shelf
In a bathroom by myself—
Oh, how I long to be home!

CHORUS 3

Oh, just to eat again
From a seat again,
Off your feet again,
Just one meal back home in the States,
Served on two or three diff'rent plates.
Oh, to be seen again
With a bean again
Fresh and green again;
To have some meat with your chow
Not from cans but from a cow—
Oh, how I long to be home!

CHORUS 4

Oh, for the news again,
To enthuse again
Over news again—
Just to know what things are about
On the day the papers come out.
Oh, to relax again
Taking cracks again
At the tax again,
To spend an hour all alone
With a private telephone—
Oh, how I long to be home!

CHORUS 5

Oh, for a play again,
Matinee again,
Where you pay again
Just to see a girl show again
Where the girls aren't played by the men.
Oh, where one sees again
A striptease again

Done by shes again.
To see a girl partly dressed
Without hair upon her chest—
Oh, how I long to be home!

CHORUS 6

Oh, not to stand again
Lifting hand again
At command again.
Just to see a guy with a bar
Thumb your nose and stay where you are.
Oh, to be back again
In a shack again
Without flak again;
To watch a plane as you stroll
Without diving in a hole—
Oh, how I long to be home.

CHORUS 7

Oh, just to be again
With a she again
Neath a tree again.
We adore the nurses and WACs,
Even in their trousers and slacks;
But to caress again
May and Bess again
In a dress again:
There's no romance when you dance
Cheek to cheek and pants to pants—
Oh, how I long to be home!

OH, FOR A DRESS AGAIN

There is some uncertainty over whether this lyric, which was probably written on Leyte in the Philippines, came before or after "Oh, to Be Home Again." In 1947 Berlin received a letter from Nola S. Forrest that stated

I was a Director of Nurses in the SWPA in 1944–45 and went to the native dances in the Bay

in the same party as you did in New Guinea. When I asked you about writing a song for the Army Nurse Corps, you asked me what I disliked the most over there and I replied, "Oh, I guess it is these heavy khaki pants." Later someone told me you had written "Oh, Give Me a Skirt Again."

Oh, for a dress again,
To caress again
In a dress again.
Covered up from your head to your toe,
You must hide what you'd like to show.
Oh, for a skirt again,
Sweeping dirt again
In a skirt again.
There's no romance
When you dance
Cheek to cheek
And pants to pants.
Oh, for an old-fashioned dress!

WHAT IS A WAR SONG?

No music. Date unknown. Lyric appeared in Hal Eaton's October 17, 1950, syndicated column.

What is a war song?
No less, no more,
Than a song that's popular
During a war.
And a soldier reacts to it,
Good or bad,
Exactly the same
As his mother and dad!
For what is a soldier?
Cool or warm,
He's just a civilian
In uniform!

OVERLEAF: *The Berlin Family: Elizabeth, Irving, Mary Ellin, Ellin, and Linda, Christmas 1942*

Other Songs of
1940–1945

A LITTLE OLD CHURCH IN ENGLAND

Published. Copyrighted February 19, 1941. Previously registered for copyright as an unpublished song October 21, 1940. "I wrote this song in October," noted Berlin in a February 17, 1941 letter to Harry Ruby, "but was not too sure about it. The subject seemed a little too morbid but after hearing Fred Waring do it before an audience, I changed my mind." That occasion was January 30, 1941, when Waring, his choir, and orchestra premiered it at the Vanderbilt Theatre in New York. Their performance was broadcast on February 1, 1941, on the radio program *ASCAP on Parade.*

A little old church in England tumbled down,
A little old-fashioned church in London town.
A pile of mortar and brick appears
Where it had peacefully stood for years.
The little old church is gone beyond repair,
But after a while a new church will be there,
And we'll hear nothing but good
Where the little old church in England stood,
Where the little old church in England stood.

EVERYBODY KNEW BUT ME

Published. Copyrighted November 7, 1945. Previously registered for copyright as an unpublished song November 27, 1940. Written aboard the United States liner *America* during a Caribbean cruise, November 10–21, 1940. Leading recording by Woody Herman and His Orchestra (Columbia).

VERSE

Love sees ev'rything right,
But love can be blind;
I've seen things with my heart
Instead of my mind.
Love sees ev'rything high
When ev'rything's low,
And the first to be hurt
Is the last one to know.

CHORUS

Ev'rybody knew but me
You were longing to be free.
I thought that I was in clover,

But my dreams were over,
And ev'rybody knew but me.
We were in a minor key,
We were bound to disagree;
And ev'rybody saw the things
That I was too much in love to see.
You were getting through
And ev'rybody knew but me.

IN OLD SAN JUAN

Registered for copyright as an unpublished song December 21, 1940. Written aboard the United States liner *America* during a Caribbean cruise, November 10–21, 1940. Typed lyric sheet dated December 17, 1940.

I found a corner of Spain
That is not European
By the blue Caribbean
In old San Juan.
I did not want to remain,
But I soon had to weaken
When a dark Puerto Rican
Gave me the come-on.
Ponce de León looked for fountains,
Fountains to make him a kid;
Ponce de León never found them,
But I did—I did.
We saw the ship sail away,
Watched it gradually vanish.
Now she's teaching me Spanish
In old San Juan.

WHEN THAT MAN IS DEAD AND GONE

Published. Copyrighted February 4, 1941. Previously registered for copyright as an unpublished song January 14, 1941. Introduced February 1, 1941, on the radio program *ASCAP on Parade.*

VERSE

Satan, Satan thought up a plan,
Dressed as a man,
Walkin' the earth, and since he began,
The world is hell for you and me,
But what a heaven it will be—

CHORUS

When that man is dead and gone,
When that man is dead and gone!
We'll go dancing down the street,
Kissing ev'ryone we meet,
When that man is dead and gone.
What a day to wake up on,
What a way to greet the dawn!
Some fine day the news will flash:
Satan with a small mustache
Is asleep beneath the lawn.
When that man is dead and gone,
When that man is dead and gone,
What a day to wake up on,
What a way to greet the dawn,
When a certain man is dead and gone!

ANY BONDS TODAY?

Published. Copyrighted June 16, 1941. Previously registered for copyright as an unpublished song May 21, 1941. Introduced by Barry Wood over the radio in late June 1941. Leading recording by the Andrews Sisters with Jimmy Dorsey and His Orchestra (Decca). Written at the request of Secretary of the Treasury Henry Morgenthau Jr. to promote the Treasury Department's Defense Bond and savings stamp drive. All royalties went to the Treasury Department. On September 22, 1941, Secretary Morgenthau thanked Berlin for the song:

Dear Mr. Berlin:
 This is just to tell you that "Any Bonds Today" is proving to be a wonderful help to us in our Defense Bond program. You have given a real lift to American morale by writing and contributing this song.
 It may interest you to know that the Cunningham Drug Stores of Detroit have asked and received permission to distribute 200,000 copies of the song through their stores at their own expense. Requests for the song are also pouring into our Defense Savings offices, and we are sending individual copies as fast as the requests come in.
 I am just about the proudest copyright owner you ever saw.

Sincerely,

VERSE

The tall man with the high hat
And the whiskers on his chin
Will soon be knocking at your door,
And you ought to be in.

The tall man with the high hat
Will be coming down your way;
Get your savings out
When you hear him shout,
"Any bonds today?"

CHORUS 1

Any bonds today?
Bonds of freedom,
That's what I'm selling—
Any bonds today?
Scrape up the most you can;
Here comes the freedom man
Asking you to buy
A share of freedom today.
Any stamps today?
We'll be blest
If we all invest
In the U. S. A.
Here comes the freedom man;
Can't make tomorrow's plan,
Not unless you buy
A share of freedom today.

CHORUS 2

Any bonds today?
Bonds of freedom,
That's what I'm selling—
Any bonds today?
Scrape up the most you can;
Here comes the freedom man
Asking you to buy
A share of freedom today.
Any bonds today?
All you give
Will be spent to live
In the Yankee way.
Scrape up the most you can;
Here comes the freedom man
Asking you to buy
A share of freedom today.

INTERLUDE

First came the Czechs
And then came the Poles
And then the Norwegians
With three million souls.
Then came the Dutch,
The Belgians and France,
Then all of the Balkans
With hardly a chance.
It's all in the Book
If only you look;
It's there if you read the text.
They fell, ev'ry one,

At the point of a gun—
America mustn't be next.

On December 10 and 11, a few days after the Japanese attack on Pearl Harbor and Germany's declaration of war against the United States, Berlin wrote two sets of patter for the song to be introduced by Bing Crosby.

December 10 version

Give us the planes,
The ships, and the tanks,
And they won't forget
To remember the Yanks.
Give us the guns,
The shot, and the shell,
And we will avenge
All the heroes who fell.
They died in the night
With no chance to fight,
But wait till the final text:
We'll wipe Mr. Jap
From the face of the map
And wait for whoever comes next.

December 11 version

Bonds for the planes
And bonds for the tanks
And bonds for the ships
Meaning "Here come the Yanks."
Bonds for the guns,
The shot, and the shell,
And bonds to avenge
All the heroes who fell;
They died in the night
With no chance to fight,
But wait till the final text:
We'll wipe Mr. Jap
From the face of the map,
And Germany has to be next.

ANY BOMBS TODAY?

Berlin wrote the following revision of "Any Bonds Today?" in January 1942 for the New York *Journal-American*'s "Buy Bombers with Defense Stamps" drive.

VERSE

The tall man with the high hat
And the whiskers on his chin

Will hop into a plane and soon
He'll be over Berlin.
The tall man with the high hat
Will be starting on his way—
Mr. Fritz, look out
When you hear him shout,
"Any bombs today?"

CHORUS

Any bombs today?
Bombs for freedom,
That's what I'm dropping—
Any bombs today?
Here goes with three or four;
Back home we've got some more
Yankee Doodle eggs
The mighty Eagle will lay.
Any bombs today?
TNT from the Treasury
Of the U.S.A.
If one should ever crash
Close to the small mustache,
Ev'ryone will breathe a sigh of freedom today.

ARMS FOR THE LOVE OF AMERICA (THE ARMY ORDNANCE SONG)

Published. Copyrighted June 16, 1941. Previously registered for copyright as an unpublished song May 31, 1941. Introduced by Barry Wood and the Lynn Murray Chorus on June 10, 1941, from the steps of the United States Capitol in Washington, D.C., for the Arsenal Day broadcast on both the NBC and CBS radio networks. Dedicated to Major General C. M. Wesson, Chief of Ordnance, United States Army. All royalties were donated to the Army Ordnance Department.

VERSE 1

On land and on the sea and in the air
We've got to be there,
We've got to be there.
America is sounding her alarms;
We've got to have arms,
We've got to have arms.

CHORUS 1

Arms for the love of America,
They speak in a foreign land.

With weapon in ev'ry hand
Whatever they try
We've got to reply
In language that they understand.
Arms for the love of America
And for the love of ev'ry mother's son
Who's depending on the work that must be done
By the man behind the man behind the gun.

VERSE 2

They're in the camps and in the training schools;
Now give them the tools—
They've got to have tools.
We called them from the factories and farms;
Now give them the arms—
They've got to have arms.

CHORUS 2

Arms for the love of America—
We've got to get in the race
And work at a lively pace.
They say over here
We've got nothing to fear,
But let's get ready just in case.
Arms for the love of America
And for the love of ev'ry mother's son—
Oh, the fight for freedom can be lost or won
By the man behind the man behind the gun.

WHEN THIS CRAZY WORLD IS SANE AGAIN

Published. Copyrighted June 20, 1941. Introduced on June 20, 1941, by Irving Berlin in Massey Hall, Toronto, Canada, over the national network of the Canadian Broadcasting Corporation. First sung in the United States by Barry Wood on July 23, 1941, on the Columbia Broadcasting System's *U.S. Treasury Hour.*

VERSE

Someday we'll all be in clover,
Someday we'll all be in tune,
Someday our fears will be over,
Someday—let's hope it is soon.

CHORUS

When this crazy world is sane again,
When the world starts mending its ways,
We'll go strolling down the lane again

As we did in happier days.
The heavens are cloudy, but storms don't last;
The present and future will soon be the past.
When this crazy world is sane again,
We will all wake up and say,
"Isn't this a lovely day?"

ANGELS OF MERCY

Published. Copyrighted December 9, 1941. Previously registered for copyright as an unpublished song November 6, 1941. Written expressly for and dedicated to the American Red Cross. All royalties for the song went to the Red Cross.

Angels of mercy,
There's so much to do;
The heavens are gray overhead.
Angels of mercy,
They're calling to you,
So march with your crosses of red.
March where the darkness
Shuts out the light;
March where there is no dawn.
Angels of mercy,
The world's covered with night,
But your mercy goes marching on.
Angels of mercy,
Through darkest night
Your mercy goes marching on.

I PAID MY INCOME TAX TODAY

Published. Copyrighted January 22, 1942. Previously registered for copyright as an unpublished song January 6, 1942. Introduced by Eddie Cantor. Written for the U.S. Treasury Department; all royalties went to the Treasury Department. Secretary of the Treasury Henry Morgenthau's appreciation of the song was expressed in his December 30, 1941, letter to Berlin:

Dear Mr. Berlin:

The more I think about your new song, the more I wonder how you ever managed to do the job so well.

It wasn't an easy assignment to make people sing about taxes, but you have done it beautifully, and you have also hit the nail on the head as far as

the Treasury policy is concerned. I know that the song will do the country a great deal of good.

We are in your debt again, not only for the song itself, but for your unfailing willingness to help. I appreciate your contribution more than I can say.

I am looking forward now to hearing the record which you are having made. In the meantime, here are my very best wishes to you for 1942.

Sincerely,

VERSE

I said to my Uncle Sam,
"Old Man Taxes, here I am."
And he was glad to see me,
Mister Small Fry, yes indeed—
Lower brackets, that's my speed,
But he was glad to see me.

CHORUS 1

I paid my income tax today
I never felt so proud before
To be right there with the millions more
Who paid their income tax today.
I'm squared up with the U.S.A.
You see those bombers in the sky?
Rockefeller helped to build them; so did I—
I paid my income tax today.

CHORUS 2

I paid my income tax today.
A thousand planes to bomb Berlin,
They'll all be paid for, and I chipped in;
That cert'nly makes me feel okay—
Ten thousand more and that ain't hay!
We must pay for this war somehow;
Uncle Sam was worried but he isn't now—
I paid my income tax today.

CHORUS 3

I paid my income tax today.
I never cared what Congress spent,
But now I'll watch over ev'ry cent,
Examine ev'ry bill they pay;
They'll have to let me have my say.
I wrote the Treasury to go slow:
"Careful, Mister Henry Junior, that's my
    dough"—
I paid my income tax today.

THE PRESIDENT'S BIRTHDAY BALL

Published. Copyrighted January 15, 1942. Previously registered for copyright as an unpublished song January 8, 1942. Introduced by Glenn Miller and His Orchestra January 8, 1942. Written at the request of Miller, who was chairman of the Committee of Dance Band Orchestras for President Franklin D. Roosevelt's Warm Springs Paralysis Fund. Royalties were donated to the Infantile Paralysis Foundation.

VERSE

It's a great day for a great cause,
And a great time will be had by all—
Take your best girl
In her best clothes
And her best smile
To the President's ball.

CHORUS

Bands are playing,
Let's go swaying—
At the President's birthday ball
They'll be welcoming one and all.
Happy birthday,
Best-on-earth day,
To the President, FDR,
From Americans near and far.
Look forward to much happier times,
Look forward as we join in the Grand March,
The March of Dimes.
Check your sorrow till tomorrow,
For the heavens will soon be bright,
And we're gonna have fun tonight—
There'll be rhythm and mirth
At the President's birthday ball.

THIS TIME

Published. Copyrighted February 10, 1942. Previously registered for copyright as an unpublished song January 30, 1942. Introduced by Kate Smith on February 13, 1942. The chorus of "This Time" became part of "This Time (Closing)" in *This Is the Army* (1942) (see page 363).

VERSE

'Twas not so long ago
We sailed to meet the foe
And thought our fighting days were done;
But now our fighting men
Are over there again
To win the war that wasn't won.

CHORUS

This time we will all make certain
That this time is the last time.
This time we will not say "Curtain"
Till we ring it down in their own hometown,
For this time we are out to finish
The job we started then,
Clean it up for all time this time,
So we won't have to do it again.

ME AND MY PIANO

Typed lyric sheet dated February 5, 1942. This lyric became "Me and My Melinda."

CHORUS

Me and my piano,
My piano and me,
We are bound up together
With sympathy.
Me and my piano,
We are seldom apart;
On the nights when I feel like
A heart-to-heart,
When I'm blue,
I express it with my hands,
And when I do,
My piano understands.
When I'm having trouble
That I cannot disclose,
When the world mustn't know of
My private woes,
My piano knows.

ME AND MY MELINDA

Published. Copyrighted February 25, 1942. Previously registered for copyright as an unpublished song February 11, 1942. Based on the earlier lyric "Me and My Piano."

VERSE

Romeo and Juliet
Were the perfect lovers;
They're between book covers
As a famous pair.
Romeo and Juliet,
When they got together
To discuss the weather,
They could not compare with—

CHORUS

Me and my Melinda,
My Melinda and me,
We are bound up together
In sympathy.
Me and my Melinda,
We are seldom apart;
On the nights when I feel like
A heart-to-heart,
When I'm blue,
We just sit there holding hands,
And when we do,
My Melinda understands.
When I'm having trouble
That I cannot disclose,
When I can't tell the world of
My private woes,
Long before I tell her
My Melinda knows.

THE YOUTH PARADE

Typed lyric sheet dated February 21, 1942. No music is known to survive. Written at the request of Mrs. Kermit Roosevelt for her organization Young America Wants to Help.

There's a job to be done;
There's a war to be won.
Young America,
Get into place—
There is much you can do
For your red, white, and blue.
Young America,
Right about face!
Hey there, mister,
Junior and his sister's on parade—

How we need 'em
While the fight for freedom's being made.
A drum rum-tum
And here they come
From the near and the far—
Don't you know who they are?
Young America,
Bringing the dawn—
They're too young for a gun,
But you'll find when we've won
Young America
Carrying on,
For the stuff from which freedom is made
You will find in the youth parade.

I THREW A KISS IN THE OCEAN

Published. Copyrighted March 16, 1942. Previously registered for copyright as an unpublished song March 6, 1942. Earlier title: "I Spoke to the Ocean." Introduced by Kate Smith on March 6, 1942. Written for the United States Navy. All royalties were donated to the United States Navy. Many years earlier Berlin used the phrase "I threw a kiss in the ocean" in the unpublished song "Don't Forget to Remember," page 255.

VERSE

You'll say it's a dream, a lovely dream;
I say it happened, strange as it may seem.

CHORUS

I spoke last night to the ocean,
I spoke last night to the sea.
And from the ocean a voice came back;
'Twas my bluejacket answering me.
Ship ahoy, ship ahoy,
I can hear you, sailor boy.
I threw a kiss in the ocean;
It floated out on the sea.
And from the ocean a kiss came back;
'Twas my bluejacket answering me.
Ship ahoy, ship ahoy—
Ship ahoy, sailor boy, ship ahoy.

TILL WE HANG THE PAPER HANGER

The music on the surviving piano-vocals is dated May 5, 1943. Schicklgruber was the last name of Adolf Hitler's father, Alois. Born in 1837, Alois changed his last name to Hitler in 1877, twelve years before his son Adolf was born.

CHORUS

No more gas—
Till we hang the paper hanger.
No more tires—
Till we get to Germany.
No more shoes—
Till we pickle Schicklgruber
And the world is free.
No more steaks—
Till we muzzle Mussolini.
No more chops—
Till the subs are off the sea.
No more bacon—
Till the Japs are taken
And the world is free.

TAKE ME WITH YOU, SOLDIER BOY

Registered for copyright as an unpublished song July 8, 1943.

Take me with you, soldier boy,
Take me when you start—
I won't take up too much space in your heart.
I'll be with you, soldier boy,
With you night and day,
And I promise not to get in your way.
I know there's a job to do,
But somehow you will find
A soldier does a better job
With a girl on his mind.
Let me be your lucky charm
When you cross the sea;
Someday I'll return you safely to me.

IF I COULD WRITE THE NATION'S LAWS

Verse (no music) written as a guest columnist for Leonard Lyons's column "The Lyons Den" when Lyons was on vacation during the late summer of 1943. (It appeared, for example, in the Pittsburgh *Post-Gazette* on September 8, 1943.) Other guest columnists were Harold Rome, Richard Rodgers, and Lorenz Hart. The title of the guests' contributions was "If I Could Write the Nation's Laws."

If I could write the nation's laws,
The laws to right its wrongs,
My legal pen would guard the men
Who write the nation's songs.

ALL OF MY LIFE

Published. Copyrighted April 13, 1944. Previously registered for copyright as an unpublished song March 17, 1944. Introduced by Kate Smith. Sung by Berlin in public for the first time at the 16th Evacuation Hospital near Santa Maria, Italy, May 4, 1944. Leading recordings by Sammy Kaye, vocal by Billy Williams (Victor); the Three Suns (Hit); and Bing Crosby, with John Scott Trotter's Orchestra (Decca).

VERSE

Someone was always in my dreams;
That someone was always you.
I never thought we'd meet someday,
But now that my dream came true:

CHORUS

I just want the right to love you
All of my life,
Just the right to take care of you
All of my life.
I just want the right to be near you,
Always to be there,
Sharing ev'ry care and strife.
Life can be as simple as a nursery rhyme,
Sunday, Monday, Tuesday, Wednesday,
All of the time.
Long as I may live
I just want the right to give

All my love with all my heart for
All of my life.

MONA

Verse written June 1, 1944, in Mona Williams's guest book at her villa on Capri, where he stayed one night.

Mona,
You own a
Beautiful shack;
I've been here a day
And I'd like to come back.
So I'm leaving this bread-and-butter letter
To thank you and say it couldn't be better,
My day in your shack by the sea
On the beautiful Isle of Capri.

JUST A BLUE SERGE SUIT

Published September 2, 1945. Previously registered for copyright as an unpublished song August 30, 1945. Based on Berlin's earlier song "Oh, to Be Home Again." According to an article in the Brooklyn *Eagle*, the song was to be introduced on Hy Gardner's *Suit Yourself* Jayzee quiz show on August 30, 1945. The show's aim was to outfit soldier contestants with civilian clothes. In a September 5, 1945, memo to his assistant Dave Dreyer, Berlin described what he was trying to convey in the song:

In "Blue Serge Suit" I chose a subject which seemed to me uppermost in minds of men and women in all branches of the service. It represents civilian life again and everything that goes with peace. In the past three years I have been to the United Kingdom, Africa, Italy and the Pacific and have come in contact with many thousands of our service men and women. The thing that was always uppermost in their minds was home. They wanted to get the job over with and return to peace. I can't think of any other subject that is as universally felt as the one I tried to express in "Blue Serge Suit." After the last war I wrote "I've Got My Captain Working for Me Now" which was a comedy angle on the private's revenge over the officer. We hadn't been in the war long enough then to feel too solemn about it nor was the last

war as grim as this one. Besides, while there were gags where the GI squawked about the lieutenant, the relationship of officers and enlisted men in this war was much closer and friendlier. In every case I found the officers worrying about their men getting first crack at everything. So a song like "Captain Working for Me Now" would not be expressing the feelings of the GI, sailor or marine. In a nutshell "Blue Serge Suit" is a symbol for civilian life and peace. Suggest you boil the above down to a much shorter statement embodying what you think is best in the idea.

For an appearance on CBS Radio's Reader's Digest show of September 23, 1945, Berlin described the song more succinctly:

Thank you, soldier, and if I've expressed *your* mood in my latest song, it's because I got to know it so well these past three years—in the United Kingdom, Africa, Italy and the Pacific, where I saw many thousands of your buddies. It wasn't hard to see that the thing you wanted most was to get the job over with, and return to peace and home. "A Blue Serge Suit" seems to me to be the symbol of civilian life and everything that goes with peace.

And now, one more word: I pray with all my heart that I shall never again have to write another war song, because never again should there be a war to write a song about. Thank you, and good night.

VERSE

The shooting is over 'cross the foam,
And Johnny will soon be marching home.
Johnny has won, laid down his gun—
What does he ask for now that his job is done?

CHORUS

Just a blue serge suit and a bright new necktie,
A room of his own with a door,
Just a bed with sheets and a home-cooked
 dinner—
That's what he's been fighting for.
Don't ask him questions, for he's not talking;
All that he wants to do is go out walking
In a blue serge suit and a peaceful mind
With the girl he left behind.

EYES TO SEE WITH

Registered for copyright as an unpublished song September 11, 1945. Probably written in the spring of 1945. In an August 14, 1945, letter to his assistant Dave Dreyer, Berlin describes the origins of the song:

Dear Dave:
 Enclosed is a photostat copy of a song that I wish you would have Helmy play for you and then completely forget about. You will note that I have put back the pick-up which starts the phrase "*We have* eyes to see with." I originally had it this way and decided to retain it.
 Here's the story behind this song. Sometime ago, Leo McCarey told me of a song he was trying to get into *The Bells of St. Mary['s]* for Bing to sing. This picture, as you probably heard or read, is a follow-up on *Going My Way*, and the reports on it are terrific. About ten days ago, Bobby Dolan again mentioned this song and he told me of a scene that Bing has with one of the children in a Convent based on the five senses. I immediately thought of a good angle on how to treat the five senses and told Dolan about it. Dolan was very enthusiastic and said he would mention the idea to McCarey. That night the idea seemed to write itself up. I sang this chorus for Bobby Dolan the next day. He thought it was wonderful. I asked Bobby then whether I was stepping on anyone's toes. He assured me that Burke and Van Heusen had not been asked to write a song for that spot. They had one song called "Bluebirds on a Blackboard," which McCarey didn't like.
 Yesterday Bobby Dolan told me he had spoken to McCarey and that he was very enthusiastic about my angle but that Burke and Van Heusen were bringing in a new song. I smelled a situation, so told Bobby that I naturally would bow out.
 Today it seems that Burke and Van Heusen have a song based on the five senses, and of course very much on the same order. I called McCarey myself and told him to forget about me, and that if he wanted the song I would be glad to let him have it for one of two deals—either 10% of the gross or for nothing. He laughed and said, "Well, you've given me enough of margin to argue." This was all done very good-naturedly, and I think no situation will come out of it. He still would like to hear my song, but I am going to step out and wait until I hear from him.
 Obviously we can't do anything about this number. It is based on the five senses idea in the picture, although, curiously enough, if you will look at an old song I wrote many years ago called "We Have Much to Be Thankful For," which was

part of the Waterson, Berlin & Snyder catalog, you will see that the same idea is embodied in that lyric.

I am sending you this to keep on file. Even if I can't use the lyric, I like the tune and I may find use for it.

Obviously you will keep the story behind this to yourself. It is a delicate situation and I wouldn't want Burke and Van Heusen to think that I tried to cut in on one of their pictures.

You might wire me your reaction to the song. Maybe it isn't as good as Bobby and I think.

My best.

We have eyes to see with,
But when the raindrops fall,
If you can't see the rainbow
You have no eyes at all.
Ears to hear with,
But when your neighbors call,
If you can't hear them knocking
You have no ears at all.
We've been blest, for the Lord gave us much—
We can taste, we can smell, we can touch.
We have five great senses,
But if your heart is small
Your senses make no sense at all.

OVERLEAF: *Fred Astaire, "Puttin' on the Ritz"*

BLUE SKIES | 1946

BLUE SKIES (1946)

A film produced for Paramount Pictures by Sol C. Siegel. Released in September 1946. Music and lyrics by Irving Berlin. Screenplay by Arthur Sheekman. Adapted by Allan Scott from an original idea by Irving Berlin. Directed by Stuart Heisler, replacing Mark Sandrich, who died in early 1945, before shooting began. Dances staged by Hermes Pan. Music arranged by Mason Van Cleave, Hugo Frey, Charles Bradshaw, Ralph Hallenbeck, Matty Matlock, Sidney Fine. Vocal arrangements by Joseph J. Lilley. Music conducted by Robert Emmett Dolan. Cast: starring Bing Crosby (Johnny Adams), Fred Astaire (Jed Potter), and Joan Caulfield (Mary O'Dare Adams) and featuring Billy DeWolfe (Tony) and Olga San Juan (Nita Nova). Original cast recording (Decca). For the lyric to "Puttin' on the Ritz (Revised Version)," see page 262.

A SERENADE TO AN OLD-FASHIONED GIRL

Published. Copyrighted June 24, 1946. Previously registered for copyright as an unpublished song September 11, 1945. Introduced by Joan Caulfield, singing dubbed by Betty Russell (Mary O'Dare Adams), and male quartet (the Guardsmen).

CHORUS

A night in June,
A silv'ry moon,
A falling star,
A steel guitar,
A plaintive tune,
A lovesick boy,
A heart awhirl,
A serenade
To an old-fashioned girl.
A perfect dream,
A matchless pearl,
A serenade
To an old-fashioned girl.
A lovely maid,
A half-drawn shade,
A serenade
To an old-fashioned girl.*

The last four lines are not in published sheet music.

I'LL SEE YOU IN C-U-B-A

Additional material for *Blue Skies*. Typed lyric sheet dated June 29, 1945. Introduced by Bing Crosby (Johnny Adams) and Olga San Juan (Nita Nova). For original song, see page 220.

PATTER FOR C-U-B-A

JOHNNY: Why don't you do your drinking like a
          Cuban
          Instead of hiding in a cellar?
          Since Pro-hi-bition tell me, pal, have
              you been
          A very frightened little feller?
          Why don't you pour it from a bottle
          'Stead of a tiny silver flask?
          Hear that pop of a cork that they
              stopped in New York—
          The finest bars are there—cigars are
              there
          That only are made in Cuba.
NITA: I'm not a drinking lady,
          I never smoked a panatela,
          But I'm a she who likes to be where it
              is gay—okay?
BOTH: So let us leave our cares behind
          Join the sì señoras where they say that
              love is blind.
          Blind—but nevertheless
          They're glad to see you—in
              C-U-B-A.

TAG

Why don't you come with us on a bus
To Miami, where you can plan a
Lovely trip on a ship,
One that carries you to Havana?
See you in C-U-B-A.

Additional material, not used in film

PATTER FOR DUET

JOHNNY: Why don't you grab your fav'rite
              señorita
          And take a trip across the ocean?
          The weather's fine, and there the wine
              is sweeter—
          And don't forget your suntan lotion.
          What if it costs a little money?
          What is a dollar or a dime?
          Hear that pop of the cork that they
              stopped in New York—

You'll love the weather and the
    clime—
You'll have a wonderful time in Cuba.
NITA: I'd love to go there with you,
          And now you've given me a reason.
          You ought to hurry home and pack,
              'cause it's the season.
          Now why don't you plan to take a
              wonderful trip?
          Just pack a grip and get on a ship
          And tell your friends you're goin' to
              spend a day or maybe a weekend
          And I'll see you in C-U-B-A.
          Why don't you take a little vacation?
              You can make a reservation,
          Or you can always hop a freighter.
          We'll be lookin' you up a little
              later—
          See you in C-U-B-A.

A COUPLE OF SONG-AND-DANCE MEN

Registered for copyright as an unpublished song September 11, 1945. Typed lyric sheet dated August 20 and 21, 1945. Introduced by Bing Crosby (Johnny Adams) and Fred Astaire (Jed Potter).

BOTH: In us you see
          A couple of song-and-dance men.
JOHNNY: I'm the song.
JED: I'm the dance.
BOTH: For laughter, joy, and happiness,
          We're advance men,
JOHNNY: With a song—
JED: And a dance.
JOHNNY: I sing for my supper.
JED: I dance for my lunch.
JOHNNY: I croon when the landlord comes around.
BOTH: For miles and miles
          The women and children pass out cold
JOHNNY: When my voice hits the air
JED: And my feet hit the ground.
JOHNNY: Last night
JED: Out in the moonlight
JOHNNY: I came to serenade
JED: A very pretty maid.
JOHNNY: I sang her to sleep with "Asleep in the
              Deep."
JED: That always makes them collapse.
JOHNNY: I saw her eyes close;
          Then she started to doze.

JED: But she arose when I sounded taps.
BOTH: Which goes to show
What women will do when we're around
JOHNNY: And my voice hits the air
JED: And my feet hit the ground.

YOU KEEP COMING BACK LIKE A SONG

Published. Copyrighted July 9, 1945. Previously registered for copyright as an unpublished song July 8, 1943. Introduced by Bing Crosby (Johnny). Leading recordings by Dinah Shore (Columbia), Jo Stafford (Capitol), and Bing Crosby (Decca).

VERSE

Can't run away from you, dear;
I've tried so hard, but I fear
You'll always follow me, near and far.
Just when I think that I'm set,
Just when I've learned to forget,
I close my eyes, dear, and there you are.

CHORUS

You keep coming back like a song,
A song that keeps saying "Remember."
The sweet used-to-be
That was once you and me
Keeps coming back like an old melody;
The perfume of roses in May
Returns to my room in December.
From out of the past
Where forgotten things belong,
You keep coming back like a song.

Earlier version of chorus

You keep coming back like a song,
A song that keeps saying "Remember."
A beautiful tune
That ended in June
Keeps coming back in December.
You're hard to forget like a song,
A song that keeps saying "Remember."
From out of the past
Where forgotten things belong,
You keep coming back like a song.

WE KEEP COMING BACK WITH A SONG

Undated parody of "You Keep Coming Back Like a Song."

We keep coming back with a song—
You heard one just last week, remember?
We're turned down and then
You say "Come back again,"
And so on the next day
We come back with ten.
We hope that you'll take one by May;
We may get a break by December.
The words may be lousy
And the music may sound wrong,
But we'll keep coming back with a song.

(RUNNING AROUND IN CIRCLES) GETTING NOWHERE

Published. Copyrighted July 1, 1946. Previously registered for copyright as an unpublished song November 30, 1945. Typed lyric sheets dated August 8 and 9, 1945. Introduced by Bing Crosby (Johnny Adams).

A greyhound who had lots of speed
Was surely bound to fail,
For morning, noon, and evening
He'd be chasing his own tail.
He was running around in circles,
Running around in circles,
Getting nowhere.
A squirrel in a treadmill cage,
Around and round he'd go;
You'd think that he'd be in a rage,
But seems he didn't know
He was running around in circles,
Running around in circles,
Getting nowhere.
The man who runs a carousel
Is often heavy-hearted;
He rides all day,
But sad to say,
He winds up where he started.
So concentrate and clear your mind
Of schemes that never last
Or you'll wake up someday and find

Your chances all have passed—
You've been running around in circles,
Running around in circles,
Getting nowhere,
Getting nowhere very fast.

THE RACE HORSE AND THE FLEA

Published in a professional edition. Copyrighted July 20, 1945. Published again in 1947. Previously registered for copyright as an unpublished song December 6, 1944. The earliest musical sketch dates from February 17, 1942. The piano-vocal score is dated November 24, 1944. Intended for Bing Crosby to sing to his character's five-year-old daughter in the film. Not used.

Here's a story of "Who gets credit?"
It happened on a track—
A race horse was about to start
When a flea jumped on his back.

All the horses were left behind him;
It looked like he would win.
But coming down the stretch he felt
Mister Flea bite on his skin.

He fell back into place
And almost lost the race,
But spite of what the flea had done
The horse could run and so he won.

The race was over, the crowd applauded,
And with a smiling face
The flea said to his friends that night,
"If I hadn't harassed him
They all would have passed him—
'Twas me who was settin' the pace.
So you see it was me, Mister Flea,
Should get the credit for the race."

The story of the flea
Applies to you and me:
It points out with tremendous force
That when you're on a winning horse
You should be glad you won,
But don't try to be like the flea
And take the credit for the race.

Just be satisfied
To take the ride

But don't try to be like the flea
And take the credit for the race.

WILHELMINA

Published in a black-and-white professional edition. Copyrighted July 9, 1945. Not used.

VERSE

Loving you so much
Keeps me out of touch.
Tell-me, dear, am I in heaven
Or am I in Dutch?

CHORUS

Wilhelmina,
Though the wedding day is set,
Wilhelmina,
Somehow I'm unhappy yet.
I'm your boy, you're my girl;
Still my brain's in a whirl—
It keeps turning like an old Dutch mill.
Wilhelmina,
When the big day comes around,
Wilhelmina,
I'm afraid you won't be found.
When the good news is spreading,
Who will be at that wedding?
I will, but Wilhelmina?
I hope that Wilhelmina will.

I'LL DANCE RINGS AROUND YOU

Published. Copyrighted July 26, 1945. Previously registered for copyright as an unpublished song June 22, 1945. Probably written in early 1945. Intended for Paul Draper and Joan Caulfield. Draper was replaced by Fred Astaire before filming began. This song was not used.

VERSE

Ring-around-a-rosy may be
Something for a tiny baby;
But I own up—

I'm a grown-up
Who would like to ring-around-a-rosy too.

CHORUS

I'll dance rings around you—
'Twon't be hard, 'cause since I found you,
I've been dancing around in circles.
I'll dance rings around you,
Yes, until the very ground you
Walk on turns to a great big circle.
Let me be your permanent caller,
'Companied by a band;
Watch the ring grow smaller and smaller
Till it fits the finger of your hand.
And
Watch that fam'ly circle
Grow from year to year,
Dancing rings around you, dear.

Earlier version

Berlin sent this version of the lyric to Mark Sandrich, the film's first director, who died in early 1945 before shooting began.

I'll dance rings around you—
'Twon't be hard, because since I found you,
I've been dancing around in circles.
I'll dance rings around you
And we'll hear them tell
How the lady fell
In a dizzy spell.
I'll be your constant caller,
Accompanied by a band;
The ring'll get smaller and smaller
Till it fits the finger of your left hand.
Then I'll dance rings around you,
Lis'ning to the sound
Of wedding bells on heaven's merry-go-round.

"The staging of this number is pretty obvious," Berlin wrote Sandrich. "A dance floor designed with a continuous circle starting from the centre. Draper can begin his dance from the largest circle and dance down to the centre where the girl would be waiting. The dance could be conceived so that it would be confined to this spiral movement. It may develop into something new. I've never seen it before. Also you may get some interesting shots from overhead.

"Another way to do it would be on a revolving stage."

IT'S A LOVELY DAY FOR A WALK

Published 1995 in the songbook *Unsung Irving Berlin.* Previously registered for copyright as an unpublished song August 9, 1945. Intended for Paul Draper and Joan Caulfield. Not used. Also intended for the unproduced musical *Stars on My Shoulders* (1948).

VERSE

Darling,
What a morning,
Darling,
What a day!
Please don't
Keep me waiting—
Let's be
On our way.
My heart's
Bursting beyond control;
Let's go
Out for a nice long stroll.

REFRAIN

Arm in arm,
Let's go walking.
Let's go walking, you and I;
There's a sun up in the sky—
It's a lovely day for a walk.

Arm in arm,
We'll be talking;
I'll be saying something sweet.
And we'll tell the folks we meet
It's a lovely day for a walk.

We won't be stopping
For window shopping,
But there's a church out in the sun.
A special feature
About the preacher
Is turning twosomes into one.

Arm in arm,
Let's go walking;
Come, let's hear that marriage talk—
And we'll tell our great-grandchildren
'Twas a lovely day for a walk.

PATTER

How do you do, do, do?
Fancy meeting you

On a day that is so divine.
Whad'ya say, say, say,
This delightful day?
Hope to hear that you're feeling fine.
Just a whiff of the great outdoors—
What a heavenly smell!
Happy walking to you and yours—
Glad to see you looking well.
Why don't you wait, wait, wait,
Kindly hesitate—
We would like to admire the view.
Gotta go bye, bye, bye—
There's a knot to tie.
Do you mind if we follow you?

REPEAT REFRAIN

HAVE YOU EVER TRIED DRINKING WATER?

Written in November 1944. Not used. Possibly intended for Billy DeWolfe and male ensemble.

VERSE

There ain't no sin
In a drop of gin
Or a glass of sherry wine.
You're not disgraced
If you have a taste
Of a cocktail when you dine.
Brandy wouldn't harm you
After it's been cut;
Scotch should not alarm you
In small doses—but

CHORUS 1

Have you ever tried drinking water?
If you haven't, then you oughta.
Have you ever tried drinking water when you're
    dry?
In the spring, in the fall,
It's the best drink of all—
It's especially good for washing down
A jigger of Scotch or rye.

CHORUS 2

Have you ever tried drinking seltzer?
Oh, you haven't? Very well, sir—
It's a beverage that you simply will adore.

When your glass starts to fizz,
It's the best drink there is—
It's especially good with aspirin
Mornings after the night before.

CHORUS 3

Have you ever tried drinking cider?
Out with Mary or with Ida?
Ev'ry farmer has jugs of cider in his yard;
On his old apple cart
Ev'ry rube in his heart
Has a very soft spot for cider—
Yes, especially if it's hard.

I WANT YOU TO MEET MY GIRL

Written July 11, 1945. Intended for Paul Draper and male ensemble. Not used. No music is known to survive.

DRAPER: I want you to meet my girl, fellers,
        I want you to meet my girl.
        Here she comes down the street—
        If you just throw some light on,
        You'll find that she's right on the beat.
        I want you to meet my girl, fellers,
        I want you to meet my girl.
        Say without any fuss
        And without much rehearsin'
        The gal's quite a person, and plus
        Ain't she a whiz?
   BOYS: She certainly is.
DRAPER: Ain't she a wow?
   BOYS: A cutie, and how!
DRAPER: Ain't she as sweet,
        Just as sweet as can be?
   BOYS: I've got a sweet tooth bothering me.
DRAPER: I want you to meet my girl, fellers,
        And after you've met my girl,
        There's an exit near, so disappear from
           view—
        Meaning I've got lots of kissing and
           hugging to do.

THE ROAD TO YESTERDAY

Typed lyric sheet dated August 27, 1945. Not used. Lyric appears to be unfinished. No music is known to survive.

Pack your grip with memories and come with me;
Come with me and journey to the used-to-be.
Close your eyes and soon we'll all be on our way
On the road to yesterday.

I'D RATHER NOT DANCE AGAIN

Registered for copyright as an unpublished song March 20, 1945. Not used in film.

VERSE

Your letter tells me, dear, that ev'rything's OK;
You say don't worry and you want me to be gay,
To go dancing and have some fun.
I'm afraid that it can't be done.

CHORUS

I'd rather not dance again,
Although you want me to.
Oh, how could I dance again
When I feel oh so blue?
I'll stay at home in my lonely apartment,
Dreaming the whole night through.
I'd rather not dance again
Till I'm dancing with you.

MENDING THE OLD WORLD (MAKING IT NEW)

There are two similar lyrics with this title. The first was dated September 14, 1945; the second is undated.

First version

CHORUS

Busy, busy, busy, busy,
Busy, busy, busy, busy
With plenty to do,
Mending the old world,
Making it new.
Busy, busy, busy, busy,
Busy, busy, busy, busy—
No time for complaint,
Giving the old world
A new coat of paint.
Nails and hammers,
Shovels and picks,
Iron and copper and steel,
Paint and brushes,
Mortar and bricks,
Shoulders and hands to the wheel,
Busy, busy, busy, busy,
Busy, busy, busy, busy
With plenty to do,
Mending the old world,
Making it new.

PATTER

There'll be houses to build
All over the town,
Roofs to put up
And floors to put down,
Cases to pack
And trucks on the road,
Trains to arrive
And vessels to load,
Motors to run
And holes to be drilled,
Cows to be milked
And soil to be tilled.
Busy, busy, busy, busy,

Busy, busy, busy, busy—
There's me and there's you,
Rolling our sleeves up,
Plenty to do.

Second version

Angels—
With plenty to do,
Mending the old world
And making it new.
Angels—
Without a complaint
Giving the old world
A new coat of paint.
Strange as it may be,
Still it seems to me
Every night
When stars are bright
I close my eyes and see
Angels—
With plenty to do,
Mending the old world
And making it new.

MY OLD PAL

Possibly intended for *Blue Skies*. Not used. Date of composition unknown. Also see "Pardners," page 396.

VERSE

Time or tide
Never could divide
The tie that binds us two.

King or queen
Couldn't come between
The team that is me and you.

CHORUS 1

My old pal,
We have always been together,
Through thick and thin, in all sorts of weather,
My old pal.
My old pal,
You would think that I'm his brother—
It's awful how we love one another,
My old pal.
When I needed fifteen dollars—
My room rent I had to pay—
He gave me the fifteen dollars
And I didn't have to pay it back until the next day.
My old pal,
When I'm out with some young Venus,
He grabs her so she can't come between us,
My old pal.

CHORUS 2

My old pal,
At the races I'm in clover—
He tells me who will win when it's over,
My old pal.
My house burned,
But he told me not to hurry,
Because he didn't want me to worry,
My old pal.
When we're out together dining,
Whatever the check may be,
He picks up the check and adds it,
Yes he adds it up before he hands it over to me.
My old pal,
When I once fell from a tanker,
He shouted "Help!" and threw me the anchor,
My old pal.

OVERLEAF: *Ethel Merman*

ANNIE GET YOUR GUN | 1946

ANNIE GET YOUR GUN (1946)

Tryout: Shubert Theatre, New Haven, March 28, 1946; Shubert Theatre, Boston, April 2, 1946; Shubert Theatre, Philadelphia, April 30, 1946. New York run: Imperial Theatre; opened May 16, 1946; 1,147 performances. Music and lyrics by Irving Berlin. Produced by Richard Rodgers and Oscar Hammerstein II. Book by Herbert and Dorothy Fields. Directed by Joshua Logan. Dances staged by Helen Tamiris. Orchestrations by Philip J. Lang, Robert Russell Bennett, and Ted Royal. Orchestra under the direction of Jay S. Blackton. Cast: starring Ethel Merman (Annie Oakley) and featuring Ray Middleton (Frank Butler), Harry Bellaver (Chief Sitting Bull), Marty May (Charlie Davenport), Lea Penman (Dolly Tate), Betty Anne Nyman (Winnie Tate), Kenny Bowers (Tommy Keeler), and William O'Neal (Colonel William F. "Buffalo Bill" Cody). Original cast recording (Decca). National tour with Mary Martin (Annie) and Earl Covert (Frank) opened in Dallas October 3, 1947. London production, starring Dolores Gray (Annie) and Bill Johnson (Frank), opened at the Coliseum Theatre June 7, 1947, and ran for 1,304 performances. The 1950 M-G-M film version starred Betty Hutton (Annie) and Howard Keel (Frank). There were notable New York stage revivals in 1966, with Merman (Annie) and Bruce Yarnell (Frank) at the New York State Theater at Lincoln Center, and 1999 with Bernadette Peters (Annie) and Tom Wopat (Frank) at the Marquis Theatre.

Irving Berlin came to write the score of *Annie Get Your Gun* because of the sudden, tragic death of Jerome Kern. When Kern died of a cerebral hemorrhage on November 11, 1945—he had collapsed on a Park Avenue sidewalk nine days earlier—he was about to start work on a new musical entitled *Annie Oakley* in collaboration with Herbert and Dorothy Fields.

The show's producers, Richard Rodgers and Oscar Hammerstein II, turned to Berlin, asking him if he would be interested in taking on the project. "After Jerry Kern died," Berlin recalled in an April 8, 1966, letter to press agent Richard Maney,

Oscar Hammerstein asked me if I would write the score for *Annie*. I had just finished three and a half years with *This Is the Army*—about two of those years were spent overseas—and about nine months after that in Hollywood with a picture called *Blue Skies* for Paramount, and I was pretty tired. However, I asked Oscar to send me the script. There was only one act at that time—a first draft called *Annie Oakley*. I read it and liked it very much but didn't think it was quite up my alley. I wasn't sure I could write the period songs

that the book required. I told Oscar how I felt and he was very understanding. I thought that was the end of it.

That week on a Friday, Dick Rodgers telephoned and said, "If you will do the score, I can get Josh Logan to direct it." That was an inducement because Josh had staged some of the numbers in *This Is the Army*. I still was reluctant but Dick said "Why don't you think about it over the weekend?"

I read the first act again and over the weekend wrote two songs, "They Say It's Wonderful" and "Doin' What Comes Natur'lly." I then met with Dick and Oscar on Monday but was still playing it very cautiously and asked to think it over another week. Dick Rodgers, very rightly, said "Why another week?" Having in mind the two songs I had already written, I said okay. It didn't take long to agree on terms. I was anxious to do it and Rodgers and Hammerstein wanted me to. The songs for the score came quickly and easily, looking back. I think the reason was because of the possibilities in the Fields' script, my association with Rodgers and Hammerstein and, above all, writing songs for Ethel Merman. At a conference with Rodgers and Hammerstein in my office I sang for them for the first time "Doin' What Comes Natur'lly," "The Girl That I Marry," "They Say It's Wonderful," "You Can't Get a Man with a Gun," "I Got Lost in His Arms," "I'm an Indian Too," and I think one other. They were very enthusiastic.

COLONEL BUFFALO BILL

Published. Copyrighted April 12, 1946. Previously registered for copyright as an unpublished song February 12, 1946. Introduced by Marty May (Charlie Davenport) and ensemble. Listed in show programs as "Buffalo Bill."

CHARLIE: Who's got the stuff that made the Wild
West wild?
Who pleases ev'ry woman, man, and
child?
Who does his best to give the customers
a thrill?
CROWD: Who?
CHARLIE: Colonel Buff'lo Bill.
Who's got the show that gets the most
applause—
Five hundred Indians and fifty squaws,
Ten feature acts, and there's the special
feature still?

CROWD: Who?
CHARLIE: Colonel Buff'lo Bill.
Did you ever see a cowboy rope a steer?
CROWD: No, we haven't.
CHARLIE: Or an Indian with feathers throw a
spear?
CROWD: No, we haven't.
CHARLIE: Or a marksman shoot an earring from an
ear?
CROWD: No, we haven't.
CHARLIE: Did you ever see a holdup?
CROWD: No, sir.
CHARLIE: Then gather closer
And let me give you some of the
atmosphere.
The hour is midnight and all is still;
We see the stagecoach climbing up a
hill,
Going along the mountain trail,
Carrying passengers and mail,
Never suspecting danger as they roll
along.
The watchful driver is in his seat,
His trusty rifle lying at his feet.
Some of the passengers inside
Seem to be dozing as they ride,
Never suspecting there is something
really wrong.
Suddenly there's a shout—
CROWD: What is it all about?
CHARLIE: What is it all about, you ask?
It's Indians!
CROWD: Indians?
CHARLIE: Indians!
CROWD: Indians?
CHARLIE: Very notable, cut-your-throatable
Indians!
CROWD: Indians?
CHARLIE: Just when they've taken ev'ryone by
force,
Who makes an entrance on a big white
horse?
Who starts a-shootin' till
There's no one left to kill?
VOICE: General Grant?
CHARLIE: No! Colonel Buff'lo Bill!
CROWD: Certainly this is quite a thrill,
Better than all the vaudeville—
Let us be on the go
And see the show
With Buff'lo Bill.

REPRISE

[In front of curtains preceding troupe's appearance in Minneapolis]

MAN: [*with throwaway announcement of show*]
Five hundred Indians, it can't be so—
That's what they always say in every show.
I've never seen him, but I'll bet that he's a pill.

CROWD: Who?

MAN: Colonel Buff'lo Bill.
Ten feature acts? I'll bet there aren't five.
Wild bucking broncos? Bet they're half alive.
I've never seen him, but I know he'd make me ill.

CHARLIE: [*who has been listening*]
Who?

MAN: Colonel Buff'lo Bill.

CHARLIE: Did you know that what you're saying hurts the sale?

MAN: No, I didn't.

CHARLIE: That it's libelous and you could go to jail?

MAN: No, I didn't.

CHARLIE: That you're liable to be tied up to a rail?

MAN: No, I didn't.

CHARLIE: Do you know what's apt to happen?

MAN: No, sir.

CHARLIE: Then gather closer
And listen while I tell you a gruesome tale.
While we were playing
In Buffalo,
A certain hick
Who hadn't seen the show
Started to say that it was bunk,
Spreading a rumor that it stunk,
Never suspecting that the news would reach my ear.
That very midnight
We found his house,
And through the window
Quiet as a mouse
Somebody saw him fast asleep;
There he was, wrapped in slumber deep,
Never suspecting there was danger lurking near.
Suddenly came a shout—

CROWD: What was it all about?

CHARLIE: What was it all about, you ask?
'Twas Indians!

CROWD: Indians?

CHARLIE: Indians.

MAN: Indians?

CHARLIE: Very notable, cut-your-throatable Indians.

CROWD: Indians!

CHARLIE: Now will you give yourself another guess?

MAN: Yes!

CHARLIE: Now will you tell them we're a big success?

MAN: Yes!

CHARLIE: Now who's the man who gives the customers a thrill?

MAN: General Grant?

CHARLIE: No—Colonel Buff'lo Bill!

CROWD: Certainly this is quite a thrill,
Better than all the vaudeville!
Let us be on the go
And see the show
With Buff'lo Bill!

I'M A BAD, BAD MAN

Published. Copyrighted April 15, 1946. Previously registered for copyright as an unpublished song January 5, 1946. Introduced by Ray Middleton (Frank Butler) and female ensemble. Danced by Duncan Noble, Paddy Stone, Parker Wilson, and ensemble.

VERSE 1

FRANK: I'm honored, I'm flattered,
This greeting really mattered—
This welcome is grand, but I'm really concerned.
I like your attention,
But this I have to mention:
You're playing with fire and you're apt to get burned.

CHORUS 1

There's a girl in Tennessee
Who's sorry she met up with me.
Can't go back to Tennessee—
I'm a bad, bad man.
There's a girl in Omaha,
But I ran faster than her pa.
Can't go back to Omaha—
I'm a bad, bad man.
There's a girl in Wyoming,
And they're combing Wyoming
To find the man in white
Who was out with her that night.
There's a girl in Arkansas,
The sheriff is her brother-in-law.
Can't go back to Arkansas—
I'm a bad, bad man.

CHORUS 2

GIRLS: You are making too much fuss,
For we don't give a tinker's cuss.
We've been out, yes, each of us,
With a bad, bad man.
We've been chasing up and down;
That other show has just left town,
And the one who played the clown
Was a bad, bad man.
You may love us and leave us
But the parting won't grieve us;
We'll turn the other cheek
When the minstrels come next week.
When the show folks come to call,
A girl may slip but she won't fall—
We'll give some but won't give all
To a bad, bad man.*

VERSE 2

FRANK: For years I have yearned to
Play towns I could return to,
And this may be it from the way that you speak.
I'm glad you're not frightened;
The atmosphere has brightened,
And now let's make plans for a wonderful week.

CHORUS 3

FRANK: Monday when my show is done,
I'll teach you how to shoot a gun;
You may find it lots of fun
With a bad, bad man.
Tuesday there's no matinee,
But I'll be in my tent all day—
You can come around and play
With a bad, bad man.
Send your mothers on Wednesday
Because Wednesday's old hens' day,
But Thursday is sublime—
I'll have lots of open time.
Friday night will be the test;
If Saturday you're still my guest,
Sunday you can come and rest
With a bad, bad man.

*Alternate version of last eight lines:
FRANK: I'm enlightened but frightened—
Though my interest you've heightened,
It might turn out to be
That you're much too much for me.
So I'll go back to my tent,
And someday when you're old and bent
Think of hours you might have spent
With a bad, bad man.

DOIN' WHAT COMES NATUR'LLY

Published. Copyrighted March 4, 1946, and April 29, 1946. Previously registered for copyright as an unpublished song January 5, 1946. Introduced by Ethel Merman (Annie Oakley) with Art Barnett (Foster Wilson) and, as Annie's brothers and sisters, Nancy Jean Raab (Minnie), Camilla De Witt (Jessie), Marlene Cameron (Nellie), Clifford Sales (Little Jake). In a letter to Dorothy (Mrs. Oscar) Hammerstein (April 25, 1983), Berlin wrote: "Oscar was wonderful to me during *Annie Get Your Gun*. I recall an incident when I decided that I couldn't do the show and said 'This is more up your alley. I can't write these hillbilly lyrics.' Oscar announced 'All you have to do is drop the G's.' That night I wrote 'Doin' What Comes Naturally' and decided to do the show."

PART 1

ANNIE: Folks are dumb where I come from;
    They ain't had any learnin'.
    Still they're happy as can be
    Doin' what comes natur'lly.
KIDS: Doin' what comes natur'lly.
ANNIE: Folks like us could never fuss
    With schools and books and learnin'.
    Still we've gone from A to Z
    Doin' what comes natur'lly.
KIDS: Doin' what comes natur'lly.
ANNIE: You don't have to know how to read or
        write
    When you're out with a feller in the pale
        moonlight.
    You don't have to look in a book to find
    What he thinks of the moon and what is
        on his mind.
    That comes natur'lly.
KIDS: That comes natur'lly.
ANNIE: My uncle out in Texas
    Can't even write his name;
    He signs his checks with X's,
    But they cash them just the same.
    If you saw my pa and ma,
    You'd know they had no learnin'.
    Still they raised a family
    Doin' what comes natur'lly.
KIDS: Doin' what comes natur'lly.

PART 2

ANNIE: Uncle Jed has never read
    An almanac on drinkin';
    Still he's always on a spree
    Doin' what comes natur'lly.

KIDS: Doin' what comes natur'lly.
ANNIE: Sister Sal, who's musical,
    Has never had a lesson;
    Still she's learned to sing off key
    Doin' what comes natur'lly.
KIDS: Doin' what comes natur'lly.
ANNIE: You don't have to go to a private school
    Not to turn up your bustle to a stubborn
        mule.
    You don't have to have a professor's
        dome
    Not to go for the honey when the bee's at
        home.
    That comes natur'lly.
KIDS: That comes natur'lly.
ANNIE: My tiny baby brother,
    Who's never read a book,
    Knows one sex from the other—
    All he had to do was look.
    Grandpa Bill lives on the hill
    With someone he just married.
    There he is at ninety-three
    Doin' what comes natur'lly.
KIDS: Doin' what comes natur'lly.

[ANNIE *turns to* WILSON *and sings:*]

ANNIE: Sister Lou ain't got a sou
    Although she goes out shopping;
    She gets all her stockings free
    Doin' what comes natur'lly.
WILSON: Doin' what comes natur'lly.
ANNIE: Cousin Nell can't add or spell,
    But she left school with honors;
    She got every known degree
    For doin' what comes natur'lly.
WILSON: Doin' what comes natur'lly.
ANNIE: You don't have to come from a great big
        town
    Not to clean out a stable in an evening
        gown.
    You don't have to mix with the
        Vanderbilts
    Not to take off your panties when you're
        wearing kilts.
    That comes natur'lly.
WILSON: That comes natur'lly.
ANNIE: My mother's cousin Carrie
    Won't ever change her name;
    She doesn't want to marry
    And her children feel the same.
    Sister Rose has lots of beaus
    Although we have no parlor;
    She does fine behind a tree
    Doin' what comes natur'lly—
    Doin' what comes natur'lly.

THE GIRL THAT I MARRY

Published. Copyrighted April 8, 1946. Previously registered for copyright as an unpublished song January 5, 1946. Introduced by Ray Middleton (Frank Butler). "You never know what the public will go for," Berlin told an interviewer for the New York *Herald-Tribune* (October 17, 1954). "I had a song in *Annie Get Your Gun* which was meant to be only an introduction to another song, 'You Can't Get a Man with a Gun.' I needed something for Frank Butler to sing to Annie Oakley telling her the kind of a woman he wanted. I called it 'The Girl That I Marry.' Nothing much happened to it at first. Then Frank Sinatra did a record of it. Before anybody knew it the record had sold a million copies and the song was a big hit."

The girl that I marry will have to be
As soft and as pink as a nursery.
The girl I call my own
Will wear satins and laces
And smell of cologne.
Her nails will be polished,
And in her hair
She'll wear a gardenia,
And I'll be there—
'Stead of flittin'
I'll be sittin'
Next to her
And she'll purr like a kitten.
A doll I can carry
The girl that I marry must be.

YOU CAN'T GET A MAN WITH A GUN

Published. Copyrighted April 5, 1946. Previously registered for copyright as an unpublished song January 24, 1946. Introduced by Ethel Merman (Annie Oakley).

VERSE

Oh, my mother was frightened by a shotgun, they
    say;
That's why I'm such a wonderful shot.
I'd be out in the cactus and I'd practice all day,
And now tell me, what have I got?

CHORUS 1

I'm quick on the trigger,
With targets not much bigger
Than a pinpoint
I'm number one.
But my score with a feller
Is lower than a cellar—
Oh, you can't get a man with a gun.
When I'm with a pistol,
I sparkle like a crystal,
Yes, I shine like the morning sun.
But I lose all my luster
When with a bronco buster—
Oh, you can't get a man with a gun.
With a gu-un, with a gu-un,
No, you can't get a man with a gun.
If I went to battle
With someone's herd of cattle,
You'd have steak when the job was done;
But if I shot the herder,
They'd holler bloody murder,
And you can't get a hug
From a mug with a slug—
Oh, you can't get a man with a gun.

CHORUS 2

I'm cool, brave, and daring
To see a lion glaring
When I'm out with my Remington;
But a look from a mister
Will raise a fever blister—
Oh, you can't get a man with a gun.
The gals with umbrellers
Are always out with fellers,
In the rain or the blazing sun;
But a man never trifles
With gals who carry rifles—
Oh, you can't get a man with a gun.
With a gu-un, with a gu-un,
No, you can't get a man with a gun.
A man's love is mighty;
He'll even buy a nightie
For a gal who he thinks is fun.
But they won't buy pajamas
For pistol-packin' mamas,
And you can't shoot a male
In the tail like a quail—
Oh, you can't get a man with a gun.

CHORUS 3

If I shot a rabbit,
Some furrier would grab it
For a coat that would warm someone;
But you can't shoot a lover
And use him for a cover—

Oh, you can't get a man with a gun.
If I shot an eagle,
Although it wasn't legal,
He'd be stuffed when the job was done;
But you can't stuff a feller
And watch him turning yeller—
Oh, you can't get a man with a gun.
With a gu-un, with a gu-un,
No, you can't get a man with a gun.
A Tom, Dick, or Harry
Will build a house for Carrie
When the preacher has made them one;
But he can't build you houses
With buckshot in his trousers,
For a man may be hot
But he's not when he's shot—
Oh, you can't get a man with a gun.

THERE'S NO BUSINESS LIKE SHOW BUSINESS

Published. Copyrighted April 12, 1946. Previously registered for copyright as an unpublished song February 12, 1946. Introduced by William O'Neal (Buffalo Bill), Marty May (Charlie Davenport), Ray Middleton (Frank Butler), and Ethel Merman (Annie Oakley). Listed in show programs as "Show Business." "One myth I would like to straighten out," Berlin wrote in a letter to noted press agent Richard Maney (April 8, 1966):

> There have been so many stories connected with "Show Business"—that I didn't like the song, that I wanted it out of the show, that at one audition I eliminated it—there is no truth to any of that. I wrote it to take care of a spot in one for a scene change indicated in the script. Buffalo Bill, Charlie and Frank Butler were trying to induce Annie to join the show and I thought of the title "There's No Business Like Show Business." I remember calling Oscar Hammerstein and telling him the title. He was crazy about it, which of course encouraged me to write it up. Once it was in the show we all knew that it was an important part of the score. Certainly no one, including myself, realized at the time that it would become the so-called theme song for show business.

Published version

VERSE 1

The butcher, the baker, the grocer, the clerk
Are secretly unhappy men because

The butcher, the baker, the grocer, the clerk
Get paid for what they do, but no applause.
They'd gladly bid their dreary jobs goodbye,
For anything theatrical, and why?

CHORUS 1

There's no bus'ness like show bus'ness,
Like no bus'ness I know.
Ev'rything about it is appealing,
Ev'rything the traffic will allow;
Nowhere could you get that happy feeling
When you are stealing that extra bow.
There's no people like show people;
They smile when they are low.
Yesterday they told you you would not go far,
That night you open and there you are,
Next day on your dressing room they've hung a
    star—
Let's go on with the show.

VERSE 2

The costumes, the scen'ry, the makeup, the props,
The audience that lifts you when you're down.
The headaches, the heartaches, the backaches, the
    flops,
The sheriff who escorts you out of town.
The opening when your heart beats like a drum,
The closing when the customers won't come.

CHORUS 2

There's no bus'ness like show bus'ness,
Like no bus'ness I know.
You get word before the show has started
That your fav'rite uncle died at dawn.
Top of that your pa and ma have parted,
You're brokenhearted, but you go on.
There's no people like show people;
They don't run out of dough.
Angels come from ev'rywhere with lots of jack,
And when you lose it, there's no attack—
Where could you get money that you don't give
    back?
Let's go on with the show.

VERSE 3

The cowboys, the tumblers, the wrestlers, the
    clowns,
The roustabouts who move the show at dawn.
The music, the spotlight, the people, the towns,
Your baggage with the labels pasted on.
The sawdust and the horses and the smell,
The towel you've taken from the last hotel.

CHORUS 3

There's no bus'ness like show bus'ness
If you tell me it's so.
Trav'ling through the country will be thrilling,
Standing out in front on opening nights,
Smiling as you watch the theatre filling,
And there's your billing out there in lights.
There's no people like show people;
They smile when they are low.
Even with a turkey that you know will fold,
You may be stranded out in the cold,
Still you wouldn't change it for a sack of gold—
Let's go on with the show.

Show version

VERSE 1

CHARLIE: The cowboys, the tumblers, the
wrestlers, the clowns,
The roustabouts who move the
show at dawn,
BUFFALO BILL: The music, the spotlight, the
people, the towns,
Your baggage with the labels
pasted on.
FRANK: The sawdust and the horses and
the smell,
The towel you've taken from the
last hotel.

CHORUS 1

CHARLIE, FRANK,
BUFFALO BILL: There's no bus'ness like show
business,
Like no bus'ness I know.
BUFFALO BILL: Ev'rything about it is appealing.
CHARLIE: Ev'rything the traffic will allow.
FRANK: Nowhere could you get that
happy feeling
When you are stealing that extra
bow.

CHARLIE, FRANK,
BUFFALO BILL: There's no people like show
people;
They smile when they are low.
CHARLIE: Yesterday they told you you
would not go far—
BUFFALO BILL: That night you open and there
you are—
FRANK: Next day on your dressing room
they've hung a star—

CHARLIE, FRANK,
BUFFALO BILL: Let's go on with the show.

VERSE 2

BUFFALO BILL: The costumes, the scen'ry, the
makeup, the props,
The audience that lifts you when
you're down.
CHARLIE: The headaches, the heartaches,
the backaches, the flops,
The sheriff who escorts you out
of town.
FRANK: The opening when your heart
beats like a drum,
The closing when the customers
won't come.

CHORUS 2

CHARLIE, FRANK,
BUFFALO BILL: There's no bus'ness like show
bus'ness,
Like no bus'ness I know.
CHARLIE: You get word before the show has
started
That your favorite uncle died at
dawn—
FRANK: Top of that your pa and ma have
parted,
You're brokenhearted, but you
go on.

CHARLIE, FRANK,
BUFFALO BILL: There's no people like show
people;
They don't run out of dough.
CHARLIE: Angels come from ev'rywhere
with lots of jack—
BUFFALO BILL: And when you lose it there's no
attack.
FRANK: Where could you get money that
you don't give back?

CHARLIE, FRANK,
BUFFALO BILL: Let's go on with the show.

CHORUS 3

ANNIE: There's no bus'ness like show
bus'ness
If you tell me it's so.
FRANK: Trav'ling through the country is
so thrilling.
BUFFALO BILL: Standing out in front on opening
nights.
CHARLIE: Smiling as you watch the benches
filling,
And there's your billing out
there in lights.
ANNIE: There's no people like show
people;
They smile when they are low.

CHARLIE: Even with a turkey that you know
will fold—
BUFFALO BILL: You may be stranded out in the
cold—
FRANK: Still you wouldn't change it for a
sack of gold.
ALL: Let's go on with the show.
Let's go on with the show.

REPRISE

ANNIE: There's no bus'ness like show
bus'ness,
Like no bus'ness I know.
All made up and soon you'll be
appearing;
Ev'ry bit of nervousness is gone.
Then the sound that's music to
your hearing—
To hear them cheerin' when you
come on.
There's no people like show
people;
They smile when they are low.
How I wish the folks at home
could only see
What's come to Annie—how
proud they'd be!
Gettin' paid for doin' what comes
natur'lly—
Let's go on with the show.

Chorus written for Mary Martin for national tour (1947)

There's no bus'ness like show bus'ness,
Like no bus'ness I know.
Playing Broadway at the famous Palace
Don't compare with this—it's simply grand.
Ask me how I feel to be in Dallas—
Like little Alice
In Wonderland.
There's no people like show people;
They smile when they are low.
Who'd have thought when I was on my mother's
knee
I'd play in Texas, but here I be,
Gettin' paid for doin' what comes natur'lly—
Let's go on with the show.

Film industry version, February 18, 1959

There's no bus'ness like show bus'ness,
Like no bus'ness I know.
Making motion pictures can be thrilling—

Personal appearance, opening nights,
Smiling as you watch the theatre filling,
And there's your billing out there in lights.
There's no people like show people;
They smile when they are low.
Yesterday they told you you would not go far;
Your picture opens and there you are;
Next day on your dressing room they've hung a
　　star—
Let's go on with the show.
Let's go on with the show.

Special lyric written for Gene Kelly, 1974

There's no bus'ness like show bus'ness,
Like no business I know.
I've been very close to entertainment
Here at Metro, where the days were long;
I discovered "Singin' in the Rain" meant
An entertainment,
Not just a song.
There's no people like show people;
They smile when they are low.
Here's a toast to stars who will forever shine—
A cup o' kindness for auld lang syne—
Not forgetting Leo, Metro's famous lion,
Let's go on with the show.

THEY SAY IT'S WONDERFUL

Published. Copyrighted March 4, 1946. Previously registered for copyright as an unpublished song January 10, 1946. Introduced by Ethel Merman (Annie Oakley) and Ray Middleton (Frank Butler).

VERSE 1

ANNIE: Rumors fly and you can't tell where they
　　　　start,
　　　　Speci'lly when it concerns a person's
　　　　heart.
　　　　I've heard tales that could set my heart
　　　　aglow—
　　　　Wish I knew if the things I hear are so.

CHORUS 1

ANNIE: They say that falling in love is wonderful,
　　　　It's wonderful, so they say.
　　　　And with a moon up above
　　　　It's wonderful, it's wonderful,
　　　　So they tell me.

I can't recall who said it,
I know I never read it;
I only know they tell me that love is grand
And
The thing that's known as romance
Is wonderful, wonderful
In ev'ry way,
So they say.

VERSE 2

FRANK: Rumors fly and they often leave a doubt,
　　　　But you've come to the right place to find
　　　　out.
　　　　Ev'rything that you've heard is really
　　　　so—
　　　　I've been there once or twice and I should
　　　　know.

CHORUS 2

FRANK: You'll find that falling in love is
　　　　wonderful,
　　　　It's wonderful.
ANNIE: So you say.
FRANK: And with a moon up above
　　　　It's wonderful, it's wonderful.
ANNIE: So you tell me.
FRANK: To leave your house some morning,
　　　　And without any warning
　　　　You're stopping people shouting that love
　　　　is grand,
　　　　And to hold a man in your arms
　　　　Is wonderful, wonderful
　　　　In ev'ry way.
ANNIE: So you say.

Show version of chorus 2

FRANK: You'll find that falling in love is
　　　　wonderful,
　　　　It's wonderful, as they say.
　　　　And with a moon up above
　　　　It's wonderful, it's wonderful,
　　　　As they tell you.
　　　　You leave your house some morning
　　　　And without any warning
　　　　You're stopping people shouting that love
　　　　is grand,
　　　　And
　　　　To hold a man in your arms
　　　　Is wonderful, wonderful
　　　　In ev'ry way.
ANNIE: I should say.

MOONSHINE LULLABY

Published. Copyrighted March 5, 1946. Previously registered for copyright as an unpublished song January 5, 1946. Introduced by Ethel Merman (Annie Oakley) and trio.

Behind the hill
There's a busy little still
Where your pappy's working in the moonlight.
Your lovin' pa
Isn't quite within the law,
So he's hiding there behind the hill.
Bye, bye, baby,
Stop your yawning.
Don't cry, baby,
Day will be dawning.
And when it does
From the mountain where he was
He'll be coming with a jug of moonshine.
So count your sheep,
Mamma's singing you to sleep
With the moonshine lullaby.
Dream of Pappy,
Very happy
With his jug of mountain rye.
So count your sheep,
Mamma's singing you to sleep
With the moonshine lullaby.

I'LL SHARE IT ALL
WITH YOU

Published. Copyrighted April 12, 1946. Previously registered for copyright as an unpublished song March 6, 1946. Introduced by Betty Anne Nyman (Winnie Tate) and Kenny Bowers (Tommy Keeler).

VERSE

TOMMY: What is mine, dear, will be yours,
　　　　When the sun shines and when it
　　　　pours—
　　　　Summer, winter, fall, and spring,
　　　　Fifty-fifty in ev'rything.
　　　　Haven't got much,
　　　　Even that much,
　　　　To my name.
　　　　Fortune's door shut;

Can't get in, but
Just the same—

CHORUS 1

My ear for music,
My feet for dancing,
My lips for kissing,
I'll share it all with you.
My sense of humor,
My disposition,
My rosy future,
I'll share it all with you.
Someday, honey,
I'll have money—
You know what that brings:
Furs and diamond rings
And besides those things
There'll be
My ear for music,
My feet for dancing,
My lips for kissing,
I'll share it all with you.

CHORUS 2

WINNIE: My head for thinking,
My face for smiling,
My hands for cooking,
I'll share it all with you.
My understanding,
My loving nature,
My good intentions,
I'll share it all with you.
I'm not twenty,
But there's plenty
Underneath my hat—
I know where I'm at
And on top of that
There'll be
My ear for music,
My feet for dancing,
My lips for kissing,
I'll share it all with you.

MY DEFENSES ARE DOWN

Published. Copyrighted April 12, 1946. Previously registered for copyright as an unpublished song February 1, 1946. Introduced by Ray Middleton (Frank Butler) and male ensemble.

VERSE

I've had my way with so many girls,
And it was lots of fun.
My system was to know many girls;
'Twould keep me safe from one—
I find it can't be done.

CHORUS

My defenses are down;
She's broken my resistance,
And I don't know where I am.
I went into the fight like a lion,
But I came out like a lamb.
My defenses are down;
She's got me where she wants me,
And I can't escape nohow.
I could speak to my heart when it weakened,
But my heart won't listen now.
Like a toothless, clawless tiger,
Like an organ grinder's bear,
Like a knight without his armor,
Like Samson without his hair,
My defenses are down;
I might as well surrender,
For the battle can't be won.
But I must confess that I like it,
So there's nothing to be done;
Yes, I must confess that I like it—
Being mis'rable is gonna be fun.

I'M AN INDIAN TOO

Published. Copyrighted April 15, 1946. Previously registered for copyright as an unpublished song February 12, 1946. Introduced by Ethel Merman (Annie Oakley). Berlin got the names of the different Indian tribes from one of his daughter Elizabeth's schoolbooks.

Published version

VERSE

Since I was a child of three,
They've had the Indian sign on me.
They'd sit and watch me as I grew;
I would dream how nice 'twould be
To have an Indian family—
And now my dreams have all come true.

CHORUS 1

Like the Seminole,
Navajo, Kickapoo,
Like the Cherokee,
I'm an Indian too,
A Sioux, ooh-ooh!
A Sioux, ooh-ooh!
Just like Battle Ax,
Hatchet Face, Eagle Nose,
Like those Indians,
I'm an Indian too,
A Sioux, ooh-ooh!
A Sioux, ooh-ooh!
Some Indian summer's day
Without a care
I may run away
With Big Chief Son of a Bear.
And I'll wear moccasins,
Wampum beads, feather hats,
Which will go to prove
I'm an Indian too,
A Sioux, ooh-ooh!
A Sioux, ooh-ooh!

CHORUS 2

Like the Chippewa,
Iroquois, Omaha,
Like the Powatan,
I'm an Indian too,
A Sioux, ooh-ooh!
A Sioux, ooh-ooh!
Just like Rising Moon,
Falling Pants, Running Nose,
Like those Indians,
I'm an Indian too,
A Sioux, ooh-ooh!
A Sioux, ooh-ooh!
Some Indian summer's day
Without a sound
I may hide away
With Big Chief Hole in the Ground.
And I'll have totem poles,
Tomahawks, small papoose,
Which will go to prove
I'm an Indian too,
A Sioux, ooh-ooh!
A Sioux!

Show version

CHORUS 1

ANNIE: Like the Seminole,
Navajo, Kickapoo,

Like those Indians,
I'm an Indian too,
A Sioux—ooh-ooh—
A Sioux.
Just like Battle Ax,
Hatchet Face, Eagle Nose,
Like those Indians,
I'm an Indian too,
A Sioux—ooh-ooh—
A Sioux.
Some Indian summer's day
Without a sound
I may hide away
With Big Chief Hole in the Ground.
And I'll have totem poles,
Tomahawks, pipes of peace,
Which will go to prove
I'm an Indian too,
A Sioux—ooh-ooh—
A Sioux.

INTERLUDE

With my chief in his teepee
We'll raise an Indian family,
And I'll be busy night and day
Looking like a flour sack,
With two papooses on my back
And three papooses on the way.

CHORUS 2

Like the Chippewa,
Iroquois, Omaha,
Like those Indians,
I'm an Indian too,
A Sioux—ooh-ooh—
A Sioux.
Just like Rising Moon,
Falling Pants, Running Nose,
Like those Indians,
I'm an Indian too,
A Sioux—ooh-ooh—
A Sioux.
Some Indian summer's day
Without a care
I may run away
With Big Chief Son of a Bear.
And I'll wear moccasins,
Wampum beads, feather hats,
Which will go to prove
I'm an Indian too,
A Sioux—ooh-ooh—
A Sioux.

[*In the mid-1980s Berlin added a half-chorus to the song. Here is the September 12, 1985, addition.*]

HALF-CHORUS

I'll travel to New York town
Dressed up in style,
And for twenty-four bucks
I'll buy Manhattan Isle,
And after that is done
I'll sell it back to Washington
And make the Congress pass a law
That the White House needs an Indian squaw
To tell the President what to do,
And he'll obey me through and through,
Because the President happens to be
An Indian too,
A Sioux—ooh-ooh!
A Sioux—ooh-ooh!

I GOT LOST IN HIS ARMS

Published. Copyrighted March 4, 1946, and April 5, 1946. Previously registered for copyright as an unpublished song January 5, 1946. Introduced by Ethel Merman (Annie Oakley) and ensemble.

VERSE

Don't ask me just how it happened;
I wish I knew.
I can't believe that it's happened,
And still it's true.

CHORUS

I got lost in his arms
And I had to stay;
It was dark in his arms
And I lost my way.
From the dark came a voice
And it seemed to say,
"There you go . . . there you go."
How I felt as I fell
I just can't recall;
But his arms held me fast
And it broke the fall,
And I said to my heart
As it foolishly kept jumping all around,
"I got lost
But look what I found."

WHO DO YOU LOVE? I HOPE

Published. Copyrighted March 5, 1946. Previously registered for copyright as an unpublished song February 12, 1946. Introduced Betty Anne Nyman (Winnie Tate) and Kenny Bowers (Tommy Keeler).

VERSE

TOMMY: I've got the question;
I've had it for days—
You've got the answer, dear.
I'll put the question
In one little phrase—
Say what I want to hear.

CHORUS 1

Who do you love? I hope—
Who would you kiss? I hope—
Who is it going to be?
I hope, I hope, I hope it's me.
Who do you want? I hope—
Who do you need? I hope—
Who is it going to be?
I hope, I hope, I hope it's me.
Is it the baker who gave you a cake?
I saw that look in his eye.
Is it the butcher who brought you a steak?
Say that it is and I'll die.
Who do you love? I hope—
Who would you kiss? I hope—
Who is it going to be?
I hope, I hope, I hope it's me.

VERSE 2

WINNIE: I heard your question;
The answer you know—
Love is my middle name.
You asked a question
That worried you so;
Mind if I do the same?

CHORUS 2

Who do you love? I hope—
Who would you kiss? I hope—
Who is it going to be?
I hope, I hope, I hope it's me.
Who do you want? I hope—
Who do you need? I hope—
Who is it going to be?

I hope, I hope, I hope it's me.
Is it the blondie who acted so shy?
You seemed to think she was quaint.*
Is it the redhead who gave you the eye?
Say that it is and I'll faint.†
Who do you love? I hope—
Who would you kiss? I hope—
Who is it going to be?
I hope, I hope, I hope it's me.

I GOT THE SUN IN THE MORNING

Published. Copyrighted April 8, 1946. Previously registered for copyright as an unpublished song under the title "I've Got the Sun in the Morning" on January 24, 1946. Introduced by Ethel Merman (Annie Oakley). Listed in programs as "Sun in the Morning."

VERSE

Taking stock of what I have and what I haven't,
What do I find?
The things I've got will keep me satisfied.
Checking up on what I have and what I haven't,
What do I find?
A healthy balance on the credit side.

CHORUS 1

Got no diamond, got no pearl,
Still I think I'm a lucky girl—
I got the sun in the morning
And the moon at night.
Got no mansion, got no yacht,
Still I'm happy with what I've got—
I got the sun in the morning
And the moon at night.
Sunshine
Gives me a lovely day,
Moonlight
Gives me the Milky Way.
Got no checkbooks, got no banks,
Still I'd like to express my thanks—
I got the sun in the morning
And the moon at night,

*Show version:
   I heard the things that she said.

†Show version:
   Say that it is and you're dead.

And with the sun in the morning
And the moon in the evening,
I'm all right.

CHORUS 2

Got no butler, got no maid,
Still I think I've been overpaid—
I've got the sun in the morning
And the moon at night.
Got no silver, got no gold,
What I've got can't be bought or sold—
I've got the sun in the morning
And the moon at night.
Sunshine
Gives me a lovely day,
Moonlight
Gives me the Milky Way.
Got no heirlooms for my kin,
Made no will but when I cash in,
I'll leave the sun in the morning
And the moon at night,
And with the sun in the morning
And the moon in the evening,
I'm all right.

CHORUS 3 (NOT USED)

Got no honey, got no jam,
Lost my feller and here I am
With just the sun in the morning
And the moon at night.
Got no future, got no plan,
Things look different without a man—
I got the sun in the morning
And the moon at night.
Sunshine
Vanished beyond recall,
Moonlight
Just isn't there at all.
No ambition, things look black,
Won't be different till he comes back
And brings the sun in the morning
And the moon at night,
And with the sun in the morning
And the moon in the evening,
I'm all right.

ANYTHING YOU CAN DO

Published. Copyrighted April 12, 1946. Previously registered for copyright as an unpublished song February 12, 1946. Introduced by Ethel Merman (Annie Oakley) and Ray Middleton (Frank Butler).

Published version

VERSE

ANNIE: I'm superior, you're inferior,
   I'm the big attraction, you're the small;
   I'm the major one, you're the minor one,
   I can beat you shootin'—that's not all.

CHORUS 1

ANNIE: Anything you can do, I can do better.
   I can do anything better than you.
FRANK: No you can't.
ANNIE: Yes I can.
FRANK: No you can't.
ANNIE: Yes I can.
FRANK: No you can't.
ANNIE: Yes I can,
   Yes I can.
   Anything you can be, I can be greater.
   Sooner or later, I'm greater than you.
FRANK: No you're not.
ANNIE: Yes I am.
FRANK: No you're not.
ANNIE: Yes I am.
FRANK: No you're not.
ANNIE: Yes I am,
   Yes I am.
FRANK: I can shoot a partridge with a single
      cartridge.
ANNIE: I can get a sparrow with a bow and arrow.
FRANK: I can do most anything.
ANNIE: Can you bake a pie?
FRANK: No.
ANNIE: Neither can I.
   Anything you can sing I can sing louder.
   I can sing anything louder than you.
FRANK: No you can't.
ANNIE: Yes I can.
FRANK: No you can't.
ANNIE: Yes I can.
FRANK: No you can't.
ANNIE: Yes I can,
   Yes I can.

CHORUS 2

ANNIE: Anything you can buy, I can buy cheaper.
I can buy anything cheaper than you.
FRANK: Fifty cents.
ANNIE: Forty cents.
FRANK: Thirty cents.
ANNIE: Twenty cents.
FRANK: No you can't.
ANNIE: Yes I can,
Yes I can.
Anything you can dig, I can dig deeper.
I can dig anything deeper than you.
FRANK: Thirty feet.
ANNIE: Forty feet.
FRANK: Fifty feet.
ANNIE: Sixty feet.
FRANK: No you can't.
ANNIE: Yes I can,
Yes I can.
FRANK: I can drink my liquor faster than a flicker.
ANNIE: I can do it quicker and get even sicker.
FRANK: I can live on bread and cheese.
ANNIE: And only on that?
FRANK: Yes.
ANNIE: So can a rat.
Any note you can reach, I can go higher.
I can sing anything higher than you.
FRANK: No you can't.
ANNIE: Yes I can.
FRANK: No you can't.
ANNIE: Yes I can.
FRANK: No you can't.
ANNIE: Yes I can,
Yes I can.

CHORUS 3

ANNIE: Anyone you can lick, I can lick faster.
I can lick anyone faster than you.
FRANK: With your fist?
ANNIE: With my feet.
FRANK: With your feet?
ANNIE: With an axe.
FRANK: No you can't.
ANNIE: Yes I can,
Yes I can.
Any school where you went, I could be
master.
I could be master much faster than you.
FRANK: Can you spell?
ANNIE: No I can't.
FRANK: Can you add?
ANNIE: No I can't.
FRANK: Can you teach?
ANNIE: Yes I can,
Yes I can.
FRANK: I could be a racer, quite a steeplechaser.

ANNIE: I can jump a hurdle even with my girdle.
FRANK: I can open any safe.
ANNIE: Without being caught?
FRANK: Yes.
ANNIE: That's what I thought.
Any note you can hold I can hold longer.
I can hold any note longer than you.
FRANK: No you can't.
ANNIE: Yes I can.
FRANK: No you can't.
ANNIE: Yes I can.
FRANK: No you can't.
ANNIE: Yes I can,
Yes I can.

Show version

CHORUS 1

ANNIE: Anything you can do I can do better.
I can do anything better than you.
FRANK: No you can't.
ANNIE: Yes I can.
FRANK: No you can't.
ANNIE: Yes I can.
FRANK: No you can't.
ANNIE: Yes I can,
Yes I can!
FRANK: Anything you can be, I can be greater.
Sooner or later, I'm greater than you.
ANNIE: No you're not.
FRANK: Yes I am.
ANNIE: No you're not.
FRANK: Yes I am.
ANNIE: No you're not.
FRANK: Yes I am,
Yes I am!
I can shoot a partridge
With a single cartridge.
ANNIE: I can get a sparrow
With a bow and arrow.
FRANK: I can live on bread and cheese.
ANNIE: And only on that?
FRANK: Yes.
ANNIE: So can a rat!
FRANK: Any note you can reach, I can go higher.
ANNIE: I can sing anything higher than you.
FRANK: No you can't.
ANNIE: Yes I can.
FRANK: No you can't.
ANNIE: Yes I can.
FRANK: No you can't.
ANNIE: Yes I can.

CHORUS 2

ANNIE: Anything you can buy, I can buy cheaper.
I can buy anything cheaper than you.
FRANK: Fifty cents.
ANNIE: Forty cents.
FRANK: Thirty cents.
ANNIE: Twenty cents.
FRANK: No you can't.
ANNIE: Yes I can,
Yes I can!
FRANK: Anything you can say, I can say softer.
ANNIE: I can say anything softer than you.
FRANK: No you can't.
ANNIE: Yes I can.
FRANK: No you can't.
ANNIE: Yes I can.
FRANK: No you can't.
ANNIE: Yes I can,
Yes I can!
FRANK: I can drink my liquor
Faster than a flicker.
ANNIE: I can do it quicker
And get even sicker.
FRANK: I can open any safe.
ANNIE: Without being caught?
FRANK: Sure.
ANNIE: That's what I thought—
You crook!
FRANK: Any note you can hold, I can hold longer.
ANNIE: I can hold any note longer than you.
FRANK: No you can't.
ANNIE: Yes I can.
FRANK: No you can't.
ANNIE: Yes I can.
FRANK: No you can't.
ANNIE: Yes I can.
Yes I ———
FRANK: No, you can't.
ANNIE: ———can
FRANK: Yes, you can!

CHORUS 3

ANNIE: Anything you can wear, I can wear better.
In what you wear I'd look better than you.
FRANK: In my coat?
ANNIE: In your vest.
FRANK: In my shoes?
ANNIE: In your hat.
FRANK: No you can't.
ANNIE: Yes I can,
Yes I can!
FRANK: Anything you can say, I can say faster.
ANNIE: I can say anything faster than you.
FRANK: No you can't.
ANNIE: Yes I can.
FRANK: No you can't.

ANNIE: Yes I can.

FRANK: No you can't,
No you can't.

ANNIE: Yes I can,
Yes I can!

FRANK: I can jump a hurdle.

ANNIE: I can wear a girdle.

FRANK: I can knit a sweater.

ANNIE: I can fill it better.

FRANK: I can do most anything.

ANNIE: Can you bake a pie?

FRANK: No.

ANNIE: Neither can I.

FRANK: Any note you can sing I can sing sweeter.

ANNIE: I can sing anything sweeter than you.

FRANK: No you can't.

ANNIE: Yes I can.

FRANK: No you can't.

ANNIE: Yes I can.

FRANK: No you can't.

ANNIE: Yes I can.

FRANK: No you can't.

ANNIE: Yes I can.

FRANK: No you can't, can't, can't.

ANNIE: Yes I can, can, can!

FRANK: No you can't!

ANNIE: Yes I can!

TAKE IT IN YOUR STRIDE (WHATEVER THE FATES DECIDE)

Registered for copyright as an unpublished song January 25, 1946. Not used. Intended for Ethel Merman (Annie Oakley). Replaced by Annie's reprise of "There's No Business Like Show Business." There are two versions; both have the same verse.

Version 1

VERSE

Hey there, you
On the top shelf—
Your skies are blue,
Pleased with yourself.
Well, don't you get too cocky;
The road is rocky away up there.
Life is sweet,
Rosy and round,
But keep your feet

Close to the ground—
The weather won't be always fair.

CHORUS 1

There'll be ups and there'll be downs;
There'll be smiles and there'll be frowns;
There'll be hopes and there'll be doubts,
Ins and outs—
But whatever the fates decide,
Take it in your stride.
There'll be rain and there'll be sun;
You'll have all and you'll have none;
Hitch your wagon to a star,
Travel far,
But you're in for a bumpy ride—
Take it in your stride.

CHORUS 2

There'll be friends both new and old;
They'll blow hot and they'll blow cold;
You'll be cheered and you'll be hissed,
Kicked and kissed—
But whatever the fates decide,
Take it in your stride.
Don't get too big for your crown;
What goes up may soon come down.
Someone's waiting down below,
Set to go,
Coming in on the rising tide—
Take it in your stride.

Version 2

CHORUS

There'll be ups and there'll be downs;
There'll be smiles and there'll be frowns—
Put the good with the bad
And just take it in your stride.
There'll be ins and there'll be outs;
You'll be sure and you'll have doubts—
Put the good with the bad
And just take it in your stride.
One day roses, next day thorns—
Learn to wear them side by side.
There'll be rain and there'll be sun;
You'll be bored and you'll have fun—
Put the good with the bad
And you'll have a pleasant ride,
Taking it in your stride.

WITH MUSIC

Registered for copyright as an unpublished song January 5, 1946. Not used. Intended for Kenny Bowers (Tommy Keeler) and Betty Anne Nyman (Winnie Tate). Replaced by "Who Do You Love? I Hope"

VERSE

TOMMY: Now that we're married, we'll get along, I know,
We'll get along whatever may come or go.
One thing we have in common will see us through:
I have an ear for music and so have you.

CHORUS 1

TOMMY: We'll settle down
With music,
Somewhere in town
With music.
Some hurdy-gurdy
Will fill the street with Verdi,
And Mister Strauss
Will fill our house
With music.
We'll greet the night
With music,
Turn down the light
With music;
While night is falling,
We'll hear the crickets calling,
And you and I
Will hush-a-bye
With music.

CHORUS 2

WINNIE: We'll stay indoors
With music,
And I'll be yours
With music.
Brahms will inspire me
To be as you desire me,
And Mister Liszt
Will see you're kissed
With music.

TOMMY: We'll greet the stork
With music,
Then pop a cork
With music.
Bach and Beethoven,
They'll both be interwoven
With things you knit

To fit for it
With music.

PARDNERS

An unused number intended for Ray Middleton (Frank Butler) and Ethel Merman (Annie Oakley). No music is known to survive. Also see "My Old Pal," page 383.

CHORUS 1

Pardners, pardners—
Fifty-fifty in everything.
Pardners, Pardners—
Share and share alike.
FRANK: When I need a hundred dollars,
There may be some bills to pay—
ANNIE: And I'll give you the hundred dollars
And you needn't give it back to me until
the next day.
BOTH: Pardners, pardners—
We'll never disagree.
FRANK: What's mine is yours.
ANNIE: What's mine is mine.
BOTH: And that's how it's always gonna be.

CHORUS 2

Pardners, pardners—
Fifty-fifty in everything.
Pardners, pardners—
Share and share alike.
ANNIE: When we're out together dining,
Right after the meal is through—
FRANK: I'll pick up the check and add it,
Yes, I'll add it up before I hand it over to
you.
BOTH: Pardners, pardners—
We'll split our salary.
ANNIE: And I've rehearsed to get there first.
BOTH: And that's how it's always gonna be.

SOMETHING BAD'S GONNA HAPPEN ('CAUSE I FEEL SO GOOD)

Written for *Annie Get Your Gun*. Not used. Lines 13–16, slightly revised, were used later in the song

"You're Just in Love" in *Call Me Madam* (1950); see page 434.

CHORUS

There's a new kind o' polish
On the sun today.
There's a blue patch of heaven
Where the sky was gray,
Never felt so contented,
But I'm knocking wood.
Something bad's gonna happen
'Cause I feel so good—
So good.
Why does the present
Seem so very pleasant?
I can't understand why it should.
I can hear people singing
Though there's no one there.
I can smell orange blossoms
Though the trees are bare.
I'm afraid to enjoy it
As I know I could.
Something bad's gonna happen,
'Cause I feel so good—
So good.

LET'S GO WEST AGAIN

Published. Copyrighted March 29, 1949. Previously registered for copyright as an unpublished song May 1, 1946. Intended for the original production. Not used. Introduced by Betty Hutton (Annie Oakley) in the film version (1950).

Let's go west again—
I won't rest again
Till we're west again,
You and I.
Let's go back where the skies are seldom gray,
Where the sun goes the end of ev'ry day—
Let's return again,
How I yearn again
To return again,
You and I.
Don't forget there was someone who knew best
Said "Go west, young man, go west."

AN OLD-FASHIONED WEDDING

Published. Copyrighted June 24, 1966. Previously registered for copyright as an unpublished song January 17, 1966, and April 18, 1966. Introduced by Ethel Merman (Annie Oakley) and Bruce Yarnell (Frank Butler) in the 1966 Lincoln Center revival.

CHORUS 1

FRANK: We'll have an old-fashioned wedding,
Blessed in the good old-fashioned way.
I'll vow to love you forever,
You'll vow to love and honor and obey.
Somewhere in some little chapel,
Someday when orange blossoms bloom,
We'll have an old-fashioned wedding,
A simple wedding for an old-fashioned
bride and groom.

CHORUS 2

ANNIE: I wanna wedding in a big church
With bridesmaids and flower girls,
A lot of ushers in tailcoats,
Reporters and photographers,
A ceremony by a bishop
Who will tie the knot and say:
"Do you agree to love and honor?"
Love and honor, yes, but not obey!
I wanna wedding ring surrounded
By diamonds in platinum,
A big reception at the Waldorf
With champagne and caviar.
I wanna wedding like the Vanderbilts
have,
Ev'rything big, not small—
If I can't have that kind of a wedding
I don't wanna get married at all.

REPEAT CHORUS 1 AND 2

[*Sung simultaneously as countermelodies.*]

WHO NEEDS THE BIRDS AND BEES?

Registered for publication as an unpublished song March 9, 1966. Previously registered for copyright as an unpublished song under the title "The Birds and Bees" on February 28, 1966. Introduced by Benay Venuta (Dolly Tate), David Manning, Donna Conforti, Jeanne Tanzy, and Holly Sherwood at the O'Keefe Center, Toronto, in May 1966. Written for the 1966 Lincoln Center revival, but was dropped before the show came to New York.

[*The following verse, set to music, can be sung or spoken.*]

DOLLY: I suppose you know about babies, too.
KIDS: Yes, we do—yes, we do.
JESSIE: A doctor brings it in a satchel—
    Of that I have the proof.
NELLIE: A stork flies over the house
    And drops the baby on the roof.
KIDS: We do—we do—we know about babies
    too.

[*The above is sung or spoken tongue-in-cheek.*]

DOLLY: I think you kids are mighty dumb—
    You don't know just where you came
      from.
    To know how folks have families,
    You must observe the birds and bees.
KIDS: Who needs the birds and bees
    To prove that people have families?
    Who needs to live in trees
    To learn about the birds and bees?
DOLLY: A rooster calls upon a hen,
    He struts up close to her, and then
    He'll scratch the ground with both his
      legs—
KIDS: And soon the chicks break through the
      eggs.
    So who needs the birds and bees
    To prove that chickens have families?
    Who needs to live in trees
    To learn about the birds and bees?

DOLLY: A pair of rabbits meet one day
    And settle on a bale of hay;
    A month goes by—what do we see?
KIDS: Instead of two there's twenty-three!
    So who needs the birds and bees
    To prove that rabbits have families?
    Who needs to live in trees
    To learn about the birds and bees?
DOLLY: When Missus Fish has done her
      bit,
    And Mister Fish swims over it,
    A school of fishes when it's done.
JAKE: [*not knowing he's singing a dirty
      line*]
    But Mister Fish ain't had no fun!
ALL: So who needs the birds and bees
    To prove that fishes have families?
    Who needs to live in trees
    To learn about the birds and bees?

EASTER PARADE | 1948

EASTER PARADE (1948)

A film produced by Arthur Freed for Metro-Goldwyn-Mayer. Released in June 1948. Music and lyrics by Irving Berlin. Screenplay by Sidney Sheldon, Frances Goodrich, and Albert Hackett (based upon an original story by Goodrich and Hackett). Additional scriptwriting Guy Bolton. Directed by Charles Walters. Musical numbers staged and directed by Robert Alton. Orchestrations by Conrad Salinger, Mason Van Cleave, Robert Franklyn, Paul Marquardt, Sidney Cutner, Leo Shuken. Vocal arrangements Robert Tucker. Music conducted by Johnny Green. Associate musical director, Roger Edens. Cast: starring Judy Garland (Hannah Brown) and Fred Astaire (Don Hewes) and featuring Peter Lawford (Johnny Harrow III) and Ann Miller (Nadine Gale). Original cast album (MGM).

Berlin wrote Francis Gilbert, his attorney, about the film on February 6, 1948:

> Incidentally, we showed the picture to Louie Mayer and some of the other front office heads this morning, and they are calling *Easter Parade* "the *Gone with the Wind* of musicals"—that may be a slight exaggeration, then again, it may very easily prove to be "one of those things." Personally, I feel it's the most satisfactory musical I've ever been connected with. I'm sure it will be a tremendous success. Also, I feel we have at least a couple of big song hits in it.

HAPPY EASTER

Published. Copyrighted April 11, 1957. Previously registered for copyright as an unpublished song November 24, 1947, and again on January 26, 1948. Introduced by Fred Astaire (Don Hewes) and ensemble.

Never saw such a lovely day—
Happy Easter, Happy Easter.
Everything seems to come your way—
Happy Easter, Happy Easter.
My oh me, what a hit you'll be,
On the well-known Avenue.
Me oh my, you're a lucky guy—
Happy Easter to you.

Judy Garland and Fred Astaire

Film version

[*Opening for* DON *and the* GIRLS *modeling hats.*]
[*We see* DON *walking down the street.*]

DON: [*whistles first two bars; then to some* PASSERBY]
Happy Easter.
PASSERBY: Happy Easter.

[DON *continues walking.*]

DON: [*whistles another two bars; then, to* SECOND PASSERBY]
Happy Easter.
SECOND PASSERBY: Happy Easter.
DON: [*sings*]
Me oh my, there's a lot to buy—
There is shopping I must do.

[*He continues walking and enters hat shop.*]

DON: [*whistles another two bars; then, to* PROPRIETRESS *of hat shop*]
Happy Easter to you.

[GIRLS *begin to model hats for him.*]

FIRST GIRL: Here's a hat that you should take home—
Happy Easter.
DON: [*over scene*]
Happy Easter.
SECOND GIRL: Here's a lid for m'lady's dome—
Happy Easter.
DON: [*over scene*]
Happy Easter.
THIRD GIRL: This was made for the hat parade
On the well-known Avenue.
FOURTH GIRL: This one's nice and it's worth the price—
Happy Easter to you.
FIFTH GIRL: Here's a hat for a pretty face—
Happy Easter.
DON: [*over scene*]
Happy Easter.
SIXTH GIRL: Here is one that is trimmed with lace—
Happy Easter.
DON: [*over scene*]
Happy Easter.
SEVENTH GIRL: Here's a touch of the quaint old Dutch—
It's an old that's always new.
EIGHTH GIRL: This in white is exactly right—
Happy Easter to you.
MILLINER: I think that is a lovely hat—
Maybe you think so too.
DON: [*coming into scene*]
I do.
ALL: Wrap it up for the chap
With a Very Happy Easter to you.
MESSENGER BOYS: [*who have arrived with the presents*]
Never saw such a lovely gal—
Happy Easter, Happy Easter.
Where oh where did you get her, pal?
Happy Easter, Happy Easter.
My oh me, what a hit she'll be
On the well-known Avenue!
Me oh my, you're a lucky guy—
Happy Easter to you.

DRUM CRAZY

Published. Copyrighted March 31, 1948. Previously registered for copyright as an unpublished song March 26, 1947. Berlin's lyric manuscript of refrain dated February 21, 1947. Introduced by Fred Astaire (Don Hewes).

VERSE

A bunny for my honey,
A dolly with a curl,
An aeroplane, an electric train,
And a teddy bear for my girl.
A kitty for my pretty,
A castle for my love—
Gee, what do I see?
Brother, if that's a drum, that's for me.

CHORUS

I'm drum crazy, yes,
I'm drum crazy, yes,
I'm plumb crazy for drums.
I've got drumsticks
Full of hot licks
And a roll loaded with soul under control.
First, soft violins,
Then sweet saxophones,
Then blue clarinets croon;
When it's my turn,
I turn into a loon—
When the drum takes the melody,
When the drum carries the tune.

IT ONLY HAPPENS WHEN I DANCE WITH YOU

Published. Copyrighted March 31, 1948. Previously registered for copyright as an unpublished song June 14, 1947. Berlin's typed lyric sheets dated April 15 and 16, 1947. Introduced by Fred Astaire (Don Hewes); danced by Astaire and Ann Miller (Nadine Gale). Reprised by Judy Garland (Hannah Brown).

CHORUS

It only happens when I dance with you—
That trip to heaven till the dance is through.
With no one else do the heavens seem quite so
    near;
Why does it happen, dear, only with you?
Two cheeks together can be so divine,
But only when those cheeks are yours and mine.
I've danced with dozens of others the whole night
    through,
But the thrill that comes with spring
When anything could happen,
That only happens with you.

Earlier version

It only happens when I dance with you—
What's more, it lingers when the dance is
    through.
I mean the scenic railway ride
That gives you butterflies inside—
That only happens when I'm dancing with you.
Those moments when your cheek is pressed to
    mine,
I feel like someone who's had too much wine.
I've danced with other girls who were attractive
    too,
But the thrill that comes with spring
When anything can happen,
That only happens with you.

A FELLA WITH AN UMBRELLA

Published. Copyrighted March 22, 1948. Previously registered for copyright as an unpublished song June 14, 1947. Introduced by Peter Lawford (Johnny Harrow III) and Judy Garland (Hannah Brown).

VERSE

HE: Who am I,
    What's my name,
    Where I'm from,
    How I came,
    Doesn't matter, dear.
    Long as I am here.

CHORUS 1

HE: I'm just a fella,
    A fella with an umbrella,
    Looking for a girl who saved her love for a
        rainy day.
    I'm just a fella,
    A fella with an umbrella,
    Glad to see the skies of blue have turned into
        skies of gray.
    Raindrops have brought us together,
    And that's what I longed to see;
    Maybe the break in the weather
    Will prove to be a break for me.
    So I'll be the fella,
    The fella with an umbrella,
    If you'll be the girl who saved her love for a
        rainy day.

CHORUS 2

SHE: I met a fella,
    A fella with an umbrella,
    Looking for a girl who saved her love for a
        rainy day.
    I met a fella,
    A fella with an umbrella,
    Waiting for the skies of blue to turn into
        skies of gray.
    Raindrops will bring us together,
    And that's what I long to see;
    Maybe a break in the weather
    Will prove to be a break for me.
    For I told the fella,
    The fella with the umbrella,
    I could be the girl who saved her love for a
        rainy day.

Chorus 2 for Judy Garland

For ev'ry fella,
Each fella with an umbrella,
There's a girl, a girl who saved her love for a rainy
    day.
For ev'ry fella,
Each fella with an umbrella,
There's a time when skies of blue must turn into
    skies of gray.

Raindrops have brought us together;
That's what they were meant to do.
Maybe the break in the weather
Will turn into a break for you.
And I'll help the fella,
The fella with an umbrella,
Help him find the girl who saved her love for a
    rainy day.

Alternate verse

Cloudy sky, looks like rain,
Got no time to explain
How I happened here—
Doesn't matter, dear.

STEPPIN' OUT WITH MY BABY

Published. Copyrighted March 31, 1948. Previously registered for copyright as an unpublished song June 26, 1947. Introduced by Fred Astaire (Don Hewes); danced by Astaire with Patricia Jackson, Bobbie Priest, Dee Turnell, and other dancers from ensemble.

VERSE

If I seem to scintillate,
It's because I've got a date,
A date with a package of
The good things that come with love.
You don't have to ask me,
I won't waste your time;
But if you should ask me
Why I feel sublime, I'm

CHORUS

Steppin' out with my baby—
Can't go wrong 'cause I'm in right.
It's for sure not for maybe
That I'm all dressed up tonight.
Steppin' out with my honey—
Can't be bad to feel so good.
Never felt quite so sunny,
And I keep on knockin' wood;
There'll be smooth sailin' 'cause I'm trimmin' my
    sails
In my top hat and my white tie and my tails.*

---
*Alternate (female) version of line:
    With a bright shine on my shoes and on my nails.

Steppin' out with my baby—
Can't go wrong 'cause I'm in right.
Ask me when will the day be—
The big day may be tonight.

A COUPLE OF SWELLS

Published. Copyrighted May 27, 1948. Previously regis-
tered for copyright as an unpublished song July 2, 1947.
Introduced by Fred Astaire (Don Hewes) and Judy Gar-
land (Hannah Brown).

VERSE 1

We're a couple of swells;
We stop at the best hotels.
But we prefer the country,
Far away from the city smells.
We're a couple of sports,
The pride of the tennis courts;
In June, July, and August,
We look cute when we're dressed in shorts.
The Vanderbilts have asked us up for tea;
We don't know how to get there, no siree.

CHORUS 1

We would drive up the Avenue,
But we haven't got the price.
We would skate up the Avenue,
But there isn't any ice.
We would ride on a bicycle,
But we haven't got a bike.
So we'll walk up the Avenue,
Yes, we'll walk up the Avenue,
And to walk up the Avenue's what we like.

VERSE 2

Wall Street bankers are we,
With plenty of currency.
We'd open up the safe, but
We forgot where we put the key.
We're the favorite lads
Of girls in the picture ads;
We'd like to tell you who
We kissed last night, but we can't be cads.
The Vanderbilts are waiting at the club,
But how are we to get there? That's the rub.

CHORUS 2

We would sail up the Avenue,
But we haven't got a yacht.

We would drive up the Avenue,
But the horse we had was shot.
We would ride on a trolley car,
But we haven't got the fare.
So we'll walk up the Avenue,
Yes, we'll walk up the Avenue,
Yes, we'll walk up the Avenue till we're there.

BETTER LUCK NEXT TIME

Published. Copyrighted March 22, 1948. Previously reg-
istered for copyright as an unpublished song June 14,
1947. Introduced by Judy Garland (Hannah Brown).

VERSE

For ev'ry rose that withers and dies,
Another blooms in its stead;
A new love waits to open its eyes
After the old love is dead.
That sounds all right in a careless rhyme,
But there's seldom a second time.

CHORUS

Better luck next time—
That could never be,
Because there ain't gonna be no next time
For me,
No siree.
Made up my mind
To make another start;
I've made my mind up,
But I can't make up my heart.
I'd like a new lucky day—
That would be nice—
But this comes just once in a lifetime,
Not twice.
So don't say, "Better luck next time"—
That could never be,
Because there ain't gonna be no next time
For me.

MR. MONOTONY and MRS. MONOTONY

Published. Copyrighted June 17, 1949. Previously regis-
tered for copyright as an unpublished song June 14,
1947. Written for Judy Garland (Hannah Brown) to sing
in *Easter Parade*. Although filmed, this number was cut
from the final print.

Even in its earliest form Berlin was undecided
whether the song should be "Mr. Monotony" or "Mrs.
Monotony." Although it was actually performed in *Miss
Liberty* as "Mrs. Monotony" (where it was introduced
during the pre-Broadway tryout by Mary McCarty
[Maisie] and ensemble, but dropped before the New
York opening), it was published as "Mr. Monotony" with
other songs from the show. Then it was sung by Ethel
Merman in the pre-Broadway tryout of *Call Me
Madam*, only to be replaced by "Something to Dance
About." Later it was considered for the 1954 film
There's No Business Like Show Business, but not used.
Finally, it was introduced by Debbie Shapiro (now
known as Debbie Gravitte) in *Jerome Robbins' Broad-
way* (1988).

Over the years this song was the subject of much
humor for Berlin and Jerome Robbins, who first staged
it for *Miss Liberty*.

On October 19, 1962, at the time of *Mr. President*'s
New York opening, Robbins sent Berlin the following
telegram:

GOOD LUCK TONIGHT AND ALL MY LOVE AND
WHATEVER THE NEW SHOW IS IF IT DOESNT IN-
CLUDE MONOTONY FORGET IT SINCERELY JERRY
ROBBINS

Berlin replied on October 30:

Getting back to your wire, I'm planning to rest
until I become restless which will be in about
three or four weeks. After then, I hope we can get
together. Nothing would please me more than to
again work with you, but this time, no "Mr. Mo-
notony." Twice is enough.

When Robbins included "Mr. Monotony" in *Jerome
Robbins' Broadway*, he sent Berlin the following letter:

Well, we finally made it. "Monotony" is in the
eleven o'clock place (these days it's ten-thirty) and
I think you would be very, very pleased. It is sung
by a great young talent named Debbie Shapiro
who tears the place down with the song alone.
Then we dance it and that goes equally well.

I'm so proud to have it in my show, dear Irv-
ing, and the audience reacts with such deep re-
spect, affection and anticipation to the number. I

wish you could see it but in case you can't I've enclosed a tape of the number.

Again my thanks and again, as always, my love to you.

Version intended for *Easter Parade*

Playing on his slide trombone,
In a certain monotone,
He was known as Mister Monotony.
Any pleasant interlude
That would mean a change of mood
Didn't go with Mister Monotony.
Sometimes he would change the key,
But the same dull melody
Would emerge from Mister Monotony.
Folks for miles would run away;
Only one preferred to stay:
She would come around and say,
"Have you got any monotony today?
Have you got any monotony today?"
They got married as they should,
And around the neighborhood
She was known as "Missus Monotony."
They were happy as could be,
And they raised a family,
Six or seven little Monotonies.
From another village came a snappy clarineter;
She heard him play and, strange to say, she liked
    him better—
'Twas the end of Mister Monotony.
Soon there came another bride,
And she snuggled to his side,
But he answered when she cried,
"Have you got any monotony today?,"
"Haven't got any monotony today—
Can't play
Today,
Haven't got any
Monotony today."

Version intended for *Miss Liberty*

At her piano all alone,
Playing in a monotone,
She was known as Missus Monotony.
Any pleasant interlude
That would mean a change of mood
Didn't go with Missus Monotony.
Sometimes she would change the key,
But the same dull melody
Would emerge from Missus Monotony.
Folks for miles would run away;
Only one preferred to stay:
He would come around and say,
"Have you got any monotony today?"

She refused to live in sin,
So one evening he gave in
And he married Missus Monotony.
They were happy as could be,
And they raised a family,
Six or seven little Monotonies.
From another village came a snappy little dancer;
She caught his eye, and after then—you know
    the answer:
'Twas the end of Missus Monotony.
Soon another feller tried
Gettin' closer to her side,
But she answered when he cried,
"Have you got any monotony today?,"
"Haven't got any monotony today—
Can't play
Today,
Haven't got any
Monotony today."

Version intended for *Call Me Madam* (1950) and *There's No Business Like Show Business* (1954)

Playing on his slide trombone,
In a certain monotone,
He is known as Mister Monotony.
Any pleasant interlude
That will mean a change of mood
Doesn't go with Mister Monotony.
Sometimes he will change the key,
But the same dull melody
Will emerge from Mister Monotony.
Folks for miles will run away;
Only one prefers to stay:
She will come around and say,
"Have you got any monotony today?"
They were married, but we find
That she quickly changed her mind;
She got tired of Mister Monotony.
While he practiced all alone
Bugle calls on his trombone,
Someone called on Missus Monotony.
From another village came a snappy clarineter;
She heard him play and right away she liked him
    better—
'Twas the end of Mister Monotony.
There's a moral in my song:
Trombone players don't last long,
And it's right to do them wrong.
When they've got any monotony to play,
And it's not any monotony that's gay,
Don't stay,
Just say,
"Haven't got any
Monotony today."

I LOVE YOU— YOU LOVE HIM

Registered for copyright as an unpublished song June 14, 1947. Not used in film. *Easter Parade* scriptwriter Frances Goodrich told Arthur Freed's biographer Hugh Fordin (*That's Entertainment*, p. 224), "Sometimes [Berlin] would come in with an idea and a song to illustrate it. For example, he had a new song 'I Love You— You Love Him,' which he had envisioned as sort of *La Ronde* with a Greek vase, etc. And we would say we couldn't work that out . . . and he'd answer, 'That's all right, I'll use it somewhere else.' What we are trying to say is that he was very flexible."

VERSE

Here we are, four of us,
Lovers in distress,
Glad there's not more of us
In this awful mess.
I'm afraid for all of us
The future looks black,
Each in love with one of us
Who doesn't love back.

CHORUS

I love you, you love him,
He loves her, she loves me—
Ev'rything is just as it shouldn't be.
You love him, he loves her,
She loves me, I love you—
There's a job we all of us have to do
To untangle an angle
We all of us have to get;
We must fix up this mixup,
For none of us will be set
Till he loves her as she loves him,
She loves him as he loves her,
And you love me as I love you.

Irving Berlin, Jinx Falkenburg, and Bob Hope prepare to land during the Berlin airlift, 1948

STARS ON MY SHOULDERS | 1948
and Other Songs of 1946–1949

STARS ON MY SHOULDERS (1948)

In late 1947 or early 1948 Berlin began work with author Norman Krasna on a new musical, *Stars on My Shoulders*, about what happens to an Eisenhower-like general after the war when, as a civilian, he is being persuaded to run for President of the United States. Rodgers and Hammerstein were approached to be the producers, and Walter Huston was to have played the leading role. Berlin completed much of the score, but according to him, there were book problems; the second act was never in satisfactory shape. The project was abandoned in early 1949, but the idea bore fruit later in the 1954 film *White Christmas*. Four songs written for *Stars on My Shoulders* were used later in other scores. For the lyrics of "The Old Man" and "What Can You Do with a General?" see *White Christmas* (1954), pages 440 and 442. For "A Man Chases a Girl (Until She Catches Him)," see *There's No Business Like Show Business* (1954), page 447. For "It Gets Lonely in the White House," see *Mr. President* (1962), page 471.

FIVE O'CLOCK IN THE AFTERNOON

No music is known to survive. This number was to have been preceded by "Have You Ever Tried Drinking Water?," written for but not used in *Blue Skies* (1946).

Five o'clock in the afternoon
Once meant a cup of tea,
But what does five in the afternoon
Now mean for you and me?
It means a cocktail or a highball for two.
Whether it's in a country town
Or whether it's New York,
Whether it's in a Bowery joint
Or in the swanky Stork,
They come to cocktails and to highballs for two.

The lowbrows and the thinkers,
The nice folks and the stinkers
Become important drinkers
No matter where they are—
The girls who plug the switches,
The poor who dig the ditches,
The wealthy sons of riches
Will gather at the bar.

BEAUTIFUL BROOKLYN

Registered for copyright as an unpublished song May 8, 1948.

CHORUS

Why should I cry
For a house in Versailles?
I've got Brooklyn—
Beautiful Brooklyn.
What could I gain
With a castle in Spain?
I've got Brooklyn—
Beautiful Brooklyn.
Just cross the bridge
And give your eyes a feast—
I mean the bridge
That goes across the East
River.
Come here and see,
Come and see why a tree
Grows in Brooklyn—
Beautiful Brooklyn,
And what's good enough for a tree
Is good enough for me.

A BEAUTIFUL DAY IN BROOKLYN

Published in *The Unsung Irving Berlin*. Sung on *Unsung Irving Berlin* (Varese-Sarabande) by Crista Moore. Copyrighted 1995. Previously registered for copyright as an unpublished song February 25, 1948.

VERSE

Poets love to sing
Of Paris in the spring;
They say it's something that you can't conceive.
I don't know a thing
Of Paris in the spring;
I've never been abroad, but I believe—

CHORUS

A beautiful day in Brooklyn is more beautiful
Than a beautiful day in any other place.
When the sun comes shining through
Over Flatbush Avenue
You wake with a smile on your face.

The weatherman doesn't have to say it's beautiful—
When you open your window, ev'rything's okay.
If a tree that grows in Brooklyn
Could speak, it would say
A beautiful day in Brooklyn
Is a most beautiful day.

FUNNY WHEN YOU'RE LEFT WITH NOTHING MORE TO SAY

Published in *The Unsung Irving Berlin*. Sung on *Unsung Irving Berlin* (Varese-Sarabande) by Liz Callaway. Copyrighted 1995. Previously registered for copyright as an unpublished song February 25, 1948.

Funny when you're left with nothing more to say;
Suddenly you find you should be on your way.
Funny how you long for some excuse
To remain a while, but it's no use—
The conversation ends and you've nothing more to say.
Funny when you're left without a thought on your mind;
Funny when you search for words you never can find.
Gone are the pretty speeches that you planned for your lucky day—
Funny when you're left with nothing more to say.

JOHN JACOB ASTOR

Registered for copyright as an unpublished song May 8, 1948.

VERSE

The Indians sold Manhattan
For a dozen drinks of rye;
That's when the boom in real estate began.
The fellows who bought Manhattan
Didn't think much of their buy;
They sold it to a very clever man.

CHORUS

John Jacob Astor
Bought up half the town;
No one was faster
With a payment down.
Properties that were passed up by the suckers
Are developments now as big as Sophie Tucker's.
John never gambled;
He had too much brains:
Stocks often vanish,
But the ground remains.
The the'ters that you see
Owned by brothers Jake and Lee
Were built on a spot
That once was a lot,
A lot that they got
From Mister Astor.
And what was Herald Square
When the buildings weren't there?
A ditch filled with pitch.
And who owned that ditch?
A son of the rich
Called Mister Astor.

IF WE WEREN'T MARRIED

Written for *Stars on My Shoulders*.

If we weren't married,
How happy we would be!
You'd call for me at eight o'clock
And keep me up till three.
We'd wind up somewhere
Where I'd leave some hairpins and a comb—
But we're married,
And the only place we can wind up is home.

If we weren't married,
How happy we would be!
I'd tremble with excitement
When you cuddled up to me.
You'd smother me with kisses
That would open up my eyes—
But we're married,
And I like it fine,
But I miss the surprise.

[*Repeat first stanza.*]

When we were single, single,
My blood would fairly tingle
When lights were burning low—
But that seems so long ago.

A ROOF OVER MY HEAD

Registered for copyright as an unpublished song May 8, 1948. There are three slightly different versions of the chorus. The first two date from 1948; the last revision is dated July 2, 1984.

VERSE

Trouble and worry and strife—
That's what I haven't got.
What do I want out of life?
Not such an awful lot.

CHORUS

A roof over my head,
A floor under my feet,
A roof over my head,
And enough to keep my baby by my side.
Enough to pay the butcher and the grocer—
Is that so very much to ask for? No sir!
A roof over my head,
A floor under my feet,
And enough to keep my baby by my side.

Alternate chorus (1948)

A roof over my head,
A floor under my feet,
A kind heaven to help me provide
A roof over my head,
A floor under my feet,
And enough to keep my baby by my side.
Enough to pay the butcher and the grocer—
Is that so very much to ask for? No sir!
A roof over my head,
A floor under my feet,
And enough to keep my baby by my side.

Alternate chorus (1984)

A roof over my head,
A floor under my feet—
I know that I'll be more than satisfied
With a roof over my head,
A floor under my feet,
And enough to keep my baby by my side.
Enough to pay the butcher and the
    grocer—
Is that so very much to ask for? No sir!
With the helping hand of heaven
I'll be able to provide
A roof over my head,

A floor under my feet,
And enough to keep my baby by my side.

MONOHAN AND CALLAHAN

Registered for copyright as an unpublished song May 8, 1948.

CHORUS 1

GERT: When you lift up a rock,
        What comes up from under?
        A Monohan.
SPIKE: A Callahan.
GERT: A Monohan.
SPIKE: When a bank has been robbed,
        Who is hiding the plunder?
GERT: A Monohan.
SPIKE: A Callahan.
GERT: Here is a picture that you simply will
        adore:
        Two men are fighting like they never
        fought before—
        One man is standing while the other's on
        the floor.
SPIKE: Who's on the floor?
GERT: A Monohan.
SPIKE: A Callahan.
GERT: A Monohan.
SPIKE: A Callahan.

{ GERT: A Monohan, not a Callahan's on the floor.
{ SPIKE: A Callahan, not a Monohan's on the floor.

CHORUS 2

SPIKE: When there's drinking to do,
        Who is first 'neath the table?
        A Callahan.
GERT: A Monohan.
SPIKE: A Callahan.
GERT: When a horse disappears,
        Who was last in the stable?
        A Monohan.
SPIKE: A Callahan.
GERT: A Monohan.

OTHER SONGS OF 1946–1949

HELP ME TO HELP MY NEIGHBOR

Published. Copyrighted January 27, 1947. Previously registered for copyright as an unpublished song January 17, 1947. Introduced by Kate Smith February 16, 1947. Written in response to a request from American Brotherhood for Brotherhood Week.

Help me to help my neighbor,
Help me to understand,
Help me to hear the pleading
Of an outstretched, empty hand.
Help me to do to others
As I'd have them do to me;
Help me to help my neighbor,
Whatever his faith may be.
Help me to see a heavy heart
Behind a smiling face;
Help me to judge as I'd be judged
If I were in his place.
The night is dark
And the way is long
On a road that has no end—
Help me to help my neighbor,
Help me to be his friend.

KATE (HAVE I COME TOO EARLY, TOO LATE?)

Published. Copyrighted June 3, 1947. Previously registered for copyright as an unpublished song May 20, 1947. Introduced by Kate Smith June 15, 1947. Leading recording by Eddy Howard and His Orchestra (Majestic).

VERSE

Here's that man again,
Waiting at your garden gate
With a bouquet—
Don't you send me away.
Have a little pity, Kate—

Poor me, can't you see
I'm in an awful state?

CHORUS

How much longer must I wait, Kate,
Till you let me know my fate, Kate?
The sun's down,
The moon's out,
There's no one in sight.
My questions need answers;
Tonight is the night.
Nine o'clock we had a date, Kate;
I've been here since half past eight, Kate.
I came a little bit early, I couldn't wait—
Have I come too early too late?

LOVE AND THE WEATHER

Published. Copyrighted May 26, 1947. Introduced by Kate Smith on June 15, 1947. Leading recordings by Jo Stafford (Columbia) and Kenny Baker (Decca).

VERSE

Unpredictable, irresponsible,
Unbelievable, unreliable,
Ever since the world began
Are Cupid and the weatherman.

CHORUS

Love and the weather,
Birds of a feather,
Can't be depended upon.
One day it's sunny;
Next day the sunshine has gone.
Love and the weather,
Always together,
Planning another surprise,
Bringing the raindrops
Just like the tears to your eyes.
There was I with love close by,
So cozy and warm;
Love walked out and so did I
Right out of the warm
Into a storm.
Moonlight romances
Have to take chances;
That's what I learned with the dawn—
Love and the weather
Can't be depended upon.

Alternate ending, March 1985

Moonlight advances
Love's golden chances;
Rain comes along and they're gone—
Love and the weather
Change from night to dawn,
Can't be depended upon.

THE FREEDOM TRAIN

Published. Copyrighted July 8, 1947. Previously registered for copyright as an unpublished song May 27, 1947. Introduced in Philadelphia September 17, 1947. Leading recording by Bing Crosby and the Andrews Sisters (Decca). Copyright assigned to the American Heritage Foundation. At some point in 1947, Berlin wrote the following notes on "The Freedom Train":

> About a year ago, Attorney General [Tom C.] Clark invited me to come to Washington to hear about his idea of sending a train through America bearing original famous documents on which our way of life is based. I got terribly excited about his idea. After that first meeting, his idea kept growing and a couple of months ago he called a meeting at the White House. I have never been to a more enthusiastic gathering. On my way back to New York I started thinking about a song called "The Freedom Train." That was on a Tuesday, May 22nd. I finished the song over the weekend and on Tuesday of the next week, Bing Crosby and The Andrews Sisters recorded it. That was a very lucky break for me because a copy of the recording was sent to Washington and Attorney General Clark was able to hear them sing it. "The Freedom Train" was played for the first time in Philadelphia, where The Freedom Train was inaugurated.

On October 7, 1947, Berlin replied to Diane Fort, a high-school student who had written to him about "The Freedom Train":

> I can only say that as an immigrant who came to this country over fifty years ago, I have had a front row seat in watching freedom at work. Everything I have and everything I am, I owe to this country, which is the main reason why I thought the Freedom Train was important enough to write a song about. I'm glad you like the song and I hope it becomes worthy of the great subject that inspired it.

Also see "This Is a Great Country," page 355.

VERSE

This song is a train song;
It's a song about a train.
Not the Atchison, Topeka,
Not the Chattanooga Choo-Choo,
Nor the one that leaves at midnight
For the state of Alabam'—
This song is a train song
Where the engineer is Uncle Sam.

CHORUS

Here comes the Freedom Train—
You better hurry down;
Just like a Paul Revere,
It's comin' into your hometown.
Inside the freedom train
You'll find a precious freight—
Those words of liberty,
The documents that made us great.
You can shout your anger from a steeple,
You can shoot the system full of holes,
You can always question "We the People,"
You can get your answer at the polls.
That's how it's always been
And how it will remain
As long as all of us
Keep riding on the Freedom Train.
You can write the President a letter;
You can even tell him to his face—
If you think that you can do it better,
Get the votes and you can take his place.
That's how it's always been
And how it will remain
As long as all of us
Keep riding on the Freedom Train.
You can hate the laws that you're obeying,
You can shout your anger to the crowd—
We may disagree with what you're saying,
But we'll fight to let you say it loud.
That's how it's always been
And how it will remain
As long as all of us
Keep riding on the Freedom Train.

MISTER JOLSON

Registered for copyright as an unpublished song November 30, 1977. Probably written in late July or early August 1947. Performed at a party for Al Jolson at the Friars Club sometime in August 1947.

VERSE 1

I have taken down some tributes for an oldtime
    pal,
The best that were on my shelf;
But there isn't any tribute I could pay to Al
That Al hasn't paid to himself.

CHORUS 1

Mister Jolson, Mister Jolson—
There will never be another Mister Jolson.
Oh, the horse and buggy have had their day,
But Jolson is here to stay.

VERSE 2

With a rabbi for a father, he's the lucky one—
His dad is a perfect lamb.
But you never could imagine that a rabbi's son
Could turn out to be such a ham.

CHORUS 2

Mister Jolson, Mister Jolson—
There will never be another Mister Jolson.
Even Eddie Cantor admits today
That Jolson is here to stay.

VERSE 3

Mister J. keeps getting younger, singing on his
    knees—
For that let us give three cheers.
He admits to being fifty, yes, and what's more he's
Been fifty the last twenty years.

CHORUS 3

Mister Jolson, Mister Jolson—
There will never be another Mister Jolson.
They say Georgie Jessel's a lousy ———,
But Jolson is still okay—
Yes, Jolson is still okay.

LYRIC IDEAS FOR PROFESSIONAL CHILDREN'S SCHOOL SHOW

During the summer of 1947 (July–September), Berlin worked with Dorothy and Herbert Fields on an idea of a musical about the Professional Children's School and the young Baby Peggy. *Small Fry* was a tentative title for the show; Betty Garrett was considered as a possible star. The idea was never developed. No music is known to survive. Here are the lyric sketches from Berlin's notes.

All Washed Up

All washed up,
Poison at the box office—
All washed up, I'm through.
When an usher on the Roxy staff
Hands you back your autograph,
You're all washed up
And there's nothing you can do.

Untitled Couplet

I intend to hang around till you grow older,
Old enough to rest your head upon my shoulder.

We're Married

We're married, married;
I can't believe we're married—
The preacher's words keep ringing in my ears.
We tarried, tarried,
But now that we're married,
Let's stay married for a hundred thousand years.

It's Better When It Comes from the Heart

That pleasant note in your throat
Is better when it comes from the heart.
That rhythmic beat in your feet
Is better when it comes from the heart.

Make It Come from Your Heart

Make it come from your heart—
A sweet pleasant note
Can emerge from your throat,
But it's sweeter when it comes from your heart.

So mind what I said:
Songs can come from your head,
But it's sweeter from the bottom of your heart.

I GAVE HER MY HEART
IN ACAPULCO

Published. Copyrighted February 3, 1948. Previously registered for copyright as an unpublished song under the title "In Acapulco" on January 7, 1948. Written while Berlin was on a holiday in Acapulco, Mexico, and introduced at Ciro's in Mexico City.

My heart kept missing a beat
As I gazed in her eyes
Under Mexican skies
In Acapulco.
I held her close in my arms
As we danced 'neath the stars
To the tune of guitars
In Acapulco.

Male version

She started teaching me Spanish;
I knew it never could last.
She only gave me one lesson—
I was learning Spanish too fast.
The dawn came over the hills,
And we soon had to part;
So I gave her my heart and whispered low,
"Please keep it till I come back
To Acapulco, Mexico."

Female version

I started teaching him English;
I knew it never could last.
I only gave him one lesson—
He was learning English too fast.
The dawn came over the hills,
And we soon had to part;
So I gave him my heart and whispered low,
"Please keep it till I come back
To Acapulco, Mexico."

LET'S KEEP IN TOUCH
WHILE WE'RE DANCING

Registered for copyright as an unpublished song December 23, 1977. Written August 16–20, 1948. Berlin reworked some of the same ideas in two later songs, "Bring Back the Days," page 488, and "I Wanna Dance with the Girl in My Arms," page 485. The "rock-and-rolling" phrase was written after 1948.

Let's keep in touch while we're dancing;
Let's dance and touch as before.
Let's cuddle close as we used to when we danced
With nothing between us but the clothes we wore.
Wrapped in my arms while we're dancing
'Stead of rock-and-rolling miles apart,
Let's keep in touch, keep in touch as we used to
When we danced cheek to cheek and heart to
    heart.

I'M BEGINNING
TO MISS YOU

Published. Copyrighted January 10, 1949. Previously registered for copyright as an unpublished song December 20, 1948.

I'm beginning to miss you when you're away,
Ev'ry moment that we're apart.
I'm beginning to want you when you're away,
And the wanting comes from my heart.
I used to think that knowing you
Could never mean a thing,
But now I stay home waiting
For the telephone to ring.
I'm beginning to love you—how do I know?
From the way I miss you when you're away.

JINGLE BELLES

Berlin's parody of "Jingle Bells," the famous Christmas classic written by James Pierpont (1822–1893) in 1857, was performed in Bob Hope's 1948 Christmas tour of Germany in support of the Berlin airlift. It is an ensemble number and is described on Berlin's lyric sheet as "Opening Chorus for the Six Rockettes."

Jingle belles, jingle belles,
From across the sea,
Oh, what fun it was to fly
In a plane to Germany.
Jingle belles, jingle belles,
From across the foam,
We came here to bring good cheer
And to give you news from home.

They've done their Christmas shopping.
There were lots of things to buy.
But folks were very low because
The prices were so high.
We're glad to send things over here.
We're cleaning out our shelves,
So please deliver everything
But hold on to yourselves.
We have our little problems,
But we aren't seeing red
In spite of what Vishinsky and
What Molotov have said.
The people went a-voting,
Nearly fifty million souls,
And Truman was elected
As predicted by the polls.

Jingle belles, jingle belles,
Here to say hello,
Oh, what fun it is for us
To be opening the show.
Jingle belles, jingle belles,
Let the show advance.
Throwing you a kiss or two
As we go into our dance.

THANKS FOR THE
MEMORY (PARODY)

Written by Berlin in late 1948 for Bob Hope's Christmas tour of Germany to support the Berlin airlift. Introduced by Bob Hope. The original song was written by Leo Robin (words) and Ralph Rainger (music) for the musical film *The Big Broadcast of 1938*, where it was introduced by Hope and Shirley Ross.

Thanks for the memory—
For saying it was set
And seeing that we met
And giving us a Christmas
That we never will forget,
We thank you so much.
Thanks for the memory—

For giving us a view
Of what you're going through
And putting on a better show
Than we could ever do,
We thank you so much.
Thanks to the fighting Air Force
That daily took its toll;
Now it's a humane Air Force
With heart and soul,
Dropping wheat and coal.
And thanks for the memory—
Before we say goodnight
And take our homeward flight
We wish you all a Christmas
That is merry and is white—
We thank you so much.

OPERATION VITTLES

Introduced by Berlin December 25, 1948, at the Titania
Palast Theatre, Berlin, in the Christmas show organized
by Bob Hope for the U.S. Air Force during the city's
blockade by the Soviets. Written especially for the flight
crews of the airlift operations, the lyric was printed in
the *Times*, the airlift newspaper in Germany.

VERSE

Not long ago
A group we called the Air Corps
Helped win the war and took a bow.
Not long ago
We cheered the fighting Air Corps—
Let's see what's happened to them now.

CHORUS

Operation Vittles—
We'll soon be on our way
With coal and wheat and hay
And everything's okay.
Operation Vittles—
As in the sky we go,
We won't forget to blow
A kiss to Uncle Joe.
We're growing fonder
Of the wild blue yonder,
Making a buck
Flying a truck.
No one here belittles
The job that must be done;
Although the war was won,
We'll be there
Earning stripes and bars
In our old freight cars
Till the airlift gets the air.

OPERATION FRÄULEIN

Berlin's parody of his own "Operation Vittles." Written
in late 1948 or early 1949.

Operation Fräulein—
The final bugle sounds,
And like a pack of hounds,
We wander out of bounds.
Operation Fräulein—
We jump upon our bikes
And meet someone who likes
A pack of Lucky Strikes.
We're growing fonder
Of a girl who's blonder
Than the brunette
We can't forget.
Operation Fräulein—
We must make Germany
A true democracy
On the square,
So a guy begats
Little Democrats
Till the airlift gets the air.

OVERLEAF: *Jerome Robbins rehearses Allyn Ann
McLerie and Tommy Rall in "Follow the Leader Jig"*

MISS LIBERTY | 1949

MISS LIBERTY (1949)

Tryout: Forrest Theatre, Philadelphia, June 13, 1949. New York run: Imperial Theatre; opened July 15, 1949; 308 performances. Music and lyrics by Irving Berlin. Produced by Irving Berlin, Robert E. Sherwood, and Moss Hart. Book by Robert E. Sherwood. Directed by Moss Hart. Dances and musical numbers staged by Jerome Robbins. Orchestrations by Don Walker. Orchestra under the direction of Jay Blackton. Cast: starring Eddie Albert (Horace Miller), Allyn Ann McLerie (Monique Dupont), Mary McCarty (Maisie Dell) and featuring Charles Dingle (James Gordon Bennett), Philip Bourneuf (Joseph Pulitzer), Ethel Griffies (the Countess), Herbert Berghof (Bartholdi), and, in dance roles, Maria Karnilova and Tommy Rall. Original cast album (Columbia).

Irving Berlin on *Miss Liberty*, Cleveland *Press*, June 7, 1949:

> As I say, I feel good about this thing. But a fellow never can tell. He works hard fixing up a lot of dishes he's sure are all good. But when the theatregoer sits down to them and gets to dessert he may have indigestion—or worse.

Letter to Herbert Bayard Swope, July 18, 1949:

> *Miss Liberty* is not quite the show I had hoped we would have, but when I think of what we had the opening night in Philadelphia, we can take a silent bow for the great job we did in fixing it up to what you saw the opening night. If it proves to be a so-called commercial hit, I'll be very grateful and feel that I got out of a tight spot.

Letter to Francis Gilbert, Berlin's attorney, August 4, 1949:

> Now about the show. I am glad you think the critics went haywire, but frankly, I didn't entirely disagree with a good deal of their criticisms. I have already told you how I feel about this show. In a nutshell, we went after something that could have been very significant but which did not come off, and I think we were fortunate in being showmen enough to wind up with a good "audience" show that will get its money back and maybe make a little. Also, if we play out this season in New York, the show will be good for a road tour and then I think it will have value as a motion picture property. But I have written *Miss Liberty* off and my mind is beginning to turn to other things. By that I don't mean to say that I won't do everything I possibly can to keep the songs alive and get as much out of the score that is possible, but *Miss Liberty* as a show is behind me now.

EXTRA! EXTRA!

Published. Copyrighted June 2, 1949. Previously registered for copyright as an unpublished song May 13, 1949. Introduced by Newsboys and ensemble.

PART A

NEWSBOYS: Extra! Extra!
Morning, noon, and night we yell
Trying very hard to sell
Mister Bennett's *Morning Herald*,
Mister Pulitzer's *Morning World*.
Extra! Extra!
Ev'ry day the same old grind—
Getting worse because we find
It's hard to sell the *Herald*
While it's easy to sell the *World*.
This isn't good for Mister Bennett,
So it's driving him nuts;
And the result is Mister Bennett
Hates Mister Pulitzer's guts.
They're a-feudin' and a-fussin'
And a-fussin' and a-feudin',
And it doesn't seem to make much
sense;
Mister Bennett is usin'
The kind of words that
We wouldn't write on a fence.
Extra! Extra!
Who will win is hard to tell.
In the meantime we must sell
Mister Bennett's *Morning Herald*,
Mister Pulitzer's *Morning World*.

BOYS: Extra!

WORLD
READERS: Gimme a *World*, gimme a *World*.

HERALD
READERS: *Herald!*

BOYS: Extra!

WORLD
READERS: Gimme a *World*, gimme a *World*.

HERALD
READERS: *Herald!*

BOYS: Extra!

WORLD
READERS: Gimme a *World*, gimme a *World*.

HERALD
READERS: *Herald!*

WORLD
READERS: Gimme a *World*, gimme a *World*.

HERALD
READERS: *Herald!*

BOYS: Extra! Extra!

PART B

HERALD
READERS: I like the *Herald*, filled with stock
market news,
Smart social items and conservative
views.
It's quite amazing how we always
agree—
I'm for the *Herald*
'Cause the *Herald*'s for me.

WORLD
READERS: Couldn't eat a meal without the
World;
That's the way we feel about the
World.
It's the people's paper, yes
indeed,
With the kind o' news we like to read.
Circulation bigger ev'ry day,
Spite of what the other papers say;
Spite of accusations that are hurled,
Never was a paper like the *World*.

PART C

The *Herald* Readers and the *World* Readers sing the two sections of Part B in counterpoint.

PART D

NEWSBOYS: Extra! Extra!
Soon we'll all be getting hell
Just because we couldn't sell
Mister Bennett's *Morning Herald*,
And our lives will be imperiled
When he hears how many we sold
Of Mister Pulitzer's *Morning World*.
Extra! Extra!

I'D LIKE MY PICTURE TOOK

Published. Copyrighted August 30, 1949. Previously registered for copyright as an unpublished song July 12, 1949. Introduced by Mary McCarty (Maisie) and Eddie Albert (Horace). Alternate title (programs): "What Do I Have to Do to Get My Picture Took?" This number replaced "What Do I Have to Do to Get My Picture in the Paper?" page 419, during the pre-Broadway tryout.

VERSE

Hey there, Mister Photographer,
That's not where you should be.

Let someone else get behind your cam'ra
And come over here with me.

CHORUS

I'd like my picture took.
What do I have to do to get my picture took?
Who do I have to be to get my picture took with
    you?
I'd like to spark with you,
Having the film developed in the dark with you.
Nothing I wouldn't do to get my picture took with
    you.
Me sittin' down,
You standin' up;
Looking at the birdie will be fun.
Hands in my lap,
Yours on your chest,
Just like Napoleon.
And someday we'll take a look
Into a fam'ly album or a mem'ry book—
'Stead of a boring ev'ning we'll be laughing at
The picture that I took with you.

THE MOST EXPENSIVE STATUE IN THE WORLD

Published. Copyrighted May 31, 1949. Previously registered for copyright as an unpublished song May 13, 1949. Introduced by Charles Dingle (Bennett), Donald McClelland (Mayor), Philip Bourneuf (Pulitzer), Emile Renan (French Ambassador) and ensemble.

PULITZER: Citizens of New York, I greet you
    With a hundred-thousand-dollar check,
    The money that my readers have
        contributed
    For the pedestal
    Of the statue.

[Crowd applauds.]

    A statue that you will love as much
        as I,
    And worthy of the pennies that you
        spent—
    A statue that you will think of when
        you buy
    The paper that I proudly represent.
MAYOR: Citizens of New York, I greet you
    With the news that soon our flag will
        be unfurled

On the most expensive statue in the
    world.
CROWD: On the most expensive statue in the
    world.
BENNETT: When it's finally installed,
    Tell us, what will it be called?
CROWD: When it's finally installed,
    Tell us, what will it be called?
MAYOR: When we finally install it,
    What's the diff'rence what we
        call it?
    It's the best that money
        can buy
    And will stand three hundred feet
        high.
    And I understand before we're
        through,
    The cost may not be known.
    A hundred thousand dollars
    For the pedestal alone.
    And our flag will soon be
        unfurled
    On the most expensive statue in the
        world.
CROWD: On the most expensive statue in the
    world.
WOMAN IN
CROWD: When it finally is claimed,
    Tell us, what will it be named?
CROWD: When it finally is claimed,
    Tell us, what will it be named?
MAYOR: When at last we come to
        claim it,
    What's the difference what we
        name it?
    What's important is the
        expense.
    What it means in dollars and cents.
PULITZER: From the French across the ocean
    It was sent to me and you.
    And now I'd like to call upon and
    hear a word or two
    From our friend the French
        ambassador.
AMBASSADOR: [spoken]
    Your Honor,
    I speak not for my government but
    my people,
    For it's not the government but the
        people
    Who give this statue,
    Creation of the genius of Bartholdi.
    May it arise in your harbor
    And give the light of Liberty,
    Equality,
    Fraternity.
CROWD: [sung]
    May it arise in our harbor

And give the light of Liberty,
    Equality,
    Fraternity.
BENNETT: When it's finally installed,
    Tell us, what will it be called?
CROWD: When it's finally installed,
    Tell us, what will it be called?
MAYOR: When we finally install it,
    What's the diff'rence what we call it?
    It's the most expensive statue in the
        world.
ALL: It's the most expensive statue in the
    world.

A LITTLE FISH IN A BIG POND

Published. Copyrighted May 18, 1949. Previously registered for copyright as an unpublished song February 7, 1949. Introduced by Mary McCarty (Maisie), Eddie Albert (Horace), and "The Sharks" (Bill Bradley, Allen Knowles, Kazimir Kokic, Robert Pagent).

CHORUS 1

HE: A little fish in a big pond
    Has plenty of room to swim,
    But swimming around are big fish
    All ready to pounce on him.
    Back to his little pond
    He starts to roam;
    The little fish spreads his fins
    And begins to swim back home.
    That's me,
    A little fish
    In a big pond, all wrong—
    That's me,
    A little fish
    Where a little fish don't belong.
    A little man in a big town
    Gets butterflies in his dome—
    I'm ready to spread my fin
    And begin to swim back home
    To the little pond
    Where a little fish
    And a little man belong.

CHORUS 2

SHE: A little fish in a big pond
    Has gotta have lots of heart,
    For swimming around are big fish;
    But if he's the least bit smart,

Back to his little pond
He doesn't go—
The little fish spreads his fins
And begins to grow, grow, grow.
That's you,
A little fish
In a big pond, all right—
Me too,
A little fish,
But we gotta stand up and fight.
A little man in a big town
Don't have to get out and roam—
Stop taking it on the chin
And begin to feel at home
In the bigger pond
Where the bigger fish
And the bigger men belong.

LET'S TAKE AN OLD-FASHIONED WALK

Published. Copyrighted May 25, 1949. Previously registered for copyright as an unpublished song February 25, 1948. Introduced by Eddie Albert (Horace), Allyn Ann McLerie (Monique), and ensemble. Leading recordings by Perry Como (RCA Victor) and Frank Sinatra and Doris Day (Columbia). Originally written for the film *Easter Parade* (1948), but replaced by "A Couple of Swells"; then intended for the unproduced musical *Stars on My Shoulders* (1948).

VERSE 1

HE: Some couples go for a buggy ride
When they start caring a lot.
Others will bicycle side by side
Out to some romantic spot.
But when you haven't a sou,
There's only one thing to do.

CHORUS

Let's take an old-fashioned walk;
I'm just bursting with talk—
What a tale could be told
If we went for an old-fashioned walk!
Let's take a stroll through the park,
Down a lane where it's dark,
And a heart that's controlled
May relax on an old-fashioned walk.
I know for a couple who seem to be miles apart,
There's nothing like walking and having a heart-
    to-heart.

I know a girl who declined,
Couldn't make up her mind—
She was wrapped up and sold
Coming home from an old-fashioned walk.

VERSE 2

SHE: I used to dream of a millionaire
Handsome and rich from the States,
Taking me out for a breath of air,
Saying, "The carriage awaits."
But since you haven't a sou,
And I have nothing to do—

REPEAT CHORUS

HOMEWORK

Published. Copyrighted May 17, 1949. Previously registered for copyright as an unpublished song February 7, 1949. Introduced by Mary McCarty (Maisie). On June 4, 1949, Cole Porter wrote Berlin that "the records [demos made by Berlin] arrived but so far I have only played one of them, which is 'Homework.' This I have played over and over again with great joy, as it is delightful and unadulterated Berlin."

VERSE

I'm so tired of working in an office,
And it's making me blue.
There is work that don't require an office
That I'm anxious to do.

CHORUS 1

Homework,
I wanna do homework—
Instead of an office
I wanna work home.
Staying
At home and crocheting
And meekly obeying
The guy who comes home.
A cozy kitchen
To be in there pitchin',
That's the thing I'm longing to do;
To be there learning
When a steak needs turning
And just what goes into a stew.
Homework,
I wanna do homework—
A genius who sits and plans

With pots and pans at home,
A genius who bakes a pie
That keeps a guy at home.

CHORUS 2

Homework,
I wanna do homework—
Instead of an office
I wanna work home.
Messing
Around with French dressing
And slightly impressing
The guy who comes home.
I long to settle
With a steaming kettle
And a frying pan and a pot
And be the keeper
Of a carpet sweeper—
That's the one ambition I've got.
Homework,
I wanna do homework—
A genius who has a way
That makes him stay at home,
A genius who has what takes
That makes or breaks a home.

CHORUS 3

Homework,
I wanna do homework.
Instead of an office
I wanna work home.
Staying
At home and crocheting
And meekly obeying
The guy who comes home.
A table wiper
Who can change a diaper
Is the thing I'd like to be best
And be the master
Of a mustard plaster
When the cold goes down to his chest.
Homework,
I wanna do homework—
A genius who does her part
So he don't start to roam,
A genius who earns her keep
That makes him sleep at home.

PARIS WAKES UP
AND SMILES

Published. Copyrighted May 17, 1949. Previously registered for copyright as an unpublished song March 3, 1949. Introduced by Johnny V. R. Thompson (Lamplighter) and Allyn Ann McLerie (Monique).

CHORUS

When the sun goes down,
Paris wakes up,
Fills up her cup
And smiles.
When the lights are low,
Paris is high,
Lights up the sky
For miles.
When they stop playing shop on the Rue de la
    Paix,
Count their stock and they lock up their styles,
When the busy town
Goes home to sup,
Paris wakes up
And smiles.

ONLY FOR AMERICANS

Published. Copyrighted May 25, 1949, and July 5, 1949. Previously registered for copyright as an unpublished song May 13, 1949. Introduced by Eddie Albert (Horace), Ethel Griffies (the Countess), and ensemble.

CHORUS 1

Only for Americans—
The midnight life in gay Paree,
The Frenchman, he would never see;
It's only for Americans.
The prices in the smart café,
The Frenchman, he would never pay;
The price that's more
Is only for
Americans from the U.S.A.
A Montmartre lady drops her hanky
And slyly winks her eye:
That's only for a Yankee;
The Frenchman wouldn't buy.
Only for Americans—
The Frenchmen on the boulevards
Don't buy those dirty postal cards;

They're only for Americans.
The little holes for peeping through
To see what naughty people do,
The French would bore;
They're only for
Americans from the U.S.A.

CHORUS 2

Only for Americans—
The shops with many real antiques,
Antiques as old as seven weeks,
They're only for Americans.
The bed on which a king made love,
Which there are sev'ral dozens of,
The French pooh-pooh,
We sell them to
Americans from the U.S.A.
Those old Napoleon brandy labels
That recently were made,
They're not for Frenchmen's tables;
They're for the Yankee trade.
Only for Americans—
The Frenchman gets his kisses free,
But those for which there is a fee
Are only for Americans.
You'll find two prices on a dress;
There's one that is extremely less—
The one that's more
Is only for
Americans from the U.S.A.

CHORUS 3

Only for Americans—
A Frenchman's food is very plain;
The fancy sauces with ptomaine
Are only for Americans.
A Frenchman seldom eats the snails
With little ulcers on their tails,
And all that cheese
Was made to please
Americans from the U.S.A.
While the American carouses
Where crimson shadows creep,
The French avoid those houses—
They go to bed to sleep.
Only for Americans—
A Frenchman wouldn't be impressed
To see a show with girls undressed;
That's only for Americans.
The French don't go to naked shows;
They've seen what's underneath the clothes.
And each encore
Is only for
Americans from the U.S.A.

CHORUS 4

Only for Americans—
The Frenchmen don't keep company
With south-of-France society;
That's only for Americans.
The Frenchman hasn't large amounts
To pay for barons, dukes, and counts
That you adore;
They're only for
Americans from the U.S.A.
We like to keep the good relations
That nothing must upset;
We give you decorations
That Frenchmen seldom get.
Only for Americans—
Our finest art is in the Louvre;
The ones the experts don't approve
Are only for Americans:
We keep an artist at the gate
To sign the paintings while you wait;
Before they're dry
They're purchased by
Americans from the U.S.A.

JUST ONE WAY TO
SAY I LOVE YOU

Published. Copyrighted May 18, 1949. Previously registered for copyright as an unpublished song under the title "I Love You" on February 7, 1949. Introduced by Eddie Albert (Horace) and Allyn Ann McLerie (Monique).

VERSE 1

HE: Why search for flowery phrases
    Quoting what poets have said?
    Why talk in circles around it—
    Why not be simple instead?
    Let's hit the nail on the head.

CHORUS

I love you, I love you—
There's no other way,
Just one way to say
I love you.
I love you, I love you,
And try as I may,
That's all I can say—
I love you.
Much more could be said
If I thought with my head,

But I only can think with my heart.
I love you, I love you
And yearn for the day,
The day when you'll say
I love you.

VERSE 2

SHE: I could be oh so indifferent
    With very little success.
    I could continue pretending
    But I'm afraid you would guess,
    So why not simply say yes?

REPEAT CHORUS

MISS LIBERTY

Published. Copyrighted June 29, 1949. Previously registered for copyright as an unpublished song February 7, 1949. Introduced by entire company.

MAYOR: Liberty, Miss Liberty,
    We welcome you here to our shores.
    Liberty, Miss Liberty,
    The key to the city is yours.
    Liberty, Miss Liberty,
    With banners and streamers unfurled,
    You're not just the symbol of
    A statue that we love
    But the most beautiful girl in the
        world.
1ST GIRL: Would you like to dine some evening
        with the Astors?*
MONIQUE: I'd love to.
2ND GIRL: Would you like to play a week at Tony
        Pastors?

*Script version of lines 10–17:
    1ST GIRL: Would you like to dine some evening with
            the Astors?
    BENNETT: She'd love to.
    2ND GIRL: Would you like to play a week at Tony
            Pastors?
    BENNETT: She'd love to.
    MINISTER: Would you like to come to Trinity on
            Sunday?
    BENNETT: Charmed.
    ADMIRAL: Would you like to launch a battleship on
            Monday?
    BENNETT: She'd love to.

MONIQUE: I'd love to.
MINISTER: Would you like to come to Trinity on
        Sunday?
MONIQUE: I'd love to.
ADMIRAL: Would you like to launch a battleship
        on Monday?
MONIQUE: I'd love to.
TWO BOYS: Here's some orchids fresh with dew
        From the President to you.
WOMAN: Here's some winter flannels from the
        nation's mothers.
COP: Here's some tickets for our ball—
        You'll be welcome at the hall.
TWO MEN: Here's some cough drops from the
        famous bearded brothers.
MAN: I represent Pratt's Astral Oil,
        The finest application for a pimple or
        a boil.
        We'll pay you handsomely for very
        little toil—
        Your picture with a bottle of Pratt's
        Astral Oil.
MONIQUE: I thank you, I thank you,
        I'm grateful, to be sure.
        Like money in the bank
        You have made me feel secure.
        Your Congress, your Senate,
        Your President, so dear,
        But mostly Mister Bennett,
        The man who brought me here.

[ALL repeat "Liberty, Miss Liberty," etc. along with "Hoorays."]

Earlier version

HORACE: Here she is, the girl that you have read
        about,
        That very famous girl who much was
        said about.
        A Reginald or Gerald
        Who reads the Morning Herald
        Has memorized the stories that were
        spread about—

CHORUS 1

Liberty, Miss Liberty,
As fair as a lady could be.
Liberty, Miss Liberty,
The sweetheart of all who are free.
Liberty, Miss Liberty,
With banners of freedom unfurled,
You're not just the symbol of
A statue that we love
But the most beautiful girl in the world.

CHORUS 2

MAYOR: Liberty, Miss Liberty,
    We welcome you here to our shores.
    Liberty, Miss Liberty,
    The key to the city is yours.
    Liberty, Miss Liberty,
    With banners and streamers unfurled,
    When the statue's down the bay
    We'll gaze at it and say
    You're the most beautiful girl in the
        world.

End of original finale

HORACE: A little fish in a big pond
        Has plenty of room to swim
MAISIE: But swimming around are big fish
        All ready to pounce on him.
HORACE: Back to his little pond
        His thoughts will roam.
        I'm feeling the strike
        Of a hook, and I'd like
        To swim back home—
MAISIE: To the little pond—
HORACE: Where the little fish—
TOGETHER: And the little man belong.

CONSUL BOWS

Not used.

MADEMOISELLE: I salute you for our government
            and our people.
            I thank you for the honor and
            the glory
            That you have brought us,
            The spirit that inspired the
            great Bartholdi—
            May it convey to our neighbors
            The love of France for
            Liberty,
            Equality,
            Fraternity.

THE TRAIN

Introduced by Allyn Ann McLerie (Monique), "the Train" (Eddie Phillips, Erik Kristen, Joseph Milan), and ensemble. Musically, this is really an extension of "Miss Liberty."

[*First town*]

CROWD: There she is!
MAYOR: Liberty, Miss Liberty—
We're happy you came to Detroit.
CROWD: Hooray! Hooray!

[*Bang! A cannon fires.*]

MAYOR: Liberty, Miss Liberty—
You honor the name of Detroit.
CROWD: Wheeeee!
MONIQUE: I thank you.
MAN: She thanks you.
TRAIN: She thanks you.
MONIQUE: I thank you
From the bottom of my heart.
CROWD: From the bottom of her heart—
MONIQUE: I thank you.
CROWD: You're welcome—
Hooray! Hooray! Hooray!

[*Bang! Another cannon.*]

MONIQUE: Goodbye!

[*Second town*]

CROWD: There she is!
CLUB WOMAN: Liberty, Miss Liberty,
We welcome you here to
Duluth.
CROWD: Hooray! Hooray!

[*Bang! Cannon fires.*]

CLUB WOMAN: Liberty, Miss—
MONIQUE: Thank you.
TRAIN: She thanks you.
MONIQUE: From the bottom of my heart!
CROWD: Hooray! Hooray! Hooray!
MONIQUE
AND TRAIN: Goodbye!

[*Third town*]

MONIQUE: From the bottom of my heart—
Goodbye! Goodbye! Goodbye!

YOU CAN HAVE HIM

Published. Copyrighted June 3, 1949. Previously registered for copyright as an unpublished song February 7, 1949. Introduced by Allyn Ann McLerie (Monique) and Mary McCarty (Maisie).

CHORUS 1

MAISIE: You can have him, I don't want him—
He's not worth fighting for;
Besides, there's plenty more
Where he came from.
I don't want him, you can have him—
I'm giving him the sack,
And he can go right back
Where he came from.
I could never make him happy;
He'd be better off with you.
I'm afraid I never loved him;
All I ever wanted to do was
Run my fingers through his curly locks,
Mend his underwear and darn his socks,
Fetch his slippers and remove his shoes,
Wipe his glasses when he read the news,
Rub his forehead with a gentle touch
Mornings after when he's had too
much,
Kiss him gently when he cuddled near,
Give him babies, one for ev'ry year—
So you see
I don't want him, you can have him,
You can have him, I don't want him,
For he's not the man for me.

CHORUS 2

MONIQUE: You can have him, I don't want him—
He's not worth fighting for;
Besides, there's plenty more
Where he came from.
I don't want him, you can have him—
He isn't my concern,
And he can just return
Where he came from.
I would look a trifle silly
Taking him away from you.
That was never my intention;
All I ever wanted to do was
Close the window while he soundly
slept,
Raid the icebox where the food is kept,
Cook a breakfast that would please him
most,
Eggs and coffee and some buttered
toast,

Wake him gently with a breakfast tray,
After breakfast clear the things away,
Bring the papers and when they've been
read,
Spend the balance of the day in bed—
So you see
I don't want him, you can have him,
You can have him, I don't want him,
For he's not the man for me.

Earlier version

You can have him, I don't want him—
He's not worth fighting for;
Besides, there's plenty more
Where he came from.
I don't want him, you can have him—
I'm giving him the sack,
And he can go right back
Where he came from.
He's just another fellow, don't forget,
An ordinary one in fact,
And what was my impression when we met?
How did I react?
I longed to run my fingers through his curly locks,
Mend his underwear and darn his socks,
Fetch his slippers and remove his shoes,
Wipe his glasses when he read the news—
So I don't want him, you can take him,
And if you do you're stuck.
Invite me to the wedding—
I'll be wishing you the best of luck.

THE POLICEMEN'S BALL

Published. Copyrighted May 18, 1949. Previously registered for copyright as an unpublished song February 7, 1949. Introduced by Mary McCarty (Maisie) and ensemble.

INTRODUCTION

Tickets for one and all
For the Policemen's Ball.

CHORUS

Fifty cents for a gent and his bundle
Will admit you to the Policemen's Ball.
Fifty cents and you're all set to trundle
Arm in arm and dance all around the hall.
Dancing round gettin' hot 'neath the collar—

If it starts to wilt from the lack of starch,
There'll be six you can buy for a dollar,
And you'll have a spare for the big Grand March.
All ev'ning they'll be tripping the light fantastic—
Watch their suspenders stretching the old elastic,
Each dressed up in a suit made of cotton,
Patent-leather shoes that are much too small.
But who cares? That'll soon be forgotten,
Dancing at the Policemen's Ball.

ME AND MY BUNDLE

Published. Copyrighted May 18, 1949. Previously registered for copyright as an unpublished song February 7, 1949. Introduced by Eddie Albert (Horace) and Allyn Ann McLerie (Monique).

VERSE

Come over here, my hunk of charm,
And wrap yourself around my arm.
I've got a pair of what we call
Those Annie Oakleys for the Ball.
I keep looking you over,
Feeling terrible proud,
And I would like to show you off
To the crowd.

CHORUS

Me an' my bundle
At Walhalla Hall,
Leading the Grand March tonight.
My pretty bundle,
The belle of the ball,
Knocking their eyes out tonight.
Hey! there,
You better not stay there.
Get out of the way there.
We've gotta have room
When we start
Doing the cake walk
And winning the prize,
All of the judges agreein'
On me an' my bundle.

Earlier version

VERSE

I'm all set for I just bought a ticket.
Soon I'll be on my way.
Fifty cents for a gent and his bundle,
That's what I had to pay.

I'm all set for the best time yet,
That'll last 'til the break of day.

CHORUS

Me and my bundle tripping the light fantastic.
Me and my bundle at the Policeman's Ball.
Watch my suspenders stretching the old elastic
As we go dancing envied by one and all.
We mean to lead the Grand March, yeseree,
And when the march is over just you wait and see.
Me and my bundle tripping the light fantastic.
There's a prize that we'll be winning and then
We'll have something to brag about when
We get too heavy to trip the light fantastic.

FALLING OUT OF LOVE CAN BE FUN

Published. Copyrighted August 30, 1949. Previously registered for copyright as an unpublished song July 12, 1949. Introduced by Mary McCarty (Maisie); added during the pre-Broadway tryout, it replaced "I'll Know Better the Next Time," also known as "The Next Time I Fall in Love," page 419.

VERSE

Crocodile tears will not be shed;
They're not for a lady like I'm.
I can recall what my aunt said
When she married for the twentieth time.

CHORUS 1

Falling out of love can be fun.
After love is over and done,
It's an awful blow, but although it's upsetting,
So much you can do while you're forgetting.
Falling out of love can be fun.
When you find your lover has gone,
Get your second wind and go on;
There's an old affair that is there for renewing—
In your grief do you know what you're doing?
Falling out of love can be fun.
Soon
You'll be swinging in a hammock on a porch,
One arm wrapped around someone else,
The other one carrying the torch.*

Alternate version of lines 13 and 14:
  One hand pressing him close to you,
  The other hand carrying the torch.

Love can give a lady a clout,
And she may be down but not out—
Get yourself a date, don't you wait
Till the count of ten,
Then
Falling out of love can be falling in love again.

CHORUS 2

Falling out of love can be fun.
Someone else may soon be the one;
By another name he's the same as his brother—
Close your eyes and one is like the other.
Falling out of love can be fun.
If he leaves you after you're wed,
And the stork is over your head,
Soon you're gonna be with a she or a laddie—
Smile as you go shopping for a daddy.
Falling out of love can be fun.
Soon
You'll be losing all your troubles and fears
One eye winking at someone else,
The other eye filling up with tears.
When you find your loving romance
Gets a sudden kick in the pants,
Get yourself surrounded and bounded
With lots of men
Then
Falling out of love can be falling in love again.

GIVE ME YOUR TIRED, YOUR POOR

Published. Copyrighted May 25, 1949. Previously registered for copyright as an unpublished song February 7, 1949. Lyric by Emma Lazarus (1849–1887), the final lines of her sonnet "The New Colossus," which had been written for the fund-raising effort to build a pedestal for Frederic Auguste Bartholdi's *Liberty Enlightening the World*, better known as the Statue of Liberty, on Bedloe's Island in New York Harbor. "The New Colossus" refers to the Colossus of Rhodes, the large bronze statue of legend that was one of the Seven Wonders of the World. Lazarus's sonnet was recited at the ceremony dedicating the Statue of Liberty in 1886. Berlin's setting of the closing words of the poem was introduced by Allyn Ann McLerie (Monique) and ensemble in *Miss Liberty*. Lazarus's poem follows:

THE NEW COLOSSUS

Not like the brazen giant of Greek fame,
With conquering limbs astride from land to
  land;

Here at our sea-washed, sunset gates shall
    stand
A mighty woman with a torch, whose flame
Is the imprisoned lightning, and her name
Mother of Exiles. From her beacon-hand
Glows world-wide welcome; her mild eyes
    command
The air-bridged harbor that twin cities frame.
"Keep, ancient lands, your storied pomp!"
    cries she
With silent lips. "Give me your tired, your
    poor,
Your huddled masses yearning to breathe
    free,
The wretched refuse of your teeming shore.
Send these, the homeless, tempest-tost to me,
I lift my lamp beside the golden door!"

THE HON'RABLE PROFESSION OF THE FOURTH ESTATE

Published. Copyrighted June 2, 1949. Previously registered for copyright as an unpublished song May 10, 1949. Introduced in the pre-Broadway tryout by Philip Bourneuf (Pulitzer), Charles Dingle (Bennett), and ensemble. Dropped before the New York opening.

CHORUS 1

PULITZER: *Times* and *Herald*, *World* and *Sun*,
    Each admits the other one is great—
    The hon'rable profession of the
        fourth estate.
REPORTERS: A profession that we love
    And delighted to be members of.
BENNETT: Out in Maine a dam has burst;
    Though the *Herald* gets there first,
        we'll wait—
    The hon'rable profession of the
        fourth estate.
REPORTERS: None of us would ever stoop
    To indulge in what we call a scoop.
PULITZER: Giving you the news as we do our
        stint—
BENNETT: Seeing that the news is well
        presented—
PULITZER: All the news that's fit and unfit to
        print—
BENNETT: All the facts as soon as they're invented.

PULITZER: If your sales are not okay,
    Who'll be very glad to say they're
        great?
    The hon'rable profession of the
        fourth estate.
REPORTERS: We will say you're doing fine
    At a dollar fifty cents a line.
ALL: From the east to the west to the
        north,
    Not the first, nor the second, nor the
        third,
    But the fourth estate.

CHORUS 2

PULITZER: When a baby starts to bounce
    Out of wedlock, who'll announce
        the date?
    The hon'rable profession of the
        fourth estate.
REPORTERS: We agree to spread the word
    When the stork becomes an early
        bird.
BENNETT: When they raided madam's flat
    Filled with husbands, who was at the
        gate?
    The hon'rable profession of the
        fourth estate.
REPORTERS: When a married man lets go,
    We believe the public ought to
        know.
PULITZER: Ev'ry now and then we send out
        some checks—
BENNETT: Paying off the folks who sue for
        libel—
PULITZER: Saturday we give you murder and
        sex—
BENNETT: Sunday we'll be quoting from the
        Bible.
PULITZER: When elections have been planned,
    Who can pick the winning candidate?
    The hon'rable profession of the
        fourth estate.
REPORTERS: When the people cast their votes,
    We can all go home and cut our
        throats.
ALL: From the east to the west to the
        north,
    Not the first, nor the second, nor the
        third,
    But the fourth estate.

CHORUS 3

PULITZER: Interviews are such a bore,
    But who'll always get your story
        straight?

    The hon'rable profession of the
        fourth estate.
REPORTERS: If you haven't news that day,
    We'll be glad to misquote what you
        say.
BENNETT: Who will publish your attack
    Saying that we've been in-ac-cu-rate?
    The hon'rable profession of the
        fourth estate.
REPORTERS: We'll be glad to print your gripes
    On the last page in the smallest type.
PULITZER: While exposing men who keep
        breaking laws—
BENNETT: What's the diff'rence if we pull a
        bloomer?
PULITZER: Never check a story; print it
        because—
BENNETT: It may just turn out to be a rumor.
PULITZER: When you're laid out stiff and cold,
    Who will meet you at the Golden
        Gate?
    The hon'rable profession of the
        fourth estate.
REPORTERS: And you must be free from sin;
    Otherwise we just won't let you in.
ALL: From the east to the west to the
        north,
    Not the first, nor the second, nor the
        third,
    But the fourth estate.

Earlier version

PULITZER: The hon'rable profession of the
        fourth estate.
    One for all and all for one,
    Tribune, *Herald*, *World*, and *Sun*
    Each admits the other one is great—
    The hon'rable profession of the
        fourth estate.
REPORTERS: A profession that we love
    And delighted to be members of.
BENNETT: The one who gets there early helps
        the one who's late.
    Out in Maine a dam has burst;
    Though the *Herald* gets there first,
    Till the others get there we will
        wait—
    The hon'rable profession of the
        fourth estate.
REPORTERS: None of us would ever stoop
    To indulge in what we call a scoop.
PULITZER: Giving you the news as we do our
        stint—
BENNETT: Seeing that the news is well
        presented—

PULITZER: All the news that's fit and unfit to
      print—
BENNETT: All the facts as soon as they're in-
      vented.
PULITZER: When the Joneses' child was born
      Right before the wedding morn,
      Who announced the birth and wed-
      ding date?
      The hon'rable profession of the
      fourth estate.
REPORTERS: We agree to spread the word
      When the stork becomes an early
      bird.
PULITZER: Ev'ry now and then we send out
      some checks—
BENNETT: Paying off the folks who sue for
      libel.
PULITZER: Saturday we give you murder and
      sex—
BENNETT: Sunday we'll be quoting from the
      Bible.
PULITZER: When the married Mr. Brown
      Met his mistress out of town,
      Who was there to meet him at the
      gate?
      The hon'rable profession of the
      fourth estate.
REPORTERS: When a married man lets go,
      We believe the public ought to know.
PULITZER: While exposing the men who keep
      breaking laws—
BENNETT: What's the difference if we pull a
      bloomer?
PULITZER: Never check a story, print it
      because—
BENNETT: It may just turn out to be a rumor.
PULITZER: In our national events
      When it comes to Presidents—
BENNETT: Who can pick the winning
      candidate?
PULITZER: The hon'rable profession of the
      fourth estate.
REPORTERS: From the east to the west to the
      north,
      Not the first, nor the second, nor the
      third, but the fourth estate.

I'LL KNOW BETTER THE NEXT TIME

Registered for copyright as an unpublished song January 17, 1957. Introduced during the pre-Broadway tryout by Mary McCarty (Maisie). Dropped before the New York opening. Replaced by "Falling Out of Love Can Be Fun." Alternate titles: "The Next Time I Fall in Love" and "Next Time." Berlin returned to this lyric again in the 1980s.

I'll know better the next time,
The next time I fall in love.
I know that I won't make the same mistake the
    next time,
Won't be a know-it-all the next time I fall in love.
Yes, yes,
I'll be smarter the next time,
As sure as the stars above.
Although he's wrong, I'll go along
With what he's thinking of,
The next time I fall in love.

PATTER

If he says black, I'll say black,
Although the color is white.
If he says left, I'll say left,
Although I know that it's right.
If he says yes, I'll say yes,
Although the answer is no.
If he says sun, I'll say sun,
Though we're covered with snow—oh,
I'll know better the next time,
As sure as the stars above.
Though wrong he'll be, I'll still agree
With what he's thinking of,
The next time I fall in love

1982 version, dated August 26

I'll know better the next time,
The next time I fall in love.
I know that I won't make the same mistake the
    next time,
Won't be a know-it-all,
Next time I fall in love.
If he says black,
I'll say black,
Although the color is white.
If he says wrong,
I'll say wrong,
Although I know that I'm right.
If he likes onions, I'll eat onions,

Although they cling to my breath.
If he likes flying, I'll start flying,
Although it scares me to death.
I'll be smarter the next time,
As sure as the stars above.
I'll yes him and caress him,
And when the lights are low,
I'll suddenly have a headache and say no,
Until the next time,
The next time I fall in love.

1985 version, dated August 23

I'll know better the next time,
The next time I fall in love.
I know that I won't make the same mistake the
    next time,
Won't be a know-it-all,
Next time I fall in love.
If he says black,
I'll say black,
Although the color is white.
If he says wrong,
I'll say wrong,
Although I know that I'm right.
If he likes snails,
I'll eat snails,
Although they cling to my breath.
If he likes planes,
I'll ride planes,
Although they scare me to death.
I'll be smarter the next time,
As sure as the stars above.
I'll yes him and caress him
And make certain
That the next time
Is the last time I fall in love.
I'll be smarter the next time,
As sure as the stars above,
I'll yes him, bless him, and caress him with a
    velvet glove,
The next time I fall in love.

WHAT DO I HAVE TO DO TO GET MY PICTURE IN THE PAPER?

Published. Copyrighted June 2, 1949. Previously registered for copyright as an unpublished song February 7, 1949. Introduced in the pre-Broadway tryout by Mary McCarty (Maisie), Eddie Albert (Horace), and dancers.

Dropped before the New York opening; replaced by "I'd Like My Picture Took."

VERSE

Hey there, Mister Photographer,
Turn your cam'ra my way.
Say there, Mister Photographer,
I've got something to say.

CHORUS

What do I have to do to get my picture in the
    paper?
What do I have to do?
Do I have to murder someone,
Must I rob a bank, or just be nice to you?
Who do I have to be to get my picture in the paper?
Who do I have to be?
Do I have to be a Morgan or a Vanderbilt
Before you notice me?
Show me a birdie that has gained renown,
I'll gladly take a look;
Now that I've caught you with your cam'ra down,
I'd like my picture took.*
What do I have to pay to get my picture in the
    paper?
What do I have to pay?
Do I have to bribe the editor,
Become his creditor,
Or just be very nice to you?

BUSINESS FOR A GOOD GIRL IS BAD

Published in a professional copy only. Copyrighted May 31, 1949. Previously registered for copyright as an unpublished song May 13, 1949. Intended for Allyn Ann McLerie (Monique) and Herbert Berghof (Bartholdi). Dropped during rehearsals.

Published version

Finding work in Paris isn't easy
For a girl who just wants to work,

Earlier version of lines 9–12:
    You photographed the ladies of renown
    Dozens of times and more;
    Now that we've caught you with your camera down,
    How about some faces that they haven't seen before?

For in ev'ry bus'ness place I find
That the boss has more than bus'ness on his mind.
Finding work is easy if a girl agrees
To fall in love with the clerk;
She must make her heart
An important part of her work.
There are lots of jobs in Paris,
But they're not for girls like I'm;
If you easily embarrass,
You're embarrassed all the time.
There's a job that I would treasure
Selling hats and hosiery;
I could have the job with pleasure,
But with pleasure not for me.
Yesterday I was on my way
To the famous Folies-Bergère;
Someone said in the news I read
That they wanted chorus girls there.
Soon I stood in an office questioned by a man;
He put me through an interview,
And this is how it ran:
"Can you kick?"
I can kick.
"How high?"
So high.
"Can you sing?"
I can sing.
"How high?"
So high.
"Can you dance?"
I can dance.
"How well?"
Quite well.
Then he said to me,
"I would like to see,"
And I danced so he could tell.
But I suddenly stopped dancing
When I saw him dim the lights.
He remarked, "I like your dancing,
But do you look good in tights?"
As he cast a wicked eye on
What I call my hips, he said,
"Here's some tights that you can try on,"
So I slapped his face and fled.
Finding work in Paris isn't easy
For a girl who won't unclad.
I prefer to keep my clothes on,
My above and my belows on,
So bus'ness for a good girl is bad.

Alternate version

MONIQUE: Finding work in Paris isn't easy
    For a girl who just wants to work,
    For in ev'ry business place I find
    That the boss has more than business
      on his mind.

Finding work is easy if a girl agrees
To fall in love with the clerk;
She must make her heart
An important part of her work.
BARTHOLDI: There are lots of jobs in Paris.
MONIQUE: But they're not for girls like I'm.
BARTHOLDI: Do you easily embarrass?
MONIQUE: I'm embarrassed all the time.
BARTHOLDI: Here's a job that you would treasure.
MONIQUE: But a model I won't be.
BARTHOLDI: You can have the job with pleasure.
MONIQUE: No, with pleasure not for me.
    Yesterday I was on my way
    To the famous Folies-Bergère;
    Someone said in the news I read
    That they wanted chorus girls there.
    Soon I stood in an office
    Questioned by a man;
    He put me through an interview.
BARTHOLDI: I know just how it ran,
    Can you kick?
MONIQUE: I can kick.
BARTHOLDI: How high?
MONIQUE: So high.
BARTHOLDI: Can you sing?
MONIQUE: I can sing.
BARTHOLDI: How high?
MONIQUE: So high.
BARTHOLDI: Can you dance?
MONIQUE: I can dance.
BARTHOLDI: How well?
MONIQUE: Quite well.
    Then he said to me,
    "I would like to see."
BARTHOLDI: And you danced so he could tell.

[*She dances sixteen bars and stops suddenly.*]

MONIQUE: But I suddenly stopped dancing
    When I saw him dim the lights;
    He remarked, "I like your dancing
    But do you look good in tights?"
BARTHOLDI: That is quite a proper question,
    And I think entirely fair.
MONIQUE: But he made the rude suggestion
    That I try them on right there.
    Finding work in Paris isn't easy
    For a girl who won't unclad;
    I prefer to keep my clothes on,
    My above and my belows on,
    So business for a good girl is bad.

FOR A GOOD GIRL IT'S BAD

Not used. Replaced by "Business for a Good Girl Is Bad." Intended for Allyn Ann McLerie (Monique).

VERSE

I've looked around for work and I can see
The jobs that I can get are not for me;
In almost every business place I find
The boss has more than business on his mind.

CHORUS

For a bad girl it's good,
For a good girl it's bad,
And a job often winds up with a slap.
There is always a place
For a young pretty face,
But the place may be on the boss's lap.
There are lots of jobs in Paris,
But they're not for girls like I'm;
If you easily embarrass,
You're embarrassed all the time.
There is always success
For the girl who says yes;
For the girl who says no, it's very sad.
It's not hard to get employment
If a girl enjoys enjoyment,
But business for a good girl is bad.
There's a job that I would treasure
In a Montmartre restaurant;
I can have the job with pleasure,
But with pleasure I don't want.
There's a sculptor I met
Who would hire me, you bet,
But it means I would have to be unclad;
I prefer to keep my clothes on,
My above and my belows on,
And business for a good girl is bad.

THE PULITZER PRIZE

Registered for copyright as an unpublished song May 26, 1949. Intended for Philip Bourneuf (Pulitzer), Charles Dingle (Bennett), and ensemble. Not used. There are several versions of this song.

PULITZER: Gentlemen of the press, I greet you.
In my final will and testament
I leave a sum of money as a donation
For the creation
Of a prize.

[*Applause.*]

Today the standard of writing isn't
high;
It badly needs a stimulant, I fear.
To raise the standard of journalism I
Intend to give some prizes ev'ry year.
Gentlemen of the press, I'm happy
To announce that when I've said my
last goodbyes,
I will leave behind a very useful prize.
REPORTERS: He will leave behind a very useful
prize.
BENNETT: When the document is framed,
Tell us, what will it be named?
REPORTERS: When the document is framed,
Tell us, what will it be named?
PULITZER: [*disregarding*]
A committee will be serving
To reward the most deserving,
And the best reporting each year
That is truthful, simple, and clear
Will receive a thousand dollars;
though it's not a large amount,
The glory and the honor are the
things that really count.
And the trustees, honest and wise,
Will install a system governing the
prize.
REPORTERS: They'll install a system governing the
prize.
BENNETT: When it's finally installed,
Tell us, what will it be called?
REPORTERS: When it's finally installed,
Tell us, what will it be called?
PULITZER: [*disregarding*]
I have gotten the impression
That our hon'rable profession
Don't behave as well as it should,
And a prize might do it some good.
By distinguished editorials these
prizes can be won;
It well could be the *Times* or be the
Tribune or the *Sun*—

[*Looking at* BENNETT:]

It could even be the *Herald*.
REPORTERS: It could even be the *Herald*.
BENNETT: Mr. Pulitzer,
I speak not for the *Herald* but the
people,
And I'd like a statement for the
people
About the prizes.

I'm certain the intent is altruistic;
Nevertheless, when the prizes are
given,
Is it possible
They'll be calling it
The Pulitzer Prize?

[*He glares at* PULITZER.]

PULITZER: That's a wonderful idea.
REPORTERS: That's a wonderful idea.
BENNETT: That's exactly what I fear.
REPORTERS: This is something we can cheer.
Arise, arise, and hail the Pulitzer
Prize!
Grateful are we who inherit it;
May the heavens please
Guide the wise trustees
Only to those who will merit it.
Arise, arise, and hail the Pulitzer
Prize!
Here's to the lucky guys
Who'll win—
BENNETT: And quickly commercialize
And happily advertise—
ALL: The Pulitzer Prize,
The Pulitzer Prize,
The Pulitzer Prize!

First earlier version

PULITZER: Journalism's gone to hell.
I've devised a plan to elevate
The hon'rable profession of the
fourth estate.
REPORTERS: He will raise the standard of
The profession that we dearly love.
BENNETT: Chances for a change are slim;
How do you intend to stimulate
The hon'rable profession of the
fourth estate?
PULITZER: For the finest work that's done
There'll be several prizes to be won.
BENNETT: This is altruistic, honest, and wise.
Still, I'd like to ask a simple question:
Will this thing be called the Pulitzer
Prize?
PULITZER: Thank you, that's an excellent
suggestion.
BENNETT: [*sarcastically spoken*]
I thought so.
PULITZER: Not with medals, but a check
Every year I mean to dec-o-rate.
REPORTERS: The hon'rable profession of the
fourth estate.
PULITZER: But they mustn't advertise
Or commercialize the Pulitzer Prize.

BENNETT: [*mockingly*]
No, they mustn't advertise
Or commercialize the Pulitzer Prize.
PULITZER: For a novel or a play
That advances the American Way.
REPORTERS: But they mustn't advertise
Or commercialize the Pulitzer Prize.
PULITZER: For the finest epic "pome"
Glorifying the American home.
BENNETT: But they mustn't advertise
Or commercialize the Pulitzer Prize.
PULITZER: For the best biography
That is written with integrity.
BENNETT: But they mustn't advertise
Or commercialize the Pulitzer Prize.
PULITZER: For a cartoon that will bite
Anyone who doesn't know wrong
from right.
ALL: But they mustn't advertise
Or commercialize the Pulitzer Prize.
But they mustn't advertise
Or commercialize the Pulitzer Prize.
But they mustn't advertise
Or commercialize the Pulitzer Prize.

Second earlier version

[*Same as first early version, alternate lyrics beginning at "Not with medals but a check."*]

PULITZER: Not with medals but a check
Every year I mean to decorate
The hon'rable profession of the
fourth estate.
REPORTERS: This is what we've waited for—
Let us give three cheers and one cheer
more.
Arise, arise, and hail the Pulitzer
Prize!
Grateful are we who inherit it;
May the heavens please
Guide the wise trustees
Only to those who will merit it.
Arise, arise, and hail the Pulitzer
Prize!
Here's to the lucky guys
Who'll win—
BENNETT: And quickly commercialize
And happily advertise—
ALL: The Pulitzer Prize,
The Pulitzer Prize,
The Pulitzer Prize!

SING A SONG OF SING SING

Registered for copyright as an unpublished song February 7, 1949. Not used. Intended for Eddie Albert (Horace), Mary McCarty (Maisie), Allyn Ann McLerie (Monique), Ethel Griffies (the Countess), and ensemble.

VERSE

GOONS: Why do you, all of you, look so worried?
Why do you look so sad?
Prison is not so bad;
I was there as a lad.

CHORUS 1

Sing a song of Sing Sing,
The summer and winter resort.
Nothing's wrong with Sing Sing,
According to ev'ry report.
They will teach you a trade;
While you're learning, you're paid
Till you serve your sentence, and then
They will set you afloat
With a ten-dollar note
And you start life over again.
Take the car to Sing Sing,
It's filled with the people you know.
While they are in Sing Sing,
They don't have to pay what they owe.
If your banker upsets you
And finally gets you
So you lie awake all night long,
Steal some horses or sheep
And they'll sing you to sleep
With a Sing Sing song.

CHORUS 2

Sing a song of Sing Sing—
The life isn't hard to endure.
Nothing's wrong with Sing Sing
That knowing the warden won't cure.
If the warden's your pal,
You can send for a gal
And although it won't be believed,
It was there in a cell
That I met Isabel
And 'twas there her child was conceived.*

—————
*Alternate version of lines 7–10:
That's what happened early one morn—
It was there in a cell
That a pris'ner met Nell;
That's how Nellie's baby was born.

Tools are stored in Sing Sing,
And jailers are seldom about;
If you're bored with Sing Sing,
You just pay your bill and check out.
If you long for your mother
One way or another,
And if your homesickness is strong,
You can get to your ma
With a file and a saw
To a Sing Sing song.

CHORUS 3

ALL: Sing a song of Sing Sing—
It sounds like a wonderful place.
We belong in Sing Sing—
Let's hope that we don't win the case.
HORACE: I'll begin as a clerk,
But I'll work and I'll work,
And I'll be promoted, I know.
MAISIE: I'll give out with some sin
Till the warden gives in,
And I'll soon be running the show.
MONIQUE: I'll elope in Sing Sing—
It sounds like a place for romance.
COUNTESS: I just hope that Sing Sing
Is warmer than prisons in France.
HORACE: But suppose that it isn'
A steam-heated prison;
The walls and the bars will be strong.
MAISIE: I'll be there with the keys
As we sing a reprise—
ALL: Of the Sing Sing song.

CHORUS 4

[*To be split among principals.*]

Sing a song of Sing Sing—
It's easy if you know the tricks.
Nothing's wrong with Sing Sing
That just a few dollars won't fix.
There's the finest of drink
To be bought in the clink;
You can get as high as the stars.
You can all get a bun,
If you'll pardon the pun,
It's a place lousy with bars.
Gangsters bound for Sing Sing
Are happy when they get inside;
They have found in Sing Sing
The safest of places to hide.
Two-Gun Tony was slated
To be liquidated,
But he didn't wait very long;
Tony murdered his wife
And he's just doing life
To a Sing Sing song.

Alternate verse

Why do you look so sad?
Prison is not so bad.
You'll find it easy to bear—
Some of my best friends are there.

THE STORY OF NELL AND THE *POLICE GAZETTE*

Registered for copyright as an unpublished song March 3, 1949. Not used. This lyric is set to the same music as "Mr. Monotony."

Listen to me while I tell
How it was that little Nell
Got her picture on the *Police Gazette*.
She came here from Kal'mazoo,
Met a whiskey salesman who
Smoked cigars and read the *Police Gazette*.
One night she came to his flat;
What she saw there as she sat
Was a sofa and a *Police Gazette*.
As the night was very cold,
She became a trifle bold,
Drank a glass of what he sold,
And the liquor
Made her thicker
With the slicker.
Two days later she came out
And the rumor spread about
Till the story reached the *Police Gazette*.
Soon their best photographer
Had a photograph of her
For the front page of the *Police Gazette*.
In a little village Nellie's father and her mother
Got on a train because it seems that Nellie's
    brother
Saw her picture on the *Police Gazette*.
Nellie's father took a stand
With a shotgun in each hand,
Told the salesman, "I demand
That you gotta do right
By Nellie tonight."
And after the wedding was set,
A very nice piece
Was in the *Police Gazette*.
The *Police Gazette*.
Told of how Nellie met
With the slick city gent,
Of the first night they spent,
How they both fell in love,

And a cute picture of
Nellie and her husband in the *Police Gazette*.

ONLY IN AMERICA

Not used. Intended for Allyn Ann McLerie (Monique). Set to the same music as "Only for Americans."

Only in America
Could someone who don't mean a thing
Receive such royal welcoming, and
Only in America
Could someone so extremely small
Be belle of the Policemen's Ball—
And more and more
My heart beats for
Americans and the U.S.A.
I came from Paris with my granny;
The sun refused to shine—
A simple Orphan Annie,
But now the world is mine.
Only in America
Could I have found my pride and joy,
The one and only certain boy, and
Only in America
Could I have met the handsome sir,
The famous Mister Pulitzer.
I'll always love
The memory of
Americans and the U.S.A.

A WOMAN'S PLACE IS IN THE HOME

Registered for copyright as an unpublished song November 30, 1977. Not used. Intended for Eddie Albert (Horace) and Mary McCarty (Maisie) to sing in the opening scene. Replaced by "Homework."

VERSE

Ever since the world began,
Women all have said,
"I'm as smart as any man,"
Pointing to her head.
No mistake there's wisdom in her dome,
But the place to use it is the home.

CHORUS 1

A woman's place is in the home;
A woman's business is the home.
A man may travel
Over sand and gravel,
But a woman's place is in the home.
A woman's job is with a pan
Instead of working on a plan;
The thing to settle
Is a steaming kettle
And a tasty supper for her man.
"Home, Sweet Home"—
That's a beautiful song.
Home, sweet home—
That's where women belong.
A man would pack his grip and roam
And even sail across the foam;
He soon would wander
To a gal who's blonder
If his woman didn't stay at home—
That's what makes it home, sweet home.

CHORUS 2

A woman's place is in the home
With children there to brush and comb.
A man goes working
In an office clerking,
But a woman's place is in the home.
The job a girl should occupy
Is doing homework for a guy,
A table wiper
Who can change a diaper
And can sing a tender lullaby.
"Home, Sweet Home"—
That's a beautiful song.
Home, sweet home—
That's where women belong.
A man was meant to learn a trade
And get a job for which he's paid,
But woman's learning
Keeps the home fires burning,
For a woman's place is in the home,
That's what makes it home, sweet home.

IF I HAD NEVER BEEN BORN

Not used. Intended for Eddie Albert (Horace) to sing early in the second act.

VERSE 1

Why am I here in a mess of trouble?
How did it come to pass?
Why is it I am the one who's stupid?
Why am I such an ass?
Maybe it all could have been avoided;
Maybe it could, but how?
All that occurred didn't have to happen;
I see it clearly now.

CHORUS 1

If I hadn't gone to France,
If I hadn't met Monique,
If I only had been strong,
If I hadn't been so weak,
If I only had the common sense to see
What a most unhappy ending there would be.
If I hadn't cabled home,
If they hadn't sent the dough,
If I hadn't spent it all,
I could pay them what I owe.
If my mother and my father hadn't met that
　　morn,
And if I had never been born,
I'd be out of this mess,
Oh yes, oh yes,
If I had never been born.

VERSE 2

Unlucky me, if I nailed a horseshoe
Somewhere upon my bed,

I'm pretty sure in a week that horseshoe'd
Fall down upon my head.
Unlucky me, someone so unlucky
It would be hard to find.
Unlucky me, what have I been saying?
I must have lost my mind.

CHORUS 2

If I hadn't gone to France,
I'd have never met Monique.
If I hadn't met Monique,
I'd be mis'rable and weak.
If I had the sense they credit to a horse,
I'd have taken an entirely diff'rent course.
If I hadn't cabled home,
They'd have never sent the fare.
If they hadn't sent the fare,
She would still be over there.
If my mother and my father hadn't met that
　　morn,
And if I had never been born,
There'd be no such happiness,
Oh yes, oh yes,
If I had never been born.

THEY SAY IT'S FULL
OF INDIANS

Not used. Possibly intended for Miss Liberty's tour of America.

VERSE

I've seen pictures and I've read
Everything that has been said

Of that brand-new country over the sea,
Very much different from Paree.

CHORUS 1

They say it's full of Indians
And cowboys and buffaloes
And grass grows under your feet,
And there are lots of millionaires
And gold mines and dollar bills
That you can find in the street.
The houses all have parlors
Where nobody sits;
The men all chew tobacco
And ev'ryone spits.
And there are all those Indians
And cowboys and buffaloes—
I wonder how it would be
For a girl like me.

CHORUS 2

They say it's full of factories,
And with so much hammering
It's hard to hear when you speak;
And with those smoking chimneys
The place gets dirtier—
They have to bathe once a week.
They take defenseless puppies
And cook them on coals;
They're very fond of hot dogs
With mustard and rolls.
And there are all those Indians
And cowboys and buffaloes—
I don't think they would agree
With a girl like me.

Galina Talva, Ethel Merman, and Russell Nype

CALL ME MADAM | 1950

CALL ME MADAM (1950)

Tryout: Shubert Theatre, New Haven, September 11, 1950; Colonial Theatre, Boston, September 19, 1950. New York run: Imperial Theatre; opened October 12, 1950; 644 performances. Music and lyrics by Irving Berlin. Produced by Leland Hayward. Book by Howard Lindsay and Russel Crouse. Directed by George Abbott. Dances and musical numbers staged by Jerome Robbins. Orchestrations by Don Walker. Additional orchestrations by Joe Glover. Vocal arrangements by Jay Blackton. Dance music arrangements by Genevieve Pitot and Jesse Meeker. Piano arrangements by Helmy Kresa. Orchestra under the direction of Jay Blackton. Cast: starring Ethel Merman (Mrs. Sally Adams) and featuring Paul Lukas (Cosmo Constantine), Russell Nype (Kenneth Gibson), Galina Talva (Princess Maria), Alan Hewitt (Pemburton Maxwell), Pat Harrington (Congressman Wilkins), Ralph Chambers (Senator Gallagher), Jay Velie (Senator Brockbank). Because Ethel Merman had an exclusive contract with Decca Records, she was replaced on the RCA original cast album by Dinah Shore. Dick Haymes joined her on the Decca recording. There was a national tour, starring Elaine Stritch; a 1952 London production, starring Billie Worth; and a 1953 film version in which Merman was joined by, among others, George Sanders, Donald O'Connor, and Vera-Ellen.

MRS. SALLY ADAMS

Registered for copyright as an unpublished song September 20, 1950. Introduced by the company.

Mrs. Sally Adams
Requests the pleasure of your company
At a supper and dance,
A farewell party
That she's giving at her house tonight.
Mrs. Sally Adams,
The queen of Washington society—
Anybody at all
Who's anybody
Will be gathered at her house tonight.
Mrs. Sally Adams,
The new ambassador to cross the sea—
Mrs. Sally Adams,
Who says, "The hell with all formality."
Mrs. Sally Adams,
Mrs. Sally Adams

Makes 'em sing at her parties,
And each guest becomes a ham,
Giving all that he's got;
It may not please the smarties,
But she doesn't give a damn
If they like it or not.
She is liable to blurt out
The thing that she should ignore,
But nobody will care—
She can iron a shirt out
That's stuffed with a senator
Or a congressman there.
God bless America
For Mrs. Sally Adams,
Who wants the pleasure of our company—
Glad are we
To accept and root for
Mrs. Sally Adams,
Queen of all the madams,
Madam Ambassador.

ACT II REPRISE

Mrs. Sally Adams
Requests the pleasure of your company
At a supper and dance,
A coming-home party
That she's giving at her house tonight.
Mrs. Sally Adams
Has lost some of her popularity,
And the chances are that
A few somebodys
Will be missing at her house tonight.
Mrs. Sally Adams
Is back among us very suddenly,
And we're very anxious to hear
What happened there across the sea.
We are simply delighted
And happy without a doubt
To be gathering there;
Ev'ryone is excited,
For maybe we'll hear about
Sally's foreign affair.
God bless America
For Mrs. Sally Adams,
Who wants the pleasure of our company—
Glad are we
To accept and root for
Mrs. Sally Adams,
Queen of all the madams,
Madam Ex-Ambassador.

THE HOSTESS WITH THE MOSTES' ON THE BALL

Published. Copyrighted September 26, 1950. Previously registered for copyright as an unpublished song on March 16, 1950, and again on June 27, 1950. Introduced by Ethel Merman (Mrs. Sally Adams). One of the first songs written for the score, completed by early March 1950.

VERSE

I was born on a thousand acres
Of Oklahoma land;
Nothing grew on the thousand acres,
For it was gravel and sand.
One day Father started digging in a field,
Hoping to find some soil.
He dug and he dug, and what do you think?
Oil, oil, oil.
The money rolled in and I rolled out
With a fortune piled so high.
Washington was my destination,
And now who am I?

CHORUS 1

I'm the chosen party giver
For the White House clientele,
And they know that I deliver
What it takes to make 'em jell,
And in Washington I'm known by one and all
As the hostess with the mostes' on the ball.
They would go to Elsa Maxwell
When they had an ax to grind;
They could always grind their ax well
At the parties she designed.
But the hatchet grinders now prefer to call
On the hostess with the mostes' on the ball.
I've a great big bar*

---

*Earlier version of lines 13–24
   I found in politics
   It's the drinks you mix
   Warms them up when they are cold,
   And a Republican
   Loves a Democrat
   When the tenth martini takes hold.
   When the Senate's acting human,
   And a certain bill is passed,
   There's a thank-you note from Truman
   For some extra votes they cast—
   On the night before, those extra votes were all
   With the hostess with the mostes' on the ball.

And good caviar,
Yes, the best that can be found,
And a large amount
In my bank account
When election time comes 'round.
If your thoughts are presidential,
You can make it, yes, indeed;
There are just three things essential:
Let me tell you all you need
Is an ounce of wisdom and a pound of gall
And the hostess with the mostes' on the ball.

CHORUS 2

Entertaining vodka drinkers
Is a job they give to me;
Making nice guys out of stinkers
Seems to be my cup of tea.
What they really need behind the iron wall
Is the hostess with the mostes' on the ball.
There's a book of regulations
As to who sits next to who,
But there may be complications
When the blue blood's not so blue;
So the priestess with the leastes' protocol
Is the hostess with the mostes' on the ball.
An ambassador
Has just reached the shore;
He's a man of many loves,
An important gent
From the Orient,
To be handled with kid gloves.
He can come and let his hair down
Have the best time of his life,
Even bring his new affair down,
Introduce her as his wife,
But she mustn't leave her panties in the hall
For the hostess with the mostes' on the ball.

CHORUS 3

I've been highly complimented,
And I thank you; what is more,
You'll be damned well represented
By your new ambassador,
For my one ambition is to make them fall
For the hostess with the mostes' on the ball.
In the handbag that I'll carry
There's a precious little note
To Their Highnesses from Harry;
Introducing me, he wrote,
"I'll appreciate a favor, large or small,
For the hostess with the mostes' on the ball."
There'll be no mistakes—
I've got what it takes
To make friends across the sea.
I'll make bein' smart
An important part

Of my foreign policy.
I'll cement our good relations
When I give my first affair;
There'll be special invitations
To the duke and duchess there.
Who's already written asking them to call?
Not the priestess
With the leastes',
But the hostess
With the mostes',
With the mostes' on the ball.

Earlier version

[*Verse is the same as later version.*]

CHORUS 1

The hostess with the mostes' on the ball,
The priestess with the leastest protocol,
I found the only recipe
For Washington society
An ounce of wisdom and a pound of gall.
They profit by my parties, you will find,
Espec'lly those who have an ax to grind;
If you want to grind your ax well,
Don't go to Elsa Maxwell—
See the hostess with the mostes' on the ball.

CHORUS 2

The hostess with the mostes' at the bar,
Her Highness with the fines' caviar:
I found success in politics
Depends upon the drinks you mix—
Keep serving till they don't know who they are.
Republicans to Democrats are cold
Until the tenth martini takes a hold;
When the Senate's acting human,
My buddy Harry Truman
Thanks the hostess with the mostes' on the ball.

CHORUS 3

The hostess with the mostes' up her sleeve,
The madam with an Adam for each Eve:
Before the guests go in to sup,
I mix the wives and husbands up
But make sure they're together when they leave.
Respect for me is what they never lose;
They're careful of the language that they use,
But the Veep in all his glory
Can tell a dirty story
To the hostess with the mostes' on the ball.

WASHINGTON SQUARE DANCE

Published. Copyrighted October 5, 1950. Previously registered for copyright as an unpublished song June 27, 1950. Introduced by Ethel Merman (Mrs. Sally Adams) and company. Originally this was the last number in the second act. First performed by Berlin for Lindsay and Crouse on May 10, 1950.

Square dance,
The Washington Square Dance—
Republicans make up with the
    Democrats,
Show those foreign diplomats
That you dare dance
The Washington Square Dance.
No matter what side you're on
Or where you stand,
Take your partner by the hand
And each pair dance
The Washington Square Dance.
The theme is a get-together policy—
Show our friends across the sea
It's a fair dance,
The Washington Square Dance.
The rules are the same as cricket, golf, or
    squash—
No fair cheating, 'cause
The Washington Square Dance
Is square.

PATTER

Bow to your partners,
Bow to your corners,
Dance till your cheeks are red as a rose
But try not to step on your partner's toes.
Now duck for the oyster,
Dig for the clam,
Duck for the oyster,
Dig for the clam,
But do your digging for Uncle Sam—
And one for the money,
Two for the show,
One for the money,
Two for the show,
And three to get ready for Uncle Joe.
Republicans over to the right,
Democrats over to the left.
The left meet the right and don't explode—
Try to find the middle of the road, and

Square dance,
The Washington Square Dance.

The rules are the same as cricket, golf, or
    squash—
No fair cheatin', cause
The Washington Square Dance
Is square.

Roll up the rug—
Everybody dance.

Hi! Hi!
Do, do, do, do,
Do, do, do, do, do, do.
Hi, babe, whaddaya say?
Change your partners—
Square dance.

Now bow to your partners,
Bow to your corners,
And dance till your cheeks are red as a rose,
But try not to step on your partner's toes.
Now duck for the oyster,
Dig for the clam,
Now duck for the oyster,
Dig for the clam,
But do your diggin' for Uncle Sam.
And one for the money,
Two for the show,
Now one for the money,
Two for the show,
Three to get ready for Uncle Joe.
Square dance,
Come on.
[Dance]
Square dance,
The Washington Square Dance.
No matter what side you're on
Or where you stand,
Take your partner by the hand
And each pair dance
The Washington Square Dance.
Be careful, you'll have to watch your step, by
    gosh—
No round heels, because
The Washington Square Dance
Is square.

For the square dance,
The Washington Square Dance,
Is square.

Earlier version (different music)

Square dance,
Washington Square Dance.
Couples will line up front and face the
    band—
Take your partner by the hand

And each pair dance
The Washington Square Dance.

Square dance,
Washington Square Dance.
Mister Ambassador, you're in the groove—
Kiss McCarthy just to prove
It's a fair dance,
The Washington Square Dance.
If only from night till dawn, let's all be on the
    square.
Hey there, Mister Senator, now that won't do—
Mustn't hold the pretty girl so close to you.
I'm afraid you've had a little too much cup—
Raise your hand much higher up.

Hey there, Senator, now that won't do—
Must not hold the girl so close to you.
You have had a little too much cup—
Raise your hand much higher up.
Gen'ral, go and get yourself a maid;
It's not cricket dancing with your aide.
Don't you know there isn't much romance
Dancing cheek to cheek and pants to pants?

Square dance,
Washington Square Dance.
Fellers with pretty partners must let go—
Change your partners just to show
It's a fair dance,
The Washington Square Dance.
If only from night till dawn,
Let's all be on the square.

Republicans over to the right,
Democrats over to the left.
The left meet the right and don't explode—
Try to find the middle of the road and
Square dance,
Washington Square Dance.
Fellow Republicans and Democrats,
Show the foreign diplomats
That you dare dance
The Washington Square Dance.

Hey there, Senator, now that's not right—
Don't you hold the lady quite so tight.
You have had a little too much cup—
Raise your hand much higher up.
Gen'ral, go and get yourself a maid—
It's not cricket dancing with your aide.
There's no pleasure in it when you dance
Cheek to cheek and pants to pants.

LICHTENBURG

Registered for copyright as an unpublished song under
the title "Cosmo's Opening (Lichtenburg Verse)" on
September 20, 1950. Introduced by Paul Lukas (Cosmo
Constantine) and singers. Alternate title: "Welcome to
Lichtenburg."

COSMO: Welcome to Lichtenburg.
    I don't think you know much about us,
    Except, of course, our famous
        Lichtenburg cheese.
    I know very well you enjoy it,
    And we would enjoy it too,
    But we can't afford it,
    For we must have dollars,
    And so we send it to you.

[Music continues under the dialogue scene that fol-
lows. At the end of the dialogue, "How they love to
play with explosives," Cosmo continues to sing:]

COSMO: But Lichtenburg won't be offended;
    We'll manage to stay alive.
    We're not very touchy,
    This quaint little duchy
    That somehow seems to survive.

CHORUS: Too small to be a city,
    Too big to be a town,
    Too poor to have an army
    And too easy to knock down.
    Too little to sell across the seas—
    Babies and cheese
    Are our main industries.
    Too slow to please the young folks,
    Too fast to please the old;
    Too many who have copper pennies,
    Too few who have gold.
    But somehow we manage to play the
        game—
    While the other lands
    Keep changing hands,
    Old Lichtenburg stays the same.

CAN YOU USE ANY MONEY TODAY?

Registered for copyright as an unpublished song March 20, 1950. Introduced by Ethel Merman (Mrs. Sally Adams). One of the first songs written for the score.

CHORUS 1

Money, money, money, money, money, money—
Can you use any money today?
Money, money, money, money, money, money—
Nice new bills that we're giving away?
There are photographs on ev'ry one,
Lincoln, Grant, and Washington,
Or you might like the ones with Henry Clay—
Can you use any money today?
Two million, four million, six million, eight
    million, ten—
Take what you want, when it's gone you can come
    back again.
Bills that haven't been printed yet,
You can have them by the sack;
Coins that haven't been minted yet
That you never have to give back.
Money, money, money, money, money, money—
Uncle Sam puts it right on the line,
And if we ever run out of checks for him to sign,
You can have mine,
All of mine,
You can have mine.

CHORUS 2

Money, money, money, money, money, money—
Can you use any dollars today?
Money, money, money, money, money, money—
We've so much that it gets in our way.
In our treasury there's a mighty sum,
Millions we've subtracted from,
The envelopes that hold our take-home pay—
Can you use any money today?
Home in the States, underground, there's a cave
    full of gold;
Back up a truck and we'll fill it with all it can hold.
Take ten million and please don't fuss
If you find it can't be spent;
You can loan it right back to us
And we'll pay you seven percent.
Money, money, money, money, money, money—
Uncle Sam puts it right on the line,
And if that feller with whiskers ever should
    decline,
You can have mine,

All of mine,
You can have mine.

MARRYING FOR LOVE

Published. Copyrighted September 7, 1950. Previously registered for copyright as an unpublished song March 16, 1950. Introduced by Paul Lukas (Cosmo Constantine) and Ethel Merman (Mrs. Sally Adams).

VERSE

HE: Ten generations of Constantines
    Lived very comf'table lives.
    They were contented to live in style
    Supported by their wives.
    Daughters of men who were wealthy
    Fitted them like a glove.
    They all married for money;
    I mean to marry for love.

CHORUS

It's an old-fashioned idea,
Marrying for love;
And that old-fashioned idea's
What I'm thinking of.
Where there's love, poets have said,
Two can live as one;
That's an old-fashioned idea,
But it's being done.
If she must have gold,
Let it be in her hair;
Rubies,
Let them be in her lips;
Diamonds,
Let them shine in her eyes.
Just an old-fashioned romance
With a moon above,
A romance, one that will end
Marrying for love—
That's the kind of love
That I'm thinking of.

SHE: It's an old-fashioned idea,
    Marrying for love;
    And that old-fashioned idea's
    What I'm thinking of.
    Where there's love, poets have said,
    Two can live as one;
    That's an old-fashioned idea,
    But it's being done.
    When I find the man

That I'm crazy about,
There's much more that
I could do without,
But I
Wouldn't do without love.
Just an old-fashioned romance
With a moon above,
A romance, one that will end
Marrying for love—
That's the kind of love
That I'm thinking of.

(DANCE TO THE MUSIC OF) THE OCARINA

Published. Copyrighted September 7, 1950. Previously registered for copyright as an unpublished song June 27, 1950. Introduced by Galina Talva (Princess Maria) and ensemble.

VERSE

[*Ocarinas play first four bars of chorus.*]

Listen to the ocarina play—

[*They repeat the same phrase.*]

Listen, don't you seem to hear it say:

CHORUS

Dance to the music of the ocarina,
Ocarina, ocarina—
Gretchen and Otto, Hans and Wilhelmina
Dance to the ocarina, dance.
Dance to the music of the sweet potata,
Sweet potata, sweet potata:
Cheeks getting redder than a ripe tomata
Dance to the ocarina, dance.
Listen and hear
The notes escaping
Out of that tiny hole—
Doesn' it please your soul?
Doesn' it say,
Dance the polka?
Step to the music of the ocarina—
Who refuses? Wilhelmina?
Wait till she listens to the ocarina;
I know that Wilhelmina will.

IT'S A LOVELY DAY TODAY

Published. Copyrighted September 19, 1950. Previously registered for copyright as an unpublished song September 15, 1950. Introduced by Russell Nype (Kenneth Gibson) and Galina Talva (Princess Maria).

CHORUS 1

HE: It's a lovely day today,
So whatever you've got to do,
You've got a lovely day
To do it in,
That's true.
And I hope whatever you've got to do
Is something that can be done by two,
For I'd really like to stay.
It's a lovely day today,
And whatever you've got to do,
I'd be so happy
To be doing it
With you.
But if you've got something
That must be done,
And it can only be
Done by one,
There is nothing more to say,
Except it's a lovely day
For saying
It's a lovely day.

CHORUS 2

SHE: It's a lovely day today,
And whatever I've got to do,
I've got a lovely day
To do it in,
That's true.
But perhaps whatever I've got to do
Is something that can be done by two
If it is then you can stay.
It's a lovely day today,
But you're probably busy too,
So I suppose there's really
Nothing we
Can do.
For if you've got something
That must be done
And it can only be
Done by one,
There is nothing more to say,
Except it's a lovely day
For saying
It's a lovely day.

CHORUS 3

HE: It's a lovely day today
If you've something that must be done,
Now don't forget two heads
Are better than
Just one.
And besides, I'm certain if you knew me,
You'd find I'm very good company—
Won't you kindly let me stay?

[*Dialogue against the next 16 bars:*]

SHE: Mr. . . . . American! Your Madam
Ambassador told me she is very
lonesome. Remember? She asked me to
come and see her. If it were known
I did, there would be a great scandal.
HE: But if you used that passage from the
palace—
SHE: Yes, that just occurred to me.
HE: And I could be there waiting for you.
SHE: That also just occurred to me.

[*Sung*]

HE: There is nothing more to say
BOTH: Except it's a lovely day
For saying
It's a lovely day.

Earlier version of chorus 2

SHE: It's a lovely day today,
And whatever I've got to do,
I've got a lovely day
To do it in,
That's true.
But I fear whatever I've got to do
Is nothing that can be done by two,
So you might be on your way.
It's a lovely day today,
And whatever your plans may be,
You've got a lovely day
To do it in
Without me.
You can crawl right back again
On your shelf—
What I must do I can
Do myself,
So there's nothing more to say,
Except it's a lovely day
For saying
It's a lovely day.

THE BEST THING FOR YOU

Published. Copyrighted September 7, 1950. Previously registered for copyright as an unpublished song March 20, 1950. Introduced by Ethel Merman (Mrs. Sally Adams) and Paul Lukas (Cosmo Constantine). First sung by Berlin for Lindsay and Crouse on March 13, 1950.

VERSE 1

SHE: Please let me say from the start,
I don't pretend to be smart.
I just suggest
What I think best,
Having your int'rest at heart.

CHORUS 1

I only want
What's the best thing for you,
And the best thing for you
Would be me.
I've been convinced
After thinking it through
That the best thing for you
Would be me.
Ev'ry day
To myself I say,
Point the way,
What will it be?
I ask myself,
What's the best thing for you?
And myself and I
Seem to agree
That the best thing for you
Would be me.

VERSE 2

HE: Thanks for the interest, my dear;
You've made it perfectly clear.
I'd like to do
What's best for you,
But I'm too selfish, I fear.

CHORUS 2

I only want
What's the best thing for me,
And the best thing for me
Would be you.
I've thought it over
And now I can see
That the best thing for me
Would be you.
Ev'ry day

To myself I say,
Point the way,
What should I do?
I ask myself,
What's the best thing for me?
And myself and I
Have the same view:
That the best thing for me
Would be you.*

While you're there brokenhearted
Suddenly he returns.*
That's something to dance about
With someone to dance it with,
Pick something to dance it to,
To a fox-trot or a waltz.

SECOND ENDING

To a fox-trot or a waltz,
To a fox-trot or a waltz.

SOMETHING TO DANCE ABOUT

Published. Copyrighted November 7, 1950. Previously registered for copyright as an unpublished song October 2, 1950. Introduced by Ethel Merman (Mrs. Sally Adams) with dancers Tommy Rall, Barbara Heath, Norma Doggett, Arthur Partington, and ensemble. Completed September 23, 1950, during the Boston tryout—the last song written for the show. The idea for this song came from Jerome Robbins, who told Berlin that early in the second act they needed "something to dance about."

VERSE

An old hand at giving parties,
And I've learned an awful lot.
The best reason for a party
And what keeps it boiling hot—
An occasion when you've got

CHORUS

Something to dance about,
Someone to dance it with,
Something to dance it to,
To a fox-trot or a waltz.
Put on your dancing shoes—
Here comes some happy news.
Break up in twos and twos
To a fox-trot or a waltz.
You and someone have parted
And your lonely heart yearns

Alternate version of lines 13–18:
  SHE: I ask myself,
      What's the best thing for you?
      And myself and I
      Seem to agree
  BOTH: That the best thing for you
      Would be me.

ONCE UPON A TIME TODAY

Published. Copyrighted September 26, 1950. Previously registered for copyright as an unpublished song August 2, 1950. Introduced by Russell Nype (Kenneth Gibson). Russel Crouse reports in his diary that he heard this song for the first time on May 22, 1950.

VERSE

I would like you to listen,
Pay attention and listen,
To a story that's old but never stale.
I would like you to listen,
Pay attention and listen,
To a twentieth-century fairy tale.

CHORUS 1

Once there was a princess,
Once there was a guy,
And they fell in love one wonderful day.
But she was a princess,
He was just a guy,
So there was the royal devil to pay.
They were ordered not to speak to one another,
And they knew the sorrow that would bring;
Still they promised not to speak to one another—
But they didn't promise not to sing.
So beneath her window
Tenderly he sang
All the things he promised never to say
Once upon a time, today.

Earlier version of lines 9–12:
  Here's a note from the Russians;
  Let the arguments cease.
  We are tired of discussions;
  Let's sit down and talk peace.

CHORUS 2

Once there was a princess,
Once there was a guy,
And they fell in love one wonderful day.
But she was a princess,
He was just a guy,
So there was the royal devil to pay.
He collected lots of ordinary phrases
Like "I love you, dear," and "You're for me,"
But he found that when he set them all to music,
They were just as good as poetry.
So beneath her window
Tenderly he sang,
"How about that happy ending in May?"
Once upon a time, today.

THEY LIKE IKE

Published. Copyrighted September 27, 1950. Previously registered for copyright as an unpublished song June 27, 1950. Introduced by Pat Harrington (Congressman Wilkins), Ralph Chambers (Senator Gallagher), and Jay Velie (Senator Brockbank). In a letter to Ed Sullivan (November 6, 1952), Berlin discussed the genesis and evolution of the song:

Dear Ed:
    Following is the story behind "I Like Ike."
    In 1948 when the talk of Eisenhower for President started, I wrote a chorus of a song called "I Like Ike" as a campaign number. The first version was a straight campaign song. I thought then that the traditional fear of a military man in the White House would be a big issue, so one of the couplets in that original version was—

    With so many treasures in our back yard,
    It's good to have a soldier standing on
        guard

    The talk about Eisenhower for President died down and I forgot about the song.
    When *Call Me Madam* came along I saw a spot in Lindsay and Crouse's script where we could use the "Ike" number as a comedy song. I then rewrote it and switched "I" to "They." The rest of the story, you know.
    Ike came to the opening night and he seemed to enjoy it. I never dreamed it would be embarrassing to him.
    In any event, the number started going better with each performance and I realized after a while that it was based on the warm feeling we all had for General Eisenhower.
    After the convention, I had to change the

lyrics and kept on changing them from then on to fit every change in the political situation.

If you do this Sunday night, I suggest having Pat Harrington, Ralph Chambers and Jay Velie do the version that they did the opening night at the Imperial Theater.

Good luck and many thanks.

Published version

VERSE 1

1ST DEMOCRAT: The Presidential year
Will soon be drawing near;
The people soon will choose
their fav'rite son.
2ND DEMOCRAT: I wonder what they'll do
In nineteen fifty-two;
I wonder who they'll send to
Washington.

CHORUS 1

REPUBLICAN: They like Ike,
And Ike is good on a mike.
They like Ike.
1ST DEMOCRAT: But Ike says he don't wanna.
REPUBLICAN: That makes Ike
The kind o' feller they like—
And what's more,
They seem to think he's gonna.
2ND DEMOCRAT: But Harry won't get out;
They're in for plenty of fights.
1ST DEMOCRAT: Harry won't get out;
He's got squatter's rights.
REPUBLICAN: But there's Ike,
And Ike is good on a mike,
And they know
The votes that he can carry.
DEMOCRATS: But don't forget there's Harry.
REPUBLICAN: But they like Ike.

VERSE 2

1ST DEMOCRAT: They won't take Saltonstall,
And Stassen's chance is small;
The same would go for
Vandenberg and Taft.
2ND DEMOCRAT: And Dewey's right in line
With William Jennings Bryan;
There isn't anyone that they can
draft.

CHORUS 2

REPUBLICAN: They like Ike,
And Ike is good on a mike.
They like Ike.
1ST DEMOCRAT: But Ike says he won't take it.
REPUBLICAN: That makes Ike
The kind o' feller they like—
And what's more,
They seem to think he'll make
it.
2ND DEMOCRAT: But Harry's on the ground,
And should Republicans win—
1ST DEMOCRAT: When they come around,
He won't let them in.
REPUBLICAN: If it's Ike,
Your Chief can get on his bike,
And his things
A moving van will carry.
DEMOCRATS: They can't do that to Harry!
REPUBLICAN: But they like Ike.

VERSE 3

1ST DEMOCRAT: For nearly twenty years
We've had the people's cheers;
The Democrats continue to
advance.
2ND DEMOCRAT: Of course, they could arrange
To make a sudden change;
But no one's 'round who seems
to have a chance.

CHORUS 3

REPUBLICAN: They like Ike,
And Ike is good on a mike.
They like Ike.
1ST DEMOCRAT: But Ike says he's not bidding.
REPUBLICAN: That makes Ike
The kind o' feller they like—
And what's more,
They seem to think he's kidding.
2ND DEMOCRAT: But Harry won't consent—
They'll get a sock in the jaw.
1ST DEMOCRAT: Republican President?
That's against the law.
REPUBLICAN: If it's Ike,
Your Chief can go on a hike,
And we boys
Will see he doesn't tarry.
DEMOCRATS: They can't do that to Harry!
REPUBLICAN: But they like Ike.

VERSE 4

1ST DEMOCRAT: With your permission, sir,
We're anxious to confer,

And we would like to do it
privately.
REPUBLICAN: Go on and make your crack—
I'll even turn my back.
But if you're speaking of the
GOP—

CHORUS 4

REPUBLICAN: They like Ike,
And Ike is good on a mike.
They like Ike.
1ST DEMOCRAT: But Ike says he'll reject it.
REPUBLICAN: That makes Ike
The kind o' feller they like—
And what's more,
They think he'll be elected.
2ND DEMOCRAT: But Harry won't give in;
Defeat he'll never admit.
1ST DEMOCRAT: No one else can win;
He won't stand for it.
REPUBLICAN: If it's Ike,
Your Chief can get on his bike
Two years more
The month of January.
TWO DEMOCRATS: They can't do that to Harry!
REPUBLICAN: But they like Ike.

VERSE 5

1ST DEMOCRAT: It seems that ev'ry spring
They all approach the ring
And cockily keep throwing in
their hats.
2ND DEMOCRAT: They always lose, but then
They come right back again—
And some of them come back as
Democrats.

CHORUS 5

REPUBLICAN: They like Ike,
And Ike is good on a mike.
They like Ike.
1ST DEMOCRAT: But Ike says he don't choose
to.
REPUBLICAN: That makes Ike
The kind o' feller they like—
And what's more,
They know he won't refuse to.
2ND DEMOCRAT: But Harry is content
To stay there living in peace.
1ST DEMOCRAT: The people pay the rent;
You can't break his lease.
REPUBLICAN: If it's Ike,
Your Chief can go on a strike,
And we boys
Will hand his hat to Harry.

TWO DEMOCRATS: You can't do that to Harry!
REPUBLICAN: But they like Ike.

Alternate lyrics

Here are some changed lines from July 1, 1952, intended for the Republican National Convention, which nominated Eisenhower for President:

Let's take Ike,
A man we all of us like—
Makes no deals;
His favors can't be curried.
And Uncle Joe is worried
'Cause we like Ike.

I LIKE IKE

Published. Copyrighted January 18, 1952. As soon as it became clear that Eisenhower would be a candidate for President in 1952, Berlin began to revise this song. In 1952 there was "I Like Ike," an Eisenhower campaign song.

I like Ike—
I'll shout it over a mike,
Or a phone,
Or from the highest steeple.
I like Ike,
And Ike is easy to like;
Stands alone,
The choice of We the People.
A leader we can call
Without political noise,
He can lead us all
As he led the boys.
Let's take Ike,
A man we all of us like,
Tried and true,
Courageous, strong, and human—
Why, even Harry Truman
Says, "I like Ike."

I STILL LIKE IKE

On March 6, 1954, ASCAP presented a show at the White House Correspondents Dinner for President Eisenhower, held at the Statler Hotel in Washington, D.C. On that occasion Berlin unveiled a new Ike song with a preamble that detailed some history of *This Is the Army*. Registered for copyright as an unpublished song March 8 and March 15, 1954.

For this occasion I've written a special song,
A simple chorus that's just thirty-six bars long.
But it needs an explanation
With words and melody;
I'll have to say it with music,
So I hope you'll be patient through this
    explanation
And bear with me.

It was just about ten years ago
'Neath London's troubled skies
I was playing in *This Is the Army*
With a hundred and sixty GIs.
And this was a special performance,
Very carefully planned,
For a certain gen'ral
Who came to London
To take over command.

After the show he sent for me
And said with warmth and poise,
"I loved the show and I'd like to go
Backstage and talk to the boys."
A sergeant shouted "Attention!"
The gen'ral put them at ease
And told them the one thing they wanted to hear
In words something like these:
"There are all kinds of soldiers in the army,
Some at the front, most in the back,
And their jobs are of equal importance
For the final attack."
And he wasn't just making a speech,
For he sent a directive next day
Recommending that every theater of war
Should see this soldier play.

It was shortly after then—
Not too long—
I thought of a simple phrase,
And later I wrote this song:

I like Ike,
And Ike is good on a mike.

And now the special chorus I've written for you,
Which I hope you like.

I still like Ike
And will like Ike
The same as I liked him at the start,
For Ike remains
A man with brains,
But what's much more,
A man with heart.
He takes his time to make his mind up,
But when he does, we most of us agree
We all trust Ike,
And there's just Ike,
Who knows what's best for you and me
And has what it takes to keep us free.

IKE FOR FOUR MORE YEARS

Published. Copyrighted August 13, 1956. Introduced by Irving Berlin August 22, 1956, at the Republican National Convention in San Francisco, which nominated Eisenhower for a second term as President.

Four more years!
Four more years!
Give us what we'd like;
What we'd like is Ike
For four more years—three cheers
For Ike for four more years!
I like Ike,
I like Ike,
Like him even more
Than I did before—
So give three rousing cheers
For Ike for four more years!

WE STILL LIKE IKE

Registered for copyright as an unpublished song May 15, 1967. Written for an unproduced television presentation of *Call Me Madam*, which was to have starred Angela Lansbury. There are two versions of this lyric, as Berlin had to alter the words to fit the ever-changing political events of 1967 and 1968. There is also an "I Still Like Ike" version of this song, which changes "We" to "I."

First version

VERSE 1

DEMOCRATS: The presidential year
Will soon be drawing near;
The Democrats look forward to the
    date.
Republicans as well

Are waiting for the bell;
We wonder who you'll choose to
    nominate.

CHORUS 1

REPUBLICANS: We still like Ike,
    And Ike is good on a mike.
    We still like Ike.
DEMOCRATS: But Ike is now a farmer.
REPUBLICANS: He likes plows
    And pigs and chickens and cows,
    And they like him,
    'Cause Ike is still a charmer.
DEMOCRATS: But Johnson couldn't lose;
    We're getting set for the day—
    When the people choose,
    We've got LBJ.
    But he likes Ike;
    He comes to him for advice.
    He likes Ike;
    He likes him like a brother.
REPUBLICANS: Compared to any other,
    We still like Ike.

VERSE 2

DEMOCRATS: There's Nixon, quite a man;
    And Romney thinks he can;
    And Rocky's just as smart as he can
        be.
    And Reagan, though he's new,
    Can get a vote or two,
    Including those from Actors'
        Equity.

CHORUS 2

REPUBLICANS: We still like Ike,
    And Ike is good on a mike.
DEMOCRATS: Ike likes golf.
REPUBLICANS: But golf is just a hobby.
DEMOCRATS: Lyndon's in;
    There's no one else that can win.
REPUBLICANS: Don't forget
    That handsome kid named Bobby.
DEMOCRATS: But Bobby wouldn't run;
    That rumor's nothing but talk.
    Bobby wouldn't run.
REPUBLICANS: He'd just have to walk.
DEMOCRATS: He's not the man;
    He'd lose if ever he ran.
REPUBLICANS: If he's out,
    You know there's always Teddy.
DEMOCRATS: But Teddy isn't ready.
REPUBLICANS: We still like Ike.

Second version

VERSE 1

Election's drawing near;
The day will soon be here.
And every politician in the land
Is saying, "I'm the gent
To be your President."
We've listened to those politicians, and—

CHORUS 1

We still like Ike,
And Ike is easy to like.
We still like Ike,
Although he's now a farmer.
He likes plows
And pigs and chickens and cows;
They like him,
'Cause Ike is still a charmer.
The Democrats pretend
They aren't worried, they say
If the war should end
They'll draft LBJ.
But he likes Ike;*
He goes to him for advice.
He likes Ike;
He likes him like a brother.
Compared to any other,
We still like Ike.

VERSE 2

Now Nixon's quite a man,
And Rocky has a plan,
And Stassen still is cocky as can be.
And Reagan, though he's new,
Can get a vote or two,
Especially from the Actors' Equity.

CHORUS 2

But we like Ike,
And Ike is easy to like.
He plays golf,
And while he's out there sunning,
He walks miles,
His face all covered with smiles,

Lines 9–13 were changed to:
    The Democrats no doubt
    Will choose somebody, but then
    LBJ is out—
    He won't run again,
    'Cause he likes Ike.

Thinking of*
The others who are running.
McCarthy says he's in;
He's just as sure as can be.
Humphrey thinks he'll win,
But there's Kennedy:
Bobby's great,
But he got in it too late—
One more choice.
There's Bobby's brother Teddy
But Teddy isn't ready
So we like Ike.

YOU'RE JUST IN LOVE

Published. Copyrighted October 10, 1950. Previously registered for copyright as an unpublished song September 20, 1950. Introduced by Ethel Merman (Mrs. Sally Adams) and Russell Nype (Kenneth Gibson). Written during the New Haven tryout; first performed, privately, by Berlin on September 15, 1950. The idea for this song came from Ethel Merman, who was so impressed with the reception that Nype had received for "It's a Lovely Day Today" that she told Berlin, according to Nype, "I want a number with the kid."

Helmy Kresa, who began making piano arrangements for Berlin with "Blue Skies" in 1926 and who became his chief arranger and head of his company's music department, recalled the writing of "You're Just in Love":

I was with him all through the New Haven and Boston try-outs. After we opened in New Haven . . . it became apparent that Russell Nype, the juvenile lead, was the surprise hit of the show. Also that Ethel Merman needed one more comedy song in the second act. At that time, we had a very successful revival of an old Berlin song "Play a Simple Melody" which is a double number—one smooth melody against a rhythmic melody. Mr. Berlin said it would be wonderful if he could write a similar song for Merman and Nype. . . . That was the middle of the first week in New Haven and for the next four or five days, especially over the weekend, Mr. Berlin worked hard on that song. He took two lines that he had from a song he wrote for *Annie Get Your Gun* entitled "Something Bad's Gonna Happen" which read, "I can hear people singing tho' there's no one there, I can smell orange blossoms tho' the trees

---

Line 7 was changed to:
    Laughing at

are bare." With that to start on, he first wrote the sweet melody and I played it over and over again for him as he wrote the rhythmic counter-melody on top of it. The following Monday the song was finished and that night I made a piano part of it. On Tuesday morning of the second week in New Haven, Mr. Berlin sang "You're Just In Love" for Hayward, Lindsay & Crouse and Abbott and they all thought it was wonderful. After lunch, Ethel Merman and Russell Nype got a demonstration of the song by Mr. Berlin and myself. They learned it very fast and sang it together right then and there in Mr. Berlin's room at the Taft Hotel. . . . After the keys were set, Jay Blackton, the musical director, had the orchestration made by Joe Glover and on the following Sunday afternoon in Boston we rehearsed the orchestration with the singers in one of the ballrooms at the Bradford Hotel. The song was put into the show on opening night in Boston.

CHORUS 1

I hear singing and there's no one there;
I smell blossoms and the trees are bare;
All day long I seem to walk on air—
I wonder why,
I wonder why.
I keep tossing in my sleep at night,
And what's more, I've lost my appetite;
Stars that used to twinkle in the skies
Are twinkling in my eyes—
I wonder why.

CHORUS 2

You don't need analyzing;
It is not so surprising
That you feel very strange but nice.
Your heart goes pitter patter;
I know just what's the matter,
Because I've been there once or twice.
Put your head on my shoulder;
You need someone who's older,
A rubdown with a velvet glove.
There is nothing you can take
To relieve that pleasant ache—
You're not sick, you're just in love.

REPEAT CHORUS 1 AND CHORUS 2

[Sung together as counter-melodies.]

"Dummy" lyric for start of chorus 1:

I hear footsteps coming down the hall,
And I know there's no one there at all;

I smell summer and I know it's fall—
I wonder why,
I wonder why.
I go walking in the street at night,
And I cross against the traffic light

[Lyric breaks off here.]

WHAT DID YOU DO TO ME?

A possible forerunner of "You're Just in Love." Date unknown, although probably from the 1920s. No music is known to survive.

VERSE

Tell me, tell me, baby,
What am I to do?
Mister Cupid paid me a call,
Making me fall for you.
Doctor says I'm lovesick,
And I guess it's true
I don't look as well as I should;
I feel bad, but it's terribly good.

CHORUS

Oh, babe, I've lost my appetite—
What did you do to me?
What did you do to me?
And I can't sleep a wink at night—
What did you do to me?
What did you do to me?
All I do is think of you, the other morning
I tried to put my right shoe on my left foot,
And you know that isn't right.
Oh, babe, I'm acting mighty queer—
What did you do to me?
What did you do to me?
My heart goes thumping when you're near and I
  fear
Something's wrong way up in my dome;
Outside of you there is nobody home—
Tell me, baby, what did you do to me, dear.

FREE

Published. Copyrighted September 7, 1950. Previously registered for copyright as an unpublished song July 21, 1950. Introduced by Ethel Merman (Mrs. Sally Adams)

and company. Dropped from the show during the pre-Broadway tryout. Berlin first played this song for Crouse on May 22, 1950. A few years later, Berlin, using the same melody, wrote a new lyric, "Snow," which was presented in the film *White Christmas* (1954). According to a later note in the New York *Herald-Tribune*, "Free" itself was introduced by Jan Peerce on the NBC *Producers' Showcase* salute to freedom of the press by the Overseas Press Club.

CHORUS

Free—
The only thing I want on earth is to be free.
Free
To disagree with those who disagree with me.
Free
To close my door at night and never turn the key.
Free
To fall asleep and know I'll slumber peacefully.
Free from bending down on my knees,
To be pushed and be shoved;
Free to work and play where I please;
Free to love and be loved.
Free—
The only thing worth fighting for is to be free.
Free—
A diff'rent world you'd see if it were left to me;
Ev'rybody would be free, free, free.

Free—
The only thing I want on earth is to be free.
Free
To disagree with those who disagree with me.
Free
To close my door at night and never turn the key.
Free
To fall asleep and know I'll slumber peacefully.
Free from bending down on my knees,
To be pushed and be shoved;
Free to work and play where I please;
Free to love and be loved.
Free—
The only thing I want on earth is to be free.
Free—
The only thing worth fighting for is to be free,
Free.*

---

*Alternate version of last five lines:
    Free—
    The only thing worth fighting for is to be free.
    A diff'rent world you'd see if it were left to me—
    Ev'rybody would be free,
    Free.

OUR DAY OF INDEPENDENCE

Registered for copyright as an unpublished song August 1, 1952. Apparently written in New Haven in mid-September 1950 during the pre-Broadway tryout. Sung during the post-Broadway run by Pat Harrington (Congressman Wilkins), Ralph Chambers (Senator Gallagher), and Jay Velie (Senator Brockbank). It replaced "They Like Ike," but after a short time was dropped and "They Like Ike" was restored to the show.

VERSE

The East, the West, the South, the North,
All over the U.S.A.,
We all agree July the Fourth
Is our greatest holiday.

CHORUS 1

On our Day of Independence,
On the Fourth of July,
We are Washington's descendants
With our flags flying high.
We fall asleep on the beaches
And burn our cheeks
And can't sit down for weeks and weeks
On our Day of Independence,
On the Fourth of July.

CHORUS 2

On our Day of Independence
To the tune of brass bands
You will find a large attendance
Round the cheap-hot-dog stands.
We stagger home in the morning
With nerves all shot
And brag about how sick we got
On our Day of Independence,
On the Fourth of July.

CHORUS 3

On our Day of Independence
When the wife starts a row,
You're about as independent
As a horse or a cow.
You try to stand on your rights
As she starts to frown;
You stand up till
She knocks you down
On our Day of Independence,
On the Fourth of July.

CHORUS 4

On our Day of Independence
Little Johnny's so cute
As he lights a Roman candle,
Points it right at your snoot.
He lights a big firecracker
Neath Grandpa's chair,
And Grandpa can
Be found nowhere
On our Day of Independence,
On the Fourth of July.

CHORUS 5

On our Day of Independence
We wind up at a ball
That the DAR is giving
At the local town hall.
You waltz around with your partner,
And as you dance,
A thousand ants
Crawl up your pants,
On our Day of Independence,
On the Fourth of July.

CHORUS 6

On our Day of Independence
To the schoolhouse we go,
Where we hear the Declaration
That they signed long ago.
You hear the great words of freedom
Those brave men wrote
And get a lump
Up in your throat
On our Day of Independence,
On the Fourth of July.

OUR TOWN

Written in March 1950. Not used. There are four versions of this song. In his diary, Russel Crouse wrote that he and Howard Lindsay first heard a version of it on March 6, 1950.

First version

Our town is not a big town;
Our town is rather small.
A room meant for two is crowded with four,
And ev'ry year they make room for one more.
Some days the skies are dreary,

But when the heavens frown,
We like to believe that some special star
Will smile down
On our town.

Second version

Our town
Is a wonderful town
When the heavens look down
On our town.
For hundreds of years
We have managed to weather the storm;
The love that the people have had for each other
Has kept them warm.
Our town
Is a wonderful town
When the sky doesn't frown
On our town.
For hundreds of years we have managed to find
A happiness all our own,
And all that we ask from the rest of the world
Is just to be left alone,
Alone
In our town.

Third version

Our town
Is a wonderful town;
Though there's much that we lack in our town—
Our system will often go wrong—
Nevertheless we muddle along.
In our town
We've a wonderful faith;
When the rest of the world seems to frown,
We like to believe that some special star
Will shine down
On our town.

Fourth version

There's no town like our town,
With its plain, simple, ev'ryday folks.
There's no gang like our gang,
With their warmhearted laughter and jokes.
Where a handshake is all you need
To prove to a friend you're a friend indeed—
There's no town like our town;
It's a bit of heaven here on earth.

CALL ME MADAM

Written for an unproduced television version of the show which was to have starred Angela Lansbury. There are two versions. The first was registered for copyright as an unpublished song June 20, 1967. Typed lyric sheet dated April 25, 1967. The second, longer version was written in 1971.

CHORUS

I'm so glad they've made me a dame,
But call me madam;
I like "dame" attached to my name,
But call me madam.
What did you do, America?
It's thanks to you, America,
A foreign countryside has made me a dame.
I like my ambassador post,
So call me madam—
That's the name that pleases me most,
So call me madam.
I'm not just a hostess, the mostes',
That once I used to be—
America made a madam out of me.

Long version

VERSE

I began as a gospel singer
In Nashville, Tennessee;
Played the nightclubs and all the theaters
And all the spots on TV.
One day I was invited to sing
For the President in the White House.
I sang and I sang—with each encore
It was "More! More! More!"
The President said when I was through,
"The country needs a woman like you
To foster good relations
With one of the foreign nations."
So now I'm on my way to a foreign shore,
With my credentials,
All the essentials,
Madam Ambassador.

CHORUS 1

From now on don't mention my name,
Just call me madam.
I've not changed; the name is the same,
But call me madam.
What did you do, America?
It's thanks to you, America,

I'm on the road that'll lead me to fame.
I like my ambassador post,
So call me madam,
That's a name that's really the most,
So call me madam.
I'm not just a singer,
The swinger
That once I used to be—
America made a madam out of me.

CHORUS 2

From now on, we're starting today,
Just call me madam.
I don't know what Mother would say,
But call me madam.
What did you do, America,
Red, white, and blue America?
You made me like the American way.
From now on wherever I roam,
They'll call me madam.
I don't say a house is a home,
But call me madam.
I'm not just a hostess, the mostes',
That once I used to be—
America made a madam out of me.

YOU'VE GOT TO BE WAY OUT TO BE IN

Written for an unproduced television version of the show, which was to have starred Angela Lansbury. Intended as a replacement for "Washington Square Dance." There are two versions. The first was registered for copyright as an unpublished song May 15, 1967. Typed lyric sheet dated April 21, 1967. The second, or revised, version was completed on July 14, 1971.

1967 version

You got to be way out to be in,
Way out to be in.
Marriage is out,
But the couples who live in sin
Are in.
You got to wear stretch pants to be in,
Mod clothes to be in.
Water is out,
But a dash of vermouth and gin
Is in.
You got to wear skirts above your knees,
Sideburns and goatees,

Shoulder-length hair for the boys,
So you can't tell the hes from the shes.
You got to like pop art to be in,
So smart to be in.
To be or not to be,
To be you got to be
Way out to be in.

1971 version

You've gotta be way out to be in,
Way out to be in.
Marriage is out,
But the couples who live in sin
Are in.
You've gotta wear hot pants to be in,
Long hair to be in.
Costumes are out,
But a show where they just wear skin
Is in.*
You've gotta know all the beautiful people—
You know the ones I mean;
Some of the beautiful people
Have the homeliest faces I've seen.
You've gotta like pop art to be in,
So smart to be in.
To be or not to be,
To be you've gotta be
Way out to be in.

NUTS TO YOU

Intended for Ethel Merman (Mrs. Sally Adams) and Paul Lukas (Cosmo Constantine). Not used. No music is known to survive.

SALLY: I'll teach you to speak American;
Not English—American.
When you're with some diplomat,
If he is very obstinate,
Instead of arguing
You simply say, "In your hat."
If he keeps interfering,
Just ask him to sup,
And while he pays the check you say,
"Stop lousing me up."

---

*Earlier version (June 23, 1971) of lines 8–10:
Water is out,
But a dash of vermouth and gin
Is in.

And then if he still is obstinate,
And he tries to frighten you
To do what you don't want to do,
Just fold your arms and listen to his point
    of view
And just say, "Nuts to you."
COSMO: Nots to you?
SALLY: Not nots to you
But nuts to you.

I SPEAK AMERICAN

Intended for Ethel Merman (Mrs. Sally Adams). Not used. No music is known to survive.

I speak American;
Not English—American.
When someone asks for something I won't do,
I don't make conversation,
A lengthy explanation;
I listen politely till they're through
And just say, "Nuts to you."
I speak American;
Not English—American.
When some bride and groom have started on their
    way,
If someone sees them heaving,
He whispers, "They're conceiving";
But speaking American, I'd say,
"They're in the hay."

LICHTENBURG CHEESE

Intended for Ethel Merman (Mrs. Sally Adams). Not used. No music is known to survive.

Lichtenburg cheese,
Lichtenburg cheese,

Crowned as renowned as
The cheese that'll please.
I'd awaken, I know,
From a coma
To smell the aroma
Of Lichtenburg cheese,
Lichtenburg cheese.

THE WILD MEN OF LICHTENBURG

Not used. No music is known to survive.

CHORUS

The wild men of Lichtenburg,
I wonder what makes them wild.
It can't be the milk they drink from the goats,
For they give that to a child;
The cheese that they eat would make them smell,
But it wouldn't make them wild.
The wild men of Lichtenburg,
I wonder what makes them stare
And gives them the hungry look in their eyes.
It is not the mountain air;
Where the men are wild, the women are wild,
Even when their nails are filed—
Maybe that's what makes them wild.

BLINTZES FROM LINDY'S

Not used. No music is known to survive. The last line might have included the words "Lichtenburg cheese."

Blintzes from Lindy's,
Roast beef from Moore's,
Sturgeon from Barney Greengrass,
Steaks from Toots Shor's,

Chicken and mushrooms from La Rue's,
Chow mein and rice from Ruby Foo's,
Hot dogs from Reuben's,
Ice cream from Sherry's,
And a fruit cake from Dean's;
Champagne, can't wait to pull the cork
With the compliments of Billingsley from the
    Stork—
And now to top the feast,
The last but not the least

[Lyric breaks off.]

WHAT THIS COUNTRY NEEDS

Not used. No music is known to survive.

What this country needs
Is less singing congressmen,
Less dancing senators,
Less parties.
We've a two-party system,
And just one more party
Is the last thing, the last sing
That this country needs.
Attacks upon our President are false,
But we're getting awf'lly tired of the Missoori
    Waltz.
More men in cutaways and less men in tweeds,
That's what this country needs.

*Bing Crosby and Danny Kaye, Vera-Ellen and
Rosemary Clooney, "Sisters"*

WHITE
CHRISTMAS
1954

WHITE CHRISTMAS (1954)

A film produced by Robert Emmett Dolan for Paramount. Released in August 1954. Music and lyrics by Irving Berlin. Screenplay by Norman Krasna, Norman Panama, and Melvin Frank, drawn in part from *Stars on My Shoulders*, Berlin's unproduced 1948 musical with Norman Krasna. Directed by Michael Curtiz. Choreography by Robert Alton and Bob Fosse (uncredited). Orchestrations by Van Cleave. Music conducted by Joseph J. Lilley. Cast: starring Bing Crosby (Bob Wallace), Danny Kaye (Phil Davis), Rosemary Clooney (Betty Haynes), and Vera-Ellen (Judy Haynes) and featuring Dean Jagger (General Waverly), Mary Wickes (Emma Allen), and George Chakiris (Vera-Ellen's unnamed dance partner in club). The score included a number of earlier Berlin songs. There was no official cast album. Bing Crosby and Danny Kaye were joined by Peggy Lee and Trudy Stevens in an album for Decca, while Rosemary Clooney and her sister Betty recorded for Columbia.

THE OLD MAN

Published August 20, 1954. Previously registered for copyright as an unpublished song February 25, 1948, and December 10, 1952. Originally intended for the unproduced musical *Stars on My Shoulders* (1948). Earlier title: "(We'll Follow) the Old Man." Introduced in *White Christmas* by the ensemble headed by Bing Crosby (Bob Wallace) and Danny Kaye (Phil Davis) and reprised by them late in the film.

CHORUS

We'll follow the Old Man
Wherever he wants to go,
Long as he wants to go
Opposite to the foe.
We'll stay with the Old Man
Wherever he wants to stay,
Long as he stays away,
From the battle's fray.
Because we love him,
We love him,
Especially when he keeps us on the ball,
And we'll tell the kiddies we answered duty's call
With the grandest son-of-a-soldier of them all.

Earlier version

VERSE

Sharp as a razor,
Cool as a clam,
Seeing the job was done;
Warm as the summer,
Meek as a lamb,
After the fight was won.
He gave us the book of rules
That was on the shelf,
But never a job that he
Hadn't done himself.

CHORUS

The old man,
The old man,
The toughest son-of-a-soldier of them all.
The old man,
The old man,
He woke us even before the bugle call.
The hard way,
The hard way,
We hated him when he kept us on the ball;
But we're here
Because we had the old man,
The grandest son-of-a-general of them all.

SISTERS

Published. Copyrighted September 14, 1954. Previously registered for copyright as an unpublished song August 3, 1953. According to a letter from Berlin to Don Hartman, this song was finished July 24, 1953. Introduced by Rosemary Clooney (Betty Haynes) and Vera-Ellen, singing voice dubbed by Trudy Stabile (Judy Haynes). Reprised by Bing Crosby (Bob Wallace) and Danny Kaye (Phil Davis), who lip-synched to a recording by Clooney and Stabile. Also reprised by Clooney and Stabile, dubbing for Vera-Ellen.

Female version

Sisters, sisters—
There were never such devoted sisters.
Never had to have a chaperone, no sir,
I'm there to keep my eye on her.
Caring, sharing
Ev'ry little thing that we are wearing.
When a certain gentleman arrived from Rome,
She wore the dress and I stayed home.
All kinds of weather, we stick together,
The same in the rain or sun.
Two diff'rent faces, but in tight places
We think and we act as one.
Those who've seen us
Know that not a thing could come between us;
Many men have tried to split us up, but no one can.
Lord help the mister who comes between me and my sister—
And Lord help the sister who comes between me and my man.

Male version

Brothers, brothers,
There were never such devoted brothers.
When there comes a glamour girl who's nice and trim,
He watches me and I watch him.
Caring, sharing
Ev'ry little thing that we are wearing.
When a certain signorina came from Rome,
He wore the blue serge; I stayed home.
All kinds of weather, we stick together,
The same in the rain and sun.
Two diff'rent faces, but in tight places
We think and we act as one.
Those who've seen us
Know that not a thing could come between us;
Many girls have tried to split us up, but no one shall.
Lord help another who comes between me and my brother—
And Lord help the brother who comes between me and my gal.

THE BEST THINGS HAPPEN WHILE YOU'RE DANCING

Published. Copyrighted August 20, 1954. Previously registered for copyright as an unpublished song July 13, 1953. Typed lyric sheet dated July 9, 1953. Introduced by Danny Kaye (Phil Davis) and ensemble; danced by Kaye and Vera-Ellen (Judy Haynes).

The best things happen while you're dancing;
Things that you would not do at home
Come natur'lly on the floor.

For dancing soon becomes romancing,
When you hold a girl in your arms
That you've never held before.
Even guys with two left feet
Come out all right if the girl is sweet,
If by chance their cheeks should meet while
 dancing,
Proving that the best things happen while you
 dance.

SNOW

Published September 14, 1954. Previously registered for copyright as an unpublished song August 14, 1953. The music for "Snow" is a revision of the music for "Free" from *Call Me Madam*; see page 435. Introduced by Bing Crosby (Bob Wallace), Danny Kaye (Phil Davis), Rosemary Clooney (Betty Haynes), and Vera-Ellen, singing voice dubbed by Trudy Stabile (Judy Haynes).

CHORUS

Snow—
It won't be long before we'll all be there with
 snow.
Snow—
I want to wash my hands, my face and hair with
 snow.
Snow—
I long to clear a path and lift a spade of snow.
Oh,
To see a great big man entirely made of snow!
Where it's snowing all winter through,
That's where I want to be.
Snowball throwing,
That's what I'll do.
How I'm longing to ski!
Snow—
Those glist'ning houses that seem to be built of
 snow.
Oh,
To see a mountain covered with a quilt of snow!
What is Christmas with no snow?
No white Christmas with no snow—snow!

TAG

I'll soon be there with snow,
To wash my hair with snow,
And with a spade of snow,
A man that's made of snow,

A house that's built of snow,
Beneath a quilt of snow.
I'd love to stay up with you, but I
Recommend a little shut-eye.
Go to sleep
And dream
Of snow.

I'D RATHER SEE A MINSTREL SHOW and MANDY

Revised versions of numbers from the *Ziegfeld Follies of 1919*. prepared for *White Christmas* (1954). Introduced by Bing Crosby (Bob Wallace), Danny Kaye (Phil Davis), Rosemary Clooney (Betty Haynes), Vera-Ellen (Judy Haynes), and ensemble. George Chakiris is the dancer who partners Vera-Ellen. The only new material, given below, was the lyric for the "Mandy" vocal arrangement.

There's a knot to be tied
Around the groom and bride,
A minister needing a job.
He's got his rent to pay,
So don't delay—
It's not a day
To linger.
Here is a string
You can use for a ring;
We advise
To "love and honor and obey"
Before he gets away—
Make it Mandy and me.

COUNT YOUR BLESSINGS INSTEAD OF SHEEP

Published August 20, 1954. Previously registered for copyright as an unpublished song September 17, 1952. Typed lyric sheet dated September 2, 1952. Inspired by Berlin's insomnia. Introduced by Bing Crosby (Bob Wallace); reprised by Rosemary Clooney (Betty Haynes).

When I'm worried and I can't sleep,
I count my blessings instead of sheep,
And I fall asleep counting my blessings.

When my bankroll is getting small,
I think of when I had none at all*
And I fall asleep counting my blessings.
I think about a nurs'ry,
And I picture curly heads,
And one by one I count them
As they slumber in their beds.†
If you're worried and you can't sleep,
Just count your blessings instead of sheep,
And you'll fall asleep counting your blessings.

Earlier version (September 2, 1952), not in published sheet music

VERSE

Couldn't sleep,
I was worried,
Wrapped in problems deep.
Took a pill,
Then another;
Still I couldn't sleep.
Called a doctor to my bed,
Asked him what to do.
Smilingly the doctor said,
"Did you ever try counting your blessings?"

CHOREOGRAPHY

Published September 14, 1954. Previously registered for copyright as an unpublished song August 3, 1953. Typed lyric sheet dated July 9, 1953. Introduced by Danny

Earlier version of line 5:
 I think of those who have less than I

†*Earlier versions (September 2, 1952, and July 17, 1953) of lines 7–10:*
 I think of someone who can't see,
 Whose eyes forever close,
 Then count the sunsets I have seen
 And I begin to doze.

 I think of those less lucky than I,
 Who may be feeling low,
 Then thank the stars way up in the sky
 And off to sleep I go.

In Clooney's reprise, lines 7–10 are sung:
 For bachelor boys who toss their heads
 When lights are burning low,
 Gold wedding rings and double beds
 And off to sleep they go.

Kaye (Phil Davis) and ensemble. Danced by Vera-Ellen (Judy Haynes) and George Chakiris and ensemble.

VERSE

The the'ter, the the'ter,
What's happened to the the'ter,
Especially where dancing is concerned?

CHORUS 1

Chaps
Who did taps
Aren't tapping anymore;
They're doing choreography.
Chicks
Who did kicks
Aren't kicking anymore;
They're doing choreography.
Queens
With routines
That would stop the show
In days that used to be,*
One and all
They're not chancing
What we used to call dancing—
Instead of dance
It's choreography.†

CHORUS 2

Jakes
Who did breaks
Aren't breaking anymore;
They're doing choreography.
Who
Did soft shoe
Doesn't do it anymore;
He's doing choreography.
Heps
Who did steps
That would stop the show
In days that used to be,
Through the air
They keep flying
Like a duck that is dying—
Instead of dance
It's choreography.

*Earlier version of lines 11 and 12:
    That would start the thunder
    In the gallery,

†Earlier version of lines 16 and 17:
    They're busy doing
    Choreography.

EXTRA CATCH LINES

One and all
Keep us guessing
What the ——— they're expressing—
Instead of dance
It's choreography.

LOVE, YOU DIDN'T DO RIGHT BY ME

Published August 20, 1954. Previously registered for copyright as an unpublished song June 26, 1953. Introduced by Rosemary Clooney (Betty Haynes).

Love, you didn't do right by me—
You planned a romance
That just hadn't a chance,
And I'm through.
Love, you didn't do right by me—
I'm back on the shelf
And I'm blaming myself,
But it's you.
My one love affair
Didn't get anywhere from the start.
To send me a Joe*
Who had winter and snow in his heart
Wasn't smart.
Love, you didn't do right by me—
As they say in the song,
You done me wrong!

Earlier version

Love, you didn't do right by me—
You gave my romance
Such a kick in the pants,
And I'm through.
Love, you didn't do right by me—
I'm back on the shelf
And I'm blaming myself,
But it's you.
That feeling inside
Wasn't easy to hide from the start;
To make me reveal
What I tried to conceal
In my heart

*The version for male singers substitutes these two lines:
    To send me a Jane
    Who had thunder and rain in her heart

Wasn't smart.
Love, you didn't do right by me—
As they say in the song,
You done me wrong.

WHAT CAN YOU DO WITH A GENERAL?

Published. Copyrighted April 21, 1949. Previously registered for copyright as an unpublished song February 25, 1948. Introduced by Bing Crosby (Bob Wallace) and ensemble. Written for the unproduced musical *Stars on My Shoulders* (1948).

VERSE

When the war was over,
There were jobs galore
For the GI Josephs
Who were in the war.
But for gen'rals, things were not so grand,
And it's not so hard to understand.

CHORUS 1

What can you do with a general
When he stops being a general?
Oh, what can you do with a general who retires?
Who's got a job for a general
When he stops being a general?
They all get a job,
But a general no one hires.
He walks into an office
In answer to an ad;
He'll take the job that's offered—
The pay is not too bad.
They ask his last position;
He answers with a punch,
"I was a general"—
And they ask him out to lunch,
And he has to meet the mob,
But he doesn't get the job.
Nobody thinks of assigning him
When they've stopped wining and dining him.
It seems this country never has enjoyed
So many one- and two- and three-
And four-star generals unemployed.*

*Extra lines deleted from middle section:
    For captains and for majors
    Demand is very large
    As ushers at the Roxy,
    With a colonel, no less, in charge.

CHORUS 2

What can you do with a general
When he stops being a general?
Oh, what can you do with a general who retires?
Who's got a job for a general
When he stops being a general?
They all get a job,
But a general no one hires.
They fill his chest with medals
While he's across the foam
And spread the crimson carpet
When he comes marching home;
The next day someone hollers
When he comes into view,
"Here comes the general!"
And they all say, "Gen'ral who?"
They're delighted that he came,
But they can't recall his name.
Somehow he's not understood enough;
They think no job could be good enough.
That's why this country never has enjoyed
So many one- and two- and three-
And four-star generals unemployed.

Earlier version of chorus 2

What can you do with a general
When he stops being a general?
Oh, what can you do with a general when he's
    through?
Captains and majors are doing good,
They've got jobs working in Hollywood,
And colonels are there, but a general just won't
    do.
He calls upon the Warners;
They're shooting battle scenes.
He'll even be an extra;
He says how much it means.
They ask his last employment;
He answers kinda cute,
"I was a general"—
And the Warners all salute,
And he has to meet the mob,
But he doesn't get the job.
Somehow he's not understood enough;
They think no job could be good enough.
That's why this country never has enjoyed
So many one- and two- and three-
And four-star generals unemployed.

GEE, I WISH I WAS BACK IN THE ARMY

Published. Copyrighted September 14, 1954. Previously registered for copyright as an unpublished song March 26, 1954. Introduced by Bing Crosby (Bob Wallace), Danny Kaye (Phil Davis), Rosemary Clooney (Betty Haynes), Vera-Ellen, singing voice dubbed by Trudy Stabile (Judy Haynes), and ensemble. Sung in public for the first time by Berlin at the White House Correspondents Dinner for President Eisenhower at the Statler Hotel, Washington, D.C., March 6, 1954. This was the same occasion on which Berlin premiered his 1954 song "I Still Like Ike."

VERSE

BOY: When I was mustered out,
    I thought without a doubt
    That I was through with all my care and
        strife.
    I thought that I was then
    The happiest of men,
    But after months of tough civilian life:

CHORUS 1

Gee, I wish I was back in the army!
The army wasn't really bad at all.
Three meals a day,
For which you didn't pay;
Uniforms for winter, spring, and fall.
There's a lot to be said for the army,
The life without responsibility.
A soldier out of luck
Was really never stuck;
There's always someone higher up
Where you can pass the buck.
Oh, gee, I wish I was back in the army!

CHORUS 2

Gee, I wish I was back in the army!
The shows we got civilians couldn't see.
How we would yell
For Dietrich and Cornell,
Crosby, Hope, and Jolson, all for free.*
There's a lot to be said for the army;
The best of doctors watched you carefully.
A dentist and a clerk,
For weeks and weeks they'd work;
They'd make a thousand-dollar job

*In the film this line was changed to:
    Jolson, Hope, and Benny, all for free.

And give it to a jerk.
Oh, gee, I wish I was back in the army!

CHORUS 3

GIRL: Gee, I wish I was back in the army!
    The army was the place to find romance.
    Soldiers and Wacs,
    The Wacs who dressed in slacks,
    Dancing cheek to cheek and pants to pants.
    There's a lot to be said for the army;
    A gal was never lost for company.
    A million handsome guys
    With longing in their eyes,
    And all you had to do was pick
    The age, the weight and size.
    Oh, gee, I wish I was back in the army!

Additional chorus (not used in the picture, prepared by Berlin for the 1954 Eisenhower dinner)

Gee, I wish I was back in the army!
In spite of all the Joe McCarthy noise,
I'll help him shout
To kick the commies out,
Including all the Fifth Amendment boys.
But when Joe gets to smearing the army,
I think of nineteen forty-two and -three—
If on that vital date
He cried "Investigate!,"
The Normandy invasion and the army came too
    late.
Oh, gee, I wish I was back in the Army!

[*When Berlin actually sang the song, he changed the lyric slightly to read:*]

Gee, I wish I was back in the Army!
In spite of the investigating noise,
I'll help them shout
To kick the commies out,
Including all the Fifth Amendment boys.
But when senators browbeat the army,
I think of nineteen forty-two and -three—
If on that vital date
They cried "Investigate!,"
The Normandy invasion and the army came too
    late.
Oh, gee, how grateful we are to the Army!

A SINGER—A DANCER

Registered for copyright as an unpublished song August 18, 1953. Typed lyric sheet dated August 13, 1953. Adapted from "Monohan and Callahan" from *Stars on My Shoulder* (1948). Written for Bing Crosby and Donald O'Connor. Dropped from the film when O'Connor withdrew and replaced when Danny Kaye joined the cast by "A Crooner—a Comic."

VERSE

CROSBY: I'm a singer.
O'CONNOR: I'm a dancer.
CROSBY: I applaud his steps.
O'CONNOR: And I adore his notes.
CROSBY: We are friendly—
O'CONNOR: While we're working.
CROSBY: When it's over, we could cut each
    other's throats.

CHORUS

CROSBY: When you lift up a rock, what comes
    out from under?
O'CONNOR: A singer.
CROSBY: A dancer.
O'CONNOR: A singer.
CROSBY: When a bank has been robbed, who is
    found with the plunder?
O'CONNOR: A singer.
CROSBY: A dancer.
O'CONNOR: A singer.
CROSBY: Here is a picture that I simply do
    adore.
O'CONNOR: Two men are fighting as they never
    fought before.
CROSBY: One man is standing while the other is
    on the floor.
O'CONNOR: Who's on the floor?
CROSBY: A dancer.
O'CONNOR: A singer.
CROSBY: A dancer.
O'CONNOR: A singer.
O'CONNOR: A singer, not a dancer's, on the floor.
CROSBY: A dancer, not a singer's, on the floor.

A CROONER—A COMIC

Registered for copyright as an unpublished song September 3, 1953. Intended for Bing Crosby (Bob Wallace) and Danny Kaye (Phil Davis). Not used. It replaced "A Singer—a Dancer," when Donald O'Connor left the cast of the film because of illness. On August 19, 1953, Berlin sent a letter to Helmy Kresa, the head of his music department, in which he discussed the cast change as follows:

> By the way, by now you've read the great news that due to Donald O'Connor's illness, we have been able to get Danny Kaye in the picture. This is really a big set-up now. Kaye is very excited about the score, and, luckily, the "A Singer—a Dancer" number now will be "A Crooner—a Comic," which makes the song much funnier. Crosby will be dressed straight and Kaye will be the red-nosed, baggy-pants, burlesque comedian. For the finish, after Crosby sings an 8-bar phrase of one of the ballads, Kaye will do some comedy gag which, of course, leaves it wide open for laughs.

VERSE

CROSBY: I'm a crooner.
KAYE: I'm a comic.
CROSBY: I applaud his jokes.
KAYE: And I adore his notes.
CROSBY: We are friendly—
KAYE: While we're working.
CROSBY: When it's over, we could cut each other's
    throats

CHORUS

CROSBY: When you lift up a rock what comes out
    from under?
KAYE: A crooner.
CROSBY: A comic.
KAYE: A crooner.
    When a bank has been robbed, who is
    found with the plunder?
CROSBY: A comic.
KAYE: A crooner.
CROSBY: A comic.
KAYE: Here is a picture that I simply do adore.
CROSBY: Two men are fighting as they never
    fought before.
KAYE: One man is standing while the other is on
    the floor.
CROSBY: Who's on the floor?
KAYE: A crooner.
CROSBY: A comic.

KAYE: A crooner.
CROSBY: A comic.
KAYE: A crooner, not a comic's, on the floor.
CROSBY: A comic, not a crooner's, on the floor.
    When a wisecrack is made, who's the
    wise guy who said it?
KAYE: A cr—comic.
CROSBY: A crooner.
KAYE: A comic.
    If the crack gathers fame, who's the one
    takes the credit?
CROSBY: A cr—comic.
KAYE: A crooner.
CROSBY: A comic.
KAYE: Picture a maiden with a lovely golden curl.
CROSBY: Two men start chasing, for she set their
    hearts awhirl.
KAYE: One man stays single while the other gets
    the girl.
CROSBY: Who gets the girl?
KAYE: The comic.
CROSBY: The crooner.
KAYE: The comic.
CROSBY: The crooner.
KAYE: The comic, not the crooner, gets the girl.
CROSBY: The crooner, not the comic, gets the—

[GIRL *enters.*]

CROSBY: How much do I love you? I'll tell you no
    lie—
    How deep is the ocean, how high is the
    sky?

[KAYE *tells a joke or does a funny bit of business—to be underscored.* GIRL *reacts.*]

CROSBY: I'll be loving you always,
    With a love that's true always.

[KAYE *again tells a joke or does a funny bit of business, to be underscored.* KAYE *and* CROSBY *get nowhere. A little fat* MUSICIAN *with a trombone to his lips comes on tooting "Blue Skies."* GIRL *leaves* CROSBY *and* KAYE *flat, walks off with the* MUSICIAN.]

CROSBY: The crooner nor the comic gets the girl—
    it always happens.
KAYE: The crooner nor the comic gets the girl.

SANTA CLAUS NUMBER

Written in early September 1953. Intended for Bing Crosby and Danny Kaye. Not sung in film.

[CROSBY *and* KAYE *dressed as Santa Clauses.*]

VERSE

CROSBY: Santa Claus is here to pay a call.
KAYE: With a precious gift for one and all.

CHORUS

CROSBY: Here's a shiny new mess kit [*old rusty
mess kit*].
KAYE: And here's a pair of shoes that fit [*size 16
GI brown shoes*].
CROSBY: Here's a set of stripes
For the sergeant types [*chevrons*].
KAYE: Here's some wool for guys who knit
[*throws ball of pink wool out*].
CROSBY: A pair of earmuffs when the bugle
sounds [*earmuffs*].
KAYE: A pass to wander out of bounds [*pass*].
CROSBY: Here's the latest fashions
In governmental rations [*small cans of
K rations, which GIs hate*].
KAYE: Here's a pretty hankie
Especially for a Yankee [*embroidered
lady's handkerchief*].
CROSBY: Here's a brand-new uniform [*tired,
wrinkled old private's coat on hanger*].
KAYE: And here is something to keep you warm
[*hot-water bag made of automobile tire*].
CROSBY: And for a general, here's an extra star
[*general's star*].
KAYE: For romance, here's a chocolate bar
[*Hershey chocolate bar*].
CROSBY: Here's a pretty pinup
To help you keep your chin up [*a
composite picture of Monroe and Russell
with exaggerated bosoms—this prop will
of course go as far as censorship will
allow*].
KAYE: Here's a suit of flannels
We got through army channels [*red
woolen long-legged drawers, regulation
government issue*].
BOTH: Now that we have paid our call,
A Merry Christmas to one and all.

WHAT DOES A SOLDIER WANT FOR CHRISTMAS?

Registered for copyright as an unpublished song
July 20, 1953. Not used. Music later used for "How Does
a Pilot Spend His Furlough?" page 461.

What does a soldier want for Christmas?
Tell me what Santa Claus can bring.
Does he want a new mess kit for Christmas,
Or a bugle on a purple string?
Would he enjoy a knitted sweater
Made with the colors of the flag?
If there's anything he wants for Christmas,
There's a Santa Claus who's holding the bag.

He wants his breakfast served in bed,
A bed with clean sheets and a spread,
Then go right back and pound his head.
He wants a bathtub to himself
And meat mixed in his chow,
Not from a can but from a cow.
He wants to march without his gun,
But not until his job is done;
And then he wants to have some fun
And hear the neighbors call him "mister"—
And for his morale,
A soldier wants to see his gal.

[*The second section ("He wants his breakfast") is first
sung separately, then as a countermelody to the "What
does a soldier . . ." section.*]

SITTIN' IN THE SUN (COUNTIN' MY MONEY)

Published. Copyrighted July 20, 1953. Previously regis-
tered for copyright as an unpublished song March 4,
1953, and June 26, 1953. On August 27, 1952, Berlin
wrote to his friend Irving Hoffman that "I just wrote my
first song for the picture *White Christmas*. This will be
sung by Bing Crosby and the title is "Sittin' in the Sun
Counting My Money." Earliest typed lyric dated Decem-
ber 4, 1952, intended for *Palm Beach*. Leading record-
ing by Louis Armstrong, accompanied by Jack Pleis'
Orchestra (Decca). Not used in *White Christmas*.

Published version

Sittin in the sun,
Countin' my money,
Fanned by a summer breeze.
Sweeter than honey
Is countin' my money,
Those greenbacks on the trees.

Comes a summer show'r,
Drops o' rain fallin'—

Sweeter than Christmas chimes,
Hearing those jingles
Upon the roof shingles,
Like pennies, nickels, and dimes.

Though it's known
That all I own
Is not a large amount,
Fields of gold
That I behold
Are in my bank account.

Sittin' in the sun,
Countin' my money,
Happy as I can be.
And to top it all,
When shadows fall,
I look to heaven and I see
There's a silver dollar in the sky
Shining down on me.

Earlier version

Sittin' in the sun,
Counting my money,
Over a hundred times.
Sweeter than honey
Is counting my money,
Pennies, nickels, and dimes.

Sittin' in the sun,
Hearing that jingle,
Sweeter than Christmas chimes.
Spirits keep mounting
While sittin' there counting
Pennies, nickels, and dimes.

There's no gold
Nor bills that fold
Among my modest pile,
And it's strange
With just small change
How broadly I can smile.

Sittin' in the sun,
Counting my money,
Happy as I can be,
Till the shadows fall,
And best of all,
A precious piece of currency
Is the silver dollar in the sky
Shining down at me.

THERE'S NO BUSINESS LIKE
SHOW BUSINESS | 1954

THERE'S NO BUSINESS LIKE SHOW BUSINESS (1954)

A film produced by Sol C. Siegel for 20th Century–Fox. Released in December 1954. Music and lyrics by Irving Berlin. Screenplay by Henry and Phoebe Ephron, based on a story by Lamar Trotti. Directed by Walter Lang. Choreography by Robert Alton and Jack Cole. Music conducted by Alfred Newman. Cast, starring Ethel Merman (Molly Donahue), Donald O'Connor (Tim Donahue), Marilyn Monroe (Vicky), Dan Dailey (Terence Donahue), Johnnie Ray (Steve Donahue), and Mitzi Gaynor (Katy Donahue) and featuring Hugh O'Brian (Charles Biggs), Frank McHugh (Eddie Duggan), Lee Patrick (Marge), Chick Chandler (Harry), Lyle Talbot (Stage Manager), and George Chakiris (dancer). Original cast album (Decca) included Dolores Gray replacing Marilyn Monroe.

The film also included many earlier Berlin songs: for "If You Believe," see page 269.

A MAN CHASES A GIRL (UNTIL SHE CATCHES HIM)

Published April 1, 1949. Previously registered for copyright as an unpublished song May 8, 1948. Written for the unproduced musical *Stars on My Shoulders* (1948). Also considered for *Call Me Madam* (1950). Introduced in *There's No Business Like Show Business* by Donald O'Connor (Tim Donahue), singing to Marilyn Monroe (Vicky).

VERSE

I don't know where I heard it
Or when it first was said,
But here's a famous saying
That hits the nail on the head.

CHORUS 1

A man chases a girl
Until she catches him;

Marilyn Monroe, "After You Get What You Want (You Don't Want It)"

He runs after a girl
Until he's caught.
He fishes for a girl
Until she's landed him—
It all comes out exactly
The way she thought.
Uncertain,
He tags along behind;
Uncertain—
Till she makes up his mind.
A man chases a girl
Until she catches him—
But don't run too fast
While you are saying no,
And once you've caught him,
Don't ever let him go.

CHORUS 2

A man chases a girl
Until she's out of breath;
He runs after a girl
Who can't be caught.
He fishes for a girl
And scares her half to death—
His one-track mind
Is filled with a single thought.
He wants her
For better or for worse;
The bridesmaids
Are waiting to rehearse.
A man chases a girl,
But she's not catching him,
For he works fast
While she may be working slow;
But once she's caught him,
She'll never let him go.

A SAILOR'S NOT A SAILOR (TILL A SAILOR'S BEEN TATTOOED)

Published. Copyrighted December 13, 1954. Previously registered for copyright as an unpublished song July 30, 1954. Introduced by Ethel Merman (Molly Donahue) and Mitzi Gaynor (Katy Donahue).

MOLLY: I'm an old salt.
KATY: I'm a young salt.
BOTH: In the navy we've been working very hard.
MOLLY: I was part of the flotilla
With Dewey in Manila.

KATY: I'm a new recruit at the Brooklyn Navy Yard.
BOTH: Tonight we're on a spree
And feeling flow'ry—
We've got a date with gals and drink and food.
KATY: Across the Brooklyn Bridge and to the Bow'ry.
MOLLY: And I'm gonna get the kid tattooed.
KATY: Tattooed?
MOLLY: Tattooed!
BOTH: A sailor's not a sailor
Till a sailor's been tattooed.
MOLLY: Here's an anchor from a tanker
That I sailed upon when first I went to sea.
Here's another of my mother,
Takes me back to when I sat upon her knee.
Here's a crimson heart with a Cupid's dart;
Here's a battle cruiser—and when I sit down,
On that, too, there's a tattoo of my hometown.
KATY: To the Bow'ry!
MOLLY: To the Bow'ry!
KATY: 'Cross the Brooklyn Bridge, and I'm just in the mood.
MOLLY: He'll be filled with diff'rent mixtures
And covered up with pictures.
KATY: I can't wait to be—
'Twill be great to be tattooed.
MOLLY: Tattooed?
KATY: Tattooed!
BOTH: A sailor's not a sailor
Till a sailor's been tattooed.

BUT I AIN'T GOT A MAN

Registered for copyright as an unpublished song June 25, 1954. Typed lyric sheet dated June 21, 1954. Written for Marilyn Monroe (Vicky). Not used in film.

CHORUS

I got the sun, the moon, the stars, the sky,
And things of a personal nature have I;
But I ain't got a man,
I ain't got a man.

They say I'm blessed with what it takes for guys,
And there is a definite gleam in my eyes—

What's the good of a gleam in your eyes
When you ain't got a man?

Love—
I'm a sitting duck, a wounded quail
Or grouse.
But—
What's the good of love without a man
Around the house?

I got the ground, the dough to build a hut;
I've talked to the architect who'll do the job, but
What's the good of a house
That is built
On a blueprint or plan
When you ain't got a man,
When you ain't got a man?

THE GAL ON THE CALENDAR

Typed lyric dated March 13, 1954. Written for Marilyn Monroe (Vicky). Not used in film.

CHORUS

I'd love to meet the gal,
The gal on the calendar.
I'd love to rendezvous
And spend an hour or two
With her.
I know that it would make you laugh
If you knew how many times
I've seen her photograph.
Of all the sweet things, I prefer
The gal on the calendar.

I CAN MAKE YOU LAUGH (BUT I WISH I COULD MAKE YOU CRY)

Published February 23, 1955. Previously registered for copyright as an unpublished song March 15, 1954. Not used in film. The lyric for the chorus is dated March 3, 1954; the lyric for the verse is dated February 15, 1955.
    Berlin wrote about this song to Louella Parsons on February 13, 1954:

I always, when I have a deadline to meet on a song, go away by myself, which I did a week ago, and I think I came up with a pretty good song and I'll give you the title and a few of the lyrics. The title is "I Can't Reach Your Heart."

I can make you laugh
But I wish I could make you cry
I can wrinkle your nose
But I wish I could dampen your eye
I can reach your funny bone
But I can't reach your heart.

VERSE

A clown in the circus,
A girl on the flying trapeze:
The clown loves her madly;
The girl simply laughs at his pleas.

CHORUS

I can make you laugh,
But I wish I could make you cry.
I can wrinkle your nose,
But I wish I could dampen your eye.
You watch me and keep smiling,
Times when we're alone;
Seems that I can't reach your heart,
But I can always reach your funny bone.

I always leave you laughing
When we say goodbye;
I can make you laugh,
But I wish I could make you cry.

WHEN IT'S PEACH BLOSSOM TIME IN LICHTENBURG

Registered for copyright as an unpublished song March 15, 1954. Typed lyric sheet dated March 13, 1954. Not used in film. This number was not originally intended for *Call Me Madam* (1950).

CHORUS

When it's peach blossom time in Lichtenburg,
In Lichtenburg
By the sea,
I will reach for a peach
As we sit on the beach,
Singing love's sweet melody.
The theme song of our operetta
Will be Romberg as Romberg can be,
And we'll make up a rhyme
To three-quarter time
With Viennese harmony
When it's peach blossom time in Lichtenburg,
Dear old Lichtenburg
By the sea.

SENTIMENTAL GUY | 1955–1956

and Other Songs of the 1950s

SENTIMENTAL GUY (1955-1956)

On November 29, 1955, there was an article in the New York *Times* that said Irving Berlin and George S. Kaufman might join S. N. Behrman to write a musical based on *The Legendary Mizners* (1953) by Alva Johnston. Behrman had acquired the rights to the book about Addison (1872–1933) and Wilson (1876–1933) Mizner. After a month Kaufman withdrew from the project, but Behrman and Berlin pressed on. Berlin finished most of the songs for the first act by the spring of 1956, and Jose Ferrer and Mary Martin were among those considered for leading roles. The show also was titled *Wise Guy* and *The Mizner Story*. Behrman worked on the second act through the fall, but the project remained unfinished. In the mid-1960s Berlin briefly considered making a movie about the Mizners and suggested casting Robert Preston as Wilson, Robert Morley as Addison, and Edie Adams as Grace Washburn, Wilson's girl. It never came to pass. The large number of songs that Berlin wrote for his collaboration with Behrman follow.

THREE MORE MINUTES TO MIDNIGHT (OPENING)

Typed lyric sheet dated January 5, 1956. Alternate title: "Opening the Mizner Story."

MRS. YERKES: Three more minutes to midnight,
Three more minutes and then
With a wistful eye
We will say goodbye
To the old year nineteen ten,
And our thanks we'll give
That we don't have to live
Through nineteen ten again.
CHORUS: The pound and the franc are immense,
But the dollar is only worth ninty-eight cents.
MRS. YERKES: Soon we will ring out the old year
With everyone's consent.
With our coupons clipped
We have all been gypped
And a good deal less was spent,
And you can't relax
When they speak of a tax
As high as one percent.

CHORUS: And the same old Tammany graft,
With the only bright spot—
President Taft.

TWO MORE MINUTES TO MIDNIGHT (OPENING CHORUS)

Registered for copyright as an unpublished song under the title "Opening the Mizner Story," May 10, 1956. Typed lyric sheet dated January 5, 1956.

[*Fifth Avenue house of* HOSTESS. *New Year's Eve 1910. Clock in center shows two minutes to midnight.* HOSTESS *and guests grouped around her, hiding two card players all through this opening chorus.*]

HOSTESS: Two more minutes to midnight,
Two more minutes and then
With a happy sigh
We will say goodbye
To the old year nineteen ten,
And our thanks we'll give
That we don't have to live
Through nineteen ten again.
CHORUS: The pound and the franc are immense,
But the dollar is just worth ninety-eight cents.
HOSTESS: Up goes the price of living—
Thirty cents for a steak.
And the servants say,
"We must have more pay,"
And a day off they must take;
And we can't afford
When we pay for their board
To answer "Let 'em eat cake."
CHORUS: Three bucks for a meal at the Ritz,
And on top of that there's the tip of two bits.
HOSTESS: Soon we'll ring out the old year
With the people's consent.
With our coupons clipped
We have all been gypped
And a good deal less was spent,
For you can't relax
With an income tax
As high as one percent.
CHORUS: What's more, there's the Tammany graft,
And the only bright spot is President Taft.
HOSTESS: [*raising champagne glass high; all follow suit*]

Here's to a happier nineteen eleven,
Twelve months of laughter and cheer.
Raise up your glasses
And point up to heaven
And drink to a Happy New Year.
ALL: Here's to a Happy New Year.

CARD SENSE

Typed lyric sheet dated April 12, 1956. Intended for Wilson Mizner to sing to "Mary's Father."

Card sense—
Card sense—
You never have to cheat
If you've got card sense.
You make the sucker feel
He's simply grand
By letting him take a pot
And show him you had the winning hand.
When you bluff with deuces,
Play them like they're aces
And be prepared to back them with your all,
But with card sense,
Card sense,
You must never try
To bluff a guy
With money enough
Who's foolish enough to call.

DALLAS and I LIKE NEW YORK

Typed lyric sheet dated February 5, 1956. Earliest version of typed lyric sheet dated January 5, 1956. A double song.

Dallas

FATHER: I wouldn't change
My home on the range
In Dallas—Dallas—
For a highfalutin' mansion
Or a palace;
I prefer my ranch house in Dallas.
I wouldn't swap

My last season's crop
And cattle—cattle—
For the swellest folks
From Boston to Seattle.
I prefer my ranch house
And cattle.

I Like New York

MIZNER: I like New York,
I like New York,
Where I can hear
The pop of a champagne cork.
I never stray
Far from Broadway,
I hate to leave Manhattan,
'Cause I like New York.

[*Then "Dallas" and "I Like New York" are sung together in counterpoint.*]

Additional lyrics to "Dallas"

I wouldn't change
My home on the range
In Dallas—Dallas.
I can take a trip through Wonderland
With Alice,
Sittin' in my ranch house in Dallas.
Though we're not cranks,
We'll argue with Yanks
In Dallas—Dallas.
I can fight the Civil War again
With malice,
Sittin' in my ranch house
In Dallas.

Earlier version of "Dallas"

I wouldn't change
My home on the range
In Dallas—Dallas—
For a highfalutin' mansion
Or a palace;
I prefer my ranch house in Dallas.
I'm mighty keen
For pastures of green
And cattle—cattle.
You can keep your swells
From Boston to Seattle
I prefer my ranch house
And cattle.
The steak you buy

To broil or fry—
I nursed it when it was
A dogie so high.
Like the people we freed,
We've learned how to read
In Dallas—Dallas.
I can take a trip through Wonderland
With Alice,
Sittin' in my ranch house
In Dallas.

LOVE LEADS TO MARRIAGE

Registered for copyright as an unpublished song May 10, 1956. Earlier title: "Love Leads to Weddings." Typed lyric sheet for "Love Leads to Weddings" dated March 5, 1956. First recording by Bill Daugherty on the 1995 Varèse Sarabande album *Unsung Irving Berlin*. Became part of *Say It with Music*, page 481.

WILSON: Love leads to marriage;
That leads to divorce;
That leads to lawyers—
Expensive, of course.
Private detectives
Who watch all your moves;
That leads to charges
Which nobody proves.
If there are children,
You hear from the court,
Father can't see them
But pays their support.
Love is the start of it;
I want no part of it.
Love leads to marriage,
Divorce and to lawyers,
Detective and charges,
Supporting of children—
A youngster in school falls
And only a fool falls in love.

YOU'RE A SUCKER FOR A DAME

Registered for copyright as an unpublished song May 10, 1956. Previously registered for copyright as an unpublished song November 29, 1955, under the title "I'm a Sucker for a Dame." Typed lyric sheet for "I'm a Sucker for a Dame" dated November 28, 1955. First recording by "Guy Haines" (Bruce Kimmel) in 1995 as part of Varèse Sarabande's album *Unsung Irving Berlin*.

VERSE

You know the big percentage in roulette,
And that is why you never place a bet.
You've talked to sev'ral horses that have won,
And once or twice you knew who'd win
Before the race was run.
You know what's coming when the cards are cut,
You're on to each and ev'ry racket, but—

CHORUS 1

You're a sucker for a dame;
The pucker of a dame
Will make you jump
Just like a chump.
When you gaze into her eyes,
The springs that make you wise
Refuse to work,
And you're a jerk.
I've seen you playing poker with three aces,
A hand of which you're very, very fond;
You knew that your opponent had three deuces—
But it happened your opponent was a blonde.
So, you just threw your cards away
And thought about the day
When you became
A sucker for a dame.

CHORUS 2

You're a softy for a dame;
You're lofty till a dame
Sets out her traps—
Then you collapse.
You can hold your own with guys,
But when a lady's eyes
Begin to pop,
You blow your top.
You're selling real estate that's underwater,
The deal is set, you're riding on a crest;
The customer comes in to sign the papers
In a sweater and a shelf upon her chest.
So you just tore your papers up
And took her out to sup,
And you became
A sucker for a dame.

THE SNOBS ON THE WRONG SIDE OF THE TRACKS

Registered for copyright as an unpublished song December 23, 1977. Typed lyric sheet dated November 29, 1955. Also see *Palm Beach* version on page 456.

CHORUS 1

ADDISON: The snobs on the wrong side of the
                   tracks,
                They work at it and never relax.
                Their noses have a higher tilt
                Than a Morgan or a Vanderbilt,
                The snobs on the wrong side of the
                   tracks.

                They give parties for some of their
                   friends;
                There's one neighbor who never attends.
                They ask the boss to drink their gin,
                But they think the foreman won't fit in,
                The snobs on the wrong side of the
                   tracks.

                They won't go to Coney Island;
                They sweat in the heat all week.
                It's cooler in Coney Island,
                But they don't think that it's chic.

                Though downtown is where most of
                   them dwell,
                They go strolling uptown where it's
                   swell.
                They pass up the neighborhood store
                Because Fifth Avenue charges more,
                The snobs on the wrong side of the
                   tracks.

CHORUS 2

WILSON: The snobs on the right side of the
                   tracks,
                They build houses where they can relax.
                They start their lives as brides and
                   grooms
                In a cottage with a hundred rooms,
                The snobs on the right side of the
                   tracks.

                Their walls are hung with oils that they
                   enjoy,
                And one, maybe two, are the McCoy.
                They fill their houses with antiques;

There are some as old as seven weeks—
The snobs on the right side of the
   tracks.

They don't ever go to dinner;
They only go out to dine.
There may be a stew for dinner,
But there must be vintage wine.

The clown that they so carefully slight
They greet when the king makes him a
   knight;
They won't see a musical show
Unless they sit in the second row,
The snobs on the right side of the
   tracks.

YOU'RE A SENTIMENTAL GUY

Published. Copyrighted 1995 by the Estate of Irving Berlin in the Berlin songbook *Unsung Irving Berlin* after having been sung by Laurie Beechman on the 1995 Varèse Sarabande recording *Unsung Irving Berlin*. Previously registered for copyright as an unpublished song July 21, 1956. Typed lyric sheet dated December 4, 1955. Music (lead sheet) dictated by Berlin to Helmy Kresa on December 3, 1955. Intended as a first-act duet for Wilson Mizner and Mary.

CHORUS 1

MARY: You're a sentimental guy—
             It's a charge that you'll deny,
             But a song of home and mother
             In a pinch could make you cry,
             And it seems my natural bent
             Is to love a sentimental guy.

             You can always knock them dead
             With some clever thing you've said,
             But your heart is not in tune
             With what is running through your head,
             And I'm perfectly content
             Just to love a sentimental guy.

             You think you're the type for Broadway;
             You prowl it from night till dawn.
             You really belong to Yonkers
             With a garden and a lawn.

             Though I never heard you say
             In the ordinary way

That you're simply wild about me,
But I know there'll come a day
When my evenings will be spent
With a very sentimental guy.

CHORUS 2

WILSON: You're as wrong as you can be
                In your estimate of me.
                When the rent for my apartment
                Is delayed a month or three,
                If some tears will save the rent,
                I'm a *very* sentimental guy.

                When I'm speaking soft and low
                To a copper that I know
                Who is taking in a pal
                And I would like him to let go,
                If a sob will get consent,
                I'm a *very* sentimental guy.

                I melt with the breath of springtime
                When grass starts to green the lawn;
                I get very sentimental
                As I take my coat to pawn.

MARY: So you think and so you say
                In your clever sort of way,
                But I know it won't be long before
                There'll come that happy day
                When my evenings will be spent
                With a very sentimental guy.

I NEVER WANT TO SEE YOU AGAIN

Registered for copyright as an unpublished song May 10, 1956. Typed lyric sheet dated April 10, 1956.

[*After* MARY *walks behind* WILSON, *who is about to call her father with the best hand, and says "I wouldn't do that," Wilson, who is furious, grabs her by the hand. They go downstage to a small set in one in front of a railing overlooking the ocean. Through this number,* WILSON *is obviously very mad.* MARY, *on the other hand, does it tongue in cheek.*]

CHORUS 1

WILSON: I never want to see you again.
MARY: Never?
WILSON: Never.

MARY: Never, never, never, never, never?
WILSON: Never, never, never, never, never.
MARY: You never want to meet me again ever?
WILSON: Ever.
MARY: Ever, ever, ever, ever, ever.
WILSON: Ever, ever, ever, ever, ever.
MARY: Suppose we were invited
To the swanky Cold Stream Guards?
WILSON: I'd walk right in and cut you
Like I would a deck of cards.
MARY: You never want to see me again?
That's as long as it can be.
WILSON: Never, never, never
Will be soon enough for me.
MARY: Never?
BOTH: Never, never, never
Will be soon enough for me.

VERSE

WILSON: You're a very possessive dame.
MARY: You're a gentleman and a scholar.
WILSON: You are playing a losing game.
MARY: You are getting hot neath the collar.
WILSON: Let me warn you I can get mad.
MARY: But to me you're not so alarming.
WILSON: I've a temper that's very bad.
MARY: You're a bully, but then you're
charming.

CHORUS 2

WILSON: I never want to see you again.
MARY: Never?
WILSON: Never.
MARY: Never, never, never, never, never?
WILSON: Never, never, never, never, never.
MARY: Suppose you heard of something I said
clever?
WILSON: Clever?
MARY: Something smart
For which they'd give me credit.
WILSON: Someone soon
Would spread the news I said it.
MARY: Suppose you swam the Channel
And you met me on the way?
WILSON: I'd go down to the bottom,
And the bottom's where I'd stay.
MARY: You never want to see me again?
That's as long as it can be.
WILSON: Never, never, never
Will be soon enough for me
MARY: Never?
BOTH: Never, never, never
Will be soon enough for me.

ANYBODY CAN WRITE

Registered for copyright as an unpublished song April 16, 1956, and May 10, 1956. Typed lyric sheet dated February 10, 1956. This lyric was revised for *Mr. President* (1962); see page 477.

VERSE

You can't be a banker unless you can count.
You can't be a jockey unless you can mount.
You can't make good lager unless you can brew.
There's only one thing anyone can do:

CHORUS 1

Anybody can write,
Anybody can write—
A pencil or pen,
Some paper, and then
You just sit down and write.
Spend a weekend in Rome;
Write a book when you're home.
It's easy for anyone
To write for the stage;
You put down these simple words
On top of a page:
"Act One, Scene One"—
And when that's done,
Write, write.
If you get that empty feeling
Looking at the ceiling,
Take a rest, then go right back
And write.

CHORUS 2

Anybody can sing,
Anybody can sing—
You just clear your throat
And ask for a note,
Then stand right up and sing.
Everyone has a voice;
You must sing—there's no choice.
You don't need an evening dress
Or white tie and tails;
You start with a practice shot
And run up the scales:
Do, re, me, fa,
Sol, la, ti, do—
Sing, sing.
If the critics who are yokels
Criticize your vocals,
Say, "To hell with the critics,"
And sing.

CHORUS 3

Anybody can dance,
Anybody can dance—
Astaire won't refuse
To loan you his shoes,
So get right up and dance.
Ev'ry body today
Learns to tap and ballet;
You don't need a floor
Or dancing shoes on your feet—
If you feel like dancing,
Do it out on the street.
Strike a pose and
On your toes and
Dance, dance—
If you slip while you are splitting
And you wind up sitting,
Get right up, brush your clothes off,
And dance.

GOLD

Typed lyric sheet dated December 1, 1955.

Gold—gold—
We traveled a lot
To gather a pot of gold.
Gold—gold—
We wanna go back
With all that a sack can hold.
Gold—gold—
There's plenty of ore
To handle before it's sold.
Gold from underneath
For your pocket and your teeth—
The very sweetest story ever told
Is gold, gold, gold.

KLONDIKE KATE

Registered for copyright as an unpublished song May 10, 1956. Typed lyric sheet dated February 23, 1956.

VERSE 1

Here's the story of Klondike Kate—
Came to Nome from the Mormon state,
Served the drinks at the Nugget Bar,

Weighed about two hundred pounds
And smoked a cigar.

CHORUS 1

Kate, Kate,
Klondike Kate
Wouldn't watch her diet,
She just slept and ate.

VERSE 2

She grew heavier pound by pound;
Miners looked and said, "She's too round."
Came a gambler who did some tricks,
Smiled at her and she fell like
A barrel of bricks.

CHORUS 2

Kate, Kate,
Klondike Kate
Fell in love and soon
She started losing weight.

VERSE 3

When the gambler man hit the trail,
She grew skinnier than a rail;
Miners looked at her with a grin,
Saying, "She was much too fat
And now she's too thin."

CHORUS 3

Kate, Kate,
Klondike Kate
They would look and say,
"There's not enough for bait."

VERSE 4

Came a miner from her hometown,
Fell in love with her all thinned down,
Popped the question and she said yes;
Bridal gown was made from half
Her favorite dress.

CHORUS 4

Kate, Kate,
Klondike Kate
Settled down and married
In the Mormon state.
Happy little wife, although
She's one of eight.
Back again to what was once
Her former weight—

Husband doesn't like it,
But it's much too late.
That's the story of
Klondike Kate.

IT TAKES MORE THAN LOVE TO KEEP A LADY WARM

There are two versions of this song; the music is different for each. The second version was registered for copyright as an unpublished song June 21, 1956. The lyric sheet of the first version is dated February 5, 1956; of the second, March 9, 1956. The song was intended as an ensemble number. No music for the first version is known to survive.

First version

When it's ten below
'Mid the ice and snow
And you find yourself out in the storm,
Though you're just a bride,
If it's cold outside,
It takes more than love to keep a lady warm.
It takes mink and fox
And some fur-lined frocks
And some sable wrapped around your form.
It takes more than charms
And a pair of arms
To keep a lady warm.

Second version

It takes more than love to keep a lady warm,
A lot more than love to keep a lady warm.
It takes more than charms and a pair of arms
When you're outdoors in a storm;
It takes more than love to keep a lady warm.
It takes earrings for each ear
And some bracelets up to here;
It takes mink or sable wrapped around your form.
When the first year ends and things get down to
    norm,
It takes more than love to keep a lady warm.*

Earlier version of last four lines:
    And some diamond rings and mink around your form.
    There's none warmer than a blushing bride,
    But when it's cold outside,
    It takes more than love to keep a lady warm.

LOVE IS FOR BOYS

Typed lyric sheet "dictated over phone from hospital," December 13, 1955. No music is known to survive.

CHORUS

Love is for boys and not for men,
As sure as the stars above.
Your headaches double,
And that's the trouble,
The trouble that comes with love.
Love is for kids with starry eyes
Who don't know it's all pretend,
But any grown-up
Should hang the phone up
When love's on the other end.

YOU'D MAKE A WONDERFUL WIFE FOR SOME MAN

Typed lyric sheet dated January 5, 1956. Note by Irving Berlin: "Mizner to Mrs. Astor trying to avoid her advances and telling her how marvelous she is—that he's never seen a woman with as much charm. Her reaction to the verse is that he is going to propose—but it leads up to this chorus."

CHORUS

You'd make a wonderful wife
For some man;
Some lucky fellow somewhere
You'd make happy.
To help you find him,
I will do all that I can,
For you'd make a wonderful wife
For some man.
I see him very clearly;
I know the very type:
He sits before a fire
And smokes a Dunhill pipe,
A credit to his country,
Respectable and good—
The kind of man I'd like to be
But somehow never could.
Oh, how I'd love to be there
When you plan
A wonderful life

For a wonderful wife
When you meet
That wonderful man.

PALM BEACH (1952)

In November 1952 Berlin began work on the score of a musical version of Cleveland Amory's book *The Last Resorts*, which Berlin tentatively titled *Palm Beach*. Apparently, the dramatic rights to the book had been acquired by Leland Hayward, and Howard Lindsay and Russel Crouse were slated to write the libretto. According to Amory, one reason the show never happened was that columnists had leaked word that one of the starring roles was to have been played by Mary Martin or Ethel Merman. This premature disclosure upset both women.

On November 19, 1952, Berlin dictated an outline for the opening scenes of the show:

This is a rough suggestion for a possible story based on the background material and some of the personalities in Cleveland Amory's *The Last Resorts*.

The show opens in 1896, full stage. This is Palm Beach and the background scene is the Poinciana Hotel. Actually it is the photograph that was given to Mrs. George C. White of Palm Beach by her cousin Colonel Philip Lydig. It is the occasion of the arrival of the Cornelius Vanderbilt Private Special Train arriving at Palm Beach. Before the train's arrival, a few Negroes cross in the traditional wheelchairs of the period. Also a few Palm Beach natives, and finally, one or two of the society people who are there at that time to meet the incoming train. The train comes in with well-known personalities who were on this particular train—Cornelius Vanderbilt, Mabel Terry, Miss Gertrude Vanderbilt, Harry Payne Whitney—and other well-known society names of the period who were not on the train. These parts will be played by chorus people and one or two minor principals. They exit from the train and go into a concerted number telling the occasion of why they are there, also establishing the theme of our show. These are the so-called wealthy, Social Register, society personalities who frequent the resorts, Newport, Bar Harbor, Southampton, etc., that are in Amory's *The Last Resorts*. They have come to Palm Beach, which promises to be the greatest of all resorts for them.

This is only a prologue but it will establish our theme and use as much of the material in New-port, Bar Harbor, etc. that we can. The possible ending for this one scene will be a number quoting Ward McAllister's famous list of "the Four Hundred"—one hundred percent Americans who count—that is, count their money in a large amount—and made the list of the four hundred people who count.

The Everglades of Palm Beach, with a view of the ocean in the background. This is a scene using Alligator Joe taking a few society people through the jungle. Among them are included Paris Singer and Addison Mizner. Out of this scene we get the character of Paris Singer, who he is, what he has done, his eccentricities, and so forth. The same goes for Addison Mizner. Also, this scene furnishes the Mizner inspiration to turn the Florida jungle into a Spanish Riviera. Some number for Singer and Mizner will close the scene in I.

The next scene is Worth Avenue, where the Everglades Club is to be built. This is some months later, and Addison Mizner is well on his way. The Florida boom is just beginning, and somewhere up north, Wilson Mizner, Addison's brother, has heard about it. Addison gets word that his brother Will is on his way and will soon arrive. Addison's reaction is mixed with affection for Wilson and apprehension of what Will's arrival can do to his promising setup. The scene will finish with a number based on the excitement of the Florida boom and particularly Addison Mizner's building progress—the Stotesbury house, the Cosden house, The Shearer house, etc.

Next is an intimate bedroom scene with Addison Mizner dressed to go to the opening of the Everglades Club, which he built. He is waiting for Wilson, who is going with him. Wilson arrives dressed for the opera, white tie, tails, and what have you. Also with the news that he has asked Jane Baker (Ethel Merman), a gal Wilson knew in the old days and one who can sing not alone good, but loud, to come to the opening with them. Addison is not too pleased. The Everglades Club is very exclusive and being the first architectural job he has done in Palm Beach, a lot depends on its success.

In the next scene, we get the relationship between the Mizner brothers. It is as hard as nails. Their insults are devastating, but we sense a great affection between these two hardboiled characters. They really love each other. Addison is fat, lovable, talented, social-conscious in a nice way. Wilson is hard as nails—tough on the surface, experienced, caustic, insulting, on the defensive, and thinks he believes his famous crack "Never give a sucker an even break"—underneath, he is a sentimental slob. A phony cripple selling pencils could empty his pockets, and an old lady selling a few flowers could bring tears to his eyes. A good song for the Mizner brothers would help a lot to close this scene.

On December 8, 1952, Berlin compiled a list of songs, scenes, and characters for *Palm Beach*:

POSSIBLE SONGS

1. Sittin' in the Sun Counting My Money
2. A Cottage with a Hundred Rooms*
3. Don't Forget to Bring Your Banjo*
4. The Snobs on the Wrong Side of the Tracks
5. My Brother*
6. Only Four Hundred People in the World Who Count

SCENES

Open with Vanderbilt train arriving in Palm Beach—1896.

A photograph of this scene is on the flyleaf of *The Last Resorts*.

Negroes with bicycle chairs. Society children who will be the grown-ups in Palm Beach when Addison Mizner takes over (1919).

Florida jungle in one before Mizner and Singer start.

Comedy scene—first meeting of the membership committee of the Everglades Club.

Scene in Bradley's gambling house.

Stotesbury birthday party.

Ed Hutton's brokerage office.

Finale first act, February 28th, closing of Palm Beach season at Poinciana Hotel with Negro help. Song—"Alexander's Ragtime Band."

POSSIBLE CHARACTERS

Addison Mizner
Wilson Mizner
Paris Singer
Ed Hutton
Clarence Jones
Mrs. Stotesbury
Isadora Duncan
The Girl Lead (Merman, Martin, or ? ?). This character could be a native Florida "cracker" whose family has lived in West Palm Beach for years. She is the girl on the wrong side of the tracks and our love story.

Lyrics numbered 2, 3, and 5 do not survive. It's possible they were never written.

THE SNOBS ON THE WRONG SIDE OF THE TRACKS

Typed lyric sheet dated December 5, 1952. Unfinished. Berlin drafted the last lines of the chorus. Also see "Sentimental Guy" (1955–56), page 452.

A man who wore a wristwatch,
Though his chest was hairy,
He either was an Englishman
Or just a sissy.
And a Vanderbilt who's rich
Must be a son of a witch
According to the snobs on the wrong side of the tracks.

ONLY FOUR HUNDRED PEOPLE IN THE WORLD WHO COUNT

Unfinished lyric. Written in December 1952.

Only four hundred people who count,
Only four hundred people who count,
Only four hundred people who count
Their money till it reaches a large amount,
And they're the Four Hundred,
A hundred percent Americans, who count.

MUSIC BOX REVUE TELEVISION SPECTACULAR (1957)

MUSIC BOX OPENING

Piano-vocal dated "January 9, 1957—Palm Beach." Typed lyric sheet dated January 10, 1957. Intended for Mary Martin, George Gobel, Perry Como, and "Ticket Taker." This project was to be a television spectacular aimed at recreating something of the spirit and substance of Berlin's *Music Box Revues*.

[*We open with a scene, which will probably have to be photographed, of the lobby of the Music Box Theater as it is today with a sign showing the present attraction* Separate Tables. *The audience is going back for the second act. The* TICKET TAKER *is on stage. A couple (*MARY MARTIN *and* GEORGE GOBEL*) walk up to him, all out of breath, dressed in the period of 1923.—IB*]

GEORGE: At last we're here at the Music Box.
MARY: At the Music Box,
TICKET
TAKER: At the Music Box.
GEORGE: [*handing two tickets to* TICKET TAKER]
We've got two seats for the Music Box.
MARY: For the Music Box tonight.
GEORGE: We know we're late, but the crowd was such—
MARY: That stubborn cop was the final touch.
GEORGE: I hope that we haven't missed too much
At the Music Box tonight.
TICKET
TAKER: [*who has been looking over the tickets*]
These tickets, sir, were sold to you in nineteen twenty-three—
They're for a *Music Box Revue.*
MARY AND
GEORGE: Well, that's what we came to see.
TICKET
TAKER: You're thirty-four years too late, sir;
I'm afraid that they're no good.
MARY AND
GEORGE: We were held up by the traffic
And we got here as fast as we could.

TICKET
TAKER: You were held up by the what?
MARY AND
GEORGE: Not by the what, by the traffic—
And we got here as fast as we could.

[*Manager enters (*PERRY COMO*).*]

GEORGE: We've got two seats for the Music Box,
PERRY: [*smiling*]
For the Music Box.
MARY: For the Music Box.
GEORGE: We've got two seats for the Music Box.
MARY: For the Music Box tonight.
PERRY: You're welcome here, and I'm glad to state
There's much to see, though you're somewhat late.
The critics said that the show is great
At the Music Box tonight.

[*During the above, the* TICKET TAKER *hands the two seats over to* PERRY.]

PERRY: These tickets, sir, were sold to you in nineteen twenty-three.
MARY AND
GEORGE: They're for a *Music Box Revue*
And that's what we came to see!!
PERRY: But you're thirty-four years later, sir;
I'm afraid that they're no good.
MARY AND
GEORGE: We were held up by the traffic—
And we got here as fast as we could.
PERRY AND
TICKET
TAKER: You were held up by the what???
MARY AND
GEORGE: Not by the what, by the traffic—
And we got here as fast as we could!!!
PERRY: Just wait a moment or two
And I'll see what I can do.

[*Curtains close as he addresses the audience who are there to see* Separate Tables.]

PERRY: Ladies and gentlemen,
It seems to be my lot
To tell you the management
Is in an awful spot.
You came to see *Separate Tables;*
I know you're drama fans.
But ladies and gentlemen,
There's a sudden change in our plans.

We've got to do a revue;
We hope it satisfies you.
We'll have to stop and change the show
From a play into a revue.
Two tickets that were sold here
Back in nineteen twenty-three
Showed up with a charming couple,
And that's what they want to see.
They were held up by the traffic,
And you know what that can be.
So you see,
You see,
We've got to do
That old revue
That introduced the song you know as
"Say It with Music."

[PERRY *sings chorus as* Music Box Revue *continues.*]

INTRODUCTION TO "EVERYBODY STEP"

Typed lyric sheet is undated; written in January 1957.

In that first revue
We had a tune they said was new
With a peppy swing
That had a certain thing
That new rhythm has.
I don't mean to boast,
But it was played from coast to coast,
And I really think
'Twas the connecting link
Between ragtime and jazz.
Here's the little tune I mean
From the big finale scene.

MONTMARTRE

Typed lyric dated January 16, 1957. A revision of a song from the *Music Box Revue of 1922*; see page 207. In this version only the chorus is new.

CHORUS

Montmartre,
Playground of France,
Montmartre,

Wrapped in romance,
Montmartre,
On with the dance.
While the melody
Whispers tenderly
With romance
Leading you on
Till the
Stars have all gone.
Young hearts
Wake with the break of each dawn
In Montmartre.

GO HOME AND TELL IT TO YOUR WIFE

Registered for copyright as an unpublished song November 19, 1977. Probably written in January 1957. Alternate title: "You Can't Do This to Me."

HE: You can't do this to me,
    You can't do this to me.
    I've given you the best years of my life—
    You can't put on your hat,
    Walk out and leave me flat.
SHE: Go home tonight and tell it to your wife.
HE: You can't do this to me,
    You can't do this to me.
    I'm hurt—we haven't even had a row.
    You can't give me the air
    And end this love affair.
SHE: Go home tonight and tell it to your frau.
HE: I guess that you've forgotten
    Those wonderful nights.
    Remember in this country
    A husband has rights.
    You can't do this to me,
    You can't do this to me—
    Remember that a home is not a house.
    You can't say that we're through
    With all I've done for you.
SHE: Go home tonight and tell it to your spouse.

WHEN LOVE WAS ALL

Registered for copyright as an unpublished song January 17, 1957. Typed lyric sheet dated January 12, 1957. Intended for Mary Martin and Perry Como.

[*Preceding this song is a short scene in the corner of their living room. They have just returned from a party and are quarreling.*]

CHORUS 1

PERRY: I recall
       When love was all,
       When love was all we needed.
       No dining where it's grand,
       Just dinner at a hot-dog stand—
       Yes, I recall
       A simple shawl
       Was all you thought you needed.
       I spend my nickels and dimes
       And often think of the times
       When all we needed was love.

CHORUS 2

MARY: I recall
      When love was all,
      When love was all we needed.
      The jerks I used to snub,
      I have to meet them at your club.
      Yes, I recall
      A new golf ball
      Was what you never needed—
      No golf all day on a course,
      No polo played from a horse,
      When all we needed was love.

CHORUS 3

PERRY: I recall
       When love was all,
       When love was all we needed.
       You never found much fault
       Before those diamonds in your vault.
MARY: [*putting her arm around him*]
      Yes, I recall
      A cottage small
      Is all we thought we needed.
      Let's kiss this quarrel away
      And go right back to the day
BOTH: When all we needed was love.

Earlier version

CHORUS 2

I recall
When love was all,
When love was all we needed.
No treasures in a vault,
No look that means it's all my fault—
Yes, I recall

A cottage small
Was all you thought we needed.
While rent takes half of my pay,
My mind goes back to the day
When all we needed was love.

CHORUS 3

I recall
When love was all,
When love was all we needed.
The jerks we used to snub,
We meet them at the country club.
Yes, I recall
A fancy ball
Was what you never needed.
We gave one Saturday last,
And I just thought of the past
When all we needed was love.

MARY AND PERRY AND GEORGE

Typed lyric sheet dated January 11, 1957.

CHORUS 1

ALL: Mary and Perry and George,
     Closer with each Valley Forge.
MARY: Just a great big family—
PERRY: Working for the NBC.
GEORGE: When it comes to salary—
MARY: It's Mary for Mary—
PERRY: And Perry's for Perry—
GEORGE: And Georgie is in there for George.

CHORUS 2

ALL: Mary and Perry and George,
     With love, each other we gorge.
MARY: Every honor each one shares.
PERRY: As for billing—poof, who cares?
GEORGE: Networks sometimes don't get theirs.
MARY: But Mary's for Mary—
PERRY: And Perry's for Perry—
GEORGE: And Georgie is in there for George.

INTERLUDE

PERRY AND
GEORGE: Mary, you're wonderful.
MARY: I think you're lambs.
ALL: We are inseparable,

But we are all hams.
   Monday rehearsal comes round,
   You'll find us there on the ground.
MARY: Gee, we have a lot of fun!
PERRY: One for all and all for one!
GEORGE: Till the night the show is done—
MARY: Then Mary's for Mary—
PERRY: And Perry's for Perry—
GEORGE: And Georgie is in there for George.

RCA: "SAY IT WITH MUSIC"

Typed lyric sheet dated January 10, 1957. A commercial.

Say it with music,
With Victor music—
Play me the song of my choice,
Brought to me by His Master's Voice,
Etc.

OLDSMOBILE: "LADY OF THE EVENING"

Typed lyric sheet dated January 11, 1957. A commercial.

Evening,
Lady of the evening—
Nothing like our Oldsmobiles
Riding
While you're groom-and-briding—
Take your honeymoon on wheels.

[*Music continues as commercial goes on.*]

COCA-COLA: "EVERYBODY STEP"

Typed lyric sheet dated January 11, 1957. A commercial.

Everybody step,
Have a drink of Coca-Cola—
It's the finest pepperola

We found.
After a Coke
You will be all feeling oke,
Step-step-stepping around.

[*Music continues as commercial goes on.*]

THE WAY IT WAS

Registered for copyright as an unpublished song November 30, 1977. Typed lyric sheet dated January 17, 1957.

As it was,
Just the way it was,
As it was
When we were sweethearts.
Our love was meant to last,
So let's go back and find the past,
The way it was,
Happy day it was,
When you used to call me sweetheart—
Patch up our shattered romance
And give the future a chance
With love
The way it was.

THE TODDLE

Typed lyric sheet dated January 23, 1957. Written in Palm Beach.

Toddle—
Ev'rybody learn to do the Toddle.
Every trav'ling salesman and his model,
Toddle to a toddling tune.
Yes sir,
Walk up to your sweetie and address her,
"May I have the next while the professor
Plays the latest toddling tune?"
That fellow leading the band,
Stick in his hand,
Gives you the beat
And, while you're led,
Loses his head
So that it goes to your feet.
Toddle—
There's been talk of censoring the Toddle,

But to me it's just a lot of twaddle—
Toddle to a toddling tune.

YOU'RE FUN TO BE WITH

Registered for copyright as an unpublished song November 30, 1977. Written in Palm Beach. Typed lyric sheet dated January 24, 1957.

You're fun to be with,
The one to be with
When gray clouds dim the skies.
When stocks are falling
And brokers calling,
You make my spirits rise.
When gloom makes up his mind
To crawl down from his shelf,
You smile and soon I find
I'm laughing at myself.
I'd miss your laughter
On mornings after
When my head weighs a ton.
You're beautiful,
You're glamorous,
You're lovable,
You're amorous,
But most of all
You're fun.

OTHER SONGS OF THE 1950s

FOR THE VERY FIRST TIME

Published. Copyrighted March 31, 1952. Previously registered for copyright as an unpublished song March 16, 1950. According to Russel Crouse's diary of 1950 concerning *Call Me Madam*, Berlin suggested the song to Lindsay and Crouse during a meeting at Lindsay's house on March 6, 1950. In an April 21, 1952 letter to Walter Preston of *Produce News*, Hy Fenster, who worked for Berlin, wrote the following account of the genesis of this song:

> Mr. Berlin had written the melody to this song some years back in hopes of placing it in one of his shows. Failing to find the proper spot for it he neglected to put a lyric to the melody. Several months ago when our professional manager remarked to him that we needed a new song to work on, Mr. Berlin replied "for the first time, I haven't got a song." Somehow the phrase "for the first time" stuck with him. While vacationing in Nassau he wrote a lyric around this idea and married it to the above mentioned melody and out came "For the Very First Time."

In an interview with the New York *Herald Tribune* (October 17, 1954), Berlin said: "Sure I haven't had a hit since I did *Call Me Madam*. I put out a couple of songs that I thought were pretty good. One of them, 'For the Very First Time,' was recorded by Tony Martin and I thought it was a good ballad. But it never got off the ground."

For the very first time
I find for the first time
I'm head over heels in love.
For the very first time
I know that the last time
Was ev'rything else but love.
For the very first time
There won't be a next time;
My romancing days are all through.
All my love-affairing
Was simply preparing
To love for the first time, you.

Earlier version (1950)

For the first time
There is music in my heart;
For the first time
I'm in love.
For the first time
I've upset the apple cart;
For the first time I'm in love.
Those other times when I was caring,
It wasn't really love, I was just preparing
For the first time.
Snuggle close and hold me fast;
This is the first time—and the last.

THE MUSTACHE IS DIFFERENT (BUT THE WORDS ARE THE SAME)

Typed lyric sheet dated August 21, 1950. No music is known to survive.

VERSE

Seated round a radio in a Texas gen'ral store,
Listenin' to the UN discussions,
Seated there, a cowboy said as he missed the
  cuspidor,
"This is what I think of the Russians."

CHORUS

"The mustache is different,
But the words are the same,
The same as ten years ago.
The voice is familiar;
They have just changed the name—
Instead of Adolf it's Joe,
Uncle Joe, Uncle Joe.
Is there any way to let your people know
The mustache is different
But the words are the same,
And 'stead of Adolf it's Joe?"

TRIBUTE TO RODGERS AND HART

In April 1951 Berlin wrote the following tribute to Richard Rodgers and Lorenz Hart for Simon & Schuster's *Rodgers and Hart Song Book*.

April 5th, 1951

Mr. Jack Goodman
Simon & Schuster Inc.
1230 Sixth Avenue
New York, N. Y.

Dear Jack:
    Here is the four line jingle which you liked for the Rodgers and Hart song book:—

    "Tuneful and tasteful
    Schmaltzy and smart
    Music by Rodgers
    Lyrics by Hart"

I'm sorry about the delay.
My best.

Sincerely,
Irving Berlin

The next day he wrote again with a revision:

Dear Jack:
    I prefer the following version because it is shorter and simpler.

    "Tuneful, tasteful
    Schmaltzy, smart
    Music—Rodgers
    Lyrics—Hart"

My best,
Irving Berlin

YOU GOTTA BELIEVE IN SANTA CLAUS

Typed lyric sheet dated September 8, 1952.

You've gotta believe in Santa Claus.
On Christmas Eve you've gotta believe
He'll come down your chimney—
But he won't pause
Unless you believe in Santa Claus.

SAYONARA

Published. Copyrighted September 9, 1957. Previously registered for copyright as an unpublished song October 7, 1953. Introduced by Miiko Taka in the 1957 Warner Bros. film *Sayonara*, which was produced by William Goetz, directed by Joshua Logan, and starred Marlon Brando.

In late 1953 Logan approached Berlin to write the score for a musical stage version of James A. Michener's best-selling 1953 novel *Sayonara*. Paul Osborn was to write the libretto. Berlin apparently wrote several songs for the project, but when the Broadway *Sayonara* failed to materialize because of legal problems, he lost interest. Eventually Logan's *Sayonara* became a film and Berlin's title song became part of it.

On February 14, 1957, Berlin wrote his friend Irving Hoffman about the song. "I made my usual good business deal with Bill Goetz," he noted, "to use this as the theme song if Josh could fit it in. I told Bill I had two prices—what it was worth and nothing—and suggested that he accept the latter which he did."

Other Berlin songs probably written for the Broadway version of *Sayonara* include "Is She the Only Girl in the World?" (see "Is He the Only Man in the World," page 471), "How Does a Pilot Spend His Furlough?" (page 461), "When a Three-Star General's Daughter Meets a Four-Star General's Son" (page 461), and "She's Graceful and Pretty" (page 461).

Sayonara,
Japanese goodbye—
Whisper sayonara,
But you mustn't cry.
No more we stop to see
Pretty cherry blossoms,
No more we 'neath the tree
Looking at the sky.
Sayonara, sayonara,
Goodbye.

Sayonara,
If it must be so,
Whisper sayonara,
Smiling as we go.
No more we stop to see
Pretty cherry blossoms,
No more we 'neath the tree
Looking at the sky.
Sayonara, sayonara,
Goodbye.

MR. PRESIDENT OF ASCAP

Registered for copyright as an unpublished song December 5, 1977. A song-speech written and performed by Berlin at a banquet at the Waldorf-Astoria Hotel in New York City on March 30, 1954, marking the fortieth anniversary of ASCAP's founding. Berlin's typed lyric sheet is dated March 25, 1954.

Mr. President
Of ASCAP,
Fellow members and honored guests,
I don't have to say what it means to me
To help you celebrate
This fortieth anniversary,
An important ASCAP date.
I'm ashamed to admit it's been much too long
Since I came to these dinners each year,
But I'm glad to note
With a lump in my throat
This wonderful change of atmosphere.

The single question in my day
Was how do you get in double A.
The grousing and squawking,
Speech making and talking,
Emotions that reached to the sky—
And let me say for the record now,
Nobody bellyached louder than I.
But we've all grown older,
With much more sense
And many more dollars
To pay the expense.
I feel safe under ASCAP's umbrella,
And I'll stay there with each writin' fella,
But tonight I would prefer
To speak to you as a publisher.

As a publisher member of ASCAP,
My, how the money rolls in!
To get that bit that I have to split
With just Irving Berlin,
That quarterly check from the publisher's share
Sends a thrill from my toes to the roots of my
    hair.
Oh, God bless America
And the quarterly check from the publisher's
    share of ASCAP.

And now to a musical interlude—
I'd like to express my gratitude
To a man in my employ.
I'm speaking of the little colored boy.

Sweetest little fella,
And can he compose!

No one's ever seen him,
But he's mighty like a rose.
He wrote "Come on and hear, come on and hear"
    and a hundred other hits.
There are times he doesn't show up, and then
The ink goes dry on my writin' pen.
And things look mighty black
Until the little boy comes back.

A few years ago he left me,
Like one of those temp'ramental molls;
It was just around that certain time
Frank Loesser wrote *Guys and Dolls*.
And now let me close my bit
With a theme song for ASCAP, and this is it:

Say it with music,
With words and music—
ASCAP, keep healthy and strong,
To say it with a beautiful song.

I'M NOT AFRAID

Published. Copyrighted May 12, 1954. Previously registered for copyright as an unpublished song April 8, 1954. Introduced by Eddie Fisher on April 9, 1954. Berlin described the genesis of the song in a letter he wrote to Congressman Francis Dorn of South Carolina. "I was a guest at an informal stag dinner at the White House on April 5th. After dinner, we heard the President make his television speech. The theme of that speech [the perils of nuclear war] inspired a song I wrote the next day called 'I'm Not Afraid.' Eddie Fisher introduced it that Friday on his television show and repeated it on April 29th."

VERSE

When the skies are not as clear
As they used to be,
There are salesmen selling fear,
But they can't reach me,
For I have faith in my country
And the men who guard our shores,
And I'm not alone,
For the faith that's mine is yours.

CHORUS

I'm not afraid
Of those who try to frighten us.
I'm not afraid
Of plots our foes have laid,

For I believe in America,
And most of us in America
Will always be Americans unafraid.

HOW DOES A PILOT SPEND HIS FURLOUGH?

Typed lyric dated May 5, 1954. Same music as the previously written "What Does a Soldier Want for Christmas?" (see page 445). Clearly intended for the unproduced musical version of James Michener's bestselling novel *Sayonara*, as a duet for the Air Force doctor and Major Lloyd Gruver. The show was never completed.

DOCTOR: How does a pilot spend his furlough?
    What does he do in Tokyo?
    Does he study maps while on his
      furlough
    While the lanterns and the lights burn
      low?
    Is he for army regulations,
    Proper and always dignified,
    Or would he prefer to spend his furlough
    Seeing Tokyo with a geisha as guide?

GRUVER: He wants his breakfast served in bed,
    A bed with clean sheets and a spread,
    And then go back and pound his head;
    He wants to sleep around the clock and
      then
    Wake up at ten—then go right back to
      sleep again.
    He softens up from being tough;
    A glass of beer is quite enough.
    He's tired of all the hero stuff—
    Instead of "Ace" just call him "Mister."
    And for his morale,
    A pilot dreams about his gal.

[*The second section ("He wants his breakfast served in bed") is first sung separately and then as a countermelody to the "How does a pilot spend his furlough?" section.*]

WHEN A THREE-STAR GENERAL'S DAUGHTER MEETS A FOUR-STAR GENERAL'S SON

Typed lyric dated May 5, 1954. Possibly intended for the unproduced musical version of *Sayonara*. Revised and registered for copyright as an unpublished song December 5, 1956, under the title "When a One-Star General's Daughter Meets a Four-Star General's Son."

CHORUS

When a three-star general's daughter
Meets a four-star general's son,
There's lots of class
And plenty of brass
But very little fun.
They don't relax while courtin',
Like other gals and guys,
For the stars are on the generals' shoulders
And not in the son's and daughter's eyes—
The stars are not in the son's and daughter's eyes.

SHE'S GRACEFUL AND PRETTY

Typed lyric sheet dated May 5, 1954. Probably intended for the unproduced musical version of *Sayonara*.

She's graceful and pretty,
Delightful and smart;
She's no fool, with a head that's cool,
And there's warmth in her heart.
A future we're planning
As husband and wife;
I'll be safe from harm
With a good-luck charm
For the rest of my life.

THE GATE TO THE ALLEY IS OPEN

Verse without music, written May 2, 1955, for a possible Tin Pan Alley section in *Variety*'s fiftieth anniversary issue. Sent to *Variety* editor-in-chief Abel Green.

The gate to the Alley is open;
None with talent are barred.
But writing a song is so easy—
That's what makes it so hard.

AESOP (THAT ABLE FABLE MAN)

Registered for copyright as an unpublished song June 16, 1955. Typed lyric sheet dated June 6, 1955. According to columnist Dorothy Kilgallen (New York *Journal-American*, June 27, 1955), "Irving Berlin has written—are you ready?—a bop song. It's about Aesop, and it's sure to make the juke boxes jingle. Irving phoned it in to his publishing firm from his house in the Catskills."

INTRODUCTION

Take the word of Aesop—
Take it while you can
From the wise old Aesop,
That able fable man.

VERSE 1

A hungry fox,
Some grapes on a vine—
He simply couldn't reach 'em;
They were way out of line.
He tried and tried,
But after an hour
He said, "I thought the grapes were ripe—
I see that they're sour."

That's the word of Aesop—
Take it while you can
From the wise old Aesop,
That able fable man.

VERSE 2

A tortoise went
To race with a hare;
The hare was kinda cocky,
Though he knew 'twasn't fair.
Way out in front,
He stopped on the run
And took a nap, but when he woke,
The tortoise had won.

That's the word of Aesop—
Take it while you can
From the wise old Aesop,
That able fable man.

VERSE 3

An angry lion,
A mouse in his claws—
The mouse said, "I'll remember you
If only you pause."
The lion let go,
Then got trapped in a net;
The mouse, he freed the lion
Because he didn't forget.

That's the word of Aesop—
Take it while you can
From the wise old Aesop,
That able fable man.

VERSE 4

A selfish dog
With straw for a bed;
The cows came in the manger,
For they had to be fed.
He barked and growled
And snapped at their feet
And didn't let them have the straw
That he couldn't eat.

That's the word of Aesop—
Take it while you can
From the wise old Aesop,
That able fable man.

VERSE 5

A precious goose,
Gold eggs she would lay;
The owner wasn't satisfied
With just one a day.
He thought inside there's more than just one—
He killed the goose that laid the eggs,
And now there are none.

That's the word of Aesop—
Take it while you can
From the wise old Aesop,
That able fable man.

'TWAS A WONDERFUL NIGHT FOR WALTZING

Registered for copyright as an unpublished song November 30, 1977. There are two versions of this lyric. The earlier typed lyric sheet is dated June 9, 1955; the later is dated December 13, 1955.

Earlier version

Violins softly played—
'Twas a wonderful night for waltzing.
In my arms, unafraid,
You were whisp'ring, "I love you so."

All alone in a crowd
On that wonderful night for waltzing,
I believed when you vowed
That you never would let me go.

Suddenly they started a new rhythm;
I couldn't keep up with it at all.
You went to change partners, so I waited,
And I was still waiting when they closed up the hall.*

Violins in my dreams
And that wonderful night for waltzing—
You were there, and it seems
You were whisp'ring, "I love you so."

Later version

Violins softly played—
'Twas a wonderful night for waltzing.
In my arms, unafraid,
You were whisp'ring, "I love you so."
I believed what you said
On that wonderful night for waltzing.

---

*Earlier version of lines 9–12:
    Suddenly they changed to a new rhythm;
    Suddenly it went right to your dome.
    You started first rocking and then rolling;
    I couldn't keep up with you, so I went home.

At the end of our dance you were called to the
    phone;
I waited and waited then went home alone.
But I'll never forget when we waltzed long ago
And you whispered, "I love you so."

PLEASE LET ME COME BACK TO YOU

Registered for copyright as an unpublished song
June 16, 1955. Typed lyric sheet and music manuscript
in the hand of Helmy Kresa are dated June 10, 1955.
Berlin then used this tune with a new lyric, "Blue
River."

One swallow doesn't make a summer;
One quarrel doesn't mean we're through;
One heartache doesn't mean it's broken—
Please let me come back to you.

One parting doesn't mean that someone
Starts going out with someone new.
One snowflake doesn't make a winter;
Please let me come back to you—do.
Please let me come back to you.

BLUE RIVER

Typed lyric sheet dated June 16, 1955. This lyric em-
ploys the melody for "Please Let Me Come Back to You"
and is a later setting of that tune.

Blue River,
Have you seen my darling,
My loved one
Who went out to sea?
Blue River,
If you see my darling,
Tell him to come back to me.
Please tell him
Ever since we parted
I'm lonely,
Lonely as can be.
Blue River,
If he's not returning,
Tell him to please wait for me,
River, tell him to please wait for me.

THE MOST

Registered for copyright as an unpublished song Sep-
tember 2, 1955. Typed lyric sheet dated September 1,
1955. A music manuscript in the hand of Helmy Kresa
is dated August 29, 1955.

I love you the most,
I need you the most,
And we'll be the most
When we are hostess and host.
Your eyes are the most,
Your lips are the most,
And I'll eat the most,
Darling, when you carve the roast.
All the fancy adjectives
That the dictionary gives,
When applied to you
Don't get to the post.
If I had a chance to shout it
From coast to coast
The least that I could say is
That you're the most.

OUT OF THIS WORLD INTO MY ARMS

Published. Copyrighted September 29, 1955. Previ-
ously registered for copyright as an unpublished song
September 1, 1955. According to *Variety* (September 7,
1955), Berlin "has whipped up 'Out of This World into
My Arms' as an out-and-out pop song which he's plan-
ning to work on." An article in the New York *Journal-
American* (September 9, 1955) stated that "Irving
Berlin's irrepressible energy has him back on Tin Pan
Alley, batting out candidates for the hit parade. The
first to make the juke boxes will be 'Out of This World
into My Arms'—and the disc artists are scrambling to
record it."

You came from
Out of this world into my arms, sweetheart,
From somewhere out of this world,
Spilling my apple cart.
You fell from high above—
Another planet, it seems—
A great big bundle of love,
The stuff that's made out of dreams.
The happy ending is here
Now that you've made the start

From somewhere
Out of this world into my arms, sweetheart.

HOW'S YOUR HEART

Typed lyric February 21, 1956. Unfinished. Intended for
the Heart Fund Association and sung by Berlin over the
telephone to Dr. Myron Prinzmetal.

How's your heart?
How's your heart?
If it's strong enough to stand the great
    outdoors,
Won't you help a heart that's weaker than
    yours?
How's your heart?
How's your heart?
If it's brave enough to roam the distant shores,
If it doesn't miss a beat though heaven pours,
Won't you help a heart that's weaker than
    yours?

THIS IS AMERICA (OPENING)

Typed lyric sheet dated July 6, 1956. *This Is America*
appears to have been an idea for a show that was not de-
veloped very far.

We're Americans—
That special band of yeggs
Who order ham and eggs
In the finest French restaurants.
We talk too much
And we tip too much
And we don't all think the same;
We bellyache about taxes
But we pay them just the same.
We love to fight among ourselves
Till it's misunderstood by some;
Then this funny breed
That disagreed
Suddenly become—
Americans.
We arrange our laws
So we can change our laws
When most of us feel the need;

We're an independent breed,
We Americans.*

> GIRLS: Our ancestors were immigrants
> Who came from foreign shores.
> BOYS: Who you gonna vote for in
> November?
> GIRLS: It's no damn business of yours.
> INTERLOCUTOR: Americans, be seated.

[*A screen is lowered showing Castle Garden at the turn of the century. Eight* IMMIGRANT COUPLES *enter.*]

ITALIAN
COUPLE: This is America,
Where gold lies at your feet.
So far we haven't found
A gold piece on the street.
We're getting homesick
And we're feeling very low,
But do we want to go back
Where we came from?
No!

GERMAN
COUPLE: This is America,
They tell us over here.
We'll miss the sauerkraut
Washed down with Pilsner beer.
It's hard to hurry
When you're used to going slow,
But do we want to go back
Where we came from?
No!

JEWISH
COUPLE: We have traveled far
From the Russian czar,
Who would tell us
What to do.
We intend to stay
Till the happy day
When the dreams we brought
Come true.

NEGRO
COUPLE: This is America;
We came here to be free.
We're bound for Alabam'
To see what we can see.
We've heard an awful lot of talk

An earlier version substitutes these lines for lines 15–19:

> We go to the polls,
> To our cubbyholes,
> Where we privately disagree;
> And when it's done,
> No matter who won,
> We continue to disagree.

About Jim Crow,
But do we want to go back
Where we came from?
No!

[*After they finish they will be surrounded by members of the minstrels as in "This Is the Army, Mr. Jones." While the minstrel group sings the same chorus, the* IMMIGRANTS *change into American dress of the period and exit singing, "But do we want to back where we came from? No!"*]

[*After this the* INTERLOCUTOR *introduces* MR. X *and* MISS Z. *Follow with gags, leading into "Anyone Can Be President."*]

ANYONE CAN BE PRESIDENT

Typed lyric sheet dated July 6, 1956. Intended for the unfinished show *This Is America.*

Anyone can be President,
That's what we've been told;
But it takes a lot of speeches
And a pot full of gold.
It takes a lot of blasting,
And you need an elephant's hide;
But anyone can be President
If beneath his elephant's hide
He's got what it takes inside.

I KEEP RUNNING AWAY FROM YOU

Published. Copyrighted July 15, 1957. Previously registered for copyright as an unpublished song April 30, 1957, and again on May 8, 1957. Later revised to become "Glad to Be Home" in *Mr. President* (1962); see page 473.

I keep running away from you,
A week, a month, or a day from you,
But all the time I'm away from you
You are there by my side—
The further away,
The closer you stay by my side.
I keep leaving you far behind,
I try to banish you from my mind,

I run away, but I always find
You are there by my side—
The further away,
The closer you stay by my side.
I try doing without you,
But wherever I go,
I keep taking you with me,
And that worries me so.
I keep running away from you,
A week, a month, or a day from you,
But all the time I'm away from you
You are there by my side—
The further away,
The closer you stay by my side.
Yes, the further I fly,
The closer you're by my side.

YOU CAN'T LOSE THE BLUES WITH COLORS

Published. Copyrighted July 29, 1957. Previously registered for copyright as an unpublished song May 1, 1957.

Dress of white, shoes of red,
But you can't lose the blues with colors.
Purple hat on my head,
But you can't lose the blues with colors.
Yellow bag trimmed with green,
But I'm blue neath the splash of colors.
On the outside a rainbow,
A smile a yard wide,
An orchid corsage with a pink ribbon tied;
But you can't cover up
What you feel deep inside—
No, you can't lose the blues with colors.

SILVER PLATTER

Registered for copyright as an unpublished song May 15, 1957. Typed lyric sheet dated May 1, 1957. Possibly intended for a musical version of Ellin Berlin's novel of the same name. The project was never completed.

Ev'rything on a silver platter—
I'll give you on a silver platter
A dream come true,
On a silver platter

With my love to you.
Ev'rything on a silver platter—
More and more as my luck grows fatter,
A world brand new
On a silver platter
With my love to you.
Oh, I just can't wait
Till my ship comes in;
No, I just can't wait
Till the moment when I begin
Giving you
Ev'rything on a silver platter.
I'll give you on a silver platter
A dream come true,
On a silver platter
With my love to you.

LOVE WITH A BEAT

Music dated May 3 and May 5, 1957. There are two versions of the lyric.

First version

Love with a beat,
Love with a beat,
Please, baby, give me love with a beat.
Love with a beat,
Love with a beat,
Please teach your heart to love with a beat.
Love with a rock,
Love with a rock
Will make your kiss twice as sweet.
Nothing else means
More to the teens
Than love, love, love, love with a beat.

Second version

Love with a beat,
Love with a beat,
Please, baby, give me love with a beat.
Kiss with a beat,
Kiss with a beat,
That's just what makes your kisses so sweet.
Nothing else means
More to the teens;
Nothing makes love so complete.
Baby, please start
Teaching your heart
To love, love, love, love with a beat.

SAM, SAM
(THE MAN WHAT AM)

Published. Copyrighted June 13, 1960. Previously registered for copyright as an unpublished song July 15, 1957. Written to celebrate the eighty-first birthday of retired New York schoolteacher Samuel Hoffman, the father of Berlin's close friend, press agent Irving Hoffman.

Sam, Sam,
The man what am,
You're just as good as new.
Eighty-one?
You've just begun
To live to a hundred and two.
Happy Birthday to you,
Happy Birthday to you.

A WORRIED OLD MAN

Irving Berlin limerick dictated to Hilda Schneider and sent to Irving Hoffman April 18, 1958.

A worried old man on the hill,
But no one believed he was ill.
They said, "You'll be sound
If you just get around"
And one night he was found—
Very still.

MORE THAN SILVER,
MORE THAN GOLD

Registered for copyright as an unpublished song November 30, 1977. Typed lyric sheet dated May 13, 1958.

More than silver,
More than gold,
More than treasures
The ground could hold
Is my love for you.
Love that's blessed from on high,
More than money can buy;

The sweetest story ever told
Is not about silver
And not about gold.

FOOTSTEPS

Typed lyric sheet dated November 3, 1958.

Footsteps on the dance floor,
Footsteps to my seat,
Footsteps while I'm thinking—
My brains are in my feet.

Footsteps reading letters,
Footsteps with the news,
Footsteps while I'm talking—
My mouth is in my shoes.

My father was a plumber
And to follow in his path
I get up every morning
And footstep to my bath.

Footsteps to my baby
Each time that we meet;
Some folks say it with flowers—
I say it with my feet.

THE MAN IN THE MOON
IS GETTING ANGRY

Typed lyric sheet dated October 1, 1959. No music is known to survive.

The man in the moon is getting angry.
It seems I heard him remark,
"If you don't stop hittin' me,
I'll stop shinin'
And you'll all be left in the dark."
For millions of years he's sprinkled moonbeams
On Lovers' Lane in the park;
So if we keep hittin' him,
He'll stop shinin',
And we'll be left in the dark,
We'll all be left in the dark.

ISRAEL

Registered for copyright as an unpublished song November 16, 1959. There are three versions of this lyric dated June 24, 1958, October 30, 1959, and November 3, 1959. Berlin wrote to Irving Hoffman on December 1, 1959: "I've reviewed my song 'Israel' and have grown quite cold on it, especially the first half. Also, I couldn't get a clearance on the title because there have been several written called 'Israel,' one by Jolson. That wouldn't worry me, but after going over it a couple of times I felt it was quite heavy."

First version, June 24, 1958

Israel,
The skies above burn bright
With the Star of David.

Born to be
A land that's free,
That nobody could ever change.
Wandering,
Through with wandering,
Nevermore to roam.
Today's the day you sing and pray
And thank God that at last you're home.

Second version, October 30, 1959

Israel,
Oh, Israel,
You said, "Welcome my homeless children."
Here we are
From near and far
To find peace in our ancient land.
Wandering,
Through with wandering,
Nevermore to roam.

Today's the day we sing and pray
And thank God that at last we're home,
Thank God that at last we're home.

Third version, November 3, 1959

Israel,
With outstretched arms
You gave hope to your homeless people.
Sunny shores
And open doors
Were there waiting for those who came.
Wandering,
Through with wandering,
Nevermore to roam.
Today's the day we sing and pray
And thank God that at last we're home,
Thank God that at last we're home.

Nanette Fabray and Robert Ryan, "In Our Hideaway"

MR. PRESIDENT | 1962

MR. PRESIDENT (1962)

Tryouts: Colonial Theatre, Boston, August 27, 1962; National Theatre, Washington, D.C., September 25, 1962. New York run: St. James Theatre, October 20, 1962, 265 performances. Produced by Leland Hayward. Book by Howard Lindsay and Russel Crouse. Directed by Joshua Logan. Choreography by Peter Gennaro. Orchestrations by Philip J. Lang. Orchestra under the direction of Jay Blackton. Cast: starring Robert Ryan (President Stephen Decatur Henderson) and Nanette Fabray (Nell Henderson) and featuring Anita Gillette (Leslie Henderson), Jack Haskell (Pat Gregory), Jack Washburn (Yussain Davair), Stanley Grover (Charley Wayne), Jerry Strickler (Larry Henderson), Charlotte Fairchild (Tippy Taylor), Wisa D'Orso (Princess Kyra), John Cecil Holm (Chester Kincaid), and David Brooks (Manager and Governor Harmon Bardahl).

MR. PRESIDENT (OPENING)

Published. Copyrighted July 31, 1962. Previously registered for copyright as an unpublished song June 6, 1962. Introduced by David Brooks (Manager). Alternate title (script): "Prologue."

MANAGER: [*Spoken*]
Good evening, ladies and gentlemen,
I'm the manager,
The manager of this show,
And I'd like to have you know
What the show is all about.
With the title *Mr. President*,
You've wondered, no doubt,
Just who it can be.
Don't jump to conclusions—
It's not who you think.
It's about an American,
Not one of the greats,
But he happens to be President
Of these United States.

[*Sung*]

Just someone doing the best he can,
A simple everyday family man.
Not the Roosevelts,
Not the Trumans,
Not the Eisenhowers, no—
This is not that kinda show.

Not the Kennedys,
No, not the Kennedys,
Just a family of four,
So it couldn't be the Kennedys—
With the Kennedys
There'd have to be more than four.
Just a simple American,
Not one of the greats,
But he happens to be President
Of these United States.

[*Stage business. Scene concludes with:*]

And now I'd like you to take a glance
At a formal, dignified White House
   dance.

LET'S GO BACK TO THE WALTZ

Published. Copyrighted June 5, 1962. Previously registered for copyright as an unpublished song May 14, 1962. Introduced by Nanette Fabray (Nell Henderson) and ensemble.

Let's go back to the waltz,
Take me back to the waltz.
Let's journey back to the past,
Back when the world wasn't
Turning so fast.
When the tempo was slow,
In the long, long ago.
How I yearn,
How I long to return
To the golden days of the waltz.

IN OUR HIDE-AWAY

Published. Copyrighted June 8, 1962. Previously registered for copyright as an unpublished song January 3, 1962. Introduced by Nanette Fabray (Nell Henderson) and Robert Ryan (President Henderson).

In our hide-away,
Far from all the fuss
That bothers us,
We'll hide away,

We two.
In our hide-away
We'll be all alone,
No telephone
To worry me
Or you.
We will have a ball,
Busy doing nothing at all.
In our hide-away,
We will lock the door
And throw away the key—
What a holiday
Our hide-away
Will be!

THE FIRST LADY

Published. Copyrighted June 7, 1962. Previously registered for copyright as an unpublished song January 3, 1962. Published again with a new verse, and a third chorus October 16, 1962. New version previously registered for copyright as an unpublished song October 1, 1962. Introduced by Nanette Fabray (Nell Henderson).

First published version

VERSE

I might have been a teacher,
A job that I'd adore;
I might have been a housewife,
A wife and nothing more.
I might have been an actress,
Who might have played Broadway.
But my husband had to be President,
And what am I today?

CHORUS 1

I'm the First Lady of the land,
The First Lady of the land—
Standing on the receiving line,
Winding up with an aching spine,
Calluses on my receiving hand,
As the First Lady of the land.
For ev'ry week a diff'rent hairdo,
Which means another dress,
Those meetings with committees,
And sparring with the press,
Those dreary formal dinners,
When I stay up till dawn,
Counting all the silver
When the guests have gone.

When they march out in single file
And I must smile, smile, smile,
I'd rather be the second or the third or the fourth
Or the fifth or the sixth or the seventh
Instead of the First Lady of the land.

CHORUS 2

I'm the First Lady of the land,
The First Lady of the land—
Entertaining at lunch or tea,
Do-do-gooders who call on me,
Telling of the noble deeds they've planned
For the First Lady of the land.
And oh, the presents that they send me,
An awful lot of junk,
An un-housebroken poodle,
A dehydrated skunk,
A turkey for Thanksgiving,
Potatoes in a sack,
But when they send a diamond,
I must send it back.
When the whole cabinet arrives
And bring their wives, wives, wives,
I'd rather be the second or the third or the fourth
Or the fifth or the sixth or the seventh
Instead of the First Lady of the land.

Second published version

VERSE

I shouldn't be complaining;
I've got the same address
As Eleanor and Mamie,
As Jacqueline and Bess.
My life is filled with glamour;
I really think it's swell.
Oh, yes, I think it's wonderful—
But then it's also hell.

CHORUS

I'm the First Lady of the land,
A large staff at my command—
Cooks and maids with their ears all bent,
Hearing gossip that they invent,
Writing books that really should be banned
On the First Lady of the land.
I run the White House on a budget
And often I'm in Dutch
And Congress starts to holler,
"She's spending much too much!"
The caviar and vodka
I always get for free—
It's given to me by the Russian embassy.
We send fresh fruit to every land,

But mine is canned, canned, canned.
I'd rather be the second or the third or the fourth
Or the fifth or the sixth or the seventh
Instead of the First Lady of the land.

Show version

VERSE (SAME AS SECOND PUBLISHED VERSION)

CHORUS 1

Being First Lady of the land,
The First Lady of the land—
Standing on the receiving line,
Winding up with an aching spine,
Calluses on my receiving hand,
As the First Lady of the land.
I run the White House on a budget
And often I'm in Dutch
And Congress starts to holler,
"She's spending much too much!"
Those dreary formal dinners
When I stay up till dawn
Counting the silver
When the guests have gone.
When they march out in single file
And I must smile, smile, smile,
I'd rather be the second or the third or the fourth
Or the fifth or the sixth or the seventh
Instead of the First Lady of the land.

CHORUS 2

I'm the First Lady of the land,
A large staff at my command—
Cooks and maids with their ears all bent,
Hearing gossip that they invent,
Writing books that really should be banned
On the First Lady of the land.
And oh, the presents that they send me
An awful lot of junk,
An un-housebroken poodle,
A dehydrated skunk,
A turkey for Thanksgiving,
Potatoes in a sack,
But when they send a diamond,
I must send it back.
When the whole cabinet arrives
And bring their wives, wives, wives,
I'd rather be the second or the third or the fourth
Or the fifth or the sixth or the seventh
Instead of the First Lady of the land.

MEAT AND POTATOES

Published. Copyrighted July 31, 1962. Previously registered for copyright as an unpublished song January 3, 1962. Introduced by Jack Haskell (Pat Gregory) and Stanley Grover (Charley Wayne).

VERSE 1

You're wrong, so wrong,
As wrong as you can be.
I'm not the man for her,
And she's not the girl for me.

CHORUS 1

Meat and potatoes,
Fried eggs and ham,
That's the kinda guy I am.
Meat and potatoes,
Blueberry pie,
That's the kinda guy am I.
She'd be yearning for a soufflé;
I'd be longing for a stew.
The girl that I marry
Will have to be
Meat and potatoes,
Potatoes and meat,
Like me.

VERSE 2

You're wrong, so wrong,
As sure as stars above.
You know the facts of life,
You don't know the facts of love.

CHORUS 2

Meat and potatoes,
Fried eggs and ham,
Mixed with love don't mean a damn.
Meat and potatoes,
Blueberry pie,
Suits a doll who loves a guy.
You'd get used to eating soufflé;
She would learn to cook a stew.
For you're just a human,
She's human too—
Meat and potatoes,
Potatoes and meat, like you.

Show version

CHORUS 2

PAT: [*Verse 1 and chorus 1 as above*]
CHARLEY: Meat and potatoes,
Fried eggs and ham,
Mixed with love don't mean a damn.
You'll find trees that grow in Brooklyn
Growing on Park Avenue.
For you're just a human,
She's human too—
Meat and potatoes,
Potatoes and meat,
Like you.

REPRISE (LAST FOUR LINES)

PAT: You'd not be happy;
I'd never do—
Meat and potatoes
Is not for a girl like you.

I'VE GOT TO BE AROUND

Published. Copyrighted June 7, 1962. Previously registered for copyright as an unpublished song January 3, 1962. Introduced by Jack Haskell (Pat Gregory).

I've got to be around,
I've got to be around;
My job is to be close at hand
And keep my eye on you.
I'd rather spend the day
At home or at a play,
Or any other thing
That would be much more fun to do.
I don't intend to reach the hall of fame
For having been a nursemaid to a dame.
You're always on a cloud,
A thing you're not allowed,
My orders are to see that you keep both feet
On the ground.
Don't ask me not to—
I've got to be around.

THE SECRET SERVICE

Published. Copyrighted June 7, 1962. Previously registered for copyright as an unpublished song January 3, 1962. Introduced by Anita Gillette (Leslie Henderson).

CHORUS 1

The Secret Service
Makes me nervous—
When I am dating,
They are waiting
To observe us.
When I get ready
To hold steady
For the kiss he'll plant,
The Secret Service
Makes me nervous
And I can't.
They're always spying,
No denying;
They're always peeping,
Gumshoe-creeping,
Private-eyeing.
When I'm beginning
To give-inning
Like a maiden aunt,
The Secret Service
Makes me nervous
And I can't.
I've been exposed beyond control,
Just like a goldfish in a bowl.
The Pres'dent's daughter
Must drink water,
No drink of scotch—
She might do what
She hadn't oughter.
When I'm ignited,
So excited
That I start to pant,
The Secret Service
Makes me nervous
When my lamps are lit,
And I say, "This is it"—
The Secret Service
Makes me nervous
And I can't.

CHORUS 2

The Secret Service
Makes me nervous—
Those White House dicks
Get all their kicks
When they observe us.
Just as I wind up,

Make my mind up
Not to say I won't,
The Secret Service
Makes me nervous
And I don't.
When things look rosy,
They get nosey;
They'll say, "There's Tootsie
Playing footsie,
Very cozy."
My pulse goes higher,
I'm on fire,
Shaking at the knees—
The Secret Service
Makes me nervous
And I freeze.
Whatever I may do or say
Will be reported the next day.
When I'm reported,
It's distorted;
They don't see clearly
When I'm merely
Being courted.
When I'm just necking,
Simply pecking
With a Cary Grant,
They stand behind me
To remind me
Who and what I am
When I don't give a damn—
The Secret Service
Makes me nervous
And I can't.

CHORUS ENCORE

The Secret Service
Makes me nervous—
Those dirty minds
Peep through the blinds
When they observe us.
When I'm proposing,
Eyelids closing
In a naughty slant,
The Secret Service
Makes me nervous—
When I lose my quirks,
All set to shoot the works,
The Secret Service
Makes me nervous
And I can't.

IT GETS LONELY IN THE WHITE HOUSE

Published. Copyrighted June 5, 1962. Previously registered for copyright May 14, 1962. Introduced by Robert Ryan (President Henderson).

CHORUS 1

It gets lonely in the White House
When your cares begin,
And the White House is a big place
To be lonely in,
When you're all alone there staring into space
And you wish the man you ran against
Could be there in your place.
It gets lonely in the White House
When you've been attacked
By the loyal opposition
Getting in the act;
If you make the wrong decision
When the final chips are down,
The White House is
The loneliest place in town.

CHORUS 2

It gets lonely in the White House
When you're sitting there
And you have to do your thinking
In a rocking chair,
When some exercise would keep you feeling well
But a journey to a golf course
And the country's gone to hell.
When the budget isn't balanced
And you're in the red
And you feel it would be better
To be dead than red,*
When your speech is optimistic
But the stocks keep tumbling down,
The White House is
The loneliest place in town.

Recently Marc Kirkeby of Sony Music discovered a tape in the Sony vaults that was labeled "Original Cast Recording Session, 7/29/62." Actually, it wasn't an original cast recording but a recording of Irving Berlin singing "It Gets Lonely in the White House." Berlin's recording includes lyrics for a third chorus not on the original cast album or in the published sheet music. This recording and lyric were brought to the editors' attention by Bert Fink of the Rodgers and Hammerstein Organization.

CHORUS 3 (BEGINNING WITH LINE 5)

You give management and labor what they like
Then the bosses push their prices up
And labor goes on strike.
It gets lonely at the White House
When you're in a mess
And you have to answer questions
When you meet the press.
When those cute reporters catch you
With your fancy trousers down,
The White House is
The loneliest place in town.

IS HE THE ONLY MAN IN THE WORLD?

Published. Copyrighted June 5, 1962. Previously registered for copyright as an unpublished song May 25, 1962. Written in 1954, possibly for the unfinished musical *Sayonara*, and registered for copyright as an unpublished song May 14, 1954, under the title "Is She the Only Girl in the World?" Introduced by Nanette Fabray (Nell Henderson) and Anita Gillette (Leslie Henderson). The music for this song was derived from the music of "Where Is the Song of Songs for Me" (page 263).

Is he the only man in the world*
That you will always love and adore?
Look just as good to you in the morning
As he did the night before?
Out of a hundred million or two,
Is he the only one for you?
If he's the only man in the world,
Come rain or shine,
Then he's a man
Like mine.

Alternate version of lines 8–11 as in script and original cast recording:
　　When a bill to lower taxes
　　Must go on the shelf
　　And you'd really like to sign it
　　And pay less yourself

**"Is She the Only Girl in the World?"* substitutes "she" and "girl" for "he" and "man" throughout.*

Additional lyrics
(script and original cast recording)

HALF-CHORUS

NELL: Out of a hundred million or two
　　　Is he the only one for you?

LESLIE: He's not the only man in the world;
　　　　Still he's divine.

NELL: That's not a man
　　　Like mine.

THEY LOVE ME

Published. Copyrighted July 31, 1962. Previously registered for copyright as an unpublished song July 5, 1962. Introduced by Nanette Fabray (Nell Henderson).

VERSE

Oh, what a trip,
What a wonderful trip—
And to think that I was worried
At the start of the trip!
I must confess that I was filled with doubt,
But there was really nothing to worry about.

CHORUS 1

They love me,
They love me—
I'm welcomed ev'rywhere with open arms.
They love me,
They love me—
I never knew I had so many charms.
In Pakistan they took me
Sailing on a lovely lake,
In India they let me see
A mongoose kill a snake,
Because they love me,
They love me,
And they want me to come back again.

CHORUS 2

They love me,
They love me—
In Tokyo they think that I'm a dream.
They claimed me
And named me
America's ambassador supreme.
They always have a banquet
On the day that I arrive;
In Borneo they made me

Eat an octopus alive,
Because they love me,
They love me,
And they want me to come back again.

CHORUS 3

They love me,
They love me—
With ev'ry place I visit it's the same:
They meet me
And greet me
With ev'ry kind of present you could
    name.
A chieftain in New Guinea
With his forehead painted red
Presented me with a poison arrow
And a shrunken head,
Because they love me,
They love me,
And they want me to come back again.

CHORUS 4

They love me,
They love me—
I smile when they present me with the key.
In Thailand,
'Twas my land,
I spent a happy day from two to three.
The day I left Arabia
My seat was full of bumps;
They made me ride a camel
Where I sat between the humps,
Because they love me,
They love me,
And they want me to come back again.

Additional lyrics

And in the Fiji Islands
Where the red banana grows
They tried to pierce a hole
And put a ring right through my nose,
Because they love me,
They love me,
And they want me to come back again.

They love me,
They love me—
With every place I visit it's the same:
They meet me
And greet me
With every kind of present you could
    name.
The elephant I rode upon
When I was in Iraq

Turned up his trunk and sneezed
And I was blown right off his back.

ENSEMBLE: We love you,
           We love you,
           And we want you to come back again.

PIGTAILS AND FRECKLES

Published. Copyrighted November 5, 1962. Introduced by Jack Haskell (Pat Gregory) and Anita Gillette (Leslie Henderson).

CHORUS

Pigtails and freckles,
Braces on your teeth—
Who would have thought
You would turn out so beautiful?
Awkward and bashful,
Scared right from the start—
Who would have thought
You would turn out so smart?
Changes, many changes,
Since I first looked at you;
Funny, very funny,
What a few years can do.
Pigtails and freckles,
Braces on your teeth—
Who would have thought
They'd become so sublime?
I would have thought,
For I thought so
All the time.

Additional lyrics
(script and original cast recording)

CHORUS 2

[*Orchestra plays melody of chorus until:*]

LESLIE: Changes, many changes,
         Every stage I went through—
PAT: Funny, very funny,
         What a few years can do.
         Pigtails and freckles,
         Braces on your teeth—
         Who would have thought
         They'd become so sublime?
         I would have thought,
         For I thought so
         All the time.

DON'T BE AFRAID OF ROMANCE

Published. Copyrighted June 7, 1962. Previously registered for copyright as an unpublished song January 3, 1962. Introduced by Jack Washburn (Yussain Davair).

Don't be afraid of romance,
Don't be so frightened—
Come on, take a chance.
Don't stop to question
Is this the real thing—
Don't be afraid to let go,
Don't run away till you know.
Romance is best while you're young;
That's when the sweetest
Of love songs are sung.
That's when your daydreams
Are filled with moonlight—
Don't be afraid when you start,
You have nothing to lose
But your heart.

LAUGH IT UP

Published. Copyrighted July 31, 1962. Previously registered for copyright as an unpublished song June 6, 1962. Introduced by Nanette Fabray (Nell Henderson), Robert Ryan (President Henderson), Anita Gillette (Leslie Henderson), and Jerry Strickler (Larry Henderson).

CHORUS 1

Though you've lost the race—
Laugh it up, laugh it up.
Wear a happy face—
Laugh it up, laugh it up.
Though your cares and woes
Overflow your cup—
Laugh it up, laugh it up.
Laugh it up.

Don't know how we lost—
Laugh it up, laugh it up.
We were double-crossed—
Laugh it up, laugh it up.
We began all wrong
With that campaign song—
Laugh it up, laugh it up.
Laugh it up.

That phony speech
How he would take care of the old,
And kissing babies
When he had a nasty cold.

Our opponent knew
What the people really needed
When they came with an empty cup;
He was smart enough
To promise more than we did—
Laugh it up, laugh it up,
Laugh it up.

CHORUS 2

When you're feeling down—
Laugh it up, laugh it up.
Like a circus clown—
Laugh it up, laugh it up.
When you're feeling like
A neglected pup—
Laugh it up, laugh it up.
Laugh it up.
If you've got troubles
That depress you night and day,
You'll find a laugh or two
Will chase them all away.

[*Orchestra picks up as song turns into dance.*]

EMPTY POCKETS FILLED WITH LOVE

Published. Copyrighted October 11, 1962. Previously registered for copyright as an unpublished song September 12, 1962. Introduced by Jack Haskell (Pat Gregory) and Anita Gillette (Leslie Henderson). Added to the show during the Boston tryout.

CHORUS 1

Empty pockets
But a heart full of love,
A heart full of love
For you.
Cash, not any,
Not one red penny,
But kisses many
For you.
Empty pockets
But a heart beating fast,
As true as the stars above.

Please say that you'll get by with
Just a guy with
Empty pockets filled with love.

INTERLUDE

I don't want silver,
I don't want gold—
I just want love,
But then I've been told—

CHORUS 2

You can't eat love,
You can't drink love,
You can't wear love
Like you would a gown.
Don't trust love,
For just love
Won't pay for caviar,
Won't buy that motorcar
Or a house in town.
You can't spend love,
You can't lend love,
You must end love
When the chips are down.
Love flies out the window
When there's nothing to eat,
Nothing to drink,
Nothing to wear but a frown
And the chips are down.

[*Chorus 1 and chorus 2 are then sung together as countermelodies.*]

GLAD TO BE HOME

Published. Copyrighted July 31, 1962. Previously registered for copyright as an unpublished song July 11, 1962. Introduced by Nanette Fabray (Nell Henderson) and ensemble.

VERSE

Thanks, many thanks,
For your wonderful welcome today;
I'm not good at making speeches,
But this much I'd like to say:

CHORUS

I'm so glad to be home again;
I promise never to roam again.*
It's oh so good to be home again,
I could cry,
I'm so happy.
I'm back where I had to be,
Awfully glad to be home.
My heart suddenly mends again
Among my neighbors and friends again,
As I start tying loose ends again,
I could cry,
I'm so happy.
There's no need of asking me,
Certainly you can see,
Just why I'm glad to be home,
Why I'm so glad to be home.

YOU NEED A HOBBY

Registered for copyright as an unpublished song October 2, 1962. Introduced by Nanette Fabray (Nell Henderson) and Robert Ryan (President Henderson). Added during the Boston tryout. According to Boston critic Elliot Norton (Boston *Advertiser*, October 25, 1962), Berlin composed it "while walking across the Public Garden between the Colonial Theater and the Ritz Carlton Hotel." Norton added, "Berlin found the words and the melody in a few moments and was singing them as he walked. He didn't need a piano."

INTRODUCTION—REPRISE OF "LAUGH IT UP"

When you're feeling down—
Laugh it up, laugh it up.
Like a circus clown—
Laugh it up, laugh it up.
When your cares and woes
Overflow your cup—
Laugh it up, laugh it up,
Laugh it up.

VERSE

PRESIDENT: You couldn't wait until the day
            When I was through,
            But doing nothing
            Is the hardest thing to do.

_____

Alternate line, as in script and original cast recording:
    With no more Capitol dome again.

NELL: That's true,
And I know what's wrong with you.

CHORUS 1

You need a hobby,
A hobby.
A man who's doing nothing
Needs a hobby—
Fly fishing
In streams and brooks,
Birdwatching,
Or collecting books.*
Go in for rowing,
Glass blowing,
Or keeping your eye
On the ball;
And when you're tired
Working at your hobby,
Come home—home—
To the best hobby of all.

CHORUS 2

NELL: You need a hobby.
PRESIDENT: What hobby?
NELL: Observing cuties
In a hotel lobby.
PRESIDENT: Teddy Roosevelt collected heads.
NELL: George Washington just slept in beds.
Go in for dancing.
PRESIDENT: Dancing?
NELL: Yes, dancing!

[Orchestral passage, followed by:]

And when you're tired
Working at your hobby,
Come home—home—
To the best hobby of all.

THE WASHINGTON TWIST

Published. Copyrighted July 31, 1962. Previously registered for copyright as an unpublished song July 5, 1962. Introduced by Anita Gillette (Leslie Henderson).

*On the original cast recording lines 5–8 are:
Thomas Edison
Played with lights;
Ben Franklin
Fooled around with kites.

CHORUS 1

Doing the Washington Twist,
Doing the twist with a twist—
No one is set
Till they finally get
On the President's favorite list.
President doubts
While the ins and the outs
Keep on doing
The Washington Twist.

CHORUS 2

Gentlemen loaded with charm,
Seemingly meaning no harm,
But while they're there
You're becoming aware
That they're quietly twisting your arm,
Gentle in tone
While promoting a loan,
Which is part of
The Washington Twist.

CHORUS 3

Congressmen's lips that are puck'ed,
Waiting for plums to be plucked,
Legal concerns
Making out their returns
With expenses they'd like to deduct,
Drinking a toast
To the host with the most
While they're doing
The Washington Twist.

**Alternate version
(script and original cast recording):**

CHORUS 1

Doing the Washington Twist—
This is a twist with a twist.
He was beguiled
By the President's child;
I was always the first on his list.
Now he begins
Getting in with the ins,
Which is part of
The Washington Twist.

CHORUS 2

Gentlemen loaded with charm,
Seemingly meaning no harm,
But while they're there
You're becoming aware
That they're quietly twisting your arm,

Drinking a toast
To the host with the most,
Which is part of
The Washington Twist.

THE ONLY DANCE I KNOW

Published. Copyrighted July 31, 1962. Previously registered for copyright as an unpublished song June 1, 1962. Introduced by Wisa D'Orso (Princess Kyra). Copyrighted under the title "Song for Belly Dancer."

VERSE

My youth was spent
In the Orient,
Where they never taught me to waltz.
You'd be surprised—
When I exercised,
It was never done to a waltz.
It was done like this,
But never to a waltz.

CHORUS 1

In ancient Siam,
Women like I am,
Indoors or on the street,
No woman dances with her feet.
Egyptian, Persian,
Only one version,
No other stands a chance—
Feet are for walking, not for dance.
To an Oriental fiddle
You can see them shake their middle;
The feet don't mean a thing—
Middles are all they swing.
Even an Egyptian mummy
Wiggles her tummy,
Wiggles it so and so—
That is the only dance I know.

CHORUS 2

A Greek or Roman
With an abdomen
Could learn to do it too;
They all could do it—so could you.
With Cleopatra,
Even Sinatra
Would have enjoyed the view.
He would enjoy it, so would you.
You don't need an Arthur Murray;
Just a fringe that's on a surrey,

Will satisfy your needs,
Dancing between the beads.
Ev'rybody shake your torso,
Sexy but more so,
Shake it, come on, let's go—
Let's do the only dance I know.

[*The script and the original cast recording omit the first eight lines of chorus 2.*]

I'M GONNA GET HIM

Published. Copyrighted July 31, 1962. Previously registered for copyright as an unpublished song May 10, 1956, when it was intended for *Sentimental Guy*. Introduced by Nanette Fabray (Nell Henderson) and Anita Gillette (Leslie Henderson).

VERSE

When I was a kid
And I wanted a doll,
I got it.
Don't ask how I did,
But when I was a kid
And I wanted a doll,
I got it.
I carefully laid out a plan;
When I was a kid
'Twas a doll,
And now it's a man.

CHORUS 1

I'm gonna get him,
I'm gonna get him—
Instead of giving up and throwing in the tow'l,
I'm gonna keep on fighting, fair or foul,
Until I get him.
I'm gonna get him—
I'm gonna wear my jewels and my ermine wrap,
And if I have to drop my shoulder strap,
I'm gonna get him,
I'm gonna get him.
And when I've got him where I think he ought
    to be,
I'm gonna love him, love him—
My mission in life will be to love him
Until he loves me.

CHORUS 2

I'm gonna get him,
I'm gonna get him—

I'll back him in a corner till he squirms and twists,
And if I must put handcuffs on his wrists,
I'm gonna get him,
I'm gonna get him.
He'll know the facts of life, and when he
    understands,
I'll put a shotgun in my father's hands,
And that'll get him.
I'm gonna get him,
And when I've got him where I think he ought
    to be,
I'm gonna hug him, hug him,
I'll hug him, and if I have to slug him,
He's gonna love me.

Show version
(script and original cast recording)*

VERSE

NELL: When you were a kid
    And you wanted a doll,
    You got it.
    You knew what to do,
    And before you were through,
    When you wanted a doll,
    You got it.
    You carefully laid out a plan—
    When you were a kid
    'Twas a doll,
    And now it's a man.

CHORUS 1

    Go out and get him,
    You gotta get him—
    Instead of giving up and throwing in the
        tow'l,
    You've got to keep on fighting, fair or foul,
    Until you get him.
LESLIE: I'm gonna get him.
    I'm gonna wear my jewels and my ermine
        wrap,
    And if I have to drop my shoulder strap,
    I'm gonna get him.
NELL: Go out and get him.
    And when you've got him where you want
        him jumping through,
    You gotta love him.
LESLIE: Love him.
NELL: Your mission in life
    Must be to love him
    Until he loves you.

CHORUS 2

LESLIE: I'm gonna get him,
    I'm gonna get him—
    I'll back him in a corner till he squirms
        and twists,
    And if I must put handcuffs on his wrists,
    I'm gonna get him.
NELL: Go out and get him.
LESLIE: Suppose he isn't int'rested in wedding
        bands?
NELL: I'll put a shotgun in your father's hands
    And that'll get him.
LESLIE: [*spoken*]
    Yeah, that'll get him.
NELL: And when you've got him
    Where you want him
    Jumping through—
LESLIE: I'm gonna hug him,
    Hug him.
NELL: You hug him,
    And if you have to slug him,
    He's gotta love you.

CHORUS 3

BOTH: Get him, get him, get him—
    Get him, get him, get him—
    That's just what to do.
NELL: Go out and get him.
LESLIE: I'm gonna get him.
NELL: Instead of giving up and saying that
        you're through,
    You gotta chase him
    Till he catches you.
LESLIE: I'm gonna get him.
NELL: Go out and get him.
LESLIE: I'll plan a private dinner
        at a small hotel,
    And when the house detective comes, I'll
        yell,
    And that'll get him.
NELL: Yes, that'll get him.
    And when you've got him
    Where you want him
    Jumping through—
LESLIE: I'm gonna pet him.
    Pet him.
NELL: And if he starts making passes,
    Let him
    Until he loves you.
BOTH: Get him, get him, get him—
    Get him, get him, get him—
    That's just what to do.

On the recordings, lines 1–13 of chorus 2 are followed by the ending (from line 18) of chorus 3.

THIS IS A GREAT COUNTRY

Published. Copyrighted July 31, 1962. Previously registered for copyright as an unpublished song February 14, 1962. Introduced by Robert Ryan (President Harrison) and entire company. Except for an identical title, this is not the same number as the 1940 song intended for *Holiday Inn* (1942); see page 355.

VERSE

Patriotism has gone out of fashion;
We seem to think our patriotic days are dead.
We used to sing of our homeland with passion,
But now we seem to shy away from it instead.
I think it's time to hit the nail right on the head.

CHORUS

This is a great country,
A great country,
So let's shout it clear and loud.
Take a look
In your hist'ry book
And you'll see why we should be proud.
Hats off to America,
The home of the free and the brave—
If this is flag waving,
Flag waving,
Do you know of a better flag to wave?
You've seen the characters in our plot,*
And you have recognized who they're not.
Not the Roosevelts,
Not the Trumans,
Not the Eisenhowers, no—
This was not that kind of show.
Not the Kennedys,
No, not the Kennedys,
Just an ordinary President singing:
Hats off to America,
The home of the free and the brave—
If this is flag waving
Flag waving,
Do you know of a better flag to wave?

ONCE EV'RY FOUR YEARS

Published. Copyrighted June 6, 1962. Previously registered for copyright as an unpublished song May 25,

1962. Introduced during the Boston tryout by the ensemble. Dropped from the show before the Washington tryout.

CHORUS 1

Once ev'ry four years,
Once ev'ry four years,
We the people
Are the finest people,
The grandest people,
The divinest people.
Once ev'ry four years,
When election appears,
We crawl out of our holes,
Go down to the polls;
They're waiting to give three cheers.
Once, only once, only
Once ev'ry four years.

CHORUS 2

Once ev'ry four years,
Once ev'ry four years—
We the people
Are the frozen people,
But when they need us,
We're the chosen people.
Once ev'ry four years,
When election appears—
When a President runs,
We're favorite sons;
The rest of the time, Bronx cheers.
Once, only once, only
Once ev'ry four years.

POOR JOE

Published. Copyrighted July 31, 1962. Previously registered for copyright as an unpublished song May 9, 1962. Dropped from the score before the Boston tryout.

VERSE 1

Listen to the story
Of a man named Joe,
A man who ruled the Russians
Many years ago,
A leader who was feared by all
The folks he led
Till the morning when they suddenly
Pronounced him dead.

CHORUS 1

Poor Joe, poor Joe—
Just exactly how it happened
We will never know.
But they gave him such a fun'ral,
Like you've never seen,
And they placed him in a tomb
Beside his pal Leneen—
Joe, poor, poor Joe.

VERSE 2

People came to see him
In the tomb each day
Until they got a message
Signed by Mister K.
He called a special meeting
And he told the clan
That their ever-lovin' Joseph
Was a bad, bad man.

CHORUS 2

Poor Joe, poor Joe—
They decided at the meeting
That he'd have to go.
There were some who thought
They treated Joseph very mean
When they took him from the tomb
Beside his pal Leneen—
Joe, poor, poor Joe.

VERSE 3

After they removed him
From his spacious tomb,
They placed him in a field
Where there was not much room.
A narrow piece of ground
Is all the Russians gave,
Just in case he thought
Of turning over in his grave.

CHORUS 3

Poor Joe, poor Joe—
Now he's resting very lonely
Where the daisies grow,
Yes, he's resting very lonely
Where the grass is green,
And he's waiting the arrival
Of his pal Leneen—
Joe, poor, poor Joe.

Last 14 lines not included in original cast recording.

ANYBODY CAN WRITE
(Revised Version)

Revised version of lyric written in 1956 for *Sentimental Guy;* see page 453. Registered for copyright as an unpublished song July 31, 1962. Typed lyric sheet of revised version dated May 3, 1962. Dropped from *Mr. President.*

VERSE

You can't be a banker unless you can count.
You can't be a jockey unless you can mount.
You can't make good lager unless you can brew.
There's only one thing anyone can do:

CHORUS 1

Anybody can write,
Anybody can write—
A pencil or pen,
Some paper, and then
You just sit down and write.
Spend a weekend in Rome;
Write a book when you're home.
It's easy to write about the trips that you've had;
You just put two simple words on top of a pad—
"Chapter One"—and when that's done,
Just write, write.
If you get that empty feeling
Looking at the ceiling,
Take a rest, then go right back and write.

CHORUS 2

Anybody can write,
Anybody can write—
If you get the call,
The call to tell all,
You just sit down and write.
Many persons of note
Published books that they wrote:
There's Truman and Eisenhower, Kennedy too,
There's Goldwater, Nixon, and that's only a few.
Sherman Adams—even madams—write, write;
Almost every politician
Writes a first edition,
Just to prove anybody can write.

One-chorus version

VERSE (SAME AS EARLIER VERSION)

CHORUS

Anybody can write,
Anybody can write—
A pencil or pen,
Some paper, and then
You just sit down and write.
Many persons of note
Published books that they wrote:
There's Truman and Eisenhower, Kennedy too,
There's Goldwater, Nixon, and that's only a few.
Sherman Adams—even madams—write, write;
Almost every politician
Writes a first edition,
Just to prove anybody can write.

Show version 1

[*The* PRESIDENT *turns down writing his memoirs. The* EDITOR *asks why.* PRESIDENT *answers, "I'll tell you in three words. I can't write." The* EDITOR *says, "Oh, yes you can."*]

VERSE (SAME AS EARLIER VERSION)

[*Sung by* EDITOR]

CHORUS 1

   EDITOR: Anybody can write,
      Anybody can write—
      A pencil or pen,
      Some paper, and then
      You just sit down and write.
PRESIDENT: I've got so much to say;
      You must show me the way.
   EDITOR: It's easy—just write a book with
      plenty of heart.
PRESIDENT: I know what you're telling me, but
      where do I start?
   EDITOR: Chapter One—and when that's done,
      Write, write.
PRESIDENT: If I get that empty feeling
      Looking at the ceiling?
   EDITOR: Take a rest and go right back and
      write.

[PRESIDENT *takes pad and pencil.*]

CHORUS 2

PRESIDENT: Anybody can write,
      Anybody can write—
      A pencil or pen,
      Some paper and then
      You just sit down and write.
   EDITOR: Many persons of note
      Published books that they wrote.

PRESIDENT: There's Truman and Eisenhower,
      Kennedy too;
      There's Goldwater, Nixon—
   EDITOR: And that's only a few.
      Sherman Adams, even madams,
      Write, write.
PRESIDENT: If my story could be brighter?
   EDITOR: Tell it to a writer.
    BOTH: Which is one way to prove you can
      write.

Show version 2

[*The* PRESIDENT *turns down writing his memoirs. The* EDITOR *exits.* NELL *enters. She asks what the* EDITOR *wanted.* PRESIDENT *says, "He wanted me to write my memoirs."* NELL *is delighted. This will give him something to do.* PRESIDENT *says he turned it down.* NELL *asks why. The* PRESIDENT *explains in three simple words—"I can't write."* NELL *says, "Yes, you can," and goes into verse.*]

VERSE (SAME AS EARLIER VERSION)

[*Sung by* NELL]

CHORUS 1

    NELL: Anybody can write,
      Anybody can write—
      A pencil or pen,
      Some paper, and then,
      You just sit down and write.
PRESIDENT: I've got so much to say,
      But I don't know the way.
    NELL: It's easy—just write a book with
      plenty of heart.
PRESIDENT: I know what you're telling me, but
      where do I start?
    NELL: Chapter One—and when that's done,
      Write, write.
PRESIDENT: If I get that empty feeling
      Looking at the ceiling?
    NELL: Take a rest and go right back and
      write.

[PRESIDENT *takes pad and pencil.*]

CHORUS 2

PRESIDENT: Anybody can write,
      Anybody can write—
      A pencil and pen,
      Some paper and then—

[*He throws down pencil and gives up.* NELL *continues to encourage him.*]

NELL: Many persons of note
Published books that they wrote.
PRESIDENT: There's Truman and Eisenhower,
Kennedy too;
There's Goldwater, Nixon—
NELL: And that's only a few.
PRESIDENT: Sherman Adams, even madams, write.
NELL: Right!
PRESIDENT: If my story could be brighter?
NELL: Tell it to a writer—
BOTH: Which will prove anybody can write.

IF YOU HAVEN'T GOT AN EAR FOR MUSIC

Published 1996 in the songbook *Unsung Irving Berlin*. Sung by Liz Larsen on the 1995 album *Unsung Irving Berlin* (Varèse Sarabande). Previously registered for copyright as an unpublished song January 3, 1962. Not used in show.

CHORUS 1

What
Good
Is
A
Fancy motor car?
If you haven't got an ear for music,
You haven't got a thing at all.
What
Good
Is
A
Ton of caviar?
If you haven't got an ear for music,
You haven't got a thing at all.
What good is a sack of gold
If a jazz band leaves you cold?
What
Good
Is
A
Mansion large or small?
If you haven't got an ear for music,
You haven't got a thing at all.

CHORUS 2

What
Good
Is

A
Sable or a mink?
If you haven't got an ear for music,
You haven't got a thing at all.
What
Good
Is
That
Extra midnight drink?
If you haven't got an ear for music,
You haven't got a thing at all.
When I journey to the moon,
I won't go without a tune.
What
Good
Is
A
Party or a ball?
If you haven't got an ear for music,
You haven't got a thing at all,
You haven't got a thing at all,
You haven't got a thing at all.

I'VE GOT AN EAR FOR MUSIC

Typed lyric sheet dated October 23, 1961. Although only the titles are similar, this number could have been a forerunner to "If You Haven't Got an Ear for Music."

I haven't got a head for figures,
I couldn't add a simple sum,
But I've got an ear for music
And I can make things hum.
I couldn't dig those politicians,
I don't know if they're right or wrong;
But I've got an ear for music,
And life is one sweet song.
Music that comes from the sweet violin,
Music that's played by a band—
I'd get along in Greece or China
Or all the other foreign lands,
For I've got an ear for music,
A language everybody understands,
Everybody understands.

WORDS WITHOUT MUSIC

Typed lyric sheet dated February 9, 1962. No music is known to survive. Possibly considered for *Mr. President*.

You speak to me
In words without music,
Beautiful words,
But words without music.
You quote poetry all night long,
But a poem is not a song,
Just words,
Words without music,
Beautiful words,
But words without music.

NEPOTISM

Typed lyric sheet dated October 30, 1961. An earlier, less developed version is dated October 20, 1961. Amy Asch, archivist for the Irving Berlin Music Company, believes that the number was intended for the character of Yussain in *Mr. President*. Berlin describes it at the top of the October 30 lyric sheet as a "possible song for the 'Rubirosa' character."

CHORUS 1

My father is the leader of my country;
My brother is the chief of the police;
My uncle is commander of the army;
The taxes are collected by my niece;
My nephew is in charge of all the air corps;
My cousin runs the navy on the sea—
On the money in the mint
There's a motto that we print:
"For the people
And by the people
And for my family."

CHORUS 2

My mother is in charge of education;
My sister runs the big electric plant;
Her husband watches over the elections,
And all the votes are counted by my aunt.
We never had an argument with labor;
They never ask a raise in salary—
For they seem to understand
We're a patriotic land,
For the people

And by the people
And for my family.

Earlier version

My father runs the country;
My brother runs the police;
The mint that prints the money
Is run by my favorite niece.
My brother runs the army;
But I disappear
To see what I can see and I can hear.

WHY SHOULDN'T
I LIKE ME?

Typed lyric sheet dated January 24, 1962. Intended for
the character of Yussain in *Mr. President*. Not used. No
music is known to survive.

I've got charm,
I am neat,
Perfect manners when I eat,

So why shouldn't I like me?
I've got poise,
I've got style,
And the most infectious smile,
So why shouldn't I like me?
If my shape isn't ugly and fat
And I'm glad to admit it,
What's wrong with that?
If I sold motor cars,
I would praise them to the stars,
So why shouldn't I praise me—
Me, me, me
Why shouldn't I like me?

OVERLEAF: *MGM production chief Robert Weitman,
Irving Berlin, producer Arthur Freed, and director
Vincente Minnelli*

SAY IT WITH MUSIC
1963–1969

SAY IT WITH MUSIC (1963–1969)

Say It with Music was Berlin's last score for a major project. Written for an unproduced Metro-Goldwyn-Mayer film, it was begun in 1963 and came to an unhappy end after years of delay and uncertainty, in the spring of 1969. Arthur Freed was the producer, and for much of the time Vincente Minnelli was to have been the director. Choreographer Jerome Robbins, arranger Roger Edens, and director Blake Edwards also were associated with *Say It with Music* at various points during its troubled odyssey. A constantly changing projected cast included, among others, Julie Andrews, Frank Sinatra, Sophia Loren, Robert Goulet, Shirley MacLaine, and Fred Astaire (though not all at the same time). Arthur Laurents was the first book writer, and most of Berlin's songs were written for Laurents's version of the script. Other librettists who worked on the project were Leonard Gershe, Garson Kanin, Betty Comden and Adolph Green, and George Wells. As executives at MGM changed, interest in film musicals waned and the popular-music world altered dramatically in the age of the Beatles. Unhappily, Berlin ended his film-musical-writing career much as he had begun it with *Reaching for the Moon* in 1930—with a major disappointment. For "Love Leads to Marriage," see page 451.

ALWAYS THE SAME

Registered for copyright as an unpublished song July 26, 1963; again on August 12, 1963; and on November 18, 1963. Typed lyric sheet is dated June 20, 1963.

VERSE

I don't know who said it
Or from where it came,
But there's an old saying,
The one where they claim
The more things change,
The more they remain the same.

CHORUS 1

The music may be diff'rent,
The lyrics and the name,
The singer may be diff'rent,
But the song is always the same.
The season may be diff'rent
When young hearts burst into flame,

But the mad desire
That starts the fire
Is the same,
Always the same.

CHORUS 2

The picture may be diff'rent,
The colors and the frame,
The artist may be diff'rent,
But the girl is always the same.
The distance may be oceans
Between a queen and a dame,
But that certain thing
That makes them swing
Is the same,
Always the same.

CHORUS 3

The hunting may be diff'rent,
The hunter and the game,
The jungle may be diff'rent,
But the chase is always the same.
The waters may be diff'rent,
With every fish you could name,
But the wish you wish
To catch that fish
Is the same,
Always the same.

CHORUS 4

The countries may be diff'rent,
The language and the name,
The leaders may be diff'rent,
But the people always the same.
The speeches may be diff'rent
When they're out searching for fame,
But the goods they sell,
The lies they tell
Are the same,
Always the same.

CHORUS 5

The bankers may be diff'rent,
The friendship that they claim,
The interest may be diff'rent,
But collat'ral always the same.
The miners may be diff'rent,
In search of gold dust to claim,
But you'll find the lust
To get that dust
Is the same,
Always the same.

Alternate lyrics

[*Another undated lyric with the same title as the more developed, finished number.*]

Alarm clocks may be different,
No matter if they came
From Tiffany's or from Macy's;
Getting up is always the same.
The bugler may be different,
The guy who gets all the blame,
But the sleepy yawn
At break of dawn
Is the same,
Always the same.

IT'S ALWAYS THE SAME

Registered for copyright as an unpublished song July 1, 1963. Typed lyric sheet dated June 25, 1963. Copyist (Helmy Kresa) piano-vocal score dated June 28, 1963.

CHORUS

The music is different,
The words and the name,
The singer is diff'rent,
But the song is the same.
The color keeps changing
From silver to flame,
But that mad desire
That can start a fire
In a royal queen or a dame
Never is diff'rent,
It's always the same

IT'S THE SAME IN EVERY LANGUAGE

Although this song was not registered for copyright until November 30, 1977, the typed lyric sheet is dated July 12, 1963. One arrangement of the music and lyrics was dated December 6, 1965.

VERSE

He was handsome,
So attractive,
And oh, what a lot of fun!
So intelligent,
And quite a linguist,
But he spoke ev'ry language
But one.

CHORUS 1

He spoke French, he spoke German,
He spoke Greek and Japanese;
He spoke Dutch, he spoke Spanish,
He spoke Welsh and Portuguese.
He spoke Czech, he spoke Russian—
But I was left behind,
For he couldn't speak English,
So I couldn't tell him
What was on my mind.

CHORUS 2

It's the same
In ev'ry language;
It's the same
In ev'ry land.
It's the same
In ev'ry nation
Without conversation
You can always,
Always,
Make them understand.

[*Both choruses are then sung together as counter-melodies.*]

Alternate version for male, July 12, 1963

VERSE

She's so beautiful,
And so attractive,
The kind of girl who could be lots of fun.
So intelligent,
And quite a linguist,
But she speaks every language but one.

CHORUS 1

She speaks French, she speaks German,
She speaks Greek and Japanese;
She speaks Dutch, she speaks Spanish,
She speaks Welsh and Portuguese.
She speaks Czech, she speaks Russian—
But I'll be left behind,
For she can't speak English,

So I just can't tell her
What's on my mind.

CHORUS 2

It's the same
In ev'ry language;
It's the same
In ev'ry land.
It's the same
In ev'ry nation—
Without conversation
You can always,
Always,
Make them understand.

[*Both choruses are then sung together as counter-melodies.*]

A MAN TO COOK FOR

Registered for copyright as an unpublished song August 5, 1963. Copyist (Helmy Kresa) piano-vocal score without lyrics dated July 30, 1963. Typed lyric sheet dated July 30, 1963.

VERSE

Year after year,
I seek a career
To brighten my life.
And it appears
The best of careers
Is being a wife.

CHORUS 1

I look for
A man to cook for,
A cozy nook for
The man I love.
I mean the good old-fashioned type
Who'll spend his nights at home
With slippers and pipe.
The one man,
Not just a fun man;
A hit-and-run man
I couldn't see.
And so I look for
A man to cook for—
That's the only man for me.

CHORUS 2

BOY: Look for
A man to cook for,
A cozy nook for
The man you love.
I mean the good old-fashioned type
Who spends his nights at home
With slippers and pipe.
The one man,
Not just a fun man;
A hit-and-run man
Would never do.
Go out and look for
A man to cook for—
That's the only man for you.
GIRL: Look for
A man to cook for,
A cozy nook for
The man I love.
And that's exactly what I plan,
But then until I find
That wonderful man . . .

[*Segues directly to "A Guy on Monday."*]

A GUY ON MONDAY

Registered for copyright as an unpublished song August 5, 1963. Typed lyric sheet dated July 30, 1963. This song was revised to become "One-Man Woman."

There'll be a guy on Monday,
Another guy on Tuesday,
And Wednesday will be Men's Day for me.
There'll be a guy on Thursday,
Another guy on Friday—
Yes, Friday will be my day for a spree.
And what a day
Will be Saturday
When I'm out with the choicest of men!
But there'll be no guys on Sunday;
I'll sit home on Sunday—
But on Monday I'll start all over again.

ONE-MAN WOMAN

Registered for copyright as an unpublished song August 19, 1963. Typed lyric sheet dated July 30, 1963.

This song was derived from "A Man to Cook For" and "A Guy on Monday."

VERSE

I look for
A man to cook for,
A cozy nook for
The man I love.
Yes, that's exactly
What I plan;
But then until I find
That wonderful man—

CHORUS

There'll be a guy on Monday,
Another guy on Tuesday,
And Wednesday will be Men's Day for me.
There'll be a guy on Thursday,
Another guy on Friday—
Yes, Friday will be my day for a spree.
And what a day
Will be Saturday,
And on Sunday there'll be someone sublime;
I'll be a one-man woman,
A one-man woman—
That is, one man,
One man at a time.

THE TEN BEST UNDRESSED WOMEN

Registered for copyright as an unpublished song July 31, 1963. Typed lyric sheet dated July 24, 1963. Music sketch is dated July 19, 1963.

I lost my heart
To a girl who is one of
The ten best
Undressed
Women.
It's very smart
For a girl to be one of
The ten best
Undressed
Women.
I've never seen her
With her ribbons and bows on;
I wonder what she looks like
With her clothes on.
But with her charms unfurled,

She's one of the
Ten best
Undressed
Women in the world.

THE PX

Registered for copyright as an unpublished song October 21, 1963. Typed lyric sheet dated September 27, 1963. This song was intended for Sophia Loren. According to a note on the typed lyric, "This is sung in Italy after the Lieutenant leaves her in bed and she reminds him not to forget to stop at the P.X."

VERSE

War would be hell for a girl like me
Living in occupied Italy;
We all would be perfect wrecks
If it wasn't for
A certain store
That the soldiers call the PX.

CHORUS 1

A soldier needs love;
A woman must eat.
It's very romantic
Whenever they meet;
But what's on her mind
While she necks?
The PX,
The PX,
The PX.
She'll kiss him goodnight;
His head's in a whirl.
The soldier is happy,
And so is the girl—
Providing
The soldier boy checks
The PX,
The PX,
The PX.
A chocolate bar,
A cigarette
For every kiss he's taken;
A jar of jam
And powdered eggs
For your breakfast
When you waken—
With bacon.
Before they can fight,
Those darling GIs

Must go to the army
To get their supplies—
But where do they go
To get sex?
The PX,
The PX,
The PX.

SECOND HALF OF CHORUS 2

He'll call at night
And bring a steak;
Your heart begins to flutter.
You're in his arms;
He whispers low,
"Won't you kindly close the shutter—
Here's butter."
A soldier boy knows
He always can get
A kiss that is dry
Or a kiss that is wet,
But they couldn't even
Get sex*
Without the PX,
The PX,
The PX.

Alternate version

VERSE

War is hell
For girls like me;
We'd all be perfect wrecks
If it wasn't for
A certain store
That the soldiers call the PX.

CHORUS

A soldier needs love;
A woman must eat.
It's very romantic
Whenever they meet;
But what's on her mind
While she necks?
The PX,
The PX,
The PX.
She'll rest in his arms;
His head's in a whirl.

---

*Alternate version of line:
  Get pecks [she illustrates]

The soldier is happy,
And so is the girl—
Providing
The soldier boy checks
The PX,
The PX,
The PX.
A chocolate bar,
Some cigarettes,
A pound or two of butter,
A can of beans,
A frozen steak,
And her heart begins to flutter—
Butter!
Before they can fight,
Those darling GIs
Must go to the army
To get their supplies—
But where do they go
To get sex?
The PX,
The PX,
The PX.

OUTSIDE OF LOVING YOU, I LIKE YOU

Registered for copyright as an unpublished song July 12, 1963. Typed lyric sheet dated June 28, 1963. Sung by Emily Loesser on the 1995 album *Unsung Irving Berlin* (Varèse Sarabande).

Outside of loving you,
I like you,
And liking you makes me
Love you more.
You're fun to be with
And disagree with
While drinking cocktails
Or sipping tea with.
Outside of kissing you,
I like you;
It sweetens the kisses
I adore.
I love
Making love to you,
But after the kissing ends,
Outside of sweethearts,
We're friends.

OUTSIDE OF LOVING HIM

A revision of "Outside of Loving You, I Like You." Typed lyric sheet dated June 28, 1979.

Outside of loving him,
I like him,
And liking him
Makes me love him more.
He's fun to be with
To disagree with
And wind up closer
Than we were before.
We fight and break up,
Then kiss and make up,
But before the loving
And kissing ends,
I like him,
I like him—
Outside of lovers,
We're friends.

WHISPER IT

Published 1996 in the songbook *Unsung Irving Berlin*. Previously registered for copyright as an unpublished song July 15, 1963. Typed lyric sheet dated July 10, 1963. Sung by Gloria Crampton on the 1995 album *Unsung Irving Berlin* (Varèse Sarabande).

You love me and I don't doubt it,
But you don't have to shout it;
Whisper it—
Whisper it in my ear.
I just love to hear you tell it,
But you don't have to yell it;
Whisper it—
Whisper it in my ear.
Pin that medal
Of merit on my chest,
But please soft-pedal
The talking bit
That goes with it.
You can shout from all the housetops,
But I won't hear
Unless you whisper it, baby,
Whisper it in my ear.

I USED TO PLAY IT BY EAR

Published 1996 in the songbook *Unsung Irving Berlin*. Previously registered for copyright as an unpublished song May 26, 1965, and again on June 18, 1965. Typed lyric sheet dated May 20, 1965. Introduced by Robert Goulet on Ed Sullivan's May 5, 1968, televised tribute to Berlin, marking the composer-lyricist's eightieth birthday.

I used to play it by ear,
That wonderful thing called love.
I never believed I'd fall in love—
Not me.
I used to think
That those who kissed and ran away
Would live to kiss again
Another day.
I used to laugh at romance,
But now that I know the score,
But now that the one I've waited for
Is here,
I know that this is the song
That the angels sing,
This is the once-in-a-lifetime thing,
This is the real McCoy,
And it's crystal clear,
What's deep in your heart
Can't be played by ear.

Earlier version

I used to play it by ear—
I've had an affair or two
But never would follow through,
Not me.
I used to think
That those who kissed and ran away
Would live to kiss again
Another day.
I used to laugh at romance;
I played with it like a toy.
But now that the real McCoy
Is here,
I know that this is the song
That the angels sing,
This is the once-in-a-lifetime thing,
This is the thing called love,
And it's crystal clear,
What's deep in your heart
Can't be played by ear.

I WANNA DANCE WITH THE GIRL IN MY ARMS

Typed lyric sheet dated January 19, 1966. No music is known to survive. Intended for Fred Astaire, who at one time was being considered for *Say It with Music*. According to a note by Berlin on his typed lyric sheet:

> Possible song for Astaire in *Say It with Music* to introduce some of the songs I had in the movies I wrote for him and his dancing partners—"Cheek to Cheek," "Let's Face the Music and Dance," "Top Hat, White Tie and Tails," "Change Partners," "Let Yourself Go," "It Only Happens When I Dance with You," etc.
>
> Astaire is in a discotheque where a lot of teenagers are doing the latest dance—The Frug, The Watusi, The Mashed Potato, etc.
>
> We then cue into the following:—

VERSE

The frug, the swim, the jerk, the monkey
As dances aren't much.
I miss the dance the way we did it
When the dancers used to touch.

CHORUS

I wanna dance
With the girl in my arms—
I wanna hold her
And feel all her charms.
I wanna hold a dancing Venus
With just a postage stamp between us.
Instead of twisting,
Rock-and-rolling miles apart,
I wanna dance
Cheek to cheek and heart to heart.

MUSICAL WOODMAN

Written to fit the countermelody ("Musical Demon") to "Play a Simple Melody." Typed lyric sheet dated August 2, 1963.

Musical woodman,
Mister Benjamin Goodman,
Won't you play me some jazz—
A composition that has

The snappy rhythm of jazz?
Oh, Mister Scotty Fitzgerald,
Write a piece for the *Herald*—
On the very first page,
A piece that tells of the age,
The age of wonderful jazz.

SAY IT WITH MUSIC

A new version for *Say It with Music*.

Why don't you
Say it with music,
Beautiful music?
You'll find that in every land
That's one language they understand—
A melody mellow
Played on a cello,
And while she listens you'll find
She knows exactly what's on your mind.

Songs of 1960–1988

YOUR LOVE IS SHOWING

Typed lyric sheet dated January 12, 1961. No music is known to survive.

Your love is showing.
I can see stardust in your eyes.
I can hear music in your sighs.
Funny how you don't realize
Your love is showing.
You're sailing along on a cloud.
You're all by yourself in a crowd.
You listen to compliments,
Warm and endearing.
You listen attentively,
But you're not hearing.
Your love is showing,
Which anyone can see.
Your love is showing,
I hope it's for me.

PUSH THE TABLE AWAY

Typed lyric sheet dated August 21, 1961. No music is known to survive.

If you want to get thinner,
Before you finish your dinner
Push the table away.
If you're pleasingly plump,
Don't be a chump
And eat everything on your tray.
Don't be a glutton
If you can't see your belly button;
Push the table away.

Harold Arlen, Adolph Green, Betty Comden, Jimmy McHugh, Ethel Merman, Irving Berlin, Ed Sullivan, Dorothy Fields, Stanley Adams, Burton Lane, Jule Styne, Sammy Cahn, and Noble Sissle celebrate Irving Berlin's eightieth birthday on the Ed Sullivan Show.

HOME AGAIN

Registered for copyright as an unpublished song November 30, 1977. Materials in Berlin's song files date this number November 3, 1961. Typed lyric sheet dated November 10, 1961.

Home again,
When we're home again,
There'll be so much to remember.
We'll talk of days gone by
And laugh at things that made us cry.
An open fire
Till we both retire,
When there's no more to remember;
Our heads as close as can be,
Wrapped up in close harmony,
A song of home, sweet home.

YOU COULD BE BEAUTIFUL

Registered for copyright as an unpublished song November 30, 1977. Typed lyric sheet dated August 4, 1963. According to a note in Berlin's files, this song was written in July 1963.

Beautiful,
You could be beautiful—
Wash the makeup from your face
And you'll be beautiful.

Wonderful,
It could be wonderful—
Without so much paint
The diff'rence would be wonderful.

Why don't you stop being so silly,
Painting the lily the way you do?
Beautiful,
You could be beautiful.

Why don't you wake up
Under that makeup
Wrapped like a flag unfurled
Is the most beautiful girl in the world.

JUST PASSING THROUGH

Typed lyric sheet dated February 16, 1965. No music is known to survive.

I was just passing through
When I ran into a Mona Lisa smile.
I was just passing through,
But I had to linger a while.
I missed my plane
When I stopped to remain,
Wondering what's behind that Mona Lisa smile.
Couldn't wait till I knew,
So I lingered a while.
There were cocktails
And then a dinner
And then some tickets to a show—
Then a taxi
To her apartment,
Where the lights were burning low.
And in the gloom
In that dim-lighted room
Through her apartment door
A man came into view,
Just as nice as could be.
He said, "Please don't mind me—
I'm her husband,
Just her husband,
And like you,
I'm just passing through."

FOR JOHNNY MERCER

This quatrain was written for Johnny Mercer and sent to him in a letter dated December 22, 1965. No music is known to survive. Mercer's annual Christmas cards were eagerly awaited and highly appreciated by all who received them.

Dear Johnny:
  Only God can make the tree
  Where presents lie for you and me,
  But only Mercer makes the rhyme
  That cheers us all at Christmas time.

Thanks for the couplet you inscribed and best Holiday wishes to you and Ginger from us.

BRING BACK THE DAYS

Typed lyric sheet dated December 28, 1965. This lyric was a forerunner of "I Wanna Dance with the Girl in My Arms," intended for the unproduced film *Say It with Music* (see page 485). Also see "Let's Keep in Touch While We're Dancing" (see page 408).

Bring back the days,
Those wonderful days,
When you danced with a girl in your arms.
Bring back the thrill,
That wonderful thrill,
When you held her and felt all her charms.
Days when we were dancing close together
Instead of exercising miles apart—
Those were the days,
Those wonderful days,
When we danced cheek to cheek
And heart to heart.

LONG AS I CAN TAKE YOU HOME

Registered for copyright as an unpublished song January 17, 1966. Typed lyric sheet dated January 10, 1966. Sung by Sal Viviano on the 1995 album *Unsung Irving Berlin* (Varèse Sarabande).

I don't care who takes you to the party, baby,
Just as long as I can take you home.
I don't care just who you go with,
Just who it may be,
I don't care how much you're with him,
Long as you wind up with me.
If he musses up your pretty hairdo, baby,
I'll be waiting with a brush and comb.
Give him all your dances at the party, baby—
But save your kisses for when I take you home.*

Alternate version of lines 9 and 10:
   I don't care how long you keep me waiting, baby;
   I won't leave till the band plays "Home, Sweet Home."

I WASN'T DOING ANYTHING WRONG

Typed lyric sheet dated January 14, 1966. No music is known to survive.

I must have been doing something wrong;
My baby walked out on me.
We had a date for twelve o'clock,
But she didn't show up till three—
In a sable coat and a diamond ring,
And I began to see the light:
I wasn't doing anything wrong;
Someone else was doing something right.

A LITTLE LOVE TO START WITH

Typed lyric sheet dated February 25, 1966. No music is known to survive.

A little love to start with,
A little love to warm your heart with,
And then—a little more.
Take your time while keeping score.

A single kiss to start with,
A single kiss to break apart with,
And then that special night
When you begin to climb
The golden steps to heaven.
Take it easy—
One kiss at a time.

TOMORROW

Typed lyric sheet dated March 21, 1966. No music is known to survive.

VERSE

Funny what a difference just a few hours make;
Everything was blacker than the night.
I felt lower than the bottom of a lake;
Now I'm feeling higher than a kite.

CHORUS

Tomorrow
There'll be bluebirds singing—
Tomorrow—
For me.
Tomorrow
There'll be joy bells ringing,
As clear as can be—
Just you wait and see,
Because tomorrow,
On a day that's sunny,
Everything will turn out
Milk and honey.
Here am I, happy and gay,
Looking forward to tomorrow today.

WAIT UNTIL YOU'RE MARRIED

Published 1996 in the album *Unsung Irving Berlin* songbook. Sung on the 1996 album *Unsung Irving Berlin* (Varèse Sarabande) by Liz Larsen and Sal Viviano. Previously registered for copyright as an unpublished song July 1, 1966. Probably intended for *East River*, an unfinished musical about immigrant life on the Lower East Side of Manhattan.

VERSE

Mama, Mama—
No more toys;
I'm old enough to play with boys.
Mama, Mama—
I'm all set
For the kisses that I haven't had yet.

CHORUS 1

You must wait until you're married
If you want a happy life.
If you want to know what bliss is,
You must save your kisses
Till you're married—married—
Till you become a wife.

CHORUS 2

I can't wait till I'm married
To unwrap my many charms.
I can't wait till I'm married
To be lost in someone's arms.
I can't wait for those kisses

Till I take that marriage vow.
I can't wait until I'm married—
I want a little love right now.

[*Both choruses are then sung together as counter-melodies.*]

DON'T CALL ME— I'LL CALL YOU

There are several versions of this lyric. The earliest typed lyric sheet is dated November 1, 1966. There are unfinished musical sketches, including one dated February 2, 1968. Other typed lyric sheets are dated November 2 and November 3, 1970.

Earliest version, November 1, 1966

Don't call me—
I'll call you.
That's what you said,
And I knew we were through.
Still I sit by the telephone,
List'ning, list'ning, list'ning.
Don't call me—
I'll call you.
Somehow my heart
Won't believe that it's true.
So I sit by the telephone,
List'ning,
And the hardest thing to do
Is to keep from calling you.

Later version, November 2–3, 1970

How much longer
Must I gaze at the phone in the hall?
How much longer
Must I wait till it rings?
He said, "Don't call me—
I'll call you."
Can't believe
That we're really through.
Oh, how much,
How much longer must I wait?
Why don't I simply dispel with it,
Say the hell with it,
Let him go?
Why don't I dress
In my best evening gown
With a guy on my arm

And go out on the town?*
But suppose while I'm doing my thing,
The phone in the hallway should ring.
Don't call me—
I'll call you.
That's what he said
So there's nothing to do
But keep waiting, wond'ring
What did I do that was wrong.
Why is it taking so long?

Later version, November 3, 1970

Don't call me—
I'll call you.
That's what he said,
And I knew we were through.
Still I'm hoping, hoping, hoping.
Don't call me—
I'll call you.
That's what he said,
So there's nothing to do
But keep list'ning—
Hearing the beat of my heart as it sings
When the telephone rings in the hall.
Why do I keep holding on
To a dream that is over and gone?
Now that it's over and gone,
I should turn on the charm
With a guy on my arm.
Why don't I start having fun with it,
Say I'm done with it,
Let him go?
Why when I'm not doing well with it—
Say the hell with it?
But I know
While I'm out somewhere doing my thing,
The phone in the hallway might ring;
I know that my chances are slight,
But maybe, just maybe he might.
So how can I say that I'm done with it—
Hit-and-run with it—
When I know there's the phone in the hall
And he's liable to call?
So I'm hoping—
List'ning—
Waiting—
Wond'ring
What did I do that was wrong?
Why is he taking so long?

Alternate, two-line version of lines 14–17:
    Dressed in my best evening gown
    With a guy on my arm on the town.

WHAT CAN YOU GIVE A MAN WHO HAS EVERYTHING

Typed lyric sheet dated December 27, 1966. No music is known to survive.

What can you give a man who has everything,
Everything money can buy?
How can you give a man who has everything
Three pairs of socks or a tie?
What can you give him for Christmas,
A gift from which he'll never part?
What can he get from a girl who has nothing to
    give,
Nothing to give but her heart?

A MAN WHO HAS EVERYTHING

Typed lyric sheet of this fragment dated December 27, 1966. No music is known to survive. Probably an earlier version of the lyric that became "What Can You Give a Man Who Has Everything."

What can you give a man who has everything,
Everything he needs but love?
Another hi-fi to play his jazz
When there isn't anyone to hear the one he has?

TO GROUCHO MARX

Berlin included this couplet in an April 4, 1967, letter to Groucho Marx. "I still get compliments on my couplet about you," he wrote. "In case you've forgotten it, here it is again for your memory book."

The world would not be in such a snarl
If Marx had been Groucho instead of Karl.

ONLY GOD CAN MAKE A TREE

A poem dated August 29, 1967. The story of how the poem was written was related in the Bartlett Tree Company's in-house newsletter of December 1967. It appeared in the publication's "Tree Topics" column. The trees in question were on the property of the Berlin family's Catskills home in Lew Beach, New York.

IRVING BERLIN WRITES TREE TOPIC POEM

Richard Kolyer, a new Bartlett Sales Representative, recently obtained an order from one of our country's most famous composers, Mr. Irving Berlin. While foreman Bill Treible was working on the job, Mr. Berlin came out to talk to the crew and even wrote a poem, printed here especially for "Tree Topics."

"It was a great privilege and pleasure to work for Mr. Berlin, who enjoyed watching our crew prune his favorite tree," said Bill Treible. "I also had an opportunity to enjoy pleasant conversation with him. During the course of one of our chats, Mr. Berlin offered to write a poem for me, which I shall always prize."

Mr. Berlin also presented Mr. Treible with an autographed copy of a song written by him more than thirty years ago—"You'd Be Surprised."

It's not every forman [sic] who can have a poem written to him by a famous song-writer, as happened to Bill Treible.

Only God can make a tree,
But it's up to men like Bill
To feed it when it's hungry,
And prune it when the branches die,
To spray it when it's buggy,
And clear it for the sunlit sky,
To keep it alive and help it survive
With the special care they take
To nurse the tree, that lovely tree,
That only God can make.

FOR BILL TREIBLE

An undated quatrain.

"Poems are made by fools like me,"
But only Bill can climb a tree

That lived a hundred years or two
And make it look as good as new.

ONE KISS LED TO ANOTHER

Typed lyric sheets dated May 31, 1968; July 30, 1968; and September 9, 1987. The 1987 revision is possibly the last editing work that Berlin did on any of his lyrics.

First version, May 31, 1968

There they were on a summer's night
With a yellow moon above;
One kiss led to another,
And they fell deeply in love.

One kiss led to another
Till their dream world came to life;
Then she went back to her mother,
And he went back to his wife.

Second version, July 30, 1968

A summer's night,
A yellow moon above—
One kiss led to another,
And they fell deeply in love.
A handsome boy,
A girl with many charms:
One kiss led to another
As they nestled in each other's arms.
When morning came the yellow moon had gone;
A night of bliss had ended with the dawn.
He kissed her as he whispered tenderly,
"I love you more than life"—
Then she went home to her mother
And he went home to his wife.
"I spent the night with a friend," she said;
Her mother saw no harm.
He woke his wife with a pleasant smile
And a mink coat on his arm.
A summer's night,
A happy ending,
Without a care or strife—
She made up with her mother,
And he made breakfast for his wife.

Third version, September 9, 1987

A summer's night, a yellow moon above—
One kiss led to another

As they fell deeply in love.
A handsome boy, a girl with many charms—
One kiss led to another
As they nestled in each other's arms.
When morning came, the yellow moon had gone;
A night of bliss had vanished with the dawn.
He kissed her as he whispered tenderly,
"I love you more than life"—
Then she went back to her mother
And he went back to his wife.

KISSES WITHOUT LOVE

Registered for copyright as an unpublished song August 2, 1968. Typed lyric sheet dated July 31, 1968.

A short romance may be lots of fun,
But it's for lovers who kiss and run.

Kisses without love
Are words without music,
Days without sunshine,
Nights without moonlight.
Kisses without love are soon forgotten,
Like the dreams you have at night
That you can't recall.
Those one-time kisses without love
Are toys without children,
Bees without honey,
Storms without rainbows.
You can have those loveless kisses,
The kind there's plenty of,
But I won't settle for anything less than love.

Additional or earlier chorus

Kisses without love
Are banks without money,
Stocks without margin,
Rings without diamonds.
Kisses without love are soon forgotten,
Like a show that closes after opening night.
Those one-time kisses without love
Are books without bedrooms,
Chins without whiskers,
Franks without mustard.
Kisses worth a dime a dozen are not worth
    thinking of,
So I won't settle for anything less than love.

WELCOME, COMRADES, WELCOME

Typed lyric sheet dated September 3, 1968. Soviet troops had invaded Czechoslovakia on August 20–21, 1968.

Welcome, comrades, welcome,
Welcome to your slaves—
Thank you for the roses
On our children's graves,
On our children's graves.
Welcome, Russian comrades,
Soldiers brave and true—
With salt in our eyes
And hope in our hearts
We welcome you,
We welcome you.

THE EVERLEIGH CLUB

Typed lyric sheet dated December 18, 1968. No music is known to survive. In a letter to Jerome Robbins dated December 20, 1968, Berlin discusses this lyric.

> Here is the Irving Wallace book which includes "Two Nice Old Ladies," the Everleigh sisters story I spoke to you about.
> As I told you, Moss Hart and I were going to do a musical based on the Everleigh sisters and their "club" [a notorious Chicago brothel] many years ago. Also, I spoke to Wallace about it when the book came out.

We live with the sisters Everleigh,
Where life is a trifle gay.
They do everything so cleverly
As we turn night into day.
We don't go to bed until reveille,
And all the reformers say
That we're bound for hell,
Because we sell
What the others are giving away.

PIGS

Typed lyric sheet dated December 26, 1968. No music is known to survive. According to a note by Berlin that preceded the lyric, this number is to be "done by two pigs—one black and one white," perhaps in reference to George Orwell's *Animal Farm*. Also see the lyric "The Revolt of the Pigs" (page 492).

VERSE

Millions of pigs both black and white
Are being offended day and night
By folks on the left and folks on the right
Calling each other pigs.
It's become a dirty name;
We resent it just the same.

CHORUS

Who's afraid of the bad George Wallace?
Who's afraid of the bad Rap Brown?
They fume and fuss,
But compared to us,
They're the biggest hams in town.

MOON LYRICS

Included in a letter from Berlin to Harry Ruby dated August 15, 1969. No music is known to survive. The letter and lyrics follow.

> August 15th, 1969
>
> Dear Harry:
> I received your letter of the 7th.
> The moon landing is indeed the greatest event that's happened in anybody's lifetime to inspire some kind of a song, but I don't know of any songwriter who can measure up to this occasion. I'm afraid that includes you.
> However, I'm sure I would love your moon song if I knew what the hell you were talking about.
> Here are some examples that I dictated without much thought:
>
> > Moon, Moon, songwriters' moon,
> > You turned out to be a bust—
> > For how can you spoon
> > Neath the light of a moon
> > That's made of rocks and dust?
>
> or:
>
> > Now that they've put a man on the moon,
> > Why don't they put a man in my arms?
> > A Tom, Dick, or Harry or Jack—
> > And they won't have to bring him back.
>
> or:
>
> > I'm in love with the man on the moon,
> > And I pray he'll be coming home soon.
> > I'm sure it's worth risking his life,
> > But I happen to be his wife,
> > So I wait for the man on the moon
> > And I pray he'll be coming home soon.
>
> Seriously, Harry, I remember being in Atlantic City in 1927 when Lindbergh crossed the ocean and landed in Paris. I was there working on the *Ziegfeld Follies* of that year. I was so overcome with emotion and really tried to write some kind of a song. It just didn't work. I could come up with nothing. And looking back, what did Tin Pan Alley come up with? The Lindy Hop and Wolfie Gilbert's "Lucky Lindy."
> The best words for a moon song that I've heard so far are those spoken by the three astronauts.
> I'm in the country and dictating this over the telephone.
> My best to you,
>
> As always,

IF YOU DON'T LIKE MY APPLES

Typed lyric sheet dated September 2, 1969. No music is known to survive. See the 1914 song "If You Don't Want My Peaches (You'd Better Stop Shaking My Tree)" (page 89).

If you don't like my apples, don't climb my tree;
If you don't like my apples, don't climb my tree;
If you don't care for applesauce, keep away from
    me.
If you don't like my marbles, you needn't play;
If you don't like my marbles, you needn't play;
If you don't like my neighborhood, you can move
    away.
I'm willing to be criticized and bossed;
I'll pay the price no matter what the cost.
But if you don't like my apples
And you don't like my marbles

And you don't like my neighborhood—
Get lost.

FLAG WAVING

Typed lyric sheet dated November 17, 1969. No music is
known to survive.

We're a land of bellyachers
With a grain of trouble makers,
Criticizing, disapproving,
Finding fault—but never moving.

The mugging and the slugging's got me down.

With taxes and the bad polluted air
I'd like to get away somewhere—but where?

Do I want to live in London, where the taxes are
     much higher
And the climate chills your bones down to your
     feet?
Do I want to live in Paris, where they sell those
     dirty postals?
We've got dirtier ones on Forty-second Street!
Do I want to join the Slovaks and the Czechs who
     lost their freedom
When the Russian tanks rolled down their avenue?
Would I settle in New Guinea, where the women
     are all topless?
We've got women who show their top and bottoms
     too.
I'm afraid I'll have to stay in the troubled U.S.A.
With the others who complain but still remain.
I'll remain and do my thing,
Wave my flag and proudly sing:

America, America,
You fill my heart with song.
You aren't always right but still
My country right or wrong.

THE REVOLT OF THE PIGS

Typed lyric sheet dated February 25, 1970. No music is
known to survive.

I had a crazy dream last night:
Millions of pigs both black and white
Were marching toward Washington,
Protesting that characters full of dope
Badly in need of water and soap
Were calling folks they didn't dig
Pig.

I HAVEN'T GOT A HOME TO GO TO

Typed lyric sheet dated August 14, 1970. No music is
known to survive.

I haven't got a home to go to anymore.
I haven't got a home to go to anymore.
My baby's mad—
The pad I had
Has a padlock on the door,
And I haven't got a home to go to anymore.
A nice day,
A crowded town,
But I'm standing alone;
The sun shines,
The heat comes down,
But I'm chilled to the bone,
'Cause the woman that I never said no to
Has a padlock on the door
And I haven't got a home to go to anymore.

OF ALL THE TIN PAN ALLEY GREATS

A typed lyric included in a letter to Harry Ruby dated
October 7, 1970.

> Now, about your poem—I like it very much. Your
> first line, "God makes us what we are," reminded
> me of a crack Saul Bornstein once made about
> me. After we separated, he told somebody, "What
> the hell is Irving so stuck-up about? God gave him
> his talent." Of course, he didn't add the fact that
> I worked God-damn hard not to let God down.
>
>   Apropos of all this, I just wrote a four line jin-
> gle for you:—
>
>> Of all the Tin Pan Alley Greats
>> Berlin is the tops.

A "colored boy" writes all his hits—
But who writes all his flops?

THE DAY AFTER TOMORROW

Typed lyric sheet dated November 21, 1970. No music is
known to survive.

The day after tomorrow
And the days after then,
The sun will shine again,
Sure as there's a God in heaven.
It's gonna take an awful lot of love
And understanding;
It's gonna take much more than love
To make that happy landing—
But the day after tomorrow
And the days after then,
I promise you the sun will shine again.

PEACE

Typed lyric sheet dated February 17, 1971. No music is
known to survive.

We march and protest
With hope in each breast,
Shouting peace to people we meet.
Let our shouting increase—
But the road to peace
Isn't a one-way street.

If the Russian soldiers
And those Russian tanks
That rolled into Czechoslovakia
Had left the tanks
And joined the ranks
Shouting "Hell no, we won't go,"
What a day that would have been,
What a giant step toward peace!
Not just peace for Americans
But the banner of peace unfurled
Not just for Americans
But peace for the rest of the world.

If the Russian youth started marching
With their pent-up hopes released,
Shouting loud and clear
So that Brezhnev could hear,
"Bring our boys back from the Middle East,"
What a day that would be,
What a giant step toward peace—
Not just for the Arabs,
Not just for the Israelis,
But the flag of peace unfurled
For the Middle East and the rest of the world.

So let's continue marching,
But let us not forget:
It's not rubbing off on the Russians;
It's not rubbing off yet—
Not yet.

LET THE GATE SWING OPEN

Typed lyric sheet dated February 23, 1971. No music is known to survive. The theme is the immigration of Soviet Jews.

Let the gate swing open,
Open wide—
There's a rainbow on the other side.
Let the gate swing open,
Wide, wide open,
And let my people go.

Can't you hear those silent voices,
Those forgotten, silent voices?
From the tomb of silent voices
Can't you hear them whisper low:

Let the gate swing open,
Open wide—
There's a rainbow on the other side.
Let the gate swing open,
Wide, wide open,
And let my people go.

THE CZARS KEPT THE GATES WIDE OPEN

Typed lyric sheet dated February 26, 1971. No music is known to survive.

It was tough living under the czars,
But the czars kept the gates wide open.
We still wear the scars
To remind us of the czars,
But the czars kept the gates wide open.
If the czars had closed the gates,
Those of us in the fifty states
Would be there with the sad three million or so
Pleading, "Let my people go."

HE DIDN'T WAKE UP ONE MORNING

Published. Copyrighted March 12, 1971. Black-and-white professional copy privately printed by Irving Berlin.

He didn't wake up one morning;
He couldn't get out of bed.
He heard his mother screaming,
"My darling boy is dead!"
He grabbed the morning paper,
Which left him in a rage—
He saw his name in a headline
On the obituary page.
He shouted, "This can't be!
They can't do this to me!"

But there he was in Campbell's
With everyone in tears;
The voice of Georgie Jessel
Was ringing in his ears:
A sugar-coated tribute
With goodness thickly sliced,
And all agreed when Jessel
Compared the guy with Christ.

But suddenly a miracle:
A voice from high above
Came down and softly whispered,
"This noble man you love
Must stay with you forever,

For it would not be fair
To send him up to heaven—
We've enough o' bastards there."

OPEN YOUR HEART

Typed lyric sheet dated April 6, 1971. No music is known to survive.

Open your eyes
And I'll show you a road
That ends like the end of a fairy tale.
Open your ears
And I'll sing you a song
That was written and sung by a nightingale.
Open your lips
And I'll press them to mine
With a kiss dipped in wine
That'll make your head spin.
Open your heart
And let me in.

SONG FOR THE RUSSIAN PEOPLE

Typed lyric sheet dated May 10, 1971, and October 4, 1971. No music is known to survive.

Later version

VERSE

There are millions of Americans who give a
    damn
Shouting, "Bring our boys home from Vietnam."
There are millions of Russians—if they'd only
    dare,
They'd be marching and singing in Red Square:

CHORUS

Bring our boys home from the Middle East,
Bring our boys home from the Middle East!
Bring our boys home from that foreign soil—
Bring them home and the hell with the oil.
Bring them home, bring them home,
Bring them home from that foreign soil.

Bring them home, bring them home—
Bring them home and the hell with the oil.

Earlier version

VERSE 1

The Russians are marching in Red Square—
How do I know it? I was there.
In a dream I had last night
They were singing with all their might:

CHORUS (SAME AS LATER VERSION)

VERSE 2

The Russians are watching Uncle Sam
Bringing the boys back from Vietnam.

[*Lyric ends here.*]

WHAT COLOR IS LOVE?

Typed lyric sheet dated June 28, 1971. Typed lyric sheet of alternate version, undated. No music is known to survive for either version. Alternate title: "The Color of Love."

Skies are blue,
Clouds are gray,
Stars are silver above.
Lilies are white,
Roses are red—
But what color is love,
What color is love?
Is it the color of a sunset
Casting its magical glow?
Is it the color of a rainbow?
I'm afraid we never will know.
Like the Unknown Soldier,
Only heaven above
Knows the color, the color of love—
Only heaven knows the color of love.

Undated version

Roses are red,
Vi'lets are blue,
Lilies are white as a dove.

Christmas is green,
Babies are pink—
But what color is love?
Is it the color of a sunset
Casting its wonderful glow?
Is it the color of a rainbow?
I'm afraid we never will know.
Roses are red,
Vi'lets are blue,
Lilies are white as a dove—
But only heaven knows the color,
The unknown color, of love.

SONG FOR THE U.N.

Published. Copyrighted October 26, 1971. Berlin's last published song. Previously registered for copyright as an unpublished song October 8, 1971. A note on the inside of the cover of the published sheet music reads: "Written on the occasion of the 25th anniversary of the United Nations and premiered at the annual United Nations concert and dinner, Washington, D.C., October 23, 1971." The event, held at the Washington Hilton's International Ballroom, was called "A Birthday Toast to the United Nations" and "A Tribute to Irving Berlin, 'Songwriter to the World,' " and featured Caterina Valente, Vincent Price, the Radio City Rockettes, the George Washington University Troubadours, and 117 Boy and Girl Scouts. In a letter of October 26, 1971, to his friend Harry Ruby, Berlin wrote:

> Through the years, I've been asked many times to write a peace song but always decided it just couldn't be done. You will see when you read the lyrics that the song is *about* a peace song that hasn't been written yet. Note the five words, "One song with one word." Even as "great" a songwriter as I couldn't possibly write a song with one word.

VERSE

Let's have a sing-along—
Just bring along your voices.
Let's get the UN to sing—
What will we sing about with so many choices?
There's only one song to sing.

CHORUS

One song,
Just one song for the UN to sing,
One song that's in your heart;

We'll hear it though we're miles apart.
Just one song,
With one word that the UN must release—
Take it and make it your national anthem,
That song of songs called Peace.
That one song of songs called Peace.

THE BATTLE HYMN OF THE UNITED NATIONS

Typed lyric sheet dated November 23, 1971, "with apologies to Julia Ward Howe." It is set to the same music as the traditional tune of Howe's "Battle Hymn of the Republic." On October 7, 1971, the one-China policy came into effect and Taiwan lost its seat in the United Nations.

Mine eyes have seen them lobbying
To get each other's vote;
I have listened to the speeches
That their special writers wrote;
They speak of peace and freedom
While they're at each other's throat—
The UN marches on.

Glory, glory, hallelujah!
Glory, glory, hallelujah!
Glory, glory, hallelujah!
The UN marches on.

There mustn't be two Chinas—
There is only room for one;
So a loyal charter member
Has to take it on the run.
You can argue with a man,
But you can't talk back to a gun—
The UN marches on.

Glory, glory, hallelujah!
Glory, glory, hallelujah!
Glory, glory, hallelujah!
The UN marches on.

Along New York's East River,
Where the busy tugboats pass,
There's a most impressive building
That's entirely made of glass,
Could be turned into apartments
For the wealthy upper class—
The UN marches on.

Please unite, United Nations!
Please unite, United Nations!
Please unite, United Nations!
It's later than you think.

WITHOUT LOVE

Typed lyric sheets dated December 7, 1972; November 17, 1977; and November 3, 1986. The 1977 and 1986 versions are aligned differently but are otherwise the same. No music is known to survive.

1972 version

Flowers wouldn't bloom in spring,
Nightingales would never sing,
Nature couldn't do her thing
Without love.
A boy and girl would feel so all alone
Without love.
Elephants would never mate,
A famous king would not give up his throne
Without love.
Hens and roosters wouldn't date,
Weddings couldn't celebrate
Without love.
The Man Upstairs
Who hears our prayers
Reminds us from above,
He could never do His job up there
Without love.

1977/1986 version

Flowers wouldn't bloom in spring,
Nightingales would never sing,
Nature wouldn't do her thing
Without love.
A boy and girl would feel so all alone
Without love.
A famous king would not give up his throne
Without love.
A summer's night beneath the moon would drag
Without love.
And Betsy Ross could not have made that flag
Without love.
The Man Upstairs reminds us from above
He could never do His job up there
Without love.
He could not perform His miracles
Without love.

YOU CAN'T DO IT
BY YOURSELF

Typed lyric sheets dated February 1, 1973; February 12, 1975; and November 3, 1986. The 1975 version is titled "He Can't Do It By Himself" and includes an undated alternate version. The 1986 version is titled "I Can't Do It By Myself." No music is known to survive.

1973 version

VERSE

You can climb the highest mountain,
You can swim the deepest river,
You can brag about the trophies on your shelf.
You can win the highest honors,
You can go from rags to riches—
But you can't,
You can't do it by yourself.

CHORUS

You can't do it by yourself—
You can't do it by yourself.
You can do, do, do most anything,
But you can't do it by yourself.
The Man Upstairs
Who hears your prayers
Can help you;
The Man Upstairs
Who really cares
Can really help you.
So look up there and whisper, "Please
Help me cross the stormy seas,"
'Cause you can't do it by yourself—
You can't do it by yourself.

1975 version

Behind every successful man there's a woman,
Pushing him, shoving him, kissing him, loving
    him,
Helping him get to the top.
That expression isn't new,
But it happens to be true—
To push him, shove him, kiss him, love him,
And help him get to the top.

He can climb the highest mountain,
Swim the deepest river,
Brag about his trophies on the shelf;
He can win the highest honors,

Go from rags to riches,
But he can't,
No he can't, do it by himself.

He's gotta have a woman,
A sweet and loving woman,
To help him get those trophies for his shelf.
Especially
If he's a he
Who would like to raise a family,
He's gotta have a woman,
A sweet and loving woman,
'Cause he can't,
No he can't, do it by himself.

1975 alternate version

Behind every successful man there's a woman,
Pushing him, shoving him, kissing him, loving
    him,
Helping him get to the top.

There has to be a woman
'Cause he can't,
No he can't, do it by himself.

He can climb the highest mountain,
Swim the deepest river,
Brag about his trophies on the shelf;
He can win the highest honors,
Go from rags to riches,
But he can't,
No he can't, do it by himself.

A man without a woman never does the best he
    can—
And that goes for a woman without a man.

She can knit a woolen sweater,
Cook a tasty dinner,
Wipe the dust that gathers on the shelf;
She can tie a baby's diaper,
But she can't get that baby by herself;
She's gotta have a man—
There has to be a man,
'Cause she can't get that baby by herself.

The Man Upstairs who hears our prayers
Designed a perfect plan:
A man's gotta have a woman,
And a woman's gotta have a man.

The Man Upstairs decided
Ever since the world began
That a man needs a woman
And a woman needs a man.

1986 version

I could climb the highest mountain,
I could swim the deepest river,
Brag about the trophies on my shelf;
I could swim the deepest ocean,
I could go from rags to riches,
But I can't,
I can't, do it by myself.
Behind every successful man there's a woman—a
    woman
Pushing him, shoving him, kissing him, loving
    him,
Helping him get to the top.
What I need is a special kind of a woman
To push me, shove me, kiss me, love me,
And help me get to the top.
I'm a family man—
I'd love to spend my nights surrounded
By a houseful of children,
Beautiful, lovable children,
Telling them what I did to get those trophies on
    my shelf.
But I can't,
No I can't, do it by myself;
Got to have that special woman,
'Cause I can't do it by myself.

TELL IT LIKE IT IS

Typed lyric sheet dated February 14, 1973. No music is
known to survive.

Tell it like it is, baby—
Tell it like it is today.
Tell 'em of the night when you walked out
And left me alone.
Tell 'em of the many times
I tried to get you on the phone.
Tell 'em of the many notes
I sent you slipped under your door,
Saying that I'm sorry,
Not knowing what I'm sorry for.
That's how it is today, baby,
So tell 'em like it is,
Tell it like it is.

Tell it like it was, baby—
Tell it like it used to be

[*Lyric breaks off here.*]

NOW THAT I'VE REACHED THREESCORE AND TEN

Typed lyric sheet dated October 15, 1974. On February 15,
1975, Harold Arlen's seventieth birthday, Berlin sent a
copy of this lyric to his close friend Arlen, saying, "It
may apply to you as it did to me when I reached that bib-
lical age." No music is known to survive.

Now that I've reached threescore and ten,
If I had my life to live over again,
Would I do the foolish things I did before?
Now that I've reached threescore and ten,
Would I run like a frightened rabbit when
That first romance came knocking at my door?
Would I right the wrongs
And heal the hurts
And learn to say I'm sorry?
Would it be more work and much less fun?
Would I do the things I left undone?
Now that at last I've reached threescore and ten,
I'm afraid I would do it all all over again.

WE'VE HAD A LOVELY EVENING

Typed lyric sheet of only four lines dated December 24,
1974. No music is known to survive.

We've had a lovely evening;
I hope you're satisfied.
And now we've reached the door of your
    apartment,
Aren't you going to ask me inside?

A LULLABY WITH A BEAT

Typed lyric sheet dated February 10, 1975. Another ver-
sion is undated. No music is known to survive.

1975 version

Rock, rock, rock-a-bye, baby—
Go to sleep, my sweet.

Daddy swings while Mama sings
A lullaby with a beat.

Some fine day when you grow older
You'll become a star,
With your hair down to your shoulder,
Strumming a guitar.

So rock, rock, rock-a-bye, baby—
Go to sleep, my sweet.
Daddy swings while Mama sings
A lullaby with a beat.

Undated version

Rock, rock, rock-a-bye, baby—
Go to sleep, my sweet.
Daddy swings while Mama sings
A lullaby with a beat.

Rock, rock, slumber, my angel—
Heaven's at your feet.
Spread your wings while Mama sings
A lullaby with a beat.

Some fine day when you grow older
You'll become a great big star,
With your hair down to your shoulder,
Strumming a bar on your guitar.

So rock, rock, rock-a-bye, baby—
Some fine day you'll write a song, maybe,
A rock and roll full of soul
That'll reach the top of the sheet,
A lullaby, a lullaby with a beat.

Rock, rock, rock-a-bye, baby—
Some fine day there'll be a song, maybe,
That'll reach the top of the sheet,
A lullaby with a beat.

THEY WON'T BE PUSHED IN THE SEA

Typed lyric sheet dated January 16, 1976. No music is
known to survive.

They won't be pushed in the sea,
They won't be pushed in the sea.
Death in the river Jordan
Is just the same, alas,

As death in a camp at Auschwitz
In a chamber filled with gas.

FREE AGAIN

Typed lyric sheet dated January 20, 1976. No music is known to survive.

Free again,
So I'm free again—
Where there used to be a couple
There's just me again.
I was happy when they gave me my decree,
Glad to be free.
Free again—
I can see again
Being free
Is not what it's cracked up to be again;
After living as a single on my own,
I'm so alone.
Though the song has ended,
The dream has gone,
Many golden memories linger on;
Sparks of love still burn in the dying ember,
And I remember
The used-to-be.
Back again,
To go back again,
To return the love I wrecked
Back on the track again—
I would gladly come back on my bended
    knee
Just to be we again,
Just you and me.

YIPPER

A quatrain for E. Y. ("Yip") Harburg. Included in a letter to Harold Arlen dated November 18, 1976. No music is known to survive.

November 18th, 1976

Dear Harold:
    I saw one of the verses from Yipper's new book in the *Times*, which I'm enclosing, where he complains that the Pentagon is spending too much of his taxes for defense.
    I thought you might be amused by the following four lines:

There's a big atomic submarine
Manned by a Russian skipper
Bound for Martha's Vineyard
Coming to get Yipper.

My best.

THE GATES ARE OPEN WIDE

Typed lyric sheet dated December 9, 1976. No music is known to survive.

The gates are wide open in America,
If there's another land for which you yearn;
The gates are wide open in America,
And they'll be open when you return.

THE RUSSIANS ARE COMING

There are two typed lyric sheets, one dated December 9, 1976, and the other undated. No music is known to survive.

1976 version

The Russians are coming,
The Russians are coming—
Listen to Paul Revere.
Let's not lose our senses
And cut our defenses.
It's too late—
The Russians are here.

Undated version

The Russians are coming,
The Russians are coming—
Listen to Paul Revere.
The Russians are coming,
The Russians are coming—
Their missiles are drawing near.
Let's not lose our senses
And cut our defenses;
Let's listen to Paul Revere.
The Russians are coming,
The Russians are coming.

Too late—
The Russians are here.

ALEXANDER SOLZHENITSYN

Typed lyric sheet dated December 13, 1976. According to Berlin, it was written after hearing a William Buckley interview with Solzhenitsyn. No music is known to survive.

Listen, my children, and lend an ear
To the bearded Russian Paul Revere.
He warns us to keep our powder dry
And watch the zipper on Russia's fly.

TO HAROLD ARLEN

Through the years Berlin enjoyed a close friendship with fellow songwriter Harold Arlen. They spoke frequently by telephone, and on birthdays and other special occasions they sent each other greetings in verse. Arlen's birthday was February 15; Berlin's was May 11. Harold Arlen was born "Hyman Arluck." "Anya" was the name of Harold Arlen's wife. "Ellin" was Ellin Berlin. "Pablo B." is a reference to Pablo Picasso and Irving Berlin. "Our friend in Martha's Vineyard" is E. Y. ("Yip") Harburg. Lyricist Stanley Adams was the president of ASCAP. "Lee and Ira" are Mrs. and Mr. Ira Gershwin. Here are excerpts from Berlin's offerings to Arlen.

January 8th, 1970

Harold the music,
Anya the word,
Ellin the Matchmaker—
Happy thirty-third.

Love,

May 12th, 1970

Dear Harold:

I swear to heaven,
Till May eleven
I didn't sneak even a tiny peek
At your birthday song.
But now that I've seen it
I've got to say

That the Arlen music
Is quite okay,
But your lyrics
Have me in hysterics.
As a lyric writer
I think that you
Are almost as good
As you know who.
Your lyrics, Mister Music Man,
Are simply for the birds;
Ac-cent-u-ate the melody—
Don't mess around with the words.
But I thank you for your kindness,
Regardless of your rhyme,
And I hope when you
Reach eighty-two
You're as big a shmuck as I'm.

As ever,

May 13th, 1970

Dear Harold:

The verses I sent you yesterday were for New Haven. Enclosed is the New York version with cuts.

Lyric writing should be treated as you would a sensitive stomach. It isn't what you put in, but what you keep out.

As always,

I swear to heaven,
Till May eleven
I didn't even sneak
A tiny little peek
At your birthday song.
But now that I've seen it
I've got to say
That the Arlen music
Is quite okay,
But as a lyricist
I'm afraid that you
Are almost as good
As you know who.
But I thank you for your kindness,
Regardless of your rhyme,
And I hope when you
Reach eighty-two
You're as big a shmuck as I'm.

May 10th, 1971

Your birthday verses, Hymie,
Were read and loved by me;
If you think eighty-three
Will stop Pablo B.
From foolin' around—try me.

May 6th, 1974

Dear Harold:

I'm sorry you haven't been well.

Why the hell didn't you call me? I'd have come over to see you and we could have spent a pleasant afternoon talking about me.

You mentioned that you haven't written my birthday poem yet. Please don't bother doing it because it gives me a chance to write it for you. It's enclosed in this letter and I hope you like it.

You don't have to send it—I have a copy.

Get well soon.

As always,

TO AN AUTHENTIC GENIUS ON HIS 86TH BIRTHDAY

BY HAROLD ARLEN

Once again a happy day
For Mr. B from Mr. A,
Hoping that you're free from care and pain.
There are many who'll agree
You're a dirty SOB,
But bei mir bist du schoen,
Bei mir bist du schoen.*

February 15th, 1976

Seventy-one
Can be fun
If you still have bullets
In your gun.

Zei mir gezunt,†

March 25th, 1976

It's lovely, I claim,
To turn on a dame
With kisses both wet and deep,
But it's nicer, I find, to turn off your mind
And sleep—sleep—sleep.

February 28th, 1977

Dear Harold:

When I seriously suggested that you consider doing a one-man "and then I wrote" show with

---

*Roughly translated: "You'll always be beautiful to me."

†Roughly translated: "I'm wishing you good health."

your wonderful catalogue, your answer was, "I've shot my wad."

Following is the verse I wrote about it which you liked and asked me to send you a copy.

I'VE SHOT MY WAD

A nightingale looked up to God
And said, "Dear God, I've shot my wad,
No longer can I do my thing,
Dear God, no longer can I sing."
And He replied, "Don't be a schmuck,
No nightingale has had such luck,
Your songs have built a golden nest
For Stanley Adams and the rest.
They're praying for the moment when
You get off your ass and sing again."

My best,
As always,

March 23rd, 1977

Every time that Brezhnev sneezes
People shake with fright,
But our friend in Martha's Vineyard
Simply says "Gezundheit."

February 15, 1978

Lucky me,
Just seventy-three—
A talk with Ira
And with Lee
And now a gift from Mister B. . . .

SAY IT WITH MUSIC
(1980 Version)

This new lyric to Berlin's 1921 song was written in December 1980 for Jack Elliott and a television show *100 Years of Music.*

Say it with music,
Beautiful music.
Somehow for so many years
This great land
Through smiles and through tears
Has said it with music,
With words and music.
Let's keep America strong
And say it with a beautiful song.

FRED ASTAIRE

Typed lyric sheet dated March 19, 1981. This song may have had the last Berlin melody. Nothing later is known to survive.

Give my regards to Fred Astaire the singer—
Fred as a singer is a real humdinger.
So many times have I been in clover,
For his heart's in the song before his feet take over.

IT TAKES MORE THAN LOVE

Typed lyric sheet dated November 24, 1981. No music is known to survive.

It takes more than love
To make a fellow happy;
It takes more than love
To give him all the breaks.
To get up early,
Cook his breakfast,
And take the kids to school,
It takes more than love—
And you've got what it takes.

THE SUN'S SHINING DOWN AT LAST

Typed lyric sheet dated January 25, 1982. No music is known to survive.

The sun's shining down at last;
The sun's shining down at last.
The skies of gray have gone away
And the sun is shining down at last.
Up with a rosy future,
Down with the gloomy past;
The skies of gray have gone away
And the sun's shining down at last.

WHY DID WE HAVE TO FALL IN LOVE?

Typed lyric sheet dated September 19, 1983. The last stanza was added to the lyric on July 22, 1985, possibly as a replacement for the fourth stanza. No music is known to survive.

We were such a happy couple,
Peaceful as the well-known dove;
But love came along and spoiled it—
Why did we have to fall in love?

We were getting along so very,
Billing and cooing like a dove;
But love came along and spoiled it—
Why did we have to fall in love?

We could spend the night romantically,
With or without a moon above;
But now every night we finish with a fight—
Why did we have to fall in love?

We were such good friends, wonderful friends,
Peaceful as a cooing dove;
But now day and night all we do is fight—
Why did we have to fall in love?

We were getting along so well,
As peaceful as a dove;
Now day and night we argue and fight—
Why did we have to fall in love?

NOT BECAUSE YOU'RE BEAUTIFUL

Typed lyric sheets dated December 14, 1983; June 22, 1984; and November 3, 1986. The 1984 version differs only slightly from the 1986 version and is not included here. No music is known to survive.

1983 version

It's not because you're beautiful;
I adore you, but it's not because you're beautiful.
And it's not because you're smart,
Or because your perfect features are a work of art.
I see you standing side by side
With the gorgeous women Ziegfeld glorified,

But if you were a country bumpkin
With a ribbon in your hair,
I would care.
But you're beautiful, beautiful, and very, very
    smart,
And all I can give is all of my love
From the bottom of my heart.

1986 version

I love you,
But it's not because you're beautiful,
Not because you happen to be beautiful.
You would stand out in a chorus side by side
With the gorgeous girls that Ziegfeld glorified;
But if you were just an ordinary plain Jane,
A girl who didn't have what's known as looks,
Who couldn't make the famous beauty contest,
Whose pictures won't appear in fashion books,
I would love you just as much and just as true
As the most attractive girl I ever knew—
But it wouldn't be because you're beautiful;
It would be because you happen to be you.

IF YOU DIDN'T KNOW HOW OLD YOU WERE

Typed lyric sheet dated May 31, 1984. See also "Old Men." No music is known to survive.

How old would you be
If you didn't know how old you are?
How old would you be
If they didn't call from near and far?
Old men,
Telling old jokes,
Drinking old wine at a bar,
Are as happy as a rooster in a hen coop,
Because they don't know how old they are.

OLD MEN

Typed lyric sheet dated May 13, 1985, two days after Berlin's ninety-seventh birthday. There is also an undated alternate version of the chorus. No music is known to survive.

VERSE

VERSE

Another birthday and you're almost in tears;
Another birthday and you're counting the
    years.
But if you didn't know how old you were,
You would join those older citizens,
That very happy bunch of

CHORUS

Old men drinking old wine,
Singing old songs at a bar.
A simple song again,
They're feeling young again,
Because they don't know how old they are.

Old men swapping old jokes
With their old friends near and far,
Happy as a rooster in a hen coop,
Because they don't know how old they are.

Alternate version of chorus

Old men drinking old wine,
Telling old jokes at a bar,
Happy as a rooster in a hen coop,
Because they don't know how old they are.

Old men dreaming old dreams,
Hearing old songs from afar,
Old-fashioned songs to be sung again—
They're young again,
Because they don't know how old they are.

VOTE, AMERICA

Typed lyric sheet dated April 1, 1986. No music is
known to survive.

Get out and vote, America—
Here comes Election Day.
Go to the polls, America—
Say what you have to say.
Get to the nearest voting booth,
And when you're alone inside,
Vote for your favorite candidate
And let your conscience be your guide.

OLD SONGS

Typed lyric sheets dated April 9, 1986, and February 18,
1987. There is also an earlier, undated version. No music
is known to survive.

1987 version

Old songs bring back the old days,
The golden old days when we were young.
Simple songs that we sang then
Keep reminding us to sing them again.
With old friends we'll sing the old songs,
Bring back the old days gone by.
There will always be old songs,
Because old songs never die.

1986 version

Old songs bring back the old days,
The golden old days when we were young.
We loved the songs that we sang then,
So let us get together and sing them again,
For old friends who miss the old days.
And when there's no sun up in the sky,
There will always be old songs,
Because old songs never die.

Undated version

VERSE

It seems to me I heard you clear your throat,
And from your throat emerged a pleasant note—
If you go into a sing-along,
Bring along some old songs.

CHORUS

Old songs bring back the old days,
Those golden old days
When we were young.
We used to sing those old songs then,
So let us get together
And sing them again.
Old friends who miss those old songs,
Those golden old songs, can rely
That there will always be old songs,
Because old songs never die.

TILL THIS CRAZY WORLD
IS SANE AGAIN

Typed lyric sheet dated April 28, 1986. No music is
known to survive.

The world is dressed in gray, my dear;
There's trouble far and wide.
We cannot run away, my dear,
And there is no place to hide.
Let's stroll down memory lane again,
Where there's a brighter view,
Till this crazy world is sane again
And the sun comes shining through.

IT'S ABOUT TIME

Typed lyric sheet dated October 21, 1986. This lyric
evolved from earlier attempts. No music is known to
survive.

It's about time—
It's about time—
It's about time.
When I take you home tonight,
As I've often done before,
You won't just say goodnight
And leave me standing at your door.
It's about time—
It's about time.

After taking you to dinner,
To a movie or a show,
It isn't fair when later down
To your place we go
To say goodnight and close the door
And leave me with a grin.
It's about time—
About time you asked me in.

I long to hold you in my arms behind closed doors
And start a fire when I press my lips to yours.
Too long I've waited for that moment sublime;
Baby, don't you think that it's about time?
It's about time—
It's about time.

MISTER ALEXANDER COH'N

Typed lyric sheet dated June 23, 1987. This tribute to producer Alexander Cohen was set to the music of "Alexander's Ragtime Band." Intended for an unproduced show of Cohen's titled *Broadway's Best*.

Come on and hear—come on and hear—
Mister Alexander Coh'n.
Come on and hear—come on and hear—
Mister Coh'n is on the phone.
He would like to do a show with a very special
    score:
Gershwin and Kern, Jerry Herman, many more,
Romberg, Cole Porter, Rodgers and
    Hammerstein—
With every song, the list is long;
You don't know just where to begin—
And three or four or maybe more
From the famous, great Berlin.
And he'd close the show with Stephen Foster's
    "Swanee River,"
Then touch his brow and take a bow
To "Alexander's Ragtime Band."

BACK AGAIN

Typed lyric sheet dated August 7, 1987. The lyric is unfinished. No music is known to survive.

Back again—
We're back again—
The love we tossed aside
Is back on the track again,
And a shining star above
Is that four-letter word "love."

A happier day,
Back to stay

[*Lyric breaks off.*]

GROWING GRAY

Typed lyric sheet dated September 2, 1987—eight months before Berlin's one-hundredth birthday. This appears to have been his last lyric. No music is known to survive.

Growing gray,
Simply growing gray,
Doesn't mean that life is over.
Old people who agree
Tell us the best is yet to be;
Your heavy load
Will find a road
To a sunny field of clover.
Just hope that heaven above
Will send you someone to love
Who'll keep the blues away
While you're growing gray.

Epilogue

This epilogue consists of undated lyrics as well as lyrics that came to the editors' attention during the production of this book.

AN ANGEL FROM HEAVEN

Written sometime after 1930. A holograph lyric manuscript is now in the Irving Berlin Collection of the Music Division of the Library of Congress. No music is known to survive.

I'm afraid that I'll stay single,
But it's not that I wanna be free.
It's because the girl that I would marry
Wouldn't marry me.

BABY

Probably written during the early 1930s. Music manuscript and typed lyric fragment are now in the Irving Berlin Collection of the Music Division of the Library of Congress.

What did I do to you,
That you should do to me
The things you do to me, Baby?
What did I say to you,
That you should say to me
The things you say to me, Baby?

CARELESS

Typed lyric sheet dated November 2, 1932. No music survives for Berlin's original lyric, which is now in the Irving Berlin Collection of the Music Division of the Library of Congress. Seven years later Lew Quadling, Eddy Howard, and Dick Jurgens submitted a song to the Irving Berlin publishing company. According to Robert Lissauer (*Lissauer's Encyclopedia of Popular Music in America*):

Irving Berlin in the library at Beekman Place.
Drawing of Berlin above the mantel by Neysa McMein

Berlin heard Dave Dreyer, his company manager, going over the melody at the piano. Liking the tune, but not the lyric or title, they foresaw a problem. If they rejected the song, they felt that Jurgens, who had a lot of air time with his band, would not play any future songs published by the Berlin company. Berlin took the song home and, overnight, wrote a new lyric with the title of "Careless." His company published the song, though Berlin received neither credit nor royalty as a writer. The financial returns were huge as it became a #1 song.

"Careless," with the help of Berlin's uncredited lyric, was hugely successful. The recording by Glenn Miller and His Orchestra, vocal by Ray Eberle (Bluebird), was number one on the popular music charts for several weeks. Also successful was the recording by Dick Jurgens and His Orchestra, vocal by Eddy Howard (Vocalion). Here is Berlin's original 1932 lyric.

VERSE

Maybe you love me too little,
Maybe I love you too much,
Maybe my heart is too brittle,
Maybe it breaks with a touch.

CHORUS

Careless,
You're getting careless—
Someday you'll let my heart slip through your
     fingers and break.
You said that you wanted me so,
And now you've got me
Just where you want me,
But you don't want me.
Careless,
You're getting careless—
You asked me for my heart and then you threw it
     away.
I know you don't mean to be mean—
You're simply careless,
And while I'm caring for you you care less each
     day.

COUNT SHEEP

Written in the late 1920s or early 1930s for "Giesdorf and Cook Sisters." Copyist manuscript (music and lyrics) is now in the Irving Berlin Collection of the Music Division of the Library of Congress.

Blue,
No wonder I'm blue
All of the time.
These tears are real—
Gee but I feel
So lowdown.
Through
Playing around,
Through
Covering ground,
Tired of it all,
I hear the call
Of a one-horse town.
Oh won't you
Let me live
A life of ease
Where lazy daisies roam?
Like a little Bo-Peep,
I wanna count sheep
Till the cows come home.
Let me hear
The buzz of bees
Around a honeycomb.
Where the daffodills sleep,
I wanna count sheep
Till the cows come home.
Making love while the moon shines
Can make an old heart new.
Making hay while the sun shines
Can make your dreams come true.
Let me find
Some peace of mind,
The only kind I've known.
Where the willow trees weep,
I wanna count sheep
Till the cows come home.

COVER GIRL

Written in the spring of 1943, this lyric, in Ira Gershwin's handwriting, was taken down by Gershwin in his Beverly Hills home during a telephone conversation with Berlin. Gershwin later verified Berlin's authorship in a conversation with Michael Feinstein, Gershwin's archivist and musical secretary. According to Feinstein, Berlin offered the lyric as a present to Gershwin because Berlin had learned that Gershwin and composer Jerome Kern had written a song titled "The Girl on the Cover" for the Gene Kelly–Rita Hayworth film *Cover Girl*, and Berlin thought it was too close to Berlin's 1915 song "The Girl on the Magazine." Gershwin told Feinstein that Berlin was in Hollywood at the time for the filming of *This Is the Army* and was contemplating a musical that he was thinking of calling *The Girl on the Maga-*

THE COMPLETE LYRICS OF IRVING BERLIN

zine Cover. While Ira Gershwin did not use Berlin's "Cover Girl" lyric, he retitled his own "Cover Girl" in deference to Berlin and to avoid any possible confusion between the Berlin and the Jerome Kern–Ira Gershwin song. The Berlin "Cover Girl" lyric is in the Ira and Leonore Gershwin Trusts Archive in San Francisco, California. No music for it is known to survive.

Cover girl,
Come out from under cover.
It's a lovely day for walking in the sun.
Won't you make
A personal appearance
For a sympathetic audience of one?
I've had an eyeful,
But that's not enough.
An eye full of love won't do.
Cover girl,
Come out from under cover.
Give me a heart full of you.

THE GARBAGE MAN

Date unknown. Typed lyric sheet is now in the Irving Berlin Collection of the Music Division of the Library of Congress. No music is known to survive.

Mr. Henry Jackson Brown—
Finest garbage man in town.
Yes sir, he was quite a man,
With a well-filled garbage can.
Soon his reputation spread,
Reached the sanitation head,
Who, with Henry so impressed,
Pinned a medal on his chest.

One day he began to brood.
In a most depressive mood,
Sat for hours with a somber face,
Silent, staring into space.
When his wife who liked perfume
Sprayed it freely through the room,
Henry crawled into a shell
For he lacked a sense of smell.

After weeks of mental pain,
He collapsed beneath the strain.
And he quickly took to bed,
Called a doctor in, who said,
"What you need is crystal clear.
But my pills won't help, I fear.
I am just a plain M.D.
This case needs psychiatry."

Came a smart psychiatrist,
And he quickly cleared the mist,
Saying, "This you can not do:
Have your cake and eat it too.
Lack of smell has made you, Brown,
Finest garbage man in town,
So get up and make your plans.
Go back to your GARBAGE cans."

THE GIRL I WANT

Written sometime after 1930. A holograph lyric manuscript is now in the Irving Berlin Collection of the Music Division of the Library of Congress. No music is known to survive.

The girl I want
Must be pretty as a picture,
Good as an angel,
Lovely as a girl could be.
But what would that kind of
Girl want with me?

THE GOLD IN A GOLDEN WEDDING DAY

Date unknown. Possibly the 1930s. Possibly 1976 for Ellin and Irving Berlin's fiftieth wedding anniversary. Typed lyric sheet is now in the Irving Berlin Collection of the Music Division of the Library of Congress. No music is known to survive.

You can't take away
The gold in a golden wedding day.
There's none in Fort Knox,
The vault where we've buried
All the gold in the U.S.A.
For fifty years it was mined
By gentle hands and hearts that were kind,
So whatever the law,
Whatever the president may say,
You can't take away
The gold in a golden wedding day.

I DON'T THINK WE'D BETTER SEND THEM BACK

Date unknown. Typed lyric sheet is now in the Irving Berlin Collection of the Music Division of the Library of Congress. No music is known to survive.

Men are stupid, men are vain,
They give you and me a pain,
Geniuses for painting futures black.
It's hell living with them,
But we can't live without them,
So I don't think we'd better send them back.
Men are monsters, men are cads,
But remember we have dads,
And without them there'd be quite a lack.
The world, someone stated,
Must be more populated,
So I don't think we'd better send them back.
When you're alone there's lots of things for you to do.
Yes, lots of things except what it takes two to do.

IT CAN'T BE DID

While this book was in production, Harvey Granat, a collector of music manuscripts, made known to the editors a lyric of this song, which included an additional verse and chorus not previously known. Granat also sent the editors a copy of a contract-like letter from Berlin dated December 9, 1909, indicating that this lyric was written four months earlier than previously believed. See page 18 for the other verses and choruses of this lyric.

VERSE 3

Julius comes from such a lovely fam'ly:
His father as a chicken thief was shot;
His brother was a bum
Who drank a lot of rum.
Thats lovely is it not!
Yes it is not.
One night Julius said come let's be married,
He wanted me to be his little Frau;
I looked at him and said,
"You're crazy in the head."
That's something that can never happen now.

CHORUS 3

"It can't be did," I told him,
But he answered, "Why not so?"
I said, "Don't talk so foolish,
There is something you don't know.
The lovely ways what you have got,
Would make me wed you on the spot,
But my husband said that I should not.
You see it can't be did."

MY FAVORITE SONG

Date unknown. Manuscript of music and lyrics is now in
the Irving Berlin Collection of the Music Division of
the Library of Congress.

My fav'rite song
Reminds me of my fav'rite girl.
My fav'rite girl
Reminds me of you.
My fav'rite song
Reminds me of a summer day,
When love was young
And heavens were blue.

MY HEART IS MENDED NOW (COME BACK AND BREAK IT)

Date unknown. Music and typed lyric sheet are now in
the Irving Berlin Collection of the Music Division of
the Library of Congress.

I took my broken heart
And put each part together.
My heart is mended now,
Come back and break it again.
My crying days are done,
I look for sunny weather.
My heart is mended now;
Come back and break it again.
You gave my heart such an awful dent,
But soon I learned
That I'm a glutton for punishment
Where you're concerned.
I took my broken heart

And put each part together.
My heart is mended now;
Come back and break it again.

NO MAN IS GOOD ENOUGH

Date unknown. A Berlin holograph manuscript of lyrics
and a music manuscript by Berlin's chief arranger,
Helmy Kresa, are now in the Irving Berlin Collection of
the Music Division of the Library of Congress.

CHORUS

No man is good enough,
Good enough for my girl.
No man, whoever that man may be.
I wonder if he knows the value of his prize—
He doesn't see his sweetheart through her father's
    eyes.
No man could measure up,
Measure up to my girl.
No man, whoever that man may be.
But if he loves you—sincerely—
Thank your stars above,
And just be worthy of his love.

SEEING THINGS THROUGH EYES OF LOVE

Date unknown. Typed lyric sheet is now in the Irving
Berlin Collection of the Music Division of the Library
of Congress.

VERSE

My Ingersoll was running slow,
Now it seems to fly.
My Chariot was swinging low,
Now I'm riding high.
The sun would never come 'round to my
    windowpane,
But now it couldn't be sunnier—let me explain.

CHORUS

I'm seeing ev'rything through eyes of love.
And what do I see,

Oh what do I see?
A crowded bus is a private car.
A hot-dog sandwich is caviar.
And a joyride in a Ford
Is an ocean trip abroad.*
For I'm seeing ev'rything through eyes of love.
A glass filled with rain
Is sparkling champagne.
A perfect little devil
Is an angel from above.
For I'm seeing things through eyes of love.

FEMALE CATCH-LINE FINISH

The papers say it's cloudy
But the skies are blue above.
For I'm seeing things through eyes of love.

THAT WONDERFUL TANGO

Date unknown, although it might be as early as
1912–1914. Music and typed lyric sheet are now in the
Irving Berlin Collection of the Music Division of the Li-
brary of Congress. Alternate title: "Tango."

In South America,
Most every orchestra
Plays a dreamy tango.
It's where they started it,
When they decided it.
Most everybody picked it up
And are doing it now.
Everybody's doing it
And I want to do it too,
I do.
I'm in love with it
And I'll be doing it soon
Before I'm through.
While they go playing it,
We go swaying it.
Oh, that wonderful tango.
Everybody thinks it's fascinating,
They do, don't you,
I do.
Tango, oh I'm wild about it,
Can't do without it,
That wonderful tango.

Alternate version of lines 6 and 7:
    And any tune that's played
    Is the Schubert "Serenade."

THIS TIME IT'S LOVE

The verse to a song that possibly dates from the early 1930s. A copyright ink piano-vocal score, with lyrics written in, is now in the Irving Berlin Collection of the Music Division of the Library of Congress. The refrain to this song has not survived or perhaps was never written.

I've been most everywhere,
Met girls both dark and fair,
And sat with them when lights were low.
I've fallen in the past,
And said I'm gone at last,
But since I met you dear, I know

ALEXANDER'S RAGTIME BAND (PARODY)

Written April 10,1972. This parody reflects a time when "Alexander's Ragtime Band" nearly went into the public domain. Along with other works of the 1906–1916 era, it was reprieved when the copyright term was extended in the late 1970s from fifty-six to seventy-five years. When "Alexander's Ragtime Band" went into the public domain on January 1, 1997, Berlin was ninety-eight years old and had outlived the copyright on this, his most famous early song.

Come on and hear, come on and hear
"Alexander's Ragtime Band,"
One of the songs that now belongs
To the people in the land.
We were pleading on our knees, we were begging
    day and night,
"Please change the law. Please extend the
    copyright."
But Congress didn't give a damn,
Honey lamb.
The pressure mob was on the job
And they cut us down to size.
We will miss the dough, but even so,
There's a consolation prize.
We're in the club with Stephen Foster's "Swanee
    River."
Come on and hear and shed a tear
For "Alexander's Ragtime Band."

WHAT CAN A SONGWRITER SAY?

Introduced by Irving Berlin on WABC's gala radio tribute of August 3, 1938, to celebrate Berlin's fiftieth birthday.

What can a songwriter say?
What can a songwriter do?
I wish I could make an appropriate speech,
But speechmaking simply is out of my reach.
So what can a songwriter say?
What can a songwriter do?
A fiddler can speak with his fiddle.
A singer can speak with his voice.
An actor can speak
With his tongue in his cheek,
But a songwriter has no choice.
Whatever his rights or his wrongs,
He can only speak with his songs.

Index

This is an alphabetical index of song titles and first lines (including first refrains) of Irving Berlin's lyrics. When the first line of a refrain begins with or is identical to the song title, the first line is not included. Alternate titles are listed except where they duplicate first lines. The index also includes individual song copyright information.

The following copyright information should be added to individual notices according to the corresponding number:

(1) Assigned to Winthrop Rutherfurd, Jr., Anne Phipps Sidamon-Eristoff and Theodore R. Jackson as Trustees of the God Bless America Fund. International Copyright Secured. All Rights Reserved. Used By Permission.

(2) International Copyright Secured. All Rights Reserved. Used By Permission.

For all other lyrics: Publishing and allied rights controlled by Irving Berlin Music Company throughout the world (administered by Williamson Music). International Copyright Secured. All Rights Reserved. Used By Permission.